THE CREEDS

OF THE

EVANGELICAL PROTESTANT CHURCHES.

Bibliotheca Symbolica Ecclesiæ Universalis.

THE CREEDS OF CHRISTENDOM,

WITH

A HISTORY AND CRITICAL NOTES.

BY

PHILIP SCHAFF, D.D., LL.D.,

PROFESSOR OF BIBLICAL LITERATURE IN THE UNION THEOLOGICAL SEMINARY, N. Y.

IN THREE VOLUMES.

FOURTH EDITION—REVISED AND ENLARGED.

VOLUME III.

THE EVANGELICAL PROTESTANT CREEDS, WITH TRANSLATIONS.

BAKER BOOK HOUSE
Grand Rapids, Michigan
1966

Reprinted by arrangement with
Harper and Row, Publishers

TABLE OF CONTENTS.

(VOL. III.)

THE CREEDS OF THE EVANGELICAL PROTESTANT CHURCHES.

PART FIRST.

THE CREEDS OF THE EVANGELICAL LUTHERAN CHURCH.

PART SECOND.

THE CREEDS OF THE EVANGELICAL REFORMED CHURCHES.

PART THIRD.

MODERN PROTESTANT CREEDS.

PART FOURTH.

RECENT CONFESSIONAL DECLARATIONS AND TERMS OF CORPORATE CHURCH UNION.

SYMBOLA EVANGELICA.

PARS PRIMA:

ECCLESIA LUTHERANA.

SYMBOLA EVANGELICA.

EVANGELICAL SYMBOLS.

PART FIRST·

Concordia.

PIA ET VNANIMI

CONSENSV REPETITA

Confeſsio Fidei & doctrinæ

ELECTORVM, PRINCIPVM,

ET ORDINVM IMPERII,

Atq3 eorundem Theologorum, qui

Auguſtanam Confeſsionem am-
plectuntur.

CVI EX SACRA SCRIPTVRA,

VNICA ILLA VERITATIS NORMA ET
regula, quorundam Articulorum, qui poſt Doctoris MARTI-
NI LVTHERI felicem ex hac vita exitum, in con-
trouerſiam venerunt, ſolida acceſsit

Declaratio.

COMMVNI CONSILIO ET MAN-
dato eorundem Electorum, Principum ac Ordinum Imperij, &
erudiendis & monendis ſubditis, Eccleſijs & Scholis ſuis,
ad memoriam poſteritatis denuò typis
vulgata.

LIPSIÆ,

ANNO M. D. LXXXIIII.

Cum gratia & priuilegio Elect. Sax.

OMNIBVS
ET SINGVLIS HAS

noſtras lecturis, nos qui ijſdem nomina noſtra ſubſcripſimus Auguſtanæ
Confeſſioni addicti Electores, Prin-
cipes, & Sacri Romani Imperij, in Germania ordines,
pro dignitate & gradu cuiuſq;, noſtra ſtudia,
amicitiam ac ſalutem cum officio con-
iunctam deferimus & nun-
ciamus.

 NGENS DEI
Opt. Max. benefici-
um eſt, quòd poſtre-
mis temporibus, & in
hac mundi ſenecta,
pro ineffabili amore,
clementia ac miſeri-
cordia ſua, humano generi lucem Euangelij & verbi ſui (per quod ſolum veram ſalutem accipimus) poſt tenebras
illas Papiſticarum ſuperſtitionum, in
Germania chariſſima patria noſtra,

A 2 puram

CONFESSIO AUGUSTANA.

THE AUGSBURG CONFESSION. A.D. 1530.

[The Latin text is from the *editio princeps*, 1531, as printed in the best editions of the 'Book of Concord,' and especially (with all the various readings) in the *Corpus Reformatorum*, ed. Bindseil, Vol. XXVI. (1858), pp. 263–336. I have inserted in brackets the most important additions of the German text, and marked in foot-notes the chief alterations of the edition of 1540. The English translation (in the style of the sixteenth century) was prepared (1868), and at my request carefully revised for this work (1874), by my friend. the Rev. Dr. CHARLES P. KRAUTH, Vice-Provost of the University of Pennsylvania, and Professor of Theology in the Evangelical Lutheran Seminary, Philadelphia. First English translation by Richard Taverner, London, 1536; recent translations, more or less complete, by S. S. Schmucker (1834) : E. Hazelius (1841), Ambrose and Socrates Henkel (1851 and 1854). See Vol. I. § 41, pp. 225 sqq.]

CONFESSIO FIDEI

Exhibita Invictissimo Imperatori Carolo V. Cæsari Augusto in Comiciis Augustæ. Anno MDXXX.[1]

———

Et loquebar de testimoniis tuis in conspectu Regum, et non confundebar.—PSALM cxix. 46.

———

PRÆFATIO AD CÆSAREM CAROLUM V.

Invictissime Imperator, Cæsar Auguste, Domine clementissime. Cum V. C. M. indixerit conventum Imperii Augustæ, ut deliberetur de auxiliis contra Turcam, atrocissimum, hæreditarium atque veterem Christiani nominis ac religionis hostem, quomodo illius scilicet furori et conatibus durabili et perpetuo belli apparatu resisti possit; deinde et de dissensionibus in causa nostræ sanctæ religionis et Christianæ fidei, et ut in hac causa religionis partium opiniones ac sententiæ inter sese in caritate, lenitate et mansuetudine mutua audiantur coram, intelligantur et ponderentur, ut illis, quæ utrinque in Scripturis secus tractata aut intellecta sunt, sepositis et correctis, res illæ ad unam simplicem veritatem et Christianam concordiam componantur et reducantur; ut de cætero a nobis una, sincera et vera religio colatur et servetur,

CONFESSION OF FAITH

Presented to the Invincible Emperor Charles V., Cæsar Augustus, at the Diet of Augsburg, Anno Domini MDXXX.[1]

———

I will speak of thy testimonies also before kings, and will not be ashamed.—PSALM cxix. 46.

———

PREFACE TO THE EMPEROR CHARLES V.

Most Invincible Emperor, Cæsar Augustus, Most Clement Master: Inasmuch as Your Imperial Majesty has summoned a Convention of the Empire at Augsburg, to deliberate in regard to aid against the Turk, the most atrocious, the hereditary, and ancient enemy of the Christian name and religion, in what way, to wit, resistance might be made to his rage and assaults, by protracted and perpetual preparation for war: Because, moreover, of dissensions in the matter of our holy religion and Christian faith, and in order that in this matter of religion the opinions and judgments of diverse parties may be heard in each other's presence, may be understood and weighed among one another, in mutual charity, meekness, and gentleness, that those things which in the writings on either side have been handled or understood amiss, being laid aside

———

[1] The title of the German edition is *Confessio odder Bekantnus des Glaubens etlicher Fürsten und Stedte: Uberantwort Kaiserlicher Majestet: zu Augspurg, Anno M.D.XXX.*

ut, quemadmodum sub uno Christo sumus et militamus: ita in una etiam Ecclesia Christiana, in unitate et concordia vivere possimus; cumque nos infra scripti Elector et Principes, cum aliis, qui nobis conjuncti sunt, peinde ut alii Electores et Principes et Status ad præfata Comitia evocati simus, ut Cæsareo mandato obedienter obsequeremur, mature venimus Augustam; et, quod citra jactantiam dictum volumus, inter primos affuimus.

Cum igitur V. C. M. Electoribus, Principibus et aliis Statibus Imperii etiam hic Augustæ sub ipsa initia horum Comitiorum inter cætera proponi fecerit, quod singuli Status Imperii vigore Cæsarei edicti suam opinionem et sententiam in Germanica et Latina lingua proponere debeant atque offerre; et habita deliberatione proxima feria quarta, rursum responsum est V. C. M. nos proxima feria sexta articulos nostræ Confessionis pro nostra parte oblaturos esse:

Ideo ut V. C. M. voluntati obsequamur, offerimus in hac religionis causa nostrorum Concionatorum et nostram Confessionem, cujusmodi doctrinam ex Scripturis Sanctis et puro verbo Dei hactenus illi in nostris terris, ducatibus, ditionibus et urbibus tradiderint, ac in Ecclesiis tractaverint. Quod si et cæteri Electores, Principes ac Status Imperii, similibus scriptis, Latinis scilicet et Germanicis, juxta prædictam Cæsaream propositionem, suas opiniones in hac causa religionis produxerint: hic nos coram V. C. M. tanquam Domino nostro clementissimo paratos offerimus, nos cum præfatis Principibus et amicis nostris de tollerabilibus modis ac viis amice conferre, ut, quantum honeste fieri potest, conveniamus, et

and corrected, these things may be harmonized and brought back to the one simple truth and Christian concord; so that hereafter the one unfeigned and true religion may be embraced and preserved by us, so that as we are subjects and soldiers of the one Christ, so also, in unity and concord, we may live in the one Christian Church: And inasmuch as we, the Elector and Princes, whose names are subscribed, together with others who are conjoined with us, in common with other Electors, and Princes, and States, have been called to the aforenamed Diet,—we have, in order to render most humble obedience to the Imperial Mandate, come early to Augsburg, and, with no desire to boast, would state that we were among the very first to be present.

When, therefore, Your Imperial Majesty, among other things, has also at Augsburg, at the very beginning of these sessions, caused the proposition to be made to the Princes and States of the Empire, that each of the States of the Empire, in virtue of the Imperial Edict, should propose and offer in the German and in the Latin language its opinion and decision; after discussion on Wednesday we replied to Your Imperial Majesty, that on the following Friday we would offer on our part the Articles of our Confession:

Wherefore, in order that we may do homage to the will of Your Imperial Majesty, we now offer in the matter of religion the Confession of our preachers and of ourselves, the doctrine of which, derived from the Holy Scriptures and pure Word of God, they have to this time set forth in our lands, dukedoms, domains, and cities, and have taught in the churches. If the other Electors, Princes, and States of the Empire, should in similar writings, to wit, in Latin and German, according to the aforementioned Imperial proposition, produce their opinions in this matter of religion: we here, in the presence of Your Imperial Majesty, our most Clement Lord, offer ourselves, prepared, in conjunction with the Princes and

re inter nos partes citra odiosam contentionem pacifice agitata, Deo dante, dissensio dirimatur, et ad unam veram concordem religionem reducatur; sicut omnes sub uno Christo sumus et militamus et unum Christum confiteri debemus, juxta tenorem edicti V. C. M. et omnia ad veritatem Dei perducantur, id quod ardentissimis votis a Deo petimus.

Si autem, quod ad cœteros Electores, Principes et Status, ut partem alteram, attinet, hæc tractatio causæ religionis, eo modo, quo V. C. M. agendam et tractandam sapienter duxit, scilicet cum tali mutua præsentatione scriptorum ac sedata collatione inter nos non processerit, nec aliquo fructu facta fuerit: nos quidem testatum clare relinquimus, hic nihil nos, quod ad Christianam concordiam (quæ cum Deo et bona conscientia fieri possit) conciliandam conducere queat, ullo modo detrectare; quemadmodum et V. C. M. deinde et cœteri Electores et Status Imperii et omnes, quicunque sincero religionis amore ac studio tenentur, quicunque hanc causam æquo animo audituri sunt, ex hac nostra et nostrorum Confessione hoc clementer cognoscere et intelligere dignabuntur.

Cum etiam V. C. M. Electoribus, Principibus et reliquis Statibus Imperii non una vice, sed sæpe clementer significaverit, et in Comitiis Spirensibus, quæ anno Domini etc. XXVI. habita sunt, ex data et præscripta forma vestræ Cæsareæ instructionis et commissionis recitari et publice prælegi fecerit: Vestram M. in hoc negocio religionis ex causis certis, quæ V. M. nomine allegatæ sunt, non velle quicquam determinare, nec concludere posse, sed apud Pontificem Romanum pro officio V. C. M. diligenter daturam operam de congregando Concilio generali. Quemad-

our friends already designated, to compare views in a kindly manner in regard to mode and ways which may be available, so that, as far as may honorably be done, we may agree, and the matter between us of both parts being peacefully discussed, with no hateful contention, by God's help the dissension may be removed, and brought back to one true accordant religion (as we are all subjects and soldiers under one Christ, so also we ought to confess one Christ, in accordance with the tenor of the decree of Your Imp. M.), and all things should be brought back to the truth of God, which with most fervent prayers we beseech God to grant.

But if, as regards the rest of the Electors, Princes, and States, those of the other party, this treatment of the matter of religion, in the manner in which Your I. M. has wisely thought fit it should be conducted and treated, to wit, with such a mutual presentation of writings and calm conference between us, should not go on, nor be attended by any result; yet shall we leave a clear testimony that in no manner do we evade any thing which can tend to promote Christian concord (any thing which God and a good conscience allow); and this Your I. M. and the other Electors and States of the Empire, and all who are moved by a sincere love of religion and concern for it, all who are willing to give an equitable hearing in this matter, will kindly gather and understand from the Confession of ourselves and of ours.

Since, moreover, Your I. M. has not once only, but repeatedly signified to the Electors, Princes, and other States of the Empire; and at the Diet of Spires, which was held in the year of our Lord 1526, caused to be recited and publicly proclaimed, in accordance with the form of Your Imperial instruction and commission given and prescribed: That Your I. M. in this matter of religion for certain reasons, stated in the name of Your Majesty, was not willing to determine, nor was able to conclude touching any thing, but that Your I. M. would diligently endeavor to have the Roman Pontiff,

modum idem latius expositum est ante annum in publico proximo conventu, qui Spiræ congregatus fuit. Ubi V. C. M. per Dominum Ferdinandum, Bohemiæ et Ungariæ Regem, amicum et Dominum clementem nostrum, deinde per Oratorem et Comissarios Cæsareos, hæc inter cætera proponi fecit, quod V. C. M. intellexisset et expendisset Locum Tenentis V. C. M. in Imperio et Præsidentis et Consiliariorum in Regimine et Legatorum ab aliis Statibus, qui Ratisbonæ convenerant, deliberationem de Concilio congregando, et quod judicaret etiam V. C. M. utile esse, ut congregaretur Concilium, et quia causæ, quæ tum tractabantur inter V. C. M. et Romanum Pontificem, vicinæ essent concordiæ et Christianæ reconciliationi, non dubitaret V. C. M. quin Romanum Pontifex adduci posset ad habendum generale Concilium: ideo significabat se V. C. M. operam daturam, ut præfatus Pontifex Maximus una cum V. C. M. tale generale Concilium primo quoque tempore emissis literis publicandum congregare consentiret.

In eventum ergo talem, quod in causa religionis dissensiones inter nos et partes amice et in caritate non fuerint compositæ, tunc coram V. C. M. hic in omni obedientia nos offerimus, ex superabundanti comparituros et causam dicturos in tali generali, libero et Christiano Concilio, de quo congregando in omnibus Comitiis Imperialibus, quæ quidem annis Imperii V. C. M. habita sunt, per Electores, Principes et reliquos Status Imperii semper concorditer actum et congruentibus suffragiis conclusum est. Ad cujus etiam generalis Concilii conventum, simul et ad V. C. M. in hac longe maxima et gravissima causa jam ante etiam debito modo et in forma juris provocavimus et appellavimus. Cui appellationi ad V. C. M. simul et Concilium adhuc adhæremus, neque eam per hunc vel alium tractatum

in accordance with his office, to assemble a General Council; as also the same matter was more amply set forth a year ago in the last public Convention, which was held at Spires, where through His Highness Ferdinand, King of Bohemia and Hungary, our friend and clement Lord, afterward through the Orator and the Imperial Commissioners, Your I. M., among other propositions, caused these to be made: that Your I. M. had known and pondered the resolution to convene a Council, formed by the Representatives of Your I. M. in the Empire, and by the Imperial President and Counselors, and by the Legates of other States convened at Ratisbon, and this Your I. M. also judged that it would be useful to assemble a Council; and because the matters which were to be adjusted at this time between Your I. M. and the Roman Pontiff were approaching agreement and Christian reconciliation, Your I. M. did not doubt that, but that the Pope could be induced to summon a General Council: Wherefore Your I. M. signified that Your I. M. would endeavor to bring it to pass that the Chief Pontiff, together with Your I. M., would consent at the earliest opportunity to issue letters for the convening of such a General Council.

In the event, therefore, that in this matter of religion the differences between us and the other party should not be settled in friendship and love, we here present ourselves before Your I. M. in all obedience, as we have done before, ready to appear and to defend our cause in such a general, free, and Christian Council, concerning the convening of which there has been concordant action and a determination by agreeing votes on the part of the Electors, Princes, and the other States of the Empire, in all the Imperial Diets which have been held in the reign of Your I. M. To this Convention of a General Council, as also to Your I. M., we have in the due method and legal form before made our protestation and appeal in this greatest and gravest of matters. To which appeal both to Your I. M.

(nisi causa inter nos et partes juxta tenorem Cæsareæ proximæ citationis amice in caritate composita, sedata, et ad Christianam concordiam reducta fuerit) deserere intendimus aut possumus; de quo hic etiam solenniter et publice protestamur.

and a Council we still adhere; nor do we intend, nor would it be possible for us to forsake it by this or any other document, unless the matter between us and the other party should, in accordance with the tenor of the latest Imperial citation, be adjusted, settled, and brought to Christian concord, in friendship and love; concerning which appeal we here also make our solemn and public protest.

PARS I.

ARTICULI FIDEI PRÆCIPUI.[1]

ART. I.—*De Deo.*

Ecclesiæ magno consensu [einträchtiglich] apud nos docent, Decretum Nicænæ Synodi, de unitate essentiæ divinæ et de tribus personis, verum et sine ulla dubitatione credendum esse. Videlicet, quod sit una essentia divina, quæ et appellatur et est Deus, æternus, incorporeus impartibilis [ohne Stück], immensa potentia, sapientia, bonitate, creator et conservator omnium rerum, visibilium et invisibilium; et tamen tres sint personæ, ejusdem essentiæ et potentiæ, et coæternæ, Pater, Filius et Spiritus Sanctus. Et nomine personæ utuntur ea significatione, qua usi sunt in hac causa Scriptores Ecclesiastici [die Väter], ut significet non partem aut qualitatem in alio, sed quod proprie subsistit.

PART FIRST.

CHIEF ARTICLES OF FAITH.

ART. I.—*Of God.*

The churches, with common consent among us, do teach that the decree of the Nicene Synod concerning the unity of the divine essence and of the three persons is true, and without doubt to be believed: to wit, that there is one divine essence which is called and is God, eternal, without body, indivisible [without part], of infinite power, wisdom, goodness, the Creator and Preserver of all things, visible and invisible; and that yet there are three persons of the same essence and power, who also are co-eternal, the Father, the Son, and the Holy Ghost. And they use the name of person in that signification in which the ecclesiastical writers [the fathers] have used it in this cause, to signify, not a part or quality in another, but that which properly subsists.

---

[1] Germ. ed. : *Artikel des Glaubens und der Lehre.*

Damnant omnes hœreses, contra hunc articulum exortas, ut Manichœos, qui duo principia ponebant, Bonum et Malum, item Valentinianos, Arianos, Eunomianos, Mahometistas et omnes horum similes. Damnant et Samosatenos, veteres et neotericos,[1] *qui, cum tantum unam personam esse contendant, de Verbo et de Spiritu Sancto astute et impie rhetoricantur, quod non sint personœ distinctœ, sed quod Verbum significet verbum vocale, et Spiritus motum in rebus creatum [geschaffene Regung in Creaturen].*

They condemn all heresies which have sprung up against this Article, as the Manichees, who set down two principles, good and evil; in the same manner the Valentinians, Arians, Eunomians, Mohammedans, and all such like. They condemn also the Samosatenes, old and new;[1] who, when they earnestly contend that there is but one person, do craftily and wickedly trifle, after the manner of rhetoricians, about the Word and Holy Ghost, that they are not distinct persons, but that the Word signifieth a vocal word, and the Spirit a motion created in things.

Art. II.—*De Peccato Originis.*

Item docent, quod post lapsum Adœ omnes homines, secundum naturam propagati, nascantur cum peccato, hoc est, sine metu Dei, sine fiducia erga Deum, et cum concupiscentia; quodque hic morbus, seu vitium originis vere sit peccatum, damnans et afferens nunc quoque œternam mortem his, qui non renascuntur per Baptismum et Spiritum Sanctum.[2]

Damnant Pelagianos et alios, qui vitium originis negant esse peccatum, et, ut extenuent gloriam meriti et beneficiorum Chri-

Art. II.—*Of Original Sin.*

Also they teach that, after Adam's fall, all men begotten after the common course of nature are born with sin; that is, without the fear of God, without trust in him, and with fleshly appetite; and that this disease, or original fault, is truly sin, condemning and bringing eternal death now also upon all that are not born again by baptism and the Holy Spirit.

They condemn the Pelagians, and others, who deny this original fault to be sin indeed; and who, so as to lessen the glory of the merits and

---

[1] The Antitrinitarian Anabaptists, Denk, Hetzer, etc., but not Servede and the Socinians, who appeared after 1530. See Zöckler, *Die Augsb. Conf.* p. 137.

[2] Much enlarged in the edition of 1540.

sti, disputant hominem propriis viribus rationis coram Deo justificari posse.[1]

benefits of Christ, argue that a man may, by the strength of his own reason, be justified before God.

Art. III.—*De Filio Dei.*

Item docent, quod Verbum, hoc est, Filius Dei, assumpserit humanam naturam in utero beatæ Mariæ virginis, ut sint duæ naturæ, divina et humana, in unitate personæ inseparabiliter conjunctæ, unus Christus, vere Deus et vere homo, natus ex virgine Maria, vere passus, crucifixus, mortuus et sepultus, ut reconciliaret nobis Patrem, et hostia esset non tantum pro culpa originis, sed etiam pro omnibus actualibus hominum peccatis.

Idem descendit ad inferos, et vere resurrexit tertia die, deinde ascendit ad cœlos, ut sedeat ad dexteram Patris, et perpetuo regnet et dominetur omnibus creaturis, sanctificet credentes in ipsum, misso in corda eorum Spiritu Sancto, qui regat [heilige, reinige, stärke], consoletur ac vivificet eos, ac defendat adversus diabolum et vim peccati.

Idem Christus palam est redi-

Art. III.—*Of the Son of God.*

Also they teach that the Word, that is, the Son of God, took unto him man's nature in the womb of the blessed Virgin Mary, so that there are two natures, the divine and the human, inseparably joined together in unity of person; one Christ, true God and true man: who was born of the Virgin Mary, truly suffered, was crucified, dead, and buried, that he might reconcile the Father unto us, and might be a sacrifice, not only for original guilt, but also for all actual sins of men.

The same also descended into hell, and truly rose again the third day. Afterward he ascended into the heavens, that he might sit at the right hand of the Father; and reign forever, and have dominion over all creatures; might sanctify those that believe in him, by sending the Holy Spirit into their hearts, who shall rule [sanctify, purify, strengthen], comfort, and quicken them, and shall defend them against the devil, and the power of sin.

The same Christ shall openly

---

[1] The edition of 1540 changes this sentence as follows: *Damnant Pelagianos, qui negant peccatum originis, et sentiunt defectus illos seu concupiscentiam esse res indifferentes seu pœnas tantum, nec esse res sua natura damnatas, et somniant hominem legi Dei satisfacere posse, et propter hanc propriam obedientiam coram Deo justum pronunciari.*

turus, ut judicet vivos et mor-
tuos, etc., juxta Symbolum Apo-
stolorum.

come again, to judge the quick and
the dead, according as the Apostles' Creed declareth these and
other things.

Art. IV.—*De Justificatione.*

Item docent, quod homines non
possint justificari [Vergebung
der Sünde und Gerechtigkeit er-
langen] coram Deo propriis viri-
bus, meritis aut operibus, sed
gratis [aus Gnaden] justificentur
propter Christum per fidem, cum
credunt se in gratiam recipi, et
peccata remitti propter Christum,
qui sua morte pro nostris pec-
catis satisfecit. Hanc fidem im-
putat Deus pro justicia coram
ipso. Rom. III. et IV.[1]

Art. IV.—*Of Justification.*

Also they teach that men can not
be justified [obtain forgiveness of
sins and righteousness] before God
by their own powers, merits, or
works; but are justified freely [of
grace] for Christ's sake through
faith, when they believe that they
are received into favor, and their
sins forgiven for Christ's sake, who
by his death hath satisfied for our
sins. This faith doth God impute
for righteousness before him. Rom.
iii. and iv.

Art. V.—*De Ministerio Ecclesiastico.*

Ut hanc fidem consequamur,
institutum est ministerium do-
cendi Evangelii et porrigendi
Sacramenta.

Nam per verbum et Sacra-
menta, tanquam per instrumenta,
donatur Spiritus Sanctus, qui
fidem efficit, ubi et quando vi-
sum est Deo, in iis, qui audiunt
Evangelium, scilicet, quod Deus
non propter nostra merita, sed
propter Christum justificet hos,
qui credunt, se propter Christum
in gratiam recipi.

Damnant Anabaptistas et alios,

Art. V.—*Of the Ministry of the Church.*

For the obtaining of this faith,
the ministry of teaching the Gospel and administering the Sacraments was instituted.

For by the Word and Sacraments, as by instruments, the Holy
Spirit is given : who worketh faith,
where and when it pleaseth God,
in those that hear the Gospel, to
wit, that God, not for our merit's
sake, but for Christ's sake, doth
justify those who believe that they
for Christ's sake are received into
favor.

They condemn the Anabaptists

---

[1] Much enlarged in the edition of 1540

qui sentiunt, Spiritum Sanctum contingere sine verbo externo hominibus per ipsorum preparationes et opera.[2]

and others,[1] who imagine that the Holy Spirit is given to men without the outward word, through their own preparations and works.

Art. VI.—*De Nova Obedientia.*

Item docent, quod fides illa debeat bonos fructus parere, et quod oporteat bona opera, mandata a Deo, facere, propter voluntatem Dei, non ut confidamus, per ea opera justificationem coram Deo mereri.

Nam remissio peccatorum et justificatio fide apprehenditur, sicut testatur et vox Christi (Luc. xvii. 10): *Cum feceritis hæc omnia, dicite, servi inutiles sumus.*

Idem docent et veteres Scriptores Ecclesiastici. Ambrosius enim inquit: Hoc constitutum est a Deo, ut qui credit in Christum, salvus sit, sine opere, sola fide, gratis accipiens remissionem peccatorum.

Art. VI.—*Of New Obedience.*

Also they teach that this faith should bring forth good fruits, and that men ought to do the good works commanded of God, because it is God's will, and not on any confidence of meriting justification before God by their works.

For remission of sins and justification is apprehended by faith, as also the voice of Christ witnesseth: 'When ye have done all these things, say, We are unprofitable servants.'

The same also do the ancient writers of the Church teach; for Ambrose saith: 'This is ordained of God, that he that believeth in Christ shall be saved, without works, by faith alone, freely receiving remission of sins.'

Art. VII.—*De Ecclesia.*

Item docent, quod una Sancta Ecclesia pepetuo mansura sit. Est autem Ecclesia congregatio Sanctorum [Versammlung aller Gläubigen],[3] in qua Evangelium

Art. VII.—*Of the Church.*

Also they teach that one holy Church is to continue forever. But the Church is the congregation of saints [the assembly of all believers], in which the Gospel is

---

[1] The Roman theologians, who teach that men receive the Holy Ghost through the Sacraments *ex opere operato.* Apol., German text, p. 71, Rechenb. edition.

[2] This Article is also much enlarged in the edition of 1540.

[3] Edition of 1540: *Congregatio membrorum Christi, hoc est, Sanctorum, qui vere credunt et*

recte [*rein*] *docetur, et recte* [*laut des Evangelii*] *admini-strantur Sacramenta.*

Et ad veram unitatem Eccle-siæ satis est consentire de do-ctrina Evangelii et administra-tione Sacramentorum. Nec ne-cesse est ubique esse similes tra-ditiones humanas, seu ritus aut ceremonias, ab hominibus insti-tutas. Sicut inquit Paulus (Eph. iv. 5, 6): *Una fides, unum Baptisma, unus Deus et Pater omnium, etc.*

rightly taught [purely preached] and the Sacraments rightly admin-istered [according to the Gospel].

And unto the true unity of the Church, it is sufficient to agree con-cerning the doctrine of the Gospel and the administration of the Sac-raments. Nor is it necessary that human traditions, rites, or ceremo-nies instituted by men should be alike every where, as St. Paul saith: 'There is one faith, one baptism, one God and Father of all.'

Art. VIII.—*Quid sit Ecclesia.*

Quanquam Ecclesia proprie sit congregatio Sanctorum et vere credentium: tamen, cum in hac vita multi hypocritæ et mali admixti sint, licet uti Sacramen-tis, quæ per malos administran-tur, juxta vocem Christi (Matt. xxiii. 2): *Sedent Scribæ et Pha-risæi in Cathedra Mosi, etc. Et Sacramenta et verbum propter ordinationem et mandatum Chri-sti sunt efficacia, etiamsi per ma-los exhibeantur.*

Damnant Donatistas et simi-les,[1] qui negabant licere uti mini-sterio malorum in Ecclesia, et

Art. VIII.—*What the Church is.*

Though the Church be properly the congregation of saints and true believers, yet seeing that in this life many hypocrites and evil persons are mingled with it, it is lawful to use the Sacraments administered by evil men, according to the voice of Christ (Matt. xxiii. 2): 'The Scribes and the Pharisees sit in Moses' seat,' and the words following. And the Sacraments and the Word are effect-ual, by reason of the institution and commandment of Christ, though they be delivered by evil men.

They condemn the Donatists and such like, who denied that it was lawful to use the ministry of evil

---

obediunt Christo; etsi in hac vita huic congregationi multi mali et hypocritæ admixti sunt usque ad novissimum judicium.

[1] The Wiclefites (*Donatistas et Viglevistas*). Apol. p. 150, Rechenb. edition.

sentiebant ministerium malorum inutile et inefficax esse.

men in the Church, and held that the ministry of evil men is useless and without effect.

Art. IX.—*De Baptismo.*

De Baptismo docent, quod sit necessarius ad salutem, quodque per Baptismum offeratur gratia Dei; et quod pueri[1] *sint baptizandi, qui per Baptismum oblati Deo recipiantur in gratiam Dei.*

Damnant Anabaptistas, qui improbant Baptismum puerorum et affirmant pueros sine Baptismo[2] *salvos fieri.*

Art. IX.—*Of Baptism.*

Of Baptism they teach that it is necessary to salvation, and that by Baptism the grace of God is offered, and that children are to be baptized, who by Baptism, being offered to God, are received into God's favor.

They condemn the Anabaptists who allow not the Baptism of children, and affirm that children are saved without Baptism.

Art. X.—*De Cœna Domini.*

De Cœna Domini docent, quod corpus et sanguis [wahrer Leib und Blut] Christi vere adsint [unter Gestalt des Brotes und Weines], et distribuantur vescentibus [da ausgetheilt und genommen wird] in Cœna Domini; et improbant secus docentes [Derhalben wird auch die Gegenlehr verworfen].[3]

Art. X.—*Of the Lord's Supper.*

Of the Supper of the Lord they teach that the [true] body and blood of Christ are truly present [under the form of bread and wine], and are [there] communicated to those that eat in the Lord's Supper [and received]. And they disapprove of those that teach otherwise [wherefore also the opposite doctrine is rejected].

Art. XI.—*De Confessione.*

De confessione docent, quod absolutio privata in Ecclesiis re-

Art. XI.—*Of Confession.*

Concerning confession, they teach that private absolution be retained

---

[1] Edition of 1540: '*Infantes.*'

[2] The edition of 1540 adds after Baptismo: '*et extra Ecclesiam Christi.*'

[3] In the edition of 1540 the tenth article reads thus: '*De cœna Domini docent quod cum pane et vino vere exhibeantur corpus et sanguis Christi vescentibus in Cœna Domini.*' The disapproval of other views is omitted. This is by far the most important departure from the original edition, and has caused much controversy. See Vol. I. p. 241.

tinenda sit, quanquam in confessione non sit necessaria omnium delictorum enumeratio. Est enim impossibilis juxta Psalmum (xix. 12): Delicta quis intelligit?

in the churches, though enumeration of all offenses be not necessary in confession. For it is impossible; according to the Psalm: 'Who can understand his errors?"

ART. XII.—*De Pœnitentia.*

De pœnitentia docent, quod lapsis post Baptismum contingere possit remissio peccatorum, quocunque tempore cum convertuntur [zu aller Zeit, so sie zur Busse kommen]; et quod Ecclesia talibus redeuntibus ad pœnitentiam absolutionem impartiri debeat.

Constat autem pœnitentia proprie his duabus partibus: Altera est contricio seu terrores incussi conscientiæ agnito peccato. Altera est fides, quæ concipitur ex Evangelio seu absolutione, et credit propter Christum remitti peccata, et consolatur conscientiam, et ex terroribus liberat. Deinde sequi debent bona opera, quæ sunt fructus pœnitentiæ.

Damnant Anabaptistas, qui negant semel justificatos posse amittere Spiritum Sanctum. Item, qui contendunt quibusdam tantam perfectionem in hac vita contingere, ut peccare non possint [dass diejenigen so einst sind fromm worden, nicht

ART. XII.—*Of Repentance.*

Touching repentance, they teach that such as have fallen after baptism may find remission of sins, at what time they are converted [whenever they come to repentance], and that the Church should give absolution unto such as return to repentance.

Now repentance consisteth properly of these two parts: One is contrition, or terrors stricken into the conscience through the acknowledgment of sin; the other is faith, which is conceived by the Gospel, or absolution, and doth believe that for Christ's sake sins be forgiven, and comforteth the conscience, and freeth it from terrors. Then should follow good works, which are fruits of repentance.

They condemn the Anabaptists, who deny that men once justified can lose the Spirit of God, and do contend that some men may attain to such a perfection in this life that they can not sin. [Here are rejected those who teach that those who have once been holy can not

wieder fallen mögen]. *Damnantur et Novatiani, qui nolebant absolvere lapsos post Baptismum redeuntes ad pœnitentiam. Rejiciuntur et isti, qui non docent remissionem peccatorum per fidem contingere, sed jubent nos mereri gratiam per satisfactiones nostras.*

fall again.] The Novatians are also condemned, who would not absolve such as had fallen after baptism, though they returned to repentance. They also that do not teach that remission of sins is obtained by faith, and who command us to merit grace by satisfactions, are rejected.

ART. XIII.—*De Usu Sacramentorum.*

De usu Sacramentorum docent, quod Sacramenta instituta sint, non modo ut sint notæ professionis inter homines, sed magis ut sint signa et testimonia voluntatis Dei erga nos, ad excitandam et confirmandam fidem in his, qui utuntur, proposita. Itaque utendum est Sacramentis ita, ut fides accedat, quæ credat promissionibus, quæ per Sacramenta exhibentur et ostenduntur.

Damnant igitur illos, qui docent, quod Sacramenta ex opere operato justificent, nec docent fidem requiri in usu Sacramentorum, quæ credat remitti peccata.

ART. XIII.—*Of the Use of Sacraments.*

Concerning the use of the Sacraments, they teach that they were ordained, not only to be marks of profession among men, but rather that they should be signs and testimonies of the will of God towards us, set forth unto us to stir up and confirm faith in such as use them. Therefore men must use Sacraments so as to join faith with them, which believes the promises that are offered and declared unto us by the Sacraments.

Wherefore they condemn those that teach that the Sacraments do justify by the work done, and do not teach that faith which believes the remission of sins is requisite in the use of Sacraments.

ART. XIV.—*De Ordine Ecclesiastico.*

De ordine Ecclesiastico [Kirchen-Regiment] docent, quod nemo debeat in Ecclesia publice docere,

ART. XIV.—*Of Ecclesiastical Orders.*

Concerning Ecclesiastical Orders [Church Government], they teach that no man should publicly

aut Sacramenta administrare, ni-
si rite vocatus [ohne ordentlichen
Beruf].

in the Church teach, or administer
the Sacraments, except he be rightly called [without a regular call].

Art. XV.—*De Ritibus Ecclesiasticis.*

De ritibus Ecclesiasticis [von
Menschen gemacht] docent, quod
ritus illi servandi sint, qui sine
peccato servari possunt, et pro-
sunt ad tranquillitatem et bonum
ordinem in Ecclesia, sicut certæ
feriæ, festa et similia. De tali-
bus rebus tamen admonentur ho-
mines, ne conscientiæ onerentur,
tanquam talis cultus ad salutem
necessarius sit.

Admonentur etiam, quod tra-
ditiones humanæ institutæ ad
placandum Deum, ad promeren-
dam gratiam et satisfaciendum
pro peccatis, adversentur Evan-
gelio et doctrinæ fidei. Quare
vota et traditiones de cibis et
diebus, etc., institutæ ad prome-
rendam gratiam, et satisfacien-
dum pro peccatis inutiles sint et
contra Evangelium.

Art. XV.—*Of Ecclesiastical Rites.*

Concerning Ecclesiastical rites
[made by men], they teach that those
rites are to be observed which may
be observed without sin,and are profitable for tranquillity and good order in the Church ; such as are set
holidays, feasts, and such like. Yet
concerning such things, men are to
be admonished that consciences are
not to be burdened as if such service were necessary to salvation.

They are also to be admonished
that human traditions, instituted to
propitiate God, to merit grace, and
make satisfaction for sins, are opposed to the Gospel and the doctrine of faith. Wherefore vows
and traditions concerning foods
and days, and such like, instituted
to merit grace and make satisfaction for sins, are useless and contrary to the Gospel.

Art. XVI.—*De Rebus Civilibus.*

De rebus civilibus docent, quod
legitimæ ordinationes civiles sint
bona opera Dei, quod Christianis
liceat gerere Magistratus, exer-
cere judicia, judicare res ex Im-
peratoriis et aliis præsentibus le-
gibus. supplicia jure constituere,

Art. XVI.—*Of Civil Affairs.*

Concerning civil affairs, they
teach that such civil ordinances as
are lawful are good works of God ;
that Christians may lawfully bear
civil office, sit in judgments, determine matters by the imperial laws,
and other laws in present force,

*jure bellare, militare, lege contra-
here, tenere proprium, jusjurandum postulantibus magistratibus
dare, ducere uxorem, nubere.
Damnant Anabaptistas, qui in-
terdicunt hæc civilia officia Christianis. Damnant et illos, qui
Evangelicam perfectionem non
collocant in timore Dei et fide,
sed in deserendis civilibus officiis, quia Evangelium tradit justiciam æternam cordis. Interim non dissipat Politiam aut
Œconomiam, sed maxime postulat conservare tanquam ordinationes Dei, et in talibus ordinationibus exercere caritatem.
Itaque necessario debent Christiani obedire magistratibus suis et
legibus; nisi cum jubent peccare,
tunc etiam magis debent obedire
Deo quam hominibus* (Acts v.
29).

appoint just punishments, engage
in just war, act as soldiers, make
legal bargains and contracts, hold
property, take an oath when the
magistrates require it, marry a wife,
or be given in marriage. They condemn the Anabaptists who forbid
Christians these civil offices. They
condemn also those that place the
perfection of the Gospel, not in the
fear of God and in faith, but in
forsaking civil offices, inasmuch as
the Gospel teacheth an everlasting
righteousness of the heart. In the
mean time, it doth not disallow
order and government of commonwealths or families, but requireth
especially the preservation and
maintenance thereof, as of God's
own ordinances, and that in such
ordinances we should exercise love.
Christians, therefore, must necessarily obey their magistrates and
laws, save only when they command any sin; for then they must
rather obey God than men (Acts
v. 29).

ART. XVII.—*De Christi Reditu ad Judicium.*

*Item docent, quod Christus ap-
parebit in consummatione mundi [am jüngsten Tag] ad judicandum, et mortuos omnes resuscitabit, piis et electis dabit
vitam æternam et perpetua gau-
dia, impios autem homines ac*

ART. XVII.—*Of Christ's Return to Judgment.*

Also they teach that, in the consummation of the world [at the last
day], Christ shall appear to judge,
and shall raise up all the dead, and
shall give unto the godly and elect
eternal life and everlasting joys;
but ungodly men and the devils

diabolos condemnabit, ut sine fine crucientur.

Damnant Anabaptistas, qui sentiunt hominibus damnatis ac diabolis finem pœnarum futurum esse. Damnant et alios, qui nunc spargunt Judaicas opiniones, quod ante resurrectionem mortuorum pii regnum mundi occupaturi sint, ubique oppressis impiis [eitel Heilige, Fromme ein weltlich Reich haben, und alle Gottlosen vertilgen werden].

shall he condemn unto endless torments.

They condemn the Anabaptists who think that to condemned men and the devils shall be an end of torments. They condemn others also, who now scatter Jewish opinions, that, before the resurrection of the dead, the godly shall occupy the kingdom of the world, the wicked being every where suppressed [the saints alone, the pious, shall have a worldly kingdom, and shall exterminate all the godless].

Art. XVIII.—*De Libero Arbitrio.*

De libero arbitrio docent, quod humana voluntas habeat aliquam libertatem ad efficiendam civilem justiciam et deligendas res rationi subjectas. Sed non habet vim sine Spiritu Sancto efficindœ justiciœ Dei seu justiciœ spiritualis, quia animalis homo non percipit ea, quœ sunt Spiritus Dei (1 Cor. ii. 14); sed hœc fit in cordibus, cum per verbum Spiritus Sanctus concipitur.

Hœc totidem verbis dicit Augustinus lib. III. Hypognosticon: Esse fatemur liberum arbitrium omnibus hominibus, habens quidem judicium rationis, non per quod sit idoneum in iis, quœ ad Deum pertinent, sine Deo aut inchoare

Art. XVIII.—*Of Free Will.*

Concerning free will, they teach that man's will hath some liberty to work a civil righteousness, and to choose such things as reason can reach unto; but that it hath no power to work the righteousness of God, or a spiritual righteousness, without the Spirit of God; because that the natural man receiveth not the things of the Spirit of God (1 Cor. ii. 14). But this is wrought in the heart when men do receive the Spirit of God through the Word.

These things are in as many words affirmed by St. Augustine, *Hypognosticon*, lib. iii.: 'We confess that there is in all men a free will, which hath indeed the judgment of reason; not that it is thereby fitted, without God, either to

aut certe peragere: sed tantum in operibus vitæ præsentis tam bonis, quam etiam malis. Bonis dico, quæ de bono naturæ oriuntur, i. e., velle laborare in agro, velle manducare et bibere, velle habere amicum, velle habere indumenta, velle fabricare domum, uxorem velle ducere, pecora nutrire, artem discere diversarum rerum bonarum, vel quicquid bonum ad præsentem pertinet vitam. Quæ omnia non sine divino gubernaculo subsistunt, imo ex ipso et per ipsum sunt et esse cœperunt. Malis vero dico, ut est, velle idolum colere, velle homicidium, etc.

Damnant Pelagianos et alios, qui docent, quod sine Spiritu Sancto, solis naturæ viribus possimus Deum super omnia diligere; item præcepta Dei facere, quoad substantiam actuum. Quanquam enim externa opera aliquo modo efficere natura possit, potest enim continere manus a furto, a cede: tamen interiores motus non potest efficere, ut timorem Dei, fiduciam erga Deum, castitatem, patientiam, etc.[1]

begin or to perform any thing in matters pertaining to God, but only in works belonging to this present life, whether they be good or evil. By good works, I mean those which are of the goodness of nature; as to will to labor in the field, to desire meat or drink, to desire to have a friend, to desire apparel, to desire to build a house, to marry a wife, to nourish cattle, to learn the art of divers good things, to desire any good thing pertaining to this present life; all which are not without God's government, yea, they are, and had their beginning from God and by God. Among evil things, I account such as these: to will to worship an image; to will manslaughter, and such like.'

They condemn the Pelagians and others, who teach that by the powers of nature alone, without the Spirit of God, we are able to love God above all things; also to perform the commandments of God, as touching the substance of our actions. For although nature be able in some sort to do the external works (for it is able to withhold the hands from theft and murder), yet it can not work the inward motions, such as the fear of God, trust in God, chastity, patience, and such like.

---

[1] The wording of this article is considerably changed in the edition of 1540.

Art. XIX.—*De Causa Peccati.*

De causa peccati docent, quod tametsi Deus creat et conservat naturam, tamen causa peccati est voluntas malorum, videlicet diaboli et impiorum, quæ non adjuvante Deo avertit se a Deo, sicut Christus ait (John viii. 44): *Cum loquitur mendacium, ex se ipso loquitur.*

Art. XIX.—*Of the Cause of Sin.*

Touching the cause of sin, they teach that, although God doth create and preserve nature, yet the cause of sin is the will of the wicked; to wit, of the devil and ungodly men; which will, God not aiding, turneth itself from God, as Christ saith: 'When he speaketh a lie, he speaketh of his own' (John viii. 44).

Art. XX.—*De Bonis Operibus.*[1]

Falso accusantur nostri, quod bona opera prohibeant. Nam scripta eorum, quæ extant de decem præceptis, et alia simili argumento testantur, quod utiliter docuerint de omnibus vitæ generibus et officiis, quæ genera vitæ, quæ opera in qualibet vocatione Deo placeant. De quibus rebus olim parum docebant Concionatores, tantum puerilia et non necessaria opera urgebant, ut certas ferias, certa jejunia, fraternitates, peregrinationes, cultus Sanctorum, rosaria, monachatum et similia. Hæc adversarii nostri admoniti nunc dediscunt, nec perinde prædicant hæc inutilia opera, ut olim. Preterea incipiunt fidei mentionem facere, de qua olim mirum erat silentium. Docent nos non tantum operibus justificari, sed conjungunt fidem

Art. XX.—*Of Good Works.*

Ours are falsely accused of forbidding good works. For their writings extant upon the Ten Commandments, and others of the like argument, do bear witness that they have to good purpose taught concerning every kind of life, and its duties; what kinds of life, and what works in every calling, do please God. Of which things preachers in former times taught little or nothing: only they urged certain childish and needless works; as, keeping of holidays, set fasts, fraternities, pilgrimages, worshiping of saints, the use of rosaries, monkery, and such like things. Whereof our adversaries having had warning, they do now unlearn them, and do not preach concerning these unprofitable works, as they were wont. Besides, they begin now to make mention of faith, concerning which

---

[1] This article is enlarged to more than double its original size in the altered edition of 1540.

et opera, et dicunt, nos fide et ope-
ribus justificari. Quæ doctrina
tolerabilior est priore, et plus
afferre potest consolationis, quam
vetus ipsorum doctrina.

Cum igitur doctrina de fide,
quam oportet in Ecclesia præ-
cipuam esse, tam diu jacuerit
ignota, quemadmodum fateri om-
nes necesse est, de fidei justitia
altissimum silentium fuisse in
concionibus, tantum doctrinam
operum versatam esse in eccle-
siis, nostri de fide sic admonue-
runt ecclesias :

Principio, quod opera nostra
non possint reconciliare Deum,
aut mereri remissionem peccato-
rum et gratiam et justificatio-
nem, sed hanc tantum fide conse-
quimur, credentes, quod propter
Christum recipiamur in gra-
tiam, qui solus positus est Medi-
ator et Propitiatorium (1 Tim. ii.
5), *per quem reconcilietur Pater.*
Itaque qui confidit, operibus se
mereri gratiam, is aspernatur
Christi meritum et gratiam, et
querit sine Christo humanis vi-
ribus viam ad Deum, cum Chri-
stus de se dixerit (John xiv. 6):
Ego sum via, veritas et vita.

there was formerly a deep silence.
They teach that we are not justified by works alone; but they con-
join faith and works, and say we
are justified by faith and works.
Which doctrine is more tolerable
than the former one, and can afford
more consolation than their old doctrine.

Whereas, therefore, the doctrine
of faith, which should be the chief
one in the Church, hath been so
long unknown, as all men must needs
grant, that there was the deepest
silence about the righteousness of
faith in their sermons, and that the
doctrine of works was usual in the
churches; for this cause our divines
did thus admonish the churches:

First, that our works can not reconcile God, or deserve remission of
sins, grace, and justification at his
hands, but that these we obtain by
faith only, when we believe that we
are received into favor for Christ's
sake, who alone is appointed the Mediator and Propitiatory, by whom
the Father is reconciled. He, therefore, that trusteth by his works to
merit grace, doth despise the merit
and grace of Christ, and seeketh by
his own power, without Christ, to
come unto the Father; whereas
Christ hath said expressly of himself, 'I am the way, the truth, and
the life' (John xiv. 6).

Hæc doctrina de fide ubique in Paulo tractatur (Eph. ii. 8): *Gratia salvi facti estis per fidem, et hoc non ex vobis, Dei donum est, non ex operibus, etc. Et ne quis cavilletur, a nobis novam Pauli interpretationem excogitari, tota hæc causa habet testimonia Patrum. Nam Augustinus multis voluminibus defendit gratiam et justitiam fidei contra merita operum. Et similia docet Ambrosius de vocatione gentium, et alibi. Sic enim inquit de vocatione gentium : Vilesceret redemptio sanguinis Christi, nec misericordiæ Dei humanorum operum prærogativa succumberet, si justificatio, quæ fit per gratiam, meritis præcedentibus deberetur, ut non munus largientis, sed merces esset operantis.*

Quanquam autem hæc doctrina contemnitur ab imperitis, tamen experiuntur piæ ac pavidæ conscientiæ, plurimum eam consolationis afferre, quia conscientiæ non possunt reddi tranquillæ per ulla opera, sed tantum fide, cum certo statuunt, quod propter Christum habeant placatum Deum ; quemadmodum Paulus docet

This doctrine of faith is handled by Paul almost every where: 'By grace ye are saved through faith, and that not of yourselves: it is the gift of God, not of works' (Eph. ii. 8, 9). And lest any here should cavil, that we bring in a new-found interpretation, this whole cause is sustained by testimonies of the Fathers. Augustine doth in many volumes defend grace, and the righteousness of faith, against the merit of works. The like doth Ambrose teach in his book, *De Vocatione Gentium*, and elsewhere; for thus he saith of the calling of the Gentiles : 'The redemption made by the blood of Christ would be of small account, and the prerogative of man's works would not give place to the mercy of God, if the justification which is by grace were due to merits going before; so as it should not be the liberality of the giver, but the wages or hire of the laborer.'

This doctrine, though it be contemned of the unskillful, yet godly and fearful consciences find by experience that it bringeth very great comfort : because that consciences can not be quieted by any works, but by faith alone, when they believe assuredly that they have a God who is propitiated for Christ's sake; as St. Paul teacheth, 'Being justified

(Rom. v. 1): *Justificati per fidem, pacem habemus apud Deum. Tota hæc doctrina ad illud certamen perterrefactæ conscientiæ referenda est, nec sine illo certamine intelligi potest. Quare male judicant de ea re homines imperiti et prophani, qui Christianam justitiam nihil esse somniant, nisi civilem et philosophicam justitiam.*

Olim vexabantur conscientiæ doctrina operum, non audiebant ex Evangelio consolationem. Quosdam conscientia expulit in desertum, in monasteria, sperantes ibi se gratiam merituros esse per vitam monasticam. Alii alia excogitaverunt opera ad promerendam gratiam et satisfaciendum pro peccatis. Ideo magnopere fuit opus, hanc doctrinam de fide in Christum tradere et renovare, ne deesset consolatio pavidis conscientiis, sed scirent fide in Christum apprehendi gratiam et remissionem peccatorum et justificationem.

Admonentur etiam homines, quod hic nomen fidei non significet tantum historiæ notitiam, qualis est in impiis et diabolo, sed significet fidem, quæ credit non tantum historiam, sed etiam

VOL. III —C

by faith, we have peace with God' (Rom. v. 1). This doctrine doth wholly belong to the conflict of a troubled conscience; and can not be understood, but where the conscience hath felt that conflict. Wherefore, all such as have had no experience thereof, and all that are profane men, who dream that Christian righteousness is naught else but a civil and philosophical righteousness, are poor judges of this matter.

Formerly men's consciences were vexed with the doctrine of works; they did not hear any comfort out of the Gospel. Whereupon conscience drove some into the desert, into monasteries, hoping there to merit grace by a monastical life. Others devised other works, whereby to merit grace, and to satisfy for sin. There was very great need, therefore, to teach and renew this doctrine of faith in Christ; to the end that fearful consciences might not want comfort, but might know that grace, and forgiveness of sins, and justification, are received by faith in Christ.

Another thing, which we teach men, is that in this place the name of FAITH doth not only signify a knowledge of the history, which may be in the wicked, and in the devil, but that it signifieth a faith

effectum historiæ, videlicet hunc articulum, remissionem peccatorum, quod videlicet per Christum habeamus gratiam, justitiam et remissionem peccatorum. Jam qui scit, se per Christum habere propitium Patrem, is vere novit Deum, scit, se ei curæ esse, invocat eum; denique non est sine Deo, sicut gentes. Nam diaboli et impii non possunt hunc articulum credere, remissionem peccatorum. Ideo Deum tanquam hostem oderunt, non invocant eum, nihil boni ab eo expectant. Augustinus etiam de fidei nomine hoc modo admonet lectorem et docet, in Scripturis nomen fidei accipi, non pro notitia, qualis est in impiis, sed pro fiducia, quæ consolatur et erigit perterrefactas mentes.

Præterea docent nostri, quod necesse sit bona opera facere, non ut confidamus per ea gratiam mereri, sed propter voluntatem Dei. Tantum fide apprehenditur remissio peccatorum ac gratia. Et quia per fidem accipitur Spiritus Sanctus, jam corda renovantur et induunt novos affectus, ut parere bona opera

which believeth, not only the history, but also the effect of the history; to wit, the article of remission of sins; namely, that by Christ we have grace, righteousness, and remission of sins. Now he that knoweth that he hath the Father merciful to him through Christ, this man knoweth God truly; he knoweth that God hath a care of him; he loveth God, and calleth upon him; in a word, he is not without God, as the Gentiles are. For the devils and the wicked can never believe this article of the remission of sins; and therefore they hate God as their enemy; they call not upon him, they look for no good thing at his hands. After this manner doth Augustine admonish the reader touching the name of Faith, and teacheth that this word Faith is taken in Scriptures, not for such a knowledge as is in the wicked, but for a trust, which doth comfort and lift up disquieted minds.

Moreover, ours teach that it is necessary to do good works; not that we may trust that we deserve grace by them, but because it is the will of God that we should do them. By faith alone is apprehended remission of sins and grace. And because the Holy Spirit is received by faith, our hearts are now renewed, and so put on new affec

possint. Sic enim ait Ambrosius: Fides bonæ voluntatis et justæ actionis genitrix est. Nam humanæ vires, sine Spiritu Sancto, plenæ sunt impiis affectibus, et sunt imbecilliores, quam ut bona opera possint efficere coram Deo. Ad hæc, sunt in potestate diaboli, qui impellit homines ad varia peccata, ad impias opiniones, ad manifesta scelera. Quemadmodum est videre in philosophis, qui et ipsi conati honeste vivere, tamen id non potuerunt efficere, sed contaminati sunt multis manifestis sceleribus. Talis est imbecillitas hominis, cum est sine fide et sine Spiritu Sancto, et tantum humanis viribus se gubernat.

Hinc facile apparet, hanc doctrinam non esse accusandam, quod bona opera prohibeat, sed multo magis laudandam, quod ostendit, quomodo bona opera facere possimus. Nam sine fide nullo modo potest humana natura primi aut secundi præcepti opera facere. Sine fide non invocat Deum, a Deo nihil expectat, non tollerat crucem, sed querit humana præsidia, confidit humanis præsidiis. Ita regnant in corde omnes cupiditates et humana consilia, cum abest fides et fiducia erga Deum.

tions, so that they are able to bring forth good works. For thus saith Ambrose: 'Faith is the begetter of a good will and of good actions.' For man's powers, without the Holy Spirit, are full of wicked affections, and are too weak to perform any good deed before God. Besides, they are in the devil's power, who driveth men forward into divers sins, into profane opinions, and into heinous crimes; as was to be seen in the philosophers, who, assaying to live an honest life, could not attain unto it, but were defiled with many heinous crimes. Such is the weakness of man, when he is without faith and the Holy Spirit, and hath no other guide but the natural powers of man.

Hereby every man may see that this doctrine is not to be accused, as forbidding good works; but rather is much to be commended, because it showeth after what sort we must do good works. For without faith the nature of man can by no means perform the works of the First or Second Table. Without faith, it can not call upon God, hope in God, bear the cross; but seeketh help from man, and trusteth in man's help. So it cometh to pass that all lusts and human counsels bear sway in the heart so long as faith and trust in God are absent.

Quare et Christus dixit: Sine me nihil potestis facere (John xv. 5). *Et Ecclesia canit: Sine tuo numine nihil est in homine, nihil est innoxium.*

Wherefore, also, Christ saith, 'Without me ye can do nothing' (John xv. 5), and the Church singeth, 'Without thy power is naught in man, naught that is innocent.'

ART. XXI.—*De Cultu Sanctorum.*[1]

De cultu Sanctorum docent, quod memoria Sanctorum proponi potest, ut imitemur fidem eorum et bona opera juxta vocationem; ut Cæsar imitari potest exemplum Davidis in bello gerendo ad depellendos Turcas a patria. Nam uterque Rex est. Sed Scriptura non docet invocare Sanctos, seu petere auxilium a Sanctis; quia unum Christum nobis proponit mediatorem, propitiatorium, pontificem et intercessorem. Hic invocandus est, et promisit, se exauditurum esse preces nostras, et hunc cultum maxime probat, videlicet, ut invocetur in omnibus afflictionibus (1 John ii. 1). *Si quis peccat, habemus advocatum apud Deum, etc.*

ART. XXI.—*Of the Worship of Saints.*

Touching the worship of saints, they teach that the memory of saints may be set before us, that we may follow their faith and good works according to our calling; as the Emperor may follow David's example in making war to drive away the Turks from his country; for either of them is a king. But the Scripture teacheth not to invocate saints, or to ask help of saints, because it propoundeth unto us one Christ the Mediator, Propitiatory, High-Priest, and Intercessor. This Christ is to be invocated, and he hath promised that he will hear our prayers, and liketh this worship especially, to wit, that he be invocated in all afflictions. 'If any man sin, we have an advocate with God, Jesus Christ the righteous' (1 John ii. 1).

ART. XXII.

Hæc fere summa est doctrinæ apud nos, in qua cerni potest, nihil inesse, quod discrepet a Scripturis, vel ab Ecclesia Catholica,

ART. XXII.

This is about the sum of doctrine among us, in which can be seen that there is nothing which is discrepant with the Scriptures, or with the

---

[1] Considerably enlarged in the edition of 1540.

vel ab Ecclesia Romana quatenus ex scriptoribus [aus der Väter Schrift] nota est. Quod cum ita sit, inclementer judicant isti qui nostros pro hæreticis haberi postulant. Sed dissensio est de quibusdam [Traditionen und] abusibus, qui sine certa autoritate in ecclesias irrepserunt, in quibus etiam, si qua esset dissimilitudo, tamen decebat hæc lenitas episcopos, ut propter Confessionem, quam modo recensuimus, tolerarent nostros, quia ne Canones quidem tam duri sunt, ut eosdem ritus ubique esse postulent, neque similes unquam omnium ecclesiarum ritus fuerunt. Quanquam apud nos magna ex parte veteres ritus diligenter servantur. Falsa enim calumnia est, quod omnes ceremoniæ, omnia vetera instituta in ecclesiis nostris aboleantur. Verum publica querela fuit, abusus quosdam in vulgaribus ritibus hærere. Hi, quia non poterant bona conscientia probari, aliqua ex parte correcti sunt.[1]

Church Catholic, or even with the Roman Church, so far as that Church is known from writers [the writings of the Fathers]. This being the case, they judge us harshly who insist that we shall be regarded as heretics. But the dissension is concerning certain [traditions and] abuses, which without any certain authority have crept into the churches; in which things, even if there were some difference, yet would it be a becoming lenity on the part of the bishops that, on account of the Confession which we have now presented, they should bear with us, since not even the Canons are so severe as to demand the same rites every where, nor were the rites of all churches at any time the same. Although among us in large part the ancient rites are diligently observed. For it is a calumnious falsehood, that all the ceremonies, all the things instituted of old, are abolished in our churches. But the public complaint was that certain abuses were connected with the rites in common use. These, because they could not with good conscience be approved, have to some extent been corrected.

---

[1] The first sentence of the conclusion of Part I. is much longer in the German text: '*Dies ist fast die Summa der Lehre, welche in unsern Kirchen zu rechtem christlichem Unterricht und Trost der Gewissen, auch zu Besserung der Gläubigen gepredigt und gelehret ist,*' etc. The rest also differs considerably.

Pars II.

ARTICULI IN QUIBUS RECENSENTUR ABUSUS MUTATI.

Cum ecclesiæ apud nos de nullo articulo fidei dissentiant ab Eccle sia Catholica [nicht gelehret wird zuwider der heiligen Schrift, oder gemeiner christlichen Kirchen], tantum paucos quosdam abusus omittant, qui novi sunt [etliche Missbräuche, welche zum Theil mit der Zeit selbst eingerissen, zum Theil mit Gewalt aufgericht] et contra voluntatem Canonum vitio temporum recepti, rogamus, ut Cæsarea Majestas clementer audiat, et quid sit mutatum, et quæ fuerint causæ, quo minus coactus sit populus illos abusus contra conscientiam observare.

Nec habeat fidem Cæsarea Majestas istis, qui, ut inflamment dia hominum adversus nostros, niras calumnias spargunt in populum. Hoc modo irritatis animis bonorum virorum initio præbuerunt occasionem huic dissidio, et eadem arte conantur nunc augere discordias. Nam Cæsarea Majestas haud dubie comperiet tolerabiliorem esse formam et doctrinæ et ceremoniarum apud nos, quam qualem homines iniqui et malevoli de-

Part Second.

ARTICLES IN WHICH ARE RECOUNTED THE ABUSES WHICH HAVE BEEN CORRECTED.

Inasmuch as the churches among us dissent in no article of faith from [the holy Scriptures, or] the Church Catholic [the Universal Christian Church], and only omit a few of certain abuses, which are novel [in part have crept in with time, in part have been introduced by violence], and, contrary to the purport of the Canons, have been received by the fault of the times, we beg that Your Imperial Majesty would clemently hear both what ought to be changed and what are the reasons that the people ought not to be forced against their consciences to observe those abuses.

Nor should Your Imperial Majesty have faith in those who, that they may inflame the hatred of men against us, scatter amazing slanders among the people. In this way, the minds of good men being angered at the beginning, they gave occasion to this dissension, and by the same art they now endeavor to increase the discords. For beyond doubt your Imperial Majesty will find that the form, both of doctrines and of ceremonies, among us is far more tolerable than that

scribunt. Porro veritas ex vulgi rumoribus aut maledictis inimicorum colligi non potest. Facile autem hoc judicari potest, nihil magis prodesse ad dignitatem ceremoniarum conservandam et alendam reverentiam ac pietatem in populo, quam si ceremoniæ rite fiant in ecclesiis.

which these wicked and malicious men describe. The truth, moreover, can not be gathered from common rumors and the reproaches of enemies. But it is easy to judge this, that nothing is more profitable to preserve the dignity of ceremonies and to nurture reverence and piety among the people than that the ceremonies should be rightly performed in the churches.

Art. I.—*De Utraque Specie.*[1]

Art. I.—*Of both Kinds [in the Lord's Supper].*

Laicis datur utraque species Sacramenti in Cœna Domini, quia hic mos habet mandatum Domini (Matt. xxvi. 27): *Bibite ex hoc omnes. Ubi manifeste præcepit Christus de poculo, ut omnes bibant; et ne quis possit cavillari, quod hoc ad sacerdotes tantum pertineat, Paulus ad Corinth.* (1 Cor. xi. 26) *exemplum recitat, in quo apparet, totam Ecclesiam utraque specie usam esse. Et diu mansit hic mos in Ecclesia, nec constat, quando aut quo autore mutatus sit; tametsi Cardinalis Cusanus recitet, quando sit approbatus.*[2] [*Und dieser Brauch ist lange Zeit in der Kirchen blieben, wie man durch*

Both kinds of the Sacrament in the Lord's Supper are given to the laity, because that this custom hath the commandment of the Lord: 'Drink ye all of this' (Matt. xxvi. 27); where Christ doth manifestly command concerning the cup that all should drink. And that no man might cavil that this doth only pertain to the priests, the example of Paul to the Corinthians witnesseth that the whole Church did use both kinds in common (1 Cor. xi. 28). And this custom remained a long time in the Church; neither is it certain when or by what authority it was changed; although the Cardinal de Cusa relates when it was approved. [And this custom remained a long

---

[1] In the edition of 1540 Melanchthon changed the order of the articles, and put the Art. *De Missa* first.

[2] The German edition omits the reference to Cardinal Nicolas de Cusa (d. 1464), but adds the clause which follows.

die Historien und der Väter Schriften beweisen kann]. *Cyprianus aliquot locis testatur, populo sanguinem datum esse. Idem testatur Hieronymus, qui ait, sacerdotes Eucharistiæ ministrant, et sanguinem Christi populis dividunt. Imo Gelasius Papa mandat, ne dividatur Sacramentum* (*Dist. II. de Consecratione. Cap. Comperimus*). *Tantum consuetudo non ita vetus aliud habet. Constat autem, quod consuetudo, contra mandata Dei introducta, non sit probanda, ut testantur Canones* (*Dist. VIII. Cap. Veritate*) *cum sequentibus. Hæc vero consuetudo non solum contra Scripturam, sed etiam contra veteres Canones et exemplum Ecclesiæ recepta est. Quare si qui maluerunt utraque specie Sacramenti uti, non fuerunt cogendi, ut aliter facerent cum offensione conscientiæ. Et quia divisio Sacramenti non convenit cum institutione Christi, solet apud nos omitti processio, quæ hactenus fieri solita est.*

time in the churches, as may be proved from history and the writings of the Fathers.] Cyprian in certain places doth witness that the blood was given to the people; the same thing doth Jerome testify, saying, ' The priests do minister the Eucharist, and communicate the blood of Christ to the people.' Nay, Pope Gelasius commandeth that the Sacrament be not divided (*Dist. II., De Consecr. Cap. Comperimus*). Only a custom, not thus ancient, doth otherwise. But it is manifest that a custom, brought in contrary to the commandments of God, is not to be approved, as the Canons do witness (*Dist.VIII., Cap. Veritate*) with the words which follow. Now this custom has been received, not only against the Scripture, but also against the ancient Canons and the example of the Church. Therefore if any would rather use both kinds in the Sacrament, they are not to be compelled to do otherwise with the offense of their conscience. And because that the division of the Sacrament doth not agree with the institution of Christ, among us it is the custom to omit that procession which hitherto hath been in use.

Art. II.—*De Conjugio Sacerdotum.*

Publica querela fuit de exemplis Sacerdotum, qui non con-

Art. II.—*Of the Marriage of Priests.*

There was a common complaint of the examples of such priests as

tinebant. Quam ob causam et Pius Papa dixisse fertur, fuisse aliquas causas, cur ademptum sit sacerdotibus conjugium, sed multo majores esse causas, cur reddi debeat; sic enim scribit Platina. Cum igitur sacerdotes apud nos publica illa scandala vitare vellent, duxerunt uxores, ac docuerunt, quod liceat ipsis contrahere matrimonium. Primum, quia Paulus dicit (1 Cor. vii. 2): *Unusquisque habeat uxorem suam propter fornicationem. Item* (9): *Melius est nubere, quam uri. Secundo, Christus inquit* (Matt. xix. 12): *Non omnes capiunt verbum hoc; ubi docet, non omnes homines ad cœlibatum idoneos esse, quia Deus creavit hominem ad procreationem* (Gen. i. 28). *Nec est humanæ potestatis, sine singulari dono et opere Dei creationem mutare. Igitur qui non sunt idonei ad cœlibatum, debent contrahere matrimonium. Nam mandatum Dei et ordinationem Dei nulla lex humana, nullum votum tollere potest. Ex his causis docent Sacerdotes, sibi licere uxores ducere. Constat etiam, in Ecclesia veteri Sacerdotes fuisse maritos. Nam et Paulus ait* (1 Tim. iii. 2), *Episcopum eligendum esse, qui sit maritus. Et in Germa-*

were not continent. For which cause Pope Pius is reported to have said, that 'there were certain causes for which marriage was forbidden to priests, but there were many weightier causes why it should be permitted again;' for so Platina writeth. Whereas, therefore, the priests among us seek to avoid these public offenses, they have married wives, and have taught that it is lawful for them to enter into marriage. First, because that Paul saith, ' To avoid fornication, let every man have his wife;' again, ' It is better to marry than to burn' (1 Cor. vii. 2, 9). Secondly, Christ saith, 'All men can not receive this word' (Matt. xix. 11); where he showeth that all men are not fit for a single life, because that God created mankind male and female (Gen. i. 28). Nor is it in man's power, without a special gift and work of God, to alter his creation. Therefore such as are not meet for a single life ought to contract marriage. For no law of man, no vow, can take away the commandment of God and his ordinance. By these reasons the priests do prove that they may lawfully take wives. And it is well known that in the ancient churches priests were married. For Paul saith, ' That a bishop must be chosen which is a husband' (1 Tim.

nia primum ante annos quad-
ringentos Sacerdotes vi coacti
sunt ad cœlibatum, qui quidem
adeo adversati sunt, ut Archie-
piscopus Moguntinus, publicatu-
rus edictum Rom. Pontificis de
ea re, pene ab iratis Sacerdoti-
bus per tumultum oppressus sit.
Et res gesta est tam incivili-
ter, ut non solum in posterum
conjugia prohiberentur, sed etiam
præsentia, contra omnia jura di-
vina et humana, contra ipsos
etiam Canones, factos non solum
a Pontificibus, sed a laudatissi-
mis Synodis, distraherentur. Et
cum senescente mundo paulatim
natura humana fiat imbecillior,
convenit prospicere, ne plura vi-
tia serpant in Germaniam. Por-
ro Deus instituit conjugium, ut
esset remedium humanœ infirmi-
tatis. Ipsi Canones veterem ri-
gorem interdum posterioribus
temporibus propter imbecillita-
tem hominum laxandum esse di-
cunt, quod optandum est, ut fiat
et in hoc negotio. Ac videntur
ecclesiis aliquando defuturi pas-
tores, si diutius prohibeatur con-
jugium.

Cum autem extet mandatum
Dei, cum mos Ecclesiæ notus

iii. 2). And in Germany, not until about four hundred years ago, were the priests by violence compelled to live a single life; who then were so wholly bent against the matter, that the Archbishop of Mentz, being about to publish the Pope of Rome's decree to that effect, was almost murdered in a tumult by the priests in their anger. And the matter was handled so rudely, that not only were marriages forbidden for the time to come, but also such as were then contracted were broken asunder, contrary to all laws divine and human, contrary to the Canons themselves, that were before made not only by Popes, but also by most famous Councils. And seeing that, as the world decayeth, man's nature by little and little waxeth weaker, it is well to look to it, that no more vices do overspread Germany. Furthermore, God ordained marriage to be a remedy for man's infirmity. The Canons themselves do say that the old rigor is now and then in latter times to be released because of the weakness of men. Which it were to be wished might be done in this matter also. And if marriage be forbidden any longer, the churches may at length want pastors.

Seeing, then, that there is a plain commandment of God; seeing the

sit, cum impurus cœlibatus plurima pariat scandala, adulteria et alia scelera, digna animadversione boni magistratus: tamen mirum est, nulla in re majorem exerceri sœvitiam, quam adversus conjugium Sacerdotum. Deus prœcepit honore afficere conjugium. Leges in omnibus rebus publicis bene constitutis, etiam apud Ethnicos, maximis honoribus ornaverunt. At nunc capitalibus pœnis excruciantur, et quidem Sacerdotes, contra Canonum voluntatem, nullam aliam ob causam, nisi propter conjugium. Paulus vocat doctrinam dœmoniorum, quœ prohibet conjugium (1 Tim. iv. 1, 3). Id facile nunc intelligi potest, cum talibus suppliciis prohibitio conjugii defenditur.

Sicut autem nulla lex humana potest mandatum Dei tollere, ita nec votum potest tollere mandatum Dei. Proinde etiam Cyprianus suadet, ut mulieres nubant, quœ non servant promissam castitatem. Verba ejus sunt hœc, Lib. I., Epistola XI.: 'Si autem perseverare nolunt, aut non possunt, melius est, ut nubant, quam ut in ignem deliciis suis cadant; certe nullum fratribus aut sororibus

use of the Church is well known; seeing that impure single life bringeth forth very many offenses, adulteries, and other enormities worthy to be punished by the godly magistrate, it is a marvel that greater cruelty should be showed in no other thing than against the marriage of priests. God hath commanded to honor marriage; the laws in all well-ordered commonwealths, even among the heathen, have adorned marriage with very great honors. But now men are cruelly put to death, yea, and priests also, contrary to the mind of the Canons, for no other cause but marriage. Paul calleth that 'a doctrine of devils' which forbiddeth marriage (1 Tim. iv. 1, 3); which may now very well be seen, since the forbidding of marriage is maintained by such punishments.

But as no law of man can take away the law of God, no more can any vow whatsoever. Therefore Cyprian also giveth counsel, that those women should marry who do not keep their vowed chastity. His words are these, in the 1st Book, the 2d Epistle: 'If they will not or are not able to endure, it is far better they should marry than that they should fall into the fire by their importunate desires. In any wise let them give no offense to their

scandalum faciant.' Et æquitate quadam utuntur ipsi Canones erga hos, qui ante justam ætatem voverunt, quomodo fere hactenus fieri consuevit.

brethren or sisters.' Yea, even the Canons show some kind of justice towards such as before their ripe years did vow chastity, as hitherto the use hath for the most part been.

ART. III.—*De Missa.*[1]

Falso accusantur Ecclesiæ nostræ, quod Missam aboleant ; retinetur enim Missa apud nos, et summa reverentia celebratur. Servantur et usitatæ ceremoniæ fere omnes, præterquam quod Latinis cantionibus [neben lateinischem Gesang] admiscentur alicubi Germanicæ, quæ additæ sunt ad docendum populum. Nam ad hoc unum opus est ceremoniis, ut doceant imperitos.

Et non modo Paulus præcipit (1 Cor. xiv. 9) *uti lingua intellecta populo in ecclesia, sed etiam ita constitutum est humano jure. Assuevit populus, ut una utantur Sacramento, si qui sunt idonei, id quoque auget reverentiam ac religionem publicarum ceremoniarum. Nulli enim admittuntur, nisi antea explorati. Admonentur etiam homines de dignitate et usu Sacramenti, quantam con-*

ART. III.—*Of the Mass.*[1]

Our churches are wrongfully accused to have abolished the Mass. For the Mass is retained still among us, and celebrated with great reverence; yea, and almost all the ceremonies that are in use, saving that with the things sung in Latin we mingle certain things sung in German at various parts of the service, which are added for the people's instruction. For therefore alone we have need of ceremonies, that they may teach the unlearned.

This is not only commanded by St. Paul, to use a tongue that the people understand (1 Cor. xiv. 9), but man's law hath also appointed it. We accustom the people to receive the Sacrament together, if so be any be found fit thereunto; and that is a thing that doth increase the reverence and due estimation of the public ceremonies. For none are admitted, except they be first proved. Besides, we put men in

---

[1] The word here denotes the public service with the holy communion. *Missa* (= *missio*, dismissal) is usually derived from the formula—*missa* or *dismissa est ecclesia*—by which in the ante-Nicene Church the catechumens were dismissed before the communion-service began, hence the division of the ancient service into two distinct parts, the *missa catechumenorum* and the *missa fidelium*.

solationem afferat pavidis con-scientiis, ut discant Deo credere, et omnia bona a Deo expectare et petere.

Hic cultus delectat Deum, talis usus Sacramenti alit pietatem erga Deum. Itaque non viden-tur apud adversarios Missæ ma-jore religione fieri, quam apud nos.

Constat autem hanc quoque publicam et longe maximam querelam omnium bonorum vi-rorum diu fuisse, quod Missæ turpiter prophanarentur, collatæ ad quæstum. Neque enim obscu-rum est, quam late pateat hic abusus in omnibus templis, a qualibus celebrentur Missæ, tan-tum propter mercedem aut sti-pendium, quam multi contra interdictum Canonum celebrent. Paulus autem graviter minatur his, qui indigne tractant Eucha-ristiam, cum ait (1 Cor. xi. 27): 'Qui ederit panem hunc, aut bi-berit calicem Domini indigne, reus erit corporis et sanguinis Domini.' Itaque cum apud nos admonerentur Sacerdotes de hoc peccato, desierunt apud nos pri-vatæ Missæ, cum fere nullæ pri-vatæ Missæ nisi quæstus causa fierent. Neque ignoraverunt hos

mind of the worthiness and use of the Sacrament, how great comfort it bringeth to timid consciences; that they may learn to believe God, and to look for and crave all good things at his hands.

This worship doth please God; such a use of the Sacrament doth nourish piety towards God. There-fore it seemeth not that Masses be more religiously celebrated among our adversaries than with us.

But it is evident that of long time this hath been the public and most grievous complaint of all good men, that Masses are basely pro-faned, being used for gain. And it is not unknown how far this abuse hath spread itself in all churches; of what manner of men Masses are used, only for a reward, or for wages; and how many do use them against the prohibition of the Canons. But Paul doth griev-ously threaten those who treat the Lord's Supper unworthily, saying, 'He that eateth this bread or drink-eth this cup of the Lord unworthi-ly, shall be guilty of the body and blood of the Lord' (1 Cor. xi. 27). Therefore, when the priests among us were admonished of this sin, pri-vate Masses were laid aside among us, seeing that for the most part there were no private Masses but only for lucre's sake. Neither were

abusus episcopi, qui si corre-
xissent eos in tempore, minus
nunc esset dissensionum. Antea
sua dissimulatione multa vitia
passi sunt in Ecclesiam serpere.
Nunc sero incipiunt queri de
calamitatibus Ecclesiæ, cum hic
tumultus non aliunde sumpse-
rit occasionem, quam ex illis
abusibus, qui tam manifesti
erant, ut tolerari amplius non
possent. Magnæ dissensiones de
Missa, de Sacramento extiterunt.
Fortasse dat pœnas orbis tam
diuturnæ prophanationis Missa-
rum, quam in Ecclesiis tot se-
culis toleraverunt isti, qui emen-
dare et poterant et debebant.
Nam in Decalogo scriptum est
(Exod. xx. 7): 'Qui Dei nomine
abutitur, non erit impunitus.'
At ab initio mundi nulla res
divina ita videtur unquam
ad quæstum collata fuisse, ut
Missa.

Accessit opinio, quæ auxit pri-
vatas Missas in infinitum, vide-
licet quod Christus sua passione
satisfecerit pro peccato originis,
et instituerit Missam, in qua
fieret oblatio pro quotidianis de-
lictis, mortalibus et venialibus.
Hinc manavit publica opinio,

the bishops ignorant of these abuses,
and if they had amended them in
time, there had now been less of dissensions. Heretofore, by their dissembling, they suffered much corruption to creep into the Church;
now they begin, though it be late,
to complain of the calamities of the
Church; seeing that this tumult was
raised up by no other mean than
by those abuses, which were so evident that they could no longer be
tolerated. There were many dissensions, concerning the Mass, concerning the Sacrament. And perhaps the world is punished for so
long a profaning of Masses, which
they, who both could and ought to
have amended it, have so many
years tolerated in the churches.
For in the Ten Commandments it
is written, 'He that taketh in vain
the name of the Lord shall not be
held guiltless' (Exod. xx. 7). And
from the beginning of the world
there neither was nor is any divine
thing which seems so to have been
employed for gain as the Mass.

There was added an opinion,
which increased private Masses infinitely: to wit, that Christ by his
passion did satisfy for original sin,
and appointed the Mass, wherein
an oblation should be made for
daily sins, both mortal and venial.
Hereupon a common opinion was

quod Missa sit opus delens pec- cata vivorum et mortuorum ex opere operato. Hic cœptum est disputari, utrum una Missa, dicta pro pluribus, tantundem valeat, quantum singulæ pro sin- gulis. Hæc disputatio peperit istam infinitam multitudinem Missarum. De his opinionibus nostri admonuerunt, quod dis- sentiant a Scripturis Sanctis, et ledant gloriam passionis Christi. Nam passio Christi fuit obla- tio et satisfactio, non solum pro culpa originis, sed etiam pro omnibus reliquis peccatis, ut ad Hebræos (x. 10) scriptum est : 'Sanctificati sumus per oblatio- nem Jesu Christi semel.' Item (Heb. x. 14): ' Una oblatione con- sumavit in perpetuum sanctifi- catos.' Item, Scriptura docet, nos coram Deo justificari per fidem in Christum, cum credi- mus, nobis remitti peccata pro- pter Christum. Jam si Missa delet peccata vivorum et mortu- orum ex opere operato, contin- git justificatio ex opere Missa- rum, non ex fide, quod Scriptu- ra non patitur. Sed Christus jubet (Luke xxii. 19) 'facere in sui memoriam,' quare Missa instituta est, ut fides in iis, qui utuntur Sacramento, recor- detur, quæ beneficia accipiat per

received, that the Mass is a work that taketh away the sins of the quick and the dead, and that for the doing of the work. Here men began to dispute whether one Mass said for many were of as great force as particular Masses said for par- ticular men. This disputation hath brought forth that infinite multi- tude of Masses. Our preachers have admonished concerning these opinions that they do depart from the holy Scriptures, and diminish the glory of the passion of Christ. For the passion of Christ was an oblation and satisfaction, not only for original sin, but also for all oth- er sins ; as it is written in the Epis- tle to the Hebrews (x. 10): ' We are sanctified by the oblation of Jesus Christ once made ;' also, ' By one oblation he hath perfected for- ever them that are sanctified ' (Heb. x. 14). The Scripture also teach- eth that we are justified before God through faith in Christ, when we be- lieve that our sins are forgiven for Christ's sake. Now, if the Mass do take away the sins of the quick and the dead, even for the work's sake that is done, then justification com- eth by the work of Masses, and not by faith ; which the Scripture can not endure. But Christ command- eth us ' to do it in remembrance of himself' (Luke xxii. 19), therefore

Christum, et erigat et consoletur pavidam conscientiam. Nam id est meminisse Christi, beneficia meminisse, ac sentire, quod vere exhibeantur nobis. Nec satis est historiam recordari, quia hanc etiam Judæi et impii recordari possunt. Est igitur ad hoc facienda Missa, ut ibi porrigatur Sacramentum his, quibus opus est consolatione, sicut Ambrosius ait : ' Quia semper pecco, semper debeo accipere medicinam.'

Cum autem Missa sit talis communicatio Sacramenti, servatur apud nos una communis Missa singulis feriis atque aliis etiam diebus, si qui Sacramento velint uti, ubi porrigitur Sacramentum his, qui petunt. Neque hic mos in Ecclesia novus est, nam veteres ante Gregorium non faciunt mentionem privatæ Missæ; de comuni Missa plurimum loquuntur. Chrysostomus ait : ' Sacerdotem quotidie stare ad altare, et alios ad communionem accersere, alios arcere.' Et ex Canonibus veteribus apparet, unum aliquem celebrasse Missam, a quo reliqui presbyteri et diaconi

the Mass has been instituted that faith in them which use the Sacrament may remember what benefits it receiveth by Christ, and that it may raise and comfort the fearful conscience. For this is to remember Christ, to wit, to remember his benefits, and to feel and perceive that they be indeed imparted unto us. Nor is it sufficient to call to mind the history; because that the Jews also and the wicked can do. Therefore the Mass must be used to this end, that there the Sacrament may be reached unto them that have need of comfort; as Ambrose saith, 'Because I do always sin, therefore I ought always to receive the medicine.'

And seeing that the Mass is such a communion of the Sacrament, we do observe one common Mass every holy day, and on other days, if any will use the Sacrament, at which times it is offered to them that desire it. Neither is this custom newly brought into the Church. For the ancients, before Gregory's time, make no mention of any private Mass; of the common Mass they speak much. Chrysostom saith that 'the priest doth daily stand at the altar, and call some unto the Communion, and put back others.' And by the ancient Canons it is evident that some one did celebrate the Mass, of whom the other elders

sumpserunt corpus Domini. Sic enim sonant verba Canonis Niceni : 'Accipiant diaconi secundum ordinem post presbyteros ab episcopo vel a presbytero sacram communionem.' Et Paulus (1 Cor. xi. 33) de communione jubet, ut alii alios expectent, ut fiat communis participatio.

Postquam igitur Missa apud nos habet exemplum Ecclesiæ, ex Scriptura et Patribus, confidimus improbari eam non posse, maxime cum publicæ ceremoniæ magna ex parte similes usitatis serventur; tantum numerus Missarum est dissimilis, quem propter maximos et manifestos abusus certe moderari prodesset. Nam olim etiam in ecclesiis frequentissimis non fiebat quotidie Missa, ut testatur Historia Tripartita Lib. IX. Cap. 38 : 'Rursus autem in Alexandria quarta et sexta feria Scripturæ leguntur, easque Doctores interpretantur, et omnia fiunt præter solennem oblationis morem.'

and deacons did receive the body of the Lord. For so the words of the Nicene Canon do sound : 'Let the deacons in their order, after the elders, receive the holy Communion of a bishop, or of an elder.' And Paul, concerning the Communion, commandeth, 'that one tarry for another' (1 Cor. xi. 33), that so there may be a common participation.

Seeing, therefore, that the Mass amongst us hath the example of the Church, out of the Scripture, and the Fathers, we trust that it can not be disapproved; especially since our public ceremonies are kept, the most part, like unto the usual ceremonies; only the number of Masses is not alike, the which, by reason of very great and manifest abuses, it were certainly far better to be moderated. For in times past also, in the churches whereunto was greatest resort, it was not the use to have Mass said every day, as the Tripartite History, lib. ix. cap. 38, doth witness. 'Again,' saith it, 'in Alexandria, every fourth and sixth day of the week, the Scriptures are read, and the doctors do interpret them; and all other things are done also, except only the celebration of the Eucharist.'

Art. IV.—*De Confessione.*

Confessio in ecclesiis apud nos non est abolita, non enim solet porrigi corpus Domini, nisi antea exploratis et absolutis. Et docetur populus diligentissime de fide absolutionis, de qua ante hæc tempora magnum erat silentium. Docentur homines, ut absolutionem plurimi faciant, quia sit vox Dei et mandato Dei pronuncietur.

Ornatur potestas clavium, et commemoratur, quantam consolationem afferat perterrefactis conscientiis, et quod requirat Deus fidem, ut illi absolutioni tanquam voci de cælo sonanti credamus, et quod illa fides in Christum vere consequatur et accipiat remissionem peccatorum.

Antea immodice extollebantur satisfactiones; fidei et meriti Christi ac justitiæ fidei nulla fiebat mentio; quare in hac parte minime sunt culpandæ ecclesiæ nostræ. Nam hoc etiam adversarii tribuere nobis coguntur, quod doctrina de pœnitentia diligentissime a nostris tractata ac patefacta sit.

Sed de confessione docent, quod enumeratio delictorum non

Art. IV.—*Of Confession.*

Confession is not abolished in our churches. For it is not usual to communicate the body of our Lord, except to those who have been previously examined and absolved. And the people are taught most carefully concerning the faith required to absolution, about which before these times there has been a deep silence. Men are taught that they should highly regard absolution, inasmuch as it is God's voice, and pronounced by God's command.

The power of the keys is honored, and mention is made how great consolation it brings to terrified consciences, and that God requires faith that we believe that absolution as a voice sounding from heaven, and that this faith in Christ truly obtains and receives remission of sins.

Aforetime satisfactions were immoderately extolled; of faith, and the merit of Christ, and justification by faith, no mention was made. Wherefore on this point our churches are by no means to be blamed. For this even our adversaries are compelled to concede in regard to us, that the doctrine of repentance is most diligently treated and laid open by us.

But of Confession our churches teach that the enumeration of sins

sit necessaria, nec sint oneran-
dæ conscientiæ cura enumerandi
omnia delicta, quia impossibile
est omnia delicta recitare, ut
testatur Psalmus (xix. 13): *'De-*
licta quis intelligit?' Item Jere-
mias (xvii. 9): *'Pravum est cor*
hominis et inscrutabile.' Quod
si nulla peccata nisi recitata
remitterentur, nunquam adquie-
scere conscientiæ possent, quia
plurima peccata neque vident,
neque meminisse possunt.

Testantur et veteres scripto-
res enumerationem non esse ne-
cessariam. Nam in Decretis
citatur Chrysostomus, qui sic
ait: 'Non tibi dico, ut te pro-
das in publicum, neque apud
alios te accuses, sed obedire te
volo prophetæ dicenti: "Revela
ante Deum viam tuam." Ergo
tua confitere peccata apud De-
um, verum judicem, cum ora-
tione. Delicta tua pronuncia
non lingua, sed conscientiæ tuæ
memoria,' etc. Et Glosa (De Pœ-
nitentia, Dist. V. Cap. Consideret),
fatetur humani juris esse confes-
sionem [dass die Beicht nicht
durch die Schrift geboten, son-
dern durch die Kirche einge-
setzt sei].

Verum confessio, cum propter
maximum absolutionis beneficium,

is not necessary, nor are consciences to be burdened with the care of enumerating all sins, inasmuch as it is impossible to recount all sins, as the Psalm (xix. 12) testifies: 'Who can understand his errors?' So also Jeremiah (xvii. 9): 'The heart is deceitful above all things, and desperately wicked. Who can know it?' But if no sins were remitted except what were recounted, consciences could never find peace, because very many sins they neither see nor can remember.

The ancient writers also testify that the enumeration is not necessary. For in the Decrees Chrysostom is cited, who speaks thus: 'I do not say to thee that thou shouldst discover thyself in public, or accuse thyself before others, but I would have thee obey the prophet when he says: "Reveal thy way unto the Lord." Therefore with prayer confess thy sins before God the true Judge. Pronounce thine errors, not with the tongue, but with the memory of thy conscience.' And the Gloss (*Of Repentance,* Dist. V., Chap. *Consideret*), admits that Confession is of human right only [is not commanded in Scripture, but has been instituted by the Church].

Nevertheless, on account of the very great benefit of absolution,

tum propter alias conscientia-
rum utilitates apud nos retine-
tur.

as well as for other uses to the conscience, Confession is retained among us.

Art. V.—*De Discrimine Ciborum.*

Art. V.—*Of the Distinction of Meats, and of Traditions.*

Publica persuasio fuit non tantum vulgi, sed etiam docentium in ecclesiis, quod discrimina ciborum et similes traditiones humanæ sint opera utilia ad promerendam gratiam et satisfactoria pro peccatis. Et quod sic senserit mundus, apparet ex eo, quia quotidie instituebantur novæ ceremoniæ, novi ordines, novæ feriæ, nova jejunia, et Doctores in templis exigebant hæc opera tanquam necessarium cultum ad promerendam gratiam, et vehementer terrebant conscientias, si quid omitterent.

Ex hac persuasione de traditionibus multa incommoda in Ecclesia secuta sunt. Primo, obscurata est doctrina de gratia et justitia fidei, quæ est præcipua pars Evangelii, et quam maxime oportet, extare et eminere in Ecclesia, ut meritum Christi bene cognoscatur, et fides, quæ credit remitti peccata propter Christum, longe supra opera collocetur. Quare et Paulus in hunc locum maxime incumbit, legem et traditiones humanas

It hath been a general opinion, not of the people alone, but also of such as are teachers in the churches, that the differences of meats, and such like human traditions, are works available to merit grace, and are satisfactions for sins. And that the world thus thought is apparent by this—that daily new ceremonies, new orders, new holidays, new fasts, were appointed; and the teachers in the churches did exact these works as a service necessary to deserve grace; and they did greatly terrify men's consciences, if aught were omitted.

Of this persuasion concerning traditions many disadvantages have followed in the Church. For first the doctrine of grace is obscured by it, and also the righteousness of faith, which is the principal part of the Gospel, and which it behooveth most of all to stand forth and to have the pre-eminence in the Church, that the merit of Christ may be well known, and faith, which believeth that sins are remitted for Christ's sake, may be exalted far above works. For which cause also Paul

removet, ut ostendat justitiam Christianam aliud quiddam esse, quam hujusmodi opera, videlicet fidem, quæ credit peccata gratis remitti propter Christum. At hæc doctrina Pauli pene tota oppressa est per traditiones, quæ pepererunt opinionem, quod per discrimina ciborum et similes cultus oporteat mereri gratiam et justitiam. In pœnitentia nulla mentio fiebat de fide, tantum hæc opera satisfactoria proponebantur, in his videbatur pœnitentia tota consistere.

Secundo, hæ traditiones obscuraverunt præcepta Dei, quia traditiones longe præferebantur præceptis Dei. Christianismus totus putabatur esse observatio certarum feriarum, rituum, jejuniorum, vestitus. Hæ observationes erant in possessione honestissimi tituli, quod essent vita spiritualis et vita perfecta. Interim mandata Dei juxta vocationem nullam laudem habebant, quod paterfamilias educabat sobolem, quod mater pariebat, quod princeps regebat rem publicam, hæc putabantur esse opera mundana et imperfecta et longe deteriora illis splendidis

lays much stress on this point: he removeth the law and human traditions, that he may show that the righteousness of Christ is a far other thing than such works as these be, namely, a faith, which believeth that sins are freely remitted for Christ's sake. But this doctrine of Paul is almost wholly smothered by traditions, which have bred an opinion, that, by making difference in meats, and such like services, a man should merit grace and justification. In their doctrine of repentance there was no mention of faith; only these works of satisfaction were spoken of: repentance seemed to consist wholly in these.

Secondly, these traditions obscured the commandments of God, because traditions were preferred far above the commandments of God. All Christianity was thought to be an observation of certain holidays, rites, fasts, and attire. These observations were in possession of a most goodly title, that they were the spiritual life and the perfect life. In the mean time God's commandments, touching every man's calling, were of small estimation: that the father brought up his children, that the mother nurtured them, that the prince governed the commonwealth. These were reputed worldly affairs, and imperfect, and far

observationibus. Et hic error valde cruciavit pias conscientias, quæ dolebant se teneri imperfecto vitæ genere, in conjugio, in magistratibus, aut aliis functionibus civilibus, mirabantur monachos et similes, et falso putabant illorum observationes Deo gratiores esse.

Tertio, traditiones attulerunt magna pericula conscientiis, quia impossibile erat omnes traditiones servare, et tamen homines arbitrabantur has observationes necessarios esse cultus. Gerson scribit, 'multos incidisse in desperationem, quosdam etiam sibi mortem conscivisse, quia senserant, se non posse satisfacere traditionibus,' et interim consolationem nullam de justitia fidei et de gratia audierant. Videmus Summistas et Theologos colligere traditiones, et quærere ἐπιεικείας, ut levent conscientias, non satis tamen expediunt, sed interdum magis injiciunt laqueos conscientiis. Et in colligendis traditionibus ita fuerunt occupatæ scholæ et conciones, ut non vacaverit attingere Scripturam, et quærere utiliorem doctrinam de fide, de cruce, de spe, de dignitate civilium rerum, de

inferior to those glittering observances. And this error did greatly torment pious consciences, which were grieved that they were held by an imperfect kind of life, in marriage, in magistracy, or in other civil functions. They had the monks, and such like, in admiration, and falsely imagined that the observances of these men were more grateful to God than their own.

Thirdly, traditions brought great danger to men's consciences, because it was impossible to keep all traditions, and yet men thought the observation of them to be necessary services. Gerson writeth that 'many fell into despair, and some murdered themselves, because they perceived that they could not keep the traditions;' and all this while they never heard the comfort of the righteousness of faith, or of grace. We see the Summists and Divines gather together the traditions, and seek qualifications of them, to unburden men's consciences; and yet all will not serve, but meantime they bring more snares upon the conscience. The schools and pulpits have been so busied in gathering together the traditions, that they had not leisure to touch the Scripture, and to seek out a more profitable doctrine—of faith, of the cross, of hope, of the dignity of civil af-

consolatione conscientiarum in ar-
duis tentationibus. Itaque Gerson
et alii quidam Theologi graviter
questi sunt, se his rixis traditio-
num impediri, quo minus ver-
sari possent in meliore genere
doctrinæ. Et Augustinus vetat
onerare conscientias hujusmodi
observationibus, et prudenter ad-
monet Januarium, ut sciat eas
indifferenter observandas esse ; sic
enim loquitur.

Quare nostri non debent vi-
deri hanc causam temere atti-
gisse, aut odio episcoporum,
ut quidam falso suspicantur.
Magna necessitas fuit, de illis
erroribus, qui nati erant ex tra-
ditionibus male intellectis, ad-
monere ecclesias. Nam Evange-
lium cogit urgere doctrinam in
ecclesiis de gratia et justitia
fidei, quæ tamen intelligi non
potest, si putent homines se me-
reri gratiam per observationes ab
ipsis electas. Sic igitur docue-
runt, quod per observationem
traditionum humanarum non
possimus gratiam mereri, aut
justificari, quare non est sen-
tiendum, quod hujusmodi obser-
vationes sint necessarius cultus.

Addunt testimonia ex Scriptu-

fairs, of the comfort of conscience
in arduous trials. Wherefore Gerson and some other Divines have
made grievous complaints, that they
were hindered by these strifes about
traditions, so that they could not be
occupied in some better kind of doctrine. And Augustine forbiddeth
that men's consciences should be
burdened with observations of this
kind, and doth very prudently warn
Januarius to know that they are to
be observed as things indifferent;
for he so speaketh.

Wherefore our ministers must
not be thought to have touched
this matter rashly, or from hatred
of the bishops, as some do falsely
surmise There was great need
to admonish the churches of those
errors, which did arise from mis-
taking of traditions; for the Gospel compelleth men to urge the doctrine of grace and of the righteousness of faith in the Church; which
yet can never be understood if men
suppose that they can merit remission of sins and justification by observances of their own choice. Thus,
therefore, they teach us that we can
not merit grace or justification by
the observation of man's traditions;
and therefore we must not think
that such observations are necessary service.

Hereunto they add testimonies

ra. Christus (Matt. xv. 3) *excu-*
sat Apostolos, qui non servaverant
usitatam traditionem, quæ tamen
videbatur de re non illicita,
sed media esse, et habere cogna-
tionem cum baptismatibus legis;
et dicit (ver. 9): '*Frustra colunt*
me mandatis hominum.' *Igitur*
non exigit cultum inutilem. Et
paulo post addit (ver. 11): ' *Om-*
ne quod intrat in os, non inqui-
nat hominem.' *Item* (Rom. xiv.
17): '*Regnum Dei non est esca*
aut potus.' Col. ii. 16 : '*Nemo ju-*
dicet vos in cibo, potu, sabbato
aut die festo.' *Item* (ver. 20 sq.):
'*Si mortui estis cum Christo ab*
elementis mundi, quare tanquam
viventes in mundo decreta faci-
tis: Ne attingas, ne gustes, ne
contrectes?'

Ait Petrus (Acts xv. 10, 11):
'*Quare tentatis Deum, impo-*
nentes jugum super cervices di-
scipulorum, quod neque nos ne-
que patres nostri portare potui-
mus, sed per gratiam Domini
nostri Jesu Christi credimus sal-
vari, quemadmodum et illi.' *Hic*
vetat Petrus onerare conscien-
tias pluribus ritibus sive Mosi,
sive aliis. Et (1 Tim. iv. 1–3) *vo-*
cat prohibitionem ciborum '*doc-*

out of the Scriptures. Christ ex-
cuseth his Apostles who kept not
the received tradition (which yet
seemed to be about a matter not
unlawful, but indifferent, and to
have some affinity with the bap-
tisms of the law), and saith, ' They
worship me in vain with the commandments of men' (Matt. xv. 9).
Christ, therefore, exacteth no unprofitable service. And a little
after, he addeth : ' Whatsoever entereth in at the mouth defileth not
the man' (ver. 11). So also (Paul):
' The kingdom of God is not meat
and drink' (Rom. xv. 17). ' Let no
man judge you in meat or drink,
or in respect of the Sabbath-days,
or of a holiday' (Col. ii. 16). Again:
' If ye be dead with Christ from
the rudiments of the world, why, as
though ye lived in the world, are
ye subject to traditions: Touch not,
taste not, handle not ?' (ver. 20, 21).

Peter saith, ' Why tempt ye God,
laying a yoke upon the necks of
the disciples, which neither we nor
our fathers were able to bear? But
we believe that through the grace
of the Lord Jesus Christ we shall
be saved, even as they' (Acts xv.
10, 11). Here Peter forbiddeth to
burden the consciences with many
rites, whether they be of Moses' or
of any others' appointing. And he
(Paul) calleth the forbidding of

trinam dæmoniorum,' quia pugnat cum Evangelio, talia opera instituere aut facere, ut per ea mereamur gratiam, aut quod non possit existere Christianismus sine tali cultu.

Hic objiciunt adversarii, quod nostri prohibeant disciplinam et mortificationem carnis, sicut Jovinianus. Verum aliud deprehendetur ex scriptis nostrorum. Semper enim docuerunt de cruce, quod Christianos oporteat tolerare afflictiones. Hæc est vera, seria et non simulata mortificatio, variis afflictionibus exerceri et crucifigi cum Christo. Insuper docent, quod quilibet Christianus debeat se corporali disciplina aut corporalibus exercitiis et laboribus sic exercere et cœrcere, ne saturitas aut desidia extimulet ad peccandum, non ut per illa exercitia mereamur gratiam, aut satis faciamus pro peccatis. Et hanc corporalem disciplinam oportet semper urgere, non solum paucis et constitutis diebus. Sicut Christus præcipit (Luke xxi. 34): '*Cavete, ne corpora vestra graventur crapula.' Item* (Matt. xvii. 21): '*Hoc genus dæmoniorum non ejicitur nisi jejunio et oratione.' Et Paulus ait* (1 Cor. ix. 27): '*Cas-*

meats 'a doctrine of devils' (1 Tim. iv. 1), because that it is against the Gospel to appoint or do such works, to the end that by them we may merit grace or justification, or as though Christianity could not exist without such service.

Here our adversaries object against us, that our ministers hinder all good discipline and mortification of the flesh, as Jovinian did. But the contrary may be seen by our men's writings. For they have always taught, touching the cross, that Christians ought to bear afflictions. This is the true, earnest, and unfeigned mortification, to be exercised with divers afflictions, and to be crucified with Christ. Moreover they teach that every Christian must so by bodily discipline, or bodily exercises and labor, exercise and keep himself under, that plenty and sloth do not stimulate him to sin; not that he may by such exercises merit grace, or satisfy for sins. And this corporal discipline should be used always, not only on a few and set days; according to the commandment of Christ: 'Take heed lest your hearts be overcharged with surfeiting' (Luke xxi. 34). Again: 'This kind (of devils) goeth not out but by prayer and fasting' (Matt. xvii. 21). And Paul saith, 'I keep under my body,

tigo corpus meum, et redigo in servitutem.' Ubi clare ostendit, se ideo castigare corpus, non ut per eam disciplinam mereatur remissionem peccatorum, sed ut corpus habeat obnoxium et idoneum ad res spirituales et ad faciendum officium juxta vocationem suam. Itaque non damnantur ipsa jejunia, sed traditiones, quæ certos dies, certos cibos præscribunt, cum periculo conscientiæ, tanquam istiusmodi opera sint necessarius cultus.

Servantur tamen apud nos pleræque traditiones, quæ conducunt ad hoc, ut res ordine geratur in Ecclesia; ut ordo lectionum in Missa et præcipuæ feriæ. Sed interim homines admonentur, quod talis cultus non justificet coram Deo, et quod non sit ponendum peccatum in talibus rebus, si omittantur sine scandalo. Hæc libertas in ritibus humanis non fuit ignota Patribus. Nam in Oriente alio tempore servaverunt Pascha quam Romæ, et cum Romani propter hanc dissimilitudinem accusarent Orientem schismatis, admoniti sunt ab aliis, tales mores non oportere ubique similes esse. Et Irenæus inquit: 'Dissonantia jejunii fidei consonantiam non solvit;' sicut

and bring it into subjection' (1 Cor. ix. 27), where he plainly showeth that he did therefore chastise his body; not that by that discipline he might merit remission of sins, but that his body might be apt and fit for spiritual things, and to do his duty according to his calling. Therefore we do not condemn fasts themselves, but the traditions which prescribe certain days and certain meats, with danger to the conscience, as though such works as these were a necessary service.

Yet most of the traditions are observed among us which tend unto this end, that things may be done orderly in the Church; as, namely, the order of Lessons in the Mass and the chiefest holidays. But, in the mean time, men are admonished that such a service doth not justify before God, and that it is not to be supposed there is sin in such things, if they be left undone, without scandal. This liberty in human rites and ceremonies was not unknown to the Fathers. For in the East they kept Easter at another time than they did in Rome; and when they of Rome accused the East of schism for this diversity, they were admonished by others that such customs need not be alike every where. And Irenæus saith: 'The disagree-

et Dist. XII.[1] *Gregorius Papa significat, talem dissimilitudinem non ledere unitatem Ecclesiæ. Et in Historia Tripartita, lib. nono, multa colliguntur exempla dissimilium rituum, et recitantur hæc verba: 'Mens Apostolorum fuit, non de diebus festis sancire, sed prædicare bonam conversationem et pietatem [Glaube und Liebe zu lehren].'*

ment about fasting doth not break off the agreement of faith.' Besides, Pope Gregory, in the 12th Distinction, intimates that such diversity doth not hurt the unity of the Church; and in the *Tripartite History*, lib. 9, many examples of dissimilar rites are gathered together, and these words are there rehearsed: 'The mind of the Apostles was, not to give precepts concerning holidays, but to preach godliness and a holy life [faith and love].'

Art. VI.—*De Votis Monachorum.*

Quid de votis monachorum apud nos doceatur, melius intelliget, si quis meminerit, qualis status fuerit monasteriorum, quam multa contra Canones in ipsis monasteriis quotidie fiebant. Augustini tempore erant libera collegia, postea, corrupta disciplina, ubique addita sunt vota, ut tanquam excogitato carcere disciplina restitueretur.

Additæ sunt paulatim supra vota aliæ multæ observationes. Et hæc vincula multis ante justam ætatem contra Canones injecta sunt.

Art. VI.—*Of Monastic Vows.*

What is taught among us touching the Vows of Monks will be better understood if one call to mind what was the state of monasteries, and how many things were every day committed in the monasteries contrary to the Canons. In Augustine's time cloister-fraternities were free; but afterwards, when discipline was corrupted, vows were every where laid upon them, that, as it were in a newly devised prison, the discipline might be restored again.

Over and besides vows, many other observances by little and little were added. And these bands and snares were cast upon many, before they came to ripe years, contrary to the Canons.

---

[1] Viz., *in Decret.* P. I. Dist. XII. cap. 10, *quod incipit a verbis:* '*Novit fraternitas tua.* Vide *Corp. jur. Can.* ed. Richter, Tom. I. p. 25 sq. (From Bindseil.)

Multi inciderunt errore in hoc vitæ genus, quibus etiam si non deessent anni, tamen judicium de suis viribus defuit. Qui sic irretiti erant, cogebantur manere, etiam si quidam beneficio Canonum liberari possent. Et hoc accidit magis etiam in monasteriis virginum, quam monachorum, cum sexui imbecilliori magis parcendum esset.

Hic rigor displicuit multis bonis viris ante hæc tempora, qui videbant puellas et adolescentes in monasteria detrudi propter victum, videbant, quam infœliciter succederet hoc consilium, quæ scandala pareret, quos laqueos conscientiis injiceret. Dolebant autoritatem Canonum in re periculosissima omnino negligi et contemni.

Ad hæc mala accedebat talis persuasio de votis, quam constat etiam olim displicuisse ipsis monachis, si qui paulo cordatiores fuerunt. Docebant vota paria esse baptismo, docebant se hoc vitæ genere mereri remissionem peccatorum et justificationem coram Deo. Imo addebant, vitam monasticam non tantum justitiam mereri coram

Many through error fell into this kind of life unawares, who, though they wanted not years, yet they wanted discretion to judge of their strength and ability. They who were once got within these nets were constrained to abide in them, though, by the benefit of the Canons, some might be set at liberty. And that fell out rather in the monasteries of nuns than of monks; although the weaker sex ought more to have been spared.

This rigor and severity displeased many good men heretofore, when they saw young maids and young men thrust into monasteries, there to get their living. They saw what an unhappy issue this counsel had, what offenses it bred, and what snares it laid upon consciences. They were grieved that the authority of the Canons was wholly neglected and contemned in a thing most dangerous.

To all these evils there was added such a persuasion concerning vows, as, it is well known, did in former times displease the monks themselves, if any of them were somewhat wiser than the rest. They taught that vows were equal to baptism; they taught that by this kind of life they merited remission of sins and justification before God; yea, they added that the

Deo, sed amplius etiam, quia servaret non modo præcepta, sed etiam consilia Evangelicá. Ita persuadebant monasticam professionem longe meliorem esse baptismo, vitam monasticam plus mereri, quam vitam magistratuum, vitam pastorum et similium, qui in mandatis Dei sine facticiis religionibus suæ vocationi serviunt.

Nihil horum negari potest, extant enim in libris eorum.

Quid fiebat postea in monasteriis? Olim erant scholæ sacrarum literarum, et aliarum disciplinarum, quæ sunt utiles Ecclesiæ, et sumebantur inde pastores et episcopi: nunc alia res est; nihil opus est recitare nota. Olim ad discendum conveniebant: nunc fingunt institutum esse vitæ genus ad promerendam gratiam et justitiam; imo prædicant esse statum perfectionis, et longe præferunt omnibus aliis vitæ generibus a Deo ordinatis.

Hæc ideo recitavimus nihil odiose exaggerantes, ut melius in-

monk's life did not only merit righteousness before God, but more than that, because it observed not only the commandments, but also the counsels of the Gospel. And thus they taught that the monk's profession was better than baptism; that the monk's life did merit more than the life of magistrates, of pastors, and such like, who, in obedience to God's commandment, followed their calling without any such religions of man's making.

None of these things can be denied: they are to be seen in their writings.

What occurred afterwards in the monasteries? In old time they were schools for the study of sacred letters, and other branches of knowledge, which were profitable to the Church; and thence were pastors and bishops taken: but now the case is altered. It is needless to rehearse what is notorious. In old time they came together into such places to learn; but now they feign that it is a kind of life taken up to merit remission of sins and justification; yea, they say it is a state of perfection, and prefer it to all other kinds of life, the kinds that God ordained.

We have therefore mentioned these things, not to excite odium,

telligi posset de hac re doctrina nostrorum.

Primum de his, qui matrimonia contrahunt, sic docent apud nos, quod liceat omnibus, qui non sunt idonei ad cœlibatum, contrahere matrimonium, quia vota non possunt ordinationem ac mandatum Dei tollere. Est autem hoc mandatum Dei (1 Cor. vii. 2): '*Propter fornicationem habeat unusquisque uxorem suam.*' *Neque mandatum solum, sed etiam creatio et ordinatio Dei cogit hos ad conjugium, qui sine singulari Dei opere non sunt excepti, juxta illud* (Gen. ii. 18)): '*Non est bonum homini esse solum.*' *Igitur non peccant isti, qui obtemperant huic mandato et ordinationi Dei.*

Quid potest contra hœc opponi? Exaggeret aliquis obligationem voti, quantum volet, tamen non poterit efficere, ut votum tollat mandatum Dei. Canones docent, 'in omni voto jus superioris excipi:' quare multo minus hœc vota contra mandata Dei valent.

Quodsi obligatio votorum nul-

exaggerating nothing, to the end that the doctrine of our churches touching this matter might be understood.

First, concerning such as contract marriage, thus they teach among us: that it is lawful for any to marry that are not adapted for a single life; forasmuch as vows can not take away God's ordinance and commandment. The commandment of God is, 'To avoid fornication, let every man have his own wife' (1 Cor. vii. 2). And not only the commandment, but also the creation and ordinance of God, compelleth such unto marriage as without the special work of God are not exempted; according to that saying, 'It is not good for man to be alone' (Gen. ii. 18). They, therefore, that are obedient to this commandment and ordinance of God do not sin.

What can be said against these things? Let a man exaggerate the bond of a vow as much as he will, yet can he never bring to pass that the vow shall take away God's commandment. The Canons teach, 'that in every vow the right of the superior is excepted:' much less, therefore, can these vows, which are contrary to God's commandment, be of force.

If so be that the obligation of

las haberet causas, cur mutari possit : nec Romani Pontifices dispensassent; neque enim licet homini obligationem, quæ simpliciter est juris divini, rescindere. Sed prudenter judicaverunt Romani Pontifices æquitatem in hac obligatione adhibendam esse. Ideo sæpe de votis dispensasse leguntur. Nota est historia de Rege Arragonum, revocato ex monasterio, et extant exempla nostri temporis.

Deinde, cur obligationem exaggerant adversarii seu effectum voti, cum interim de ipsa voti natura sileant, quod debet esse in re possibili,[1] quod debet esse voluntarium, sponte et consulto conceptum. At quomodo sit in potestate hominis perpetua castitas, non est ignotum. Et quotusquisque sponte et consulto vovit? Puellæ et adolescentes, priusquam judicare possunt, persuadentur ad vovendum, interdum etiam coguntur.

Quare non est æquum tam rigide de obligatione disputare, cum omnes fateantur contra

vows has no causes why it might be changed, then could not the Roman Pontiffs have dispensed therewith. For neither is it lawful for man to disannul that bond which doth simply belong to the law of God. But the Roman Pontiffs have judged very prudently, that in this obligation there must equity be used; therefore they often, as we read, have dispensed with vows. The history of the King of Arragon, being called back out of a monastery, is well known; and there are examples in our own time.

Secondly, why do our adversaries exaggerate the obligation or the effect of the vow; when in the mean time they speak not a word of the very nature of a vow, that it ought to be in a thing possible, ought to be voluntary, and taken up of a man's own accord, and with deliberation? But it is not unknown how far perpetual chastity is in the power of a man. And how many a one amongst them is there that doth vow of his own accord and well advised? Maidens and youths, before they know how to judge, are persuaded, yea, sometimes also compelled to vow.

Wherefore it is not meet to dispute so rigorously of the obligation, seeing that all men confess that it is

---

[1] The *ed. princeps* reads *possibi*—a typographical error.

voti naturam esse, quod non sponte, quod inconsulto admittitur.

Plerique Canones rescindunt vota ante annum XV. contracta, quia ante illam ætatem non videtur tantum esse judicii, ut de perpetua vita constitui possit. Alius Canon, plus concedens hominum imbecillitati, addit annos aliquot, vetat enim ante annum XVIII. votum fieri. Sed utrum sequemur? maxima pars habet excusationem, cur monasteria deserant, quia plurimi ante hanc ætatem voverunt.

Postremo, etiam si voti violatio reprehendi posset, tamen non videtur statim sequi, quod conjugia talium personarum dissolvenda sint. Nam Augustinus negat debere dissolvi, XXVII. quæst. I. Cap. Nuptiarum; cujus non est levis auctoritas, etiamsi alii postea aliter senserunt.

Quanquam autem mandatum Dei de conjugio videatur plerosque liberare a votis, tamen afferunt nostri et aliam rationem de votis, quod sint

against the nature of a vow, that it is not done of a man's own accord, nor advisedly.

The Canons for the most part disannul vows which are made before fifteen years of age; because that before one come to that age there seemeth not to be so much judgment that determination may be made concerning a perpetual life. Another Canon, permitting more to the weakness of men, doth add some years more; for it forbiddeth a vow to be made before one be eighteen years of age. But which of these shall we follow? The greatest part have this excuse for forsaking monasteries, because most of them vowed before they came to this age.

Last of all, even though the breaking of a vow were to be reprehended, yet it seems not to follow directly that the marriages of such persons are to be dissolved. For Augustine, in his 27th quest. 1st chap. *Of Marriages*, doth deny that they ought to be dissolved; and his authority is not lightly to be esteemed, although others afterwards have thought otherwise.

And although the commandment of God touching wedlock doth free most men from vows; yet our teachers do also bring another reason concerning vows, to show that they are

irrita, quia omnis cultus Dei, ab hominibus sine mandato Dei institutus et electus ad promerendam justificationem et gratiam, impius est, sicut Christus ait (Matt. xv. 9): '*Frustra colunt me mandatis hominum.*' *Et Paulus ubique docet, justitiam non esse quærendam ex nostris observationibus et cultibus, qui sint excogitati ab hominibus, sed contingere eam per fidem credentibus, se recipi in gratiam a Deo propter Christum.*

Constat autem monachos docuisse, quod facticiæ religiones satisfaciant pro peccatis, mereantur gratiam et justificationem. Quid hoc est aliud, quam de gloria Christi detrahere, et obscurare ac negare justitiam fidei? Sequitur igitur, ista vota usitata impios cultus fuisse; quare sunt irrita. Nam votum impium et factum contra mandata Dei non valet, neque enim debet votum vinculum esse iniquitatis, ut Canon dicit.

Paulus dicit (Gal. v. 4): '*Evacuati estis a Christo, qui in lege justificamini, a gratia excidistis.*' *Ergo etiam, qui votis justificari volunt, evacuantur a*
Vol. III.—E

void: because that all the worship of God, instituted of men without the commandment of God, and chosen to merit remission of sins and justification, is wicked; as Christ saith: 'In vain they do worship me, teaching for doctrines the commandments of men' (Matt. xv. 9). And Paul doth every where teach that righteousness is not to be sought of our own observances, and services which are devised by men; but that it cometh by faith to those that believe that they are received into favor by God for Christ's sake.

But it is evident that the monks did teach that these counterfeited religions satisfy for sins, and merit grace and justification. What else is this than to detract from the glory of Christ, and to obscure and deny the righteousness of faith? Wherefore it followeth that these common vows were wicked services, and are therefore void. For a wicked vow, and that which is made against the commandments of God, is one of no force; neither, as the Canon saith, ought a vow to be a bond of iniquity.

Paul saith, 'Christ is become of no effect unto you, whosoever of you are justified by the law; ye are fallen from grace' (Gal. v. 4). They, therefore, who wish to be

Christo, et a gratia excidunt. Nam et hi, qui votis tribuunt justificationem, tribuunt propriis operibus hoc, quod proprie ad gloriam Christi pertinet. Neque vero negari potest, quin monachi docuerint, se per vota et observationes suas justificari et mereri remissionem peccatorum, imo affinxerunt absurdiora, dixerunt se aliis mutuari sua opera. Hæc si quis velit odiose exaggerare, quam multa possit colligere, quorum jam ipsos monachos pudet.

Ad hæc persuaserunt hominibus, facticias religiones esse statum Christianæ perfectionis. An non est hoc justificationem tribuere operibus? Non est leve scandalum in Ecclesia, populo proponere certum cultum ab hominibus excogitatum sine mandato Dei, et docere, quod talis cultus justificet homines: quia justitia fidei, quam maxime oportet tradi in Ecclesia, obscuratur, cum illæ mirificæ religiones angelorum, simulatio paupertatis et humilitatis, et cœlibatus offunduntur oculis hominum.

Præterea obscurantur præcepta

justified by vows, are made void of Christ, and fall from grace. For they also who attribute justification to their vows, attribute to their own works what properly belongs to the glory of Christ. Nor truly can it be denied that the monks taught that they are justified by their vows and observances, and merit the remission of sins; nay, they invented yet greater absurdities, and said they could transfer their good works to others. If any man wished to expand these things, so as to excite odium, how many things might he rehearse whereof the monks themselves are now ashamed!

Moreover, they would persuade men that these invented religious orders are a state of Christian perfection. Or is this not attributing justification to works? It is no light offense in the Church to propound unto the people a certain service devised by men, without the commandment of God, and to teach that such a service doth justify men; because that the righteousness of faith, which ought especially to be taught in the Church, is obscured when those marvelous religions of angels, the pretense of poverty and humility, and of celibacy, are cast before men's eyes.

Moreover, the commandments of

Dei et verus cultus Dei, cum audiunt homines, solos monachos esse in statu perfectionis, quia perfectio Christiana est serio timere Deum, et rursus concipere magnam fidem, et confidere propter Christum, quod habeamus Deum placatum, petere a Deo, et certo expectare auxilium in omnibus rebus gerendis, juxta vocationem; interim foris diligenter facere bona opera, et servire vocationi. In his rebus est vera perfectio et verus cultus Dei, non est in cœlibatu, aut mendicitate, aut veste sordida.

Verum populus concipit multas perniciosas opiniones ex illis falsis preconiis vitæ monasticæ. Audit sine modo laudari cœlibatum : ideo cum offensione conscientiæ versatur in conjugio. Audit solos mendicos esse perfectos : ideo cum offensione conscientiæ retinet possessiones, negotiatur. Audit consilium Evangelicum esse de non vindicando : ideo alii in privata vita non verentur ulcisci, audiunt enim consilium esse, non præceptum. Alii omnes magistratus et civilia officia judicant indigna esse Christianis.

God, and the true worship of God, are obscured when men hear that monks alone are in that state of perfection; because that Christian perfection is this, to fear God sincerely, and again, to conceive great faith, and to trust assuredly that God is pacified towards us, for Christ's sake; to ask, and certainly to look for, help from God in all our affairs, according to our calling; and outwardly to do good works diligently, and to attend to our vocation. In these things doth true perfection and the true worship of God consist: it doth not consist in singleness of life, in beggary, or in vile apparel.

The people doth also conceive many pernicious opinions from these false commendations of the monastic life. They hear celibacy praised above measure; therefore with offense of conscience they live in marriage. They hear that mendicants only are perfect; therefore with offense of conscience they keep their possessions, and buy and sell. They hear that the Gospel only giveth counsel not to take revenge; therefore some in private life are not afraid to avenge themselves; for they hear that it is a counsel, not a commandment. Others do think that all magistracy and civil offices are unworthy Christian men.

Leguntur exempla hominum, qui deserto conjugio, deserta reipublicæ administratione, abdiderunt se in monasteria. Id vocabant fugere ex mundo, et quærere vitæ genus, quod Deo magis placeret, nec videbant, Deo serviendum esse in illis mandatis, quæ ipse tradidit, non in mandatis, quæ sunt excogitata ab hominibus. Bonum et perfectum vitæ genus est, quod habet mandatum Dei. De his rebus necesse est admonere homines. Et ante hæc tempora reprehendit Gerson errorem monachorum de perfectione, et testatur, suis temporibus novam vocem fuisse, quod vita monastica sit status perfectionis.

We read examples of men who, forsaking wedlock, and leaving the government of the commonwealth, have hid themselves in monasteries. This they called flying out of the world, and seeking a kind of life which is more acceptable to God: neither did they see that God is to be served in those commandments which he himself hath delivered, not in the commandments which are devised by men. That is a good and perfect kind of life which hath the commandment of God for it. It is necessary to admonish men of these things. And before these times Gerson did reprehend this error of the monks concerning perfection; and witnesseth, that in his time this was a new saying, that the monastical life is a state of perfection.

Tam multæ impiæ opiniones hærent in votis, quod justificent, quod sint perfectio Christiana, quod servent consilia et præcepta, quod habeant opera supererogationis. Hæc omnia cum sint falsa et inania, faciunt vota irrita.

Thus many wicked opinions do cleave fast unto vows: as that they merit remission of sins and justification, that they are Christian perfection, that they do keep the counsels and commandments, that they have works of supererogation. All these things (seeing they be false and vain) do make vows to be of none effect.

Art. VII.—*De Potestate Ecclesiastica.*

Art. VII.—*Of Ecclesiastical Power.*

Magnæ disputationes fuerunt de potestate Episcoporum, in

There have been great controversies touching the power of Bishops;

*quibus nonnulli incommode com-
miscuerunt potestatem Ecclesiasticam et potestatem gladii.*

*Et ex hac confusione maxima
bella, maximi motus extiterunt,
dum Pontifices, freti potestate
clavium, non solum novos cultus
instituerunt reservatione casu-
um, violentis excommunicationi-
bus conscientias oneraverunt, sed
etiam regna mundi transferre et
imperatoribus adimere imperium
conati sunt.*

*Hœc vitia multo ante repre-
henderunt in Ecclesia homines
pii et eruditi. Itaque nostri ad
consolandas conscientias coacti
sunt ostendere discrimen ecclesi-
asticœ potestatis et potestatis gladii, et docuerunt utramque propter mandatum Dei religiose
venerandam et honore afficien-
dam esse, tanquam summa Dei
beneficia in terris.*

*Sic autem sentiunt, potesta-
tem clavium seu potestatem Episcoporum, juxta Evangelium, potestatem esse seu mandatum Dei,
prœdicandi Evangelii, remittendi
et retinendi peccata, et administrandi Sacramenta. Nam cum*

in which many have incommodi-
ously mingled together the Ecclesiastical power and the power of
the sword.

And out of this confusion there
have sprung very great wars and
tumults, while that the Pontiffs,
trusting in the power of the keys,
have not only appointed new kinds
of service, and burdened men's consciences by reserving of cases, and
by violent excommunications; but
have also endeavored to transfer
worldly kingdoms from one to another, and to despoil emperors of
their power and authority.

These faults did godly and learned men long since reprehend in
the Church; and for that cause
our teachers were compelled, for
the comfort of men's consciences,
to show the difference between the
ecclesiastical power and the power of the sword. And they have
taught that both of them, because
of God's commandment, are duti-
fully to be reverenced and honored,
as the chiefest blessings of God
upon earth.

Now their judgment is this: that
the power of the keys, or the power
of the Bishops, by the rule of the
Gospel, is a power or commandment from God, of preaching the
Gospel, of remitting or retaining
sins, and of administering the Sac-

hoc mandato Christus mittit Apostolos (John xx. 21 sqq.): *'Sicut misit me Pater, ita et ego mitto vos. Accipite Spiritum Sanctum: quorum remiseritis peccata, remittuntur eis, et quorum retinueritis peccata, retenta sunt.'* Mark xvi. 15: *'Ite, prædicate Evangelium omni creaturæ,'* etc.

Hæc potestas tantum exercetur docendo seu prædicando verbum, et porrigendo Sacramenta, vel multis vel singulis juxta vocationem, quia conceduntur non res corporales, sed res æternæ, justitia æterna, Spiritus Sanctus, vita æterna. Hæc non possunt contingere nisi per ministerium verbi et Sacramentorum; sicut Paulus dicit (Rom. i. 16): *'Evangelium est potentia Dei ad salutem omni credenti.'*

Itaque cum potestas ecclesiastica concedat res æternas, et tantum exerceatur per ministerium verbi: non impedit politicam administrationem; sicut ars canendi nihil impedit politicam administrationem. Nam politica administratio versatur circa alias res, quam Evangelium: magistratus defendit non mentes, sed corpora et res corporales

raments. For Christ doth send his Apostles with this charge: 'As the Father hath sent me, even so send I you. Receive ye the Holy Ghost: whosesoever sins ye remit, they are remitted unto them; and whosesoever sins ye retain, they are retained' (John xx. 21–23). 'Go, and preach the Gospel to every creature,' etc. (Mark xvi. 15).

This power is put in execution only by teaching or preaching the Word and administering the Sacraments, either to many or to single individuals, in accordance with their call. For thereby not corporal things, but eternal, are granted; as an eternal righteousness, the Holy Ghost, life everlasting. These things can not be got but by the ministry of the Word and of the Sacraments, as Paul saith, 'The Gospel is the power of God to salvation to every one that believeth' (Rom. i. 16).

Seeing, then, that the ecclesiastical power concerneth things eternal, and is exercised only by the ministry of the Word, it hindereth not the political government any more than the art of singing hinders political government. For the political administration is occupied about other matters than is the Gospel. The magistracy defends not the minds, but the bodies, and

adversus manifestas injurias, et coërcet homines gladio et corporalibus pœnis, ut justitiam civilem et pacem retineat.

Non igitur commiscendæ sunt potestates ecclesiastica et civilis: ecclesiastica suum mandatum habet Evangelii docendi et administrandi Sacramenta. Non irrumpat in alienum officium, non transferat regna mundi, non abroget leges magistratuum, non tollat legitimam obedientiam, non impediat judicia de ullis civilibus ordinationibus aut contractibus, non præscribat leges magistratibus de forma rei publicæ; sicut dicit Christus (John xviii. 36): *'Regnum meum non est de hoc mundo.' Item* (Luke xii. 14): *'Quis constituit me judicem aut divisorem super vos?' Et Paulus ait* (Phil. iii. 20): *'Nostra politia in cœlis est.'* 2 Cor. x. 4: *'Arma militiæ nostræ non sunt carnalia, sed potentia Dei, ad destruendas cogitationes,' etc. Ad hunc modum discernunt nostri utriusque potestatis officia, et jubent utramque honore afficere et agnoscere, utramque Dei donum et beneficium esse.*

Si quam habent Episcopi po-

bodily things, against manifest injuries; and coerces men by the sword and corporal punishments, that it may uphold civil justice and peace.

Wherefore the ecclesiastical and civil powers are not to be confounded. The ecclesiastical power hath its own commandment to preach the Gospel and administer the Sacraments. Let it not by force enter into the office of another; let it not transfer worldly kingdoms; let it not abrogate the magistrates' laws; let it not withdraw from them lawful obedience; let it not hinder judgments touching any civil ordinances or contracts; let it not prescribe laws to the magistrate touching the form of the republic; as Christ saith, 'My kingdom is not of this world' (John xviii. 36). Again, 'Who made me a judge or a divider over you?' (Luke xii. 14). And Paul saith, 'Our conversation [citizenship] is in heaven' (Phil. iii. 20). 'The weapons of our warfare are not carnal, but mighty through God, casting down imaginations,' etc. (2 Cor. x. 4). In this way do our teachers distinguish between the duties of each power one from the other, and do warn all men to honor both powers, and to acknowledge both to be the [highest] gift and blessing of God.

If so be that the Bishops have

testatem gladii, hanc non habent Episcopi ex mandato Evangelii, sed jure humano donatam a regibus et imperatoribus, ad administrationem civilem suorum bonorum. Hæc interim alia functio est, quam ministerium Evangelii.

Cum igitur de jurisdictione Episcoporum quæritur, discerni debet imperium ab ecclesiastica jurisdictione. Porro secundum Evangelium, seu, ut loquuntur, de jure divino, nulla jurisdictio competit Episcopis, ut Episcopis, hoc est, his, quibus est commissum ministerium Verbi et Sacramentorum, nisi remittere peccata, item, cognoscere doctrinam, et doctrinam ab Evangelio dissentientem rejicere, et impios, quorum nota est impietas, excludere a communione Ecclesiæ, sine vi humana, sed Verbo. Hic necessario et de jure divino debent eis Ecclesiæ præstare obedientiam, juxta illud (Luke x. 16): '*Qui vos audit, me audit.*'

Verum cum aliquid contra Evangelium docent aut statuunt, tunc habent Ecclesiæ mandatum Dei, quod obedientiam prohibet (Matt. vii. 15): '*Cavete a Pseudo-*

any power of the sword, they have it not as Bishops by the commandment of the Gospel, but by man's law given unto them of kings and emperors, for the civil government of their goods. This, however, is a kind of function diverse from the ministry of the Gospel.

Therefore, when the question touches the jurisdiction of Bishops, government must be distinguished from ecclesiastical jurisdiction. Again, by the Gospel, or, as they term it, by divine right, Bishops, as Bishops—that is, those who have the administration of the Word and Sacraments committed to them— have no other jurisdiction at all, but only to remit sin, also to take cognizance of [to judge in regard to] doctrine, and to reject doctrine inconsistent with the Gospel, and to exclude from the communion of the Church, without human force, but by the Word [of God], those whose wickedness is known. And herein of necessity the churches ought by divine right to render obedience unto them; according to the saying of Christ, ' He that heareth you heareth me' (Luke x. 16).

But when they teach or determine any thing contrary to the Gospel, then have the churches a commandment of God, which forbiddeth obedience to them: ' Beware

prophetis.' Gal. i. 8: '*Si An- gelus de cœlo aliud Evangelium evangelizaverit, anathema sit.*' 2 Cor. xiii. 8: '*Non possumus ali- quid contra veritatem, sed pro veritate.*' Item (10): '*Data est nobis potestas ad œdificationem, non ad destructionem.*' Sic et Canones præcipiunt (*II. Quæst. VII. Cap. Sacerdotes, et Cap. Oves*). *Et Augustinus contra Petiliani Epistolam inquit :* '*Nec Catholicis Episcopis con- sentiendum est, sicubi forte fal- luntur, aut contra Canonicas Dei Scripturas aliquid senti- unt.*'

Si quam habent aliam vel po- testatem, vel jurisdictionem in cognoscendis certis causis, vide- licet matrimonii, aut decima- rum, etc., hanc habent humano jure ; ubi cessantibus Ordina- riis coguntur Principes, vel in- viti, suis subditis jus dicere, ut pax retineatur.

Præter hæc disputatur, utrum Episcopi seu Pastores habeant jus instituendi ceremonias in Eccle- sia, et leges de cibis, feriis, gra- dibus ministrorum, seu ordini- bus, etc., condendi. Hoc jus qui tribuunt Episcopis, allegant testi- monium (John xvi. 12): '*Adhuc*

of false prophets' (Matt. vii. 15). 'If an angel from heaven preach any other Gospel, let him be ac- cursed' (Gal. i. 8). 'We can not do any thing against the truth, but for the truth' (2 Cor. xiii. 8). Also, 'This power is given us to edify, and not to destroy' (2 Cor. xiii. 10). So do the Canons command (II. Quæst. 7, *Cap. Sacerdotes*, and *Cap. Oves*). And Augustine, in his *Treatise against Petilian's Epistle*, saith, 'Neither must we subscribe to Catholic Bishops, if they chance to err, or determine any thing contrary to the canon- ical divine Scriptures.'

If so be that they have any other power or jurisdiction, in hearing and understanding certain cases, as namely, of Matrimony, and Tithes, etc., they hold it by human right. But when the ordinaries fail [to attend to this office], princes are constrained, whether they wish to do so or not, to declare the law to their subjects, for maintaining of peace.

Besides these things, there is a controversy whether Bishops or Pas- tors have power to institute cere- monies in the Church, and to make laws concerning meats, and holi- days, and degrees, or orders of min- isters, etc. They that ascribe this power to the Bishops allege this

multa habeo vobis dicere, sed non potestis portare modo. Cum autem venerit ille Spiritus veritatis, docebit vos omnem veritatem.' Allegant etiam exemplum Apostolorum, qui prohibuerunt abstinere a sanguine et suffocato. Allegant Sabbatum mutatum in diem Dominicum, contra Decalogum ut videtur. Nec ullum exemplum magis jactatur, quam mutatio Sabbati. Magnam contendunt Ecclesiæ potestatem esse, quod dispensaverit de præcepto Decalogi.

Sed de hac quæstione nostri sic docent, quod Episcopi non habent potestatem statuendi aliquid contra Evangelium, ut supra ostensum est, docent idem Canones IX. Distinct. Porro contra Scripturam est, traditiones condere aut exigere, ut per eam observationem satis faciamus pro peccatis, aut mereamur gratiam et justitiam. Leditur enim gloria meriti Christi, cum talibus observationibus conamur mereri justificationem. Constat autem propter hanc persuasionem, in Ecclesia pene in infinitum crevisse traditiones, oppressa interim doctrina de fide

testimony for it : ' I have yet many things to say unto you, but ye can not bear them now; but when that Spirit of truth shall come, he shall teach you all truth' (John xvi. 12, 13). They allege also the examples of the Apostles, who commanded to abstain from blood, and that which was strangled (Acts xv. 29). They allege the change of the Sabbath into the Lord's day, contrary, as it seemeth, to the Decalogue; and they have no example more in their mouths than the change of the Sabbath. They will needs have the Church's power to be very great, because it hath dispensed with a precept of the Decalogue.

But of this question ours do thus teach : that the Bishops have no power to ordain any thing contrary to the Gospel, as was showed before. The same also do the Canons teach : *Distinct.* 9. Moreover, it is against the Scripture to ordain or require the observation of any traditions, to the end that we may merit remission of sins, and satisfy for sins by them. For the glory of Christ's merit suffers when we seek by such observances to merit justification. And it is very apparent, that through this persuasion traditions grew into an infinite number in the Church. In the mean while, the doctrine concerning faith, and the

et justitia fidei, quia subinde plures feriæ factæ sunt, jejunia indicta, ceremoniæ novæ, novi honores sanctorum instituti sunt, quia arbitrabantur se autores talium rerum his operibus mereri gratiam. Sic olim creverunt Canones pœnitentiales, quorum adhuc in satisfactionibus vestigia quædam videmus.

Item, autores traditionum faciunt contra mandatum Dei, cum collocant peccatum in cibis, in diebus et similibus rebus, et onerant Ecclesiam servitute legis, quasi oporteat apud Christianos ad promerendam justificationem cultum esse similem Levitico, cujus ordinationem commiserit Deus Apostolis et Episcopis. Sic enim scribunt quidam, et videntur Pontifices aliqua ex parte exemplo legis Mosaicæ decepti esse. Hinc sunt illa onera, quod peccatum mortale sit, etiam sine offensione aliorum, in feriis laborare manibus, quod sit peccatum mortale omittere horas Canonicas, quod certi cibi polluant conscientiam, quod jejunia sint opera placantia Deum, quod peccatum in casu reservato non possit remitti, nisi accesserit autoritas reservantis, cum quidem ipsi Canones non de reservatione

righteousness of faith, was quite suppressed, for thereupon there were new holidays made, new fasts appointed, new ceremonies, new worships for saints, instituted; because that the authors of such things supposed by these works to merit grace. After the same manner heretofore did the Penitential Canons increase, whereof we still see some traces in satisfactions.

Moreover, the authors of traditions do contrary to the command of God when they find matters of sin in foods, in days, and like things, and burden the Church with the servitude of the law, as if there ought to be among Christians, in order to merit justification, a service like the Levitical, the ordination of which God has committed to the Apostles and Bishops. For this some of them write, and the Pontiffs in some measure seem to be misled by the example of the Law of Moses. From hence are those burdens, that it is mortal sin, even without offense to others, to do manual labor on the festivals, that it is a mortal sin to omit the Canonical Hours, that certain foods defile the conscience, that fastings are works which appease God; that sin, in a reserved case, can not be pardoned, but by the authority of him that reserved it; whereas the Canons speak only of

culpæ, sed de reservatione pœnæ ecclesiasticæ loquantur.

Unde habent jus Episcopi has traditiones imponendi Ecclesiis ad illaqueandas conscientias, quum Petrus (Acts xv. 10) *vetet ' imponere jugum discipulis,' quum Paulus* (2 Cor. xiii. 10) *dicat, potestatem ipsis datam esse ' ad ædificationem, non ad destructionem.' Cur igitur augent peccata per has traditiones?*

Verum extant clara testimonia, quæ prohibent condere tales traditiones ad promerendam gratiam, aut tanquam necessarias ad salutem. Paulus (Col. ii. 16): *' Nemo vos judicet in cibo, potu, parte diei festi, novilunio aut Sabbatis.' Item* (20): *' Si mortui estis cum Christo ab elementis mundi, quare tanquam viventes in mundo, decreta facitis? non attingas, non gustes, non contrectes; quæ omnia pereunt usu, et sunt mandata et doctrinæ hominum, quæ habent speciem sapientiæ.' Item, ad Titum* (i. 14) *aperte prohibet traditiones: ' Non attendentes Judaicis fabulis et mandatis hominum aversantium veritatem.' Et Christus* (Matt. xv. 14) *inquit de his, qui exigunt traditiones: 'Sinite illos, cæci sunt et duces*

reserving of ecclesiastical penalty, and not of the reserving of the fault.

Whence, then, have the Bishops power and authority of imposing these traditions upon the churches, for the ensnaring of men's consciences, when Peter forbids (Acts xv. 10) ' to put a yoke upon the neck of the disciples,' and St. Paul says (2 Cor. xiii. 10) that the power given him was to edification, not to destruction? Why, therefore, do they increase sins by these traditions?

For there are divers clear testimonies which prohibit the making of such traditions, either to merit grace, or as things necessary to salvation. Paul saith to the Colossians, ' Let no man judge you in meat, or in drink, or in respect of a holiday, or of the new moon, or of the Sabbath days' (Col. ii. 16). Again, ' If ye be dead with Christ from the rudiments of the world, why, as though living in the world, are ye subject to ordinances (Touch not, taste not, handle not; which all are to perish with the using) after the commandments and doctrines of men? which things indeed have a show of wisdom' (Col. ii. 20–23). And to Titus he doth plainly forbid traditions; for he saith, ' Not giving heed to Jewish fables, and to commandments of men, that turn from the truth' (Tit. i. 14). And Christ saith of them

cæcorum.' Et improbat tales cul-
tus (13): ' *Omnis plantatio, quam*
non plantavit Pater meus cœles-
tis, eradicabitur.'

Si jus habent Episcopi one-
randi ecclesias infinitis tradi-
tionibus, et illaqueandi conscien-
tias, cur toties prohibet Scriptu-
ra condere et audire traditiones?
cur vocat eas (1 Tim. iv. 1) *do-*
ctrinas dæmoniorum? num fru-
stra hæc præmonuit Spiritus
Sanctus?

Relinquitur igitur, cum ordi-
nationes institutæ tanquam neces-
sariæ, aut cum opinione prome-
rendæ gratiæ, pugnent cum Evan-
gelio, quod non liceat ullis Epi-
scopis tales cultus instituere aut
exigere. Necesse est enim in ec-
clesiis [*in der Christenheit*] *reti-*
neri doctrinam de libertate Chri-
stiana, quod non sit necessaria
servitus legis ad justificationem;
sicut in Galatis scriptum est
(v. 1): ' *Nolite iterum jugo ser-*
vitutis subjici.' Necesse est reti-
neri præcipuum Evangelii lo-
cum, quod gratiam per fidem in
Christum, gratis consequamur,
non propter certas observationes,
aut propter cultus ab hominibus
institutos.

which urge traditions, 'Let them
alone; they be blind leaders of the
blind' (Matt. xv. 14). And he condemneth such services: 'Every
plant which my heavenly Father
hath not planted shall be rooted
up' (ver. 13).

If Bishops have authority to burden the churches with innumerable
traditions, and to snare men's consciences, why doth the Scripture so
oft forbid to make and to listen to
traditions? Why doth it call them
the doctrines of devils? (1 Tim. iv.
1.) Hath the Holy Ghost warned
us of them to no purpose?

It remaineth, then, that (seeing
ordinances, instituted as necessary,
or with the opinion of meriting
grace, are repugnant to the Gospel)
it is not lawful for any Bishops
to institute or exact such worship.
For it is necessary that the doctrine
of Christian liberty should be maintained in the churches [Christen-
dom]; that the bondage of the law
is not necessary unto justification,
as it is written to the Galatians:
'Be not entangled again with the
yoke of bondage' (Gal. v. 1). It is
necessary that the chiefest point of
all the Gospel should be holden
fast, that we do freely obtain grace,
by faith in Christ, not because of
certain observances, or of services
devised by men.

Quid igitur sentiendum est de die Dominico et similibus ritibus templorum? Ad hæc respondent [die Unsern], quod liceat Episcopis seu Pastoribus facere ordinationes, ut res ordine gerantur in Ecclesia, non ut per illas mereamur gratiam, aut satis faciamus pro peccatis, aut obligentur conscientiæ, ut judicent esse necessarios cultus, ac sentiant se peccare, cum sine offensione aliorum violant. Sic Paulus ordinat (1 Cor. xi. 15) 'ut in congregatione mulieres velent capita' (1 Cor. xiv. 30), 'ut ordine audiantur in Ecclesia interpretes,' etc.

Tales ordinationes convenit ecclesias propter caritatem et tranquillitatem servare eatenus, ne alius alium offendat, ut ordine et sine tumultu omnia fiant in ecclesiis (1 Cor. xiv. 40, comp. Phil. ii. 14): verum ita, ne conscientiæ onerentur, ut ducant res esse necessarias ad salutem, ac judicent se peccare, cum violant eas sine aliorum offensione, sicut nemo dixerit peccare mulierem, quæ in publicum non velato capite procedit, sine offensione hominum.

Talis est observatio diei Do-

What is, then, to be thought of the Lord's day, and of like rites of temples? Hereunto they [ours] answer, that it is lawful for Bishops or Pastors to make ordinances, whereby things may be done in order in the Church; not that by them we may merit grace, or satisfy for sins, or that men's consciences should be bound to esteem them as necessary services, and think that they sin when they violate them, without the offense of others. So Paul ordained, 'that women should cover their heads in the congregation' (1 Cor. xi. 6); 'that the interpreters of Scripture should be heard in order in the Church' (1 Cor. xiv. 27), etc.

Such ordinances it behooveth the churches to keep for charity and quietness' sake, so that one offend not another, that all things may be done in order, and without tumult in the churches (1 Cor. xiv. 40 and Phil. ii. 14), but so that consciences be not burdened, so as to account them as things necessary to salvation, and think they sin when they violate them, without offense of others; as no one would say that a woman sins if she went into public with her head uncovered, provided it were without the offense of men.

Such is the observation of the

minici, Paschatis, Pentecostes et similium feriarum et rituum. Nam qui judicant Ecclesiæ autoritate pro Sabbato institutam esse diei Dominici observationem, tanquam necessariam, longe errant. Scriptura abrogavit Sabbatum, quæ docet omnes ceremonias Mosaicas, post revelatum Evangelium omitti posse. Et tamen, quia opus erat constituere certum diem, ut sciret populus, quando convenire deberet, apparet Ecclesiam [die christliche Kirche] ei rei destinasse diem Dominicum, qui ob hanc quoque causam videtur magis placuisse, ut haberent homines exemplum Christianæ libertatis, et scirent, nec Sabbati nec alterius diei observationem necessariam esse [dass weder die Haltung des Sabbaths, noch eines andern Tages vonnöthen sei].[1]

Extant prodigiosæ disputationes de mutatione legis, de ceremoniis novæ legis, de mutatione Sabbati, quæ omnes ortæ sunt

Lord's day, of Easter, of Pentecost, and like holidays and rites. For they that think that the observation of the Lord's day was appointed by the authority of the Church, instead of the Sabbath, as necessary, are greatly deceived. The Scripture, which teacheth that all the Mosaical ceremonies can be omitted after the Gospel is revealed, has abrogated the Sabbath. And yet, because it was requisite to appoint a certain day, that the people might know when they ought to come together, it appears that the [Christian] Church did for that purpose appoint the Lord's day: which for this cause also seemed to have been pleasing, that men might have an example of Christian liberty, and might know that the observation, neither of the Sabbath, nor of another day, was of necessity.

There are certain marvelous disputations touching the changing of the law, and the ceremonies of the new law, and the change of the Sab-

---

[1] This view of the Christian Sabbath, which was held by all the Reformers, and still prevails on the Continent of Europe, overlooks the important fact that the Sabbath has a moral as well as a ceremonial aspect, and is a part of the *Decalogue*, which the Lord did not come 'to destroy, but to fulfill' (Matt. v. 17, 18; comp. xxii. 37–40; Rom. iii. 31; x. 4). As a periodical day of rest for the body, and worship for the soul, the Sabbath is founded in the physical and moral constitution of man, and reflects the rest of God after the work of creation (Gen. ii. 3). Under this view it is of primitive origin, like the institution of marriage, and of perpetual obligation, like the other commandments of the *Decalogue*. A lax theory of the Sabbath naturally leads to a lax practice, and tends to destroy the blessing of this holy day. The Anglo-American churches have an unspeakable advantage over those of the Continent of Europe in their higher theory and practice of Sabbath observance, which dates from the close of the sixteenth century. Even Puritan rigor is better than the opposite extreme.

ex falsa persuasione, quod oporteat in Ecclesia cultum esse similem Levitico, et quod Christus commiserit Apostolis et Episcopis excogitare novas ceremonias, quæ sint ad salutem necessariæ. Hi errores serpserunt in
Ecclesiam, cum justitia fidei non
satis clare doceretur. Aliqui
disputant, diei Dominici observationem non quidem juris divini esse, sed quasi juris divini;
præscribunt de feriis, quatenus
liceat operari. Hujusmodi disputationes quid sunt aliud, nisi
laquei conscientiarum? Quanquam enim conentur epiikeizare
[zu lindern und epiiciren] traditiones, tamen nunquam potest
æquitas deprehendi [so kann
man doch keine ἐπιείκειαν oder
Linderung treffen], donec manet
opinio necessitatis, quam manere
necesse est, ubi ignorantur justitia fidei et libertas Christiana.

Apostoli jusserunt (Acts xv.
20) 'abstinere a sanguine.' Quis
nunc observat? Neque tamen
peccant, qui non observant, quia
ne ipsi quidem Apostoli voluerunt onerare conscientias tali
servitute, sed ad tempus prohibuerunt propter scandalum. Est
enim perpetuo voluntas Evangelii [das Hauptstück christlicher
Lehre] consideranda in decreto.

bath: which all arose from the false
persuasion, that there should be a
service in the Church, like to the
Levitical; and that Christ committed to the Apostles and Bishops the devising new ceremonies,
which should be necessary to salvation. These errors crept into the
Church, when the righteousness of
faith was not plainly enough taught.
Some dispute that the observation
of the Lord's day is not indeed of
the law of God, but as it were of
the law of God; and touching holidays, they prescribe how far it is
lawful to work in them. What else
are such disputations but snares for
men's consciences? For though
they seek to moderate traditions,
yet the equity of them can never
be perceived so long as the opinion
of necessity remaineth; which must
needs remain, where the righteousness of faith and Christian liberty
are not known.

The Apostles commanded 'to
abstain from blood' (Acts xv. 20).
Who observeth that nowadays?
And yet they do not sin that observe it not. For the Apostles
themselves would not burden men's
consciences with such a servitude;
but they forbade it for a time, because of scandal. For in the decree, the will of the Gospel is always to be considered

Vix ulli Canones servantur accurate, et multi quotidie exolescunt apud illos etiam, qui diligentissime defendunt traditiones. Nec potest conscientiis consuli, nisi hæc æquitas servetur [wo diese Linderung nicht gehalten wird], ut sciamus eos sine opinione necessitatis servari, nec lædi conscientias, etiamsi traditiones exolescant.

Facile autem possent Episcopi legitimam obedientiam retinere, si non urgerent servare traditiones, quæ bona conscientia servari non possunt. Nunc imperant cœlibatum, nullos recipiunt, nisi jurent se puram Evangelii doctrinam nolle docere. Non petunt Ecclesiæ, ut Episcopi honoris sui jactura sarciant concordiam, quod tamen decebat bonos Pastores facere. Tantum petunt, ut injusta onera remittant, quæ nova sunt, et præter consuetudinem Ecclesiæ Catholicæ [wider den Gebrauch der christlichen gemeinen Kirchen] recepta. Fortassis initio quædam constitutiones habuerunt probabiles causas, quæ tamen posterioribus temporibus non congruunt. Apparet etiam quasdam errore receptas esse; quare Pontificiæ clementiæ esset,

Scarcely any Canons are precisely kept; and many grow out of use daily, yea, even among them that do most busily defend traditions. Neither can there be sufficient care had of men's consciences, except this equity be kept, that men should know that such rites are not to be observed with any opinion of necessity, and that men's consciences are not hurt, though traditions grow out of use.

The Bishops might easily retain lawful obedience, if they would not urge men to observe such traditions as can not be kept with a good conscience. Now they command single life; and they admit none, except they will swear not to teach the pure doctrine of the Gospel. The churches do not desire of the Bishops that they would repair peace and concord with the loss of their honor (which yet good pastors ought to do): they only desire that they would remit unjust burdens, which are both new and received contrary to the custom of the Catholic [Christian Universal] Church. It may well be that some constitutions had some probable reasons when they began, which yet will not agree to latter times. It is evident that some were received through error. Wherefore it were a matter for the pontifical;

illas nunc mitigare, quia talis mutatio non labefacit Ecclesiæ unitatem. Multæ enim traditiones humanæ tempore mutatæ sunt, ut ostendunt ipsi Canones. Quod si non potest impetrari, ut relaxentur observationes, quæ sine peccato non possunt præstari, oportet nos regulam Apostolicam sequi (Acts v. 29), *quæ præcipit, 'Deo magis obedire, quam hominibus.'*

Petrus (1 Pet. v. 3) *vetat Episcopos dominari, et ecclesiis imperare. Nunc non id agitur, ut dominatio eripiatur Episcopis, sed hoc unum petitur, ut patiantur Evangelium pure doceri, et relaxent paucas quasdam observationes, quæ sine peccato servari non possunt. Quod si nihil remiserint, ipsi viderint, quomodo Deo rationem reddituri sint, quod pertinacia sua causam schismati præbent* [*Spaltung und Schisma, das sie doch billig sollen verhüten helfen*].

gentleness to mitigate them now; for such a change would not overthrow the unity of the Church. For many human traditions have been changed in time, as the Canons themselves declare. But if it can not be obtained that those observances may be relaxed which can not be kept without sin, then must we follow the Apostles' rule, which willeth 'to obey God rather than men' (Acts v. 29).

Peter forbiddeth Bishops to be lords, and to be imperious over the churches (1 Pet. v. 3). Now our meaning is not to have rule taken from the Bishops; but this one thing only is requested at their hands, that they would suffer the Gospel to be purely taught, and that they would relax a few observances, which can not be held without sin. But if they will remit none, let them look how they will give account to God for this, that by their obstinacy they afford cause of schism [division and schism, which it were yet fit they should aid in avoiding].

EPILOGUS.

Hi sunt præcipui articuli, qui videntur habere controversiam. Quanquam enim de pluribus abusibus dici poterat, tamen, ut fugeremus prolixitatem, præcipua complexi sumus, ex quibus cætera facile judicari possunt. Magnæ querelæ fuerunt de indulgentiis, de peregrinationibus, de abusu excommuni-

CONCLUSION.

These are the principal articles which seem to be matters of controversy. For although we might speak of more abuses, yet that we may avoid undue length we have embraced a few, whereby it is easy to judge of the others. Great have been the complaints about indulgences, about pilgrimages, about the abuse of

cationis. Parochiæ multipliciter vexabantur per Stationarios. Infinitæ contentiones erant pastoribus cum monachis, de jure parochiali, de confessionibus, de sepulturis, de extraordinariis concionibus, et de aliis innumerabilibus rebus. Hujusmodi negotia prætermisimus, ut illa, quæ sunt in hac causa præcipua, breviter proposita, facilius cognosci possent. Neque hic quicquam ad ullius contumeliam dictum aut collectum est. Tantum ea recitata sunt, quæ videbantur necessario dicenda esse, ut intelligi possit in doctrina ac ceremoniis apud nos nihil esse receptum contra Scripturam aut Ecclesiam Catholicam [gemeiner christlichen Kirchen], quia manifestum est, nos diligentissime cavisse, ne qua nova et impia dogmata in ecclesias nostras serperent [sich einflechte, einreisse und überhand nehme].

Hos articulos supra scriptos voluimus exhibere juxta edictum C. M. in quibus confessio nostra exstaret, et eorum, qui apud nos docent, doctrinæ summa cerneretur. Si quid in hac confessione desiderabitur, parati sumus latiorem informationem, Deo volente, juxta Scripturas exhibere [der daran Mangel hält, dem ist man ferner Bericht mit Grund göttlicher heiliger Schrift zu thun erbötig].

Cæsareæ Majestatis Vestræ,

fideles et subditi:

JOANNES, *Dux Saxoniæ, Elector.*
GEORGIUS, *Marchio Brandenburgensis.*
ERNESTUS, *Dux Luneburgensis.*
PHILIPPUS, *Landgravius Hessorum.*
JOANNES FRIDERICUS, *Dux Saxoniæ.*
FRANCISCUS, *Dux Luneburgensis.*
VOLFGANGUS, *Princeps ab Anhalt.*
SENATUS *Magistratusque Nurnbergensis.*
SENATUS *Reutlingensis.*

excommunication. The parishes have been vexed in manifold ways by the *stationarii.* Endless contentions have arisen between the pastors and the monks about parochial law, about confession, about burials, about sermons on extraordinary occasions, and about other things without number. Things of this sort we pass over, that those which are chief in this matter, being briefly set forth, may more easily be noted. Nor has any thing been here said or adduced for the purpose of casting reproach on any one. Those things only have been enumerated which it seemed necessary to say, that it might be understood that in doctrine and ceremonials among us there is nothing received contrary to Scripture or to the Catholic [Universal Christian] Church, inasmuch as it is manifest that we have diligently taken heed that no new and godless doctrines should creep into our churches.

In accordance with the Edict of His Imperial Majesty, we wish to present these articles above written, in which is our Confession, and in which is seen a summary of the doctrine of those who teach among us. If any thing be lacking in this Confession, we are prepared, God willing, to present ampler information, in accordance with the Scriptures.

Your Imperial Majesty's

most faithful and humble,

JOHN, Duke of Saxony, Elector.
GEORGE, Margrave of Brandenburg.
ERNEST, Duke of Luneburg.
PHILIP, Landgrave of Hesse.
JOHN FREDERICK, Duke of Saxony.
FRANCIS, Duke of Luneburg.
WOLFGANG, Prince of Anhalt.
SENATE and MAGISTRACY of Nuremberg.
SENATE of Reutlingen.

LUTHER'S SMALL CATECHISM. A.D. 1529.

[The German text is taken from the third edition, which appeared in Wittenberg, 1531, and was accurately republished by Dr. Schneider, Berlin, 1853. The orthography is modernized, and some words (as *Erstes Hauptstück, Gebot*) are inserted in parentheses from the later editions. The English translation is more literal than those in use among the Lutheran churches in America. On Luther's *Catechisms*, see Vol. I. § 43, pp. 245 sqq.]

Dr. Martin Luther's
Enchiridion : Der Kleine Catechismus.

Dr. Martin Luther's Enchiridion, or Small Catechism.

(Das Erste Hauptstück.)

PART I.

Die Zehn Gebote,

THE TEN COMMANDMENTS,

wie sie ein Hausvater seinem Gesinde einfältiglich fürhalten soll.

As they should be clearly and simply explained to every household by the head of the family.

Das Erste (Gebot).

THE FIRST COMMANDMENT.

Du sollst nicht andere Götter haben.

Thou shalt have no other gods.

Was ist das? Antwort:

What does this mean? Answer:

Wir sollen Gott über alle Dinge fürchten, lieben und vertrauen.

We should fear and love God, and trust in him, above all things.

Das Zweite (Gebot).

THE SECOND COMMANDMENT.

Du sollst den Namen deines Gottes nicht unnützlich führen.

Thou shalt not take the name of thy God in vain.

Was ist das? Antwort:

What does this mean? Answer:

Wir sollen Gott fürchten und lieben, daß wir bei seinem Namen nicht fluchen, schwören, zaubern, lügen oder trügen; sondern denselbigen in allen Nöthen anrufen, beten, loben und danken.

We should so fear and love God as not to curse, swear, conjure, lie, or deceive, by his name; but call upon it in every time of need, pray, praise, and give thanks.

Das Dritte (Gebot).

THE THIRD COMMANDMENT.

Du sollst den Feiertag heiligen.

Thou shalt keep holy the Sabbath day.

Was ist das? Antwort:

What does this mean? Answer:

Wir sollen Gott fürchten und lieben, daß wir die Predigt und sein Wort

We should so fear and love God as not to despise preaching and his

nicht verachten; sondern dasselbige heilig halten, gerne hören und lernen.

Word, but deem it holy, and willingly hear and learn it.

Das Vierte (Gebot).

Du sollst deinen Vater und deine Mutter ehren.[1]

Was ist das? Antwort:

Wir sollen Gott fürchten und lieben, daß wir unsere Eltern und Herren nicht verachten noch erzürnen; sondern sie in Ehren halten, ihnen dienen, gehorchen, sie lieb und werth haben.

THE FOURTH COMMANDMENT.

Thou shalt honor thy father and thy mother.[1]

What does this mean? Answer:

We should so fear and love God as not to despise nor provoke our parents and rulers, but honor, serve, obey, love, and esteem them.

Das Fünfte (Gebot).

Du sollst nicht tödten.

Was ist das? Antwort:

Wir sollen Gott fürchten und lieben, daß wir unserm Nächsten an seinem Leibe keinen Schaden noch Leid thun; sondern ihm helfen und fördern in allen Leibesnöthen.

THE FIFTH COMMANDMENT.

Thou shalt not kill.

What does this mean? Answer:

We should so fear and love God as not to do our neighbor any injury or harm in his body, but help and befriend him in all bodily troubles.

Das Sechste (Gebot).

Du sollst nicht ehebrechen.

Was ist das? Antwort:

Wir sollen Gott fürchten und lieben, daß wir keusch und züchtig leben in Worten und Werken, und ein Jeglicher sein Gemahl lieben und ehren.

THE SIXTH COMMANDMENT.

Thou shalt not commit adultery.

What does this mean? Answer:

We should so fear and love God as to be chaste and pure in our words and deeds, and that husband and wife should love and honor each other.

Das Siebente (Gebot).

Du sollst nicht stehlen.

Was ist das? Antwort:

Wir sollen Gott fürchten und lieben, daß wir unsers Nächsten Geld oder

THE SEVENTH COMMANDMENT.

Thou shalt not steal.

What does this mean? Answer:

We should so fear and love God as not to take our neighbor's money

---

[1] In the edition of 1542 the blessing is added: 'That thy days may be long upon the land which the Lord thy God giveth thee.'

Gut nicht nehmen, noch mit fälscher Waare oder Handel an uns bringen; sondern ihm sein Gut und Nahrung helfen beßern und behüten.

or property, nor get it by false ware or dealing, but help him to improve and protect his property and livelihood.

Das Achte (Gebot).

Du sollst nicht falsch Zeugniß reden wider deinen Nächsten.

Was ist das? Antwort:

Wir sollen Gott fürchten und lieben, daß wir unsern Nächsten nicht fälschlich belügen, verrathen, afterreden, oder bösen Leumund machen; sondern sollen ihn entschuldigen und Gutes von ihm reden, und Alles zum Besten kehren.[1]

THE EIGHTH COMMANDMENT.

Thou shalt not bear false witness against thy neighbor.

What does this mean? Answer:

We should so fear and love God as not to belie, betray, or slander our neighbor, nor injure his character, but defend him, speak well of him, and make the best of all he does.[1]

Das Neunte (Gebot).

Du sollst nicht begehren deines Nächsten Haus.

Was ist das? Antwort:

Wir sollen Gott fürchten und lieben, daß wir unserm Nächsten nicht mit List nach seinem Erbe oder Hause stehen, und mit einem Schein des Rechts an uns bringen; sondern ihm dasselbige zu behalten förderlich und dienstlich sein.

THE NINTH COMMANDMENT.

Thou shalt not covet thy neighbor's house.

What does this mean? Answer:

We should so fear and love God as not to try to defraud our neighbor of his inheritance or home, nor obtain it under pretext of a legal right, but aid and assist him to keep it.

Das Zehnte (Gebot).

Du sollst nicht begehren deines Nächsten Weib, Knecht, Magd, Vieh, oder was sein ist.

Was ist das? Antwort:

Wir sollen Gott fürchten und lieben, daß wir unserm Nächsten nicht

THE TENTH COMMANDMENT.

Thou shalt not covet thy neighbor's wife, nor his man-servant, nor his maid-servant, nor his cattle, nor any thing that is his own.

What does this mean? Answer:

We should so fear and love God as not to detach, extort, or alienate

---

[1] Or, 'Put the most charitable construction on all his actions.'—Edition of the Lutheran Board of Publications, Philadelphia.

sein Weib, Gesinde oder Vieh abspan=
nen, abbringen oder abwendig machen;
sondern dieselbigen anhalten, daß sie
bleiben und thun was sie schuldig sind.

Was saget nun Gott von diesen Geboten
allen? Antwort:

Er saget also:

Ich der HERR dein Gott bin
ein eifriger Gott, der über die,
so mich hassen, die Sünde der
Väter heimsuchet an den Kin=
dern bis ins dritte und vierte
Glied; aber denen, so mich lie=
ben und meine Gebote halten,
thue ich wohl in tausend Glied.

Was ist das? Antwort:

Gott dräuet zu strafen Alle, die
diese Gebote übertreten; darum sollen
wir uns fürchten vor seinem Zorn, und
nicht wider solche Gebote thun. Er
verheißet aber Gnade und alles Gutes
Allen, die solche Gebote halten; darum
sollen wir ihn auch lieben und ver=
trauen, und gerne thun nach seinen
Geboten.

from our neighbor his wife, servants, or cattle, but induce them to
stay and do their duty.

What does God say about all these Commandments?

He says this:

*I the Lord thy God am a jeal-
ous God, visiting the iniquity of
the fathers upon the children unto
the third and fourth generation
of them that hate me, and showing
mercy unto thousands of them that
love me and keep my commandments.*

What does this mean? Answer:

God threatens to punish all who
transgress these Commandments:
we should, therefore, fear his anger, and do nothing against such
Commandments. But he promises
grace and every blessing to all who
keep them: we should, therefore,
love and trust in him, and gladly
obey his Commandments.

(Das Zweite Hauptstück.)

Der Glaube,

wie ein Hausvater denselbigen seinem Gesinde
aufs einfältigste vorhalten soll.

Der Erste Artikel.

Von der Schöpfung.

Ich glaube an Gott den Va=
ter allmächtigen, Schöpfer Him=
mels und der Erden.

PART II.

THE CREED,

*As it should be clearly and simply explained
to every household by the head of the family.*

THE FIRST ARTICLE.

Of Creation.

*I believe in God the Father
Almighty, Maker of heaven and
earth.*

Was ist das? Antwort:

Ich glaube, daß mich Gott geschaffen hat sammt allen Creaturen, mir Leib und Seele, Augen, Ohren und alle Glieder, Vernunft und alle Sinne gegeben hat und noch erhält; dazu Kleider und Schuh, Essen und Trinken, Haus und Hof, Weib und Kind, Acker, Vieh und alle Güter; mit aller Nothdurft und Nahrung dieses Leibes und Lebens reichlich und täglich versorget, wider alle Fährlichkeit beschirmet, und vor allem Uebel behütet und bewahret; und das alles aus lauter väterlicher, göttlicher Güte und Barmherzigkeit, ohne alle mein Verdienst und Würdigkeit; deß alles ich ihm zu danken und zu loben, und dafür zu dienen und gehorsam zu sein schuldig bin. Das ist gewißlich wahr.

What does this mean? Answer:

I believe that God has created me and all that exists; that he has given and still preserves to me body and soul, eyes, ears, and all my limbs, my reason and all my senses; and also clothing and shoes, food and drink, house and home, wife and child, land, cattle, and all my property; that he provides me richly and daily with all the necessaries of life, protects me from all danger, and preserves and guards me against all evil; and all this out of pure paternal, divine goodness and mercy, without any merit or worthiness of mine; for all which I am in duty bound to thank, praise, serve, and obey him. This is most certainly true.

Der Zweite Artikel.
Von der Erlösung.

Und an Jesum Christum, seinen einigen Sohn, unsern HERRN, der empfangen ist vom heiligen Geiste, geboren von der Jungfrau Maria, gelitten unter Pontio Piláto, gekreuziget, gestorben und begraben, niedergefahren zur Hölle, am dritten Tage auferstanden von den Todten, aufgefahren gen Himmel, sitzend zur Rechten Gottes

THE SECOND ARTICLE.
Of Redemption.

And in Jesus Christ his only Son, our Lord; who was conceived by the Holy Ghost, born of the Virgin Mary; suffered under Pontius Pilate; was crucified, dead, and buried; he descended into hell; the third day he rose again from the dead; he ascended into heaven, and sitteth on the right hand of God the Father Almighty; from thence he shall

des allmächtigen Vaters, von dannen er kommen wird, zu richten die Lebendigen und die Todten.

Was ist das? Antwort:

Ich glaube, daß Jesus Christus, wahrhaftiger Gott vom Vater in Ewigkeit geboren und auch wahrhaftiger Mensch von der Jungfrau Maria geboren, sei mein HERR, der mich verlornen und verdammten Menschen erlöset hat, erworben, gewonnen [und][1] von allen Sünden, vom Tode und von der Gewalt des Teufels, nicht mit Gold oder Silber, sondern mit seinem heiligen, theuren Blute, und mit seinem unschuldigen Leiden und Sterben; auf daß ich sein eigen sei, und in seinem Reiche unter ihm lebe, und ihm diene in ewiger Gerechtigkeit, Unschuld und Seligkeit; gleichwie er ist auferstanden vom Tode, lebet und regieret in Ewigkeit. Das ist gewißlich wahr.

Der Dritte Artikel.
Von der Heiligung.

Ich glaube an den heiligen Geist, eine heilige christliche[2] Kirche, die Gemeine der Heiligen, Vergebung der Sünden, Auferstehung des Fleisches, und ein ewiges Leben. Amen.

come to judge the quick and the dead.

What does this mean? Answer:

I believe that Jesus Christ, true God, begotten of the Father from eternity, and also true man, born of the Virgin Mary, is my Lord; who has redeemed me, a lost and condemned man, secured and delivered me [even][1] from all sins, from death, and from the power of the devil, not with gold or silver, but with his holy, precious blood, and with his innocent sufferings and death; in order that I might be his own, live under him in his kingdom, and serve him in everlasting righteousness, innocence, and blessedness, even as he is risen from the dead, and lives and reigns forever. This is most certainly true.

THE THIRD ARTICLE.
Of Sanctification.

I believe in the Holy Ghost; one holy Christian[2] Church; the Communion of Saints; the Forgiveness of Sins; the Resurrection of the Body; and the Life Everlasting. Amen.

---

[1] This *und* (which, if not a typographical error, must have the force of *und zwar*, even) is found in all the editions of Luther, but is now usually omitted as superfluous.

[2] Luther omitted the word *Catholic*, and substituted for it *Christian*. The Heidelberg Catechism combines the two: '*allgemeine christliche Kirche.*'

Was ist das? Antwort:

Ich glaube, daß ich nicht aus eigener Vernunft noch Kraft an Jesum Christ meinen Herrn glauben oder zu ihm kommen kann; sondern der heilige Geist hat mich durchs Evangelium berufen, mit seinen Gaben erleuchtet, im rechten Glauben geheiliget und erhalten; gleich= wie er die ganze Christenheit auf Erden berufet, sammlet, erleuchtet, heiliget, und bei Jesu Christo erhält im rechten eini= gen Glauben; in welcher Christenheit er mir und allen Gläubigen täglich alle Sünden reichlich vergiebt; und am jüngsten Tage mich und alle Todten auferwecken wird, und mir sammt allen Gläubigen in Christo ein ewiges Leben geben wird. Das ist gewißlich wahr.

What does this mean? Answer:

I believe that I can not, by my own reason or strength, believe in Jesus Christ my Lord, or come to him; but the Holy Ghost has called me through the Gospel, enlightened me by his gifts, and sanctified and preserved me in the true faith; just as he calls, gathers, enlightens, and sanctifies the whole Christian Church on earth, and preserves it in union with Jesus Christ in the one true faith; in which Christian Church he daily forgives richly all my sins, and the sins of all be-lievers; and will raise up me and all the dead at the last day, and will grant everlasting life to me and to all who believe in Christ. This is most certainly true.

(Das Dritte Hauptstück.)

Das Vaterunser,

wie ein Hausvater dasselbige seinem Gesinde aufs einfältigste fürhalten soll.

Vater unser,[1] der du bist im Himmel.

PART III.

THE LORD'S PRAYER,

As it should be clearly and simply explained to every household by the head of the family.

Our Father, who art in heaven.

Was ist das? Antwort:

Gott will damit uns locken, daß wir glauben sollen, Er sei unser rechter Vater, und wir seine rechten Kinder, auf daß wir getrost und mit aller

What does this mean? Answer:

God would thereby affectionate-ly encourage us to believe that he is truly our Father, and that we are truly his children, so that we may

---

[1] Luther, in his Catechism, retained the old form (*Paternoster*), but in his translation of the Bible he chose the modern *Unser Vater* (*Our Father*). In the first two editions (1529) the explanation of the address does not occur.

Zuverſicht ihn bitten ſollen, wie die lieben Kinder ihren lieben Vater.

cheerfully and with all confidence pray to him, even as dear children ask their dear father.

Die Erſte Bitte.

Geheiliget werde dein Name.

Was iſt das? Antwort:

Gottes Name iſt zwar an ihm ſelbſt heilig; aber wir bitten in dieſem Gebet, daß er bei uns auch heilig werde.

Wie geſchieht das? Antwort:

Wo das Wort Gottes lauter und rein gelehret wird, und wir auch heilig, als die Kinder Gottes, darnach leben: des [dazu] hilf uns, lieber Vater im Himmel! Wer aber anders lehret und lebet, denn das Wort Gottes lehret, der entheiliget unter uns den Namen Gottes. Davor behüte uns, himmliſcher Vater!

THE FIRST PETITION.

Hallowed be thy name.

What does this mean? Answer:

The name of God is indeed in itself holy; but we pray in this petition that it may be hallowed also by us.

How can this be done? Answer:

When the Word of God is taught in its truth and purity, and we, as the children of God, lead holy lives accordingly. To this may our blessed Father in heaven help us! But whoever teaches and lives otherwise than as God's Word teaches, profanes the name of God among us. From this preserve us, heavenly Father!

Die Andere [Zweite] Bitte.

Dein Reich komme.

Was iſt das? Antwort:

Gottes Reich kommt wohl ohne unſer Gebet von ihm ſelbſt; aber wir bitten in dieſem Gebet, daß es auch zu uns komme.

Wie geſchieht das? Antwort:

Wenn der himmliſche Vater uns ſeinen heiligen Geiſt giebt, daß wir ſeinem heiligen Worte durch ſeine Gnade glauben, und göttlich leben, hier zeitlich und dort ewiglich.

THE SECOND PETITION.

Thy kingdom come.

What does this mean? Answer:

The kingdom of God comes indeed of itself, without our prayer; but we pray in this petition that it may come also to us.

How can this be done? Answer:

When our heavenly Father gives us his Holy Spirit, so that by his grace we believe his holy Word, and live a godly life here in time, and hereafter in eternity.

Die Dritte Bitte.

Dein Wille geschehe, wie im Himmel, also auch auf Erden.

Was ist das? Antwort:

Gottes guter, gnädiger Wille geschieht wohl ohne unser Gebet; aber wir bitten in diesem Gebet, daß er auch bei uns geschehe.

Wie geschieht das? Antwort:

Wenn Gott allen bösen Rath und Willen bricht und hindert, so uns den Namen Gottes nicht heiligen und sein Reich nicht kommen lassen wollen, als da ist des Teufels, der Welt und unsers Fleisches Wille, sondern stärket und behält uns fest in seinem Wort und Glauben bis an unser Ende; das ist sein gnädiger, guter Wille.

Die Vierte Bitte.

Unser täglich Brot gieb uns heute.

Was ist das? Antwort:

Gott giebt täglich Brot auch wohl ohne unsere Bitte, allen bösen Menschen; aber wir bitten in diesem Gebet, daß er uns erkennen lasse und mit Danksagung empfahen unser täglich Brot.

Was heißt denn täglich Brot? Antwort:

Alles, was zur Leibes Nahrung und Nothdurft gehört, als Essen, Trinken, Kleider, Schuh, Haus, Hof, Acker,

The Third Petition.

Thy will be done on earth, as it is in heaven.

What does this mean? Answer:

God's good, gracious will is done indeed without our prayer; but we pray in this petition that it may be done also by us.

How can this be done? Answer:

When God breaks and brings to naught every evil counsel and will which would hinder us from hallowing the name of God, and prevent his kingdom from coming to us (such as the will of the devil, of the world, and of our own flesh); but makes us strong and steadfast in his Word and faith even unto our end: this is his gracious, good will.

The Fourth Petition.

Give us this day our daily bread.

What does this mean? Answer:

God gives indeed, without our prayer, even to the wicked their daily bread; but we pray in this petition that he would make us sensible [of his benefits] and enable us to receive our daily bread with thanksgiving.

What is, then, our daily bread? Answer:

All that pertains to the nourishment and needs of the body, as drink, food, clothing, shoes, house,

Vieh, Geld, Gut, fromm Gemahl, fromme Kinder, fromm Gesinde, fromme und treue Oberherren, gut Regiment, gut Wetter, Friede, Gesundheit, Zucht, Ehre, gute Freunde, getreue Nachbarn, und deßgleichen.

home, land, cattle, money, property, pious husband or wife, pious children, pious servants, pious and faithful rulers, good government, good seasons, peace, health, education, honor, good friends, trusty neighbors, and the like.

Die Fünfte Bitte.

Und verlaße [vergieb] uns unsre Schuld, als wir verlaßen [vergeben] unsern Schuldigern.

Was ist das? Antwort:

Wir bitten in diesem Gebet, daß der Vater im Himmel nicht ansehen wolle unsre Sünde, und um derselbigen willen solche Bitte nicht versagen: denn wir sind der keines werth, das wir bitten, haben's auch nicht verdienet; sondern er wolle es uns alles aus Gnaden geben; denn wir täglich viel sündigen, und wohl eitel Strafe verdienen. So wollen wir zwar wiederum auch herzlich vergeben, und gerne wohlthun [denen], die sich an uns versündigen.

THE FIFTH PETITION.

And forgive us our debts, as we forgive our debtors.

What does this mean? Answer:

We pray in this petition that our Father in heaven would not look upon our sins, nor on account of them deny our request; for we are not worthy of any thing for which we pray, and have not merited it; but that he would grant us all things through grace; for we daily sin much, and deserve nothing but punishment. We will, therefore, also on our part, heartily forgive and willingly do good to those who sin against us.

Die Sechste Bitte.

Und führe uns nicht in Versuchung.

Was ist das? Antwort:

Gott versucht zwar niemand; aber wir bitten in diesem Gebet, daß uns Gott wolle behüten und erhalten, auf daß uns der Teufel, die Welt und

THE SIXTH PETITION.

And lead us not into temptation.

What does this mean? Answer:

God indeed tempts no one, but we pray in this petition that God would so guard and preserve us that the devil, the world, and our

unſer Fleiſch nicht betrüge und ver=
führe in Mißglauben, Verzweiflung
und andere große Schande und Laſter;
und ob wir damit angefochten würden,
daß wir doch endlich gewinnen und den
Sieg behalten.

own flesh may not deceive us, nor
lead us into misbelief, despair, and
other great shame and vice; and
that, though we may be thus tempted, we may nevertheless finally prevail and gain the victory.

Die Siebente Bitte.

The Seventh Petition.

Sondern erlöſe uns von dem
Uebel.

But deliver us from evil.

Was iſt das? Antwort:

What does this mean? Answer:

Wir bitten in dieſem Gebet, als in
der Summa, daß uns der Vater im
Himmel von allerlei Uebel Leibes und
der Seele, Gutes und Ehre erlöſe, und
zuletzt, wenn unſer Stündlein kommt,
ein ſeliges Ende beſchere, und mit
Gnaden von dieſem Jammerthal zu
ſich nehme in den Himmel.

We pray in this petition, as in a
summary, that our Father in heaven
may deliver us from all manner of
evil—in body or soul, property or
honor—and, at last, when our time
comes, may grant us a happy end,
and graciously take us from this
world of sorrow to himself in
heaven.

Amen.[1]

Amen.[1]

Was iſt das? Antwort:

What does this mean? Answer:

Daß ich ſoll gewiß ſein, ſolche
Bitten ſind dem Vater im Himmel
angenehm und erhöret; denn er ſelbſt
hat uns geboten, alſo zu beten, und
verheißen, daß er uns will erhören.
Amen, Amen, das heißt, Ja, Ja, es
ſoll alſo geſchehen.

That I should be sure that such
petitions are pleasing to our Father
in heaven, and are heard by him;
for he himself has commanded us
thus to pray, and has promised that
he will hear us. Amen, Amen:
that is, Yea, yea, so shall it be.

---

[1] Many modern editions insert the doxology before *Amen*, with this question: , Wie lautet
der Beſchluß? Denn dein iſt das Reich, und die Kraft, und die Herrlichkeit, in Ewigkeit. Amen.,
—'What is the conclusion? For thine is the kingdom, and the power, and the glory, forever.
Amen.'

(Das Vierte Hauptstück.)

Das Sakrament der heiligen Taufe

wie dasselbige ein Hausvater seinem Gesinde soll einfältiglich fürhalten.

Zum Ersten.

Was ist die Taufe? Antwort:

Die Taufe ist nicht allein schlecht Wasser, sondern sie ist das Wasser in Gottes Gebot gefasset, und mit Gottes Wort verbunden.

Welches ist denn solch Wort Gottes? Antwort:

Da unser Herr Christus spricht, Matthäi am letzten:

Gehet hin in alle Welt,[1] lehret alle Heiden [Völker], und taufet sie im Namen des Vaters, und des Sohnes, und des heiligen Geistes.

Zum Andern.

Was giebt oder nützet die Taufe? Antwort:

Sie wirkt Vergebung der Sünden, erlöset vom Tode und Teufel, und giebt die ewige Seligkeit Allen, die es glauben, wie die Worte und Verheißungen Gottes lauten.

Welches sind denn solche Worte und Verheißungen Gottes? Antwort:

Da unser Herr Christus spricht, Marci am letzten:

Wer da glaubet und getauft

PART IV.

THE SACRAMENT OF HOLY BAPTISM,

As it should be clearly and simply explained to every household by the head of the family.

I.

What is Baptism? Answer:

Baptism is not simply common water, but it is the water comprehended in God's command, and connected with God's Word.

What is that Word of God? Answer:

It is that which our Lord Christ speaks in the last chapter of Matthew [xxviii. 19]:

'*Go ye [into all the world], and teach all nations, baptizing them in the name of the Father, and of the Son, and of the Holy Ghost.*'

II.

What does Baptism give, or of what use is it? Answer:

It worketh forgiveness of sins, delivers from death and the devil, and gives everlasting salvation to all who believe, as the Word and promise of God declare.

What are such words and promises of God? Answer:

Those which our Lord Christ speaks in the last chapter of Mark: '*He that believeth and is bap-*

---

[1] The words *in alle Welt* are inserted from Mark xvi. 15.

wird, der wird selig; wer aber nicht glaubet, der wird verdammt.

tized, shall be saved; but he that believeth not, shall be damned.'

Zum Dritten.

Wie kann Wasser solche große Dinge thun? Antwort:

Wasser thut's freilich nicht, sondern das Wort Gottes, so mit und bei dem Wasser ist, und der Glaube, so solchem Worte Gottes im Wasser trauet; denn ohne Gottes Wort ist das Wasser schlecht Wasser, und keine Taufe; aber mit dem Worte Gottes ist's eine Taufe, das ist ein gnaden reich Wasser des Lebens und ein Bad der neuen Geburt im heiligen Geiste; wie S. Paulus sagt zu Tito am dritten Kapitel:

Durch das Bad der Wiedergeburt und Erneuerung des heiligen Geistes, welchen er ausgegossen hat über uns reichlich durch Jesum Christum, unsern Heiland, auf daß wir durch desselben Gnade gerechtfertiget, Erben seien des ewigen Lebens, nach der Hoffnung. Das ist gewißlich wahr.

III.

How can water do such great things? Answer:

It is not water, indeed, that does it, but the Word of God which is with and in the water, and faith, which trusts in the Word of God in the water. For without the Word of God the water is nothing but water, and no baptism; but with the Word of God it is a baptism—that is, a gracious water of life and a washing of regeneration in the Holy Ghost, as St. Paul says, Titus, third chapter [iii. 5–7]:

'By the washing of regeneration, and renewing of the Holy Ghost, which he shed on us abundantly through Jesus Christ our Saviour; that being justified by his grace, we should be made heirs according to the hope of eternal life.' This is certainly true. [Or, *'This is a faithful saying,'* ver. 8.]

Zum Vierten.

Was bedeutet denn solch Wassertaufen? Antwort:

Es bedeutet, daß der alte Adam in uns durch tägliche Reue und Buße soll ersäufet werden, und sterben mit allen Sünden und bösen Lüsten; und

IV.

What does such baptizing with water signify? Answer:

It signifies that the old Adam in us is to be drowned by daily sorrow and repentance, and perish with all sins and evil lusts; and

wiederum täglich herauskommen und auferstehen ein neuer Mensch, der in Gerechtigkeit und Reinigkeit für [vor] Gott ewiglich lebe.

that the new man should daily come forth again and rise, who shall live before God in righteousness and purity forever.

Wo steht das geschrieben? Antwort:

Where is it so written? Answer:

S. Paulus zu den Römern am sechsten spricht:

St. Paul, in the 6th chapter of Romans, says:

Wir sind sammt Christo durch die Taufe begraben im [in den] Tod, daß gleichwie Christus ist von den Todten auferwecket durch die Herrlichkeit des Vaters, also sollen wir auch in einem neuen Leben wandeln.

'*We are buried with Christ by baptism into death; that like as he was raised up from the dead by the glory of the Father, even so we also should walk in newness of life.*'

Wie man die Einfältigen soll lehren beichten.[1]

HOW THE UNLEARNED SHOULD BE TAUGHT TO CONFESS.[1]

Was ist die Beichte? Antwort:

What is confession? Answer:

Die Beichte begreift zwei Stücke in sich: eins, daß man die Sünden bekenne; das andre, daß man die Absolution oder Vergebung vom Beichtiger empfahe, als von Gott selbst, und ja nicht daran zweifle, sondern fest glaube, die Sünden seien dadurch vergeben für [vor] Gott im Himmel.

Confession comprehends two parts: one, that we confess our sins; the other, that we receive absolution or forgiveness from the father confessor, as from God himself, in no wise doubting, but firmly believing that our sins are thereby forgiven before God in heaven.

Welche Sünden soll man denn beichten? Antwort:

What sins should we confess? Answer:

Für [vor] Gott soll man aller Sünden sich schuldig geben, auch die wir

Before God we should accuse ourselves of all manner of sins,

---

[1] This section on *Confession* appears first in the third edition before Part V., and preparatory to it. So also in the editions of 1539 and 1542. (See Harnack, p. lvi. and p. 53.) In later editions it is enlarged (by inserting the passages Matt. xvi. 19 and John xx. 22, 23, and other additions), and is counted as a separate Part (V.) on *The Office of the Keys* (Von der Beichte oder dem Amt der Schlüssel). or added as an Appendix after Part V. See Vol. I. § 43, p. 248.

nicht erkennen, wie wir im Vaterunser thun; aber für [vor] dem Beichtiger sollen wir allein die Sünden bekennen, die wir wissen und fühlen im Herzen.

even of those which we do not ourselves perceive; as we do in the Lord's Prayer. But to the confessor we should confess those sins only which we know and feel in our hearts.

Welche sind die? Antwort:

Da siehe deinen Stand an nach den Zehn Geboten, ob du Vater, Mutter, Sohn, Tochter, Herr, Frau, Knecht seiest; ob du ungehorsam, untreu, unfleißig, zornig, unzüchtig, hitzig gewesen seiest; ob du Jemand Leide gethan habest mit Worten oder Werken; ob du gestohlen, versäumt, verwahrlost, Schaden gethan habest.

Which are these? Answer:

Here consider your condition, according to the Ten Commandments, whether you are a father or mother, a son or daughter, a master or mistress, a man-servant or maid-servant; whether you have been disobedient, unfaithful, lazy, angry, unchaste, spiteful; whether you have injured any one by words or deeds; whether you have stolen, neglected, or wasted any thing, or done any harm.

Lieber stelle mir eine kurze Weise zu beichten. Antwort:[1]

So sollst du zum Beichtiger sprechen:

Würdiger, lieber Herr, ich bitte euch, wollet meine Beichte hören, und mir die Vergebung zusprechen um Gottes willen.

Show me a short way to confess. Answer:[1]

Speak thus to the confessor:

Worthy, dear sir, I beseech you to hear my confession, and absolve me for God's sake.

Sage an:

Ich armer Sünder bekenne mich vor Gott aller Sünden schuldig; insonderheit bekenne ich vor euch, daß ich ein Knecht, Magd, etc. bin; aber ich diene leider untreulich meinem Herrn: denn da und da habe ich nicht gethan,

Say:

I, poor sinner, confess before God that I am guilty of all manner of sin; in particular I confess before you that I am a man-servant, maid-servant, etc.; but, alas! I serve my master unfaithfully, for I

---

[1] This and the following forms of Confession and Absolution are omitted in the translations of the 'Evang. Luth. Ministerium of Pennsylvania,' and even in the 'Church Book' of the General Council of the Ev. Luth. Church in America (1873). The reason of the omission is obvious.

was sie mich hießen; habe sie erzürnt und zu fluchen bewegt, habe versäumt und Schaden lassen geschehn; bin auch in Worten und Werken schambar [schamlos] gewesen, habe mit meines Gleichen gezürnt, wider meine Frau gemurrt und geflucht, etc. Das alles ist mir leid, und bitte um Gnade; ich will mich bessern.

Ein Herr oder Frau sage also:

Insonderheit bekenne ich für [vor] euch, daß ich mein Kind und Gesinde, Weib nicht treulich gezogen habe zu Gottes Ehren; ich habe geflucht, böse Exempel mit unzüchtigen Worten und Werken gegeben, meinem Nachbar Schaden gethan, übel nachgeredet, zu theuer verkauft, falsche und nicht ganze Waare gegeben.

[Und was er mehr wider die Gebote Gottes und seinen Stand gethan, etc. Wenn aber Jemand sich nicht befindet beschweret mit solcher oder größeren Sünden, der soll nicht sorgen oder weiter Sünden suchen noch erdichten, und damit eine Marter aus der Beichte machen; sondern erzähle eine oder zwei, die du weißt, also:]

Insonderheit bekenne ich, daß ich einmal geflucht; item, einmal unhübsch mit Worten gewesen, einmal dies N. versäumt habe, etc.

[Und lasse es genug sein. Weißt du aber gar keine (welches doch nicht wohl sollte möglich sein), so sage auch keine insonderheit, sondern nimm die Vergebung auf die gemeine Beichte, so du für [vor] Gott thust gegen den Beichtiger.]

have not done what they told me; I have moved them to anger and to cursing, have neglected my duty, and let things go to waste; I have also been immodest in words and deeds, have quarreled with my equals, have grumbled and sworn at my wife, etc. For all this I am sorry, and plead for mercy; I will do so no more.

A master or mistress should say thus:

In particular I confess before you, that I have not brought up my child, household, and wife to the glory of God; I have cursed, have set a bad example with unchaste words and actions, have injured my neighbor, have slandered, overcharged, given spurious goods and short measure.

[And so on with any thing he has done contrary to the commands of God, and to his position, etc. If, however, the conscience of any one of you is not troubled with such or greater sins, do not worry, or hunt up, or invent other sins, and thereby make a torture out of confession, but mention one or two you know of. Thus:]

In particular, I confess that I have once sworn; also, I have once used improper language, once neglected some duty, etc.

[And then stop. But if you should know of no sin (which, however, is hardly possible), then mention none in particular, but receive absolution after the general confession which you make to God before the confessor.]

Darauf soll der Beichtiger sagen:

Gott sei dir gnädig, und stärke deinen Glauben. Amen.

Weiter:

Glaubst du auch, daß meine Vergebung Gottes Vergebung sei?

Antwort:

Ja, lieber Herr.

Darauf spreche er:

Wie du glaubst, so geschehe dir! Und ich aus dem Befehl unsers HERRN Jesu Christi vergebe dir deine Sünden, im Namen des Vaters und des Sohnes und des heiligen Geistes. Amen.

Gehe hin im Frieden.

[Welche aber große Beschwerung des Gewissens haben, oder betrübt und angefochten sind, die wird ein Beichtvater wohl wissen mit mehr Sprüchen zu trösten und zum Glauben reizen. Das soll allein eine gemeine Weise der Beichte sein für die Einfältigen.]

(Das Fünfte Hauptstück.)[1]

Das Sacrament des Altars,

wie ein Hausvater dasselbige seinem Gesinde einfältiglich fürhalten soll.

Was ist das Sacrament des Altars? Antwort:

Es ist der wahre Leib und Blut unsers Herrn Jesu Christi, unter dem Brot und Wein, uns Christen zu essen und zu trinken von Christo selbst eingesetzt.

Then shall the father confessor say:

God be merciful unto thee, and strengthen thy faith. Amen.

Further:

Dost thou believe that my forgiveness is the forgiveness of God?

Answer:

Yes. dear sir.

Then let him say:

As thou believest, so be it unto thee. And I, by command of our Lord Jesus Christ, forgive thee thy sins in the name of the Father, and of the Son, and of the Holy Ghost. Amen.

Depart in peace.

[Those, however, who are much troubled in conscience, or who are in distress or temptation, a father confessor will know how to comfort with Scripture passages, and stir up to faith. This is only a general method of confession for the unlearned.]

PART V.[1]

THE SACRAMENT OF THE ALTAR,

As it should be clearly and simply explained to every household by the head of the family.

What is the Sacrament of the Altar? Answer:

It is the true body and blood of our Lord Jesus Christ, under the bread and wine, given unto Christians to eat and to drink, as it was instituted by Christ himself.

---

[1] In the 'Book of Concord,' and in many editions of the Catechism, this section is numbered as Part VI., and the preceding insertion, or appendix, as Part V.

Wo steht das geschrieben? Antwort:

So schreiben die heiligen Evangelisten, Matthäus, Markus, Lukas—und S. Paulus:

Unser HERR Jesus Christus, in der Nacht, da er verrathen ward, nahm er das Brot, dankte und brach's, und gab's seinen Jüngern, und sprach: Nehmet hin, esset; das ist mein Leib, der für euch gegeben wird; solches thut zu meinem Gedächtniß.

Desselbigen gleichen nahm er auch den Kelch nach dem Abendmahl, dankte und gab ihnen den, und sprach: Nehmet hin und trinket alle daraus; dieser Kelch ist das neue Testament in meinem Blute, das für euch vergossen wird zur Vergebung der Sünden; solches thut, so oft ihr's trinket, zu meinem Gedächtniß.

Was nützet denn solch Essen und Trinken? Antwort:

Das zeigen uns diese Worte: Für euch gegeben und vergossen zur Vergebung der Sünden; nämlich, daß uns im Sacrament Vergebung der Sünden, Leben und Seligkeit durch solche Worte gegeben wird; denn wo Vergebung der Sünden ist, da ist auch Leben und Seligkeit.

Wie kann leiblich Essen und Trinken solche große Dinge thun? Antwort:

Essen und Trinken thut's freilich nicht, sondern die Worte, so da stehen:

Where is it so written? Answer:

The holy Evangelists, Matthew, Mark, and Luke, together with St. Paul, write thus:

'*Our Lord Jesus Christ, the same night in which he was betrayed, took bread; and when he had given thanks, he brake it, and gave it to the disciples, and said, Take, eat; this is my body, which is given for you; this do, in remembrance of me.*

'*After the same manner also he took the cup, when he had supped, gave thanks, and gave it to them, saying, Drink ye all of it: this cup is the New Testament in my blood, which is shed for you, for the remission of sins: this do ye, as oft as ye drink it, in remembrance of me.*'

What is the use, then, of such eating and drinking? Answer:

It is pointed out to us in the words: '*Given, and shed for you, for the remission of sins.*' Namely, through these words, the remission of sins, life and salvation are given us in the Sacrament: for where there is remission of sins, there are also life and salvation.

How can bodily eating and drinking do such great things? Answer:

Eating and drinking, indeed, do not do them, but the words which

Für euch gegeben und vergossen zur Vergebung der Sünden. Welche Worte sind neben dem leiblichen Essen und Trinken als das Hauptstück im Sacrament; und wer denselbigen Worten glaubt, der hat, was sie sagen, und wie sie lauten, nämlich Vergebung der Sünden.

Wer empfähet denn solch Sacrament würdiglich? Antwort:

Fasten und leiblich sich bereiten ist wohl eine feine äußerliche Zucht; aber der ist recht würdig und wohl geschickt, wer den Glauben hat an diese Worte: Für euch gegeben und vergossen zur Vergebung der Sünden. Wer aber diesen Worten nicht glaubt, oder zweifelt, der ist unwürdig und ungeschickt; denn das Wort: Für euch fordert eitel gläubige Herzen.

stand here: '*Given, and shed for you, for the remission of sins.*' Which words, besides the bodily eating and drinking, are the main point in the sacrament; and he who believes these words has that which they declare and mean, namely, forgiveness of sins.

Who, then, receives this Sacrament worthily? Answer:

Fasting and bodily preparation are, indeed, a good external discipline, but he is truly worthy and well prepared who has faith in these words: '*Given, and shed for you, for the remission of sins.*' But he who does not believe these words, or who doubts, is unworthy and unfit, for the words '*for you*' require truly believing hearts.

FORMULA CONCORDIÆ.

(*Die Concordien-Formel.*)

THE FORMULA OF CONCORD. A.D. 1576 (1584).

(THE EPITOME.)

[The Formula of Concord was originally written in the German language, 1576, and published at Dresden, 1580. It was translated into Latin by Lucas Osiander, 1580; but the translation was very defective, and was revised by two of the authors—first by Selnecker for the German-Latin edition of the Book of Concord, 1582, then more fully by Chemnitz, 1583; and in this doubly improved form it became the authorized text, published in the first *authentic Latin* edition of the Book of Concord, Leipzig, 1584. We give this text, with a new English translation made for this work from the German and Latin compared, and adapted to the style of the age of composition. The EPITOME contains, in clear and concise form, all that is necessary for this collection; and hence we omit the lengthy SOLID REPETITION AND DECLARATION, which merely repeats more fully the same articles, and fortifies them by ample quotations from the Scriptures, the fathers, the older Lutheran symbols, and the private writings of Luther, with an appendix of patristic testimonies for the doctrine of the *communicatio idiomatum.* See Vol. I. § 45, pp. 258 sqq.]

EPITOME ARTICULORUM

de quibus

CONTROVERSIÆ

ortæ sunt inter Theologos Augustanæ Confessionis, qui in repetitione sequenti, secundum verbi Dei præscriptum, pie declarati sunt et conciliati.[1]

DE COMPENDIARIA REGULA ATQUE NORMA,

ad quam omnia dogmata exigenda, et quæ inciderunt certamina, pie declaranda et componenda sunt.

I. *Credimus, confitemur et docemus, unicam regulam et normam [die einige Regel und Richtschnur], secundum quam omnia dogmata,*

EPITOME OF THE ARTICLES

touching which

CONTROVERSIES

have arisen among the divines of the Augsburg Confession, which in the following restatement have been in godly wise, according to the express word of God, set forth and reconciled.

OF THE COMPENDIOUS RULE AND NORM,

according to which all dogmas ought to be judged, and all controversies which have arisen ought to be piously set forth and settled.

I. We believe, confess, and teach that the only rule and norm, according to which all dogmas and all doctors ought to be esteemed

---

[1] The German title of the First Part: 'SUMMARISCHER BEGRIFF DER STREITIGEN ARTIKEL *zwischen den Theologen Augsburgischer Confession in nachfolgender Wiederholung nach Anleitung Gottes Worts christlich erkläret und verglichen.*' The Second Part has the title: '*Gründliche, lautere, richtige und endliche* WIEDERHOLUNG *und* ERKLÄRUNG *etlicher Artikel Augsburgischer Confession,*' etc., or '*Solida, plana ac perspicua* REPETITIO *et* DECLARATIO *quorundam Articulorum Aug. Confessionis,*' etc.

omnesque Doctores æstimari et ju-dicari oporteat, nullam omnino aliam esse, quam Prophetica et Apostolica scripta cum Veteris, tum Novi Testamenti, sicut scriptum est (Psa. cxix. 105): '*Lucerna pedibus meis verbum tuum, et lumen semitis meis.*' *Et Divus Paulus inquit* (Gal. i. 8): '*Etiamsi Angelus de cœlo aliud prædicet Evangelium, anathema sit.*'

Reliqua vero sive Patrum sive Neotericorum scripta, quocunque veniant nomine, sacris literis nequaquam sunt æquiparanda, sed universa illis ita subjicienda sunt, ut alia ratione non recipiantur, nisi testium loco, qui doceant, quod etiam post Apostolorum tempora, et in quibus partibus orbis doctrina illa Prophetarum et Apostolorum sincerior conservata sit.[1]

II. *Et quia statin post Apostolorum tempora, imo etiam cum adhuc superstites essent, falsi doctores et hæretici exorti sunt, contra quos in primitiva Ecclesia Symbola sunt composita, id est, breves et categoricæ Confessiones, quæ unanimem Catholicæ Christianæ fidei Consensum et Confessionem Orthodoxo-*

and judged, is no other whatevei than the prophetic and apostolic writings both of the Old and of the New Testament, as it is written (Psalm cxix. 105): 'Thy word is a lamp unto my feet, and a light unto my path.' And St. Paul saith (Gal. i. 8): 'Though an angel from heaven preach any other gospel unto you, let him be accursed.'

But other writings, whether of the fathers or of the moderns, with whatever name they come, are in nowise to be equalled to the Holy Scriptures, but are all to be esteemed inferior to them, so that they be not otherwise received than in the rank of witnesses, to show what doctrine was taught after the Apostles' times also, and in what parts of the world that more sound doctrine of the Prophets and Apostles has been preserved.

II. And inasmuch as immediately after the times of the Apostles, nay, even while they were yet alive, false teachers and heretics arose, against whom in the primitive Church symbols were composed, that is to say, brief and explicit confessions, which contained the unanimous consent of the Catholic Christian faith, and the confession

---

[1] '*Als Zeugen, welcher Gestalt nach der Apostel Zeit und an welchen Orten solche Lehre der Propheten und Apostel erhalten worden.*'

rum et veræ Ecclesiæ complecte-
bantur (ut sunt SYMBOLUM APO-
STOLICUM, NICÆNUM, *et* ATHANASIA-
NUM): *profitemur publice, nos illa*
amplecti, et rejicimus omnes hæ-
reses, omniaque dogmata, quæ con-
tra illorum sententiam unquam
in Ecclesiam Dei sunt invecta.

III. *Quod vero ad schismata*
in negotiis fidei attinet, quæ in
nostra tempora inciderunt, judi-
camus, unanimem Consensum et
Declarationem Christianæ no-
stræ fidei et Confessionis, in
primis contra Papatum, et hu-
jus falsos ac idolatricos cultus
et superstitiones, et alias sectas,
esse nostri temporis Symbolum,
AUGUSTANAM *illam primam, et*
non mutatam CONFESSIONEM, *quæ*
Imperatori Carolo V. Augustæ
anno XXX. in magnis Imperii
Comitiis exhibita est; similiter
et APOLOGIAM [*derselben* APOLO-
GIE]; *et* ARTICULOS SMALCALDICOS
anno XXXVII. conscriptos [AR-
TIKELN *so zu* SCHMALKALDEN *Anno*
37 *gestellet*], *et præcipuorum Theo-*
logorum illius temporis subscrip-
tione comprobatos.

Et quia hæc religionis causa
etiam ad Laicos, quos vocant,
spectat, eorumque perpetua salus
agitur: profitemur publice, nos
etiam amplecti MINOREM *et* MA-
JOREM D. LUTHERI CATECHISMOS

of the orthodox and true Church
(such as are the APOSTLES', the NI-
CENE, and the ATHANASIAN CREEDS):
we publicly profess that we embrace them, and reject all heresies
and all dogmas which have ever
been brought into the Church of
God contrary to their decision.

III. And as concerns the schisms
in matters of faith, which have
come to pass in our times, we
judge the unanimous consent and
declaration of our Christian faith,
especially against the papacy and
its idolatrous rites and superstitions, and against other sects, to
be the Symbol of our own age,
called The First, Unaltered AUGS-
BURG CONFESSION, which in the
year 1530 was exhibited to the
Emperor Charles the Fifth at the
Diet of the Empire; and likewise
the APOLOGY [of the Augsburg
Confession]; and the SMALCALD
ARTICLES drawn up in the year
1537, and approved by the subscription of the principal divines
of that time.

And inasmuch as this matter
of religion appertains also to the
laity, as they are called, and their
eternal salvation is at stake, we publicly profess that we also receive
DR. LUTHER'S SMALLER and LARGER

[*zu dem* KLEINEN *und* GROSSEN KATECHISMO DOCTOR LUTHERS], *ut ii Tomis Lutheri sunt inserti: quod eos quasi Laicorum Biblia* [*Laienbibel*] *esse censeamus, in quibus omnia illa breviter comprehenduntur, quæ in Sacra Scriptura fusius tractantur, et quorum cognitio homini Christiano ad æternam salutem est necessaria.*

Ad has rationes, paulo ante monstratas, omnis doctrina in religionis negotio conformanda est, et, si quid iis contrarium esse deprehenditur, id rejiciendum atque damnandum est: quippe quod cum unanimi fidei nostræ declaratione pugnet.

Hoc modo luculentum discrimen inter sacras Veteris et Novi Testamenti literas, et omnia aliorum scripta retinetur: et sola Sacra Scriptura judex, norma et regula [*der einige Richter, Regel und Richtschnur*] *agnoscitur, ad quam, ceu ad Lydium lapidem* [*als dem einigen Probierstein*], *omnia dogmata exigenda sunt et judicanda, an pia, an impia, an vera, an vero falsa sint.*

Cœtera autem Symbola, et alia scripta, quorum paulo ante mentionem fecimus, non obtinent autoritatem judicis; hæc enim dignitas solis sacris literis debetur: sed duntaxat pro religione

CATECHISMS as they are included in Luther's works, because we judge them to be, as it were, the Bible of the laity, in which all those things are briefly comprehended which in the Holy Scripture are treated more at length, and the knowledge of which is necessary to a Christian man for his eternal salvation.

To these principles, as set forth a little above, every religious doctrine ought to be conformed; and, if any thing is discovered to be contrary to them, that is to be rejected and condemned, as being at variance with the unanimous declaration of our faith.

In this way a clear distinction is retained between the sacred Scriptures of the Old and New Testaments, and all other writings; and Holy Scripture alone is acknowledged as the [only] judge, norm, and rule, according to which, as by the [only] touchstone, all doctrines are to be examined and judged, as to whether they be godly or ungodly, true or false.

But the other symbols and other writings, of which we made mention a little while ago, do not possess the authority of a judge—for this dignity belongs to Holy Scripture alone; but merely give testi-

nostra testimonium dicunt eam-que explicant, ac ostendunt, quo-modo singulis temporibus sacræ literæ in articulis controversis in Ecclesia Dei a Doctoribus, qui tum vixerunt, intellectæ et explicatæ fuerint, et quibus ra-tionibus dogmata cum Sacra Scriptura pugnantia rejecta et condemnata sint.

mony to our religion, and set it forth to show in what manner from time to time the Holy Scriptures have been understood and explain-ed in the Church of God by the doctors who then lived, as respects controverted articles, and by what arguments, dogmas at variance with the Holy Scriptures have been re-jected and condemned.

Art. I.

DE PECCATO ORIGINIS.

Status Controversiæ.

An peccatum originale sit pro-prie et absque omni discrimine ipsa hominis corrupti natura, substantia et essentia, aut certe principalis et præstantissima pars ipsius substantiæ; utpote ipsa rationalis anima in summo suo gradu et in summis ipsius viribus considerata? An vero inter hominis substantiam, natu-ram, essentiam, corpus et ani-mam, etiam post lapsum humani generis, et inter originale pecca-tum aliquod sit discrimen, ita, ut aliud sit ipsa natura, et aliud ipsum peccatum originis, quod in natura corrupta hæret, et natu-ram etiam depravat?

Art. I.

CONCERNING ORIGINAL SIN.

Statement of the Controversy.

Whether Original Sin is proper-ly and without any distinction the very nature, substance, and essence of corrupt man, or at the least the principal and pre-eminent part of his substance, namely, the ra-tional soul itself, considered in its highest degree and in its chief pow-ers? Or whether between the sub-stance, nature, essence, body, and soul of man, even after the fall of mankind on the one hand, and Original Sin on the other, there be some distinction, so that the nature itself is one thing, and Original Sin another thing, which adheres in the corrupt nature, and also corrupts the nature?

*Sincera doctrina, fides et confessio, cum su-
periore norma et compendiosa declaratione
consentiens.*

I. *Credimus, docemus et confitemur, quod sit aliquod discrimen
inter ipsam hominis naturam,
non tantum, quemadmodum initio a Deo purus, et sanctus, et
absque peccato homo conditus est,
verum etiam, qualem jam post
lapsum naturam illam habemus,
discrimen, inquam, inter ipsam
naturam, quæ etiam post lapsum
est permanetque Dei creatura, et
inter peccatum originis, et quod
tanta sit illa naturæ et peccati originalis differentia, quanta est inter
opus Dei, et inter opus Diaboli.*

II. *Credimus, docemus et confitemur, quod summo studio hoc
discrimen sit conservandum, propterea quod illud dogma, nullum videlicet inter naturam hominis corrupti et inter peccatum
originis esse discrimen, cum præcipuis Fidei nostræ articulis (de
creatione, de redemtione, de sanctificatione et resurrectione carnis
nostræ) pugnet, neque salvis hisce
articulis stare possit.*

*Deus enim non modo Adami
et Hevæ corpus et animam ante
lapsum, verum etiam corpora et
animas nostras post lapsum cre-
vit; etsi hæc jam sunt cor-*

*The pure doctrine, faith and confession, agree-
ing with our above-stated norm and compendious declaration.*

I. We believe, teach, and confess
that there is a distinction between
the nature of man itself, not only
as man was created of God in the
beginning pure and holy and free
from sin, but also as we now possess it after our nature has fallen;
a distinction, namely, between the
nature itself, which even after the
fall is and remains God's creature,
and Original Sin; and that this difference between nature and Original Sin is as great as between the
work of God and the work of the
devil.

II. We believe, teach, and confess that this distinction should be
maintained with the greatest care,
because the dogma that there is no
distinction between the nature of
fallen man and Original Sin is inconsistent with the chief articles
of our faith (of Creation, of Redemption, of Sanctification, and the
Resurrection of our flesh), and can
not be maintained except by im-
pugning these articles.

For God not only created the
body and soul of Adam and Eve
before the fall, but has also created
our bodies and souls since the fall,
although these are now corrupt.

rupta. Et sane hodie Dominus animas et corpora nostra creaturas et opus suum esse agnoscit, sicut scriptum est (Job x. 8): '*Manus tuæ fecerunt me, et plasmaverunt me totum in circuitu.*'

Et Filius Dei unione personali illam humanam naturam, sed sine peccato, assumsit, et non alienam, sed nostram carnem sibi adjungens arctissime copulavit, ejusque assumtæ carnis ratione vere frater noster factus est; ut Scriptura testatur (Heb. ii. 14): '*Posteaquam pueri commercium habent cum carne et sanguine, et ipse similiter particeps factus est eorundem.*' *Item* (ii. 16): '*Non Angelos assumit, sed semen Abrahæ assumit, unde et debuit per omnia fratribus assimilari, excepto peccato.*'

Eandem humanam nostram naturam (opus videlicet suum) Christus redemit, eandem (quæ ipsius opus est) sanctificat, eandem a mortuis resuscitat, et ingenti gloria (opus videlicet suum) ornat: peccatum autem originale non creavit, non assumsit, non redemit, non sanctificat, non resuscitabit in electis, neque unquam gloria cælesti ornabit aut salvabit, sed in beata illa resurrectione plane

And to-day no less God acknowledges our minds and bodies to be his creatures and work; as it is written (Job x. 8): 'Thy hands have made me and fashioned me together round about.'

And the Son of God, by a personal union, has assumed this nature, yet without sin; and uniting not other flesh, but our flesh to himself, hath most closely conjoined it, and in respect of this flesh thus assumed he has truly become our brother; as the Scripture bears witness (Heb. ii. 14): 'Forasmuch then as the children are partakers of flesh and blood, he also himself likewise took part of the same.' Also (ii. 16): 'For verily he took not on him angels; but he took on him the seed of Abraham. Wherefore in all things it behooved him to be made like unto his brethren, yet without sin.'

This same human nature of ours (that is his own work) Christ has redeemed, the same (inasmuch as it is his own work) he sanctifies, the same doth he raise from the dead, and with great glory (as being his own work) doth he crown it. But Original Sin he has not created, has not assumed, has not redeemed, doth not sanctify, will not raise again in the elect, nor will ever save and crown with heavenly

abolitum erit [*sondern in der Auferstehung gar vertilget sein wird*].

Ex his, quæ a nobis allata sunt, discrimen inter corruptam naturam, et inter corruptionem, quæ naturæ infixa est, et per quam natura est corrupta, facile agnosci potest.

III. *Vicissim autem credimus, docemus atque confitemur, peccatum originis non esse levem, sed tam profundam humanæ naturæ corruptionem, quæ nihil sanum, nihil incorruptum, in corpore et anima hominis, atque adeo in interioribus et exterioribus viribus ejus reliquit. Sicut Ecclesia canit: 'Lapsus Adæ vi pessima humana tota massa, natura et ipsa essentia corrupta, luce cassa,'[1] etc. Hoc quantum sit malum, verbis revera est inexplicabile, neque humanæ rationis acumine indagari, sed duntaxat per verbum Dei revelatum agnosci potest. Et sane affirmamus, quod hanc naturæ corruptionem ab ipsa natura nemo, nisi solus Deus, separare queat; id quod per mortem in beata illa resurrec-*

glory, but in that blessed resurrection it shall be utterly abolished and done away.

From these considerations which have been advanced by us, the distinction between our corrupt nature and the corruption which is implanted in the nature, and through which the nature is corrupt, can be easily discerned.

III. But, on the other hand, we believe, teach, and confess that Original Sin is no trivial corruption, but is so profound a corruption of human nature as to leave nothing sound, nothing uncorrupt in the body or soul of man, or in his mental or bodily powers. As reads the hymn of the Church:

'Through Adam's fall is all corrupt,
Nature and essence human.'[1]

How great this evil is, is in truth not to be set forth in words, nor can it be explored by the subtlety of human reason, but can only be discerned by means of the revealed word of God. And we indeed affirm that no one is able to dissever this corruption of the nature from the nature itself, except God alone, which will fully come to pass by means of death in the resurrection

---

[1] '*Durch Adam's Fall ist ganz verderbt*
Menschlich Natur und Wesen.'

The beginning of a hymn by Lazarus Spengler, of Nuremberg (d. 1534), composed in 1525. See Schaff's *German Hymn-Book*, No. 62.

tione plene fiet. Ibi enim ea ipsa natura nostra, quam nunc circumferimus, absque peccato originis, et ab eodem omnino separata et remota resurget, et æterna felicitate fruetur. Sic enim scriptum est (Job xix. 26): '*Pelle mea circumdabor, et in carne mea videbo Deum, quem ego visurus sum mihi, et oculi mei eum conspecturi sunt.*'

unto blessedness. For then that very same nature of ours, which we now bear about, will rise again free from Original Sin, and wholly severed and disjoined from the same, and will enjoy eternal felicity. For thus it is written (Job xix. 26): 'I shall be compassed again with my skin, and in my flesh shall I see God; whom I shall see for myself, and mine eyes shall behold, and not another.'

NEGATIVA.

Rejectio falsorum dogmatum, quæ commemoratæ sanæ doctrinæ repugnant.

I. *Rejicimus ergo et damnamus dogma illud, quo asseritur, peccatum originale tantummodo reatum et debitum esse, ex alieno delicto, absque ulla naturæ nostræ corruptione, in nos derivatum.*

II. *Item, concupiscentias pravas non esse peccatum, sed concreatas naturæ conditiones, et proprietates quasdam essentiales: aut defectus illos, et malum ingens a nobis paulo ante commemoratum, non esse peccatum, propter quod homo, Christo non insertus, sit filius iræ.*

III. *Rejicimus etiam Pelagianam hæresin, qua asseritur, hominis naturam post lapsum incorruptam esse, et quidem in spi-*

NEGATIVE.

Rejection of false dogmas, which are opposite to the sound doctrine as set forth above.

I. We therefore reject and condemn that dogma by which it is asserted that Original Sin is merely the liability and debt of another's transgression, transmitted to us apart from any corruption of our nature.

II. Also, that depraved concupiscences are not sin, but certain concreate conditions and essential properties of the nature, or that those defects and that huge evil just set forth by us is not sin on whose account man, if not grafted into Christ, is a child of wrath.

III. We also reject the Pelagian heresy, in which it is asserted that the nature of man after the fall is incorrupt, and that, moreover, in

ritualibus rebus totam bonam et puram in viribus suis naturalibus mansisse.

IV. *Item, peccatum originis externum, levem, et nullius prope momenti esse nœvum, aut aspersam quandam maculam, sub qua nihilominus natura bonas suas vires etiam in rebus spiritualibus retinuerit.*

V. *Item, peccatum originale tantum esse externum impedimentum bonarum spiritualium virium, et non esse despoliationem et defectum earundem, sicuti cum magnes allii succo illinitur, vis ejus naturalis attrahendi ferrum non tollitur, sed tantum impeditur, aut sicut macula de facie, aut color de pariete abstergi facile potest.*

VI. *Item, hominis naturam et essentiam non prorsus esse corruptam: sed aliquid boni adhuc in homine reliquum, etiam in rebus spiritualibus, videlicet, bonitatem, capacitatem, aptitudinem, facultatem, industriam, aut vires, quibus in rebus spiritualibus inchoare aliquid boni, operari, aut cooperari valeat.*

VII. *Contra autem rejicimus etiam falsum dogma Manichœorum, cum docetur, peccatum originis tanquam quiddam essentiale atque substantiale a Satana in naturam esse infusum, et cum eadem*

spiritual things it has remained wholly good and pure in its natural powers.

IV. Also, that Original Sin is an external, trivial, and almost insignificant birth-mark, or a certain stain dashed upon the man, under the which, nevertheless, nature hath retained her powers unimpaired even in spiritual things.

V. Also, that Original Sin is only an external impediment of sound spiritual powers, and is not a despoliation and defect thereof, even as, when a magnet is smeared with garlic-juice, its natural power of drawing iron is not taken away, but is only impeded; or as a stain can be easily wiped off from the face, or paint from a wall.

VI. Also, that man's nature and essence are not utterly corrupt, but that there is something of good still remaining in man, even in spiritual things, to wit, goodness, capacity, aptitude, ability, industry, or the powers by which in spiritual things he has strength to undertake, effect, or co-effect somewhat of good.

VII. But, on the other hand, we reject also the false dogma of the Manichæans, where it is taught that Original Sin is, as it were, something essential and substantial, infused by Satan into the nature, and mingled

permixtum, quemadmodum vene-
num et vinum miscentur.

VIII. *Item, non ipsum anima-*
lem hominem, sed aliquid aliud,
et peregrinum quiddam, quod sit
in homine, peccare, ideoque non
ipsam naturam, sed tantummodo
peccatum originale, in natura
existens, accusari.

IX. *Rejicimus etiam atque dam-*
namus, ut Manichœum errorem,
quando docetur, originale pecca-
tum proprie, et quidem nullo po-
sito discrimine, esse ipsam homi-
nis corrupti substantiam, natu-
ram et essentiam, ita ut inter na-
turam corruptam post lapsum,
per se ipsam consideratam, et in-
ter peccatum originis nulla pror-
sus sit differentia, neque ulla dis-
tinctio cogitari, aut saltem pecca-
tum illud a natura cogitatione
discerni possit.

X. *D. Lutherus quidem origi-*
nis illud malum, peccatum na-
turœ, personale, essentiale vocat:
sed non eam ob causam, quasi
natura, persona, aut essentia ho-
minis, absque omni discrimine,
sit ipsum peccatum originis: sed
ideo ad hunc modum loquitur, ut
hujusmodi phrasibus discrimen
inter peccatum originale, quod
humanœ naturœ infixum est, et
inter alia peccata, quœ actualia
vocantur, melius intelligi possit.

with the same, as wine and poison
are mixed.

VIII. Also, that it is not the natural man himself, but something
alien and strange, which is in man,
that sins, and that therefore not his
nature itself, but only Original Sin
existing in his nature is liable to
arraignment.

IX. We reject also and condemn,
as a Manichæan error, the teaching
that Original Sin is properly, and
without any distinction, the very
substance, nature, and essence of
fallen man, so that between his
corrupt nature after the fall, considered in itself, and Original Sin
there is no difference at all, and
that no distinction can be conceived
by which Original Sin can be distinguished from man's nature even
in thought.

X. Dr. Luther, it is true, calls
this original evil a sin of nature,
personal, essential; but not for
the reason that the nature, person, or essence of man, without
any distinction, is itself Original
Sin, but he speaks after this manner in order that by phrases of
this sort the distinction between
Original Sin, which is infixed in
human nature, and other sins,
which are called actual, may be
better understood.

XI. *Peccatum enim originis non est quoddam delictum, quod actu perpetratur, sed intime inhæret infixum ipsi naturæ, substantiæ et essentiæ hominis. Et quidem, si maxime nulla unquam prava cogitatio in corde hominis corrupti exoriretur, si nullum verbum otiosum proferretur, si nullum malum opus aut facinus designaretur: tamen natura nihilominus corrupta est per originale peccatum, quod nobis ratione corrupti seminis agnatum est, quod ipsum etiam scaturigo est omnium aliorum actualium peccatorum, ut sunt pravæ cogitationes, prava colloquia, prave et scelerate facta. Sic enim scriptum legimus* (Matt. xv. 19): '*Ex corde oriuntur cogitationes malæ.*' *Et alibi* (Gen. vi. 5; viii. 21): '*Omne figmentum cordis tantummodo malum est, a pueritia.*'

XII. *Est etiam diligenter observanda varia significatio vocabuli* '*naturæ,*' *cujus æquivocatione Manichæi abutentes, errorem suum occultant, multosque simplices homines in errorem inducunt. Quandoque enim* '*natura*' *ipsam hominis substantiam significat, ut, cum dicimus: Deus humanam naturam creavit. Interdum vero per vocabulum naturæ intelligitur*

XI. For Original Sin is not a particular transgression which is perpetrated in act, but intimately inheres, being infixed in the very nature, substance, and essence of man. And, indeed, if no depraved thought at all should ever arise in the heart of fallen man, if no idle word were uttered, if no evil work or deed were perpetrated by him: yet, nevertheless, the nature is corrupted by Original Sin, which is innate in us by reason of the corrupted seed from which we spring, and is, moreover, a fountain of all other actual sins, such as evil thoughts, evil discoursings, evil and abominable deeds. For thus it is written, as we read in Matthew xv. 19: 'For out of the heart proceed evil thoughts.' And elsewhere (Gen. vi. 5; viii. 21): 'Every imagination of the thought of man's heart is only evil from his youth.'

XII. We must also diligently observe the various significations of the word *nature*, which equivocal meaning the Manichæans abusing, thereby disguise their error, and lead many simple men astray. For sometimes *nature* signifies the very substance of man, as when we say: God created human nature. Sometimes, on the other hand, by the word *nature* there is understood

ingenium, conditio, defectus, aut vitium alicujus rei, in ipsa natura insitum et inhærens, ut cum dicimus: Serpentis natura est icere, hominis natura est peccare et peccatum. Et in hac posteriore significatione vocabulum (naturæ) non ipsam hominis substantiam, sed aliquid, quod in natura aut substantia fixum inhæret, denotat.

XIII. Quod vero ad Latina vocabula substantiæ et accidentis attinet, cum ea non sint Scripturæ Sacræ vocabula, præterea etiam a plebe non intelligantur, abstinendum est ab illis in publicis sacris concionibus, ubi inlocta plebs docetur; et hac in re simplicium et rudiorum merito habenda est ratio.

In scholis autem, et apud homines doctos (quibus horum vocabulorum significatio nota est, et qui iisdem recte atque citra abusum uti possunt, proprie discernentes essentiam alicujus rei ab eo, quod aliunde ei accidit et per accidens inhæret) in disputatione de peccato originis retinenda sunt.

Nam hisce vocabulis discrimen inter opus Dei, et inter opus Diaboli quam maxime per-

the temper, condition, defect, or vice of any thing implanted and inhering in the nature, as when we say: The serpent's nature is to strike, man's nature is to sin and is sin. And in this latter signification the word *nature* denotes, not the very nature of man, but something which inheres and is fixed in his nature or substance.

XIII. But as respects the Latin words *substantia* and *accidens*, since these are not expressions of Holy Scripture, and moreover are not understood by the common people, we ought to abstain from them in public preaching devoted to the instruction of the unlearned multitude, and in this matter account should rightly be taken of the more simple and untaught.

But in schools and among learned men (to whom the signification of these words is known, and who can use them correctly and without danger of misuse, properly discriminating the essence of any thing from that which has been added to it from without, and inheres in it by way of accident) they are to be retained in the discussion concerning Original Sin.

For by means of these terms the distinction between the work of God and the work of the devil can

spicue explicari potest. Diabolus enim substantiam nullam creare, sed tantummodo per accidens, permittente Domino, substantiam a Deo creatam depravare potest.

be set forth with the greatest clearness. For the devil can not create any substance, but can only, by way of accident, under the permission of the Lord, deprave a substance created by God.

Art. II.

DE LIBERO ARBITRIO.

Status Controversiæ.

Cum hominis voluntas quadruplicem habeat considerationem [in vier ungleichen Ständen]: primo, ante lapsum; secundo, post lapsum; tertio, post regenerationem; quarto, post resurrectionem carnis: nunc quæstio præcipua est tantum de voluntate et viribus hominis in secundo statu, quasnam vires post lapsum primorum parentum nostrorum, ante regenerationem, ex seipso habeat, in rebus spiritualibus: an propriis viribus, antequam per Spiritum Dei fuerit regeneratus, possit sese ad gratiam Dei applicare et præparare [sich zur Gnade Gottes schicken und bereiten],[1] et num gratiam divinam (quæ illi per Spiritum Sanctum in verbo et Sacramentis divinitus institutis offertur) accipere et apprehendere possit, nec ne.

Art. II.

OF FREE WILL.

Statement of the Controversy.

Since the will of man is to be considered under a fourfold view [in four dissimilar states]: first, before the fall; secondly, since the fall; thirdly, after regeneration; fourthly, after the resurrection of the body: the chief present inquiry regards the will and powers of man in the second state, what manner of powers since the fall of our first parents he has of himself in spiritual things antecedently to regeneration: whether by his own proper powers, before he has been regenerated by the Spirit of God, he can apply and prepare himself unto the grace of God, and whether he can receive and apprehend the divine grace (which is offered to him through the Holy Ghost in the word and sacraments divinely instituted), or not?

---

[1] The synergistic term used by Melanchthon in his later period. See Vol. I. pp. 262 and 270.

AFFIRMATIVA.

AFFIRMATIVE.

Sincera doctrina de hoc articulo, cum immota regula verbi divini congruens.

The sound doctrine concerning this article, agreeable to the steadfast rule of the divine Word.

I. *De hoc negotio hæc est fides, doctrina et confessio nostra: quod videlicet hominis intellectus et ratio in rebus spiritualibus prorsus sint cæca, nihilque propriis viribus intelligere possint. Sicut scriptum est* (1 Cor. ii. 14): '*Animalis homo non percipit ea, quæ sunt Spiritus; stultitia illi est, et non potest intelligere, quia de spiritualibus examinatur*' [*wann er wird von geistlichen Sachen gefraget*].[1]

I. Concerning this matter, the following is our faith, doctrine, and confession, to wit: that the understanding and reason of man in spiritual things are wholly blind, and can understand nothing by their proper powers. As it is written (1 Cor. ii. 14): 'The natural man perceiveth not the things of the Spirit of God: for they are foolishness unto him: neither can he know them, because he is examined concerning spiritual things.'[1]

II. *Credimus, docemus et confitemur etiam, voluntatem hominis nondum renatam, non tantum a Deo esse aversam, verum etiam inimicam Deo factam, ita, ut tantummodo ea velit et cupiat, iisque delectetur, quæ mala sunt et voluntati divinæ repugnant. Scriptum est enim* (Gen. viii. 21): '*Sensus et cogitatio humani cordis in malum prona sunt ab adolescentia sua.*' *Item* (Rom. viii. 7): '*Affectus carnis inimicitia est adversus Deum, neque*

II. We believe, teach, and confess, moreover, that the yet unregenerate will of man is not only averse from God, but has become even hostile to God, so that it only wishes and desires those things, and is delighted with them, which are evil and opposite to the divine will. For it is written (Gen. viii. 21): 'For the imagination and thought of man's heart are prone to evil from his youth.' Also (Rom. viii. 7): 'The carnal mind is enmity against God: for it is not

---

[1] We usually transfer the Scripture passages from our Authorized English Version. But this would not answer here, nor in several other cases. The German text of the Formula deviates in 1 Cor. ii. 14 from Luther's Version (*es muss geistlich gerichtet sein*), and the Latin text deviates from the Vulgate and accords with the German. Tyndale (1534) and the Rheims Version (1582) translate ὅτι πνευματικῶς ἀνακρίνεται, 'because he is spiritually examined;' the Authorized Version, 'because they are spiritually discerned.'

enim legi subjicitur, ac ne po-
test id quidem.'

Itaque credimus, quantum abest,
ut corpus mortuum seipsum vivi-
ficare, atque sibiipsi corporalem
vitam restituere possit, tantum
abesse, ut homo, qui ratione pec-
cati spiritualiter mortuus est,
seipsum in vitam spiritualem re-
vocandi ullam facultatem habeat;
sicut scriptum est (Eph. ii. 5):
'Cum essemus mortui in peccatis,
convivificavit nos cum Christo,' etc.
(2 Cor. iii. 5): *'Itaque etiam ex no-*
bismetipsis, tanquam ex nobis, non
sumus idonei, ut aliquid boni [et-
was Guts][1] *cogitemus; quod vero*
idonei sumus, id ipsum a Deo est.'

III. *Conversionem autem ho-*
minis operatur Spiritus Sanctus
non sine mediis, sed ad eam effi-
ciendam uti solet prædicatione
et auscultatione verbi Dei, sicut
scriptum est (Rom. i. 16): *'Evan-*
gelion est potentia Dei ad salu-
tem omni credenti.' Et (Rom. x.
17): *'Fides est ex auditu verbi*
Dei.' Et sane vult Dominus,
ut ipsius verbum audiatur, ne-
que ad illius prædicationem
aures obdurentur (Psa. xcv. 8).
Huic verbo adest præsens Spiri-
tus Sanctus, et corda hominum
aperit, ut, sicut Lydia in Actis

subject to the law, neither indeed
can be.'

Therefore we believe that by
how much it is impossible that
a dead body should vivify itself
and restore corporal life to itself,
even so impossible is it that man,
who by reason of sin is spiritually dead, should have any faculty
of recalling himself into spiritual life; as it is written (Eph. ii.
5): 'Even when we were dead in
sins, he hath quickened us together with Christ.' (2 Cor. iii. 5):
'Not that we are sufficient of
ourselves to think any thing good[1]
as of ourselves; but that we are
sufficient is itself of God.'

III. Nevertheless the Holy Spirit
effects the conversion of man not
without means, but is wont to use
for effecting it preaching and the
hearing of the Word of God, as it is
written (Rom. i. 16): 'The gospel
is a power of God unto salvation
to every one that believeth.' And
(Rom. x. 17): 'Faith cometh by
hearing of the Word of God.' And
without question it is the will of
the Lord that his Word should be
heard, and that our ears should not
be stopped when it is preached
(Psa. xcv. 8). With this Word is
present the Holy Spirit, who opens

---

[1] The paraphrastic addition 'good' of the German and Latin text is wanting in the Greek
and in Luther's Version.

Apostolicis (xvi. 14), *diligenter attendant, et ita convertantur, sola gratia et virtute Spiritus Sancti, cujus unius et solius opus est hominis conversio. Si enim Spiritus Sancti gratia absit* (Rom. ix. 16), *nostrum velle et currere* (1 Cor. iii. 7), *nostrum plantare, seminare et rigare, prorsus frustranea sunt; si videlicet ille incrementum non largiatur, sicut Christus inquit* (John xv. 5): *'Sine me nihil potestis facere.' Et his quidem paucis verbis Christus libero arbitrio omnes vires derogat, omniaque gratiæ divinæ adscribit* (1 Cor. i. 29; 2 Cor. xii. 5; Jer. ix. 23): *'Ne quis coram Deo habeat, de quo glorietur.'*

the hearts of men, in order that, as Lydia did (Acts xvi. 14), they may diligently attend, and thus may be converted by the sole grace and power of the Holy Spirit, whose work, and whose work alone, the conversion of man is. For if the grace of the Holy Spirit is absent, our willing and running, our planting, sowing, and watering, are wholly in vain (Rom. ix. 16; 1 Cor. iii. 7); if, that is, he do not give the increase, as Christ says (John xv. 5): 'Without me ye can do nothing.' And, indeed, in these few words Christ denies to free-will all power whatever, and ascribes all to divine grace, 'that no one may have whereof he may glory before God' (1 Cor. i. 29; 2 Cor. xii. 5; Jer. ix. 23).

NEGATIVA.

Rejectio contrariæ et falsæ doctrinæ.

Repudiamus igitur et damnamus omnes, quos recitabimus, errores, cum verbi divini regula non congruentes.

I. *Primo delirum Philosophorum Stoicorum dogma, quemadmodum et Manichæorum furorem, qui docuerunt, omnia, quæ eveniant, necessario fieri, et aliter fieri prorsus non posse, et hominem omnia coactum facere, etiam ea, quæ in rebus externis agat, eumque ad designanda mala*

NEGATIVE.

Rejection of contrary and false doctrine.

We repudiate, therefore, and condemn all the errors which we will now recount, as not agreeing with the rule of the divine word:

I. First, the insane dogma of the Stoic philosophers, as also the madness of the Manichæans, who taught that all things which come to pass take place by necessity, and can not possibly be otherwise; and that man does all things by constraint, even those things which he transacts in outward matters, and that he is

opera et scelera (qualia sunt libi-dines vagæ, rapinæ, cædes, furta, et similia) cogi.

II. *Repudiamus etiam crassum illum Pelagianorum errorem, qui asserere non dubitarunt, quod homo propriis viribus, sine gratia Spiritus Sancti, sese ad Deum convertere, Evangelio credere, legi divinæ ex animo parere, et hac ratione peccatorum remissionem ac vitam æternam ipse promereri valeat.*

III. *Præter hos errores rejicimus et Semipelagianorum falsum dogma, qui docent, hominem propriis viribus inchoare posse suam conversionem: absolvere autem sine Spiritus Sancti gratia non posse.*

IV. *Item, cum docetur, licet homo non renatus, ratione liberi arbitrii, ante sui regenerationem infirmior quidem sit, quam ut conversionis suæ initium facere, atque propriis viribus sese ad Deum convertere, et legi Dei toto corde parere valeat: tamen, si Spiritus Sanctus prædicatione verbi initium fecerit, suamque gratiam in verbo homini obtulerit, tum hominis voluntatem, propriis et naturalibus suis viribus quodammodo aliquid, licet id modiculum, infirmum et lan-*

compelled to the committing of evil works and crimes, such as unlawful lusts, acts, rapine, murders, thefts, and the like.

II. We repudiate, also, that gross error of the Pelagians, who have not hesitated to assert that man by his own powers, without the grace of the Holy Spirit, has ability to convert himself to God, to believe the gospel, to obey the divine law from his heart, and in this way to merit of himself the remission of sins and eternal life.

III. Besides these errors, we reject also the false dogma of the Semi-Pelagians, who teach that man by his own powers can commence his conversion, but can not fully accomplish it without the grace of the Holy Spirit.

IV. Also the teaching that, although unregenerate man, in respect of free-will, is indeed, antecedently to his regeneration, too infirm to make a beginning of his own conversion, and by his own powers to convert himself to God, and obey the law of God with all his heart; yet if the Holy Spirit, by the preaching of the word, shall have made a beginning, and offered his grace in the word to man, that then man, by his own proper and natural powers, can, as it were, give some assistance and co-operation, though it be but

guidum admodum sit, conversionem adjuvare, atque cooperari, et seipsam ad gratiam applicare, præparare, eam apprehendere, amplecti, et Evangelio credere posse.

V. *Item, hominem, post regenerationem, legem Dei perfecte observare atque implere posse, eamque impletionem esse nostram coram Deo justitiam, qua vitam æternam promereamur.*

VI. *Rejicimus etiam damnamusque Enthusiastarum[1] errorem, qui fingunt, Deum immediate, absque verbi Dei auditu, et sine Sacramentorum usu, homines ad se trahere, illuminare, justificare et salvare.*

VII. *Item, Deum in conversione et regeneratione hominis substantiam et essentiam veteris Adami, et præcipue animam rationalem penitus abolere, novamque animæ essentiam ex nihilo, in illa conversione et regeneratione creare.*

VIII. *Item, cum hi sermones citra declarationem usurpantur, quod videlicet hominis voluntas, ante conversionem, in ipsa conversione, et post conversionem, Spiritui Sancto repugnet, et quod*

slight, infirm, and languid, towards his conversion, and can apply and prepare himself unto grace, apprehend it, embrace it, and believe the gospel.

V. Also that man, after regeneration, can perfectly observe and fulfill the law of God, and that this fulfilling is our righteousness before God, whereby we merit eternal life.

VI. We also reject and condemn the error of the Enthusiasts,[1] who feign that God immediately, apart from the hearing of the Word of God, and without the use of the sacraments, draws men to himself, enlightens them, justifies and saves them.

VII. Also, that God in the regeneration of man utterly abolishes the substance and essence of the old Adam, and especially the rational soul, and creates from nothing in that conversion and regeneration a new essence of the soul.

VIII. Also, when such statements as these are used without explanation, that the will of man, before conversion, in conversion itself, and after conversion, is set against the Holy Ghost, and that the Holy

---

[1] '*Enthusiastæ*' *vocantur, qui neglecta prædicatione verbi divini cælestes revelationes Spiritus exspectant.*

[1] *Enthusiasts* are those who, neglecting the preaching of the divine Word, yet expect celestial revelations of the Spirit.

Spiritus Sanctus iis detur, qui ex proposito et pertinaciter ipsi resistunt. Nam Deus in conversione ex nolentibus volentes facit, et in volentibus habitat, ut Augustinus loqui solet.

Quod vero ad dicta quædam, tum Patrum, tum Neotericorum quorundam Doctorum attinet: Deus trahit, sed volentem trahit: et hominis voluntas in conversione non est otiosa, sed agit aliquid: judicamus hæc formæ sanorum verborum non esse analoga. Afferuntur enim hæc dicta ad confirmandam falsam opinionem de viribus humani arbitrii in hominis conversione, contra doctrinam, quæ soli gratiæ divinæ id opus attribuit. Ideoque ab ejusmodi sermonibus, quando de conversione hominis ad Deum agitur, abstinendum censemus.

Contra autem recte docetur, quod Dominus in conversione, per Spiritus Sancti tractionem (id est, motum et operationem) ex hominibus repugnantibus et nolentibus volentes homines faciat, et quod post conversionem in quotidianis pœnitentiæ exercitiis hominis renati voluntas non sit otiosa, sed omnibus Spiritus Sancti operibus, quæ ille per nos efficit, etiam cooperetur.

Ghost is given to those who of set purpose and obstinately resist him. For God in conversion *of unwilling men makes willing men, and dwells in the willing,* as Augustine is wont to speak.

But as concerns certain dicta, both of the Fathers and of certain modern doctors, such as the following: *God draws, but draws a willing man,* and *man's will in conversion is not idle, but effects somewhat*—we judge that these are not agreeable to the form of sound words. For these dicta are advanced for the confirming of the false opinion of the powers of the human will in the conversion of man, contrary to the doctrine which attributes that work to divine grace alone. And therefore we judge that we ought to abstain from expressions of such sort in treating of the conversion of man to God.

But, on the other hand, it is rightly taught that the Lord in conversion, through the drawing (that is, the movement and operation) of the Holy Spirit, of resisting and unwilling makes willing men, and that after conversion, in the daily exercises of penitence the will of man is not idle, but co-operates also with all the works of the Holy Spirit which he effects through us.

IX. *Item, quod D. Lutherus scripsit, hominis voluntatem in conversione pure passive se habere: id recte et dextre est accipiendum, videlicet, respectu divinæ gratiæ in accendendis novis motibus, hoc est, de eo intelligi oportet, quando Spiritus Dei per verbum auditum, aut per usum Sacramentorum hominis voluntatem aggreditur, et conversionem atque regenerationem in homine operatur. Postquam enim Spiritus Sanctus hoc ipsum jam operatus est atque effecit, hominisque voluntatem sola sua divina virtute et operatione immutavit atque renovavit: tunc revera hominis nova illa voluntas instrumentum est et organon Dei Spiritus Sancti, ut ea non modo gratiam apprehendat, verum etiam in operibus sequentibus Spiritui Sancto cooperetur.*

Relinquuntur igitur ante conversionem hominis duæ tantum efficientes causæ (ad conversionem efficaces), nimirum Spiritus Sanctus, et verbum Dei, quod est instrumentum Spiritus Sancti, quo conversionem hominis efficit.[1] Hoc verbum homo certe audire debet, sed tamen ut illud ipsum

IX. Also, whereas Dr. Luther has written that the will of man in conversion is *purely passive*, that is to be received rightly and fitly, to wit: in respect of divine grace in kindling new motions, that is, it ought to be understood of the moment when the Spirit of God, through the hearing of the Word or through the use of the sacraments, lays hold of the will of man, and works conversion and regeneration in man. For after the Holy Spirit has already wrought and effected this very thing, and has changed and renewed the will of man by his own divine virtue and working alone, then, indeed, this new will of man is the instrument and organ of God the Holy Ghost, so that it not only lays hold of grace, but also co-operates, in the works which follow, with the Holy Spirit.

There are, therefore, left before the conversion of man two efficient causes only (efficacious to conversion), that is to say, the Holy Spirit and the Word of God, which is the instrument of the Holy Spirit whereby he effects the conversion of man.[1] This Word man is, without question, bound to hear; but,

---

[1] Against Melanchthon, who in his later years taught that there are three causes of conversion closely combined, namely, the Holy Spirit (the creative cause), the Word of God (the instrumental cause), and *the consenting will* of man. See Vol. I. p. 262.

*vera fide amplectatur, nequa-
quam suis viribus propriis, sed
sola gratia et operatione Dei
Spiritus Sancti obtinere potest.*

nevertheless, he is in nowise by his
own powers able to obtain the benefit of embracing it in true faith,
but only by the grace and working
of God the Holy Ghost.

Art. III.

DE JUSTITIA FIDEI CORAM DEO.

Status Controversiæ.

*Unanimi consensu (ad normam
verbi divini, et sententiam Augustanæ Confessionis) in Ecclesiis nostris docetur, nos peccatores longe miserrimos sola in
Christum fide coram Deo justificari et salvari, ita ut Christus
solus nostra sit justitia. Hic
autem Jesus Christus, Salvator
noster, et justitia nostra, verus
Deus est et verus homo: etenim
divina et humana naturæ in
ipso sunt personaliter unitæ.
Quæsitum igitur fuit: secundum quam naturam Christus
nostra sit justitia? Et hac occasione duo errores, et quidem inter se pugnantes, Ecclesias quasdam perturbarunt.*

*Una enim pars sensit, Chris-
tum tantummodo secundum divinam naturam esse nostram justitiam, si videlicet ille per fidem
in nobis habitet: etenim omnia*

Art. III.

OF THE RIGHTEOUSNESS OF FAITH BEFORE GOD.

Statement of the Controversy.

By unanimous consent (according to the rule of the divine Word
and the judgment of the Augsburg
Confession), it is taught in our
churches that we most wretched
sinners are justified before God and
saved alone by faith in Christ, so
that Christ alone is our righteousness. Now this Jesus Christ, our
Saviour and our righteousness, is
true God and true man; for the
divine and human natures in him
are personally united (Jer. xxiii. 6;
1 Cor. i. 30; 2 Cor. v. 21). It has
therefore been asked: According
to which nature is Christ our righteousness? And by occasion of this,
two errors, and these contrary the
one to the other, have disturbed
certain churches.

For one part has held that
Christ is our righteousness only
according to the divine nature, if,
that is, he dwell by faith in us;
for that all the sins of men, com-

hominum peccata, collata nimi-
rum cum illa per fidem inhabi-
tante Divinitate, esse instar unius
guttulæ aquæ, cum magno mari
comparatæ. Contra hanc opinio-
nem alii quidam asseruerunt,
Christum esse nostram coram
Deo justitiam, duntaxat secun-
dum humanam naturam.

pared with that Godhead thus indwelling by faith, are like one
drop of water compared with the
broad sea. Against this opinion
others, indeed, have asserted that
Christ is our righteousness before
God, only according to his human
nature.

AFFIRMATIVA.

Sincera doctrina piarum Ecclesiarum, utrique
commemorato errori opposita.

AFFIRMATIVE.

The sound doctrine of godly churches opposed
to both of the fore-mentioned errors.

I. *Ad refellendum utrumque*
errorem, credimus, docemus et
confitemur unanimiter, quod
Christus vere sit nostra justitia,
sed tamen neque secundum so-
lam divinam naturam, neque
secundum solam humanam na-
turam: sed totus Christus, se-
cundum utramque naturam, in
sola videlicet obedientia sua,
quam Patri ad mortem usque
absolutissimam Deus et homo
præstitit, eaque nobis peccatorum
omnium remissionem et vitam
æternam promeruit. Sicut scrip-
tum est: 'Sicut per inobedien-
tiam unius hominis peccatores
constituti sunt multi: ita et per
unius obedientiam justi constitu-
entur multi' (Rom. v. 19).

I. To overthrow both errors we
unanimously believe, teach, and confess that Christ is truly our righteousness, but yet neither according to the divine nature alone, nor
according to the human nature
alone, but the whole Christ according to both natures, to wit:
in his sole, most absolute obedience which he rendered to the
Father even unto death, as God
and man, and thereby merited for
us the remission of all our sins
and eternal life. As it is written: 'As by one man's disobedience many were made sinners,
so by the obedience of one shall
many be made righteous' (Rom.
v. 19).

II. *Credimus igitur, docemus*
et confitemur, hoc ipsum nostram
esse coram Deo justitiam, quod

II. We believe, therefore, teach,
and confess that this very thing is
our righteousness before God, name-

Dominus nobis peccata remittit, ex mera gratia, absque ullo respectu præcedentium, præsentium, aut consequentium nostrorum operum, dignitatis, aut meriti. Ille enim donat atque imputat nobis justitiam obedientiæ Christi; propter eam justitiam a Deo in gratiam recipimur, et justi reputamur.

III. *Credimus etiam, docemus et confitemur, solam fidem esse illud medium et instrumentum, quo Christum Salvatorem, et ita in Christo justitiam illam, quæ coram judicio Dei consistere potest, apprehendimus: propter Christum enim fides illa nobis ad justitiam imputatur* (Rom. iv. 5).

IV. *Credimus præterea, docemus et confitemur, fidem illam justificantem non esse nudam notitiam historiæ de Christo, sed ingens atque tale Dei donum, quo Christum, Redemtorem nostrum, in verbo Evangelii recte agnoscimus, ipsique confidimus: quod videlicet propter solam ipsius obedientiam, ex gratia, remissionem peccatorum habeamus, sancti et justi coram Deo Patre reputemur, et æternam salutem consequamur.*

V. *Credimus, docemus et confitemur, vocabulum 'justificare'*

ly, that God remits to us our sins of mere grace, without any respect of our works, going before, present, or following, or of our worthiness or merit. For he bestows and imputes to us the righteousness of the obedience of Christ; for the sake of that righteousness we are received by God into favor and accounted righteous.

III. We believe, also, teach, and confess that Faith alone is the means and instrument whereby we lay hold on Christ the Saviour, and so in Christ lay hold on that righteousness which is able to stand before the judgment of God; for that faith, for Christ's sake, is imputed to us for righteousness (Rom. iv. 5).

IV. We believe, moreover, teach, and confess that this justifying faith is not a bare knowledge of the history of Christ, but such and so great a gift of God as that by it we rightly recognize Christ our Redeemer in the word of the gospel, and confide in him: to wit, that for his obedience' sake alone we have by grace the remission of sins, are accounted holy and righteous before God the Father, and attain eternal salvation.

V. We believe, teach, and confess that the word *justify* in this

phrasi Scripturæ Sacræ, in hoc articulo, idem significare, quod absolvere a peccatis, ut ex dicto Salomonis (Prov. xvii. 15) *intelligi potest: 'Qui justificat impium, et qui condemnat justum, abominabilis est uterque apud Deum.' Item* (Rom. viii. 33): *'Quis accusabit electos Dei? Deus est qui justificat.'*

Et, si quando pro vocabulo justificationis vocabula regenerationis et vivificationis usurpantur (quod in Apologia Augustanæ Confessionis factum est), sunt ea in illa superiore significatione accipienda. Nam alias eæ voces de hominis renovatione intelligendæ sunt, quæ a fidei justificatione recte discernitur.

VI. *Credimus, docemus et confitemur etiam, etsi vere in Christum credentes et renati multis infirmitatibus et nævis usque ad mortem sunt obnoxii: non tamen illis vel de justitia, quæ per fidem ipsis imputatur, vel de æterna salute esse dubitandum, quin potius firmiter illis statuendum esse [vor gewiss halten sollen], quod propter Christum, juxta promissionem et inmotum verbum Evangelii, Deum sibi placatum habeant.*

article, conformably to the usage of Holy Scripture, signifies the same as to absolve from sin, as may be understood by the word of Solomon (Prov. xvii. 15): 'He that justifieth the wicked, and he that condemneth the just, even they both are abomination to the Lord.' Also (Rom. viii. 33): 'Who shall lay any thing to the charge of God's elect? It is God that justifieth.'

And if at any time for the word Justification the words Regeneration and Vivification are used (as is done in the Apology of the Augsburg Confession), these words are to be taken in the above-stated signification. For elsewhere these words are to be understood of the renewing of man, which is rightly distinguished from the justification of faith.

VI. We believe, teach, and confess, moreover, that, although they that truly believe in Christ and are born again are even to the hour of death obnoxious to many infirmities and stains, yet they ought not to doubt either of the righteousness which is imputed to them through faith or concerning their eternal salvation, but rather are they firmly to be convinced that, for Christ's sake, according to the promise and unshaken word of the gospel, they have God reconciled to them.

VII. *Credimus, docemus et confitemur, quod ad conservandam puram doctrinam de justitia fidei coram Deo, necessarium sit, ut particulæ exclusivæ (quibus Apostolus Paulus Christi meritum ab operibus nostris prorsus separat, solique Christo eam gloriam tribuit) quam diligentissime retineantur, ut cum Paulus scribit: ex gratia, gratis, sine meritis, absque lege, sine operibus, non ex operibus. Quæ omnia hoc ipsum dicunt: 'Sola fide in Christum justificamur et salvamur'* (Eph. ii. 8; Rom. i. 17; iii. 24; iv. 3 sqq.; Gal. iii. 11; Heb. xi.).

VIII. *Credimus, docemus et confitemur, etsi antecedens contritio et subsequens nova obedientia ad articulum justificationis coram Deo non pertinent: non tamen talem fidem justificantem esse fingendam, quæ una cum malo proposito peccandi, videlicet, et contra conscientiam agendi, esse et stare possit. Sed postquam homo per fidem est justificatus, tum veram illam et vivam fidem esse per caritatem efficacem* (Gal. v. 6), *et bona opera semper fidem justificantem sequi, et una cum ea, si modo vera et viva fides est, certissime deprehendi. Fides enim vera nunquam sola est, quin caritatem et spem semper secum habeat.*

VII. We believe, teach, and confess that, for the preserving of the pure doctrine of the righteousness of faith before God, it is necessary that the exclusive particles (by which the apostle Paul separates the merit of Christ utterly from our works, and attributes that glory to Christ alone) should be most diligently retained, as when Paul writes: '*Of grace, freely, without our deserts, without law, without works, not of works.*' All which expressions amount to this: '*By faith in Christ alone are we justified and saved*' (Eph. ii. 8; Rom. i. 17; iii. 24; iv. 3 sqq.; Gal. iii. 11; Heb. xi.).

VIII. We believe, teach, and confess that, although antecedent contrition and subsequent new obedience do not appertain to the article of justification before God, yet we are not to imagine any such justifying faith as can exist and abide with a purpose of evil, to wit: of sinning and acting contrary to conscience. But after that man is justified by faith, then that true and living faith works by love (Gal. v. 6), and good works always follow justifying faith, and are most certainly found together with it, provided only it be a true and living faith. For true faith is never alone, but hath always charity and hope in its train.

ANTITHESIS, SEU NEGATIVA.

Rejectio contrariæ et falsæ doctrinæ.

ANTITHESIS, OR NEGATIVE.

Rejection of opposite and false doctrine.

Repudiamus ergo et damnamus omnia falsa dogmata, quæ jam recitabimus.

I. *Christum esse justitiam nostram solummodo secundum divinam naturam.*

II. *Christum esse justitiam nostram tantummodo juxta humanam naturam.*

III. *In dictis Propheticis et Apostolicis, ubi de justificatione fidei agitur, vocabula 'justificare' et 'justificari' non idem esse ac a peccatis absolvere et absolvi, et remissionem peccatorum consequi: sed nos per caritatem, a Spiritu Sancto infusam, per virtutes et per opera, quæ a caritate promanant, reipsa coram Deo justos fieri.*

IV. *Fidem non respicere in solam Christi obedientiam, sed in divinam ejus naturam; quatenus videlicet ea in nobis habitet atque efficax sit, ut per eam inhabitationem peccata nostra tegantur.*

V. *Fidem esse talem fiduciam in obedientiam Christi, quæ possit in eo etiam homine permanere et consistere, qui vera pœnitentia careat, et ubi caritas non sequatur, sed qui contra conscientiam in peccatis perseveret.*

We repudiate, therefore, and condemn all the false dogmas, which we will now recount:

I. That Christ is our righteousness only according to his divine nature.

II. That Christ is our righteousness only according to his human nature.

III. That in the prophetic and apostolic declarations, which treat of the righteousness of faith, the words *justify* and *to be justified* are not the same as to absolve and be absolved from sins, and to obtain remission of sins, but that we, through love infused by the Holy Ghost, through the virtues and through the works which flow forth from charity, become in very deed righteous before God.

IV. That faith does not have respect to the sole obedience of Christ, but to his divine nature, so far as that dwells and is efficacious in us, so that by that indwelling our sins are covered.

V. That faith is such a confidence in the obedience of Christ as can abide and have a being even in that man who is void of true repentance, and in whom it is not followed by charity, but who contrary to conscience perseveres in sins.

VI. *Non ipsum Deum, sed tantum dona Dei in credentibus habitare.*

VII. *Fidem ideo salutem nobis conferre, quod novitas illa, quæ in dilectione erga Deum et proximum consistit, per fidem in nobis inchoetur.*

VIII. *Fidem in justificationis negotio primas quidem partes tenere, sed tamen etiam renovationem et caritatem ad justitiam nostram coram Deo pertinere, ita ut renovatio et caritas quidem non sit principalis causa nostræ justitiæ: sed tamen justitiam nostram coram Deo (si absint renovatio et caritas) non esse integram et perfectam.*

IX. *Credentes in Christum coram Deo justos esse et salvos, simul per imputatam Christi justitiam, et per inchoatam novam obedientiam, vel, partim quidem per imputationem justitiæ Christi, partim vero per inchoatam novam obedientiam.*

X. *Promissionem gratiæ nobis applicari per fidem in corde, et præterea etiam per confessionem, quæ ore fit, et per alias virtutes.*

XI. *Fidem non justificare sine bonis operibus, itaque bona opera necessario ad justitiam requiri, et*

VI. That not God himself dwells, but only the gifts of God dwell in believers.

VII. That faith bestows salvation upon us for the reason that that renewal which consists in love towards God and our neighbor, commences in us through faith.

VIII. That faith in the matter of justification holds, indeed, the first place, but that renewal and charity also appertain to our righteousness before God, so that renewal and charity, indeed, are not the principal cause of our righteousness, but yet that our righteousness before God (if renewal and charity be wanting) is not whole and perfect.

IX. That believers in Christ are righteous and saved before God, both through the imputed righteousness of Christ and through the new obedience which is begun in them, or partly, indeed, through the imputation of the righteousness of Christ, and partly through the new obedience which is begun in them.

X. That the promised grace is appropriated to us by the faith of the heart, and also by the confession of the mouth, and moreover, also, by other virtuous acts.

XI. That faith does not justify without good works, that therefore good works are necessarily required

absque eorum præsentia hominem justificari non posse.

for righteousness, and that independently of their being present man can not be justified.

ART. IV.

DE BONIS OPERIBUS.

STATUS CONTROVERSIÆ.

In doctrina de bonis operibus duæ controversiæ in quibusdam Ecclesiis ortæ sunt.

I. *Primum schisma inter Theologos quosdam factum est, cum alii assererent, bona opera necessaria esse ad salutem, impossibile esse salvari sine bonis operibus, et neminem unquam sine bonis operibus salvatum esse: alii vero docerent, bona opera ad salutem esse perniciosa.*

II. *Alterum schisma inter Theologos nonnullos super vocabulis 'necessarium' et 'liberum' ortum est. Altera enim pars contendit, vocabulum 'necessarium' non esse usurpandum de nova obedientia: eam enim non a necessitate quadam et coactione, sed a spontaneo spiritu [aus freiwilligen Geiste] promanare. Altera vero pars vocabulum 'necessarium' prorsus retinendum censuit: propterea, quod illa obedientia non in nostro arbitrio posita et libera sit, sed homines renatos illud obsequium debere præstare.*

ART. IV.

OF GOOD WORKS.

STATEMENT OF THE CONTROVERSY.

Respecting the doctrine of Good Works, two controversies have arisen in certain churches:

I. The first schism among certain theologians arose when some asserted, that good works are necessary to salvation, and that it is impossible to be saved without good works, and that no one was ever saved without good works; while others taught that good works are detrimental to salvation.

II. The other schism has arisen between certain divines concerning the terms *necessary* and *free*. For the one part contends that the term *necessary* should not be used concerning the new obedience, for that this flows not from any necessity or constraint, but from a voluntary spirit. But the other part judges that the term *necessary* should by all means be retained, inasmuch as this obedience is not left to our mere will, and therefore is not free, but that regenerate men are bound to render such service.

Et dum de commemoratis illis vocabulis disputatum est, tandem etiam de reipsa fuit disceptatum. Alii enim contenderunt, Legem apud Christianos prorsus non esse docendam, sed tantummodo doctrina Evangelii homines ad bona opera invitandos esse: alii hanc opinionem impugnarunt.

And out of this discussion concerning the aforementioned terms there arose at length a dispute concerning the material fact. For some have contended that the law ought not to be taught at all among Christians, but that men should be invited to good works by the doctrine of the gospel alone. Others have impugned this opinion.

AFFIRMATIVA.

Sincera Ecclesiæ doctrina de hac controversia.

Ut hæ controversiæ solide et dextre explicentur atque decidantur, hæc nostra fides, doctrina et confessio est.

   I. Quod bona opera veram fidem (si modo ea non sit mortua, sed viva fides) certissime atque indubitato sequantur, tanquam fructus bonæ arboris.

   II. Credimus etiam, docemus et confitemur, quod bona opera penitus excludenda sint, non tantum cum de justificatione fidei agitur, sed etiam cum de salute nostra æterna disputatur, sicut Apostolus perspicuis verbis testatur, cum ait (Rom. iv. 6): '*Sicut et David dicit, beatitudinem hominis, cui Deus accepto fert*

AFFIRMATIVE.

The sound doctrine of the Church concerning this controversy.

In order that these controversies may be solidly and judiciously explained and decided, the following is our faith, doctrine, and confession:

   I. That good works[1] must certainly and without all doubt follow a true faith (provided only it be not a dead but a living faith), as fruits of a good tree.

   II. We believe, also, teach, and confess that good works are wholly to be excluded, not only when the righteousness of faith is treated of, but also when the matter of our eternal salvation is discussed, as the apostle bears witness in clear words, when he says (Rom. iv. 6): 'Even as also David describeth the blessedness of the man to whom God im-

---

[1] 'Good works do spring out necessarily of a true and lively faith; insomuch that by them a lively faith may be as evidently known as a tree discerned by the fruit.'—*XII. Article of the Church of England.*

justitiam sine operibus. Beati, quorum remissæ sunt iniquitates, et quorum tecta sunt peccata. Beatus vir, cui non imputavit Dominus peccatum, etc. Et alibi (Eph. ii. 8 sq.): '*Gratia,*' *inquit,* '*estis salvati, per fidem, et hoc non ex vobis, Dei enim donum est, non ex operibus, ne quis glorietur.*'

III. *Credimus, docemus et confitemur, omnes quidem homines, præcipue vero eos, qui per Spiritum Sanctum regenerati sunt et renovati, ad bona opera facienda debitores esse.*

IV. *Et in hac sententia vocabula illa* '*necessarium,*' '*debere,*' '*oportere*' ['*nöthig,*' '*sollen,*' *und* '*müssen*'] *recte usurpantur, etiam de renatis hominibus, et cum forma sanorum verborum non pugnant.*

V. *Sed tamen per vocabula* '*necessitas,*' '*necessarium,*' *quando videlicet de renatis est sermo, non intelligenda est coactio, sed tantum debita illa obedientia, quam vere credentes, quatenus renati sunt, non ex coactione, aut compulsu legis, sed libero et spontaneo spiritu præstant, quandoquidem non amplius sub lege sunt, sed sub gratia* (Rom. vi. 14; vii. 6; viii. 14).

VI. *Credimus igitur, docemus et confitemur, cum dicitur. rena-*

puteth righteousness without works, saying, Blessed are they whose iniquities are forgiven, and whose sins are covered. Blessed is the man to whom the Lord hath not imputed sin.' And elsewhere (Eph. ii. 8 sq.): ' By grace,' saith he, ' are ye saved through faith; and that not of yourselves, for it is the gift of God—not of works, lest any man should boast.'

III. We believe, teach, and confess that all men, indeed, but chiefly those who through the Holy Spirit are regenerated and renewed, are debtors to do good works.

IV. And in this decision those words—'necessary,' ' ought,' ' it behooves'—are rightly used even of regenerate men, and are not inconsistent with the form of sound words.

V. But, nevertheless, by the terms *necessity, necessary,* when we speak of the regenerate, we are not to understand constraint, but only that bounden obedience which true believers, so far as they are regenerate, render, not of constraint or compulsion of the law, but of a free and spontaneous spirit: inasmuch as they are no longer under the law, but under grace (Rom. vi. 14; vii. 6; viii. 14).

VI. We believe, therefore, teach, and confess that when it is said

*tos bene operari libero et spon-
taneo spiritu, id non ita accipiendum esse, quod in hominis
renati arbitrio relictum sit, bene
aut male agere, quando ipsi visum fuerit, ut nihilominus tamen fidem retineat, etiamsi in
peccatis ex proposito perseveret.*

VII. *Hoc tamen non aliter,
quam de spiritu hominis jam
liberato intelligendum est, sicut
hanc rem ipse Christus, ejusque
Apostoli declarant* (Rom. viii.
15): *quod videlicet spiritus hominis liberatus bene operetur,
non formidine pœnæ, ut servus, sed justitiæ amore, qualem
obedientiam filii præstare solent.*

VIII. *Hanc vero libertatem spiritus in electis Dei filiis non
perfectam, sed multiplici infirmitate adhuc gravatam agnoscimus, quemadmodum D. Paulus
super ea re de sua ipsius persona conqueritur* (Rom. vii. 14
sqq.; Gal. v. 17).

IX. *Illam tamen infirmitatem
Dominus electis suis non imputat, idque propter Mediatorem
Christum. Sic enim scriptum
est* (Rom. viii. 1): *'Nihil jam
damnationis est his, qui in Christo Jesu sunt.'*

X. *Credimus præterea, docemus et confitemur, fidem et salu-*

that the regenerate do good works
of a free and spontaneous spirit,
this is not to be so understood as
that it is left to the regenerate man's
option to do well or ill whenever
it may seem good to him, so that
he retains faith, even though of set
purpose he persevere in sins.

VII. That this, nevertheless, is not
to be understood except of the spirit
of man when set free, even as Christ
himself and his apostles set forth
this matter, to wit: that the liber-
ated spirit of man does good works,
not, as a slave, from fear of punishment, but from love of righteousness, such as is the obedience which
children are wont to render (Rom.
viii. 15).

VIII. But we acknowledge that
this liberty of spirit in the elect
children of God is not perfect,
but is as yet weighed down with
manifold infirmity, as St. Paul la-
ments concerning himself about
this matter (Rom. vii. 14–25; Gal.
v. 17).

IX. This infirmity, nevertheless,
the Lord, for the sake of Christ
the Mediator, does not impute to
his elect. For so it is written
(Rom. viii. 1): 'There is therefore
now no condemnation to them
which are in Christ Jesus.'

X. We believe, moreover, teach,
and confess that faith and salvation

tem in nobis conservari, aut retineri, non per opera, sed tantum per Spiritum Dei, et per fidem (qua scilicet salus custoditur), bona autem opera testimonia esse, quod Spiritus Sanctus praesens sit, atque in nobis habitet.

are preserved or retained in us not by works, but only by the spirit of God and by faith (by which, namely, salvation is guarded), and that good works are a testimony that the Holy Spirit is present and dwells in us.

Negativa.

Falsa doctrina, superiori repugnans.

I. *Rejicimus igitur et damnamus subsequentes phrases, cum docetur : bona opera necessaria esse ad salutem ; neminem unquam sine bonis operibus salvatum ; impossibile esse sine bonis operibus salvari.*[1]

II. *Repudiamus et damnamus nudam hanc, offendiculi plenam, et Christianae disciplinae perniciosam phrasin : bona opera noxia esse ad salutem.*[2]

His enim postremis temporibus non minus necessarium est, ut homines ad recte et pie vivendi rationem bonaque opera invitentur atque moneantur, quam necessarium sit, ut ad declarandam fidem atque gratitudinem suam erga Deum in bonis operibus sese exerceant : quam necessarium est, cavere, ne bona opera negotio justificationis admisceantur. Non minus enim homines Epicurea persuasione de fide,

Negative.

False doctrine opposed to that above stated.

I. We reject, therefore, and condemn the following phrases, when it is taught : That good works are necessary to salvation ; that no one has ever been saved without good works ; that it is impossible to be saved without good works.

II. We repudiate and condemn this bald phrase, full of offense and pernicious to Christian discipline : That good works are detrimental to salvation.

For in these last times it is not less necessary that men should be admonished to a right and pious manner of living and to good works, and reminded how necessary it is that they should exercise themselves to declare and set forth their faith and gratitude towards God by good works, than it is necessary to beware lest good works be mingled in the matter of justification. For men may incur damnation no less by an Epicurean persuasion concern-

---

[1] Against Major.   [2] Against Amsdorf.

quam *Pharisaica et Papistica fiducia in propria opera et merita damnationem incurrere possunt.*

III. *Præterea reprobamus atque damnamus dogma illud, quod fides in Christum non amittatur, et Spiritus Sanctus nihilominus in homine habitet, etiamsi sciens volensque peccet; et quod sancti atque electi [die Heiligen und Auserwählten] Spiritum Sanctum retineant, tametsi in adulterium, aut in alia scelera prolabantur, et in iis perseverent.*

ing faith than by a Pharisaic and Papistic confidence in their own works and merits.

III. Moreover, we repudiate and condemn that dogma that faith in Christ is not lost, and that the Holy Spirit, even though a man sin wittingly and willingly, nevertheless dwells in him; and that the holy and elect retain the Holy Spirit, even though they fall into adultery or other crimes, and persevere in the same.

ART. V.

DE LEGE ET EVANGELIO.

STATUS CONTROVERSIÆ.

Quæsitum fuit: an Evangelium proprie sit tantummodo concio de gratia Dei, quæ remissionem peccatorum nobis annunciet: an vero etiam sit concio pœnitentiæ, arguens peccatum incredulitatis, quippe quæ non per Legem, sed per Evangelion duntaxat arguatur.

ART. V.

OF THE LAW AND THE GOSPEL.

STATEMENT OF THE CONTROVERSY.

It has been inquired: Whether the gospel is properly only a preaching of the grace of God, which announces to us the remission of sins, or whether it is also a preaching of repentance, rebuking the sin of unbelief, as one which is not rebuked by the Law, but only by the Gospel.

AFFIRMATIVA.

Sincera doctrina, cum norma verbi Dei congruens.

I. *Credimus, docemus et confitemur, discrimen Legis et Evangelii, ut clarissimum quoddam lumen [ein besonder herrlich Licht],*

AFFIRMATIVE.

Sound doctrine agreeing with the rule of the Word of God.

I. We believe, teach, and confess that the distinction of the Law and of the Gospel, as a most excellently clear light, is to be retained with

singulari diligentia in Ecclesia Dei retinendum esse, ut verbum Dei, juxta admonitionem D. Pauli, recte secari queat.

II. *Credimus, docemus et confitemur, Legem esse proprie doctrinam divinitus revelatam, quæ doceat, quid justum Deoque gratum sit; quæ etiam, quicquid peccatum est, et voluntati divinæ adversatur, redarguat.*

III. *Quare, quicquid extat in sacris literis, quod peccata arguit, id revera ad Legis concionem pertinet.*

IV. *Evangelion vero proprie doctrinam esse censemus, quæ doceat, quid homo credere debeat, qui Legi Dei non satisfecit, et idcirco per eandem damnatur: videlicet, quod illum credere oporteat, Jesum Christum omnia peccata expiasse, atque pro iis satisfecisse, et remissionem peccatorum, justitiam coram Deo consistentem et vitam æternam, nullo interveniente peccatoris illius merito, impetrasse.*

V. *Cum autem vocabulum 'Evangelii' non semper in una eademque significatione in Sacra Scriptura usurpetur, unde et dissensio illa primum orta est: credimus, docemus et confitemur, si vocabulum 'Evangelii' de tota Christi doctrina accipiatur, quam*

special diligence in the Church of God, in order that the Word of God, agreeably to the admonition of St. Paul, may be rightly divided.

II. We believe, teach, and confess that the Law is properly a doctrine divinely revealed, which teaches what is just and acceptable to God, and which also denounces whatever is sinful and opposite to the divine will.

III. Wherefore, whatever is found in the Holy Scriptures which convicts of sins, that properly belongs to the preaching of the Law.

IV. The Gospel, on the other hand, we judge to be properly the doctrine which teaches what a man ought to believe who has not satisfied the law of God, and therefore is condemned by the same, to wit: that it behooves him to believe that Jesus Christ has expiated all his sins, and made satisfaction for them, and has obtained remission of sins, righteousness which avails before God, and eternal life without the intervention of any merit of the sinner.

V. But inasmuch as the word *Gospel* is not always used in Holy Scripture in one and the same signification, whence also that dissension first arose, we believe, teach, and confess that if the term *Gospel* is understood of the whole doctrine of Christ, which he set forth in his

ipse in Ministerio suo (quemad-
modum et ejus Apostoli) profes-
sus est (in qua significatione
Mark i. 15 *et* Acts xx. 21 *vox*
illa usurpatur), recte dici et do-
ceri, Evangelium esse concionem
de pœnitentia et remissione pec-
catorum.

VI. *Quando vero Lex et Evan-*
gelion, sicut et ipse Moises, ut
Doctor Legis, et Christus, ut
Doctor Evangelii, inter se confe-
runtur: credimus, docemus et
confitemur, quod Evangelion non
sit concio pœnitentiæ, arguens
peccata: sed quod proprie nihil
aliud sit, quam laetissimum
quoddam nuncium, et concio ple-
na consolationis, non arguens aut
terrens, quandoquidem conscien-
tias contra terrores Legis sola-
tur, easque in meritum solius
Christi respicere jubet, et dul-
cissima prædicatione, de gratia
et favore Dei, per meritum Chri-
sti impetrato, rursus erigit.

VII. *Quod vero ad revelatio-*
nem peccati attinet, sic sese res
habent. Velum illud Moisis om-
nium hominum oculis est obduc-
tum, quam diu solam Legis con-
cionem, nihil autem de Christo
audiunt. Itaque peccata sua ex
Lege non vere agnoscunt: sed
aut hypocritæ fiunt, qui justitiæ
propriæ opinione turgent, quales

ministry, as did also his apostles
after him (in which signification
the word is used in Mark i. 15
and Acts xx. 21), it is rightly said
and taught that the Gospel is a
preaching of repentance and remission of sins.

VI. But when the Law and the
Gospel are compared together, as
well as Moses himself, the teacher
of the Law, and Christ the teacher
of the Gospel, we believe, teach,
and confess that the Gospel is not a
preaching of repentance, convicting
of sins, but that it is properly nothing else than a certain most joyful
message and preaching full of consolation, not convicting or terrify-
ing, inasmuch as it comforts the conscience against the terrors of the
Law, and bids it look at the merit
of Christ alone, and by a most sweet
preaching of the grace and favor of
God, obtained through Christ, lifts
it up again.

VII. But as respects the revelation of sin, the matter stands thus:
That veil of Moses is drawn over all
men's eyes, so long as they hear only
the preaching of the Law, and hear
nothing of Christ. Therefore they
do not, by the Law, truly come to
know their sins, but either become
hypocrites, swelling with an opinion
of their own righteousness, as were

olim *erant Pharisæi, aut in peccatis suis desperant, quod Judas proditor ille fecit. Eam ob causam Christus sumsit sibi Legem explicandam spiritualiter* (Matt. v. 21 sqq.; Rom. vii. 14), *et hoc modo ira Dei de cœlo revelatur super omnes peccatores* (Rom. i. 18), *ut, vera Legis sententia intellecta, animadvertatur, quanta sit illa ira. Et sic demum peccatores ad Legem remissi vere et recte peccata sua agnoscunt. Talem vero peccatorum agnitionem solus Moises nunquam ex ipsis extorquere potuisset.*

Etsi igitur concio illa de passione et morte Christi Filii Dei, severitatis et terroris plena est, quæ iram Dei adversus peccata ostendit, unde demum homines ad Legem Dei propius adducuntur, postquam velum illud Moisis ablatum est, ut tandem exacte agnoscant, quanta videlicet Dominus in Lege sua a nobis exigat, quorum nihil nos præstare possumus, ita, ut universam nostram justitiam in solo Christo quærere oporteat :

VIII. *Tamen, quam diu nobis Christi passio et mors iram Dei ob oculos ponunt, et hominem perterrefaciunt, tam diu non sunt proprie concio Evangelii,*

aforetime the Pharisees, or grow desperate in their sins, as did the traitor Judas. On this account Christ took upon him to explain the Law spiritually (Matt. v. 21 sqq.; Rom. vii. 14), and in this manner is the wrath of God revealed from heaven against all sinners (Rom. i. 18), in order that, by perceiving the true meaning of the Law, it may be understood how great is that wrath. And thus at length sinners, being remanded to the Law, truly and rightly come to know their own sins. But such an acknowledgment of sins Moses alone could never have extorted from them.

Although, therefore, this preaching of the passion and death of Christ, the Son of God, is full of severity and terror, inasmuch as it sets forth the anger of God against sin, from whence men at length are brought nearer to the Law of God, after that veil of Moses is taken away, that at length they may exactly perceive how great things God exacts from us in his Law, none of which we are able to perform, so that it behooves us to seek the whole of our righteousness in Christ alone:

VIII. Nevertheless, so long as the passion and death of Christ place before the eyes the wrath of God and terrify man, so long they are not properly the preaching of the

sed Legis et Moisis doctrina, et sunt alienum opus Christi, per quod accedit ad proprium suum officium, quod est, prædicare de gratia Dei, consolari et vivificare. Hæc propria sunt prædicationis Evangelicæ.

Gospel, but the teaching of the Law and Moses, and are Christ's strange work, through which he proceeds to his proper office, which is to declare the grace of God, to console and vivify. These things are the peculiar function of the evangelical preaching.

NEGATIVA.

Contraria et falsa doctrina, quæ rejicitur.

Rejicimus igitur, ut falsum et periculosum dogma, cum asseritur : quod Evangelion proprie sit concio pœnitentiæ, arguens, accusans et damnans peccata, quodque non sit tantummodo concio de gratia Dei. Hac enim ratione Evangelion rursus in Legem transformatur, meritum Christi et sacræ literæ obscurantur, piis mentibus vera et solida consolatio eripitur, et Pontificiis erroribus et superstitionibus fores aperiuntur.

NEGATIVE.

Contrary and false doctrine, which is rejected.

We reject, therefore, as a false and perilous dogma, the assertion that the Gospel is properly a preaching of repentance, rebuking, accusing, and condemning sins, and that it is not solely a preaching of the grace of God. For in this way the Gospel is transformed again into Law, the merit of Christ and the Holy Scriptures are obscured, a true and solid consolation is wrested away from godly souls, and the way is opened to the papal errors and superstitions.

ART. VI.

DE TERTIO USU LEGIS.

STATUS CONTROVERSIÆ.

Cum constet, Legem Dei propter tres causas hominibus datam esse, primo, ut externa quædam disciplina conservetur, et feri atque intractabiles homines quasi repagulis quibusdam cœrceantur,

ART. VI.

OF THE THIRD USE OF THE LAW.

STATEMENT OF THE CONTROVERSY.

Since it is established that the Law of God was given to men for three causes : first, that a certain external discipline might be preserved, and wild and intractable men might be restrained, as it were,

secundo, ut per Legem homines ad agnitionem suorum peccatorum adducantur, tertio, ut homines jam renati, quibus tamen omnibus multum adhuc carnis adhæret, eam ipsam ob causam certam aliquam regulam habeant, ad quam totam suam vitam formare possint et debeant, etc., orta est inter paucos quosdam Theologos controversia, super tertio usu Legis: videlicet, an Lex etiam renatis inculcanda, et ejus observatio apud eos urgenda sit, an non. Alii urgendam Legem censuerunt: alii negarunt.

by certain barriers; secondly, that by the Law men might be brought to an acknowledgment of their sins; thirdly, that regenerate men, to all of whom, nevertheless, much of the flesh still cleaves, for that very reason may have some certain rule after which they may and ought to shape their life, etc., a controversy has arisen among some few theologians concerning the third use of the Law, to wit: whether the Law is to be inculcated upon the regenerate also, and its observation urged upon them or not? Some have judged that the Law should be urged, others have denied it.

AFFIRMATIVA.

Sincera et pia doctrina de hac controversia.

AFFIRMATIVE.

The souna and godly doctrine concerning this controversy.

I. *Credimus, docemus et confitemur, etsi vere in Christum credentes, et sincere ad Deum conversi, a maledictione et coactione Legis per Christum liberati sunt [gefreiet und ledig gemacht], quod ii tamen propterea non sint absque Lege, quippe quos Filius Dei eam ob causam redemit, ut Legem Dei diu noctuque meditentur, atque in ejus observatione sese assidue exerceant* (Psa. i. 2; cxix. 1). *Etenim ne primi quidem nostri parentes, etiam ante lapsum, prorsus sine Lege vixerunt, quæ certe cordibus*

I. We believe, teach, and confess that although they who truly believe in Christ, and are sincerely converted to God, are through Christ set free from the curse and constraint of the Law, they are not, nevertheless, on that account without Law, inasmuch as the Son of God redeemed them for the very reason that they might meditate on the Law of God day and night, and continually exercise themselves in the keeping thereof (Psa. i. 2; cxix. 1 sqq.). For not even our first parents, even before the fall, lived

ipsorum tum inscripta erat, quia Dominus eos ad imaginem suam creaverat (Gen. i. 26 sqq.; ii. 16 sqq.; iii. 3).

II. *Credimus, docemus et confitemur, concionem Legis non modo apud eos, qui fidem in Christum non habent, et pœnitentiam nondum agunt, sed etiam apud eos, qui vere in Christum credunt, vere ad Deum conversi et renati, et per fidem justificati sunt, sedulo urgendam esse.*

III. *Etsi enim renati, et spiritu mentis suœ renovati sunt: tamen regeneratio illa et renovatio, in hac vita non est omnibus numeris absoluta, sed duntaxat inchoata. Et credentes illi, spiritu mentis suœ perpetuo luctantur cum carne, hoc est, cum corrupta natura, quœ in nobis ad mortem usque hœret* (Gal. v. 17; Rom. vii. 21, 23). *Et propter veterem Adamum, qui adhuc in hominis intellectu, voluntate, et in omnibus viribus ejus infixus residet, opus est, ut homini Lex Dei semper prœluceat, ne quid privatœ devotionis affectu in negotio religionis confingat, et cultus divinos verbo Dei non institutos eligat. Item, ne vetus Adam pro suo ingenio agat, sed potius contra suam voluntatem, non*

wholly without Law, which was certainly at that time graven on their hearts, because the Lord had created them after his own image (Gen. i. 26 sq.; ii. 16 sqq.; iii. 3).

II. We believe, teach, and confess that the preaching of the Law should be urged not only upon those who have not faith in Christ, and do not yet repent, but also upon those who truly believe in Christ, are truly converted to God, and regenerated and are justified by faith.

III. For, although they are regenerate and renewed in the spirit of their mind, yet this regeneration and renewal is in this life not absolutely complete, but only begun. And they that believe according to the spirit of their mind have perpetually to struggle with their flesh, that is, with corrupt nature, which inheres in us even till death (Gal. v. 17; Rom. vii. 21, 23). And on account of the old Adam, which still remains fixed in the intellect and will of man and in all his powers, there is need that the law of God should always shine before man, that he may not frame any thing in matter of religion under an impulse of self-devised devotion, and may not choose out ways of honoring God not instituted by the Word of God. Also, lest the old Adam

modo admonitionibus et minis Legis, verum etiam pœnis et plagis coerceatur, ut Spiritui obsequatur, seque ipsi captivum tradat (1 Cor. ix. 27; Rom. vi. 12; Gal. vi. 14; Psa. cxix. 1 sqq.; Heb. xii. 1; xiii. 21).

should act according to his own bent, but that he may the rather be constrained against his own will, not only by the admonitions and threats of the Law, but also by punishments and plagues, in order that he may give obedience to the Spirit, and render himself up captive to the same (1 Cor. ix. 27; Rom. vi. 12; Gal. vi. 14; Psalm cxix. 1 sqq.; Heb. xii. 1; xiii. 21).

IV. *Jam quod ad discrimen operum Legis et fructuum Spiritus attinet, credimus, docemus et confitemur, quod opera illa, quæ secundum præscriptum Legis fiunt, eatenus opera Legis sint et appellentur, quatenus ea solummodo urgendo, et minis pœnarum atque iræ divinæ, ab homine extorquentur.*

IV. As respects now the distinction between the works of the Law and the fruits of the Spirit, we believe, teach, and confess that those works, which are done according to the commandment of the Law, are and are called works of the Law so far as they are extorted from man only by sharp urgency, and by the threats of punishment and of the divine wrath.

V. *Fructus vero Spiritus sunt opera illa, quæ Spiritus Dei, in credentibus habitans, per homines renatos operatur, et quæ a credentibus fiunt, quatenus renati sunt, ita quidem sponte ac libere, quasi nullum præceptum unquam accepissent, nullas minas audivissent, nullamque remunerationem expectarent. Et hoc modo filii Dei in Lege vivunt, et secundum normam Legis divinæ vitam suam instituunt; hanc vivendi rationem*

V. But the fruits of the Spirit are those works which the Spirit of God, dwelling in believers, effects through regenerate men, and which are done by believers so far as they are regenerate, and therefore freely and spontaneously, as if they had never received any precept, had never heard any threats, and expected no remuneration. And in this way do the children of God live in the Law, and fashion their life according to the rule of the divine Law, which way of living

D. Paulus vocare solet in suis Epistolis Legem Christi et Legem mentis (Rom. vii. 25 ; viii. 2, 7 ; Gal. vi. 2).

VI. *Ad hunc modum una eademque Lex est manetque, immota videlicet Dei voluntas, sive pœnitentibus sive impœnitentibus, renatis aut non renatis proponatur. Discrimen autem, quo ad obedientiam, duntaxat in hominibus est : quorum alii non renati Legi obedientiam qualemcunque a Lege requisitam præstant, sed coacti et inviti id faciunt (sicut etiam renati faciunt, quatenus adhuc carnales sunt): credentes vero in Christum, quatenus renati sunt, absque coactione, libero et spontaneo spiritu, talem obedientiam præstant, qualem alias nullæ quantumvis severissimæ Legis comminationes extorquere possent.*

St. Paul is wont to call in his epistles the Law of Christ and the Law of the mind (Rom. vii. 25 ; viii. 2, 7 ; Gal. vi. 2).

VI. After this manner the Law is and remains one and the same, to wit: the unchangeable will of God, whether it be set forth before the penitent or the impenitent, the regenerate or the unregenerate. But the distinction, as to obedience, is only in men, of whom some, not being regenerate, render to the Law a certain manner of obedience required by the Law, but do this constrainedly and unwillingly (as also the regenerate do, so far as they are yet carnal); but believers in Christ, so far as they are regenerate, do without compulsion, with a free and unconstrained mind, render such an obedience as otherwise no threatenings of the Law, however grievous, would be able to extort.

NEGATIVA.

Falsæ doctrinæ rejectio.

Repudiamus itaque ut perniciosum et falsum dogma, quod Christianæ disciplinæ et veræ pietati adversatur, cum docetur, quod Lex Dei (eo modo, quo supra dictum est) non sit piis et vere credentibus, sed tantum impiis, infidelibus et non agentibus pœni-

NEGATIVE.

Rejection of false doctrine.

We repudiate, therefore, as a false and pernicious dogma, contrary to Christian discipline and true piety, the teaching that the Law of God (in such wise as is described above) is not to be set forth before the godly and true believers, but only before the ungodly, unbelievers, and

tentiam, proponenda, atque apud hos solos sit urgenda.

impenitent, and to be urged upon these alone.

ART. VII.

DE CŒNA DOMINI.

Etsi Cingliani Doctores non in eorum Theologorum numero, qui Augustanam Confessionem agnoscunt et profitentur [Augsburgische Confessionsverwandte], habendi sunt, quippe qui tum, cum illa Confessio exhiberetur, ab eis secessionem fecerunt : tamen cum nunc sese in eorum cœtum callide ingerant, erroremque suum sub prœtextu piœ illius Confessionis quam latissime spargere conentur, etiam de hac controversia Ecclesiam Dei erudiendam judicavimus.

ART. VII.

OF THE LORD'S SUPPER.

Although the Zwinglian doctors are not to be reckoned as in the number of those theologians who acknowledge and profess the Augsburg Confession, inasmuch as, when that Confession was set forth, they seceded from them; yet, since they are at this present craftily intruding themselves into their company, and endeavoring to disseminate their error as widely as possible, under cover of that godly Confession, we have judged that the Church of God ought to be instructed concerning this controversy also.

STATUS CONTROVERSIÆ,

Quæ est inter nos et Sacramentarios in hoc articulo.

Quæritur, an in Sacra Cœna verum corpus et verus sanguis Domini nostri Jesu Christi vere et substantialiter sint prœsentia, atque cum pane et vino distribuantur, et ore sumantur, ab omnibus illis, qui hoc Sacramento utuntur, sive digni sint, sive indigni, boni aut mali, fideles aut infideles, ita tamen, ut fideles

STATEMENT OF THE CONTROVERSY

Which exists between us and the Sacramentarians in this article.

It is asked whether in the Holy Supper the true body and true blood of our Lord Jesus Christ are truly and substantially present, and are distributed with the bread and wine, and are taken with the mouth by all those who use this sacrament, be they worthy or unworthy, good or bad, believers or unbelievers, in such wise, nevertheless, as that be-

e Cœna Domini consolationem et vitam percipiant, infideles autem eam ad judicium sumant. Cingliani hanc præsentiam et dispensationem corporis et sanguinis Christi in Sacra Cœna negant: nos vero eandem asseveramus.

Ad solidam hujus controversiœ explicationem primum sciendum est, duo esse Sacramentariorum genera. Quidam enim sunt Sacramentarii crassi admodum: hi perspicuis et claris verbis id aperte profitentur, quod corde sentiunt, quod videlicet in Cœna Domini nihil amplius quam panis et vinum sint præsentia, ibique distribuantur et ore percipiantur. Alii autem sunt versuti et callidi, et quidem omnium nocentissimi Sacramentarii: hi de negotio Cœnœ Dominicœ loquentes, ex parte nostris verbis splendide admodum utuntur, et præ se ferunt, quod et ipsi veram præsentiam veri, substantialis atque vivi corporis et sanguinis Christi in Sacra Cœna credant, eam tamen præsentiam et manducationem dicunt esse spiritualem, quœ fiat fide. Et hi posteriores Sacramentarii sub his splendidis verbis eandem crassam, quam priores habent, opinionem occultant et retinent:

lievers derive consolation and life from the Supper of the Lord, but unbelievers take it unto condemnation? The Zwinglians deny this presence and dispensation of the body and blood of Christ in the Holy Supper, but we affirm the same.

For a solid explication of this controversy, it is first to be understood that there are two sorts of sacramentarians. For some are exceedingly gross sacramentarians; these in perspicuous and plain words openly profess that which they think in their heart, to wit: that in the Lord's Supper there is nothing more present than bread and wine, which alone are there distributed and received with the mouth. But others are astute and crafty, and thereby the most harmful of all the sacramentarians; these, when talking of the Lord's Supper, make in part an exceedingly high-sounding use of our mode of speaking, declaring that they too believe in a *true* presence of the *true*, substantial, and living body and blood of Christ in the Holy Supper, which presence and manducation, nevertheless, they say to be spiritual, such as takes place by faith. And yet these latter sacramentarians, under these high-sounding phrases, hide and hold

quod videlicet præter panem et vinum nihil amplius in Cœna Domini sit præsens, et ore sumatur. Vocabulum enim (spiritualiter) nihil aliud ipsis significat, quam Spiritum Christi, seu virtutem absentis corporis Christi, ejusque meritum, quod præsens sit: ipsum vero Christi corpus nullo prorsus modo esse præsens, sed tantummodo id sursum in supremo cœlo contineri sentiunt, et affirmant, oportere nos cogitationibus fidei sursum assurgere, inque cœlum ascendere, et ibidem (nulla autem ratione cum pane et vino Sacræ Cœnæ) illud corpus et sanguinem Christi quærendum esse.

fast the same gross opinion which the former have, to wit: that, besides the bread and wine, there is nothing more present or taken with the mouth in the Lord's Supper. For the term (*spiritualiter*) signifies nothing more to them than the Spirit of Christ or the virtue of the absent body of Christ and his merit, which is present; but they think that the body of Christ itself is in no way whatever present, but is contained above in the highest heaven, and they affirm that it behooves us by the meditations of faith to rise on high and ascend into heaven, and that this body and blood of Christ are to be sought there, and in nowise in union with the bread and wine of the Holy Supper.

AFFIRMATIVA.

Confessio sinceræ doctrinæ, de Cœna Domini, contra Sacramentarios.

I. *Credimus, docemus et confitemur, quod in Cœna Domini corpus et sanguis Christi vere et substantialiter sint præsentia, et quod una cum pane et vino vere distribuantur atque sumantur.*

II. *Credimus, docemus et confitemur, verba Testamenti Christi non aliter accipienda esse, quam sicut verba ipsa ad literam sonant: ita, ne panis absens Christi corpus, et vinum*

AFFIRMATIVE.

Confession of the sound doctrine of the Supper of the Lord against the Sacramentarians.

I. We believe, teach, and confess that in the Lord's Supper the body and blood of Christ are truly and substantially present, and that they are truly distributed and taken together with the bread and wine.

II. We believe, teach, and confess that the words of the Testament of Christ are not to be otherwise received than as the words themselves literally sound, so that the bread does not signify the absent

absentem Christi sanguinem significent, sed ut propter sacramentalem unionem, panis et vinum vere sint corpus et sanguis Christi.

III. *Jam quod ad Consecrationem attinet, credimus, docemus et confitemur, quod nullum opus humanum, neque ulla Ministri Ecclesiæ pronunciatio præsentiæ corporis et sanguinis Christi in Cœna causa sit, sed quod hoc soli omnipotenti virtuti Domini nostri Jesu Christi sit tribuendum.*

IV. *Interim tamen unanimi consensu credimus, docemus et confitemur, in usu Cœnæ Dominicæ verba institutionis Christi nequaquam omittenda, sed publice recitanda esse, sicut scriptum est* (1 Cor. x. 16): '*Calix benedictionis, cui benedicimus, nonne communicatio sanguinis Christi est?*' etc. *Illa autem benedictio fit per recitationem verborum Christi.*

V. *Fundamenta autem, quibus in hoc negotio contra Sacramentarios nitimur, hæc sunt, quæ etiam D. Lutherus in majore sua de Cœna Domini Confessione posuit:*

Primum fundamentum est articulus fidei nostræ Christianæ, videlicet Jesu Christus est verus,

body of Christ and the wine the absent blood of Christ, but that on account of the sacramental union the bread and wine are truly the body and blood of Christ.

III. Moreover, as concerns the consecration, we believe, teach, and confess that no human work, nor any utterance of the minister of the Church, is the cause of the presence of the body and blood of Christ in the Supper, but that this is to be attributed to the omnipotent power of our Lord Jesus Christ alone.

IV. Nevertheless, we believe, teach, and confess, by unanimous consent, that in the use of the Lord's Supper the words of the institution of Christ are by no means to be omitted, but are to be publicly recited, as it is written (1 Cor. x. 16): 'The cup of blessing which we bless, is it not the communion of the blood of Christ?' etc. And this benediction takes place by the recitation of the words of Christ.

V. Now the foundations on which we rest in this controversy with the sacramentarians are the following, which, moreover, Dr. Luther has laid in his Larger Confession concerning the Supper of the Lord:

The first foundation is an article of our Christian faith, to wit: Jesus Christ is true, essential, natu-

essentialis, naturalis, perfectus Deus et homo in unitate perso-næ, inseparabilis et indivisus.

Secundum, quod dextera Dei ubique est: ad eam autem Christus, ratione humanitatis suæ, vere et reipsa, collocatus est, ideoque præsens gubernat, in manu sua, et sub pedibus suis, ut Scriptura loquitur (Eph. i. 22), *habet omnia, quæ in cœlo sunt et in terra. Ad eam Dei dexteram nullus alius homo, ac ne Angelus quidem, sed solus Mariæ Filius collocatus est, unde et ea, quæ diximus, præstare potest.*

Tertium, quod verbum Dei non est falsum, aut mendax.

Quartum, quod Deus varios modos novit, et in sua potestate habet, quibus alicubi esse potest, neque ad unicum illum alligatus est, quem Philosophi localem aut circumscriptum appellare solent.

VI. *Credimus, docemus et confitemur, corpus et sanguinem Christi non tantum spiritualiter per fidem, sed etiam ore, non tamen Capernaitice, sed supernaturali et cœlesti modo, ratione sacramentalis unionis, cum pane et vino sumi. Hoc enim verba Christi perspicue testantur, quibus præcipit, accipere, edere, bibere: idque ab Apostolis factum*

ral, perfect God and man in unity of person, inseparable and undivided.

Secondly: that the right hand of God is every where, and that Christ, in respect of his humanity, is truly and in very deed seated thereat, and therefore as present governs, and has in his hand and under his feet, as the Scripture saith (Eph. i. 22), all things which are in heaven and on earth. At this right hand of God no other man, nor even any angel, but the Son of Mary alone, is seated, whence also he is able to effect those things which we have said.

Thirdly: that the Word of God is not false or deceiving.

Fourthly: that God knows and has in his power various modes in which he can be any where, and is not confined to that single one which philosophers are wont to call local or circumscribed.

VI. We believe, teach, and confess that the body and blood of Christ are taken with the bread and wine, not only spiritually through faith, but also by the mouth, nevertheless not Capernaitically, but after a spiritual and heavenly manner, by reason of the sacramental union. For to this the words of Christ clearly bear witness, in which he enjoins us to

esse, Scriptura commemorat, dicens (Mark xiv. 23): '*Et biberunt ex eo omnes.*' *Et Paulus inquit* (1 Cor. x. 16): '*Panis, quem frangimus, est communicatio corporis Christi;*' *hoc est, qui hunc panem edit, corpus Christi edit.* *Idem magno consensu præcipui ex antiquissimis Ecclesiæ Doctoribus, Chrysostomus, Cyprianus, Leo Primus, Gregorius, Ambrosius, Augustinus, testantur.*

VII. Credimus, docemus et confitemur, quod non tantum vere in Christum credentes, et qui digne ad Cœnam Domini accedunt, verum etiam indigni et infideles verum corpus et sanguinem Christi sumant: ita tamen, ut nec consolationem, nec vitam inde percipiant, sed potius, ut illis sumtio ea ad judicium et damnationem cedat, si non convertantur et pœnitentiam agant (1 Cor. xi. 27, 29).

Etsi enim Christum, ut Salvatorem, a se repellunt, tamen eundem, licet maxime inviti, ut severum Judicem, admittere coguntur. Is vero non minus præsens judicium suum in convivis illis impœnitentibus exercet, quam præsens consolationem et vitam in cordibus vere credentium et dignorum convivarum operatur.

take, to eat, to drink; and that this was done by the Apostles the Scripture makes mention, saying (Mark xiv. 23): 'And they all drank of it.' And Paul says: 'The bread which we break is the communion of the body of Christ;' that is, he that eats this bread eats the body of Christ. To the same with great consent do the chief of the most ancient doctors of the Church, Chrysostom, Cyprian, Leo the First, Gregory, Ambrose, Augustine, bear witness.

VII. We believe, teach, and confess that not only true believers in Christ, and such as worthily approach the Supper of the Lord, but also the unworthy and unbelieving receive the true body and blood of Christ; in such wise, nevertheless, that they derive thence neither consolation nor life, but rather so as that receiving turns to their judgment and condemnation, unless they be converted and repent (1 Cor. xi. 27, 29).

For although they repel from them Christ as a Saviour, nevertheless they are compelled, though extremely unwilling, to admit him as a stern Judge. And he no less present exercises his judgment over these impenitent guests than as present he works consolation and life in the hearts of true believers and worthy guests.

VIII. *Credimus, docemus et confitemur, unum tantum genus esse indignorum convivarum: ii sunt soli illi, qui non credunt. De his scriptum est* (John iii. 18): '*Qui non credit, jam judicatus est.*' *Et hoc judicium indigno Sacræ Cœnæ usu cumulatur et aggravatur* [gehäufet, grösser und schwerer wird] (1 Cor. xi. 29).

IX. *Credimus, docemus et confitemur, quod nullus vere credentium, quam diu vivam fidem retinet, Sacram Domini Cœnam ad judicium sumat, quantacunque fidei imbecillitate laboret. Cœna enim Domini inprimis propter infirmos in fide, pœnitentes tamen, instituta est, ut ex ea veram consolationem et imbecillis fidei suæ confirmationem percipiant* (Matt. ix. 12; xi. 5, 28).

X. *Credimus, docemus et confitemur, totam dignitatem convivarum cœlestis hujus Cœnæ in sola sacratissima obedientia et absolutissimo Christi merito consistere. Illud autem nobis vera fide applicamus, et de applicatione hujus meriti per Sacramentum certi reddimur, atque in animis nostris confirmamur. Nequaquam autem dignitas illa ex*

VIII. We believe, teach, and confess that there is one kind only of unworthy guests: they are those only who do not believe. Of these it is written (John iii. 18): 'He that believeth not is condemned already.' And this judgment is enhanced and aggravated by an unworthy use of the holy Supper (1 Cor. xi. 29).

IX. We believe, teach, and confess that no true believer, so long as he retains a living faith, receives the holy Supper of the Lord unto condemnation, however much weakness of faith he may labor under. For the Lord's Supper has been chiefly instituted for the sake of the weak in faith, who nevertheless are penitent, that from it they may derive true consolation and a strengthening of their weak faith (Matt. ix. 12; xi. 5, 28).

X. We believe, teach, and confess that the whole worthiness of the guests at this heavenly Supper consists alone in the most holy obedience and most perfect merit of Christ. And this we apply to ourselves by true faith, and are rendered certain of the application of this merit, and are confirmed in our minds by the sacrament. But in no way does that worthiness depend

virtutibus nostris, aut ex internis vel externis nostris præparationibus pendet.

upon our virtues, or upon our inward or outward preparations.

NEGATIVA.

Contrariæ et damnatæ Sacramentariorum doctrinæ rejectio.

NEGATIVE.

Rejection of the contrary and condemned doctrine of the Sacramentarians.

Rejicimus atque damnamus unanimi consensu omnes erroneos, quos jam recitabimus, articulos, ut qui commemoratæ piæ doctrinæ, simplicitati fidei et sinceræ confessioni de Cœna Domini repugnant.

We reject and condemn, by unanimous consent, all the erroneous articles which we will now recount, as being opposite to the above-stated godly doctrine, to the simplicity of faith, and to the sound confession concerning the Supper of the Lord:

I. *Papisticam Transsubstantiationem : cum videlicet in Papatu docetur, panem et vinum in Sacra Cœna substantiam atque naturalem suam essentiam amittere, et ita annihilari, atque elementa illa ita in Christi corpus transmutari, ut præter externas species nihil de iis reliquum maneat.*

I. The papistical transubstantiation, when, to wit, in the Papal Church it is taught that the bread and wine in the holy Supper lose their substance and natural essence, and are thus annihilated, and those elements so transmuted into the body of Christ, that, except the outward species, nothing remains of them.

II. *Papisticum Missæ sacrificium, quod pro peccatis vivorum et mortuorum offertur.*

II. The papistical sacrifice of the Mass, which is offered for the sins of the living and the dead.

III. *Sacrilegium, quo Laicis una tantum pars Sacramenti datur, cum nimirum, contra expressa verba Testamenti Christi, calice illis interdicitur, atque ita sanguine Christi spoliantur.*

III. The sacrilege whereby one part of the sacrament only is given to the laity, the cup being forbidden them, against the express words of the Testament of Christ, and they are thus despoiled of the blood of Christ.

IV. *Dogma, quo docetur, quod*

IV. The dogma whereby it is

verba Testamenti Jesu Christi non simpliciter intelligenda et fide amplectenda sint, uti sonant; ea enim obscura esse, ideoque verum eorum sensum ex aliis Scripturæ locis petendum esse.

V. Corpus Christi in Sacra Cœna non ore una cum pane sumi: sed tantum panem et vinum ore accipi: corpus vero Christi spiritualiter duntaxat, fide nimirum, sumi.

VI. Panem et vinum in Cœna Domini tantummodo symbola seu tesseras esse, quibus Christiani mutuo sese agnoscant.

VII. Panem et vinum tantum esse figuras, similitudines et typos corporis et sanguinis Christi, longissimo intervallo a nobis absentis.

VIII. Panem et vinum tantummodo signa, memoriæ conservandæ gratia, instituta esse, quæ sigillorum et pignorum rationem habeant, quibus nobis confirmetur, quod fides, cum in cœlum illa ascendit et evehitur, ibi tam vere corporis et sanguinis Christi particeps fiat, quam vere nos in Sacra Cœna panem manducamus et vinum bibimus.

IX. Fidem nostram de salute

taught that the words of the Testament of Jesus Christ are not to be understood and embraced by faith in simplicity as they sound, on the ground that they are obscure, and that therefore their true sense is to be sought from other places of Scripture.

V. That the body of Christ in the holy Supper is not received by the mouth together with the bread, but that only bread and wine are received by the mouth, while the body of Christ is taken only spiritually, to wit, by faith.

VI. That the bread and wine in the Lord's Supper are only symbols or tokens whereby Christians mutually recognize each other.

VII. That the bread and wine are only figures, similitudes, and types of the body and blood of Christ, who himself is very far distant from us.

VIII. That the bread and wine are only signs, instituted for a memorial, and having the character of seals and pledges, by which it is made sure to us that faith, when she ascends and is transported into heaven, there as truly becomes participant of the body and blood of Christ, as we do truly in the holy Supper eat the bread and drink the wine.

IX. That our faith concerning

certam reddi et confirmari in Cœna Domini, non nisi signis illis externis, pane et vino : nequaquam autem vere præsentibus vero corpore et sanguine Christi.

X. *In Sacra Cœna duntaxat virtutem, operationem et meritum absentis corporis et sanguinis Christi dispensari.*

XI. *Christi corpus ita cœlo inclusum esse, ut nullo prorsus modo, simul, eodem tempore, pluribus aut omnibus locis in terris præsens esse possit, ubi Cœna Domini celebratur.*

XII. *Christum substantialem corporis et sanguinis sui præsentiam neque promittere neque exhibere potuisse, quandoquidem id proprietas humanæ ipsius naturæ assumtæ nequaquam ferre aut admittere possit.*

XIII. *Deum ne quidem universa sua omnipotentia (horrendum dictu et auditu) efficere posse, ut corpus Christi, uno eodemque tempore in pluribus, quam uno tantum loco, substantialiter præsens sit.*

XIV. *Non omnipotens illud verbum Testamenti Christi, sed fidem præsentiæ corporis et sanguinis Christi in Sacra Cœna causam esse.*

XV. *Fideles corpus et sangui-*

our salvation is rendered certain and confirmed in the Supper of the Lord only by those external signs, bread and wine, but in nowise by the true body and blood of Christ truly present.

X. That in the holy Supper, only the virtue, operation, and merit of the absent body of Christ are dispensed.

XI. That Christ's body is so confined in heaven that it can in no mode whatever be likewise at one and the same time in many places, or in all the places where the Lord's Supper is celebrated.

XII. That Christ could neither promise nor impart the substantial presence of his body and blood, inasmuch as the essential property of the human nature itself which he had assumed could by no means bear or admit of this.

XIII. That God, even with all his omnipotence (a thing fearful to say and fearful to hear), can not effect that the body of Christ should be substantially present· at one and the same time in more places than one.

XIV. That not that omnipotent word of the Testament of Christ, but faith is the cause of the presence of the body and blood of Christ in the holy Supper.

XV. That the faithful ought not

nem Christi non in pane et vino
Cœnæ Dominicæ quærere, sed oculos in cœlum attollere, et ibi corpus Christi quærere debere.

XVI. Infideles et impœnitentes
Christianos in Cœna Domini non
verum corpus et sanguinem Christi, sed panem tantum et vinum
sumere.

XVII. Dignitatem convivarum
in hac cœlesti Cœna non ex sola
vera in Christum fide, sed etiam
ex præparatione hominum externa pendere.

XVIII. Eos etiam, qui veram
et vivam in Christum fidem habent, eamque retinent, nihilominus hoc sacramentum ad judicium sumere posse, propterea
quod in externa sua conversa-
tione adhuc imperfecti sint.

XIX. Externa visibilia elementa panis et vini in sacramento
adoranda esse.

XX. Præter hæc justo Dei
judicio relinquimus omnes curiosas, sannis virulentis tinc-
tas, et blasphemas quæstiones,
quæ honeste, pie, et sine gravi
offensione recitari nequeunt, aliosque sermones, quando de supernaturali et cœlesti mysterio
hujus sacramenti crasse, carnaliter, Capernaitice, et plane
abominandis modis, blaspheme,
et maximo cum Ecclesiæ offen-

to seek the body and blood of Christ
in the Lord's Supper, but to lift
their eyes to heaven, and there
seek the body of Christ.

XVI. That unbelieving and impenitent Christians in the Lord's
Supper do not receive the true
body and blood of Christ, but only
bread and wine.

XVII. That the worthiness of
the guests at this heavenly Supper
does not depend alone upon true
faith in Christ, but upon the outward preparation of men.

XVIII. That even those who
have and hold fast a true and living faith in Christ are capable of
taking this sacrament to their condemnation, inasmuch as in their
external course of life they are
yet imperfect.

XIX. That the external, visible
elements of bread and wine in the
sacrament are to be adored.

XX. Over and above these, we
leave to the just judgment of God
all curious and blasphemous questions imbued with virulent poison
of mockeries, such as can not be
set forth without grave offense to
seemliness and piety, and other
pratings, wherein the Sacramentarians speak of the supernatural and
heavenly mystery of this sacrament
grossly, carnally, Capernaitically,
and in utterly abominable fashion,

diculo, Sacramentarii loquuntur.

XXI. *Prorsus etiam rejicimus atque damnamus Capernaiticam manducationem corporis Christi, quam nobis Sacramentarii contra suæ conscientiæ testimonium, post tot nostras protestationes, malitiose affingunt, ut doctrinam nostram apud auditores suos in odium adducant, quasi videlicet doceamus, corpus Christi dentibus laniari, et instar alterius cujusdam cibi, in corpore humano digeri. Credimus autem et asserimus, secundum clara verba Testamenti Christi, veram, sed supernaturalem manducationem corporis Christi, quemadmodum etiam vere, supernaturaliter tamen, sanguinem Christi bibi docemus. Hæc autem humanis sensibus aut ratione nemo comprehendere potest, quare in hoc negotio, sicut et in aliis fidei articulis, intellectum nostrum in obedientiam Christi captivare oportet. Hoc enim mysterium in solo Dei verbo revelatur, et sola fide comprehenditur.*

blasphemously, and to the most grievous offense of the Church.

XXI. We also utterly reject and condemn the Capernaitic manducation of the body of Christ, which, after so many protestations on our part, the Sacramentarians maliciously feign against us, contrary to the testimony of their own conscience, in order that they may bring our doctrine into discredit with their hearers, as if, forsooth, we taught that the body of Christ is torn by the teeth and digested in the human body like any other food. But we believe and assert, according to the plain words of the Testament of Christ, a true but supernatural manducation of the body of Christ, even as also we teach that the blood of Christ is truly, but nevertheless supernaturally, drunk. But these things no one is able with human senses or reason to comprehend; wherefore in this matter, as also in other articles of the faith, it behooves that our understanding be brought into captivity to the obedience of Christ. For this mystery is revealed in the Word of God alone, and is comprehended by faith alone.

Art. VIII.

DE PERSONA CHRISTI.

Ex controversia superiore de Cœna Domini inter sinceros Theologos Augustanæ Confessionis, et Calvinistas, qui alios etiam quosdam Theologos perturbarunt, dissensio orta est de persona Christi, de duabus in Christo naturis, et de ipsarum proprietatibus.

Status Controversiæ.

Principalis hujus dissidii quæstio fuit, an divina et humana natura et utriusque proprietates propter unionem personalem, realiter, hoc est, vere et reipsa in persona Christi invicem communicent, et quousque illa communicatio extendatur?

Sacramentarii affirmarunt, divinam et humanam naturas in Christo eo modo personaliter unitas esse, ut neutra alteri quicquam realiter, hoc est, vere et reipsa, quod cujusque naturæ proprium sit, communicet: sed nomina tantum nuda communicari. Unio (inquiunt illi) facit tantum nomina communia, ut videlicet Deus dicatur homo, et homo Deus appelletur, ita tamen,

Art. VIII.

OF THE PERSON OF CHRIST.

From the above-mentioned controversy concerning the Lord's Supper between the sincere divines of the Augsburg Confession and the Calvinists, who had, moreover, unsettled certain other theologians, there has arisen a dissension concerning the person of Christ, concerning the two natures in Christ, and concerning the attributes of these.

Statement of the Controversy.

The principal question of this controversy has been whether the divine and the human nature in the attributes of each are in mutual communication REALLY, that is, truly and in very fact and deed, in the person of Christ, and how far that communication extends.

The Sacramentarians have affirmed that the divine and human natures are in such wise personally united in Christ that neither communicates to the other really, that is, truly and in very deed, any thing which is proper to either nature, but that bare names only are communicated. The union, say they, makes only the names common, so that, to wit, God is termed man, and man is called God, yet

ut Deus nihil cum humanitate commune habeat, et vicissim humanitas nihil cum Divinitate, quo ad ipsius majestatem et proprietates, realiter, hoc est, revera et reipsa commune habeat. Contrariam vero huic dogmati sententiam D. Lutherus, et qui cum ipso faciunt, adversus Sacramentarios propugnarunt.

so that God has nothing common with humanity, and on the other hand humanity has nothing really, that is, in very deed and very fact, common with Divinity, as to the majesty and attributes thereof. But Dr. Luther and those who hold with him have firmly maintained against the Sacramentarians the opinion contrary to this dogma.

AFFIRMATIVA.

Sincera doctrina Ecclesiæ Dei de Persona Christi.

Ad explicandam hanc controversiam et juxta analogiam fidei nostræ Christianæ decidendam, fidem, doctrinam et confessionem nostram piam perspicue profitemur, videlicet :

I. *Quod divina et humana natura in Christo personaliter unitæ sint, ita prorsus, ut non sint duo Christi, unus Filius Dei, alter Filius hominis, sed ut unus et idem sit Dei et hominis Filius* (Luke i. 35 ; Rom. ix. 5).

II. *Credimus, docemus et confitemur, divinam et humanam naturas, non in unam substantiam commixtas, nec unam in alteram mutatam esse, sed utramque naturam retinere suas proprietates essentiales, ut quæ alte-*

AFFIRMATIVE.

The sound doctrine of the Church of God touching the Person of Christ.

For the better setting forth of this controversy, and deciding it according to the analogy of our Christian faith, we distinctly profess our godly faith, doctrine, and confession in the terms following, to wit :

I. That the divine and the human nature in Christ are personally united, and so completely that there are not two Christs—one the Son of God, the other the Son of man— but that one and the same is Son of God and Son of Man (Luke i. 35 ; Rom. ix. 5).

II. We believe, teach, and confess that the divine and human natures are not mingled into one substance, nor one changed into the other, but that each nature retains its own essential attributes, as being such as can not be-

rius naturæ proprietates fieri nequeant.

III. *Proprietates divinæ naturæ sunt: esse omnipotentem, æternam, infinitam, et secundum naturæ naturalisque suæ essentiæ proprietatem, per se, ubique præsentem esse, omnia novisse, etc. Hæc omnia neque sunt, neque unquam fiunt humanæ naturæ proprietates.*

IV. *Humanæ autem naturæ proprietates sunt: corpoream esse creaturam, constare carne et sanguine, esse finitam et circumscriptam, pati, mori, ascendere, descendere, de loco ad locum moveri, esurire, sitire, algere, æstu affligi, et si quæ sunt similia. Hæc neque sunt, neque unquam fiunt proprietates divinæ naturæ.*

V. *Cum vero divina et humana naturæ personaliter, hoc est, ad constituendum unum ὑφιστάμενον, sint unitæ, credimus, docemus et confitemur, unionem illam hypostaticam non esse talem copulationem aut combinationem, cujus ratione neutra natura cum altera personaliter, hoc est, propter unionem personalem, quicquam commune habeat, qualis combinatio fit, cum duo asseres conglutinantur, ubi neuter alteri quicquam confert, aut aliquid ab altero accipit: quin potius hic summa communio est, quam Deus cum*

come the attributes of the other nature.

III. The attributes of the divine nature are: To be omnipotent, eternal, infinite, and, by attribute of nature and of its natural essence, to be every where present, to know all things, etc. All these things neither are nor ever become the attributes of the human nature.

IV. The attributes of the human nature are: To be a corporeal creature, to consist of flesh and blood, to be finite and circumscribed, to suffer, to die, to ascend, to descend, to move from place to place, to hunger, to thirst, to suffer with cold, to be overcome by heat, and the like. These neither are nor ever become attributes of the divine nature.

V. And inasmuch as the divine and human natures are personally united, that is, so as to constitute one ὑφιστάμενον, we believe, teach, and confess that this hypostatic union is not such a conjunction or combination as that thereby neither nature had any thing personally—that is, on account of the personal union—common with the other, such as the combination that takes place when two boards are glued together, where neither confers any thing on the other nor receives any thing from the other. But, rather, here is the highest communion which God

assumto homine vere habet, et ex personali unione, et summa ac ineffabili communione, quæ inde consequitur, totum illud promanat, quicquid humani de Deo, et quicquid divini de homine Christo dicitur et creditur. Et hanc unionem atque communionem naturarum antiquissimi Ecclesiæ Doctores similitudine ferri candentis, itemque unione corporis et animæ in homine, declararunt.

VI. *Hinc etiam credimus, docemus atque confitemur, quod Deus sit homo, et homo sit Deus, id quod nequaquam ita se haberet, si divina et humana natura prorsus inter se nihil revera et reipsa communicarent.*

Quomodo enim homo, Mariæ Filius, Deus aut Filius Dei altissimi vere appellari posset, aut esset, si ipsius humanitas cum Filio Dei non esset personaliter unita, atque ita realiter, hoc est, vere et reipsa, nihil prorsus, excepto solo nudo nomine, cum ipso commune haberet?

VII. *Eam ob causam credimus, docemus et confitemur, quod virgo Maria non nudum aut merum hominem duntaxat, sed verum Dei Filium conceperit et genuerit : unde recte Mater Dei et appellatur et revera est.*

---

truly has with the man assumed, and from the personal union and highest and ineffable communion, which thence follows, flows all of human that is said and believed of God, and all of divine that is said and believed of the man Christ. And this union and communion of the natures the most ancient doctors of the Church have illustrated by the similitude of glowing iron, and also of the union of body and soul in man.

VI. Hence also we believe, teach, and confess that God is man and man is God, which would by no means be the truth if the divine and the human nature had no mutual intercommunication in very deed and truth.

For how could a man, the son of Mary, be truly called God or the Son of God Most High, if his humanity were not personally united with the Son of God, and so had nothing really that is, in very deed and truth, common with him, the bare name alone excepted?

VII. For this reason we believe, teach, and confess that the Virgin Mary did not conceive and bear a mere man and no more, but the true Son of God; whence she is both rightly called and in very deed is the Mother of God.

VIII. *Inde porro credimus, docemus et confitemur, quod non nudus homo tantum pro nobis passus, mortuus et sepultus sit, ad inferos descenderit, a mortuis resurrexit, ad cœlos ascenderit, et ad majestatem et omnipotentem Dei virtutem evectus fuerit: sed talis homo, cujus humana natura cum Filio Dei tam arctam ineffabilemque unionem et communicationem habet, ut cum eo una sit facta persona.*

IX. *Quapropter vere Filius Dei pro nobis est passus, sed secundum proprietatem humanæ naturæ, quam in unitatem divinæ suæ personæ assumsit, sibique eam propriam fecit, ut videlicet pati, et, Pontifex noster summus, reconciliationis nostræ cum Deo causa esse posset. Sic enim scriptum est* (1 Cor. ii. 8): '*Dominum gloriæ crucifixerunt.*' *Et* (Acts xx. 28): '*Sanguine Dei redempti sumus.*'

X. *Ex eodem etiam fundamento credimus, docemus, et confitemur, Filium hominis ad dextram omnipotentis majestatis et virtutis Dei realiter, hoc est, vere et reipsa, secundum humanam suam naturam, esse exaltatum, cum homo ille in Deum assumtus fuerit, quamprimum in utero matris a Spiritu Sancto est conceptus, ejusque hu-*

Vol. III.—L

VIII. Therefore, furthermore, we believe, teach, and confess that it is not a mere man only that has suffered, died and been buried for us, that has descended into Hell, has risen from the dead, has ascended into heaven, and has been raised to the majesty and omnipotent power of God; but a man, such that his human nature has with the Son of God a union and communication so strict and ineffable that he has become one person with him.

IX. Wherefore the Son of God has truly suffered for us, but according to the attribute of human nature, which he assumed into the unity of his divine person and made it proper to himself, so that he might be able to suffer and to become our great high-priest, the cause of our reconciliation with God. For so is it written (1 Cor. ii. 8): 'They crucified the Lord of glory.' And (Acts xx. 28): 'We are redeemed by the blood of God.'

X. On the same ground, also, we believe, teach, and confess that the Son of Man is really, that is, truly and in very deed, according to his human nature, exalted to the right hand of the omnipotent majesty and power of God, since that man was assumed into God when he was conceived by the Holy Ghost in the womb of his mother, and his hu-

manitas jam tum cum Filio Dei al-lissimi personaliter fuerit unita.

XI. *Eamque majestatem, ra-tione unionis personalis, semper Christus habuit, sed in statu suæ humiliationis sese exinani-vit, qua de causa revera ætate, sapientia, et gratia apud Deum atque homines profecit. Quare majestatem illam non semper, sed quoties ipsi visum fuit, exe-cruit, donec formam servi, non autem naturam humanam, post resurrectionem plene et prorsus deponeret, et in plenariam usur-pationem, manifestationem et de-clarationem divinæ majestatis collocaretur, et hoc modo in glo-riam suam ingrederetur* (Phil. ii. 6 sqq.). *Itaque jam non tantum ut Deus, verum etiam ut homo, omnia novit, omnia potest, om-nibus creaturis præsens est, et omnia, quæ in cælis, in terris, et sub terra sunt, sub pedibus suis, et in manu sua habet. Hæc ita se habere, Christus ipse testatur, inquiens* (Matt. xxviii. 18; John xiii. 3): '*Mihi data est omnis potestas in cælo et in terra.' Et Paulus* (Eph. iv. 10) *ait: 'Ascen-dit super omnes cælos, ut omnia impleat. Hanc suam potestatem ubique præsens exercere potest, neque quicquam illi aut impos-sibile est, aut ignotum.*

manity was then personally united with the Son of God Most High.

XI. And that majesty, in virtue of the personal union, Christ has al-ways had, but in the state of his hu-miliation he divested himself of it, for which cause he truly grew in age, wisdom, and favor with God and men. Wherefore he did not always make use of that majesty, but as oft-en as seemed good to him, until after the resurrection, he fully and for-ever laid aside the form of a serv-ant, but not the human nature, and was established in the plenary use, manifestation, and revelation of the divine majesty, and in this manner entered into his glory (Phil. ii. 6 sqq.). Therefore now not only as God, but also as man, he knows all things, can do all things, is present to all creatures, has under his feet and in his hand all things which are in heaven, in the earth, and under the earth. That this is so, Christ himself bears witness, saying (Matt. xxviii. 18; John xiii. 3): 'All power in heaven and in earth is given unto me.' And Paul saith (Eph. iv. 10): 'He as-cended up far above all heavens, that he might fill all things.' This his power, being every where pres-ent, he can exercise, nor is any-thing to him either impossible or unknown.

XII. *Inde adeo, et quidem facillime, corpus suum verum et sanguinem suum in Sacra Cœna præsens distribuere potest. Id vero non fit secundum modum et proprietatem humanæ naturæ, sed secundum modum et proprietatem dextræ Dei, ut Lutherus secundum analogiam fidei nostræ Christianæ, in Catechesi comprehensæ, loqui solet. Et hæc Christi in Sacra Cœna præsentia neque physica aut terrena est, neque Capernaitica: interim tamen verissima et quidem substantialis est. Sic enim verba Testamenti Christi sonant: Hoc est, est, est corpus meum, etc.*

Hac nostra fide, doctrina et confessione persona Christi non solvitur, quod olim Nestorius fecit. Is enim veram communicationem idiomatum seu proprietatum utriusque naturæ in Christo negavit, et hac ratione Christi personam solvit: quam rem D. Lutherus in libello suo de Conciliis perspicue declaravit. Neque hac pia nostra doctrina duæ in Christo naturæ, earumque proprietates confunduntur, aut in unam essentiam commiscentur (in quo errore Eutyches fuit), neque humana natura in persona Christi negatur, aut aboletur, neque altera natura in

XII. Hence also, and indeed most easily, can he, being present, impart his true body and his blood in the Holy Supper. Now this is not done according to the mode and attribute of human nature, but according to the mode and attribute of the right hand of God, as Luther, according to the analogy of our Christian faith, as contained in the Catechism, is wont to speak. And this presence of Christ in the Holy Supper is neither physical or earthly, nor Capernaitic; nevertheless it is most true and indeed substantial. For so read the words of the Testament of Christ: ' *This is, is, is my body,*' etc.

By this our faith, doctrine, and confession, the person of Christ is not severed, as of old Nestorius severed it. For he denied a true communication of the *idiomata* or attributes of both natures in Christ, and in this way separated the person of Christ: which thing Dr. Luther has perspicuously set forth in his book on the Councils. Nor by this godly doctrine of ours are the two natures in Christ and their attributes confounded, or mingled into one essence (as Eutyches erroneously taught), nor is the human nature in the person of Christ denied or abolished, nor the one nature changed into the other; but Christ

alteram mutatur : sed Christus verus Deus et homo in una indivisa persona est, permanetque in omnem æternitatem. Hoc post illud Trinitatis summum est mysterium, ut Apostolus (1 Tim. iii. 16) *testatur, in quo solo tota nostra consolatio, vita et salus posita est.*

is and abides to all eternity true God and man in one undivided person. Next to the mystery of the Trinity this is the chiefest mystery, as the Apostle bears witness (1 Tim. iii. 16); on which alone all our consolation, life, and salvation depend.

Contrariæ et falsæ doctrinæ de persona Christi rejectio.

Rejection of contrary and false doctrine touching the person of Christ.

Repudiamus igitur atque damnamus omnes erroneos, quos jam recitabimus, articulos, eo quod Verbo Dei et sinceræ fidei nostræ Christianæ repugnent, cum videlicet sequentes errores docentur :

We repudiate, therefore, and condemn all the erroneous articles which we will now recount, inasmuch as they are opposed to the Word of God and to our sound Christian faith—the errors following, to wit:

I. *Quod Deus et homo in Christo non constituant unam personam, sed quod alius sit Dei Filius, et alius hominis Filius, ut Nestorius deliravit.*

I. That God and man do not constitute one person in Christ, but that the Son of God is one and the Son of Man another, as Nestorius insanely feigned.

II. *Quod divina et humana naturæ in unam essentiam commixtæ sint, et humana natura in Deitatem mutata sit, ut Eutyches furenter dixit.*

II. That the divine and human natures are commingled into one essence, and the human nature is changed into Deity, as Eutyches has madly affirmed.

III. *Quod Christus non sit verus, naturalis et æternus Deus, ut Arius blasphemavit.*

III. That Christ is not true, natural, and eternal God, as Arius blasphemously declared.

IV. *Quod Christus non veram humanam naturam anima rationali et corpore constantem habuerit, ut Marcion finxit.*

IV. That Christ did not have a true human nature, consisting of a rational soul and of a body, as Marcion feigned.

V. *Quod unio personalis faciat tantum communia nomina et communes titulos.*

VI. *Quod phrasis tantum et modus quidam loquendi sit, cum dicitur: Deus est homo, et homo est Deus; siquidem Divinitas nihil cum humanitate, et humanitas nihil cum Deitate realiter, hoc est, vere et reipsa, commune habeat.*

VII. *Quod tantum sit verbalis, sine re ipsa, idiomatum communicatio, cum dicitur: Filium Dei pro peccatis mundi mortuum esse: Filium hominis omnipotentem factum esse.*

VIII. *Quod humana in Christo natura, eo modo, quo est Divinitas, facta sit essentia quædam infinita, et ex hac essentiali, communicata, in humanam naturam effusa, et a Deo separata virtute et proprietate, eo modo, quo divina natura, ubique præsens sit.*

IX. *Quod humana natura divinæ, ratione substantiæ atque essentiæ suæ, vel proprietatum divinarum essentialium, exæquata sit.*

X. *Quod humana natura in Christo in omnia loca cœli et terræ localiter expansa sit; quod*

V. That the personal union makes only common names and common titles.

VI. That it is only a phrase, and a certain mode of speaking, when it is said: God is man, and man is God; since divinity has nothing really, that is, truly and in deed, common with humanity, and humanity nothing common with Deity.

VII. That it is only a verbal *communicatio idiomatum*, without any corresponding fact, when it is said: The Son of God has died for the sins of the world; the Son of man has become omnipotent.

VIII. That the human nature in Christ has become a certain infinite essence, in the same way in which the divinity is one, and that from this essential, communicated virtue and property, effused into human nature and separate from God, it is every where present in like mode and manner with the divine nature.

IX. That the human nature has been made equal to the divine. in respect of its substance and essence, or of the essential divine attributes.

X. That the human nature in Christ is locally spread out into all places of heaven and earth; some-

ne quidem divinæ naturæ est tri-buendum.

XI. *Quod Christo impossibile sit, propter humanæ naturæ pro-prietatem, ut simul in pluribus, quam in uno loco, nedum ubique, suo cum corpore esse possit.*

XII. *Quod sola humanitas pro nobis passa sit, nosque redemerit, et quod Filius Dei in passione nullam prorsus cum humanitate (reipsa) communicationem habue-rit, perinde ac si id negotium nihil ad ipsum pertinuisset.*

XIII. *Quod Filius Dei tan-tummodo Divinitate sua nobis in terris, in verbo, sacramentis, in omnibus denique ærumnis nostris, præsens sit, et quod hæc præsentia prorsus ad humanitatem nihil pertineat. Christo enim, post-quam nos passione et morte sua redemerit, secundum humanita-tem suam nihil amplius nobis-cum in terris esse negotii.*

XIV. *Quod Filius Dei, qui hu-manam naturam assumsit, jam post depositam servi formam, non omnia opera omnipotentiæ suæ, in et cum humanitate sua, et per eam, efficiat, sed tantum aliqua, et quidem in eo tantum loco, ubi humana natura est lo-caliter.*

XV. *Quod secundum humani-tatem, omnipotentiæ aliarumque*

thing that is not to be attributed even to the divine nature.

XI. That it is impossible for Christ, on account of the propriety of his human nature, to be in more places than one, not to say every where, with his body.

XII. That the humanity alone suffered for us and redeemed us; and that the Son of God in the passion had no communication at all (in very deed) with the human-ity, even as if that matter had in nowise appertained to him.

XIII. That the Son of God is present to us on earth in the word, the sacraments, and in all our troubles, only by his divinity, and that this presence appertains noth-ing at all to the humanity. For that Christ, after he had redeemed us by his passion and death, had no longer, according to his humanity, any concern with us on earth.

XIV. That the Son of God, who assumed human nature, henceforth, after having laid aside the form of a servant, does not accomplish all the works of his omnipotence in and with his humanity, and by means of it, but only some of them, and these only in that place where the human nature locally is.

XV. That, according to the hu-manity, he is not at all capable of

proprietatum divinæ naturæ prorsus non sit capax. Idque asserere audent contra expressum testimonium Christi (Matt. xxviii. 18): '*Mihi data est omnis potestas in cœlo et in terra.*' *Et contradicunt Paulo, qui ait* (Col. ii. 9): '*In ipso inhabitat tota Divinitatis plenitudo corporaliter.*'

XVI. *Quod Christo secundum humanitatem data quidem sit maxima potestas in cœlo et in terra, videlicet major et amplior, quam omnes angeli et creaturæ acceperint: sed tamen ita, ut cum omnipotentia Dei nullam habeat communicationem, neque omnipotentia illi data sit. Itaque mediam quandam potentiam, inter omnipotentiam Dei, et inter aliarum creaturarum potentiam, fingunt, datam Christo secundum humanam ejus naturam per exaltationem; quæ minor quidem sit, quam Dei omnipotentia, major tamen omnium aliarum creaturarum potestate.*

XVII. *Quod Christo secundum spiritum suum humanum certi limites positi sint, quantum videlicet ipsum scire oporteat, et quod non plus sciat, quam ipsi conveniat, et ad executionem sui officii, Judicis nimirum, necessario requiratur.*

XVIII. *Quod Christus ne hodie*

omnipotence and other properties of the divine nature. And this they dare to assert against the express testimony of Christ (Matt. xxviii. 18): 'All power is given unto me in heaven and in earth.' And they contradict Paul, who says (Col. ii. 9): 'In him dwelleth all the fullness of the Godhead bodily.'

XVI. That to Christ, according to the humanity, there is given, indeed, the greatest power in heaven and in earth; that is, a power greater and more ample than all angels and creatures have received, but in such wise, nevertheless, that it has no communication with the omnipotence of God, nor that omnipotence has been given to him. And so they feign a certain middle power between the omnipotence of God and the power of other creatures, given to Christ according to his human nature by exaltation; which is less, indeed, than the omnipotence of God, yet greater than the power of all other creatures.

XVII. That to Christ, according to his human spirit, certain limits are appointed as to how much it behooves him to know, and that he knows no more than is suitable for him, and is necessarily required for the execution of his office, to wit, as Judge.

XVIII. That Christ has not even

quidem perfectam habeat cogni-
tionem Dei, et omnium ipsius
operum ; cum tamen de Christo
scriptum sit (Col. ii. 3) : ' *In ipso*
omnes thesauros sapientiæ et sci-
entiæ absconditos esse.'

XIX. *Quod Christo secundum*
humanitatis suæ spiritum im-
possibile sit scire, quid ab æter-
no fuerit, quid jam nunc ubique
fiat, et quid in omnem æternita-
tem sit futurum.

XX. *Rejicimus etiam damna-*
musque, quod dictum Christi
(Matt. xxviii. 18) : ' *Mihi data*
est omnis potestas in cœlo et in
terra ;' horribili et blasphema in-
terpretatione a quibusdam depra-
vatur in hanc sententiam : quod
Christo secundum divinam suam
naturam in resurrectione et as-
censione ad cœlos iterum resti-
tuta fuerit omnis potestas in cœlo
et in terra, perinde quasi, dum
in statu humiliationis erat, eam
potestatem, etiam secundum Di-
vinitatem, deposuisset et exuisset.
Hac enim doctrina non modo
verba Testamenti Christi falsa
explicatione pervertuntur : verum
etiam dudum damnatæ Aria-
næ hæresi via de novo sternitur,
ut tandem æterna Christi Divi-
nitas negetur, et Christus totus,
quantus est, una cum salute no-
stra amittatur, nisi huic impiæ

now a perfect knowledge of God
and of all his works. Whereas it
is written of Christ (Col. ii. 3) : ' In
him are hid all the treasures of wisdom and knowledge.'

XIX. That to Christ, according
to his human spirit, it is impossible to know what has been from
all eternity, what now takes place
every where, and what will be to
all eternity.

XX. We also reject and condemn
the way in which the saying of
Christ (Matt. xxviii. 18), ' All power
is given unto me in heaven and in
earth,' is by some, through a horrible and blasphemous interpretation, corruptly wrested to this effect:
That to Christ, according to his
divine nature, there was restored
again at the resurrection and ascension all power in heaven and
on earth ; as if, forsooth, while he
was in the state of humiliation he
had laid aside and put off that
power even according to the divine nature. For by this doctrine
not only are the words of the Testament of Christ perverted by a
false interpretation, but also a way
is prepared anew for the long-since
condemned Arian heresy ; so that
at length the eternal divinity of
Christ will be denied, and all there
is of Christ, together with our sal-

doctrinæ ex solidis Verbi Dei et fidei nostræ Catholicæ fundamentis constanter contradicatur.

vation, will be lost, unless this ungodly doctrine be steadfastly contradicted according to the solid grounds of the Word of God and of our Catholic faith.

Art. IX.

DE DESCENSU CHRISTI AD INFEROS.

Status Controversiæ.

Disceptatum fuit super hoc articulo inter quosdam theologos, qui Augustanam Confessionem profitentur : quando et quomodo Dominus noster Jesus Christus, ut testatur fides nostra Catholica, ad inferos descenderit, an id ante, vel post mortem ejus factum sit. Præterea quæsitum fuit, num anima tantum, an divinitate sola, an vero anima et corpore descenderit, idque an spiritualiter, an vero corporaliter sit factum. Disputatum etiam est, num hic articulus ad passionem, an verum ad gloriosam victoriam et triumphum Christi sit referendus.

Cum autem hic fidei nostræ articulus, sicut et præcedens, neque sensibus neque ratione nostra comprehendi queat, sola autem fide acceptandus sit : unanimi consensu consulimus, de hac re non esse disputandum, sed quam simplicissime hunc articulum credendum et docendum esse. Atque

Art. IX.

OF THE DESCENT OF CHRIST INTO HELL.

Statement of the Controversy.

There has been a dispute touching this article among certain divines who profess the Augsburg Confession : when and how our Lord Jesus Christ, as our Catholic faith attests, descended into hell? whether this came to pass before or after his death? Moreover, it has been asked whether he descended in soul only or in divinity only, or indeed in soul and body, and whether this came to pass spiritually or corporally? It has also been disputed whether this article is to be referred to the passion, or to the glorious victory and triumph of Christ.

Now, inasmuch as this article of our faith, as also the foregoing, can be comprehended neither by our senses nor by our reason, but is to be received by faith alone, we have by unanimous consent agreed that this matter should not be disputed about, but should be believed and taught as simply as possible. And

*in hoc negotio sequamur piam
D. Lutheri doctrinam, qui; hunc
articulum in concione, Torgœ
habita (Anno, etc. XXXIII.),
pie admodum explicuit, omnes
inutiles et curiosas quæstiones
præcidit, atque ad piam fidei
simplicitatem omnes Christianos
adhortatus est.*

in this respect let us follow the godly teaching of Dr. Luther, who, in
his discourse held at Torgau in the
year 1533, unfolded this article in
a most godly wise, cutting short all
curious questions, and exhorting all
Christians to the pious simplicity
of faith.

*Satis enim nobis esse debet, si
sciamus, Christum ad inferos
descendisse, infernum omnibus
credentibus destruxisse, nosque
per ipsum e potestate mortis et
Satanæ, ab æterna damnatione,
atque adeo e faucibus inferni
ereptos. Quo autem modo hæc
effecta fuerint, non curiose scru-
temur, sed hujus rei cognitionem
alteri seculo reservemus, ubi non
modo hoc mysterium, sed alia
multa, in hac vita simpliciter a
nobis credita, revelabuntur, quæ
captum cœcæ nostra rationis excedunt.*

For it ought to be enough for
us to know that Christ descended
into hell, that he destroyed hell for
all believers, and that we through
him have been snatched from the
power of death and Satan, from
eternal damnation, and even from
the jaws of hell. But in what way
these things have been brought to
pass let us not curiously inquire,
but let us reserve the knowledge of
this thing to another world, where
not only this mystery, but many
other things also which in this life
have been simply believed by us,
shall be revealed, things which exceed the reach of our blind reason.

Art. X.

DE CEREMONIIS ECCLESIASTICIS,

*Quæ vulgo Adiaphora seu res mediæ et
indifferentes vocantur.*

*Orta est etiam inter theologos
Augustanæ Confessionis controversia de ceremoniis seu ritibus Ecclesiasticis, qui in Verbo
Dei neque præcepti sunt, neque*

Art. X.

OF ECCLESIASTICAL CEREMONIES,

*Which are commonly called Adiaphora, or
things indifferent.*

There has also arisen among the
divines of the Augsburg Confession
a controversy touching ecclesiastical
ceremonies or rites, which are neither enjoined nor forbidden in the

prohibiti, sed ordinis tantum et decori gratia in Ecclesiam sunt introducti.

Word of God, but have been introduced into the Church merely for the sake of order and seemliness.

Quæsitum fuit, num persecutionis tempore, et in casu confessionis (etiamsi adversarii nobiscum in doctrina consentire nolint) nihilominus salva conscientia aliquæ abrogatæ ceremoniæ, quæ per se indifferentes, et a Deo neque mandatæ neque prohibitæ sint, postulantibus id et urgentibus adversariis, iterum in usum revocari possint, et an hoc modo cum Pontificiis in ejusmodi ceremoniis et adiaphoris conformari recte queamus. Una pars hoc fieri posse affirmavit, altera vero negavit.

It has been asked whether in time of persecution and a case of confession (even though our adversaries will not agree with us in doctrine), nevertheless with a safe conscience, certain ceremonies already abrogated, which are of themselves indifferent, and neither commanded nor forbidden by God, may, on the urgent demand of our adversaries, again be re-established in use, and whether we can in this way rightly conform with the Papists in ceremonies and adiaphora of this sort. The one part has affirmed that this might be done, the other has denied it.

Sincera doctrina et confessio de hoc Articulo.

1. *Ad hanc controversiam dirimendam unanimi consensu credimus, docemus, et confitemur, quod ceremoniæ sive ritus Ecclesiastici (qui Verbo Dei neque præcepti sunt, neque prohibiti, sed tantum decori et ordinis causa instituti) non sint per se cultus divinus, aut aliqua saltem pars cultus divini. Scriptum est enim* (Matt. xv. 9): '*Frustra*

Sound doctrine and confession touching this Article.

I. For the better taking away of this controversy we believe, teach, and confess, with unanimous consent, that ceremonies or ecclesiastical rites (such as in the Word of God are neither commanded nor forbidden, but have only been instituted for the sake of order and seemliness) are of themselves neither divine worship, nor even any part of divine worship. For it is written

colunt me, docentes doctrinas, mandata hominum.'

II. *Credimus, docemus, et confitemur, Ecclesiæ Dei, ubivis terrarum, et quocunque tempore, licere, pro re nata, ceremonias tales mutare, juxta eam rationem, quæ Ecclesiæ Dei utilissima, et ad ædificationem ejusdem maxime accommodata judicatur.*

III. *Ea tamen in re omnem levitatem fugiendam et offendicula cavenda, in primis vero infirmorum in fide rationem habendam, et iis parcendum esse censemus.*

IV. *Credimus, docemus, et confitemur, quod temporibus persecutionum, quando perspicua et constans confessio a nobis exigitur, hostibus Evangelii in rebus adiaphoris non sit cedendum. Sic enim Apostolus inquit* (Gal. v. 1): *'Qua libertate Christus nos liberavit, in ea state, et nolite iterum jugo servitutis subjici.' Et alibi* (2 Cor. vi. 14): *'Nolite jugum ducere cum infidelibus,' etc. 'Quæ enim est societas luci ad tenebras?' etc. Item* (Gal. ii. 5): *'Quibus neque ad horam cessimus subjectione, ut veritas Evangelii permaneret apud vos. In*

(Matt. xv. 9): 'In vain they do worship me, teaching for doctrines the commandments of men.'

II. We believe, teach, and confess that it is permitted to the Church of God any where on earth, and at whatever time, agreeably to occasion, to change such ceremonies, in such manner as is judged most useful to the Church of God and most suited to her edification.

III. We judge, nevertheless, that in this matter all levity should be avoided and matters of offense be guarded against, and that especially account should be taken of the weak in the faith, and forbearance shown towards them (1 Cor. viii. 9; Rom. xiv. 13).

IV. We believe, teach, and confess that in times of persecution, when a clear and steadfast confession is required of us, we ought not to yield to the enemies of the Gospel in things indifferent. For thus speaks the Apostle (Gal. v. 1): 'Stand fast, therefore, in the liberty wherewith Christ hath made us free, and be not entangled again with the yoke of bondage.' And elsewhere (2 Cor. vi. 14): 'Be not unequally yoked together with unbelievers,' etc. 'For what concord hath light with darkness?' Also (Gal. ii. 5): 'To whom we gave place by subjection, no, not for an hour; that

tali enim rerum statu non agitur jam amplius de adiaphoris, sed de veritate Evangelii, et de libertate Christiana sarta tectaque conservanda, et quomodo cavendum sit, ne manifeste idololatria confirmetur, et infirmi in fide offendantur. In hujusmodi rebus nostrum certe non est, aliquid adversariis largiri: sed officium nostrum requirit, ut piam et ingenuam confessionem edamus, et ea patienter feramus, quæ Dominus nobis ferenda imposuerit, et hostibus Verbi Dei in nos permiserit.

the truth of the Gospel might remain with you.' For in such a state of things it is no longer a question of adiaphora, but of the restoration and maintenance of the truth of the Gospel and of Christian liberty, and of how care may be taken lest idolatry be manifestly strengthened and the weak in the faith be caused to stumble. In matters of this sort it is certainly not our part to concede any thing to our adversaries, but our duty requires that we should show forth a godly and frank confession, and patiently bear those things which the Lord may have laid upon us to bear, and may have suffered our enemies to do against us.

V. *Credimus, docemus, et confitemur, quod Ecclesia alia aliam damnare non debeat, propterea, quod hæc vel illa plus minusve externarum ceremoniarum, quas Dominus non instituit, observet; si modo in doctrina ejusque articulis omnibus, et in vero Sacramentorum usu sit inter eas consensus. Hoc enim vetus et verum dictum est: Dissonantia jejunii non dissolvit consonantiam fidei.*

V. We believe, teach, and confess that one Church ought not to condemn another because it observes more or less of external ceremonies, which the Lord has not instituted, provided only there be consent between them in doctrine and all the articles thereof, and in the true use of the sacraments. For so runneth the old and true saying: 'Dissimilarity of fasting does not destroy similarity of faith.'

NEGATIVA.

Falsæ doctrinæ de hoc Articulo rejectio.

Repudiamus atque damnamus hæc falsa et Verbo Dei contraria dogmata :

NEGATIVE.

Rejection of false doctrine touching this Article.

We repudiate and condemn the following false dogmas as repugnant to the Word of God:

I. *Quod humanæ traditiones et constitutiones, in Ecclesiasticis rebus, per se, pro cultu Dei, aut certe pro parte divini cultus sint habendæ.*

II. *Quando ejusmodi ceremoniæ et constitutiones Ecclesiæ Dei coactione quadam tanquam necessariæ obtruduntur, et quidem contra libertatem Christianam, quam Ecclesia Christi in rebus ejusmodi externis habet.*

III. *Cum asseritur, quod tempore persecutionis, quando clara confessio requiritur, hostibus Evangelii in observatione ejusmodi rerum adiaphorarum gratificari, et cum ipsis pacisci et consentire liceat : quæ res cum detrimento veritatis cælestis conjuncta est.*

IV. *Cum externæ ceremoniæ, quæ indifferentes sunt, ea opinione abrogantur, quasi Ecclesiæ Dei liberum non sit, pro re nata, ut judicaverit ad ædificationem utile esse, hanc vel illam ceremoniam, ratione libertatis Christianæ, usurpare.*

I. That human traditions and constitutions in things ecclesiastical are of themselves to be accounted as divine worship, or at least as a part of divine worship.

II. When ceremonies and constitutions of this kind are by a sort of coercion obtruded upon the Church as necessary, and that contrary to the Christian liberty which the Church of Christ has in external matters of this sort.

III. When it is asserted that in time of persecution, when a clear confession is required, it is permitted to gratify the enemies of the Gospel in the observation of adiaphora of this sort, and to covenant and agree with them, which thing is attended with detriment of the heavenly truth.

IV. When external ceremonies, which are indifferent, are abrogated under the opinion that it is not free to the Church of God, as occasion demands, to use this or that ceremony by the privilege of its Christian liberty as it shall judge to be useful to edification.

ART. XI.

DE ÆTERNA PRÆDESTINATIONE ET ELECTIONE DEI.

De hoc articulo non quidem publice mota est controversia inter Augustanæ Confessionis Theologos: sed tamen cum hic articulus magnam piis mentibus consolationem adferat, si recte et dextre explicetur, visum est eundem in hoc scripto declarare, ne forte temporis progressu disputationes aliquæ cum offendiculo conjunctæ de hac re exoriantur.

AFFIRMATIVA.

Sincera doctrina de hoc Articulo.

I. *Primum omnium est, quod accurate observari oportet, discrimen esse inter præscientiam [Vorsehung], et prædestinationem, sive æternam electionem [ewige Wahl] Dei.*

II. *Præscientia enim Dei nihil aliud est, quam quod Deus omnia noverit, antequam fiant, sicut scriptum est* (Dan. ii. 28): '*Est Deus in cœlo, revelans mysteria, qui indicavit tibi Rex Nabuchodonosor, quæ ventura sunt in novissimis temporibus.*'

III. *Hæc Dei præscientia simul ad bonos et malos pertinet, sed interim non est causa mali, neque est causa peccati, quæ hominem*

ART. XI.

OF THE ETERNAL PREDESTINATION AND ELECTION OF GOD.

Touching this article there has not, indeed, arisen any public controversy among the divines of the Augsburg Confession; but nevertheless, inasmuch as this article brings great consolation to pious minds, if it be rightly and skillfully expounded, it has seemed good to set forth the same in this writing, lest perchance, in process of time, certain disputations leading to offense should arise thereupon.

AFFIRMATIVE.

Sound doctrine touching this Article.

I. First of all, it ought to be most accurately observed that there is a distinction between the foreknowledge and the predestination or eternal election of God.

II. For the foreknowledge of God is nothing else than this, that God knows all things before they come to pass, as it is written (Dan. ii. 28): 'There is a God in heaven that revealeth secrets, and maketh known to the king Nebuchadnezzar what shall be in the latter days.'

III. This foreknowledge of God extends both to good and evil men; but nevertheless it is not the cause of evil, nor is it the cause of sin,

*ad scelus impellat. Peccatum
enim ex diabolo, et ex hominis
prava et mala voluntate oritur.
Neque hæc Dei præscientia causa
est, quod homines pereant; hoc
enim sibi ipsis imputare debent:
sed præscientia Dei disponit [ord-
net] malum, et metas illi constituit, quousque progredi et quam
diu durare debeat, idque eo dirigit, ut, licet per se malum sit,
nihilominus electis Dei ad salutem cedat.*

IV. *Prædestinatio vero, seu
æterna Dei electio, tantum ad
bonos et dilectos filios Dei pertinet; et hæc est causa ipsorum
salutis. Etenim eorum salutem
procurat, et ea, quæ ad ipsam
pertinent, disponit. Super hanc
Dei prædestinationem salus nostra ita fundata est, ut inferorum portæ eam evertere nequeant* (John x. 28; Matt. xvi. 18).

V. *Hæc Dei prædestinatio non
in arcano Dei consilio est scru-
tanda, sed in Verbo Dei, in quo
revelatur quærenda est.*

VI. *Verbum autem Dei deducit nos ad Christum, is est liber
ille vitæ, in quo omnes inscripti et
electi sunt, qui salutem æternam
consequuntur. Sic enim scriptum
est* (Eph. i. 4): '*Elegit nos in Christo, ante mundi constitutionem.*'

impelling man to crime. For sin
arises from the devil, and from the
depraved and evil will of man.
Nor is this foreknowledge of God
the cause why men perish, for this
they ought to impute to themselves.
But the foreknowledge of God dis
poses evil and sets bounds to it, how
far it may proceed and how long
endure, and directs it in such wise
that, though it be of itself evil, it
nevertheless turns to the salvation
of the elect of God.

IV. But the predestination or
eternal election of God extends
only to the good and beloved children of God, and this is the cause
of their salvation. For it procures
their salvation, and appoints those
things which pertain to it. Upon
this predestination of God our salvation is so founded that the gates
of hell can not prevail against it
(John x. 28; Matt. xvi. 18).

V. This predestination of God is
not to be searched out in the hidden
counsel of God, but is to be sought
in the Word of God, in which it is
revealed.

VI. But the Word of God leads
us to Christ, he is that book of life
in which all are inscribed and elected who attain eternal salvation.
For thus it is written (Eph. i. 4):
'He hath chosen us in Christ before the foundation of the world.'

VII. *Christus vero omnes peccatores ad se vocat, et promittit
illis levationem, et serio vult [ist
ihm Ernst], ut.omnes homines ad
se veniant, et sibi consuli et subveniri sinant. His sese Redemptorem in verbo offert, et vult, ut
verbum audiatur, et ut aures non
obdurentur, nec verbum negliga-
tur et contemnatur. Et promittit se largiturum virtutem et
operationem Spiritus Sancti et
auxilium divinum, ut in fide
constantes permaneamus, et vitam
æternam consequamur.*

VIII. *De nostra igitur electione
ad vitam æternam neque ex rationis nostræ judicio, neque ex
lege Dei judicandum est, ne vel
dissolutæ et Epicureæ vitæ nos
tradamus, vel in desperationem
incidamus. Qui enim rationis
suæ judicium in hoc negotio sequuntur, in horum cordibus hæ
perniciosæ cogitationes (quibus
ægerrime resistere possunt) exci-
tantur: Si (inquiunt) Deus me
ad æternam salutem elegit, non
potero damnari, quicquid etiam
designavero. Contra vero, si non
sum electus ad vitam æternam,
nihil plane mihi profuerit, quan-
tumcunque boni fecero, omnes
enim conatus mei irriti erunt [es
ist doch alles umsonst].*

VII. But Christ calls all sinners
to him, and promises to give them
rest. And he earnestly wishes that
all men may come to him, and suffer themselves to be cared for and
succored. To these he offers himself in the Word as a Redeemer, and
wishes that the Word may be heard,
and that their ears may not be hardened, nor the Word be neglected and
contemned. And he promises that
he will bestow the virtue and operation of the Holy Spirit and divine
aid, to the end that we may abide
steadfast in the faith and attain
eternal life.

VIII. Therefore we are to judge
neither by the judgment of our
own reason nor by the law of God,
concerning our election to eternal
life, lest we either give ourselves
over to a dissolute and Epicurean
life or fall into desperation. For
they who follow the judgment of
their own reason in this matter, in
their hearts arise these mischievous
thoughts, which it is hard indeed
for them to resist: If (say they)
God has elected me to eternal salvation, I can not be damned, let me
do what evil I will. But, on the
other hand, if I am not elected to
eternal life, all the good that I may
do will advantage me nothing at
all, for all my endeavors will be in
vain.

IX. *Vera igitur sententia de præ-destinatione ex Evangelio Christi discenda est. In eo enim perspicue docetur, quod Deus omnes sub incredulitatem concluserit, ut omnium misereatur, et quod nolit quenquam perire, sed potius ut omnes convertantur, et in Christum credant* (Rom. xi. 32; Ezek. xviii. 23; xxxiii. 11; 2 Pet. iii. 9; 1 John ii. 2).

X. *Qui igitur voluntatem Dei revelatam inquirunt, eoque ordine progrediuntur, quem D. Paulus in Epistola ad Romanos secutus est (qui hominem prius deducit ad pœnitentiam, ad agnitionem peccatorum, ad fidem in Christum, ad obedientiam mandatorum Dei, quam de æternæ præ-destinationis mysterio loquatur), iis doctrina de prædestinatione Dei salutaris est, et maximam consolationem affert.*

XI. *Quod vero scriptum est* (Matt. xxii. 14), '*Multos quidem vocatos, paucos vero electos esse;*' *non ita accipiendum est, quasi Deus nolit, ut omnes salventur; sed damnationis impiorum causa est, quod Verbum Dei aut prorsus non audiant, sed contumaciter contemnant, aures obdurent, et cor indurent, et hoc modo Spi-ritui Sancto viam ordinariam*

IX. The true opinion, therefore, concerning predestination is to be learned from the Gospel of Christ. For in it is clearly taught that 'God hath concluded all under unbelief, that he might have mercy upon all;' and that 'he is not willing that any should perish, but rather that all should be converted and believe in Christ' (Rom. xi. 32; Ezek. xviii. 23; xxxiii. 11; 2 Pet. iii. 9; 1 John ii. 2).

X. Whoever, therefore, inquire into the revealed will of God, and proceed in that order which St. Paul has followed in the Epistle to the Romans (who first leads man to repentance, to the acknowledgment of his sins, to obedience to the commandments of God, before he speaks of the mystery of eternal predestination), to them the doctrine of the predestination of God is salutary, and affords very great consolation.

XI. But as to the declaration (Matt. xxii. 14), 'Many are called, but few are chosen,' it is not to be so understood as if God were unwilling that all should be saved, but the cause of the damnation of the ungodly is that they either do not hear the Word of God at all, but contumaciously contemn it, stop their ears, and harden their hearts, and in this way foreclose to the

præcludant, ut opus suum in eis efficere nequeat, aut certe quod verbum auditum flocci pendant [in Wind schlagen], atque abjiciant. Quod igitur pereunt, neque Deus, neque ipsius electio, sed malitia eorum in culpa est (2 Pet. ii. 1 sqq.; Luke ii. 49, 52; Heb. xii. 25 sqq.).

XII. *Huc usque homo pius in meditatione articuli de æterna Dei electione tuto progredi potest, quatenus videlicet ea in Verbo Dei est revelata. Verbum Dei enim nobis Christum, librum vitæ, proponit: is nobis per Evangelii prædicationem aperitur et evolvitur, sicut scriptum est* (Rom. viii. 30): '*Quos elegit, hos vocavit.' In Christo igitur electio æterna Dei Patris est quærenda. Is in æterno suo consilio decrevit, quod præter eos, qui Filium ejus Jesum Christum agnoscunt et in eum vere credunt, neminem salvum facere velit. Reliquæ cogitationes ex animis piorum penitus excutiendæ sunt, qui non a Deo, sed ex af flatu Satanæ proficiscuntur, quibus humani generis hostis hoc agit, ut dulcissimam illam consolationem vel enervet, vel penitus e medio tollat, quam ex saluberrima hac doctrina haurire possumus, qua videlicet certi*

Spirit of God his ordinary way, so that he can not accomplish his work in them, or at least when they have heard the Word, make it of no account, and cast it away. Neither God nor his election, but their own wickedness, is to blame if they perish (2 Pet. ii. 1 sqq.; Luke ii. 49, 52; Heb. xii. 25 sqq.).

XII. So far, therefore, may a godly man proceed with safety in meditation upon the article of the eternal election of God, even as far, that is, as it is revealed in the Word of God. For the Word of God proposes to us Christ, the Book of Life which through the preaching of the Gospel is opened and spread out before us, as it is written (Rom. viii. 30): 'Whom he did predestinate, them he also called.' In Christ, therefore, is the eternal election of God the Father to be sought. He in his eternal counsel has decreed that besides those who acknowledge his Son Jesus Christ, and truly believe on him, he will save no one. Other surmisings should be wholly dismissed from the minds of the godly, because they are not of God, but of the inspiration of Satan, whereby the enemy of mankind is endeavoring either to weaken or wholly to take away that most sweet consolation which we may draw from this most wholesome doctrine:

reddimur, quod mera gratia, sine ullo nostro merito, in Christo ad vitam æternam electi simus, et quod nemo ex ipsius manibus rapere nos possit. Et hanc clementissimam electionem non nudis verbis, sed interposito jurejurando Dominus contestando confirmavit, et venerabilibus Sacramentis nobis obsignavit, quorum in summis tentationibus meminisse, et ex iis consolationem petere debemus, ut ignita Diaboli tela extinguamus.

XIII. *Interim tamen summo studio in eo elaboremus, ut ad normam voluntatis divinæ vitam nostram instituamus, et vocationem nostram [ut D. Petrus (2 Pet. i. 20) loquitur] firmam faciamus, neque a Dei revelato verbo latum unguem recedamus; illud enim nunquam nos fallet.*

XIV. *Hac brevi explicatione æternæ electionis divinæ honos suus Deo plene et in solidum tribuitur: quod videlicet, secundum voluntatis suæ propositum, mera misericordia, sine ullo nostro merito salvos nos faciat. Neque tamen hac doctrina, vel gravioribus illis animi perturbationibus, et pusillanimitati, vel Epicurismo [zur Kleinmüthigkeit oder rohem, wildem Leben] ansa præbetur.*

inasmuch as by it we are rendered certain that by mere grace, without any merit of our own, we are chosen in Christ to eternal life, and that no one can pluck us out of his hands. And this most merciful election the Lord hath attested and confirmed, not by mere words, but by the mediation of an oath, and hath sealed to us by the holy sacraments, which we ought to call to mind in our deepest temptations, and seek consolation from them, that we may quench all the fiery darts of the Devil.

XIII. Yet none the less ought we to take the utmost pains to fashion our life agreeably to the norm of the divine will, and *to make our calling and election sure,* as St. Peter says (2 Pet. i. 10), nor to recede a hair-breadth from the revealed Word of God; for that will never fail us.

XIV. This brief explication of the eternal election of God, attributes fully and completely to God his own proper honor, showing that he saves us according to the purpose of his own will, of mere compassion, without any merit of our own. While by this doctrine no handle is given to vehement disturbances of mind and faint-heartedness, nor to Epicureanism.

Negativa.

Falsæ doctrinæ de hoc Articulo rejectio.

Credimus igitur et sentimus, quando doctrina de electione Dei ad vitam æternam eo modo proponitur, ut perturbatæ piæ mentes ex ea consolationem nullam capere queant, sed potius per eam in animi angustias [Kleinmüthigkeit] aut desperationem conjiciantur, aut impænitentes in dissoluta sua vita confirmentur, quod articulus hic non ad normam verbi et voluntatis Dei, sed juxta humanæ rationis judicium, et quidem impulsu Satanæ, male et perperam tractetur. 'Quæcunque enim scripta sunt' [inquit (Rom. xv. 4) apostolus] 'ad nostram doctrinam scripta sunt, ut per patientiam et consolationem Scripturarum spem habeamus.' Rejicimus itaque omnes, quos jam enumerabimus, errores.

I. *Quod Deus nolit, ut omnes homines pænitentiam agant, et Evangelio credant.*

II. *Quando Deus nos ad se vocat, quod non serio hoc velit, ut omnes homines ad ipsum veniant.*

III. *Quod nolit Deus, ut omnes salventur, sed quod quidam, non ratione peccatorum suorum, verum solo Dei consilio, proposito et voluntate, ad exitium*

NEGATIVE.

Rejection of false doctrine touching this Article.

We believe, therefore, and judge that when the doctrine of God's election of men to eternal life is so propounded that godly minds can derive no consolation from it under anxiety, but are by it the rather thrown into distress of mind or desperation, or the impenitent are confirmed in their dissolute life, that this article is not then handled agreeably to the rule of the word and will of God, but according to the judgment of human reason, and that badly and falsely by the instigation of Satan. 'For whatsoever things were written aforetime' [says the apostle (Romans xv. 4)] 'were written for our learning, that we through patience and comfort of the Scriptures might have hope.' We therefore reject all the errors which we will now enumerate:

I. That God is unwilling that all men should repent and believe the Gospel.

II. That when God calls us to him, he does not earnestly wish that all men should come to him.

III. That God is not willing that all men should be saved, but that some men are destined to destruction, not on account of their sins, but by the mere counsel, purpose,

destinati sint, ut prorsus salutem consequi non possint.

IV. *Quod non sola Dei misericordia et sanctissimum Christi meritum, sed etiam in nobis ipsis aliqua causa sit electionis divinæ, cujus causæ ratione Deus nos ad vitam æternam elegerit.*

Hæc dogmata omnia falsa sunt, horrenda et blasphema, iisque piis mentibus omnis prorsus consolatio eripitur, quam ex Evangelio et sacramentorum usu capere deberent, et idcirco in Ecclesia Dei nequaquam sunt ferenda.

Hæc brevis est et simplicissima articulorum controversorum explicatio, de quibus inter theologos Augustanæ Confessionis aliquandiu disceptatum et discrepantibus inter se sententiis disputatum est. Et ex hac declaratione homo pius, quamtumvis simplex, secundum analogiam Verbi Dei et Catechismi simplicem doctrinam deprehendere potest, quid verum sit, quid falsum. Non enim tantummodo sincera doctrina diserte est recitata, verum etiam contraria et falsa doctrina repudiata est et rejecta, et controversiæ illæ, offendiculorum plenæ, solide sunt decisæ atque dijudicatæ [*und also die eingefallene ärgerlichen Spaltungen gründlich entschieden seind*].

and will of God, so that they can not in any wise attain to salvation.

IV. That the mercy of God and the most holy merit of Christ is not the sole cause of the divine election, but that there is also some cause in us, on account of which cause God has chosen us to eternal life.

All these dogmas are false, horrid, and blasphemous, and by them all consolation is utterly taken away from godly minds, such as they ought to receive from the Gospel and the use of the sacraments, and therefore they are by no means to be borne with in the Church of God.

This is a brief and most simple explication of the controverted articles, touching which there has been, for some time, discussion among the divines of the Augsburg Confession, and touching which they have disputed among themselves with varying opinions. And from this statement and exposition a man, however unlearned, is able, according to the analogy of the Word of God, and according to the simple doctrine of the Catechism, to discover what is true and what is false. For not only has the genuine doctrine been distinctly set forth, but also the contrary and false doctrine has been repudiated and rejected, and controversies full of occasions of offense have been solidly decided and settled.

Faxit Deus omnipotens, Pater Domini nostri Jesu Christi, ut per gratiam Spiritus Sancti omnes in ipso consentientes et concordes simus, atque in consensu pio, qui ipsi probetur, constanter perseveremus. Amen.

May Almighty God, the Father of our Lord Jesus Christ, grant that by the grace of the Holy Spirit we may all be harmonious and of one accord in him, and may steadfastly persevere in a godly agreement, which may be approved by him. Amen.

Art. XII.

DE ALIIS HÆRESIBUS ET SECTIS

[*Von anderen Rotten und Secten*],

quæ nunquam Augustanam Confessionem sunt amplexæ.

Art. XII.

OF OTHER HERESIES AND SECTS,

which have never embraced the Augsburg Confession.

Ne tacita cogitatione hæreses illæ et sectæ nobis tribuantur, propterea, quod earum in commemorata declaratione expressam mentionem non fecimus: visum est, articulos earum ad calcem (ut dicitur) hujus scripti nude recitare, in quibus nostri temporis hæretici a veritate dissentiunt, et sinceræ nostræ religioni et confessioni contrarium docent.

Lest such heresies and sects should tacitly be attributed to us, for the reason that we have not made express mention of them in the statement given above, it has seemed good simply to recite this document at the end of their articles of belief, wherein the heretics of our time dissent from the truth, and teach contrary to our sound confession and doctrine.

ERRORES ANABAPTISTARUM.

Anabaptistæ in multas sectas [viel Haufen] sunt divisi, quarum aliæ plures, aliæ pauciores errores defendunt: generatim [ingemein] tamen omnes talem doctrinam profitentur, quæ neque in Ecclesia, neque in politia [noch in der Polizei und weltlichem Regiment], neque in œconomia [Haushaltung] tolerari potest.

ERRORS OF THE ANABAPTISTS.

The Anabaptists are divided into many sects, of which some maintain more, some fewer errors. Nevertheless, in a general way, they all profess such a doctrine as can be tolerated neither in the Church, nor by the police and in the commonwealth, nor in daily [domestic and social] life.

Articuli Anabaptistici, qui in Ecclesia ferri non possunt.

I. *Quod Christus carnem et sanguinem suum, non e Maria virgine assumserit, sed e cœlo attulerit.*

II. *Quod Christus non sit verus Deus, sed tantummodo cæteris sanctis sit superior, quia plura Spiritus Sancti dona acceperit, quam alius quispiam homo sanctus.*

III. *Quod justitia nostra coram Deo, non in solo Christi merito, sed in renovatione atque adeo in nostra propria probitate, in qua ambulemus, consistat. Ea vero Anabaptistarum justitia magna ex parte electitia et humanitus excogitata quadam sanctimonia constat, et revera nil aliud est, quam novus quidam monachatus.*

IV. *Quod infantes non baptizati coram Deo non sint peccatores, sed justi et innocentes, et in illa sua innocentia, cum usum rationis nondum habeant, sine baptismo (quo videlicet, ipsorum opinione, non egeant) salutem consequantur. Et hoc modo rejiciunt totam de peccato originali doctrinam, reliqua etiam, quæ ex ea dependent.*

V. *Quod infantes baptizandi non sint, donec usum rationis*

Anabaptist Articles which can not be endured in the Church.

I. First, that Christ did not assume his flesh and blood of the Virgin Mary, but brought them from heaven.

II. That Christ is not true God, but is merely superior to other saints, because he has received more gifts of the Holy Spirit than any other holy man whatsoever.

III. That our righteousness before God does not consist in the merit of Christ alone, but in our renewal, and thus in our own uprightness in which we walk. Now this righteousness of the Anabaptists consists in great part in a certain arbitrary and humanly devised sanctimony, and in truth is nothing else than some new sort of monkery.

IV. That infants not baptized are not sinners before God, but just and innocent, and in this their innocence, when they have not as yet the use of reason, may, without baptism (of which, to wit, in the opinion of the Anabaptists, they have no need), attain unto salvation. And in this way they reject the whole doctrine of original sin, and all the consequences that follow therefrom.

V. That infants ought not to be baptized until they attain the use

consequantur, et fidem suam ipsi profiteri possint.

VI. *Quod Christianorum liberi eam ob causam, quia parentibus Christianis et fidelibus orti sunt (etiam præter et ante susceptum baptismum), revera sancti, et in filiorum Dei numero sint habendi. Qua de causa etiam neque Pædobaptismum magnificaciunt, neque id operam dant, ut infantes baptizentur, quod cum expressis verbis promissionis divinæ* (Gen. xvii. 7 sqq.) *pugnat: ea enim tantum ad eos pertinet, qui fœdus Dei observant, illudque non contemnunt.*

VII. *Quod ea non sit vera et Christiana Ecclesia, in qua aliqui adhuc peccatores reperiuntur.*

VIII. *Quod conciones non sint audiendæ ullæ in iis templis, in quibus aliquando Missæ Pontificiæ sunt celebratæ.*

IX. *Quod homo pius nihil prorsus commercii habere debeat cum Ecclesiæ ministris, qui Evangelion Christi juxta Augustanæ Confessionis sententiam docent, et Anabaptistarum conciones ac errores reprehendunt, et quod ejusmodi Ecclesiæ ministris neque servire, neque operam locare liceat, sed quod iidem ut perversores*

of reason, and are able themselves to profess their faith.

VI. That the children of Christians, on the ground that they are sprung of Christian and believing parents (even apart from and before the receiving of baptism), are in very deed holy, and to be accounted as belonging to the children of God, for which reason they neither make much account of the baptism of children, nor take care to have their children baptized, which conflicts with the express words of the divine promise (Gen. xvii. 7 sqq.): for this only holds good to those who *observe the covenant of God, and do not contemn it.*

VII. That that is not a true Christian Church in which any sinners are yet found.

VIII. That we ought not to listen to any sermons in those churches in which the Papist masses have ever been celebrated.

IX. That a godly man ought to have no dealings at all with the ministers of the Church who teach the Gospel of Christ according to the tenor of the Augsburg Confession, and rebuke the preachings and errors of the Anabaptists; and that it is not lawful either to serve or to do any work for such ministers of the Church, but that they are to be

verbi divini vitandi et fugiendi sint.

avoided and shunned as perverters of the divine Word.

Articuli Anabaptistici, qui in Politia [in der Polizei] sunt intolerabiles.

Anabaptist Articles which are intolerable in the Commonwealth.

I. *Quod Magistratus officium non sit, sub Novo Testamento, genus vitæ, quod Deo placeat.*

I. That the office of the magistrate is not, under the New Testament, a condition of life that pleases God.

II. *Quod homo Christianus salva et illæsa conscientia officio Magistratus fungi non possit.*

II. That a Christian man can not discharge the office of a magistrate with a safe and quiet conscience.

III. *Quod homo Christianus illæsa conscientia officium Magistratus, rebus ita ferentibus, adversus improbos administrare et exequi, et subditi potestatem illam, quam Magistratus a Deo accepit, ad defensionem implorare non possint.*

III. That a Christian man can not with a safe conscience administer and execute the office of a magistrate, if matters so require, against the wicked, nor subjects implore for their defense that power which the magistrate has received of God.

IV. *Quod homo Christianus sana conscientia jusjurandum præstare, et juramento interposito obedientiam et fidem suo Principi aut Magistratui promittere nequeat.*

IV. That a Christian man can not with a safe conscience take an oath, nor swear obedience and fidelity to his prince or magistrate.

V. *Quod Magistratus, sub Novo Testamento, bona conscientia homines facinorosos capitali supplicio afficere non possit.*

V. That the magistrate, under the New Testament, can not with a good conscience punish criminals with death.

Articuli Anabaptistici, qui in Œconomia [Haushaltung] ferri non possunt.

Anabaptist Articles which can not be tolerated in daily life.

I. *Quod homo pius non possit conscientia salva proprium tenere*

I. That a godly man can not with safe conscience hold or pos-

et possidere, sed quod is, quic-quid omnino facultatum habeat, id totum in commune conferre [in die Gemein zu geben] debeat.

II. *Quod homo Christianus illæsa conscientia neque cauponariam, neque mercaturam exercere, aut arma conficere possit [kein Gastgeber, Kaufmann oder Messerschmidt sein könne].*

III. *Quod conjugibus, propter diversam religionem, divortium facere, et cum alia persona, quæ in religione non dissentiat, matrimonium contrahere liceat.*

sess any property, but that whatever means he may possess, he is bound to bestow them all as common good.

II. That a Christian man can not with a safe conscience either keep an inn, or carry on trade, or forge weapons.

III. That it is permitted married people who think differently in religion to divorce themselves, and to contract matrimony with some other persons who agree with them in religion.

ERRORES SCHWENCOFELDIANORUM.

I. *Quod omnes illi, qui Christum, secundum carnem, creaturam esse dicunt, non habeant veram regnantis cœlestis Regis agnitionem.*

II. *Quod caro Christi per exaltationem eo modo omnes proprietates divinas acceperet, ut Christus, quatenus homo est, potentia, virtute, majestate, gloria, Patri et τῷ Λόγῳ, per omnia, in gradu et statu essentiæ, omnino æqualis sit, ita, ut jam utriusque in Christo naturæ una sit essentia, eædem proprietates, eadem voluntas eademque gloria; et quod caro Christi ad Sacrosanctæ Trinitatis essentiam pertineat.*

ERRORS OF THE SCHWENKFELDIANS.

I. That all those who affirm Christ, according to the flesh, to be a creature, have no true knowledge of the heavenly king and his reign.

II. That the flesh of Christ through its exaltation has in such wise received all the divine attributes, that Christ, as he is man, is altogether like to the Father and to the Word [Logos] in power, might, majesty, in all things, in grade and state of essence, so that henceforth there is one essence of both natures in Christ, and the same attributes, the same will, and the same glory; and that the flesh of Christ pertains to the essence of the Blessed Trinity.

III. *Quod ministerium verbi, prœdicatum et auditu perceptum verbum, non sit instrumentum illud, per quod Deus Spiritus Sanctus homines doceat, salutaremque Christi agnitionem largiatur, et conversionem, veram pœnitentiam, fidem et novam obedientiam in ipsis efficiat.*

IV. *Quod aqua Baptismi non sit medium, per quod Dominus adoptionem in filiis Dei obsignet, et regenerationem efficiat.*

V. *Quod panis et vinum in Sacra Cœna non sint organa, per quœ et cum quibus Christus corpus et sanguinem suum distribuat.*

VI. *Quod homo pius, vere per Spiritum Dei regeneratus, legem Dei in hac vita perfecte servare et implere valeat.*

VII. *Quod non sit vera Ecclesia Christi, in qua non vigeat publica excommunicatio, et solennis aliquis excommunicationis modus, seu, ut vulgo dicitur, processus ordinarius.*

VIII. *Quod is Ecclesiœ minister alios homines cum fructu docere, aut vera Sacramenta dispensare non possit, qui ipse non sit vere renovatus, renatus et vere justus.*

III. That the ministry of the Word, the Word preached and heard, is not that instrument whereby God the Holy Ghost teaches men, and bestows the salutary knowledge of Christ, and effects conversion, true repentance, faith, and new obedience in them.

IV. That the water of baptism is not a means whereby the Lord seals adoption in the children of God and effects regeneration.

V. That the bread and wine in the Holy Supper are not organs by which and with which Christ dispenses his body and blood.

VI. That a godly man, truly regenerated by the Spirit of God, has power perfectly to keep and fulfill the law of God in this life.

VII. That that is no true Church of Christ in which there is not in full force public excommunication, and some formal mode, or, as is commonly said, ordinary process of excommunication.

VIII. That a minister of the Church who is not truly renewed, regenerate, and truly righteous, can not fruitfully teach men, or dispense true sacraments.

Error Novorum Arianorum.

Quod Christus non sit verus, substantialis, naturalis Deus

Error of the New Arians.

That Christ is not true, substantial, natural God, of the same es

[*wahrhaftiger, wesentlicher, natürlicher Gott*], *ejusdem cum Patre et Spiritu Sancto essentiæ: sed divina tantum majestate ita cum Patre ornatus, ut Patre sit inferior.*

sence with the Father and the Holy Ghost; but that he has merely been in such-wise adorned with divine majesty with the Father, as that he is nevertheless inferior to the Father.

Error Antitrinitariorum.

Hæc prorsus nova est hæresis, quæ antehac Ecclesiis Christi ignota fuit, eorum videlicet, qui opinantur, docent et profitentur, non esse unicam tantum divinam et æternam Patris, Filii, et Spiritus Sancti essentiam: sed quemadmodum Pater, Filius, et Spiritus Sanctus tres sunt distinctæ personæ, ita unamquamque personam habere distinctam, et a reliquis personis Divinitatis separatam essentiam. Et horum alii sentiunt, quod singulæ personæ in singulis essentiis æquali sint potestate, sapientia, majestate, et gloria: sicut alias tres numero differentes homines, ratione essentiæ suæ, sunt a se invicem disjuncti et separati. Alii sentiunt tres illas personas et essentias ita inæquales esse, ratione essentiæ et proprietatum, ut solus Deus Pater verus sit Deus.

Hos, atque his similes errores omnes, ut eos etiam, qui ab his dependent, et ex his consequuntur, rejicimus atque damnamus:

Error of the Antitrinitarians.

This is a heresy entirely new, which hitherto has been unknown to the churches of Christ—the heresy, namely, of such as imagine, teach, and profess that there is not one sole divine and eternal essence only of Father, Son, and Holy Ghost; but as Father, Son, and Holy Ghost are three distinct persons, so each person has a distinct essence, separate from the other persons of the Godhead. And some of these may think that the separate persons, in their separate essences, are of equal power, wisdom, majesty, and glory, as, for instance, three men, differing numerically in respect of their essence, are mutually separate and disjoined. Others think that these three persons and essences are so unequal in respect of essence and attributes, as that God the Father alone is true God.

All these errors, and the errors like to these, and also those which depend on these and follow from them, we reject and condemn, as

utpote, qui falsi sint atque hæ-retici [als unrecht, falsch, ketze-risch], et qui Verbo Dei, tribus approbatis Symbolis [den dreien Symbolis],[1] Augustanæ Confessioni, ejusdem Apologiæ, Smalcaldicis Articulis, et Catechismis Lutheri repugnent: quos etiam errores omnes pii summi atque infimi cavere et vitare debent, nisi æternæ suæ salutis jacturam facere velint [so lieb ihnen ihrer Seelen Heil und Seligkeit ist].

Quod autem hæc sit omnium nostrum fides, doctrina et confessio (de qua in novissimo illo die Judici Domino nostro Jesu Christo rationem reddere parati sumus), et quod contra hanc doctrinam nihil vel occulte vel aperte dicere aut scribere, sed per gratiam Dei in ea constanter perseverare velimus: in ejus rei fidem, re bene meditata, in vero Dei timore et invocatione nominis ejus [wohlbedächtig in wahrer Furcht und Anrufung Gottes] hanc epitomen propriis manibus subscripsimus.[2]

being false and heretical, and as being inconsistent with the Word of God, with the three approved Symbols,[1] the Augsburg Confession, with the Apology of the same, the Smalcald Articles, and the Catechisms of Luther; which errors also all the godly, high and low alike, ought to beware of and avoid, unless they wish to hazard their own eternal salvation.

Now that this is the faith, doctrine, and confession of us all (concerning which we are prepared to render account at the last day to our Lord Jesus Christ the Judge), and that against this doctrine we are minded to speak or write nothing either hiddenly or openly, but by the grace of God steadfastly to persevere therein: in attestation of this thing, having well advised of the matter, in the true fear of God and calling upon his name, we have with our own hands subscribed this Epitome.[2]

---

[1] That is, the Apostles', the Nicene, and the Athanasian Creeds, which are incorporated in the Lutheran Book of Concord.

[2] The list of subscribers is added to the Preface of the Book of Concord, and embraces eighty-six names, headed by three Electors—John of the Palatinate, Augustus of Saxony, and John George of Brandenburg.

ARTICULI VISITATORII.

THE SAXON VISITATION ARTICLES. A.D. 1592.

[The Four Articles of Visitation, prepared by Ægidius Hunnius and other Lutheran divines against Crypto-Calvinism in Electoral Saxony, 1592, never acquired general authority, and have now ceased to be binding even in Saxony. But they are historically important as a condensed and authoritative statement of the differences between orthodox Lutheranism and Calvinism concerning the doctrines of the sacraments, the person of Christ, and predestination. It should not be forgotten that they are the product of a fierce polemical age, which could hardly do justice to an opponent. Calvinists would not accept the views in the extreme form here ascribed to them, least of all the horrible doctrine 'that God *created* the greater portion of mankind for eternal damnation.' Luther (in his book against Erasmus) taught the same doctrine on the subject of predestination as Calvin.

The German and Latin texts are taken from Müller's edition of the *Symbolical Books of the Lutheran Church*, pp. 779–784. The Latin text is also given in Hase's *Libri Symb.* Comp. Vol. I. p. 345.]

Christliche Visitations-Artikel

im ganzen Churkreis Sachsen, etc.

Der erste Artikel.

Von dem heiligen Nachtmahl.

Die reine und wahrhaftige Lehre unser Kirchen vom heiligen Nachtmahl:

I. Daß die Worte Christi: **Nehmet und esset, das ist mein Leib; trinket, das ist mein Blut,** einfältig und nach dem Buchstaben, wie sie lauten, zu verstehen sind.

II. Daß im Sacrament zwei Dinge sind, gegeben und mit einander empfangen werden: ein irdisches, das ist Brot und Wein; und ein himmlisches, das ist der Leib und Blut Christi.

III. Daß solches hiernieden auf Erden geschieht, und nicht droben im Himmel.

ARTICULI VISITATORII

A. C. 1592 *in Electoratu et Provinciis superioris Saxoniæ publicati, etc.*

ART. I.

De Sacra Cœna.

Pura et vera doctrina nostrarum ecclesiarum de Sacra Cœna:

I. Quod verba Christi: ACCIPITE ET COMEDITE, HOC EST CORPUS MEUM; BIBITE, HIC EST SANGUIS MEUS, *simpliciter et secundum litteram*, sicut sonant, intelligenda sint.

II. Quod in sacramento duæ res sint, quæ exhibentur et simul accipiuntur: *una terrena*, quæ est panis et vinum; et *una cœlestis*, quæ est corpus et sanguis Christi.

III. Quod hæc Unio, Exhibitio et Sumptio fiat hic inferius in terris, non superius in cœlis.

THE VISITATION ARTICLES

For the Electorate and Provinces of Upper Saxony, published A.D. 1592.

ART. I.

Of the Lord's Supper.

The pure and true Doctrine of our Churches on the Lord's Supper.

I. That the words of Christ, 'Take and eat, this is my Body;' 'Drink, this is my Blood,' are to be understood in the simple and literal sense, as they sound.

II. That, in the Sacrament, there are two things which are exhibited and received together: one, earthly, which is bread and wine; the other, heavenly, which is the body and blood of Christ.

III. That these things [this union, exhibition, and sumption] take place here below on the earth, and not above in heaven

IV. Daß es der rechte natürliche Leib Christi sei, der am Kreuz gehangen, und das rechte, natürliche Blut, das aus Christi Seite geflossen.

IV. Quod exhibeatur et accipiatur *verum et naturale corpus Christi*, quod in cruce pependit, *et verus ac naturalis sanguis*, qui ex Christi latere fluxit.

IV. That the true and natural body of Christ which hung on the cross, and the true and natural blood, which flowed from the side of Christ, are exhibited and received.

V. Daß der Leib und Blut Christi nicht nur mit dem Glauben geistlich, welches auch außerhalb dem Abendmahl geschehen kann, sondern allda mit Brot und Wein mündlich, doch unerforschlicher und übernatürlicher Weise empfangen werde, zu einem Pfand und Versicherung der Auferstehung unserer Leiber von den Todten.

V. Quod corpus et sanguis Christi non fide tantum *spiritualiter*, quod etiam extra cœnam fieri potest, sed cum pane et vino *oraliter*, modo tamen imperscrutabili et supernaturali illic in cœna accipiantur, idque in pignus et certificationem resurrectionis nostrorum corporum ex mortuis.

V. That the body and blood of Christ are received in the Supper, not only spiritually, which might be done out of the Supper; but by the mouth, with the bread and wine; yet in an inscrutable and supernatural manner; and this for a pledge and ascertainment of the resurrection of our bodies from the dead.

VI. Daß die mündliche Nießung des Leibes und Blutes Christi nicht allein von den Würdigen geschehe, sondern, auch von den Unwürdigen, die ohne Buße und wahren Glauben hinzugehen; doch zu ungleichem Ende: von den Würdigen zur Seligkeit, von den Unwürdigen aber zum Gericht.

VI. Quod oralis perceptio corporis et sanguinis Christi non solum fiat a *dignis*, verum etiam ab *indignis*, qui sine pœnitentia et vera fide accedunt; eventu tamen diverso. A *dignis* enim percipitur ad salutem, ab *indignis* autem ad iudicium.

VI. That the body and blood of Christ are received orally, not only by the worthy, but also by the unworthy, who approach them without repentance and true faith; though with different effect. By the worthy, they are received for salvation; by the unworthy, for judgment.

Der andere Artikel.
Von der Person Christi.

Die reine und wahrhaftige Lehre unserer Kirchen dieses Artikels von der Person Christi:

I. In Christo sind zwei unterschiedene Naturen, die göttliche und die mensch-

ART. II.
De Persona Christi.

Pura et vera doctrina nostrarum ecclesiarum de hoc articulo de Persona Christi.

I. In Christo sunt duæ distinctæ naturæ, *divina et humana*. Hæ manent in

ART. II.
Of the Person of Christ.

The pure and true Doctrine of our Churches on the Article of the Person of Christ.

I. In Christ there are two distinct natures, the divine and the human. These re-

liche; diese bleiben in Ewigkeit unvermenget und ungetrennet.

II. Diese beide Naturen sind persönlich also mit einander vereiniget, daß nur ein Christus, eine Person ist.

III. Um dieser persönlichen Vereinigung willen wird recht gesagt, ist auch in der That und Wahrheit also, daß Gott Mensch, und Mensch Gott ist, daß Maria den Sohn Gottes geboren, und Gott uns durch sein eigen Blut erlöset hat.

IV. Durch diese persönliche Vereinigung und darauf erfolgte Erhöhung ist Christus nach dem Fleisch zur Rechten Gottes gesetzet, und hat empfangen alle Gewalt im Himmel und auf Erden, ist auch aller göttlichen Majestät, Ehre, Kraft und Herrlichkeit theilhaftig worden.

æternum *inconfusæ et inseparabiles* (seu indivisæ).

II. Hæ duæ naturæ *personaliter* ita sunt unitæ, ut *unus* tantum sit *Christus*, et *una* persona.

III. Propter hanc personalem unionem recte dicitur, atque in re et veritate ita se habet, quod *Deus Homo* et *Homo Deus* sit, quod Maria *Filium Dei* genuerit, et quod Deus nos *per proprium suum sanguinem* redemerit.

IV. Per hanc unionem personalem et, quæ eam secuta est, exaltationem Christus *secundum carnem* ad *dexteram Dei* collocatus est, et accepit *omnem potestatem* in cœlo et in terra, factusque est particeps *omnis divinæ majestatis, honoris, potentiæ et gloriæ.*

main eternally unmixed and inseparable (or undivided).

II. These two natures are personally so united that there is but one Christ and one person.

III. On account of this personal union it is rightly said, and in fact and truth it really is, that God is man, and man is God; that Mary begat the Son of God, and that God redeemed us by his own proper blood.

IV. By this personal union, and the exaltation which followed it, Christ, according to the flesh, is placed at the right hand of God, and has received all power in heaven and in earth, and is made partaker of all the divine majesty, honor, power, and glory.

Der dritte Artikel.

Von der heiligen Taufe.

Die reine, wahrhaftige Lehre unserer Kirchen von diesem Artikel der heiligen Taufe:

I. Daß nur eine Taufe sei und eine Abwaschung, nicht welche die Unsauberkeit des Leibes pfleget hinweg zu nehmen, sondern uns von Sünden wäschet.

II. Durch die Taufe als das

Art. III.

De S. Baptismo.

Pura et vera doctrina nostrarum ecclesiarum de hoc articulo s. baptismatis.

I. Quod *unum* tantum baptisma sit et una ablutio, non quæ sordes corporis tollere solet, sed quæ nos a peccatis abluit.

II. Per baptismum tan-

Art. III.

Of Holy Baptism.

The pure and true Doctrine of our Churches on this Article of Holy Baptism.

I. That there is but one Baptism, and one Ablution: not that which is used to take away the filth of the body, but that which washes us from our sins.

II. By Baptism, as a bath

Bad der Wiedergeburt und Erneuerung des heiligen Geistes machet uns Gott selig, und wirket in uns solche Gerechtigkeit und Reinigung von Sünden, daß, wer in solchem Bund und Vertrauen bis an das Ende beharret, nicht verloren wird, sondern das ewige Leben hat.

III. Alle, die in Christum Jesum getauft sind, die sind in seinen Tod getauft, und durch die Taufe mit ihm in seinen Tod begraben, und haben Christum angezogen.

IV. Die Taufe ist das Bad der Wiedergeburt, darum, daß in derselben wir von neuem geboren, und mit dem Geist der Kindheit versiegelt und begnadet werden.

V. Es sei denn, daß jemand geboren werde aus dem Wasser und Geist, so kann er nicht in das Reich Gottes kommen. Doch ist der Nothfall hiemit nicht gemeinet.

VI. Was vom Fleisch geboren ist, das ist Fleisch, und von Natur sind wir alle Kinder des Zornes Gottes; denn aus sündlichem Samen sind wir gezeuget und in Sünden werden wir alle empfangen.

quam lavacrum illud regenerationis et renovationis Spiritus Sancti salvos nos facit Deus et operatur in nobis talem justitiam et purgationem a peccatis, ut, qui in eo fœdere et fiducia usque ad finem perseverat, non pereat, sed habeat vitam æternam.

III. Omnes, qui in Christum Jesum baptizati sunt, in mortem ejus baptizati sunt, et per baptismum cum ipso in mortem ejus consepulti sunt, et Christum induerunt.

IV. Baptismus est lavacrum illud regenerationis, propterea, quia in eo renascimur denuo et Spiritu adoptionis obsignamur ex gratia (sive gratis).

V. Nisi quis renatus fuerit ex aqua et Spiritu, non potest introire in regnum cœlorum. Casus tamen necessitatis hoc ipso non intenditur.

VI. Quidquid de carne nascitur, caro est, et natura sumus omnes filii iræ divinæ, quia ex semine peccaminoso sumus geniti et in peccatis concipimur omnes.

of the regeneration and renovation of the Holy Ghost, God saves us, and works in us such justice and purgation from our sins, that he who perseveres to the end in that covenant and hope does not perish, but has eternal life.

III. All who are baptized in Jesus Christ are baptized in his death; and by baptism are buried with him in his death, and have put on Christ.

IV. Baptism is the bath of regeneration, because in it we are born again, and sealed by the Spirit of adoption through grace (or gratuitously).

V. Unless a person be born again of water and Spirit, he can not enter into the kingdom of heaven. This is not intended, however, for cases of necessity.

VI. Whatever is born of the flesh is flesh; and, by nature, all of us are children of divine wrath: because we are born of sinful seed, and we are all born in sin.

Der vierte Artikel.

Von der Gnadenwahl und ewigen Vorsehung Gottes.

Die reine und wahrhaftige Lehre unserer Kirchen von diesem Artikel.

I. Daß Christus für alle Menschen gestorben, und als das Lamm Gottes der ganzen Welt Sünde getragen hat.

II. Daß Gott niemand zur Verdammniß geschaffen, sondern will, daß allen Menschen geholfen werde und sie zur Erkenntniß der Wahrheit kommen. Befiehlet allen, daß sie seinen Sohn Christum in dem Evangelio hören sollen, und verheißt dadurch Kraft und Wirkung des heiligen Geistes zur Bekehrung und Seligkeit.

III. Daß viele Menschen durch ihre eigene Schuld verdammt werden, die entweder das Evangelium von Christo nicht hören wollen oder aus der Gnade wieder ausfallen. durch Irrthum wider das Fundament oder durch Sünde wider das Gewißen.

IV. Daß alle Sünder, so Buße thun, zu Gnaden angenommen, und keiner ausgeschloßen werde, wenn seine Sünden gleich blutroth wären. Sintemal Gottes Barmherzigkeit viel größer ist denn aller Welt Sünde, und Gott sich aller seiner Werke erbarmet.

Art. IV.

De Prædestinatione et Æterna Providentia Dei.

Pura et vera doctrina nostrarum ecclesiarum de hoc articulo.

I. Quod Christus pro omnibus hominibus mortuus sit, et ceu agnus Dei totius mundi peccata sustulerit.

II. Quod Deus neminem ad condemnationem condiderit, sed velit, ut omnes homines salvi fiant et ad agnitionem veritatis perveniant; propterea omnibus mandat, ut Filium suum Christum in evangelio audiant, et per hunc auditum promittit virtutem et operationem Spiritus Sancti ad conversionem et salutem.

III. Quod multi homines propria culpa pereant: alii, qui evangelium de Christo nolunt audire, alii, qui iterum excidunt gratia, sive per errores contra fundamentum sive per peccata contra conscientiam.

IV. Quod omnes peccatores, pœnitentiam agentes, in gratiam recipiantur, et nemo excludatur, etsi peccata ejus rubeant ut sanguis; quandoquidem Dei misericordia major est quam peccata totius mundi, et Deus omnium suorum operum misereatur.

Art. IV.

On Predestination and the Eternal Providence of God.

The pure and true Doctrine of our Churches on this Article.

I. That Christ died for all men, and, as the Lamb of God, took away the sins of the whole world.

II. That God created no man for condemnation; but wills that all men should be saved and arrive at the knowledge of truth. He therefore commands all to hear Christ, his Son, in the gospel; and promises, by his hearing, the virtue and operation of the Holy Ghost for conversion and salvation.

III. That many men, by their own fault, perish: some, who will not hear the gospel concerning Christ; some, who again fall from grace, either by fundamental error, or by sins against conscience.

IV. That all sinners who repent will be received into favor; and none will be excluded, though his sins be red as blood; since the mercy of God is greater than the sins of the whole world, and God hath mercy on all his works.

Falſche und irrige Lehre der Calviniſten

SEQUITUR FALSA ET ERRONEA DOCTRINA CALVINISTARUM

THE FALSE AND ERRONEOUS DOCTRINE OF THE CALVINISTS

Vom heiligen Nachtmahl.

De Sacra Cœna.

On the Lord's Supper.

I. Daß obgeſetzte Worte Chriſti figürlicher Weiſe zu verſtehen ſein, und nicht, wie ſie lauten.

I. Quod supra posita verba Christi figurate intelligenda sint, et non secundum litteram, sicut sonant.

I. That the before-cited words of Christ are to be understood figuratively, and not according to the letter, as they sound.

II. Daß im Abendmahl nur bloße Zeichen ſein, aber der Leib Chriſti ſei ſo weit von dem Brot, als der höchſte Himmel von der Erden.

II. Quod in cœna tantum nuda signa sint, corpus autem Christi tam procul a pane, quam supremum cœlum a terra.

II. That bare signs only are in the Supper; but the body of Christ is as far from the bread as the highest heaven from the earth.

III. Daß Chriſtus allda gegenwärtig ſei nur mit ſeiner Kraft und Wirkung, und nicht mit ſeinem Leibe; gleichwie die Sonne mit ihrem Scheine und Wirkung hiernieden auf Erden gegenwärtig und kräftig iſt, aber die Sonne ſelbſt iſt droben im Himmel.

III. Quod Christus illic præsens sit tantum virtute et operatione sua, et non corpore suo. Quemadmodum sol splendore et operatione sua in terris præsens et efficax est, corpus autem solare superius in cœlo existit.

III. That Christ is present therein, by his virtue and operation only, and not in his body; as the sun, by his splendor and operation, is present and effective on earth; but the body of the sun exists above in heaven.

IV. Daß es ein typicum corpus, ein figürlicher Leib ſei, der nur bedeutet und fürgebildet werde.

IV. Corpus Christi esse typicum corpus, quod pane et vino tantum significetur et præfiguretur.

IV. That the body of Christ is therein a typified body, which is only signified and prefigured by the bread and wine.

V. Daß er allein mit dem Glauben, welcher ſich hinauf in den Himmel ſchwinget, und nicht mündlich empfangen werde.

V. Quod sola fide, quæ in cœlum se elevet, et non ore accipiatur.

V. That the body is received by faith alone, which raiseth itself to heaven, and not by the mouth.

VI. Daß ihn alleine die Würdigen empfahen; die Unwürdigen aber, ſo ſolchen Glauben nicht haben, der hinauf in den Himmel ſteigen kann, nichts denn Brot und Wein empfahen.

VI. Quod soli digni illud accipiant; indigni autem, qui talem fidem evolantem sursum in cœlos non habent, nihil præter panem et vinum accipiant.

VI. That the worthy only receive it; that the unworthy, who have not the faith which ariseth to the heavens, receive nothing besides bread and wine.

Falsche und irrige Lehre der Calvinisten

FALSA ET ERRONEA DOCTRINA CALVINISTARUM

THE FALSE AND ERRONEOUS DOCTRINE OF THE CALVINISTS

Von der Person Christi,

so vornehmlich wider den dritten und vierten Artikel reiner Lehre streiten.

I. Erstlich, daß Gott Mensch ist und der Mensch Gott sei, das sei ein figürliche Rede.

II. Daß die Menschheit mit der Gottheit nicht in der That und Wahrheit, sondern allein nach dem Namen und Worten Gemeinschaft habe.

III. Daß Gott unmüglich sei mit aller seiner Allmacht zu verschaffen, daß Christi natürlicher Leib auf einmal mehr denn an Einem Orte sei.

IV. Daß Christus nach seiner Menschheit durch sein Erhöhung allein erschaffene Gaben und gemeßene Gewalt empfangen habe, und nicht alles wiße und vermöge.

V. Daß Christus nach seiner Menschheit abwesend regiere, gleichwie der König in Hispanien über die neuen Inseln regieret.

VI. Daß ein verdammliche Abgötterei sei, wann man das Vertrauen und den Glauben des Herzens auf Christum nicht allein nach seiner Gottheit, sondern auch nach seiner Menschheit setzet, und die Ehre der Anrufung darauf richtet.

De Persona Christi,

quæ potissimum III. et IV. Articulo purioris doctrinæ repugnat.

I. Quod Deus Homo, et Homo Deus est, esse figuratam locutionem.

II. Quod humana natura cum divina non in re et veritate, sed tantum nomine et verbis communionem habeat.

III. Quod Deo impossibile sit ex tota omnipotentia sua præstare, ut corpus Christi naturale simul et instante in pluribus quam in unico loco sit.

IV. Quod Christus secundum humanam naturam per exaltationem suam tantum creata dona et finitam potentiam acceperit, non omnia sciat aut possit.

V. Quod Christus secundum humanitatem absens regnet, sicut rex Hispaniæ novas insulas regit.

VI. Quod damnabilis idolatria sit, si fiducia et fides cordis in Christum non solum secundum divinam, sed etiam secundum humanam ipsius naturam collocetur, et honor adorationis ad utramque dirigatur.

On the Person of Christ:

Which differs, in particular, from the Third and Fourth Article of the more pure doctrine.

I. That God is man, and man God, is a figurative mode of speech.

II. That human nature hath communion with the divine, not in fact and truth, but in name and words only.

III. That it is impossible to God, by all his omnipotence, to effect that the natural body of Christ, which is in one place, should, at the same time and instant, be in several.

IV. That, according to his human nature, Christ hath, by his exaltation, received only created good and finite power; and doth not know and can not do all things.

V. That, according to his humanity, Christ reigns, where he is absent, as the King of Spain governs his new islands.

VI. That it is a damnable idolatry to place the hope and faith of the heart in Christ, not only according to his divine, but also according to his human nature, and to direct the honor of adoration to both.

Falſche und irrige Lehre der Calviniſten

FALSA ET ERRONEA DOCTRINA CALVINISTARUM

THE FALSE AND ERRONEOUS DOCTRINE OF THE CALVINISTS

Von der heiligen Taufe.

I. Die Taufe ſei ein äußerlich Waßerbad, damit eine innerliche Abwaſchung von Sünden alleine bedeutet werde.

II. Die Taufe wirke oder gebe nicht die Wiedergeburt, den Glauben, Gnade Gottes und Seligkeit, ſondern bezeichne und verſiegle alleine dieſelbige.

III. Nicht alle, die mit Waßer getauft werden, erlangen hiemit die Gnade Chriſti oder Gabe des Glaubens, ſondern allein die Auserwählten.

IV. Die Wiedergeburt geſchehe nicht in und bei der Taufe, ſondern erſt hernacher bei erwachſenen Jahren, in etlichen auch wol gar im Alter.

V. Die Seligkeit hange nicht an der Taufe, daher denn auch die Nothtaufe in der Kirchen nicht ſoll geſtattet werden, ſondern wenn man den Kirchendienſt nicht haben mag, ſoll das Kindlein immer ohne Taufe ſterben.

VI. Der Chriſten Kinder ſind heilig für der Taufe und von Mutterleibe an, ja noch in ihrer Mutter Leib in dem Bunde des ewigen Lebens; ſonſt könnte ihnen die heilige

De Sacro Baptismo.

I. Baptismum esse externum lavacrum aquæ, per quod interna quædam ablutio a peccatis tantum significetur.

II. Baptismum non operari neque conferre regenerationem, fidem, gratiam Dei et salutem, sed tandum significare et obsignare ista.

III. Non omnes, qui aqua baptizantur, consequi eo ipso gratiam Christi aut donum fidei, sed tantum electos.

IV. Regenerationem non fieri in vel cum baptismo, sed postea demum crescente ætate, imo et multis in senectute demum contingere.

V. Salutem non dependere a baptismo, atque ideo baptismum in casu necessitatis non permittendum esse in ecclesia, sed in defectu ordinarii ministri ecclesiæ permittendum esse, ut infans sine baptismo moriatur.

VI. Christianorum infantes iam ante baptismum esse sanctos, ab utero matris, imo adhuc in utero materno constitutos esse in fœdere vitæ æternæ; cete-

On Holy Baptism.

I. That Baptism is an external washing of water, by which a certain internal ablution from sin is merely signified.

II. That Baptism does not work nor confer regeneration, faith, the grace of God, and salvation, but only signifies and seals them.

III. That not all who are baptized in water, but the elect only, obtain by it the grace of Christ and the gifts of faith.

IV. That regeneration doth not take place in and with Baptism, but afterwards, at a more advanced age—yea, with many not before old age.

V. That salvation doth not depend on Baptism, and therefore in cases of necessity should not be required in the Church; but when the ordinary minister of the Church is wanting, the infant should be permitted to die without Baptism.

VI. The infants of Christians are already holy before Baptism in the womb of the mother, and even in the womb of the mother are received into the covenant of eternal life: otherwise the Sacrament of Bap-

Taufe nicht mitgetheilet werden.

roqui sacrum baptisma ip-
sis conferri non posse.

tism could not be conferred
on them.

Falſche und irrige Lehre
der Calviniſten

FALSA ET ERRONEA DOCTRI-
NA CALVINISTARUM

THE FALSE AND ERRONEOUS
DOCTRINE OF THE CAL-
VINISTS

Von der Gnadenwahl und Fürſehung Gottes.

De Prædestinatione et Providentia Dei

On Predestination and the Providence of God.

I. Daß Chriſtus nicht für alle
Menſchen, ſondern alleine für
die Auserwählten geſtorben ſei.

I. Christum non pro om-
nibus hominibus, sed pro
solis electis mortuum esse.

I. That Christ did not
die for all men, but only
for the elect.

II. Daß Gott den meiſten
Theil der Menſchen zum ewigen Verdammnis geſchaffen,
und wolle nicht haben, daß ſie
bekehret und ſelig werden.

II. Deum potissimam
partem homin ım ad dam-
nationem æternam creasse,
et nolle, ut potissima pars
convertatur et vivat.

II. That God created the
greater part of mankind
for eternal damnation, and
wills not that the greater
part should be converted
and live.

III. Daß die Auserwählten
und Neugebornen nicht können
den Glauben und heiligen Geiſt
verlieren und verdammt werden, wenn ſie gleich allerlei
große Sünde und Laſter be-
gehen.

III. Electos et regenitos
non posse fidem et Spiri-
tum Sanctum amittere aut
damnari, quamvis omnis
generis grandia peccata et
flagitia committant.

III. That the elected and
regenerated can not lose
faith and the Holy Spirit,
or be damned, though they
commit great sins and
crimes of every kind.

IV. Die, ſo nicht erwählet
ſind, müßen verdammet werden, und können nicht zur Seligkeit kommen, wenn ſie gleich
tauſendmal getauft würden
und täglich zum Abendmahl
giengen, auch ſo heilig und
unſträflich lebten, als es immer möglich.

IV. Eos vero, qui electi
non sunt, necessario dam-
nari, nec posse pervenire
ad salutem, etiamsi millies
baptizarentur et quotidie
ad eucharistiam accede-
rent, præterea vitam tam
sancte atque inculpate du-
cerent, quantum unquam
fieri potest.

IV. That those who are
not elect are necessarily
damned, and can not arrive
at salvation, though they
be baptized a thousand
times, and receive the Eucharist every day, and lead
as blameless a life as ever
can be led.

SYMBOLA EVANGELICA.

PARS SECUNDA:

ECCLESIA REFORMATA.

SYMBOLA EVANGELICA.

EVANGELICAL SYMBOLS.

PART SECOND:

CORPVS ET SYNTAGMA
CONFESSIONVM
FIDEI

QVÆ IN DIVERSIS REGNIS
ET NATIONIBVS, ECCLESIARVM

nomine fuerunt authenticè editæ : in celeberrimis
Conuentibus exhibitæ, publicáque
auctoritate comprobatæ.

QVIBVS ANNECTITVR, IN OMNIBVS CHRISTIANÆ
Religionis Articulis, CATHOLICVS CONSENSVS,
ex Sententiis Veterum, qui PATRES
vocantur, defumptus.

CONFESSIONVM ENVMERATIONEM ET HARMONIAM:
atque huius Catholici Veterum cum illis Confenfus, ordinem indicant
paginæ primæ fingularum partium huius Syntagmatis,
in Tres Partes diftributi.

EDITIO NOVA,
In qua quid præftitum fit, docet pagina fequens.

GENEVÆ,
Sumptibus Petri Chouët.

M. DC. LIV.
[The first edition appeared A.D. 1612.]

PRÆFATIO.

*X*HIBENTVR *hoc in Volumine, celeberrimæ
Confessiones Fidei ex optimis quibusque edi-
tionibus omni ex parte integræ. Non pri-
uatum aut alicuius priuati scriptum, sed
publicum ad omnes & singulos pertinens:
in quo Ecclesiæ Dei audientiam sibi fieri
postulant, vt ex ipsarum vocibus dignoscatur*
earum doctrina: *nihil enim, nisi abscondi veretur Religionis
veritas, ne damnetur ignorata. Fuerat quidem earum Harmonia, ante triginta annos edita: sed per varias sectiones intersecta.
Nunc verò illæ tanquam corpus integrum, conspiciendæ repræsentantur, & quàm in illa editione plures. Venustiùs autem &
vtiliùs cernitur ipsum corpus totum, quàm partes eius diuulsæ.
Earum quoque nexus & harmonia facilè deprehendetur vel ex
integra lectione, vel ex Concordantia per singulos articulos hic
illis annexa: quibus etiam in hoc Syntagmate adiungitur ex
Sententiis veterum, qui Patres vocantur, Catholicus Consensus:
Anno quidem 1595 à me editus, nunc rursus multò locupletior
factus, ac quibusdam Articulis auctus: cuius institutum declarat
quæ in illo est ad Illustrissimum Principem præfixa Epistola.*

*At verò cur illæ Confessiones fidei constitutæ in diuersis
Regnis & Nationibus, causæ fuere complures perquam necessariæ, quæ in ipsarum Præfationibus declarantur. Nam per
illas, tanquam ex Tabulis authenticis quid in Ecclesiis doceretur, manifestum fuit, aduersus calumnias & iniqua præiudi-
cia: vnde & in celeberrimis Conuentibus exhibitæ fuerunt*

¶ 2

HARMONIA

CONFESSIONVM

FIDEI,

Orthodoxarum, & Reformatarum Ecclefiarum, quæ in præcipuis quibufque Europæ Regnis, Nationibus, & Prouinciis, facram Euangelij doctrinam purè profitentur: quarum catalogum & ordinem fequentes paginæ indicabunt.

Additæ funt ad calcem breuifsimæ obferuationes: quibus, tum illuftrantur obfcura, tum quæ in fpeciem pugnare inter fe videri poffunt, perfpicuè, atque modeftifsimè conciliantur: & fi quæ adhuc controuerfa manent, fyncerè indicantur.

Quæ omnia, Ecclefiarum Gallicarum, & Belgicarum nomine, fubiiciuntur libero & prudenti reliquarum omnium, iudicio.

GENEVÆ,

Apud Petrum Santandreanum.

M. D. LXXXI.

PRAEFATIO NOMI-
NE ECCLESIARVM GALLI-
CARVM ET BELGICARVM, QVÆ
Reformationem Euangelicam
profitentur.

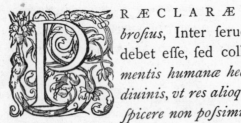

RÆCLARÆ *quodam loco dicit Am-brosius*, Inter seruos Christi contentio non debet esse, sed collatio. *Quum enim sit ea mentis humanæ hebetudo in rebus præsertim diuinis, vt res alioqui maximè claras sæpe per-spicere non possimus, quin ex mutua* συζητήσει, *& amica fraternaque disceptatione plurimum lucis assequamur, negari nullo modo potest. Imprim'sque illud vtile & necessarium videtur alios ab aliis acui, vt quæ singulis Ecclesiæ membris pri-uatim Dominus contulit, ea ad totius corporis commodum commu-nicentur, &, omni deposito sinistro affectu, Christus, qui est patris Sapientia, vnicus magister ac Ecclesiæ doctor audiatur: vtque est pacis princeps, ita suo spiritu nostros animos conglutinet, vt, si fieri possit, in Domino vnum idémque omnes sentiamus. Conten-dere verò, rixari, & ferociter ac proteruè digladiari, tantùm ab-est vt deceat à Deo institutos homines, vt ne modestis aut humanis quidẽ cõueniat. Quòd si in omnibus, vel etiã minimis vitæ hu-*

* ij

ARTICULI SIVE CONCLUSIONES LXVII. H. ZWINGLII.

A.D. 1523.

THE SIXTY-SEVEN ARTICLES OR CONCLUSIONS OF ULRICH ZWINGLI.

[These Theses of Ulrich Zwingli (1484–1531) were publicly discussed and successfully defended at the religious conference in Zurich, Jan. 29, 1523, and prepared the way for the introduction of the Reformation in German Switzerland. They exhibit the first creed of the Reformed Churches (seven years older than the Lutheran Confession of Augsburg). Their form, consisting of brief, concise propositions, is much better adapted for a creed than the lengthy argumentative discussions of many later and more authoritative confessions. They never acquired a strictly symbolical authority, not even in Zurich, but may justly claim a place in this Collection on the ground of their historical importance. We give the original in High-German, with some of the old readings in foot-notes, together with the Latin translation (instead of the less intelligible Swiss dialect in which Zwingli wrote them, and which is reproduced by Niemeyer, pp. 1 sqq.). For an abridgment in English, see the *History of Creeds*, Vol. I. pp. 363 sqq.]

Diese nachbestimmten siebenundsechzig Artikel und Meinungen bekenne ich Huldrich Zwingly in der löblichen Stadt Zürich geprebigt zu haben aus Grund der Schrift, die θεόπνευστος (d. i. von Gott eingegeben[1]) heißt, und erbiete[2] mich, mit ihr genannte Artikel zu beschirmen und zu erobern, und wenn ich jetzt berührte Schrift nicht recht verstünde, mich besfern Verstandes, doch aus ehegedachter Schrift, berichten zu lassen.

I. Alle, welche sagen, das Evangelium sei nichts[3] ohne die Bewährung der Kirche, irren, und schmähen Gott.

II. Die Summe des Evangeliums ist, daß unser Herr Jesus Christus, wahrer Gottessohn, uns den Willen seines himmlischen Vaters kund gethan, und uns mit seiner Unschuld vom Tode erlöset und Gott versöhnet hat.

III. Daher ist Christus der alleinige Weg zur Seligkeit Aller, die je waren, sind und sein werden.

IV. Wer eine andere Thür sucht

ELENCHUS ARTICULORUM

IN DISPUTATIONEM PRIMAM PROMULGATORUM

AB

HULDRICO ZWINGLIO.

I. *Quicunque Evangelion nihil esse dicunt, nisi ecclesiæ calculus et adprobatio accedat, errant, et Deum blasphemant.*

II. *Summa Evangelii est, quod Christus Filius Dei vivi notefecit nobis voluntatem Patris cœlestis, et quod innocentia sua nos de morte æterna redemit, et Deo reconciliavit.*

III. *Hinc sequitur Christum esse unicam viam ad salutem omnium, qui fuerunt, sunt et erunt.*

IV. *Quicunque aliud ostium vel*

---

[1] ungesprochen.   [2] entbeüt.   [3] nüt.

oder zeigt, der irrt, ja, ist ein Seelen= mörder und ein Dieb.

V. Daher Alle, die andere Lehre dem Evangelium gleich oder höher achten,[1] irren, und wissen nicht, was Evangelium ist.

VI. Denn Christus Jesus ist der Wegführer und Hauptmann, dem gan= zen[2] menschlichen Geschlechte von Gott verheißen und gegeben:[3]

VII. Daß er ein ewiges Heil und Haupt sei aller Gläubigen, die sein Leib[4] sind, der aber todt ist und nichts vermag ohne ihn.

VIII. Daraus[5] folgt, zuerst, daß Alle, die in dem Haupte leben, Glieder und Kinder Gottes sind, und das ist die Kirche oder Gemeinschaft[6] der Heiligen, eine Hausfrau Christi, ecclesia catholica.

IX. Zum andern, daß, wie die leiblichen Glieder ohne Leitung[7] des Hauptes nichts vermögen, also an dem Leibe Christi Niemand etwas vermag ohne sein Haupt, Christus.

X. Wie der Mensch taub [toll] ist, wenn die Glieder etwas ohne das Haupt wirken, sich selbst reißen, verwun= den, beschädigen, also, wenn die Glieder Christi etwas ohne ihr Haupt Chri= stum sich unterstehen, sind sie taub [toll], schlagen und beschweren sich selbst mit unweisen Gesetzen.

XI. Daher wir sehen, daß der so=

quærit vel ostendit, errat; quin animarum latro est et fur.

V. *Quicunque ergo alias doctrinas Evangelio vel æquant vel præferunt, errant, nec intelligunt quid sit Evangelion.*

VI. *Nam Christus Jesus dux est et imperator, a Deo toti generi humano et promissus et præstitus:*

VII. *Ut sit ipse salus et caput omnium credentium, qui corpus eius sunt, quod quidem absque ipso mortuum est, et nihil potest.*

VIII. *Ex his sequitur, quod omnes, qui in isto capite vivunt, sunt membra et Filii Dei. Et hæc est ecclesia seu communio sanctorum, sponsa Christi, ecclesia catholica.*

IX. *Quemadmodum membra corporis sine administratione capitis nihil possunt, sic in corpore Christi nemo quidquam potest sine capite eius, Christo.*

X. *Quum membra absque capite aliquid operantur, ut, dum sese lacerant aut perdunt, demens est homo: sic, dum membra Christi sine capite Christo aliquid tentant, insana sunt, sese gravant et perdunt imprudentibus legibus.*

XI. *Colligimus hinc Ecclesia-*

---

[1] messent.   [3] gelapstet.   [5] Uss dem.   [7] Verwalten.
[2] allem.   [4] Leichnam.   [6] Gemeynsame.

genannten Geiftlichen Satzungen von ihrer Pracht, Reichthum, Ständen, Titeln und Gesetzen eine Urfache aller Unfinnigkeit find, da fie mit dem Haupte nicht übereinftimmen.[1]

XII. Alfo toben fie noch, nicht von des Hauptes wegen (denn das befleißigt man fich aus Gottes Gnade zu diefer Zeit hervorzubringen), fondern weil man fie nimmer will laffen toben, fondern auf das Haupt allein hören.[2]

XIII. Wo man darauf hört,[3] da erlernt man lauter und flar den Willen Gottes, und wird der Menfch durch feinen Geift zu ihm gezogen und in ihn verwandelt.

XIV. Darum alle Chriftenmenfchen ihren höchften Fleiß anwenden[4] follen, daß das Evangelium Chrifti allein geprediget werde allenthalben.

XV. Denn in dem Glauben an daſſelbe ſteht unſer Heil, und im Unglauben daran unſere Verdammniß; denn alle Wahrheit iſt klar in ihm.

XVI. Im Evangelium lernt man, daß Menſchenlehre und Satzungen zur Seligfeit nichts nützen:

Merck Bapſt.[5]

XVII. Daß Chriſtus ein einiger, ewiger, oberſter Prieſter iſt, daraus ermeſſen wird, daß, die ſich für oberſte Prieſter ausgegeben haben, der Ehre

sticorum (quos vocant) traditiones et leges, quibus fastum, divitias, honores, titulos legesque suas fulciunt et defendunt, causam esse omnis insaniæ; nam capiti Christo non consonant.

XII. Adhuc ergo insaniunt non pro capite, quod per gratiam Dei pii omnes summo studio conantur erigere, sed quod non permittuntur insanire et furere. Volunt enim pii soli capiti Christo auscultare.

XIII. Verbo Dei quum auscultant homines, pure et synceriter voluntatem Dei discunt. Deinde per Spiritum Dei in Deum trahuntur et veluti transformantur

XIV. Summo igitur studio hoc unum in primis curent omnes Christiani ut Evangelium Christi unice et synceriter ubique prædicetur.

XV. Qui credit Evangelio, salvus erit; qui non credit, condemnabitur. Nam in Evangelio omnis veritas clarescit.

XVI. In Evangelio discimus, hominum doctrinas et traditiones ad salutem nihil esse utiles:

XVII. Christus unicus æternus et summus est sacerdos. Qui ergo se pro summis sacerdotibus venditant, gloriæ et potentiæ Christi

---

[1] mittheilend.
[2] dem haubt einig lofen (i. e., listen, hear).
[3] Wo dem gelofet würt.
[4] anferen.
[5] That is, *Mind Pope* (what follows).

und Gewalt Christi widerstreben, ja, sie verwerfen.[1]

adversantur, et Christum rejiciunt.

Von der Messe.

XVIII. Daß Christus, der sich selbst Ein Mal aufgeopfert hat, in Ewigkeit ein immerwährendes und bezahlendes Opfer ist für aller Gläubigen Sünden. Daraus ermessen wird, daß die Messe nicht ein Opfer, sondern des Opfers Wiedergedächtniß sei, und Versicherung[2] der Erlösung, die Christus uns bewiesen hat.

XVIII. *Christus qui sese semel in cruce obtulit hostia est et victima satisfaciens in æternum pro peccatis omnium fidelium. Ex quo colligitur, missam non esse sacrificium, sed sacrificii in cruce semel oblati commemorationem et quasi sigillum redemptionis per Christum exhibitæ.[3]*

Fürbitte der Heiligen.

XIX. Daß Christus ein einiger Mittler ist zwischen Gott und uns.

XIX. *Christus unicus est Mediator inter Deum et nos.*

XX. Daß uns Gott alle Dinge will in seinem Namen geben. Daraus folgt,[4] daß wir außer dieser Zeit keines Mittlers bedürfen, als seiner.

XX. *Omnia nobis per Christum et in nomine Christi præstat Deus. Hinc sequitur, nobis extra hanc vitam intercessore præter Christum nullo opus esse.*

XXI. Daß, wenn wir für einander auf Erden bitten, wir das dergestalt thun, daß wir vertrauen, allein durch Christum werden uns alle Dinge gegeben.

XXI. *Quum mutuo pro nobis hic in terris oramus, in hoc[5] facere debemus, quod per solum Christum omnia nobis dari confidamus.*

Gute Werke.

XXII. Daß Christus unsere Gerechtigkeit ist; woraus wir ermessen, daß unsere Werke so viel gut sind, so viel sie Christi sind; so viel sie aber unser, nicht recht, nicht gut sind.

XXII. *Christus est nostra institia. Hinc consequitur, opera nostra eatenus esse bona, quatenus sunt Christi; quatenus vero nostra, non esse vere bona.*

Wie der Geistlichen Gut Christi sey.

XXIII. Daß Christus die Habe und Pracht dieser Welt verwirft; woraus wir ermessen, daß die, welche Reich-

XXIII. *Quod Christus substantiam hujus mundi et fastum contemnit, docet, quod hi, qui sub*

---

[1] verschupffen.   [2] Sicherung.   [3] *effectæ.*   [4] entspringt.   [5] *ita.*

thümer an sich ziehen in seinem Namen,
ihn gräßlich schmähen, wenn sie ihn
zu einem Deckmantel ihres Geizes und
Muthwillens machen.

Speise-Verbot.

XXIV. Daß ein jeder Christ zu
den Werken, die Gott nicht geboten hat,
unverbunden ist; er darf allezeit alle
Speisen essen. Daraus erlernt wird,
daß Käse= und Butterbriefe[1] ein rö=
mischer Betrug[2] sind.

Von Feiertag und Wallfahrt.

XXV. Daß Zeit und Ort den Chri=
stenmenschen unterworfen sind, und der
Mensch nicht ihnen. Daraus gelernt
wird, daß die, welche an Zeit und Ort
binden, die Christen ihrer Freiheit be=
rauben.

Kutten=Kleidung, Zeichen, etc.

XXVI. Daß Gott nichts mißfälli=
ger ist, als Gleißen. Daher erlernt
wird, daß Alles, so sich schön macht
vor den Menschen, eine schwere Gleiß=
nerei und Verruchtheit ist. Hier fallen
Kutten, Zeichen, Platten, etc.

Orden und Secten.

XXVII. Daß alle Christenmenschen
Brüder Christi und unter einander sind,
und Keinen auf Erden Vater nennen[4]
sollen. Da fallen hin Orden, Secten,
Rotten, etc.

*Christi titulo divitias ad se ra-
piunt, ipsum magna infamia affi-
ciunt, quum cupiditatis suæ et
luxus eum patronum faciunt.*

XXIV. *Christianorum nullus
ad ea opera, quæ Christus non
præcepit, adstringitur; quolibet
tempore, quolibet cibo vesci potest.
Consequitur ergo literas, quas pro
caseo et butyro dant pontificii, Ro-
manas esse imposturas.*

XXV. *Tempus et locus in po-
testate.sunt hominis, non homo in
illorum potestate. Qui ergo tempus et locum[3] alligant, Christiana
libertate pios fraudant et spo-
liant.*

XXVI. *Nihil magis displicet
Deo quam hypocrisis. Hinc discimus hypocrisim esse gravem, et
impudentem audaciam quidquid
sanctum se simulat coram hominibus. Hic cadunt cuculli, signa,
rasus vertex, etc.*

XXVII. *Omnes Christiani fratres sunt Christi, et fratres inter
sese, patrem ergo super terram[5]
vocare non debent. Hic cadunt
factiones et sectæ.*

---

[1] käss und ancken, brieff.
[2] Römische Geschwindigkeit.
[3] *tempore et loco.*
[4] uffblasen.
[5] *in terris.*

Der Geistlichen Ehe.

XXVIII. Daß Alles, was Gott erlaubt, oder nicht verboten hat, recht ist; daher erlernt wird, daß die Ehe allen Menschen geziemt.

Der unreine Geistliche nehme ein Weib.

XXIX. Daß Alle, die man Geistliche nennt, sündigen, wenn sie, nachdem sie inne geworden sind, daß ihnen Gott, Reinigkeit zu halten, versagt hat, sich nicht durch die Ehe sicher stellen.[1]

Gelübde der Reinigkeit.

XXX. Daß die, welche Reinigkeit verheißen, närrisch oder kindisch zu viel übernehmen. Daraus erlernt wird, daß, die solche Gelübde annehmen, freventlich an den frommen Menschen handeln.

Von dem Bann.

XXXI. Daß den Bann kein einzelner Mensch Jemand auflegen mag, sondern die Kirche, das ist die Gemeinschaft derer, unter denen der des Bannes Würdige wohnt, sammt deren Wächter, das ist der Pfarrherr.

XXXII. Daß man allein den bannen mag, der ein öffentliches Aergerniß giebt.[2]

Von unrechtfertigem Gut.

XXXIII. Daß ungerechtes Gut nicht Tempeln, Klöstern, Mönchen, Pfaffen, Nonnen, sondern den Dürftigen gegeben werden solle, wenn es

---

XXVIII. *Quidquid Deus non vetat et permittit, juste fit. Ex quo discimus matrimonium omnibus ex œquo convenire.*

XXIX. *Qui Ecclesiastici vulgo seu spirituales vocantur, peccant, dum, posteaquam senserint castitatem sibi a Deo negatam, non uxores ducunt aut nubunt.*

XXX. *Qui vovent castitatem, stulta præsumptione et puerili arrogantia tenentur. Qui ergo ab eis vota hujusmodi vel exquirunt vel oblata recipiunt, injuriam eis faciunt et tyrannidem in simplices exercent.*

XXXI. *Excommunicationem nemo privatus ferre potest, sed ecclesia in qua excommunicandus habitat una cum episcopo.*

XXXII. *Nemo potest nec debet excommunicari, quam is, qui sceleribus suis publice offendit.*

XXXIII. *Ablata injuste non templis, monasteriis, non monachis aut sacerdotibus, sed paupe ribus danda sunt, si iis quibus*

---

[1] verbüttent.   [2] offentlich verergeret.

dem rechten Besitzer nicht wieder zugewendet werden mag.

Von der Obrigkeit.

XXXIV. Die sogenannte geistliche Gewalt hat keinen Grund ihrer Pracht aus der Lehre Christi.

Weltliche Gewalt von Gott.

XXXV. Aber die weltliche hat Kraft und Befestigung aus der Lehre und That Christi.

XXXVI. Alles, wovon der sogenannte geistliche Stand vorgiebt, es gehöre ihm zu von Rechts wegen und zum Schutze des Rechts, gehört den weltlichen [Obrigkeiten] zu, wenn sie Christen sein wollen.

XXXVII. Ihnen sind auch alle Christen schuldig gehorsam zu sein, Niemand ausgenommen;

XXXVIII. Sofern sie nichts gebieten, das wider Gott ist.

XXXIX. Darum sollen alle ihre Gesetze dem göttlichen Willen gleichförmig sein, also, daß sie den Bedrückten beschirmen, ob er schon nicht klagte.

XL. Sie mögen allein mit Recht tödten, auch allein die, welche ein öffentliches Aergerniß geben, ohne Gott zu erzürnen, er heiße denn ein anderes.

XLI. Wenn sie recht mit Rath und Hülfe dienen denen, für die sie Rechen-

ablata sunt restitui commode non possunt.

XXXIV. *Potestas quam sibi Papa et Episcopi, cæterique quos spiritales vocant, arrogant, et fastus, quo turgent, ex sacris literis et doctrina Christi firmamentum non habet.*

XXXV. *Magistratus publicus firmatur verbo et facto Christi.*

XXXVI. *Jurisdictio aut juris administratio, quam sibi dicti spirituales arrogant, tota magistratus sæcularis est, si modo velit esse Christianus.*

XXXVII. *Magistratibus publicis omnes Christiani obedire debent nemine excepto.*

XXXVIII. *Modo contra Deum nihil præcipiant!*

XXXIX. *Leges magistratuum ad regulam divinæ voluntatis sunt conformandæ, ut oppressus et vim passos defendant et ab injuria asserant, etiam si nemo queratur.*

XL. *Magistratus jure duntaxat occidere possunt, atque eos tantum qui publice offendunt, idque inoffenso Deo, nisi Deus aliud præcipiat.*

XLI. *Quum illis, pro quibus rationem reddere coguntur, con-*

schaft geben werden vor Gott, so sind auch diese schuldig, ihnen leibliche Handreichung zu thun.

XLII. Wenn sie aber untreu und nicht nach[1] der Richtschnur Christi verfahren würden, mögen sie mit Gott entsetzt werden.[2]

XLIII. Summa: Dessen Reich ist das allerbeste und festeste, der allein mit Gott herrschet, und dessen das allerböseste und unsicherste, der nach seinem Gemüthe herrschet.

Vom Gebet.

XLIV. Wahre Anbeter rufen Gott im Geist und in der Wahrheit an, ohne alles Geschrei vor den Menschen.

XLV. Gleißner thun ihre Werke, daß sie von den Menschen gesehen werden, nehmen auch den Lohn in dieser Zeit ein.

XLVI. So muß ja folgen, daß Tempelgesang oder Geschrei, ohne Andacht und nur um Lohn, entweder Ruhm sucht von den Menschen oder Gewinn.

Von Aergerniß.

XLVII. Leiblichen Tod soll der Mensch eher leiden, als daß er einen Christenmenschen ärgerte oder in Schande brächte.

XLVIII. Wer aus Blödigkeit oder Unwissenheit sich will ohne Ursache ärgern, den soll man nicht frank oder

silia et auxilia legitime administrant, debent et illi ipsi magistratibus subsidia corporalia.

XLII. *Quando vero perfide et extra regulam Christi egerint, possunt cum Deo deponi.*

XLIII. *Hujus regnum optimum est et firmissimum qui ex Deo et cum Deo regnat; hujus vero pessimum et infirmissimum qui sua libidine.*

XLIV. *Veri adoratores invocant Deum in spiritu et veritate, corde orantes, non clamore coram hominibus.*

XLV. *Hypocritæ omnia opera sua faciunt ut videantur ab hominibus; propterea mercedem suam hic recipiunt.*

XLVI. *Cantiones ergo, seu verius boatus, qui in templis sine devotione pro mercede fiunt, aut laudem aut quæstum ab hominibus quærunt.*

XLVII. *Potius mortem eligere debet homo, quam Christianum offendere aut pudefacere.*

XLVIII. *Qui ex infirmitate aut ignorantia absque causa vult offendi, non patiamur ut is infir-*

---

[1] usser (ausser).

[2] This article asserts the right of revolution.

Rein laffen bleiben, fondern ihn ftarf machen, daß er nicht für Sünde hält, was nicht Sünde ift.

XLIX. Größeres Aergerniß weiß ich nicht, als daß man den Pfaffen, Eheweiber zu haben, nicht nachläßt, aber Huren zu haben, um Geldes willen vergönnt. Pfui der Schande![1]

Vom Nachlaffen der Sünde.

L. Gott läßt allein die Sünden nach, durch Chriftum Jefum, seinen Sohn, unfern Herrn allein.

LI. Wer folches der Creatur beilegt,[2] entzieht Gott feine Ehre und giebt fie dem, der nicht Gott ift; das ift eine wahre Abgötterei.

LII. Darum die Beichte, die dem Priefter oder dem Nächften gefchieht, nicht für ein Nachlaffen der Sünde, fondern für ein um Rathfragen[3] aus=gegeben werden foll.

LIII. Aufgelegte Bußwerfe fommen von menfchlichen Rathfchlägen (aus=genommen der Bann), nehmen die Sünde nicht hinweg, werden aufge=legt Andern zu einem Schrecken.

Das Leiden Chrifti büßt die Sünde.

LIV. Chriftus hat alle unfre Schmerzen und Arbeit getragen. Wer nun den Bußwerfen beilegt, was al=lein Chrifti ift, der irrt und fchmähet Gott.

mus et ignorans maneat; sed demus operam ut rite edoctus firmus tandem evadat, nec peccatum ducat quod peccatum non est.

XLIX. Maius et gravius scandalum non puto, quam quod sacerdotibus matrimonio legitimo interdicitur; concubinas et scorta habere accepta ab eis pecunia permittitur.

L. Solus Deus peccata remittit, idque per solum Christum Jesum Dominum nostrum.

LI. Qui remissionem peccatorum creaturæ tribuit, Deum gloria sua spoliat et idololatra est.

LII. Confessio ergo, quæ sacerdoti aut proximo fit, non pro remissione peccatorum, sed pro consultatione haberi debet.

LIII. Opera satisfactionis a sacerdote imposita humanæ sunt traditionis (excepta excommunicatione); peccatum non tollunt, sed aliis in terrorem imponuntur.

LIV. Christus dolores nostros et omnes labores nostros tulit; qui vero operibus pœnitentialibus tribuit, quod Christi solius est, errat et Deum blasphemat.

---

[1] Pfuch der schand! [2] zugibt. [3] rathferschung.

Vorbehalten der Sünde.

LV. Wer einerlei Sünde dem reui=
gen Menschen nachzulaffen sich wei=
gerte, wäre nicht an Gottes, noch
Petri, sondern an des Teufels Statt.

LVI. Wer etliche Sünden allein
um Geldes willen nachläßt, ist Si=
mon's und Bileam's Gesell und des
Teufels eigentlicher Bote.

Vom Fegfeuer.

LVII. Die wahre heilige Schrift
weiß von keinem Fegfeuer nach dieser
Zeit.

LVIII. Das Urtheil über die Ab=
geschiedenen ist allein Gott bekannt.

LIX. Und je weniger uns Gott hat
davon wissen lassen, desto weniger sollen
wir davon zu wissen versuchen.

LX. Wenn der Mensch, für die Ver=
storbenen besorgt, Gott anruft, ihnen
Gnade zu beweisen, das verwerfe ich
nicht; doch davon die Zeit bestimmen
(sieben Jahre um eine Todsünde), und
um Gewinnes willen lügen, ist nicht
menschlich, sondern teuflisch.

Von der Priesterschaft und ihrer Weihe.

LXI. Von dem Character (der
Weihe), den die Priester in der letzten
Zeit ersonnen haben,[1] weiß die göttliche
Schrift nichts.

LXII. Sie erkennt auch keine
Priester, als die das Gotteswort ver=
kündigen.

LXIII. Denen heißt sie Ehre er=

LV. *Qui vel unicum peccatum
pœnitenti remittere negat, is non
Dei nec Petri, sed Diaboli vicem
tenet.*

LVI. *Qui quædam tantum peccata idque pro mercede aut pecunia remittunt, Simonis et Balaami
socii sunt, et veri Satanœ legati.*

LVII. *Scriptura sacra purgatorium post hanc vitam nullum
novit.*

LVIII. *Defunctorum judicium
soli Deo cognitum est.*

LIX. *Quo minus de hisce rebus
nobis revelat Deus, hoc minus nobis pervestigandœ sunt.*

LX. *Si quis, pro mortuis sol-
licitus, apud Deum gratiam eis
implorat aut precatur, non damno; sed tempus de hoc definire
(septennium pro peccato mortali),
et propter quœstum mentiri, non
humanum est, sed diabolicum.*

LXI. *De charactere, quem postremis hisce temporibus excogita-
runt sacrifici, nihil novit divina
Scriptura.*

LXII. *Scriptura alios presbyteros aut sacerdotes non novit quam
eos qui verbum Dei annunciant.*

LXIII. *Illis vero presbyteris, de*

---

[1] seind ynnen worden.

bieten, d. i. leibliche Nahrung dar=
reichen.

Von Abstellung der Mißbräuche.

LXIV. Alle, die ihren Irrthum
erkennen, soll man nichts lassen ent=
gelten, sondern sie in Frieden sterben
lassen, und hernach das der Kirche
gewidmete Gut christlich verwalten.

LXV. Die sich [ihren Irrthum]
nicht erkennen wollen, mit denen wird
Gott wohl handeln; darum man ihren
Leibern keine Gewalt anthun soll, es
wäre denn, daß sie so ungebührlich
verführen, daß man das nicht unter=
lassen könnte.

LXVI. Es sollen alle geistlichen
Vorgesetzten sich sogleich herablassen,
und einzig das Kreuz Christi, nicht
die Kisten aufrichten, oder sie gehen
unter; die Art steht am Baum.

LXVII. Wenn Jemand begehrte,
ein Gespräch mit mir zu haben von
Zinsen, Zehenten, ungetauften Kin=
dern, von der Firmelung, entbiete ich
mich willig, zu antworten.

quibus diximus, qui Verbum Dei
prædicant, Scriptura divina jubet,
ut necessaria ministrentur.

LXIV. *Qui errorem agnoscunt,
illis nihil damni inferendum, fe-
rantur autem donec in pace dece-
dant, deinde sacerdotiorum bona
juxta Christianam caritatem ordinentur.*

LXV. *Qui errorem non agnoscunt nec ponunt, Deo sunt relin-
quendi, nec vis corporibus illorum inferenda nisi tam enormi-
ter ac tumultuose se gerant, ut
parcere illis magistratui salva
publica tranquillitate non liceat.*

LXVI. *Humilient se illico quicunque in Ecclesia sunt præfecti,
crucemque Christi (non cistam)
erigant; aut perditio eorum
adest, nam securis radici arboris
est admota.*

LXVII. *Si cui libet disserere
mecum de decimis, reditibus, de
infantibus non baptizatis, de con-
firmatione, non detrectabo collo-
quium.*

Hier unternehme Keiner zu streiten mit Sophisterei oder Menschentand,
sondern komme, die Schrift zum Richter zu haben (die Schrift athmet den
Geist Gottes), damit man die Wahrheit entweder finde, oder, wenn sie
gefunden ist, wie ich hoffe, behalte.

Amen. Das walte Gott!

THESES BERNENSES. A.D. 1528.

The Ten Conclusions of Berne.

These Ten Conclusions were carefully prepared by Berthold Haller and Francis Kolb, Reformed ministers at Berne, and, at their request, revised and published by Zwingli (in German, Latin, and French) for a large religious Conference held in the capital of Switzerland, Jan. 7-26, 1528. They were approved by all the leading Swiss Reformers, and also by Ambrosius Blaarer of Constance, Bucer and Capito of Strasburg, and others, who attended the Conference. The result of the Conference was the complete triumph of the Reformation in Berne. They are a model of brevity. Niemeyer gives the German original in the Swiss dialect from the Zurich edition of 1528. An English version is given in Vol. I. p. 365.

Ueber diese nachfolgenden Schlußreden wollen wir, Franciscus Kolb und Berchtoldus Haller, beide Prediger zu Bern, sammt andern, die das Evangelium bekennen, einem Jeden mit Gott Antwort und Bericht geben, aus heiliger biblischer Schrift, Neuen und Alten Testaments, auf angesetzten Tag zu Bern, Sonntag nach dem Feste der Beschneidung Christi, im Jahre 1528.

De sequentibus Conclusionibus nos Franciscus Kolb *et* Berchtoldus Haller, *ambo pastores Ecclesiæ Bernensis, simul cum aliis orthodoxiæ professoribus unicuique rationem reddemus, ex scriptis biblicis, Veteris nimirum et N. Testamenti libris, die designato, nimirum primo post dominicam primam circumcisionis, anno* MDXXVIII.

I. Die heilige christliche Kirche,[1] deren einiges Haupt Christus, ist aus dem Worte Gottes geboren; in demselben bleibt sie, und hört nicht die Stimme eines Fremden.

II. Die Kirche Christi macht nicht Gesetze und Gebote ohne Gottes Wort; deßhalb alle Menschensatzungen, die man Kirchengebote nennt, uns nicht weiter binden, als sie in Gottes Wort gegründet und geboten sind.

III. Christus ist unsre einige Weisheit, Gerechtigkeit, Erlösung und Bezahlung für aller Welt Sünde; deßhalb ein anderes Verdienst der Seligkeit und Genugthuung für die Sünde bekennen, ist Christum verleugnen.

I. *Sancta Christiana Ecclesia, cujus unicum caput est Christus, nata est ex Dei Verbo, in eoque permanet, nec vocem audit alieni.*

II. *Ecclesia Christi non condit leges et mandata extra Dei Verbum; ea propter omnes traditiones humanæ, quas Ecclesiasticas vocant, non ulterius nos obligant, quam quatenus in Dei Verbo sunt fundatæ et præceptæ.*

III. *Christus est unica sapientia, justitia, redemptio et satisfactio pro peccatis totius mundi; idcirco aliud salutis et satisfactionis meritum pro peccato confiteri, est Christum abnegare.*

---

[1] Kilch.

IV. Daß der Leib und das Blut Christi wesentlich und leiblich in dem Brote der Danksagung empfangen wird, kann mit biblischer Schrift nicht bewiesen werden.

V. Die Messe, wie sie jetzt im Gebrauche ist, darin man Christum Gott dem Vater für die Sünden der Lebenden Todten aufopfere, ist der Schrift zuwider, dem allerheiligsten Opfer, Leiden und Sterben Christi eine Lästerung, und um der Mißbräuche willen ein Gräuel vor Gott.

VI. Wie Christus allein für uns gestorben ist, so soll er, als alleiniger Mittler und Fürsprecher zwischen Gott dem Vater und uns Gläubigen, angerufen werden. Deßhalb ist das Anrufen aller andern Mittler und Fürsprecher außerhalb dieser Zeit ohne Grund der Schrift vorgeschrieben.

VII. Nach dieser Zeit wird kein Fegefeuer in der Schrift gefunden. Deßhalb sind alle Todtendienste, als Vigilien, Seelenmessen, Septimen, Trigesimen,[1] Jahrzeiten,[2] Lampen,[3] Kerzen und dergleichen vergeblich.

VIII. Bilder machen zur Verehrung ist wider Gottes Wort des Neuen und Alten Testaments. Deßhalb sind sie abzuthun, wo sie mit Gefahr der Verehrung aufgestellt sind.

IV. *Quod corpus et sanguis Christi essentialiter et corporaliter in pane Eucharistiæ percipiatur, ex Scriptura Sacra non potest demonstrari.*

V. *Missa, ut hodie in usu est, in qua Christus Deo Patri offertur pro peccatis vivorum et mortuorum, Scripturæ est contraria, in sanctissimum sacrificium, passionem et mortem Christi blasphema et propter abusus coram Deo abominabilis.*

VI. *Quemadmodum Christus solus pro nobis mortuus est, ita etiam solus ut mediator et advocatus inter Deum Patrem et nos fideles adorandus est. Idcirco alios mediatores extra hanc vitam existentes ad adorandum proponere cum fundamento Verbi Dei pugnat.*

VII. *Esse locum post hanc vitam, in quo purgentur animæ, in Scriptura non reperitur; proin omnia officia pro mortuis instituta, ut vigiliæ, missæ pro defunctis, exequiæ, septimæ, trigesimæ, anniversariæ, lampades, cerei et id genus alia frustanea sunt.*

VIII. *Imagines fabricare cultus gratia, Dei Verbo, Veteris et Novi Testamenti libris comprehenso repugnat. Idcirco si sub periculo adorationis proponantur, abolendæ.*

---

[1] Tryßgost.　　　[2] Jarzyt.　　　[3] Amplen.

IX. Die heilige Ehe ist in der Schrift keinem Stande verboten, sondern, Hurerei und Unkeuschheit zu vermeiden, allen Ständen geboten.

IX. *Matrimonium nulli ordini hominum in Scriptura interdictum est, sed scortationis et impuritatis vitandœ causa omnium ordinum hominibus præceptum et permissum.*

X. Da ein öffentlicher Hurer nach der Schrift im wahren Banne ist, so folgt, daß Unkeuschheit und Hurerei des Aergernisses wegen keinem Stande schädlicher ist, als dem Priesterstande.

X. *Quia manifestus scortator juxta Scripturam excommunicandus; sequitur, scortationem aut impurun cœlibatum propter scandalum nulli ordini hominum magis quam sacerdotali damnosum esse.*

Alles Gott und seinem heiligen Worte zur Ehre'

CONFESSIO HELVETICA PRIOR (SIVE BASILEENSIS POSTERIOR).

THE FIRST HELVETIC CONFESSION. A.D. 1536.

[This Confession was composed by a number of Swiss divines (Bullinger, Grynæus, Myconius, and others), delegated and assembled for the purpose, in the city of Basle, A.D. 1536. It is the first Confession which represented the faith of all the Reformed cantons of Switzerland; the preceding ones had merely a local authority. It is called the FIRST HELVETIC CONFESSION to distinguish it from the SECOND HELVETIC CONFESSION (1566), which acquired still greater authority. It is also less aptly called the SECOND CONFESSION OF BASLE (CONF. BASILEENSIS POSTERIOR), from the place of its composition and publication, in distinction from the FIRST CONFESSION OF BASLE, or of MÜHLHAUSEN (1534), which continued in force in these two cities. See the *History*, Vol. I. §§ 53 and 54. The Latin text was published first under the title: *Ecclesiarum per Helvetiam Confessio Fidei summaria et generalis*. It is reproduced in the *Corpus et Syntagma*, and in Niemeyer's *Collectio* (pp. 115–122). The German text in the Swiss dialect was prepared by Leo Judæ, and is of equal authority with the Latin, although it is a free and enlarged translation. I give it in High-German, which is more intelligible. It appeared with the following title and introductory note:

'Ein gemeine bekantnus der helgen waren vnd vralten Chrijtlichen gloubens vnd vnsern mittburgern vnd Chrijtlichen gloubgnoffen, etc. Zurich. Bern. Bajell. Straßburg. Cojtenz. Santgalln. Schaffhujn. Müllhujn. Biel. etc. zbafell vffgericht georbnet vnd gmacht vff wytern bjcheib, etc. Jm 1536. 1. 2. 3. et 4. Februariy.

'Ein kurtze vnd gemeine bekantnuß des gloubens der kelchen ſo in einer Eidtgnoſchafft das Evangelium Chrijti angenomen habenb, allen glöbigen vnd fromen zu erwegen, zu beſchatzn vnd zu vrteilen bargejtelt. 1 Pet. iii.; 1 Joh. iv.']

I. Von der heiligen Schrift.

Die heilige, göttliche, biblijche Schrift, die da ist das Wort Gottes, von dem heiligen Geijte eingegeben, und durch die Propheten und Apojtel der Welt vorgetragen, ist die allerältejte, vollkommenjte und höchjte Lehre, und begreift allein alles das, was zur wahren Erkenntniß, Liebe und Ehre Gottes, zu rechter, wahrer Frömmigkeit und Anrichtung eines frommen, ehrbaren und gottjeligen Lebens dienet.[1]

II. Von Auslegung der Schrift.

Dieje heilige, göttliche Schrift ſoll nicht anders, als aus ihr ſelbjt aus=

I. DE SCRIPTURA SACRA.

Scriptura canonica Verbum Dei, Spiritu Sancto tradita, et per prophetas apostolosque mundo proposita, omnium perfectissima et antiquissima Philosophia, pietatem omnem, omnem vitæ rationem sola perfecte continet.[1]

II. DE INTERPRETATIONE SCRIPTURÆ.

Hujus interpretatio ex ipsa sola petenda est, ut ipsa inter-

---

[1] 2 Pet. i.; 2 Tim. iii.

gelegt und erklärt werden durch die Richt=
schnur des Glaubens und der Liebe.[1]

pres sit sui, caritatis fideique
regula moderante.[1]

III. Von den alten Lehrern.

Wo nun die heiligen Väter und alten
Lehrer, welche die Schrift erklärt und
ausgelegt haben, von dieser Richtschnur
nicht abgewichen sind,[2] wollen wir sie
nicht allein für Ausleger der Schrift,
sondern für auserwählte Werkzeuge,
durch die Gott geredet und gewirkt hat,
erkennen und halten.

III. De Antiquis Patribus.

A quo interpretationis genere,
quatenus sancti patres non di-
scessere, eos non solum ut inter-
pretes Scripturæ recipimus, sed
ut organa Dei electa venera-
mur.

IV. Von Menschenlehren.

Was sonst menschliche Lehren und
Satzungen sind, sie seien so schön,
hübsch, angesehen und lange gebraucht,
als sie nur wollen, die uns von Gott
und dem wahren Glauben abführen,
halten wir für eitel und kraftlos,
wie es der heilige Matth. 15 selbst
bezeugt, da er spricht: Sie ehren mich
vergebens, wenn sie lehren die Lehren
der Menschen.[3]

IV. De Traditionibus Hominum.

Per cœtera de traditionibus
hominum quantumvis speciosis
et receptis, quæcumque nos ab-
ducunt, sic illud Domini re-
spondemus, Frustra me colunt docentes doctrinas hominum.[3]

V. Was der Zweck der heiligen Schrift sei, und worauf sie zuletzt hinweise.

Die ganze biblische Schrift sieht al=
lein darauf, daß der Mensch verstehe,
daß ihm Gott günstig sei und wohl=
wolle, und daß er diese seine Gutwillig=
keit durch Christum, seinen Sohn, dem

V. Scopus Scripturæ.

Status hujus Scripturæ cano-
nicæ totius is est, bene Deum
hominum generi velle, et eam
benevolentiam per Christum Fi-
lium suum declarasse. Quæ fide

---

[1] Joh. v.; Rom. xii.; 1 Cor. xiii.   *Sic Christus facit* Matt. iv.
[2] über dise richtschur nit gehowen habend.
[3] Esa. xxix.; Matt. xv.; Marc vii.; 1 Tim. iv.; Tit. i.

ganzen menſchlichen Geſchlecht öffent=
lich dargeſtellt und bewieſen habe, die
aber allein durch den Glauben zu uns
komme, allein durch den Glauben emp=
fangen, und durch die Liebe gegen den
Nächſten gezeigt und bewieſen werde.[1]

VI. Von Gott.

Von Gott halten wir alſo, daß ein eini=
ger, wahrer, lebendiger und allmächtiger
Gott ſei, einig im Weſen, dreifaltig in
der Perſon, der alle Dinge durch ſein
Wort, das iſt, durch ſeinen Sohn, aus
nichts geſchaffen habe, und alle Dinge
durch ſeine Vorſehung recht, wahrhaft
und weiſe regiere, verwalte und erhalte.[2]

VII. Von dem Menſchen.

Der Menſch, das vollkommenſte
Bild Gottes auf Erden, unter allen
ſichtbaren Geſchöpfen das edelſte und
vornehmſte, iſt aus Leib und Seele
zuſammengeſetzt; der Leib iſt ſterblich,
die Seele unſterblich. Dieſer Menſch,
der von Gott recht und wohl geſchaffen
war, iſt durch ſeine eigne Schuld in
die Sünde gefallen, und hat das ganze
menſchliche Geſchlecht mit ſich in dieſen
Fall gezogen, und ſolchem Elend unter=
würfig gemacht.[3]

VIII. Von der Erbſünde.

Dieſe Erbſünde[4] und urſprüngliche

---

*sola ad nos perveniat recipia-
turque, caritate vero erga prox-
imos exprimatur.*[1]

VI. Deus.

De Deo sic sentimus, unum
substantia : trinum *personis, omnipotentem esse. Qui ut condiderit per verbum, id est, Filium
suum, omnia ex nihilo, sic providentia sua juste vereque et
sapientissime gubernet : servet :
foveat omnia.*

VII. Homo et Vires ejus.

*Homo perfectissima Dei in
terris imago, primasque creaturarum visibilium habens, ex anima et corpore constans, quorum
hoc mortale, illud immortale est,
quum esset sancte a Deo conditus, sua culpa in vitium prolap-
sus, in eandem secum ruinam
genus humanum totum traxit, ac
eidem calamitati obnoxium reddidit.*[3]

VIII. Originale Peccatum.

Atque hæc lues, quam origina-

Gen. iii. ; Joh. iii. ; Rom. viii. ; Eph. ii. ; 1 Joh. iv.
Deut. vi. ; Matt. xxviii. ; Gen. i. : Act. xvii.

[3] Gen. i.-iii. ; Rom. v.
[4] eerbſucht (Erbſeuche).

Sünde hat das ganze menschliche Geschlecht so durchdrungen, und hat es so verwüstet und vergiftet, daß dem Menschen, der ein Kind des Zornes und ein Feind Gottes geworden war, Niemand als Gott durch Christum helfen oder ihn wiederherstellen konnte, und was in ihm Gutes übrig geblieben ist, das wird durch tägliche Mängel und Gebrechen [prästen] für und für geschwächt, so daß es noch ärger wird; denn die Kraft der Sünde und des Gebrechens [prästen] in uns ist so mächtig, daß weder die Vernunft dem, was sie erkannt, nachkommen, noch der Verstand das göttliche Fünklein pflanzen und weiterbringen kann.[1]

lem *vocant, genus totum humanum sic pervasit, ut nulla ope iræ filius, inimicusque Dei nisi divina per Christum curari potuerit. Nam si quid frugis hic bonæ superstes est, vitiis nostris assidue debilitatum, in pejus vergit. Superat enim mali vis, et nec rationem persequi, nec mentis divinitatem excolere sinit.*[1]

IX. Von der freien Willkür, die man den freien Willen nennt.

Deßhalb schreiben wir dem Menschen eine freie Willkür also zu, weil wir an uns selbst befinden, daß wir mit Wissen und Willen Gutes und Böses thun. Das Böse können wir von uns selbst thun, das Gute aber können wir weder annehmen, noch vollbringen, wir seien denn durch die Gnade Christi erleuchtet, erwecket und getrieben; denn Gott ist der, der in uns das Wollen und Vollbringen wirkt, nach seinem guten Willen; aus Gott ist unser Heil, aus uns aber ist nichts, als Sünde und Verdammniß.[2]

IX. LIBERUM ARBITRIUM.

Unde sic homini liberum arbitrium tribuimus, ut qui scientes et volentes agere nos bona et mala experimur, mala quidem agere sponte nostra queamus, bona vero amplecti et persequi, nisi gratia Christi illustrati, Spiritu ejus impulsi, non queamus. Deus enim is est, qui operatur in nobis et velle et perficere pro bona sua voluntate. Et ex Deo salus, e nobis perditio est.[2]

---

[1] Eph. ii.; Psa. l.; Rom. viii.   [2] Phil. ii.; Hos. xiii.

X. Wie Gott den Menschen durch seinen ewigen Rathschluß wiedergebracht habe.

Wiewohl nun der Mensch durch diese seine Schuld und Uebertretung zur ewigen Verdammniß verurtheilt und in den gerechten Zorn Gottes gefallen ist, so hat doch Gott, der gnädige Vater, nie aufgehört, Sorge für ihn zu tragen, welches wir aus der ersten Verheißung und aus dem ganzen Gesetz (durch welches die Sünde erweckt, nicht erlöscht wird), und aus dem Herrn Christo, der dazu verordnet und gegeben ist, klar und offenbar genug merken und verstehen können.[1]

XI. Von dem Herrn Christo, und was wir durch ihn haben.

Dieser Herr Christus, ein wahrer Sohn Gottes, wahrer Gott und Mensch, hat in der Zeit, die Gott von Ewigkeit dazu bestimmt hat, die wahre menschliche Natur, mit Leib und Seele angenommen, hat zwei unterschiedene, unvermischte Naturen in einer einigen unzertrennlichen Person, welche Annehmung menschlicher Natur darum geschehen ist, daß er uns, die todt waren, wieder lebendig und zu Miterben Gottes machte, weßhalb er auch unser Bruder geworden ist.[2]

Dieser Herr Christus, der Sohn des wahren, lebendigen Gottes, hat

X. CONSILIUM DEI ÆTERNUM DI REPARATIONE HOMINIS.

Hujus igitur hominis hac culpa damnationi addicti, et in indignationem justam incurrentis, nunquam tamen curam gerere Deus Pater desiit. Id quod ex primis promissionibus, legeque tota (quæ peccatum excitat, non extinguit) et a Christo in hoc destinato præstitoque perspicuum est.[1]

XI. JESUS CHRISTUS ET QUÆ PER CHRISTUM.

Hic Christus verus Dei Filius, verusque Deus, et homo verus, quum juxta præfinitum tempus hominem totum, id est, anima et corpore constantem assumpsisset, in una individuaque persona duas, sed impermixtas naturas obtinens, ut vitæ mortuos nos restitueret, et Dei cohæredes faceret, frater noster factus est.[2]

Is sacrosanctam divinitatis unione carnem, nostræ (peccato

---

[1] Eph. i. · Gen. iii.; Rom. vii.

[2] Joh. i.; Gal. iv.; Joh. xvi.; Heb. ii.

das Fleisch, das durch die Vereinba=
rung mit der Gottheit heilig ist, unserm
Fleisch in allen Dingen gleich, ausge=
nommen die Sünde, weil es ein reines,
unbeflecktes Opfer sein sollte, aus der
unbefleckten Jungfrau Maria durch
Mitwirkung Gottes des heiligen Geistes
angenommen, für uns in den Tod
gegeben, zu einer Bezahlung, Begnadi=
gung und Abwaschung aller Sünden.[1]

Und damit wir eine vollkommne
Hoffnung und Vertrauen unsers un=
sterblichen Lebens haben möchten, hat
er sein Fleisch, das vom Tode zum
Leben wieder auferweckt, zur Rechten
seines allmächtigen Vaters gesetzt.[2]

Dieser Herr Christus, der den Tod,
die Sünde und alle höllische Gewalt
überwunden und besiegt hat, ist unser
Vorgänger, unser Führer und unser
Haupt; er ist der rechte Hohepriester,
der da sitzt zur Rechten Gottes, und
unsre Sache überall beschirmt und
führt, bis er uns zu dem Bilde, zu
dem wir geschaffen sind, reformire und
zurückbringe, und in die Gemeinschaft
seines göttlichen Wesens einführe.[3]

Auf diesen Herrn Jesum Christum
warten wir, daß er kommen werde am
Ende der Welt, als ein wahrer, gerechter
Richter, der das wahre Urtheil über
alles Fleisch, von ihm zum Urtheil
auferweckt, fällen wird; die Frommen
und Gläubigen wird er in den Himmel

*solum excepto, quoniam illibatam
esse hostiam oportebat) per omnia similem, ex intacta Virgine
Maria, Spiritu Sancto cooperante, sumens, in mortem ad universi peccati expiationem tradidit.*[1]

*Idem ut esset plena nobis per-
fectaque immortalitatis nostræ
spes et fiducia, suam ipse carnem,
de morte suscitatam, in cœlum ad
omnipotentis Patris dexteram collocavit.*[2]

*Hic morte, peccato, inferis-
que omnibus triumphatis, victor
duxque, et caput nostrum, ac
pontifex vere summus [ad dexteram Patris], sedens, causam
nostram perpetuo tuetur agitque,
dum ad imaginem ad quam conditi eramus, reformet.*[3]

*Hunc venturum ad sæculorum
omnium finem, verum rectum-
que judicem, ac sententiam in
omnem carnem, ad id judicium
prius suscitatam, laturum, ac
pios supra ethera evecturum, impios corpore et anima ad æter-*

---

[1] Heb. v.; Luc. ii.; 1 Joh. ii.   [2] 1 Cor. xv.; Act. i.   [3] Eph. i.; Rom. viii.; Eph. iv.

führen, und die Ungläubigen wird er mit Leib und Seele in die ewige Verdammniß stoßen und verdammen.[1]

Dieser Herr Jesus, wie er allein unser Mittler, Fürsprecher, Opfer, Hoher Priester, Herr und König ist, also erkennen wir ihn allein, und glauben von ganzem Herzen, daß er allein unsre Versöhnung, unsre Erlösung, Heiligung, Bezahlung, Weisheit, Schirm und Rettung sei. Hier verwerfen wir alles das, was sich als Mittel, Opfer und Versöhnung unsers Lebens und Heils darstellt, und erkennen keines, als allein den Herrn Christum.[2]

num exitium damnaturum, expectamus.[1]

Qui ut solus est mediator, intercessor, hostia, idemque et pontifex, dominusque, et rex noster, ita hunc solum agnoscimus ac toto corde credimus conciliationem, redemptionem, sanctificationem, expiationem, sapientiam, protectionem, assertionem nostram solum: omne hîc simpliciter vitæ salutisque nostræ medium, præter hunc solum Christum, rejicientes.[2]

XII. Was der Zweck der evangelischen Lehre sei.

Deßhalb soll in aller evangelischen Lehre das das höchste und vornehmste Hauptstück sein, das in allen Predigten nachdrücklich getrieben und in die Herzen der Menschen eingedrückt werden soll, nämlich, daß wir allein durch die einige Barmherzigkeit Gottes und durch das Verdienst Christi erhalten und selig werden. Damit aber die Menschen verstehen, wie nothwendig ihnen Christus zum Heil und zur Seligkeit sei, soll man ihnen die Größe und Schwere der Sünde durch das Gesetz und den Tod Christi auf's Hellste und Klarste anzeigen, vorbilden und vor Augen stellen.[3]

XII. Scopus Evangelicæ Doctrinæ.

Itaque in omni doctrina evangelica primum ac præcipuum hoc ingeri debet, sola nos Dei misericordia et Christi merito servari. Quo ut intelligant homines quam opus habeant, peccata eis per legem et mortem Christi luculentissime semper sunt indicanda.[3]

---

[1] Dan. vii.; Joh. v.   [2] 1 Tim. ii.; Heb. vii.; Rom. iii.; 1 Cor. i.   [3] 1 Tim. i.; Rom. v

XIII. Wie uns die Gnade Chri=
sti und sein Verdienst mitge=
theilt werden, und welche
Frucht daraus folge.

Solche hohe und große Wohlthaten
göttlicher Gnade und die wahre Heili=
gung des Geistes Gottes erlangen wir
nicht durch unsre Verdienste oder Kräfte,
sondern durch den Glauben, der eine
lautere Gabe und Geschenk Gottes ist.[1]

[XIV.] Was der Glaube sei.[2]

Derselbe Glaube ist ein gewisser,
fester, ja unbezweifelter Grund und
eine Ergreifung aller der Dinge, die
man von Gott hofft, welcher daraus die
Liebe und demnach allerlei Tugenden
und guter Werke Frucht wachsen macht.
Und wiewohl die Frommen und Gläu=
bigen sich in solchen Früchten des Glau=
bens ohne Unterlaß üben, so schreiben
wir doch die Frommmachung und das
erlangte Heil nicht solchen Werken,
sondern nur der Gnade Gottes zu.

Dieser Glaube, der sich nicht seiner
Werke, wiewohl er unzählbare gute
Werke wirkt, sondern der Barmherzig=
keit Gottes tröstet, ist der rechte, wahre
Dienst, mit dem man Gott gefällt.[3]

XIV. [XV.] Von der Kirche.

Wir halten dafür, daß aus den le=

XIII. Christianus et Officia
ejus.

*Ista vero tum divina beneficia,
ac veram Spiritus Dei sanctificationem, fide mero Dei dono,
haud ullis aut viribus aut meritis nostris consequimur.*[1]

XIV. De Fide.[2]

*Quæ fides certa et indubita
omnium sperandarum de Dei be-
nevolentia rerum substantia est et
apprehensio. Ex sese caritatem
ac mox præclaros virtutum omnium fructus pullulat. Non quidquam tamen his officiis, licet piorum, sed ipsi simpliciter justificationem et partam salutem gratiæ
Dei tribuimus.*

*Atque sic quidem solus verus
Dei cultus est, fides inquam nulla
operum fiducia, operum fæcun-
dissima.*[3]

XV. Ecclesia.

Et ex talibus lapidibus super

---

[1] Rom. iii.; Gal. ii.; Eph. ii.
[2] From this Article the numbering differs; the German has twenty-seven, the Latin twenty-eight Articles. See Niemeyer, p. 109. But in the *Corpus et Syntagma Conf.* the Latin has likewise only twenty-seven Articles.
[3] Heb. xi.; Gal. v.

bendigen Steinen, die auf diesen lebendigen Felsen gebauet sind, eine heilige,
allgemeine Kirche, die Gemeinschaft
und Versammlung aller Heiligen, die
Christi Braut und Gemahl ist, welche
er durch sein Blut reinige, und endlich
dem Vater ohne Tadel ganz unbe-
fleckt darstelle, gebaut und versammelt
werde.

Und wiewohl diese Kirche und Versammlung Christi allein den Augen
Gottes offen und bekannt ist, so wird
sie doch durch äußere Zeichen, Gebräuche
und Ordnungen, die von Christo selbst
eingesetzt und geordnet sind, und durch
das Wort Gottes, als durch eine allgemeine, öffentliche und ordentliche Zucht,
nicht allein gesehen und erkannt, sondern
auch also gesammelt und gebaut, daß
zu dieser Kirche Niemand (ordentlich
zu reden und ohne besondre von Gott
geoffenbarte Freiheit) ohne diese Dinge
gezählt wird.[1]

vivam hanc petram, hoc pacto,
inedificatis, ecclesiam construi,
sanctamque sanctorum omnium
collectionem et immaculatam
Christi sponsam esse tenemus,
quam Christus sanguine suo lavet et purificet, et tandem Patri
suo eam sine macula et ruga
statuat et tradat.

Quæ quidem quum solius sit
Dei oculis nota, externis tamen
quibusdam ritibus, ab ipso Christo institutis, et Verbi Dei velut
publica legittimaque disciplina,
non solum cernitur cognoscitur-
que, sed ita constituitur, ut in
hanc sine his nemo (nisi singulari Dei privilegio) censeatur.[1]

XV. [XVI.] Von den Dienern des Wortes Gottes und dem Dienste der Kirche.

Deßhalb bekennen wir auch, daß die
Diener der Kirche Mitarbeiter Gottes
sind, wie sie der heilige Paulus nennt,
durch die er seinen Gläubigen Erkenntniß seiner selbst und Vergebung der
Sünden zutheilt und darbietet, die
Menschen zu sich bekehrt, aufrichtet,

XVI. De Ministerio Verbi.

Atque hanc ob causam ministros ecclesiæ cooperarios esse
Dei (quod et Paulus agnoscit)
fatemur, per quos ille et cognitionem sui, et peccatorum remissionem administret, homines ad
se convertat, erigat, consoletur,

---

[1] 1 Pet. ii.; Matt. xvi.; Eph. v.; Marc. xvi.; Matt. xxviii.; Act. x.

tröstet, ja, auch schreckt und richtet, doch in dem Verstande, daß wir in dem Allen alle Wirkung und Kraft dem Herrn Gott allein, dem Diener aber das Zudienen zuschreiben; denn gewiß ist es, daß diese Kraft und Wirkung keinem Geschöpfe jemals beigelegt werden soll, noch kann, sondern Gott theilt sie aus nach seinem freien Willen, denen er will.[1]

terreat etiam et judicet. *Ita tamen, ut virtutem et efficaciam in his omnem Domino, ministerium ministris tamen adscribamus. Nam hanc virtutem efficaciamque nulli omnino creaturæ alligari, sed libera Dei dignatione dispensari [quomodo et] quibus ipse velit, certum est.*[1] [*Nihil enim est, qui rigat, neque qui plantat, sed qui dat incrementum Deus.*][2]

XVI. [XVII.] Von der Macht der Kirche.

Die Macht, das Wort Gottes zu predigen und die Schäflein des Herrn zu weiden, welches eigentlich zu reden das Amt der Schlüssel ist, schreibt allen Menschen vor Eine Form zu leben, sie seien hoch oder niedern Standes. Dieß Ansehn soll, als ein Befehl Gottes, hoch, theuer und unverletzt sein; es soll auch Niemand diese Macht zur Verwaltung übertragen werden, er sei denn zuvor durch die göttliche Stimme und Wahl, durch diejenigen, die von der Kirche durch wohlerwogene Rathschläge als Ausschuß dazu bestimmt und erwählt sind, tauglich und geschickt dazu erfunden und erkannt.[3]

XVII. Potestas Ecclesiastica.

Ipsa autem verbi, et pascendi gregis Dominici auctoritas, quæ proprie clavium potestas est, cunctis, summis æque et imis præscribens, sacrosancta inviolabilisque esse, et vel divino Dei, vel certo et consulto ecclesiæ suffragio, electis tantum ad ministrandum committi debet.[3]

---

[1] 1 Cor. iii. ; 2 Cor. vi. ; Joh. xx. ; Luc. i. ; 1 Cor. xiv.

[2] [The bracketed sentence in the Latin text is not found in Niemeyer, and has been inserted from the *Corpus et Syntagma Conf.* (1654), p. 69. So also *quomodo et*, for which Niemeyer reads *iis.*]

[3] Matt. xvi. ; Joh. xx. ; Hierem. i. ; 1 Thess. iv. ; Act. xiii.

XVII. [XVIII.] Von der Erwäh= lung der Diener der Kirche.

Dieß Amt und dieser Dienst soll Niemand befohlen oder vertraut wer= den, er sei denn zuvor in der Heiligen Schrift und der Erkenntniß des Willens Gottes wohlberichtet, in Frömmigkeit und Unschuld des Lebens unsträflich, und im Fleiß und Ernst, die Ehre und den Namen Christi zu fördern, eifrig und inbrünstig erfunden und erkannt worden, nämlich durch die Diener und Vorsteher der Kirche; auch die, welche aus der christlichen Obrigkeit, als von der Kirche wegen, zu solchem Amt er= wählt sind. Und weil dasselbe eine rechte, wahre Wahl Gottes ist, sollen sie durch das Urtheil der Kirche und Auflegung der Hände der Aelteren als billig und recht erkannt und angenommen werden.[1]

XVIII. ELECTIO MINISTRORUM.

Est enim functio hæc nulli, quem non et legis divinæ peritia, et vitæ innocentia, et Christi no- minis studio singulari esse com- pererint et judicarint ministri ecclesiæ, et iis, quibus id negotii per Christianum magistratum ecclesiæ nomine commissum est, concedenda. Quæ quum vera Dei electio sit, ecclesiæ tamen suffragio et manuum presbyterorum [sacer- dotis] impositione recte compro- batur.[1]

XVIII. [XIX.] Wer der Hirt und das Haupt der Kirche sei.

Christus selbst ist allein das wahre und rechte Haupt und der Hirt seiner Kirche; derselbe giebt seiner Kirche Hirten und Lehrer, die aus seinem Befehl das Wort und das Amt der Schlüssel ordentlich und rechtmäßig, wie oben gemeldet, führen. Deßhalb wir diejenigen, die allein mit dem Namen Bischöfe sind, und das Haupt zu Rom weder bekennen, noch anneh= men.[2]

XIX. PASTOR QUIS.

Christus ipse verum suæ eccle- siæ caput ac pastor solus est is ecclesiæ suæ pastores dat et doc- tores, qui in ecclesia externa hac clavium potestate legitime sic concredita recte et legitime utan- tur. Unde illos titulotenus tan- tum pastores, caputque romanum minime agnoscimus.[2]

---

[1] 1 Tim iii.; Luc. xii.; Act. i.; Tit. i.; Act. vi.; Heb. vi.
[2] Joh. x.; Eph. i. 5, 4; Joh. xxi.

XIX. [XX.] Was das Amt sei der Diener und der Kirche.

Das Allerhöchste und Vornehmste in diesem Amte ist, daß die Diener der Kirche Reue und Leid über die Sünde, Aenderung des Lebens und Verzeihung der Sünde predigen, und das Alles durch Christum; ferner, daß sie unaufhörlich für das Volk bitten, der Heiligen Schrift und dem Worte Gottes in Lesen und heiliger Betrachtung ernstlich und fleißig obliegen, mit dem Worte Gottes, als mit dem Schwerte des Geistes, in alle Wege den Teufel mit tödtlichem Hasse verfolgen und seine Kraft unterdrücken und schwächen, daß sie die gesunden Bürger Christi beschirmen, die bösen aber warnen, zurückdrängen und entfernen, und wenn sie in ihrem Frevel und ihren unverschämten Lastern die Kirche Christi wollten für und für ärgern und verwüsten, sollen sie durch diejenigen, die von den Dienern des Wortes und christlicher Obrigkeit dazu verordnet sind, ausgestoßen, oder auf andere fügliche und schickliche Weise gestraft und gebessert werden, bis sie ihren Irrthum bekennen, sich ändern und gesund werden; dann aber soll der Bürger Christi, der also ungesund und krank gewesen und ausgeschlossen ist, wieder in die Kirche aufgenommen

XX. MINISTRORUM OFFICIA.

Summum functionis hujus munus est, pœnitentiam et peccatorum per Christum remissionem prædicare : pro populo incessanter orare, sanctis studiis verboque Dei indefesse invigilare, atque Verbo Dei velut gladio Spiritus, et arte omnigena Satanam internecino semper odio persequi ac debilitare, Christi cives sanos quidem tueri, vitiosos autem monere, reprehendere, coërcere, et grassantes longius, ecclesiœ, id est, Christi confœderatorum conspiratione consensuque pio, tota ditione aut ejicere ac proscribere, aut alia ratione commoda emendare tantisper,[1] dum resipiscant et salvi fiant. Is enim ad ecclesiam civi Christi morbido regressus est, si conversis animis studiisque (quo omnis hœc disciplina spectat) errorem agnoscens confiteatur suum, et disciplinam sanam ultro jam requirat, ac

---

[1] Corp. et Synt. reads after *longius :* '*Conspiratione pia eorum, qui ex ministris magistratuque delecti sunt, disciplina excludere, vel alia ratione commoda multare tantisper.*' etc.

werden, wenn er sich bekehrt und mit großem Ernst seine Sünde und seinen Irrthum bekennt und gesteht (denn dazu soll diese Strafe dienen) und Arzenei für seine Krankheit willig sucht, sich in geistliche Zucht begiebt, und mit neuem Fleiß und Ernst in der Frömmigkeit alle Frommen erfreut.[1]

XX. [XXI.] Von der Kraft und Wirkung der Sacramente.

Der Zeichen, die man Sacramente nennt, sind zwei, nämlich die Taufe und das Nachtmahl des Herrn. Diese Sacramente sind bedeutsame, heilige Zeichen hoher, heimlicher Dinge; sie sind aber nicht bloße und leere Zeichen, sondern bestehen in Zeichen und wesentlichen Dingen. Denn in der Taufe ist das Wasser das Zeichen; das Wesentliche aber und Geistliche ist die Wiedergeburt und die Aufnahme in das Volk Gottes. Im Nachtmahl oder Danksagung sind Brot und Wein Zeichen; das Wesentliche aber und Geistliche ist die Gemeinschaft des Leibes und Blutes Christi, das Heil, das am Kreuz erobert ist, und Vergebung der Sünden, welche wesentliche, unsichtbare und geistliche Dinge im Glauben empfangen werden, so wie die Zeichen leiblich, und in diesen geistlichen, wesentlichen Dingen besteht die ganze Kraft, Wirkung und Frucht der Sacramente.

studio pietatis novo pios omnes exhilaret.[1]

XXI. DE VI ET EFFICACIA SACRAMENTORUM.

Signa, quæ [*in ecclesia Christi*] *et* sacramenta *vocantur, duo sunt,* baptismus, *et* eucharistia. *Hæc rerum arcanarum symbola non nudis signis, sed signis simul et rebus constant. In baptismo enim aqua signum est, at res ipsa regeneratio adoptioque in populum Dei. In eucharistia panis et vinum signa sunt, res autem communicatio corporis Domini, parta salus, et peccatorum remissio. Quæ quidem, ut ore corporis signa, sic fide spiritus percipiuntur. Nam in rebus ipsis totus fructus sacramentorum est.*

---

[1] Luc. xxiv.; Hierem. xi.; Act. vi.; 1 Tim. iv.; Eph. vi.; 2 Tim. iv.; Ezech. xxxiv.; 1 Cor. v.; 2 Thess. iii.

Deßhalb bekennen wir, daß die Sa=
cramente nicht allein äußere Zeichen
sind christlicher Gesellschaft, sondern
wir bekennen sie für Zeichen göttlicher
Gnade, durch welche die Diener der
Kirche mit dem Herrn in der Absicht
und zu dem Ende, wie er es uns selbst
verheißt, anbietet und kräftiglich ver=
schafft, wirken, jedoch, wie oben von
den Dienern des Wortes gesagt ist,
nämlich, daß alle heiligende und selig=
machende Kraft Gott, dem Herrn,
allein zugeschrieben wird.

*Unde asserimus sacramenta
non solum tesseras quasdam societatis Christianæ, sed et gratiæ
divinæ symbola esse, quibus ministri, Domino, ad eum finem
quem ipse promittit offert et
efficit, cooperentur, sic tamen,
qualiter de verbi ministerio dictum est, ut omnis virtus salvifica uni Domino transscriba-
tur.*

XXI. [XXII.] Von der Taufe.

Die Taufe ist nach der Einsetzung
des Herrn ein Bad der Wiedergeburt,[1]
welches der Herr seinen Auserwählten
mit einem sichtbaren Zeichen durch den
Dienst der Kirche, wie oben gesagt und
erläutert ist, anbietet und darstellt.

In diesem heiligen Bade taufen wir
unsre Kinder darum, weil es unbillig
wäre, daß wir diejenigen, die von uns,
einem Volke Gottes, geboren sind, der
Gemeinschaft des Volkes Gottes sollten
berauben, die doch durch das göttliche
Wort dazu bestimmt und diejenigen
sind, von denen man vermuthen soll,
sie seien von Gott erwählt.[2]

XXII. Baptisma.

*Baptisma quidem ex institu-
tione Domini lavacrum regenerationis quam Dominus electis
suis, visibili signo per ecclesiæ
ministerium (qualiter supra expositum est) exhibeat.*

*Quo quidem sancto lavacro in-
fantes nostros idcirco tingimus,
quoniam e nobis (qui populus
Domini sumus) genitos populi
Dei consortio rejicere nefas est,
tantum non divina voce huc designatos, præsertim quum de eorum electione pie est præsumen-
dum.[2]*

---

[1] widergeberliche abweschung.
[2] Tit. iii. ; Act. x. ; Gen. xvii. ; 1 Cor. vii. ; Luc. xviii.

XXII. [XXIII.] Vom Nachtmahl des Herrn, oder von der Danksagung.

Vom heiligen Nachtmahl halten wir also, daß der Herr in demselben seinen Leib und sein Blut, das ist, sich selbst den Seinen wahrlich anbietet, und zu solcher Frucht zu genießen giebt, daß er je mehr und mehr in ihnen, und sie in ihm leben. Nicht, daß der Leib und das Blut des Herrn mit Brot und Wein natürlich vereinbart oder räumlich darein verschlossen werde, oder daß eine leibliche, fleischliche Gegenwärtigkeit hier gesetzt werde, sondern daß Brot und Wein nach der Einsetzung des Herrn hochbedeutende, heilige, wahre Zeichen seien, durch die von dem Herrn selbst, vermittelst des Dienstes der Kirche, die wahre Gemeinschaft des Leibes und Blutes Christi den Gläubigen gereicht und angeboten werde, nicht zur vergänglichen Speise des Bauches, sondern zur Speise und Nahrung des geistlichen und ewigen Lebens.[1]

Dieser hohen und heiligen Speise gebrauchen wir oft, daß wir, dadurch erinnert, den Tod und das Blut des gekreuzigten Christus mit den Augen des Glaubens erblicken, und unser Heil mit einem Vorgeschmack des himmlischen Wesens und mit einer wahren Empfindung des ewigen Lebens betrachten.

XXIII. Eucharistia.

Cœnam vero mysticam, in qua Dominus corpus et sanguinem suum, id est, seipsum suis vere ad hoc offerat, ut magis magisque in illis vivat, et illi in ipso. Non quod pani et vino corpus et sanguis Domini vel naturaliter uniantur: vel hic localiter includantur, vel ulla huc carnali præsentia statuantur. Sed quod panis et vinum ex institutione Domini symbola sint, quibus ab ipso Domino per ecclesiæ ministerium vera corporis et sanguinis ejus communicatio, non in periturum ventris cibum, sed in æternæ vitæ alimoniam exhibeatur.[1]

Hoc sacro cibo idcirco utimur sæpe, quoniam hujus monitu in crucifixi mortem sanguinemque, fidei oculis intuentes, ac salutem nostram, non sine cœlestis vitæ gustu, et vero vitæ æternæ sensu, meditantes, hoc spirituali, vivifico intimoque pabulo, ineffabili

---

[1] Matt. xxvi. ; Joh. vi. 14; 1 Cor. x.

Mit dieser geistlichen, lebendig machen=
den, inneren Speise werden wir mit
unaussprechlicher Süßigkeit ergötzt und
erquickt, und mit hoher Freude erfüllt,
daß wir in dem Tode Christi unser
Leben finden. Deßhalb wir ganz und
gar vor Freude in unserm Herzen froh=
locken, und mit allen unsern Kräften
desto mehr für eine so theure und hohe
Wohlthat, die er uns bewiesen hat,
uns in Danksagung ergießen.

Deßhalb beschuldigt man uns sehr
unbillig, daß wir auf die hohen Wahr=
zeichen wenig Werth legen; denn diese
heiligen Zeichen und Sacramente sind
heilige und ehrwürdige Dinge, da sie
von Christo, dem hohen Priester, ein=
gesetzt und gebraucht sind. So reichen
sie in der Art, wie oben davon geredet
ist, die geistlichen Dinge, die sie bedeu=
ten, dar und bieten sie an. Sie geben
von den geschehenen Dingen Zeugniß.
Sie geben uns ein Bild und eine
Erinnerung so hoher, heiliger Dinge,
und mit einer besondern Aehnlichkeit
der Dinge, die sie bedeuten, bringen
sie ein großes und herrliches Licht in
die heiligen, göttlichen Angelegenheiten.
Ueberdieß geben sie etwas Hülfe und
Unterstützung dem Glauben, und sind
gleichsam ein Eid, mit dem sich die
Gläubigen ihrem Haupte und der
Kirche verpflichten und verbinden.
So hoch und theuer halten wir die
heiligen, hochbedeutenden Wahrzei=
chen; jedoch schreiben wir die leben=

*cum suavitate reficimur, ac in-
enarrabili verbis lœtitia, propter
inventam vitam, exultamus, to-
tique ac viribus omnino omnibus nostris, in gratiarum actionem pro tam mirando Christi
erga nos beneficio, effundimur.*

*Itaque immerito fit nostro
maximo, quod quidam parum
nos tribuere sacris symbolis putant. Sunt enim hæc res sanctæ
venerandæque, utpote, a summo
sacerdote Christo institutæ et sus-
ceptæ, suo quo diximus modo
res significatas exhibentes, testimonium rei gestæ præbentes, res
tam arduas repræsentantes, et
mirabili quadam rerum signifi-
catarum analogia clarissimam
mysteriis istis lucem afferentes.
Ad hæc auxilium opemque ipsi
suppeditant fidei, ac jurisjuran-
di denique vice initiatum capiti
Christi et ecclesiæ adstringunt.
Tam sancte de sacris symbolis
sentimus. At vero vivificantis
et sanctificantis vim et virtutem
tribuimus ei perpetuo, qui vita*

dig machende und heiligende Kraft in alle Wege allein dem zu, der allein das Leben ist; dem sei Lob in Ewigkeit. Amen.

est, cui sit laus in sæcula sæculorum. Amen.

XXIII. [XXIV.] Von der heiligen Versammlung und der Zusammenkunft der Gläubigen.

XXIV. CŒTUS SACRI.

Wir halten dafür, daß die heiligen Versammlungen und Zusammenkünfte der Gläubigen so sollen begangen werden, daß man vor allen Dingen dem Volke das Wort Gottes an einem gemeinen und dazu bestimmten Orte vortrage, daß die Geheimnisse der Schrift durch geschickte Diener täglich ausgelegt und erklärt werden, daß man das Nachtmahl des Herrn und heilige Danksagung halte, damit der Gläubigen Glaube für und für geübt werde, daß man mit ernstlichem Gebet für alles Anliegen aller Menschen ernstlich anhalte.

Cœtus autem sacros sic peragendos esse censemus, ut ante omnia verbum Dei in publicum plebi quottidie propronatur, Scripturæ abdita per idoneos ministros quottidie eruantur edisseranturque: sacra Eucharistia celebranda piorum subinde fides exerceatur, precationi pro omnibus omnium necessitatibus assidue instetur.

Andere Ceremonien, die unzählbar sind, als Kelche, Meßgewänder, Chorröcke, Kutten, Platten, Fahnen, Kerzen und Altäre, Gold und Silber, wie fern sie die wahre Religion und den rechten Gottesdienst zu stören und umzukehren dienen, und besonders die Götzen und Bilder, die zur Verehrung und zum Aergerniß gebraucht werden, und was solcher ungöttlichen Dinge mehr sind, die wollen wir aus unsrer heiligen Gemeinde weit hinweggetrieben haben.[1]

Ceteras vero cerimoniarum ambages inutiles et innumerabiles, vasa, vela, vestes, faces, aras, aurum, argentum, quatenus pervertendæ religioni serviunt, idola præsertim et imagines, quæ ad cultum et scandalum prostant et id genus omnia prophana, a sacro nostro cœtu procul arcemus.[1]

---

[1] Act. ii.; 1 Tim. ii.; 1 Cor. xiv.; Ex. xx.; 1 Joh. v.; 1 Pet. iv.; Es. xl.

XXIV. [XXV.] Von den Dingen, die weder geboten, noch verboten, sondern Mitteldinge und frei sind.

Alle Dinge, die man Mitteldinge nennt, wie sie es denn (eigentlich zu reden) sind, kann ein frommer, gläubiger Christ zu allen Zeiten und an allen Orten frei gebrauchen, doch daß er es thue nach rechter Einsicht und mit Liebe; denn der Gläubige soll aller Dinge also gebrauchen, daß die Ehre Gottes befördert, und die Kirche und der Nächste nicht geärgert werde.[2]

XXV. [XXVI.] De Mediis.[1]

Quæ media *vocantur, et sunt proprie, iis uti vir pius quamquam libere ubique et omni tempore potest, tamen scienter, et ex charitate, nempe ad edificationem omnibus utetur solum.*[2]

XXV. [XXVI.] Von denen, die durch falsche Lehren die Kirche Christi trennen oder sich von ihr absondern und rotten.

Alle diejenigen, die sich von der heiligen Gemeinschaft und Gesellschaft der Kirche trennen und absondern, fremde, ungöttliche Lehren in die Kirche einführen, oder solcher Lehre anhangen, —Gebrechen, die zu unsrer Zeit sich am meisten bei den Wiedertäufern zeigen,— wenn sie die Warnung der Kirche und christlichen Unterricht nicht hören und befolgen, sondern hartnäckig auf ihrem Streit und Irrthum mit Verletzung und Verführung der Kirche bestehn und verharren wollen,—sollen durch

XXVI. [XXV.] De Hæreticis et Schismaticis.

Arcemus item quotquot ab ecclesiæ sancta societate discedentes, aliena dogmata vel ingerunt vel sectantur. Quo malo Catabaptistæ *hodie cum primis laborant. Quos si obstinate monitioni ecclesiæ et Christianæ eruditioni non obsecundant, per magistratum coërcendos, ne contagione*

---

[1] In the Latin text of the *Corpus et Syntagma* and of Niemeyer the order of this and the following section is reversed.

[2] Rom. xiv.; 1 Cor. iii., viii., x.

die oberſte Gewalt geſtraft und unter=
drückt werden, damit ſie die Heerde
Gottes mit ihrer falſchen Lehre nicht
vergiften und verletzen oder beflecken.[1]

XXVI. [XXVII.] Von der welt= lichen Obrigkeit.

Da alle Gewalt und Obrigkeit von
Gott iſt, ſo iſt ihr höchſtes und vor=
nehmſtes Amt, wenn ſie nicht eine
Tyrannin ſein will, daß ſie die wahre
Ehre Gottes und den rechten Gottes=
dienſt, mit Strafe und Ausrottung
aller Gotteslästerung, ſchirme und för=
dere, und möglichen Fleiß anwende,
daß ſie dasjenige, was der Diener der
Kirche und Verkündiger des Evange=
liums aus dem Worte Gottes lehrt
und vorträgt, fördere und vollſtrecke.
Damit aber ſolche Religion, wahrer
Gottesdienſt und Ehrbarkeit aufgehe
und wachſe, wird die Obrigkeit vor=
nehmlich allen Fleiß dahin wenden, daß
das lautre Wort Gottes der Gemeine
treulich vorgetragen, und Niemand da=
ran verhindert werde, daß die Schulen
wohl eingerichtet, die gemeine Bürger=
ſchaft wohl gelehret, fleißig unterrichtet
und geſtraft werde, daß man fleißig
Sorge trage für die Diener der Kirche
und die Armen in der Kirche, daß die=
ſelben nach der Billigkeit und ziemlicher
Nothdurft verſehen werden; denn dazu
ſollen die Güter der Kirche dienen.

XXVII. De Magistratu.

*Magistratus omnis a Deo
quum sit, officium ejus (nisi tyrannidem exercere mavult), præcipuum est, religionem omni
blasphemia reprimenda defendere et procurare, ac qualiter
ex Verbo Domini propheta docet,
pro virili exequi. Qua quidem
in parte præcipue illi advigilan-
dum, ut purum Verbum Dei
pure et synceriter ac vere populo predicetur, nec ulli hominum veritas evangelica præclu-
datur. Mox curabit ut inventus
et pubes tota civium recta et sedula institutione ac disciplina
formetur, ut justa sit ministrorum ecclesiæ provisio, pauperum-
que solicita cura. Huc enim
ecclesiasticæ facultates spectant.*

gregem Dei inficiant, judicamus.[1]

---

[1] Esa. v.; Act. iii.; Rom. xii.

Weiter soll die Obrigkeit das Volk nach billigen, göttlichen Gesetzen regieren, Gericht und Recht halten und handhaben, den allgemeinen Frieden und Wohlstand erhalten, den allgemeinen Nutzen schützen und schirmen, und die Uebertreter nach Beschaffenheit ihrer Missethat an Gut, Leib und Leben, wie billig strafen. Und wenn sie das thut, dienet sie Gott, ihrem Herrn, wie sie schuldig und verpflichtet ist.

Solcher Obergewalt sollen wir Alle, obwohl wir in Christo frei sind, mit Leib, Hab und Gut gehorsam und gewärtig sein, und mit Liebe von Herzen und aus Glauben uns ihr unterthänig beweisen, Treue und Eid thun und leisten, wenn ihr Geheiß und Gebot nicht offenbar wider den ist, um deß willen wir ihr Ehre anthun und gehorsam sind.[1]

Deinde secundum leges æquas judicare populum: tueri pacem publicam: rempublicam fovere, sontes pro delicti ratione mulctare, opibus, corpore, vita. Quæ quum facit debitum Deo cultum præstat.

Huïc nos (etiam si in Christo liberi sumus) et corpore et facultatibus omnibus nostris, et animi studio [vera] cum fide, sancte subjiciendos esse (quantisper hujus imperia cum eo, propter quem hunc veneramur, palam non pugnant), scimus.[1]

XXVII. [XXVIII.] Von der heiligen Ehe.

XXVIII. DE SANCTO CONJUGIO.

Wir halten dafür, daß der eheliche Stand allen Menschen, die dazu tauglich und geschickt und von Gott sonst nicht berufen sind, außerhalb der Ehe keusch zu leben, von Gott eingesetzt und verordnet sei, daß kein Orden oder Stand so heilig und ehrbar sei, daß ihm der eheliche Stand zuwider wäre und verboten werden sollte. Und wie nun solche Ehe vor der Kirche mit einer herrlichen

Conjugium hominibus omnibus aptis et alio non vocatis divinitus institutum, nullius ordinis sanctimoniæ repugnare censemus. Quod ut ecclesia hortatione solenni precationeque inaugurat et sancit, ita magistratus interest, ut digne et ineatur et colatur

---

[1] Rom. xiii.; 1 Cor. ix.; 1 Tim. v.: 1 Cor. xvi.: Matt. xxii.; Act. iv.

öffentlichen Ermahnung und einem | *nec nisi justis ex causis solva-*
Gelübde bestätigt wird, also soll auch | *tur.*
die Obrigkeit Acht haben und dafür
sorgen, daß die Ehe rechtlich und or=
dentlich eingegangen und recht und
ehrbar gehalten, auch nicht leicht, ohne
wichtige und rechtmäßige Ursachen,
getrennt und geschieden werde.

Deßhalb können wir die Klöster | *Proinde cœlibatum istum mo-*
und die unsaubere und unordentliche | *nasticum et eorum (quos spiri-*
Keuschheit aller vermeinter Geistlichen | *tuales vocant) impuram castita-*
und derselben faules und unnützes | *tem, et totum hoc ignavum vitæ*
Leben, das etliche Leute aus unbegrün= | *genus, superstitiosorum hominum*
detem Eifer eingesetzt und angeordnet | *abominabile commentum, procul*
haben, nicht loben, sondern verwerfen | *rejicimus, æque et ecclesiæ et rei-*
es als ein scheußliches und gräuliches | *publicæ repugnans.*[1]
Ding, von Menschen wider Gottes
Ordnung erdichtet und erfunden.[1]

Ist durch oben gemeldeter Städte Boten bestätigt und einhellig angenom=
men.

Basel, 1536, am 26. März.

---

[1] Matt. xix.; Heb. xiii.; 1 Cor. vii.; 1 Tim. iii.; Matt. v.; 1 Tim. iv.; 2 Thess. iii.

CATECHISMUS GENEVENSIS, CONSENSUS TIGURINUS, CONSENSUS GENEVENSIS.

These three documents, drawn up by Calvin, would follow next in chronological order, but do not come within the scope of our selection, partly on account of their length (the Latin text alone would fill about two hundred pages—see Niemeyer, pp. 123–310), partly for intrinsic reasons. The CATECHISM OF GENEVA (1541) is no more in use, having been superseded by the Heidelberg and Westminster Catechisms, included in this volume. The CONSENSUS OF ZURICH (1549), and the CONSENSUS OF GENEVA (1552), especially the latter, are not so much confessions of faith as elaborate theological and polemical essays on two doctrines—the one on the Lord's Supper, the other on Predestination—for the purpose of harmonizing and defending the teaching of the Swiss Churches. On both these doctrines the Second Helvetic, the Gallican, the Belgic, the Scotch, and other Reformed Confessions, which we give in full, are sufficiently explicit and more authoritative.

For a history and summary of these documents, see the first volume, pp. 467 sqq.

CONFESSIO HELVETICA POSTERIOR, A.D. 1566.

THE SECOND HELVETIC CONFESSION.

[This Helvetic Confession is called the *second* or *later* Helv. Conf., to distinguish it from the *Confessio Helvetica Prior* (or *Basileensis Posterior*, 1536). It was written by Henry Bullinger, of Zürich (Zwingli's successor), 1562, and first published 1566 in Latin, also in German and French. It is the most elaborate and most catholic among the Swiss Confessions. (Hagenbach calls it a '*wahres dogmatisches Meister-stück.*') It was adopted, or at least highly approved, by nearly all the Reformed Churches on the Continent and in England and Scotland. Hence it must have a place in this selection. But it is rather a theological treatise than a popular creed ; and on account of its great length I am obliged to omit a translation, referring the reader to the summary given in the first volume. There is an English translation by Owen Jones (*The Church of the Living God; also the Swiss and Belgian Confessions of Faith*, London, 1865), and another by Prof. Jeremiah Good, D.D. (of Tiffin, Ohio), Phila. 1873.

For the text I have compared the following Latin editions: 1. The edition of Zürich, 1651, as reprinted in the *Corpus et Syntagma Confessionum Fidei* (Geneva, 1654, pp. 1–61). 2. The edition in the Oxford *Syllage Confessionum*, 2d ed. 1827, pp. 9–115, printed in very superior style, but with some omissions. 3. J. P. Kindler's *Confessio Helvetica Posterior*, with a preface by Winer, Solisbaci, 1825 (pp. 102) ; from this edition I have adopted the division of chapters into sections, and the references to the Augsburg Confession. 4. The edition of Niemeyer, in his *Collectio Conf. Reform.*, Leipz. 1840, pp. 462–536, who gives the text of the edition of 1568, with unimportant variations of a Zürich MS., and the editions of Oxford and of Kindler. 5. The German text in Böckel's *Bekenntniss-Schriften der evang.-reformirten Kirche*, Leipz. 1847, pp. 281–347. The editions of Fritzsche and Böhl were not at hand. Some editions add the Imperial Edict against heretics from the Justinian Code, and the Symbolum of Pope Damasus from the works of Jerome. The title and preface are copied from the Zürich edition, 1651, in the *Corpus et Syntagma Confessionum*, 1654.]

CONFESSIO

ET

EXPOSITIO SIMPLEX

ORTHODOXÆ FIDEI, ET DOGMA-
TVM CATHOLICORVM SYNCERÆ RELI-
gionis Chriſtianæ.

Concorditer ab Eccleſiæ Chriſti Miniſtris, qui ſunt in Heluetia, Tiguri, Bernæ, Glaronæ,[1] Baſileæ,[1] Scaphusij, Abbatiſcellæ,[1] Sangalli, Curiæ Rhetorum, & apud Confœderatos, Mylhuſij item, & Biennæ: quibus adiunxerunt ſe Geneuenſis & Neocomenſis Eccleſiæ Miniſtri, vnà cum aliis Euangelij Præconibus in Polonia, Hungaria & Scotia:

EDITA IN HOC, VT VNIVERSIS TESTEN-
tur fidelibus, quod in vnitate veræ & antiquæ Chriſti Eccleſiæ,
perſtent, neque vlla noua, aut erronea dogmata ſpargant,
atque ideò etiam nihil conſortij cum vllis Seĉtis
aut Hæreſibus habeant.

Ad Rom. cap. X. verſ. 10.
Corde creditur ad iuſtitiam, ore autem confeſsio fit ad ſalutem.

TIGVRI.
Typis IOH. IACOBI BODMERI.

Anno MDCLI.

---

[1] Glarus, Basel, and Appenzell are not mentioned in the first editions, as they subscribed at a later period.

PRÆFATIO.

Universis Christi Fidelibus per Germaniam atque exteras etiam Nationes.

Ministri Subscriptarum Ecclesiarum per Helvetiam

Gratiam et Pacem a Deo Patre, per Jesum Christum, Dominum nostrum, precamur.

Conscriptæ sunt hactenus, et eduntur hoc præcipue tempore in publicum, a regnis, nationibus, et civitatibus, multæ ac variæ Confessiones et Expositiones fidei, quibus extremo hoc seculo, in tam infelici perniciosarum proventu hæresium, quæ passim exoriuntur, docent, atque testantur, se in Ecclesiis suis orthodoxe simpliciterque sentire, credere atque docere, de omnibus in universum et singulis Christianæ fidei et religionis nostræ dogmatibus, denique, se et ab hæresium sectarumve communione esse quam alienissimos. Nos ergo, tametsi antea hoc ipsum fecerimus in nostris scriptis in publicum editis, quia tamen illa in oblivionem forte abierunt, variisque in locis, et prolixius etiam rem exponunt, quam ut omnibus inquirere ac perlegere vacet, præclaro aliorum fidelium exemplo excitati, brevi hac expositione conamur complecti, et omnibus Christi fidelibus proponere doctrinam, œconomiamque Ecclesiarum nostrarum, quam illæ mox ab initio Reformationis, multos jam per annos, multaque per discrimina rerum ad hunc usque diem, summo cum consensu, et docuerunt, et nunc quoque custodiunt. Eadem opera attestamur etiam omnibus consensum nostrum unanimem, quem dedit nobis Dominus, ut in nostris Ecclesiis, quibus nos ministrare voluit Dominus, idem loquamur omnes, nec sint inter nos dissidia, sed simus integrum corpus, eadem mente eademque sententia. Attestamur item, nos minime talia in Ecclesiis nostris spargere dogmata, qualia adversarii nonnulli nostri nobis, apud eos maxime, ad quos scripta nostra non perveniunt, et qui doctrinæ nostræ imperiti sunt, falso et præter meritum tribuere, obtrudereque nituntur. Ergo manifestissime ex his nostris æqui deprehendent lectores, nihil nos quoque habere communionis cum ullis sectis atque hæresibus, quarum, hoc consilio, in singulis prope capitibus, mentionem facimus, easque rejicientes perstringimus. Colligent itaque et illud, nos a sanctis Christi Ecclesiis Germaniæ, Galliæ, Angliæ, aliarumque in orbe Christiano nationum, nephario schismate nos non sejungere atque abrumpere: sed cum ipsis omnibus et singulis, in hac confessa veritate Christiana, probe consentire, ipsasque caritate sincera complecti.

Tametsi vero in diversis Ecclesiis quædam deprehenditur varietas, in loqutionibus, et modo expositionis doctrinæ, in ritibus item vel ceremoniis, eaque recepta pro Ecclesiarum quarumlibet ratione, opportunitate et ædificatione, nunquam tamen ea, ullis in Ecclesia temporibus, materiam dissensionibus et schismatibus, visa est suppeditare. Semper enim hac in re, Christi Ecclesiæ usæ sunt libertate. Id quod in historia Ecclesiastica videre licet. Abunde piæ vetustati satis erat, mutuus ille in præcipuis fidei dogmatibus, inque sensu orthodoxo et caritate fraterna, consensus.

Quo circa speramus Christi Ecclesias, ubi viderint deprehenderintque nos in sancti et æterni Dei doctrina, in sensu item orthodoxo et caritate fraterna, cum ipsis, imprimis vero cum veteri Apostolica Ecclesia, per omnia consentire, libenter ipsas quoque in unitate fidei atque doctrinæ, sensuque orthodoxo, et fraterna caritate consensuras nobiscum. Cum hanc Confessionem in hoc quoque ediderimus præcipue, ut Ecclesiarum pacem concordiamque cum

mutua caritate, apud Germaniæ exterasque Ecclesias quæramus, nobis conciliemus, concilia-
tamque retineamus. Ubi sane illas ipsas Ecclesias, ea dilectione, sinceritate, integritateque
præditas esse, nobis certo persuademus, ut si quid forte nostrarum rerum hactenus minus recte
intellectum sit a nonnullis, porro, audita hac simplici Confessione nostra, illæ nos neatiquam
numeraturæ sint inter hæreticos, neque Ecclesias nostras, quæ veræ Christi Ecclesiæ sunt,
damnaturæ, ut impias.

Ante omnia vero protestamur, nos semper esse paratissimos, omnia et singula hic a nobis
proposita, si quis requirat, copiosius explicare, denique meliora ex verbo Dei docentibus, non
sine gratiarum actione, et cedere et obsequi in Domino, Cui laus et gloria. Acta 1 Martii,
Anno 1566.

SUBSCRIPSERUNT omnes omnium Ecclesiarum Christi in Helvetia Ministri, qui sunt Tiguri,
Bernæ, Glaronæ, Basileæ, Scaphusii, Abbatiscellæ, Sangalli, Curiæ Rhetorum, et apud Confœderatos, in Ecclesiis Evangelium profitentibus cis et ultra Alpes, Mylhusii item et Biennæ,
quibus adjunxerunt se et Ministri Ecclesiæ, quæ est Genevæ, et Neocomi, etc. Sed et con-
senserunt in ipsam jam editam Ministri Ecclesiæ Polonicæ, quæ est in Ducatu Zathoriensi,
et Ossviecimensi, Scoticarum quoque Ecclesiarum Ministri, qui Nonis Sept. Anno D. 1566,
scriptis ad Clarissimum Virum, DN. Theodorum Bezam literis, inter alia dicunt; *Subscripsimus omnes, qui in hoc cœtu interfuimus, et hujus Academiæ sigillo publico obsignavimus.*
Præterea Debrecini in Hungaria, edita et impressa est Confessio, una cum articulis quibusdam, Septemb. 1, Anno D. 1567, et inscripta Serenissimo Principi et Domino, Domino Johanni II., Dei gratia electo Hungariæ Regi, etc. In qua inter alia hæc leguntur verba:
Omnes Ecclesiæ Ministri, qui in Conventu sancto ad 24 Febr., Anno Domini 1567, *Debre-
cinum convocato, cis et ultra Tibyscum, inter reliquas Confessiones recepimus et subscripsimus
Helveticæ Confessioni, Anno Domini* 1566 *editæ, cui et Ecclesiæ Genevensis Ministri subscripserunt.*

EDICTUM IMPERATORIUM.

DE EO, QUINAM HABENDI SINT, VEL CATHOLICI, VEL HÆRETICI,

Ex *Cod. Justin. Imper.* et *Tripart. Hist.* libro nono capite 7.

Impp. Gratianus, Valentinianus et Theodosius, Aug. Populo urbis Constantinopolitanæ.
Cunctos populos, quos clementiæ nostræ regit imperium, in ea volumus religione versari,
quam divinum Petrum Apostolum tradidisse Romanis, religio usque nunc ab ipso insinuata
declarat, quamque Pontificem Damasum sequi claret, et Petrum Alexandriæ Episcopum,
virum Apostolicæ sanctitatis: Hoc est, ut secundum Apostolicam disciplinam Evangelicamque
doctrinam, Patris, et Filii, et Spiritus Sancti, unam Deitatem sub pari majestate, et sub pia
trinitate credamus. Hanc legem sequentes, Christianorum Catholicorum nomen jubemus
amplecti: reliquos vero dementes væsanosque judicantes, hæretici dogmatis infamiam susti-
nere, divina primum vindicta, post etiam motu animi nostri, quem ex cœlesti arbitrio sump-
serimus ultione plectendos. Data 3 Calend. Martias Thessalonicæ, Gratiano 5. Valent. et
Theod. Aug. Coss.

Cæterum Evangelica et Apostolica historia una cum 2 Pet. Epistolis docent nos, qualem
religionem S. Petrus Apostolus tradiderit omnibus Ecclesiis per Orientem et Occidentem,
nedum Romanæ. Fides vero et doctrina Damasi Pontificis, qualis fuerit, colliquescit ex
ipsius Symbolo.

SYMBOLUM DAMASI.

Ex 2. Tomo *Operum* S. Hieron.

CREDIMUS in unum Deum Patrem omnipotentem, et in unum Dominum nostrum Jesum
Christum, Dei Filium, et in Spiritum Sanctum. Deum non tres Deos, sed Patrem, Filium, et
Spiritum Sanctum, unum Deum colimus et confitemur: non sic unum Deum quasi solitarium,

nec eundem qui ipse sibi pater sit, ipse et filius : sed Patrem esse, qui genuit, et Filium esse, qui genitus sit: Spiritum vero sanctum non genitum, neque ingenitum, non creatum neque factum, sed de Patre Filioque procedentem, Patri et Filio coæternum, et coæqualem, et coopera-torem.   Quia scriptum est, *Verbo Domini cœli firmati sunt,* id est, a Filio Dei et Spiritu oris ejus omnis virtus eorum.   Et alibi, *Emitte Spiritum tuum, et creabuntur, et renovabis faciem terræ.*   Ideoque in nomine Patris, et Filii, et Spiritus Sancti unum confitemur Deum, quod nomen est potestatis, non proprietatis.   Proprium nomen est Patri, Pater, et proprium nomen est Filio, Filius ; et proprium nomen Spiritui Sancto, Spiritus Sanctus.   In hac trinitate unum Deum colimus : quia ex uno Patre quod est, unius cum Patre naturæ est, unius substantiæ et unius potestatis.   Pater Filium genuit, non voluntate, nec necessitate, sed natura.   Filius ultimo tempore ad nos salvandos et ad implendas Scripturas descendit a Patre, qui nunquam desiit esse cum Patre.   Et conceptus est de Spiritu Sancto, et natus ex Virgine.   Carnem, et animam, et sensum, hoc est perfectum suscepit hominem; nec amisit, quod erat, sed cœpit esse quod non erat, ita tamen ut perfectus in suis sit, et verus in nostris.   Nam qui Deus erat, homo natus est, et qui homo natus est, operatur ut Deus, et qui operatur ut Deus, ut homo moritur, et qui ut homo moritur, ut Deus resurgit.

Qui devicto mortis imperio, cum ea carne, qua natus et passus et mortuus fuerat, et resur-rexit, ascendit ad Patrem, sedetque ad dexteram ejus in gloria, quam semper habuit et habet. In hujus morte et sanguine credimus emundatos nos, et ab eo resuscitandos die novissimo, in hac carne, qua nunc vivimus.   Et habemus spem nos consequuturos præmium boni meriti, aut pœnam pro peccatis æterni supplicii.   Hæc lege, hæc crede, hæc retine, huic fidei animam tuam subjuga, et vitam consequeris, et præmium a Christo.

Eadem porro docuit et credidit, cum beato Damaso et Athanasio, S. Petrus Alexandrinus Episcopus, sicut facile colligitur ex *Trip. Hist.* Lib. VII. cap. 37, et Lib. VIII. cap. 14.

Cum autem nos omnes simus hujus fidei religionisque, speramus nos ab omnibus habendos, non pro hæreticis, sed pro Catholicis et Christianis, etc.

INDEX CAPITUM.

CONFESSIO ET EXPOSITIO BREVIS ET SIMPLEX SINCERÆ RELIGIONIS CHRISTIANÆ, ETC.

CAP. I.

DE SCRIPTURA SANCTA, VERO DEI VERBO. [CONF. AUG., ART. V.]

1. Credimus et confitemur, Scripturas Canonicas sanctorum Prophetarum et Apostolorum utriusque Testamenti ipsum verum esse verbum Dei, et auctoritatem sufficientem ex semetipsis, non ex hominibus habere. Nam Deus ipse loquutus est Patribus, Prophetis, et Apostolis, et loquitur adhuc nobis per Scripturas Sanctas.

2. Et in hac Scriptura Sancta habet universalis Christi Ecclesia plenissime exposita, quæcunque pertinent cum ad salvificam fidem, tum ad vitam Deo placentem recte informandam, quo nomine distincte a Deo præceptum est, ne ei *aliquid vel addatur vel detrahatur* (Deut. iv. 2; Apoc. xxii. 18, 19).

3. Sentimus ergo, ex hisce Scripturis petendam esse veram sapientiam et pietatem, ecclesiarum quoque reformationem et gubernationem, omniumque officiorum pietatis institutionem, probationem denique dogmatum reprobationemque aut errorum confutationem omnium, sed et admonitiones omnes juxta illud Apostoli: *Omnis Scriptura divinitus inspirata utilis est ad doctrinam, ad redargutionem,* etc. (2 Tim. iii. 16, 17), et iterum, *Hæc tibi scribo,* inquit ad Timotheum apostolus (in 1 Epist. iii. 15), *ut noris, quomodo oporteat, te versari in domo Dei,* etc. Et idem ille rursus ad Thess.: *Cum* (ait) *acciperetis sermonem a nobis, accepistis non sermonem hominum, sed sicut erat vere, sermonem Dei,* etc. (1 Thess. ii. 13). Nam ipse in Evangelio dixit Dominus: *Non vos estis loquentes illi, sed Spiritus Patris mei loquitur in vobis. Ergo, qui vos audit, me audit; qui autem vos spernit, me spernit* (Matt. x. 20; Luc. x. 16; Joh. xiii. 20).

4. Proinde cum hodie hoc Dei verbum per prædicatores legitime vocatos annunciatur in Ecclesia, credimus ipsum Dei verbum annunciari et a fidelibus recipi, neque aliud Dei verbum vel fingendum, vel cœlitus esse exspectandum: atque in præsenti spectandum esse ipsum verbum, quod annunciatur, non annunciantem ministrum, qui, etsi sit

malus et peccator, verum tamen et bonum manet nil.ilominus verbum
Dei.

5. Neque arbitramur, prædicationem illam externam tanquam inutilem ideo videri, quoniam pendeat institutio veræ religionis ab interna Spiritus illuminatione: propterea, quod scriptum sit: *Non eru-
diet quis proximum suum. Omnes enim cognoscent me* (Jer. xxxi.
34), et: *Nihil est, qui rigat aut qui plantat, sed qui incrementum
dat, Deus* (1 Cor. iii. 7). Quamquam enim *nemo veniat ad Christum,
nisi trahatur a Patre cœlesti* (Joh. vi. 44), ac intus illuminetur per
Spiritum, scimus tamen, Deum omnino velle prædicari verbum Dei,
etiam foris. Equidem potuisset per Spiritum Sanctum, aut per ministerium angeli absque ministerio S. Petri instituisse Cornelium in Actis
Deus, ceterum rejicit hunc nihilominus ad Petrum, de quo angelus
loquens: *Hic*, inquit, *dicet tibi, quid oporteat te facere* (Act. x. 6).

6. Qui enim intus illuminat, donato hominibus Spiritu Sancto,
idem ille præcipiens dixit ad discipulos suos: *Ite in mundum universum, et prædicate evangelium omni creaturæ* (Marc. xvi. 15).
Unde Paulus Lydiæ apud Philippos purpurariæ prædicavit verbum
exterius, interius autem *aperuit mulieri cor Dominus* (Act. xvi. 14):
Idemque Paulus collocata gradatione eleganti (ad Rom. x. 13–17),
tandem infert: *Ergo fides ex auditu est; auditus autem per verbum Dei.*

7. Agnoscimus interim, Deum illuminare posse homines etiam sine
externo ministerio, quos et quando velit, id quod ejus potentiæ est.
Nos autem loquimur de usitata ratione instituendi homines, et præcepto et exemplo tradita nobis a Deo.

8. Execramur igitur omnes hæreses Artemonis, Manichæorum, Va-
lentinianiorum, Cerdonis et Marcionitarum, qui negarunt Scripturas
a Spiritu Sancto profectas: vel quasdam illarum non receperunt, vel
interpolarunt et corruperunt.

9. Interim nihil dissimulamus, quosdam Veteris Testamenti libros
a veteribus nuncupatos esse *apocryphos*, ab aliis *ecclesiasticos*, utpote
quos in ecclesiis legi voluerunt quidem, non tamen proferri ad auctoritatem ex his fidei confirmandam. Sicuti et Augustinus in lib. *de civitate Dei* (xviii. 38) commemorat, in libris Regum adduci Prophetarum
quorundam nomina et libros, sed addit, hos non esse in canone, ac
sufficere ad pietatem eos libros, quos habemus.

CAP. II.

DE INTERPRETANDIS SCRIPTURIS SANCTIS, ET DE PATRIBUS, CONCILIIS, ET TRADITIONIBUS.

1. Scripturas Sanctas, dixit Apostolus Petrus, *non esse interpretationis privatæ* (2 Pet. i. 20). Proinde non probamus interpretationes quaslibet; unde nec pro vera aut genuina Scripturarum interpretatione agnoscimus eum, quem vocant sensum Romanæ ecclesiæ, quem scilicet simpliciter Romanæ ecclesiæ defensores omnibus obtrudere contendunt recipiendum: sed illam duntaxat Scripturarum interpretationem pro orthodoxa et genuina agnoscimus, quæ ex ipsis est petita Scripturis (ex ingenio utique ejus linguæ, in qua sunt scriptæ, secundum circumstantias item expensæ, et pro ratione locorum vel similium vel dissimilium, plurium[1] quoque et clariorum expositæ), cum regula fidei et caritatis congruit, et ad gloriam Dei hominumque salutem eximie facit.

2. Proinde non aspernamur sanctorum Patrum Græcorum Latinorumque interpretationes, neque reprobamus eorundem disputationes ac tractationes rerum sacrarum cum Scripturis consentientes: a quibus tamen recedimus modeste, quando aliena a Scripturis aut his contraria adferre deprehenduntur. Nec putamus, illis ullam a nobis hac re injuriam irrogari, cum omnes uno ore nolint sua scripta æquari canonicis, sed probare jubeant, quatenus vel consentiant cum illis, vel dissentiant, jubeantque consentientia recipere, recedere vero a dissentientibus.

3. Eodem in ordine collocantur etiam conciliorum definitiones vel canones.

4. Quapropter non patimur, nos in controversiis religionis vel fidei causis urgeri nudis Patrum sententiis aut conciliorum determinationibus, multo minus receptis consuetudinibus, aut etiam multitudine idem sentientium, aut longi temporis præscriptione. Ergo non alium sustinemus in causa fidei judicem, quam ipsum Deum, per Scripturas Sanctas pronunciantem, quid verum sit, quid falsum, quid sequendum sit, quidve fugiendum. Ita judiciis nonnisi spiritualium hominum, ex verbo Dei petitis, acquiescimus. Jeremias certe cæterique prophetæ sacerdotum concilia, contra legem Dei instituta, damnarunt graviter, ac monuerunt diligenter, ne audiamus Patres, aut insistamus viæ il-

---

[1] Kindler and Niemever read *plurimum.*

lorum, qui, in suis ambulantes adinventionibus, a lege Dei deflexerunt.

5. Pariter repudiamus traditiones humanas, quæ, tametsi insigniantur speciosis titulis, quasi divinæ apostolicæque sint, viva voce Apostolorum et ceu per manus virorum Apostolicorum succedentibus Episcopis, ecclesiæ traditæ; compositæ tamen cum Scripturis, ab his discrepant, discrepantiaque illa sua ostendunt, se minime esse Apostolicas. Sicut enim Apostoli inter se diversa non docuerunt, ita et Apostolici non contraria Apostolis ediderunt. Quinimo impium esset adseverare, Apostolos viva voce contraria scriptis suis tradidisse.

6. Paulus disserte dicit: *Eadem se in omnibus ecclesiis docuisse* (1 Cor. iv. 17); et iterum *non alia*, inquit, *scribimus vobis, quam quæ legitis aut etiam agnoscitis* (2 Cor. i. 13). Alibi rursus testatur: *Se et discipulos suos* (i. e., viros Apostolicos), *eadem ambulare via et eodem spiritu pariter facere omnia* (2 Cor. xii. 18). Habuerunt quondam et Judæi suas traditiones seniorum, sed refutatæ sunt graviter a Domino, ostendente, quod earum observatio legi Dei officiat, *et his Deus frustra colatur* (Matt. xv. 8, 9; Marc. vii. 6, 7).

CAP. III.

De Deo, Unitate ejus et Trinitate. [Conf. Aug., Art. I.]

1. Deum credimus et docemus unum esse essentia vel natura, per se subsistentem, sibi ad omnia sufficientem, invisibilem, incorporeum, immensum, æternum, creatorem rerum omnium, tum visibilium tum invisibilium, summum bonum, vivum, et omnia vivificantem et conservantem, omnipotentem et summe sapientem, clementem, sive misericordem, justum atque veracem.

2. Pluralitatem vero Deorum abominamur, quod diserte scriptum sit, *Dominus Deus tuus unus est* (Deut. vi. 4). *Ego sum Dominus Deus tuus, non sint tibi dii alieni ante faciem meam* (Exod. xx. 2, 3). *Ego Dominus et nullus ultra, præter me non est Deus. An non ego Dominus et non est alius præter me solum? Deus justus et salvans, nullus præter me* (Isa. xlv. 5). *Ego Jehovah, Jehovah Deus, misericors, clemens et longanimis, immensæ bonitatis et veritatis* (Exod. xxxiv. 6).

3. Eundem nihilominus Deum immensum, unum et indivisum, credimus et docemus personis inseperabiliter et inconfuse esse distinctum,

Patrem, Filium, et Spiritum Sanctum, ita ut Pater ab æterno Filium generavit, Filius generatione ineffabili genitus sit, Spiritus Sanctus vero procedat ab utroque, idque ab æterno, cum utroque adorandus: ita ut sint tres non quidem Dii sed tres Personæ consubstantiales, coæternæ et coæquales, distinctæ quoad hypostases, et ordine alia aliam præcedens, nulla tamen inæqualitate. Nam quoad naturam vel essentiam ita sunt conjunctæ, ut sint unus Deus, essentiaque divina communis sit Patri, Filio, et Spiritui Sancto.

4. Distinctionem enim personarum manifestam tradidit nobis Scriptura, angelo ad divam virginem inter alia dicente: *Spiritus Sanctus superveniet in te et virtus Altissimi obumbrabit tibi, et quod nascetur sanctum, vocabitur Filius Dei* (Luc. i. 35). Sed et in baptismo Christi auditur vox cœlitus delata super Christo dicens: *Hic est Filius meus dilectus* (Matt. iii. 16, 17; Joh. i. 32). Adparebat et Spiritus Sanctus in specie columbæ. Cumque ipse juberet baptizare Dominus, jussit baptizare *in nomine Patris, et Filii, et Spiritus Sancti* (Matt. xxviii. 19). Item alibi in Evangelio dixit: *Spiritum Sanctum mittet Pater nomine meo* (Joh. xiv. 26). Idem iterum: *Cum,* inquit, *venerit Paracletus, quem ego mittam vobis a Patre, Spiritus veritatis, qui a Patre procedit, ille testimonium perhibebit de me,* etc. (Joh. xv. 26). Breviter recipimus Symbolum Apostolorum, quod veram nobis fidem tradit.

5. Damnamus ergo Judæos et Mahumetistas, omnesque sacrosanctam et adorandam hanc trinitatem blasphemantes. Damnamus item omnes hæreses atque hæreticos, docentes, Filium et Spiritum Sanctum nuncupatione esse Deum; item creatum ac serviens aut alteri officiale esse in trinitate, esse in ea denique inæquale, majus aut minus, corporeum aut corporaliter effigiatum, moribus vel voluntate diversum, aut confusum vel solitarium, quasi Filius et Spiritus Sanctus affectiones et proprietates sint unius Dei Patris, ut Monarchici senserunt, Noëtiani, Praxeas, Patripassiani, Sabellius, Samosatenus, Aëtius, Macedonius, Anthropomorphitæ, Arius, et similes.

CAP. IV.

De Idolis vel Imaginibus Dei, Christi et Divorum.

1. Quoniam vero Deus Spiritus est invisibilis et immensa essentia, non potest sane ulla arte aut imagine exprimi, unde non veremur, cum Scriptura simulacra Dei mera nuncupare mendacia.

2. Rejicimus itaque non modo gentium idola, sed et Christianorum simulacra. Tametsi enim Christus humanam assumserit naturam, non ideo tamen assumsit, ut typum præferret statuariis atque pictoribus. *Negavit se venisse ad solvendum legem et prophetas* (Matt. v. 17); *at lege et prophetis prohibitæ sunt imagines* (Deut. vi. 23; Isa. xl. 18). Negavit, corporalem suam ecclesiæ profuturam præsentiam; Spiritu suo se nobis perpetuo adfuturum promisit (Joh. xvi. 7; 2 Cor. v. 5).

3. Quis ergo crederet, umbram vel simulacrum corporis aliquam conferre piis utilitatem? *Cumque maneat in nobis per Spiritum suum, sumus utique templa Dei* (1 Cor. iii. 16). *Quid autem convenit templo Dei cum simulacris?* (2 Cor. vi. 16). Et quando beati spiritus ac divi cœlites, dum hic viverent, omnem cultum sui averterunt et statuas oppugnarunt (Act. xiv. 15; Apoc. xiv. 7; xxii. 8, 9), cui verisimile videatur, divis cœlitibus et angelis suas placere imagines, ad quas genua flectunt homines, detegunt capita, aliisque prosequuntur honoribus?

4. Ut vero instituantur homines in religione, admoneanturque rerum divinarum et salutis suæ, *prædicare jussit evangelium Dominus* (Marc. xvi. 15), non pingere et pictura laicos erudire: sacramenta quoque instituit, nullibi statuas constituit.

5. Sed et passim, quoquo vertamus oculos, occurrunt res creatæ a Deo vivæ et veræ in oculos nostros, quæ, si observentur, ut par est, longe evidentius movent adspectantem, quam omnes omnium hominum imagines vel picturæ vanæ, immobiles, marcidæ atque mortuæ. De quibus vere dixit Propheta: *Oculos habent et non vident,* etc. (Psa. cxv. 5, 6, 7).

6. Idcirco adprobamus Lactantii, veteris scriptoris, sententiam, dicentis: 'Non est dubium, quin religio nulla sit, ubicunque simulacrum est.' Recte item fecisse adserimus beatum episcopum Epiphanium, qui in foribus ecclesiæ inveniens velum, habens depictam imaginem quasi Christi vel sancti cujuspiam, scidit atque sustulit: quod contra auctoritatem Scripturarum vidisset, in Ecclesia Christi hominis pendere imaginem. Ideoque præcipiebat, ne deinceps in Ecclesia Christi ejusmodi vela, quæ contra religionem nostram veniunt, adpenderentur, sed tolleretur potius illa scrupulositas, quæ indigna sit Ecclesia Christi et populis fidelibus. Præterea adprobamus hanc S. Augustini de vera religione sententiam: 'Non sit nobis religio humanorum operum cul-

tus. Meliores enim sunt ipsi artifices, qui talia fabricantur, quos tamen colere non debemus (Epist. 55).

CAP. V.

DE ADORATIONE, CULTU ET INVOCATIONE DEI PER UNICUM MEDIATOREM JESUM CHRISTUM. ⌊CONF. AUG., ART. XXI.]

1. Deum verum docemus solum adorare et colere. Hunc honorem communicamus nemini, juxta mandatum Domini: *Dominum Deum tuum adorabis, et illum solum coles,* vel, *et huic uni servies* (Matt. iv. 10). Certe omnes Prophetæ gravissime invecti sunt contra populum Israelis, quandocunque deos alienos, non unum solum Deum verum adorarunt et coluerunt.

2. Adorandum autem colendumque docemus Deum, sicuti ipse nos colere docuit, *in spiritu* videlicet *et veritate* (Joh. iv. 29), non cum ulla superstitione, sed cum sinceritate, secundum verbum ejus, ne aliquando ad nos etiam dicat: *Quis requisivit hæc ex manibus vestris?* (Isa. lxvi. 3; Jer. vi. 20.) Nam et Paulus: *Deus non colitur,* ait, *humanis manibus, tanquam, qui ipse aliquo indigeat* (Act. xvii. 25).

3. Eundem solum invocamus in omnibus discriminibus et casibus vitæ nostræ, idque per interventum unici mediatoris et intercessoris nostri Jesu Christi. Diserte enim præceptum est nobis: *Invoca me in die tribulationis, et eruam te, et glorificabis me* (Psa. l. 15). Sed et liberalissime nobis promissum est a Domino dicente: *Quidquid petieritis a Patre meo, dabit vobis* (Joh. xvi. 23); item: *Venite ad me, quotquot laboratis et onerati estis, et ego reficiam vos* (Matt. xi. 28). Et cum scriptum sit: *Quomodo invocabunt eum, in quem non crediderunt?* (Rom. x. 14.) Nos vero cum in solum Deum credamus, solum certe invocamus, et quidem per Christum. *Unus enim Deus,* ait Apostolus, *et unus mediator Dei et hominum Jesus Christus* (1 Tim. ii. 5), item, *Si quis peccaverit, advocatum habemus apud Patrem Jesum Christum justum* (1 Joh. ii. 1).

4. Proinde sanctos cœlites sive divos nec adoramus, neque colimus nec invocamus, neque illos coram Patre pro intercessoribus aut mediatoribus nostris agnoscimus. Sufficit enim nobis Deus et Mediator Christus, neque honorem soli Deo et Filio ejus debitum aliis commu

nicamus; quod ille diserte dixerit: *Gloriam meam alteri non dabo*
(Isa. xlii. 8), et quod Petrus dixit: *Non aliud hominibus nomen da-*
tum est, in quo oporteat salvos fieri, nisi nomen Christi (Act. iv. 12).
In quo sane, qui per fidem adquiescunt, non quærunt extra Christum
quidquam.

5. Interim divos nec contemnimus, nec vulgariter de eis sentimus.
Agnoscimus enim, eos esse viva Christi membra, amicos Dei, qui carnem et mundum gloriose vicerunt. Diligimus ergo illos ut fratres, et
honoramus etiam, non tamen cultu aliquo, sed honorabili de iis existi-
matione, denique laudibus justis. Imitamur item eos. Nam imitatores
fidei virtutumque ipsorum, consortes item æternæ salutis esse, illis æternum apud Deum cohabitare et cum eis in Christo exsultare, desideriis
votisque ardentissimis exoptamus. Atque hac in parte adprobamus
illam S. Augustini de vera religione sententiam: 'Non sit nobis religio cultus hominum mortuorum. Quia si pie vixerint, non sic ha-
bentur, ut tales quærant honores, sed illum a nobis coli volunt, quo
illuminante, lætantur, meriti sui nos esse conservos. Honorandi ergo
sunt propter imitationem, non adorandi propter religionem,' etc.

6. Multo vero minus credimus, reliquias divorum adorandas esse aut
colendas. Veteres isti sancti satis honorasse videbantur mortuos suos,
si honeste mandassent terræ reliquias, postquam astra petiisset spiritus: ac omnium nobilissimas reliquias majorum æstimabant esse virtutes, doctrinam et fidem: quas ut commendabant cum laude mortuorum, ita eas exprimere adnitebantur, dum vivebant in terris.

7. Illi ipsi veteres non jurarunt, nisi per nomen solius Dei Jehovah,
sicuti lege divina est præceptum: qua sicut vetitum est jurare *per*
nomina alienorum deorum (Exod. xxiii. 13; Deut. x. 20), sic nos juramenta per divos requisita non præstamus. Rejicimus ergo in his omnibus doctrinam divis cœlitibus plus nimium tribuentem.

CAP. VI.

DE PROVIDENTIA DEI.

1. Dei hujus sapientis, æterni et omnipotentis providentia credimus
cuncta in cœlo et in terra et in creaturis omnibus conservari et gubernari. David enim testificatur et ait: *Excelsus super omnes gentes*
Dominus, et super cœlos gloria ejus. Quis sicut Dominus Deus

noster, qui in altis habitat, et se demittit, ut inspiciat, quæ sunt in cœlo et in terra? (Psa. cxiii. 5, 6). Idem rursus: *Omnes vias meas prævidisti, quia non est verbum in lingua mea, quod non universum noveris, Domine* (Psa. cxxxix. 3, 4). Testificatur et Paulus, et ait: *Per ipsum vivimus, movemur et sumus* (Act. xvii. 28). Et: *Ex illo et per illum et in illum omnia* (Rom. xi. 36).

2. Verissime ergo et secundum Scripturam pronunciavit Augustinus (in libro De agone Christi, cap. viii.): '*Dominus dixit, nonne duo passeres asse veniunt, et unus eorum non cadit in terram sine voluntate Patris vestri?* (Matt. x. 29). Ita vero loquens ostendere voluit, quidquid vilissimum homines putant, omnipotentia Domini gubernari. Sic enim et *volatilia cœli ab eo pasci, et lilia agri ab eo vestiri,* veritas loquitur, *quæ capillos etiam nostros numeratos esse dicit,* etc. (Matt. vi. 26–29).'

3. Damnamus ergo Epicureos, providentiam Dei abnegantes, omnesque illos, qui blaspheme dicunt, Deum versari circa cardines cœli, et nos atque nostra nec videre nec curare. Damnavit hos etiam David, propheta regius, qui dixit: *Quousque Domine! quousque impii exsultabunt? Dicunt: Dominus non videt, neque intelligit Deus Jacob. Intelligite stupidi in populo et stulti! quando demum sapietis? Is, qui aurem condidit, an non audiret? et qui oculum finxit, quomodo non videret?* (Psa. xciv. 7–9).

4. Interim vero media, per quæ operatur divina providentia, non aspernamur, ut inutilia, sed his hactenus nos accomodandos esse docemus, quatenus in verbo Dei nobis commendantur. Unde illorum voces temerarias improbamus, qui dicunt: si providentia Dei omnia geruntur, inutiles certe sunt conatus nostri et studia nostra: satis fuerit, si omnia divinæ permittamus providentiæ gubernanda, nec erit, quod porro simus solliciti de re ulla, aut quidquam faciamus. Tametsi enim Paulus agnosceret, se in Dei providentia navigare, qui ipse dixerat, *oportet te et Romæ testificari* (Act. xxiii. 11): qui insuper promiserat dixeratque: *Jactura nulla erit ullius animæ, nec cadet pilus de capite vestro* (Act. xxvii. 22, 34); nihilominus meditantibus fugam nautis, dicit idem ille Paulus centurioni et militibus: *Nisi hi in navi manserint, vos servari non poteritis* (ver. 31). Deus enim, qui cuilibet rei suum destinavit finem, is et principium et media, per quæ ad finem usque pervenitur, ordinavit. Ethnici fortunæ res attribuunt cœcæ, vel

incerto casui. S. Jacobus non vult, ut dicamus, *hodie et cras in illam urbem proficiscemur et negotiabimur,* sed addit: *Pro eo, quod dicere debueritis, si Dominus voluerit et vixerimus, hoc vel illud faciemus* (Jac. iv. 13, 15); et Augustinus: 'Omnia quæ vanis videntur in rerum natura temere fieri, non faciunt, nisi verbum ejus' (Enarrat. in Psa. cxlviii.). Ita videbatur forte fortuna fieri, quod Saul quærens Patris asinas, incidit in prophetam Samuelem, sed antea dixerat Dominus ad prophetam: *Cras mittam ad te virum de tribu Benjamin* (1 Sam. ix. 16).

CAP. VII.

De Creatione Rerum Omnium, de Angelis, Diabolo, et Homine.

1. Deus hic bonus et omnipotens creavit omnia, cum visibilia, tum invisibilia, per Verbum suum coæternum, eademque quoque conservat per Spiritum suum coæternum, testificante Davide atque dicente: *Verbo Dei cœli facti sunt, et in Spiritu oris ejus omnis virtus eorum* (Psa. xxxiii. 6). *Omnia autem, quæ condidit Deus, erant,* ut Scriptura ait, *valde bona* (Gen. i. 31), et ad utilitatem usumque hominis condita.

2. Cuncta vero illa dicimus ab uno profecta esse principio. Damnamus ergo Manichæos et Marcionitas, qui impie fingebant duas substantias atque naturas boni et mali, duo item principia, et duos sibi adversos Deos, bonum et malum.

3. Inter omnes creaturas præstant angeli atque homines. De angelis pronunciat Scriptura divina: *Qui creat angelos suos spiritus, et ministros suos flammam ignis* (Psa. civ. 4); item: *Nonne omnes sunt administratorii spiritus, qui in ministerium emittuntur, propter eos, qui hæredes sunt salutis?* (Heb. i. 14).

Dominus vero Jesus ipse testificatur de diabolo: *Ille,* inquit, *homicida erat ab initio, et in veritate non stetit, quia non est veritas in eo; cum loquitur mendacium, ex propriis loquitur, quia mendax est, atque ejus rei pater* (Joh. viii. 44).

4. Docemus ergo, angelos alios quidem perstitisse in obedientia, ac ad fidele Dei et hominum ministerium esse deputatos: alios vero sua sponte lapsos, et in exitium esse præcipitatos, factosque esse omnis boni fideliumque hostes, etc.

5. Jam vero de homine dicit Scriptura, quod ab initio conditus sit

bonus, ad imaginem et similitudinem Dei; quod Deus collocaverit eum in paradisum, subjeceritque ei omnia (Gen. i. 27, 28; ii. 8; v. 1). Id, quod David magnifice celebrat in Psa. viii. Addidit ei insuper conjugem ac benedixit eis (ii. 22 sqq.).

6. Dicimus autem, constare hominem duabus ac diversis quidem substantiis, in una persona, anima immortali, utpote quæ separata a corpore, nec dormit, nec interit, et corpore mortali, quod tamen in ultimo judicio a mortuis resuscitabitur, ut totus homo inde, vel in vita, vel in morte, æternum maneat.

7. Damnamus omnes, qui irrident aut subtilibus disputationibus in dubium vocant immortalitatem animarum, aut animam dicunt dormire, aut partem esse Dei. Breviter, damnamus omnes omnium opiniones, quotquot diversa sentiunt de creatione, de angelis, et dæmonibus, et homine, ab iis, quæ nobis tradita sunt per Scripturas Sanctas, in Apostolica Christi Ecclesia.

CAP. VIII.

DE LAPSU HOMINIS, ET PECCATO [CONF. AUG. 2, ART. XIX.], ET CAUSA PECCATI.

1. Fuit homo ab initio a Deo conditus ad imaginem Dei, in justitia et sanctitate veritatis, bonus et rectus. Sed instinctu serpentis, et sua culpa a bonitate et rectitudine deficiens, peccato, morti, variisque calamitatibus factus est obnoxius. Et qualis factus est a lapsu, tales sunt omnes, qui ex ipso prognati sunt, peccato, inquam, morti, variisque obnoxii calamitatibus.

2. Peccatum autem intelligimus esse nativam illam hominis corruptionem, ex primis illis nostris parentibus, in nos omnes derivatam vel propagatam, qua concupiscentiis pravis immersi, et a bono aversi, ad omne vero malum propensi, pleni omni nequitia, diffidentia, contemtu et odio Dei, nihil boni ex nobis ipsis facere, imo ne cogitare quidem possumus.

3. Quinimo accedentibus jam etiam annis, cogitationibus, dictis et factis pravis contra legem Dei admissis, corruptos fructus, mala arbore dignos, proferimus (Matt. xii. 33): quo nomine, merito nostro, iræ Dei obnoxii, pœnis subjicimur justis; adeoque a Deo abjecti essemus omnes, nisi reduxisset nos Christus liberator.

4. Per mortem itaque intelligimus non tantum corpoream mortem, quæ omnibus nobis semel, propter peccata, est obeunda, sed etiam supplicia sempiterna, peccatis et corruptioni nostræ debita. Nam Apostolus: *Eramus mortui,* inquit, *delictis ac peccatis, et eramus naturâ filii iræ, sicut et ceteri. Sed Deus, qui dives est misericordia, cum essemus mortui per delicta, convivificavit nos una cum Christo* (Eph. ii. 1, 3, 4, 5). Item: *Sicut per unum hominem peccatum in mundum introiit, ac per peccatum mors, et ita in omnes homines mors transiit, in quo omnes peccarunt* (Rom. v. 12).

5. Agnoscimus ergo, in omnibus hominibus esse originale peccatum; agnoscimus, omnia alia peccata, quæ ex hoc oriuntur, et dici, et vere esse peccata, qualicunque nomine nuncupentur, sive mortalia, sive venialia, sive illud quoque, quod vocatur *peccatum in Spiritum Sanctum, quod nunquam remittitur* (Marc. iii. 29; 1 Joh. v. 16).

6. Fatemur etiam, peccata non esse æqualia, licet ex eodem corruptionis et incredulitatis fonte exoriantur, sed alia aliis esse graviora. Sicut Dominus dixit: *Sodomæ tolerabilius futurum, quam urbi rejicienti verbum evangelii* (Matt. x. 14, 15; xi. 24; 1 Joh. v. 16, 17).

7. Damnamus ergo omnes, qui his contraria docuerunt, imprimis vero Pelagium et omnes Pelagianos, una cum Jovinianistis, peccata cum Stoicis paria facientibus. Sentimus per omnia in hac causa cum S. Augustino, qui sua ex Scripturis Sanctis protulit atque defendit.

8. Damnamus præterea Florinum et Blastum, contra quos et Irenæus scripsit, et omnes, qui Deum faciunt auctorem peccati. Cum diserte scriptum sit: *Tu non es Deus, qui velit iniquitatem. Odisti omnes, qui operantur iniquitatem, perdes omnes, qui loquuntur mendacium* (Psa. v. 5–7). Et iterum: *Cum loquitur diabolus mendacium, ex propriis loquitur, quia mendax est, et pater ejus rei* (Joh. viii. 44). Sed et in nobis ipsis satis est vitii corruptionisque, ut nihil necesse sit, Deum infundere nobis novam aut auctiorem pravitatem.

9. Proinde quando dicitur in Scripturis Deus indurare, excœcare, et tradere in reprobum sensum, intelligendum id est, quod justo judicio Deus id faciat, tanquam judex et ultor justus. Denique quotiescunque Deus aliquid mali in Scriptura facere dicitur atque videtur, non ideo dicitur, quod homo malum non faciat, sed quod Deus fieri sinat et non prohibeat, justo suo judicio, qui prohibere potuisset, si voluisset; vel, quod malo hominum bene utatur, ut peccatis fratrum Josephi: vel

quod ipse peccata gubernet, ne latius, quam par est, erumpant atque grassentur. S. Augustinus, in Enchiridio suo, 'Miro modo, inquit, et ineffabili non fit præter voluntatem ejus, quod etiam fit contra volun-tatem ejus. Quia non fieret, si fieri non sineret. Nec utique nolens sinit, sed volens. Nec sineret bonus fieri male, nisi omnipotens etiam de malo facere posset bene.' Hæc ille.[1]

10. Reliquas quæstiones, an Deus voluerit labi Adamum, aut impu-lerit ad lapsum, aut quare lapsum non impediverit, et similes quæs-tiones deputamus inter curiosas (nisi forte cum hæreticorum aut alio-qui importunorum hominum improbitas cogit ista etiam ex verbo Dei explicare, sicut fecerunt non raro pii ecclesiæ doctores), scientes Domi-num prohibuisse, ne homo ederet de fructu prohibito, et transgressio-nem punivisse; sed et mala non esse, quæ fiunt, respectu providentiæ Dei, voluntatis ac potestatis Dei, sed respectu Satanæ et voluntatis nostræ, voluntati Dei repugnantis.

CAP. IX.

DE LIBERO ARBITRIO ADEOQUE VIRIBUS HOMINIS. [CONF. AUG., ART. XVIII.]

1. Docemus in hac causa, quæ semper in Ecclesia multas peperit conflictationes, conditionem vel statum hominis triplicem esse conside-randum. Principio qualis fuerit homo ante lapsum, rectus nimirum et liber, qui et in bono manere et ad malum potuerit declinare; declina-verit autem ad malum, implicaveritque peccato et morti, et se, et omne genus mortalium, sicuti dictum est antea.

2. Deinde considerandum est, qualis fuerit homo post lapsum. Non sublatus est quidem homini intellectus, non erepta ei voluntas, et pror-sus in lapidem vel truncum[2] est commutatus; ceterum illa ita sunt im-mutata et inminuta in homine, ut non possint amplius, quod potuerunt ante lapsum. Intellectus enim obscuratus est, voluntas vero ex libera facta est voluntas serva. Nam servit peccato, non nolens, sed volens.

3. Etenim voluntas non noluntas dicitur. Ergo quoad malum sive peccatum, homo non coactus vel a Deo vel a diabolo, sed sua sponte,

---

· *Hæc ille* are not in the Zurich MS.

[2] Expressions of Luther and Flacius, afterwards sanctioned by the Formula of Concord, Art. II.

malum facit; et hac parte liberrimi est arbitrii. Quod vero non raro cernimus, pessima hominis facinora et consilia impediri a Deo, ne finem suum consequantur, non tollit homini libertatem in malo, sed Deus potentia sua prævenit, quod homo alias libere instituit, sicut fratres Josephi Josephum libere instituunt tollere; sed non possunt, quod Dei consilio aliud visum esset.

4. Quantum vero ad bonum et ad virtutes, intellectus hominis non recte judicat de divinis ex semetipso. Requirit enim Scriptura Evangelica et Apostolica regenerationem *abs quolibet* nostrûm, qui salvari velimus. Unde nativitas prior ex Adamo ad salutem nihil nobis confert. Paulus, *animalis homo*, ait, *non percipit ea, quæ sunt Spiritus Dei*, etc. (1 Cor. ii. 14). Idem: *Negat alicubi nos idoneos esse, ex nobis ipsis cogitare aliquid boni* (2 Cor. iii. 5).

5. Constat vero, mentem vel intellectum ducem esse voluntatis, cum autem cœcus sit dux, claret, quousque et voluntas pertingat. Proinde nullum est ad bonum homini arbitrium liberum, nondum renato, vires nullæ ad perficiendum bonum. Dominus in Evangelio dicit: *Amen, amen dico vobis, quod omnis, qui facit peccatum, servus est peccati* (Joh. viii. 34). Et Paulus Apostolus: *Affectus carnis*, inquit, *inimicitia est adversus Deum, nam legi Dei non subditur, imo ne potest quidem* (Rom. viii. 7).

6. Porro terrenarum rerum intelligentia in lapso homine non est nulla. Reliquit enim Deus ex misericordia ingenium, multum tamen distans ab eo, quod inerat ante lapsum. Jubet Deus excolere ingenium, et addit dona simul et profectum. Et manifestum est, quam nihil proficiamus in artibus omnibus sine benedictione Dei. Scriptura certe omnes artes ad Deum refert. Nam et ethnici retulerunt artium origines ad inventores Deos.

7. Postremo videndum, an regenerati sint liberi arbitrii, et quatenus. In regeneratione intellectus illuminatur, per Spiritum Sanctum, ut et mysteria et voluntatem Dei intelligat. Et voluntas ipsa non tantum mutatur per Spiritum, set etiam instruitur facultatibus, ut sponte velit et possit bonum (Rom. viii. 5, 6). Nisi hoc dederimus, negabimus Christianam libertatem, et inducemus legalem servitutem. Sed et Propheta facit Deum loquentem: *Dabo legem meam in mentes illorum, et in cordibus eorum inscribam eas* (Jer. xxxi. 33). Dominus quoque dicit in Evangelio: *Si Filius vos liberaverit, vere liberi estis*

(Joh. viii. 36; Ezek. xxxvi. 26). Paulus quoque ad Philippenses (i. 24): *Vobis, donatum est,* inquit, *pro Christo, non solum, ut in eum credatis, sed etiam ut pro illo patiamini.* Et iterum: *Persuasum habeo, quod is, qui cœpit in vobis bonum opus, perficiet usque ad diem Domini Jesu* (Phil. i. 6); item: *Deus est, qui agit in vobis, et ut velitis, et ut efficiatis* (Phil. ii. 13).

8. Ubi interim duo observanda esse docemus: *Primum,* regeneratos in boni electione et operatione, non tantum agere passive, sed active. Aguntur enim a Deo, ut agant ipsi, quod agunt. Recte enim Augustinus adducit illud, quod Deus dicitur noster adjutor. Nequit autem adjuvari, nisi is, qui aliquid agit. Manichæi spoliabant hominem omni actione, et veluti saxum et truncum faciebant.

9. *Secundum,* in regeneratis remanere infirmitatem. Cum enim inhabitet in nobis peccatum, et caro in renatis obluctetur spiritui, in finem usque vitæ nostræ, non expedite omnino perficiunt regenerati, quod instituerant. Confirmantur hæc ab Apostolo ad Rom. vii. et Gal. v.

10. Proinde infirmum est nostrum illud liberum arbitrium, propter reliquias remanentis in nobis, ad finem usque vitæ nostræ, veteris Adami, agnatæque corruptionis humanæ. Interim cum carnis vires et reliquiæ veteris hominis non ita sint efficaces, ut extinguant penitus Spiritus operationem; idcirco fideles liberi dicuntur, ita tamen, ut agnoscant infirmitatem, et nihil glorientur de libero arbitrio. Semper enim animis fidelium obversari debet, quod toties inculcat beatus Augustinus ex Apostolo: *Quid habes, quod non accepisti, et si accepisti, quid gloriaris, quasi non acceperis?* (1 Cor. iv. 7). His accedit, quod non statim evenit, quod institueramus. Eventus enim rerum positi sunt in manu Dei. Unde Paulus orat Dominum, ut prosperet iter suum (Rom. i. 10). Unde vel hac causa infirmum est liberum arbitrium.

11. Ceterum nemo negat, in externis, et regenitos et non regenitos habere liberum arbitrium; habet enim homo hanc constitutionem cum animantibus aliis (quibus non est inferior) communem, ut alia velit, alia nolit. Ita loqui potest, aut tacere, domo egredi, vel domi manere, etc. Quamvis semper et hic potentia Dei observanda sit: quæ effecit, ut Balaam eo non posset pertingere, quo volebat (Num. xxiv.), neque Zacharias, rediens ex templo, loqui posset, prout volebat (Luc. i. 22).

12. Damnamus hac in causa Manichæos, qui negant, homini bono ex libero arbitrio fuisse initium mali. Damnamus etiam Pelagianos, qui dicunt, hominem malum sufficienter habere liberum arbitrium, ad faciendum præceptum bonum. Redarguuntur utrique a Scriptura Sancta, quæ illis dicit: *Fecit Deus hominem rectum* (Eccles. vii. 29), his vero dicit: *Si Filius vos liberaverit, vere liberi estis* (Joh. viii. 36).

CAP. X.

DE PRÆDESTINATIONE DEI ET ELECTIONE SANCTORUM.

1. Deus ab æterno prædestinavit vel elegit libere et mera sua gratia, nullo hominum respectu, sanctos, quos vult salvos facere in Christo, juxta illud Apostoli: *Deus elegit nos in ipso, antequam jacerentur fundamenta mundi* (Eph. i. 4), et iterum: *Qui salvos fecit nos, et vocavit vocatione sancta, non secundum opera nostra, sed secundum suum propositum et gratiam, quæ data quidem est nobis, per Jesum Christum, ante tempora æterna, sed palam facta est nunc per apparitionem Servatoris nostri Jesu Christi* (2 Tim. i. 9, 10).

2. Ergo non sine medio, licet non propter ullum meritum nostrum, sed in Christo et propter Christum, nos elegit Deus, ut qui jam sunt in Christo insiti per fidem, illi ipsi etiam sint electi, reprobi vero, qui sunt extra Christum, secundum illud Apostoli: *Vos ipsos tentate, num sitis in fide. An non cognoscitis vosmet ipsos, quod Jesus Christus in vobis est? nisi sicubi reprobi estis* (2 Cor. xiii. 5).

3. Denique electi sunt sancti in Christo per Deum ad finem certum, quem et ipsum exponit Apostolus et ait: *Elegit nos in ipso, ut essemus sancti et irreprehensibiles coram illo per caritatem; qui prædestinavit nos, ut adoptaret in filios per Jesum Christum, in sese, ut laudetur gloria gratiæ suæ* (Eph. i. 4, 5, 6).

4. Et quamvis Deus norit, qui sint sui, et alicubi mentio fiat paucitatis electorum, bene sperandum est tamen de omnibus, neque temere reprobis quisquam est adnumerandus. Paulus certe ad Philippenses: *Gratias ago*, inquit, *pro omnibus vobis* (loquitur autem de tota Ecclesia Philippensi), *quod veneritis in communionem evangelii, persuasum habens, quod is, qui cœpit opus bonum in vobis, perficiet, sicut justum est, ut hoc sentiam de vobis omnibus* (Phil. i. 3–7).

5. Et cum (Luc. xiii.) rogaretur Dominus: an pauci sint, qui sal-

ventur? non respondet Dominus ac dicit, paucos aut plures fore servandos, aut perdendos, sed hortatur potius, ut quisque contendat ingredi per portam arctam. Quasi dixerit, vestrum non est, de his curiosius inquirere, sed magis adniti, ut per rectam viam cœlum ingrediamini.

6. Proinde non probamus impias quorundam voces, qui dicunt: pauci sunt electi, et cum mihi non constet, an sim in illo paucorum numero, genium meum non fraudabo. Alii dicunt: si prædestinatus vel electus sum a Deo, nihil impediet me a salute certo jam definita, quicquid tandem designavero. Si vero sum de reproborum numero, nulla me vel fides vel pœnitentia juvabit, cum definitio Dei mutari non possit. Itaque inutiles sunt doctrinæ et admonitiones omnes. Nam contra hos pugnat illud Apostoli: *Oportet servum Domini propensum esse ad docendum, erudientem eos, qui obsistunt, si quando det Deus illis pœnitentiam, ad agnoscendum veritatem, ut resipiscant a laqueo diaboli, capti ab eo ad ejus voluntatem* (2 Tim. ii. 24–26).

7. Sed et Augustinus de bono perseverantiæ cap. xiv. et conseq. ostendit, utrumque esse prædicandum et liberæ electionis prædestinationisque gratiam, et admonitiones et doctrinas salutares. Improbamus itaque illos, qui extra Christum quærunt: an sint electi? Et quid ante omnem æternitatem de ipsis statuerit Deus?

8. Audienda est enim prædicatio Evangelii, eique credendum est: et pro indubitato habendum, si credis ac sis in Christo, electum te esse. Pater enim prædestinationis suæ æternam sententiam, sicut modo ex Apostolo (2 Tim. i.) exposui, in Christo nobis aperuit. Docendum ergo et considerandum ante omnia, quantus amor Patris erga nos in Christo nobis sit revelatus; audiendum, quid nobis quotidie in Evangelio ipse Dominus prædicet, quomodo vocet et dicat: *Venite ad me omnes, qui laborati et onerati estis, ego vos reficiam* (Matt. xi. 28). *Sic Deus dilexit mundum, ut unigenitum dederit pro mundo, ut omnis, qui credit in eum non pereat, sed habeat vitam æternam* (Joh. iii. 16). Item: *Non est voluntas Patris, ut quisquam de his pusillis pereat* (Matt. xviii. 14).

9. Christus itaque sit speculum, in quo prædestinationem nostram contemplemur. Satis perspicuum et firmum habebimus testimonium, nos in libro vitæ inscriptos esse, si communicaverimus cum Christo, et is in vera fide noster sit, nos ejus simus. Consoletùr nos in tentatione

præstinationis, qua vix alia est periculosior, quod promissiones Dei
sunt universales fidelibus, quod ipse ait: *Petite et accipietis.* *Omnis*
qui petit, accipit (Luc. xi. 9, 10).

10. Quod denique cum universa Dei Ecclesia oramus: 'Pater noster, qui es in cœlis;' et quod baptismo sumus insiti corpori Christi, et
pascimur in Ecclesia ejus carne et sanguine frequenter ad vitam æternam. His confirmati cum *timore et tremore,* juxta Pauli præceptum,
nostram salutem operari jubemur (Phil. ii. 12).

CAP. XI.

DE JESU CHRISTO, VERO DEO ET HOMINE, UNICO MUNDI SALVATORE.
[CONF. AUG., ART. III.]

1. Credimus præterea et docemus, Filium Dei Dominum nostrum
Jesum Christum ab æterno prædestinatum vel præordinatum esse a
Patre salvatorem mundi: credimusque hunc esse genitum, non tantum, cum ex virgine Maria carnem adsumsit, nec tantum ante jacta
fundamenta mundi, sed ante omnem æternitatem, et quidem a Patre,
ineffabiliter. Nam Esaias dixit: *Generationem ejus quis enarrabit?*
(liii. 8); et Micheas: *Et egressus ejus a diebus æternitatis* (v. 2).
Nam et Joannes in Evangelio dixit: *In principio erat verbum, et*
verbum erat apud Deum, et Deus erat verbum (i. 1).

2. Proinde Filius est Patri juxta divinitatem coæqualis et consub-
itantialis, Deus verus, non nuncupatione, aut adoptione, aut ulla dignatione, sed substantia atque natura (Phil. ii. 6), sicut Joannes Apostolus
iterum dixit: *Hic est verus Deus, et vita æterna* (1 Joh. v. 20); et
Paulus quoque: *Filium,* ait, *constituit hæredem omnium, per quem*
et secula fecit : idem est splendor gloriæ et character substantiæ ejus,
portans omnia verbo potentiæ suæ (Heb. i. 2, 3). Nam in Evangelio
ipse quoque Dominus dixit: *Pater glorifica tu me apud temet ipsum*
gloria, quam habui, priusquam hic mundus esset, apud te (Joh. xvii.
5). Nam et alibi in Evangelio scribitur: *Judæi quærebant occidere*
Jesum, quod Patrem suum dixisset Deum, æqualem se ipsum faciens
Deo (Joh. v. 18).

3. Abominamur ergo Arii et omnium Arianorum impiam contra
Filium Dei doctrinam, imprimis vero Michælis Serveti, Hispani et
Servetanorum omnium blasphemias, quas contra Dei Filium Satan per

illos, veluti ex inferis hausit et in orbem audacissime et impiissime dispergit.

4. Eundem quoque æterni Dei æternum Filium credimus et docemus hominis factum esse filium, ex semine Abrahæ atque Davidis, non ex viri coitu, quod Ebion dixit, sed conceptum purissime ex Spiritu Sancto, et natum ex Maria semper virgine : sicut diligenter nobis historia explicat evangelica (Matt. i.). Et Paulus ait: *Nullibi angelos adsumit, sed semen Abrahæ* (Heb. ii. 16). Joannes item Apostolus, *qui non credit, Jesum Christum in carne venisse, ex Deo non est* (1 Joh. iv. 3). Caro ergo Christi nec phantastica fuit, nec cœlitus adlata, sicuti Valentinus et Marcion somniabant.

5. Præterea anima fuit Domino nostro Jesu Christo non absque sensu et ratione, ut Apollinaris sentiebat, neque caro absque anima, ut Eunomius docebat, sed anima cum ratione sua, et caro cum sensibus suis, per quos sensus veros dolores tempore passionis suæ sustinuit; sicuti et ipse testatus est, et dixit: *Tristis est anima mea usque ad mortem* (Matt. xxvi. 36–38), *et nunc anima mea turbata est* (Joh. xii. 27).

6. Agnoscimus ergo in uno atque eodem Domino nostro Jesu Christo duas naturas vel substantias, divinam et humanam (Heb. iv. 14); et has ita dicimus conjunctas et unitas esse, ut absorptæ, aut confusæ, aut inmixtæ non sint, sed salvis potius et permanentibus naturarum proprietatibus, in una persona, unitæ vel conjunctæ; ita ut unum Christum Dominum, non duos veneremur: unum inquam verum Deum, et hominem, juxta divinam naturam Patri, juxta humanam vero nobis hominibus consubstantialem, et per omnia similem, peccato excepto (Heb. iv. 15).

7. Etenim, ut Nestorianum dogma ex uno Christo duos faciens, et unionem personæ dissolvens, abominamur: ita Eutychetis et Monothelitarum vel Monophysicorum vesaniam, expungentem naturæ humanæ proprietatem execramur[1] penitus.

8. Ergo minime docemus, naturam in Christo divinam passam esse, aut Christum secundum humanam naturam adhuc esse in hoc mundo, adeoque esse ubique. Neque enim vel sentimus, vel docemus, veritatem corporis Christi a clarificatione desiisse, aut deificatam, adeoque sic deificatam esse, ut suas proprietates, quoad corpus et animam depo-

---

[1] *Execramur* is omitted in Kindler's edition.

suerit, ac prorsus in naturam divinam abierit, unaque duntaxat substantia esse cœperit.

9. Et proinde Schwenkfeldii similiumque leptologorum inargutas argutias, intricatas, obscurasque, et parum sibi constantes hac de re dissertationes, haudquaquam probamus aut recipimus, neque Schwenkfeldiani sumus.

10. Præterea credimus, *Dominum nostrum Jesum Christum vere passum et mortuum esse pro nobis,* sicut Petrus ait, *carne* (1 Pet. iv. 8). Abominamur Jacobitarum et omnium Turcarum, passionem Domini exsecrantium, impiissimam vesaniam. Interim non negamus et *Dominum gloriæ* juxta verba Pauli, *crucifixum esse pro nobis* (2 Cor. ii. 8). Nam communicationem idiomatum, ex Scripturis petitam, et ab universa vetustate in explicandis componendisque Scripturarum locis in speciem pugnantibus, usurpatam, religiose et reverenter recipimus et usurpamus.

11. Credimus et docemus, eundem Dominum nostrum Jesum Christum vera sua carne, in qua crucifixus et mortuus fuerat, a mortuis resurrexisse, et non aliam pro sepulta excitasse, aut spiritum pro carne suscepisse, sed veritatem corporis retinuisse. Ergo dum discipuli ejus arbitrarentur, se Domini spiritum videre, exhibet eis manus atque pedes, stigmatibus utique clavorum et vulnerum notatas, et addit: *Adspicite manus meas et pedes meos : quia ego ipse sum. Contrectate me et videte : quia spiritus carnem et ossa non habet, sicut videtis me habere* (Luc. xxiv. 39).

12. In eadem illa carne sua credimus adscendisse Dominum nostrum Jesum Christum, supra omnes cœlos adspectabiles, in ipsum cœlum supremum, sedem videlicet Dei et beatorum, ad dextram Dei Patris, quæ, etsi et gloriæ majestatisque consortium æquale significet, accipitur tamen et pro loco certo, de quo in Evangelio loquens Dominus dicit, *se abiturum et suis paraturum locum* (Joh. xiv. 2). Sed et Apostolus Petrus : *Oportet Christum,* inquit, *cœlum accipere, usque ad tempus restitutionis omnium* (Act. iii. 21).

13. [Conf. Aug., Art. XVII.] Ex cœlis autem idem ille redibit in judicium, tum, quando summa erit in mundo consceleratio, et antichristus, corrupta religione vera, superstitione impietateque omnia opplevit, et sanguine atque flamma ecclesiam crudeliter vastavit. Redibit autem Christus, adserturus suos, et aboliturus adventu suo anti-

christum, judicaturusque vivos et mortuos. Resurgent enim mortui, et qui illa die (quæ omnibus incognita est creaturis) superstites futuri sunt, mutabuntur in momento oculi, fidelesque omnes una obviam Christo rapientur in aëra, ut inde cum ipso ingrediantur in sedes beatas sine fine victuri (Act. xvii. 31; 1 Thess. iv. 15–17; Marc. xiii. 32; 1 Cor. xv. 51; Matt. xxv. 41). Increduli vero vel impii descendent cum dæmonibus ad tartara, in sempiternum arsuri, atque ex tormentis numquam liberandi.

14. Damnamus ergo omnes negantes veram carnis resurrectionem (2 Tim. ii. 18), aut qui cum Joanne Hierosolymitano, contra quem scripsit Hieronymus, non recte sentiunt de clarificatis corporibus. Damnamus eos, qui senserunt, et dæmones et impios omnes aliquando servandos, et pœnarum finem futurum. Simpliciter enim pronuncia-vit Dominus: *Ignis eorum numquam exstinguitur, et vermis eorum non moritur* (Marc. ix. 44). Damnamus præterea Judaica somnia, quod ante judicii diem aureum in terris sit futurum seculum, et pii regna mundi occupaturi, oppressis suis hostibus impiis. Nam Evangelica veri-tas (Matt. xxiv. et xxv.; Luc., item xviii.) et Apostolica doctrina (2 Thess ii., et in 2 Tim. iii. et iv. capite) longe aliud perhibere inveniuntur.

15. Porro passione vel morte sua omnibusque adeo, quæ a suo in carne adventu nostra causa fecit et pertulit, reconciliavit omnibus fidelibus Dominus noster Patrem cœlestem, expiavit peccatum, exarmavit mortem, condemnationemque et inferos confregit, ac resurrectione sua ex mor-tuis vitam immortalitatemque reduxit ac restituit (Rom. iv. 25; x. 4; 1 Cor. xv. 17; Joh. vi. 45; xi. 25, 26). Ipse enim est justitia nostra, vita et resurrectio, denique plenitudo et absolutio fidelium omnium, salusque et sufficientia abundantissima. Apostolus enim, *sic placuit Patri,* inquit, *omnem in ipso habitare plenitudinem, et in ipso estis completi* (Col. i. 19 et ii. 10).

16. Docemus enim ac credimus, hunc Jesum Christum, Dominum nostrum, unicum et æternum generis humani adeoque totius mundi esse Servatorem, in quo per fidem servati sint, quotquot ante legem, sub lege, et sub Evangelio salvati sunt, et quotquot adhuc in finem usque seculi salvabuntur. Nam ipse Dominus in Evangelio dicit: *Qui non intrat per ostium in stabulum ovium, sed adscendit ali-unde, ille fur est et latro. Ego sum ostium ovium* (Joh. x. 1, 2). Item alibi in eodem Evangelio (viii. 56): *Abraham vidit diem meum, et*

gavisus est.   Sed et Petrus Apostolus: *Non est in quoquam alio,* inquit, *nisi in Christo salus. Neque aliud nomen est sub cœlo datum
inter homines, in quo oporteat nos salvos fieri* (Act. iv. 12 et x. 43).
*Credimus ergo per gratiam Domini Jesu Christi nos servatum iri,
sicuti et Patres nostros* (Act. xv. 11).   Nam et Paulus ait: *Omnes
Patres nostros eandem escam spiritualem edisse; et omnes eundem
potum spiritualem bibisse; bibisse autem de spirituali ipsos conse-
quente petra, petram vero Christum fuisse* (1 Cor. x. 3, 4).   Ideoque
legimus, et Joannem dixisse, *Christum esse agnum illum, qui occisus
sit ab origine mundi* (Apoc. xiii. 8); et Baptistam testatum: *Christum
esse agnum illum Dei, qui tollat peccatum mundi* (Joh. i. 29).

17. Unde pleno ore profitemur, et prædicamus, Jesum Christum
unicum esse mundi Redemptorem et Salvatorem, regem et pontificem
maximum, Messiam verum et exspectatum illum, inquam, sanctum
benedictum, quem omnes legis typi et vaticinia prophetarum præ-
figurarint atque promiserint, Deus autem præstiterit ac miserit illum
nobis, ut alius porro non sit ullus nobis exspectandus.   Nec restat jam
aliud, quam ut omnes omnem gloriam Christo tribuamus, in ipsum
credamus, et in ipso solo adquiescamus, omnibus aliis vitæ præsidiis
spretis atque abjectis.   Nam gratia Dei exciderunt, et Christum in-
anem sibi reddunt, quotquot salutem in alia re ulla, quam in uno
Christo quærunt (Gal. v. 4).

18. Et ut paucis multa hujus causæ dicamus, quæcunque de incar-
nationis Domini nostri Jesu Christi mysterio definita sunt ex Scripturis
Sanctis, et comprehensa symbolis ac sententiis quatuor primarum et
præstantissimarum synodorum, celebratarum Niceæ, Constantinopoli,
Ephesi et Chalcedone, una cum beati Athanasii symbolo, et omnibus
his similibus symbolis, credimus corde sincero, et ore libero ingenue
profitemur, condemnantes omnia his contraria.

Atque ad hunc modum retinemus inviolatam sive integram fidem
Christianam, orthodoxam atque Catholicam: scientes, symbolis prædictis nihil contineri, quod non sit conforme verbo Dei, et prorsus faciat ad sinceram fidei explicationem.

CAP. XII.

De Lege Dei.

1. Docemus, lege Dei exponi nobis voluntatem Dei, quid a nobis fieri velit aut nolit, quid bonum et justum, quidve malum sit et injustum. Bonam igitur et sanctam confitemur esse legem. Et hanc quidem alias digito Dei *inscriptam esse in corda hominum, vocarique legem naturæ* (Rom. ii. 15), alias autem digito insculptam esse in tabulas Mosis geminas, et libris Mosis copiosius expositam (Exod. xx.; Deut. v.). Distinguimus illam, perspicuitatis gratia, in moralem, quæ comprehenditur decalogo vel geminis tabulis, per Mosis libros expositis, in ceremonialem item, quæ de cæremoniis cultuque Dei constituit, et in judicialem, quæ versatur circa politica atque œconomica.

2. Credimus, hac Dei lege omnem Dei voluntatem, et omnia præcepta necessaria, ad omnem vitæ partem, plenissime tradi. Alioqui enim non vetuisset Dominus, *huic legi nihil vel addi vel adimi* (Deut. iv. 2); non præcepisset, *recta ad hanc incedi, neque in dextram vel sinistram deflexo itinere, declinare* (Isa. xxx. 21).

3. Docemus, legem hanc non datam esse hominibus, ut ejus justificemur observatione: sed ut ex ejus indicio infirmitatem potius, peccatum atque condemnationem agnoscamus, et de viribus nostris desperantes, convertamur ad Christum in fide. Aperte enim Apostolus: *Lex iram*, ait, *operatur* (Rom. iv. 15). *Per legem agnitio peccati* (Rom. iii. 20). *Si data fuisset lex, quæ posset justificare, vel vivificare, vere ex lege esset justitia: sed conclusit Scriptura* (legis nimirum) *omnia sub peccatum, ut promissio ex fide Jesu daretur credentibus. Itaque lex pædagogus noster ad Christum fuit, ut ex fide justificaremur* (Gal. iii. 21, 22, 24). Neque vero potuit aut potest ulla caro legi Dei satisfacere, et hanc adimplere, ob imbecillitatem in carne nostra, ad extremum usque spiritum in nobis hærentem aut remanentem. Rursus enim Apostolus: *Quod lex præstare non poterat*, inquit, *quia imbecillis erat per carnem, hoc Deus, proprio Filio misso sub specie carnis peccato obnoxiæ, præstitit* (Rom. viii. 3). *Idcirco Christus est perfectio legis et adimpletio nostra* (Rom. x. 4), qui ut *execrationem legis sustulit, dum factus est pro nobis maledictio, vel execratio* (Gal. iii. 13), ita communicat nobis per fidem adimpletionem suam, nobisque ejus imputatur justitia et obedientia.

4. Hactenus itaque abrogata est lex Dei, quatenus nos amplius non damnat, nec iram in nobis operatur. Sumus enim sub gratia, et non sub lege. Præterea implevit Christus omnes legis figuras. Unde umbræ cesserunt, corpore adveniente, ut jam in Christo et veritatem habeamus et omnem plenitudinem. Attamen legem non ideo fastidientes rejicimus. Meminimus enim verborum Domini, dicentis: *Non veni legem et prophetas solvere, sed implere* (Matt. v. 17). Scimus, lege nobis tradi formulas virtutum atque vitiorum. Scimus, Scripturam legis, si exponatur per Evangelium, Ecclesiæ esse utilem, et idcirco ejus lectionem non exterminandam esse ex Ecclesia. Licet enim velo obtectus fuerit Mosis vultus, Apostolus tamen perhibet, velum per Christum tolli atque aboleri. Damnamus omnia, quæ hæretici veteres et neoterici contra legem Dei docuerunt.

CAP. XIII.

De Evangelio Jesu Christi, de Promissionibus, item Spiritu et Litera.

1. Evangelium quidem opponitur legi. Nam lex iram operatur, et maledictionem adnunciat; Evangelium vero gratiam et benedictionem prædicat. Sed et Joannes dicit: *Lex per Mosen data est, gratia et veritas per Jesum Christum exorta est* (Joh. i. 17; nihilominus tamen certissimum est, eos, qui ante legem et sub lege fuerunt, non omnino destitutos fuisse Evangelio. Habuerunt enim promissiones evangelicas insignes, quales hæ sunt: *Semen mulieris conculcabit caput serpentis* (Gen. iii. 15). *In semine tuo benedicentur omnes gentes* (Gen. xxii. 18). *Non auferetur sceptrum de Juda, nisi prius venerit Silo* (Gen. xlix. 10). *Prophetam excitabit Dominus de medio fratrum,'* etc. (Deut. xviii. 18).

2. Et quidem agnoscimus, Patribus duo fuisse promissionum genera, sicuti et nobis, revelata. Aliæ enim erant rerum præsentium vel terrenarum, quales sunt promissiones de terra Canaan, de victoriis, et quales hodie adhuc sunt de pane quotidiano. Aliæ vero erant tunc, et sunt etiam nunc, rerum cœlestium et æternarum, gratiæ videlicet divinæ, remissionis peccatorum, et vitæ æternæ, per fidem in Jesum Christum. Habuerunt autem veteres non tantum externas vel terrenas, sed spirituales etiam cœlestesque promissiones, in Christo. Nam

de salute, ait Petrus, *exquisiverunt et scrutati sunt prophetœ, qui de ventura in nos gratia vaticinati sunt,* etc. (1 Pet. i. 10). Unde et Paulus Apostolus dixit: *Evangelium Dei ante promissum esse per prophetas Dei, in Scripturis sanctis* (Rom. i. 2). Inde nimirum claret, veteres non prorsus destitutos fuisse omni Evangelio.

3. Et, quamvis ad hunc modum patres nostri in Scripturis prophetarum habuerint Evangelium, per quod salutem in Christo per fidem consecuti sunt, Evangelium tamen proprie illud dicitur lætum et felix nuncium, quod nobis primum per Joannem Baptistam, deinde per ipsum Christum Dominum, postea per Apostolos ejus Apostolorumque successores prædicatum est mundo, Deum jam præstitisse, quod ab exordio mundi promisit, ac misisse, imo donavisse nobis Filium unicum, et in hoc reconciliationem cum Patre, remissionem peccatorum, omnem plenitudinem, et vitam æternam. Historia ergo descripta a quatuor Evangelistis, explicans, quomodo hæc sint facta vel adimpleta a Christo, quæ docuerit et fecerit Christus; et quod in ipso credentes omnem habent plenitudinem, recte nuncupatur Evangelium. Prædicatio item et Scriptura Apostolica, qua nobis exponunt Apostoli, quomodo nobis a Patre datus sit Filius, et in hoc vitæ salutisque omnia, recte dicitur doctrina Evangelica, sic, ut ne hodie quidem, si sincera sit, appellationem tam præclaram amittat.

4. Illa ipsa Evangelii prædicatio nuncupatur item ab Apostolo spiritus et ministerium spiritus, eo, quod efficax et viva fiat per fidem in auribus, imo cordibus credentium, per Spiritum Sanctum illuminantem. Nam litera, quæ opponitur spiritui, significat quidem omnem rem externam, sed maxime doctrinam legis, sine spiritu et fide in animis, non viva fide credentium, operantem iram, et excitantem peccatum. Quo nomine et ministerium mortis ab Apostolo nuncupatur. Huc enim illud Apostoli pertinet, *Litera cccidit, spiritus vivificat* (2 Cor. iii. 6). Et pseudoapostoli prædicabant Evangelium, lege admixta, corruptum, quasi Christus sine lege non possit servare. Quales fuisse dicuntur Ebionæi, ab Ebione hæretico descendentes, et Nazaræi, qui et Minæi antiquitus vocabantur. Quos omnes nos damnamus, pure prædicantes Evangelium, docentesque per Spiritum [al. Christum] solum, et non per legem justificari credentes. De qua re mox sequetur sub titulo justificationis copiosior expositio.

5. Et quamvis Evangelii doctrina collata cum Pharisæorum doc-

trina legis, visa sit, cum primum prædicaretur per Christum, nova esse
doctrina, quod et Jeremias de Novo Testamento vaticinatus sit, revera tamen illa, non modo vetus erat, et est adhuc (nam nova dicitur
et hodie a Papistis, collata cum doctrina jam Papistarum recepta) vetus
doctrina, sed omnium in mundo antiquissima.

6. Deus enim *ab æterno prædestinavit* mundum servare per Christum, et hanc suam prædestinationem et consilium sempiternum *aperuit mundo per Evangelium* (2 Tim. i. 9, 10). Unde claret religionem
doctrinamque Evangelicam, inter omnes, quotquot fuerunt unquam,
sunt atque erunt, omnium esse antiquissimam.

7. Unde dicimus, omnes eos errare turpiter, et indigna æterno Dei
consilio loqui, qui Evangelicam doctrinam et religionem nuncupant
nuper exortam, et vix XXX. annorum fidem. In quos competit illud
Jesaiæ Prophetæ: *Væ his, qui dicunt, malum esse bonum, et bonum
malum, qui ponunt tenebras lucem, et lucem tenebras, amarum dulce,
et dulce amarum* (Isa. v. 20).

CAP. XIV.

De Pœnitentia et Conversione Hominis.   [Conf. Aug., Art. XI., XII.]

1. Habet Evangelium conjunctam sibi doctrinam de pœnitentia. Ita
enim dixit in Evangelio Dominus: *Oportet prædicari in nomine meo
pœnitentiam et remissionem peccatorum in omnes gentes* (Luc.
xxiv. 47).

2. Per pœnitentiam autem intelligimus mentis in homine peccatore
resipiscentiam, verbo Evangelii et Spiritu Sancto excitatam, fideque
vera acceptam, qua protinus homo peccator, agnatam sibi corruptionem peccataque omnia sua, per Verbum Dei accusata, agnoscit, ac de
his ex corde dolet, eademque coram Deo non tantum deplorat et
fatetur ingenue cum pudore, sed etiam cum indignatione execratur,
cogitans jam sedulo de emendatione, et perpetuo innocentiæ virtutumque studio, in quo sese omnibus diebus vitæ reliquis sancte exerceat.

3. Et hæc quidem est vera pœnitentia, sincera nimirum ad Deum
et omne bonum conversio, sedula vero a diabolo et ab omni malo aver-
sio. Diserte vero dicimus, hanc pœnitentiam merum esse Dei donum,

et non virium nostrarum opus. Jubet enim Apostolus: *Fidelem ministrum diligenter erudire obsistentes veritati, si quando Deus his det pœnitentiam ad agnoscendum veritatem* (2 Tim. ii. 25).

4. Jam vero peccatrix illa Evangelica, *quæ lacrymis rigat pedes Domini,* ac Petrus, *amare flens deploransque Domini sui abnegationem,* manifeste ostendunt, qualis esse debeat pœnitentis animus, serio deplorans commissa peccata (Luc. vii. 38; xxii. 62).

5. Sed et filius ille concoctor, et publicanus ille in Evangelio, cum Pharisæo collatus, præeunt nobis formulis adcommodatissimis peccata nostra Deo confitendi. Ille dicebat: *Pater, peccavi in cœlum et coram te! Jam non sum dignus vocari filius tuus, fac me sicut unum de mercenariis tuis* (Luc. xv. 18, 19). Hic vero non audens elevare oculos in cœlum, pectus suum tundendo, clamabat: *Deus propitius esto mihi peccatori* (Luc. xviii. 13). Nec dubitamus, illos in gratiam a Deo esse receptos. Etenim Joannes Apostolus: *Si confiteamur peccata nostra,* inquit, *fidelis est et justus, ut remittat nobis peccata nostra, et emundet nos ab omni iniquitate. Si dixerimus: non peccavimus, mendacem facimus eum, et sermo ejus non est in nobis* (1 Joh. i. 9, 10).

6. Credimus autem, hanc confessionem ingenuam, quæ soli Deo fit, vel privatim inter Deum et peccatorem, vel palam in templo, ubi generalis illa peccatorum confessio recitatur, sufficere, nec necessarium esse ad remissionem peccatorum consequendam, ut quis peccata sua confiteatur sacerdoti, susurrando in aures ipsius, ut vicissim cum impositione manuum ejus audiat ab ipso absolutionem; quod ejus rei nec præceptum ullum, nec exemplum exstet in Scripturis Sanctis. David protestatur et ait: *Delictum meum cognitum tibi feci, et injustitiam meam non abscondi. Dixi, confitebor contra me injustitiam meam Domino; et tu remisisti impietatem peccati mei* (Psa. xxxii. 5). Sed et Dominus orare nos docens, simul et confiteri peccata, dixit: *Sic orabitis: Pater noster, qui es in cœlis, remitte nobis debita nostra; sicut et nos remittimus debitoribus nostris* (Matt. vi. 12).

7. Necesse est ergo, ut Deo Patri nostro confiteamur peccata nostra, et cum proximo nostro, si ipsum offendimus, redeamus in gratiam. De quo confessionis genere loquens Jacobus Apostolus: *Confitemini,* inquit, *alterutrum peccata vestra* (Jac. v. 16). Si quis vero peccatorum mole et tentationibus perplexis oppressus, velit consilium, insti-

tutionem, et consolationem privatim, vel a ministro ecclesiæ, aut alio aliquo fratre, in lege Dei docto, petere, non improbamus, quemadmodum et generalem et publicam illam in templo ac cœtibus sacris recitari solitam (cujus et superius meminimus) peccatorum confessionem utpote Scripturis congruam, maxime approbamus.

8. De clavibus regni Dei, traditis a Domino Apostolis, multi admiranda garriunt, et ex his cudunt enses, lanceas, sceptra et coronas, plenamque in maxima regna, denique in animas et corpora potestatem. Nos simpliciter judicantes, secundum Verbum Dei dicimus: omnes ministros legitime vocatos habere et exercere claves vel usum clavium, cum Evangelium adnunciant, id est, populum suæ fidei creditum docent, hortantur, consolantur et increpant, inque disciplina retinent. Ita enim regnum cœlorum aperiunt obsequentibus, et inobsequentibus claudunt. Has claves promisit Apostolis Dominus (Matt. xvi. 19) et præstitit (Joh. xx. 23, Marc. xvi. 15, et Luc. xxiv. 47) dum ablegat discipulos et jubet eos universo mundo prædicare Evangelium, et condonare peccata. Apostolus in Ep. I. ad Cor. (v. 18, 19) dicit: Dominum ministris dedisse *reconciliationis ministerium;* et quale hoc sit, mox explicat et ait: *Sermonem vel doctrinam reconciliationis.* Et adhuc clarius sua illa exponens addit: *Ministros Christi, nomine Christi fungi legatione, tanquam ipso Deo, per ministros adhortante populos, ut reconcilientur Deo,* nimirum per fidelem obedientiam. Exercent ergo claves, cum suadent fidem et pœnitentiam. Sic illi reconciliant Deo. Sic remittunt peccata. Sic aperiunt regnum cœlorum, et credentes introducunt: multum distantes ab istis, de quibus dixit in Evangelio Dominus: *Væ vobis legisperitis, quia tulistis clavem scientiæ, ipsi non introistis, et eos, qui introibant, vetuistis* (Luc. xi. 52).

9. Rite itaque et efficaciter ministri absolvunt, dum Evangelium Christi, et in hoc remissionem peccatorum, quæ singulis promittitur fidelibus, sicuti et singuli sunt baptizati, prædicant, et ad singulos peculiariter pertinere testantur. Nec putamus absolutionem hanc efficaciorem fieri, per hoc, quod in aurem alicui aut super caput alicujus singulariter inmurmuratur. Censemus tamen, sedulo adnunciandam esse hominibus remissionem peccatorum in sanguine Christi, admonendosque singulos, quod ad ipsos pertineat remissio peccatorum.

10. Ceterum quam vigilantes sedulosque oporteat esse pœnitentes in studio vitæ novæ, et in conficiendo vetere et excitando novo homine,

docent nos exempla Evangelica. Dominus enim ad paralyticum, quem sanaverat, dicit: *Ecce sanus factus es, ne posthac pecces, ne quid deterius tibi contingat* (Joh. v. 14). Ad adulteram liberatam idem dixit: *Vade, et ne posthac peccaveris* (Joh. viii. 11). Quibus sane verbis non significavit, fieri posse, ut homo aliquando non peccet, dum adhuc in hac carne vivit, sed vigilantiam accuratumque studium commendat, ut modis in quam omnibus adnitamur, et precibus a Deo petamus, ne relabamur in peccata, ex quibus veluti resurreximus, et ne vincamur a carne, mundo et diabolo. Zachæus publicanus in gratiam receptus a Domino clamat in Evangelio: *Ecce, dimidium bonorum meorum, Domine, do pauperibus, et si quem defraudavi, reddo quadruplum* (Luc. xix. 8). Ad eundem ergo modum prædicamus restitutionem et misericordiam, adeoque eleemosynam vere pœnitentibus esse necessariam; et in universum Apostoli verbis hortamur omnes, ac dicimus: *Ne regnet peccatum in mortali vestro corpore, ut obediatis ei per cupiditates ejus; neque adcommodetis membra vestra arma injustitiæ peccato, sed accommodetis vosmet ipsos Deo, velut ex mortuis viventes, et membra vestra arma justitiæ Deo* (Rom. vi. 12, 13).

11. Proinde damnamus omnes impias quorundam Evangelica prædicatione abutentium voces, et dicentium: facilis est ad Deum reditus. Christus expiavit omnia peccata; facilis est peccatorum condonatio. Quid ergo peccare nocebit? Nec magnopere curanda est pœnitentia, etc. Docemus interim semper, et omnibus peccatoribus aditum patere ad Deum, et hunc omnia omnibus fidelibus condonare peccata, *excepto uno illo peccato, in Spiritum Sanctum* (Marc. iii. 29).

12. Ideoque damnamus et veteres et novos Novatianos, atque Catharos. Damnamus imprimis lucrosam papæ de pœnitentia doctrinam; et contra simoniam ejus simoniacasque ejus indulgentias illud usurpamus Simonis Petri judicium: *Pecunia tua tecum sit in perditionem: quoniam donum Dei existimasti parari pecuniis. Non est tibi pars neque sors in ratione hac. Cor enim tuum non est rectum coram Deo* (Act. viii. 20, 21).

13. Improbamus item illos, qui suis satisfactionibus existimant, se pro commissis satisfacere peccatis. Nam docemus, Christum unum, morte vel passione sua, esse omnium peccatorum satisfactionem, pro-

pitiationem vel expiationem (Isa. liii. 5; 1 Cor. i. 30; 1 Joh. ii. 2). Interim tamen, quod et ante diximus, mortificationem carnis urgere non desinimus: addimus tamen, hanc non obtrudendam esse Deo superbe pro peccatorum satisfactione, sed præstandam humiliter, pro ingenio filiorum Dei, ut obedientiam novam, gratitudinis ergo, pro consecuta, per mortem et satisfactionem Filii Dei, liberatione, et plenaria satisfactione.

CAP. XV.

De vera Fidelium Justificatione. [Conf. Aug., Art. IV.]

1. Justificare significat Apostolo in disputatione de justificatione, peccata remittere, a culpa et pœna absolvere, in gratiam recipere, et justum pronunciare. Etenim ad Romanos dicit Apostolus: *Deus est, qui justificat, quis ille, qui condemnet?* (Rom. viii. 33) opponuntur justificare et condemnare. Et in Actis App. dicit Apostolus: *Per Christum adnunciatur nobis remissio peccatorum: et ab omnibus, a quibus non potuistis per legem Mosis justificari, per hunc omnis, qui credit, justificatur* (Act. xiii. 38, 39). Nam in lege quoque et prophetis legimus: *Si lis fuerit orta inter aliquos, et venerint ad judicium, judicent eos judices justificentque justum, et impient vel condemnent impium* (Deut. xxv. 1). Et: *Væ illis, qui justificant impium pro muneribus* (Isa. v. 23).

2. Certissimum est autem, omnes nos esse natura peccatores et impios, ac coram tribunali Dei convictos impietatis et reos mortis. Justificari autem, id est, absolvi a peccatis et morte, a judice Deo, solius Christi gratia, et nullo nostro merito aut respectu. Quid enim apertius, quam quod Paulus dixit? *Omnes peccaverunt, et destituuntur gloria Dei. Justificantur autem gratis per illius gratiam, per redemptionem, quæ est in Christo Jesu* (Rom. iii. 23, 24).

3. Etenim Christus peccata mundi in se recepit et sustulit, divinæque justitiæ satisfecit. Deus ergo propter solum Christum passum et resuscitatum, propitius est peccatis nostris, nec illa nobis imputat, imputat autem justitiam Christi pro nostra: ita, ut jam simus non solum mundati a peccatis et purgati, vel sancti, sed etiam donati justitia Christi, adeoque absoluti a peccatis, morte vel condemnatione, justi denique ac hæredes vitæ æternæ. Proprie ergo loquendo, Deus solus nos justificat, et duntaxat propter Christum justificat, non im-

putans nobis peccata, sed imputans ejus nobis justitiam (2 Cor. v. 21; Rom. iv. 24, 25).

4. Quoniam vero nos justificationem hanc recipimus, non per ulla opera, sed per fidem in Dei misericordiam et Christum, ideo docemus et credimus cum Apostolo, hominem peccatorem justificari sola fide in Christum, non lege, aut ullis operibus. Dicit enim Apostolus: *Arbitramur, fide justificari hominem absque operibus legis* (Rom. iii. 28). Item: *Si Abraham ex operibus justificatus fuit, habet, quod glorietur, sed non apud Deum. Quid enim Scriptura dicit? Credidit Abraham Deo, et imputatum est ei ad justitiam. At ei, qui non operatur, sed credit in eum, qui justificat impium, imputatur fides sua ad justitiam* (Rom. iv. 2–5). Et iterum: *Gratia estis servati per fidem, idque non ex vobis, Dei donum est. Non ex operibus, ne quis glorietur,* etc. (Eph. ii. 8, 9). Ergo, quia fides Christum justitiam nostram recipit, et gratiæ Dei in Christo omnia tribuit, ideo fidei tribuitur justificatio, maxime propter Christum, et non ideo, quia nostrum opus est. Donum enim Dei est. Ceterum nos Christum fide recipere multis ostendit Dominus, apud Joan. cap. vi. ubi pro credere ponit manducare, et pro manducare credere. Nam sicut manducando cibum recipimus, ita credendo participamus Christum.

5. Itaque justificationis beneficium non partimur, partim gratiæ Dei, vel Christo, partim nobis, aut dilectioni operibusve, vel merito nostro, sed insolidum gratiæ Dei in Christo per fidem tribuimus. Sed et non possent Deo placere dilectio et opera nostra, si fierent ab injustis; proinde oportet nos prius justos esse, quam diligamus aut faciamus opera justa. Justi vere efficimur, quemadmodum diximus, per fidem in Christum, mera gratia Dei, qui peccata nobis non imputat, sed justitiam Christi, adeoque fidem in Christum ad justitiam nobis imputat. Apostolus præterea apertissime dilectionem derivat ex fide, dicens: *Finis præcepti est caritas, ex puro corde, conscientia bona, et fide non ficta* (1 Tim. i. 5).

6. Quapropter loquimur in hac causa non de ficta fide, de inani et otiosa, aut mortua, sed de fide viva vivificanteque, quæ propter Christum, qui vita est et vivificat, quem comprehendit, viva est et dicitur, ac se vivam esse vivis declarat operibus. Nihil itaque contra hanc nostram doctrinam pugnat Jacobus, qui de fide loquitur inani et mortua, quam quidam jactabant, Christum autem intra se viventem per

fidem non habebant. Idem ille dixit, opera justificare, non contra dicens Apostolo (rejiciendus alioqui), sed ostendens Abrahamum vivam justificantemque fidem suam declaravisse per opera (Jac. ii.). Id quod omnes pii faciunt, qui tamen soli Christo, nullis suis operibus fidunt. Iterum enim Apostolus dixit: *Vivo jam non ego, sed vivit in me Christus. Vitam autem, quam nunc vivo in carne, per fidem vivo Filii Dei, qui dilexit me, et tradidit semetipsum pro me. Non adspernor gratiam Dei. Nam si per legem est justitia: igitur Christus frustra mortuus est,* etc. (Gal. ii. 20, 21).

CAP. XVI.

DE FIDE, ET BONIS OPERIBUS, EORUMQUE MERCEDE, ET MERITO HOMINIS.
[CONF. AUG., ART. VI., XX.]

1. Fides enim Christiana non est opinio ac humana persuasio, sed firmissima fiducia et evidens ac constans animi adsensus, denique certissima comprehensio veritatis Dei, propositæ in Scripturis et Symbolo Apostolico, atque adeo Dei ipsius summi boni, et præcipue promissionis divinæ, et Christi, qui omnium promissionum est colophon.

2. Hæc autem fides merum est Dei donum, quod solus Deus ex gratia sua, electis suis, secundum mensuram, et quando, cui, et quantum ipse vult, donat, et quidem per Spiritum Sanctum, mediante prædicatione Evangelii, et oratione fideli. Hæc etiam sua habet incrementa; quæ nisi et ipsa darentur a Deo, non dixissent Apostoli: *Domine! adauge nobis fidem* (Luc. xvii. 5).

3. Et hæc quidem omnia, quæ hactenus de fide diximus, ante nos ita docuerunt Apostoli. Paulus enim: *Est autem fides,* inquit, *eorum, quæ sperantur,* ὑπόστασις, *vel subsistentia firma, et earum rerum, quæ non videntur,* ἔλεγχος, *id est, evidens ei certa rei comprehensio* (Heb. xi. 1). Et idem iterum: *Quotquot sunt promissiones Dei,* inquit, *per Christum sunt etiam et per ipsum Amen* (2 Cor. i. 20). Ad Philipp. idem ait, *donatum esse ipsis ut credant in Christum* (Phil. i. 29). Item: *Deus unicuique partitus est mensuram fidei* (Rom. xii. 3; 2 Thess. iii. 2). Rursus: *Non omnium est fides,* ait, *neque obediunt omnes Evangelio* (Rom. x. 16). Sed et Lucas testatur et ait: *Et crediderunt, quotquot erant ordinati ad vitam* (Act. xiii. 48). Unde idem iterum fidem nuncupat, *fidem electorum Dei* (Tit. i. 1). Et

iterum: *Fides est ex auditu, auditus autem per verbum Dei* (Rom. x. 17). Alibi sæpe jubet orare pro fide.

4. Idem ille Apostolus *fidem* vocat *efficacem* et *sese exserentem per dilectionem* (Gal. v. 6). Illa conscientiam quoque pacificat, et liberum ad Deum aditum aperit, ut cum fiducia ad ipsum accedamus, et obtineamus ab eo utilia et necessaria. Eadem retinet nos in officio, quod Deo debemus et proximo, et in adversis patientiam firmat, et confessionem veram format atque facit, et, ut uno verbo omnia dicam, omnis generis bonos fructus et bona opera progignit (Gal. v. 22 sqq.).

5. Docemus enim, vere bona opera enasci ex viva fide, per Spiritum Sanctum, et a fidelibus fieri secundum voluntatem vel regulam Verbi Dei. Nam Petrus Apostolus: *Omni adhibito studio*, inquit, *subministrate in fide vestra virtutem, in virtute vero scientiam, in scientia vero temperantiam*, etc. (2 Pet. i. 5–7). Diximus autem antea, legem Dei, quæ voluntas Dei est, formulam nobis præscribere bonorum operum. Et Apostolus ait: *Hæc est voluntas Dei, sanctificatio vestra, ut abstineatis ab immunditie, et ne quis opprimat aut fraudet in negotio fratrem suum* (1 Thess. iv. 4–6). Etenim non probantur Deo opera, et nostro arbitrio delecti cultus, quos Paulus nuncupat: ἐθελοθρησκείας (Col. ii. 18). De quibus et Dominus in Evangelio: *Frustra me colunt*, ait, *docentes doctrinas præcepta hominum* (Matt. xv. 9).

6. Improbamus ergo hujusmodi opera: adprobamus et urgemus illa, quæ sunt ex voluntate et mandato Dei. Illa ipsa fieri debent, non ut his promereamur vitam æternam. Donum Dei enim est, ut Apostolus ait, vita æterna, neque ad ostentationem, quam rejecit Dominus (Matt. vi.), neque ad quæstum, quem et ipsum rejecit (Matt. xxiii.), sed ad gloriam Dei, ad ornandam vocationem nostram, gratitudinemque Deo præstandam, et ad utilitatem proximi. Rursus enim Dominus noster in Evangelio dicit: *Sic luceat lux vestra coram hominibus, ut videant vestra opera bona, et glorificent Patrem, qui in cœlis est* (Matt. v. 16). Sed et Apostolus Paulus: *Ambulate digne vocatione vestra* (Eph. iv. 1). Item: *Quidquid egeritis*, inquit, *aut sermone aut facto, omnia in nomine Jesu facite, gratias agentes Deo et Patri per illum* (Col. iii. 17). Idem: *Nemo, quod suum est, quærat, sed quisque quod alterius* (Phil. ii. 4). Et: *Discant et nostri, bona opera tueri ad necessarios usus, ut non sint infrugiferi* (Tit. iii. 14).

7. Quamvis ergo doceamus cum Apostolo, hominem gratis justificari per fidem in Christum, et non per ulla opera bona, non ideo tamen vilipendimus aut condemnamus opera bona. Cum sciamus, hominem nec conditum nec regenitum esse per fidem, ut otietur, sed potius, ut indesinenter, quæ bona et utilia sunt, faciat. Etenim in Evangelio dicit Dominus: *Bona arbor bonum fructum adfert* (Matt. xii. 33). Et iterum: *Quid in me manet, plurimum fructum adfert* (Joh. xv. 5). Denique Apostolus: *Dei sumus creatura,* ait, *conditi in Christo Jesu ad opera bona, quœ prœparavit Deus, ut in eis ambulemus* (Eph. ii. 10). Et iterum: *Qui tradidit semetipsum pro nobis, ut redimeret ab omni iniquitate et mundaret sibi populum peculiarem, sectatorem bonorum operum* (Tit. ii. 14).

8. Damnamus itaque omnes, qui bona opera contemnunt, non curanda et inutilia esse blaterant. Interim, quod et antea dictum est, non sentimus, per opera bona nos servari, illaque ad salutem ita esse necessaria, ut absque illis nemo unquam sit servatus. Gratia enim soliusque Christi beneficio servamur. Opera necessario ex fide progignuntur. At improprie his salus attribuitur: quæ propriissime adscribitur gratiæ. Notissima enim est illa Apostoli sententia: *Si per gratiam, jam non ex operibus: quandoquidem gratia, jam non est gratia. Sin ex operibus, jam non ex gratia; quandoquidem jam opus, non est opus* (Rom. xi. 6).

9. Placent vero adprobanturque a Deo opera, quæ a nobis fiunt per fidem. Quia illi placent Deo, propter fidem in Christum, qui faciunt opera bona, quæ insuper per Spiritum Sanctum ex gratia Dei sunt facta. S. Petrus enim: *In quavis gente,* inquit, *qui timet ipsum et operatur justitiam, is acceptus est illi* (Act. x. 35). Et Paulus: *Non desinimus orare pro vobis, ut ambuletis digne Domino, ut per omnia placeatis, in omni opere bono fructificantes* (Col. i. 9, 10). Itaque veras, non falsas aut philosophicas virtutes, vere bona opera et genuina Christiani hominis officia sedulo docemus, et quanta possumus, diligentia vehementiaque omnibus inculcamus, vituperantes omnium illorum et desidiam et hypocrisin, qui ore Evangelium laudant et profitentur, vita autem turpi dedecorant, proponentes hac in causa horribiles Dei minas, amplas denique promissiones Dei, et liberalia præmia, exhortando, consolando, et objurgando.

10. Etenim docemus, Deum bona operantibus amplam dare merce-

dem, juxta illam prophetæ sententiam: *Cohibe vocem tuam a fletu: quoniam erit merces operi tuo* (Jer. xxxi. 16). In Evangelio quoque dixit Dominus: *Gaudete et exultate, quia merces vestra multa est in cœlis* (Matt. v. 12). *Et qui dederit uni ex minimis meis poculum aquæ frigidæ, amen dico vobis, non perdet mercedem suam* (Matt. x. 42). Referimus tamen mercedem hanc, quam Dominus dat, non ad meritum hominis accipientis, sed ad bonitatem, vel liberalitatem, et veritatem Dei promittentis atque dantis, qui, cum nihil debeat cuiquam, promisit tamen, se suis cultoribus fidelibus mercedem daturum: qui interim dat eis etiam, ut ipsum colant. Sunt multa præterea indigna Deo, et imperfecta plurima inveniuntur in operibus etiam sanctorum: quia vero Deus recipit in gratiam et complectitur propter Christum operantes, mercedem eis promissam persolvit. Alioqui enim justitiæ nostræ comparantur panno menstruato (Isa. lxiv. 6). Sed et Dominus dicit in Evangelio: *Cum feceritis omnia, quæ præcepta sunt vobis, dicite, servi inutiles sumus: quod debuimus facere, fecimus* (Luc. xvii. 10).

11. Tametsi ergo doceamus, mercedem dari a Deo nostris benefactis, simul tamen docemus cum Augustino, coronare Deum in nobis non merita nostra, sed dona sua. Et proinde quidquid accipimus mercedis, dicimus gratiam quoque esse, et magis quidem gratiam quam mercedem: quod, quæ bona facimus, per Deum magis, quam per nos ipsos facimus: et quod Paulus dicat: *Quid habes, quod non accepisti? Si vero accepisti, quid gloriaris, quasi non acceperis?* (1 Cor. iv. 7). Et quod hinc collegit beatus martyr Cyprianus: In nullo nobis gloriandum esse, quando nostrum nihil sit. Damnamus ergo illos, qui merita hominum sic defendunt, ut[1] evacuent gratiam Dei.

CAP. XVII.

DE CATHOLICA ET SANCTA DEI ECCLESIA, ET UNICO CAPITE ECCLESIÆ.
[CONF. AUG., ART. VII., VIII.]

1. Quando autem Deus ab initio salvos voluit fieri homines, et ad agnitionem veritatis venire, oportet omnino semper fuisse, nunc esse, et ad finem usque seculi futuram esse Ecclesiam, id est, e mundo evo-

---

[1] Kindler reads *et* for *ut*—a typographical error.

catum vel collectum cœtum fidelium, sanctorum, inquam, omnium communionem, eorum videlicet, qui Deum verum, in Christo Servatore, per verbum et Spiritum Sanctum vere cognoscunt et rite colunt, denique omnibus bonis per Christum gratuito oblatis fide participant. Sunt isti omnes unius civitatis cives, viventes sub eodem Domino, sub iisdem legibus, in eadem omnium bonorum participatione. Sic enim hos *concives sanctorum et domesticos Dei* appellavit Apostolus (Eph. ii. 19): Sanctos appellans fideles in terris, sanguine Filii Dei sanctificatos (1 Cor. vi. 11). De quibus omnino intelligendus est Symboli articulus: Credo sanctam Ecclesiam Catholicam, sanctorum communionem.

2. Et cum semper unus modo sit Deus, unus Mediator Dei et hominum Jesus Messias, unus item gregis universi pastor, unum hujus corporis caput, unus denique Spiritus, una salus, una fides, unum testamentum vel fœdus; necessario consequitur unam duntaxat esse Ecclesiam: quam propterea Catholicam nuncupamus, quod sit universalis, et diffundatur per omnes mundi partes, et ad omnia se tempora extendat, nullis vel locis inclusa vel temporibus. Damnamus ergo Donatistas, qui Ecclesiam in nescio quos Africæ coarctabant angulos. Nec Romanensem adprobamus clerum, qui solam prope Romanam Ecclesiam venditat pro Catholica.

3. Diducitur quidem Ecclesia in partes vel species varias, non quod divisa aut divulsa sit in semetipsa, sed magis propter membrorum in ipsa diversitatem distincta. Aliam enim faciunt Ecclesiam militantem, aliam vero triumphantem. Militat illa adhuc in terris, et certat cum carne, cum mundo, et principe mundi hujus, diabolo, cum peccato atque morte. Hæc vero rude jam donata, in cœlo triumphat de istis devictis omnibus, et exultat coram Domino: nihilominus habent illæ inter sese communionem, vel conjunctionem.

4. Et militans in terris Ecclesia semper plurimas habuit particulares ecclesias, quæ tamen omnes ad unitatem Catholicæ Ecclesiæ referuntur. Hæc aliter fuit instituta ante legem inter patriarchas, aliter sub Mose per legem, aliter a Christo per Evangelium. Vulgo numerantur fere duo populi, Israelitarum videlicet et gentium, vel eorum, qui ex Judæis et gentibus collecti sunt in Ecclesiam, testamenta item duo, vetus et novum. Omnium tamen horum populorum una fuit et est societas, una salus in uno Messia, in quo ceu membra unius corporis

sub unum caput connectuntur omnes, in eadem fide, etiam de eodem cibo et potu spirituali participantes. Agnoscimus hic tamen diversa fuisse tempora, diversa symbola promissi et exhibiti Messiæ, sublatisque cærimonialibus, lucem nobis illustriorem lucere, et dona auc tiora donari, et libertatem esse pleniorem.

5. Hæc Ecclesia Dei sancta vocatur domus Dei viventis, exstructa ex lapidibus vivis et spiritualibus, et imposita super petram immotam, super fundamentum, quo aliud collocari non potest: et ideo nuncupatur etiam columna et basis veritatis (1 Tim. iii. 15). Non errat illa, quamdiu innititur petræ Christo et fundamento Prophetarum et Apostolorum. Nec mirum, si erret, quoties deserit illum, qui solus est veritas. Vocatur Ecclesia etiam virgo ac sponsa Christi, et quidem unica et dilecta. Apostolus enim: *Adjunxi vos*, inquit, *uni viro, ut virginem castam exhiberetis Christo* (2 Cor. xi. 2). Vocatur Ecclesia grex ovium sub uno pastore Christo, idque apud Ezechielem in Cap. XXXIV. et apud Joannem in Cap. X. Vocatur item corpus Christi, quia fideles sunt viva Christi membra, sub capite Christo.

6. Caput est, quod in corpore eminentiam habet, et unde corpus vitam haurit, cujus spiritu regitur in omnibus, unde et incrementa et, ut crescat, habet. Unicum item est corporis caput, et cum corpore habet congruentiam. Ergo Ecclesia non potest ullum aliud habere caput, quam Christum. Nam ut Ecclesia est corpus spirituale, ita caput habeat sibi congruens spirituale, utique oportet. Nec alio potest regi spiritu, quam Christi. Paulus quoque: *Ipse est caput*, inquit, *corporis ecclesiæ, qui est principium, primogenitus ex mortuis, ut sit ipse in omnibus primas tenens* (Col. i. 18). Et idem iterum: *Christus est*, inquit, *caput ecclesiæ, qui idem salutem dat corpori* (Eph. r. 23). Et rursus: *Qui est caput ecclesiæ*, ait, *quæ corpus illius, complementum ejus, qui omnia in omnibus adimplet* (Eph. i. 22, 23). Item: *Adolescamus in illum per omnia, qui est caput, nempe Christus, in quo totum corpus, si compingatur, incrementum capit* (Eph. iv. 15, 16).

7. Non probamus ergo doctrinam cleri Romani, facientis suum illum Romanum Pontificem Catholicæ in terris ecclesiæ militantis pastorem universalem et caput summum, adeoque verum Christi vicarium, qui habeat in Ecclesia plenitudinem, ut vocant, potestatis, et dominium supremum.

8. Docemus enim, Christum Dominum esse et manere unicum pastorem universalem, summum item Pontificem coram Deo Patre, ac in Ecclesia ipsum omnia pontificis vel pastoris obire munia, ad finem usque sæculi, ideoque nullo indigere vicario, qui absentis est. Christus vero præsens est ecclesiæ, et caput vivificum. Hic Apostolis suis Apostolorumque successoribus primatum et dominium in Ecclesia severissime prohibuit. [Quicunque ergo huic illustri veritati contradicentes reluctantur, et in Ecclesiam Christi diversam inducunt gubernationem, quis non videat, eos illis potius esse adcensendos, de quibus Apostoli Christi vaticinantur, Petrus (2 Pet. ii.), et Paulus (Act. xx., 2 Cor. xi., et 2 Thess. ii.), et aliis quoque in locis?][1]

9. Sublato autem capite Romano; nullam inducimus in Ecclesiam Christi ἀταξίαν, vel perturbationem: cum doceamus, gubernationem Ecclesiæ, ab Apostolis traditam, nobis sufficere ad retinendam in justo ordine Ecclesiam, quæ ab initio, dum hujusmodi capite Romano, quale hodie dicitur Ecclesiam conservare in ordine, caruit, atactica vel inordinata non fuit. Servat quidem caput Romanum tyrannidem suam, et corruptelam inductam in Ecclesiam: sed impedit interim, oppugnat, et, quantis potest viribus, exscindit justam ecclesiæ reformationem.

10. Objicitur nobis, varia esse in ecclesiis nostris certamina atque dissidia, posteaquam se a Romana separarunt Ecclesia, proinde non esse eas Ecclesias veras. Quasi vero nullæ unquam fuerint in Ecclesia Romana sectæ, nulla unquam dissidia atque certamina, et quidem de religione, non tam in scholis, quam in cathedris sacris, in medio populi instituta. Agnoscimus sane, dixisse Apostolum: *Deus non est Deus dissensionis, sed pacis* (1 Cor. xiv. 33). Et: *Cum sit in vobis æmulatio et contentio, an non carnales estis?* (1 Cor. iii. 3). Negari tamen non potest, Deum fuisse in Ecclesia Apostolica, et Apostolicam Ecclesiam fuisse Ecclesiam veram, in qua tamen fuerunt concertationes et dissidia. Reprehendit enim Petrum Apostolum Apostolus Paulus, ab hoc dissidet Barnabas (Gal. ii.). Certamen grave exo-

---

[1] The passage inclosed in brackets was substituted by Bullinger for the following passage: '*Quæ vero Romanenses fingunt de ministeriali capite et titulo servi servorum Dei, minime recipimus. Experimur enim voces illas inanes jactari, et papam sese constituere adversarium Christi et efferre se adversus Deum, adeo ut in templo Dei sedeat ostentans se ipsum esse Deum.* 2 Thess. ii.' See Niemeyer, p. 501.

ritur in Ecclesia Antiochena inter eos, qui unum Christum prædicabant: sicut commemorat Lucas in Actis Apost., Cap. XV. Gravia semper fuerunt in Ecclesia certamina, et dissenserunt inter sese de rebus
non levibus doctores ecclesiæ præclarissimi, ut ex his contentionibus
interim Ecclesia non id esse desineret, quod erat. Ita enim placet Deo,
dissidiis ecclesiasticis uti, ad gloriam nominis sui, ad illustrandam denique veritatem, et ut qui probati sunt, manifesti fiant.

11. Ceterum, ut non agnoscimus aliud caput Ecclesiæ quam Christum, ita non agnoscimus quamlibet Ecclesiam, quæ se venditat pro
vera, veram esse Ecclesiam; sed illam docemus veram esse Ecclesiam,
in qua signa vel notæ inveniuntur Ecclesiæ veræ, imprimis vero Verbi
Dei legitima vel sincera prædicatio, prout nobis est tradita in libris
Prophetarum et Apostolorum, qui omnes ad Christum deducunt, qui
in Evangelio dixit: *Oves meæ vocem meam audiunt, et ego cognosco
eas, et sequuntur me, et ego vitam æternam do eis. Alienum autem
non sequuntur, sed fugiunt, ab eo, quia non noverunt vocem alienorum* (Joh. x. 4, 5, 27, 28).

12. Et qui tales sunt in Ecclesia, hi unam habent fidem, unum spiritum, et idcirco unum solum Deum adorant, solum hunc in spiritu et
veritate colunt, hunc ex toto corde et omnibus viribus solum diligunt,
solum per Christum mediatorem et intercessorem unicum invocant,
extra Christum fidemque in ipsum nullam quærunt justitiam et vitam;
quia Christum solum caput et fundamentum Ecclesiæ agnoscunt, ac
super hoc impositi quotidie se pœnitentia reparant, patientia impositam
ipsis crucem ferunt, sed et caritate non ficta cum omnibus Christi
membris connexi, hac se declarant discipulos esse Christi, perseve-
rando in vinculo pacis atque unitatis sanctæ; simul et participant
sacramentis a Christo institutis, et ab Apostolis traditis: neque his
aliter utuntur, quam uti acceperunt a Domino. Notum est enim omnibus illud Apostoli: *Ego enim accepi a Domino, quod et tradidi
vobis* (1 Cor. xi. 23). Proinde damnamus illas ecclesias, ut alienas
a vera Christi Ecclesia, quæ tales non sunt, quales esse debere audivi-
mus, utcunque interim jactent successionem episcoporum, unitatem,
et antiquitatem. Quinimo præcipiunt nobis Apostoli, ut fugiamus
idololatriam et Babylonem, et ne participemus cum hac, nisi et plaga-
rum Dei participes esse velimus (1 Cor. x. 14, 21; 1 Joh. v. 21; Apoc.
xviii. 4; 1 Cor. vi. 9).

13. Communionem vero cum Ecclesia Christi vera tanti facimus, ut negemus eos coram Deo vivere posse, qui cum vera Dei Ecclesia non communicant, sed ab ea se separant. Nam ut extra arcam Noë non erat ulla salus, pereunte mundo in diluvio, ita credimus, extra Christum, qui se electis in Ecclesia fruendum præbet, nullam esse salutem certam: et proinde docemus, vivere volentes non oportere separari a vera Christi Ecclesia.

14. Signis tamen commemoratis non ita arcte includimus Ecclesiam, ut omnes illos extra Ecclesiam esse doceamus, qui vel sacramentis non participant, non quidem volentes, neque per contemtum, sed necessitate potius inevitabili coacti, nolentes ab iis abstinent, aut iis carent: vel in quibus aliquando deficit fides, non tamen penitus exstinguitur, aut prorsus desinit: vel in quibus infirmitatis vitia atque errores inveniuntur. Scimus enim, Deum aliquot habuisse in mundo amicos, extra Israelis rempublicam. Scimus, quid populo Dei evenerit in captivitate Babylonica, in qua sacrificiis suis caruerunt annis septuaginta; scimus, quid evenerit S. Petro negatori, et quid quotidie evenire soleat electis Dei fidelibus, errantibus et infirmis. Scimus præterea, quales Apostolorum temporibus fuerint Galatarum et Corinthiorum ecclesiæ, in quibus multa et gravia accusat Apostolus scelera, et tamen nuncupat easdem sanctas Christi ecclesias.

15. Quinimo fit aliquando, ut Deus justo judicio veritatem verbi sui, fidemque Catholicam, et cultum Dei legitimum sic obscurari et convelli sinat, ut prope videatur exstincta, et nulla amplius superesse Ecclesia: sicuti factum videmus Eliæ et aliis temporibus. Interim habet Deus in hoc mundo et in hisce tenebris suos illos veros adoratores, nec paucos, sed septem millia ac plures (1 Reg. xix. 18; Apoc. vii. 4, 9). Nam et Apostolus clamat: *Solidum fundamentum Dei stat, habens signaculum hoc, novit Dominus, qui sunt sui!* etc. (2 Tim. ii. 19). Unde et Ecclesia invisibilis appellari potest, non, quod homines sint invisibiles, ex quibus Ecclesia colligitur, sed quod oculis nostris absconsa, Deo autem soli nota, judicium humanum sæpe subterfugiat.

16. Rursus non omnes, qui numerantur in Ecclesia, sancti et viva atque vera sunt ecclesiæ membra. Sunt enim hypocritæ multi, qui foris Verbum Dei audiunt, et sacramenta palam percipiunt, Deum quoque per Christum invocare solum, Christum confiteri, justitiam suam unicam, Deum item colere, et caritatis officia exercere, patien-

tiaque in calamitatibus ad tempus perdurare videntur; sed intus vera
Spiritus illuminatione, et fide animique sinceritate, et finali perseverantia destituuntur. Qui etiam, quales sint, tandem deteguntur fere.
Joannes enim Apostolus: *Exierunt ex nobis,* inquit, *sed non erant ex
nobis.* Nam si fuissent ex nobis, *permansissent utique nobiscum*
(1 Joh. ii. 19). Et tamen, dum hi simulant pietatem, licet ex Ecclesia
non sint, numerantur tamen in Ecclesia: sicuti proditores in republica,
priusquam detegantur, numerantur et ipsi inter cives, et quemadmodum lolium vel zizania et palea inveniuntur in tritico, aut sicut strumæ
et tumores inveniuntur in integro corpore, cum revera morbi et de-
formitates sint verius corporis, quam membra vera. Proinde Ecclesia
Dei recte comparatur sagenæ, quæ omnis generis pisces attrahit, et
agro, in quo inveniuntur et zizania et triticum. Ubi maxime cavere
oportet, ne ante tempus judicemus, et excludere abjicereque, aut ex-
cindere conemur eos, quos Dominus excludi abjicique non vult, aut
quos sine jactura Ecclesiæ separare non possumus. Rursus vigilandum est, ne, stertentibus piis, impii proficiendo damnum dent Ecclesiæ
(Matt. xiii. 25).

17. Observandum præterea diligenter docemus, in quo potissimum
sit sita veritas et unitas Ecclesiæ, ne temere schismata excitemus, et in
Ecclesia foveamus. Sita est illa non in cærimoniis et ritibus externis,
sed magis in veritate et unitate fidei Catholicæ. Fides Catholica non
est nobis tradita humanis legibus, sed Scriptura divina, cujus compendium est Symbolum Apostolicum. Unde legimus, apud veteres rituum
fuisse diversitatem variam, sed eam liberam, qua nemo unquam existi-
mavit dissolvi unitatem ecclesiasticam. In dogmatibus itaque et in
vera concordique prædicatione Evangelii Christi, et in ritibus a Domino diserte traditis, dicimus veram Ecclesiæ constare concordiam;
ubi illam maxime Apostoli sententiam urgemus. *Quotquot itaque
perfecti sumus, hoc sentiamus. Quod si quid aliter sentitis, hoc
quoque vobis Deus revelabit. Attamen in eo, ad quod pervenimus,
eadem incedamus regula, et itidem simus affecti* (Phil. iii. 15, 16).

CAP. XVIII.

DE MINISTRIS ECCLESIÆ, IPSORUMQUE INSTITUTIONE ET OFFICIIS. [CONF. AUG., ART. XIV.]

1. Deus ad colligendam vel constituendam sibi Ecclesiam, eanaemque gubernandam et conservandam, semper usus est ministris, iisque utitur adhuc, et utetur porro, quoad Ecclesia in terris fuerit. Ergo ministrorum origo, institutio et functio vetustissima et ipsius Dei, non nova aut hominum est ordinatio. Posset sane Deus sua potentia immediate sibi adjungere ex hominibus Ecclesiam, sed maluit agere cum hominibus per ministerium hominum. Proinde spectandi sunt ministri, non ut ministri duntaxat per se, sed sicut ministri Dei, utpote per quos Deus salutem hominum operatur. Unde cavendum monemus, ne ea, quæ sunt conversionis nostræ et institutionis, ita occultæ virtuti Spiritus Sancti attribuamus, ut ministerium ecclesiasticum evacuemus. Nam convenit nos semper esse memores verborum Apostoli: *Quomodo credent, de quo non audierunt? quomodo autem audient absque prædicante? Ergo fides est ex auditu, auditus autem per Verbum Dei* (Rom. x. 14, 17). Et quod Dominus dixit in Evangelio: *Amen, amen, dico vobis, qui recipit, quemcunque misero, me recipit, qui autem me recipit, recipit eum, qui me misit* (Joh. xiii. 20). Et quod vir Macedo per visionem Paulo in Asia agenti apparens, submonuit et dixit: *Profectus in Macedoniam, sucurre nobis* (Act. xvi. 9). Alibi enim idem Apostolus dixit: *Dei sumus cooperarii, Dei agricolatio et ædificatio estis* (1 Cor. iii. 9).

2. Rursus tamen et hoc cavendum est, ne ministris et ministerio nimium tribuamus, memores etiam hic verborum Domini, dicentis in Evangelio: *Nemo venit ad me, nisi Pater meus traxerit eum* (Joh. vi. 44), et verborum Apostoli: *Quis igitur est Paulus? quis autem Apollo, nisi ministri, per quos credidistis, et ut cuique Dominus dedit? Ego plantavi, Apollo rigavit: sed Deus dedit incrementum. Itaque non qui plantat, est aliquid, neque qui rigat, sed qui dat incrementum Deus* (1 Cor. iii. 5–7). Credamus ergo, Deum Verbo suo nos docere foris per ministros suos, intus autem commovere electorum suorum corda ad fidem per Spiritum Sanctum; ideoque omnem gloriam totius hujus beneficii referendam esse ad Deum. Sed ea de re dictum est et primo capite hujus expositionis.

3. Et quidem ab initio mundi usus est Deus omnium præstantissimis in mundo (simplicibus quidem pluribus in mundana sapientia vel philosophia, sed excellentissimis in vera theologia) hominibus, Patriarchis videlicet, cum quibus non raro collocutus est per angelos. Fuerunt enim Patriarchæ sui seculi Prophetæ sive Doctores, quos Deus hoc nomine aliquot voluit secula vivere, ut essent veluti Patres et lumina orbis. Secutus est illos Moses cum Prophetis[1] per universum mundum celeberrimis.

4. Quid quod post hos misit Pater cœlestis Filium suum unigenitum, doctorem mundi absolutissimum, in quo est abscondita divina illa sapientia, et in nos derivata, per sacratissimam simplicissimamque et omnium perfectissimam doctrinam. Allegit enim ille sibi discipulos, quos fecit Apostolos. Hi vero exeuntes in mundum universum collegerunt ubique ecclesias per prædicationem Evangelii, deinde vero per omnes mundi ecclesias ordinarunt pastores atque doctores, ex præcepto Christi, per quorum successores hucusque Ecclesiam docuit ac gubernavit. Itaque ut Deus veteri populo dedit Patriarchas una cum Mose et Prophetis: ita novi testamenti populo misit suum unigenitum Filium una cum Apostolis et doctoribus ecclesiæ.

5. Porro ministri novi populi variis nuncupantur appellationibus. Dicuntur enim Apostoli, Prophetæ, Evangelistæ, Episcopi, Presbyteri, Pastores atque Doctores (1 Cor. xii. 3; Eph. iv. 11). Apostoli nullo certo consistebant loco, sed per orbem varias colligebant ecclesias. Quæ, ubi jam constitutæ erant, desierunt esse Apostoli, ac subierunt quique in sua ecclesia in locum istorum pastores. Prophetæ quondam, præscii futurorum, vates erant: sed et Scripturas interpretabantur, quales etiam hodie adhuc inveniuntur. Evangelistæ appellabantur scriptores Evangelicæ historiæ, sed et præcones Evangelii Christi; quomodo et Paulus Timotheum jubet implere opus Evangelistæ. Episcopi vero sunt inspectores vigilesque Ecclesiæ, qui victum et necessaria ecclesiæ dispensant. Presbyteri sunt seniores, et quasi senatores patresque Ecclesiæ, gubernantes ipsam consilio salubri. Pastores ovile Domini et custodiunt, et ei de rebus prospiciunt necessariis. Doctores erudiunt, et veram fidem pietatemque docent. Licebit ergo nunc ecclesiarum ministros nuncupare Episcopos, Presbyteros, Pastores atque Doctores.

6. Subsequentibus porro temporibus, multo plures in Ecclesiam Dei

---

[1] For *Prophetis* Niemeyer reads *prophetia*.

inductæ sunt nuncupationes ministrorum in Ecclesia. Alii enim ordinati sunt Patriarchæ, alii Archiepiscopi, alii Suffraganei, item Metropolitani, Archipresbyteri, Diaconi quoque, Subdiaconi, Acoluthi, Exorcistæ, Cantores, Janitores, et nescio, qui alii, ut Cardinales, Præpositi, et Priores, Patres minores et majores, ordines majores et minores. At de his omnibus nihil sumus nos soliciti, quales olim fuerint, aut nunc sint. Sufficit nobis Apostolica de ministris doctrina.

7. [Conf. Aug., de Abus. 6.] Ita cum sciamus certo, monachos et monachorum ordines vel sectas neque a Christo, neque ab Apostolis esse institutas; docemus, nihil eas ecclesiæ Dei utiles esse, imo perniciosas. Tametsi enim quondam (cum essent solitarii, et manibus sibi victum quærerent, nec ullis essent oneri, sed pastoribus ecclesiarum ubique parerent, ut laici) fuerint tolerabiles, tamen nunc, quales sint, videt et sentit universus orbis. Prætexunt nescio quæ vota et vivunt votis suis vitam prorsus contrariam : ut prorsus optimi eorum inter eos numerari mereantur, de quibus dixit Apostolus : *Audimus quosdam versantes inter vos inordinate, nihil operis facientes, sed curiose agentes. Tales ergo nos in nostris ecclesiis nec habemus, nec in ecclesiis Christi habendos esse docemus* (2 Thess. iii. 11, 12).

8. Nemo autem honorem ministerii ecclesiastici usurpare sibi, id est, ad se largitionibus, aut ullis artibus, aut arbitrio proprio, rapere debet. Vocentur et eligantur electione ecclesiastica et legitima ministri ecclesiæ : id est, eligantur religiose ab Ecclesia, vel ad hoc deputatis ab Ecclesia, ordine justo, et absque turba, seditionibus et contentione. Eligantur autem non quilibet, sed homines idonei, eruditione justa et sacra, eloquentia pia, prudentiaque simplici, denique moderatione et honestate vitæ insignes, juxta canonem Apostolicum, qui ab Apostolo contexitur in 1 ad Tim. iii. et ad Tit. i. Et qui electi sunt, ordinentur a senioribus cum orationibus publicis, et impositione manuum. Damnamus hic omnes, qui sua sponte currunt, cum non sint electi, missi, vel ordinati (Jer. xxiii. 32). Damnamus ministros ineptos, et non instructos donis pastori necessariis.

9. Interim agnoscimus, quorundam in veteri Ecclesia pastorum simplicitatem innocuam plus aliquando profuisse ecclesiæ, quam quorundam eruditionem variam, exquisitam, delicatamque, sed paulo fastuosiorem. Unde ne hodie quidem rejicimus simplicitatem quorundam probam, nec tamen omnino imperitam.

10. Nuncupant sane Apostoli Christi omnes in Christum credentes sacerdotes, sed non ratione ministerii, sed quod per Christum omnes fideles facti reges et sacerdotes, offerre possumus spirituales Deo hostias (Exod. xix. 6; 1 Pet. ii. 9; Apoc. i. 6). Diversissima ergo inter se sunt sacerdotium et ministerium. Illud enim commune est Christianis omnibus, ut modo diximus, hoc non item. Nec e medio sustulimus ecclesiæ ministerium, quando repudiavimus ex Ecclesia Christi sacerdotium papisticum.

11. Equidem in Novo Testamento Christi non est amplius tale sacerdotium, quale fuit in populo veteri, quod unctionem habuit externam, vestes sacras et cærimonias plurimas: quæ typi fuerunt Christi, qui illa omnia veniens et adimplens abrogavit. *Manet autem ipse solus sacerdos in æternum* (Ebr. v. 6); cui ne quid derogemus, nemini inter ministros sacerdotis vocabulum communicamus. Ipse enim Dominus noster non ordinavit ullos in Ecclesia Novi Testamenti sacerdotes, qui accepta potestate a suffraganeo, offerant quotidie hostiam, ipsam inquam carnem et ipsum sanguinem Domini pro vivis et mortuis, sed qui doceant et sacramenta administrent. Paulus enim simpliciter et breviter, quid sentiamus de Novi Testamenti vel de Ecclesiæ Christianæ ministris, et quid eis tribuamus, exponens: *Sic nos æstimet homo*, inquit, *ut ministros Christi, et dispensatores mysteriorum Dei* (1 Cor. iv. 1). Proinde vult Apostolus, ut de ministris sentiamus, tanquam de ministris. Ὑπηρέτας vero nuncupavit Apostolus subremigatores, qui ad nauclerum unice respiciunt, vel homines non sibi, nec suo arbitrio, sed aliis viventes, Dominis inquam suis, a quorum mandatis omnino dependent. Nam minister Ecclesiæ totus et in omnibus suis officiis non suo arbitrio indulgere, sed illud duntaxat exsequi jubetur, quod in mandatis habet a suo Domino. Et in præsenti, quis sit Dominus, exprimitur, Christus, cui in omnibus ministerii negotiis sunt mancipati ministri.

12. Adjicit præterea, quo ministerium plenius explanet, ministros Ecclesiæ œconomos esse vel dispensatores mysteriorum Dei. Mysteria vero Dei multis in locis, imprimis ad Eph. iii. 3 appellavit Paulus Evangelium Christi. Mysteria nuncupavit etiam vetustas Christi sacramenta. Proinde in hoc sunt vocati ministri Ecclesiæ, ut Evangelium Christi adnuncient fidelibus, et sacramenta administrent. Alibi enim legimus in Evangelio *de fideli servo et prudente, quod eum Dominus*

constituit super familiam suam, ut tempore opportuno det ei cibum suum (Luc. xii. 42). Rursus proficiscitur alibi in Evangelio peregre homo, relinquens domum, et in hac dat servis suis potestatem vel substantiam suam, et suum cuique opus (Matt. xxv. 14 sqq.).

13. [Conf. Aug., de Abus. 7.] Nunc ergo commode dicemus etiam quædam de potestate et officio ministrorum Ecclesiæ. De potestate hac operosius quidam disputarunt, subdideruntque suæ potestati omnia in terris summa, idque contra mandatum Domini, qui suis dominium prohibuit, humilitatem autem maximopere commendavit (Luc. xxii. 25 ; Matt. xviii. 1 sqq.; xx. 25). Revera alia quidem potestas est mera et absoluta, quæ et juris vocatur. Ea potestate Christo Domino universorum subjecta sunt omnia: sicuti ipse testatus est et dixit : *Data est mihi potestas in cœlo et in terra* (Matt. xxviii. 18). Et iterum : *Ego sum primus et novissimus, ecce sum vivens in sæcula sæculorum, et habeo claves inferni et mortis* (Apoc. i. 17, 18). Item : *Ipse habet clavem David, qui aperit, et nemo claudit, claudit, et nemo aperit* (Apoc. iii. 7).

14. Hanc potestatem sibi servat Dominus, nec in alium quemquam transfert, ut ipse deinceps otiosus adsistat, operantibus ministris spectator. Jesaias enim : *Clavem domus David*, inquit, *ponam super humerum ejus* (Jes. xxii. 22), et iterum : *Cujus imperium erit super humerum ejus* (Jer. ix. 6). Nam gubernationem non injicit aliis in suos humeros, sed servat et utitur adhuc potestate sua, gubernans omnia. Alia porro potestas est officii vel ministerialis, limitata ab eo, qui plena utitur potestate. Ea ministerio, quam imperio similior est. Concedit enim Dominus aliquis œconomo suo potestatem in domum suam, quo nomine et claves dat, quibus intromittat in domum, vel ex domo excludat, quos Dominus vel intromitti vult, vel excludi. Juxta hanc potestatem facit minister ex officio, quod a Domino jussus est facere : et Dominus ratum habet, quod facit, ipsumque ministri sui factum, perinde ut suum vult æstimari atque agnosci.

15. Quo nimirum pertinent illæ Evangelicæ sententiæ : *Dabo tibi claves regni cœlorum, et, quicquid adligaveris aut solveris in terra, adligatum aut solutum erit in cœlis* (Matt. xvi. 19). Item : *Quorumcunque remiseritis peccata, remittentur eis, et quorumcunque retinueritis peccata, retenta erunt* (Joh. xx. 23). Nisi vero minister res omnes ita expediverit, sicut jussus est a Domino suo, sed limites fidei transilierit, sane irritum habetur a Domino, quod fecit. Proinde potestas eccle-

siastica ministrorum Ecclesiæ est functio illa, qua ministri Ecclesiam
Dei gubernant quidem, verum omnia in Ecclesia sic faciunt, quemadmodum verbo suo præscripsit Dominus: quæ cum facta sunt, fideles
tanquam ab ipso Domino facta reputant. Et de clavibus antea quoque
dictum est nonnihil.

16. Data est autem omnibus in Ecclesia ministris una et æqualis
potestas sive functio. Certe ab initio Episcopi vel Presbyteri Ecclesiam communi opera gubernaverunt; nullus alteri se prætulit, aut sibi
ampliorem potestatem dominiumve in coëpiscopos usurpavit. Memores
enim verborum Domini: *Qui voluerit inter vos primus esse, sit vester
servus* (Luc. xxii. 26); continuerunt se in humilitate, et mutuis officiis
juverunt se invicem in gubernanda et conservanda Ecclesia. Interea
propter ordinem servandum, unus aut certus aliquis ministrorum cœtum
convocavit, et in cœtu res consultandas proposuit, sententias item aliorum collegit, denique, ne qua oriretur confusio, pro virili cavit.

17. Sic legitur fecisse in Actis App. S. Petrus, qui tamen ideo nec
aliis fuit præpositus, nec potestate majore ceteris præditus. Rectissime
enim Cyprianus, martyr, de simplicitate clericorum: Hoc erant utique,
inquit, et ceteri Apostoli, quod fuit Petrus, pari consortio præditi et
honoris et potestatis; sed exordium ab unitate proficiscitur, ut Ecclesia
una monstretur. Refert item S. Hieronymus non disparia in Comment. ad Ep. ad Tit. Pauli, et dicit: Antequam diaboli instinctu studia
in religione fierent, communi Presbyterorum consilio Ecclesiæ guber-
nabantur, postquam vero unusquisque eos, quos baptizaverat, suos puta-
bat, non Christi, decretum est, ut unus de Presbyteris electus super-
poneretur ceteris, ad quem omnis ecclesiæ cura pertineret, et schismatum semina tollerentur. Hoc tamen decretum Hieronymus non pro
divino venditat. Mox enim subjicit: Sicut Presbyteri sciunt, se ex
ecclesiæ consuetudine, ei, qui sibi præpositus fuerit, esse subjectos: ita
Episcopi noverint, se magis consuetudine, quam dispositionis Dominicæ
veritate, Presbyteris esse majores, et in commune debere Ecclesiam re-
gere. Hæc ille. Ideoque nemo jure prohibuerit ad veterem Ecclesiæ
Dei constitutionem redire, et illam præ humana consuetudine recipere.

18. Officia ministrorum sunt varia, quæ tamen plerique ad duo re-
stringunt, in quibus omnia alia comprehenduntur, ad doctrinam Christi Evangelicam, et ad legitimam sacramentorum administrationem.
Ministrorum enim est congregare cœtum sacrum. in hoc exponere Ver-

bum Dei, et universam doctrinam accommodare ad rationem usumque
Ecclesiæ, ut ea, quæ docentur, prosint auditoribus, et ædificent fideles.
Ministrorum, inquam, est, docere imperitos, hortari item, et urgere ad
progrediendum in via Domini cessantes, aut etiam tardius procedentes,
consolari item et confirmare pusillanimes, munireque contra Satanæ
tentationes varias, corripere peccantes, revocare in viam errantes, lapsos erigere, contradicentes revincere, lupos denique ab ovili Dominico
abigere, scelera item et sceleratos prudenter et graviter increpare,
neque connivere aut tacere ad conscelerationem : sed et sacramenta
administrare, usumque eorum justum commendare, et omnes ad illa
percipienda per sanam doctrinam præparare, in unitate quoque sancta
fideles conservare, et schismata prohibere, denique catechisare rudes,
pauperum necessitatem commendare ecclesiæ, ægrotantes et variis im-
pexos tentationibus visitare, instruere, et in via vitæ retinere : præterea
orationes publicas, vel supplicationes necessitatis tempore, una cum jejunio, id est, abstinentia sancta procurare ; et omnia quæ pertinent ad
ecclesiarum tranquillitatem, pacem et salutem, quam diligentissime
curare.

19. Ut autem hæc omnia rectius faciliusque possit minister præstare,
requiritur ab eo imprimis, ut sit Dei timens, oret sedulo, lectioni sacræ
intendat, et in omnibus et semper vigilet, et puritate vitæ omnibus
præluceat.

20. Cumque omnino oporteat esse in Ecclesia disciplinam, et apud
veteres quondam usitata fuerit excommunicatio, fuerintque judicia
ecclesiastica in populo Dei, in quibus per viros prudentes et pios exer-
cebatur hæc disciplina, ministrorum quoque fuerit, ad ædificationem,
disciplinam moderari hanc, pro conditione temporum, status publici,
ac necessitate. Ubi semper tenenda est regula, omnia fieri debere ad
ædificationem, decenter, honeste, sine tyrannide et seditione. Apostolus enim testatur : *Sibi a Deo traditam esse in Ecclesia potestatem
ad ædificationem et non ad destructionem* (2 Cor. x. 8). Nam ipsemet
Dominus vetuit, lolium in agro Dominico eradicari, quando periculum
sit, ne et triticum evellatur (Matt. xiii. 29).

21. Ceterum exsecramur in præsenti Donatistarum errorem, qui doctrinam et administrationem sacramentorum, vel efficacem vel ineffica-
cem, ex mala vel bona ministrorum vita æstimant. Scimus enim,
vocem Christi audiendam esse vel ex malorum ministrorum ore.

Quando ipse Dominus dixit: *Quæ dicunt, facite, secundum opera autem eorum nolite facere* (Matt. xxiii. 3). Scimus, sacramenta ex institutione et per Verbum Christi sanctificari, et efficacia esse piis, tametsi offerantur ab indignis ministris. De qua re ex Scripturis multa contra Donatistas disputavit beatus Dei servus Augustinus.

22. Atqui debet interim justa esse inter ministros disciplina. Inquirendum enim diligenter in doctrinam et vitam ministrorum, in synodis. Corripiendi sunt peccantes a senioribus, et in viam reducendi, si sunt sanabiles, aut deponendi, et velut lupi abigendi sunt per veros Pastores a grege Dominico, si sunt incurabiles. Si enim sint pseudo-doctores, minime ferendi sunt. Neque vero et œcumenica improbamus concilia, si ad exemplum celebrentur Apostolicum, ad Ecclesiæ salutem, non perniciem.

23. Ministri quoque fideles omnes, ut boni operarii, mercede sua digni sunt, nec peccant, quando stipendium omniaque interim necessaria pro se et sua familia accipiunt. Nam Apostolus ostendit, hæc jure dari ab Ecclesia, et accipi a ministris, in 1 ad Cor. ix. et 1 ad Tim. v. et alibi quoque. Confutati sunt autem Apostolica doctrina et Anabaptistæ, qui ministros ex ministerio suo viventes damnant, et conviciis proscindunt.

CAP. XIX.

De Sacramentis Ecclesiæ Christi. [Conf. Aug., Art. XIII.]

1. Prædicationi verbi sui adjunxit Deus mox ab initio, in Ecclesia sua, sacramenta vel signa sacramentalia. Ita enim clare testatur universa Scriptura sacra. Sunt autem sacramenta symbola mystica, vel ritus sancti aut sacræ actiones, a Deo ipso institutæ, constantes verbo suo, signis, et rebus significatis, quibus in Ecclesia summa sua beneficia, homini exhibita, retinet in memoria, et subinde renovat, quibus item promissiones suas obsignat, et quæ ipse nobis interius præstat, exterius repræsentat, ac veluti oculis contemplanda subjicit, adeoque fidem nostram, Spiritu Dei in cordibus nostris operante, roborat et auget: quibus denique nos ab omnibus aliis populis et religionibus separat, sibique soli consecrat et obligat, et quid a nobis requirat, significat.

2. Et sunt quidem alia veteris, alia novi populi sacramenta. Veteris populi sacramenta fuerunt circumcisio, et agnus paschalis, qui immo-

labatur: quo nomine ad sacrificia refertur, quæ fuerunt celebrata ab origine mundi. Novi populi sacramenta sunt baptismus, et cœna Dominica. Sunt, qui septem sacramenta novi populi numerent. Ex quibus nos pœnitentiam, ordinationem ministrorum, non papisticam quidem illam, sed Apostolicam, et matrimonium agnoscimus instituta esse Dei utilia, sed non sacramenta. Confirmatio et extrema unctio inventa sunt hominum, quibus nullo cum damno carere potest Ecclesia. Neque illa nos in nostris ecclesiis habemus. Nam habent illa quædam, quæ minime probare possumus. Nundinationem omnem, quam exercent Romanenses in dispensatione sacramentorum, omnino execramur.

3. Auctor autem sacramentorum omnium non est homo ullus, sed Deus solus. Homines sacramenta instituere non possunt. Nam pertinent illa ad cultum Dei. At hominum non est, instituere et formare cultum Dei; sed traditum a Deo recipere et custodire. Præterea habent symbola promissiones adjunctas, quæ requirunt fidem. Fides autem solo Dei Verbo innititur. Et Verbum Dei habetur instar tabularum vel literarum, sacramenta vero instar sigillorum: quæ literis Deus adpendit solus. Et ut Deus sacramentorum auctor est, ita perpetuo operatur in Ecclesia, in qua rite peraguntur sacramenta: adeo ut fideles, cum a ministris sacramenta percipiunt, agnoscant, operari Deum in suo instituto, ideoque sacramenta perinde, ac ex ipsius Dei manu percipere, et ipsis ministri vitium (si quod insigne ipsi insit) non obesse, quando agnoscant, sacramentorum integritatem dependere ab institutione Domini. Unde etiam discriminant aperte in administratione sacramentorum inter Dominum ipsum, et Domini ministrum, confitentes, sacramentorum res dari ab ipso Domino, symbola autem a Domini ministris.

4. Ceterum præcipuum illud, quod in omnibus sacramentis proponitur a Deo, et attenditur a piis omnibus omnium temporum (quod alii nuncupant substantiam et materiam sacramentorum) Christus est Servator, hostia illa unica, agnus item ille Dei mactatus ab origine mundi, petra quoque illa, de qua omnes majores nostri biberunt, per quem electi omnes circumciduntur sine manibus, per Spiritum Sanctum, abluunturque a peccatis suis omnibus, et aluntur vero corpore et sanguine Christi ad vitam æternam.

5. Et quantum quidem attinet ad illud, quod in sacramentis est præcipuum et res ipsa, paria sunt utriusque populi sacramenta. Nam

Christus unicus Mediator et Servator fidelium utrobique est illud præcipuum et ipsa res sacramentorum. Unus et idem Deus, utrobique
horum est auctor. Utrique populo data sunt illa, ut signa adeoque
obsignationes gratiæ et promissionum Dei, quæ in memoriam reducant,
reparentque maxima Dei beneficia, quibus item fideles ab omnibus
aliis orbis religionibus sejungerentur, denique quæ spiritualiter per
fidem perciperentur, et percipientes obstringerent Ecclesiæ, et ipsos
sui admonerent officii. In his inquam et similibus non disparia sunt
utriusque populi sacramenta, quæ tamen in signis sunt diversa.

6. Et quidem constituimus etiam in his ampliorem differentiam.
Nostra enim firmiora et magis durabilia sunt, utpote quæ in finem
usque seculi nunquam mutabuntur. Sed et rem et promissionem completam vel perfectam in Christo testantur, quam complendam illa sig-
nificabant. Simpliciora item sunt nostra et minus operosa, minus item
sumptuosa et cærimoniis involuta. Pertinent præterea ad ampliorem
populum, per totum terrarum orbem dispersum: cumque etiam illus-
triora sint, et majorem (per Spiritum Sanctum) excitent fidem, inse-
quitur etiam uberior spiritus copia.

7. Certe cum Christus verus Messias nobis sit exhibitus, et abundantiá
gratiæ[1] effusa in populum Novi Testamenti, abrogata sunt utique, ac
desierunt veteris populi sacramenta, et subrogata sunt Novi Testamenti
symbola, in locum circumcisionis, baptismus, et in locum agni Paschalis sacrificiorumque, cœna Dominica.

8. Sicut autem quondam sacramenta constabant verbo, signo et re
significata, ita nunc quoque iisdem veluti partibus absolvuntur. Nam
Verbo Dei fiunt, quæ antea non fuerunt, sacramenta. Consecrantur
enim Verbo et sanctificata esse ostenduntur ab eo, qui instituit. Et
sanctificare vel consecrare est, rem aliquam Deo sacrisque usibus de-
dicare, h. e. a communi vel profano usu segregare et sacro usui desti-
nare. Sunt enim in sacramentis signa petita ex usu vulgari, res externæ et visibiles. In baptismo enim signum est elementum aquæ,
ablutioque illa visibilis, quæ fit per ministrum. Res autem significata
est regeneratio vel ablutio a peccatis. In cœna vero Domini signum
est panis et vinum, sumptum ex communi usu cibi et potus. Res
autem significata est ipsum traditum Domini corpus, et sanguis ejus

---

[1] Kindler reads '*et abundans gratia.*'

effusus pro nobis, vel communio corporis et sanguinis Domini. Proinde aqua, panis et vinum sua natura, et extra institutionem divinam ac usum sanctum, duntaxat id sunt, quod esse dicuntur, et experimur. Ceterum, si accedat Domini Verbum, cum invocatione divini nominis, et renovatione primæ institutionis et sanctificationis, signa ista consecrantur, et sanctificata a Christo esse ostenduntur. Manet enim semper efficax in Ecclesia Dei prima Christi institutio et consecratio sacramentorum adeo ut, qui non aliter celebrent sacramenta, quam ipse Dominus ab initio instituit, fruantur etiam nunc prima illa consecratione omnium præstantissima. Et ideo recitantur in celebratione sacramentorum ipsa verba Christi.

9. Et quoniam Verbo Dei discimus, quod signa hæc in alium finem sint instituta a Domino, quam usurpentur vulgo, ideo docemus, signa nunc in usu sacro usurpare rerum signatarum vocabula, nec appellari amplius aquam tantum, panem et vinum, sed etiam regenerationem vel lavacrum renovationis, item corpus et sanguinem Domini, vel symbola aut sacramenta corporis et sanguinis Domini; non quod symbola mutentur in res significatas, et desinant esse id, quod sunt sua natura. Alioqui enim sacramenta non essent, quæ re significata duntaxat constarent, signa non essent : sed ideo usurpant signa rerum nomina, quod rerum sacrarum sint symbola mystica, et signa et res significatæ inter se sacramentaliter conjungantur, conjungantur inquam, vel uniantur per significationem mysticam, et voluntatem vel consilium ejus, qui sacramenta instituit.

10. Non enim aqua, panis et vinum sunt signa vulgaria, sed sacra. Et qui instituit aquam baptismi, non ea voluntate consilioque instituit, ut fideles aqua duntaxat baptismi perfundantur : et qui jussit in cœna sacra panem edere, et vinum bibere, non hoc voluit, ut fideles panem et vinum tantum percipiant sine mysterio, sicut domi suæ panem manducant, sed ut rebus quoque significatis spiritualiter communicent, et vere per fidem abluantur a peccatis, et Christo participent.

11. Idcirco minime probamus eos, qui sanctificationem sacramentorum attribuunt, nescio, quibus characteribus, et recitationi, vel virtuti verborum pronuntiatorum a consecratore,[1] et qui habeat intentionem consecrandi, aut rebus aliis adventitiis, quæ neque Christi, neque Apo-

---

[1] Niemeyer : '*a consecrato.*'

stolorum, vel verbo, vel exemplo nobis traduntur. Neque probamus eorum quoque doctrinam, qui de sacramentis perinde loquuntur, ut signis communibus, non sanctificatis aut efficacibus. Neque eos probamus, qui propter invisibilia aspernantur in sacramentis visibilia, adeoque signa sibi credunt fore supervacanea, quod rebus se jam frui arbitrantur, quales Messaliani fuisse dicuntur. Neque vero approbamus istorum quoque doctrinam, qui docent, gratiam et res significatas signis ita alligari et includi, ut quicunque signis exterius participent, etiam interius gratiæ rebusque significatis participes sint, quales quales sint.

12. Interim sicut a dignitate vel indignitate ministrorum non æstimamus integritatem sacramentorum, ita neque a conditione sumentium. Agnoscimus enim sacramentorum integritatem ex fide vel veritate meraque bonitate Dei dependere. Sicut enim Verbum Dei manet verum Verbum Dei, quo non tantum verba nuda recitantur, dum prædicatur, sed simul a Deo offeruntur res verbis significatæ, vel adnunciatæ, tametsi impii vel increduli verba audiant, et intelligant, rebus tamen significatis non perfruantur: eo quod vera fide non recipiant: Ita sacramenta verbo, signis et rebus significatis constantia, manent vera et integra sacramenta, non tantum significantia res sacras, sed Deo offerente etiam res significatas, tametsi increduli res oblatas non percipiant. Fit hoc non dantis aut offerentis Dei vitio, sed hominum sine fide illegitimeque accipientium culpa: *Quorum incredulitas fidem Dei irritam non facit* (Rom. iii. 3).

13. Porro cum mox ab initio, quando expositum est, quid sint sacramenta, pariter et obiter explicatum sit, ad quid sint instituta; non est, quod semel dicta cum molestia repetantur. Consequenter ergo sigillatim dicemus de novi populi sacramentis.

CAP. XX.

De Sancto Baptismo. [Conf. Aug., Art. IX.]

1. Baptismus a Deo institutus et consecratus est, primusque baptizavit Joannes, qui Christum aqua in Jordano tinxit. Inde defluxit ad Apostolos, qui et ipsi aqua baptizarunt. Jussit hos manifeste Dominus Evangelium prædicare, *et baptizare in nomine Patris et Filii et Spiritus Sancti* (Matt. xxviii. 19); et Petrus ad Judæos interrogantes, quid facere deberent? dixit in Actis: *Baptizetur unusquisque ves-*

trum in nomine Jesu Christi, ad remissionem peccatorum, et acci-
pietis donum Spiritus Sancti (Act. ii. 37, 38). Unde a nonnullis
baptismus nuncupatus est signum initiale populi Dei, utpote quo ini-
tiantur Deo electi Dei.

2. Unus est duntaxat baptismus in Ecclesia Dei, et satis est semel
baptizari vel initiari Deo. Durat autem semel susceptus baptismus
per omnem vitam, et est perpetua obsignatio adoptionis nostræ. Etenim baptizari in nomine Christi est: inscribi, initiari et recipi in fœdus
atque familiam adeoque in hæreditatem filiorum Dei, imo, jam nunc
nuncupari nomine Dei, id est, appellari filium Dei, purgari item a
sordibus peccatorum, et donari varia Dei gratia ad vitam novam et
innocentem. Baptismus ergo in memoria retinet et reparat ingens
Dei beneficium generi mortalium præstitum.

3. Nascimur enim omnes in peccatorum sordibus, et sumus filii iræ.
Deus autem, qui dives est misericordia, purgat nos a peccatis gratuito,
per sanguinem Filii sui, et in hoc adoptat nos in filios, adeoque fœdere sancto nos sibi connectit, et variis donis ditat, ut possimus novam
vivere vitam. Obsignantur hæc omnia baptismo. Nam intus regene-
ramur, purificamur, et renovamur a Deo per Spiritum Sanctum: foris
autem accipimus obsignationem maximorum donorum in aqua, qua
etiam maxima illa beneficia repræsentantur et veluti oculis nostris
conspicienda proponuntur. Ideoque baptizamur, id est, abluimur, aut
adspergimur aqua visibili. Aqua enim sordes mundat, deficientia et
æstuantia recreat et refrigerat corpora. Gratia vero Dei hæc animabus præstat, et quidem invisibiliter vel spiritualiter.

4. Separat item Deus nos baptismi symbolo ab omnibus alienis religionibus et populis, et sibi consecrat ceu peculium: nos itaque, dum
baptizamur, confitemur fidem nostram et obstringimur Deo ad obedientiam et mortificationem carnis vitæque novitatem, adeoque inscribi-
mur in sanctam Christi militiam, ut toto vitæ cursu pugnemus contra
mundum, et Satanam, atque carnem propriam. Baptizamur præterea
in unum Ecclesiæ corpus, ut cum omnibus membris Ecclesiæ pulchre
in una et eadem religione mutuisque officiis consentiamus.

5. Credimus perfectissimam esse baptizandi formam, qua Christus
ipse baptizatus est, et qua baptizarunt Apostoli. Ergo, quæ humana
inventione postea adjecta et usurpata sunt in Ecclesia, non arbitramur
necessaria esse ad perfectionem baptismi: cujus generis est exorcismus,

usus item ardentis luminis, olei, salis, sputi, et similium rerum, ut, quod baptismus singulis annis pluribus cærimoniis bis consecratur. Nos enim credimus, unum Ecclesiæ baptismum in prima Dei institutione sanctificatum esse, et consecrari per verbum, efficacemque esse nunc etiam propter primam Dei benedictionem.

6. Docemus, baptismum in Ecclesia non administrari debere a mulierculis, vel ab obstetricibus. Paulus enim removit mulierculas ab officiis ecclesiasticis. Baptismus autem pertinet ad officia ecclesiastica. Damnamus Anabaptistas, qui negant baptizandos esse infantulos recens natos a fidelibus. Nam juxta doctrinam Evangelicam horum est regnum Dei, et sunt in fœdere Dei; cur itaque non daretur eis signum fœderis Dei? cur non per sanctum baptisma initiarentur, qui sunt peculium et in Ecclesia Dei? Damnamus Anabaptistas et in aliis ipsorum dogmatibus, quæ contra Verbum Dei peculiaria habent. Non sumus ergo Anabaptistæ, neque cum eis in ulla re ipsorum communicamus.

CAP. XXI.

DE SACRA CŒNA DOMINI. [CONF. AUG., ART. X.]

1. Cœna Domini, quæ et mensa Domini, et eucharistia, id est, gratiarum actio nuncupatur, ideo cœna nuncupatur vulgo, quod a Christo in ultima illa cœna sua instituta sit, eamque adhuc repræsentet, ac in ipsa spiritualiter cibentur et potentur fideles. Auctor enim cœnæ Dominicæ non est angelus aut homo ullus, sed ipse Dei Filius, Dominus noster Jesus Christus, qui primus eam Ecclesiæ suæ consecravit. Durat autem ea consecratio vel benedictio adhuc apud omnes eos, qui non aliam cœnam, sed illam ipsam celebrant, quam Dominus instituit; ad quam verba cœnæ Domini recitant, et in omnibus ad unum Christum vera fide respiciunt, et cujus veluti manibus accipiunt, quod per ministerium ministrorum Ecclesiæ accipiunt.

2. Retinere vult Dominus ritu hoc sacro in recenti memoria maximum generi mortalium præstitum beneficium, nempe quod, tradito corpore, et effuso suo sanguine, omnia nobis peccata nostra condonavit, ac a morte æterna et potestate diaboli nos redemit, jam pascit nos sua carne et potat suo sanguine, quæ vera fide spiritualiter percepta, alunt nos ad vitam æternam. Et hoc tantum beneficium renovatur toties,

quoties cœna Domini celebratur. Dixit enim Dominus: *Hoc facite in mei commemorationem.* Obsignatur item hac cœna sancta, quod revera corpus Domini pro nobis traditum et sanguis ejus in remissionem peccatorum nostrorum effusus est, ne quid fides nostra vacillet.

3. Et quidem visibiliter hoc foris sacramento per ministrum repræsentatur, et veluti oculis contemplandum exponitur, quod intus in anima invisibiliter per ipsum Spiritum Sanctum præstatur. Foris offertur a ministro panis, et audiuntur voces Domini: *Accipite, edite, hoc est corpus meum, accipite et dividite inter vos, bibite ex hoc omnes, hic est sanguis meus.* Ergo accipiunt fideles, quod datur a ministro Domini, et edunt panem Domini, ac bibunt de poculo Domini: intus interim opera Christi per Spiritum Sanctum percipiunt etiam carnem et sanguinem Domini, et pascuntur his in vitam æternam. Etenim caro et sanguis Christi verus cibus et potus est ad vitam æternam; et Christus ipse, quatenus pro nobis traditus et Salvator noster est, illud præcipuum cœnæ est, nec patimur, quicquam aliud in locum ejus substitui.

4. Ut autem rectius et perspicacius intelligatur, quo modo caro et sanguis Christi sint cibus et potus fidelium, percipianturque a fidelibus ad vitam æternam, paucula hæc adjiciemus. Manducatio non est unius generis. Est enim manducatio corporalis, qua cibus in os percipitur ab homine, dentibus atteritur et in ventrem deglutitur. Hoc manducationis genere intellexerunt olim Capernaitæ sibi manducandam carnem Domini, sed refutantur ab ipso, Joann. cap. vi. Nam ut caro Christi corporaliter manducari non potest citra flagitium aut truculentiam, ita non est cibus ventris. Id quod omnes fateri coguntur. Improbamus canonem in decretis itaque pontificum: Ego Berengarius, etc. (De Consecratione, Distinct. 2). Neque enim credidit vetustas pia, neque nos credimus, corpus Christi manducari ore corporis corporaliter vel essentialiter.

5. Est et spiritualis manducatio corporis Christi, non ea quidem, qua existimemus cibum mutari in spiritum, sed qua, manente in sua essentia et proprietate corpore et sanguine Domini, ea nobis communicantur spiritualiter, utique non corporali modo, sed spirituali, per Spiritum Sanctum, qui videlicet ea, quæ per carnem et sanguinem Domini pro nobis in mortem tradita parata sunt, ipsam, inquam, remissionem peccatorum, liberationem et vitam æternam, applicat et confert nobis, ita

ut Christus in nobis vivat et nos in ipso vivamus, efficitque, ut ipsum, quo talis fit cibus et potus spiritualis noster, id est, vita nostra, vera fide percipiamus.

6. Sicut enim cibus et potus corporalis corpora nostra non tantum reficiunt ac roborant, sed et in vita conservant: ita et caro Christi tradita pro nobis, et sanguis ejus effusus pro nobis, non tantum reficiunt et roborant animas nostras, sed etiam in vita conservant, non quatenus quidem corporaliter eduntur et bibuntur, sed quatenus spiritualiter nobis a Spiritu Dei communicantur, dicente Domino: *Et panis, quem ego dabo, caro mea est, quam dabo pro mundi vita.* Item: *Caro* (nimirum corporaliter manducato) *non prodest quidquam, spiritus est, qui vivificat.* Et: *Verba, quæ loquor vobis, spiritus et vita sunt* (Joh. vi. 51, 63). Et sicut oportet cibum in nosmetipsos edendo recipere, ut operetur in nobis, suamque in nobis efficaciam exserat, cum extra nos positus nihil nobis prosit: ita necesse est, nos fide Christum recipere, ut noster fiat, vivatque in nobis et nos in ipso. Dicit enim: *Ego sum panis vitæ. Qui venit ad me, non esuriet, et qui credit in me, non sitiet unquam.* Item: *Qui ederit me, vivet et ipse propter me: ac manet in me et ego in ipso* (Joh. vi. 51, 52).

7. Ex quibus omnibus claret, nos per spiritualem cibum minime intelligere imaginarium, nescio quem, cibum, sed ipsum Domini corpus pro nobis traditum, quod tamen percipiatur a fidelibus, non corporaliter, sed spiritualiter per fidem. In qua re sequimur per omnia doctrinam ipsius Salvatoris Christi Domini apud Joh. vi. Et hic esus carnis et potus sanguinis Domini ita est necessarius ad salutem, ut sine ipso nullus servari possit. Fit autem hic esus et potus spiritualis etiam extra Domini cœnam, et quoties, aut ubicunque homo in Christum crediderit. Quo fortassis illud Augustini pertinet: quid paras dentem et ventrem? crede, et manducasti.

8. Præter superiorem manducationem spiritualem est et sacramentalis manducatio corporis Domini, qua fidelis non tantum spiritualiter et interne participat vero corpore et sanguine Domini, sed foris etiam accedendo ad mensam Domini accipit visibile corporis et sanguinis Domini sacramentum. Prius quidem, dum credidit fidelis, vivificum alimentum percepit, et ipso fruitur adhuc, sed ideo, dum nunc sacramentum quoque accipit, non nihil accipit. Nam in continuatione communicationis corporis et sanguinis Domini pergit, adeoque magis

magisque incenditur et crescit fides, ac spirituali alimonia reficitur.
Dum enim vivimus, fides continuas habet accessiones. Et qui foris
vera fide sacramentum percipit, idem ille non signum duntaxat percipit, sed re ipsa quoque, ut diximus, fruitur. Præterea idem ille institutioni et mandato Domini obedit, lætoque animo gratias pro redemptione sua totiusque generis humani agit, ac fidelem mortis Dominicæ memoriam peragit, atque coram Ecclesia, cujus corporis membrum sit, attestatur; obsignatur item percipientibus sacramentum,
quod corpus Domini non tantum in genere pro hominibus sit traditum, et sanguis ejus effusus, sed peculiariter pro quovis fideli com-
municante, cujus cibus et potus sit ad vitam æternam.

9. Cæterum qui nulla cum fide ad hanc sacram Domini mensam
accedit, sacramento duntaxat communicat, et rem sacramenti, unde
est vita et salus, non percipit. Et tales indigne edunt de mensa Domini. Qui autem indigne edunt de pane Domini et de poculo ejus
bibunt, rei fiunt corporis et sanguinis Domini, et ad judicium sibi
edunt et bibunt. Nam cum vera fide non accedant, mortem Christi
contumelia adficiunt, et ideo damnationem sibi ipsis edunt et bibunt.

10. Ergo corpus Domini et sanguinem ejus cum pane et vino non
ita conjungimus, ut panem ipsum dicamus esse corpus Christi, nisi
ratione sacramentali, aut sub pane corporaliter latitare corpus Christi:
ut etiam sub speciebus panis adorari debeat, aut quicunque signum
percipiat, idem et rem percipiat ipsam. Corpus Christi in cœlis est
ad dextram Patris. Sursum ergo elevanda sunt corda, et non defi-
genda in panem, nec adorandus Dominus in pane. Et tamen non est
absens Ecclesiæ suæ celebranti cœnam Dominus. Sol absens a nobis
in cœlo, nihilominus efficaciter præsens est nobis: quanto magis sol
justitiæ Christus, corpore in cœlis absens nobis, præsens est nobis, non
corporaliter quidem, sed spiritualiter per vivificam operationem, et ut
ipse se nobis præsentem futurum exposuit in ultima cœna (Joh. xiv.,
xv., xvi.). Unde consequens est, nos non habere cœnam sine Christo,
interim tamen habere cœnam incruentam et mysticam, sicuti universa
nuncupavit vetustas.

11. Admonemur præterea celebratione cœnæ Dominicæ, ut memores simus, cujus corporis membra facti simus, et idcirco concordes
simus cum omnibus fratribus, ut sancte vivamus, et non polluamus
nos flagitiis et peregrinis religionibus, sed in vera fide in finem usque

vitæ perseverantes, studeamus excellere sanctimonia vitæ. Decet ergo, ut accessuri ad cœnam, prius nos ipsos juxta præceptum Apostoli probemus, imprimis quali simus fide præditi, an credamus, Christum venisse, servandis peccatoribus et ad pœnitentiam vocandis, et an quisque credat, se in horum esse numero, qui per Christum liberati servantur, et an mutare vitam pravam instituerit, ac vivere sancte, perseverareque, auxiliante Domino, in vera religione et in concordia cum fratribus, dignasque Deo pro liberatione agere gratias, etc.

12. Ritum, modum vel formam cœnæ, illam existimamus esse simplicissimam et præstantissimam, quæ proxime accedit ad primam Domini institutionem et apostolicam doctrinam: quæ videlicet constat annuntiatione verbi Dei, precibus piis, ipsa actione dominica et repetitione ejus, manducatione corporis et potu sanguinis domini, memoria item mortis dominicæ salubri, et gratiarum actione fideli, nec non sancta consociatione in corporis ecclesiastici unionem. Improbamus itaque illos, qui alteram speciem, poculum, inquam, domini, fidelibus subtraxerunt. Graviter enim hi peccant contra institutionem domini, dicentis: *Bibite ex hoc omnes :* Id quod ad panem, non ita expresse dixit.

13. Missa qualis aliquando apud veteres fuerit, tolerabilis an intolerabilis, modo non disputamus; hoc autem libere dicimus, missam, quæ hodie in usu est per universam Romanam Ecclesiam, plurimas et justissimas quidem ob causas in ecclesiis nostris esse abrogatam, quas sigillatim ob brevitatem nunc non commemoramus. Certe approbare non potuimus, quod ex actione salubri, spectaculum inane est factum, quod item facta est meritoria, vel celebrata pro pretio, quodque in ea sacerdos dicitur conficere ipsum Domini corpus, et hoc offerre realiter pro remissione peccatorum vivorum et mortuorum, adde et in honorem et celebrationem, vel memoriam sanctorum in cœlis, etc.

CAP. XXII.

DE CŒTIBUS SACRIS ET ECCLESIASTICIS.

1. Tametsi omnibus sacras literas privatim legere domi, et instruendo ædificare mutuum in vera religione liceat; ut tamen legitime adnuncietur verbum Dei populo, et preces ac supplicationes fiant publice, sacramenta item celebrentur legitime, et collecta Ecclesiæ

fiat in pauperes et omnes Ecclesiæ necessarios sumtus faciendos, aut usus sustentandos, necessarii sunt omnino cœtus sacri, vel ecclesiastici fidelium conventus. Constat enim, in Ecclesia Apostolica et primitiva hujusmodi cœtus esse ab omnibus piis frequentatos.

2. Quotquot hos aspernantur, et ab his sese segregant, religionem veram contemnunt, urgendique sunt a pastoribus et piis magistratibus, ne contumacius se segregare, et cœtus sacros aversari pergant. Sint vero cœtus ecclesiastici non occulti et obscuri, sed publici atque frequentes, nisi, persecutio hostium Christi et Ecclesiæ non sinat esse publicos. Scimus enim, quales fuerint quondam primitivæ Ecclesiæ cœtus in abditis locis, sub tyrannide Romanorum principum.

3. Sint autem loca, in quibus coëunt fideles, honesta et Ecclesiæ Dei per omnia commoda. Deligantur ergo ædes amplæ, aut templa. Repurgentur tamen ab iis rebus omnibus, quæ Ecclesiam non decent. Instruantur autem omnia pro decoro, necessitate et honestate pia, ne quid desit, quod requiritur ad ritus et usus Ecclesiæ necessarios.

4. Sicut autem credimus, Deum non habitare in templis manu factis, ita propter verbum Dei et usus sacros scimus, loca Deo cultuique ejus dedicata non esse profana sed sacra, et qui in his versantur, reverenter et modeste conversari debere, utpote qui sint in loco sacro, coram Dei conspectu et sanctorum angelorum ejus. Longe itaque a templis et oratoriis Christianorum repellendus, est omnis vestium luxus, omnis superbia, et omnia, quæ humilitatem, disciplinam et modestiam dedecent christianam. Ac verus templorum ornatus non constat ebore, auro et gemmis, sed frugalitate, pietate, virtutibusque eorum, qui versantur in templo. Omnia autem decenter et ordine fiant in Ecclesia, omnia denique fiant ad ædificationem. Taceant ergo omnes peregrinæ linguæ in cœtibus sacris. Omnia proponantur lingua vulgari, et quæ eo in loco ab hominibus in cœtu intelligatur.

CAP. XXIII.

DE PRECIBUS ECCLESIÆ, CANTU ET HORIS CANONICIS.

1. Licet sane privatim precari quavis lingua quam quis intelligat, sed publicæ preces in sacris cœtibus vulgari lingua vel omnibus cognita fieri debent. Oratio fidelium omnis per solum Christi interventum soli Deo fundatur ex fide et caritate. Divos cœlites invocare,

aut his uti pro intercessoribus, prohibet sacerdotium Christi Domini
et vera religio. Orandum est autem pro magistratu, pro regibus aut
omnibus in eminentia constitutis, pro ministris Ecclesiæ et omnibus
necessitatibus ecclesiarum. In calamitatibus vero et potissimum Ecclesiæ, absque intermissione, et privatim et publice precandum est.

2. Sponte item precandum est, non coacte, neque pro ullo pretio.
Neque decet orationem superstitiose adstrictam esse loco, quasi alibi
non liceat, nisi in templo precari. Neque oportet preces publicas,
quoad formam et tempus, in omnibus ecclesiis esse pares. Libertate
enim sua utantur Ecclesiæ quælibet. Socrates in historia, In omnibus, ubique regionibus, inquit, non poteris invenire duas ecclesias,
quæ orando plene consentiant. Hujusmodi discrepantiæ autores eos
esse puto, qui singulis temporibus ecclesiis præfuerunt. Si tamen
sunt congruentes, maximopere commendandum id et aliis imitandum
videtur.

3. Sed et modum esse decet, ut in re quavis, ita et in precibus publicis, ne nimis sint prolixæ et molestæ. Cedant ergo potiores partes
in cœtibus sacris doctrinæ evangelicæ, caveaturque, ne nimis prolixis
precibus fatigetur in cœtu populus, ut cum audienda est prædicatio
Evangelii, vel egredi ex cœtu, vel hunc in universum solvi cupiant
defatigati. Talibus in concione nimis videtur prolixum esse, quod alias
succinctum est satis. Nam et concionatores modum tenere decet.

4. Sic et cantus in cœtu sacro est moderandus, ubi is est in usu.
Cantus, quem Gregorianum nuncupant, plurima habet absurda: unde
rejectus est merito a nostris et pluribus ecclesiis. Si ecclesiæ sunt,
quæ orationem fidelem legitimamque habent, cantum autem nullum
habent, condemnari non debent. Non enim canendi commoditatem
omnes habent ecclesiæ. Ac certum est ex testimoniis vetustatis, ut
cantus usum fuisse vetustissimum in orientalibus ecclesiis, ita sero tandem receptum esse ab occidentalibus.

5. Horas canonicas, id est, preces ad certas in die horas compositas,
a Papistis cantatas aut recitatas, nescivit vetustas: quod ex ipsis hora-
rum lectionibus et argumentis pluribus demonstrari potest. Sed et
absurda non pauca habent, ut nihil dicam aliud, proinde omittuntur
recte ab ecclesiis substituentibus in locum ipsarum res salutares Ecclesiæ Dei universæ.

CAP. XXIV.

DE FERIIS, JEJUNIIS, CIBORUMQUE DELECTU. [CONF. AUG., DE ABUS. 5.]

1. Quamquam religio tempori non alligetur, non potest tamen absque justa temporis distinctione vel ordinatione plantari et exerceri. Deligit ergo quævis ecclesia sibi tempus certum ad preces publicas et Evangelii prædicationem, nec non sacramentorum celebrationem. Non licet autem cuivis pro suo arbitrio Ecclesiæ ordinationem hanc convellere. Ac nisi otium justum concedatur religionis externæ exercitio, abstrahuntur certe ab eo negotiis suis homines.

2. Unde videmus in ecclesiis vetustis, non tantum certas fuisse horas in septimana constitutas cœtibus, sed ipsam diem dominicam ab ipsis Apostolorum temporibus, iisdem sacroque otio fuisse consecratam: quod etiam nunc recte propter cultum et caritatem, ab ecclesiis nostris custoditur. Observationi Judaicæ et superstitionibus nihil hic permittimus. Neque enim alteram diem altera sanctiorem esse credimus, neque otium Deo per se probari existimamus, sed et dominicam non sabbatum libera observatione celebramus.

3. Præterea si ecclesiæ pro Christiana libertate memoriam dominicæ nativitatis, circumcisionis, passionis et resurrectionis, ascensionis item in cœlum, et missionis Sancti Spiritus in discipulos religiose celebrent, maximopere approbamus. Festa vero hominibus aut divis instituta non probamus. Et sane pertinent feriæ ad tabulam legis primam, et sunt solius Dei: denique habent feriæ divis institutæ et a nobis abrogatæ, absurda, inutilia, minimeque toleranda plurima. Interim fatemur non inutiliter sanctorum memoriam, suo loco et tempore in sacris concionibus populo commendari, et omnibus sancta exempla sanctorum imitanda proponi.

4. Quanto vero gravius accusat Christi Ecclesia crapulam, ebrietatem, et omnem libidinem ac intemperantiam, tanto vehementius commendat nobis jejunium Christianum. Est enim jejunium aliud nihil, quam abstinentia et temperantia piorum, disciplina item, custodia, et castigatio carnis nostræ, pro necessitate præsenti suscepta, qua humiliamur coram Deo, et carni sua fomenta detrahimus, quo facilius libentiusque spiritui pareat. Proinde non jejunant, qui istorum nullam rationem habent, sed jejunare se credunt, si semel in die farciant ventrem, et certo vel præscripto tempore a certis abstineant cibis, existi-

mantes, hoc opere operato se Deo placere et bonum opus facere. Jejunium est adminiculum orationis sanctorum ac virtutum omnium. Non placuit Deo (ut videre est in Prophetarum libris), jejunium, quo a cibo non a sceleribus jejunabant Judæi.

5. Est autem publicum jejunium, et privatum. Celebrarunt olim jejunia publica calamitosis temporibus rebusque Ecclesiæ afflictis. Abstinebant in universum a cibo ad vesperam usque. Totum autem hoc tempus impendebant precibus sacris cultuique Dei et pœnitentiæ. Parum hæc abfuerunt a luctu: et frequens fit horum mentio in Prophetis, præcipue apud Joëlem (cap. ii.). Celebrari debet hujusmodi jejunium etiam hodie in rebus Ecclesiæ difficilibus. Privata jejunia suscipiuntur abs quovis nostrum, prout quisque senserit detrahi spiritui. Hactenus enim fomenta carni detrahit.

6. Omnia jejunia proficisci debent ex libero, spontaneoque spiritu et vere humiliato, nec composita esse ad plausum vel gratiam hominum consequendam, multo minus eo, ut per ipsa velit homo justitiam demereri. Jejunet autem in hunc finem quilibet, ut fomenta carni detrahat, et ferventius Deo inserviat.

7. Quadragesimale jejunium vetustatis habet testimonia, sed nulla ex literis Apostolicis: ergo non debet, nec potest imponi fidelibus. Certum est, quondam varias fuisse jejuniorum formas vel consuetudines. Unde Irenæus, scriptor vetustissimus, Quidam, inquit, putant uno tantum die observari debere jejunium, alii duobus, alii vero pluribus, nonnulli etiam quadraginta diebus. Quæ varietas observantiæ, non nostris nunc demum temporibus cœpit, sed multo ante nos, ex illis, ut opinor, qui non simpliciter, quod ab initio traditum est, tenentes, in alium morem, vel per negligentiam, vel per imperitiam postmodum decidere. Sed et Socrates historicus, Quia lectio nulla, inquit, de hoc invenitur antiqua, puto, Apostolos hoc singulorum reliquisse sententiæ, ut unusquisque operetur, non timore et necessitate, quod bonum est.

8. Jam vero, quoad delectum ciborum attinet, in jejuniis arbitramur omne id detrahendum esse carni, unde redditur ferocior, et quo delectatur impensius, unde existunt fomenta carni, sive pisces sint, sive carnes, sive aromata, delitiæve aut præstantia vina. Alioqui scimus, creaturas Dei omnes conditas esse in usus et servitia hominum. *Omnia, quæ condidit Deus, bona sunt* (Gen. i. 31), et citra delectum, cum

timore Dei et justa moderatione usurpanda. Apostolus enim, *Omnia*, inquit, *mundis munda sunt* (Tit. i. 15). Item : *Omne, quod in macello venditur, edite, nihil interrogantes propter conscientiam* (1 Cor. x. 25). Idem Apostolus nominat *doctrinam eorum, qui jubent abstinere a cibis, doctrinam dæmoniorum. Cibos enim creasse Deum ad sumendum cum gratiarum actione fidelibus, et his, qui cognoverunt veritatem, quod quidquid creavit Deus, bonum sit, et nihil rejiciendum, si sumatur cum gratiarum actione*, etc. (1 Tim. iv. 1, 3, 4). Idem ad Colossenses reprobat eos, qui nimia abstinentia, sibi comparare volunt existimationem sanctitatis (Coloss. ii. 21, 23). Nos itaque in universum reprobamus Tatianos et Encratitas, omnes denique Eustathii discipulos, contra quos congregata est Gangrensis synodus.

CAP. XXV.

De Catechesi, et Ægrotantium Consolatione vel Visitatione.

1. Dominus veteri suo populo injunxit, maximam curam ut impenderent ab infantia recte instituendæ juventuti, adeoque mandavit diserte in lege sua, erudirent et sacramentorum mysteria interpretarentur. Cum autem ex Evangelicis et Apostolicis literis constet, Deum non minorem rationem habere novi sui populi pubis, cum palam testetur et dicat, *Sinite pueros venire ad me, talium enim est regnum cœlorum* (Marc. x. 14), consultissime faciunt ecclesiarum pastores, qui juventutem mature et diligenter catechisant, prima fidei fundamenta jacientes, ac rudimenta religionis nostræ fideliter docentes, explicando decalogum mandatorum Dei, symbolum item Apostolorum, orationem quoque dominicam, et sacramentorum rationem, cum aliis ejus generis primis principiis, et religionis nostræ capitibus præcipuis. . Fidem vero et diligentiam hic suam in adducendis ad catechismum liberis præstet Ecclesia, cupiens et gaudens liberos suos recte institui.

2. Cum vero nunquam gravioribus tentationibus expositi sunt homines, quam dum infirmitatibus exercentur aut ægrotant, morbis cum animi tum corporis fracti, nunquam sane convenit pastores ecclesiarum saluti sui gregis invigilare accuratius, quam in hujusmodi morbis et infirmitatibus. Visitent ergo mature ægrotantes, vocentur item mature ab ægrotantibus, siquidem res ipsa postulaverit : consolentur autem illos, et in vera fide confirment, muniant denique contra perniciosas

Satanæ suggestiones: instituant item preces apud ægrotantem dome-
sticas, ac si necesse sit, precentur pro ægrotantis salute etiam in cœtu
publico curentque, quo feliciter ex hoc seculo migret. Papisticam
visitationem cum sua illa unctione extrema, diximus superius, nos non
approbare, quod absurda habeat, et a scriptura canonica non appro-
betur.

CAP. XXVI.

DE SEPULTURA FIDELIUM, CURAQUE PRO MORTUIS GERENDA, DE PUR-GATORIO, ET APPARITIONE SPIRITUUM.

1. Fidelium corpora, ut Spiritus Sancti templa, et quæ in ultimo
die recte creduntur resurrectura, jubet scriptura honeste absque super--
stitione humo mandare, sed et honestam eorum, qui sancte in Domino
obdormiverunt, mentionem facere, relictisque eorum, ut viduis et pu-
pillis, omnia pietatis officia præstare: aliam non docemus pro mortuis
curam gerere. Improbamus ergo maxime Cynicos, corpora mortuorum negligentes, aut quam negligentissime contemptissimeque in terram abjicientes, nunquam vel verbum bonum de defunctis facientes,
aut relictos ipsorum ne tantillum quidem curantes.

2. Improbamus rursus nimis et præpostere officiosos in defunctos,
qui instar Ethnicorum suos deplangunt mortuos (luctum moderatum,
quem Apostolus (1 Thess. iv.) concessit, non vituperamus, inhumanum
esse judicantes, prorsus nihil dolere), et pro mortuis sacrificant, et
preculas certas, non sine pretio, demurmurant, hujusmodi suis officiis
liberaturi suos illos ex tormentis, quibus a morte inmersos, et inde
rursus liberari posse hujusmodi næniis arbitrantur.

3. Credimus enim, fideles recta a morte corporea migrare ad Christum, ideoque viventium suffragiis aut precibus pro defunctis, denique
illis suis officiis nihil indigere. Credimus item, infideles recta præcipitari in tartara, ex quibus nullus impiis aperitur, ullis viventium officiis, exitus.

4. Quod autem quidam tradunt de igne purgatorio, fidei Christianæ:
Credo remissionem peccatorum et vitam æternam, purgationique plenæ
per Christum, et Christi Domini hisce sententiis adversatur: *Amen,
amen dico vobis, qui sermonem meum audit, et credit ei qui misit
me, habet vitam æternam, et in judicium non veniet, sed transivit a
morte in vitam* (Joh. v. 24). Item, *Qui lotus est, non opus habet,*

nisi ut pedes lavet, sed est mundus totus, et vos mundi estis (Joh. xiii. 10).

5. Jam quod traditur de spiritibus vel animabus mortuorum apparentibus aliquando viventibus, et petentibus ab eis officia, quibus liberentur, deputamus apparitiones eas inter ludibria, artes et deceptiones diaboli, qui, ut potest se transfigurare in angelum lucis, ita satagit fidem veram vel evertere, vel in dubium revocare. Dominus in veteri testamento vetuit veritatem sciscitari a mortuis, et ullum cum spiritibus habere commercium (Deut. xviii. 10, 11). Epuloni vero poenis mancipato, sicut narrat veritas evangelica, negatur ad fratres suos reditus: pronunciante interim divino oraculo, atque dicente, *Habent Mosen et Prophetas, audiant illos. Si Mosen et Prophetas non audiunt, neque si quis ex mortuis resurrexit, credent* (Luc. xvi. 31).

CAP. XXVII.

DE RITIBUS ET CÆREMONIIS, ET MEDIIS. [CONF. AUG., ART. XV.]

1. Veteri populo traditæ sunt quondam cæremoniæ, ut pædagogia quædam, iis qui sub lege veluti sub pædagogo et tutore quodam custodiebantur, sed adveniente Christo liberatore, legeque sublata, *fideles sub lege amplius non sumus* (Rom. vi. 14), disparueruntque cæremoniæ, quas in Ecclesia Christi adeo retinere aut reparare noluerunt Apostoli, ut aperte sint testati *se nullum onus velle imponere Ecclesiæ* (Act. xv. 28). Proinde Judaismum videremur reducere aut restituere, si in Ecclesia Christi, ad morem veteris Ecclesiæ, cæremonias, ritusve multiplicaremus. Ideoque minime approbamus eorum sententiam, quibus visum est Ecclesiam Christi cohiberi oportere, ceu pædagogia quadam, multis variisque ritibus. Nam si populo Christiano Apostoli cæremonias vel ritus divinitus traditos imponere noluerunt, quis ergo sanæ mentis obtrudet illi adinventiones adinventas humanitus? Quanto magis accedit cumulo rituum in Ecclesia, tanto magis detrahitur non tantum libertati Christianæ, sed et Christo et ejus fidei: dum vulgus ea quærit in ritibus, quæ quæreret in solo Dei Filio Jesu Christo per fidem. Sufficiunt itaque piis pauci, moderati, simplices, nec alieni a verbo Dei ritus.

2. Quod si in ecclesiis dispares inveniuntur ritus, nemo ecclesias existimet ex eo esse dissidentes. Socrates, Impossibile fuerit, inquit,

omnes ecclesiarum, quæ per civitates et regiones sunt, ritus conscribere. Nulla religio eosdem ritus custodit, etiamsi eandem de illis doctrinam amplectatur. Etenim, qui ejusdem sunt fidei, de ritibus inter se dissentiunt. Hæc ille. Et nos hodie ritus diversos in celebratione cœnæ Domini et in aliis nonnullis rebus habentes in nostris ecclesiis, in doctrina tamen et fide non dissidemus, neque unitas societasque ecclesiarum nostrarum ea re discinditur. Semper vero ecclesiæ in hujusmodi ritibus, sicut mediis, usæ sunt libertate. Id quod nos hodie quoque facimus.

3. At cavendum interim monemus, ne inter media deputentur, ut quidem solent missam et usum imaginum in templo pro mediis reputare, quæ revera non sunt media. *Indifferens* (dixit ad Augustinum Hieron.) *illud est, quod nec bonum nec malum est, ut sive feceris, sive non feceris, nec justitiam habeas nec injustitiam.* Proinde cum ἀδιάφορα rapiuntur ad fidei confessionem, libera esse desinunt: sicuti Paulus ostendit, licitum esse carnibus vesci, si quis non submoneat, idolis esse litatas, alioqui fore illicitas, quod qui his vescitur, jam vescendo, idololatriam approbare videatur (1 Cor. viii. 10).

CAP. XXVIII.
DE BONIS ECCLESIÆ.

1. Opes habet Ecclesia Christi ex munificentia principum ac liberalitate fidelium, qui facultates suas Ecclesiæ donarunt. Opus enim habet Ecclesia facultatibus, et habuit ab antiquo facultates ad res Ecclesiæ necessarias sustinendas. Ac verus usus opum Ecclesiæ quondam fuit, et nunc est, conservare doctrinam in scholis, et cœtibus sacris, cum universo cultu, ritibus et ædificio sacro, conservare denique doctores, discipulos atque ministros, cum rebus aliis necessariis, et imprimis pauperibus juvandis atque alendis. Deligantur autem viri timentes Deum, prudentes, et in œconomia insignes, qui legitime bona dispensent ecclesiastica.

2. Si vero opes Ecclesiæ per injuriam temporis, et quorundam audaciam, inscitiam, aut avaritiam translatæ sunt in abusum, reducantur a viris piis et prudentibus ad sanctum usum. Neque enim connivendum est ad abusum maxime sacrilegum. Docemus itaque reformandas esse scholas et collegia corrupta in doctrina, in cultu, et in mori-

bus, ordinandamque esse pie, bona fide, atque prudenter pauperum subventionem.

CAP. XXIX.

De Cœlibatu, Conjugio, et Œconomia.   [Conf. Aug., De Abus. 2.]

1. Qui cœlitus donum habent cœlibatus, ita ut ex corde, vel toto animo, puri sint ac continentes, nec urantur graviter, serviant in ea vocatione Domino, donec senserint se divino munere præditos, et ne efferant se cæteris, sed serviant Domino assidue, in simplicitate et humilitate.   Aptiores autem hi sunt curandis rebus divinis, quam qui privatis familiæ negotiis distrahuntur.   Quod si adempto rursus dono, ustionem senserint durabilem, meminerint verbi Apostolici: *Melius est nubere, quam uri* (1 Cor. vii.).

2. Conjugium enim (incontinentiæ medicina et continentia ipsa est) institutum est ab ipso Domino Deo, qui ei liberalissime benedixit, ac virum ac fœminam inseparabiliter sibi mutuum adhærere, et una in summa dilectione, concordiaque vivere voluit (Matt. xiii.).   Unde scimus Apostolum dixisse: *Honorabile est conjugium inter omnes et cubile impollutum* (Heb. xiii. 4).   Et iterum: *Si virgo nupserit, non peccavit* (1 Cor. vii.).   Damnamus ergo polygamiam, et eos, qui secundas damnant nuptias.   Docemus, contrahenda esse conjugia legitime in timore Domini, et non contra leges, prohibentes aliquot in conjugio gradus, ne incestæ fiant nuptiæ.   Contrahantur cum consensu parentum, aut qui sunt loco parentum, ac in illum maxime finem, ad quem Dominus conjugia instituit et confirmentur publice in templo cum precatione et benedictione.   Colantur denique sancte, cum maxima conjugum fide, pietate et dilectione, nec non puritate. · Caveantur itaque rixæ, dissidia, libidines et adulteria.   Constituantur legitima in Ecclesia judicia, et judices sancti, qui tueantur conjugia, et omnem impudicitiam impudentiamque coërceant, et apud quos controversiæ matrimoniales transigantur.

3. Educentur quoque liberi a parentibus, in timore Domini: provideant item parentes liberis, memores Apostolicæ sententiæ: *Qui suis non prospicit, fidem abnegavit, et infideli est deterior* (1 Tim. v. 8).   Imprimis autem doceant suos, quibus sese alant, artes honestas. abstrahant ab otio, et veram in his omnibus fiduciam in Deum inse

rant, ne diffidentia aut securitate nimia aut avaritia fœda diffluant, nec ad ullum fructum perveniant.

4. Estque certissimum opera illa, quæ in vera fide fiunt a parentibus, per conjugii officia et œconomiam, esse coram Deo sancta et vere bona opera, et placere hæc Deo non minus, quam preces, jejunia, atque eleemosynas. Sic enim docuit et Apostolus in epistolis suis, præcipue vero ad Tim. et Titum. Numeramus autem cum eodem Apostolo inter dogmata Satanica illorum doctrinam, qui matrimonium prohibent, aut palam vituperant, vel oblique perstringunt, quasi non sanctum vel mundum sit.

5. Execramur autem cœlibatum immundum, libidines et fornicationes tectas et apertas hypocritarum, simulantium continentiam, cum omnium sint incontinentissimi. Hos omnes judicabit Deus. Divitias, et divites, si pii sunt et recte utantur divitiis, non reprobamus. Reprobamus autem sectam Apostolicorum, etc.

CAP. XXX.

DE MAGISTRATU. [CONF. AUG., ART. XVI.]

1. Magistratus omnis generis ab ipso Deo est institutus ad generis humani pacem ac tranquillitatem, ac ita, ut primum in mundo locum obtineat. Si hic sit adversarius Ecclesiæ, et impedire et obturbare potest plurimum. Si autem sit amicus, adeoque membrum Ecclesiæ, utilissimum excellentissimumque membrum est Ecclesiæ, quod ei permultum prodesse, eam denique peroptime juvare potest.

2. Ejus officium præcipuum est, pacem et tranquillitatem publicam procurare et conservare. Quod sane nunquam fecerit felicius, quam cum fuerit vere timens Dei ac religiosus, qui videlicet ad exemplum sanctissimorum regum principumque populi Domini, veritatis prædicationem et fidem sinceram promoverit, mendacia et superstitionem omnem cum omni impietate et idololatria exciderit ecclesiamque Dei defenderit. Equidem docemus religionis curam imprimis pertinere ad magistratum sanctum.

3. Teneat ergo ipse in manibus verbum Dei, et ne huic contrarium doceatur, procuret, bonis item legibus ad verbum Dei compositis moderetur populum, sibi a Deo creditum, eundemque in disciplina, officio, obedientiaque contineat. Judicia exerceat juste judicando, ne respi

ciat personam, aut munera accipiat; viduas, pupillos et afflictos asse-
rat, injustos, impostores et violentos coërceat atque adeo et exscindat.
Neque enim frustra accepit a Deo gladium (Rom. xiii. 4). Stringat
ergo hunc Dei gladium in omnes maleficos, seditiosos, latrones vel
homicidas, oppressores, blasphemos, perjuros et in omnes eos, quos
Deus punire ac etiam cædere jussit. Coërceat et hæreticos (qui vere
hæretici sunt) incorrigibiles, Dei majestatem blasphemare et Ecclesiam
Pei conturbare, adeoque perdere non desinentes.

4. Quod si necesse sit, etiam bello populi conservare salutem, bellum,
in nomine Dei suscipiat, modo prius pacem modis omnibus quæsierit,
nec aliter nisi bello suos servare possit. Et dum hæc ex fide facit
magistratus, illis ipsis operibus, ut vere bonis, Deo inservit, ac benedictionem a Domino accipit. Damnamus Anabaptistas, qui, ut Christianum negant fungi posse officio magistratus, ita etiam negant, quemquam a magistratu juste occidi, aut magistratum bellum gerere posse,
aut juramenta magistratui præstanda esse, etc.

5. Sicut enim Deus salutem populi sui operari vult per magistratum,
quem mundo veluti patrem dedit: ita subditi omnes, hoc Dei beneficium in magistratu agnoscere jubentur. Honorent ergo et revereantur
magistratum, tanquam Dei ministrum: ament eum, faveant ei, et orent
pro illo, tanquam pro Patre: obediant item omnibus ejus justis et
æquis mandatis: denique pendant vectigalia atque tributa, et quæ
hujus generis debita sunt, fideliter atque libenter. Et si salus publica
patriæ vel justitia requirat, et magistratus ex necessitate bellum suscipiat, deponant etiam vitam, et fundant sanguinem pro salute publica
magistratusque, et quidem in Dei nomine, libenter, fortiter et alacriter.
Qui enim magistratui se opponit, iram Dei gravem in se provocat.

Damnamus itaque omnes magistratus contemptores, rebelles, reipublicæ hostes, et seditiosos nebulones, denique omnes, quotquot officia
debita præstare, vel palam, vel arte renuunt.

Oramus Deum Patrem nostrum in cœlis clementissimum, ut principibus populi, nobis quoque et universo populo suo benedicat, per
Jesum Christum, Dominum et Servatorem nostrum unicum, cui laus
et gloria ac gratiarum actio in secula seculorum. Amen.

THE HEIDELBERG CATECHISM. A.D. 1563.

[The German text is that of the *third* edition, including the 80th Question (republished, with the old orthography, by Niemeyer, *Collectio Conf.* p. 390, and in the Tercentenary Edition of the German Reformed Church of the United States, 1863), compared with the *first* edition (accurately republished by A. Wolters, *Der Heidelb. Katechismus in seiner Urgestalt*, 1864), but in modern spelling, and with some accepted verbal improvements (such as, in Qu. 1, *beides im* for *beyde in*, *vollkommen* for *volkomlich*). The same text, with critical notes, various readings, and Scripture proofs, is given in the revised issue of my Tercentenary Edition (*Der Heidelb. Katechismus nach der Ausg. v. 1563 revidirt*, etc., Phila., 1866), for which I had the advantage of using the only extant copy of the *editio princeps*, then in possession of my friend, the late Rev. Dr. Treviranus, of Bremen, and bearing the name of its original owner (Prof. H. Wilcken, in Heidelberg, 1563).

The English version, which is much better than the one in common use, was prepared by an able committee, consisting of Rev. Drs. Gerhart, Nevin, Harbaugh, Kessler, Zacharias, and others, in the name and by direction of the Synod of the German Reformed Church of the United States, held in Harrisburg, Pa., 1859, and was published in very superior style, as a Tercentenary Edition, together with the German and Latin texts (of the third edition), and a valuable introduction by Dr. John W. Nevin, New York, 1863 (pp. 277). It is here inserted by permission of the translators. The German title below is an imitation of the title-page of the first edition, except the electoral arms. See a full fac-simile in my German edition, 1866.]

Catechismus

Oder

Christlicher Underricht/ wie der in Kirchen vnd Schulen der Churfürstlichen Pfaltz getrieben wirdt.

Gedruckt in der Churfürstlichen Stad Heydelberg/ durch Johannem Mayer. 1563.

Frage 1.

Was ist dein einiger Trost im Leben und im Sterben?

Antwort.

Daß ich mit Leib und Seele, beides im Leben und im Sterben, nicht mein, sondern meines getreuen Heilandes Jesu Christi eigen bin, der mit seinem

Catechism

or

CHRISTIAN INSTRUCTION

as conducted in the Churches and Schools

of the

ELECTORAL PALATINATE.

Printed in the Electoral City

of Heidelberg by

JOHN MAYER.

1563.

QUESTION 1.

What is thy only comfort in life and in death?

ANSWER.

That I, with body and soul, both in life and in death, am not my own, but belong to my faithful Saviour Jesus Christ, who with his

theuren Blute für alle meine Sünden vollkommen bezahlet, und mich aus aller Gewalt des Teufels erlöset hat; und also bewahret, daß ohne den Willen meines Vaters im Himmel kein Haar von meinem Haupte kann fallen, ja auch mir alles zu meiner Seligkeit dienen muß. Darum er mich auch durch seinen heiligen Geist des ewigen Lebens versichert, und ihm forthin zu leben von Herzen willig und bereit macht.

precious blood has fully satisfied for all my sins, and redeemed me from all the power of the devil; and so preserves me that without the will of my Father in heaven not a hair can fall from my head; yea, that all things must work together for my salvation. Wherefore, by his Holy Spirit, he also assures me of eternal life, and makes me heartily willing and ready henceforth to live unto him.

Frage 2.

Wie viele Stücke sind dir nöthig zu wissen, daß du in diesem Troste seliglich leben und sterben mögest?

Antwort.

Drei Stücke: Erstlich, wie groß meine Sünde und Elend seien. Zum Andern, wie ich von allen meinen Sünden und Elend erlöset werde. Und zum Dritten, wie ich Gott für solche Erlösung soll dankbar sein.

QUESTION 2.

How many things are necessary for thee to know, that thou in this comfort mayest live and die happily?

ANSWER.

Three things: First, the greatness of my *sin* and *misery*. Second, how I am *redeemed* from all my sins and misery. Third, how I am to be *thankful* to God for such redemption.

Der erste Theil.
Von des Menschen Elend.

Frage 3.
Woher erkennest du dein Elend?

Antwort.
Aus dem Gesetz Gottes.

Frage 4.
Was erfordert denn das göttliche Gesetz von uns?

Antwort.
Dieß lehret uns Christus in einer

THE FIRST PART.
OF MAN'S MISERY.

QUESTION 3.
Whence knowest thou thy misery?

ANSWER.
Out of the Law of God.

QUESTION 4.
What does the Law of God require of us?

ANSWER.
This Christ teaches us in sum,

Summa, Matthäi am 22ſten: Du
ſollſt lieben Gott, deinen Herrn,
von ganzem Herzen, von ganzer
Seele, von ganzem Gemüth und
allen Kräften: dieß iſt das vornehmſte und größte Gebot. Das
andere aber iſt dem gleich: Du
ſollſt deinen Nächſten lieben als
dich ſelbſt.—In dieſen zweien
Geboten hanget das ganze Geſetz
und die Propheten.

Frage 5.
Kannſt du dieß Alles vollkommen halten?

Antwort.
Nein: denn ich bin von Natur geneigt, Gott und meinen Nächſten zu
haſſen.

Frage 6.
Hat denn Gott den Menſchen alſo böſe und
verkehrt erſchaffen?

Antwort.
Nein: ſondern Gott hat den Menſchen gut und nach ſeinem Ebenbild
erſchaffen, das iſt, in wahrhaftiger Gerechtigkeit und Heiligkeit; auf daß er
Gott ſeinen Schöpfer recht erkenne,
und von Herzen liebe, und in ewiger
Seligkeit mit ihm lebe,[1] Ihn zu loben
und zu preiſen.

Frage 7.
Woher kommt denn ſolche verderbte Art
des Menſchen?

Antwort.
Aus dem Fall und Ungehorſam un-

Matt. 22: *Thou shalt love the
Lord thy God with all thy heart,
and with all thy soul, and with
all thy mind, and with all thy
strength. This is the first and
great commandment; and the second is like unto it: Thou shalt
love thy neighbor as thyself.—On
these two commandments hang all
the law and the prophets.*

QUESTION 5.
Canst thou keep all this perfectly?

ANSWER.
No; for I am by nature prone
to hate God and my neighbor.

QUESTION 6.
Did God create man thus wicked and perverse?

ANSWER.
No; but God created man good,
and after his own image—that is,
in righteousness and true holiness; that he might rightly know
God his Creator, heartily love
him, and live with him in eternal
blessedness, to praise and glorify
him.

QUESTION 7.
Whence, then, comes this depraved nature
of man?

ANSWER.
From the fall and disobedience

---

[1] See here the critical note in my German edition, p. 5.

ferer erſten Eltern, Adam und Eva, im
Paradies, da unſere Natur alſo ver=
giftet worden, daß wir Alle in Sünden
empfangen und geboren werden.

Frage 8.

Sind wir aber dermaßen verderbt, daß wir
ganz und gar untüchtig ſind zu einigem Guten
und geneigt zu allem Böſen?

Antwort.

Ja: es ſei denn, daß wir durch den
Geiſt Gottes wiedergeboren werden.

Frage 9.

Thut denn Gott dem Menſchen nicht Un=
recht, daß er in ſeinem Geſetz von ihm fordert,
was er nicht thun kann?

Antwort.

Nein: denn Gott hat den Menſchen
alſo erſchaffen, daß er es konnte thun.
Der Menſch aber hat ſich und alle
ſeine Nachkommen, aus Anſtiftung des
Teufels, durch muthwilligen Ungehor=
ſam derſelbigen Gaben beraubet.

Frage 10.

Will Gott ſolchen Ungehorſam und Abfall
ungeſtraft laſſen hingehen?

Antwort.

Mit nichten: ſondern Er zürnet
ſchrecklich, beides über angeborne und
wirkliche Sünden, und will ſie aus ge=
rechtem Urtheil zeitlich und ewig ſtrafen,
wie Er geſprochen hat: Verflucht
ſei jedermann, der nicht bleibet
in allem dem, das geſchrieben
ſtehet im Buch des Geſetzes, daß
er's thue.

of our first parents, Adam and Eve,
in Paradise, whereby our nature
became so corrupt that we are all
conceived and born in sin.

QUESTION 8.

But are we so far depraved that we are
wholly unapt to any good, and prone to all
evil?

ANSWER.

Yes; unless we are born again
by the Spirit of God.

QUESTION 9.

Does not God, then, wrong man by requiring of him in his law that which he can not
perform?

ANSWER.

No; for God so made man that
he could perform it; but man,
through the instigation of the
devil, by willful disobedience deprived himself and all his posterity
of this power.

QUESTION 10.

Will God suffer such disobedience and
apostasy to go unpunished?

ANSWER.

By no means; but he is terribly
displeased with our inborn as well
as actual sins, and will punish
them in just judgment in time
and eternity, as he has declared:
*Cursed is every one that con-
tinueth not in all things which
are written in the book of the
law, to do them.*

Frage 11.

Iſt denn Gott nicht auch barmherzig?

Antwort.

Gott iſt wohl barmherzig, Er iſt aber auch gerecht. Derhalben erfordert ſeine Gerechtigkeit, daß die Sünde, welche wider die allerhöchſte Majeſtät Gottes begangen iſt, auch mit der höchſten, das iſt, der ewigen Strafe, an Leib und Seele geſtraft werde.

Der andere [zweite] Theil.

Von des Menſchen Erlöſung.

Frage 12.

Dieweil wir denn nach dem gerechten Ur= theil Gottes zeitliche und ewige Strafe verdie= net haben: wie möchten wir dieſer Strafe entgehen, und wiederum zu Gnaden kommen?

Antwort.

Gott will, daß ſeiner Gerechtigkeit genug geſchehe; deßwegen müſſen wir derſelben entweder durch uns ſelbſt, oder durch einen Andern vollkommene Bezahlung thun.

Frage 13.

Können wir aber durch uns ſelbſt Bezah= lung thun?

Antwort.

Mit nichten: ſondern wir machen auch die Schuld noch täglich größer.

Frage 14.

Kann aber irgend eine bloße Creatur für uns bezahlen?

Antwort.

Nein: denn erſtlich will Gott an keiner andern Creatur ſtrafen, was der

QUESTION 11.

Is, then, God not also merciful?

ANSWER.

God is indeed merciful, but he is likewise just; wherefore his justice requires that sin, which is committed against the most high majesty of God, be also punished with extreme, that is, with everlasting punishment both of body and soul.

THE SECOND PART.

OF MAN'S REDEMPTION.

QUESTION 12.

Since, then, by the righteous judgment of God we deserve temporal and eternal punishment, what is required that we may escape this punishment and be again received into favor?

ANSWER.

God wills that his justice be satisfied; therefore must we make full satisfaction to the same, either by ourselves or by another.

QUESTION 13.

Can we ourselves make this satisfaction?

ANSWER.

By no means; on the contrary, we daily increase our guilt.

QUESTION 14.

Can any mere creature make satisfaction for us?

ANSWER.

None; for, first, God will not punish, in any other creature, that

Mensch verschuldet hat. Zum andern, so kann auch keine bloße Creatur die Last des ewigen Zornes Gottes wider die Sünde ertragen, und andere davon erlösen.

Frage 15.

Was müssen wir denn für einen Mittler und Erlöser suchen?

Antwort.

Einen solchen, der ein wahrer und gerechter Mensch, und doch stärker denn alle Creaturen, das ist, zugleich wahrer Gott sei.

Frage 16.

Warum muß Er ein wahrer und gerechter Mensch sein?

Antwort.

Darum, weil die Gerechtigkeit Gottes erfordert, daß die menschliche Natur, die gesündiget hat, für die Sünde bezahle, aber Einer, der selbst ein Sünder wäre, nicht könnte für Andere bezahlen.

Frage 17.

Warum muß Er zugleich wahrer Gott sein?

Antwort.

Daß er aus Kraft seiner Gottheit die Last des Zornes Gottes an seiner Menschheit ertragen, und uns die Gerechtigkeit und das Leben erwerben und wieder geben möchte.

Frage 18.

Wer ist aber derselbe Mittler, der zugleich wahrer Gott und ein wahrer gerechter Mensch ist?

Antwort.

Unser Herr Jesus Christus, der

of which man has made himself guilty; and, further, no mere creature can sustain the burden of God's eternal wrath against sin, and redeem others therefrom.

QUESTION 15.

What manner of mediator and redeemer, then, must we seek?

ANSWER.

One who is a true and sinless man, and yet more powerful than all creatures; that is, one who is at the same time true God.

QUESTION 16.

Why must he be a true and sinless man?

ANSWER.

Because the justice of God requires that the same human nature which has sinned should make satisfaction for sin; but no man, being himself a sinner, could satisfy for others.

QUESTION 17.

Why must he be at the same time true God?

ANSWER.

That by the power of his Godhead he might bear, in his manhood, the burden of God's wrath, and so obtain for and restore to us righteousness and life.

QUESTION 18.

But who, now, is that mediator, who is at the same time true God and a true, sinless man?

ANSWER.

Our Lord *Jesus Christ,* who is

uns zur vollkommenen Erlösung und Gerechtigkeit geschenkt ist.

Frage 19.

Woher weißt du das?

Antwort.

Aus dem heiligen Evangelio, welches Gott selbst anfänglich im Paradies hat geoffenbaret, in der Folge durch die heiligen Erzväter und Propheten lassen verkündigen, und durch die Opfer und andere Ceremonien des Gesetzes vorgebildet, endlich aber durch seinen eingeliebten Sohn erfüllet.

Frage 20.

Werden denn alle Menschen wiederum durch Christum selig, wie sie durch Adam sind verloren worden?

Antwort.

Nein: sondern allein diejenigen, die durch wahren Glauben ihm werden einverleibt, und alle seine Wohlthaten annehmen.

Frage 21.

Was ist wahrer Glaube?

Antwort.

Es ist nicht allein eine gewisse Erkenntniß, dadurch ich Alles für wahr halte, was uns Gott in seinem Worte hat geoffenbaret, sondern auch ein herzliches Vertrauen, welches der heilige Geist durch's Evangelium in mir wirket, daß nicht allein Andern, sondern auch mir Vergebung der Sünden, ewige Gerechtigkeit und Seligkeit von Gott geschenket sei, aus lauter Gnaden, allein um des Verdienstes Christi willen.

freely given unto us for complete redemption and righteousness.

QUESTION 19.

Whence knowest thou this?

ANSWER.

From the Holy Gospel, which God himself first revealed in Paradise, afterwards proclaimed by the holy Patriarchs and Prophets, and foreshadowed by the sacrifices and other ceremonies of the law, and finally fulfilled by his well-beloved Son.

QUESTION 20.

Are all men, then, saved by Christ, as they have perished by Adam?

ANSWER.

No; only such as by true faith are ingrafted into him, and receive all his benefits.

QUESTION 21.

What is true faith?

ANSWER.

It is not only a certain knowledge whereby I hold for truth all that God has revealed to us in his Word, but also a hearty trust which the Holy Ghost works in me by the Gospel, that not only to others, but to me also, forgiveness of sins, everlasting righteousness and salvation, are freely given by God, merely of grace, only for the sake of Christ's merits.

Frage 22.

Was ist aber einem Christen nöthig zu glauben?

Antwort.

Alles, was uns im Evangelio verheißen wird, welches uns die Artikel unseres allgemeinen ungezweifelten christlichen Glaubens in einer Summa lehren.

Frage 23.

Wie lauten dieselben?

Antwort.

Ich glaube in Gott Vater, den Allmächtigen, Schöpfer Himmels und der Erden.

Und in Jesum Christum, seinen eingebornen Sohn, unsern Herrn; der empfangen ist von dem heiligen Geiste, geboren aus Maria der Jungfrau; gelitten unter Pontio Pilato, gekreuziget, gestorben und begraben; abgestiegen zu der Hölle; am dritten Tage wieder auferstanden von den Todten; aufgefahren gen Himmel; sitzet zu der Rechten Gottes, des allmächtigen Vaters; von dannen Er kommen wird zu richten die Lebendigen und die Todten.

Ich glaube in den heiligen Geist; eine heilige, allgemeine christliche Kirche; die Gemeinschaft der Heiligen; Vergebung der Sünden; Auferstehung des Fleisches, und ein ewiges Leben.

QUESTION 22.

What is it, then, necessary for a Christian to believe?

ANSWER.

All that is promised us in the Gospel, which the articles of our catholic, undoubted Christian faith teach us in sum.

QUESTION 23.

What are these Articles?

ANSWER.

I believe in God the Father Almighty, Maker of heaven and earth.

And in Jesus Christ, his only-begotten Son, our Lord: who was conceived by the Holy Ghost, born of the Virgin Mary; suffered under Pontius Pilate, was crucified, dead, and buried; he descended into Hades; the third day he rose from the dead; he ascended into Heaven, and sitteth at the right hand of God the Father Almighty; from thence he shall come to judge the quick and the dead.

I believe in the Holy Ghost; the holy Catholic Church; the communion of saints; the forgiveness of sins; the resurrection of the body, and the life everlasting.

Frage 24.

Wie werden diese Artikel abgetheilt?

Antwort.

In drei Theile: Der erste ist von Gott dem Vater und unserer Erschaffung. Der andere von Gott dem Sohne und unserer Erlösung. Der dritte von Gott dem heiligen Geiste und unserer Heiligung.

Frage 25.

Dieweil nur ein einig göttlich Wesen ist, warum nennest du drei, den Vater, Sohn und heiligen Geist?

Antwort.

Darum, weil sich Gott also in seinem Wort geoffenbaret hat, daß diese drei unterschiedlichen Personen der einige wahrhaftige ewige Gott sind.

Von Gott dem Vater.

Frage 26.

Was glaubest du, wenn du sprichst: Ich glaube in Gott Vater, den Allmächtigen, Schöpfer Himmels und der Erden?

Antwort.

Daß der ewige Vater unsers Herrn Jesu Christi, der Himmel und Erde, sammt allem, was darinnen ist, aus nichts erschaffen, auch dieselbigen noch durch seinen ewigen Rath und Fürsehung erhält und regieret, um seines Sohnes Christi willen mein Gott und mein Vater sei, auf welchen ich also vertraue, daß ich nicht zweifle, Er werde mich mit aller Nothdurft Leibes und der Seele versorgen, auch alles

QUESTION 24.

How are these Articles divided?

ANSWER.

Into three parts: The first is of *God the Father* and our *creation;* the second, of *God the Son* and our *redemption;* the third, of *God the Holy Ghost* and our *sanctification.*

QUESTION 25.

Since there is but one Divine Being, why speakest thou of three, Father, Son, and Holy Ghost?

ANSWER.

Because God has so revealed himself in his Word that these three distinct Persons are the one, true, eternal God.

OF GOD THE FATHER.

QUESTION 26.

What dost thou believe when thou sayest: *I believe in God the Father Almighty, Maker of Heaven and Earth?*

ANSWER.

That the eternal Father of our Lord Jesus Christ, who of nothing made heaven and earth, with all that in them is, who likewise upholds and governs the same by his eternal counsel and providence, is for the sake of Christ his Son my God and my Father, in whom I so trust as to have no doubt that he will provide me with all things necessary for body and soul; and fur-

Uebel, so Er mir in diesem Jammer=
thal zuschicket, mir zu gut wenden,
dieweil Er's thun kann, als ein all=
mächtiger Gott, und auch thun will,
als ein getreuer Vater.

Frage 27.

Was verstehst du unter der Fürsehung
Gottes?

Antwort.

Die allmächtige und gegenwärtige
Kraft Gottes, durch welche Er Himmel
und Erde, sammt allen Creaturen,
gleich als mit seiner Hand noch erhält,
und also regieret, daß Laub und Gras,
Regen und Dürre, fruchtbare und un=
fruchtbare Jahre, Essen und Trinken,
Gesundheit und Krankheit, Reichthum
und Armuth, und alles nicht von
ohngefähr, sondern von seiner väter=
lichen Hand uns zukomme.

Frage 28.

Was für Nutzen bekommen wir aus der
Erkenntniß der Schöpfung und Fürsehung
Gottes?

Antwort.

Daß wir in aller Widerwärtigkeit
geduldig, in Glückseligkeit dankbar, und
auf's Zukünftige guter Zuversicht zu
unserm getreuen Gott und Vater sein
sollen, daß uns keine Creatur von
seiner Liebe scheiden wird, dieweil alle
Creaturen also in seiner Hand sind,
daß sie sich ohne seinen Willen auch
nicht regen noch bewegen können.

---

ther, that whatever evil he sends
upon me in this vale of tears, he
will turn to my good; for he is able
to do it, being Almighty God, and
willing also, being a faithful Father.

QUESTION 27.

What dost thou understand by the Providence of God?

ANSWER.

The almighty and every where
present power of God, whereby, as
it were by his hand, he still upholds heaven and earth, with all
creatures, and so governs them
that herbs and grass, rain and
drought, fruitful and barren years,
meat and drink, health and sick-
ness, riches and poverty, yea, all
things, come not by chance, but
by his fatherly hand.

QUESTION 28.

What does it profit us to know that God
has created, and by his providence still upholds all things?

ANSWER.

That we may be patient in adversity, thankful in prosperity, and
for what is future have good confidence in our faithful God and
Father that no creature shall separate us from his love, since all
creatures are so in his hand that
without his will they can not so
much as move.

Von Gott dem Sohn.

OF GOD THE SON.

Frage 29.

Warum wird der Sohn Gottes Jesus, das ist, Seligmacher, genannt?

Antwort.

Darum, weil er uns selig macht von unsern Sünden, und weil bei keinem Andern einige Seligkeit zu suchen noch zu finden ist.

Frage 30.

Glauben denn die auch an den einigen Seligmacher Jesum, die ihre Seligkeit und Heil bei Heiligen, bei sich selbst, oder anderswo suchen?

Antwort.

Nein: sondern sie verläugnen mit der That den einigen Seligmacher und Heiland Jesum, ob sie sich sein gleich rühmen. Denn entweder Jesus nicht ein vollkommener Heiland sein kann, oder die diesen Heiland mit wahrem Glauben annehmen, müssen alles in Ihm haben, das zu ihrer Seligkeit vonnöthen ist.

Frage 31.

Warum ist Er Christus, das ist, ein Gesalbter, genannt?

Antwort.

Weil Er von Gott dem Vater verordnet und mit dem heiligen Geiste gesalbet ist zu unserm obersten Propheten und Lehrer, der uns den heimlichen Rath und Willen Gottes von unserer Erlösung vollkommen offenbaret; und zu unserm einigen Hohenpriester, der uns mit dem einigen Opfer seines Leibes erlöset hat, und immerdar

QUESTION 29.

Why is the Son of God called *Jesus*, that is, *Saviour?*

ANSWER.

Because he saves us from our sins; and no salvation is to be either sought or found in any other.

QUESTION 30.

Do such, then, believe in the only Saviour Jesus who seek their salvation and welfare of saints, of themselves, or any where else?

ANSWER.

No; although they may make their boast of him, yet in act they deny the only Saviour Jesus. For either Jesus is not a complete Saviour, or they who by true faith receive this Saviour must have in him all that is necessary to their salvation.

QUESTION 31.

Why is he called *Christ*, that is, *Anointed?*

ANSWER.

Because he is ordained of God the Father, and anointed with the Holy Ghost, to be our chief Prophet and Teacher, who fully reveals to us the secret counsel and will of God concerning our redemption; and our only High Priest, who by the one sacrifice of his body has redeemed us, and ever liveth

mit seiner Fürbitte vor dem Vater vertritt; und zu unserm ewigen König, der uns mit seinem Wort und Geist regieret, und bei der erworbenen Erlösung schützet und erhält.

Frage 32.

Warum wirst aber du ein Christ genannt?

Antwort.

Weil ich durch den Glauben ein Glied Christi, und also seiner Salbung theilhaftig bin, auf daß auch ich seinen Namen bekenne, mich Ihm zu einem lebendigen Dankopfer darstelle, und mit freiem Gewissen in diesem Leben wider die Sünde und Teufel streite, und hernach in Ewigkeit mit Ihm über alle Creaturen herrsche.

Frage 33.

Warum heißt Er Gottes eingeborner Sohn, so doch wir auch Gottes Kinder sind?

Antwort.

Darum, weil Christus allein der ewige natürliche Sohn Gottes ist, wir aber um seinetwillen aus Gnaden zu Kindern Gottes angenommen sind.

Frage 34.

Warum nennest du Ihn unsern Herrn?

Antwort.

Weil Er uns mit Leib und Seele von der Sünde und aus aller Gewalt des Teufels nicht mit Gold oder Silber, sondern mit seinem theuren Blut ihm zum Eigenthum erlöset und erkaufet hat.

to make intercession for us with the Father; and our eternal King, who governs us by his Word and Spirit, and defends and preserves us in the redemption obtained for us.

Question 32.

But why art *thou* called a Christian?

Answer.

Because by faith I am a member of Christ, and thus a partaker of his anointing; in order that I also may confess his name, may present myself a living sacrifice of thankfulness to him, and may with free conscience fight against sin and the devil in this life, and hereafter, in eternity, reign with him over all creatures.

Question 33.

Why is he called God's *only-begotten Son*, since we also are the children of God?

Answer.

Because Christ alone is the eternal natural Son of God; but we are children of God by adoption through grace for his sake.

Question 34.

Why callest thou him *our Lord?*

Answer.

Because, not with silver or gold, but with his precious blood, he has redeemed and purchased us, body and soul, from sin and from all the power of the devil, to be his own.

Frage 35.

Was heißt, daß Er empfangen ist von dem heiligen Geist, geboren aus Maria der Jungfrau?

Antwort.

Daß der ewige Sohn Gottes, der wahrer und ewiger Gott ist und bleibet, wahre menschliche Natur aus dem Fleisch und Blut der Jungfrau Maria, durch Wirkung des heiligen Geistes, an sich genommen hat, auf daß Er auch der wahre Same Davids sei, seinen Brüdern in allem gleich, ausgenommen die Sünde.

Frage 36.

Was für Nutzen bekommst du aus der heiligen Empfängniß und Geburt Christi?

Antwort.

Daß Er unser Mittler ist, und mit seiner Unschuld und vollkommenen Heiligkeit meine Sünde, darin ich bin empfangen, vor Gottes Angesicht bedecket.

Frage 37.

Was verstehst du unter dem Wörtlein: Gelitten?

Antwort.

Daß Er an Leib und Seele die ganze Zeit seines Lebens auf Erden, sonderlich aber am Ende desselben, den Zorn Gottes wider die Sünde des ganzen menschlichen Geschlechts getragen hat, auf daß Er mit seinem Leiden, als mit dem einigen Sühnopfer, unsern Leib und Seele von der ewigen Verdammniß erlösete, und uns Gottes Gnade, Gerechtigkeit und ewiges Leben erwürbe.

QUESTION 35.

What is the meaning of *Conceived by the Holy Ghost, born of the Virgin Mary?*

ANSWER.

That the eternal Son of God, who is and continues true and eternal God, took upon him the very nature of man, of the flesh and blood of the Virgin Mary, by the operation of the Holy Ghost, so that he also might be the true seed of David, like unto his brethren in all things, sin excepted.

QUESTION 36.

What benefit dost thou receive from the holy conception and birth of Christ?

ANSWER.

That he is our Mediator, and with his innocence and perfect holiness covers, in the sight of God, my sin wherein I was conceived.

QUESTION 37.

What dost thou understand by the word *Suffered?*

ANSWER.

That all the time he lived on earth, but especially at the end of his life, he bore, in body and soul, the wrath of God against the sin of the whole human race, in order that by his passion, as the only atoning sacrifice, he might redeem our body and soul from everlasting damnation, and obtain for us the grace of God, righteousness, and eternal life.

Frage 38.

Warum hat Er unter dem Richter Pontio Pilato gelitten?

Antwort.

Auf daß Er unschuldig unter dem weltlichen Richter verdammet würde, und uns damit von dem strengen Urtheil Gottes, das über uns ergehen sollte, erledigte.

Frage 39.

Ist es etwas mehr, daß Er ist gekreuziget worden, denn so Er eines andern Todes gestorben wäre?

Antwort.

Ja: denn dadurch bin ich gewiß, daß Er die Vermaledeiung, die auf mir lag, auf sich geladen habe, dieweil der Tod des Kreuzes von Gott verflucht war.

Frage 40.

Warum hat Christus den Tod müssen leiden?

Antwort.

Darum, weil wegen der Gerechtigkeit und Wahrheit Gottes nicht anders für unsere Sünden möchte bezahlet werden, denn durch den Tod des Sohnes Gottes.

Frage 41.

Warum ist Er begraben worden?

Antwort.

Damit zu bezeugen, daß Er wahrhaftig gestorben sei.

Frage 42.

Weil denn Christus für uns gestorben ist, wie kommt's, daß wir auch sterben müssen?

Antwort.

Unser Tod ist nicht eine Bezahlung für unsere Sünde, sondern nur eine

---

QUESTION 38.

Why did he suffer under *Pontius Pilate*, as judge?

ANSWER.

That he, being innocent, might be condemned by the temporal judge, and thereby deliver us from the severe judgment of God to which we were exposed.

QUESTION 39.

Is there any thing more in his having been *crucified* than if he had died some other death?

ANSWER.

Yes; for thereby I am assured that he took on himself the curse which lay upon me, because the death of the cross was accursed of God.

QUESTION 40.

Why was it necessary for Christ to suffer death?

ANSWER.

Because, by reason of the justice and truth of God, satisfaction for our sins could be made no otherwise than by the death of the Son of God.

QUESTION 41.

Why was he buried?

ANSWER.

To show thereby that he was really dead.

QUESTION 42.

Since, then, Christ died for us, why must we also die?

ANSWER.

Our death is not a satisfaction for our sin, but only a dying to

Absterbung der Sünden, und Eingang zum ewigen Leben.

Frage 43.

Was bekommen wir mehr für Nutzen aus dem Opfer und Tod Christi am Kreuz?

Antwort.

Daß durch seine Kraft unser alter Mensch mit Ihm gekreuziget, getödtet und begraben wird, auf daß die bösen Lüste des Fleisches nicht mehr in uns regieren, sondern daß wir uns selbst Ihm zur Danksagung aufopfern.

Frage 44.

Warum folget: Abgestiegen zu der Hölle?[1]

Antwort.

Daß ich in meinen höchsten Anfechtungen versichert sei, mein Herr Christus habe mich durch seine unaussprechliche Angst, Schmerzen und Schrecken, die Er auch an seiner Seele am Kreuz und zuvor erlitten, von der höllischen Angst und Pein erlöset.

Frage 45.

Was nützet uns die Auferstehung Christi?

Antwort.

Erstlich hat Er durch seine Auferstehung den Tod überwunden, daß Er uns der Gerechtigkeit, die Er uns durch seinen Tod erworben hat, könnte theilhaftig machen. Zum andern werden auch wir jetzt durch seine Kraft er-

sins and entering into eternal life.

QUESTION 43.

What further benefit do we receive from the sacrifice and death of Christ on the cross?

ANSWER.

That by his power our old man is with him crucified, slain, and buried; that so the evil lusts of the flesh may no more reign in us, but that we may offer ourselves unto him a sacrifice of thanksgiving.

QUESTION 44.

Why is it added: *He descended into Hades?*[1]

ANSWER.

That in my greatest temptations I may be assured that Christ, my Lord, by his inexpressible anguish, pains, and terrors which he suffered in his soul on the cross and before, has redeemed me from the anguish and torment of hell.

QUESTION 45.

What benefit do we receive from the *resurrection* of Christ?

ANSWER.

First, by his resurrection he has overcome death, that he might make us partakers of the righteousness which by his death he has obtained for us. Secondly, we also are now by his power

---

[1] In the Apostles' Creed, *Hell* has the meaning of *Hades*, or the state and place of departed spirits; but the Heidelberg Catechism explains the descent figuratively of the vicarious sufferings on the cross.

wecket zu einem neuen Leben. Zum dritten ist uns die Auferstehung Christi ein gewisses Pfand unserer seligen Auferstehung.

Frage 46.

Wie verstehst du [dieß], daß Er ist gen Himmel gefahren?

Antwort.

Daß Christus vor den Augen seiner Jünger ist von der Erde aufgehoben gen Himmel, und uns zu gut daselbst ist, bis daß Er wiederkommt zu richten die Lebendigen und die Todten.

Frage 47.

Ist denn Christus nicht bei uns bis an's Ende der Welt, wie Er uns verheißen hat?

Antwort.

Christus ist wahrer Mensch und wahrer Gott: nach seiner menschlichen Natur ist Er jetzt nicht auf Erden, aber nach seiner Gottheit, Majestät, Gnade und Geist weicht Er nimmer von uns.

Frage 48.

Werden aber auf diese Weise die zwei Naturen in Christo nicht von einander getrennt, so die Menschheit nicht überall ist, da die Gottheit ist?

Antwort.

Mit nichten: denn weil die Gottheit unbegreiflich und allenthalben gegenwärtig ist, so muß folgen, daß sie wohl außerhalb ihrer angenommenen Menschheit, und dennoch nichts desto weniger auch in derselben ist, und persönlich mit ihr vereiniget bleibt.

raised up to a new life. Thirdly the resurrection of Christ is to us a sure pledge of our blessed resurrection.

QUESTION 46.

How dost thou understand the words, *He ascended into Heaven?*

ANSWER.

That Christ, in sight of his disciples, was taken up from the earth into heaven, and in our behalf there continues, until he shall come again to judge the living and the dead.

QUESTION 47.

Is not, then, Christ with us even unto the end of the world, as he has promised?

ANSWER.

Christ is true Man and true God: according to his human nature, he is now not upon earth; but according to his Godhead, majesty, grace, and Spirit, he is at no time absent from us.

QUESTION 48.

But are not, in this way, the two natures in Christ separated from one another, if the Manhood be not wherever the Godhead is?

ANSWER.

By no means; for since the Godhead is incomprehensible and every where present, it must follow that it is indeed beyond the bounds of the Manhood which it has assumed, but is yet none the less in the same also, and remains personally united to it.

Frage 49.

Was nützet uns die Himmelfahrt Christi?

Antwort.

Erstlich, daß Er im Himmel vor dem Angesicht seines Vaters unser Fürsprecher ist. Zum andern, daß wir unser Fleisch im Himmel zu einem sichern Pfand haben, daß Er, als das Haupt, uns, seine Glieder, auch zu sich werde hinauf nehmen. Zum dritten, daß Er uns seinen Geist zum Gegenpfand herab sendet, durch welches Kraft wir suchen, was droben ist, da Christus ist, sitzend zur Rechten Gottes, und nicht, das auf Erden ist.

Frage 50.

Warum wird hinzugesetzt, daß Er sitze zur Rechten Gottes?

Antwort.

Weil Christus darum gen Himmel gefahren ist, daß Er sich daselbst erzeige als das Haupt seiner christlichen Kirche, durch welches der Vater alles regieret.

Frage 51.

Was nützet uns diese Herrlichkeit unsers Hauptes Christi?

Antwort.

Erstlich, daß Er durch seinen heiligen Geist in uns, seine Glieder, die himmlischen Gaben ausgeußt; darnach, daß Er uns mit seiner Gewalt wider alle Feinde schützet und erhält.

Frage 52.

Wes tröstet dich die Wiederkunft Christi,

QUESTION 49.

What benefit do we receive from Christ' ascension into heaven?

ANSWER.

First, that he is our Advocate in the presence of his Father in heaven. Secondly, that we have our flesh in heaven, as a sure pledge that he, as the Head, will also take us, his members, up to himself. Thirdly, that he sends us his Spirit, as an earnest, by whose power we seek those things which are above, where Christ sitteth on the right hand of God, and not things on the earth.

QUESTION 50.

Why is it added, *And sitteth at the right hand of God?*

ANSWER.

Because Christ ascended into heaven for this end, that he might there appear as Head of his Church, by whom the Father governs all things.

QUESTION 51.

What benefit do we receive from this glory of our Head, Christ?

ANSWER.

First, that by his Holy Spirit he sheds forth heavenly gifts in us, his members; then, that by his power he defends and preserves us against all enemies.

QUESTION 52.

What comfort is it to thee that Christ

zu richten die Lebendigen und die Todten?

shall come again to judge the quick and the dead?

Antwort.

Daß ich in aller Trübsal und Verfolgung mit aufgerichtetem Haupt eben des Richters, der sich zuvor dem Gerichte Gottes für mich dargestellt und alle Vermaledeiung von mir hinweggenommen hat, aus dem Himmel gewärtig bin, daß Er alle seine und meine Feinde in die ewige Verdammniß werfe, mich aber, sammt allen Auserwählten, zu sich in die himmlische Freude und Herrlichkeit nehme.

ANSWER.

That in all my sorrows and persecutions, with uplifted head, I look for the self-same One who has before offered himself for me to the judgment of God, and removed from me all curse, to come again as Judge from heaven; who shall cast all his and my enemies into everlasting condemnation, but shall take me, with all his chosen ones, to himself, into heavenly joy and glory.

Von Gott dem Heiligen Geiste.

Frage 53.

Was glaubest du vom Heiligen Geiste?

Antwort.

Erstlich, daß Er gleich ewiger Gott mit dem Vater und dem Sohne ist. Zum andern, daß Er auch mir gegeben ist, mich durch einen wahren Glauben Christi und aller seiner Wohlthaten theilhaftig macht, mich tröstet und bei mir bleiben wird bis in Ewigkeit.

Frage 54.

Was glaubest du von der heiligen allgemeinen Christlichen Kirche?

Antwort.

Daß der Sohn Gottes aus dem ganzen menschlichen Geschlechte sich eine auserwählte Gemeine zum ewigen Leben, durch seinen Geist und Wort, in Einigkeit des wahren Glaubens,

OF GOD THE HOLY GHOST.

QUESTION 53.

What dost thou believe concerning the *Holy Ghost?*

ANSWER.

First, that he is co-eternal God with the Father and the Son. Secondly, that he is also given unto me, makes me by a true faith partaker of Christ and all his benefits, comforts me, and shall abide with me forever.

QUESTION 54.

What dost thou believe concerning the *Holy Catholic Church?*

ANSWER.

That out of the whole human race, from the beginning to the end of the world, the Son of God, by his Spirit and Word, gathers, defends, and preserves for himself unto ever-

von Anbeginn der Welt bis an's Ende versammle, schütze und erhalte; und daß ich derselben ein lebendiges Glied bin, und ewig bleiben werde.

Frage 55.
Was verstehest du unter der Gemeinschaft der Heiligen?

Antwort.
Erstlich, daß alle und jede Gläubigen als Glieder an dem Herrn Christo und allen seinen Schätzen und Gaben Gemeinschaft haben. Zum andern, daß ein jeder seine Gaben zu Nutz und Heil der andern Glieder willig und mit Freuden anzulegen sich schuldig wissen soll.

Frage 56.
Was glaubest du von der Vergebung der Sünden?

Antwort.
Daß Gott um der Genugthuung Christi willen aller meiner Sünden, auch der sündlichen Art, mit der ich mein Leben lang zu streiten habe, nimmermehr gedenken will, sondern mir die Gerechtigkeit Christi aus Gnaden schenket, daß ich in's Gericht nimmermehr soll kommen.

Frage 57.
Wes tröstet dich die Auferstehung des Fleisches?

Antwort.
Daß nicht allein meine Seele nach diesem Leben alsbald zu Christo, ihrem Haupt, genommen wird, sondern auch, daß dieß mein Fleisch, durch die Kraft

lasting life, a chosen communion in the unity of the true faith; and that I am, and forever shall remain, a living member of the same.

QUESTION 55.
What dost thou understand by the *communion of saints?*

ANSWER.
First, that believers, all and every one, as members of Christ, have part in him and in all his treasures and gifts. Secondly, that each one must feel himself bound to use his gifts, readily and cheerfully, for the advantage and welfare of other members.

QUESTION 56.
What dost thou believe concerning the *forgiveness of sins?*

ANSWER.
That God, for the sake of Christ's satisfaction, will no more remember my sins, neither the sinful nature with which I have to struggle all my life long; but graciously imparts to me the righteousness of Christ, that I may nevermore come into condemnation.

QUESTION 57.
What comfort does the *resurrection of the body* afford thee?

ANSWER.
That not only my soul, after this life, shall be immediately taken up to Christ its Head, but also that this my body, raised by the power

Christi auferwecket, wieder mit meiner Seele vereiniget, und dem herrlichen Leibe Christi gleichförmig werden soll.

Frage 58.

Wes tröstet dich der Artikel vom ewigen Leben?

Antwort.

Daß, nachdem ich jetzt den Anfang der ewigen Freude in meinem Herzen empfinde, ich nach diesem Leben vollkommene Seligkeit besitzen werde, die kein Auge gesehen, kein Ohr gehöret, und in keines Menschen Herz gekommen ist, Gott ewiglich darin zu preisen.

Frage 59.

Was hilft es dir aber nun, wenn du dieß Alles glaubest?

Antwort.

Daß ich in Christo vor Gott gerecht, und ein Erbe des ewigen Lebens bin.

Frage 60.

Wie bist du gerecht vor Gott?

Antwort.

Allein durch wahren Glauben in Jesum Christum: also, daß, ob mich schon mein Gewissen anklagt, daß ich wider alle Gebote Gottes schwerlich gesündiget, und derselben keines je gehalten habe, auch noch immerdar zu allem Bösen geneigt bin, doch Gott ohne all mein Verdienst aus lauter Gnaden, mir die vollkommene Genugthuung, Gerechtigkeit und Heiligkeit Christi schenket und zurechnet, als hätte ich nie eine Sünde begangen noch gehabt, und selbst allen den

---

of Christ, shall again be united with my soul, and made like unto the glorious body of Christ.

QUESTION 58.

What comfort hast thou from the article of the life everlasting?

ANSWER.

That, inasmuch as I now feel in my heart the beginning of eternal joy, I shall after this life possess complete bliss, such as eye hath not seen, nor ear heard, neither hath entered into the heart of man, therein to praise God forever.

QUESTION 59.

But what does it help thee now that thou believest all this?

ANSWER.

That I am righteous in Christ before God, and an heir of eternal life.

QUESTION 60.

How art thou righteous before God?

ANSWER.

Only by true faith in Jesus Christ; that is, although my conscience accuse me that I have grievously sinned against all the commandments of God, and have never kept any of them, and that I am still prone always to all evil, yet God, without any merit of mine, of mere grace, grants and imputes to me the perfect satisfaction, righteousness, and holiness of Christ, as if I had never committed nor had any sin, and had myself accom-

Gehorsam vollbracht, den Christus für mich hat geleistet, wenn ich allein solche Wohlthat mit gläubigem Herzen annehme.

plished all the obedience which Christ has fulfilled for me, if only I accept such benefit with a believing heart.

Frage 61.

Warum sagst du, daß du allein durch den Glauben gerecht seiest?

QUESTION 61.

Why sayest thou that thou art righteous only by faith?

Antwort.

Nicht daß ich von wegen der Würdigkeit meines Glaubens Gott gefalle, sondern darum, daß allein die Genugthuung, Gerechtigkeit, und Heiligkeit Christi meine Gerechtigkeit vor Gott ist, und ich dieselbe nicht anders, denn allein durch den Glauben annehmen, und mir zueignen kann.

ANSWER.

Not that I am acceptable to God on account of the worthiness of my faith; but because only the satisfaction, righteousness, and holiness of Christ is my righteousness before God, and I can receive the same and make it my own in no other way than by faith only.

Frage 62.

Warum können aber unsere guten Werke nicht die Gerechtigkeit vor Gott oder ein Stück derselben sein?

QUESTION 62.

But why can not our good works be the whole or part of our righteousness before God?

Antwort.

Darum, weil die Gerechtigkeit, so vor Gottes Gericht bestehen soll, durchaus vollkommen und dem Gesetz ganz gleichförmig sein muß, aber auch unsere besten Werke in diesem Leben alle unvollkommen und mit Sünden befleckt sind.

ANSWER.

Because the righteousness which can stand before the judgment-seat of God must be perfect throughout, and wholly conformable to the divine law; whereas even our best works in this life are all imperfect and defiled with sin.

Frage 63.

Verdienen aber unsere guten Werke nichts, so sie doch Gott in diesem und dem zukünftigen Leben will belohnen?

QUESTION 63.

How is it that our good works merit nothing, while yet it is God's will to reward them in this life and in that which is to come?

Antwort.

Diese Belohnung geschieht nicht aus Verdienst, sondern aus Gnaden.

ANSWER.

The reward comes not of merit, but of grace.

Frage 64.

Macht aber diese Lehre nicht sorglose und verruchte Leute?

Antwort.

Nein : denn es unmöglich ist, daß die, so Christo durch wahren Glauben sind eingepflanzet, nicht Frucht der Dankbarkeit sollen bringen.

QUESTION 64.

But does not this doctrine make men careless and profane?

ANSWER.

No ; for it is impossible that those who are implanted into Christ by true faith should not bring forth fruits of righteousness.

Von den heiligen Sacramenten.

OF THE HOLY SACRAMENTS.

Frage 65.

Dieweil denn allein der Glaube uns Christi und aller seiner Wohlthaten theilhaftig macht, woher kommt solcher Glaube?

Antwort.

Der Heilige Geist wirket denselben in unsern Herzen durch die Predigt des heiligen Evangeliums, und bestätigt ihn durch den Brauch der heiligen Sacramente.

QUESTION 65.

Since, then, we are made partakers of Christ and all his benefits by faith only, whence comes this faith?

ANSWER.

The Holy Ghost works it in our hearts by the preaching of the holy Gospel, and confirms it by the use of the holy Sacraments.

Frage 66.

Was sind die Sacramente?

Antwort.

Es sind sichtbare heilige Wahrzeichen und Siegel, von Gott dazu eingesetzt, daß er uns durch den Brauch derselben die Verheißung des Evangeliums desto besser zu verstehen gebe und versiegele : nämlich, daß er uns von wegen des einigen Opfers Christi, am Kreuz vollbracht, Vergebung der Sünden und ewiges Leben aus Gnaden schenke.

QUESTION 66.

What are the Sacraments?

ANSWER.

The Sacraments are visible, holy signs and seals, appointed of God for this end, that by the use thereof he may the more fully declare and seal to us the promise of the Gospel; namely, that he grants us out of free grace the forgiveness of sins and everlasting life, for the sake of the one sacrifice of Christ accomplished on the cross.

Frage 67.

Sind denn beide, das Wort und die Sacramente, dahin gerichtet, daß sie unsern Glauben

QUESTION 67.

Are both these, then, the Word and the Sacraments, designed to direct our faith to

auf das Opfer Jesu Christi am Kreuz, als auf den einigen Grund unserer Seligkeit, weisen?

Antwort.

Ja freilich: denn der Heilige Geist lehret im Evangelio, und bestätigt durch die heiligen Sacramente, daß unsere ganze Seligkeit stehe in dem einigen Opfer Christi, für uns am Kreuz geschehen.

Frage 68.

Wie viel Sacramente hat Christus im Neuen Testament eingesetzt?

Antwort.

Zwei: die heilige Taufe und das heilige Abendmahl.

Von der heiligen Taufe.

Frage 69.

Wie wirst du in der heiligen Taufe erinnert und versichert, daß das einige Opfer Christi am Kreuz dir zu gut komme?

Antwort.

Also, daß Christus dieß äußerliche Wasserbad eingesetzt, und dabei verheißen hat, daß ich so gewiß mit seinem Blut und Geist von der Unreinigkeit meiner Seele, das ist, allen meinen Sünden gewaschen sei, so gewiß ich äußerlich mit dem Wasser, welches die Unsauberkeit des Leibes pflegt hinzunehmen, gewaschen bin.

Frage 70.

Was heißt mit dem Blut und Geist Christi gewaschen sein?

Antwort.

Es heißt Vergebung der Sünden

the sacrifice of Jesus Christ on the cross as the only ground of our salvation?

ANSWER.

Yes, truly; for the Holy Ghost teaches in the Gospel, and by the holy Sacraments assures us, that our whole salvation stands in the one sacrifice of Christ made for us on the cross.

QUESTION 68.

How many Sacraments has Christ appointed in the New Testament?

ANSWER.

Two: holy Baptism and the holy Supper.

OF HOLY BAPTISM.

QUESTION 69.

How is it signified and sealed unto thee in holy Baptism that thou hast part in the one sacrifice of Christ on the cross?

ANSWER.

Thus: that Christ has appointed this outward washing with water, and has joined therewith this promise, that I am washed with his blood and Spirit from the pollution of my soul, that is, from all my sins, as certainly as I am washed outwardly with water whereby commonly the filthiness of the body is taken away.

QUESTION 70.

What is it to be washed with the blood and Spirit of Christ?

ANSWER.

It is to have the forgiveness of

von Gott aus Gnaden haben, um des
Blutes Christi willen, welches er in
seinem Opfer am Kreuz für uns vergossen hat; darnach auch durch den
Heiligen Geist erneuert, und zu einem
Glied Christi geheiliget sein, daß wir
je länger je mehr der Sünde absterben,
und in einem gottseligen, unsträflichen
Leben wandeln.

Frage 71.

Wo hat Christus verheißen, daß wir so gewiß mit seinem Blut und Geist, als mit dem
Taufwasser, gewaschen sind?

Antwort.

In der Einsetzung der Taufe, welche
also lautet: Gehet hin, und lehret alle Völker, und taufet sie
im Namen des Vaters, und
des Sohnes, und des Heiligen
Geistes: wer da glaubet und getauft wird, der wird selig werden; wer aber nicht glaubet, der
wird verdammt werden. Diese
Verheißung wird auch wiederholt, da
die Schrift die Taufe das Bad der
Wiedergeburt und Abwaschung der
Sünden nennet.

Frage 72.

Ist denn das äußerliche Wasserbad die Abwaschung der Sünden selbst?

Antwort.

Nein; denn allein das Blut Jesu
Christi, und der Heilige Geist reiniget
uns von allen Sünden.

Frage 73.

Warum nennet denn der Heilige Geist die

---

sins from God, through grace, for
the sake of Christ's blood, which
he shed for us in his sacrifice on
the cross; and also to be renewed
by the Holy Ghost, and sanctified
to be members of Christ, that so
we may more and more die unto
sin, and lead holy and unblamable
lives.

QUESTION 71.

Where has Christ promised that we are as
certainly washed with his blood and Spirit as
with the water of Baptism?

ANSWER.

In the institution of Baptism,
which runs thus: *Go ye, therefore,
and teach all nations, baptizing
them in the name of the Father,
and of the Son, and of the Holy
Ghost. He that believeth and is
baptized, shall be saved; but he
that believeth not, shall be damned.*
This promise is also repeated where
the Scripture calls Baptism the
washing of regeneration and the
washing away of sins.

QUESTION 72.

Is, then, the outward washing of water itself the washing away of sins?

ANSWER.

No; for only the blood of Jesus Christ and the Holy Spirit
cleanse us from all sin.

QUESTION 73

Why, then, doth the Holy Ghost call Bap-

Taufe das Bad der Wiedergeburt und die Abwaschung der Sünden?

Antwort.

Gott redet also nicht ohne große Ursache: nämlich, nicht allein, daß Er uns damit will lehren, daß, gleichwie die Unsauberkeit des Leibes durch Wasser, also unsere Sünden durch's Blut und Geist Christi hinweg genommen werden; sondern vielmehr, daß Er uns durch dieß göttliche Pfand und Wahrzeichen will versichern, daß wir so wahrhaftig von unsern Sünden geistlich gewaschen sind, als wir mit dem leiblichen Wasser gewaschen werden.

Frage 74.

Soll man auch die jungen Kinder taufen?

Antwort.

Ja: denn dieweil sie sowohl als die Alten in den Bund Gottes und seine Gemeine gehören, und ihnen in dem Blut Christi die Erlösung von Sünden und der Heilige Geist, welcher den Glauben wirket, nicht weniger denn den Alten zugesagt wird; so sollen sie auch durch die Taufe, als des Bundes Zeichen, der christlichen Kirche eingeleibt und von der Ungläubigen Kindern unterschieden werden, wie im alten Testament durch die Beschneidung geschehen ist, an welcher Statt im neuen Testament die Taufe ist eingesetzt.

tism the washing of regeneration and the washing away of sins?

ANSWER.

God speaks thus not without great cause: namely, not only to teach us thereby that like as the filthiness of the body is taken away by water, so our sins also are taken away by the blood and Spirit of Christ; but much more, that by this divine pledge and token he may assure us that we are as really washed from our sins spiritually as our bodies are washed with water.

QUESTION 74.

Are infants also to be baptized?

ANSWER.

Yes; for since they, as well as their parents, belong to the covenant and people of God, and both redemption from sin and the Holy Ghost, who works faith, are through the blood of Christ promised to them no less than to their parents, they are also by Baptism, as a sign of the covenant, to be ingrafted into the Christian Church, and distinguished from the children of unbelievers, as was done in the Old Testament by Circumcision, in place of which in the New Testament Baptism is appointed.

Vom Heiligen Abendmahl Jesu Christi.	**OF THE HOLY SUPPER OF THE LORD.**

Frage 75.

Wie wirst du im Heiligen Abendmahl erinnert und versichert, daß du an dem einigen Opfer Christi am Kreuz und allen seinen Gütern Gemeinschaft habest?

Antwort.

Also, daß Christus mir und allen Gläubigen von diesem gebrochenen Brot zu essen, und von diesem Kelch zu trinken befohlen hat, zu seinem Gedächtniß, und dabei verheißen: Erstlich, daß sein Leib so gewiß für mich am Kreuz geopfert und gebrochen, und sein Blut für mich vergossen sei, so gewiß ich mit Augen sehe, daß das Brot des Herrn mir gebrochen, und der Kelch mir mitgetheilet wird; und zum andern, daß Er selbst meine Seele mit seinem gekreuzigten Leib und vergossenen Blut so gewiß zum ewigen Leben speise und tränke, als ich aus der Hand des Dieners empfange und leiblich genieße das Brot und den Kelch des Herrn, welche mir als gewisse Wahrzeichen des Leibes und Bluts Christi gegeben werden.

Frage 76.

Was heißt den gekreuzigten Leib Christi essen und sein vergossenes Blut trinken?

Antwort.

Es heißt nicht allein mit gläubigem Herzen das ganze Leiden und Sterben Christi annehmen, und dadurch Vergebung der Sünden und ewiges Leben

QUESTION 75.

How is it signified and sealed unto thee in the Holy Supper that thou dost partake of the one sacrifice of Christ on the cross and all his benefits?

ANSWER.

Thus, that Christ has commanded me and all believers to eat of this broken bread, and to drink of this cup, and has joined therewith these promises: First, that his body was offered and broken on the cross for me, and his blood shed for me, as certainly as I see with my eyes the bread of the *Lord* broken for me, and the cup communicated to me; and, further, that with his crucified body and shed blood he himself feeds and nourishes my soul to everlasting life, as certainly as I receive from the hand of the minister, and taste with my mouth, the bread and cup of the *Lord*, which are given me as certain tokens of the body and blood of Christ.

QUESTION 76.

What is it to eat the crucified body and drink the shed blood of Christ?

ANSWER.

It is not only to embrace with a believing heart all the sufferings and death of Christ, and thereby to obtain the forgiveness of sins

bekommen, sondern auch daneben durch den Heiligen Geist, der zugleich in Christo und in uns wohnet, also mit seinem gebenedeiten Leibe je mehr und mehr vereiniget werden, daß wir, obgleich Er im Himmel, und wir auf Erden sind, dennoch Fleisch von seinem Fleisch und Bein von seinen Beinen sind, und von Einem Geiste (wie die Glieder unsers Leibes von Einer Seele) ewig leben und regieret werden.

and life eternal, but moreover, also, to be so united more and more to his sacred body by the Holy Ghost, who dwells both in Christ and in us, that although he is in heaven, and we on the earth, we are nevertheless flesh of his flesh and bone of his bones, and live and are governed forever by one Spirit, as members of the same body are by one soul.

Frage 77.

Wo hat Christus verheißen, daß Er die Gläubigen so gewiß mit seinem Leib und Blut speise und tränke, als sie von diesem gebrochenen Brot essen, und von diesem Kelch trinken?

QUESTION 77.

Where has Christ promised that he will thus feed and nourish believers with his body and blood, as certainly as they eat of this broken bread and drink of this cup?

Antwort.

In der Einsetzung des heiligen Abendmahls, welche also lautet: Unser Herr Jesus, in der Nacht, da Er verrathen ward, nahm Er das Brot, dankete, und brach's, und sprach: ,Nehmet, esset, das ist mein Leib, der für euch gebrochen wird; solches thut zu meinem Gedächtniß.' Desselben gleichen auch den Kelch, nach dem Abendmahl, und sprach: ,Dieser Kelch ist das Neue Testament in meinem Blut; solches thut, so oft ihr's trinket, zu meinem Gedächtniß.' Denn so oft ihr von diesem Brot esset, und von diesem Kelch trinket, sollt ihr des Herrn Tod verkündigen, bis daß Er kommt. Und diese Verheißung wird auch wie-

ANSWER.

In the institution of the Supper, which runs thus: *The Lord Jesus, the same night in which he was betrayed, took bread; and when he had given thanks, he brake it, and said: 'Take, eat, this is my body, which is broken for you; this do in remembrance of me.' After the same manner also he took the cup, when he had supped, saying: 'This cup is the New Testament in my blood; this do ye as often as ye drink it, in remembrance of me. For as often as ye eat this bread, and drink this cup, ye do show the Lord's death till he come.'* And this promise is repeated also by St. Paul, where he says: *The cup of*

verholet durch St. Paulum, da er
spricht: Der Kelch der Danksagung, damit wir danksagen, ist er
nicht die Gemeinschaft des Bluts
Christi? Das Brot, das wir
brechen, ist das nicht die Gemeinschaft des Leibes Christi? Denn
Ein Brot ist's, so sind wir viele
Ein Leib, dieweil wir alle Eines
Brots theilhaftig sind?

blessing which we bless, is it not
the communion of the blood of
Christ? The bread which we
break, is it not the communion
of the body of Christ? For we,
being many, are one bread, and
one body; for we are all par-
takers of that one bread.

Frage 78.

Wird denn aus Brot und Wein der wesentliche Leib und Blut Christi?

QUESTION 78.

Do, then, the bread and wine become the
real body and blood of Christ?

Antwort.

Nein: sondern wie das Wasser in
der Taufe nicht in das Blut Christi
verwandelt, oder die Abwaschung der
Sünden selbst wird, deren es allein
ein göttlich Wahrzeichen und Versicherung ist: also wird auch das heilige
Brot im Abendmahl nicht der Leib
Christi selbst, wiewohl es, nach Art
und Brauch der Sacramente, der Leib
Christi genennet wird.

ANSWER.

No; but as the water in Baptism
is not changed into the blood of
Christ, nor becomes the washing
away of sins itself, being only the
divine token and assurance thereof,
so also in the Lord's Supper the sacred bread does not become the body
of Christ itself, though agreeably to
the nature and usage of sacraments
it is called the body of Christ.

Frage 79.

Warum nennet denn Christus das Brot
seinen Leib, und den Kelch sein Blut, oder das
Neue Testament in seinem Blute, und St.
Paulus die Gemeinschaft des Leibes und
Blutes Jesu Christi?

QUESTION 79.

Why, then, doth Christ call the bread his
body, and the cup his blood, or the New
Testament in his blood; and St. Paul, the
communion of the body and blood of
Christ?

Antwort.

Christus redet also nicht ohne große
Ursache: nämlich, daß Er uns nicht
allein damit will lehren, daß, gleich
wie Brot und Wein das zeitliche Leben
erhalten, also sei auch sein gekreuzigter

ANSWER.

Christ speaks thus not without
great cause: namely, not only to
teach us thereby that like as
bread and wine sustain this temporal life, so also his crucified

Leib und vergoffen Blut die wahre Speife und Trank unferer Seelen zum ewigen Leben, fondern vielmehr, daß Er uns durch dieß fichtbare Zeichen und Pfand will verfichern, daß wir fo wahrhaftig feines wahren Leibes und Blutes durch Wirkung des Heiligen Geiftes theilhaftig werden, als wir diefe heiligen Wahrzeichen mit dem leiblichen Mund zu feinem Gedächtniß empfangen, und daß all fein Leiden und Gehorfam fo gewiß unfer eigen fei, als hätten wir felbft in unferer eigenen Perfon alles gelitten und genug gethan.

body and shed blood are the true meat and drink of our souls unto life eternal; but much more, by this visible sign and pledge to assure us that we are as really partakers of his true body and blood, through the working of the Holy Ghost, as we receive by the mouth of the body these holy tokens in remembrance of him; and that all his sufferings and obedience are as certainly our own as if we had ourselves suffered and done all in our own persons.

(Frage 80.

Was ift für ein Unterfchied zwifchen dem Abendmahl des Herrn und der päpftlichen Meffe?

(QUESTION 80.

What difference is there between the Lord's Supper and the Popish Mass?

Antwort.

Das Abendmahl bezeuget uns, daß wir vollkommene Vergebung aller unferer Sünden haben durch das einige Opfer Jefu Chrifti, fo Er felbft einmal am Kreuz vollbracht hat; [und daß wir durch den Heiligen Geift Chrifto werden eingeleibet, der jetzt mit feinem wahren Leib im Himmel zur Rechten des Vaters ift, und dafelbft will angebetet werden]. Die Meffe aber lehret, daß die Lebendigen und die Todten nicht durch das Leiden Chrifti Vergebung der Sünden haben, es fei denn, daß Chriftus noch täglich für fie von den Meßprieftern geopfert werde; [und daß Chriftus leiblich unter der Geftalt Brots und Weins fei, und derhalben

ANSWER.

The Lord's Supper testifies to us that we have full forgiveness of all our sins by the one sacrifice of Jesus Christ, which he himself has once accomplished on the cross; [and that by the Holy Ghost we are ingrafted into Christ, who with his true body is now in heaven at the right hand of the Father, and is to be there worshiped]. But the Mass teaches that the living and the dead have not forgiveness of sins through the sufferings of Christ unless Christ is still daily offered for them by the priests; [and that Christ is bodily under the form of bread and wine, and

darin foll angebetet werden]. Und
ift alfo die Meffe im Grunde nichts
anders, denn eine Verläugnung des
einigen Opfers und Leidens Jefu
Chrifti [und eine vermaledeite Ab=
götterei].)¹

Frage 81.

Welche follen zum Tifche des Herrn kom=
men?

Antwort.

Die fich felbft um ihrer Sünden
willen mißfallen, und doch vertrauen,
daß diefelbigen ihnen verziehen, und
die übrige Schwachheit mit dem Lei=
den und Sterben Chrifti bedeckt fei,
begehren auch je mehr und mehr ihren
Glauben zu ftärken, und ihr Leben zu
beffern. Die Unbußfertigen aber und
Heuchler effen und trinken fich felbft
das Gericht.

Frage 82.

Sollen aber zu diefem Abendmahl auch
zugelaffen werden, die fich mit ihrem Bekennt=
niß und Leben als Ungläubige und Gottlofe
erzeigen?

Antwort.

Nein: denn es wird alfo der Bund
Gottes gefchmähet, und fein Zorn über
die ganze Gemeine gereizet. Derhal=
ben die chriftliche Kirche fchuldig ift,
nach der Ordnung Chrifti und feiner
Apoftel, folche bis zur Befferung ihres

is therefore to be worshiped in
them]. And thus the Mass at bottom is nothing else than a denial
of the one sacrifice and passion
of Jesus Christ [and an accursed
idolatry].)¹

QUESTION 81.

Who are to come unto the table of the
Lord?

ANSWER.

Those who are displeased with
themselves for their sins, yet trust
that these are forgiven them, and
that their remaining infirmity is
covered by the passion and death
of Christ; who also desire more
and more to strengthen their faith
and amend their life. But the impenitent and hypocrites eat and
drink judgment to themselves.

QUESTION 82.

Are they, then, also to be admitted to this
Supper who show themselves to be, by their
confession and life, unbelieving and ungodly?

ANSWER.

No; for by this the covenant of
God is profaned, and his wrath pro-
voked against the whole congregation; wherefore the Christian Church
is bound, according to the order of
Christ and his Apostles, by the office

---

¹ This 80th Question, as is now ascertained beyond controversy, is no part of the original
Heidelberg Catechism, and was inserted by express order of the Elector Frederick III., as a
counterblast to the anathemas of the Council of Trent (which closed December 4, 1563). It
appeared in part in the second edition, and the passages in brackets were added in the third,
with the remark at the close: 'What in the first edition was overlooked, especially on p. 55
[the place for the 80th Question in the first edition], has now been added by command of his
Electoral Grace.' For further information on this famous Question, which caused even a
temporary prohibition of the Catechism in the German Empire, see Vol. I., and my German
edition of the Heidelberg Catechism.

Lebens durch das Amt der Schlüssel
auszuschließen.

Frage 83.
Was ist das Amt der Schlüssel?

Antwort.

Die Predigt des heiligen Evangeli=
ums, und die christliche Bußzucht, durch
welche beide Stücke das Himmelreich
den Gläubigen aufgeschlossen und den
Ungläubigen zugeschlossen wird:

Frage 84.
Wie wird das Himmelreich durch die Pre=
digt des heiligen Evangeliums auf= und zu=
geschlossen?

Antwort.

Also, daß nach dem Befehl Christi
allen und jeden Gläubigen verkündigt
und öffentlich bezeuget wird, daß ihnen,
so oft sie die Verheißung des Evange=
liums mit wahrem Glauben annehmen,
wahrhaftig alle ihre Sünden von Gott,
um des Verdienstes Christi willen, ver=
geben sind; und' hinwiederum allen
Ungläubigen und Heuchlern, daß der
Zorn Gottes und die ewige Verdamm=
niß auf ihnen liegt, so lange sie sich
nicht bekehren. Nach welchem Zeug=
niß des Evangelii Gott beide in diesem
und dem zukünftigen Leben urtheilen
will.

Frage 85.
Wie wird das Himmelreich auf= und zuge=
schlossen durch die christliche Bußzucht?

Antwort.

Also, daß nach dem Befehl Christi
diejenigen, so unter dem christlichen

of the keys to exclude such person
until they amend their life.

QUESTION 83.
What is the Office of the Keys?

ANSWER.

The preaching of the holy Gospel and Church discipline; by
which two things the kingdom of
heaven is opened to believers and
shut against unbelievers.

QUESTION 84.
How is the kingdom of heaven opened
and shut by the preaching of the holy Gospel?

ANSWER.

In this way: that, according to
the command of Christ, it is proclaimed and openly witnessed to
believers, one and all, that as often
as they accept with true faith the
promise of the Gospel, all their sins
are really forgiven them of God
for the sake of Christ's merits; and
on the contrary, to all unbelievers
and hypocrites, that the wrath of
God and eternal condemnation
abide on them so long as they are
not converted: according to which
witness of the Gospel will be the
judgment of God, both in this life
and in that which is to come.

QUESTION 85.
How is the kingdom of heaven shut and
opened by Church discipline?

ANSWER.

In this way: that, according to
the command of Christ, if any un-

Namen unchriſtliche Lehre oder Wandel führen, nachdem ſie etlichemal brü-
derlich vermahnet ſind, und von ihren
Irrthümern oder Laſtern nicht abſte-
hen, der Kirche, oder denen, ſo von der
Kirche dazu verordnet ſind, angezeiget,
und ſo ſie ſich an derſelben Vermah-
nung auch nicht kehren, von ihnen durch
Verbietung der heiligen Sacramente
aus der chriſtlichen‘ Gemeine, und von
Gott ſelbſt aus dem Reiche Chriſti
werden ausgeſchloſſen; und wiederum
als Glieder Chriſti und der Kirche
angenommen, wenn ſie wahre Beſſe-
rung verheißen und erzeigen‘

der the Christian name show themselves unsound either in doctrine
or life, and after repeated brotherly admonition refuse to turn from
their errors or evil ways, they are
complained of to the Church or to
its proper officers, and, if they neglect to hear them also, are by them
excluded from the holy Sacraments
and the Christian communion, and
by God himself from the kingdom
of Christ; and if they promise and
show real amendment, they are
again received as members of Christ
and his Church.

Der dritte Theil.
Von der Dankbarkeit.

Frage 86.

Dieweil wir denn aus unſerm Elend, ohne
all unſer Verdienſt, aus Gnaden durch Chriſtum
erlöſet ſind, warum ſollen wir gute Werke thun?

Antwort.

Darum, daß Chriſtus, nachdem Er
uns mit ſeinem Blut erkauft hat, uns
auch durch ſeinen Heiligen Geiſt erneuert zu ſeinem Ebenbild, daß wir
mit unſerm ganzen Leben uns dankbar
gegen Gott für ſeine Wohlthat erzeigen,
und Er durch uns geprieſen werde.
Darnach auch, daß wir bei uns ſelbſt
unſers Glaubens aus ſeinen Früchten
gewiß ſeien, und mit unſerm gottſeligen
Wandel unſern Nächſten auch Chriſto
gewinnen.

THE THIRD PART.
OF THANKFULNESS.

QUESTION 86.

Since, then, we are redeemed from our
misery by grace through Christ, without any
merit of ours, why must we do good works?

ANSWER.

Because Christ, having redeemed
us by his blood, renews us also by
his holy Spirit after his own image, that with our whole life we
may show ourselves thankful to
God for his blessing, and that he
may be glorified through us; then,
also, that we ourselves may be assured of our faith by the fruits
thereof, and by our godly walk may
win our neighbors also to Christ.

Frage 87.

Können denn die nicht selig werden, die sich von ihrem undankbaren, unbußfertigen Wandel zu Gott nicht bekehren?

Antwort.

Keineswegs; denn, wie die Schrift sagt: Kein Unkeuscher, Abgöttischer, Ehebrecher, Dieb, Geiziger, Trunkenbold, Lästerer, Räuber und dergleichen, wird das Reich Gottes erben.

Frage 88.

In wie viel Stücken stehet die wahrhaftige Buße oder Bekehrung des Menschen?

Antwort.

In zwei Stücken: in Absterbung des alten, und Auferstehung des neuen Menschen.

Frage 89.

Was ist die Absterbung des alten Menschen?

Antwort.

Sich die Sünde von Herzen lassen leid sein, und dieselbe je länger je mehr hassen und fliehen.

Frage 90.

Was ist die Auferstehung des neuen Menschen?

Antwort.

Herzliche Freude in Gott durch Christum, und Lust und Liebe haben, nach dem Willen Gottes in allen guten Werken zu leben.

Frage 91.

Welches sind aber gute Werke?

Antwort.

Allein die aus wahrem Glauben nach dem Gesetz Gottes ihm zu Ehren

QUESTION 87.

Can they, then, not be saved who do not turn to God from their unthankful, impenitent life?

ANSWER.

By no means; for, as the Scripture saith, no unchaste person, idolater, adulterer, thief, covetous man, drunkard, slanderer, robber, or any such like, shall inherit the kingdom of God.

QUESTION 88.

In how many things does true repentance or conversion consist?

ANSWER.

In two things: the dying of the old man, and the quickening of the new.

QUESTION 89.

What is the dying of the old man?

ANSWER.

Heartfelt sorrow for sin; causing us to hate and turn from it always more and more.

QUESTION 90.

What is the quickening of the new man?

ANSWER.

Heartfelt joy in God; causing us to take delight in living according to the will of God in all good works.

QUESTION 91.

But what are good works?

ANSWER.

Those only which are done from true faith, according to the law of

geschehen, und nicht die auf unser Gutdünken oder Menschen-Satzung gegründet sind.

Frage 92.
Wie lautet das Gesetz des Herrn?

Antwort.
Gott redet alle diese Worte:

Das Erste Gebot.

Ich bin der Herr, dein Gott, der Ich dich aus Aegyptenland, aus dem Diensthause, geführet habe. Du sollst keine anderen Götter vor Mir haben.

Das Andere Gebot.

Du sollst dir kein Bildniß, noch irgend ein Gleichniß machen, weder deß, das oben im Himmel, noch deß, das unten auf Erden, oder deß, das im Wasser unter der Erde ist; du sollst sie nicht anbeten, noch ihnen dienen. Denn Ich, der Herr, dein Gott, bin ein starker, eifriger Gott, der die Missethat der Väter heimsucht an den Kindern bis in's dritte und vierte Glied, derer, die Mich hassen, und thue Barmherzigkeit an vielen Tausenden, die Mich lieben und Meine Gebote halten.

Das Dritte Gebot.

Du sollst den Namen des Herrn, deines Gottes, nicht mißbrauchen, denn der Herr wird den nicht ungestraft lassen, der seinen Namen mißbraucht.

God, for his glory; and not such as rest on our own opinion or the commandments of men.

QUESTION 92.
What is the law of God?

ANSWER.
God spake all these words, saying:

FIRST COMMANDMENT.

I am the Lord thy God, which have brought thee out of the land of Egypt, out of the house of bondage. Thou shalt have no other gods before me.

SECOND COMMANDMENT.

Thou shalt not make unto thee any graven image, or any likeness of any thing that is in heaven above, or that is in the earth beneath, or that is in the water under the earth; thou shalt not bow down thyself to them, nor serve them. For I the Lord thy God am a jealous God, visiting the iniquity of the fathers upon the children unto the third and fourth generation of them that hate me; and showing mercy unto thousands of them that love me and keep my commandments.

THIRD COMMANDMENT.

Thou shalt not take the name of the Lord thy God in vain; for the Lord will not hold him guiltless that taketh his name in vain.

Das Vierte Gebot.

Gedenke des Sabbathtages, daß du ihn heiligest. Sechs Tage sollst du arbeiten, und alle deine Werke thun: aber am siebenten Tage ist der Sabbath des Herrn, deines Gottes; da sollst du keine Arbeit thun, noch dein Sohn, noch deine Tochter, noch dein Knecht, noch deine Magd, noch dein Vieh, noch der Fremdling, der in deinen Thoren ist; denn in sechs Tagen hat der Herr Himmel und Erde gemacht, und das Meer, und alles, was darinnen ist, und ruhete am siebenten Tage: darum segnete der Herr den Sabbathtag, und heiligte ihn.

Das Fünfte Gebot.

Du sollst deinen Vater und deine Mutter ehren, auf daß du lange lebest im Lande, das dir der Herr, dein Gott, giebt.

Das Sechste Gebot.

Du sollst nicht tödten.

Das Siebente Gebot.

Du sollst nicht ehebrechen.

Das Achte Gebot.

Du sollst nicht stehlen.

Das Neunte Gebot.

Du sollst kein falsch Zeugniß reden wider deinen Nächsten.

Das Zehnte Gebot.

Laß dich nicht gelüsten deines Nächsten Hauses; laß dich nicht gelüsten deines Nächsten Weibes,

FOURTH COMMANDMENT.

Remember the Sabbath day to keep it holy. Six days shalt thou labor, and do all thy work: but the seventh day is the Sabbath of the Lord thy God; in it thou shalt not do any work, thou, nor thy son, nor thy daughter, thy man-servant, nor thy maid-servant, nor thy cattle, nor the stranger that is within thy gates. For in six days the Lord made heaven and earth, the sea, and all that in them is, and rested the seventh day; wherefore the Lord blessed the Sabbath day, and hallowed it.

FIFTH COMMANDMENT.

Honor thy father and thy mother; that thy days may be long upon the land which the Lord thy God giveth thee.

SIXTH COMMANDMENT.

Thou shalt not kill.

SEVENTH COMMANDMENT.

Thou shalt not commit adultery.

EIGHTH COMMANDMENT.

Thou shalt not steal.

NINTH COMMANDMENT.

Thou shalt not bear false witness against thy neighbor.

TENTH COMMANDMENT.

Thou shalt not covet thy neighbor's house; thou shalt not covet thy neighbor's wife, nor his man-

noch seines Knechts, noch seiner Magd, noch seines Ochsens, noch seines Esels, noch alles, was dein Nächster hat.

Frage 93.
Wie werden diese Gebote getheilet?

Antwort.

In zwei Tafeln: deren die erste in vier Geboten lehret, wie wir uns gegen Gott sollen halten; die andere in sechs Geboten, was wir unserm Nächsten schuldig sind.

Frage 94.
Was fordert der Herr im ersten Gebot?

Antwort.

Daß ich, bei Verlierung meiner Seelen Heil und Seligkeit, alle Abgötterei, Zauberei, abergläubische Segen, Anrufung der Heiligen oder anderer Creaturen, meiden und fliehen soll, und den einigen wahren Gott recht erkennen, ihm allein vertrauen, in aller Demuth und Geduld, von ihm allein alles Gute gewarten, und ihn von ganzem Herzen lieben, fürchten, und ehren; also, daß ich ehe alle Creaturen übergebe, denn in dem Geringsten wider seinen Willen thue.

Frage 95.
Was ist Abgötterei?

Antwort.

An Statt des einigen wahren Gottes, der sich in seinem Wort hat offenbaret, oder neben demselben, etwas anderes dichten oder haben, darauf der Mensch sein Vertrauen setzt.

---

servant, nor his maid-servant, nor his ox, nor his ass, nor any thing that is thy neighbor's.

QUESTION 93.
How are these Commandments divided?

ANSWER.

Into two tables: the first of which teaches us, in four commandments, what duties we owe to God; the second, in six, what duties we owe to our neighbor.

QUESTION 94.
What does God require in the first commandment?

ANSWER.

That, on peril of my soul's salvation, I avoid and flee all idolatry, sorcery, enchantments, invocation of saints or of other creatures; and that I rightly acknowledge the only true God, trust in him alone, with all humility and patience expect all good from him only, and love, fear, and honor him with my whole heart; so as rather to renounce all creatures than do the least thing against his will.

QUESTION 95.
What is idolatry?

ANSWER.

It is, instead of the one true God who has revealed himself in his Word, or along with the same, to conceive or have something else on which to place our trust.

Frage 96.
Was will Gott im andern Gebot?

Antwort.

Daß wir Gott in keinem Wege verbilden, noch auf irgend eine andere Weise, denn Er in seinem Wort befohlen hat, verehren sollen.

Frage 97.
Soll man denn gar kein Bildniß machen?

Antwort.

Gott kann und soll keineswegs abgebildet werden; die Creaturen aber, ob sie schon mögen abgebildet werden, so verbietet doch Gott derselben Bildniß zu machen und zu haben, daß man sie verehre, oder ihm damit diene.

Frage 98.
Mögen aber nicht die Bilder als der Laien Bücher in den Kirchen geduldet werden?

Antwort.

Nein : denn wir sollen nicht weiser sein denn Gott, welcher seine Christenheit nicht durch stumme Götzen, sondern durch die lebendige Predigt seines Worts will unterwiesen haben.

Frage 99.
Was will das dritte Gebot?

Antwort.

Daß wir nicht allein mit Fluchen, oder mit falschem Eid, sondern auch mit unnöthigem Schwören den Namen Gottes nicht lästern oder mißbrauchen, noch uns mit unserm Stillschweigen und Zusehen, solcher schrecklichen Sün-

QUESTION 96.

What does God require in the second commandment?

ANSWER.

That we in nowise make any image of God, nor worship him in any other way than he has commanded in his Word.

QUESTION 97.

Must we, then, not make any image at all?

ANSWER.

God may not and can not be imaged in any way; as for creatures, though they may indeed be imaged, yet God forbids the making or keeping any likeness of them, either to worship them, or by them to serve himself.

QUESTION 98.

But may not pictures be tolerated in churches as books for the laity?

ANSWER.

No; for we should not be wiser than God, who will not have his people taught by dumb idols, but by the lively preaching of his Word.

QUESTION 99.

What is required in the third commandment?

ANSWER.

That we must not by cursing, or by false swearing, nor yet by unnecessary oaths, profane or abuse the name of God; nor even by our silence and connivance be partakers of these horrible sins in

den theilhaftig machen; und in Summa, daß wir den heiligen Namen Gottes anders nicht, denn mit Furcht und Ehrerbietung gebrauchen, auf daß er von uns recht bekennet, angerufen, und in allen unsern Worten und Werken gepriesen werde.

Frage 100.

Ist denn mit Fluchen und Schwören Gottes Namen lästern so eine schwere Sünde, daß Gott auch über die zürnet, die, so viel an ihnen ist, dieselbe nicht helfen wehren und verbieten?

Antwort.

Ja freilich: denn keine Sünde größer ist, noch Gott heftiger erzürnet, denn Lästerung seines Namens: darum er sie auch mit dem Tode zu strafen befohlen hat.

Frage 101.

Mag man aber auch gottselig bei dem Namen Gottes einen Eid schwören?

Antwort.

Ja: wenn es die Obrigkeit von ihren Unterthanen oder sonst die Noth erfordert, Treue und Wahrheit zu Gottes Ehre und des Nächsten Heil dadurch zu erhalten und zu fördern. Denn solches Eidschwören ist in Gottes Wort gegründet, und derhalben von den Heiligen im alten und neuen Testament recht gebraucht worden.

Frage 102.

Mag man auch bei den Heiligen, oder andern Creaturen einen Eid schwören.

Antwort.

Nein: denn ein rechtmäßiger Eid

others; and in sum, that we use the holy name of God no otherwise than with fear and reverence, so that he may be rightly confessed and worshiped by us, and be glorified in all our words and works.

QUESTION 100.

Is, then, the profaning of God's name, by swearing and cursing, so grievous a sin that his wrath is kindled against those also who seek not, as much as in them lies, to hinder and forbid the same?

ANSWER.

Yes, truly; for no sin is greater or more provoking to God than the profaning of his name. Wherefore he even commanded it to be punished with death.

QUESTION 101.

But may we not swear by the name of God in a religious manner?

ANSWER.

Yes; when the magistrate requires it, or it may be needful otherwise to maintain and promote fidelity and truth, to the glory of God and our neighbor's good. For such swearing is grounded in God's Word, and therefore was rightly used by the saints in the Old and New Testament.

QUESTION 102.

May we swear by the saints or any other creatures?

ANSWER.

No; for a lawful oath is a call

ist eine Anrufung Gottes, daß Er, als der einige Herzenskündiger, der Wahrheit Zeugniß wolle geben, und mich strafen, so ich falsch schwöre, welche Ehre denn keiner Creatur gebühret.

Frage 103.
Was will Gott im vierten Gebot?

Antwort.
Gott will erstlich, daß das Predigtamt und Schulen erhalten werden, und ich, sonderlich am Feiertag, zu der Gemeine Gottes fleißig komme, das Wort Gottes zu lernen, die heiligen Sacramente zu gebrauchen, den Herrn öffentlich anzurufen, und das christliche Almosen zu geben. Zum andern, daß ich alle Tage meines Lebens von meinen bösen Werken feire, den Herrn durch seinen Geist in mir wirken lasse, und also den ewigen Sabbath in diesem Leben anfange.

Frage 104.
Was will Gott im fünften Gebot?

Antwort.
Daß ich meinem Vater und Mutter, und allen, die mir vorgesetzt sind, alle Ehre, Liebe und Treue beweisen, und mich aller guten Lehre und Strafe mit gebührlichem Gehorsam unterwerfen, und auch mit ihren Gebrechen Geduld haben soll, dieweil uns Gott durch ihre Hand regieren will.

ing upon God, as the only searcher of hearts, to bear witness to the truth, and to punish me if I swear falsely; which honor is due to no creature.

QUESTION 103.
What does God require in the fourth commandment?

ANSWER.
In the first place, that the ministry of the Gospel and schools be maintained; and that I, especially on the day of rest, diligently attend church, to learn the Word of God, to use the holy Sacraments, to call publicly upon the Lord, and to give Christian alms. In the second place, that all the days of my life I rest from my evil works, allow the Lord to work in me by his Spirit, and thus begin in this life the everlasting Sabbath.

QUESTION 104.
What does God require in the fifth commandment?

ANSWER.
That I show all honor, love, and faithfulness to my father and mother, and to all in authority over me; submit myself with due obedience to all their good instruction and correction, and also bear patiently with their infirmities, since it is God's will to govern us by their hand.

Frage 105.
Was will Gott im sechsten Gebot?

QUESTION 105.
What does God require in the sixth commandment?

Antwort.

Daß ich meinen Nächsten weder mit Gedanken, noch mit Worten oder Geberden, viel weniger mit der That, durch mich selbst oder Andere, schmähen, hassen, beleidigen oder tödten; sondern alle Rachgierigkeit ablegen, auch mich selbst nicht beschädigen, oder muthwillig in Gefahr begeben soll. Darum auch die Obrigkeit, dem Todtschlag zu wehren, das Schwert trägt.

ANSWER.

That I neither in thought, nor in word or look, much less in deed, revile, hate, insult, or kill my neighbor, whether by myself or by another; but lay aside all desire of revenge: moreover, that I harm not myself, nor willfully run into any danger. Wherefore, also, to restrain murder, the magistrate is armed with the sword.

Frage 106.
Redet doch dieß Gebot allein vom Tödten.

QUESTION 106.
But this commandment speaks only of killing.

Antwort.

Es will uns aber Gott durch Verbietung des Todtschlags lehren, daß Er die Wurzel des Todtschlags, als Neid, Haß, Zorn, Rachgierigkeit, hasset, und daß solches alles vor ihm ein heimlicher Todtschlag sei.

ANSWER.

In forbidding this, however, God means to teach us that he abhors the root of murder—namely, envy, hatred, anger, and desire of revenge; and that all these are in his sight hidden murder.

Frage 107.
Ist's aber damit genug, daß wir unsern Nächsten, wie gemeldet, nicht tödten?

QUESTION 107.
Is it, then, enough that we do not kill our neighbor in any such way?

Antwort.

Nein: denn indem Gott Neid, Haß und Zorn verdammt, will Er von uns haben, daß wir unsern Nächsten lieben, als uns selbst, gegen ihn Geduld, Friede, Sanftmuth, Barmherzigkeit und Freundlichkeit erzeigen, seinen Schaden, so viel uns möglich, abwenden, und auch unsern Feinden Gutes thun.

ANSWER.

No; for in condemning envy, hatred, and anger, God requires us to love our neighbor as ourselves, to show patience, peace, meekness, mercy, and kindness towards him, and, so far as we have power, to prevent his hurt; also, to do good even unto our enemies.

Frage 108.
Was will das siebente Gebot?

Antwort.

Daß alle Unkeuschheit von Gott vermaledeiet sei, und daß wir darum ihr von Herzen feind sein, und keusch und züchtig leben sollen, es sei im heiligen Ehestand, oder außerhalb desselben.

Frage 109.
Verbietet Gott in diesem Gebot nichts mehr denn Ehebruch und dergleichen Schanden?

Antwort.

Dieweil beide unser Leib und Seele ein Tempel des Heiligen Geistes sind: so will Er, daß wir sie beide sauber und heilig bewahren; verbietet derhalben alle unkeusche Thaten, Geberden, Worte, Gedanken, Lust, und was den Menschen dazu reizen mag.

Frage 110.
Was verbietet Gott im achten Gebot?

Antwort.

Er verbietet nicht allein den Diebstahl und Räuberei, welche die Obrigkeit straft; sondern Gott nennet auch Diebstahl alle böse Stücke und Anschläge, damit wir unseres Nächsten Gut gedenken an uns zu bringen, es sei mit Gewalt oder Schein des Rechtes, als unrechtem Gewicht, Elle, Maß, Waare, Münze, Wucher, oder durch einiges Mittel, das von Gott verboten ist; dazu auch allen Geiz und unnütze Verschwendung seiner Gaben.

QUESTION 108.
What does the seventh commandment teach us?

ANSWER.

That all unchastity is accursed of God; and that we should therefore loathe it from the heart, and live chastely and modestly, whether in holy wedlock or single life.

QUESTION 109.
Does God in this commandment forbid nothing more than adultery, and such like gross sins?

ANSWER.

Since our body and soul are both temples of the Holy Ghost, it is his will that we keep both pure and holy; for which reason he forbids all unchaste actions, gestures, words, thoughts, desires, and whatever may entice thereto.

QUESTION 110.
What does God forbid in the eighth commandment.

ANSWER.

Not only such theft and robbery as are punished by the magistrate, but God views as theft also all wicked tricks and devices whereby we seek to draw to ourselves our neighbor's goods, whether by force or with show of right, such as unjust weights, ells, measures, wares, coins, usury, or any means forbidden of God; so, moreover, all covetousness, and all useless waste of his gifts.

Frage 111.

Was gebietet dir aber Gott in diesem Gebot?

Antwort.

Daß ich meines Nächsten Nutzen, wo ich kann und mag, fördere, gegen ihn also handele, wie ich wollte, daß man mit mir handelte, und treulich arbeite, auf daß ich dem Dürftigen in seiner Noth helfen möge.

Frage 112.

Was will das neunte Gebot?

Antwort.

Daß ich wider Niemand falsch Zeugniß gebe, Niemand seine Worte verkehre, kein Afterreder und Lästerer sei, Niemand unverhört und leichtlich verdammen helfe; sondern allerlei Lügen und Trügen, als eigene Werke des Teufels, bei schwerem Gottes-Zorn vermeide, in Gerichts- und allen andern Handlungen die Wahrheit liebe, aufrichtig sage und bekenne, auch meines Nächsten Ehre und Glimpf, nach meinem Vermögen, rette und fördere.

Frage 113.

Was will das zehnte Gebot?

Antwort.

Daß auch die geringste Lust oder Gedanken wider irgend ein Gebot Gottes in unser Herz nimmermehr kommen; sondern wir für und für von ganzem Herzen aller Sünde feind sein, und Lust zu aller Gerechtigkeit haben sollen.

QUESTION 111.

But what does God require of thee in this commandment?

ANSWER.

That I further my neighbor's good where I can and may, deal with him as I would have others deal with me, and labor faithfully that I may be able to help the poor in their need.

QUESTION 112.

What is required in the ninth commandment?

ANSWER.

That I bear false witness against no one; wrest no one's words; be no backbiter or slanderer; join in condemning no one unheard and rashly: but that I avoid, on pain of God's heavy wrath, all lying and deceit, as being the proper works of the devil; in matters of judgment and justice, and in all other affairs, love, honestly speak and confess the truth; and, so far as I can, defend and promote my neighbor's good name.

QUESTION 113.

What is required in the tenth commandment?

ANSWER.

That not even the least inclination or thought against any of God's commandments ever enter into our heart; but that, with our whole heart, we continually hate all sin, and take pleasure in all righteousness.

Frage 141.

Können aber die, so zu Gott bekehret sind, solche Gebote vollkommen halten?

Antwort.

Nein; sondern es haben auch die Allerheiligsten, so lange sie in diesem Leben sind, nur einen geringen Anfang dieses Gehorsams; doch also, daß sie mit ernstlichem Vorsatz, nicht allein nach etlichen, sondern nach allen Geboten Gottes anfangen zu leben.

Frage 115.

Warum läßt uns denn Gott also scharf die zehn Gebote predigen, wenn sie in diesem Leben Niemand halten kann.

Antwort.

Erstlich, auf daß wir unser ganzes Leben lang unsere sündliche Art je länger je mehr erkennen, und [so viel]¹ desto begieriger Vergebung der Sünden und Gerechtigkeit in Christo suchen. Darnach, daß wir ohne Unterlaß uns befleißigen, und Gott bitten um die Gnade des Heiligen Geistes, daß wir je länger je mehr zu dem Ebenbilde Gottes erneuert werden, bis wir das Ziel der Vollkommenheit nach diesem Leben erreichen.

QUESTION 114.

Can those who are converted to God keep these commandments perfectly?

ANSWER.

No; but even the holiest men, while in this life, have only a small beginning of this obedience, yet so that with earnest purpose they begin to live, not only according to some, but according to all the commandments of God.

QUESTION 115.

Why, then, doth God so strictly enjoin upon us the ten commandments, since in this life no one can keep them?

ANSWER.

First, that all our life long we may learn more and more to know our sinful nature, and so the more earnestly seek forgiveness of sins and righteousness in Christ; secondly, that we may continually strive and beg from God the grace of the Holy Ghost, so as to become more and more changed into the image of God, till we attain finally to full perfection after this life.

---

¹ The words 'so viel' are to be found in all the German editions, but they are superseded by the following word 'desto;' they were, therefore, omitted in the Latin and English translations.

Vom Gebet.

Frage 116.

Warum ist den Christen das Gebet nöthig?

Antwort.

Darum, weil es das vornehmste Stück der Dankbarkeit ist, welche Gott von uns fordert, und weil Gott seine Gnade und Heiligen Geist allein denen will geben, die ihn mit herzlichem Seufzen ohne Unterlaß darum bitten, und ihm dafür danken.

Frage 117.

Was gehört zu einem solchen Gebet, das Gott gefalle, und von ihm erhört werde?

Antwort.

Erstlich, daß wir allein den einigen wahren Gott, der sich uns in seinem Wort hat geoffenbaret, um alles, das er uns zu bitten befohlen hat, von Herzen anrufen. Zum andern, daß wir unsere Noth und Elend recht gründlich erkennen, uns vor dem Angesicht seiner Majestät zu demüthigen. Zum dritten, daß wir diesen festen Grund haben, daß Er unser Gebet, unangesehen, daß wir's unwürdig sind, doch um des Herrn Christi willen gewißlich wolle erhören, wie Er uns in seinem Wort verheißen hat.

Frage 118.

Was hat uns Gott befohlen, von ihm zu bitten?

Antwort.

Alle geistliche und leibliche Nothdurft, welche der Herr Christus begriffen hat

OF PRAYER.

QUESTION 116.

Why is prayer necessary for Christians?

ANSWER.

Because it is the chief part of the thankfulness which God requires of us, and because God will give his grace and Holy Spirit only to such as earnestly and without ceasing beg them from him and render thanks unto him for them.

QUESTION 117.

What belongs to such prayer as God is pleased with and will hear?

ANSWER.

First, that from the heart we call only upon the one true God, who has revealed himself to us in his Word, for all that he has commanded us to ask of him; secondly, that we thoroughly know our need and misery, so as to humble ourselves before the face of his divine majesty; thirdly, that we be firmly assured that, notwithstanding our unworthiness, he will, for the sake of Christ our Lord, certainly hear our prayer, as he has promised us in his Word.

QUESTION 118.

What has God commanded us to ask of him?

ANSWER.

All things necessary for soul and body, which Christ our Lord has

in dem Gebet, das Er uns selbst ge=
lehret.

comprised in the prayer taught us
by himself.

Frage 119.

Wie lautet das Gebet des Herrn?

QUESTION 119.

What is the *Lord's Prayer?*

Antwort.

Unser Vater, der du bist in den
Himmeln:[1] Geheiliget werde dein
Name. Dein Reich komme. Dein
Wille geschehe auf Erden, wie
im Himmel. Unser täglich Brot
gieb uns heute. Und vergieb uns
unsere Schulden, wie auch wir
vergeben unsern Schuldigern.
Und führe uns nicht in Versu=
chung, sondern erlöse uns vom
Bösen. Denn dein ist das Reich,
und die Kraft, und die Herrlich=
keit in Ewigkeit. Amen.

ANSWER.

*Our Father who art in heav-
en: Hallowed be thy name. Thy
kingdom come. Thy will be done
in earth, as it is in heaven. Give
us this day our daily bread.
And forgive us our debts, as we
forgive our debtors. And lead
us not into temptation, but deliver us from evil: For thine is
the kingdom, and the power, and
the glory, forever. Amen.*

Frage 120.

Warum hat uns Christus befohlen, Gott
also anzureden: Unser Vater?

QUESTION 120.

Why has Christ commanded us to address
God thus: *Our Father?*

Antwort.

Daß Er gleich im Anfang unsers
Gebets in uns erwecke die kindliche
Furcht und Zuversicht gegen Gott,
welche der Grund unseres Gebetes sein
soll, nämlich, daß Gott unser Vater
durch Christum worden sei, und wolle
uns viel weniger versagen, warum wir
ihn im Glauben bitten, denn unsere
Väter uns irdische Dinge abschlagen.

ANSWER.

To awaken in us, at the very beginning of our prayer, that filial
reverence and trust toward God
which are to be the ground of our
prayer; namely, that God has become our Father through Christ,
and will much less deny us what
we ask of him in faith than our
parents refuse us earthly things.

---

[1] The plural form '*Himmeln*,' as given in the editions of 1563, 1684, and 1724, follows closely the Greek original, Matt. vi. 9 (ἐν τοῖς οὐρανοῖς; Latin, *in cælis*), though it is un-usual in German.

Frage 121.

Warum wird hinzugethan: Der du bist in den Himmeln?

Antwort.

Auf daß wir von der himmlischen Majestät Gottes nichts Irdisches gedenken, und von seiner Allmächtigkeit alle Nothdurft Leibes und der Seele gewarten.

Frage 122.

Was ist die erste Bitte?

Antwort.

Geheiliget werde dein Name; das ist: Gieb uns erstlich, daß wir dich recht erkennen, und dich in allen deinen Werken, in welchen leuchtet deine Allmächtigkeit, Weisheit, Güte, Gerechtigkeit, Barmherzigkeit und Wahrheit, heiligen, rühmen und preisen. Darnach auch, daß wir unser ganzes Leben, Gedanken, Worte und Werke dahin richten, daß dein Name um unsertwillen nicht gelästert, sondern geehret und gepriesen werde.

Frage 123.

Was ist die andere Bitte?

Antwort.

Dein Reich komme; das ist: Regiere uns also durch dein Wort und Geist, daß wir uns dir je länger je mehr unterwerfen; erhalte und mehre deine Kirche, und zerstöre die Werke des Teufels und alle Gewalt, die sich wider dich erhebt, und alle bösen Rathschläge, die wider dein heiliges Wort erdacht werden, bis die Vollkommenheit deines Reichs herzukom=

QUESTION 121.

Why is it added: *Who art in heaven?*

ANSWER.

That we may have no earthly thought of the heavenly majesty of God, and may expect from his almighty power all things necessary for body and soul.

QUESTION 122.

What is the first petition?

ANSWER.

Hallowed be thy name. That is: Enable us rightly to know thee, and to hallow, magnify, and praise thee in all thy works, in which shine forth thy power, wisdom, goodness, justice, mercy, and truth; and likewise so to order our whole life, in thought, word, and work, that thy name may not be blasphemed, but honored and praised on our account.

QUESTION 123.

What is the second petition?

ANSWER.

Thy kingdom come. That is: So govern us by thy Word and Spirit that we may submit ourselves unto thee always more and more; preserve and increase thy Church; destroy the works of the devil, every power that exalteth itself against thee, and all wicked devices formed against thy holy Word, until the full coming of thy

me, darin du wirst Alles in Allen sein.

kingdom, wherein thou shalt be all in all.

Frage 124.
Was ist die dritte Bitte?

QUESTION 124.
What is the third petition?

Antwort.

Dein Wille geschehe auf Erden, wie im Himmel; das ist: Verleihe, daß wir und alle Menschen unserem eigenen Willen absagen, und deinem allein guten Willen, ohne alles Widersprechen, gehorchen; daß also Jedermann sein Amt und Beruf so willig und treulich ausrichte, wie die Engel im Himmel.

ANSWER.

Thy will be done in earth as it is in heaven. That is: Grant that we and all men may renounce our own will, and yield ourselves, without gainsaying, to thy will, which alone is good; that so every one may fulfill his office and calling as willingly and truly as the angels do in heaven.

Frage 125.
Was ist die vierte Bitte?

QUESTION 125.
What is the fourth petition?

Antwort.

Gieb uns heute unser täglich Brot; das ist: Wollest uns mit aller leiblichen Nothdurft versorgen, auf daß wir dadurch erkennen, daß Du der einige Ursprung alles Guten bist, und daß ohne deinen Segen weder unsere Sorgen und Arbeit, noch deine Gaben uns gedeihen, und wir derhalben unser Vertrauen von allen Creaturen abziehen, und allein auf dich setzen.

ANSWER.

Give us this day our daily bread. That is: Be pleased to provide for all our bodily need, that we may thereby know that thou art the only fountain of all good, and that without thy blessing neither our care and labor nor thy gifts can profit us, and may therefore withdraw our trust from all creatures, and place it alone in thee.

Frage 126.
Was ist die fünfte Bitte?

QUESTION 126.
What is the fifth petition?

Antwort.

Vergieb uns unsere Schulden, wie auch wir vergeben unseren Schuldigern; das ist: Wollest uns armen Sündern alle unsere Missethat, auch das Böse, so uns noch immerdar anhänget, um des Bluts Christi willen

ANSWER.

And forgive us our debts as we forgive our debtors. That is: Be pleased, for the sake of Christ's blood, not to impute to us, miserable sinners, our manifold transgressions, nor the evil which still

nicht zurechnen, wie auch wir dieß Zeugniß deiner Gnade in uns finden, daß unser ganzer Vorsatz ist, unserem Nächsten von Herzen zu verzeihen.

always cleaves to us; as we also find this witness of thy grace in us, that it is our full purpose heartily to forgive our neighbor.

Frage 127.
Was ist die sechste Bitte?

Question 127.
What is the sixth petition?

Antwort.

Und führe uns nicht in Versuchung, sondern erlöse uns vom Bösen; das ist: Dieweil wir aus uns selbst so schwach sind, daß wir nicht einen Augenblick bestehen können, und dazu unsere abgesagten Feinde, der Teufel, die Welt, und unser eigen Fleisch, nicht aufhören uns anzufechten: so wollest Du uns erhalten und stärken durch die Kraft deines Heiligen Geistes, auf daß wir ihnen mögen festen Widerstand thun, und in diesem geistlichen Streit nicht unterliegen, bis daß wir endlich den Sieg vollkommen behalten.

Answer.

And lead us not into temptation, but deliver us from evil. That is: Since we are so weak in ourselves that we can not stand a moment, while our deadly enemies—the devil, the world, and our own flesh—assail us without ceasing, be pleased to preserve and strengthen us by the power of thy Holy Spirit, that we may make firm stand against them, and not sink in this spiritual war, until we come off at last with complete victory.

Frage 128.
Wie beschließest du dieß Gebet?

Question 128.
How do you close this Prayer?

Antwort.

Denn dein ist das Reich, und die Kraft, und die Herrlichkeit in Ewigkeit; das ist: Solches alles bitten wir darum von Dir, weil Du, als unser König, und aller Dinge mächtig, uns alles Gute geben willst und kannst, und daß dadurch nicht wir, sondern Dein heiliger Name ewig soll gepriesen werden.

Answer.

For thine is the kingdom, and the power, and the glory, forever. That is: All this we ask of thee, because as our King, having power over all things, thou art both willing and able to give us all good, and that thereby not we but thy holy name may be glorified forever.

Frage 129.

Was bedeutet das Wörtlein: Amen?

Antwort.

Amen heißt: das soll wahr und gewiß sein; denn mein Gebet viel gewisser von Gott erhöret ist, denn ich in meinem Herzen fühle, daß ich solches von ihm begehre.[1]

QUESTION 129.

What is the meaning of the word *Amen?*

ANSWER.

Amen means: So shall it truly and surely be. For my prayer is much more certainly heard of God than I feel in my heart that I desire these things of him.

---

[1] The first edition of 1563 (pp. 84–94), as also the third (Niemeyer, p. 424), conclude with a 'List of such important proof-texts as have been explained in the preceding Catechism.' The List contains the summary of the divine law in the words of our Lord, Matt. xxii. 37–40, as a mirror of repentance, with the threat, Deut. xxvii. 26; then the Apostles' Creed, the words of institution for Holy Baptism and the Lord's Supper, the Ten Commandments, and the Lord's Prayer. The large and fine pulpit edition in the '*Kurpfälzischen Kirchenordnung*' of 1724 adds to it 'A Short Summary of the Catechism,' and a number of Scripture passages for all sorts and conditions of men. The second and third editions of 1563 close with a remark already noticed with reference to the 80th Question, which was wanting in the first edition. Most editions are fortified with Scripture proofs, a careful selection of which has been made for my German tercentenary edition.

CONFESSIO FIDEI GALLICANA.

The French Confession of Faith. A.D. 1559.

[This Confession was prepared by CALVIN and his pupil, DE CHANDIEU, revised and approved by a synod at Paris, 1559, delivered by Beza to Charles IX. at Poissy, 1561, adopted by the Synod of La Rochelle, 1571 (hence also called the 'Confession of Rochelle'), and solemnly sanctioned by Henry IV.

The French original, with the old spelling, is printed in Beza's *Histoire ecclésiastique des églises réformées*, in Niemeyer's *Collectio* (pp. 313–326), and by Dr. Heppe, in the *Zeitschrift für die historische Theologie*, Gotha, 1875, pp. 524 sqq., from a MS. copy in Geneva. A Latin version of 1566 in the *Corpus et Syntagma Confess.*, and in Niemeyer (pp. 329–339). A German translation, Heidelberg, 1562, and in Böckel.

We give the authoritative text, in modern spelling, from the edition published by the *Société des livres religieux*, at Toulouse, 1864: *Confession de foi et discipline ecclésiastique des églises réformées de France.* The Preface we have supplied in its original form, as reprinted by Niemeyer, and in Calvin's *Opera*, Vol. IX. p. 737. The shorter French recension, which has only thirty-five Articles, is reprinted in Calvin's *Opera*, Vol. IX. pp. 738–752, with the changes of the later edition.

The English translation was kindly prepared for this work by Miss EMILY O. BUTLER, of New York. An older version is in Quick's *Synodicon*, 1692, Vol. I.]

LES FRANÇOIS QUI DESIRENT VIVRE SELON LA PURETÉ DE L'EVANGILE DE NOSTRE SEIGNEUR IÉSUS CHRIST.

Au Roy.

Sire, nous rendons grâces à Dieu, de ce que n'ayans eu iusques icy aucun accés à vostre Maiesté, pour luy faire entendre la rigueur des persécutions que nous avons endurées, et endurons iournellement pour vouloir suyure la pureté de l'Evangile, et le repos de nostre conscience: maintenant il nous fait cet heur de veoir qu'avez la volonté de connoitre le mérite de nostre cause, suyvant l'Edit dernier donné à Amboise au moys de Mars, l'An présent 1559, qu'il a pleu à vostre Maiesté faire publier. Qui est la cause qu'à présent nous osons ouvrir la bouche: laquelle nous a esté parcidevant fermée par l'iniustice et violence de plusieurs voz officiers, estans plustost incitez de haine contre nous, que de bonne affection à vostre service. Et à fin, Sire, que nous puissions pleinement informer vostre Maiesté de ce qui concerne cette cause, nous vous supplions très-humblement de voir et entendre nostre Confession de Foy, laquelle nous vous présentons: espérans qu'elle nous sera défence suffisante contre tous les blasmes et opprobres, dont iusques icy avons esté chargez à grand tort par ceux qui ont tousiours fait mestier de nous condamner, premier que nostre cause leur fust conneü. En la-

THE FRENCH SUBJECTS WHO WISH TO LIVE IN THE PURITY OF THE GOSPEL OF OUR LORD JESUS CHRIST.

To the King.

Sire, we thank God that hitherto having had no access to your Majesty to make known the rigor of the persecutions that we have suffered, and suffer daily, for wishing to live in the purity of the Gospel and in peace with our own consciences, he now permits us to see that you wish to know the worthiness of our cause, as is shown by the last Edict given at Amboise in the month of March of this present year, 1559, which it has pleased your Majesty to cause to be published. This emboldens us to speak, which we have been prevented from doing hitherto through the injustice and violence of some of your officers, incited rather by hatred of us than by love of your service. And to the end, Sire, that we may fully inform your Majesty of what concerns this cause, we humbly beseech that you will see and hear our Confession of Faith, which we present to you, hoping that it will prove a sufficient answer to the blame and opprobrium unjustly laid upon us by those who have always made a point of condemning us without having any knowledge of our cause. In the which, Sire, we can affirm that there is nothing contrary to

quelle, Sire, nous pouvons protester qu'il n'y a aucune chose qui répugne à la parole de Dieu, ne qui contrevienne à l'hommage que nous vous devons.

Car les articles de nostre Foy qui sont descrits assez au long en nostre Confession, reviennent tous à ce poinct, que puisque Dieu nous a suffisamment déclaré sa volonté par ses Prophètes et Apostres, et mesmes par la bouche de son fils nostre Seigneur Iésus Christ nous devons cet honneur et révérence à la parole de Dieu de n'y rien aioutter du nostre: mais de nous conformer entièrement à la reigle qui nous y est prescritte. Et pour ce que l'Eglise Romaine, laissant l'usage et coustume de la primitive Eglise, a introduit nouveaux commandemens et nouvelle forme du service de Dieu: nous estimons estre très-raisonnable de préférer les commandemens de Dieu, qui est la vérité mesme, aux commandemens des hommes: qui de leur nature sont enclins à mensonge et vanité. Et quoy que noz adversaires prétendent à l'encontre de nous, si pouvons nous dire devant Dieu et les hommes, que nous ne souffrons pour autre raison que pour maintenir nostre Seigneur Iésus Christ estre nostre Seul Sauveur et Rédempteur, et sa doctrine seule doctrine de vie et de salut.

Et cette est la seule cause, Sire, pour laquelle les bourreaux ont en tant de fois les mains souillées du sang de voz poures suiets, lesquels n'espargnent point leurs vies pour maintenir cette mesme confession de Foy, ont bien peu faire entendre à tous qu'ils estoyent poussez d'autre esprit que de celuy des hommes, qui naturellement ont plus de soucy de leurs repos et commoditez, que de l'honneur et gloire de Dieu.

Et partant, Sire, suyvant, la bonté et douceur de laquelle promettez user envers voz poures suiets, nous supplions très-humblement vostre Maiesté nous faire cette miséricorde, que de prendre en main la connoissance de la cause, pour laquelle estans poursvivis à toute heure ou de mort, ou de bannissement, nous perdons

the Word of God, or to the homage which we owe to you.

For the articles of our faith, which are all declared at some length in our Confession, all come to this: that since God has sufficiently declared his will to us through his Prophets and Apostles, and even by the mouth of his Son, our Lord Jesus Christ, we owe such respect and reverence to the Word of God as shall prevent us from adding to it any thing of our own, but shall make us conform entirely to the rules it prescribes. And inasmuch as the Roman Church, forsaking the use and customs of the primitive Church, has introduced new commandments and a new form of worship of God, we esteem it but reasonable to prefer the commandments of God, who is himself truth, to the commandments of men, who by their nature are inclined to deceit and vanity. And whatever our enemies may say against us, we can declare this before God and men, that we suffer for no other reason than for maintaining our Lord Jesus Christ to be our only Saviour and Redeemer, and his doctrine to be the only doctrine of life and salvation.

And this is the only reason, Sire, why the executioners' hands have been stained so often with the blood of your poor subjects, who, sparing not their lives to maintain this same Confession of Faith, have shown to all that they were moved by some other spirit than that of men, who naturally care more for their own peace and comfort than for the honor and glory of God.

And therefore, Sire, in accordance with your promises of goodness and mercy toward your poor subjects, we humbly beseech your Majesty graciously to examine the cause for which, being threatened at all times with death or exile, we thus lose the power of rendering the humble service that we owe you. May it

par ce moyen la puissance de vous faire le très-humble service que nous vous devons. Qu'il plaise donq à vostre Maiesté, Sire, à lieu des feus et glaives dont on a usé parcidevant, faire décider nostre confession de Foy par la parole de Dieu : donnant permission et sevreté pour ce faire. Et nous espérons que vous-mesmes serez iuge de nostre innocence, connoissant qu'il n'y a en nous ny hérésie, ny rébellion aucune : mais que nous tendons seulement à ce but, de pouvoir vivre en saine conscience, servans à Dieu selon ses commandemens, et honorans vostre Maiesté en toute obéissance et servitude.

Et par ce que nous avons nécessairement besoin d'estre, par la prédication de la parole de Dieu, retenus en nostre devoir et office tant envers luy : qu'envers vous : nous vous supplions très-humblement, Sire, qu'il nous soit permis d'estre quelquefois assemblez tant pour estre exhortez par la parole de Dieu à sa crainte, que pour estre conformez par l'administration des Sacremens que nostre Seigneur Iésus Christ a instituez en son Eglise. Et s'il plaist à vostre Maiesté nous donner lieu, auquel un chacun puisse voir ce qui se fait en noz assemblées, la seule veue nous absoudra de l'accusation de tant de crimes énormes, dont nosdittes assemblées ont esté diffamées parcidevant. Car on n'y pourra veoir que toute modestie et chasteté, et on n'y pourra ovyr que louanges de Dieu, exhortations à son service, et prières pour la conservation de vostre Maiesté et de vostre Royaume. Que s'il ne vous plaist nous faire tant de grâce, au moins qu'il nous soit permis de poursvyvre particulièrement entre nous avec repos l'ordre qui y est estably.

Vous supplions très-humblement, Sire, de croyre, que oyant lire cette supplication qui vous est maintenant présentée, vous oyez les cris et gémissemens d'une infinité de voz poures suiets qui implorent vostre miséricorde : à ce qu'elle esteigne les feus que la cruauté de voz iuges a allumez en vostre Royaume. Et ainsi qu'il nous soit loisible, servans à vostre Maiesté

please your Majesty, then, instead of the fire and sword which have been used hitherto, to have our Confession of Faith decided by the Word of God : giving permission and security for this. And we hope that you yourself will be the judge of our innocence, knowing that there is in us no rebellion or heresy whatsoever, but that our only endeavor is to live in peace of conscience, serving God according to his commandments, and honoring your Majesty by all obedience and submission.

And because we have great need, by the preaching of the Word of God, to be kept in our duty to him, as well as to yourself, we humbly beg, Sire, that we may sometimes be permitted to gather together, to be exhorted to the fear of God by his Word, as well as to be confirmed by the administration of the Sacraments which the Lord Jesus Christ instituted in his Church. And if it should please your Majesty to give us a place where any one may see what passes in our assemblies, we shall thereby be absolved from the charge of the enormous crimes with which these same assemblies have been defamed. For nothing will be seen but what is decent and well-ordered, and nothing will be heard but the praise of God, exhortations to his service, and prayers for the preservation of your Majesty and of your kingdom. And if it do not please you to grant us this favor, at least let it be permitted us to follow the established order in private among ourselves.

We beseech you most humbly, Sire, to believe that in listening to this supplication which is now presented to you, you listen to the cries and groans of an infinite number of your poor subjects, who implore of your mercy that you extinguish the fires which the cruelty of your judges has lighted in your kingdom. And that we may thus be permitted, in

de servir à celuy qui vous a élevé en vostre dignité et grandeur.

Et s'il ne vous plaist, Sire, d'ouyr nostre voix, qu'il vous plaise d'ouyr celle du Fils de Dieu, lequel vous ayant donné puissance sur noz biens, sur noz corps et sur nostre propre vie : vous demande que la puissance et domination sur noz ames et consciences (lesquelles il s'est acquises au pris de son sang) luy soyent réservées.

Nous le supplions, Sire, qu'il vous conduise tousiours par son Esprit, accroissant avec vostre aage, vostre grandeur et puissance, vous donnant victoire contre tous voz ennemis, establissant pour iamais en toute équité et iustice le throsne de vostre Maiesté : devant laquelle aussi il luy plaise nous faire trouver grâce, pour resentir quelque fruit de nostre présente supplication, à fin qu'ayons changé noz peines et afflictions à quelque repos et liberté, nous changeons aussi noz pleurs et larmes à une perpétuelle action de grâces à Dieu, et à vostre Maiesté, pour avoir fait chose à luy trèsagréable, très-digne de vostre bonté et iustice, et très-nécessaire pour la conservation de voz plus humbles et plus obéissans suiets et serviteurs.

serving your Majesty, to serve him who has raised you to your power and dignity.

And if it should not please you, Sire, to listen to our voice, may it please you to listen to that of the Son of God, who, having given you power over our property, our bodies, and even our lives, demands that the control and dominion of our souls and consciences, which he purchased with his own blood, be reserved to him.

We beseech him, Sire, that he may lead you always by his Spirit, increasing with your age, your greatness and power, giving you victory over all your enemies, and establishing forever, in all equity and justice, the throne of your Majesty: before whom, may it please him that we find grace, and some fruit of this our present supplication, so that having exchanged our pains and afflictions for some peace and liberty, we may also change our tears and lamentations into a perpetual thanksgiving to God, and to your Majesty for having done that which is most agreeable to him, most worthy of your goodness and mercy, and most necessary for the preservation of your most humble and obedient subjects and servants.

CONFESSION DE FOI,

faite d'un commun accord par les François, qui desirent vivre selon la pureté de l'évangile de notre Seigneur Jésus-Christ. A.D. 1559.

ART. I. *Nous croyons et confessons qu'il y a un seul Dieu, qui est une seule et simple essence,*[1] *spirituelle,*[2] *éternelle,*[3] *invisible,*[4] *immuable,*[5] *infinie,*[6] *incompréhen-*

CONFESSION OF FAITH,

made in one accord by the French people, who desire to live according to the purity of the Gospel of our Lord Jesus Christ. A.D. 1559.

ART. I. We believe and confess that there is but one God, who is one sole and simple essence, spiritual, eternal, invisible, immutable, infinite, incomprehensible, ineffa-

---

[1] Deut. iv. 35, 39 ; 1 Cor. viii. 4, 6.
[2] Gen. i. 3 ; Jean iv. 24 ; 2 Cor. iii. 17.
[3] Exode iii. 15, 16, 18.

[4] Rom. i. 20 ; 1 Tim. i. 47.
[5] Mal. iii. 6.
[6] Rom. xi. 33 ; Actes vii. 48.

sible,[1] ineffable, qui peut toutes choses, qui est toute sage,[2] toute bonne,[3] toute juste,[4] et toute miséricordieuse.[5]

Iı. *Ce Dieu se manifeste tel aux hommes,[6] premièrement par ses œuvres, tant par la création que par la conservation et conduite d'icelles. Secondement et plus clairement, par sa Parole,[7] laquelle au commencement révélée par oracles,[8] a été puis après rédigée par écrit[9] aux livres que nous appelons l'Ecriture sainte.[10]*

III. *Toute cette Ecriture sainte est comprise aux livres canoniques du Vieux et du Nouveau Testament, desquels le nombre s'ensuit : les cinq livres de Moïse, savoir :* Genèse, Exode, Lévitique, Nombres, Deutéronome. *Item,* Josué, Juges, Ruth, *le premier et le second livres de* Samuel, *le premier et le second livres des* Rois, *le premier et le second livres des* Chroniques, *autrement dits Paralipomenon ; le premier livre d'*Esdras. *Item,* Néhémie, *le livre d'*Esther, Job, *les* Psaumes *de David, les* Proverbes *ou sentences de Salomon ; le livre de l'*Ecclésiaste, *dit le* Prêcheur ; *le* Cantique de

ble, omnipotent; who is all-wise, all-good, all-just, and all-merciful.

II. As such this God reveals himself to men; firstly, in his works, in their creation, as well as in their preservation and control. Secondly, and more clearly, in his Word, which was in the beginning revealed through oracles, and which was afterward committed to writing in the books which we call the Holy Scriptures.

III. These Holy Scriptures are comprised in the canonical books of the Old and New Testaments, as follows: the five books of Moses, namely: Genesis, Exodus, Leviticus, Numbers, Deuteronomy; then Joshua, Judges, Ruth, the first and second books of Samuel, the first and second books of the Kings, the first and second books of the Chronicles, otherwise called Paralipomenon, the first book of Ezra; then Nehemiah, the book of Esther, Job, the Psalms of David, the Proverbs or Maxims of Solomon; the book of Ecclesiastes, called the Preacher, the Song of Solomon; then the book of Isaiah, Jeremiah, Lamen-

---

[1] Jér. x. 7, 10; Luc. i. 37.
[2] Rom. xvi. 27.
[3] Matt. xix. 17.
[4] Jér. xii. 1.
[5] Exode xxxiv. 6, 7.
[6] Rom. i. 20.
[7] Héb. i. 4.
[8] Gen. xv. 1.
[9] Exode xxiv. 3, 4.
[10] Rom. i. 2.

Salomon. Item, *le livre d'*Esaïe, Jérémie, Lamentations *de Jérémie,* Ezéchiel, Daniel, Osée, Joël, Amos, Abdias, Jonas, Michée, Nahum, Abakuk, Sophonie, Aggée, Zacharie, Malachie. Item, *le saint Evangile selon saint* Matthieu, *selon saint* Marc, *selon saint* Luc, *et selon saint* Jean. Item, *le second livre de saint Luc, autrement dit les* Actes *des Apôtres.* Item, *les Epîtres de saint Paul, aux* Romains *une, aux* Corinthiens *deux, aux* Galates *une, aux* Ephésiens *une, aux* Philippiens *une, aux* Colossiens *une, aux* Thessaloniciens *deux, à* Timothée *deux, à* Tite *une, à* Philémon *une.* Item, *l'Epître aux* Hébreux, *l'Epître de saint* Jacques, *la première et la seconde Epîtres de saint* Pierre, *la première, la deuxième, et la troisième Epîtres de saint* Jean, *l'Epître de saint* Jude. Item, *l'*Apocalypse *ou Révélation de saint Jean.*

IV. *Nous connaissons ces livres être canoniques, et la règle très-certaine de notre foi,*[1] *non tant par le commun accord et consentement de l'Eglise, que par le témoignage et persuasion intérieure du Saint-Esprit, qui nous les fait discerner d'avec les autres livres ecclésiastiques, sur lesquels, encore*

tations of Jeremiah, Ezekiel, Daniel, Hosea, Joel, Amos, Obadiah, Jonah, Micah, Nahum, Habakkuk, Zephaniah, Haggai, Zechariah, Malachi; then the Holy Gospel according to St. Matthew, according to St. Mark, according to St. Luke, and according to St. John; then the second book of St. Luke, otherwise called the Acts of the Apostles; then the Epistles of St. Paul: one to the Romans, two to the Corinthians, one to the Galatians, one to the Ephesians, one to the Philippians, one to the Colossians, two to the Thessalonians, two to Timothy, one to Titus, one to Philemon; then the Epistle to the Hebrews, the Epistle of St. James, the first and second Epistles of St. Peter, the first, second, and third Epistles of St. John, the Epistle of St. Jude; and then the Apocalypse, or Revelation of St. John.

IV. We know these books to be canonical, and the sure rule of our faith, not so much by the common accord and consent of the Church, as by the testimony and inward illumination of the Holy Spirit, which enables us to distinguish them from other ecclesiastical books upon which, however useful,

---

[1] Psa. xix. 9; xii. 7.

qu'ils soient utiles, on ne peut fonder aucun article de foi.

V. *Nous croyons que la Parole qui est contenue en ces livres, est procédée de Dieu,[1] duquel seul elle prend son autorité,[2] et non des hommes. Et d'autant qu'elle est la règle de toute vérité,[3] contenant tout ce qui est nécessaire pour le service de Dieu et de notre salut, il n'est pas loisible aux hommes, ni même aux Anges, d'y ajouter, diminuer ou changer.[4] D'où il s'ensuit que ni l'antiquité, ni les coutumes, ni la multitude, ni la sagesse humaine, ni les jugements, ni les arrêts, ni les édits, ni les décrets, ni les conciles, ni les visions, ni les miracles, ne doivent être opposés à cette Ecriture sainte,[5] mais, au contraire, toutes choses doivent être examinées, réglées et réformées selon elle.[6] Et suivant cela, nous avouons les trois symboles, savoir : des Apôtres, de Nicée, et d'Athanase, parce qu'ils sont conformes à la parole de Dieu.*

VI. *Cette Ecriture sainte nous enseigne qu'en cette seule et simple essence divine, que nous avons confessée, il y a trois personnes, le Père, le Fils, et le Saint-Esprit.[7]*

we can not found any articles of faith.

V. We believe that the Word contained in these books has proceeded from God, and receives its authority from him alone, and not from men. And inasmuch as it is the rule of all truth, containing all that is necessary for the service of God and for our salvation, it is not lawful for men, nor even for angels, to add to it, to take away from it, or to change it. Whence it follows that no authority, whether of antiquity, or custom, or numbers, or human wisdom, or judgments, or proclamations, or edicts, or decrees, or councils, or visions, or miracles, should be opposed to these Holy Scriptures, but, on the contrary, all things should be examined, regulated, and reformed according to them. And therefore we confess the three creeds, to wit: the Apostles', the Nicene, and the Athanasian, because they are in accordance with the Word of God.

VI. These Holy Scriptures teach us that in this one sole and simple divine essence, whom we have confessed, there are three persons: the Father, the Son, and the Holy

---

[1] 2 Tim. iii. 15, 16; 2 Pierre i. 21.
[2] Jean iii. 31, 34; 1 Tim. i. 15.
[3] Jean xv. 11; Actes xx. 27.
[4] Deut. xii. 32; iv. 1; Gal. i. 8, Apoc. xxii. 18, 19.

[5] Matt. xv. 9, Actes v. 28, 29.
[6] 1 Cor. xi. 1, 2, 23.
[7] Deut. iv. 12; Matt. xxviii. 19; 2 Cor. xiii. 14; 1 Jean v. 7 [?]; Jean i. 1, 17, 32.

Le Père, première cause, principe et origine de toutes choses. Le Fils, sa parole et sapience éternelle. Le Saint-Esprit, sa vertu, puissance et efficace. Le Fils éternellement engendré du Père. Le Saint-Esprit procédant éternellement de tous deux, les trois personnes non confuses, mais distinctes, et toutefois non divisées, mais d'une même essence, éternité, puissance et égalité. Et en cela avouons ce qui a été déterminé par les conciles anciens, et détestons toutes sectes et hérésies qui ont été rejetées par les saints docteurs, comme saint Hilaire, saint Athanase, saint Ambroise, et saint Cyrille.

VII. Nous croyons que Dieu en trois personnes coopérantes, par sa vertu, sagesse et bonté incompréhensible, a créé toutes choses, nonseulement le ciel, la terre et tout ce qui y est contenu; mais aussi les esprits invisibles,[1] desquels les uns sont déchus et trébuchés en perdition,[2] les autres ont persisté en obeissance.[3] Que les premiers s'étant corrompus en malice, sont ennemis de tout bien, par conséquent de toute l'Eglise.[4] Les seconds ayant été préservés par la grâce de Dieu, sont ministres pour

Spirit. The Father, first cause, principle, and origin of all things. The Son, his Word and eternal wisdom. The Holy Spirit, his virtue, power, and efficacy. The Son begotten from eternity by the Father. The Holy Spirit proceeding eternally from them both; the three persons not confused, but distinct, and yet not separate, but of the same essence, equal in eternity and power. And in this we confess that which hath been established by the ancient councils, and we detest all sects and heresies which were rejected by the holy doctors, such as St. Hilary, St. Athanasius, St. Ambrose, and St. Cyril.

VII. We believe that God, in three co-working persons, by his power, wisdom, and incomprehensible goodness, created all things, not only the heavens and the earth and all that in them is, but also invisible spirits, some of whom have fallen away and gone into perdition, while others have continued in obedience. That the first, being corrupted by evil, are enemies of all good, consequently of the whole Church. The second, having been preserved by the grace of God, are ministers to glorify God's name,

---

[1] Gen. i. 1; Jean i. 3; Jude vi.; Col. i. 16; Héb. i. 2.
[2] 2 Pierre ii. 4.
[3] Psa. ciii. 20, 21.
[4] Jean viii. 44.

glorifier le nom de Dieu, et servir au salut de ses élus.[1]

VIII. *Nous croyons que non-seulement il a créé toutes choses, mais qu'il les gouverne et conduit,*[2] *disposant, ordonnant selon sa volonté, de tout ce qui advient au monde;*[3] *non pas qu'il soit auteur du mal, ou que la coulpe lui en puisse être imputée,*[4] *vu que sa volonté est la règle souveraine et infaillible de toute droiture et équité;*[5] *mais il a des moyens admirables de se servir tellement des diables et des méchants, qu'il sait convertir en bien le mal qu'ils font, et duquel ils sont coupables.*[6] *Et ainsi en confessant que rien ne se fait sans la providence de Dieu, nous adorons en humilité les secrets qui nous sont cachés, sans nous enquérir par - dessus notre mesure; mais plutôt appliquons à notre usage ce qui nous est montré en l'Ecriture sainte pour être en repos et sûreté,*[7] *d'autant que Dieu, qui a toutes choses sujettes à soi, veille sur nous d'un soin paternel, tellement qu'il ne tombera point un cheveu de notre tête sans sa volonté.*[8] *Et cependant il tient les diables et tous nos ennemis bridés, en sorte qu'ils ne nous peuvent faire aucune nuisance sans son congé.*[9]

and to promote the salvation of his elect.

VIII. We believe that he not only created all things, but that he governs and directs them, disposing and ordaining by his sovereign will all that happens in the world; not that he is the author of evil, or that the guilt of it can be imputed to him, as his will is the sovereign and infallible rule of all right and justice; but he hath wonderful means of so making use of devils and sinners that he can turn to good the evil which they do, and of which they are guilty. And thus, confessing that the providence of God orders all things, we humbly bow before the secrets which are hidden to us, without questioning what is above our understanding; but rather making use of what is revealed to us in Holy Scripture for our peace and safety, inasmuch as God, who has all things in subjection to him, watches over us with a Father's care, so that not a hair of our heads shall fall without his will. And yet he restrains the devils and all our enemies, so that they can not harm us without his leave.

---

[1] Héb. i. 7, 14.
[2] Psa. civ.
[3] Prov. xvi. 4; Matt. x. 29; Rom. ix. 11; Actes xvii. 24, 26, 28.
[4] 1 Jean ii. 16; Osée xiii. 9; 1 Jean iii. 8.
[5] Psa. v. 5; cxix.; Job i. 22.
[6] Actes ii. 23, 24, 27.
[7] Rom. ix. 19, 20; xi. 33.
[8] Matt. x. 30; Luc xxi. 18.
[9] Job i. 12; Gen. iii. 15.

IX. *Nous croyons que l'homme ayant été créé pur et entier, et conforme à l'image de Dieu, est, par sa propre faute, déchu de la grâce qu'il avait reçue,[1] et ainsi s'est aliéné de Dieu, qui est la fontaine de justice et de tous biens, en sorte que sa nature est du tout corrompue. Et étant aveuglé en son esprit, et dépravé en son cœur, a perdu toute intégrité sans avoir rien de reste.[2] Et bien qu'il ait encore quelque discrétion du bien et du mal,[3] nonobstant nous disons, que ce qu'il a de clarté, se convertit en ténèbres quand il est question de chercher Dieu, tellement qu'il n'en peut nullement approcher par son intelligence et raison.[4] Et bien qu'il ait une volonté par laquelle il est incité à faire ceci ou cela, toutefois elle est du tout captive sous péché, en sorte qu'il n'a nulle liberté à bien, que celle que Dieu lui donne.[5]*

X. *Nous croyons que toute la lignée d'Adam est infectée de telle contagion, qui est le péché originel, et un vice héréditaire, et non pas seulement une imitation, comme les Pélagiens ont voulu dire, lesquels nous détestons en leurs erreurs. Et n'estimons pas qu'il soit besoin de s'enquérir comme le péché vient d'un homme à l'autre, vu que c'est*

IX. We believe that man was created pure and perfect in the image of God, and that by his own guilt he fell from the grace which he received, and is thus alienated from God, the fountain of justice and of all good, so that his nature is totally corrupt. And being blinded in mind, and depraved in heart, he has lost all integrity, and there is no good in him. And although he can still discern good and evil, we say, notwithstanding, that the light he has becomes darkness when he seeks for God, so that he can in nowise approach him by his intelligence and reason. And although he has a will that incites him to do this or that, yet it is altogether captive to sin, so that he has no other liberty to do right than that which God gives him.

X. We believe that all the posterity of Adam is in bondage to original sin, which is an hereditary evil, and not an imitation merely, as was declared by the Pelagians, whom we detest in their errors. And we consider that it is not necessary to inquire how sin was conveyed from one man to another, for what God had given Adam

---

[1] Gen. i. 26; Ecclés. vii. 10; Rom. v. 12; Ephés. ii. 2, 3.
[2] Gen. vi. 5; viii. 21.
[3] Rom. i. 21; ii. 18–20.
[4] 1 Cor. ii. 14.
[5] Jean i. 4, 5, 7; viii. 36; Rom. viii. 6, 7

assez, que ce que Dieu lui avait
donné n'était pas pour lui seul,
mais pour toute sa lignée ; et ainsi, qu'en la personne d'icelui nous
avons été dénués de tous biens, et
sommes trébuchés en toute pauvreté
et malédiction.[1]

XI. Nous croyons aussi que ce
vice est vraiment péché, qui suffit à
condamner tout le genre humain,
jusqu'aux petits enfants dès le ventre de la mère, et que pour tel il est
réputé devant Dieu ;[2] même qu'a-
près le baptême, c'est toujours péché
quant à la coulpe, bien que la condamnation en soit abolie aux enfants de Dieu, ne la leur imputant
point par sa bonté gratuite.[3] Outre
cela, que c'est une perversité produisant toujours des fruits de malice et de rébellion,[4] tels que les plus
saints, encore qu'ils y résistent, ne
laissent point d'être entachés d'infirmités et de fautes pendant qu'ils
habitent en ce monde.[5]

XII. Nous croyons que de cette
corruption et condamnation géné-
rale, en laquelle tous les hommes
sont plongés, Dieu retire ceux lesquels en son conseil éternel et immuable il a élus par sa seule bonté
et miséricorde en notre Seigneur
Jésus-Christ, sans considération de

was not for him alone, but for
all his posterity ; and thus in his
person we have been deprived of
all good things, and have fallen
with him into a state of sin and
misery.

XI. We believe, also, that this
evil is truly sin, sufficient for the
condemnation of the whole human
race, even of little children in the
mother's womb, and that God considers it as such ; even after baptism it is still of the nature of sin,
but the condemnation of it is
abolished for the children of
God, out of his mere free grace
and love. And further, that it is a
perversity always producing fruits
of malice and of rebellion, so
that the most holy men, although
they resist it, are still stained
with many weaknesses and imperfections while they are in this
life.

XII. We believe that from this
corruption and general condemnation in which all men are plunged,
God, according to his eternal and
immutable counsel, calleth those
whom he hath chosen by his goodness and mercy alone in our Lord
Jesus Christ, without consideration

---

[1] Gen. viii. 21; Rom. v. 12; Job
　　xiv. 4.
[2] Psa. li. 7: Rom. iii. 9–13; v. 12.

[3] Rom. vii.
[4] Rom. vii. 5.
[5] Rom. vii. 18, 19; 2 Cor. xii. 7.

leurs œuvres,[1] *laissant les autres en cette même corruption et condamnation, pour démontrer en eux sa justice, comme aux premiers il fait luire les richesses de sa miséricorde.*[2] *Car les uns ne sont point meilleurs que les autres, jusqu'à ce que Dieu les discerne, selon son conseil immuable qu'il a déterminé en Jésus-Christ devant la création du monde ; et nul aussi ne se pourrait introduire à un tel bien de sa propre vertu, vu que de notre nature nous ne pouvons avoir un seul bon mouvement, ni affection, ni pensée, jusqu'à ce que Dieu nous ait prévenus et nous y ait disposés.*[3]

XIII. *Nous croyons qu'en icelui Jésus-Christ tout ce qui était requis à notre salut nous a été offert et communiqué. Lequel nous étant donné à salut, nous à été quant et quant fait sapience, sanctification et rédemption : en sorte qu'en déclinant de lui, on renonce à la miséricorde du Père, où il nous convient avoir refuge unique.*[4]

XIV. *Nous croyons que Jésus-Christ étant la sagesse de Dieu, et son Fils éternel, a revêtu notre chair, afin d'être Dieu et homme en une personne,*[5] *même homme semblable à nous, passible en corps et en âme,*

of their works, to display in them the riches of his mercy; leaving the rest in this same corruption and condemnation to show in them his justice. For the ones are no better than the others, until God discerns them according to his immutable purpose which he has determined in Jesus Christ before the creation of the world. Neither can any man gain such a reward by his own virtue, as by nature we can not have a single good feeling, affection, or thought, except God has first put it into our hearts.

XIII. We believe that all that is necessary for our salvation was offered and communicated to us in Jesus Christ. He is given to us for our salvation, and 'is made unto us wisdom, and righteousness, and sanctification, and redemption:' so that if we refuse him, we renounce the mercy of the Father, in which alone we can find a refuge.

XIV. We believe that Jesus Christ, being the wisdom of God and his eternal Son, has put on our flesh, so as to be God and man in one person; man, like unto us, capable of suffering in body and

---

[1] Rom. iii. 2 ; ix. 23 ; 2 Tim. ii. 20 ; Tite iii. 5, 7 ; Ephés. i. 4 ; 2 Tim. i. 9.

[2] Exode ix. 16 ; Rom. ix. 22.

[3] Jér. x. 23 ; Ephés. i. 4, 5.

[4] 1 Cor. i. 30 ; Ephés. i. 6, 7 ; Col. i. 13, 14 ; Tite ii. 14.

[5] Jean i. 14 ; Philip. ii. 6.

sinon en tant qu'il a été pur de toute macule.[1] *Et quant à son humanité, qu'il a été vraie semence d'Abraham et de David,*[2] *bien qu'il ait été conçu par la vertu secrète du Saint-Esprit.*[3] *En quoi nous détestons toutes les hérésies qui ont anciennement troublé les Eglises ; et notamment aussi les imaginations diaboliques de Servet, lequel attribue au Seigneur Jésus une divinité fantastique, d'autant qu'il le dit être idée et patron de toutes choses, et le nomme Fils personnel ou figuratif de Dieu ; et finalement lui forge un corps de trois éléments incréés, ainsi mêle et détruit toutes les deux natures.*

XV. *Nous croyons qu'en une même personne, savoir, Jésus-Christ, les deux natures sont vraiment et inséparablement conjointes et unies, demeurant néanmoins chacune nature en sa propriété distincte :*[4] *tellement que comme en cette conjonction la nature divine retenant sa propriété, est demeurée incréée, infinie et remplissant toutes choses ; aussi la nature humaine est demeurée finie, ayant sa forme, mesure et propriété ;*[5] *et même bien que Jésus-Christ en ressuscitant ait donné l'immortalité à son corps,*

soul, yet free from all stain of sin. And as to his humanity, he was the true seed of Abraham and of David, although he was conceived by the secret power of the Holy Spirit. In this we detest all the heresies that have of old troubled the Church, and especially the diabolical conceits of Servetus, which attribute a fantastical divinity to the Lord Jesus, calling him the idea and pattern of all things, and the personal or figurative Son of God, and, finally, attribute to him a body of three uncreated elements, thus confusing and destroying the two natures.

XV. We believe that in one person, that is, Jesus Christ, the two natures are actually and inseparably joined and united, and yet each remains in its proper character : so that in this union the divine nature, retaining its attributes, remained uncreated, infinite, and all-pervading ; and the human nature remained finite, having its form, measure, and attributes ; and although Jesus Christ, in rising from the dead, bestowed immortality upon his body, yet he did not take from

---

[1] Héb. ii. 17 ; 2 Cor. v. 21.
[2] Actes xiii. 23 ; Rom. i. 3 ; viii. 3 ; ix. 5 ; Philip. ii. 7 ; Héb. ii. 14, 16 ; v.
[3] Matt. i. 18 ; Luc i. 35.

[4] Matt. i. ; Luc i. ; Jean i. 14 ; 1 Tim. ii. 5 ; iii. 16 ; Héb. v. 8.
[5] Luc xxiv. 38, 39 ; Rom. i. 4 ; Philip. ii. 6–11.

toutefois il ne lui a pas ôté la vérité de sa nature. Et ainsi, nous le considérons tellement en sa divinité, que nous ne le dépouillons point de son humanité.

XVI. Nous croyons que Dieu envoyant son Fils, a voulu montrer son amour et bonté inestimable envers nous, en le livrant à la mort, et le ressuscitant pour accomplir toute justice et pour nous acquérir la vie céleste.[1]

XVII. Nous croyons que par le sacrifice unique que le Seigneur Jésus a offert en la croix,[2] nous sommes réconciliés à Dieu pour être tenus et réputés justes devant lui, parce que nous ne lui pouvons être agréables, ni être participants de son adoption, sinon d'autant qu'il nous pardonne nos fautes, et les ensevelit.[3] Ainsi nous protestons que Jésus-Christ est notre lavement entier et parfait, qu'en sa mort nous avons entière satisfaction, pour nous acquitter de nos forfaits et iniquités dont nous sommes coupables, et ne pouvons être délivrés que par ce remède.[4]

XVIII. Nous croyons que toute notre justice est fondée en la rémission de nos péchés, comme aussi c'est notre seule félicité, comme dit David.[5] C'est pourquoi nous rejetons

it the truth of its nature, and we so consider him in his divinity that we do not despoil him of his humanity.

XVI. We believe that God, in sending his Son, intended to show his love and inestimable goodness towards us, giving him up to die to accomplish all righteousness, and raising him from the dead to secure for us the heavenly life.

XVII. We believe that by the perfect sacrifice that the Lord Jesus offered on the cross, we are reconciled to God, and justified before him; for we can not be acceptable to him, nor become partakers of the grace of adoption, except as he pardons [all] our sins, and blots them out. Thus we declare that through Jesus Christ we are cleansed and made perfect; by his death we are fully justified, and through him only can we be delivered from our iniquities and transgressions.

XVIII. We believe that all our justification rests upon the remission of our sins, in which also is our only blessedness, as saith the Psalmist (Psa. xxxii. 2).

---

[1] Jean iii. 16; xv. 13.
[2] 2 Cor. v. 19; Héb. v. 7–9.
[3] 1 Pierre ii. 24, 25.

[4] Héb. ix. 14; Ephés. v. 26; 1 Pierre i. 18, 19.
[5] Psa. xxxii. 2; Jean xvii. 23; Rom. iv. 7, 8; viii. 1–3; 2 Cor. ᵂ 19, 20.

tous autres moyens de nous pouvoir justifier devant Dieu ;[1] et sans présumer de nulles vertus, ni mérites, nous nous tenons simplement à l'obéissance de Jésus-Christ, laquelle nous est allouée, tant pour couvrir toutes nos fautes, que pour nous faire trouver grâce et faveur devant Dieu. Et de fait, nous croyons qu'en déclinant de ce fondement, tant peu que ce soit, nous ne pourrions trouver ailleurs aucun repos, mais serions toujours agités d'inquiétude : d'autant que jamais nous ne sommes paisibles avec Dieu, jusqu'à ce que nous soyons bien résolus d'être aimés en Jésus-Christ, vu que nous sommes dignes d'être haïs en nousmêmes.

XIX. Nous croyons que c'est par ce moyen que nous avons liberté et privilége d'invoquer Dieu, avec pleine fiance qu'il se montrera notre Père.[2] Car nous n'aurions aucun accès au Père, si nous n'étions adressés par ce médiateur. Et pour être exaucés en son nom, il convient tenir notre vie du lui, comme de notre chef.

XX. Nous croyons que nous sommes faits participants de cette justice par la seule foi, comme il est dit qu'il a souffert pour nous acquérir le salut, afin que quiconque

We therefore reject all other means of justification before God, and without claiming any virtue or merit, we rest simply in the obedience of Jesus Christ, which is imputed to us as much to blot out all our sins as to make us find grace and favor in the sight of God. And, in fact, we believe that in falling away from this foundation, however slightly, we could not find rest elsewhere, but should always be troubled. Forasmuch as we are never at peace with God till we resolve to be loved in Jesus Christ, for of ourselves we are worthy of hatred.

XIX. We believe that by this means we have the liberty and privilege of calling upon God, in full confidence that he will show himself a Father to us. For we should have no access to the Father except through this Mediator. And to be heard in his name, we must hold our life from him as from our chief.

XX. We believe that we are made partakers of this justification by faith alone, as it is written: 'He suffered for our salvation, that whosoever believeth on

---

[1] 1 Tim. ii. 5; 1 Jean ii. 1; Rom. v. 19; Actes iv. 12.

[2] Rom. v. 12; viii. 15; Gal. iv. 4–7; Ephés. ii. 13–15.

croira en lui, ne périsse point.[1] *Et que cela se fait, d'autant que les promesses de vie qui nous sont données en lui, sont appropriées à notre usage, et en sentons l'effet quand nous les acceptons, ne doutant point qu'étant assurés par la bouche de Dieu, nous ne serons point frustrés.*[2] *Ainsi la justice que nous obtenons par la foi, dépend des promesses gratuites par lesquelles Dieu nous déclare et testifie qu'il nous aime.*[3]

XXI. *Nous croyons que nous sommes illuminés en la foi par la grâce secrète du Saint-Esprit, tellement que c'est un don gratuit et particulier que Dieu départ à ceux que bon lui semble, en sorte que les fidèles n'ont de quoi s'en glorifier, étant obligés au double, de ce qu'ils ont été préférés aux autres.*[4] *Même que la foi n'est pas seulement baillée pour un coup aux élus pour les introduire au bon chemin, mais pour les y faire continuer aussi jusqu'au bout.*[5] *Car comme c'est à Dieu de faire le commencement, aussi c'est à lui de parachever.*[6]

XXII. *Nous croyons que, par cette foi, nous sommes régénérés en nouveauté de vie, étant naturelle-*

him should not perish.' And this is done inasmuch as we appropriate to our use the promises of life which are given to us through him, and feel their effect when we accept them, being assured that we are established by the Word of God and shall not be deceived. Thus our justification through faith depends upon the free promises by which God declares and testifies his love to us.

XXI. We believe that we are enlightened in faith by the secret power of the Holy Spirit, that it is a gratuitous and special gift which God grants to whom he will, so that the elect have no cause to glory, but are bound to be doubly thankful that they have been preferred to others. We believe also that faith is not given to the elect only to introduce them into the right way, but also to make them continue in it to the end. For as it is God who hath begun the work, he will also perfect it.

XXII. We believe that by this faith we are regenerated in newness of life, being by nature sub-

---

[1] Rom. iii.; Gal. ii.; iii. 24; Jean iii. 15.
[2] Matt. xvii. 20; Jean iii. 16, 17; x. 4.
[3] Rom. i. 17; iii. 24, 25, 27, 30; iv. 1–3; Gal. ii. 20, 21.

[4] Ephés. ii. 8; 1 Thess. i. 5; 1 Cor. ii. 12; 2 Pierre i. 3, 4.
[5] 1 Cor. i. 8, 9.
[6] Philip. ii, 13; i. 6.

ment asservis à péché.[1] *Or, nous recevons par foi la grâce de vivre saintement, et en la crainte de Dieu, en recevant la promesse qui nous est donnée par l'Evangile, savoir, que Dieu nous donnera son Saint-Esprit. Ainsi la foi non-seulement ne refroidit pas l'affection de bien et saintement vivre, mais l'engendre et excite en nous, produisant nécessairement les bonnes œuvres.*[2] *Au reste, bien que Dieu, pour accomplir notre salut, nous régénère, nous réformant à bien faire,*[3] *ioutefois nous confessons que les bonnes œuvres que nous faisons par la conduite de son Esprit, ne viennent point en compte pour nous justifier, ou mériter que Dieu nous tienne pour ses enfants, parce que nous serions toujours flottants en doute et inquiétude, si nos consciences ne s'appuyaient sur la satisfaction par laquelle Jésus-Christ nous a acquittés.*[4]

XXIII. *Nous croyons que toutes les figures de la loi ont pris fin à la venue de Jésus-Christ.*[5] *Mais bien que les cérémonies ne soient plus en usage, néanmoins la substance et vérité nous en est demeurée en la personne de celui auquel gît tout accomplissement.*[6] *Au sur-*

ject to sin. Now we receive by faith grace to live holily and in the fear of God, in accepting the promise which is given to us by the Gospel, namely: that God will give us his Holy Spirit. This faith not only doth not hinder us from holy living, or turn us from the love of righteousness, but of necessity begetteth in us all good works. Moreover, although God worketh in us for our salvation, and reneweth our hearts, determining us to that which is good, yet we confess that the good works which we do proceed from his Spirit, and can not be accounted to us for justification, neither do they entitle us to the adoption of sons, for we should always be doubting and restless in our hearts, if we did not rest upon the atonement by which Jesus Christ hath acquitted us.

XXIII. We believe that the ordinances of the law came to an end at the advent of Jesus Christ; but, although the ceremonies are no more in use, yet their substance and truth remain in the person of him in whom they are fulfilled. And, moreover, we must seek aid from

---

[1] Rom. vi. 1, 2; vii. 1, 2; Col. i. 13; iii. 10; 1 Pierre i. 3.
[2] Jacq. ii.; Gal. v. 6; 1 Jean ii. 3, 4; v. 18.
[3] Deut xxx. 6; **Jean iii. 5.**
[4] Luc xvii. 10; Psa. xvi. 2; Rom. iii.; Tite iii. 5; Rom. iv.
[5] Rom. x. 4; Gal. iii., iv.; Col. ii. 17.
[6] 2 Tim. iii. 16; 2 Pierre i. 19; iii. 2.

plus, il nous faut aider de la loi et des prophètes, tant pour régler notre vie, que pour être confirmés aux promesses de l'Evangile.

XXIV. *Nous croyons, puisque Jésus-Christ nous est donné pour seul avocat,[1] et qu'il nous commande de nous retirer privément en son nom vers son Père;[2] et même qu'il ne nous est pas licite de prier, sinon en suivant la forme que Dieu nous a dictée par sa Parole;[3] que tout ce que les hommes ont imaginé de l'intercession des Saints trépassés, n'est qu'abus et fallace de Satan, pour faire dévoyer les hommes de la forme de bien prier.[4] Nous rejetons aussi tous autres moyens que les hommes présument avoir pour se racheter envers Dieu, comme dérogeants au sacrifice de la mort et passion de Jésus-Christ.*

Finalement, nous tenons le purgatoire pour une illusion procédée de cette même boutique, de laquelle sont aussi procédés les vœux monastiques, pélerinages, défenses du mariage, et de l'usage des viandes, l'observation cérémonielle des jours la confession auriculaire, les indulgences et toutes autres telles choses, par lesquelles on pense mériter grâce et salut.[5] Lesquelles

the law and the prophets for the ruling of our lives, as well as for our confirmation in the promises of the gospel.

XXIV. We believe, as Jesus Christ is our only advocate, and as he commands us to ask of the Father in his name, and as it is not lawful for us to pray except in accordance with the model God hath taught us by his Word, that all imaginations of men concerning the intercession of dead saints are an abuse and a device of Satan to lead men from the right way of worship. We reject, also, all other means by which men hope to redeem themselves before God, as derogating from the sacrifice and passion of Jesus Christ.

Finally, we consider purgatory as an illusion proceeding from the same shop, from which have also sprung monastic vows, pilgrimages, the prohibition of marriage, and of eating meat, the ceremonial observance of days, auricular confession, indulgences, and all such things by which they hope to merit forgiveness and salvation. These things

---

[1] 1 Tim. ii. 5; Actes iv. 12; 1 Jean ii. 1, 2.
[2] Jean xvi. 23, 24.
[3] Matt. vi. 9; Luc xi. 1.

[4] Actes x. 25, 26; xiv. 14; Apoc. xix. 10.
[5] Matt. xv. 11; Actes x. 14, 15; Rom. iv. 1–4; Gal. iv. 9, 10; Col. ii. 18–23; 1 Tim. iv. 2–5.

choses nous rejetons, non-seulement pour la fausse opinion du mérite qui y est attaché, mais aussi parce que ce sont des inventions humaines, qui imposent joug aux consciences.

XXV. Or, parce que nous ne jouissons de Jésus-Christ que par l'Evangile,[1] nous croyons que l'ordre de l'Eglise, qui a été établi en son autorité, doit être sacré et inviolable, et partant que l'Eglise ne peut subsister sinon qu'il y ait des pasteurs qui aient la charge d'enseigner,[2] lesquels on doit honorer et écouter en révérence quand ils sont dûment appelés, et exercent fidèlement leur office.[3] Non pas que Dieu soit attaché à telles aides ou moyens inférieurs, mais parce qu'il lui plaît nous entretenir sous telle bride. En quoi nous détestons tous Fantastiques qui voudraient bien, en tant qu'en eux est, anéantir le ministère et prédication de la parole de Dieu et des sacrements.

XXVI. Nous croyons donc que nul ne se doit retirer à part, et se contenter de sa personne, mais que tous ensemble doivent garder et entretenir l'union de l'Eglise, se soumettant à l'instruction commune et au joug de Jésus-Christ ;[4] et ce en quelque lieu où Dieu aura établi un vrai ordre de l'Eglise,

we reject, not only for the false idea of merit which is attached to them, but also because they are human inventions imposing a yoke upon the conscience.

XXV. Now as we enjoy Christ only through the gospel, we believe that the order of the Church, established by his authority, ought to be sacred and inviolable, and that, therefore, the Church can not exist without pastors for instruction, whom we should respect and reverently listen to, when they are properly called and exercise their office faithfully. Not that God is bound to such aid and subordinate means, but because it pleaseth him to govern us by such restraints. In this we detest all visionaries who would like, so far as lies in their power, to destroy the ministry and preaching of the Word and sacraments.

XXVI. We believe that no one ought to seclude himself and be contented to be alone ; but that all jointly should keep and maintain the union of the Church, and submit to the public teaching, and to the yoke of Jesus Christ, wherever God shall have established a true order of the Church, even

---

[1] Rom. i. 16, 17; x. 3.
[2] Matt. xviii. 20; Ephés. i. 22, 23.
[3] Matt. x. 40; Jean xiii. 20; Rom. x. 15.
[4] Psa. v. 8; xxii. 23; xlii. 5; Ephés. iv. 11; Héb. ii. 12

encore que les magistrats et leurs édits y soient contraires, que tous ceux qui ne s'y rangent, ou s'en séparent, contrarient à l'ordonnance de Dieu.[1]

XXVII. Toutefois, nous croyons qu'il convient discerner soigneusement, et avec prudence, quelle est la vraie Eglise, parce que par trop on abuse de ce titre.[2] Nous disons donc, suivant la parole de Dieu, que c'est la compagnie des fidèles qui s'accordent à suivre cette Parole et la pure religion qui en dépend, et qui profitent en elle tout le temps de leur vie, croissant et se confirmant en la crainte de Dieu, selon qu'ils ont besoin de s'avancer et de marcher toujours plus outre.[3] Même quoiqu'ils s'efforcent, qu'il leur convient avoir incessamment recours à la rémission de leurs péchés,[4] néanmoins nous ne nions point que parmi les fidèles il n'y ait des hypocrites et réprouvés, desquels la malice ne peut effacer le titre de l'Eglise.[5]

XXVIII. Sous cette créance nous protestons que là où la parole de Dieu n'est point reçue, et où on ne fait nulle profession de s'assujettir à elle, et où il n'y a nul usage des sacrements, à parler proprement, on

if the magistrates and their edicts are contrary to it. For if they do not take part in it, or if they separate themselves from it, they do contrary to the Word of God.

XXVII. Nevertheless we believe that it is important to discern with care and prudence which is the true Church, for this title has been much abused. We say, then, according to the Word of God, that it is the company of the faithful who agree to follow his Word, and the pure religion which it teaches; who advance in it all their lives, growing and becoming more confirmed in the fear of God according as they feel the want of growing and pressing onward. Even although they strive continually, they can have no hope save in the remission of their sins. Nevertheless we do not deny that among the faithful there may be hypocrites and reprobates, but their wickedness can not destroy the title of the Church.

XXVIII. In this belief we declare that, properly speaking, there can be no Church where the Word of God is not received, nor profession made of subjection to it, nor use of the sacraments.

---

[1] Actes iv. 19, 20; Héb. x. 25.
[2] Jér. vii. 4, 8, 11, 12; Matt. iii. 9; vii. 22; xxiv. 5.

[3] Ephés. ii. 20; iv. 11, 12; 1 Tim. iii. 15;
[4] Rom. iii. 3. [Deut. xxxi. 12.
[5] Matt. xiii. 30; 1 Tim. i. 18–20.

ne peut juger qu'il y ait aucune Eglise.[1] Partant, nous condamnons les assemblées de la papauté, vu que la pure vérité de Dieu en est bannie, esquelles les sacrements sont corrompus, abâtardis, falsifiés ou anéantis du tout ; et esquelles toutes superstitions et idolâtries ont la vogue. Nous tenons donc que tous ceux qui se mêlent en tels actes, et y communiquent, se séparent et se retranchent du corps de Jésus-Christ.[2] Toutefois, parce qu'il reste encore quelque petite trace de l'Eglise en la papauté, et même que la vertu et substance du baptême y est demeurée, joint que l'efficace du baptême ne dépend pas de celui qui l'administre, nous confessons ceux qui y sont baptisés n'avoir besoin d'un second baptême.[3] Cependant à cause des corruptions qui y sont, on n'y peut présenter les enfants sans se polluer.

XXIX. Quant est de la vraie Eglise, nous croyons qu'elle doit être gouvernée selon la police que notre Seigneur Jésus-Christ a établie.[4] C'est qu'il y ait des pasteurs, des surveillants et des diacres, afin que la pure doctrine ait son cours, que les vices soient corrigés et réprimés, et que les pauvres

Therefore we condemn the papal assemblies, as the pure Word of God is banished from them, their sacraments are corrupted, or falsified, or destroyed, and all superstitions and idolatries are in them. We hold, then, that all who take part in these acts, and commune in that Church, separate and cut themselves off from the body of Christ. Nevertheless, as some trace of the Church is left in the papacy, and the virtue and substance of baptism remain, and as the efficacy of baptism does not depend upon the person who administers it, we confess that those baptized in it do not need a second baptism. But, on account of its corruptions, we can not present children to be baptized in it without incurring pollution.

XXIX. As to the true Church, we believe that it should be governed according to the order established by our Lord Jesus Christ. That there should be pastors, overseers, and deacons, so that true doctrine may have its course, that errors may be corrected and suppressed, and the poor and all

---

[1] Matt. x. 14, 15 ; Jean x. 1 ; 1 Cor. iii. 12, 13.

[2] 2 Cor. vi. 14–16 ; 1 Cor. vi. 15.

[3] Matt. iii. 11 ; xxviii. 19 ; Marc i. 8; Actes i. 5 ; xi. 15–17 ; xix. 4–6.

[4] Actes vi. 3–5 ; Ephés. iv. 11–13 ; 1 Tim. iii. ; Tite i., ii. ; Matt. xviii. 17.

et tous autres affligés soient se-
courus en leurs nécessités ; et que
les assemblées se fassent au nom de
Dieu, esquelles grands et petits
soient édifiés.

XXX. *Nous croyons tous vrais*
pasteurs, en quelque lieu qu'ils
soient, avoir même autorité et égale
puissance sous un seul chef, seul
souverain et seul universel évêque,
Jésus-Christ ;[1] *et pour cette cause,*
que nulle Eglise ne doit prétendre
aucune domination ou seigneurie
sur l'autre.

XXXI. *Nous croyons que nul ne*
se doit ingérer de son autorité pro-
pre pour gouverner l'Eglise, mais
que cela se doit faire par élection,
en tant qu'il est possible et que Dieu
le permet.[2] *Laquelle exception nous*
y ajoutons notamment, parce qu'il
a fallu quelquefois, et même de no-
tre temps (auquel l'état de l'Eglise
était interrompu), que Dieu ait
suscité des gens d'une façon ex-
traordinaire pour dresser l'Eglise
de nouveau, qui était en ruine et
désolation. Mais, quoi qu'il en soit,
nous croyons qu'il se faut toujours
conformer à cette règle. Que tous
pasteurs, surveillants et diacres
aient témoignage d'être appelés à
leur office.[3]

who are in affliction may be
helped in their necessities ; and
that assemblies may be held in
the name of God, so that great
and small may be edified.

XXX. We believe that all true
pastors, wherever they may be,
have the same authority and
equal power under one head, one
only sovereign and universal bishop, Jesus Christ ; and that consequently no Church shall claim
any authority or dominion over
any other.

XXXI. We believe that no person should undertake to govern the
Church upon his own authority,
but that this should be derived
from election, as far as it is possible, and as God will permit.
And we make this exception especially, because sometimes, and
even in our own days, when the
state of the Church has been in-
terrupted, it has been necessary
for God to raise men in an extraordinary manner to restore the
Church which was in ruin and des-
olation. But, notwithstanding, we
believe that this rule must always
be binding : that all pastors, overseers, and deacons should have evidence of being called to their office.

---

[1] Matt. xx. 26, 27 ; xviii. 2–4 ; 1 Cor. iii. 1–6 ; Ephés. i. 22 ; Col. i. 18, 19.
[2] Matt. xxviii. 18, 19 ; Marc xvi. 15 ; Jean xv. 16 ; Actes i. 21–26 ; vi. 1, 2 ; Rom. x. 15 ;
[3] Gal. i. 15 ; 1 Tim. iii. 7–10, 15.   [Tite i. 5–7.

XXXII. *Nous croyons aussi qu'il est bon et utile que ceux qui sont élus pour être superintendants, avisent entre eux quel moyen ils devront tenir pour le régime de tout le corps,[1] et toutefois qu'ils ne déclinent nullement de ce qui nous en a été donné par notre Seigneur Jésus-Christ.[2] Ce qui n'empêche point qu'il n'y ait quelques ordonnances particulières en chacun lieu, selon que la commodité le requerra.*

XXXIII. *Cependant nous excluons toutes inventions humaines, et toutes lois qu'on voudrait introduire sous ombre du service de Dieu, par lesquelles on voudrait lier les consciences;[3] mais seulement recevons ce qui fait et est propre pour nourrir la concorde, et tenir chacun depuis le premier jusqu'au dernier en obéisance. En quoi nous avons à suivre ce que notre Seigneur Jésus a déclaré quant à l'excommunication;[4] laquelle nous approuvons et confessons être nécessaire avec toutes ses appartenances.*

XXXIV. *Nous croyons que les sacrements sont ajoutés à la Parole pour plus ample confirmation, afin de nous être gages et marreaux de*

XXXII. We believe, also, that it is desirable and useful that those elected to be superintendents devise among themselves what means should be adopted for the government of the whole body, and yet that they should never depart from that which was ordained by our Lord Jesus Christ. Which does not prevent there being some special ordinances in each place, as convenience may require.

XXXIII. However, we reject all human inventions, and all laws which men may introduce under the pretense of serving God, by which they wish to bind consciences; and we receive only that which conduces to concord and holds all in obedience, from the greatest to the least. In this we must follow that which the Lord Jesus Christ declared as to excommunication, which we approve and confess to be necessary with all its antecedents and consequences.

XXXIV. We believe that the sacraments are added to the Word for more ample confirmation, that they may be to us pledges and

---

[1] Actes xv. 2, 6, 7, 25, 28 ; Rom. xii. 6–8 ; 1 Cor. xiv. 12 ; 2 Cor. xii. 7, 8.
[2] 1 Pierre v. ; 1 Cor. xiv. 40.
[3] Rom. xvi. 17, 18 ; 1 Cor. iii. 11 ; Col. ii. 6–8 ; Gal. v. 1.
[4] Matt. xviii. 17 ; 1 Cor. v. 5 ; 1 Tim. i. 9, 10.

la grâce de Dieu, et par ce moyen aider et soulager notre foi, à cause de l'infirmité et rudesse qui est en nous,[1] et qu'ils sont tellement signes extérieurs, que Dieu opère par eux en la vertu de son Esprit, afin de ne nous y rien signifier en vain.[2] Toutefois, nous tenons que toute leur substance et vérité est en Jésus-Christ;[3] et si on les sépare, ce n'est plus rien qu'ombrage et fumée.

XXXV. *Nous en confessons seulement deux, communs à toute l'Eglise, desquels le premier, qui est le baptême, nous est donné pour témoignage de notre adoption; parce que là nous sommes entés au corps de Christ, à fin d'être lavés et nettoyés par son sang, et puis renouvelés en sainteté de vie par son Saint-Esprit.[4] Nous tenons aussi, bien que nous ne soyons baptisés qu'une fois, que le profit qui nous est là signifié s'étend à la vie et à la mort, à fin que nous ayons une signature permanente, que Jésus-Christ nous sera toujours justice et sanctification.[5] Or, bien que ce soit un sacrement de foi et de pénitence, néanmoins parce que Dieu reçoit en son Eglise les petits enfants avec leurs pères, nous disons que par l'autorité de Jésus-Christ les petits*

seals of the grace of God, and by this means aid and comfort our faith, because of the infirmity which is in us, and that they are outward signs through which God operates by his Spirit, so that he may not signify any thing to us in vain. Yet we hold that their substance and truth is in Jesus Christ, and that of themselves they are only smoke and shadow.

XXXV. We confess only two sacraments common to the whole Church, of which the first, baptism, is given as a pledge of our adoption; for by it we are grafted into the body of Christ, so as to be washed and cleansed by his blood, and then renewed in purity of life by his Holy Spirit. We hold, also, that although we are baptized only once, yet the gain that it symbolizes to us reaches over our whole lives and to our death, so that we have a lasting witness that Jesus Christ will always be our justification and sanctification. Nevertheless, although it is a sacrament of faith and penitence, yet as God receives little children into the Church with their fathers, we say, upon the authority of Jesus

---

[1] 1 Cor. x.; xi. 23–34; Exode xii. 13; Matt. xxvi. 26, 27; Rom. iv. 11; Actes xxii. 16.

[2] Gal. iii. 27; Ephés. v. 26.

[3] Jean vi. 50–57; iii. 12.

[4] Rom. vi. 3; Tite iii. 5, 6; Actes xxii. 16.

[5] Matt. iii. 11, 12; Marc xvi. 16; Rom. vi. 1–4.

enfante engendrés des fidèles doivent être baptisés.[1]

XXXVI. *Nous confessons que la sainte Cène (qui est le second sacrement) nous est un témoignage de l'union que nous avons avec Jésus-Christ,*[2] *d'autant qu'il n'est pas seulement une fois mort et ressuscité pour nous, mais aussi nous repaît et nourrit vraiment de sa chair et de son sang, à ce que nous soyons un avec lui, et que sa vie nous soit commune.*[3] *Or, bien qu'il soit au ciel jusqu'à ce qu'il vienne pour juger tout le monde,*[4] *toutefois nous croyons que par la vertu secrète et incompréhensible de son Esprit, il nous nourrit et vivifie de la substance de son corps et de son sang.*[5] *Nous tenons bien que cela se fait spirituellement, non pas pour mettre au lieu de l'effet et de la vérité, imagination, ni pensée; mais d'autant que ce mystère surmonte en sa hautesse la mesure de notre sens, et tout ordre de nature. Bref, parce qu'il est céleste, il ne peut être appréhendé que par la foi.*

XXXVII. *Nous croyons (ainsi qu'il a été dit), que tant en la cène qu'au baptême, Dieu nous donne réellement et par effet ce qu'il y figure. Et partant, nous joignons*

Christ, that the children of believing parents should be baptized.

XXXVI. We confess that the Lord's Supper, which is the second sacrament, is a witness of the union which we have with Christ, inasmuch as he not only died and rose again for us once, but also feeds and nourishes us truly with his flesh and blood, so that we may be one in him, and that our life may be in common. Although he be in heaven until he come to judge all the earth, still we believe that by the secret and incomprehensible power of his Spirit he feeds and strengthens us with the substance of his body and of his blood. We hold that this is done spiritually, not because we put imagination and fancy in the place of fact and truth, but because the greatness of this mystery exceeds the measure of our senses and the laws of nature. In short, because it is heavenly, it can only be apprehended by faith.

XXXVII. We believe, as has been said, that in the Lord's Supper, as well as in baptism, God gives us really and in fact that which he there sets forth to us;

---

[1] Matt. xix. 14; 1 Cor. vii. 14. 1 Cor. x. 16, 17: xi. 24.   [3] Jean vi. 56, 57; xvii. 11, 22.   [5] 1 Cor. x. 16: Jean vi.
[4] Marc xvi. 19; Actes iii. 21.

avec les signes la vraie possession et jouissance de ce qui nous est là présenté. Et ainsi, tous ceux qui apportent à la table sacrée de Christ une pure foi, comme un vaisseau, reçoivent vraiment ce que les signes y testifient ; c'est que le corps et le sang de Jésus-Christ ne servent pas moins de manger et de boire à l'âme, que le pain et le vin font au corps.[1]

XXXVIII. *Ainsi nous tenons que l'eau étant un élément caduc, ne laisse pas de nous testifier en vérité le lavement intérieur de notre âme au sang de Jésus-Christ, par l'efficace de son Esprit,*[2] *et que le pain et le vin nous étant donnés en la cène, nous servent vraiment de nourriture spirituelle, d'autant qu'ils nous montrent comme à l'œil la chair de Jésus-Christ nous être notre viande, et son sang notre breuvage.*[3] *Et rejetons les Fantastiques et Sacrementaires, qui ne veulent recevoir tels signes et marques, vu que notre Seigneur Jésus prononce : Ceci est mon corps, et cette coupe est mon sang.*[4]

XXXIX. *Nous croyons que Dieu veut que le monde soit gouverné par lois et police,*[5] *afin qu'il y ait quelque bride pour réprimer les appétits désordonnés du monde. Et*

and that consequently with these signs is given the true possession and enjoyment of that which they present to us. And thus all who bring a pure faith, like a vessel, to the sacred table of Christ, receive truly that of which it is a sign; for the body and the blood of Jesus Christ give food and drink to the soul, no less than bread and wine nourish the body.

XXXVIII. Thus we hold that water, being a feeble element, still testifies to us in truth the inward cleansing of our souls in the blood of Jesus Christ by the efficacy of his Spirit, and that the bread and wine given to us in the sacrament serve to our spiritual nourishment, inasmuch as they show, as to our sight, that the body of Christ is our meat, and his blood our drink. And we reject the Enthusiasts and Sacramentarians who will not receive such signs and marks, although our Saviour said : 'This is my body, and this cup is my blood.'

XXXIX. We believe that God wishes to have the world governed by laws and magistrates, so that some restraint may be put upon its disordered appetites.

---

[1] 1 Cor. xi. ; Jean vi.   [3] Jean vi. ; 1 Cor. xi.   [5] Exode xviii. 20, 21 ; Matt.
[2] Rom. vi. 3.   [4] Matt. xxvi. 26 ; 1 Cor. xi.   xvii. 24–27 ; Rom. xiii.

ainsi qu'il a établi les royaumes, républiques et toutes autres sortes de principautés, soit héréditaires ou autrement, et tout ce qui appartient à l'Etat de justice, et en veut être reconnu auteur : à cette cause il a mis le glaive en la main des magistrats pour réprimer les péchés commis non-seulement contre la seconde table des commandements de Dieu, mais aussi contre la première. Il faut donc, à cause de lui, que non-seulement on endure que les supérieurs dominent,[1] mais aussi qu'on les honore et prise en toute révérence, les tenant pour ses lieutenants et officiers, lesquels il a commis pour exercer une charge légitime et sainte.

XL. Nous tenons donc qu'il faut obéir à leurs lois et statuts,[2] payer tributs, impôts et autres devoirs, et porter le joug de subjection d'une bonne et franche volonté, encore qu'ils fussent infidèles, moyennant que l'empire souverain de Dieu demeure en son entier.[3] Ainsi nous détestons ceux qui voudraient rejeter les supériorités, mettre communauté et confusion de biens, et renverser l'ordre de la justice.

And as he has established kingdoms, republics, and all sorts of principalities, either hereditary or otherwise, and all that belongs to a just government, and wishes to be considered as their Author, so he has put the sword into the hands of magistrates to suppress crimes against the first as well as against the second table of the Commandments of God. We must therefore, on his account, not only submit to them as superiors, but honor and hold them in all reverence as his lieutenants and officers, whom he has commissioned to exercise a legitimate and holy authority.

XL. We hold, then, that we must obey their laws and statutes, pay customs, taxes, and other dues, and bear the yoke of subjection with a good and free will, even if they are unbelievers, provided that the sovereign empire of God remain intact. Therefore we detest all those who would like to reject authority, to establish community and confusion of property, and overthrow the order of justice.

---

[1] 1 Pierre ii. 13, 14 ; 1 Tim. ii. 2.   [2] Matt. xvii. 24.   [3] Actes iv. 17–20; xviii. 9.

CONFESSIO BELGICA.

THE BELGIC CONFESSION. A.D. 1561. REVISED 1619.

[The Belgic Confession, composed in French by GUY DE BRÈS (died a martyr, 1567) for the Churches in Flanders and the Netherlands, 1561, was adopted by a Reformed Synod at Emden, 1571, and by the National Synod of Dort, 1619, which subjected the text to a careful revision by a comparison of French, Dutch, and Latin copies.

The French text is taken from the authentic MS. of 1580, with the revision of Dort, as reprinted by the *Société évangélique Belge*, at Brussels, 1850, under the title, *La Confession de foi des églises réformées Wallonnes et Flamandes,* including a table of various readings. The headings of articles are supplemented from the Latin editions.

The English text (made from the Latin) is the one authorized by the 'Reformed (Dutch) Church in America,' and printed in its *Constitution,* etc. (New York, 103 Fulton Street). An older English version in the English *Harmony of Confessions,* Cambridge, 1586, and a recent one by Owen Jones, in *Church of the Living God,* etc. London, 1865, pp. 203–237.

A Latin translation, probably made by Beza, or under his direction, appeared in the *Harmonia Confessionum,* Geneva, 1581, and in the first edition of the *Corpus et Syntagma Confessionum,* Geneva, 1612; another, by Festus Hommius, Leyden, 1618; this was revised by the Synod of Dort, reprinted (as revised) in the second edition of the *Corp. et Syntag.* (1654), and (in its original form), with various readings, in Niemeyer's *Collectio* (pp. 360–389). It is also given in the Oxford *Sylloge Confessionum* (pp. 327–354). The Latin texts in these editions differ considerably.

There are several Dutch and German editions, and a Greek version (ἐκκλησιῶν τῆς Βελγικῆς ἐξομολόγησις), made by Jac. Revius (Lugd. Batav. 1635, and Amstelod. 1638). The Greek edition before me (Utrecht, 1660) gives the Greek and Latin in parallel columns, and contains also the Heidelberg Catechism in Latin, with the Greek version of Fred. Sylburg.]

LA CONFESSION DE FOI

DES

ÉGLISES RÉFORMÉES WALLONNES ET FLAMANDES.

[*De l'ancien text du manuscrit authentique de* 1580, *avec la révision de Dortrecht de* 1619.]

ART. I

DE NATURA DEI.

Nous croyons tous de cœur et confessons de bouche, qu'il y a une seule et simple essence[1] spirituelle,[2] laquelle nous appelons Dieu éternel,[3] incompréhensible,[4] invisible,[5] immuable,[6] infini;[7] lequel est tout puissant, tout sage,[8] juste,[9] et bon,[10]

THE CONFESSION OF FAITH

OF THE

REFORMED CHURCH.

Revised in the National Synod, held at Dordrecht, in the Years 1618 *and* 1619.

ART. I.

THERE IS ONE ONLY GOD.

We all believe with the heart, and confess with the mouth, that there is one only simple and spiritual Being, which we call God; and that he is eternal, incomprehensible, invisible, immutable, infinite, almighty, perfectly wise,

---

[1] Eph. iv. 6; Deut. vi. 4; 1 Tim. ii. 5; 1 Cor. viii. 6.
[2] Jean iv. 24.
[3] Es. xl. 28.

[4] Rom. xi. 33.
[5] Rom. i. 20.
[6] Mal. iii. 6.
[7] Es. xliv. 6.

[8] 1 Tim. i. 17.
[9] Jér. xii. 1.
[10] Matt. xix. 17.

et source très-abondante de tous biens.[1]

just, good, and the overflowing fountain of all good.[2]

ART. II.

DE COGNITIONE DEI.

Nous le connaissons par deux moyens. Premièrement: Par la création, conservation et gouvernement du monde universel,[3] *d'autant que c'est devant nos yeux comme un beau livre, auquel toutes créatures, petites et grandes, servent de lettres pour nous faire contempler les choses invisibles de Dieu, savoir sa puissance éternelle et sa divinité, comme dit l'Apôtre saint Paul (Rom. i. 20). Toutes lesquelles choses sont suffisantes pour convaincre les hommes, et les rendre inexcusables.*

Secondement: Il se donne à connaître à nous plus manifestement et évidemment par sa sainte et divine Parole,[4] *tout autant pleinement qu'il nous est de besoin en cette vie pour sa gloire et le salut des siens.*

ART. II.

BY WHAT MEANS GOD IS MADE KNOWN UNTO US.

We know him by two means: first, by the creation, preservation, and government of the universe; which is before our eyes as a most elegant book, wherein all creatures, great and small, are as so many characters leading us to contemplate *the invisible things of God*, namely, *his eternal power and Godhead*, as the Apostle Paul saith (Rom. i. 20). All which things are sufficient to convince men, and leave them without excuse.

Secondly, he makes himself more clearly and fully known to us by his holy and divine Word; that is to say, as far as is necessary for us to know in this life, to his glory and our salvation.

ART. III.

DE SACRA SCRIPTURA.

Nous confessons que cette Parole de Dieu n'a point été envoyée

ART. III.

OF THE WRITTEN WORD OF GOD.

We confess that this Word of God was not sent nor delivered

---

[1] Jacq. i. 17; 1 Chron. xxix. 10, 11, 12.
[2] English *Harm. of Conf.*: 'A most plentiful well-spring of all good things.'
[3] Psa. xix. 2; Eph. iv. 6.
[4] Psa. xix. 8; 1 Cor. xii. 6.

ni apportée par volonté humaine :
mais les saints hommes de Dieu
ont parlé étant poussés du Saint-
Esprit, comme dit saint Pierre.[1]
Puis après, par le soin singulier
que notre Dieu a de nous et de
notre salut, il a commandé à ses
serviteurs les Prophètes[2] et Apôtres[3]
de rédiger ses oracles par écrit : et
lui-même a écrit de son doigt les
deux Tables de la Loi.[4] Pour cette
cause, nous appelons tels écrits :
Écritures saintes et divines.

by the will of man, but that holy
men of God spake as they were
moved by the Holy Ghost, as the
Apostle Peter saith. And that
afterwards God, from a special
care which he has for us and our
salvation, commanded his servants,
the Prophets and Apostles, to commit his revealed Word to writing;
and he himself wrote with his own
finger the two tables of the law.
Therefore we call such writings
holy and divine Scriptures.

ART. IV.

DE CANONICIS LIBRIS VETERIS ET NOVI
TESTAMENTI.

ART. IV.

CANONICAL BOOKS OF THE HOLY SCRIPT-
URES.

Nous comprenons l'Écriture
Sainte aux deux volumes du Vieux
et du Nouveau Testament, qui sont
livres canoniques, auxquels il n'y
a rien à répliquer. Le nombre en
est tel en l'Église de Dieu.

We believe that the Holy Scriptures are contained in two books,
namely, the Old and New Testaments, which are canonical, against
which nothing can be alleged.
These are thus named in the Church
of God.

Dans l'Ancien Testament : Les
cinq livres de Moïse, le livre de
Josué, des Juges, Ruth, les deux
livres de Samuël, et deux des Rois,
les deux livres des Chroniques dits
Paralipomènes, le premier d'Esdras, Néhémie, Ester, Job, les
Psaumes de David, les trois livres
de Salomon, savoir : les Proverbes,
l'Écclésiaste, et le Cantique ; les
quatre grands Prophètes : Esaïe,

The books of the Old Testament are : the five books of Moses,
viz., Genesis, Exodus, Leviticus,
Numbers, Deuteronomy; the book
of Joshua, Judges, Ruth, two books
of Samuel, and two of the Kings,
two books of the Chronicles, commonly called Paralipomenon, the
first of Ezra, Nehemiah, Esther;
Job, the Psalms of David, the
three books of Solomon, namely,

---

[1] 2 Pier. i. 21.
[2] Exod. xxiv. 4; Psa. cii. 19; Hab. ii. 2.

[3] 2 Tim. iii. 16; Apoc. i. 11.
[4] Exod. xxxi. 18.

Jérémie, Ezéchiel, et Daniel. Puis les autres douze petits Prophètes: Osée, Joël, Amos, Abdias, Jonas, Michée, Nahum, Habacuc, Sophonie, Aggée, Zacharie, Malachie.

Dans le Nouveau Testament: *les quatre Évangélistes, saint Matthieu, saint Marc, saint Luc, saint Jean; les Actes des Apôtres, les quatorze Épîtres de saint Paul: aux Romains, deux aux Corinthiens, aux Galates, Éphésiens, Philippiens, Colossiens, deux aux Thessaloniciens, deux à Timothée, à Tite, Philémon, aux Hébreux; et les sept Épîtres des autres Apôtres, savoir une de saint Jacques, deux de saint Pierre, trois de saint Jean, et une de saint Jude; enfin l'Apocalypse de saint Jean Apôtre.*

ART. V.

DE AUCTORITATE SACRÆ SCRIPTURÆ.

Nous recevons tous ces livres-là seulement, pour saints et canoniques, pour régler, fonder et établir notre foi, et croyons pleinement toutes les choses qui y sont contenues, non pas tant parce que l'Église les reçoit et approuve tels, mais principalement parce que le Saint-Esprit nous rend témoign-

the Proverbs, Ecclesiastes, and the Song of Songs; the four great Prophets: Isaiah, Jeremiah, Ezekiel, and Daniel; and the twelve lesser Prophets, viz., Hosea, Joel, Amos, Obadiah, Jonah, Micah, Nahum, Habakkuk, Zephaniah, Haggai, Zechariah, and Malachi.

Those of the New Testament are: the four Evangelists, viz., Matthew, Mark, Luke, and John; the Acts of the Apostles; the fourteen Epistles of the Apostle Paul, viz., one to the Romans, two to the Corinthians, one to the Galatians, one to the Ephesians, one to the Philippians, one to the Colossians, two to the Thessalonians, two to Timothy, one to Titus, one to Philemon, and one to the Hebrews; the seven Epistles of the other Apostles, viz., one of James, two of Peter, three of John, one of Jude; and the Revelation of the Apostle John.

ART. V.

WHENCE DO THE HOLY SCRIPTURES DERIVE THEIR DIGNITY AND AUTHORITY.

We receive all these books, and these only, as holy and canonical, for the regulation, foundation, and confirmation of our faith; believing, without any doubt, all things contained in them, not so much because the Church receives and approves them as such, but more especially because the Holy Ghost

age en notre cœur, qu'ils sont de Dieu, et aussi qu'ils sont approuvés tels par eux-mêmes; car les aveugles mêmes peuvent apercevoir que les choses adviennent qui y sont prédites.

witnesseth in our hearts that they are from God, whereof they carry the evidence in themselves. For the very blind are able to perceive that the things foretold in them are fulfilling.

Art. VI.

DE DISCRIMINE LIBRORUM CANONICORUM ET APOCRYPHORUM.

Nous mettons différence entre ces saints livres et les livres apocryphes, qui sont le troisième et quatrième livre d'Esdras, le livre de Tobie, Judith, Sapience, Ecclésiastique, Baruc, ce qui a été ajouté à l'histoire d'Ester, le cantique des trois Enfants en la fournaise, l'histoire de Susanne, l'histoire de l'idole Bel et du Dragon, l'Oraison de Manassé, et les deux livres des Maccabées, lesquels l'Église peut bien lire et y prendre instruction dans les choses conformes aux livres canoniques; mais ils n'ont point telle force et vertu que par un témoignage qui en est tiré, on puisse arrêter quelque chose de la foi ou religion chrétienne, tant s'en faut qu'ils puissent ramoindrir l'autorité des autres saints livres.

Art. VI.

THE DIFFERENCE BETWEEN THE CANONICAL AND APOCRYPHAL BOOKS.

We distinguish these sacred books from the apocryphal, viz., the third and fourth book of Esdras, the books of Tobias, Judith, Wisdom, Jesus Syrach, Baruch, the appendix to the book of Esther, the Song of the Three Children in the Furnace, the History of Susannah, of Bell and the Dragon, the Prayer of Manasses, and the two books of Maccabees. All which the Church may read and take instruction from, so far as they agree with the canonical books; but they are far from having such power and efficacy as that we may from their testimony confirm any point of faith or of the Christian religion; much less to detract from the authority of the other sacred books.

Art. VII.

DE PERFECTIONE SACRÆ SCRIPTURÆ.

Nous croyons que cette Écriture Sainte contient parfaitement la volonté divine, et que tout ce que

Art. VII.

THE SUFFICIENCY OF THE HOLY SCRIPTURES TO BE THE ONLY RULE OF FAITH.

We believe that these Holy Scriptures fully contain the will of God, and that whatsoever man ought to

l'homme doit croire pour être sauvé, y est suffisamment enseigné.[1] *Car puisque toute la manière du service que Dieu requiert de nous y est très au long décrite, les hommes, même fussent-ils Apôtres, ne doivent enseigner autrement*[2] *que ce qui nous a été enseigné par les Saintes Écritures, encore même que ce fût un ange du Ciel, comme dit saint Paul:*[3] *car puisqu'il est défendu d'ajouter ni diminuer à la Parole de Dieu,*[4] *cela démontre bien que la doctrine est très-parfaite et accomplie en toutes sortes. Aussi ne faut-il pas comparer les écrits des hommes, quelque saints qu'ils aient été, aux écrits divins,*[5] *ni la coutume à la vérité de Dieu*[6] *(car la vérité est par-dessus tout), ni le grand nombre, ni l'ancienneté, ni la succession des temps ni des personnes, ni les conciles, décrets, ou arrêts: car tous hommes d'eux-mêmes sont menteurs,*[7] *et plus vains que la vanité même. C'est pourquoi nous rejetons de tout notre cœur tout ce qui ne s'accorde*

believe unto salvation, is sufficiently taught therein. For since the whole manner of worship which God requires of us is written in them at large, it is unlawful for any one, though an Apostle, to teach otherwise than we are now taught in the Holy Scriptures: *nay, though it were an angel from heaven,* as the Apostle Paul saith. For since it is forbidden *to add unto or take away any thing from the Word of God,* it doth thereby evidently appear that the doctrine thereof is most perfect and complete in all respects. Neither may we compare any writings of men, though ever so holy, with those divine Scriptures; nor ought we to compare custom, or the great multitude, or antiquity, or succession of times or persons, or councils, decrees, or statutes, with the truth of God, for the truth is above all: for all men are of themselves liars, and more vain than vanity itself. Therefore we reject with all our hearts whatsoever doth not agree with this infallible rule, which the

---

[1] Rom. xv. 4; Jean iv. 25; 2 Tim. iii. 15, 16, 17; 1 Pier. i. 1; Prov. xxx. 5; Gal. xxx. 15; Apoc. xxii. 18; Jean xv. 15; Act. ii. 27.

[2] 1 Pier. iv. 11; 1 Cor. xv. 2, 3; 2 Tim. iii. 14; 1 Tim. i. 3; 2 Jean 10.

[3] Gal. i. 8, 9; 1 Cor. xv. 2; Act. xxvi. 22; Rom. xv. 4; 1 Pier. iv. 11; 2 Tim. iii. 14.

[4] Deut. xii. 32; Prov. xxx. 6; Apoc. xxii. 18; Jean iv. 25.

[5] Matt. xv. 3; xvii. 5; Marc vii. 7; Es. i. 12; 1 Cor. ii. 4.

[6] Es. i. 12; Rom. iii. 4; 2 Tim. iv. 3, 4.

[7] Psa. lxii. 10

à cette règle infaillible,[1] comme nous sommes enseignés de faire par les Apôtres, disant : Éprouvez les ésprits s'ils sont de Dieu,[2] et : Si quelqu'un vient à vous et n'apporte point cette doctrine, ne le recevez point en votre maison.[3]

Apostles have taught us, saying, *Try the spirits whether they are of God;* likewise, *If there come any unto you, and bring not this doctrine, receive him not into your house.*

Art. VIII.

DE SACROSANCTA TRINITATE PERSONARUM IN UNICA ESSENTIA DIVINA.

Art. VIII.

GOD IS ONE IN ESSENCE, YET DISTINGUISHED IN THREE PERSONS.

Suivant cette vérité et Parole de Dieu, nous croyons en un seul Dieu qui est une seule essence,[4] en laquelle il y a trois personnes[5] réellement, et à la vérité, et éternellement distinguées selon leurs propriétés incommunicables, savoir : le Père, le Fils, et le Saint-Esprit ;[6] le Père étant cause, origine et commencement de toutes choses, tant visibles qu'invisibles.[7] Le Fils qui est la Parole,[8] la Sagesse,[9] et l'Image du Père.[10] Le Saint-Esprit, la Vertu et Puissance éternelle[11] procédante du Père et du Fils.[12] Et cependant une telle distinction ne fait pas que Dieu soit divisé en trois, puisque l'Écriture nous enseigne que le Père, le Fils, et le Saint-Esprit ont chacun sa personne

According to this truth and this Word of God, we believe in one only God, who is one single essence, in which are three persons, really, truly, and eternally distinct, according to their incommunicable properties; namely, the Father, and the Son, and the Holy Ghost. The Father is the cause, origin, and beginning of all things, visible and invisible; the Son is the Word, Wisdom, and Image of the Father; the Holy Ghost is the eternal Power and Might, proceeding from the Father and the Son. Nevertheless God is not by this distinction divided into three, since the Holy Scriptures teach us that the Father, and the Son, and the Holy Ghost have each his personality, distinguished by their properties; ·

---

[1] Gal. vi. 16; 1 Cor. iii. 11; 2 Thess. ii. 2.
[2] 1 Jean iv. 1.
[3] 2 Jean 10.
[4] Es. xliii. 10.
[5] 1 Jean v. 7; Héb. i. 3.
[6] Matt. xxviii. 19.

[7] 1 Cor. viii. 6; Col. i. 16.
[8] Jean i. 1, 2; Apoc. xix. 13; Prov. viii. 12.
[9] Prov. viii. 12, 22, etc.
[10] Col. i. 15; Héb. i. 3.
[11] Matt. xii. 28.
[12] Jean xv. 26; Gal. iv. 6.

distincte par des propriétés ; de sorte, toutefois, que ces trois personnes ne sont qu'un seul Dieu. Il est donc manifeste que le Père n'est point le Fils, et que le Fils n'est point le Père : semblablement que le Saint-Esprit n'est pas le Père ni le Fils. Cependant ces personnes ainsi distinctes ne sont pas divisées, ni confondues, ni mêlées : car le Père n'a point pris chair ni aussi le Saint-Esprit, mais ç'a été seulement le Fils.[1] Le Père n'a jamais été sans son Fils ni sans son Saint-Esprit, parce que tous trois sont d'éternité égale, en une même essence. Il n'y a point de premier ni de dernier, car tous trois sont un en vérité et puissance, en bonté et miséricorde.

but in such wise that these three persons are but one only God. Hence, then, it is evident that the Father is not the Son, nor the Son the Father, and likewise the Holy Ghost is neither the Father nor the Son. Nevertheless these persons thus distinguished are not divided nor intermixed ; for the Father hath not assumed the flesh, nor hath the Holy Ghost, but the Son only. The Father hath never been without his Son, or without his Holy Ghost. For they are all three co-eternal and co-essential. There is neither first nor last ; for they are all three one, in truth, in power, in goodness, and in mercy.

Art. IX.

DE SACROSANCTA TRINITATE SCRIPTURÆ TESTIMONIA.

Art. IX.

THE PROOF OF THE FOREGOING ARTICLE OF THE TRINITY OF PERSONS IN ONE GOD.

Nous connaissons toutes ces choses tant par les témoignages de la Sainte Écriture, que par les effets, et principalement par ceux-là que nous sentons en nous. Les témoignages des Écritures Saintes qui nous enseignent de croire cette sainte Trinité sont écrits en plusieurs lieux de l'Ancien Testament, qui n'ont point besoin de dénombrement, mais de choix et de

All this we know, as well from the testimonies of Holy Writ as from their operations, and chiefly by those we feel in ourselves. The testimonies of the Holy Scriptures, that teach us to believe this Holy Trinity, are written in many places of the Old Testament, which are not so necessary to enumerate as to choose them out with discretion and judgment. In Genesis i. 26, 27,

---

[1] Phil. ii. 6. 7: Gal. iv. 4 ; Jean i. 14.

discrétion. Au livre de la Genèse Dieu dit : Faisons l'homme à notre image, et selon notre semblance, etc.[1] Dieu donc créa l'homme à son image : il les créa, dis-je, mâle et femelle. Voici Adam est fait comme l'un de nous.[2] Il appert par cela, qu'il y a pluralité de personnes en la Divinité, quand il dit : Faisons l'homme à notre image ; et puis il montre l'unité quand il dit : Dieu créa, etc. Il est vrai qu'il ne dit point là combien il y a de personnes ; mais ce qui nous est obscur en l'Ancien Testament nous est très-clair au Nouveau.

Car quand notre Seigneur fût baptisé au Jourdain,[3] la voix du Père a été entendue, disant : Celui-ci est mon Fils bien-aimé ; le Fils est vu en l'eau, et le Saint-Esprit apparaît en forme de colombe. De même au baptême de tous fidèles cette façon a été ordonnée de Christ : Baptisez toutes les nations au nom du Père et du Fils et du Saint-Esprit.[4] En l'Évangile selon Saint Luc, l'ange Gabriel parle ainsi à Marie, mère de notre Seigneur : Le Saint-Esprit surviendra en toi et la vertu du Souverain te couvrira de son ombre, c'est pourquoi ce qui naîtra de toi

God saith : *Let us make man in our image, after our likeness*, etc. *So God created man in his own image, male and female created he them.* And Gen. iii. 22 : *Behold, the man has become as one of us.* From this saying, *Let us make man in our image*, it appears that there are more persons than one in the Godhead ; and when he saith *God created*, this signifies the unity. It is true he doth not say how many persons there are, but that which appears to us somewhat obscure in the Old Testament is very plain in the New.

For when our Lord was baptized in Jordan, the voice of the Father was heard, saying, *This is my beloved Son :* the Son was seen in the water ; and the Holy Ghost appeared in the shape of a dove. This form is also instituted by Christ in the baptism of all believers. *Baptize all nations, in the name of the Father and of the Son, and of the Holy Ghost.* In the Gospel of Luke the angel Gabriel thus addressed Mary, the mother of our Lord : *The Holy Ghost shall come upon thee, and the power of the Highest shall overshadow thee, therefore also*

---

[1] Gen. i. 26, 27.   [2] Gen. iii. 22.   [3] Matt. iii. 16, 17.   [4] Matt. xxviii. 19.

*saint, sera appelé le Fils de Dieu.[1]
Et ailleurs il est dit : La grâce de
notre Seigneur Jésus-Christ, et la
charité de Dieu, et la communication du Saint-Esprit soient avec
vous.[2] Il y en a trois qui donnent
témoignage au Ciel, le Père, la
Parole, et le Saint-Esprit et ces
trois sont un.[3] Dans tous ces passages nous sommes à plein enseignés des trois personnes en une
seule essence divine. Et quoique
cette doctrine surpasse l'entendement humain, cependant nous la
croyons maintenant par la Parole, attendant d'en avoir pleine
connaissance et jouissance au
ciel.[4]*

*Or il faut aussi noter les offices
et effets particuliers des trois personnes envers nous. Le Père est
appelé notre Créateur par sa vertu.[5] Le Fils est notre Sauveur et
Rédempteur par son sang.[6] Le
Saint-Esprit est notre sanctifica-
teur par sa demeurance en nos
cœurs.[7]*

*Cette doctrine de la sainte Tri-
nité a toujours été maintenue en
la vraie Église, depuis le temps
des Apôtres jusqu'à présent, contre
les Juifs, les Mahométans, et con-*

that holy thing which shall be born
of thee shall be called the Son of
God. Likewise, *The grace of our
Lord Jesus Christ, and the love of
God, and the communion of the
Holy Ghost be with you.* And
*There are three that bear record in
heaven, the Father, the Word, and
the Holy Ghost, and these three
are one.* In all which places we
are fully taught that there are three
persons in one only divine essence.
And although this doctrine far surpasses all human understanding,
nevertheless we now believe it by
means of the Word of God, but
expect hereafter to enjoy the perfect knowledge and benefit thereof
in heaven.

Moreover we must observe the
particular offices and operations of
these three persons towards us.
The Father is called our Creator
by his power; the Son is our Saviour and Redeemer by his blood;
the Holy Ghost is our Sanctifier
by his dwelling in our hearts.

This doctrine of the Holy Trinity hath always been defended and
maintained by the true Church,
since the times of the Apostles to
this very day, against the Jews,

---

[1] Luc i. 35.
[2] 2 Cor. xiii. 13.
[3] 1 Jean v. 7 [?].
[4] Psa. xlv. 8; Es. lxi. 1.

[5] Eccl. xii. 3; Mal. ii. 10; 1 Pier. i. 2.
[6] 1 Pier. i. 2; 1 Jean i. 7; iv. 14.
[7] 1 Cor. vi. 11; 1 Pier. i. 2; Gal. iv. 6;
    Tit. iii. 5; Rom. viii. 9; Jean xiv. 16.

tre quelques faux Chrétiens et Hérétiques, comme Marcion, Manès, Praxéas, Sabellius, Paul de Samosate, Arius et autres semblables, lesquels à bon droit ont été condamnés par les Saints Pères.

Ainsi nous recevons volontiers en cette matière les trois symboles, celui des Apôtres, ceux de Nicée et d'Athanase, et semblablement ce qui en a été déterminé par les Anciens conformément à ceux-ci.

Mohammedans, and some false Christians and heretics, as Marcion, Manes, Praxeas, Sabellius, Samosatenus, Arius, and such like, who have been justly condemned by the orthodox fathers.

Therefore, in this point, we do willingly receive the three creeds, namely, that of the Apostles, of Nice, and of Athanasius; likewise that which, conformable thereunto, is agreed upon by the ancient fathers.

Art. X.

DE ÆTERNA DEITATE FILII DEI, DOMINI NOSTRI JESU CHRISTI.

Art. X.

JESUS CHRIST IS TRUE AND ETERNAL GOD.

Nous croyons que Jésus-Christ, quant à sa nature divine, est Fils unique de Dieu,[1] éternellement engendré,[2] n'étant ni fait ni créé (car il serait créature), d'une essence avec le Père,[3] coéternel,[4] la marque engravée de la personne du Père, et la splendeur de sa gloire,[5] étant en tout semblable à Lui ;[6] lequel est Fils de Dieu non point seulement depuis qu'il a pris notre nature, mais de toute éternité ;[7] comme ces témoignages nous enseignent, étant rapportés l'un à l'autre. Moyse dit que Dieu a créé le monde ;[8] Saint-Jean dit que toutes choses

We believe that Jesus Christ, according to his divine nature, is the only begotten Son of God, begotten from eternity, not made nor created (for then he would be a creature), but co-essential and co-eternal with the Father, *the express image of his person, and the brightness of his glory*, equal unto him in all things. Who is the Son of God, not only from the time that he assumed our nature, but from all eternity, as these testimonies, when compared together, teach us. Moses saith that *God created the world ;* and John saith that *all*

---

[1] Jean i. 18, 49.
[2] Jean i. 14; Col. i. 15.
[3] Jean x. 30; Phil ii. 6.
[4] Jean i. 2; xvii. 5; Apoc. i. 8.
[5] Héb. i. 3.

[6] Phil. ii. 6.
[7] Jean viii. 23, 58; ix. 35, 36, 37; Act. viii. 37; Rom. ix. 5.
[8] Gen. i. 1.

ont été créées par la Parole, laquelle il appelle Dieu.[1] L'Apôtre dit que Dieu a fait les siècles par son Fils.[2] Saint-Paul dit encore que Dieu a créé toutes choses par Jésus-Christ.[3] Il faut donc que celui qui est nommé Dieu, Parole, Fils, et Jésus-Christ, ait déjà été lorsque toutes choses ont été créées par lui.[4] C'est pourquoi le prophète Michée dit : Son issue est dès les jours d'éternité.[5] Et l'Apôtre : Il est sans commencement de jours, sans fin de vie.[6] Il est donc le vrai Dieu éternel, le Tout-Puissant, lequel nous invoquons, adorons et servons.

things were made by that Word, which he calleth God; and the Apostle saith that God made the worlds by his Son; likewise, that God created all things by Jesus Christ. Therefore it must needs follow that he—who is called God, the Word, the Son, and Jesus Christ—did exist at that time when all things were created by him. Therefore the Prophet Micah saith: His goings forth have been from of old, from everlasting. And the Apostle: He hath neither beginning of days nor end of life. He therefore is that true, eternal, and almighty God, whom we invoke, worship, and serve.

Art. XI.

DE PERSONA ET ÆTERNA DEITATE SPIRITUS SANCTI.

Nous croyons et confessons aussi que le Saint-Esprit procède éternellement du Père[7] et du Fils,[8] n'étant ni fait, ni créé, ni aussi engendré, mais seulement procédant des deux; lequel est la troisième personne de la Trinité en ordre, d'une même essence et majesté et gloire avec le Père et le Fils, étant vrai et éternel

Art. XI.

THE HOLY GHOST IS TRUE AND ETERNAL GOD.

We believe and confess also that the Holy Ghost from eternity proceeds from the Father and Son; and therefore is neither made, created, nor begotten, but only proceedeth from both; who in order is the third person of the Holy Trinity; of one and the same essence, majesty, and glory with the Father and the Son; and therefore

---

[1] Jean i. 3.
[2] Héb. i. 2.
[3] Col. i. 16.
[4] Col. i. 16.

[5] Mich. v. 2.
[6] Héb. vii. 3.
[7] Psa. xxxiii. 6, 17; Jean xiv. 16.
[8] Gal. iv. 6; Rom. viii. 9 ; Jean xv. 26.

Dieu, comme nous enseignent les Écritures Saintes.[1]

is the true and eternal God, as the Holy Scripture teaches us.

Art. XII.

DE CREATIONE MUNDI, ET DE ANGELIS.

Nous croyons que le Père a créé de rien le ciel et la terre, et toutes créatures, quand bon lui a semblé, par sa Parole, c'est-à-dire par son Fils,[2] *donnant à chaque créature leur être, forme et figures, et divers offices pour servir à leur Créateur: et que maintenant même il les soutient et gouverne toutes selon sa providence éternelle et par sa vertu infinie,*[3] *pour servir à l'homme,*[4] *afin que l'homme serve à son Dieu.*[5] *Il a aussi créé les anges bons*[6] *pour être ses messagers*[7] *et pour servir à ses élus:*[8] *desquels les uns sont trébuchés de l'excellence en laquelle Dieu les avait créés, en perdition éternelle;*[9] *et les autres ont persisté et demeuré en leur premier état, par la grâce de Dieu.*[10] *Les diables et esprits malins sont tellement corrompus, qu'ils sont ennemis de Dieu et de tout bien, épiant l'Église comme brigands, de tout leur pouvoir,*[11]

Art. XII.

OF THE CREATION.

We believe that the Father, by the Word—that is, by his Son—created of nothing the heaven, the earth, and all creatures, as it seemed good unto him, giving unto every creature its being, shape, form, and several offices to serve its Creator; that he doth also still uphold and govern them by his eternal providence and infinite power for the service of mankind, to the end that man may serve his God. He also created the angels good, to be his messengers and to serve his elect: some of whom are fallen from that excellency, in which God created them, into everlasting perdition; and the others have, by the grace of God, remained steadfast, and continued in their primitive state. The devils and evil spirits are so depraved that they are enemies of God and every good thing to the utmost of their power, as murderers watching to ruin the Church

---

[1] Gen. i. 2; Es. xlviii. 16; lxi. 1; Act. v. 3, 4; xxviii. 25; 1 Cor. iii. 16; vi. 19; Psa. cxxxix. 7.
[2] Gen. i. 1; Es. xl. 26; Héb. iii. 4; Apoc. iv. 11; 1 Cor. viii. 6; Jean i. 3; Col. i. 16.
[3] Héb. i. 3; Psa. civ. 10, etc.; Act. xvii. 25.
[4] 1 Tim. iv. 3, 4; Gen. i. 29, 30; ix. 2, 3; Psa. civ. 14, 15.
[5] 1 Cor. iii. 22; vi. 20; Matt. iv. 10.
[6] Col. i. 16.
[7] Psa. ciii. 20; xxxiv. 8; cxlviii. 2.
[8] Héb. i. 14; Psa. xxxiv. 8.
[9] Jean viii. 44; 2 Pier. ii. 4; Luc viii. 31; Jud. 6.
[10] Matt. xxv. 31.
[11] 1 Pier. v. 8; Job i. 7.

et aussi chaque membre, pour tout détruire et gâter par leurs tromperies ;[1] c'est pourquoi, par leur propre malice, ils sont condamnés à perpétuelle damnation, attendant de jour en jour leurs tourments.[2] Et sur ceci nous détestons l'erreur des Sadducéens qui nient qu'il y ait des esprits et des anges,[3] et aussi l'erreur des Manichéens qui disent que les diables ont leur origine d'eux-mêmes, étant mauvais de leur propre nature sans avoir été corrompus.

and every member thereof, and by their wicked stratagems to destroy all; and are therefore, by their own wickedness, adjudged to eternal damnation, daily expecting their horrible torments. Therefore we reject and abhor the error of the Sadducees, who deny the existence of spirits and angels; and also that of the Manichees, who assert that the devils have their origin of themselves, and that they are wicked of their own nature, without having been corrupted.

Art. XIII.

DE PROVIDENTIA DEI.

Art. XIII.

OF DIVINE PROVIDENCE.

Nous croyons que ce bon Dieu, après avoir créé toutes choses, ne les a pas abandonnées à l'aventure ni à fortune ; mais les conduit et gouverne de telle façon, selon sa sainte volonté,[4] que rien n'advient en ce monde sans son ordonnance,[5] quoique toutefois Dieu ne soit point auteur ni coupable du mal qui arrive ; car sa puissance et bonté est tellement grande et incompréhensible, que même il or-

We believe that the same God, after he had created all things, did not forsake them, or give them up to fortune or chance, but that he rules and governs them, according to his holy will, so that nothing happens in this world without his appointment; nevertheless, God neither is the author of, nor can be charged with, the sins which are committed. For his power and goodness are so great and incom-

---

[1] Gen. iii. 1; Matt. xiii. 25; 2 Cor. ii. 11; xi. 3, 14.
[2] Matt. xxv. 41; Luc viii. 30, 31.
[3] Act. xxiii. 8.
[4] Jean v. 17; Héb. i. 3; Prov. xvi. 4; Psa. civ. 9, etc.; Psa. cxxxix. 2, etc.
[5] Jacq. iv. 15; Job i. 21; 1 Rois xxii. 20; Act. iv. 28; 1 Sam. ii. 25; Psa. cxv. 3; xlv. 7; Am. iii. 6; Deut. xix. 5; Prov. xxi. 1; Psa. cv. 25; Es. x. 5, 6, 7; 2 Thess. ii. 11; Ezéch. xiv. 9; Rom. i. 28; Gen. xlv. 8; l. 20; 2 Sam. xvi. 10; Gen. xxvii. 20; Psa. lxxv. 7, 8; Es. xlv. 7; Prov. xvi. 4; Lam. iii. 37, 38; 1 Rois xxii. 34, 38; Exod. xxi. 13.

donne et fait très-bien et justement son œuvre, quand même le diable et les méchants font injustement.[1] Et quant à ce qu'il fait outrepassant le sens humain, nous ne voulons nous en enquérir curieusement plus que notre capacité ne porte, mais, en toute humilité et révérence, nous adorons les justes jugements de Dieu qui nous sont cachés,[2] nous contentant d'être disciples de Christ, pour apprendre seulement ce qu'il nous montre par sa Parole, et ne point outrepasser ces bornes.

Cette doctrine nous apporte une consolation indicible, puisque nous sommes enseignés par elle, que rien ne nous peut arriver à l'aventure, mais par l'ordonnance de notre bon Père céleste, lequel veille pour nous par un soin paternel, tenant toutes créatures sujettes à lui ;[3] de sorte que pas un des cheveux de notre tête (car ils sont tous nombrés) ni même un petit oiseau, ne peut tomber en terre, sans la volonté de notre Père.[4] En quoi nous nous reposons, sachant qu'il tient les diables en bride, et tous nos ennemis, qui ne nous peuvent nuire sans sa permission et bonne volonté.

prehensible, that he orders and executes his work in the most excellent and just manner even when the devil and wicked men act unjustly. And as to what he doth surpassing human understanding we will not curiously inquire into it further than our capacity will admit of ; but with the greatest humility and reverence adore the righteous judgments of God which are hid from us, contenting ourselves that we are disciples of Christ, to learn only those things which he has revealed to us in his Word without transgressing these limits.

This doctrine affords us unspeakable consolation, since we are taught thereby that nothing can befall us by chance, but by the direction of our most gracious and heavenly Father, who watches over us with a paternal care, keeping all creatures so under his power that not a hair of our head (for they are all numbered), nor a sparrow, can fall to the ground, without the will of our Father, in whom we do entirely trust ; being persuaded that he so restrains the devil and all our enemies that, without his will and permission, they can not hurt us.

---

[1] Matt. viii. 31, 32 ; Jean iii. 8.
[2] Rom. xi. 33, 34.
[3] Matt. viii. 31 ; Job. i. 12 ; ii. 6.
[4] Matt. x. 29, 30.

Sur cela nous rejetons l'erreur damnable des Épicuriens, qui disent que Dieu ne se mêle de rien et laisse aller toutes choses à l'aventure.

And therefore we reject that damnable error of the Epicureans, who say that God regards nothing, but leaves all things to chance.

Art. XIV.

DE HOMINIS CREATIONE, LAPSU ET CORRUPTIONE.

Art. XIV.

OF THE CREATION AND FALL OF MAN, AND HIS INCAPACITY TO PERFORM WHAT IS TRULY GOOD.

Nous croyons que Dieu a créé l'homme du limon de la terre, et l'a fait et formé à son image et ressemblance,[1] bon, juste et saint, pouvant par son vouloir accorder en tout au vouloir de Dieu;[2] mais quand il a été en honneur, il n'en a rien su; et n'a pas reconnu son excellence,[3] mais s'est volontairement assujetti au péché, et par conséquent à mort et à malédiction, en prêtant l'oreille à la parole du diable.[4] Car il a transgressé le commandement de vie qu'il avait reçu,[5] et s'est retranché de Dieu, qui était sa vraie vie, par son péché,[6] ayant corrompu toute sa nature,[7] par où il s'est rendu coupable de mort corporelle et spirituelle,[8] et étant devenu méchant, pervers, corrompu en toutes ses voies, a perdu tous ses excellents dons qu'il avait reçus de Dieu,[9]

We believe that God created man out of the dust of the earth, and made and formed him after his own image and likeness, good, righteous, and holy, capable in all things to will agreeably to the will of God. But being in honor, he understood it not, neither knew his excellency, but willfully subjected himself to sin, and consequently to death and the curse, giving ear to the words of the devil. For the commandment of life, which he had received, he transgressed; and by sin separated himself from God, who was his true life, having corrupted his whole nature, whereby he made himself liable to corporal and spiritual death. And being thus become wicked, perverse, and corrupt in all his ways, he hath lost all his excellent gifts which he had received from God, and

---

[1] Gen. i. 26; Eccl. vii. 29; Eph. iv. 24.
[2] Gen. i. 31; Eph. 4. 24.
[3] Psa. xlix. 21; Es. lix. 2.
[4] Gen. iii. 6, 17.
[5] Gen. i. 3, 7.

[6] Es. lix. 2.
[7] Eph. iv. 18.
[8] Rom. v. 12; Gen. ii. 17; iii. 19.
[9] Rom. iii. 10, etc.

et il ne lui en est demeuré de reste
que de petites traces,[1] qui sont suffisantes pour rendre l'homme inexcusable,[2] d'autant que tout ce
qui est de lumière en nous est con-
verti en ténèbres,[3] comme l'Écriture nous enseigne, disant : La
lumière luit dans les ténèbres et
les ténèbres ne l'ont point comprise,[4] où saint Jean appelle les
hommes ténèbres.

Par quoi nous rejetons tout ce
qu'on enseigne du franc arbitre
de l'homme, parce qu'il n'est que
serf de péché,[5] et ne peut aucune
chose, s'il ne lui est donné du
Ciel;[6] car qui est-ce qui se van-
tera de pouvoir faire quelque
bien, comme de soi-même, puisque
Christ dit : Nul ne peut venir
à moi si mon Père qui m'a envoyé, ne l'attire?[7] Qui alléguera
sa volonté, entendant que l'affection de la chair est inimitié contre
Dieu?[8] Qui parlera de sa connaissance, voyant que l'homme sen-
suel ne comprend point les choses
qui sont de l'Esprit de Dieu?[9]
Bref, qui mettra en avant une
seule pensée? vu qu'il entend que
nous ne sommes pas capables de
penser quelque chose comme de

only retained a few remains thereof, which, however, are sufficient
to leave man without excuse; for
all the light which is in us is
changed into darkness, as the
Scriptures teach us, saying: The
light shineth in darkness, and the
darkness comprehendeth it not:
where St. John calleth men darkness.

Therefore we reject all that is
taught repugnant to this concerning the free will of man, since man
is but a slave to sin; and has nothing of himself unless it is given
him from heaven. For who may
presume to boast that he of himself can do any good, since Christ
saith, No man can come to me, except the Father which hath sent
me draw him? Who will glory
in his own will, who understands
that to be carnally minded is
enmity against God? Who can
speak of his knowledge, since the
natural man receiveth not the
things of the Spirit of God? In
short, who dare suggest any thought,
since he knows that we are not
sufficient of ourselves to think any
thing as of ourselves, but that our

---

[1] Act. xiv. 16, 17; xvii. 27.
[2] Rom. i. 20, 21; Act. xvii. 27.
[3] Eph. v. 8; Matt. vi. 23.
[4] Jean i. 5.
[5] Es. xxvi. 12; Psa. xciv. 11; Jean viii. 34; Rom. vi. 17; vii. 5, 17.
[6] Jean iii. 27; Es. xxvi. 12.
[7] Jean iii. 27; vi. 44, 65.
[8] Rom. viii. 7.
[9] 1 Cor. ii. 14; Psa. xciv. 11.

nous-mêmes mais que notre ca-
pacité est de Dieu ?[1] *C'est pour-*
quoi ce que dit l'Apôtre doit à bon
droit demeurer ferme et arrêté,
que Dieu fait en nous le vouloir
et le faire selon son bon plaisir.[2]
Car il n'y a ni entendement ni vo-
lonté conforme à celle de Dieu si
Christ n'y a opéré, ce qu'il nous
enseigne, disant : Sans moi vous
ne pouvez rien faire.[3]

sufficiency is of God? And therefore what the Apostle saith ought
justly to be held sure and firm,
that *God worketh in us both to
will and to do of his good pleasure.* For there is no will nor understanding, conformable to the divine will and understanding, but
what Christ hath wrought in man:
which he teaches us when he saith,
Without me ye can do nothing.

ART. XV.

DE PECCATO ORIGINALI.

Nous croyons que par la déso-
béissance d'Adam, le péché origi-
nel a été répandu par tout le genre
humain ;[4] *lequel péché est une cor-*
ruption de toute la nature, et un
vice héréditaire, duquel même sont
entachés les petits enfants au ven-
tre de leur mère :[5] *et qui produit*
en l'homme toute sorte de péché, y
servant de racine,[6] *dont il est tant*
vilain et énorme devant Dieu qu'il
est suffisant pour condamner le
genre humain,[7] *et n'est pas aboli*
même par le baptême, ou déraciné
du tout, vu que toujours les bouil-
lons en sortent comme d'une mal-
heureuse source ; quoique toutefois
il ne soit point imputé à condam-

ART. XV.

OF ORIGINAL SIN.

We believe that, through the disobedience of Adam, original sin is
extended to all mankind; which is
a corruption of the whole nature,
and an hereditary disease, wherewith infants themselves are infected even in their mother's womb,
and which produceth in man all
sorts of sin, being in him as a root
thereof; and therefore is so vile
and abominable in the sight of
God that it is sufficient to condemn all mankind. Nor is it by
any means abolished or done away
by baptism; since sin always issues
forth from this woful source, as
water from a fountain: notwithstanding it is not imputed to the

---

[1] 2 Cor. iii. 5.
[2] Phil. ii. 13.
[3] Jean xv. 5.
[4] Rom. v. 12, 13; Psa. li. 7; Rom. iii. 10; Gen. vi. 3; Jean iii. 6; Job xiv. 4.
[5] Es. xlviii. 8; Rom. v. 14.
[6] Gal. v. 19; Rom. vii. 8, 10, 13, 17, 18, 20, 23.
[7] Eph. ii. 3, 5.

nation aux enfants de Dieu, mais pardonné par sa grâce et miséricorde, non point afin qu'ils s'endorment, mais afin que le sentiment de cette corruption fasse souvent gémir les fidèles, désirant d'être délivrés du corps de cette mort.[1] Sur cela nous rejetons l'erreur des Pélagiens qui disent que ce péché n'est autre chose qu'une imitation.

children of God unto condemnation, but by his grace and mercy is forgiven them. Not that they should rest securely in sin, but that a sense of this corruption should make believers often to sigh, desiring to be delivered from this body of death. Wherefore we reject the error of the Pelagians, who assert that sin proceeds only from imitation.

Art. XVI.

DE PRÆDESTINATIONE DIVINA.

Nous croyons que toute la race d'Adam étant ainsi précipitée en perdition et ruine par la faute du premier homme, Dieu s'est démontré tel qu'il est, savoir miséricordieux et juste :[2] miséricordieux, en retirant et sauvant de cette perdition ceux qu'en son conseil éternel et immuable il a élus et choisis par sa pure bonté en Jésus-Christ notre Seigneur, sans aucun égard de leurs œuvres ;[3] juste, en laissant les autres en leur ruine et trébuchement où ils se sont précipités.[4]

Art. XVI.

OF ETERNAL ELECTION.

We believe that all the posterity of Adam, being thus fallen into perdition and ruin by the sin of our first parents, God then did manifest himself such as he is; that is to say, MERCIFUL AND JUST: MERCIFUL, since he delivers and preserves from this perdition all whom he, in his eternal and unchangeable council, of mere goodness hath elected in Christ Jesus our Lord, without any respect to their works: JUST, in leaving others in the fall and perdition wherein they have involved themselves.

---

[1] Rom. vii. 18, 24.

  Rom. ix. 18, 22, 23 ; iii. 12.

[3] Rom. ix. 15, 16 ; xi. 32 ; Eph. ii. 8, 9, 10 ; Psa. c. 3 ; 1 Jean iv. 10 ; Deut. xxxii. 8 ; 1 Sam. xii. 22 ; Psa. lxv. 5 ; Mal. i. 2 ; 2 Tim. i. 9 ; Rom. viii. 29 ; ix. 11, 21 ; xi. 5, 6 ; Eph. i. 4 ; Tit. iii. 4, 5 ; Act. ii. 47 ; xiii. 48 ; 2 Tim. ii. 19, 20 ; 1 Pier. i. 2 ; Jean vi. 27 ; xv. 16 ; xvii. 9.

[4] Rom. ix. 17, 18 ; 2 Tim. ii. 20.

Art. XVII.

DE REPARATIONE GENERIS HUMANI PER FILIUM DEI.

Nous croyons que notre bon Dieu par sa merveilleuse sagesse et bonté, voyant que l'homme s'était ainsi précipité en la mort, tant corporelle que spirituelle, et rendu entièrement malheureux, s'est lui-même mis à le chercher, lorsque l'homme s'enfuyait de lui tout tremblant,[1] et l'a consolé, lui faisant promesse de lui donner son Fils, fait de femme, pour briser la tête du serpent, et le faire bien-heureux.[2]

Art. XVIII.

DE INCARNATIONE FILII DEI.

Nous confessons donc que Dieu a accompli la promesse qu'il avait faite aux anciens Pères, par la bouche de ses saints Prophètes,[3] en envoyant son propre Fils unique et éternel au monde, au temps ordonné par lui; lequel a pris la forme de serviteur, fait à la ressemblance des hommes,[4] prenant vraiment à soi une vraie nature humaine, avec toutes ses infirmités (excepté le péché),[5] étant conçu dans

Art. XVII.

OF THE RECOVERY OF FALLEN MAN.

We believe that our most gracious God, in his admirable wisdom and goodness, seeing that man had thus thrown himself into temporal and spiritual death, and made himself wholly miserable, was pleased to seek and comfort him when he trembling fled from his presence, promising him that he would give his Son, who should *be made of a woman, to bruise the head of the serpent,* and would make him happy.

Art. XVIII.

OF THE INCARNATION OF JESUS CHRIST.

We confess, therefore, that God did fulfill the promise which he made to the fathers by the mouth of his holy prophets when he sent into the world, at the time appointed by him, his own only-begotten and eternal Son, *who took upon him the form of a servant, and became like unto men,* really assuming the true human nature, with all its infirmities, sin excepted, being conceived in the womb

---

[1] Gen. iii. 8, 9, 19 ; Es. lxv. 1, 2.
[2] Héb. ii. 14; Gen. xxii. 18; Es. vii. 14 ; Jean vii. 42 ; 2 Tim. ii. 8; Héb. vii. 14; Gen. iii. 15 ; Gal. iv. 4.
[3] Es. xi. 1; Luc i. 55; Gen. xxvi. 4; 2 Sam vii. 12; Psa. cxxxii. 11; Act. xiii 23.
[4] 1 Tim. ii. 5; iii. 16; Phil. ii. 7.
[5] Héb. ii. 14, 15; iv. 15.

le sein de la bienheureuse vierge Marie, par la vertu du Saint-Esprit sans œuvre d'homme;[1] et non seulement il a pris la nature humaine quant au corps, mais aussi une vraie âme humaine,[2] afin qu'il fût vrai homme: car puisque l'âme était aussi bien perdue que le corps il fallait qu'il prît à soi tous les deux pour les sauver ensemble. C'est pourquoi nous confessons—contre l'hérésie des Anabaptistes, niant que Christ a pris chair humaine de sa mère—que Christ a participé à la même chair et sang des enfants,[3] qu'il est fruit des reins de David selon la chair;[4] fait de la semence de David selon la chair;[5] fruit du ventre de la vierge Marie;[6] fait de femme;[7] germe de David;[8] rejeton de la racine de Jessé;[9] sorti de Juda;[10] descendu des Juifs selon la chair;[11] de la semence d'Abraham, puis qu'il a pris la semence d'Abraham,[12] et a été fait semblable à ses frères, excepté le péché;[13] de sorte qu'il est par ce moyen vraiment notre Emmanuel, c'est-à-dire Dieu avec nous.[14]

of the blessed Virgin Mary, by the power of the Holy Ghost, without the means of man; and did not only assume human nature as to the body, but also a true human soul, that he might be a real man. For since the soul was lost as well as the body, it was necessary that he should take both upon him, to save both. Therefore we confess (in opposition to the heresy of the Anabaptists, who deny that Christ assumed human flesh of his mother) that Christ is become *a partaker of the flesh and blood of the children;* that he is a *fruit of the loins of David* after the flesh; *made of the seed of David according to the flesh;* a *fruit of the womb* of the Virgin Mary; *made of a woman;* a *branch* of David; a *shoot of the root of Jesse; sprung from the tribe of Judah; descended from the Jews according to the flesh: of the seed of Abraham, since he took upon him the seed of Abraham, and became like unto his brethren in all things, sin excepted;* so that in truth he is our IMMANUEL, that is to say, *God with us.*

---

[1] Luc i. 31, 34, 35.
[2] Matt. xxvi. 38; Jean xii. 27.
[3] Héb. ii. 14.
[4] Act. ii. 30.
[5] Psa. cxxxii. 11; Rom. i. 3.
[6] Luc i. 42.
[7] Gal. iv. 4.
[8] Jér. xxxiii. 15.
[9] Es. xi. 1.
[10] Héb. vii. 14.
[11] Rom. ix. 5.　　[i. 1; Gal. iii. 16.
[12] Gen. xxii. 18; 2 Sam. vii. 12; Matt.
[13] Héb. ii. 15, 16, 17.
[14] Es. vii. 14; Matt. i. 23.

Art. XIX.

DE UNIONE HYPOSTATICA, SEU PERSONALI, DUARUM NATURARUM IN CHRISTO.

Nous croyons que par cette conception la personne du Fils a été unie et conjointe inséparablement avec la nature humaine, de sorte qu'il n'y a point deux Fils de Dieu ni deux personnes, mais deux natures unies en une seule personne, chaque nature retenant ses propriétés distinctes. Ainsi que la nature divine est toujours demeurée incréée, sans commencement de jours ni fin de vie,[1] remplissant le ciel et la terre : la nature humaine n'a pas perdu ses propriétés, mais est demeurée créature, ayant commencement de jours, étant d'une nature finie et retenant tout ce qui convient à un vrai corps.[2] Et encore que par sa résurrection il lui ait donné immortalité, néanmoins il n'a pas changé la vérité de sa nature humaine ; attendu que notre salut et résurrection dépendent aussi de la vérité de son corps. Mais ces deux natures sont tellement unies ensemble en une personne, qu'elles n'ont pas même été séparées par sa mort. Ce qu'il a donc en mourant recommandé à son Père c'était un

Art. XIX.

OF THE UNION AND DISTINCTION OF THE TWO NATURES IN THE PERSON OF CHRIST.

We believe that by this conception the person of the Son is inseparably united and connected with the human nature; so that there are not two Sons of God, nor two persons, but two natures united in one single person; yet each nature retains its own distinct properties. As then the divine nature hath always remained uncreated, without beginning of days or end of life, filling heaven and earth, so also hath the human nature not lost its properties, but remained a creature, having beginning of days, being a finite nature, and retaining all the properties of a real body. And though he hath by his resurrection given immortality to the same, nevertheless he hath not changed the reality of his human nature; forasmuch as our salvation and resurrection also depend on the reality of his body. But these two natures are so closely united in one person, that they were not separated even by his death. Therefore that which he, when dying, commended into the hands of his Father, was a real human spirit,

---

[1] Héb. vii. 3.
[2] 1 Cor. xv. 13, 21; Phil. iii. 21; Matt. xxvi. 11; Act. i. 2, 11; iii. 21; Luc xxiv. 39; Jean xx. 25, 27.

vrai esprit humain, lequel sortit de son corps,[1] *mais cependant la nature divine demeura toujours unie à l'humaine, même étant gisante au tombeau ; et la divinité ne laissait d'être en lui, comme elle était en lui quand il était petit enfant, quoique pour un peu de temps elle ne se démontrât pas ainsi.*

Voilà pourquoi nous le confessons être vrai Dieu et vrai homme : vrai Dieu pour vaincre la mort par sa puissance, et vrai homme, afin qu'il pût mourir pour nous selon l'infirmité de sa chair.

departing from his body. But in the mean time the divine nature always remained united with the human, even when he lay in the grave; and the Godhead did not cease to be in him, any more than it did when he was an infant, though it did not so clearly manifest itself for a while.

Wherefore we confess that he is VERY GOD and VERY MAN: very God by his power to conquer death, and very man that he might die for us according to the infirmity of his flesh.

ART. XX.

DE MODO REDEMPTIONIS, PER DECLARATIONEM JUSTITIÆ ET MISERICORDIÆ DEI IN CHRISTO.

ART. XX.

GOD HATH MANIFESTED HIS JUSTICE AND MERCY IN CHRIST.

Nous croyons que Dieu étant très-parfaitement miséricordieux et aussi très-juste, a envoyé son Fils prendre la nature en laquelle la désobéissance avait été commise, pour porter, en elle, la punition du péché par sa très-rigoureuse mort et passion.[2] *Dieu donc a déclaré sa justice envers son Fils, chargé de nos péchés,*[3] *et a répandu sa bonté et miséricorde sur nous, coupables et dignes de damnation, nous donnant son Fils à la mort,*

We believe that God, who is perfectly merciful and also perfectly just, sent his Son to assume that nature in which the disobedience was committed, to make satisfaction in the same, and to bear the punishment of sin by his most bitter passion and death. God therefore manifested his justice against his Son when he laid our iniquities upon him, and poured forth his mercy and goodness on us, who were guilty and worthy of dam-

---

[1] Luc xxiii. 46; Matt. xxvii. 50.
[2] Héb. ji. 14; Rom. viii. 3, 32, 33.
[3] Es. liii. 6; Jean i. 29; 1 Jean iv. 9.

par un très-parfait amour, et le ressuscitant pour notre justification;[1] *afin que par lui nous eussions immortalité et vie éternelle.*

nation, out of mere and perfect love, giving his Son unto death for us, and raising him for our justification, that through him we might obtain immortality and life eternal.

ART. XXI.

DE SATISFACTIONE CHRISTI PRO PECCATIS NOSTRIS.

Nous croyons que Jésus-Christ est grand Sacrificateur éternellement, avec serment, selon l'ordre de Melchisédec,[2] *et s'est présenté en notre nom devant son Père, pour apaiser sa colère avec pleine satisfaction,*[3] *en s'offrant lui-même sur l'autel de la croix, et répandant son précieux sang pour la purification de nos péchés, comme les Prophètes avaient prédit : car il est écrit que le châtiment qui nous procure la paix a été mis sur le Fils de Dieu, et que nous sommes guéris par ses plaies ; qu'il a été mené à la morte comme un agneau, mis au rang des pécheurs ;*[4] *condamné comme malfaiteur par Ponce Pilate, quoiqu'il le prononçât innocent.*[5] *Il a donc payé ce qu'il n'avait point ravi,*[6] *et a souffert, lui juste pour les injustes,*[7] *même en son corps*

ART. XXI.

OF THE SATISFACTION OF CHRIST, OUR ONLY HIGH-PRIEST, FOR US.

We believe that Jesus Christ is ordained with an oath to be an everlasting High-Priest, after the order of Melchisedec : who hath presented himself in our behalf before his Father, to appease his wrath by his full satisfaction, by offering himself on the tree of the cross, and pouring out his precious blood to purge away our sins ; as the prophets had foretold. For it is written, *He was wounded for our transgressions, he was bruised for our iniquities : the chastisement of our peace was upon him, and with his stripes we are healed ; he was brought as a lamb to the slaughter, and numbered with the transgressors ;* and condemned by Pontius Pilate as a malefactor, though he had first declared him innocent. Therefore, *he restored that which he took not away,* and

---

[1] Rom. iv. 25.
[2] Psa. cx. 4; Héb. v. 10.
[3] Col. i. 14; Rom. v. 8, 9; Col. ii. 14; Héb. ii. 17: ix. 14; Rom. iii. 24; viii. 2; Jean xv. 3; Act. ii. 24; xiii. 28; Jean ü. 16; 1 Tim. ii. 6.

[4] Es. liii. 5, 7, 12.
[5] Luc xxiii. 22, 24; Act. xiii. 28; Psa. xxii. 16; Jean xviii. 38; Psa. lxix. 5; 1 Pier. iii. 18.
[6] Psa. lxix. 5.
[7] 1 Pier. iii. 18.

et en son âme, de sorte que sentant l'horrible punition due à nos péchés, sa sueur devint comme grumeaux de sang découlant en terre.[1] Il a crié: Mon Dieu, mon Dieu, pourquoi m'as-tu délaissé?[2] et a enduré tout cela pour la rémission de nos péchés. C'est pourquoi, à bon droit, nous disons avec saint Paul, que nous ne connaissons autre chose sinon Jésus-Christ et Jésus-Christ crucifié;[3] nous estimons toutes choses comme de l'ordure, en comparaison de l'excellence de la connaissance de notre Seigneur Jésus-Christ;[4] nous trouvons toutes consolations en ses plaies, et n'avons besoin de chercher ni inventer d'autre moyen pour nous réconcilier avec Dieu, que ce seul et unique sacrifice une fois fait, lequel rend les fidèles parfaits à perpétuité;[5] c'est aussi la cause pourquoi il a été appelé par l'ange de Dieu, Jésus, c'est-à-dire Sauveur, vu qu'il devait sauver son peuple de ses péchés.[6]

suffered the just for the unjust, as well in his body as in his soul, feeling the terrible punishment which our sins had merited; insomuch *that his sweat became like unto drops of blood falling on the ground.* He called out, *My God, my God, why hast thou forsaken me?* And hath suffered all this for the remission of our sins. Wherefore we justly say with the Apostle Paul, *that we know nothing but Jesus Christ, and him crucified; we count all things but loss and dung for the excellency of the knowledge of Christ Jesus our Lord:* in whose wounds we find all manner of consolation. Neither is it necessary to seek or invent any other means of being reconciled to God, than this only sacrifice, once offered, by which believers are made perfect forever. This is also the reason why he was called by the angel of God, JESUS, that is to say, SAVIOUR, because he should save his people from their sins.

ART. XXII.

DE FIDE JUSTIFICANTE, ET DE JUSTIFICATIONE FIDEI.

Nous croyons que pour obtenir la vraie connaissance de ce grand mystère, le Saint-Esprit allume en

ART. XXII.

OF OUR JUSTIFICATION THROUGH FAITH IN JESUS CHRIST.

We believe that, to attain the true knowledge of this great mystery, the Holy Ghost kindleth in

---

[1] Luc xxii. 44.
[2] Psa. xxii. 2; Matt. xxvii. 46.
[3] 1 Cor. ii. 2.

[4] Phil. iii. 8.
[5] Héb. ix. 25, 26; x. 14.
[6] Matt. i. 21; Act. iv. 12.

nos cœurs une vraie foi, laquelle embrasse Jésus-Christ avec tous ses mérites, et le fait sien,[1] et ne cherche plus rien hors de lui.[2] Car il faut nécessairement que ce qui est requis pour notre salut ne .oit point tout en Jésus-Christ; ou, si tout y est, que celui qui a Jésus-Christ par la foi, ait tout son salut.[3] De dire donc que Christ ne suffit point, mais qu'il y faut quelque autre chose avec, c'est un blasphème trop énorme contre Dieu; car il s'ensuivrait que Jésus-Christ ne serait que demi Sauveur. C'est pourquoi, à juste cause, nous disons avec saint Paul, que nous sommes justifiés par la seule foi, ou par la foi sans les œuvres.[4] Cependant nous n'entendons pas à proprement parler, que ce soit la foi même qui nous justifie; car elle n'est que l'instrument par lequel nous embrassons Christ notre justice: mais Jésus-Christ nous allouant tous ses mérites et tant de saintes œuvres qu'il a faites pour nous et en notre nom, est notre justice,[5] et la foi est l'instrument qui nous tient avec lui en la com-

our hearts an upright faith, which embraces Jesus Christ with all his merits, appropriates him, and seeks nothing more besides him. For it must needs follow, either that all things which are requisite to our salvation are not in Jesus Christ, or if all things are in him, that then those who possess Jesus Christ through faith have complete salvation in Him. Therefore, for any to assert that Christ is not sufficient, but that something more is required besides him, would be too gross a blasphemy; for hence it would follow that Christ was but half a Saviour. Therefore we justly say with Paul, *that we are justified by faith alone,* or *by faith without works.* However, to speak more clearly, we do not mean that faith itself justifies us, for it is only an instrument with which we embrace Christ our Righteousness. But Jesus Christ, imputing to us all his merits, and so many holy works, which he hath done for us and in our stead, is our Righteousness. And faith is an instrument that keeps us in communion with him in all his benefits, which, when they

---

[1] Eph. iii. 16, 17; Psa. li. 13; Eph. i. 17, 18; 1 Cor. ii. 12.

[2] 1 Cor. ii. 2; Act. iv. 12; Gal. ii. 21; Jér. xxiii. 6; 1 Cor. i. 30; Jér. xxxi. 10.

[3] Matt. i. 21; Rom. iii. 27; viii. 1, 33.

[4] Rom. iii. 27; Gal. ii. 6; 1 Pier. i. 4, 5; Rom. x. 4.

[5] Jér. xxiii. 6; 1 Cor. i. 30; 2 Tim. i. 2; Luc i. 77; Rom. iii. 24, 25; iv. 5; Psa. xxxii. 1, 2; Phil. iii. 9; Tit. iii. 5; 2 Tim. i. 9.

munion de tous ses biens : lesquels étant fait nôtres, nous sont plus que suffisants pour nous absoudre de nos péchés.

ART. XXIII.

DE JUSTITIA NOSTRA QUA CORAM DEO CON-
SISTIMUS.

Nous croyons que notre béati-tude gît en la rémission de nos péchés à cause de Jésus-Christ, et qu'en cela est contenue notre jus-tice devant Dieu, comme David et saint Paul nous enseignent, déclarant la béatitude de l'homme, à qui Dieu alloue justice sans œuvres.[1] *Et le même Apôtre dit que nous sommes justifiés gratuite-ment ou par grâce, par la rédemp-tion qui est en Jésus-Christ.*[2] *C'est pourquoi nous tenons ce fondement ferme à jamais, don-nant toute gloire à Dieu,*[3] *en nous humiliant et reconnaissant tels que nous sommes, sans rien pré-sumer de nous mêmes ni de nos mérites,*[4] *et nous nous appuyons et reposons en la seule obéissance de Christ crucifié ;*[5] *laquelle est nôtre, quand nous croyons en lui.*[6] *Elle est suffisante pour cou-vrir toutes nos iniquités, et nous*

become ours, are more than suffi-cient to acquit us of our sins.

ART. XXIII.

OUR JUSTIFICATION CONSISTS IN THE FOR-
GIVENESS OF SIN AND THE IMPUTATION
OF CHRIST'S RIGHTEOUSNESS.

We believe that our salvation consists in the remission of our sins for Jesus Christ's sake, and that therein our righteousness before God is implied ; as David and Paul teach us, declaring this to be the happiness of man, that God im-putes righteousness to him without works. And the same Apostle saith, *that we are justified freely by his grace, through the redemp-tion which is in Jesus Christ.* And therefore we always hold fast this foundation, ascribing all the glory to God, humbling ourselves before him, and acknowledging ourselves to be such as we really are, without presuming to trust in any thing in ourselves, or in any merit of ours, relying and resting upon the obedience of Christ cru-cified alone, which becomes ours when we believe in him. This is sufficient to cover all our iniquities,

---

[1] Luc i. 77 ; Col. i. 14 ; Psa. xxxii. 1, 2 ;
   Rom. iv. 6, 7.
[2] Rom. iii. 23, 24 ; Act. iv. 12.
[3] Psa. cxv. 1 ; 1 Cor. iv. 7 ; Rom. iv. 2.

[4] 1 Cor. iv. 7 ; Rom. iv. 2 ; 1 Cor. i. 29, 31.
[5] Rom. v. 19.
[6] Héb. xi. 6, 7 ; Eph. ii. 8 ; 2 Cor v. 19 ;
   1 Tim. ii. 6.

rendre assurés, éloignant de notre conscience la crainte, l'horreur et l'épouvantement, pour nous approcher de Dieu[1] sans faire comme notre premier père Adam, lequel tremblant se voulait couvrir avec des feuilles de figuier.[2] Et de fait s'il nous fallait comparaître devant Dieu étant appuyés tant peu que ce soit sur nous, ou sur quelque autre créature, hélas! nous serions engloutis.[3] C'est pourquoi chacun doit dire avec David : O Seigneur, n'entre point en jugement avec tes serviteurs, car devant toi homme qui vive ne sera justifié.[4]

and to give us confidence in approaching to God; freeing the conscience of fear, terror, and dread, without following the example of our first father, Adam, who, trembling, attempted to cover himself with fig-leaves. And, verily, if we should appear before God, relying on ourselves or on any other creature, though ever so little, we should, alas! be consumed. And therefore every one must pray with David : *O Lord, enter not into judgment with thy servant : for in thy sight shall no man living be justified.*

Art. XXIV.

DE SANCTIFICATIONE, ET DE BONIS OPERIBUS.

Nous croyons que cette vraie foi étant engendrée en l'homme par l'ouïe de la Parole de Dieu et par l'opération du Saint-Esprit,[5] le régénère, et le fait un nouvel homme, le faisant vivre d'une nouvelle vie,[6] l'affranchissant de la servitude du péché.[7] Ainsi tant s'en faut que cette foi justifiante refroidisse les hommes de vivre bien et saintement,[8] que tout

Art. XXIV.

OF MAN'S SANCTIFICATION AND GOOD WORKS.

We believe that this true faith, being wrought in man by the hearing of the Word of God and the operation of the Holy Ghost, doth regenerate and make him a new man, causing him to live a new life, and freeing him from the bondage of sin. Therefore it is so far from being true, that this justifying faith makes men remiss in a pious and holy life, that on

---

[1] Rom. v. 1; Eph. iii. 12; 1 Jean ii. 1.
[2] Gen. iii. 7.
[3] Es. xxxiii. 14; Deut. xxvii. 26; Jacq. ii. 10.
[4] Psa. cxxx. 3; Matt. xviii. 23–26; Psa. cxliii. 2; Luc xvi. 15.

[5] 1 Pier. i. 23; Rom. x. 17; Jean v. 24.
[6] 1 Thess. i. 5; Rom. viii. 15; Jean vi. 29; Col. ii. 12; Phil. i. 1, 29; Eph. ii. 8.
[7] Act. xv. 9; Rom. vi. 4, 22; Tit. ii. 12; Jean viii. 36.
[8] Tit. ii. 12.

au rebours, sans elle jamais ils ne feront rien pour l'amour de Dieu, mais seulement pour l'amour d'eux-mêmes et craignant d'être condamnés. Il est donc impossible que cette sainte foi soit oisive en l'homme, vu que nous ne parlons pas de la foi vaine,[1] mais de celle que l'Écriture appelle foi opérante par la charité,[2] laquelle induit l'homme à s'exercer dans les œuvres que Dieu a commandées par sa Parole; lesquelles œuvres procédant de la bonne racine de foi, sont bonnes et reçues devant Dieu, puisqu'elles sont toutes sanctifiées par sa grâce. Cependant elles ne viennent point en compte pour nous justifier:[3] car c'est par la foi en Christ que nous sommes justifiés même avant de faire de bonnes œuvres;[4] autrement elles ne pourraient être bonnes, non plus que le fruit d'un arbre ne peut être bon, que premièrement l'arbre ne soit bon.[5]

Nous faisons donc de bonnes œuvres, mais non point pour mériter (car que mériterions-nous?) mais plutôt nous sommes redevables à Dieu pour les bonnes œuvres que nous faisons, et non pas

the contrary without it they would never do any thing out of love to God, but only out of self-love or fear of damnation. Therefore it is impossible that this holy faith can be unfruitful in man: for we do not speak of a vain faith, but of such a faith as is called in Scripture *a faith that worketh by love,* which excites man to the practice of those works which God has commanded in his Word. Which works, as they proceed from the good root of faith, are good and acceptable in the sight of God, forasmuch as they are all sanctified by his grace: howbeit they are of no account towards our justification. For it is by faith in Christ that we are justified, even before we do good works, otherwise they could not be good works any more than the fruit of a tree can be good before the tree itself is good.

Therefore we do good works, but not to merit by them (for what can we merit?)—nay, we are beholden to God for the good works we do, and not he to us, *since it is he that worketh in us both to will*

---

[1] Tit. iii. 8; Jean xv. 5; Héb. xi. 6; 1 Tim. i. 5.
[2] 1 Tim. i. 5; Gal. v. 6; Tit iii. 8.
[3] 2 Tim. i. 9; Rom. ix. 32; Tit. iii. 5.

[4] Rom. iv. 4; Gen. iv. 4.
[5] Héb. xi. 6; Rom. xiv. 23; Gen. iv. 4; Matt. vii. 17.

Lui envers nous,[1] puisque c'est lui qui met en nous le vouloir et le faire selon son bon plaisir,[2] regardant à ce qui est écrit : Quand vous aurez fait tout ce qui vous est commandé, dites : Nous sommes des serviteurs inutiles, ce que nous devions faire nous l'avons fait.[3]

Nous ne voulons pas cependant nier que Dieu ne rémunère les bonnes œuvres, mais c'est par sa grâce qu'il couronne ses dons.[4] Au reste, quoique nous fassions de bonnes œuvres, nous n'y fondons point notre salut :[5] car nous ne pouvons faire aucune œuvre qui ne soit souillée par notre chair, et aussi digne de punition,[6] et quand nous en pourrions montrer une, la mémoire d'un seul péché suffit pour la rejeter devant Dieu : de cette manière nous serions toujours en doute et flottant çà et là sans aucune certitude ; et nos pauvres consciences seraient toujours tourmentées, si elles ne se reposaient sur le mérite de la mort et passion de notre Sauveur.[7]

and to do of his good pleasure. Let us therefore attend to what is written : *When ye shall have done all those things which are commanded you, say we are unprofitable servants : we have done that which was our duty to do.*

In the mean time we do not deny that God rewards good works, but it is through his grace that he crowns his gifts. Moreover, though we do good works, we do not found our salvation upon them; for we can do no work but what is polluted by our flesh, and also punishable ; and although we could perform such works, still the remembrance of one sin is sufficient to make God reject them. Thus, then, we should always be in doubt, tossed to and fro without any certainty, and our poor consciences would be continually vexed if they relied not on the merits of the suffering and death of our Saviour.

ART. XXV.

DE ABROGATIONE LEGIS CEREMONIALIS, ET DE CONVENIENTA V. ET N. TESTAMENTI.

Nous croyons que les cérémonies et figures de la Loi ont cessé à la

ART. XXV.

OF THE ABOLISHING OF THE CEREMONIAL LAW.

We believe that the ceremonies and figures of the law ceased at the

---

[1] 1 Cor. iv. 7 ; Es. xxvi. 12 ; Gal. iii. 5 ; 1 Thess. ii. 13.
[2] Phil. ii. 13.
[3] Luc xvii. 10.
[4] Matt. x. 42 ; xxv. 34, 35 ; Apoc. iii. 12, 21 ; Rom. ii. 6 ; Apoc. ii. 11 ; 2 Jean viii. ; Rom. xi. 6.
[5] Eph. ii. 9, 10.
[6] Es. lxiv. 6.
[7] Es. xxviii. 16 ; Rom. x. 11 ; Hab. ii. 4.

venue de Christ,¹ et toutes ombres ont pris fin, de sorte que l'usage en doit être ôté entre les Chrétiens.² Toutefois la vérité et la substance nous en demeurent en Jésus-Christ, en qui elles ont leur accomplissement ; cependant nous usons encore des témoignages pris de la Loi et des Prophètes pour nous confirmer en l'Évangile,³ et aussi pour régler notre vie en toute honnêteté, à la gloire de Dieu, suivant sa volonté.

Art. XXVI.

DE INTERCESSIONE CHRISTI.

Nous croyons que nous n'avons d'accès vers Dieu, sinon par un seul Médiateur et Avocat Jésus-Christ, le juste,⁴ qui pour cette cause a été fait Homme, unissant ensemble la nature divine et humaine, afin que nous hommes ayons entrée vers la majesté divine : autrement nous n'y aurions point d'entrée. Mais ce Médiateur que le Père nous a donné entre lui et nous, ne nous doit pas épouvanter par sa grandeur, pour nous en faire chercher un autre à notre fantaisie :⁵ car il n'y a personne ni au ciel ni en terre entre les créatures, qui nous

coming of Christ, and that all the shadows are accomplished ; so that the use of them must be abolished among Christians : yet the truth and substance of them remain with us in Jesus Christ, in whom they have their completion. In the mean time we still use the testimonies taken out of the law and the prophets, to confirm us in the doctrine of the gospel, and to regulate our life in all honesty to the glory of God, according to his will.

Art. XXVI.

OF CHRIST'S INTERCESSION.

We believe that we have no access unto God save alone through the only Mediator and Advocate, Jesus Christ the righteous, who therefore became man, having united in one person the divine and human natures, that we men might have access to the divine Majesty, which access would otherwise be barred against us. But this Mediator, whom the Father hath appointed between him and us, ought in nowise to affright us by his majesty, or cause us to seek another according to our fancy. For there is no creature, either in heaven or on earth, who loveth us more than

---

¹ Rom. x. 4.
² Gal. v. 2–4 ; iii. 1 ; iv. 10, 11 ; Col. ii. 16, 17.

³ 2 Pier. i. 19.
⁴ 1 Tim. ii. 5 ; 1 Jean ii. 1 ; Rom. viii. 33.
⁵ Os. xiii. 9 ; Jér. ii. 13, 33.

aime plus que Jésus-Christ,[1] lequel, bien qu'il fût en la forme de Dieu, s'est anéanti lui-même, prenant la forme d'homme et de serviteur pour nous,[2] et s'est fait en tout semblable à ses frères. Si donc il nous fallait trouver un autre intercesseur qui nous ait en affection, qui trouverions-nous qui nous aime plus que celui qui a mis sa vie pour nous, lors même que nous étions ses ennemis?[3] Et s'il en faut trouver un qui ait crédit et puissance, qui est celui qui en a autant que celui qui est assis à la droite du Père, et qui a toute puissance au ciel et en la terre?[4] Et qui sera plutôt exaucé que le propre Fils de Dieu bien aimé?

La seule défiance donc a amené cette coutume de déshonorer les saints au lieu de les honorer, faisant ce que jamais ils n'ont fait ni demandé ; mais l'ont rejeté constamment, et selon leur devoir, comme il appert par leurs écrits.[5] Il ne faut pas ici alléguer que nous ne sommes pas dignes : car il n'est point ici question de présenter nos prières sur notre dignité mais seulement sur l'ex-

Jesus Christ ; *who, though he was in the form of God, yet made himself of no reputation, and took upon him the form of a man and of a servant for us, and was made like unto his brethren in all things.* If, then, we should seek for another mediator, who would be well affected towards us, whom could we find who loved us more than he who laid down his life for us, even when we were his enemies? And if we seek for one who hath power and majesty, who is there that hath so much of both as *he who sits at the right hand of his Father,* and who hath *all power in heaven and on earth?* And who will sooner be heard than the own well-beloved Son of God?

Therefore it was only through diffidence that this practice of dishonoring instead of honoring the saints was introduced, doing that which they never have done nor required, but have, on the contrary, steadfastly rejected, according to their bounden duty, as appears by their writings. Neither must we plead here our unworthiness; for the meaning is not that we should offer our prayers to God on account

---

[1] Jean x. 11 ; 1 Jean iv. 10 ; Rom. v. 8 ; Eph. iii. 19 ; Jean xv. 13.
[2] Phil. ii. 7.
[3] Rom. v. 8.
[4] Marc xvi. 19 ; Col. iii. 1 ; Rom. viii. 33 ; Matt. xi. 27 ; xxvii. 18.
[5] Act. x. 26 : xiv. 15.

cellence et la dignité de Jésus-Christ,[1] duquel la justice est nôtre par la foi.

C'est pourquoi, à bon droit, l'Apôtre nous voulant ôter cette folle crainte, ou plutôt défiance, nous dit que Jésus-Christ a été fait en tout semblable à ses frères, afin qu'il fût souverain sacrificateur, miséricordieux et fidèle pour purifier les péchés du peuple : car parce qu'il a souffert étant tenté, il est aussi puissant pour secourir ceux qui sont tentés.[2] Et puis après, afin de nous donner meilleur courage d'approcher près de lui, il dit : Nous donc ayant un souverain sacrificateur, Jésus Fils de Dieu, qui est entré aux cieux, tenons la confession : car nous n'avons point un souverain sacrificateur qui ne puisse avoir compassion de nos infirmités, mais qui a été tenté de même que nous en toutes choses excepté le péché ; allons donc avec confiance au trône de la grâce, afin que nous obtenions miséricorde, et trouvions grâce pour être aidés.[3] Le même Apôtre dit que nous avons liberté d'entrer au lieu saint par le sang

of our own worthiness, but only on account of the excellence and worthiness of our Lord Jesus Christ, whose righteousness is become ours by faith.

Therefore the Apostle, to remove this foolish fear or, rather, distrust from us, justly saith that *Jesus Christ was made like unto his brethren in all things, that he might be a merciful and faithful high-priest, to make reconciliation for the sins of the people. For in that he himself hath suffered, being tempted, he is able to succor them that are tempted.* And further to encourage us, he adds: *Seeing, then, that we have a great high-priest that is passed into the heavens, Jesus the Son of God, let us hold fast our profession. For we have not a high-priest which can not be touched with the feeling of our infirmities ; but was in all points tempted like as we are, yet without sin. Let us therefore come boldly unto the throne of grace, that we may obtain mercy, and find grace to help in time of need.* The same Apostle saith : *Having boldness to enter into the holiest by the blood of Jesus, let us draw near with a true heart in full assurance of faith,* etc. Likewise, *Christ hath*

---

[1] Dan. ix. 17, 18 ; Jean xvi. 23 ; Eph. iii. 12 ; Act. iv. 12 ; 1 Cor. i. 31 ; Eph. ii. 18.
[2] Héb. ii. 17, 18.
[3] Héb. iv. 14–16.

de Jésus : Allons donc, dit-il, en certitude de foi, etc.[1] *Et encore : Christ a perpétuelle sacrificature ; c'est pourquoi il peut sauver en plein ceux qui s'approchent de Dieu par lui, toujours vivant pour intercéder pour eux.*[2] *Que faut-il davantage? puisque Christ lui-même prononce : Je suis la voie, la vérité, la vie : nul ne peut venir à mon Père, sinon par moi.*[3] *A quel propos chercherons-nous un autre avocat ?*[4] *puisqu'il a plu à Dieu de nous donner son Fils pour être notre Avocat.*[5] *Ne le laissons point là pour en prendre un autre, ou plutôt chercher sans jamais trouver : car quand Dieu nous l'a donné, il savait bien que nous étions pécheurs.*

C'est pourquoi, suivant le commandement de Christ, nous invoquons le Père céleste par Christ notre seul Médiateur, comme nous sommes enseignés par l'Oraison Dominicale,[6] *étant assurés que tout ce que nous demanderons au Père en son nom, nous l'obtiendrons.*[7]

an unchangeable priesthood, wherefore he is able also to save them to the uttermost that come unto God by him, seeing he ever liveth to make intercession for them. What more can be required ? since Christ himself saith : *I am the way, and the truth, and the life ; no man cometh unto the Father but by me.* To what purpose should we then seek another advocate, since it hath pleased God to give us his own Son as our Advocate ? Let us not forsake him to take another, or rather to seek after another, without ever being able to find him ; for God well knew, when he gave him to us, that we were sinners.

Therefore, according to the command of Christ, we call upon the heavenly Father through Jesus Christ, our only Mediator, as we are taught in the Lord's Prayer ; being assured that whatever we ask of the Father in his name will be granted us.

Art. XXVII.

DE ECCLESIA CATHOLICA.

Nous croyons et confessons une seule Église catholique ou univer-

Art. XXVII.

OF THE CATHOLIC CHRISTIAN CHURCH.

We believe and profess one catholic or universal Church, which is

---

[1] Héb. x. 19, 22.
[2] Héb. vii. 24, 25.
[3] Jean xiv. 6.
[4] Psa. xliv. 21.

[5] 1 Tim. ii. 5 ; 1 Jean ii. 1 ; Rom. viii. 33.
[6] Luc xi. 2.
[7] Jean iv. 17 ; xvi. 23 ; xiv. 13.

selle,[1] *laquelle est une sainte con-*
grégation et assemblée des vrais
fidèles Chrétiens, attendant tout
leur salut en Jésus-Christ, étant
lavés par son sang, et sanctifiés et
scellés par le Saint-Esprit.

Cette Église a été dès le com-
mencement du monde, et sera
ainsi jusqu'à la fin,[2] comme il
appert en ce que Christ est Roi
éternel, qui ne peut être sans su-
jets.[3] Et cette sainte Église est
maintenue de Dieu contre la rage
de tout le monde,[4] encore que
pour quelque temps elle soit bien
petite en apparence, aux yeux
des hommes, et comme éteinte;[5]
comme le Seigneur pendant un
temps si dangereux qu'était celui
d'Achab, s'est réservé sept mille
hommes, qui n'ont pas ployé le
genou devant Baal.[6]

Aussi cette sainte Église n'est
point située, attachée ni limitée
en un certain lieu, ou à certains
personnages; mais elle est répan-
due et dispersée par tout le monde,
étant toutefois jointe et unie de
cœur et de volonté,[7] en un même
esprit par la vertu de la foi.[8]

a holy congregation and assembly
of true Christian believers, expecting all their salvation in Jesus
Christ, being washed by his blood,
sanctified and sealed by the Holy
Ghost.

This Church hath been from the
beginning of the world, and will
be to the end thereof; which is
evident from this, that Christ is an
eternal king, which, without subjects, he can not be. And this holy
Church is preserved or supported
by God against the rage of the
whole world; though she sometimes (for a while) appear very
small, and, in the eyes of men, to
be reduced to nothing: as during
the perilous reign of Ahab, when
nevertheless *the Lord reserved unto*
him seven thousand men, who had
not bowed their knees to Baal.

Furthermore, this holy Church
is not confined, bound, or limited
to a certain place or to certain persons, but is spread and dispersed
over the whole world; and yet is
joined and united with heart and
will, by the power of faith, in one
and the same spirit.

---

[1] Es. ii. 2; Psa. xlvi. 5; cii. 14; Jér.
xxxi. 36.
[2] Matt. xxviii. 20; 2 Sam. vii. 16.
[3] Luc i. 32, 33; Psa. lxxxix. 37, 38;
cx. 2-4.
[4] Matt. xvi. 18; Jean xvi. 33; Gen.
xxii. 17; 2 Tim. ii. 19.
[5] Luc xii. 32; Es. i. 9; Apoc. xii. 6, 14;
Luc xvii. 21; Matt. xvi. 18.
[6] Rom. xii. 4; xi. 2, 4; 1 Rois xix. 18;
Es. i. 9; Rom. ix. 29.
[7] Act. iv. 32.
[8] Eph. iv. 3, 4.

Art. XXVIII.

DE COMMUNIONE SANCTORUM CUM VERA ECCLESIA.

Nous croyons que puisque cette sainte assemblée et congrégation, est l'assemblée des sauvés, et qu'il n'y a point de salut hors d'elle,[1] *que nul, de quelque état et qualité qu'il soit, ne se doit retirer à part pour se contenter de sa personne,*[2] *mais tous ensemble s'y doivent ranger et unir, entretenant l'unité de l'Église,*[3] *en se soumettant à son instruction et discipline, ployant le col sous le joug de Jésus-Christ,*[4] *et servant à l'édification des frères, selon les dons que Dieu a mis en eux, comme membres communs d'un même corps;*[5] *et, afin que cela se puisse mieux garder, c'est le devoir de tous fidèles, selon la Parole de Dieu, de se séparer de ceux qui ne sont point de l'Église*[6] *pour se ranger à cette assemblée, en quelque lieu que Dieu l'ait mise,*[7] *encore que les magistrats, et les édits des Princes fussent contraires, et que la mort et punition corporelle en dépendît.*[8]

Art. XXVIII.

EVERY ONE IS BOUND TO JOIN HIMSELF TO THE TRUE CHURCH.

We believe, since this holy congregation is an assemblage of those who are saved, and out of it there is no salvation, that no person of whatsoever state or condition he may be, ought to withdraw himself, to live in a separate state from it; but that all men are in duty bound to join and unite themselves with it; maintaining the unity of the Church; submitting themselves to the doctrine and discipline thereof; bowing their necks under the yoke of Jesus Christ; and as mutual members of the same body, serving to the edification of the brethren, according to the talents God has given them. And that this may be better observed, it is the duty of all believers, according to the Word of God, to separate themselves from those who do not belong to the Church, and to join themselves to this congregation, wheresoever God hath established it, even though the magistrates and edicts of princes be against it; yea, though they should suffer death or bodily punishment.

---

[1] 1 Pier. iii. 20; Joel ii. 32.
[2] Act. ii. 40; Es. lii. 11.
[3] Psa. xxii. 23; Eph. iv. 3, 12; Héb. ii. 12.
[4] Psa. ii. 10–12; Matt. xi. 29. Eph. iv. 12, 16; 1 Cor. xii. 12. etc.

[6] Act. ii. 40; Es. lii. 11; 2 Cor. vi. 17; Apoc. xviii. 4.
[7] Matt. xii. 30: xxiv. 28; Es. xlix. 22; Apoc. xvii. 14.
[8] Dan. iii. 17, 18; vi. 8–10; Apoc. xiv. 14; Act. iv. 17, 19; xvii. 7; xviii 13.

Ainsi tous ceux qui s'en re-tirent, ou ne s'y rangent, contra-rient à l'ordonnance de Dieu.

Therefore all those who sepa-rate themselves from the same, or do not join themselves to it, act contrary to the ordinance of God.

ART. XXIX.

DE NOTIS VERÆ ECCLESIÆ.

Nous croyons qu'il faut bien diligemment discerner, et avec bonne prudence par la Parole de Dieu, quelle est la vraie Église, à cause que toutes les sectes qui sont aujourd'hui au monde se couvrent de ce nom d'Église.

Nous ne parlons pas ici de la compagnie des hypocrites qui sont mêlés parmi les bons en l'Église, et cependant n'en sont point, bien qu'ils y soient présents quant au corps ;[1] mais nous parlons de distinguer le corps et la com-munion de la vraie Église d'avec toutes autres sectes qui se disent être l'Église.

Les marques pour connaître la vraie Église sont telles : Si l'Église use de la pure pré-dication de l'Évangile ;[2] si elle use de la pure administration des sacrements, comme Christ les a ordonnés ;[3] si la discipline ecclésiastique est en usage pour

ART. XXIX.

OF THE MARKS OF THE TRUE CHURCH, AND WHEREIN SHE DIFFERS FROM THE FALSE CHURCH.

We believe that we ought dili-gently and circumspectly to dis-cern from the Word of God which is the true Church, since all sects which are in the world assume to themselves the name of the Church.

But we speak here not of the company of hypocrites, who are mixed in the Church with the good, yet are not of the Church, though externally in it ; but we say that the body and communion of the true Church must be dis-tinguished from all sects who call themselves the Church.

The marks by which the true Church is known are these : If the pure doctrine of the gospel is preached therein ; if she maintains the pure administration of the sac-raments as instituted by Christ ; if church discipline is exercised in punishing of sin ; in short, if all

---

[1] Matt. xiii. 22 ; 2 Tim. ii. 18–20 ; Rom. ix. 6.
[2] Jean x. 27 ; Eph. ii. 20 ; Act. xvii 11, 12 ; Col. i. 23 ; Jean viii. 47.
[3] Matt. xxviii. 19 ; Luc xxii. 19, etc. ; 1 Cor. xi. 23, etc.

corriger les vices.[1] *Bref, si on se règle selon la pure Parole de Dieu, rejetant toutes choses contraires à elle,[2] tenant Jésus-Christ pour le seul chef.[3] Par cela on peut être assuré de connaître la vraie Église, et n'est le devoir d'aucun d'en être séparé. Et quant à ceux qui sont de l'Église, on les peut connaître par les marques des Chrétiens ; savoir par la foi,[4] et quand, ayant reçu un seul sauveur Jésus-Christ,[5] ils fuient le péché et suivent justice,[6] aimant le vrai Dieu et leurs prochains, sans se détourner à droite ou à gauche, crucifiant leur chair avec ses faits ;[7] non pas toutefois qu'il n'y ait une grande infirmité en eux, mais ils combattent contre par l'Esprit, tous les jours de leur vie,[8] ayant continuellement recours au sang, à la mort, passion et obéissance du Seigneur Jésus, par lequel ils ont rémission de leurs péchés en la foi en lui.[9]*

Quant à la fausse Église, elle s'attribue à elle et à ses ordonnances plus d'autorité qu'à la Parole de Dieu.[10] Elle ne veut pas

things are managed according to the pure Word of God, all things contrary thereto rejected, and Jesus Christ acknowledged as the only Head of the Church. Hereby the true Church may certainly be known, from which no man has a right to separate himself. With respect to those who are members of the Church, they may be known by the marks of Christians, namely, by faith; and when they have received Jesus Christ the only Saviour, they avoid sin, follow after righteousness, love the true God and their neighbor, neither turn aside to the right or left, and crucify the flesh with the works thereof. But this is not to be understood as if there did not remain in them great infirmities; but they fight against them through the Spirit all the days of their life, continually taking their refuge in the blood, death, passion, and obedience of our Lord Jesus Christ, *in whom they have remission of sins through faith in him.*

As for the false Church, she ascribes more power and authority to herself and her ordinances than to the Word of God, and will not

---

[1] Matt. xviii. 15–18 ; 2 Thess. iii. 14, 15.
[2] Matt. xxviii. 2 ; Gal. i. 6–8.
[3] Eph. i. 22, 23 ; Jean x. 4, 5, 14.
[4] Eph. i. 13 ; Jean xvii. 20.
[5] 1 Jean iv. 2.

[6] 1 Jean iii. 8–10.
[7] Rom. vi. 2 ; Gal. v. 24.
[8] Rom. vii. 6, 17, etc. ; Gal. v. 17.
[9] Col. i. 14.
[10] Col. ii. 18, 19.

s'assujettir au joug de Christ.[1] *Elle n'administre point les sacrements selon que Christ a ordonné par sa Parole ; mais elle y ajoute et diminue, comme il lui plaît ; elle se fonde sur les hommes plus que sur Jésus-Christ ; elle persécute ceux qui vivent saintement selon la Parole de Dieu,*[2] *et qui la reprennent de ses vices, de ses avarices de ses idolâtries.*[3] *Ces deux Églises sont aisées à connaître pour les distinguer l'une de l'autre.*

submit herself to the yoke of Christ. Neither does she administer the Sacraments, as appointed by Christ in his Word, but adds to and takes from them as she thinks proper; she relieth more upon men than upon Christ; and persecutes those who live holily according to the Word of God, and rebuke her for her errors, covetousness, and idolatry. These two Churches are easily known and distinguished from each other.

Art. XXX.
DE REGIMINE ECCLESIÆ.

Art. XXX.
CONCERNING THE GOVERNMENT OF, AND OFFICES IN, THE CHURCH.

Nous croyons que cette vraie Église doit être gouvernée selon la police spirituelle que notre Seigneur nous a enseignée par sa Parole : savoir qu'il y ait des Ministres ou Pasteurs pour prêcher la Parole de Dieu et administrer les sacrements ;[4] *qu'il y ait aussi des Surveillants et des Diacres, pour être avec les Pasteurs, comme le sénat de l'Église,*[5] *et par ce moyen conserver la vraie religion, et faire que la vraie doctrine ait son cours, et aussi que les hommes vicieux soient corrigés spirituellement, et tenus sous*

We believe that this true Church must be governed by the spiritual policy which our Lord has taught us in his Word—namely, that there must be Ministers or Pastors to preach the Word of God, and to administer the Sacraments; also elders and deacons, who, together with the pastors, form the council of the Church; that by these means the true religion may be preserved, and the true doctrine every where propagated, likewise transgressors punished and restrained by spiritual means; also that the poor and distressed may be relieved and

[1] Psa. ii. 3.
[2] Apoc. xii. 4 ; Jean xvi. 2.
[3] Apoc. xvii. 3, 4, 6.

[4] Eph. iv. 11 ; 1 Cor. iv. 1, 2 ; 2 Cor. v. 20 ; Jean xx. 23 ; Act. xxvi. 17, 18 ; Luc x. 16.
[5] Act. vi. 3 ; xiv. 23.

bride ;[1] *afin aussi que les pauvres et tous affligés soient secourus et consolés, selon qu'ils en ont besoin. Par ce moyen toutes choses iront bien et par bon ordre en l'Église, quand de tels personnages seront élus fidèles et selon la règle qu'en donne saint Paul à Timothée.*[2]

comforted, according to their necessities. By these means every thing will be carried on in the Church with good order and decency, when faithful men are chosen, according to the rule prescribed by St. Paul to Timothy.

ART. XXXI.

DE VOCATIONE MINISTRORUM ECCLESIÆ.

Nous croyons que les Ministres de la Parole de Dieu,[3] *les Anciens, et les Diacres,*[4] *doivent être élus en leurs offices par élection légitime de l'Église, avec l'invocation du nom de Dieu, avec ordre, comme la Parole de Dieu enseigne. Chacun donc doit bien se donner garde de s'ingérer par moyens illicites, mais doit attendre le temps qu'il soit appelé de Dieu,*[5] *afin qu'il ait le témoignage de sa vocation, pour être certain et assuré qu'elle est du Seigneur.*

Et quant aux Ministres de la Parole, en quelque lieu qu'ils soient, ils ont une même puissance et autorité, étant tous Ministres de Jésus-Christ,[6] *seul Évêque universel et seul Chef de l'Église.*[7]

ART. XXXI.

OF THE MINISTERS, ELDERS, AND DEACONS.

We believe that the Ministers of God's Word, and the Elders and Deacons, ought to be chosen to their respective offices by a lawful election of the Church, with calling upon the name of the Lord, and in that order which the Word of God teacheth. Therefore every one must take heed not to intrude himself by indecent means, but is bound to wait till it shall please God to call him; that he may have testimony of his calling, and be certain and assured that it is of the Lord.

As for the Ministers of God's Word, they have equally the same power and authority wheresoever they are, as they are all Ministers of Christ, the only universal Bishop, and the only Head of the Church.

---

[1] Matt. xviii. 17; 1 Cor. v. 4, 5.
[2] 1 Tim. iii. 1, etc. ; Tit. i. 5, etc.
[3] 1 Tim. v. 22.
[4] Act. vi. 3.

[5] Jér. xxiii. 21; Héb. v. 4; Act. i. 23; xiii. 2.
[6] 1 Cor. iv. 1; iii. 9; 2 Cor. v. 20; Act. xxvi. 16, 17.　　　　[22; Col. i. 18.
[7] 1 Pier. ii. 25; v. 4; Es. lxi. 1; Eph. i.

De plus, afin que la saint or-
donnance de Dieu ne puisse être
violée ou venir à mépris, nous di-
sons que chacun doit avoir les
Ministres de la Parole et les An-
ciens de l'Église, en singulière
estime, pour l'œuvre qu'ils font,
et être en paix avec eux, sans
murmure, débat, ou contention,[1]
autant que faire se peut.

Moreover, that this holy ordinance of God may not be violated
or slighted, we say that every one
ought to esteem the Ministers of
God's Word and the Elders of the
Church very highly for their work's
sake, and be at peace with them
without murmuring, strife, or contention, as much as possible.

Art. XXXII.

DE POTESTATE ECCLESIÆ IN CONDENDIS
LEGIBUS ECCLESIASTICIS, ET IN ADMINI-
STRANDA DISCIPLINA.

Art. XXXII.

OF THE ORDER AND DISCIPLINE OF THE
CHURCH.

Nous croyons cependant que
bien qu'il soit utile et bon aux
gouverneurs de l'Église d'établir
et disposer certain ordre entre
eux, pour l'entretien du corps de
l'Église, ils se doivent toutefois
bien garder de décliner de ce que
Christ notre seul Maître nous a
ordonné.[2] *C'est pourquoi nous*
rejetons toutes inventions hu-
maines, et toutes lois qu'on vou-
drait introduire pour servir
Dieu, et par elles lier et étreindre
les consciences en quelque sorte
que ce soit.[3]

In the mean time we believe
though it is useful and beneficial
that those who are rulers of the
Church institute and establish certain ordinances among themselves
for maintaining the body of the
Church; yet they ought studiously
to take care that they do not depart
from those things which Christ,
our only master, hath instituted.
And, therefore, we reject all human inventions, and all laws which
man would introduce into the worship of God, thereby to bind and
compel the conscience in any manner whatever.

Nous recevons donc seulement
ce qui est propre pour garder
et nourrir concorde et union, et

Therefore we admit only of that
which tends to nourish and preserve
concord and unity, and to keep all

---

[1] 1 Thess. v. 12, 13; 1 Tim. v. 17; Héb. xiii. 17.
[2] Col. ii. 6, 7.
[3] 1 Cor. vii. 23; Matt. xv. 9; Es. xxix. 13; Gal. v. 1; Rom. xvi. 17, 18.

entretenir tout en l'obéissance de Dieu : à quoi est requise l'excommunication faite selon la Parole de Dieu[1] avec ce qui en dépend.

men in obedience to God. For this purpose excommunication or church discipline is requisite, with the several circumstances belonging to it, according to the Word of God.

Art. XXXIII.
DE SACRAMENTIS.

Nous croyons que notre bon Dieu ayant égard à notre rudesse et infirmité, nous a ordonné des Sacrements, pour sceller en nous ses promesses,[2] et nous être gages de la bonne volonté et grace de Dieu envers nous, et aussi pour nourrir et soutenir notre foi ; lesquels il a ajoutés à la parole de l'Évangile, pour mieux représenter à nos sens extérieurs, tant ce qu'il nous donne à entendre par sa Parole, que ce qu'il fait intérieurement en nos cœurs, en ratifiant en nous le salut qu'il nous communique. Car ce sont signes et sceaux visibles de la chose intérieure et invisible, moyennant lesquels Dieu opère en nous par la vertu du Saint-Esprit. Les signes donc ne sont pas vains et vides pour nous tromper et décevoir ; car ils ont Jésus-Christ pour leur vérité, sans lequel ils ne seraient rien.[3]

Art. XXXIII.
OF THE SACRAMENTS.

We believe that our gracious God, on account of our weakness and infirmities, hath ordained the Sacraments for us, thereby to seal unto us his promises, and to be pledges of the good will and grace of God towards us, and also to nourish and strengthen our faith, which he hath joined to the word of the gospel, the better to present to our senses, both that which he signifies to us by his Word, and that which he works inwardly in our hearts, thereby assuring and confirming in us the salvation which he imparts to us. For they are visible signs and seals of an inward and invisible thing, by means whereof God worketh in us by the power of the Holy Ghost. Therefore the signs are not in vain or insignificant, so as to deceive us. For Jesus Christ is the true object presented by them, without whom they would be of no moment.

---

[1] Matt. xviii. 17; 1 Cor. v. 5; 1 Tim. i. 20.
[2] Rom. iv. 11; Gen. ix. 13; xvii. 11.
[3] Col. ii. 11, 17; 1 Cor. v. 7.

De plus, nous nous contentons du nombre des sacrements que Christ notre Maître nous a ordonnés : lesquels ne sont que deux seulement, savoir le sacrement du Baptême et de la Sainte Cène de Jésus-Christ.[1]

Moreover, we are satisfied with the number of Sacraments which Christ our Lord hath instituted, which are two only, namely, the Sacrament of Baptism, and the Holy Supper of our Lord Jesus Christ.

ART. XXXIV.
DE BAPTISMO.

Nous croyons et confessons que Jésus-Christ, qui est la fin de la Loi,[2] *par son sang répandu, a mis fin à toute autre effusion de sang qu'on pourrait ou voudrait faire pour propitiation, ou satisfaction des péchés, et ayant aboli la circoncision qui se faisait par sang, a ordonné au lieu d'elle le sacrement du Baptême*[3] *par lequel nous sommes reçus en l'Église de Dieu, et séparés de tous autres peuples et de toutes religions étrangères, pour être entièrement dédiés à lui, portant sa marque et son enseigne : et nous sert de témoignage qu'il nous sera Dieu à jamais, nous étant Père propice. Il a donc commandé de baptiser tous ceux qui sont siens. au nom du Père et du Fils et du Saint-Esprit,*[4] *avec eau pure : nous signifiant par cela que comme l'eau lave les ordures du*

ART. XXXIV.
OF HOLY BAPTISM.

We believe and confess that Jesus Christ, who is the end of the law, hath made an end, by the shedding of his blood, of all other sheddings of blood which men could or would make as a propitiation or satisfaction for sin ; and that he, having abolished circumcision, which was done with blood, hath instituted the Sacrament of Baptism instead thereof, by which we are received into the Church of God, and separated from all other people and strange religions, that we may wholly belong to him whose ensign and banner we bear, and which serves as a testimony unto us that he will forever be our gracious God and Father. Therefore he has commanded all those who are his to be baptized with pure water, *in the name of the Father, and of the Son, and of the Holy Ghost :* thereby signifying

---

[1] Matt. xxvi. 36 ; xxviii. 19.
[2] Rom. x. 4.

[3] Col. ii. 11 ; 1 Pier. iii. 21 ; 1 Cor. x. 2.
[4] Matt. xxviii. 19.

corps quand elle est répandue sur nous, laquelle aussi est vue sur le corps du baptisé, et l'arrose ; ainsi le sang de Christ par le Saint-Esprit, fait le même intérieurement en l'âme, l'arrosant et nettoyant de ses péchés et nous régénérant d'enfants de colère en enfants de Dieu :[1] non pas que l'eau matérielle fasse cela, mais c'est l'arrosement du précieux sang du Fils de Dieu,[2] lequel est notre Mer Rouge, par laquelle il nous faut passer pour sortir de la tyrannie de Pharaon, qui est le diable, et entrer en la terre spirituelle de Canaan. Ainsi les Ministres nous donnent de leur part le Sacrement et ce qui est visible :[3] mais notre Seigneur donne ce qui est signifié par le Sacrement, savior les dons et grâces invisibles, lavant, purifiant, et nettoyant nos âmes, de toutes ordures et iniquités,[4] renouvelant nos cœurs et les remplissant de toute consolation, nous donnant vraie assurance de sa bonté paternelle, nous revêtant du nouvel homme et nous dépouillant du vieil homme avec tous ses faits.[5]

Pour cette cause, nous croyons que quiconque prétend parvenir à

to us, that as water washeth away the filth of the body, when poured upon it, and is seen on the body of the baptized, when sprinkled upon him, so doth the blood of Christ, by the power of the Holy Ghost, internally sprinkle the soul, cleanse it from its sins, and regenerate us from children of wrath unto children of God. Not that this is effected by the external water, but by the sprinkling of the precious blood of the Son of God ; who is our Red Sea, through which we must pass to escape the tyranny of Pharaoh, that is, the devil, and to enter into the spiritual land of Canaan. Therefore, the Ministers, on their part, administer the Sacrament, and that which is visible, but our Lord giveth that which is signified by the Sacrament, namely, the gifts and invisible grace ; washing, cleansing, and purging our souls of all filth and unrighteousness ; renewing our hearts and filling them with all comfort ; giving unto us a true assurance of his fatherly goodness ; putting on us the new man, and putting off the old man with all his deeds.

Therefore, we believe that every man who is earnestly studious of

---

[1] 1 Cor. vi. 11 ; Tit. iii. 5 ; Héb. ix. 14 ; 1 Jean i. 7 ; Apoc. i. 6.

[2] Jean xix. 34.

[3] Matt. iii. 11 ; 1 Cor. iii. 5, 7 ; Rom. vi. 3.

[4] Eph. v. 26 ; Act. xxii. 16 ; 1 Pier. iii. 21.

[5] Gal. iii. 27 ; 1 Cor. xii. 13 ; Eph. iv. 22-24.

la vie éternelle doit être une fois baptisé d'un seul baptême, sans jamais le réitérer :[1] *car aussi nous ne pouvons naître deux fois. Et toutefois ce baptême ne profite pas seulement quand l'eau est sur nous, et que nous la recevons, mais profite tout le temps de notre vie.*[2] *Sur ceci nous détestons l'erreur des Anabaptistes, qui ne se contentent pas d'un seul baptême une fois reçu, et en outre condamnent le baptême des petits enfants des fidèles, lesquels nous croyons devoir être baptisés et scellés du signe de l'alliance ;*[3] *comme les petits enfants étaient circoncis en Israël,*[4] *sur les mêmes promesses qui sont faites à nos enfants. Et aussi à la vérité Christ n'a pas moins répandu son sang pour laver les petits enfants des fidèles, qu'il a fait pour les grands ;*[5] *c'est pourquoi ils doivent recevoir le signe et le sacrement de ce que Christ a fait pour eux : comme en la loi le Seigneur commandait qu'on leur communiquât le sacrement de la mort et passion de Christ, quand ils étaient nouveau-nés, en offrant pour eux un agneau qui était le sacrement de Jésus-Christ.*[6] *Et*

obtaining life eternal ought to be but once baptized with this only Baptism, without ever repeating the same : since we can not be born twice. Neither doth this Baptism only avail us at the time when the water is poured upon us and received by us, but also through the whole course of our life. Therefore we detest the error of the Anabaptists, who are not content with the one only baptism they have once received, and moreover condemn the baptism of the infants of believers, who, we believe, ought to be baptized and sealed with the sign of the covenant, as the children in Israel formerly were circumcised upon the same promises which are made unto our children. And, indeed, Christ shed his blood no less for the washing of the children of the faithful than for adult persons ; and, therefore, they ought to receive the sign and sacrament of that which Christ hath done for them ; as the Lord commanded in the law, that they should be made partakers of the sacrament of Christ's suffering and death shortly after they were born, by offering for them a lamb, which was a sacrament of Jesus Christ. More-

---

[1] Marc xvi. 16 ; Matt. xxviii. 19 ; Eph. iv. 5 ; Héb. vi. 2.
[2] Act. ii. 38 ; viii. 16.
[3] Matt. xix. 14 ; 1 Cor. vii. 14.
[4] Gen. xvii. 11, 12.
[5] Col. ii. 11, 12.
[6] Jean i. 29 ; Lév. xii. 6.

de plus ce que faisait la circon-cision au peuple judaïque, le Baptême fait le même envers nos enfants : c'est la cause pourquoi saint Paul appelle le Baptême la Circoncision de Christ.[1]

over, what Circumcision was to the Jews, that Baptism is to our children. And for this reason Paul calls Baptism the *Circumcision of Christ.*

Art. XXXV.

DE CŒNA DOMINI.

Art. XXXV.

OF THE HOLY SUPPER OF OUR LORD JESUS CHRIST.

Nous croyons et confessons que notre Sauveur Jésus-Christ a ordonné et institué le sacrement de la sainte Cène,[2] *pour nourrir et sustenter ceux qu'il a déjà régénérés et entés en sa famille, qui est son Église. Or ceux qui sont régénérés ont en eux deux vies ;*[3] *l'une corporelle et temporelle, laquelle ils ont apportée dès leur première naissance, et est commune à tous ; l'autre est spirituelle et céleste, laquelle leur est donnée en la seconde naissance,*[4] *qui se fait par la parole de l'Évangile,*[5] *en la communion du corps de Christ, et cette vie n'est commune qu'aux élus de Dieu.*[6] *Ainsi Dieu nous a donné pour l'entretien de la vie corporelle et terrestre un pain terrestre et matériel, qui est propre à cela, lequel pain est commun à tous, comme aussi est la vie ; mais*

We believe and confess that our Saviour Jesus Christ did ordain and institute the Sacrament of the Holy Supper, to nourish and support those whom he hath already regenerated and incorporated into his family, which is his Church. Now those who are regenerated have in them a twofold life, the one bodily and temporal, which they have from the first birth, and is common to all men ; the other spiritual and heavenly, which is given them in their second birth, which is effected by the word of the gospel, in the communion of the body of Christ ; and this life is not common, but is peculiar to God's elect. In like manner God hath given us, for the support of the bodily and earthly life, earthly and common bread, which is subservient thereto, and is common to

---

[1] Col. ii. 11.
[2] Matt. xxvi. 26; Marc xiv. 22; **Luc** xxii. 19 ; 1 Cor. xi. 23–25.
[3] Jean iii. 6.

[4] Jean iii. 5.
[5] Jean v. 23, 25.
[6] 1 Jean v. 12; Jean x. 28.

pour entretenir la vie spirituelle et céleste qui se trouve dans les fidèles, il leur a envoyé un pain vivant qui est descendu du ciel, savoir Jésus-Christ,[1] lequel nourrit et entretient la vie spirituelle des fidèles, étant mangé, c'est-à-dire appliqué et reçu par la foi en l'esprit.[2] Pour nous figurer ce pain spirituel et céleste, Christ a ordonné un pain terrestre et visible qui est sacrement de son corps, et le vin pour sacrement de son sang,[3] pour nous certifier qu'aussi véritablement que nous prenons et tenons le sacrement en nos mains, et le mangeons et buvons en nos bouches, dont puis après notre vie est sustentée, aussi vraiment par la foi (qui est la main et la bouche de notre âme) nous recevons le vrai corps et le vrai sang de Christ, notre seul Sauveur, en nos âmes, pour notre vie spirituelle.[4]

Or c'est une chose assurée que Jésus-Christ ne nous a pas recommandé ses Sacrements pour néant : partant il fait en nous tout ce qu'il nous représente par ces signes sacrés ; encore que la manière outrepasse notre entendement, et nous soit incom-

all men, even as life itself. But for the support of the spiritual and heavenly life which believers have, he hath sent a living bread, which descended from heaven, namely, Jesus Christ, who nourishes and strengthens the spiritual life of believers, when they eat him, that is to say, when they apply and receive him by faith, in the Spirit. Christ, that he might represent unto us this spiritual and heavenly bread, hath instituted an earthly and visible bread as a Sacrament of his body, and wine as a Sacrament of his blood, to testify by them unto us, that, as certainly as we receive and hold this Sacrament in our hands, and eat and drink the same with our mouths, by which our life is afterwards nourished, we also do as certainly receive by faith (which is the hand and mouth of our soul) the true body and blood of Christ our only Saviour in our souls, for the support of our spiritual life.

Now, as it is certain and beyond all doubt that Jesus Christ hath not enjoined to us the use of his Sacraments in vain, so he works in us all that he represents to us by these holy signs, though the manner surpasses our understanding, and can not be comprehended by

---

[1] Jean vi. 32, 33, 51.
[2] Jean vi. 63.

[3] Marc vi. 26.
[4] 1 Cor. x. 16, 17; Eph. iii. 17; Jean vi. 35.

préhensible, comme l'opération de l'Esprit de Dieu est secrète et incompréhensible. Cependant nous ne nous trompons pas en disant que ce qui est mangé est le propre et naturel corps de Christ, et son propre sang ce qui est bu;[1] mais la manière par laquelle nous le mangeons, n'est pas la bouche mais l'esprit par la foi. Ainsi Jésus-Christ demeure toujours assis à la droite de Dieu son Père dans les cieux,[2] et ne laisse pas pour cela de se communiquer à nous par la foi. Ce banquet est une table spirituelle en laquelle Christ se communique à nous avec tous ses biens, et nous fait jouir en elle, tant de lui-même que du mérite de sa mort et passion,[3] nourrissant, fortifiant et consolant notre pauvre âme désolée, par le manger de sa chair, et la soulageant et recréant par le breuvage de son sang.[4]

En outre, bien que les sacrements soient conjoints à la chose signifiée, ils ne sont pas toutefois reçus de tous avec ces deux choses: le méchant prend bien le sacrement à sa condamnation;[5] mais il ne reçoit pas la vérité du sacre-

us, as the operations of the Holy Ghost are hidden and incomprehensible. In the mean time we err not when we say that what is eaten and drunk by us is the proper and natural body and the proper blood of Christ. But the manner of our partaking of the same is not by the mouth, but by the Spirit through faith. Thus, then, though Christ always sits at the right hand of his Father in the heavens, yet doth he not, therefore, cease to make us partakers of himself by faith. This feast is a spiritual table, at which Christ communicates himself with all his benefits to us, and gives us there to enjoy both himself and the merits of his sufferings and death, nourishing, strengthening, and comforting our poor comfortless souls, by the eating of his flesh, quickening and refreshing them by the drinking of his blood.

Further, though the Sacraments are connected with the thing signified, nevertheless both are not received by all men: the ungodly indeed receives the Sacrament to his condemnation, but he doth not receive the truth of the

---

[1] Jean vi. 55, 56; 1 Cor. x. 16.
[2] Act. iii. 21; Marc xvi. 19; Matt. xxvi. 11.
[3] Matt. xxvi. 26, etc.; Luc xxii. 19, 20; 1 Cor. x. 2–4
[4] Es. lv. 2; Rom. viii. 22, 23.
[5] 1 Cor. xi. 29; 2 Cor. vi. 14. 15; 1 Cor. ii. 14.

ment; comme Judas et Simon le magicien recevaient bien tous deux le sacrement, mais non pas Christ, qui y est signifié: ce qui est seulement communiqué aux fidèles. Finalement nous recevons ce saint sacrement en l'assemblée du peuple de Dieu avec humilité et révérence,[1] en faisant entre nous une sainte mémoire de la mort de Christ notre Sauveur avec actions de grâces, et y faisons confession de notre foi et religion chrétienne. C'est pourquoi nul ne se doit présenter qu'il ne se soit bien éprouvé soi-même, de peur qu'en mangeant de ce pain, et buvant de cette coupe, il ne mange et boive son jugement.[2] Bref, nous sommes par l'usage de ce saint sacrement émus à un ardent amour envers Dieu et nos prochains.

En quoi nous rejetons toutes les brouilleries et inventions damnables que les hommes ont ajoutées et mêlées aux sacrements, comme profanations, et disons qu'on se doit contenter de l'ordre que Christ et ses Apôtres nous en ont enseigné, et parler comme ils en ont parlé.

Sacrament. As Judas and Simon the sorcerer both, indeed, received the Sacrament, but not Christ, who was signified by it, of whom believers only are made partakers. Lastly, we receive this holy Sacrament in the assembly of the people of God, with humility and reverence, keeping up among us a holy remembrance of the death of Christ our Saviour, with thanksgiving, making there confession of our faith and of the Christian religion. Therefore no one ought to come to this table without having previously rightly examined himself; lest by eating of this bread and drinking of this cup he eat and drink judgment to himself. In a word, we are excited by the use of this holy Sacrament to a fervent love towards God and our neighbor.

Therefore, we reject all mixtures and damnable inventions, which men have added unto and blended with the Sacraments, as profanations of them, and affirm that we ought to rest satisfied with the ordinance which Christ and his Apostles have taught us, and that we must speak of them in the same manner as they have spoken.

---

[1] Act. ii. 42; xx. 7.

[2] 1 Cor. xi. 27, 28.

ART. XXXVI.

DE MAGISTRATU.

Nous croyons que notre bon Dieu, à cause de la dépravation du genre humain, a ordonné des Rois, Princes, et Magistrats;[1] voulant que le monde soit gouverné par lois et polices, afin que le débordement des hommes soit réprimé, et que tout se fasse avec bon ordre entre les hommes. Pour cette fin il a mis le glaive dans les mains du Magistrat pour punir les méchants, et maintenir les gens de bien : et non seulement leur office est de prendre garde et veiller sur la police, mais aussi de maintenir le sacré ministère, pour ôter et ruiner toute idolâtrie et faux service de Dieu;[2] pour détruire le royaume de l'antechrist et avancer le royaume de Jésus-Christ, faire prêcher la Parole de l'Évangile partout, afin que Dieu soit honoré et servi de chacun, comme il le requiert par sa Parole.[3]

ART. XXXVI.

OF MAGISTRATES.

We believe that our gracious God, because of the depravity of mankind, hath appointed kings, princes, and magistrates, willing that the world should be governed by certain laws and policies; to the end that the dissoluteness of men might be restrained, and all things carried on among them with good order and decency. For this purpose he hath invested the magistracy with the sword, *for the punishment of evil doers, and for the praise of them that do well.* And their office is, not only to have regard unto and watch for the welfare of the civil state, but also that they protect the sacred ministry, and thus may remove and prevent all idolatry and false worship; that the kingdom of antichrist may be thus destroyed, and the kingdom of Christ promoted. They must, therefore, countenance the preaching of the word of the gospel every where, that God may be honored and worshiped by every one, as he commands in his Word.[3]

---

[1] Ex. xviii. 20, etc.; Rom. xiii. 1; Prov. viii. 15; Jér. xxi. 12; xxii. 2, 3; Psa. lxxxii. 1, 6; ci. 2, etc.; Deut. i. 15, 16; xvi. 18; xvii. 15; Dan. ii. 21, 37; v. 18.

[2] Es. xlix. 23, 25; 1 Rois xv. 12; 2 Rois xxiii. 2–4, etc.

[3] [This section, like the corresponding sections in other Reformed Confessions, is framed on the theory of a union of Church and State, and is applicable to Free Churches only so far as they may justly claim from the civil government legal protection in all their rights.—ED.]

De plus chacun, de quelque qualité, condition, ou état qu'il soit, doit être soumis aux Magistrats,[1] et payer les tributs;[2] les avoir en honneur et révérence, et leur obéir en toutes choses qui ne sont point contraires à la Parole de Dieu ;[3] priant pour eux en leurs oraisons, afin que le Seigneur les veuille diriger en toutes leurs voies, et que nous menions une vie paisible et tranquille en toute piété et honnêteté.[4]

Et sur ceci nous détestons l'erreur des Anabaptistes et autres mutins, et en général de tous ceux qui veulent rejeter les autorités et Magistrats, et renverser la justice,[5] établissant communautés de biens, et confondant l'honnêteté que Dieu a mise entre les hommes.[6]

Moreover, it is the bounden duty of every one, of what state, quality, or condition soever he may be, to subject himself to the magistrates; to pay tribute, to show due honor and respect to them, and to obey them in all things which are not repugnant to the Word of God; to supplicate for them in their prayers, that God may rule and guide them in all their ways, and that we may lead a quiet and peaceable life in all godliness and honesty.

Wherefore we detest the error of the Anabaptists and other seditious people, and in general all those who reject the higher powers and magistrates, and would subvert justice, introduce a community of goods, and confound that decency and good order which God hath established among men.

Art. XXXVII.

DE JUDICIO EXTREMO, RESURRECTIONE CARNIS, ET VITA ÆTERNA.

Art. XXXVII.

OF THE LAST JUDGMENT.

Finalement nous croyons selon la Parole de Dieu, que quand le temps ordonné du Seigneur sera venu (lequel est inconnu a toutes créatures)[7] et le nombre des Elus sera accompli, notre Seigneur Jésus-Christ viendra du Ciel cor-

Finally, we believe, according to the Word of God, when the time appointed by the Lord (which is unknown to all creatures) is come, and the number of the elect complete, that our Lord Jesus Christ will come from heaven, corporally

---

[1] Tit. iii. 1 ; Rom. xiii. 1.
[2] Marc xii. 17 ; Matt. xvii. 24.
[3] Act. iv. 17–19 ; v. 29 ; Os. v. 11.
[4] Jér. xxix. 7 ; 1 Tim. ii. 1, 2.

[5] 2 Pier. ii. 10.
[6] Jud. 8 et 10.
[7] Matt. xxiv. 36 ; xxv. 13 ; 1 Thess. v. 1, 2 ; Apoc. vi. 11 ; Act. i. 7 ; 2 Pier. iii. 10.

porellement et visiblement, comme il y est monté,[1] *avec grande gloire et majesté, pour se déclarer être le juge des vivants et des morts,*[2] *mettant en feu et en flamme ce vieux monde pour le purifier;*[3] *et alors comparaîtront personnellement devant ce grand juge toutes créatures humaines, tant hommes que femmes et enfants, qui auront été depuis le commencement du monde jusqu'à la fin,*[4] *y étant citées par la voix d'archange et par le son de la trompette divine;*[5] *car tous ceux qui auront auparavant été morts ressusciteront de la terre, l'esprit étant joint et uni avec son propre corps dans lequel il a vécu.*[6] *Et quant à ceux qui vivront alors, ils ne mourront point comme les autres, mais seront changés, en un clin d'œil, de corruption en incorruption.*[7]

Alors les livres seront ouverts (c'est-à-dire les consciences) et les morts seront jugés selon les choses qu'ils auront faites en ce monde, soit bien, soit mal;[8] *même les*

and visibly, as he ascended with great glory and majesty, to declare himself Judge of the quick and the dead, burning this old world with fire and flame to cleanse it. And then all men will personally appear before this great Judge, both men and women and children, that have been from the beginning of the world to the end thereof, being summoned by the voice of the archangel, and by the sound of the trumpet of God. For all the dead shall be raised out of the earth, and their souls joined and united with their proper bodies in which they formerly lived. As for those who shall then be living, they shall not die as the others, but be changed in the twinkling of an eye, and from corruptible become incorruptible.

Then the books (that is to say, the consciences) shall be opened, and the dead judged according to what they shall have done in this world, whether it be good or evil. Nay,

---

[1] Act. i. 11.

[2] 2 Thess. i. 7, 8; Act. xvii. 31; Matt. xxiv. 30; xxv. 31; Jud. 15; 1 Pier. iv. 5; 2 Tim. iv. 1.

[3] 2 Pier. iii. 7, 10; 2 Thess. i. 8.

[4] Apoc. xx. 12, 13; Act. xvii. 31; Héb. vi. 2; ix. 27; 2 Cor. v. 10; Rom. xiv. 10.

[5] 1 Cor. xv. 42; Apoc. xx. 12, 13; 1 Thess. iv. 16.

[6] Jean v. 28, 29; vi. 54; Dan. xii. 2; Job xix. 26, 27.

[7] 1 Cor. xv. 51–53.

[8] Apoc. xx. 12, 13; 1 Cor. iv. 5; Rom. xiv. 11, 12; Job xxxiv. 11; Jean v. 24; Dan. xii. 2; Psa. lxii. 13; Matt. xi. 22; xxiii. 33; Jean v. 29; Rom. ii. 5, 6; 2 Cor. v. 10; Héb. vi. ix. 27.

hommes rendront compte de toutes paroles oiseuses qu'ils auront prononcées, lesquelles le monde n'estime que jeux et passetemps:[1] *et lors les actions et pensées secrètes et les hypocrisies des hommes seront découvertes publiquement devant tous.*[2]

C'est pourquoi, à bon droit, le souvenir de ce jugement est horrible et épouvantable aux iniques et méchants,[3] *et fort désirable et de grande consolation aux bons et élus ; puisque alors sera accomplie leur rédemption totale, et qu'ils recevront là les fruits des labeurs et travaux qu'ils auront soutenus :*[4] *leur innocence sera ouvertement connue de tous, et ils verront la vengeance horrible que Dieu fera des méchants*[5] *qui les auront tyrannisés, affligés et tourmentés en ce monde,*[6] *lesquels seront convaincus par le propre témoignage de leurs consciences*[7] *et seront rendus immortels, de telle façon que ce sera pour être tourmentés au feu éternel,*[8] *qui est préparé au diable et à ses anges.*[9]

Et au contraire les fidèles et élus seront couronnés de gloire et

all men shall give an account of every idle word they have spoken, which the world only counts amusement and jest; and then the secrets and hypocrisy of men shall be disclosed and laid open before all.

And, therefore, the consideration of this judgment is justly terrible and dreadful to the wicked and ungodly, but most desirable and comfortable to the righteous and the elect; because then their full deliverance shall be perfected, and there they shall receive the fruits of their labor and trouble which they have borne. Their innocence shall be known to all, and they shall see the terrible vengeance which God shall execute on the wicked, who most cruelly persecuted, oppressed, and tormented them in this world; and who shall be convicted by the testimony of their own consciences, and, being immortal, shall be tormented in that everlasting fire which is prepared for the devil and his angels.

But on the contrary, the faithful and elect shall be crowned with

---

[1] Rom. ii. 5; Jud. 15; Matt. xii. 36.
[2] 1 Cor. iv. 5; Rom. ii. 1, 2, 16; Matt. vii. 1, 2.
[3] Apoc. vi. 15, 16; Héb. x. 27.
[4] Luc xxi. 28; 1 Jean iii. 2; iv. 17; Apoc. xiv. 7; 2 Thess. i. 5, 7; Luc xiv. 14.

[5] Dan. vii. 26.
[6] Matt. xxv. 46; 2 Thess. i. 6-8; **Mal** iv. 3.
[7] Rom. ii. 15.
[8] Apoc. xxi. 8; 2 Pier. ii. 9.
[9] Mal. iv. 1; Matt. xxv. 41.

d'honneur ;[1] *le Fils de Dieu con-fessera leur nom devant Dieu son Père et ses saints Anges élus ;*[2] *toutes larmes seront essuyées de leurs yeux ;*[3] *leur cause à présent condamnée par plusieurs Juges et Magistrats comme hérétique et méchante sera connue être la cause du Fils de Dieu ;*[4] *et pour récompense gratuite le Seigneur leur fera posséder une gloire telle que jamais cœur d'homme ne pourrait penser.*[5]

C'est pourquoi nous attendons ce grand jour avec désir, pour jouir à plein des promesses de Dieu en Jésus-Christ notre Seigneur.[6]

glory and honor; and the Son of God will confess their names before God his Father, and his elect angels; all tears shall be wiped from their eyes; and their cause, which is now condemned by many judges and magistrates as heretical and impious, will then be known to be the cause of the Son of God. And, for a gracious reward, the Lord will cause them to possess such a glory as never entered into the heart of man to conceive.

Therefore we expect that great day with a most ardent desire, to the end that we may fully enjoy the promises of God in Christ Jesus our Lord.   Amen.

Even so, come Lord Jesus.   Rev. xxii. 20.[7]

---

[1] Matt. xxv. 34; xiii. 43.
[2] Matt. x. 32.
[3] Es. xxv. 8; Apoc. xxi. 4.
[4] Es. lxvi. 5.
[5] Es. lxiv. 4; 1 Cor. ii. 9.

[6] Héb. x. 36–38.
[7] [From the Latin edition, which closes—
'*Apocal.* xxii. 20: *Etiam veni Domine Jesu.*']

CONFESSIO FIDEI SCOTICANA I.

THE SCOTCH CONFESSION OF FAITH. A.D. 1560.

[The English and Latin texts are an exact reprint from (Dunlop's) *Collection of Confessions of Faith, Catechisms, Directories, Books of Discipline, etc., of Publick Authority in the Church of Scotland* (Edinb. 1719, 1722, 2 vols.), Vol. II. pp. 13 sqq. The English original is given in the old spelling from a copy in Sir John Skene's edition of the Acts of Parliament, compared with many other editions. The Scripture passages are from Tyndale's and Coverdale's Version, then generally used among Protestants in England and Scotland. The Latin translation was made by PATRICK ADAMSON, at the desire of the Kirk, and printed by Robert Lekprevik, Andreapoli, 1572. Another but less accurate Latin translation is found in the *Syntagma Confessionum* (1654), pp. 110 sqq., and in Niemeyer's *Collectio*, pp. 340 sqq. For a German translation, see Böckel's *Bekenntniss-Schriften*, pp. 645 sqq.]

THE

CONFESSION

OF THE

Faith and Doctrine,

Belevit and professit be the

PROTESTANTIS of Scotland,

Exhibitit to the Estaitis of the same in Parliament, and be their publick Votis authorisit, as a Doctrine groundit upon the infallibil Worde of God, *Aug.* 1560. And afterwards stablished and publicklie confirmed be sundrie Acts of Parliaments, and of lawful General Assemblies.

CONFESSIO

FIDEI & DOCTRINÆ

Per ECCLESIAM Reformatam

Regni *SCOTIÆ* professæ,

Exhibitæ ordinibus Regni ejusdem in publicis Parliamenti, ut vocant, Comitiis, & eorum communi consensu approbatæ, uti certissimis fundamentis verbi Dei innixæ & consentaneæ, 1560; deinde in conventu ordinum, lege confirmatæ & stabilitæ, 1567.

THE PREFACE.

The Estaitis of *Scotland* with the Inhabitants of the same professand *Christ Jesus* his haly Evangel, to their natural Countrymen, and unto all uther realmes professand the same Lord *Jesus* with them, wish Grace, Mercie and Peace fra God the Father of our Lord *Jesus Christ*, with the Spirit of richteous Judgement, for Salvatioun.

Lang have we thristed, dear Brethren, to have notified to the Warld the Sum of that Doctrine quhilk we professe, and for the quhilk we have susteined Infamie and Danger: Bot sik hes bene the Rage of Sathan againis us, and againis *Christ Jesus* his eternal Veritie

PRÆFATIO.

Ordines ac cives Regni Scotorum *qui* Christum *profitentur, cæteris* Scotis, *regnis item et nationibus exteris eundem* Christum Jesum *profitentibus gratiam, misericordiam et pacem a Deo Patre Domini nostri* Jesu Christi, *una cum spiritu Justitiæ, ac recto Judicio.*

Jampridem optabamus, Fratres charissimi, ut ejus quam profitemur, ac propter quam ignominiæ et periculis toties objecti fuimus doctrinæ ratio, si fieri posset, orbi terrarum clara existeret. Sed is fuit Sathanæ furor, non modo adversus nos sed adversus ipsum Jesum

latlie now againe boin amangst us, that to this daie na Time hes been graunted unto us to cleir our Consciences, as maist gladlie we wald have done. For how we have been tossit heir-tofoir, the maist part of *Europe*, as we suppose, dois understand.

But seing that of the infinit Gudnes of our God (quha never sufferis his afflickit utter-lie to be confoundit) abone Expectation we have obteined sum Rest and Libertie, we culd not bot set furth this brefe and plaine Confessioun of sik Doctrine as is proponed unto us, and as we beleeve and professe; part-lie for Satisfactioun of our Brethren quhais-hartis, we nathing doubt, have been and zit ar woundit be the despichtful rayling of sik as zit have not learned to speke well: And partlie for stapping the mouthis of impudent blasphemers, quha bauldlie damne that quhilk they have nouther heard nor zit understude.

Not that we judge that the cankred malice of sik is abill to be cured be this our simple con-fession; na, we knaw that the sweet savoure of the evangel is and sal be deathe unto the sonnes of perditioun. Bot we have chief re-spect to our weak and infirme brethren, to quham we wald communicate the bottom of our hartes, leist that they be troubiled or car-ried awaie be diversity of rumoris, quhilk Sa-than spredis againist us to the defeating of this our maist godlie interprize: Protestand that gif onie man will note in this our confes-sioun onie Artickle or sentence repugnand to Gods halie word, that it wald pleis him of his gentleness and for christian charities sake to admonish us of the same in writing; and we upon our honoures and fidelitie, be Gods grace do promise unto him satisfactioun fra the mouth of God, that is, fra his haly scriptures, or else reformation of that quhilk he sal prove to be amisse. For God we take to recorde in our consciences, that fra our heartis we ab-

Christum, *et æternam ejus nuper hic renatam veritatem, ut ad hunc usque diem non licuerit, id quod unice optabamus, nostram vobis, hisce de rebus dilucide explicare sententiam. Major enim, ut arbitramur,* Europæ *pars non ignorat quibus toto superiore anno fuerimus afflicti calamitatibus.*

Nunc autem cum immensa Dei bonitate (qui sæpe premi, nunquam penitus opprimi suos patitur), tranquillitatis, et libertatis non ni-hil illuxerit, non potuimus nobis temperare, quo minus hanc brevem, et dilucidam ede-remus Confessionem ejus doctrinæ quæ nobis promulgata fuit, quamque nos et persuasam habemus et profitemur: partim ut medicaremur fratrum nostrorum animis, in quibus adhuc proculdubio inhærebant vestigia vulnerum, quæ ex eorum, qui nondum recte loqui didice-runt, scurrilibus acceperant convitiis: partim ut os obstrueremus quibusdam impudenter blas-phemis, qui, quæ nec audierunt unquam, nec satis intellexerunt, ea confidenter damnare non erubescunt.

Neque tamen id eo facimus, quod aliquan-do fore speremus, ut inveterata illa pestis hac nostra simplici et nuda confessione sanari possit; præsertim cum non ignoremus sua-vem evangelii odorem filiis perditionis leti-ferum futurum: sed quod fratrum infirmorum rationem habendam duceremus; cum quibus sententiam nostram, velut ex intimis animi penetralibus prolatam, communicandam esse putavimus; ne videlicet perturbarentur, aut etiam auferrentur variorum rumorum ventis, quos Sathan adversus nos excitarat, ut nos-trum illud sanctum, ac pium eluderet consilium. Denunciamus igitur, omnesque adeo rogamus, si quis aut caput aliquod, aut etiam sententiam cum sancto Dei verbo pugnantem hic animad-verterit, ut pro sua humanitate, proque eo amore, quo Christum, Christique gregem prose-quitur, nos per literas admoneat: id qui fece-rit, sancte ei repromittimus nos eidem aut ex ore Dei, hoc est, ex sacræ ͧscripturæ oraculo satisfacturos; aut quod secus a nobis dictum

horre all sectis of heresie and all teachers of erronious doctrine : and that with all humilitie we imbrace the purity of *Christs* Gospell, quhilk is the onelie fude of our sauls, and therefoir sa precious unto us, that we ar determined to suffer the extremest of wardlie daunger, rather than that we will suffer our selves to be defraudit of the sam. For heirof we ar maist certainlie perswadit, that quhasumever denieis Christ Jesus, or is aschamit of him in the presence of men, sal be denyit befoir the Father, and befoir his haly Angels. And therefoir be the assistance of the michtie Spirit of the same our Lord Jesus Christ, we firmelie purpose to abide to the end in the confessioun of this our faith, as be Artickles followis.

demonstraverit, emendaturos. Deum enim nostrorum consiliorum conscium attestamur, quod ab omni prava hæresi, atque adeo erroneæ assertionis authoribus animo abhorremus; quod cum summa humilitate evangelii Christi puritatem amplectimur, qui unicus est nostrorum animorum cibus, atque ideo eo usque carus, ut decreverimus omnia quæ possunt humanitus evenire potius experiri, quam ut nos eo cibo fraudari patiamur. Persuasissimum enim id habemus, quod quemcunque Christi puduerit, aut qui eum coram hominibus negaverit, hunc ille coram Patre, sanctisque ejus angelis negabit. Atque ideo ejusdem Domini nostri omnipotentis Jesu Christi præsenti ope freti, in animo habemus in hujus nostræ fidei, cujus capita sequuntur, confessione perseverare.

ART. I.

OF GOD.

We confesse and acknawledge ane onelie God, to whom only we must cleave, whom onelie we must serve, whom onelie we must worship, and in whom onelie we must put our trust.[1] Who is Eternall, Infinit, Unmeasurable, Incomprehensible, Omnipotent, Invisible :[2] ane in substance, and zit distinct in thre personnis, the Father, the Sone, and the holie Gost.[3] Be whom we confesse and beleve all thingis in hevin and eirth, aswel Visible as Invisible, to have been created, to be reteined in their being, and to

ART. I.

DE DEO.

Confitemur atque agnoscimus unicum Deum, cui uni adhærere, uni servire, quem unum colere debeamus, in quo uno collocemus omnem spem salutis. Eundem etiam credimus æternum, infinitum, immensum, incomprehensibilem, omnipotentem, invisibilem; essentia quidem unum, in tres autem distinctum personas, Patrem, Filiu: , ac Spiritum sanctum. Per hunc Deum asseveramus atque etiam credimus quæcunque visibilia aut invisibilia cœlo terraque continentur creata esse, constare, et inscrutabili

---

[1] Deut. vi. 4; 1 Cor. viii. 6; Deut. iv. 35; Esai. xliv. 5, 6.
[2] 1 Tim. i. 17; 1 Kings viii. 27; 2 Chron. vi. 18; Psalm cxxxix. ſ, 8; Gen. xvii. 1; 1 Tim. vi. 15, 16; Exod. iii. 14; v. 15.
[3] Matt. xxviii. 19; 1 John v. 7.

be ruled and guyded be his inscrutable Providence, to sik end, as his Eternall Wisdome, Gudnes, and Justice hes appoynted them, to the manifestatioun of his awin glorie.[1]

ejus providentia regi et gubernari; omniaque eo referri, quo ejus æternæ sapientiæ, bonitati et justitiæ visum est; nempe ad gloriæ majestatisque ipsius illustrationem.

Art. II.

OF THE CREATIOUN OF MAN.

We confesse and acknawledge this our God to have created man, to wit, our first father *Adam*, to his awin image and similitude, to whome he gave wisdome, lordship, justice, free-wil, and cleir knawledge of himselfe, sa that in the haill nature of man there culd be noted no imperfectioun.[2] Fra quhilk honour and perfectioun, man and woman did bothe fal: the woman being deceived be the Serpent, and man obeying the voyce of the woman, both conspyring against the Soveraigne Majestie of God, who in expressed words had before threatned deith, gif they presumed to eit of the forbidden tre.[3]

Art. II.

DE CREATIONE HOMINIS.

Credimus item et confitemur ab hoc nostro Deo, hominem, id est, humani generis primum parentem Adamum, ad imaginem et similitudinem ipsius fuisse creatum, Item ab eodem sapientia, imperio, justitia, libertate arbitrii, et perspicua ipsius cognitione donatum: adeo ut in universa hominis natura nil animadverti posset, quod non omni ex parte foret absolutum. Ab hac autem dignitate, et naturæ perfectione vir mulierque exciderunt; vir a muliere, mulier a serpente decepta: vir mulieris voci obtemperans, uterque conjuratione inita adversus Dei majestatem, qui aperte antea mortem iis comminatus fuerat, si de arbore ve tita gustassent.

Art. III.

OF ORIGINAL SINNE.

Be quhilk transgressioun, commonlie called Original sinne, wes

Art. III.

DE PECCATO ORIGINALI.

Hac imperii contemptione, quod originale peccatum vulgo dici solet,

---

[1] Gen. i. 1; Acts xvii. 28; Prov. xvi. 4.
[2] Gen. i. 26, 27, 28, etc.; Col. iii. 10; Eph. iv. 24.
[3] Gen. iii. 6; ii. 17.

the Image of God utterlie defaced in man, and he and his posteritie of nature become enimies to God, slaves to Sathan, and servandis unto sin.[1] In samekle that deith everlasting hes had, and sall have power and dominioun over all that have not been, ar not, or sal not be regenerate from above: quhilk regeneratioun is wrocht be the power of the holie Gost, working in the hartes of the elect of God, ane assured faith in the promise of God, reveiled to us in his word, be quhilk faith we apprehend Christ Jesus, with the graces and benefites promised in him.[2]

imago Dei in homine penitus obliterata fuit: eaque contemptio, ipsum hominem totamque ejus posteritatem ita Deo inimicam, Sathanæ mancipium, et peccato reddidit obnoxiam, ut sempiterna mors dominata fuerit, atque adeo in posterum dominatura sit in omnes, qui non fuerint, sunt, aut erunt divinitus regenerati. Hæc autem regeneratio est actio Spiritus sancti, qui in corda eorum quos Deus elegit, constantem inserit fidem de promissis, quæ Deus verbo suo nobis revelavit: qua fide Jesum Christum, omnemque gratiam et beneficentiam in Christo nobis promissam apprehendimus.

Art. IV.

OF THE REVELATIOUN OF THE PROMISE.

For this we constantlie beleeve, that God, after the feirfull and horrible defectioun of man fra his obedience, did seek *Adam* againe, call upon him, rebuke his sinne, convict him of the same, and in the end made unto him ane most joyful promise, to wit, *That the seed of the woman suld break down the serpents head*, that is, he suld destroy the works of the Devill. Quhilk promise, as it was repeated, and made mair cleare from time to time; so was it imbraced with joy,

Art. IV.

DE REVELATIONE PROMISSORUM.

Constanter enim credimus, quod post formidabilem illam atque horrendam hominis ab obedientia Dei defectionem, rursus Deus Adamum requisierit, vocaverit nominatim, accusaverit, convicerit: denique promissione illa gaudii plena eum sic consolans promisit, Futurum ut semen mulieris caput serpentis contereret, hoc est, universa diaboli opera destrueret ac everteret. Hæc promissio, ut aliis atque aliis temporibus sæpe repetita fuit, ac dilucidius explicata, ita cum summa

---

[1] Psalm li. 5; Rom. v. 10; vii. 5; 2 Tim. ii. 26; Eph. ii. 1, 2, 3.
[2] Rom. v. 14, 21; vi. 23; John iii. 5; Rom. v. 1; Phil. i. 29.

and maist constantlie received of al the faithfull, from *Adam* to *Noe,* from *Noe* to *Abraham,* from *Abraham* to *David,* and so furth to the incarnatioun of *Christ Jesus,* all (we meane the faithfull Fathers under the Law) did see the joyfull daie of *Christ Jesus,* and did rejoyce.[1]

lætitia recepta, et constanter credita est ab omnibus fidelibus, ab Adamo *ad* Noam, *a* Noa *ad* Abrahamum, *ab* Abrahamo *ad* Davidem, *ac reliquis deinceps patribus, qui vixerunt sub lege fideles usque ad incarnationem* Christi. *Hi inquam omnes jucundissimos* Jesu Christi *dies viderunt, et gavisi sunt.*

Art. V.

OF THE CONTINUANCE, INCREASE, AND PRESERVATIOUN OF THE KIRK.

Art. V.

DE PERPETUA SUCCESSIONE, INCREMENTO ET CONSERVATIONE ECCLESIÆ.

We maist constantly beleeve, that God preserved, instructed, multiplied, honoured, decored, and from death called to life, his Kirk in all ages fra *Adam,* till the cumming of *Christ Jesus* in the flesh.[2] For *Abraham* he called from his Fathers cuntry, him he instructed, his seede he multiplied;[3] the same he marveilouslie preserved, and mair marveilouslie delivered from the bondage and tyrannie of *Pharaoh*;[4] to them he gave his lawes, constitutions and ceremonies;[5] them he possessed in the land of *Canaan;*[6] to them after Judges,[7] and after *Saul,*[8] he gave *David* to be king,[9] to whome hee made promise, that of the fruite of his loynes suld ane

Illud quoque constanter persuasum habemus, quod Deus cunctis deinceps ætatibus, ab Adamo *ad* Jesu Christi *adventum in carnem, ecclesiam suam conservaverit, erudierit, multiplicaverit, honore affecerit, decoraverit, et a morte ad vitam evocaverit. Evocavit enim* Abrahamum *e patria, ac majorum suorum sedibus: eum erudiit, semen ejus multiplicavit, multiplicatum mirabiliter conservavit; mirabilius etiam e servitute ac tyrannide* Pharaonis *exemit. His (posteros* Abrahami *intelligimus) leges suas, instituta, et ceremonias dedit. Hos ad possidendam terram* Canaan *introduxit. His judices, his* Saulem, *his* Davidem *regem dedit: cui*

---

[1] Gen. iii. 9; iii. 15; xii. 3; xv. 5, 6; 2 Sam. vii. 14; Esai. vii. 14; ix. 6; Hag. ii. 7, 9; John viii. 56.

[2] Ezek. xvi. 6–14.   [4] Exod. i. etc.   [6] Jos. i. 3; xxiii. 4.   [8] 1 Sam. x.

[3] Gen. xii. etc.   [5] Exod. xx. etc.   [7] Judges i. etc.   [9] 1 Sam. xvi. 13.

sit for ever upon his regall seat.[1] To this same people from time to time he sent prophets, to reduce them to the right way of their God:[2] from the quhilk oftentimes they declined be idolatry.[3] And albeit that for their stubborne contempt of Justice, he was compelled to give them in the hands of their enimies,[4] as befoir was threatned be the mouth of *Moses*,[5] in sa meikle that the haly cittie was destroyed, the temple burnt with fire,[6] and the haill land left desolate the space of lxx years:[7] zit of mercy did he reduce them againe to *Jerusalem*, where the cittie and temple were reedified, and they against all temptations and assaultes of Sathan did abide, till the *Messias* come, according to the promise.[8]

promisit e fructu lumborum ejus futurum, qui perpetuo super regium ejus thronum sederet. Ad hanc ipsam gentem diversis subinde temporibus misit prophetas, qui eam in viam Dei sui reducerent: a qua sæpe ad idolorum cultus deflexerant. Et quanquam ob protervum justitiæ contemptum sæpe eos potestati inimicorum permiserat (quemadmodum antea per Mosen *comminatus erat) adeo ut sancta civitas eversa fuerit, templum incensum, ac universa eorum regio per spatium septuaginta annorum in vastam redacta solitudinem: nihilominus misericordia adductus, eos* Hierosolymam *reduxit; ac civitate instaurata, templo restituto, juxta promissionem eis factam, adversus omnes artes atque oppugnationes Satanæ adventum ibi* Messiæ *expectaverunt.*

Art. VI.

OF THE INCARNATION OF CHRIST JESUS.

Quhen the fulnes of time came, God sent his Sonne, his eternall Wisdome, the substance of his awin glory in this warld, quha tuke the nature of man-head of the substance of woman, to wit, of a virgine, and that be operatioun of the holie Ghost: and so was borne the just

Art. VI.

DE INCARNATIONE JESU CHRISTI.

Cum plenitudo temporis venisset, Deus Filium suum, æternam suam sapientiam, et gloriæ suæ substantiam misit in hunc mundum. Isque Filius, co-operante Spiritu Sancto, humanam assumpsit naturam ex feminæ, ejusdemque virginis, substantia. Atque ita editum

---

[1] 2 Sam. vii. 12.
[2] 2 Kings xvii. 13.
[3] 2 Kings xvii. 14, 15, etc.
[4] 2 Kings xxiv. 3, 4.
[5] Deut. xxviii. 36, etc.
[6] Jer. xxx; Ezra i. etc.; Hag. i. 14: ii. 7. 8, 9; Zech. iii. 8
[6] 2 Kings xxv.
[7] Dan. ix. 2.

seede of *David*, the Angell of the great counsell of God, the very *Messias* promised, whome we confesse and acknawledge *Emmanuel*, very God and very man, two perfit natures united, and joyned in one persoun.[1] Be quhilk our Confessioun we condemne the damnable and pestilent heresies of *Arius*, *Marcion*, *Eutyches*, *Nestorius*, and sik uthers, as either did denie the eternitie of his God-head, or the veritie of his humaine nature, or confounded them, or zit devided them.

est *justum illud semen* Davidis, *Angelus ille magni consilii. Idem verus fuit* Christus *in lege promissus; quem nos agnoscimus et confitemur* Emmanuel, *verum Deum, verum hominem, unamque, quæ ex duabus perfectis naturis constet, personam. Hac itaque nostra confessione damnamus perniciosam et pestilentem* Arii, Marchionis, Eutychis, Nestorii, *et aliorum id genus hominum, hæresim, qui aut æternitatem divinitatis ejus negant, aut humanæ naturæ veritatem; aut utramque in eo naturam confundunt, aut separant.*

Art. VII.

WHY IT BEHOOVED THE MEDIATOR TO BE VERY GOD AND VERY MAN.

We acknawledge and confesse, that this maist wonderous conjunction betwixt the God-head and the man-head in *Christ Jesus*, did proceed from the eternall and immutable decree of God, from quhilk al our salvatioun springs and depends.[2]

Art. VII.

CUR OPORTEAT MEDIATOREM ET PACIFICATOREM VERUM ESSE DEUM ET VERUM HOMINEM.

Agnoscimus item et fatemur, hanc maxime admirabilem divinitatis cum humanitate conjunctionem, ab æterno et immutabili Dei decreto profectam: unde omnis nostra salus emanat ac pendet.

Art. VIII.

OF ELECTION.

For that same eternall God and Father, who of meere grace elected

Art. VIII.

DE ELECTIONE.

Idem enim sempiternus Deus, ac Pater, qui ex mera sua gratia

---

[1] Gal. iv. 4; Luke i. 31; Matt. i. 18; ii. 1; Rom. i. 3; Matt. i. 23; John i. 45; 1 Tim. ii. 5.   [2] Eph. i. 3, 4, 5, 6.

us in *Christ Jesus* his Sonne, befoir the foundatioun of the warld was laide,[1] appointed him to be our Head,[2] our Brother,[3] our Pastor, and great Bischop of our sauls.[4] Bot because that the enimitie betwixt the justice of God and our sins was sik, that na flesh be it selfe culd or might have attained unto God :[5] It behooved that the Sonne of God suld descend unto us, and tak himselfe a bodie of our bodie, flesh of our flesh, and bone of our bones, and so become the Mediator betwixt God and man,[6] giving power to so many as beleeve in him, to be the sonnes of God;[7] as himselfe dois witnesse, *I passe up to my Father, and unto zour Father, to my God, and unto zour God.*[8] Be quhilk maist holie fraternitie, quhatsaever wee have tynt in *Adam*, is restored unto us agayne.[9] And for this cause, ar we not affrayed to cal God our Father,[10] not sa meikle because he hes created us, quhilk we have common with the reprobate ;[11] as for that, that he hes given to us his onely Sonne, to be our brother,[12] and given unto us grace, to acknawledge and imbrace him for our onlie

nos in Christo Jesu *Filio suo elegit, antequam mundi jacta essent fundamenta, eum nobis caput, fratrem, pastorem, ac magnum animorum nostrorum pontificem designavit. Sed quia tam aversa, atque inimica peccatis nostris erat Dei justitia, ut nulla per se caro ad Deum pervenire posset, Deum Filium oportuit ad nos descendere, et corpus e nostro corpore, carnem e carne, os ex ossibus assumere, atque ita idoneum mediatorem et pacificatorem inter Deum et hominem fieri ; qui potestatem daret iis qui in eum crederent, ut filii Dei fierent, quemadmodum ipse testificatur,* Vado ad Patrem meum, et Patrem vestrum, Deum meum, et Deum vestrum : *ac per hanc sanctissimam fraternitatem, quicquid in* Adamo *amiseramus, iterum nobis est restitutum ; ideoque Deum patrem nostrum appellare non dubitamus, non tam quod ab eo creati sumus id enim nobis cum reprobis est commune, quam quod indulserit, ut unicus ejus Filius frater nobis fieret ; idque nobis gratificatus est, ut hunc unum interpretem et pacificatorem, ut est*

---

[1] Eph. i. 11; Matt. xxv. 34.
[2] Eph. i. 22, 23.
[3] Heb. ii. 7, 8, 11, 12.
[4] Heb. xiii. 20; 1 Pet. ii. 25: **v. 4.**
[5] Psalm cxxx. 3; cxliii. 2.
[6] 1 Tim. ii. 5.
[7] John i. 12.
[8] John xx. 17.
[9] Rom. v. 17, 18, 19.
[10] Rom. viii. 15; Gal. iv. 5, 6.
[11] Acts xvii. 26.
[12] Heb. ii. 11, 12. See above, note 3.

Mediatour, as before is said. It behooved farther the Messias and Redemer to be very God and very man, because he was to underlie the punischment due for our transgressiouns, and to present himselfe in the presence of his Fathers Judgment, as in our persone, to suffer for our transgression and inobedience,[1] be death to overcome him that was author of death. Bot because the onelie God-head culd not suffer death,[2] neither zit culd the onlie man-head overcome the sam in, he joyned both togither in one persone, that the imbecillitie of the ane, suld suffer and be subject to death, quhilk we had deserved: And the infinit and invincible power of the uther, to wit, of the Godhead, suld triumph and purchesse to us life, libertie, and perpetuall victory:[3] And so we confesse, and maist undoubtedly beleeve.

superius memoratum, agnosceremus et amplecteremur. Præterea necesse erat, ut qui verus Messias et redemptor esset futurus, idem verus homo et verus esset Deus: quippe qui pœnas esset pensurus, quas nostro delicto commeriti eramus; et ante tribunal patris sese repræsentaturus esset, ut in pœna luenda pro nostro delicto et inobedientia, nostram sustineret personam, ac morte sua mortis autorem superaret. Et quia nec sola divinitas pati, nec sola humanitas vincere mortem poterat, utramque in unam coaptavit personam: ut alterius infirmitas morti, quam commerueramus esset obnoxia; alterius, id est divinitatis, invicta et immensa vis, de morte triumpharet, nobisque vitam, libertatem, ac perpetuam pareret victoriam. Atque sic confitemur, maximeque indubitanter credimus.

Art. IX.

OF CHRIST'S DEATH, PASSION, AND BURIAL.

That our Lord *Jesus* offered himselfe a voluntary Sacrifice unto his Father for us,[4] that he suffered contradiction of sinners, that he was wounded and plagued for our transgressiouns,[5] that hee being the

Art. IX.

DE MORTE PASSIONE, ET SEPULTURA CHRISTI.

Item asseveramus, et pro certo persuasum habemus quod Dominus noster Jesus Christus Patri sese victimam ultro pro nobis obtulerit: quod a peccatoribus contumeliis sit vexatus, quod pro nostris

---

[1] 1 Pet. iii. 18; Esa. liii. 8.
[2] Acts ii. 24.
[3] 1 John i. 2; Acts xx. 28; 1 Tim. iii. 16; John iii. 16.

[4] Heb. x. 4, 5, 6, 7, 8, 9, 10, 11, 12.
[5] Esa. liii. 5; Heb. xii. 3.

cleane innocent Lambe of God,[1] was damned in the presence of an earthlie Judge,[2] that we suld be absolved befoir the tribunal seat of our God.[3] That hee suffered not onlie the cruell death of the Crosse, quhilk was accursed be the sentence of God;[4] bot also that he suffered for a season the wrath of his Father,[5] quhilk sinners had deserved. Bot zit we avow that he remained the only welbeloved and blessed Sonne of his Father, even in the middest of his anguish and torment, quhilk hee suffered in bodie and saule, to mak the full satisfaction for the sinnes of the people.[6] After the quhilk we confesse and avow, that there remaines na uther Sacrifice for sinne,[7] quhilk gif ony affirme, we nathing dout to avow, that they ar blasphemous against *Christs* death, and the everlasting purgatioun and satisfactioun purchased to us be the same.

Art. X.

OF THE RESURRECTION.

We undoubtedly beleeve, that in sa mekle as it wes impossible, that the dolours of death sulde reteine in bondage the Author of life,[8] that our Lord Jesus crucified, dead and

peccatis vulnera passus, quod cum purus et innocens Dei agnus esset, ad tribunal terreni judicis fuerit damnatus, ut nos ante tribunal Dei nostri absolveremur : quod non modo mortem incruce atrocem, et Dei ore execratam subierit ; sed, quam peccatores meruerant, iram patris ad tempus tulerit. Nihilo tamen minus asseveramus, quod in medio etiam dolore et cruciatu, quos animo pariter et corpore pertulit (ut peccata hominum plene lueret), semper unice charus et benedictus patri filius esse perseveravit, Deinde fatemur atque etiam affirmamus, nullum post illud pro peccato restare sacrificium. Si qui autem contra affirment, nihil dubitamus eos blasphemos adversus Christi *mortem, et æternam ejus purgationem, ac satisfactionem, per quam sua morte patrem nobis placavit, asserere.*

Art. X.

DE RESURRECTIONE.

Pro certo etiam credimus, quod quatenus fieri non poterat, ut mortis dolores perpetuam haberent potestatem adversus autorem vitæ, Dominus Jesus, *qui cruci affixus,*

---

[1] John i. 29.
[2] Matt. xxvii. 11, 26; Mark xv.; Luke xxiii.
[3] Gal. iii. 13.
[4] Deut. xxi. 23.

[5] Matt. xxvi. 38, 39.
[6] 2 Cor. v. 21.
[7] Heb. ix. 12; x. 14.
[8] Acts ii. 24.

buryed, quha descended into hell, did ryse agayne for our Justificatioun,[1] and destroying of him quha wes the Author of death, brocht life againe to us, that wer subject to death, and to the bondage of the same.[2] We knaw that his Resurrectioun wes confirmed be the testimonie of his verie Enemies,[3] be the resurrectioun of the dead, quhais Sepultures did oppen, and they did ryse, and appeared to mony, within the Cittie of *Jerusalem*.[4] It wes also confirmed be the testimonie of his Angels,[5] and be the senses and judgements of his Apostles, and of uthers, quha had conversatioun, and did eate and drink with him, after his Resurrection.[6]

mortuus et sepultus fuerat, quiqua ad inferos descenderat, iterum surrexit, ut nos justificaret: et autore mortis (cui æque ac morti eramus obnoxii) devicto, vitam nobis restituit. Scimus etiam resurrectionem ejus fuisse confirmatam acerbissimorum ipsius inimicorum testimoniis; item resurrectione mortuorum, qui apertis sepulchris revixerunt, ac in urbe Hierosolyma *compluribus se videndos exhiberunt: Confirmata est etiam testimoniis angelorum, item apostolorum, qui eum viderunt et contrectarunt; aliorum item complurium, qui post resurrectionem, consuetudine ejus usi familiariter, cum eo ederunt et biberunt.*

Art. XI.

OF THE ASCENSION.

We nathing doubt, bot the self same bodie, quhilk was borne of the Virgine, was crucified, dead, and buried, and quhilk did rise againe, did ascend into the heavens, for the accomplishment of all thinges:[7] Quhere in our names, and for our comfort, he hes received all power in heaven and eirth,[8] quhere he sittes at the richt hand of the Father, inaugurate in his kingdome,

Art. XI.

DE ASCENSIONE.

Neque dubitamus quin idem corpus, quod ex virgine natum, cruci affixum, mortuum, et resuscitatum fuerat, in cœlum ascenderit, ut omnia impleret nostro nomine, et ad nostri consolationem accepit omnium potestatem in cœlo et in terra; et regno suscepto sedet ad dextram patris, patronus et unicus intercessor pro nobis. Atque hanc gloriam, honorem et prærogativam

---

[1] Acts iii. 26; Rom. vi. 5, 9; iv. 25.
[2] Heb. ii. 14, 15.
[3] Matt. xxviii. 4.
[4] Matt. xxvii. 52, 53.
[5] Matt. xxviii. 5, 6.
[6] John xx. 27; xxi. 7, 12, 13; Luke xxiv. 41, 42, 43.
[7] Luke xxiv. 51; Acts i. 9.
[8] Matt. xxviii. 18.

Advocate and onlie Mediator for us.[1] Quhilk glorie, honour, and prerogative, he alone amonges the brethren sal posses, till that all his Enimies be made his futestule,[2] as that we undoubtedlie beleeve they sall be in the finall Judgment: To the Execution whereof we certainelie beleve, that the same our Lord JESUS sall visiblie returne, as that hee was sene to ascend.[3] And then we firmely beleve, that the time of refreshing and restitutioun of all things sall cum,[4] in samekle that thir, that fra the beginning have suffered violence, injurie, and wrang, for richteousnes sake, sal inherit that blessed immortalitie promised fra the beginning.[5]

Bot contrariwise the stubburne, inobedient, cruell oppressours, filthie personis, idolaters, and all such sortes of unfaithfull, sal be cast in the dungeoun of utter darkenesse, where their worme sall not die, nether zit their fyre sall bee extinguished.[6] The remembrance of quhilk day, and of the Judgement to be executed in the same, is not onelie to us ane brydle, whereby our carnal lustes are refrained, bot alswa sik inestimable comfort, that nether may the threatning of worldly

ille unus e fratribus tenebit, donec ponat inimicos suos scabellum pedum suorum. Ibique credimus usque ad ultimum judicium, futurum; ad quod exercendum, credimus constanter eundem Dominum nostrum Jesum Christum *visibilem, et qualis erat cum ascenderat, venturum: ac tum omnia instauratum et redintegratum iri, usque adeo, ut qui tolerarant [passi sunt] vim, contumelias, injurias, justitiæ ergo [propter justitiam], beatæ illius quæ ab initio promissa est immortalitatis fient heredes.*

Contra protervi, inobedientes, crudeles, violenti, impuri, idololatræ, ac cætera impiorum genera conjicientur in carcerem tenebrarum exteriorum, ubi nec vermis eorum morietur, nec ignis extinguetur: cujus judicii exercendi dies, ejusque memoria non solum nobis pro fræno est ad voluptates carnis coercendas, sed inestimabilis etiam animi confirmatio, quæ nos ita corroboret, ut neque minis principum terrenorum, neque mortis hujus momentaneæ admoto metu, nec

---

[1] 1 John ii. 1; 1 Tim. ii. 5.
[2] Psalm cx. 1; Matt. xxii. 44; Luke xx. 42, 43.
[3] Acts i. 11.
[4] Acts iii. 19.
[5] Matt. xxv. 34; 2 Thess. i. 4, etc.
[6] Rev. xxi. 27; Esa. lxvi. 24; Matt. xxv. 41; Mark ix. 44, 46, 48; Matt. xxii. 13.

Princes, nether zit the feare of temporal death and present danger, move us to renounce and forsake that blessed societie, quhilk we the members have with our Head and onelie Mediator CHRIST JESUS:[1] Whom we confesse and avow to be the Messias promised, the onlie Head of his Kirk, our just Lawgiver, our onlie hie Priest, Advocate, and Mediator.[2] In quhilk honoures and offices, gif man or Angell presume to intruse themself, we utterlie detest and abhorre them, as blasphemous to our Soveraigne and supreme Governour CHRIST JESUS.

præsentia ulla periculi commoveamur, ut beatam illam dirimamus societatem quæ nobis, utpote membris, conflata est cum capite nostro, et unico intercessore Jesu Christo. Quem nos profitemur et asseveramus esse Messiam in lege promissum, unicum ecclesiæ suæ caput, justum nostrum legislatorem, unicum nobis summum pontificem, patronum, et pacificatorem. Ejus hos honores, atque hæc munera si quis hominum aut angelorum arroganter et superbe sibi attribuat, eum nos aspernamur, et detestamur velut blasphemum adversus supremum nostrum rectorem Jesum Christum.

ART. XII.

OF FAITH IN THE HOLY GOSTE.

This our Faith and the assurance of the same, proceeds not fra flesh and blude, that is to say, fra na natural poweris within us, bot is the inspiration of the holy Gost:[3] Whome we confesse GOD equall with the Father and with his Sonne,[4] quha sanctifyis us, and bringis us in al veritie be his awin operation, without whome we sulde remaine for ever enimies to God, and ignorant of his Sonne *Christ Jesus ;* for

ART. XII.

DE FIDE IN SPIRITUM SANCTUM.

Hæc nostra fides, ejusque certitudo, non a carne et sanguine proficiscitur, hoc est, a nulla quæ in nobis est vi et potentia naturali, sed ab inspiratione et instinctu Sancti Spiritus, quem nos item Deum confitemur æqualem Patri et Filio : qui nos sanctificat, qui omnem in nobis veritatem operatur, sine quo perpetuo maneremus inimici Deo, et Jesum Christum *Filium ejus ignoraremus. Natura*

---

[1] 2 Pet. iii. 11; 2 Cor. v. 9, 10, 11; Luke xxi. 27, 28; John xiv. 1, etc.

[2] Esa. vii. 14; Eph. i. 22; Col. i. 18; Heb. ix. 11, 15; x. 21; 1 John. ii. 1; 1 Tim. ii. 5. See note 1, p. 13.

[3] Matt. xvi. 17; John xiv. 26; xv. 26; xvi. 13.

[4] Acts. v. 3, 4.

of nature we are so dead, so blind, and so perverse, that nether can we feill when we ar pricked, see the licht when it shines, nor assent to the will of God when it is reveiled, unles the Spirit of the Lord *Jesus* quicken that quhilk is dead, remove the darknesse from our myndes, and bowe our stubburne hearts to the obedience of his blessed will.[1] And so as we confesse, that God the Father created us, when we were not,[2] as his Sonne our Lord *Jesus* redeemed us, when wee were enimies to him;[3] so also do we confesse that the holy Gost doth sanctifie and regenerat us, without all respect of ony merite proceeding from us, be it before, or be it after our Regeneration.[4] To speak this ane thing zit in mair plaine words: As we willingly spoyle our selves of all honour and gloir of our awin Creation and Redemption,[5] so do we also of our Regeneration and Sanctification, for of our selves we ar not sufficient to think one gude thocht, bot he quha hes begun the wark in us, is onlie he that continewis us in the same,[6] to the praise and glorie of his undeserved grace.[7]

enim ita sumus mortui, obcœcati, depravati, ut neque stimulis confessi quicquam sentiamus, neque lumen oblatum videamus, neque cum voluntas Dei revelata est nobis, ei assentiamur ; nisi Dei Spiritus, et mortuos ad vitam revocet, et a mentis nostrœ oculis tenebras discutiat, et contumaces flectat animos, ut sanctœ ipsius voluntati pareamus. Et quemadmodum confitemur a Deo patre nos creatos, cum antea nihil essemus, ab Jesu Christo *redemptos, cum inimici essemus; similiter fatemur nos a Spiritu Sancto renatos, et sanctificatos esse, nulla ratione habita meritorum nostrorum, sive quæ regenerationem præcesserint, sive quæ sequantur. Atque ut hanc rem paulo explicatius dicamus, quemadmodum non inviti nosmetipsos omni creationis et redemptionis nostrœ gloria spoliamus; ita regenerationis et sanctificationis nostrœ ne minimam quidem partem nobis nostrisque meritis arrogamus : nam naturœ nostrœ sponte, ne ad cogitandum quidem quicquam boni sumus idonei ; sed is qui bene operari in nobis cœpit, idem solus etiam opus continuat ad gloriam et laudem nominis sui ; quippe qui sua munera nobis gratis impartitur, non meritis vendit.*

---

[1] Col. ii. 13; Eph. ii. 1; John ix. 39; Rev. iii. 17; Matt. xvii. 17; Mark ix. 19; Luke ix 41; John vi. 63; Mic. vii. 8; 1 Kings viii. 57, 58.

[2] Psalm c. 3.

[3] Rom. v. 10.

[4] John iii. 5; Tit. iii. 5; Rom v. 8.

[5] Phil. iii. 9.

[6] Phil. i. 6; 2 Cor. iii. 5.

[7] Eph. i. 6.

Art. XIII.

OF THE CAUSE OF GUDE WARKIS.

Sa that the cause of gude warkis, we confesse to be not our free wil, bot the Spirit of the Lord *Jesus*, who dwelling in our hearts be trewe faith, bringis furth sik warkis, as God hes prepared for us to walke in. For this wee maist boldelie affirme, that blasphemy it is to say, that *Christ* abydes in the heartes of sik, as in whome there is no spirite of sanctification.[1] And therefore we feir not to affirme, that murtherers, oppressers, cruell persecuters, adulterers, huremongers, filthy persouns, Idolaters, drunkards, thieves, and al workers of iniquity, have nether trew faith, nether ony portion of the Spirit of the Lord JESUS, so long as obstinatlie they continew in their wickednes. For how soone that ever the Spirit of the Lord JESUS, quhilk Gods elect children receive be trew faith, taks possession in the heart of ony man, so soone dois he regenerate and renew the same man. So that he beginnis to hait that quhilk before he loved, and begins to love that quhilk befoir he hated; and fra thine cummis that continuall battell, quhilk is betwixt the flesh and the Spirit in Gods children, till the flesh and

Art. XIII.

DE CAUSA BONORUM OPERUM.

Itaque bonorum in nobis operum causam esse asserimus, non arbitrii nostri libertatem, sed Spiritum Domini nostri Jesu Christi, *qui in cordibus nostris per veram habitat fidem, eaque dedit opera bona, quæ a Deo præparata sunt, ut in eis ambularemus. Quamobrem blasphemum esse dictu constanter asseveramus, in cordibus eorum in quibus Spiritus sanctificationis non est,* Christum *inhabitare. Idcirco etiam non veremur affirmare in homicidis, in violentis, in his qui veritatem per vim opprimere contendunt, in adulteris, in fornicatoribus, aut alioqui impuris, in idololatris, in ebriosis, in latronibus, alterive cuivis flagitio aut sceleri deditis, neque veram inesse fidem, neque ullam Spiritus Domini* Jesu *scintillam, quamdiu in sua nequitia obstinate perseverant. Quia cum primum Spiritus Domini nostri* Jesu Christi (*quem electi Dei filii per fidem accipiunt) hominis cujuspiam cor possidet, eum continuo hominem regenerat, ac renovat, adeo ut quæ antea oderat, amare incipiat, quæ antea amaverat, odisse. Hinc autem in filiis Dei perpetuum illud bellum Spiritus adversus carnem proficiscitur; dum*

---

[1] Eph. ii. 10; Phil. ii. 13; John xv. 5; Rom. viii. 9.

natural man, according to the awin corruption, lustes for things pleisand and delectable unto the self, and grudges in adversity, is lyfted up in prosperity, and at every moment is prone and reddie to offend the majestie of God.[1] Bot the spirite of God, quhilk gives witnessing to our spirite, that we are the sonnes of God,[2] makis us to resist filthie plesures, and to groane in Gods presence, for deliverance fra this bondage of corruption;[3] and finally to triumph over sin, that it reygne not in our mortal bodyis.[4] This battell hes not the carnal men, being destitute of Gods Spirite, bot dois followe and obey sinne with greedines, and without repentance, even as the Devill, and their corrupt lustes do prick them.[5] Bot the sonnes of God, as before wes said, dois fecht against sinne; dois sob and murne, when they perceive themselves tempted in iniquitie; and gif they fal, they rise againe with earnest and unfained repentance:[6] And thir thingis they do not be their awin power, bot be the power of the Lord *Jesus*, without whom they were able to do nothing.[7]

caro ac homo animalis suæ corruptioni consentiens, suæ naturæ consentaneas appetit voluptates, rebus adversis contrahitur, secundis attollitur, ac singulis momentis pronus ad offensionem divinæ majestatis inclinat. At quod inhonestis voluptatibus obsistimus, quod ante Deum ingemiscentes ab hac servitute corruptionis liberari flagitemus, denique quod ita de peccato triumphemus, ut in hoc mortali corpore regnum non obtineat, id a Spiritu Dei est, qui spiritui nostro testificatur quod filii Dei sumus. Homines autem carni obnoxii, qui Spiritu Dei carent, hoc etiam bello carent; vitiositati suæ obsequuntur; et quo Satan, et prava libido impellit, eo avide sine ulla pœnitentia ruunt. Filii vero Dei, ut ante dictum est, adversus peccatum pugnant, suspirant, et ingemiscunt, quoties vitiorum illecebris sese titillari ac sollicitari sentiunt: et si quando cadunt, per veram et minime dissimulatam pœnitentiam resurgunt; ac ne id quidem faciunt suis viribus, sed Christi Jesu Domini nostri, sine quo nihil omnino possent.

---

[1] Rom. vii. 15, 16, 17, 18, 19, 21, 22, 23, 24, 25; Gal. v. 17.
[2] Rom. viii. 16.
[3] Rom. vii. 24. See above, note 1. Rom. viii. 22.
[4] Rom. vi. 12.
[5] Eph. iv. 17, etc.
[6] 2 Tim. ii. 26.
[7] John xv. 5. See note 1, p. 16.

Art. XIV.

WHAT WARKIS ARE REPUTIT GUDE BEFOIR GOD.

We confesse and acknawledge, that God hes given to man his holy Law, in quhilk not only ar forbidden all sik warkes as displeis and offend his godly Majestie, but alswa ar commanded al sik as pleis him, and as he hes promised to rewaird.[1] And thir warkes be of twa sortes. The ane are done to the honour of God, the uther to the profite of our Nichtbouris; and both have the reveiled will of God for their assurance. To have ane God, to worschip and honour him. to call upon him in all our troubles, reverence his holy name, to heare his word, to beleve the same, to communicate with his holy Sacraments,[2] are the warkes of the first Tabill. To honour Father, Mother, Princes, Rulers, and superiour powers; to love them, to support them, zea to obey their charges (not repugning to the commaundment of God), to save the lives of innocents, to represse tyrannie, to defend the oppressed, to keepe our bodies cleane and halie, to live in sobernes and temperance, to deall justlie with all men both in word and deed; and finally, to represse all appetite of our Nichtbouris hurt,[3]

Art. XIV.

QUÆ OPERA APUD DEUM HABENTUR BONA.

Fatemur item et pro certo tenemus, quod sanctissimas Deus leges homini dederit, quæ non modo vetent opera omnia quæ divinam ejus offendunt majestatem; sed ea jubeant quibus gaudet, quæque se remuneraturum pollicetur. Eorum autem operum duo sunt genera; altera ad Dei referuntur honorem, altera ad proximi utilitatem: utraque fidem et authoritatem assumunt ex voluntate Dei nobis revelata. Deum venerari, honore prosequi, eum in omni labore et molestia invocare, sanctum nomen ejus revereri, verbum audire, audito parere, communione sacramentorum ejus uti; hæc sunt quæ priore tabula præcipiuntur opera. At patrem, matrem, reges, magistratus, omnesque qui jus et potestatem in nos habent, honore afficere; eos amare, iis opitulari, dictis, factis audientes esse, quoties cum Dei præceptis non pugnant; vitæ bonorum adesse, tyrannidem opprimere, ab infirmioribus vim improborum defendere, corpus nostrum sanctum ac purum servare, sobrieque et temperanter vivere, in omnibus dictis factisque jure æquabili cum omnibus uti, et omnem proximi

---

[1] Exod. xx. 1, etc.; Deut. v. 6, etc.; Deut. iv. 8.

[2] Luke xvii. 4, 75; Mic. vi. 8.

[3] Eph. vi. 1, 7; Ezech. xxii. 1, etc.; 1 Cor. vi. 19, 20; 1 Thess. iv. 3, 4, 5, 6, 7; Jer. xxii. 3, etc.; Esa. l. 1.

are the gude warkes of the secund Tabill, quhilk are maist pleising and acceptabill unto God, as thir warkes that are commanded be himselfe. The contrary quhairof is sinne maist odious, quhilk alwayes displeisis him, and provokes him to anger: As not to call upon him alone, when we have need; not to hear his word with reverence, to contemne and despise it; to have or worschip idols, to maintene and defend Idolatrie; lichtlie to esteeme the reverend name of God; to prophane, abuse, or contemne the Sacraments of *Christ Jesus;* to disobey or resist ony that God hes placed in authoritie (quhil they passe not over the bounds of their office);[1] to murther, or to consent thereto, to beare hatred, or to let innocent blude bee sched, gif wee may withstand it.[2] And finally, the transgression of ony uther commandement in the first or secund Tabill, we confesse and affirme to be sinne,[3] by the quhilk Gods anger and displesure is kindled against the proud unthankfull warld. So that gude warkes wc affirme to be thir onlie, that are done in faith,[4] and at Gods commandment,[5] quha in his Lawe hes expressed what the

offendendi libidinem cohibere: hæc sunt opera posterioris tabulæ, Deo imprimis grata ac accepta, utpote ab ipso imperata. Horum autem contraria in vitiorum genere sunt, Deo invisa, ingrata, eumque ad iram incitantia; quale est, non eum solum invocare cum res postulat; nolle verbum ejus reverenter audire, aut etiam aspernari ac parvi pendere; idola aut venerari aut apud se habere; cultum idolorum fovere ac tueri; nomen Dei venerabile parvi facere; prophanare, abuti, aut contemnere sacramenta a Domino instituta; non parere, ac etiam resistere iis quibus authoritas data est divinitus, præsertim quamdiu intra juris et muneris sui terminos sese continent; cædem facere, aut quo fiat coire et consentire; odium conceptum continere; pati ut innoxius fundatur sanguis cum impedire possis: ac breviter, quicquid adversus præcepta prioris aut posterioris tabulæ committitur, id peccatum esse asseveramus, ac tale peccatum quod iram, odiumque Dei adversus hominum ingratitudinem accendat. Itaque juxta nostram sententiam, ea opera bona sunt, quæ ex fide proficiscuntur, ac fiunt juxta præcepta

---

[1] 1 Thess. iv. 6; Rom. xiii. 2.
[2] Ezech. xxii 13, etc.
    Jonn iii. 4.

[4] Rom. xiv. 23; Heb. xi. 6.
[5] 1 Sam. xv. 22; 1 Cor. x. 31.

thingis be that pleis him. And evill warkis wc affirme not only thir that expressedly ar done against Gods commaundement:[1] bot thir alswa that in matteris of Religioun, and worschipping of God, hes na uther assurance bot the inventioun and opinioun of man: quhilk God fra the beginning hes ever rejected, as be the Prophet *Esay*,[2] and be our Maister CHRIST JESUS we ar taught in thir words, *In vaine do they worschip me, teaching the doctrines the precepts of men.*[3]

Dei, qui, lege lata, quid fieri vellet diserte cavit. Contra, ea opera dicimus mala, non modo quæ aperte cum verbo Dei pugnant; sed ea etiam quæ in rebus quæ ad pietatem ac Dei cultum spectant, nullum aliud habent firmamentum, nisi ab hominis opinione et commento; hujus enim generis opera Deus ab initio usque semper rejecit et adversatus est, uti ex Esaia *propheta, et his* Christi *verbis edocti sumus,* Frustra me colunt, docentes doctrinas et præcepta hominum.

ART. XV.

OF THE PERFECTIOUN OF THE LAW, AND THE IMPERFECTIOUN OF MAN.

The Law of God we confesse and acknawledge maist just, maist equall, maist halie, and maist perfite, commaunding thir thingis, quhilk being wrocht in perfectioun, were abill to give life, and abill to bring man to eternall felicitie.[4] Bot our nature is sa corrupt, sa weake, and sa unperfite, that we ar never abill to fulfill the warkes of the Law in perfectioun.[5] Zea, gif we say we have na sinne, evin after we ar regenerate, we deceive our selves, and the veritie of God is not in us.[6]

ART. XV.

LEGEM ESSE NUMERIS OMNIBUS PERFECTAM, HOMINES AUTEM IMPERFECTOS.

Legem Dei maxime justam, æquabilem, et perfectam agnoscimus et fatemur, ea jubentem quæ, si perfecte pleneque præstarentur, vitam dare possent, et ad æternam nos perducere fœlicitatem. Sed nostra natura adeo est corrupta et infirma, ut nunquam ad opera legis perfecte præstanda simus idonei; nam si peccatum nos habere etiam post regenerationem negemus, nosmetipsos decipimus, et veritas Dei non est in nobis. Propterea necesse erat, ut Christum, *qui legis*

---

[1] 1 John iii. 4.
[2] Esa. xxix. 13.
[3] Matt. xv. 9, Mark vii. 7.
[4] Lev. xviii. 5; Gal. iii. 12; 1 Tim. i. 8; Rom. vii. 12; Psa. xix. 7, 8, 9, 11.
[5] Deut. v. 29; Rom. x. 3.
[6] 1 Kings viii. 46; 2 Chron. vi. 36; Prov. xx. 9; Eccles. vii. 22; 1 John i. 8.

And therfore, it behovis us to apprehend *Christ Jesus* with his justice and satisfaction, quha is the end and accomplishment of the Law, be quhome we ar set at this liberty, that the curse and malediction of God fall not upon us, albeit we fulfill not the same in al pointes.[1] For God the Father beholding us, in the body of his Sonne *Christ Jesus*, acceptis our imperfite obedience, as it were perfite,[2] and covers our warks, quhilk ar defyled with mony spots,[3] with the justice of his Sonne. We do not meane that we ar so set at liberty, that we awe na obedience to the Law (for that before wee have plainly confessed), bot this we affirme, that na man in eird (*Christ Jesus* onlie except) hes given, gives, or sall give in worke, that obedience to the Law, quhilk the Law requiris. Bot when we have done all things, we must falle down and unfeinedly confesse, that we are unprofitable servands.[4] And therefore, quhosoever boastis themselves of the merits of their awin works, or put their trust in the works of Supererogation, boast themselves in that quhilk is nocht, and put their trust in damnable Idolatry.

est finis et consummatio, cum sua justitia et satisfactione apprehenderemus; qui in libertatem nos asseruit, ne in execrationem ac maledictionem Dei incideremus, etiamsi opera in lege jussa non omni ex parte plene perfecteque faceremus: Deus enim Pater, in corpore Filii sui Jesu Christi *nos intuens, imperfectam nostram obedientiam boni consulit, et pro perfecta habet; operibusque nostris, quæ multis maculis polluta sunt, Filii sui justitiam prætendit. Neque tamen ita nos emancipatos dicimus, ut nullam legi obedientiam debeamus, obedientiam enim deberi supra aperte sumus confessi: illud autem affirmamus, neminem unquam præter unum* Christum *ita legi paruisse, parere, aut pariturum esse, quemadmodum lex exigit: sed cum omnia fecerimus, procumbamus oportet, ac fateamur ingenue servos nos inutiles esse. Quapropter quicunque operum suorum merita ostentat, aut in operibus supererogationis ullam collocat fiduciam, is se sciat id jactare quod omnino nihil est, et spem salutis in idololatria exitiabili collocare.*

---

[1] Rom. x. 4; Gal. iii. 13; Deut. xxvii. 26.
[2] Phil. ii. 15.
[3] Esa. lxiv. 6.
[4] Luke xvii. 10.

Art. XVI.

OF THE KIRK.

As we beleve in ane God, Father, Sonne, and haly Ghaist; sa do we maist constantly beleeve, that from the beginning there hes bene, and now is, and to the end of the warld sall be, ane Kirk, that is to say, ane company and multitude of men chosen of God, who richtly worship and imbrace him be trew faith in *Christ Jesus*,[1] quha is the only head of the same Kirk, quhilk alswa is the bodie and spouse of *Christ Jesus*, quhilk Kirk is catholike, that is, universal, because it conteinis the Elect of all ages, of all realmes, nations, and tongues, be they of the *Jewes*, or be they of the Gentiles, quha have communion and societie with God the Father, and with his Son *Christ Jesus*, throw the sanctificatioun of his haly Spirit:[2] and therefore it is called the communioun, not of prophane persounes, bot of Saincts, quha as citizenis of the heavenly *Jerusalem*,[3] have the fruitioun of the maist inestimable benefites, to wit, of ane God, ane Lord *Jesus*, ane faith, and ane baptisme:[4] Out of the quhilk Kirk, there is nouther lyfe, nor eternall felicitie. And therefore we utterly

Art. XVI.

DE ECCLESIA.

Quemadmodum credimus in unum Deum, Patrem, Filium, et Spiritum Sanctum; ita firmissime tenemus, quod ab usque rerum initio fuerit, nunc extet, ac futura sit usque ad mundi finem una ecclesia, id est, unus cœtus et multitudo hominum a Deo electorum, qui recte ac pie Deum venerantur et amplectuntur per veram fidem in Jesum Christum, *qui solus est caput ejus ecclesiæ, quæ et ipsa corpus est et sponsa* Christi. *Eademque est catholica, hoc est, universalis; quia omnium ætatum, nationum, gentium et linguarum electos continet, sive illi* Judæi *sint, seu gentes; iisque communio est et societas cum Deo Patre, cumque ejus Filio* Jesu Christo *per sanctificationem Sancti Spiritus: atque ideo non hominum prophanorum vocatur communio, sed sanctorum, qui etiam* Hierosolymæ *cœlestis sunt cives, fruunturque bonis maxime inæstimabilibus, nempe uno Deo, uno Domino nostro* Jesu, *una fide, et uno baptismo. Extra hanc ecclesiam nulla est vita, nulla æterna fœlicitas; idcirco plane ex diametro abhorremus ab eorum blasphemiis, qui asserunt, cujusvis*

---

[1] Matt. xxviii. 20; Eph. i. 4.
[2] Col. i. 18; Eph. v. 23, 24, etc.; Rev. vii. 9.
[3] Eph. ii. 19.
[4] Eph. iv. 5.

abhorre the blasphemie of them that affirme, that men quhilk live according to equitie and justice, sal be saved, quhat Religioun that ever they have professed. For as without *Christ Jesus* there is nouther life nor salvation;[1] so sal there nane be participant therof, bot sik as the Father hes given unto his Sonne *Christ Jesus*, and they that in time cum unto him, avowe his doctrine, and beleeve into him,[2] we comprehend the children with the faithfull parentes.[3] This Kirk is invisible, knawen onelie to God, quha alane knawis whome he hes chosen;[4] and comprehends as weill (as said is) the Elect that be departed, commonlie called the *Kirk Triumphant*, and they that zit live and fecht against sinne and *Sathan* as sall live hereafter.[5]

sectæ, aut religionis professores fore salvos, modo vitæ suæ actiones ad justitiæ et æquitatis normam conformaverint: nam uti absque Jesu Christo *nulla est vita, nulla salus; ita salutis ejus nemo erit particeps, nisi quem Pater dederit Filio suo* Jesu Christo, *quique ad eum dum tempus habet, adveniet, ejus doctrinam profitebitur, et in eum credet; cum adultis autem parentibus, pueros etiam comprehendi intelligo. Hæc ecclesia invisibilis est, uni Deo cognita, qui solus novit quos elegerit. Hæc æque continet electos, qui jam decesserunt, quos vulgo ecclesiam* triumphantem *appellant, ac eos qui nunc vivunt, et adversus peccatum et* Satanam *præliantur, eosque qui post nos futuri sunt.*

Art. XVII.

OF THE IMMORTALITIE OF THE SAULES.

The Elect departed are in peace and rest fra their labours:[6] Not that they sleep, and come to a certaine oblivion, as some Phantastickes do affirme; bot that they are delivered fra all feare and torment, and all temptatioun, to quhilk we and all Goddis Elect are subject

Art. XVII.

DE IMMORTALITATE ANIMARUM.

Electi qui jam decesserunt, laboribus liberi, pace et tranquillitate fruuntur; non quod dormiant, aut oblivione sopiantur, ut fanatici quidam affirmant; sed quod ab omni metu, cruciatu, et tentatione sint exempti, quibus nos ac cæteri omnes electi Dei sumus obnoxii quamdiu

---

[1] John iii. 36.
[2] John vi. 37, 39, 65; xvii. 6.
[3] Acts ii. 39.

[4] 2 Tim. ii. 19; John xiii. 18.
[5] Eph. i. 10; 1 Col. i. 20; Heb. xii. 4.
[6] Rev. xiv. 13.

in this life,[1] and therfore do beare the name of the *Kirk Militant :* As contrariwise, the reprobate and unfaithfull departed have anguish, torment, and paine, that cannot be expressed.[2] Sa that nouther are the ane nor the uther in sik sleepe that they feele not joy or torment, as the Parable of *Christ Jesus* in the 16th of *Luke*,[3] his words to the thiefe,[4] and thir wordes of the saules crying under the Altar,[5] *O Lord, thou that art righteous and just, How lang sall thou not revenge our blude upon thir that dwellis in the Eird?* dois testifie.

hac vita fruimur, ideoque nomine ecclesiæ militantis *censemur : contra vero, reprobi et infideles qui decesserunt, in iis molestiis et cruciatibus degunt, quæ verbis exprimi non possunt. Neque enim aut illi ita sunt sopiti, ut omni sensu, aut hi, ut sensu pœnarum careant ; ut indicat* Jesu Christi *parabola quæ* Lucæ *XVI. est, item ut illa testificantur animarum verba sub altari clamantium,* O Domine, qui sanctus es et justus, quoad usque non judicas et vindicas sanguinem nostrum de iis qui habitant in terra?

Art. XVIII.

OF THE NOTIS, BE THE QUHILK THE TREWE KIRK IS DECERNIT FRA THE FALSE, AND QUHA SALL BE JUDGE OF THE DOCTRINE.

Because that *Sathan* from the beginning hes laboured to deck his pestilent Synagoge with the title of the Kirk of God, and hes inflamed the hertes of cruell murtherers to persecute, trouble, and molest the trewe Kirk and members thereof, as *Cain* did *Abell*,[6] *Ismael Isaac*,[7] *Esau Jacob*,[8] and the haill Priesthead of the *Jewes Christ Jesus* himselfe, and his Apos-

Art. XVIII.

QUIBUS INDICIIS VERA ECCLESIA DISTINGUATUR A FALSA, ET QUIS IN ECCLESIASTICÆ DOCTRINÆ CONTROVERSIIS SIT JUDEX.

Quia Satan ab initio semper laboravit, ut pestilentem synagogam veræ Dei ecclesiæ titulo insigniret, animosque crudelium homicidarum accendit, ut veram ecclesiam ejusque membra premerent, turbarent, et infestarent (velut Cain Abel, Ismaal Isaac, Esau Jacob, *totusque sacerdotum* Judaicorum *ordo, primum* Christum *ipsum, deinde Apostolos ejus capitali odio sunt persecuti)*

---

[1] Esa. xxv. 8 ; Rev. vii. 14, 15, 16, 17 ; xxi. 4.
[2] Rev. xvi. 10, 11 ; Esa. lxvi. 24 ; Mark ix. 44, 46, 48.
[3] Luke xvi. 23, 24, 25.
[4] Luke xxiii. 43.

[5] Rev. vi. 9, 10.
[6] Gen. iv. 8.
[7] Gen. xxi. 9.
[8] Gen. xxvii. 41.

tles after him.[1] It is ane thing maist requisite, that the true Kirk be decerned fra the filthie Synagogues, be cleare and perfite notes, least we being deceived, receive and imbrace, to our awin condemnatioun, the ane for the uther. The notes, signes, and assured takens whereby the immaculate Spouse of *Christ Jesus* is knawen fra the horrible harlot, the Kirk malignant, we affirme, are nouther Antiquitie, Title usurpit, lineal Descence, Place appointed, nor multitude of men approving ane error. For *Cain*, in age and title, was preferred to *Abel* and *Seth*:[2] *Jerusalem* had prerogative above all places of the eird,[3] where alswa were the Priests lineally descended fra *Aaron*, and greater number followed the Scribes, Pharisies, and Priestes, then unfainedly beleeved and approved *Christ Jesus* and his doctrine:[4] And zit, as we suppose, no man of sound judgment will grant, that ony of the forenamed were the Kirk of God. The notes therefore of the trew Kirk of God we beleeve, confesse, and avow to be, first, the trew preaching of the Worde of God, into the quhilk God hes revealed himselfe unto us, as the writings of the Prophets and

imprimis necessarium videtur, veram ecclesiam ab impura synagoga certis et manifestis distinguere indiciis; ne in eum incidamus errorem, ut alteram pro altera cum nostro amplectamur exitio. Notas autem et indicia, quibus intemerata Christi sponsa ab impura illa et abominanda meretrice (ecclesiam impiorum intellige) discerni possit, asseveramus, neque ab antiquitatis prærogativa repetendas, nec usurpatis falso titulis, nec a successione perpetua episcoporum, nec a certi loci designatione, nec a multitudine hominum in eundem errorem consentientium. Cain enim ætate et primogenituræ prærogativa Abel et Seth anteibat; item Hierosolyma, cætera totius orbis oppida; huc accedebat in sacerdotibus, ab Aarone usque, perpetua familiæ et successionis series; majorque erat eorum numerus qui scribas et Pharisæos sectabantur, quam qui Jesum Christum ejusque doctrinam ex animo probabant: neque tamen arbitramur quemquam, cui purum et solidum sit judicium, commissurum ut ulli ex iis quas modo commemoravi ecclesiis Dei nomen attribuat. Igitur, quam nos veram Dei ecclesiam credimus et fatemur ejus primum est indicium, vera Verbi

---

[1] Matt. xxiii. 34; John xv. 18, 19, 20, 24; xi. 47, 53; Acts iv. 1, 2, 3; v. 17, 18.

[2] Gen. iv.   [3] Psa. xlviii. 2, 3; Matt. v. 35.   [4] John xii. 42.

Apostles dois declair. Secundly, the right administration of the Sacraments of *Christ Jesus*, quhilk man be annexed unto the word and promise of God, to seale and confirme the same in our hearts.[1] Last, Ecclesiastical discipline uprightlie ministred, as Goddis Worde prescribes, whereby vice is repressed, and vertew nurished.[2] Wheresoever then thir former notes are seene, and of ony time continue (be the number never so fewe, about two or three), there, without all doubt, is the trew Kirk of *Christ:* Who, according unto his promise, is in the middis of them.[3] Not that universall, of quhilk we have before spoken, bot particular, sik as wes in *Corinthus*,[4] *Galatia*,[5] *Ephesus*,[6] and uther places, in quhilk the ministrie wes planted be *Paull*, and were of himselfe named the kirks of God. And sik kirks, we the inhabitantis of the Realme of *Scotland*, professoris of *Christ Jesus*, professis our selfis to have in our citties, townes, and places reformed, for the doctrine taucht in our Kirkis, conteined in the writen Worde of God, to wit, in the buiks of the Auld and New Testamentis,

Divini prædicatio, per quod Verbum Deus ipse sese nobis revelavit, quemadmodum scripta Prophetarum et Apostolorum nobis indicant; proximum indicium est, legitima sacramentorum Jesu Christi *administratio, quæ cum verbo et promissionibus divinis conjungi debent, ut ea in mentibus nostris obsignent et confirment. Postremum est, ecclesiasticæ disciplinæ severa, et ex Verbi Divini præscripto, observatio, per quam vitia reprimantur, et virtutes alantur. Ubicunque hæc indicia apparuerint, atque ad tempus perseveraverint, quantumvis exiguus fuerit numerus, procul dubio ibi est ecclesia* Christi, *qui, juxta suam promissionem, in medio eorum est. Non illam dicimus universalem ecclesiam, de qua superius facta est mentio, sed particularem; tales erant* Corinthia, Gallo-græca, *et* Ephesina, *aliæque complures, in quibus verbi ministerium a* Paulo *fuerat plantatum, quasque ipse Dei ecclesias vocat. Hujusmodi ecclesias, qui in regno* Scotorum *nomen* Christi *profitemur, in oppidis, vicis, aliisque locis in quibus veræ pietatis cultus est restitutus, nos habere asseveramus:*

---

[1] Eph. ii. 20; Acts ii. 42; John x. 27; xviii. 37; 1 Cor. i. 23, 24; Matt. xxviii. 19, 20; Mark xvi. 15, 16; 1 Cor. xi. 23, 24, 25, 26; Rom. iv. 11.

[2] Matt. xviii. 15, 16, 17, 18; 1 Cor. v. 4, 5.

[3] Matt. xviii. 19, 20.

[4] 1 Cor. i. 2; 2 Cor. i. 2.

[5] Gal. i. 2.

[6] Acts. xx. 17.

in those buikis we meane quhilk of the ancient have been reputed canonicall. In the quhilk we affirme, that all thingis necessary to be beleeved for the salvation of mankinde is sufficiently expressed.[1] The interpretation quhairof, we confesse, neither appertaines to private nor publick persone, nether zit to ony Kirk, for ony preheminence or prerogative, personallie or locallie, quhilk ane hes above ane uther, bot apperteines to the Spirite of God, be the quhilk also the Scripture was written.[2] When controversie then happines, for the right understanding of ony place or sentence of Scripture, or for the reformation of ony abuse within the Kirk of God, we ought not sa meikle to luke what men before us have said or done, as unto that quhilk the haly Ghaist uniformelie speakes within the body of the Scriptures, and unto that quhilk *Christ Jesus* himselfe did, and commanded to be done.[3] For this is ane thing universallie granted, that the Spirite of God, quhilk is the Spirite of unitie, is in nathing contrarious unto himselfe.[4] Gif then the interpretation, determination, or sentence of ony Doctor, Kirk, or Councell, repugne to the plaine Worde of God, written in

ea enim in iis doctrina traditur quæ Dei Verbo scripto continentur; novi et veteris Testamenti eos intelligimus libros, qui ab infantia usque ecclesiæ semper habiti sunt canonici. Quibus in libris omnia quæ ad humani generis salutem sunt necessaria, asserimus sufficienter esse expressa. Hujus Scripturæ interpretandi potestas penes nullum est hominem, sive is privatam, sive publicam gerat personam; nec penes ullam est ecclesiam, quacunque illa, sive loci seu personæ prærogativa sibi blandiatur: sed penes Spiritum Dei, cujus instinctu illa ipsa Scriptura confecta est. Igitur, cum de Scripturæ sensu et interpretatione, aut loci alicujus, aut sententiæ quæ in ea contineatur controversia oritur, aut cum de collapsæ disciplinæ emendatione agitur in ecclesia, spectare debemus non tam quid homines qui nos antecesserunt dixerint aut fecerint, quam quid perpetuo sibi consentiens Spiritus Sanctus in Scripturis loquatur; præterea, quid Christus *ipse fecerit aut fieri jusserit: illud enim omnes uno fatentur ore, Spiritum Dei (qui et unitatis item est spiritus) nunquam secum pugnare. Itaque, si qua cujusvis doctoris, aut ecclesiæ, aut concilii interpretatio, decretum aut opinio, cum expresso*

---

[1] John xx. 31; 2 Tim. iii. 16, 17.
[2] 2 Pet. i. 20. 21.

[3] John v. 39.
[4] Eph. iv. 3, 4.

ony uther place of the Scripture, it is a thing maist certaine, that there is not the true understanding and meaning of the haly Ghaist, although that Councels, Realmes, and Nations have approved and received the same. For we dare non receive or admit ony interpretation quhilk repugnes to ony principall point of our faith, or to ony uther plaine text of Scripture, or zit unto the rule of charitie.

Dei Verbo quod in alia Scripturæ parte continetur, pugnaverit, luce clarius est, eam nec esse veram explicationem, nec mentem Spiritus Sancti, quantumvis eam concilia, regna, et nationes probaverint ac receperint. Nos enim nullam interpretationem recipere aut admittere audemus, quæ pugnet aut cum aliquo ex præcipuis fidei nostræ capitibus, aut cum perspicua Scriptura, aut cum caritatis regula.

Art. XIX.

OF THE AUTHORITIE OF THE SCRIPTURES.

As we beleeve and confesse the Scriptures of God sufficient to instruct and make the man of God perfite, so do we affirme and avow the authoritie of the same to be of God, and nether to depend on men nor angelis.[1] We affirme, therefore, that sik as allege the Scripture to have na uther authoritie bot that quhilk it hes received from the Kirk, to be blasphemous against God, and injurious to the trew Kirk, quhilk alwaies heares and obeyis the voice of her awin Spouse and Pastor;[2] bot takis not upon her to be maistres over the samin.

Art. XIX.

DE SCRIPTURÆ AUTORITATE.

Quemadmodum credimus et confitemur, ex Scripturis divinis Dei cognitionem abunde hominibus tradi; ita affirmamus atque asseveramus, a nullo hominum aut angelorum, sed a Deo solo Scripturæ autoritatem pendere. Igitur qui tantam esse Scripturæ autoritatem volunt, quantam illi ecclesiæ concedunt suffragia, eos constanter asserimus adversus Deum blasphemos esse, adversus veram ecclesiam contumeliosos; quæ sui sponsi, suique pastoris vocem audit, eique obtemperat, neque tantum sibi assumit ut domina ejus videri velit.

---

[1] 2 Tim. iii. 16, 17.　　　　[2] John x. 27.

ART. XX.

OF GENERALL COUNCELLIS, OF THEIR POWER, AUTHORITIE, AND CAUSE OF THEIR CONVENTION.

As we do not rashlie damne that quhilk godly men, assembled togither in generall Council lawfully gathered, have proponed unto us; so without just examination dare we not receive quhatsoever is obtruded unto men under the name of generall Councellis: For plaine it is, as they wer men, so have some of them manifestlie erred, and that in matters of great weight and importance.[1] So farre then as the councell previs the determination and commandement that it gives bee the plaine Worde of God, so soone do we reverence and imbrace the same. Bot gif men, under the name of a councel, pretend to forge unto us new artickles of our faith, or to make constitutionis repugning to the Word of God; then utterlie we must refuse the same as the doctrine of Devils, quhilk drawis our saules from the voyce of our onlie God to follow the doctrines and constitutiones of men.[2] The cause then quhy that generall Councellis convened, was nether to make ony perpetual Law, quhilk God before had not maid, nether zit to

ART. XX.

DE CONCILIIS GENERALIBUS, DEQUE EORUM POTESTATE, AUTORITATE ET CAUSIS CUR COGANTUR.

Quemadmodum quæ ab hominibus piis, legitime ad generale concilium convocatis nobis proposita sunt, ea non temere aut præcipitanter damnamus; ita nec sine justa examinatione recipere audemus, quicquid generalis concilii nomine nobis obtruditur: quippe cum homines eos fuisse constet, qui in manifestos inciderint errores, idque in rebus non minimi momenti. Itaque sicubi concilium perspicuo verbi divini testimonio sua decreta confirmat, statim ea reveremur atque amplectimur: sed si homines nova fidei dogmata, constitutionesve cum Verbo Dei pugnantes edant, iisque interim nomen concilii prætendant, ea nos penitus rejicimus atque recusamus tanquam doctrinam diabolicam, quæ a Dei Verbo ad constitutiones et doctrinas hominum animas nostras avocent. Causa igitur cur generalia concilia cogerentur non ea fuit, ut leges quas Deus non jussisset velut perpetuo duraturas rogarent; neque ut nova de fide dogmata comminiscerentur, neque ut Verbum Dei autoritate sua confirmarent; multo etiam minus ut pro

---

[1] Gal. ii. 11, 12, 13, 14.   [2] 1 Tim. iv. 1, 2, 3.

forge new Artickles of our beleife, nor to give the Word of God authoritie; meikle les to make that to be his Word, or zit the trew interpretation of the same, quhilk wes not before be his haly will expressed in his Word :[1] Bot the cause of Councellis (we meane of sik as merite the name of Councellis) wes partlie for confutation of heresies,[2] and for giving publick confession of their faith to the posteritie following, quhilk baith they did by the authoritie of Goddis written Word, and not by ony opinion or prerogative that they culd not erre, be reasson of their generall assemblie : And this we judge to have bene the chiefe cause of general Councellis. The uther wes for gude policie, and ordour to be constitute and observed in the Kirk, quhilk, as in the house of God,[3] it becummis *al things to be done decently and in ordour*.[4] Not that we think that any policie and an ordour in ceremonies can be appoynted for al ages, times, and places : For as ceremonies, sik as men have devised, ar bot temporall ; so may and aucht they to be changed, when they rather foster superstition then that they edifie the Kirk using the same.

Verbo Dei, aut verbi divini interpretatione nobis obtruderent, quod neque Deus antea voluisset, nec per scripturas suas nobis indicasset : sed cogebantur concilia (de iis loquimur quæ hoc nomine censeri merentur) partim ut hæreses confutarent, partim, ut publicam fidei suæ confessionem ad posteros transmitterent : atque horum utrunque faciebant ex verbi divini scripti autoritate, non autem quod putarent, hujus conventionis causa hac se prærogativa donatum iri, ut errare non possent. Atque hanc præcipuam illis fuisse causam existimamus publicorum conventuum. Erat et altera illa ad disciplinam ordinandam, ut in ecclesia, quæ Dei familia est, omnia honeste atque ordine gererentur : nec hoc tamen in eum sensum accipi volumus, ut credamur existimare unam aliquam legem, et ceremoniarum ritum præscribi posse, qui omnibus et locis et sæculis convenire possit ; nam ut ceremoniæ omnes ab hominibus excogitatæ temporariæ sunt, ita cum temporum momentis mutari possunt, et mutari etiam debent, quoties earum usus superstitionem potius alat, quam ecclesiam ædificet.

---

[1] Col. ii. 16, 18, 19, 20, 21, 22.
[2] Acts xv.
[3] 1 Tim. iii. 15; Heb. iii. 2.
[4] 1 Cor. xiv. 40.

Art. XXI.

OF THE SACRAMENTIS.

As the Fatheris under the Law, besides the veritie of the Sacrifices, had twa chiefe Sacramentes, to wit, Circumcision and the Passeover, the despisers and contemners whereof were not reputed for Gods people;[1] sa do we acknawledge and confesse that we now in the time of the Evangell have twa chiefe Sacramentes, onelie instituted be the Lord *Jesus*, and commanded to be used of all they that will be reputed members of his body, to wit, Baptisme and the Supper or Table of the Lord *Jesus*, called the Communion of his Body and his Blude.[2] And thir Sacramentes, as weil of Auld as of New Testament, now instituted of God, not onelie to make ane visible difference betwixt his people and they that wes without his league: Bot also to exerce the faith of his Children, and, be participation of the same Sacramentes, to seill in their hearts the assurance of his promise, and of that most blessed conjunction, union and societie, quhilk the elect have with their head *Christ Jesus*. And this we utterlie damne the vanitie of thay

Art. XXI.

DE SACRAMENTIS.

Quemadmodum patres, qui sub lege vivebant, præter eam veritatem quæ sacrificiis repræsentabatur, etiam duo præcipua habebant sacramenta, nempe circumcisionem et pascha; quæ quicunque sprevisset, in populo Dei non censebatur: ita nunc quoque, evangelii tempore, nos duo quidem sacramenta, eaque sola agnoscimus, atque a Christo instituta fatemur; usumque horum omnibus imperatum, qui inter corporis ejus membra censeri volunt: ea sunt baptismus, et cœna seu mensa Domini Jesu, quæ et communio corporis et sanguinis ejus nuncupatur. Hæc autem sacramenta, tam Veteris quam Novi Testamenti, instituta credimus a Deo, non modo ut visibile discrimen essent, quo populus Dei ab iis discerneretur qui fœdere nobiscum inito non continebantur: sed etiam ut filiorum suorum fidem erga se Deus exerceret; et per horum sacramentorum participationem obsignaret in mentibus nostris promissionum suarum fiduciam, ejus item felicissimæ conjunctionis, unionis et societatis, quæ est omnibus electis cum capite suo

---

[1] Gen. xvii. 10, 11; Exod. xxi.; Gen. xvii. 14; Numb. ix. 13.
[2] Matt. xxviii. 19; Mark xvi. 15, 16; Matt. xxvi. 26, 27, 28; Mark xiv. 22, 23, 24; Luke xxii. 19, 20; 1 Cor. xi. 23, 24, 25, 26.

that affirme Sacramentes to be nathing ellis bot naked and baire signes. No, wee assuredlie beleeve that be Baptisme we ar ingrafted in *Christ Jesus*, to be made partakers of his justice, be quhilk our sinnes ar covered and remitted. And alswa, that in the Supper richtlie used, *Christ Jesus* is so joined with us, that hee becummis very nurishment and fude of our saules.[1] Not that we imagine anie transubstantiation of bread into *Christes* body, and of wine into his naturall blude, as the *Papistes* have perniciouslie taucht and damnablie beleeved; bot this unioun and conjunction, quhilk we have with the body and blude of *Christ Jesus* in the richt use of the Sacraments, wrocht be operatioun of the haly Ghaist, who by trew faith carryis us above al things that are visible, carnal, and earthly, and makes us to feede upon the body and blude of *Christ Jesus*, quhilk wes anes broken and shed for us, quhilk now is in heaven, and appearis in the presence of his Father for us :[2] And zit notwithstanding the far distance of place quhilk is betwixt his body now glorified in heaven and us now mortal in this eird, zit we man assuredly beleve that the bread quhilk

Jesu Christo. *Itaque manifestissimæ vanitatis eos damnamus, qui affirmant sacramenta nihil aliud esse præterquam nuda signa : sed persuasissimum habemus, per baptismum nos in* Christum *inseri,* Christi *justitiæ participes fieri, per quam peccata nostra tegantur, propter quam veniam et gratiam impetremus. Item quod in cœna recto et legitimo usu* Christus *ita nobiscum sese jungat, ut fiat animarum nostrarum verus victus, verum alimentum. Neque confestim ullam naturæ panis in corpus* Christi, *aut vini in ejus sanguinem transsubstantiationem imaginamur, quemadmodum* Papistæ *perniciosissime docuerunt et crediderunt : sed hanc unionem et conjunctionem, quæ nobis est ex vero sacramentorum usu cum* Christi *corpore, Spiritus Sanctus in nobis operatur ; qui nos veræ fidei alis evehit ultra omnia corporea et terrena, aut quæ oculis cerni possint ; nobisque proponit epulandum verum corpus* Christi, *quod semel pro nobis fractum est, et verum sanguinem qui pro nobis fusus est ; illud inquam corpus, quod pro nobis in cœlis ante* Patrem *nunc apparet. Id autem corpus ipsum, jam gloriosum et immortale, quod nunc in cœlis est, quanquam*

---

[1] 1 Cor. x. 16; Rom. vi. 3, 4, 5; Gal. iii. 27.
[2] Mark xvi. 19; Luke xxiv. 51; Acts i. 11; iii. 21.

wee break, is the communion of
Christes bodie, and the cupe quhilk
we blesse, is the communion of his
blude.[1] So that we confesse, and
undoubtedlie beleeve, that the faithfull, in the richt use of the Lords
Table, do so eat the bodie and
drinke the blude of the Lord *Jesus*,
that he remaines in them, and they
in him : Zea, they are so maid flesh
of his flesh, and bone of his bones ;[2]
that as the eternall God-head hes
given to the flesh of *Christ Jesus*
(quhilk of the awin conditioun and
nature wes mortal and corruptible[3])
life and immortalitie ; so dois *Christ
Jesus* his flesh and blude eattin and
drunkin be us, give unto us the same
prerogatives.   Quhilk, albeit we
confesse are nether given unto us
at that time onelie, nether zit be the
proper power and vertue of the Sacrament onelie ; zit we affirme that
the faithfull, in the richt use of the
Lords Table, hes conjunctioun with
Christ Jesus,[4] as the naturall man
can not apprehend : Zea, and farther we affirme, that albeit the faithfull, oppressed be negligence and
manlie infirmitie, dois not profite
sameikle as they wald, in the verie
instant action of the Supper ; zit
sall it after bring frute furth, as
livelie seid sawin in gude ground.

*tanto distet a nobis intervallo, qui
nunc mortales in terra degimus ;
hoc tamen constanter tenemus, panem quem frangimus communionem
esse corporis* Jesu Christi, *et calicem
cui benedicimus, sanguinis ejus item
esse communionem. Itaque confitemur, et procul dubio credimus, quod
fideles, in recto cœnæ dominicæ usu,
ita corpus Domini* Jesu *edant, et
sanguinem bibant, ut ipsi in* Christo
maneant, et Christus *in eis : quin
et caro de carne ejus, et os ex ossibus ejus ita fiunt, ut quemadmodum
carni* Christi, *quæ suapte natura
mortalis erat et corruptibilis, divinitas vitam et immortalitatem lar-
gita est ; ita ut carnem* Jesu Christi
*edimus, et bibimus ejus sanguinem,
eisdem et nos prærogativis dona-
mur ; quas ut non eo solum tempore nobis donari fatemur, neque
vi solum et potestate sacramentorum, sic in recto cœnæ dominicæ
usu, talem fidelibus cum* Christo
*conjunctionem esse affirmamus, qua-
lem humana mens capere nequeat.
Quin illud quoque affirmamus, quanquam fideles, aut negligentia, aut
infirmitate conditionis humanæ im-
pediti, in ipso actionis ejus momento eum quem vellent fructum e
cœna domini non percipiant ; ve-
rumtamen, velut vitale semen in*

---

[1] 1 Cor. x. 16.   [3] Matt. xxvii. 50 ; Mark xv. 37 ; Luke xxiii. 46 ; John xix. 30.
[2] Eph. v. 30.   [4] John vi. 51, etc.

For the haly Spirite, quhilk can never be divided fra the richt institution of the Lord *Jesus*, wil not frustrat the faithfull of the fruit of that mysticall action : Bot all thir, we say, cummis of trew faith, quhilk apprehendis *Christ Jesus*, who only makis this Sacrament effectuall unto us. And therefore, whosoever sclanders us, as that we affirme or beleeve Sacraments to be naked and bair Signes, do injurie unto us, and speaks against the manifest trueth. Bot this liberallie and franklie we confesse, that we make ane distinctioun betwixt *Christ Jesus* in his eternall substance, and betwixt the Elements of the Sacramentall Signes. So that wee will nether worship the Signes, in place of that quhilk is signified be them, nether zit doe we dispise, and interpret them as unprofitable and vaine, bot do use them with all reverence, examining our selves diligentlie before that so we do ; because we are assured be the mouth of the Apostle, *That sik as eat of that bread, and drink of that coup unworthelie, are guiltie of the bodie and blude of* Christ Jesus.[1]

uberem terram jactum aliquando in frugem erumpet. Spiritus enim Sanctus, qui a vera Christi *institutione nunquam potest excludi, non committet, ut hujus mysticæ actionis fructu fideles frustrentur. Hæc autem omnia manare dicimus e veræ fidei fontibus, per quam* Jesum Christum *apprehendimus, qui unus sacramentorum suorum effectum in nobis producit. Itaque, quicunque nos calumniantur, tanquam sacramenta dicamus aut credamus nuda modo signa esse, non modo adversus nos, sed adversus veritatem sunt contumeliosi. Illud autem ingenue confitemur, nos magnum discrimen facere inter elementa signorum sacramentalium, et æternam* Jesu Christi *substantiam. Neque enim eum signis exhibemus honorem, qui rei quæ per ea significatur est exhibendus : neque rursus ea contemnimus, aut vana et inutilia esse arbitramur ; sed post diligentem nostri examinationem, illis reverenter utimur ; persuasum enim habemus ex verbis apostoli,* Quicunque ex illo pane edit, aut ex illo calice bibit indigne, eum esse reum corporis et sanguinis *Jesu Christi.*

---

[1] 1 Cor. xi. 28, 29.

Art. XXII.

OF THE RICHT ADMINISTRATIOUN OF THE SACRAMENTIS.

That Sacramentis be richtlie ministrat, we judge twa things requisite: The ane, that they be ministrat be lauchful Ministers, whom we affirme to be only they that ar appoynted to the preaching of the word, into quhais mouthes God hes put sum Sermon of exhortation, they being men lauchfullie chosen thereto be sum Kirk. The uther, that they be ministrat in sik elements, and in sik sort, as God hes appoynted; else, we affirme, that they cease to be the richt Sacraments of *Christ Jesus*. And therfore it is that we flee the doctrine of the *Papistical* Kirk, in participatioun of their sacraments; first, because their Ministers are na Ministers of *Christ Jesus; zea* (quhilk is mair horrible) they suffer wemen, whome the haly Ghaist will not suffer to teache in the Congregatioun, to baptize: And secundly, because they have so adulterate both the one Sacrament and the uther with their awin inventions, that no part of *Christs* action abydes in the originall puritie: For Oyle, Salt, Spittill, and sik lyke in Baptisme, ar bot mennis inventiounis. Adoration, Veneration, bearing throw streitis and townes, and keiping of bread in boxis or

Art. XXII.

DE RECTA ADMINISTRATIONE SACRAMENTORUM.

Ad rectam sacramentorum administrationem duo arbitramur esse necessaria; alterum, ut ea ministratio per legitimos fiat ministros: legitimos autem eos esse asserimus, quibus verbi prædicatio commissa est, in quorum ora Deus exhortationis indidit sermonem, modo legitime ab aliqua electi sint ecclesia: alterum autem, ut sub ea elementorum forma, et in eum morem administrentur quem Deus instituit; alioqui enim vera Christi *sacramenta esse desinunt. Eaque causa est, cur in sacramentorum participatione, a* papisticæ ecclesiæ communione *abhorremus, primum, quod eorum ministri* Christi *ministri non sunt; et (quod longe detestabilius est) fœminis, quas Spiritus Sanctus ne docere quidem in ecclesia patitur, illi permittunt, ut etiam baptismum administrent. Deinde, quod utrunque sacramentum ita suis commentis adulterarint, ut ejus ceremoniæ, quæ a* Christo *peracta est, nulla pars antiquam et genuinam suam retineat puritatem: nam oleum, sal, sputum, cæteraque id genus in baptismo, mera sunt hominum commenta: panis veneratio, adoratio, per urbes et vicos gestatio, in pixide conservatio, non est sacra-*

buistis, ar prophanatioun of *Christs* Sacramentis, and na use of the same: For *Christ Jesus* saide, *Take, eat,* &c., *do ze this in remembrance of me.*[1] Be quhilk words and charge he sanctifyed bread and wine, to the Sacrament of his halie bodie and blude, to the end that the ane suld be eaten, and that all suld drinke of the uther, and not that thay suld be keiped to be worshipped and honoured as God, as the *Papistes* have done heirtofore. Who also committed Sacrilege, steilling from the people the ane parte of the Sacrament, to wit, the blessed coupe. Moreover, that the Sacramentis be richtly used, it is required, that the end and cause why the Sacramentis were institute, be understanded and observed, asweil of the minister as of the receiveris: For gif the opinion be changed in the receiver, the richt use ceassis; quhilk is maist evident be the rejection of the sacrifices: As also gif the teacher planely teache fals doctrine, quhilk were odious and abhominable before God (albeit they were his awin ordinance) because that wicked men use them to an uther end than God hes ordaned. The same affirme we of the Sacraments in the *Papistical* kirk; in

mentorum Christi *usus, sed prophanatio :* Christus *enim dixit,* Accipite, comedite, etc., hoc facite in mei memoriam. *His verbis, atque hoc mandato, panem et vinum in corporis et sanguinis sui sacramenta sanctificavit, ut alterum ederetur, alterum biberetur ab omnibus, non autem ut servarentur ad venerationem, utque instar Dei adorarentur, quod hactenus a* papistis *est factum. Iidem quoque sacrilegio se alligarunt, cum alteram sacramenti partem, hoc est, sacrum calicem, populo substraxerunt. Prœterea, ad rectum sacramentorum usum illud quoque est necessarium, ut intelligatur quem ad finem tam minister, quam qui sacramenta accipit, ea referant : nam qui sacramentum accipit, si secus atqui oportet de fine ejus senserit, ibi sacramenti quoque usus et fructus cessat ; quod et in sacrificiorum rejectione est evidens : item si doctor falsam doctrinam palam obtrudat, quamquam sacramenta sint a Deo instituta, tamen quia impii alio quam quo Deus voluit ea referant, ei sunt ingrata et detestabilia. Id autem usuvenire asserimus in sacramentis ecclesiœ* papisticœ; *tota enim ceremonia a* Christo *instituta, tam in forma exteriore, quam in fine et fructus*

---

[1] Matt. xxvi. 26; Mark xiv. 22; Luke xxii. 19; 1 Cor. xi. 24.

quhilk, we affirme, the haill action of the Lord *Jesus* to be adulterated, asweill in the external forme, as in the end and opinion. Quhat *Christ Jesus* did, and commanded to be done, is evident be the Evangelistes and be Saint *Paull*: quhat the Preist dois at his altar we neid not to rehearse. The end and cause of *Christs* institution, and why the selfesame suld be used, is expressed in thir words, *Doe ze this in remembrance of me, als oft as ze sall eit of this bread, and drinke of this coupe, ze sall shaw furth,* that is, extoll, preach, magnifie and praise *the Lords death, till he cum.*[1] Bot to quhat end, and in what opinioun the Preistes say their Messe, let the wordes of the same, their awin Doctouris and wrytings witnes: To wit, that they, as Mediatoris betwix *Christ* and his Kirk, do offer unto God the Father, a Sacrifice propitiatorie for the sinnes of the quick and the dead. Quhilk doctrine, as blasphemous to *Christ Jesus,* and making derogation to the sufficiencie of his only Sacrifice, once offered for purgatioun of all they that sall be sanctifyed,[2] we utterly abhorre, detest and renounce.

opinione, penitus est adulterata; quid Jesus Christus *egerit, quid fieri præceperit, id perspicuum est ex evangelistis et* Paulo; *quid sacerdos agat ad aram, nihil opus est commemorare. Finis et causa cur* Christus *ea instituerit, et cur nos item eisdem et eodem modo uti debeamus, his verbis diserte exprimitur,* Hoc facite in mei memoriam, quoties de hoc pane ederitis, et de hoc calice bibetis, annunciabitis, *hoc est, efferetis, vulgabitis, prædicabitis, et prosequemini laudibus* mortem Domini donec veniat. *Sed quid sacerdotes missando spectent, quam opinionem de missa velint haberi, ipsa missæ verba, ipsi doctores eorum judicabunt, quippe qui, tanquam conciliatores ecclesiæ cum* Christe, *sacrificium Deo Patri offerant propitiatorium pro peccatis vivorum et mortuorum:* Hanc nos eorum doctrinam velut contumeliosam adversus Jesum Christum *rejïcimus et detestamur; quippe quæ unico sacrificio, semel ab eo pro omnibus qui sanctificabuntur oblato, detrahat, et velut parum efficax in eum usum coarguat.*

---

[1] 1 Cor. xi. 25, 26.

[2] Heb. ix. 27, 28; x. 14.

Art. XXIII.

TO WHOME SACRAMENTIS APPER-
TEINE.

We confesse & acknawledge that Baptisme apperteinis asweil to the infants of the faithfull, as unto them that be of age and discretion: And so we damne the error of the *Anabaptists*, who denies baptisme to apperteine to Children, before that they have faith and understanding.[1] Bot the Supper of the Lord, we confesse to appertaine to sik onely as be of the houshald of Faith, and can trie and examine themselves, asweil in their faith, as in their dewtie towards their Nichtbouris; sik as eite and drink at that haly Table without faith, or being at dissension and division with their brethren, do eat unworthelie:[2] And therefore it is, that in our Kirk our Ministers tak publick & particular examination, of the knawledge and conversation of sik as are to be admitted to the Table of the Lord *Jesus.*

Art. XXIV.

OF THE CIVILE MAGISTRATE.

We confesse and acknawledge Empyres, Kingdomes, Dominiounis, and Citties to be distincted and ordained be God; the powers and

Art. XXIII.

QUIBUS COMMUNICARI SACRAMENTA
DEBEANT.

Baptismum existimamus non minus communicandum infantibus fidelium, quam iis quibus est rationis et judicii usus: itaque damnamus errorem Anabaptistarum, *qui ante fidem et rationis usum negant ad pueros pertinere baptismum. Cœnœ autem dominicœ participes esse debere eos modo credimus, qui in familia fidei contineantur; quique sese ipsi probare et examinare possint, non modo in iis quœ proprie ad fidei causam spectant, sed etiam quœ ad officium erga proximum pertineant. At qui edunt et bibunt ex hac sacra mensa, interim fidei vacui, aut a fraterna caritate alieni, hi indigne edunt. Hanc igitur ob causam, in nostris ecclesiis ministri et publice et privatim de fide et vita eorum cognoscunt, qui ad mensam domini* Jesu Christi *accedunt.*

Art. XXIV.

DE MAGISTRATU CIVILI.

Agnoscimus item et confitemur imperia, regna, dominatus, et civitates, divisas et institutas esse a Deo: item imperatoribus in sua

---

[1] Col. ii. 11, 12; Rom. iv. 11; Gen. xvii. 10; Matt. xxviii. 19. [2] 1 Cor. xi. 28, 29.

authoritie in the same, be it of Emperours in their Empyres, of Kingis in their Realmes, Dukes and Princes in their Dominionis, and of utheris Magistrates in the Citties, to be Gods haly ordinance, ordained for manifestatioun of his awin glory, and for the singular profite and commoditie of mankind :[1] So that whosoever goeth about to take away, or to confound the haill state of Civile policies, now long established; we affirme the same men not onely to be enimies to mankinde, but also wickedly to fecht against Goddis expressed will.[2] Wee farther confesse and acknawledge, that sik persouns as are placed in authoritie ar to be loved, honoured, feared, and halden in most reverent estimatioun ;[3] because that they are the Lieu-tennents of God, in whose Sessiouns God himself dois sit and judge :[4] Zea, even the Judges & Princes themselves, to whome be God is given the sword, to the praise and defence of gude men, and to revenge and punish all open malefactors.[5] Mairover, to Kings, Princes, Rulers and Magistrates, wee affirme that chieflie and most principallie the conservation and purgation of the Religioun apperteinis; so that

imperia, regibus in regna, ducibus et principibus in dynastias, aliisque magistratibus in suas civitates, jus et potestatem esse ex ordinatione et instituto Dei, ad gloriæ ipsius manifestationem, et singularem humani generis utilitatem et commoditatem. Itaque quicunque id agit, ut jamdiu corroboratum inter homines civilem ordinem aut tollat aut conturbet, eum nos asserimus non modo humani generis esse inimicum, sed adversus expressam Dei voluntatem impium gerere bellum. Præterea asserimus atque affirmamus, iis qui autoritate justa funguntur, omnem laudem, honorem, et reverentiam esse deferendam : propterea, quod cum vices Dei inter homines gerant, in eorum conciliis Deus ipse assideat, ac de ipsis judicibus et principibus (quibus gladium dedit, ut bonos tueantur, et in noxios animadvertant) ipse judicabit. Præterea affirmamus regum, principum, aliorumque magistratuum, vel præcipuum esse munus ut religionem puram tueantur, adulteratam maculis purgent ; neque enim ad civilis modo ordinis conservationem, sed ad religionis etiam tutelam sunt instituti, ut idololatriam, omnemque superstitionem in ea oborientem

---

[1] Rom. xiii. 1 ; Titus iii. 1 ; 1 Pet. ii. 13. 14.
[2] R m xiii. 2.
[3] Rom. xiii. 7 ; 1 Pet. ii. 17.
[4] Psa. viii. 1.
[5] 1 Pet. ii. 14.

not onlie they are appointed for Civill policie, bot also for maintenance of the trew Religioun, and for suppressing of Idolatrie and Superstitioun whatsoever: As in *David*,[1] *Josaphat*,[2] *Ezechias*,[3] *Josias*,[4] and utheris highlie commended for their zeale in that caise, may be espyed.

And therefore wee confesse and avow, that sik as resist the supreme power, doing that thing quhilk appertains to his charge, do resist Goddis ordinance; and therefore cannot be guiltles. And farther we affirme, that whosoever denies unto them ayde, their counsell and comfort, quhiles the Princes and Rulers vigilantly travell in execution of their office, that the same men deny their helpe, support and counsell to God, quha, be the presence of his Lieu-tennent, dois crave it of them.

opprimant: quod in Davide, Josaphat, Ezechia, Josia, *aliisque regibus intueri licet, qui ob vehemens studium in puritate religionis tuenda, singularem consequuti sunt laudem.*

Ideoque profitemur et palam affirmamus, quicunque magistratui in mora est quo minus suum exerceat munus, is ordinationi Dei resistit, neque a scelere excusari potest. Præterea affirmamus, quicunque auxilium, consilium, operamque suam negat magistratui, ad officium vigilanter et ex fide faciendum, idem suum auxilium, consilium, et operam Deo negat, qui per magistratum, qui vices ejus in terris explet, ea ipsa a nobis exposcit.

Art. XXV.

OF THE GUIFTES FREELY GIVEN TO THE KIRK.

Albeit that the Worde of God trewly preached, and the Sacraments richtlie ministred, and Discipline executed according to the Worde of God, be the certaine and infallible Signes of the trew Kirk, we meane not that everie particu-

Art. XXV.

DE BENEFICIIS LIBERALITER ECCLESIÆ CONCESSIS.

Quanquam verbi divini syncera prædicatio, sacramentorum legitima ministratio, et disciplina convenienter verbo Dei exercita, sint certa et minime fallacia veræ ecclesiæ indicia; non continuo tamen quicunque in hunc cœtum nomen dedit,

---

[1] 1 Chron. xxii., xxiii., xxiv., xxv., and xxvi.
[2] 2 Chron. xvii. 6, etc.; xix. 8, etc.
[3] 2 Chron. xxix., xxx., and xxxi.
[4] 2 Chron. xxxiv. and xxxv.

lar persoun joyned with sik compeny, be ane elect member of *Christ Jesus* :[1] For we acknawledge and confesse, that Dornell, Cockell, and Caffe may be sawen, grow, and in great aboundance lie in the middis of the Wheit, that is, the Reprobate may be joyned in the societie of the Elect, and may externally use with them the benefites of the worde and Sacraments : Bot sik being bot temporall professoures ·in mouth, but not in heart, do fall backe, and continew not to the end.[2] And therefore have they na fruite of *Christs* death, Resurrection nor Ascension. Bot sik as with heart unfainedly beleeve, and with mouth bauldly confesse the Lord *Jesus*, as before we have said, sall most assuredly receive their guiftes :[3] First, in this life, remission of sinnes, and that be only faith in *Christs* blude ; in samekle, that albeit sinne remaine and continuallie abyde in thir our mortall bodies, zit it is not imputed unto us, bot is remitted, and covered with *Christs* Justice.[4] Secundly, in the general Judgement, there sall be given to every man and woman resurrection of the flesh :[5] For the Sea sall give her dead ; the Earth, they that therin be inclosed ; zea, the Eternall our God sall stretche

sit electum Jesu Christi *membrum : scimus enim lolium, zizania, aliasque id genus frugum pestes, una cum tritico seri, copioseque posse crescere ; hoc est, impios posse in eundem cum electis cœtum coire, et assidue cum eisdem verbi et sacramentorum beneficiis uti : verum hujuscemodi homines, qui ad tempus, neque id quidem ex animo, veritatem profitentur, retro abeunt, neque ad finem usque perseverant ; ideoque nullus ex morte, resurrectione, et ascensione,* Christi *fructus ad eos pertinet. At qui et animo persuasum habent, et ore constanter confitentur Dominum* Jesum Christum, *eo quo superius diximus modo, hæc haud dubie recipient beneficia : primum, in hac vita peccatorum condonationem, idque duntaxat in sanguine* Christi ; *adeo ut quanquam peccatum remaneat, et continenter habitet in hoc mortali nostro corpore, non tamen imputabitur nobis, sed condonabitur, atque operietur* Christi *justitia. Deinde in generali illo judicio redivivum cuique suum restituetur corpus ; mare enim suos reddet mortuos, terra item quos sinu suo clausos tenet ; ac sempiternus ille noster Deus manum suam super pulverem extendet, surgentque*

---

[1] Matt. xiii. 24, etc
[2] Matt. xiii. 20, 21.
[3] Rom. x. 9, 13.
[4] Rom. vii. ; 2 Cor. v. 21.
[5] John v. 28, 29.

out his hand on the dust, and the dead sall arise uncorruptible,[1] and that in the substance of the selfe same flesh that every man now beiris,[2] to receive according to their warkis, glory or punishment:[3] For sik as now delyte in vanity, cruelty, filthynes, superstition or Idolatry, sal be adjudged to the fire unquencheable: In quhilk they sall be tormented for ever, asweill in their awin bodyes, as in their saules, quhilk now they give to serve the Devill in all abhomination. Bot sik as continew in weil doing to the end, bauldely professing the Lord *Jesus*, we constantly beleve, that they sall receive glorie, honor, and immortality, to reigne for ever in life everlasting with *Christ Jesus*,[4] to whose glorified body all his Elect sall be made lyke,[5] when he sall appeir againe in judgement, and sall rander up the kingdome to God his Father, who then sall bee, and ever sall remaine all in all things God blessed for ever:[6] To whome, with the Sonne and with the haly Ghaist, be all honour and glorie, now and ever. *So be it.*

mortui in eo ipso quod quisque tulerat corpore, sed jam immortali et incorruptibili, ut recipiant, juxta opera sua, aut gloriam aut pœnam ; nam crudeles, flagitiosi, idololatrœ, quique rerum partim inanium, partim etiam impiarum studio in hac vita tenebantur, ad ignis inextincti supplicium damnabuntur: ibique sempiternis cruciabuntur pœnis non modo corpora, sed etiam animœ, quas in servitutem diabolo in omnem immunditiœ et nequitiœ usum addixerant. At qui in bonorum operum exercitio ad finem usque perseverabunt, Christumque *fidenter profitebuntur, eos persuasissimum habemus in gloriam, honorem, et immortalitatem assumptum iri, ut vivi perpetuo regnent cum* Christo; *cujus corpori glorioso omnes electi ejus conformabuntur, cum is rursus in judicio comparebit, regnumque Deo Patri tradet, qui tum erit, et in perpetuum perseverabit in omnibus et per omnia Deus in œternum benedictus: cui, cum Filio et Spiritu Sancto, omnis honor et gloria, et nunc et in œternum.* Amen.

Arise (O Lord) and let thy enimies be confounded ; let them

Exurge Domine, et confundantur inimici tui. Fugiant a facie

---

[1] Rev. xx. 13; 1 Cor. xv. 52, 53, 54.
[2] Job xix. 25, 26, 27.
[3] Matt. xxv. 31, to the end of the chapter.
[4] Rev. xiv. 10; Rom. ii. 6, 7, 8, 9, 10.
[5] Phil. iii. 21.
[6] 1 Cor. xv. 24, 28.

flee from thy presence that hate thy godlie Name. Give thy servands strenth to speake thy word in bauldnesse, and let all Natiouns cleave to thy trew knawledge. Amen.

tua qui oderunt sanctum nomen tuum. Da servis tuis virtutem, ut cum omni fiducia verbum tuum eloquantur; omnesque nationes veritatem tuam agnoscant et amplectantur. *Amen.*

Thir Acts and Artickles ar red in the face of Parliament, and ratifyed be the thre Estatis, at Edinburgh the 17 day of August, the Zeir of GOD 1560 Zeiris.

CONFESSIO FIDEI SCOTICANÆ II.

The Second Scotch Confession, or the National Covenant A.D. 1580.

[This Confession is a strong anti-papal appendix to the former, and was subscribed by the King, the Council and Court, at Holyrood House, 1580, by persons of all ranks in 1581, again in 1590 and 1638. The text, with the quaint old spelling, is likewise taken from Dunlop's *Collection* of Scotch Confessions, Vol. II. pp. 103 sqq. and 811 sqq. The Latin version is said to have been made by John Craig, who wrote the Scotch, and is superior to the one in the *Syntagma Confess.* (pp. 126 sqq.), which Niemeyer (pp. 357 sqq.) has reproduced.]

The Confession of Faith of the Kirk of Scotland;

OR,

THE NATIONAL COVENANT.

We all, and every ane of us underwritten, protest, That after lang and dew examination of our awne consciences in matters of trew and false religion, we ar now throughlie resovit in the trewth be the Word and spreit of God : and theirfoir we believe with our heartis, confesse with our mouthis, subscrive with our handis, and constantlie affirme before God and the haill warld, That this only is the trew Christian Faith and Religion, pleasing God, and bringing salvation to man, quhilk is now, be the mercie of God, revealed to the warld be the preaching of the blessed Evangell ; and is received, believed, and defendit by mony and sundrie notabil kirkis and realmes, but chiefly be the Kirke of *Scotland*, the Kings Majestie and three Estatis of this Realme, as Godis eternall trewth, and only ground of our salvation ; as mair particularlie is expressed in

Confessio Fidei Ecclesiæ Scoticanæ;

LATINE REDDITA.

Nos universi et singuli subscribentes profitemur, postquam de religionis controversiis diu multumque apud nos deliberatum esset, cunctis ad lydium veritatis divinæ lapidem accuratius examinatis, in veritatis certa persuasione, per Dei Verbum et Spiritum Sanctum, animos nostros acquiescere : ideoque corde credimus, ore profitemur, consignatis chirographis testamur et constanter asserimus, Deo teste invocato, et universo genere humano in conscientiam appellato, hanc unicam esse fidem et religionem Christianam Deo acceptam, hominique salutarem, quæ nunc ex immensa Dei misericordia per evangelii prædicationem mundo patefacta, a multis ecclesiis gentibusque clarissimis, præsertim ab ecclesia Scoticana, rege nostro serenissimo tribusque regni hujus ordinibus, ut æterna Dei veritas et unicum salutis nostræ fundamentum recepta, credita

the Confession of our Faith, stablished, and publickly confirmed by sundrie Actis of Parliaments, and now of a lang tyme hath been openlie professed by the Kings Majesty, and haill body of this Realme both in brugh and land. To the quhilk Confession and forme of Religion we willingly agree in our consciences in all pointis, as unto Godis undouted trewth and veritie, groundit only upon his written word.

And theirfoir we abhorre and detest all contrare Religion and Doctrine; but chiefly all kynde of *Papistrie* in generall and particular headis, even as they ar now damned and confuted by the word of God and kirk of *Scotland*. But in special, we detest and refuse the usurped authoritie of that *Romane* Antichrist upon the scriptures of God, upon the Kirk, the civill Magistrate, and consciences of men: All his tyranous lawes made upon indifferent thingis againis our Christian libertie: His erroneous doctrine againis the sufficiencie of the written word, the perfection of the law, the office of *Christ*, and his blessed Evangell: His corrupted doctrine concerning originall sinne, our natural inhabilitie and rebellion to Godis Law, our justification by faith onlie, our unperfect sanctifi-

et propugnata est; explicata etiam uberius, in Fidei confessione, plurimis comitiorum publicorum actis confirmata, regisque serenissimi et universorum hujus regni civium publica multorum jam annorum professione approbata. Cui nos Confessioni cultusque divini formulæ, ut veritati divinæ certissima sacrarum autoritate subnixæ, lubentissimis animis in singulis assentimur.

Omniaque ideo contraria de religione dogmata aversamur; præsertim vero papismum universum et singula ejus capita, quemadmodum hodie . Dei verbo confutata et ab ecclesia Scoticana *damnata sunt. Nominatim detestamur antichristi istius* Romani *in sacras scripturas, in ecclesias, in magistratum politicum, et in hominum conscientias sacrilege vendicatam autoritatem, nefarias omnes de rebus adiaphoris leges, libertati Christianæ derogantes: impium de sacrarum literarum, de legis, de officii* Christi, *de beati evangelii imperfectione dogma: perversam de peccato originis, de naturæ nostræ impotentia et in legem divinam contumacia, de justificatione per solam fidem: de imperfecta nostra sanctitate et obedientia legi præstanda; de natura, numero et usu*

cation and obedience to the law; the nature, number, and use of the holy sacraments: His fyve bastard sacraments; with all his ritis, ceremonies, and false doctrine, added to the ministration of the trew sacraments without the Word of God: His cruell judgement againis infants departing without the sacrament: His absolute necessitie of baptisme: His blasphemous opinion of transubstantiation, or reall presence of *Christis* body in the elements, and receiving of the same by the wicked, or bodies of men: His dispensations with solemnit aithis, perjuries, and degrees of marriage forbidden in the Word: His crueltie againis the innocent divorcit: His divilish messe: His blasphemous priesthead: His prophane sacrifice for the sinnis of the deade and the quicke: His canonization of men, calling upon angelis or sanctis depairted; worshipping of imagerie, reliques, and crocis; dedicating of kirkis, altares, dayes; vowes to creatures: His purgatory, prayers for the dead; praying or speaking in a strange language: His processions and blasphemous letany: His multitude of advocatis or mediatours with his manifold orders, and auricular confessions: His despered and uncertain Repentance: His

sacramentorum doctrinam : quinque adulterina sacramenta ; omnesque ritus, ceremonias falsasque traditiones genuinorum sacramentorum administrationi, citra autoritatem verbi divini, accumulatas : crudelem de infantibus ante baptismum morte prœreptis sententiam : districtam et absolutam baptismi necessitatem : blasphemam de transsubstantiatione, et corporali prœsentia Christi in cœnœ dominicœ elementis, cujus etiam impii fiant participes, atque orali ejusdem manducatione doctrinam : juramentorum perjuriorumque gratiam faciendi arrogatam potestatem : matrimonii in Verbo Dei interdictis permissionem : crudelitatem erga innocentes matrimonii nexu solutos : diabolicam missam : sacrilegum sacerdotium : abominandum pro vivorum mortuorumque peccatis sacrificium : hominum indigetationem seu canonizationem, angelorum mortuorumque invocationem ; crucis, imaginum reliquiarumque venerationem ; in creaturarum honorem dicata fana et altaria, dies sacratos, vota nuncupata : purgatorium ; pro defunctis deprecationem : ignotœ linguœ in precibus sacrisque usum, sacrilegas supplicationum pompas, blasphemam litaniam : mediatorum turbam, ordinum ecclesiasticorum multiplicem

general and doutsum Faith: His Satisfactionis of men for their sinnis: His justification by warkis, *opus operatum*, warkis of supererogation, merites, pardons, peregrinations, and stations: His holie water, baptising of bellis, conjuring of spreits, crocing, saining, anointing, conjuring, hallouing of Godis gude creatures, with the superstitious opinion joyned therewith: His warldlie monarchie and wicked hierarchie: His three solemnet vowes, with all his shavellings of sundrie sortis: His erroneous and bloodie Decreets made at *Trente*, with all the Subscryvars and approvers of that cruell and bloodie Band conjured againis the Kirk of God. And finallie, We detest all his vain allegories, ritis, signes, and traditions brought in the Kirk, without or againis the Word of God and doctrine of this trew reformed Kirk; to the quhilk we joyn our selves willinglie in Doctrine, Faith, Religion, Discipline, and use of the holy sacraments, as livelie members of the same, in *Christ* our head: Promising and swearing be the GREAT NAME OF THE LORD OUR GOD, That we sall contenow in the obedience of the Doctrine and Discipline of this Kirk,[1] and sall defend

varietatem, auricularem confessionem: incertam et desperationis plenam pœnitentiam, generalem et ancipitem fidem: peccatorum per satisfactiones humanas expiatonem, justificationem ex operibus, opus operatum, operum supererogationem, merita, indulgentias, peregrinationes et stationes, aquam lustralem: campanarum baptizationem, exorcismos; bonas Dei creaturas cruce obsignandi, lustrandi, ungendi, conjurandi et consecrandi superstitionem: politicam ipsius monarchiam, impiam hierarchiam: tria vota solennia, variasque rasuræ sectas: impia et sanguinaria concilii Tridentini *decreta, omnesque atrocissimæ istius in Christi ecclesiam conjurationis populares et fautores: denique inanes omnes adversamur allegorias, omnesque ritus et signa, traditiones omnes, præter aut contra autoritatem Verbi Dei ecclesiæ obtrusas, et doctrinæ hujus ecclesiæ veræ reformatæ repugnantes. Cur nos ecclesiæ reformatæ, in doctrinæ capitibus, fide, religione, disciplina, et usu sacramentorum, ut vita illius sub Christo capite membra, libentes nos aggregamus: sancte promittentes magnumque et termendum DO-MINI DEI NOSTRI NOMEN*

---

[1] The Confession, which was subscribed at *Halyrudhouse* the 25 of *February*, 1587–8, by the King, *Lennox*, *Huntlye*, the Chancelour, and about 95 other Persons, hath here added, *Agreeing to the word.* Sir *John Maxwel* of *Pollock* hath the original Parchement.

the same according to our vocation
and power, all the dayes of our
lyves; under the pains conteined
in the law, and danger baith of
bodie and saul in the day of Godis
fearfull Judgment.

And seing that monie ar stirred
up be *Sathan*, and that *Roman*
Antichrist, to promise, sweare, sub-
scryve, and for a tyme use the holie
sacraments in the Kirk deceitfullie,
againis their awne conscience, mind-
ing heirby, first under the external
cloke of Religion, to corrupt and
subvert secretlie Godis trew Religion within the Kirk; and afterward, when tyme may serve, to become open enemies and persecuters
of the same, under vain houpe of
the Papis dispensation, devysed
againis the Word of God, to his
greater confusion, and their double
condemnation in the day of the
Lord *Jesus:* We theirfoir, willing
to take away all suspicion of hypoc-
risie, and of sic double dealing with
God and his Kirk, protest, and call
the Searcher of all heartis for
witness, that our mindis and heartis
do fullilie agree with this our Confession, promeis, aith, and subscription: sa that we ar not movit with
ony warldlie respect, but ar perswadit onlie in our conscience,

*jurantes, nos in ecclesiæ hujus doc-
trina et disciplina constanter per-
severaturos, et pro cujusque vocatione
ac viribus ad extremum spiritum de-
fensuros; sub pœna omnium in lege
maledictionum, æternique cum animæ tum corporis exitii periculo in
tremendo illo Dei judicio.*

*Quumque sciamus non paucos, a
Satana et antichristo* Romano *su-
bornatos, promissionibus, subscriptionibus et juramentis se obstringere, et in usu sacramentorum cum
ecclesia orthodoxa ad tempus sub-
dole contra conscientiam communi-
care; versute constituentes, obtento
interim religionis velo, in ecclesia
verum Dei cultum adulterare et
clanculum ac per cuniculos labe-
factare; tandem per occasionem
apertis inimicitiis oppugnare, vana
spe proposita veniæ dandæ a pon-
tifice* Romano, *cujus rei potestatem
contra veritatem divinam sibi arro-
gat, ipsi perniciosam, ejusque as-
seclis multo magis exitiosam: Nos
igitur ut simulationis erga Deum
ejusque ecclesiam et insinceri animi suspicionem omnem amoliamur,
CORDIUM OMNIUM IN-
SPECTOREM testamur, huic
nostræ confessioni, promissioni, juramento et subscriptioni animos
nostros usquequaque respondere:
nulloque rerum terrestrium momento, sed indubia et certa notitia.*

through the knawledge and love of Godis trew Religion prented in our heartis be the Holie Spreit, as we sal answer to him in the day when the secreits of heartis sal be disclosed.

And because we perceave that the quyetness and stabilitie of our Religion and Kirk doth depend upon the safety and good behaviour of the Kingis Majestie, as upon ane comfortable instrument, of Godis mercie granted to this countrey, for the meinteining of his Kirk and ministration of justice amongs us; We protest and promeis solemnetlie with our heartis, under the same aith, hand-wreit, and paines, that we sall defend his personne and authoritie with our geare, bodies, and lyves, in the defence of *Christis* Evangell, libertie of our countrey, ministration of justice, and punishment of iniquitie, againis all enemies, within this realme or without, as we desire OUR GOD to be a strong and mercifull defendar to us in the day of our death, and coming of OUR LORD *JESUS CHRIST;* To whom, with the Father and the Holie Spreit, be all honour and glorie eternallie. *Amen.*

ex amore veritatis divinæ per Spiritum Sanctum in cordibus nostris inscriptæ, ad eam nos inductos esse; ita DEUM propitium habeamus eo die quo cordium omnium arcana palam fient.

Cum vero nobis constet, per eximiam Dei gratiam huic regno præfectum esse regem nostrum serenissimum, ad ecclesiam in eo conservandam et justitiam nobis administrandam; cujus incolumitate et bono exemplo, secundum Deum, religionis et ecclesiæ tranquillitas et securitas nitatur: sancte, ex animo, eodem adacti sacramento, eademque pœna proposita pollicemur, et consignatis chirographis promittimus, sacratissimi regis nostri incolumitatem et autoritatem in beato Christi evangelio defendendo, in libertate patriæ asserenda, in justitia administranda, in improbis puniendis, adversus hostes quoscunque internos sive externos, quovis etiam bonorum et vitæ discrimine, nos constanter propugnaturos. Ita DEUM NOSTRUM OPTIMUM MAXIMUM potentem et propitium conservatorem habeamus in mortis articulo, et adventu DOMINI NOSTRI JESU CHRISTI, cui cum Patre et Spiritu Sancto, sit omnis honos et gloria in æternum. Amen.

ARTICULI XXXIX. ECCLESIÆ ANGLICANÆ. A.D. 1562.

THE THIRTY-NINE ARTICLES OF RELIGION OF THE CHURCH OF ENGLAND
PUBLISHED A.D. 1571,

Together with the Revision of the Same, as set forth by the

PROTESTANT EPISCOPAL CHURCH IN THE UNITED STATES OF AMERICA,
A.D. 1801.

[1. The *Latin* text of the Elizabethan Articles, adopted in 1562, is a reprint of the *editio princeps* of Reginald Wolfe, royal printer, London, 1563, issued by express authority of the Queen, and reproduced by Charles Hardwick, in his *History of the Articles of Religion*, new edition, Cambridge, 1859, pp. 277 sqq. (Hardwick gives also, in four parallel columns, the English edition of 1571, and the Forty-two Articles of 1553, Latin and English, with the textual variations of the Parker MS. of 1571, and other printed editions.)

2. The *English* text is reprinted, with the old spelling, from the authorized London edition of John Cawood, 1571, as found in Hardwick, l. c.

The question of the comparative authority of the Latin and English texts is answered by Burnet, Waterland, and Hardwick, to the effect that both are equally authentic, but that in doubtful cases the Latin must determine the sense. The Articles were passed, recorded, and ratified in the year 1562 (1563), in *Latin* only; but these Latin Articles were revised and translated by the Convocation of 1571, and both the Latin and English texts, adjusted as nearly as possible, were published in the same year by the royal authority. Subscription was hereafter required to the English Articles, called the Articles of 1562, by the famous Act of the XIII. of Elizabeth. See Hardwick, l. c. p. 159.

3. The *American* Revision of the Articles, as adopted by the General Convention of the Protestant Episcopal Church in the United States, held in Trenton, New Jersey, Sept. 12, 1801, is taken from the standard American edition of *The Book of Common Prayer* (published by the Harpers, New York, 1844, and by the New York Bible and Common Prayer-Book Society, 1873, pp. 512 sqq.). It has been compared with the Journal of the Convention, edited by Dr. W. STEVENS PERRY, in *Journals of the General Convention of the Protestant Episcopal Church in the United States*, 1785–1835 (Claremont, N. H., 1874), Vol. I. pp. 279 sqq.

4. To facilitate the comparison, the words in which the English and American editions differ are printed in italics. The chief differences are the omission of the Athanasian Creed, in Art. VIII.; the omission of Art. XXI., on the Authority of General Councils; and the entire reconstruction of Art. XXXVII., on the Power of the Civil Magistrate.]

The English editions of the Articles are usually preceded by the following Royal Declaration, which is the work of Archbishop Laud (1628):

'Being by God's Ordinance, according to Our just Title, *Defender of the Faith, and Supreme Governour of the Church, within these Our Dominions,* We hold it most agreeable to this Our Kingly Office, and Our own religious Zeal, to conserve and maintain the Church committed to Our Charge, in the Unity of true Religion, and in the Bond of Peace; and not to suffer unnecessary Disputations, Altercations, or Questions to be raised, which may nourish Faction both in the Church and Commonwealth. We have therefore, upon mature Deliberation, and with the Advice of so many of Our Bishops as might conveniently be called together, thought fit to make this Declaration following:

'That the Articles of the Church of *England* (which have been allowed and authorized heretofore, and which Our Clergy generally have subscribed unto) do contain the true Doctrine of the *Church* of *England* agreeable to God's Word, which We do therefore ratify and confirm, requiring all Our loving Subjects to continue in the uniform Proffession thereof, and prohibiting the least difference from the said Articles; which to that End We command to be new printed, and this Our Declaration to be published therewith.

'That We are Supreme Governour of the Church of *England:* And that if any Difference arise about the external Policy, concerning the *Injunctions, Canons,* and other *Constitutions* whatsoever thereto belonging, the Clergy in their Convocation is to order and settle them, having first obtained leave under Our Broad Seal so to do: and We approving their said Ordinances and Constitutions, providing that none be made contrary to the Laws and Customs of the Land.

'That out of Our Princely Care that the Churchmen may do the Work which is proper unto them, the Bishops and Clergy, from time to time in Convocation, upon their humble Desire, shall have Licence under Our Broad Seal to deliberate of, and to do all such Things, as, being made plain by them, and assented unto by Us, shall concern the settled Continuance of the Doctrine and Discipline of the Church of *England* now established; from which We will not endure any varying or departing in the least Degree.

'That for the present, though some differences have been ill raised, yet We take comfort in this, that all Clergymen within Our Realm have always most willingly subscribed to the Articles established; which is an argument to Us, that they all agree in the true, usual, literal meaning of the said Articles; and that even in those curious points, in which the present differences lie, men of all sorts take the Articles of the Church of *England* to be for them; which is an argument again, that none of them intend any desertion of the Articles established.

'That, therefore, in these both curious and unhappy differences, which have for so many hundred years, in different times and places, exercised the Church of Christ, We will, that all further curious search be laid aside, and these disputes shut up in God's promises, as they be generally set forth to us in the holy Scriptures, and the general meaning of the Articles of the Church of *England* according to them. And that no man hereafter shall either print or preach to draw the Article aside any way, but shall submit to it in the plain and full meaning thereof: and shall not put his own sense or comment to be the meaning of the Article, but shall take it in the literal and grammatical sense.

'That if any publick Reader in either of Our Universities, or any Head or Master of a College, or any other person respectively in either of them, shall affix any new sense to any Article, or shall publickly read, determine, or hold any publick Disputation, or suffer any such to be held either way, in either the Universities or Colleges respectively; or if any Divine in the Universities shall preach or print any thing either way, other than is already established in Convocation with our Royal Assent, he, or they the Offenders, shall be liable to our displeasure, and the Church's censure in Our Commission Ecclesiastical, as well as any other: And we will see there shall be due Execution upon them.'

EDITIO LATINA PRINCEPS, 1563 [1562].	ENGLISH EDITION, 1571.	AMERICAN REVISION, 1801.
Articuli, de quibus in Synodo Londinensi anno Domini, iuxta ecclesiæ Anglicanæ computationem, M.D.LXII. ad tollendam opinionum dissensionem, et firmandum in uera Religione consensum, inter Archiepiscopos Episcoposque utriusque Prouinciæ, nec non etiam uniuersum Clerum conuenit.	Articles whereupon it was agreed by the Archbishoppes and Bishoppes of both prouinces and the whole cleargie, in the Conuocation holden at London in the yere of our Lorde God. 1562. according to the computation of the Churche of Englande, for the auoiding of the diuersities of opinions, and for the stablishyng of consent touching true Religion.	Articles of Religion; as established by the Bishops, the Clergy, and Laity of the Protestant Episcopal Church in the United States of America, in Convention, on the twelfth day of September, in the year of our Lord 1801.
I.	I.	I.
De Fide in Sacrosanctam Trinitatem.	*Of fayth in the holy Trinitie.*	*Of Faith in the Holy Trinity.*
Vnvs est uiuus et uerus Deus æternus, incorporeus, impartibilis, impassibilis, immensæ potentiæ, sapientiæ ac bonitatis: creator et conseruator omnium tum uisibilium tum inuisibilium. Et in Vnitate huius diuinæ naturæ tres sunt Personæ,	There is but one lyuyng and true God, euerlastyng, without body, partes, or passions, of infinite power, wysdome, and goodnesse, the maker and preseruer of al things both visible and inuisible. And in vnitie of this Godhead	There is but one living and true God, everlasting, without body, parts, or passions; of infinite power, wisdom, and goodness; the Maker, and Preserver of all things both visible and invisible. And in unity of this Godhead there be

ED. LAT. 1563.	ENGLISH ED. 1571.	AMERICAN REVIS. 1801.
eiusdem essentiæ, potentiæ, ac æternitatis, Pater, Filius, et Spiritus sanctus.	there be three persons, of one substaunce, power, and eternitie, the father, the sonne, and the holy ghost.	three Persons, of one substance, power, and eternity: the Father, the Son, and the Holy Ghost.

II.

Verbum Dei uerum hominem esse factum.

Filius, qui est uerbum Patris ab æterno à Patre genitus uerus et æternus Deus, ac Patri consubstantialis, in utero Beatæ uirginis ex illius svbstantia naturam humanam assumpsit: ita ut duæ naturæ, diuina et humana integrè atque perfectè in unitate personæ, fuerint inseparabiliter coniunctæ: ex quibus est vnus CHRISTVS, verus Deus et verus Homo: qui uerè passus est, crucifixus, mortuus, et sepultus, ut Patrem nobis reconciliaret, essetque [hostia] non tantùm pro culpa originis, uerum etiam pro omnibus actualibus hominum peccatis.

II.

Of the worde or sonne of God which was made very man.

The Sonne, which is the worde of the Father, begotten from euerlastyng of the Father, the very and eternall GOD, of one substaunce with the Father, toke man's nature in the wombe of the blessed Virgin, of her substaunce: so that two whole and perfect natures, that is to say, the Godhead and manhood, were ioyned together in one person, neuer to be diuided, whereof is one Christe, very GOD and very man, who truely suffered, was crucified, dead, and buried, to reconcile his father to vs, and to be a sacrifice, not only for originall gylt, but also for all[1] actuall sinnes of men.

II.

Of the Word or Son of God, which was made very Man.

The Son, which is the Word of the Father, begotten from everlasting of the Father, the very and eternal God, *and* of one substance with the Father, took Man's nature in the womb of the blessed Virgin, of her substance: so that two whole and perfect Natures, that is to say, the Godhead and Manhood, were joined together in one Person, never to be divided, whereof is one Christ, very God, and very Man; who truly suffered, was crucified, dead, and buried, to reconcile his Father to us, and to be a sacrifice, not only for original guilt, but also for actual sins of men.

III.

De Descensu Christi ad Inferos.

Qvemmadmodum Christus pro nobis mortuus est et sepultus, ita est etiam credentus ad Inferos descendisse.

III.

Of the goyng downe of Christe into hell.

As Christe dyed for vs, and was buryed: so also *it is* to be beleued that he went downe into hell.

III.

Of the going down of Christ into Hell.

As Christ died for us, and was buried, so also *it* to be believed that he went down into Hell.

---

[1] The omission of '*all*' dates from the year 1630, and the revised text of the Westminster Assembly of Divines, 1647. It appears in the edition of 1628, and is restored in modern English editions. See Hardwick, p. 279.

ED. LAT. 1563.	ENGLISH ED. 1571.	AMERICAN REVIS. 1801.

IV.

Resurrectio Christi.

Christus vere a mortuis resurrexit, suumque corpus cum carne, ossibus, omnibusque ad integritatem humanæ naturæ pertinentibus, recepit, cum quibus in cœlum ascendit, ibique residet, quoad extremo die ad iudicandos [omnes] homines reuersurus sit.

IV.

Of the Resurrection of Christe.

Christe dyd truly *aryse* agayne from death, and toke agayne his body, with flesh, bones, and all thinges apperteyning to the perfection of man's nature, wherewith he ascended into heauen, and there sitteth, vntyll he returne to iudge all men at the last day.

IV.

Of the Resurrection of Christ.

Christ did truly *rise* again from death, and took again his body, with flesh, bones, and all things appertaining to the perfection of Man's nature; wherewith he ascended into Heaven, and there sitteth, until he return to judge all Men at the last day.

V.

De Spiritu sancto.

Spiritus sanctus, à patre et filio procedens, eiusdem est cum patre et filio essentiæ, maiestatis, et gloriæ, uerus, ac æternus Deus.

V.

Of the holy ghost.

The holy ghost, proceedyng from the Father and the Sonne, is of one substaunce, maiestie, and glorie, with the Father and the Sonne, very and eternall God.

V.

Of the Holy Ghost.

The Holy Ghost, proceeding from the Father and the Son, is of one substance, majesty, and glory, with the Father and the Son, very and eternal God.

VI.

Divinæ Scripturæ doctrina sufficit ad salutem.

Scriptura sacra continet omnia quæ sunt ad salutem necessaria, ita ut quicquid in ea nec legitur, neque inde probari potest, non sit à quoquam exigendum, ut tanquam Articulus fidei credatur, aut ad necessitatem salutis requiri putetur.

Sacræ Scripturæ nomine eos Canonicos libros Veteris et Novi testamenti intelligi-

VI.

Of the sufficiencie of the Holy Scriptures for saluation.

Holy Scripture conteyneth all thinges necessarie to saluation: so that whatsoeuer is not read therein, nor may be proued therby, is not to be required of anye man, that it shoulde be beleued as an article of the fayth, or be thought requisite [as] necessarie to saluation.

In the name of holy Scripture, we do vnderstande those Canonicall

VI.

Of the Sufficiency of the Holy Scriptures for Salvation.

Holy Scripture containeth all things necessary to salvation: so that whatsoever is not read therein, nor may be proved thereby, is not to be required of any man, that it should be believed as an article of the Faith, or be thought requisite *or* necessary to salvation.

In the name of *the* Holy Scripture we do understand those canonical Books of

ED. LAT. 1563.	ENGLISH ED. 1571.	AMERICAN REVIS. 1801.
mus, de quorum autoritate in Ecclesia nunquam dubitatum est.	bookes of the olde and newe Testament, of whose aucthoritie was neuer any doubt in the Churche.	the Old and New Testament, of whose authority was never any doubt in the Church.
Catalogus librorum sacræ Canonicæ scripturæ Veteris Testamenti.	*Of the names and number of the Canonicall Bookes.*	*Of the Names and Number of the Canonical Books.*
Genesis.	Genesis.	Genesis,
Exodus.	Exodus.	Exodus,
Leuiticus.	Leuiticus.	Leviticus,
Numeri.	Numerie.	Numbers,
Deuteronom.	Deuteronomium.	Deuteronomy,
Iosue.	Iosue.	Joshua,
Iudicum.	Iudges.	Judges,
Ruth.	Ruth.	Ruth,
2 *Regum.*	The .1. boke of Samuel.	The First Book of Samuel,
Paralipom. 2.	The .2. boke of Samuel.	The Second Book of Samuel,
2 *Samuelis.*	The .1. booke of Kinges.	The First Book of Kings,
Esdræ. 2.	The .2. booke of Kinges.	The Second Book of Kings,
Hester.	The .1. booke of Chroni.	The First Book of Chronicles,
Iob.	The .2. booke of Chroni.	The Second Book of Chronicles,
Psalmi.	The .1. booke of Esdras.	The First Book of Esdras,
Prouerbia.	The .2. booke of Esdras.	The Second Book of Esdras,
Ecclesiastes.	The booke of Hester.	The Book of Esther,
Cantica.	The booke of Iob.	The Book of Job,
Prophetæ maiores.	The Psalmes.	The Psalms,
Prophetæ minores.	The Prouerbes.	The Proverbs,
	Ecclesia, or preacher.	Ecclesiastes or Preacher.
	Cantica, or songes of Sa.	Cantica, or Songs of Solomon,
	4. Prophetes the greater.	Four Prophets the greater,
	12. Prophetes the lesse.	Twelve Prophets the less.
Alios autem Libros (ut ait Hieronymus) legit quidem Ecclesia ad exempla uitæ et formandos mores, illos ta-	And the other bookes, (as Hierome sayth) the Churche doth reade for example of lyfe and in-	And the other Books (as Hierome saith) the Church doth read for example of life and instruction of man-

Ed. Lat. 1563.	English Ed. 1571.	American Revis. 1801.
men ad dogmata confirmanda non adhibet : ut sunt	struction of manners : but yet doth it not applie them to establishe any doctrene. Such are these followyng.	ners : but yet doth it not apply to them to establish any doctrine : such are these following :
Tertius et quartus Esdræ. Sapientia. Iesus filius Syrach. Tobias. Iudith. Libri Machabæorum. 2.	The third boke of Esdras. The fourth boke of Esdras. The booke of Tobias. The booke of Iudith. The rest of the booke of Hester. The booke of Wisdome. Iesus the sonne of Sirach. Baruch, the prophet. Song of the .3. Children. The storie of Susanna. Of Bel and the Dragon. The prayer of Manasses. The .1. boke of Machab. The .2. Booke of Macha.	The Third Book of Esdras, The Fourth Book of Esdras, The Book of Tobias, The Book of Judith, The rest of the Book of Esther, The Book of Wisdom, Jesus the Son of Sirach, Baruch the Prophet, The Song of the Three Children, The Story of Susanna, Of Bel and the Dragon, The Prayer of Manasses, The First Book of Maccabees, The Second Book of Maccabees.
Noui Testamenti Libros omnes (ut uulgo recepti sunt) recipimus et habemus pro Canonicis.	All the bookes of the newe Testament, as they are commonly receaued, we do receaue and accompt them for Canonicall.	All the Books of the New Testament, as they are commonly received, we do receive, and account them Canonical.

VII.
De Veteri Testamento.

Testamentum vetus Nouo contrarium non est, quandoquidem tam in veteri quàm nouo, per Christum, qui vnicus est mediator Dei et hominum, Deus et Homo, æterna vita humano generi est proposita. Quare malè sen-

VII.
Of the Olde Testament.

The olde Testament is not contrary to the newe, for both in the olde and newe Testament euerlastyng lyfe is offered to mankynde by Christe, who is the onlye mediatour betweene God and man.

VII.
Of the Old Testament.

The Old Testament is not contrary to the New : for both in the Old and New Testament everlasting life is offered to Mankind by Christ, who is the only Mediator between God and Man, being both God and

Ed. Lat. 1563.	English Ed. 1571.	American Revis. 1801.

tiunt, qui veteres tantùm in promissiones temporarias sperasse confingunt. Quanquam Lex à Deo data per Mosen, quoad Ceremonias et ritus, Christianos non astringat, neque ciuilia eius præcepta in aliqua Republica necessariò recipi debeant: nihilominus tamen ab obedientia mandatorum, quæ Moralia vocantur, nullus quantumuis Christianus, est solutus.

Wherefore they are not to be hearde whiche faigne that the olde fathers dyd looke only for transitorie promises. Although the lawe geuen from God by Moses, as touchyng ceremonies and rites, do not bynde Christian men, nor the ciuile preceptes thereof, ought of necessitie to be receaued in any common wealth: yet notwithstandyng, no Christian man whatsoeuer, is free from the obedience of the commaundementes, which are called morall.

Man. Wherefore they are not to be heard, which feign that the old Fathers did look only for transitory promises. Although the Law given from God by Moses, as touching Ceremonies and Rites, do not bind Christian men, nor the Civil precepts thereof ought of necessity to be received in any commonwealth; yet notwithstanding, no Christian man whatsoever is free from the obedience of the Commandments which are called Moral.

VIII.
Symbola tria.

Symbola tria, Nicænum, Athanasij, et quod vulgo Apostolicum appellatur, omnino recipienda sunt et credenda. Nam firmissimis Scripturarum testimonijs probari possunt.

VIII.
Of the three Credes.

The *three Credes*, Nicene Crede, *Athanasian Crede*, and that whiche is commonlye called the Apostles' Crede, ought *throughlye* to be receaued and beleued: for they may be proued by moste certayne warrauntes of holye scripture.

VIII.
Of the Creeds.

The Nicene Creed, and that which is commonly called the Apostles' Creed, ought *thoroughly* to be received and believed: for they may be proved by most certain warrants of Holy Scripture.

IX.
Peccatum Ooriginale.

Peccatum originis non est (vt fabulantur Pelagiani) in imitatione Adami situm, sed est vitium et deprauatio naturæ cuiuslibet hominis ex Adamo naturaliter propagati, qua fit, vt ab originali iustitia quàm longis-

IX.
Of originall or birth sinne.

Originall sinne standeth not in the following of Adam (as the Pelagians do vaynely talke) but it is the fault and corruption of the nature of euery man, that naturally is engendered of the ofspring

IX.
Of Original or Birth-Sin.

Original sin standeth not in the following of Adam (as the Pelagians do vainly talk); but it is the fault and corruption of the Nature of every man, that naturally is engendered of the offspring

ED. LAT. 1563.

*sime distet, ad malum sua
natura propendeat, et caro
semper aduersus spiritum
concupiscat. Vnde in vno
quoque nascentium, iram Dei
atque damnationem meretur.
Manet etiam in renatis hæc
naturæ deprauatio; qua fit,
ut affectus carnis, græce
φρόνημα σαρκὸς, (quod alij
sapientiam, alij sensum, alij
affectum, alij studium [car-
nis] interpretantur) legi Dei
non subjiciatu. Et quanquàm
renatis et credentibus nulla
propter Christum est con-
demnatio, peccati tamen in
sese rationem habere Concupiscentiam fatetur Apostolus.*

ENGLISH ED. 1571.

of Adam, whereby man is
very farre gone from originall ryghteousness, and is
of his owne nature en-
clined to euyll, so that the
fleshe lusteth alwayes contrary to the spirite, and
therefore in euery person
borne into this worlde, it
deserueth Gods wrath and
damnation. And this in-
fection of nature doth re-
mayne, yea in them that
are regenerated, whereby
the luste of the fleshe,
called in Greke φρόνημα
σαρκὸς, which some do ex-
pounde the wisdome, some
sensualitie, some the affection, some the desyre of
the fleshe, is not subiect
to the lawe of God. And
although there is no con-
demnation for them that
beleue and are baptized:
yet the Apostle doth con-
fesse that concupiscence
and luste hath of it selfe
the nature of synne.

AMERICAN REVIS. 1801.

of Adam; whereby man is
very far gone from original
righteousness, and is of his
own nature inclined to
evil, so that the flesh lusteth always contrary to the
spirit; and therefore in
every person born into
this world, it deserveth
God's wrath and damna-
tion. And this infection
of nature doth remain, yea
in them that are regener-
ated; whereby the lust of
the flesh, called in Greek
φρόνημα σαρκὸς (which some
do expound the wisdom,
some sensuality, some the
affection, some the desire,
of the flesh), is not subject
to the Law of God. And
although there is no con-
demnation for them that
believe and are baptized;
yet the Apostle doth con-
fess, that concupiscence
and lust hath of itself
the nature of sin.

X.

De Libero Arbitrio.

*Ea est hominis post lap-
sum Adæ conditio, ut sese
naturalibus suis viribus et
bonis operibus ad fidem et
invocationem Dei conuertere
ac præparare non possit:
Quare absque gratia Dei,
quæ per Christum est, nos
præueniente, ut uelimus, et
cooperante dum volumus, ad*

X.

Of free wyll.

The condition of man
after the fall of Adam is
suche, that he can not
turne and prepare hym
selfe by his owne naturall
strength and good workes,
to fayth and calling vpon
God: Wherefore we haue
no power to do good
workes pleasaunt and ac-

X.

Of Free-Will.

The condition of Man
after the fall of Adam is
such, that he can not turn
and prepare himself, by
his own natural strength
and good works, to faith,
and calling upon God.
Wherefore we have no
power to do good works
pleasant and acceptable to

Ed. Lat. 1563.	English Ed. 1571.	American Revis. 1801.
pietatis opera facienda, quæ Deo grata sint et accepta, nihil valemus.	ceptable to God, without the grace of God by Christe preuentyng us, that we may haue a good wyll, and workyng with vs, when we haue that good wyll.	God, without the grace of God by Christ preventing us, that we may have a good will, and working with us, when we have that good will.

XI.

De Hominis Iustificatione.

Tantùm propter meritum Domini ac Seruatoris nostri Iesu Christi, per fidem, non propter opera et merita nostra, iusti coram Deo reputamur: Quare sola fide nos iustificari, doctrina est saluberrima, ac consolationis plenissima: ut in Homilia de Iustificatione hominis fusiùs explicatur.

XI.

Of the iustification of man.

We are accompted righteous before God, only for the merite of our Lord and sauiour Jesus Christe, by faith, and not for our owne workes or deseruynges. Wherefore, that we are iustified by fayth onely, is a most wholesome doctrine, and very full of comfort, as more largely is expressed in the Homilie of iustification.

XI.

Of the Justification of Man.

We are accounted righteous before God, only for the merit of our Lord and Saviour Jesus Christ by Faith, and not for our own works or deservings. Wherefore, that we are justified by Faith only, is a most wholesome Doctrine, and very full of comfort, as more largely is expressed in the Homily of Justification.

XII.

De bonis Operibus.

Bona opera quæ sunt fructus fidei et iustificatos sequuntur, quanquam peccata nostra expiari et diuini iudicij seueritatem ferre non possunt, Deo tamen grata sunt et accepta in Christo, atque ex uera et uiua fide necessario profluunt, ut plane ex illis, æque fides uiua cognosci possit, atque arbor ex fructu iudicari.

XII.

Of good workes.

Albeit that good workes which are the fruites of fayth, and folowe after iustification, can not put away our sinnes, and endure the seueritie of Gods iudgement: yet are they pleasing and acceptable to God in Christe, and do spring out necessarily of a true and liuely fayth, in so muche that by them, a lyuely fayth may be as euidently knowen, as a tree discerned by the fruit.

XII.

Of Good Works.

Albeit that Good Works, which are the fruits of Faith, and follow after Justification, can not put away our sins, and endure the severity of God's judgment; yet are they pleasing and acceptable to God in Christ, and do spring out necessarily of a true and lively Faith; insomuch that by them a lively Faith may be as evidently known as a tree discerned by the fruit.

ED. LAT. 1563.	ENGLISH ED. 1571.	AMERICAN REVIS. 1801.

XIII.

Opera ante Iustificationem.

Opera quæ fiunt ante gratiam Christi, et spiritus eius afflatum, cum ex fide Iesu Christi non prodeant, minimè Deo grata sunt: neque gratiam (ut multi uocant) de congruo merentur: Imo cum non sint facta ut Deus illa fieri uoluit et præcepit, peccati rationem habere non dubitamus.

XIII.

Of workes before iustification.

Workes done before the grace of Christe, and the inspiration of his spirite, are not pleasaunt to God forasmuche as they spring not of fayth in Jesu Christ, neither do they make men meete to receaue grace, or (as the schole aucthours saye) deserue grace of congruitie: yea rather for that they are not done as GOD hath wylled and commaunded them to be done, we doubt not but they haue the nature of synne.

XIII.

Of Works before Justification.

Works done before the grace of Christ, and the Inspiration of his Spirit, are not pleasant to God, forasmuch as they spring not of faith in Jesus Christ; neither do they make men meet to receive grace, or (as the School-authors say) deserve grace of congruity: yea rather, for that they are not done as God hath willed and commanded them to be done, we doubt not but they have the nature of sin.

XIV.

Opera Supererogationis.

Opera quæ supererogationis appellant, non possunt sine arrogantia et impietate prædicari. Nam illis declarant homines non tantum se Deo reddere quæ tenentur sed plus in eius gratiam facere quam deberent: cum apertè Christus dicat: Cum feceritis omnia quæcunque præcepta sunt uobis, dicite: Serui inutiles sumus.

XIV.

Of workes of supererogation.

Voluntarie workes besydes, ouer and aboue Gods commaundementes, which they call workes of supererogation, can not be taught without arrogancie and impietie. For by them men do declare that they do not onely render vnto God as muche as they are bounde to do, but that they do more for his sake than of bounden duetie is required: Whereas Christe sayth playnly, When ye have done al that are commaunded to you, say, We be vnprofitable seruantes.

XIV.

Of Works of Supererogation.

Voluntary Works besides, over and above, God's Commandments, which they call Works of Supererogation, can not be taught without arrogancy and impiety: for by them men do declare, that they do not only render unto God as much as they are bound to do, but that they do more for his sake, than of bounden duty is required: whereas Christ saith plainly, When ye have done all that are commanded to you, say, We are unprofitable servants.

ED. LAT. 1563.	ENGLISH ED. 1571.	AMERICAN REVIS. 1801.
XV.	**XV.**	**XV.**
Nemo præter Christum sine peccato.	*Of Christe alone without sinne.*	*Of Christ alone without Sin.*
Christus in nostræ naturæ ueritate per omnia similis factus est nobis, excepto peccato, à quo prorsus erat immunis, tum in carne tum in spiritu. Venit, ut Agnus absque macula esset, qui mundi peccata per immolationem sui semel factam, tolleret: et peccatum (ut inquit Ioannes) in eo non erat. Sed nos reliqui, etiam baptizati, et in Christo regenerati, in multis tamen offendimus omnes: Et si dixerimus quia peccatum non habemus, nos ipsos seducimus, et veritas in nobis non est.	Christe in the trueth of oure nature, was made lyke vnto vs in al thinges (sinne only except) from which he was clearley voyde, both in his fleshe, and in his spirite. He came to be the lambe without spot, who by the sacrifice of hym self once made, shoulde take away the sinnes of the worlde: and sinne, (as S. John sayeth) was not in hym. But al we the rest, (although baptized, and borne agayne in Christ) yet offende in many thinges, and if we say we haue no sinne, we deceaue our selues, and the trueth is not in vs.	Christ in the truth of our nature was made like unto us in all things, sin only except, from which he was clearly void, both in his flesh, and in his spirit. He came to be the Lamb without spot, who, by sacrifice of himself once made, should take away the sins of the world; and sin (as Saint John saith) was not in him. But all we the rest, although baptized, and born again in Christ, yet offend in many things; and if we say we have no sin, we deceive ourselves, and the truth is not in us.
XVI.	**XVI.**	**XVI.**
De Lapsis post Baptismum.	*Of sinne after Baptisme.*	*Of Sin after Baptism.*
Non omne peccatum Mortale post baptismum uoluntarie perpetratum, est peccatum in Spiritum sanctum et irremissibile. Proinde lapsis à baptismo in peccata, locus pœnitentia non est negandus. Post acceptum spiritum sanctum, possumus à gratia data recedere atque peccare, denuóque per gratiam Dei resurgere ac resipiscere. Ideóque illi damnandi sunt, qui se quamdiu	Not euery deadly sinne willingly committed after baptiste, is sinne agaynst the holy ghost, and vnpardonable. Wherefore the graunt of repentaunce is not to be denyed to such as fall into sinne after baptisme. After we have receaued the holy ghost, we may depart from grace geuen, and fall into sinne, and by the grace of God (we may) aryse agayne,	Not every deadly sin willingly committed after Baptism is sin against the Holy Ghost, and unpardonable. Wherefore the grant of repentance is not to be denied to such as fall into sin after Baptism. After we have received the Holy Ghost, we may depart from grace given, and fall into sin, and by the grace of God we may arise again, and amend our lives. And

Ed. Lat. 1563.	English Ed. 1571.	American Revis. 1801.
hic viuant, amplius non posse peccare affirmant, aut verè resipiscentibus pœnitentiæ locum denegant.	and amend our lyues. And therefore, they are to be condemned, whiche say they can no more sinne as long as they lyue here, or denie the place of forgeuenesse to such as truely repent.	therefore they are to be condemned, which say, they can no more sin as long as they live here, or deny the place of forgiveness to such as truly repent.

XVII.	**XVII.**	**XVII.**
De Prædestinatione et Electione.	*Of predestination and election.*	*Of Predestination and Election.*
Prædestinatio ad uitam, est æternum Dei propositum, quo ante iacta mundi fundamenta, suo consilio, nobis quidem occulto, constanter decreuit, eos quos in Christo elegit ex hominum genere, à maledicto et exitio liberare, atque ut uasa in honorem efficta, per Christum ad æternam salutem adducere: Vnde qui tam præclaro Dei beneficio sunt donati, illi spiritu eius opportuno tempore operante, secundum propositum eius uocantur: uocationi per gratiam parent: iustificantur gratis: adoptantur in filios; vnigeniti Iesu Christi imagini efficiuntur conformes: in bonis operibus sanctè ambulant: et demùm ex Dei misericordia pertingunt ad sempiternam fœlicitatem.	Predestination to lyfe, is the euerlastyng purpose of God, whereby (before the foundations of the world were layd) he hath constantly decreed by his councell secrete to vs, to deliuer from curse and damnation, those whom he hath chosen in Christe out of mankynd, and to bryng them by Christe to euerlastyng saluation, as vessels made to honour. Wherefore they which be indued with so excellent a benefite of God, be called accordyng to Gods purpose by his spirite workyng in due season: they through grace obey the callyng: they be iustified freely: they be made sonnes of God by adoption: they be made lyke the image of his onelye begotten sonne Jesus Christe: they walke religiously in good workes, and at length by Gods mercy, they attaine to euerlastyng felicitie.	Predestination to Life is the everlasting purpose of God, whereby (before the foundations of the world were laid) he hath constantly decreed by his counsel secret to us, to deliver from curse and damnation those whom he hath chosen in Christ out of mankind, and to bring them by Christ to everlasting salvation, as vessels made to honour. Wherefore, they which be endued with so excellent a benefit of God, be called according to God's purpose by his Spirit working in due season: they through Grace obey the calling: they be justified freely: they be made sons of God by adoption: they be made like the image of his only-begotten Son Jesus Christ: they walk religiously in good works, and at length, by God's mercy, they attain to everlasting felicity.

ED. LAT. 1563.

Quemadmodum Prædestinationis et Electionis nostræ in Christo pia consideratio, dulcis, suauis et ineffabilis consolationis plena est verè pijs et his qui sentiunt in se uim spiritus CHRISTI, facta carnis et membra quæ adhuc sunt super terram mortificantem, animumque ad cœlestia et superna rapientem, tum quia fidem nostram de æterna salute consequenda per Christum plurimum stabilit atque confirmat, tum quia amorem nostrum in Deum uehementer accendit; ita hominibus curiosis, carnalibus, et spiritu Christi destitutis, ob oculos perpetuò versari Prædestinationis Dei sententiam, pernitiosissimum, est præcipitium, unde illos Diabolus protrudit, uel in desperationem, uel in æquè pernitiosam impurissimæ vitæ securitatem.

Deinde promissiones diuinas sic amplecti oportet, ut nobis in Sacris literis generaliter propositæ sunt: Et Dei voluntas in nostris actionibus ea sequenda est,

ENGLISH ED. 1571.

As the godly consyderation of predestination, and our election in Christe, is full of sweete, pleasaunt, and vnspeakeable comfort to godly persons, and such as feele in themselues the working of the spirite of Christe, mortifying the workes of the fleshe, and their earthlye members, and drawing vp their mynde to hygh and heauenly thinges, as well because it doth greatly establyshe and confirme their fayth of eternal saluation to be enjoyed through Christe, as because it doth feruently kindle their loue towardes God. So, for curious and carnal persons, lacking the spirite of Christe, to haue continually before their eyes the sentence of Gods predestination, is a most daungerous downefall, whereby the deuyll doth thrust them either into desperation, or into rechelesnesse of most vncleane liuing, no lesse perilous then desperation.

Furthermore,[1] we must receaue Gods promises in such wyse, as they be generally set foorth to vs in holy scripture: and in our doynges, that wyl of God is to

AMERICAN REVIS. 1801.

As the godly consideration of Predestination, and our Election in Christ, is full of sweet, pleasant, and unspeakable comfort to godly persons, and such as feel in themselves the working of the Spirit of Christ, mortifying the works of the flesh, and their earthly members, and drawing up their mind to high and heavenly things, as well because it doth greatly establish and confirm their faith of eternal Salvation to be enjoyed through Christ, as because it doth fervently kindle their love towards God: So, for curious and carnal persons, lacking the Spirit of Christ, to have continually before their eyes the sentence of God's Predestination, is a most dangerous downfall, whereby the Devil doth thrust them either into desperation, or into wretchlessness of most unclean living, no less perilous than desperation.

Furthermore, we must receive God's promises in such wise, as they be generally set forth to us in Holy Scripture; and, in our doings, that Will of God is

---

[1] In the Forty-two Articles of 1553 there is the addition: 'Although the decrees of predestination are unknown unto us.'

ED. LAT. 1563.	ENGLISH ED. 1571.	AMERICAN REVIS. 1801.
quam in uerbo Dei habemus disertè reuelatam.	be folowed, which we haue expreslye declared vnto vs in the worde of God.	to be followed, which we have expressly declared unto us in the Word of God.

XVIII.

Tantum in nomine Christi speranda est æterna salus.

Svnt illi anathematizandi qui dicere audent, vnumquemque in Lege aut secta quam profitetur, esse seruandum: modo iuxta illam et lumen naturæ accurate vixerit: cùm sacræ literæ tantum Iesu Christi nomen prædicent, in quo saluos fieri homines oporteat.

XVIII.

Of obtaynyng eternall saluation, only by the name of Christe.

They also are to be had accursed, that presume to say, that euery man shal be saued by the lawe or sect which he professeth, so that he be diligent to frame his life accordyng to that lawe, and the light of nature. For holy scripture doth set out vnto vs onely the name of Jesus Christe, whereby men must be saued.

XVIII.

Of obtaining eternal Salvation only by the Name of Christ.

They also are to be had accursed that presume to say, That every man shall be saved by the Law or Sect which he professeth, so that he be diligent to frame his life according to that Law, and the light of Nature. For Holy Scripture doth set out unto us only the Name of Jesus Christ, whereby men must be saved.

XIX.

De Ecclesia.

Ecclesia Christi uisibilis. est cœtus fidelium, in quo uerbum Dei purum prædicatur, et sacramenta, quoad ea quæ necessario exiguntur, iuxta Christi institutum rectè administrantur.

Sicut errauit ecclesia Hierosolymitana, Alexandrina et Antiochena: ita et errauit Ecclesia Romana, non solùm quoad agenda et cæremoniarum ritus, uerum in hijs etiam quæ credenda sunt.

XIX.

Of the Church.

The visible Church of Christe, is a congregation of faythfull men in the which the pure worde of God is preached, and the Sacramentes be duely ministred, accordyng to Christes ordinaunce in all those thynges that of necessitie are requisite to the same.

As the Church of Hierusalem, Alexandria, and Antioche haue erred: so also the Church of Rome hath erred, not only in their liuing and maner of ceremonies, but also in matters of fayth.

XIX.

Of the Church.

The visible Church of Christ is a congregation of faithful men, in the which the pure Word of God is preached, and the Sacraments be duly ministered according to Christ's ordinance, in all those things that of necessity are requisite to the same.

As the Church of Jerusalem, Alexandria, and Antioch, have erred; so also the Church of Rome hath erred, not only in their living and manner of Ceremonies, but also in matters of Faith.

ED. LAT. 1563	ENGLISH ED. 1571.	AMERICAN REVIS. 1801.
XX.	**XX.**	**XX.**
De Ecclesiæ autoritate.	*Of the aucthoritie of the Church.*	*Of the Authority of the Church.*
Habet Ecclesia Ritus statuendi ius, et in fidei controuersijs autoritatem, quamuis Ecclesiæ non licet quicquam instituere, quod verbo Dei scripto aduersetur, nec unum scripturæ locum sic exponere potest, ut alteri contradicat. Quare licet Ecclesia sit diuinorum librorum testis et conseruatrix, attamen vt aduersus eos nihil decernere, ita præter illos nihil credendum de necessitate salutis debet obtrudere.	The Church hath power to decree Rites or Ceremonies, and aucthoritie in controuersies of fayth : And yet it is not lawfull for the Church to ordayne any thyng that is contrarie to Gods worde written, neyther may it so expounde one place of scripture, that it be repugnaunt to another. Wherefore, although the Churche be a witnesse and a keper of holy writ: yet, as it ought not to decree any thing agaynst the same, so besides the same, ought it not to enforce any thing to be beleued for necessitie of saluation.	The Church hath power to decree Rites or Ceremonies, and authority in Controversies of Faith : and yet it is not lawful for the Church to ordain any thing that is contrary to God's Word written, neither may it so expound one place of Scripture, that it be repugnant to another. Wherefore, although the Church be a witness and a keeper of Holy Writ, yet, as it ought not to decree any thing against the same, so besides the same ought it not to enforce any thing to be believed for necessity of Salvation.
XXI.	**XXI.**	**XXI.**
De autoritate Conciliorum Generalium.	*Of the aucthoritie of generall Counselles.*	*Of the Authority of General Councils.*[1]
Generalia Concilia sine iussu et uoluntate principum congregari non possunt, et vbi conuenerint, quia ex hominibus constant, qui non omnes spiritu et uerbis Dei reguntur, et errare possunt, et interdum errarunt, etiam in hijs quæ ad normam pietatis pertinent: ideo quæ ab illis constituuntur,	*Generall Counsels may not be gathered together without the commaundement and wyll of princes. And when they be gathered together (forasmuche as they be an assemblie of men, whereof all be not gouerned with the spirite and word of God) they may erre, and sometyme haue erred, euen in thinges par-*	

---

[1] The Twenty-first of the English Articles is omitted in the Amer. ed., because it is partly of a local and civil nature, and is provided for, as to the remaining parts of it, in other Articles.

ED. LAT. 1563.	ENGLISH ED. 1571.	AMERICAN REVIS. 1801.

ut ad salutem necessaria, neque robur habent, neque autoritatem, nisi ostendi possint è sacris literis esse desumpta.

teynyng vnto God. Wherfore, thinges ordayned by them as necessary to saluation, haue neyther strength nor aucthoritie, vnlesse it may be declared that they be taken out of holy Scripture.

XXII.
De Purgatorio.

Doctrina Romanensium de Purgatorio, de Indulgentijs, de veneratione et adoratione tum Imaginum tum Reliquiarum, nec non de inuocatione Sanctorum, res est futilis, inaniter conficta, et nullis Scripturarum testimonijs innititur, imo verbo Dei contradicit.

XXII.
Of Purgatorie.

The Romishe doctrine concernyng purgatorie, pardons, worshipping and adoration, as well of images, as of reliques, and also inuocation of Saintes, is a fonde thing, vainly inuented, and grounded vpon no warrantie of Scripture, but rather repugnaunt to the worde of God.

XXII.
Of Purgatory.

The Romish Doctrine concerning Purgatory, Pardons, Worshipping and Adoration, as well of Images as of Relics, and also Invocation of Saints, is a fond thing, vainly invented, and grounded upon no warranty of Scripture, but rather repugnant to the Word of God.

XXIII.
Nemo in Ecclesia ministret nisi uocatus.

Non licet cuiquam sumere sibi munus publicè prædicandi, aut administrandi Sacramenta in Ecclesia, nisi prius fuerit ad hæc obeunda legitimè uocatus et missus. Atque illos, legitimè uocatos et missos existimare debemus, qui per homines, quibus potestas uocandi Ministros atque mittendi in uineam Domini publicè concessa est in Ecclesia, cooptati fuerint et asciti in hoc opus.

XXIII.
Of ministryng in the congregation.

It is not lawful for any man to take vpon hym the office of publique preachyng, or ministring the Sacramentes in the congregation, before he be lawfully called and sent to execute the same. And those we ought to iudge lawfully called and sent, whiche be chosen and called to this worke by men who haue publique aucthoritie geuen vnto them in the congregation, to call and sende ministers into the Lordes vineyarde.

XXIII.
Of Ministering in the Congregation.

It is not lawful for any man to take upon him the office of public preaching, or ministering the Sacraments in the Congregation, before he be lawfully called, and sent to execute the same. And those we ought to judge lawfully called and sent, which be chosen and called to this work by men who have public authority given unto them in the Congregation, to call and send Ministers into the Lord's vineyard.

ED. LAT. 1563.	ENGLISH ED. 1571.	AMERICAN REVIS. 1801.

XXIV.

Agendum est in Ecclesia lingua quæ sit populo nota.

Lingua populo non intellecta publicas in ecclesia preces peragere, aut Sacramenta administrare, verbo Dei et primitiuæ Ecclesiæ consuetudini planè repugnat.

XXIV.

Of speakyng in the congregation, in such a tongue as the people vnderstandeth.

It is a thing playnely repugnaunt to the worde of God, and the custome of the primitiue Churche, to haue publique prayer in the Churche, or to minister the Sacramentes in a tongue not vnderstanded of the people.

XXIV.

Of Speaking in the Congregation in such a Tongue as the people understandeth.

It is a thing plainly repugnant to the Word of God, and the custom of the Primitive Church, to have public Prayer in the Church, or to minister the Sacraments, in a tongue not understood of the people.

XXV.

De Sacramentis.

Sacramenta à Christo instituta, non tantum sunt notæ professionis Christianorum, sed certa quædam potius testimonia, et efficacia signa gratiæ, atque bonæ in nos uoluntatis Dei, per quæ inuisibiliter ipse in nobis operatur, nostrámque fidem in se, non solum excitat, uerumetiam confirmat.

Duo à Christo Domino nostro in Euangelio instituta sunt Sacramenta, scilicet Baptismus et Cœna Domini.

Quinque illa uulgo nominata Sacramenta, scilicet, Confirmatio, Pœnitentia, Ordo, Matrimonium, et Extrema unctio, pro sacramentis euangelicis habenda non sunt, ut quæ partim à praua Apostolorum imitatione pro-

XXV.

Of the Sacramentes.

Sacramentes ordayned of Christe, be not onely badges or tokens of Christian mens profession : but rather they be certaine sure witnesses and effectuall signes of grace and Gods good wyll towardes vs, by the which he doth worke inuisiblie in vs, and doth not only quicken, but also strengthen and confirme our fayth in hym.

There are two Sacramentes ordayned of Christe our Lorde in the Gospell, that is to say, Baptisme, and the Supper of the Lorde.

Those fyue, commonly called Sacramentes, that is to say, Confirmation, Penaunce, Orders, Matrimonie, and extreme Vnction, are not to be compted, for Sacramentes of the gospel, being such as haue growen

XXV.

Of the Sacraments.

Sacraments ordained of Christ be not only badges or tokens of Christian men's profession, but rather they be certain sure witnesses, and effectual signs of grace, and God's good will towards us, by the which he doth work invisibly in us, and doth not only quicken, but also strengthen and confirm our Faith in him.

There are two Sacraments ordained of Christ our Lord in the Gospel, that is to say, Baptism, and the Supper of the Lord.

Those five commonly called Sacraments, that is to say, Confirmation, Penance, Orders, Matrimony, and Extreme Unction, are not to be counted for Sacraments of the Gospel, being such as have grown

Ed. Lat. 1563.	English Ed. 1571.	American Revis. 1801.
fluxerunt, partim uitæ status sunt in scripturis quidem probati, sed sacramentorum eandem cum baptismo et cœna Domini rationem non habentes: quomodo nec Pœnitentia, ut quæ signum aliquod uisibile seu cæremoniam a Deo institutam non habeat.	partly of the corrupt folowing of the Apostles, partly are states of life alowed in the scriptures: but yet haue not lyke nature of Sacramentes with Baptisme and the Lordes Supper, for that they haue not any visible signe or ceremonie ordayned of God.	partly of the corrupt following of the Apostles, partly are states of life allowed in the Scriptures; but yet have not like nature of Sacraments with Baptism, and the Lord's Supper, for that they have not any visible sign or ceremony ordained of God.
Sacramenta non in hoc instituta sunt à Christo, ut spectarentur, aut circumferentur, sed ut ritè illis uteremur: et in hijs duntaxat qui dignè percipiunt, salutarem habent effectum: qui uerò indigne percipiunt, damnationem (ut inquit Paulus) sibi ipsis acquirunt.	The Sacramentes were not ordayned of Christ to be gased vpon, or to be caryed about; but that we shoulde duely use them. And in such only, as worthyly receaue the same, they haue a wholesome effect or operation: But they that receaue them vnworthyly, purchase to them selues damnation, as S. Paul sayth.	The Sacraments were not ordained of Christ to be gazed upon, or to be carried about, but that we should duly use them. And in such only as worthily receive the same, they have a wholesome effect or operation: but they that receive them unworthily, purchase to themselves damnation, as Saint Paul saith.
## XXVI.	## XXVI.	## XXVI.
Ministrorum malitia non tollit efficaciam institutionum diuinarum.	*Of the unworthynesse of the ministers, which hinder not the effect of the Sacramentes.*	*Of the Unworthiness of the Ministers, which hinders not the effect of the Sacraments.*
Qvamuis in Ecclesia uisibili bonis mali semper sint admixti, atque interdum ministerio uerbi et sacramentorum administrationi præsint, tamen cùm non suo sed Christi nomine agant, eiúsque mandato et autoritate ministrent, illorum ministerio uti licet, cum in verbo Dei audiendo, tum in sacramentis percipiendis. Neque per illorum malitiam effec-	Although in the visible Churche the euyl be euer myngled with the good, and sometime the euyll haue cheefe aucthoritie in the ministration of the worde and Sacramentes: yet forasmuch as they do not the same in their own name but in Christes, and do minister by his commission and aucthoritie, we may vse their minis-	Although in the visible Church the evil be ever mingled with the good, and sometimes the evil have chief authority in the Ministration of the Word and Sacraments, yet forasmuch as they do not the same in their own name, but in Christ's, and do minister by his commission and authority, we may use their Ministry, both in

ED. LAT. 1563.

tus institutorum Christi tollitur, aut gratia donorum Dei minuitur, quoad eos qui fide et ritè sibi oblata percipiunt, quæ propter institutionem CHRISTI et promissionem efficacia sunt, licet per malos administrentur.

Ad Ecclesiæ tamen disciplinam pertinent, ut in malos ministros inquiratur, accusentúrque ab hijs, qui eorum flagitia nouerint, atque tandem iusto conuicti iudicio, deponantur.

XXVII.

De Baptismo.

Baptismus non est tantùm professionis signum ac discriminis nota, qua Christiani à non Christianis discernantur, sed etiam est signum Regenerationis, per quod tanquam per instrumentum rectè baptismum suspitientes, ecclesiæ inseruntur, promissiones de Remissione peccatorum atque Adoptione nostra in filios Dei, per Spiritum sanctum uisi-

ENGLISH ED. 1571.

trie, both in hearing the word of God, and in *the* receauing *of* the Sacramentes. Neither is yᵉ effect of Christes ordinaunce taken away by their wickednesse, nor the grace of Gods gyftes diminished from such as by fayth and ryghtly do receaue the Sacramentes ministered vnto them, which be effectuall, because of Christes institution and promise, although they be ministred by euyll men.

Neuerthelesse, it apperteyneth to the discipline of the Churche, that enquirie be made of euyl ministres, and that they be accused by those that haue knowledge of their offences: and finally, beyng founde gyltie by iust iudgement, be deposed.

XXVII.

Of Baptisme.

Baptisme is not onely a signe of profession, and marke of difference, whereby Christian men are discerned from other that be not christened: but is also a signe of regeneration or newe byrth, whereby as by an instrument, they that receaue baptisme rightly, are grafted into the Church: the promises of the forgcuenesse of sinne, and of

AMERICAN REVIS. 1801.

hearing the Word of God, and in receiving the Sacraments. Neither is the effect of Christ's ordinance taken away by their wickedness, nor the grace of God's gifts diminished from such as by faith, and rightly, do receive the Sacraments ministered unto them; which be effectual, because of Christ's institution and promise, although they be ministered by evil men.

Nevertheless, it appertaineth to the discipline of the Church, that inquiry be made of evil Ministers, and that they be accused by those that have knowledge of their offences; and finally, being found guilty, by just judgment be deposed.

XXVII.

Of Baptism.

Baptism is not only a sign of profession, and mark of difference, whereby Christian men are discerned from others that be not christened, but *it* is also a sign of Regeneration or New-Birth, whereby, as by an instrument, they that receive Baptism rightly are grafted into the Church; the promises of the forgiveness of sin, and

ED. LAT. 1563.	ENGLISH ED. 1571.	AMERICAN REVIS. 1801.

biliter obsignantur, fides con-firmatur, et ui diuinæ in-uocationis, gratia augetur.

our adoption to be the sonnes of God, by the holy ghost, are visibly signed and sealed: fayth is confyrmed: and grace increased by vertue of prayer vnto God.

of our adoption to be the sons of God by the Holy Ghost, are visibly signed and sealed; Faith is con-firmed, and Grace increased by virtue of prayer unto God.

Baptismus paruulorum omnino in ecclesia retinen-dus est, ut qui cum Chri-sti institutione optimè con-gruat.

The baptisme of young children, is in any wyse to be retayned in the Churche, as most agre-able with the institution of Christe.

The Baptism of young Children is in any wise to be retained in the Church, as most agreeable with the institution of Christ.

XXVIII.
De Cœna Domini.

Cœna Domini non est tantùm signum mutuæ be-neuolentiæ Christianorum inter sese, uerum potiùs est sacramentum nostræ per mortem Christi redemptio-nis. Atque adeo ritè, dignè et cum fide sumentibus, pa-nis quem frangimus, est communicatio corporis Chri-sti: similiter poculum bene-dictionis, est communicatio sanguinis Christi.

XXVIII.
Of the Lordes Supper.

The Supper of the Lord, is not only a signe of the loue that Christians ought to haue among them selues one to another: but rather it is a Sacrament of our redemption by Christes death. Insomuch that to suche as ryghtlie, worthy-ly, and with fayth receaue the same the bread whiche we breake is a parttak-yng of the body of Christe, and likewyse the cuppe of blessing, is a parttakyng of the blood of Christe.

XXVIII.
Of the Lord's Supper.

The Supper of the Lord is not only a sign of the love that Christians ought to have among themselves one to another; but rather it is a Sacrament of our Redemption by Christ's death: insomuch that to such as rightly, worthily, and with faith, receive the same, the Bread which we break is a partaking of the Body of Christ; and like-wise the Cup of Blessing is a partaking of the Blood of Christ.

Panis et vini transub-stantiatio in Eucharistia, ex sacris literis probari non potest, sed apertis scriptu-ræ verbis aduersatur, sacra-menti naturam euertit, et

Transubstantiation (or the chaunge of the sub-staunce of bread and wine) in the Supper of the Lorde, can not be proued by holye writ, but is repugnaunt to the playne wordes of script-ure, ouerthroweth the nat-ure of a Sacrament, and

Transubstantiation (or the change of the substance of Bread and Wine) in the Supper of the Lord, can not be proved by Holy Writ; but is repugnant to the plain words of Script-ure, overthroweth the nat-ure of a Sacrament, and *multarum superstitionum dedit occasionem.*[1]

hath geuen occasion to many superstitions.

hath given occasion to many superstitions.

Corpus Christi datur, accipitur, et manducatur in cœna, tantùm cœlesti et spirituali ratione. Medium autem quo Corpus Christi accipitur et manducatur in cœna, fides est.

The body of Christe is geuen, taken, and eaten in the Supper only after an heauenly and spirituall maner: And the meane whereby the body of Christe is receaued and eaten in the Supper, is fayth.

The Body of Christ is given, taken, and eaten, in the Supper, only after an heavenly and spiritual manner. And the mean whereby the Body of Christ is received and eaten in the Supper, is Faith.

Sacramentum Eucharistiæ ex institutione Christi non seruabatur, circumferebatur, eleuabatur, nec adorabatur.

The Sacrament of the Lordes Supper was not by Christes ordinaunce reserued, caryed about, lyfted vp, or worshipped.

The Sacrament of the Lord's Supper was not by Christ's ordinance reserved, carried about, lifted up, or worshiped.

[XXIX.[2]

XXIX.

XXIX.

Of the wicked which do not eate the body of Christe in the vse of the Lordes Supper.

Of the Wicked, which eat not the Body of Christ in the use of the Lord's Supper.

[*Impii, et fide viua destituti, licet carnaliter et visibiliter (vt Augustinus loquitur) corporis et sanguinis Christi sacramentum dentibus premant, nullo tamen modo Christi participes efficiuntur. Sed potius tantæ rei sacramentum seu sym-*

The wicked, and suche as be voyde of a liuelye fayth, although they do carnally and visibly presse with their teeth (as Saint Augustine sayth) the Sacrament of the body and blood of Christ: yet in no wyse are the partakers of

The Wicked, and such as be void of a lively faith, although they do carnally and visibly press with their teeth (as Saint Augustine saith) the Sacrament of the Body and Blood of Christ; yet in no wise are they partakers of Christ:

---

[1] The following clause against the real presence and ubiquity of Christ's body was here added in the Parker Latin MS., but struck out in the Synod: ' *Christus in cœlum ascendens, corpori suo Immortalitatem dedit, Naturam non abstulit humane enim nature veritatem (iuxta Scripturas), perpetuo retinet, quam uno et definito Loco esse, et non in multa, vel omnia simul loca diffundi oportet. Quum igitur Christus in celum sublatus, ibi usque ad finem seculi permansurus, atque inde, non aliunde (ut loquitur Augustinus) venturus sit, ad iudicandum viuos et mortuos, non debet quisquam fidelium, et carnis eius, et sanguinis, realem, et corporalem (ut loquuntur) presentiam in Eucharistia vel credere, vel profiteri. Corpus tamen Christi datur.*' etc.

[2] This Article, which agrees with the Zwinglian and Calvinistic theory against the Lutheran, is wanting in all the printed copies until 1571, and has here been supplied from the Parker MS. See Hardwick, p. 315, note 3, and p. 143.

ED. LAT. 1563.	ENGLISH ED. 1571.	AMERICAN REVIS. 1801.

bolum ad judicium sibi man- ducant et bibunt.]

Christe, but rather to their condemnation do eate and drinke the signe or Sacrament of so great a thing.

but rather, to their condemnation, do eat and drink the sign or Sacrament of so great a thing.

XXIX. [XXX.]
De Vtraque Specie.

Calix Domini Laicis non est denegandus: utraque enim pars dominici sacramenti ex Christi institutione et præcepto, omnibus Christianis ex æquo administrari debet.

XXX.
Of both kindes.

The cuppe of the Lorde is not to be denyed to the laye people. For both the partes of the Lordes Sacrament, by Christes ordinaunce and commaundement, ought to be ministred to all Christian men alike.

XXX.
Of both Kinds.

The Cup of the Lord is not to be denied to the Lay-people: for both the parts of the Lord's Sacrament, by Christ's ordinance and commandment, ought to be ministered to all Christian men alike.

XXX. [XXXI.]
De unica Christi oblatione in Cruce perfecta.

Oblatio Christi semel facta, perfecta est redemptio, propitiatio, et satisfactio pro omnibus peccatis totius mundi, tam originalibus quam actualibus. Neque præter illam unicam est ulla alia pro peccatis expiatio. Vnde missarum sacrificia, quibus uulgo dicebatur, Sacerdotem offerre Christum in remissionem pœna aut culpæ pro uiuis et defunctis, blasphema figmenta sunt, et pernitiosæ imposturæ.

XXXI.
Of the one oblation of Christe finished vppon the Crosse.

The offering of Christ once made, is *the* perfect redemption, propiciation, and satisfaction for all the sinnes of the whole worlde, both originall and actuall, and there is none other satisfaction for sinne, but that alone. Wherefore the sacrifices of Masses, in the which it was commonly said that the Priestes did offer Christe for the quicke and the dead, to haue remission of payne or gylt, were blasphemous fables, and daungerous deceits.

XXXI.
Of the one Oblation of Christ finished upon the Cross.

The Offering of Christ once made is *that* perfect redemption, propitiation, and satisfaction, for all the sins of the whole world, both original and actual; and there is none other satisfaction for sin, but that alone. Wherefore the sacrifices of Masses, in the which it was commonly said that the Priest did offer Christ for the quick and the dead, to have remission of pain or guilt, were blasphemous fables, and dangerous deceits.

XXXI. [XXXII.]
De Coniugio Sacerdotum.

Episcopis, Presbyteris, et Diaconis, nullo mandato di-

XXXII.
Of the mariage of Priestes.

Byshops, Priestes, and Deacons, are not com-

XXXII.
Of the Marriage of Priests.

Bishops, Priests, and Deacons, are not com-

Ed. Lat. 1563.	English Ed. 1571.	American Revis. 1801.
uino praeceptum est, ut aut caelibatum uoueant, aut à matrimonio abstineant. Licet igitur etiam illis, vt caeteris omnibus Christianis, vbi hoc ad pietatem magis facere iudicauerint, pro suo arbitratu matrimonium contrahere.	maunded by Gods lawe eyther to vowe the estate of single lyfe, or to abstayne from mariage. Therefore it is lawfull *also* for them, as for all other Christian men, to mary at ther owne discretion, as they shall iudge the same to serue better to godlynesse.	manded by God's Law, either to vow the estate of single life, or to abstain from marriage : therefore it is lawful for them, as for all other Christian men, to marry at their own discretion, as they shall judge the same to serve better to godliness.
XXXII. [XXXIII.] **Excommunicati uitandi sunt.** *Qvi per publicam Ecclesiae denuntiationem ritè ab unitate ecclesiae praecisus est et excommunicatus, is ab uniuersa fidelium multitudine, donec per poenitentiam publicè reconciliatus fuerit, arbitrio Iudicis competentis, habendus est tanquam Ethnicus et Publicanus.*	**XXXIII.** *Of excommunicate persons, howe they are to be auoided.* That person whiche by open denuntiation of the Churche, is rightly cut of from the vnitie of the Churche, and excommunicated, ought to be taken of the whole multitude of the faythfull as an Heathen and Publicane, vntill he be openly reconciled by penaunce, and receaued into the Churche by a iudge that hath aucthoritie *thereto*.	**XXXIII.** *Of excommunicate Persons, how they are to be avoided.* That person which by open denunciation of the Church is rightly cut off from the unity of the Church, and excommunicated, ought to be taken of the whole multitude of the faithful, as a Heathen and Publican, until he be openly reconciled by penance, and received into the Church by a judge that hath authority *thereunto*.
XXXIII. [XXXIV.] **Traditiones Ecclesiasticae.** *Traditiones atque caeremonias easdem, non omnino necessarium est esse ubique aut prorsus consimiles. Nam et uariae semper fuerunt, et mutari possunt, pro regionum, temporum, et morum diuersitate, modo nihil contra uerbum Dei instituatur.*	**XXXIV.** *Of the traditions of the Churche.* It is not necessarie that traditions and ceremonies be in al places one, or vtterly like, for at all times they haue ben diuerse, and may be chaunged accordyng to the diuersitie of countreys, times, and mens maners, so that nothing be ordeyned against Gods worde.	**XXXIV.** *Of the Traditions of the Church.* It is not necessary that Traditions and Ceremonies be in all places one, or utterly like; for at all times they have been divers, and may be changed according to the diversity of countries, times, and men's maners, so that nothing be ordained against God's Word.

ED. LAT. 1563.	ENGLISH ED. 1571.	AMERICAN REVIS. 1801.
Traditiones et cæremonias ecclesiasticas quæ cum uerbo Dei non pugnant, et sunt autoritate publica institutæ atque probatæ, quisquis priuato consilio uolens et data opera publicè uiolauerit, is, ut qui peccat in publicum ordinem ecclesiæ, quique lædit autoritatem Magistratus, et qui infirmorum fratrum conscientias uulnerat, publicè, ut cæteri timeant, arguendus est.	Whosoeuer through his priuate iudgement, wyllyngly and purposely doth openly breake the traditions and ceremonies of the Church, which be not repugnaunt to the worde of God, and be ordayned and approued by common aucthoritie, ought to be rebuked openly (that other may feare to do the lyke), as he that offendeth agaynst the Common order of the Churche and hurteth the aucthoritie of the Magistrate, and woundeth the consciences of the weake brethren.	Whosoever, through his private judgment, willingly and purposely, doth openly break the Traditions and Ceremonies of the Church, which be not repugnant to the Word of God, and be ordained and approved by common authority, ought to be rebuked openly (that others may fear to do the like), as he that offendeth against the common order of the Church, and hurteth the authority of the Magistrate, and woundeth the consciences of the weak brethren.
Quælibet ecclesia particularis, siue nationalis autoritatem habet instituendi, mutandi, aut abrogandi cæremonias aut ritus Ecclesiasticos, humana tantum autoritate institutos, modò omnia ædificationem fiant.	Euery particuler or nationall Churche, hath aucthoritie to ordaine, chaunge, and abolishe ceremonies or rites of the Churche ordeyned onlye by mans aucthoritie, so that all thinges be done to edifiyng.	Every particular or national Church hath authority to ordain, change, and abolish, Ceremonies or Rites of the Church ordained only by man's authority, so that all things be done to edifying.

XXXIV. [XXXV.]	XXXV.	XXXV.
Catalogus Homiliarum.	*Of Homilies.*	*Of the Homilies.*
Tomus secundus Homiliarum, quarum singulos titulos huic Articulo subiunximus, continet piam et salutarem doctrinam, et hijs temporibus necessariam, non minus quàm prior Tomus Homiliarum quæ æditæ sunt tempore Edwardi sexti. Itaque eas in ecclesijs per ministros diligenter et clarè, ut à populo	The seconde booke of Homilies, the seuerall titles whereof we haue ioyned vnder this article, doth conteyne a godly and wholesome doctrine, and necessarie for these tymes, as doth the former booke of Homilies, which were set foorth in the time of Edwarde the sixt: and	The Second Book of Homilies, the several titles whereof we have joined under this Article, doth contain a godly and wholesome Doctrine, and necessary for these times, as doth the former Book of Homilies, which were set forth in the time of Edward the Sixth; and there-

ED. LAT. 1563.	ENGLISH ED. 1571.	AMERICAN REVIS. 1801.
intelligi possint, recitandas, esse iudicamus.	therefore we iudge them to be read in Churches by the Ministers diligently, and distinctly, that they may be vnderstanded by the people.	fore we judge them to be read in Churches by the Ministers, diligently and distinctly, that they may be understanded of the people.
[XXXIV.]		
Catalogus Homiliarum.	*Of the names of the Homilies.*	*Of the Names of the Homilies.*
De recto ecclesiæ usu.	1 Of the right vse of the Churche.	1. Of the right Use of the Church.
Aduersus Idololatriæ pericula.	2 Agaynst perill of Idolatrie.	2. Against Peril of Idolatry.
De reparandis ac purgandis ecclesijs.	3 Of repayring and keping cleane of Churches.	3. Of repairing and keeping clean of Churches.
De bonis operibus.	4 Of good workes, first of fastyng.	4. Of good Works: first of Fasting.
De ieiunio.		
In gulæ atque ebrietatis uitia.	5 Agaynst gluttony and drunkennesse.	5. Against Gluttony and Drunkenness.
In nimis sumptuosos uestium apparatus.	6 Agaynst excesse of apparell.	6. Against Excess of Apparel.
De oratione siue precatione.	7 Of prayer.	7. Of Prayer.
De loco et tempore orationi destinatis.	8 Of the place and time of prayer.	8. Of the Place and Time of Prayer.
De publicis precibus ac Sacramentis, idiomate uulgari omnibusque noto, habendis.	9 That common prayer and Sacramentes ought to be ministred in a knowen tongue.	9. That Common Prayers and Sacraments ought to be ministered in a known tongue.
De sacrosancta uerbi divini autoritate.	10 Of the reuerente estimation of Gods worde.	10. Of the reverend Estimation of God's Word.
De eleemosina.	11 Of almes doing.	11. Of Alms-doing.
De Christi natiuitate.	12 Of the Natiuitie of Christe.	12. Of the Nativity of Christ.
De dominica passione.	13 Of the passion of Christe.	13. Of the Passion of Christ.
De resurrectione Domini.	14 Of the resurrection of Christe.	14. Of the Resurrection of Christ.
De digna corporis et sanguinis dominici in cæna Domini participatione.	15 Of the worthie receauing of the Sacrament of the body and blood of Christe.	15. Of the worthy receiving of the Sacrament of the Body and Blood of Christ.
De donis spiritus sancti.		
In diebus, qui uulgo Rogationum dicti sunt, concio.	16 Of the gyftes of the holy ghost.	16. Of the Gifts of the Holy Ghost.
De matrimonij statu.	17 For the Rogation dayes.	17. For the Rogation-days
De otio seu socordia.		
De pœnitentia.		

Ed. Lat. 1563.	English Ed. 1571.	American Revis. 1801.
	18 Of the state of Matrimonie.	18. Of the State of Matrimony.
	19 Of repentaunce.	19. Of Repentance.
	20 Agaynst Idlenesse.	20. Against Idleness.
	21 Agaynst rebellion.	21. Against Rebellion.

[*This Article is received in this Church, so far as it declares the Books of Homilies to be an explication of Christian doctrine, and instructive in piety and morals. But all references to the constitution and laws of England are considered as inapplicable to the circumstances of this Church; which also suspends the order for the reading of said Homilies in churches, until a revision of them may be conveniently made, for the clearing of them, as well from obsolete words and phrases, as from the local references.*]

XXXV. [XXXVI.]	XXXVI.	XXXVI.
	Of consecration of Bishops and ministers.	*Of Consecration of Bishops and Ministers.*

Libellus de Consecratione Archiepiscoporum & Episcoporum, & de ordinatione Presbyterorum & Diaconorum æditus nuper temporibus Edwardi sexti, & autoritate Parlamenti illis ipsis temporibus confirmatus, omnia ad eiusmodi consecrationem & ordinationem necessaria continet, & nihil habet quod ex se sit aut superstitiosum aut impium.

The booke of Consecration of *Archbyshops, and* Byshops, and orderyng of Priestes and Deacons, *lately set foorth in the time of Edwarde the sixt,* and con-fyrmed at the same tyme by aucthoritie of Parliament, doth conteyne all thinges necessarie to suche consecration and orderyng: neyther hath it any thing, that of it selfe is superstitious

The Book of Consecration of Bishops, and Ordering of Priests and Deacons, *as set forth by the General Convention of this Church in 1792,* doth contain all things necessary to such Consecration and Ordering; neither hath it any thing that, of itself, is superstitious *and* ungodly. And, therefore, whosoever are consecrated or ordered

ED. LAT. 1563.	ENGLISH ED. 1571.	AMERICAN REVIS. 1801.

Itaque quicunque iuxta ritus illius libri consecrati aut ordinati sunt ab Anno secundo prædicti Regis Edwardi, usque ad hoc tempus, aut in posterum iuxta eosdem ritus consecrabuntur aut ordinabuntur ritè, ordine, atque legitimè, statuimus esse & fore consecratos & ordinatos.

or vngodly. And therefore, whosoeuer are consecrate or ordered accordyng *to the rites of that booke, sence the seconde yere of the aforenamed king Edwarde, vnto this time or hereafter shal be consecrated or ordered accordyng to the same rites,* we decree all such to be ryghtly, orderly, and lawfully consecrated and ordered.

according to *said Form,* we decree all such to be rightly, orderly, and lawfully consecrated and ordered.

XXXVI. [XXXVII.]
De ciuilibus Magistratibus.

XXXVII.
Of the ciuill Magistrates.

XXXVII.
Of the Power of *the Civil Magistrates.*

Regia Maiestas in hoc Angliæ Regno ac cæteris eius Dominijs, iure summam habet potestatem, ad quam omnium statuum huius Regni, siue illi ecclesiastici sunt siue non, in omnibus causis suprema gubernatio pertinet, & nulli externæ iurisdictioni est subiecta, nec esse debet.

Cum Regiæ Maiestati summam gubernationem tribuimus, quibus titulis intelligimus animos quorundam calumniatorum offendi: non damus Regibus nostris aut uerbi Dei aut sacramentorum administrationem, quod etiam Iniunctiones ab Elizabetha Regina nostra nuper æditæ, apertissimè testantur: sed eam tantùm prærogatiuam, quam in sacris scripturis à Deo ipso omnibus pijs

The Queenes Maiestie hath the cheefe power in this Realme of Englande, and other her dominions, vnto whom the cheefe gouernment of all estates of this Realme, whether they be Ecclesiasticall or Ciuile, in all causes doth apparteine, and is not, nor ought to be subiect to any forraigne iurisdiction.

Where we attribute to the Queenes Maiestie the cheefe gouernment, by whiche titles we vnderstande the mindes of some slanderous folkes to be offended: we geue not to our princes the ministring either of God's word, or of Sacraments, the which thing the iniunctions also lately set forth by Elizabeth our Queene, doth most plainlie testifie: But that only prerogatiue whiche we see to

The Power of the Civil Magistrate extendeth to all men, as well Clergy as Laity, in all things temporal; but hath no authority in things purely spiritual. And we hold it to be the duty of all men who are professors of the Gospel, to pay respectful obedience to the Civil Authority, regularly and legitimately constituted.

ED. LAT. 1563.	ENGLISH ED. 1571.	AMERICAN REVIS. 1801.

Principibus, uidemus semper fuisse attributam, hoc est, ut omnes status atque ordines fidei suæ à Deo commissos, siue illi ecclesiastici sint, siue ciuiles, in officio contineant, & contumaces ac delinquentes, gladio ciuili coërceant.

haue ben geuen alwayes to all godly Princes in holy Scriptures by God him selfe, that is, that they should rule all estates and degrees committed to their charge by God, whether they be Ecclesiasticall or Temporall, and restraine with the ciuill sworde the stubberne and euyll doers.

Romanus Pontifex nullam habet iurisdictionem in hoc regno Angliæ.

The bishop of Rome hath no iurisdiction in this Realme of Englande.

Leges Ciuiles possunt Christianos propter capitalia et grauia crimina morte punire.

The lawes of the Realme may punishe Christian men with death, for heynous and greeuous offences.

Christianis licet et ex mandato Magistratus arma portare, et iusta bella administrare.

It is lawfull for Christian men, at the commaundement of the Magistrate, to weare weapons, and serue in the warres.

XXXVII. [XXXVIII.]

Christianorum bona non sunt communia.

Facultates & bona Christianorum non sunt communia quoad ius & possessionem, vt quidam Anabaptistæ falso iactant. Debet tamen quisque de hijs quæ possidet, pro facultatum ratione, pauperibus eleemosynas benigne distribure.

XXXVIII.

Of Christian mens goodes, which are not common.

The ryches and goodes of Christians are not common, as touching the ryght, title, and possession of the same, as certayne Anabaptistes do falsely boast. Notwithstandyng euery man ought of suche thinges as he possesseth, liberally to geue almes to the poore, accordyng to his habilitie.

XXXVIII.

Of Christian Men's Goods, which are not common.

The Riches and Goods of Christians are not common, as touching the right, title, and possession of the same; as certain Anabaptists do falsely boast. Notwithstanding, every man ought, of such things as he possesseth, liberally to give alms to the poor, according to his ability.

XXXVIII. [XXXIX.]

Licet Christianis Iurare.

Qvemadmodum iuramen-

XXXIX.

Of a Christian mans othe.

As we confesse that vayne

XXXIX.

Of a Christian Man's Oath.

As we confess that vain

ED. LAT. 1563.	ENGLISH ED. 1571.	AMERICAN REVIS. 1801.

tum uanum & temerarium à Domino nostro Iesu Christo, & Apostolo eius Iacobo, Christianis hominibus interdictum esse fatemur: ita Christianam religionem minimè prohibere censemus, quin iubente Magistratu, in causa fidei & charitatis, iurare liceat, modò id fiat iuxta, Prophetæ doctrinam, in iustitia, in iudicio, & ueritate.[1]

and rashe swearing is forbidden Christian men by our Lord Jesus Christe, and James his Apostle: So we iudge that Christian religion doth not prohibite, but that a man may sweare when the Magistrate requireth, in a cause of faith and charitie, so it be done accordyng to the prophetes teaching, in iustice, iudgement, and trueth.[1]

and rash Swearing is forbidden Christian men by our Lord Jesus Christ, and James his Apostle, so we judge, that Christian Religion doth not prohibit, but that a man may swear when the Magistrate requireth, in a cause of faith and charity, so it be done according to the Prophets' teaching, in justice, judgment, and truth.

[The remainder of the English editions is omitted in the American Revision.]

The Ratification.

Hos Articulos fidei Christianæ, continentes in uniuersum nouemde cimpaginas in autographo, quod asseruatur apud Reuerendissimum in Christo patrem, Dominum Matthæum Centuariensem Archiepiscopum, totius Angliæ Primatem & Metropolitanum, Archiepiscopi & Episcopi utriusque Prouinciæ regni Angliæ, in sacra prouinciali Synodo legitimè congregati, unanimi assensu recipiunt & profitentur, & ut ueros atque Orthodoxos, manuum suarum subscriptionibus approbant, uicesimo nono die mensis Ianuarij: Anno Domini,

This Booke of Articles before rehearsed, is agayne approued, and allowed to be holden and executed within the Realme, by the ascent and consent of our Soueraigne Ladye Elizabeth, by the grace of GOD, of Englande, Fraunce, and Irelande Queene, defender of the fayth, &c. Which Articles were deliberately read, and confirmed agayne by the subscription of the handes of the Archbyshop and Byshoppes of the vpper house, and by the subscription of the whole Cleargie in the neather house in their Conuoca-

---

[1] In the Forty-two Articles of Edward VI. there are four additional Articles—on the Resurrection of the Dead, the State of the Souls of the Departed, Millenarians, and the Eternal Damnation of the Wicked.

Ed. Lat. 1563.	English Ed. 1571.	American Revis. 1801.
secundum computationem ecclesiæ Anglicanæ, millesimo quingentesimo sexagesimo secundo: uniuersusque Clerus Inferioris domus, eosdem etiam unanimiter & recepit & professus est, ut ex manuum suarum subscriptionibus patet, quas obtulit & deposuit apud eundem Reuerendissimum, quinto die Februarij, Anno prædicto. *Quibus omnibus articulis, Serenesima princeps Elizabeth, Dei gratia Angliæ, Franciæ, & Hiberniæ Regina, fidei Defensor, &c. per seipsam diligenter prius lectis & examinatis, Regium suum assensum præbuit.*	tion, in the yere of our Lorde GOD. 1571. [*A Table of the Articles.*] [1] 1 Of fayth in the Trinitie. 2 Of Christe the sonne of GOD. 3 Of his goyng downe into hell. 4 Of his Resurrection. 5 Of the holy ghost. 6 Of the sufficiencie of the Scripture. 7 Of the olde Testament. 8 Of the three Credes. 9 Of originall sinne. 10 Of free wyll. 11 Of Iustification. 12 Of good workes. 13 Of workes before iustification. 14 Of workes of supererogation. 15 Of Christe alone without sinne. 16 Of sinne after Baptisme. 17 Of predestination and election. 18 Of obtayning saluation by Christe. 19 Of the Churche. 20 Of the aucthoritie of the Churche. 21 Of the aucthoritie of generall Counsels. 22 Of Purgatorie. 23 Of ministring in the congregation. 24 Of speaking in the congregation.	

---

[1] This heading is inserted in the later English editions after the *Ratification.*

ED. LAT. 1563.	ENGLISH ED. 1571.	AMERICAN REVIS. 801.
	25 Of the Sacramentes.	
	26 Of the vnworthynesse of the Ministers.	
	27 Of Baptisme.	
	28 Of the Lordes supper.	
	29 Of the wicked whiche eate not the body of Christe.	
	30 Of both kyndes.	
	31 Of Christes one oblation.	
	32 Of the mariage of Priestes.	
	33 Of excommunicate persons.	
	34 Of traditions of the Churche.	
	35 Of Homilies.	
	36 Of consecration of Ministers.	
	37 Of ciuill Magistrates.	
	38 Of christian mens goods.	
	39 Of a christian mans othe.	
	40 Of the ratification.	

Excusum Londini apud REGINALDVM Wolfium, Regiæ Maiest. in Latinis typographum. ANNO DOMINI. 1563.

¶ Imprinted at London in Powles Churchyard, by Richarde Iugge and Iohn Cawood, Printers to the Queenes Maiestie, in Anno Domini 1571.

   * Cum priuilegio Regiæ maiestatis.

THE ANGLICAN CATECHISM. A.D. 1549, 1662.

[The Catechism of the Church of England, and of the Protestant Episcopal Church in the United States of America, is found in all editions of 'The Book of Common Prayer,' between the Baptismal Service and the Order of Confirmation. It was a part of the first Prayer-book of Edward VI. (1549), headed 'Confirmacion,' but has undergone several modifications. The Preface to the Commandments with their full text was added in 1552. The explanation of the Sacraments was added in 1604 by Bishop Overall, at that time Dean of St. Paul's and Prolocutor of the Convocation. The last revision of the Prayer-book in 1661 (published 1662) introduced the heading 'A Catechism,' and a few changes in the answer on baptism. The American text, in the explanation of the Commandments, substitutes 'the civil authority' for 'the king and all that are put in authority under him,' and omits several directions in the rubrics. These and other changes are indicated by italics.

The authentic text is found in the *Black-letter Prayer-book*, so called, which contains the original marginal MS. notes and alterations of 1661, and was annexed to the Act of Uniformity. It was supposed to be lost, but recovered in 1867 in the Library of the House of Lords, and reproduced in photozincographic fac-simile for the Royal Commissioners on Ritual, with a Preface by Dean Stanley, London, 1871, large 4to. Besides this, I have compared the reprint of the Prayer-book of 1662, published in London, 1853, pp. 251–258, and *The Book of Common Prayer, with notes legal and historical*, by Archibald John Stephens, Lond. 1854, Vol. III. pp. 1449–1477.]

A CATECHISM;

THAT IS TO SAY,

AN INSTRUCTION, TO BE LEARNED OF EVERY PERSON BEFORE HE BE BROUGHT TO BE CONFIRMED BY THE BISHOP.

Question. What is your name?

Answer. N. or *M.*

Ques. Who gave you this name?

Ans. My *Godfathers and Godmothers*[1] in my Baptism; wherein I was made a member of Christ, the child of God, and an inheritor of the kingdom of heaven.

Ques. What did your *Godfathers and Godmothers*[2] then for you?

Ans. They did promise and vow three things in my name. First, that I should renounce the devil and all his works, the pomps and vanity of this wicked world, and all the sinful lusts of the flesh. Secondly, that I should believe all the Articles of the Christian Faith. And, thirdly, that I should keep God's holy will and commandments, and walk in the same all the days of my life.

Ques. Dost thou not think that thou art bound to believe and to do as they have promised for thee?

Ans. Yes, verily; and by God's help so I will. And I heartily

---

[1] The American Episcopal Prayer-book reads *My Sponsors,* for *My Godfathers and Godmothers.*

[2] Amer. ed.: *Sponsors.*

thank our heavenly Father that he hath called me to this state of salvation through Jesus Christ our Saviour. And I pray unto God to give me his grace, that I may continue in the same unto my life's end.

Catechist. Rehearse the Articles of thy Belief.

Answer. I believe in God the Father Almighty, Maker of heaven and earth :

And in Jesus Christ his only Son our Lord, who was conceived by the Holy Ghost, born of the Virgin Mary, suffered under Pontius Pilate, was crucified, dead, and buried ; he descended into hell ; the third day he rose again from the dead ; he ascended into heaven, and sitteth at the right hand of God the Father Almighty ; from thence he shall come to judge the quick and the dead.

I believe in the Holy Ghost ; the holy Catholic Church ; the communion of saints ; the forgiveness of sins ; the resurrection of the body ; and the life everlasting. Amen.

Ques. What dost thou chiefly learn in these Articles of thy Belief ?

Ans. First, I learn to believe in God the Father, who hath made me, and all the world.

Secondly, in God the Son, who hath redeemed me, and all mankind.

Thirdly, in God the Holy Ghost, who sanctifieth me, and all the *elect*[1] people of God.

Ques. You said that your *Godfathers and Godmothers*[2] did promise for you that you should keep God's Commandments. Tell me how many there be ?

Ans. Ten.

Ques. Which *be*[3] they ?

Ans. The same which God spake in the twentieth chapter of Exodus, saying, I am the Lord thy God, who brought thee out of the land of Egypt, out of the house of bondage.

I. Thou shalt have none other gods but me.

II. Thou shalt not make to thyself any graven image, nor the likeness of any thing that is in heaven above, or in the earth beneath, or in the water under the earth. Thou shalt not bow down to them, nor

---

[1] Amer. ed. omits *elect*.   [2] Amer. ed. : *Sponsors.*   [3] Amer. ed. : *are.*

worship them: for I the Lord thy God am a jealous God, and visit the
sins of the fathers upon the children unto the third and fourth generation of them that hate me; and show mercy unto thousands in them
that love me, and keep my commandments.

III. Thou shalt not take the name of the Lord thy God in vain: for
the Lord will not hold him guiltless that taketh his name in vain.

IV. Remember that thou keep holy the Sabbath-day. Six days shalt
thou labor, and do all that thou hast to do; but the seventh day is the
Sabbath of the Lord thy God. In it thou shalt do no manner of work,
thou, and thy son, and thy daughter, thy man-servant, and thy maid-
servant, thy cattle, and the stranger that is within thy gates. For in
six days the Lord made heaven and earth, the sea, and all that in them
is, and rested the seventh day; wherefore the Lord blessed the seventh
day, and hallowed it.

V. Honor thy father and thy mother, that thy days may be long in
the land which the Lord thy God giveth thee.

VI. Thou shalt do no murder.

VII. Thou shalt not commit adultery.

VIII. Thou shalt not steal.

IX. Thou shalt not bear false witness against thy neighbor.

X. Thou shalt not covet thy neighbor's house, thou shalt not covet
thy neighbor's wife, nor his servant, nor his maid, nor his ox, nor his
ass, nor any thing that is his.

Ques. What dost thou chiefly learn by these Commandments?

Ans. I learn two things: my duty towards God, and my duty towards my neighbor.

Ques. What is thy duty towards God?

Ans. My duty towards God is to believe in him, to fear him, and to
love him with all my heart, with all my mind, with all my soul, and
with all my strength; to worship him, to give him thanks, to put my
whole trust in him, to call upon him, to honor his holy name and his
Word, and to serve him truly all the days of my life.

Ques. What is thy duty towards thy neighbor?

Ans. My duty towards my neighbor is to love him as myself, and to
do to all men as I would they should do unto me: to love, honor, and
succor my father and mother: to honor and obey *the King* [*Queen*],

Vol. III.—L l

and all that are put in authority under him [*her*] :[1] to submit myself to all my governors, teachers, spiritual pastors and masters: to order myself lowly and reverently to all my betters: to hurt nobody by word nor deed: to be true and just in all my dealing: to bear no malice nor hatred in my heart: to keep my hands from picking and stealing, and my tongue from evil-speaking, lying, and slandering: to keep my body in temperance, soberness, and chastity: not to covet nor desire other men's goods; but to learn and labor truly to get mine own living, and to do my duty in that state of life unto which it shall please God to call me.

Catechist. My good *child*,[2] know this, that thou art not able to do these things of thyself, nor to walk in the commandments of God, and to serve him, without his special grace; which thou must learn at all times to call for by diligent prayer. Let me hear, therefore, if thou canst say the Lord's Prayer.

Answer. Our Father, *which*[3] art in heaven, hallowed be thy name. Thy kingdom come. Thy will be done in earth, as it is in heaven. Give us this day our daily bread. And forgive us our trespasses, as we forgive *them that*[4] trespass against us. And lead us not into temptation; but deliver us from evil. Amen.

Ques. What desirest thou of God in this Prayer?

Ans. I desire my Lord God our heavenly Father, who is the giver of all goodness, to send his grace unto me, and to all people; that we may worship him, serve him, and obey him, as we ought to do. And I pray unto God, that he will send us all things that be needful both for our souls and bodies; and that he will be merciful unto us, and forgive us our sins; and that it will please him to save and defend us in all dangers, *ghostly and bodily*;[5] and that he will keep us from all sin and wickedness, and from our *ghostly*[6] enemy, and from everlasting death. And this I trust he will do of his mercy and goodness, through our Lord Jesus Christ. And therefore I say, Amen, so be it.

---

[1] Amer. ed.: *The civil authority.* The editions before 1661 read instead: 'The King and his Ministers.'

[2] Substituted for the original *son* in the edition of 1552.

[3] Amer. ed.: *who.*

[4] Amer. ed.: *those who.*

[5] Amer. ed.: *both of soul and body.*

[6] Amer. ed.: *spiritual.*

Ques. How many Sacraments hath Christ ordained in his Church?

Ans. Two only, as generally necessary to salvation: that is to say, Baptism, and the Supper of the Lord.

Ques. What meanest thou by this word *Sacrament?*

Ans. I mean an outward and visible sign of an inward and spiritual grace given unto us, ordained by Christ himself as a means whereby we receive the same, and a pledge to assure us thereof.

Ques. How many parts are there in a Sacrament?

Ans. Two: the outward visible sign, and the inward spiritual grace.

Ques. What is the outward visible sign or form in Baptism?

Ans. Water; wherein the person *is baptized* [1] IN THE NAME OF THE FATHER, AND OF THE SON, AND OF THE HOLY GHOST.

Ques. What is the inward and spiritual grace?

Ans. A death unto sin, and a new birth unto righteousness: for, being by nature born in sin, and the children of wrath, we are hereby made the children of grace.

Ques. What is required of persons to be baptized?

Ans. Repentance, whereby they forsake sin; and Faith, whereby they steadfastly believe the promises of God made to them in that Sacrament.

Ques. Why, then, are infants baptized, when by reason of their tender age they can not perform them?

Ans. Because they promise them both by their Sureties; [2] which promise, when they come to age, themselves are bound to perform.

Ques. Why was the Sacrament of the Lord's Supper ordained?

Ans. For the continual remembrance of the sacrifice of the death of Christ, and of the benefits which we receive thereby.

Ques. What is the outward part or sign of the Lord's Supper?

Ans. Bread and wine, which the Lord hath commanded to be received.

Ques. What is the inward part, or thing signified?

Ans. The body and blood of Christ, which are verily and indeed taken and received by the faithful in the Lord's Supper.

---

[1] Edition of 1604: *the person baptized is dipped, or sprinkled with it.* The change was made in 1661.

[2] Ed. of 1604: *Yes; they do perform them by their Sureties, who promise and vow them both in their names:* which, etc.

Ques. What are the benefits whereof we are partakers thereby?

Ans. The strengthening and refreshing of our souls by the body and blood of Christ, as our bodies are by the bread and wine.

Ques. What is required of them who come to the Lord's Supper?

Ans. To examine themselves, whether they repent them truly of their former sins, steadfastly purposing to lead a new life; have a lively faith in God's mercy through Christ, with a thankful remembrance of his death; and be in charity with all men.

¶ The *Curate*[1] of every parish shall diligently, upon Sundays and Holy-days,[2] *after the second Lesson at Evening Prayer,* openly in the church instruct and examine so many children of his parish sent unto him, as he shall think convenient, in some part of this Catechism.

¶ And all Fathers, Mothers, Masters, and *Dames,*[3] shall cause their children, servants, and apprentices (which have not learned their Catechism), to come to the church at the time appointed, and obediently to hear, and be ordered by the *Curate,*[4] until such time as they have learned all that is here appointed for them to learn.

¶ So soon as children are come to a competent age, and can say, *in their mother tongue,* the Creed, the Lord's Prayer, and the Ten Commandments, and *also* can answer to the other Questions of this short Catechism, they shall be brought to the Bishop. *And every one shall have a Godfather or a Godmother as a witness of their Confirmation.*

¶ And whensoever the Bishop shall give knowledge for children to be brought unto him for their Confirmation, the *Curate*[4] of every parish shall either bring, or send in writing, with his hand subscribed thereunto, the names of all such persons within his parish as he shall think fit to be presented to the Bishop to be confirmed. *And, if the Bishop approve of them, he shall confirm them in manner following.*

---

[1] The American edition reads *Minister* for *Curate,* and omits the other words printed in *italics.*

[2] The American edition adds: *or on some other convenient occasion.*

[3] The American edition reads *Mistresses* for *Dames.*

[4] The American edition reads *Minister.*

THE LAMBETH ARTICLES. A.D. 1595.

[The Lambeth Articles are a Calvinistic Appendix to the Thirty-nine Articles. They were composed by Dr. Whitaker, Regius Professor of Divinity at Cambridge, whose original draft (Hardwick, pp. 344-347) was still more '*ad mentem Calvini*,' in opposition to the nine propositions of Barret (see Strype's *Whitgift*, Vol. III. p. 320). They were formally approved by the Archbishop of Canterbury (Dr. Whitgift), the Archbishop of York (Dr. Matthew Hutton, who indorsed the first article with '*verissimum*,' and approved the rest), and a number of prelates convened at Lambeth Palace, London, Nov. 20, 1595, but not sanctioned by Queen Elizabeth (who was rather displeased with the convening of a synod without her royal permission), and met with considerable opposition. They were accepted by the Dublin Convocation of 1615, and engrafted on the Irish Articles. During the Arminian reaction under the Stuarts they lost their authority.

The Latin text is taken from Strype's *Life and Acts of John Whitgift*, Vol. II. p. 280 (Oxford edition, 1822). Strype copied it from the authentic MS. of the Lord Treasurer (probably presented to him by Dr. Whitaker).

The English text is from Thomas Fuller's *Church History of Britain*, Vol. III. p. 147 (London edition of 1837, or Vol. V. p. 220 of the Oxford University Press ed. 1845).]

ARTICULI APPROBATI A REVERENDISSIMIS DOMINIS D.D. JOANNE ARCHI-EPISCOPO CANTUARIENSI, ET RICHARDO EPISCOPO LONDINENSI, ET ALIIS THEOLOGIS, LAMBETHÆ, NOVEMBRIS 20, ANNO 1595.

1. *Deus ab æterno prædestinavit quosdam ad vitam, et quosdam ad mortem reprobavit.*

1. God from eternity hath predestinated certain men unto life; certain men he hath reprobated.

2. *Causa movens aut efficiens prædestinationis ad vitam non est prævisio fidei, aut perseverantiæ, aut bonorum operum, aut ullius rei, quæ insit in personis prædestinatis, sed sola voluntas beneplaciti Dei.*

2. The moving or efficient cause of predestination unto life is not the foresight of faith, or of perseverance, or of good works, or of any thing that is in the person predestinated, but only the good will and pleasure of God.

3. *Prædestinatorum præfinitus et certus numerus est qui nec augeri nec minui potest.*

3. There is predetermined a certain number of the predestinate, which can neither be augmented nor diminished.

4. *Qui non sunt prædestinati ad salutem necessario propter peccata sua damnabuntur.*

4. Those who are not predestinated to salvation shall be necessarily damned for their sins.

5. *Vera, viva [et] justificans fides, et Spiritus Dei sanctificans non extinguitur, non excidit, non*

5. A true, living, and justifying faith, and the Spirit of God justifying [sanctifying], is not extin-

evanescit in electis, aut finaliter aut totaliter.

6. *Homo vere fidelis, id est, fide justificante præditus, certus est plerophoria fidei, de remissione peccatorum suorum, et salute sempiterna sua per Christum.*

7. *Gratia salutaris non tribuitur, non communicatur, non conceditur universis hominibus, qua servari possint, si voluerint.*

8. *Nemo potest venire ad Christum, nisi datum ei fuerit, et nisi Pater eum traxerit. Et omnes homines non trahuntur a Patre, ut veniant ad Filium.*

9. *Non est positum in arbitrio aut potestate uniuscuiusque hominis servari.*

guished, falleth not away; it vanisheth not away in the elect, either finally or totally.

6. A man truly faithful, that is, such a one who is endued with a justifying faith, is certain, with the full assurance of faith, of the remission of his sins and of his everlasting salvation by Christ.

7. Saving grace is not given, is not granted, is not communicated to all men, by which they may be saved if they will.

8. No man can come unto Christ unless it shall be given unto him, and unless the Father shall draw him; and all men are not drawn by the Father, that they may come to the Son.

9. It is not in the will or power of every one to be saved.

NOTE.

It is interesting to compare with these Lambeth Articles the brief and clear statement of Calvin's doctrine of predestination, which was discovered by the Strasburg editors in an autograph of Calvin, without date, in the Library of Geneva (Cod. 145, fol. 100), and published in *Opera*, Vol. IX. p. 713, as follows:

'ARTICULI DE PRÆDESTINATIONE.

'*Ante creatum primum hominem statuerat Deus æterno consilio quid de toto genere humano fieri vellet.*

'*Hoc arcano Dei consilio factum est ut Adam ab integro naturæ suæ statu deficeret ac sua defectione traheret omnes suos posteros in reatum æternæ mortis.*

'*Ab hoc eodem decreto pendet discrimen inter electos et reprobos; quia alios sibi adoptavit in salutem, alios æterno exitio destinavit.*

'*Tametsi justæ Dei vindictæ vasa sunt reprobi, rursum electi vasa misericordiæ, causa tamen discriminis non alia in Deo quærenda est quam mera ejus voluntas, quæ summa est justitiæ regula.*

'*Tametsi electi fide percipiunt adoptionis gratiam, non tamen pendet electio a fide, sed tempore et ordine prior est.*

'*Sicut initium et perseverantia fidei a gratuita Dei electione fluit, ita non alii vere illuminantur in fidem, nec alii Spiritu regenerationis donantur, nisi quos Deus elegit : reprobos vero vel in sua cæcitate manere necesse est, vel excidere a parte fidei, si qua in illis fuerit.*

'*Tametsi in Christo eligimur, ordine tamen illud prius est ut nos Dominus in suis censeat, quam ut faciat Christi membra.*

'*Tametsi Dei voluntas summa et prima est rerum omnium causa, et Deus diabolum et impios omnes suo arbitrio subjectos habet, Deus tamen neque peccati causa vocari potest, neque mali autor, neque ulli culpæ obnoxius est.*

'*Tametsi Deus peccato vere infensus est et damnat quidquid est injustitiæ in hominibus, quia illi displicet, non tamen nuda ejus permissione tantum, sed nutu quoque et arcano decreto gubernantur omnia hominum facta.*

'*Tametsi diabolus et reprobi Dei ministri sunt et organa, et arcana ejus judicia exsequuntur, Deus tamen incomprehensibili modo sic in illis et per illos operatur ut nihil ex eorum vitio labis contrahat, quia illorum malitia juste recteque utitur in bonum finem, licet modus sæpe nobis sit absconditus.*

'*Inscite vel calumniose faciunt qui Deum fieri dicunt autorem peccati, si omnia eo volente et ordinante fiant : quia inter manifestam hominum pravitatem et arcana Dei judicia non distinguunt.*'

Hooker's modification of the Lambeth Articles, see in Vol. I. § 84.

THE IRISH ARTICLES OF RELIGION.   A.D. 1615.

[The Irish Articles—probably composed by the learned Archbishop James Ussher (then Professor of Divinity in Dublin), and adopted by the Archbishops, Bishops, and Convocation of the Irish Episcopal Church, and approved by the Viceroy in 1615, four years before the Synod of Dort—although practically superseded by the Thirty-nine Articles, are important as a testimony of the prevailing Calvinism of the leading divines in that Church, which had previously been expressed also in the nine *Lambeth Articles*. They are still more important as the connecting link between the Thirty-nine Articles and the Westminster Confession, and as the chief source of the latter. The agreement of the two formularies in the order of subjects, the headings of chapters, and in many single phrases, as well as in spirit and sentiment, is very striking. See the comparison in Dr. Alex. F. Mitchell's *Minutes of the Westminster Assembly of Divines*, Edinb. 1874, Introd. pp. xlvi. sqq. On the history and authority of the Irish Articles see Hardwick's *History of the Articles of Religion*, 2d ed. pp. 181 sqq.

The text is taken from the original edition of 1615, as appended to Dr. Elrington's *Life of Archbishop Ussher* (in *Works of the Most Rev. James Ussher*, Dublin, 1847, Vol. I. Appendix IV.), and reprinted in Hardwick's *History*, Append. Sixth, pp. 351 sqq. He added a few references to the Lambeth Articles. The spelling is here modernized.]

ARTICLES OF RELIGION,

Agreed upon by the Archbishops and Bishops, and the rest of the Clergy of Ireland, in the Convocation holden at Dublin in the Year of our Lord God 1615, for the Avoiding of Diversities of Opinions, and the Establishing of Consent touching True Religion.

OF THE HOLY SCRIPTURE AND THE THREE CREEDS.

1. The ground of our religion and the rule of faith and all saving truth is the Word of God, contained in the holy Scripture.

2. By the name of holy Scripture we understand all the Canonical Books of the Old and New Testament, viz.:

Of the Old Testament.

The Five Books of Moses.	Job.
Joshua.	Psalms.
Judges.	Proverbs.
Ruth.	Ecclesiastes.
The First and Second of Samuel.	The Song of Solomon.
The First and Second of Kings.	Isaiah.
The First and Second of Chronicles.	Jeremiah, his Prophecy and Lamentation.
Ezra.	Ezekiel.
Nehemiah.	Daniel.
Esther.	The Twelve lesser Prophets.

Of the New Testament.

The Gospels according to	Luke,
Matthew,	John,
Mark,	The Acts of the Apostles.

The Epistle of St. Paul to the Romans.	Titus.
II. Corinthians.	Philemon.
Galatians.	Hebrews.
Ephesians.	The Epistle of St. James.
Philippians.	St. Peter II.
Colossians.	St. John III.
II. Thessalonians.	St. Jude.
II. Timothy.	The Revelation of St. John.

All which we acknowledge to be given by the inspiration of God, and in that regard to be of most certain credit and highest authority.

3. The other Books, commonly called *Apocryphal*, did not proceed from such inspiration, and therefore are not of sufficient authority to establish any point of doctrine; but the Church doth read them as Books containing many worthy things for example of life and instruction of manners.

Such are these following:

The Third Book of Esdras.	Baruch, with the Epistle of Jeremiah.
The Fourth Book of Esdras.	The Song of the Three Children.
The Book of Tobias.	Susanna.
The Book of Judith.	Bell and the Dragon.
Additions to the Book of Esther.	The Prayer of Manasses.
The Book of Wisdom.	The First Book of Maccabæus.
The Book of Jesus, the Son of Sarah, called Ecclesiasticus.	The Second Book of Maccabæus.

4. The Scriptures ought to be translated out of the original tongues into all languages for the common use of all men: neither is any person to be discouraged from reading the Bible in such a language as he doth understand, but seriously exhorted to read the same with great humility and reverence, as a special means to bring him to the true knowledge of God and of his own duty.

5. Although there be some hard things in the Scripture (especially such as have proper relation to the times in which they were first uttered, and prophecies of things which were afterwards to be fulfilled), yet all things necessary to be known unto everlasting salvation are clearly delivered therein; and nothing of that kind is spoken under dark mysteries in one place which is not in other places spoken more familiarly and plainly, to the capacity both of learned and unlearned.

6. The holy Scriptures contain all things necessary to salvation, and

are able to instruct sufficiently in all points of faith that we are bound to believe, and all good duties that we are bound to practice.

7. All and every the Articles contained in the *Nicene Creed*, the *Creed of Athanasius*, and that which is commonly called the *Apostles' Creed*, ought firmly to be received and believed, for they may be proved by most certain warrant of holy Scripture.

OF FAITH IN THE HOLY TRINITY.

8. There is but one living and true God, everlasting, without body, parts, or passions; of infinite power, wisdom, and goodness; the maker and preserver of all things, both visible and invisible. And in unity of this Godhead, there be three persons of one and the same substance, power, and eternity: the Father, the Son, and the Holy Ghost.

9. The essence of the Father doth not beget the essence of the Son; but the person of the Father begetteth the person of the Son, by communicating his whole essence to the person begotten from eternity.

10. The Holy Ghost, proceeding from the Father and the Son, is of one substance, majesty, and glory with the Father and the Son, very and eternal God.

OF GOD'S ETERNAL DECREE AND PREDESTINATION.

11. God from all eternity did, by his unchangeable counsel, ordain whatsoever in time should come to pass; yet so, as thereby no violence is offered to the wills of the reasonable creatures, and neither the liberty nor the contingency of the second causes is taken away, but established rather.

12. By the same eternal counsel God hath predestinated some unto life, and reprobated some unto death: of both which there is a certain number, known only to God, which can neither be increased nor diminished.[1]

13. Predestination to life is the everlasting purpose of God whereby, before the foundations of the world were laid, he hath constantly decreed in his sacred counsel to deliver from curse and damnation those whom he hath chosen in Christ out of mankind, and to bring them by Christ unto everlasting salvation, as vessels made to honor.

---

[1] Lambeth Articles, i., iii.

14. The cause moving God to predestinate unto life is not the fore-seeing of faith, or perseverance, or good works, or of any thing which is in the person predestinated, but only the good pleasure of God himself.[1] For all things being ordained for the manifestation of his glory, and his glory being to appear both in the works of his mercy and of his justice, it seemed good to his heavenly wisdom to choose out a certain number towards whom he would extend his undeserved mercy, leaving the rest to be spectacles of his justice.

15. Such as are predestinated unto life be called according unto God's purpose (his spirit working in due season), and through grace they obey the calling, they be justified freely; they be made sons of God by adoption; they be made like the image of his only-begotten Son Jesus Christ; they walk religiously in good works; and at length, by God's mercy, they attain to everlasting felicity. But such as are not predestinated to salvation shall finally be condemned for their sins.[2]

16. The godlike consideration of predestination and our election in Christ is full of sweet, pleasant, and unspeakable comfort to godly persons, and such as feel in themselves the working of the spirit of Christ, mortifying the works of the flesh and their earthly members, and drawing up their minds to high and heavenly things: as well because it doth greatly confirm and establish their faith of eternal salvation, to be enjoyed through Christ, as because it doth fervently kindle their love towards God; and, on the contrary side, for curious and carnal persons lacking the spirit of Christ to have continually before their eyes the sentence of God's predestination is very dangerous.

17. We must receive God's promises in such wise as they be generally set forth unto us in holy Scripture; and in our doings that will of God is to be followed which we have expressly declared unto us in the Word of God.

OF THE CREATION AND GOVERNMENT OF ALL THINGS.

18. In the beginning of time, when no creature had any being, God, by his word alone, in the space of six days, created all things, and afterwards, by his providence, doth continue, propagate, and order them according to his own will.

---

[1] Lambeth Articles, ii.   [2] Ibid. iv.

19. The principal creatures are angels and men.

20. Of angels, some continued in that holy state wherein they were created, and are by God's grace forever established therein; others fell from the same, and are reserved in chains of darkness unto the judgment of the great day.

21. Man being at the beginning created according to the image of God (which consisted especially in the wisdom of his mind and the true holiness of his free will), had the covenant of the law ingrafted in his heart, whereby God did promise unto him everlasting life upon condition that he performed entire and perfect obedience unto his Commandments, according to that measure of strength wherewith he was endued in his creation, and threatened death unto him if he did not perform the same.

OF THE FALL OF MAN, ORIGINAL SIN, AND THE STATE OF MAN BEFORE JUSTIFICATION.

22. By one man sin entered into the world, and death by sin; and so death went over all men, forasmuch as all have sinned.

23. Original sin standeth not in the imitation of Adam (as the Pelagians dream), but is the fault and corruption of the nature of every person that naturally is engendered and propagated from Adam: whereby it cometh to pass that man is deprived of original righteousness, and by nature is bent unto sin. And therefore, in every person born into the world, it deserveth God's wrath and damnation.

24. This corruption of nature doth remain even in those that are regenerated, whereby the flesh always lusteth against the spirit, and can not be made subject to the law of God. And howsoever, for Christ's sake, there be no condemnation to such as are regenerate and do believe, yet doth the Apostle acknowledge that in itself this concupiscence hath the nature of sin.

25. The condition of man after the fall of Adam is such that he can not turn and prepare himself, by his own natural strength and good works, to faith, and calling upon God. Wherefore, we have no power to do good works, pleasing and acceptable unto God, without the grace of God preventing us, that we may have a good will, and working with us when we have that good will.

26. Works done before the grace of Christ and the inspiration of

his Spirit are not pleasing unto God, forasmuch as they spring not of faith in Jesus Christ, neither do they make men meet to receive grace, or (as the School Authors say) deserve grace of congruity: yea, rather, for that they are not done in such sort as God hath willed and commanded them to be done, we doubt not but they are sinful.

27. All sins are not equal, but some far more heinous than others; yet the very least is of its own nature mortal, and, without God's mercy, maketh the offender liable unto everlasting damnation.

28. God is not the author of sin: howbeit, he doth not only permit, but also by his providence govern and order the same, guiding it in such sort by his infinite wisdom as it turneth to the manifestation of his own glory and to the good of his elect.

OF CHRIST, THE MEDIATOR OF THE SECOND COVENANT.

29. The Son, which is the Word of the Father, begotten from everlasting of the Father, the true and eternal God—of one substance with the Father—took man's nature in the womb of the blessed Virgin, of her substance, so that two whole and perfect natures—that is to say, the Godhead and manhood—were inseparably joined in one person, making one Christ very God and very man.

30. Christ, in the truth of our nature, was made like unto us in all things—sin only excepted—from which he was clearly void, both in his life and in his nature. He came as a lamb without spot to take away the sins of the world, by the sacrifice of himself once made, and sin (as *St. John* saith) was not in him. He fulfilled the law for us perfectly: For our sakes he endured most grievous torments immediately in his soul, and most painful sufferings in his body. He was crucified, and died to reconcile his Father unto us, and to be a sacrifice not only for original guilt, but also for all our actual transgressions. He was buried, and descended into hell, and the third day rose from the dead, and took again his body, with flesh, bones, and all things appertaining to the perfection of man's nature: wherewith he ascended into Heaven, and there sitteth at the right hand of his Father, until he return to judge all men at the last day.

OF THE COMMUNICATING OF THE GRACE OF CHRIST.

31. They are to be condemned that presume to say that every man

shall be saved by the law or sect which he professeth, so that he be diligent to frame his life according to that law and the light of nature. For holy Scripture doth set out unto us only the name of Jesus Christ whereby men must be saved.

32. None can come unto Christ unless it be given unto him, and unless the Father draw him. And all men are not so drawn by the Father that they may come unto the Son. Neither is there such a sufficient measure of grace vouchsafed unto every man whereby he is enabled to come unto everlasting life.[1]

33. All God's elect are in their time inseparably united unto Christ by the effectual and vital influence of the Holy Ghost, derived from him as from the head unto every true member of his mystical body. And being thus made one with Christ, they are truly regenerated, and made partakers of him and all his benefits.

OF JUSTIFICATION AND FAITH.

34. We are accounted righteous before God only for the merit of our Lord and Saviour Jesus Christ, applied by faith, and not for our own works or merits. And this righteousness, which we so receive of God's mercy and Christ's merits, embraced by faith, is taken, accepted, and allowed of God, for our perfect and full justification.

35. Although this justification be free unto us, yet it cometh not so freely unto us that there is no ransom paid therefore at all. God showed his great mercy in delivering us from our former captivity without requiring of any ransom to be paid or amends to be made on our parts; which thing by us had been impossible to be done. And whereas all the world was not able of themselves to pay any part towards their ransom, it pleased our heavenly Father of his infinite mercy, without any desert of ours, to provide for us the most precious merits of his own Son, whereby our ransom might be fully paid, the law fulfilled, and his justice fully satisfied. So that Christ is now the righteousness of all them that truly believe in him. He, for them, paid their ransom by his death. He, for them, fulfilled the law in his life; that now, in him, and by him, every true Christian man may be called a fulfiller of the law: forasmuch as that which our infirmity

---

[1] Lambeth Articles, vii., viii., ix.

was not able to effect, Christ's justice hath performed. And thus the justice and mercy of God do embrace each other: the grace of God not shutting out the justice of God in the matter of our justification, but only shutting out the justice of man (that is to say, the justice of our own works) from being any cause of deserving our justification.

36. [1]When we say that we are justified by faith only, we do not mean that the said justifying faith is alone in man without true repentance, hope, charity, and the fear of God (for such a faith is dead, and can not justify); neither do we mean that this, our act, to believe in Christ, or this, our faith in Christ, which is within us, doth of itself justify us or deserve our justification unto us (for that were to account ourselves to be justified by the virtue or dignity of something that is within ourselves); but the true understanding and meaning thereof is, that although we hear God's Word, and believe it—although we have faith, hope, charity, repentance, and the fear of God within us, and add never so many good works thereunto—yet we must renounce the merit of all our said virtues, of faith, hope, charity, and all our other virtues and good deeds which we either have done, shall do, or can do, as things that be far too weak and imperfect and insufficient to deserve remission of our sins and our justification, and therefore we must trust only in God's mercy and the merits of his most dearly beloved Son, our only Redeemer, Saviour, and Justifier, Jesus Christ. Nevertheless, because faith doth directly send us to Christ for our justification, and that by faith given us of God we embrace the promise of God's mercy and the remission of our sins (which thing none other of our virtues or works properly doth), therefore the Scripture useth to say that *faith without works*—and the ancient fathers of the Church to the same purpose—that *only faith* doth justify us.

37. By justifying faith we understand not only the common belief of the articles of Christian religion, and the persuasion of the truth of God's Word in general, but also a particular application of the gracious promises of the gospel to the comfort of our own souls, whereby we lay hold on Christ, with all his benefits; having an earnest trust and confidence in God, that he will be merciful unto us for his only Son's

---

[1] Comp. Homily *Of Salvation*, Part II. p. 24, ed. Camb.

sake. So that a true believer may be certain, by the assurance of faith, of the forgiveness of his sins, and of his everlasting salvation by Christ.[1]

38. A true, lively, justifying faith and the sanctifying spirit of God is not extinguished nor vanished away in the regenerate, either finally or totally.[2]

OF SANCTIFICATION AND GOOD WORKS.

39. All that are justified are likewise sanctified, their faith being always accompanied with true repentance and good works.

40. Repentance is a gift of God, whereby a godly sorrow is wrought in the heart of the faithful for offending God, their merciful Father, by their former transgressions, together with a constant resolution for the time to come to cleave unto God and to lead a new life.

41. Albeit that good works, which are the fruits of faith, and follow after justification, can not make satisfaction for our sins and endure the surety of God's judgment; yet are they pleasing to God, and accepted of him in Christ, and do spring from a true and lively faith, which by them is to be discerned, as a tree by the fruit.

42. The works which God would have his people to walk in are such as he hath commanded in his holy Scripture, and not such works as men have devised out of their own brain, of a blind zeal and devotion, without the warrant of the Word of God.

43. The regenerate can not fulfill the law of God perfectly in this life. For in many things we offend all; and if we say we have no sin, we deceive ourselves, and the truth is not in us.

44. Not every heinous sin willingly committed after baptism is sin against the Holy Ghost, and unpardonable. And therefore to such as fall into sin after baptism, place for repentance is not to be denied.

45. Voluntary works, besides over and above God's commandments, which they call works of supererogation, can not be taught without arrogancy and impiety; for by them men do declare that they do not only render unto God as much as they are bound to do, but that they do more for his sake than of bounden duty is required.

OF THE SERVICE OF GOD.

46. Our duty towards God is to believe in him, to fear him, and to

---

[1] Lambeth Articles, vi.   [2] Ibid. v.

love him with all our heart, with all our mind, and with all our soul, and with all our strength; to worship him, and to give him thanks; to put our whole trust in him, to call upon him, to honor his holy name and his Word, and to serve him truly all the days of our life.[1]

47. In all our necessities we ought to have recourse unto God by prayer: assuring ourselves that whatsoever we ask of the Father, in the name of his Son (our only Mediator and Intercessor) Christ Jesus, and according to his will, he will undoubtedly grant it.

48. We ought to prepare our hearts before we pray, and understand the things that we ask when we pray: that both our hearts and voices may together sound in the ears of God's majesty.

49. When almighty God smiteth us with affliction, or some great calamity hangeth over us, or any other weighty cause so requireth, it is our duty to humble ourselves in fasting, to bewail our sins with a sorrowful heart, and to addict ourselves to earnest prayer, that it might please God to turn his wrath from us, or supply us with such graces as we greatly stand in need of.

50. [2]Fasting is a withholding of meat, drink, and all natural food, with other outward delights, from the body, for the determined time of fasting. As for those abstinences which are appointed by public order of our State, for eating of fish and forbearing of flesh at certain times and days appointed, they are noways meant to be religious fasts, nor intended for the maintenance of any superstition in the choice of meats, but are grounded merely upon politic considerations, for provision of things tending to the better preservation of the commonwealth.

51. We must not fast with this persuasion of mind, that our fasting can bring us to heaven, or ascribe holiness to the outward work wrought; for God alloweth not our fast for the work sake (which of itself is a thing merely indifferent), but simply respecteth the heart, how it is affected therein. It is, therefore, requisite that first, before all things, we cleanse our hearts from sin, and then direct our fast to such ends as God will allow to be good: that the flesh may thereby be chastised, the spirit may be more fervent in prayer, and that our fasting may be a testimony of our humble submission to God's majesty, when we ac-

---

[1] From the *Catechism.*   [2] Comp. Homily *Of Fasting*, p. 284.

knowledge our sins unto him, and are inwardly touched with sorrowful-
ness of heart, bewailing the same in the affliction of our bodies.

52. All worship devised by man's phantasy besides or contrary to
the Scriptures (as wandering on pilgrimages, setting up of candles, stations, and jubilees, Pharisaical sects and feigned religions, praying upon
beads, and such like superstition) hath not only no promise of reward
in Scripture, but contrariwise threatenings and maledictions.

53. All manner of expressing God the Father, the Son, and the Holy
Ghost in an outward form is utterly unlawful; as also all other images
devised or made by man to the use of religion.

54. All religious worship ought to be given to God alone: from
whom all goodness, health, and grace ought to be both asked and
looked for, as from the very author and giver of the same, and from
none other.

55. The name of God is to be used with all reverence and holy respect, and therefore all vain and rash swearing is utterly to be condemned. Yet, notwithstanding, upon lawful occasions, an oath may
be given and taken, according to the Word of God: *justice, judgment,
and truth.*

56. The first day of the week, which is the *Lord's day*, is wholly
to be dedicated unto the service of God; and therefore we are bound
therein to rest from our common and daily business, and to bestow that
leisure upon holy exercises, both public and private.

OF THE CIVIL MAGISTRATE.

57. The King's majesty under God hath the sovereign and chief
power within his realms and dominions, over all manner of persons,
of what estate, either ecclesiastical or civil, soever they be; so as no
other foreign power hath, or ought to have, any superiority over
them.

58. We do profess that the supreme government of all estates within the said realms and dominions, in all cases, as well ecclesiastical as
temporal, doth of right appertain to the King's highness. Neither do
we give unto him hereby the administration of the Word and Sacraments, or the power of the Keys, but that prerogative only which we see
to have been always given unto all godly princes in holy Scripture by
God himself; that is, that he should contain all estates and degree

committed to his charge by God, whether they be ecclesiastical or civil, within their duty, and restrain the stubborn and evil-doers with the power of the civil sword.

59. The Pope, neither of himself, nor by any authority of the Church or See of Rome, or by any other means with any other, hath any power or authority to depose the King, or dispose any of his kingdoms or dominions; or to authorize any other prince to invade or annoy him or his countries; or to discharge any of his subjects of their allegiance and obedience to his Majesty; or to give license or leave to any of them to bear arms, raise tumult, or to offer any violence or hurt to his royal person, state, or government, or to any of his subjects within his Majesty's dominions.

60. That princes which be excommunicated or deprived by the Pope may be deposed or murdered by their subjects, or any other whatsoever, is impious doctrine.

61. The laws of the realm may punish Christian men with death for heinous and grievous offenses.

62. It is lawful for Christian men, at the commandment of the magistrate, to bear arms and to serve in just wars.

OF OUR DUTY TOWARDS OUR NEIGHBORS.

63. [1]Our duty towards our neighbors is, to love them as ourselves, and to do to all men as we would they should do to us; to honor and obey our superiors; to preserve the safety of men's persons, as also their chastity, goods, and good names; to bear no malice nor hatred in our hearts; to keep our bodies in temperance, soberness, and chastity; to be true and just in all our doings; not to covet other men's goods, but labor truly to get our own living, and to do our duty in that estate of life unto which it pleaseth God to call us.

64. For the preservation of the chastity of men's persons, wedlock is commanded unto all men that stand in need thereof. Neither is there any prohibition by the Word of God but that the ministers of the Church may enter into the state of matrimony: they being nowhere commanded by God's law either to vow the estate of single life or to abstain from marriage. Therefore it is lawful also for them, as well

---

[1] Comp. *Catechism.*

as for all other Christian men, to marry at their own discretion, as they shall judge the same to serve better to godliness.

65. The riches and goods of Christians are not common, as touching the right, title, and possession of the same: as certain Anabaptists falsely affirm. Notwithstanding every man ought of such things as he possesseth liberally to give alms to the poor, according to his ability.

66. Faith given, is to be kept, even with heretics and infidels.

67. The Popish doctrine of Equivocation and Mental Reservation is ungodly, and tendeth plainly to the subversion of all human society.

OF THE CHURCH AND OUTWARD MINISTRY OF THE GOSPEL.

68. There is but one Catholic Church (out of which there is no salvation), containing the universal company of all the saints that ever were, are, or shall be, gathered together in one body, under one head, Christ Jesus: part whereof is already in heaven *triumphant*, part as yet *militant* here upon earth. And because this Church consisteth of all those, and those alone, which are elected by God unto salvation, and regenerated by the power of his Spirit, the number of whom is known only unto God himself: therefore it is called the *Catholic* or universal, and the *Invisible* Church.

69. But particular and visible Churches (consisting of those who make profession of the faith of Christ, and live under the outward means of salvation) be many in number: wherein the more or less sincerely, according to Christ's institution, the Word of God is taught, the Sacraments are administered, and the authority of the Keys is used, the more or less pure are such Churches to be accounted.

70. Although in the visible Church the evil be ever mingled with the good, and sometimes the evil have chief authority in the ministration of the Word and Sacraments: yet, forasmuch as they do not the same in their own name, but in Christ's, and minister by his commission and authority, we may use their ministry both in hearing the Word and in receiving the Sacraments. Neither is the effect of Christ's ordinance taken away by their wickedness, nor the grace of God's gifts diminished from such as by faith and rightly do receive the Sacraments ministered unto them; which are effectual, because of Christ's institution and promise, although they be ministered by evil men. Nevertheless it appertaineth to the discipline of the Church that inquiry be

made of evil ministers, and that they be accused by those that have knowledge of their offenses, and finally, being found guilty, by just judgment be deposed.

71. It is not lawful for any man to take upon him the office of public preaching or ministering the Sacraments in the Church, unless he be first lawfully called and sent to execute the same. And those we ought to judge lawfully called and sent which be chosen and called to this work by men who have public authority given them in the Church to call and send ministers into the Lord's vineyard.

72. To have public prayer in the Church, or to administer the Sacraments in a tongue not understood of the people, is a thing plainly repugnant to the Word of God and the custom of the Primitive Church.

73. That person which by public denunciation of the Church is rightly cut off from the unity of the Church, and excommunicate, ought to be taken of the whole multitude of the faithful as a heathen and publican, until by repentance he be openly reconciled and received into the Church by the judgment of such as have authority in that behalf.

74. God hath given power to his ministers, not simply to forgive sins (which prerogative he hath reserved only to himself), but in his name to declare and pronounce unto such as truly repent and unfeignedly believe his holy Gospel the absolution and forgiveness of sins. Neither is it God's pleasure that his people should be tied to make a particular confession of all their known sins unto any mortal man : howsoever, any person grieved in his conscience upon any special cause may well resort unto any godly and learned minister to receive advice and comfort at his hands.

OF THE AUTHORITY OF THE CHURCH, GENERAL COUNCILS, AND BISHOP OF ROME.

75. It is not lawful for the Church to ordain any thing that is contrary to God's Word : neither may it so expound one place of Scripture that it be repugnant to another. Wherefore, although the Church be a witness and a keeper of holy Writ, yet as it ought not to decree any thing against the same, so besides the same ought it not enforce any thing to be believed upon necessity of salvation.

76. General councils may not be gathered together without the com-

mandment and will of princes; and when they be gathered together (forasmuch as they be an assembly of men not always governed with the Spirit and Word of God) they may err, and sometimes have erred, even in things pertaining to the rule of piety. Wherefore things ordained by them as necessary to salvation have neither strength nor authority, unless it may be shown that they be taken out of holy Scriptures.

77. Every particular Church hath authority to institute, to change, and clean to put away ceremonies and other ecclesiastical rites, as they be superfluous or be abused; and to constitute other, making more to seemliness, to order, or edification.

78. As the Churches of *Jerusalem*, *Alexandria*, and *Antioch* have erred, so also the Church of *Rome* hath erred, not only in those things which concern matter of practice and point of ceremonies, but also in matters of faith.

79. The power which the Bishop of *Rome* now challengeth to be supreme head of the universal Church of Christ, and to be above all emperors, kings, and princes, is a usurped power, contrary to the Scriptures and Word of God, and contrary to the example of the Primitive Church; and therefore is for most just causes taken away and abolished within the King's Majesty's realms and dominions.

80. The Bishop of *Rome* is so far from being the supreme head of the universal Church of Christ, that his works and doctrine do plainly discover him to be *that man of sin*, foretold in the holy Scriptures, *whom the Lord shall consume with the spirit of his mouth, and abolish with the brightness of his coming.*

OF THE STATE OF THE OLD AND NEW TESTAMENT.

81. In the Old Testament the Commandments of the Law were more largely, and the promises of Christ more sparingly and darkly propounded, shadowed with a multitude of types and figures, and so much the more generally and obscurely delivered as the manifesting of them was further off.

82. The Old Testament is not contrary to the New. For both in the Old and New Testament everlasting life is offered to mankind by Christ, who is the only Mediator between God and man, being both God and man. Wherefore they are not to be heard which feign that

the old fathers did look only for transitory promises. For they looked for all benefits of God the Father through the merits of his Son Jesus Christ, as we now do: only they believed in Christ which should come, we in Christ already come.

83. The New Testament is full of grace and truth, bringing joyful tidings unto mankind that whatsoever formerly was promised of Christ is now accomplished; and so, instead of the ancient types and ceremonies, exhibiteth the things themselves, with a large and clear declaration of all the benefits of the Gospel. Neither is the ministry thereof restrained any longer to one circumcised nation, but is indifferently propounded unto all people, whether they be Jews or Gentiles. So that there is now no nation which can truly complain that they be shut forth from the communion of saints and the liberties of the people of God.

84. Although the Law given from God by Moses as touching ceremonies and rites be abolished, and the civil precepts thereof be not of necessity to be received in any commonwealth, yet, notwithstanding, no Christian man whatsoever is freed from the obedience of the Commandments which are called Moral.

OF THE SACRAMENTS OF THE NEW TESTAMENT.

85. The Sacraments ordained by Christ be not only badges or tokens of Christian men's profession, but rather certain sure witnesses and effectual or powerful signs of grace and God's good will towards us, by which he doth work invisibly in us, and not only quicken, but also strengthen and confirm our faith in him.

86. There be two Sacraments ordained of Christ our Lord in the Gospel: that is to say, *Baptism* and the *Lord's Supper*.

87. Those five which by the Church of *Rome* are called Sacraments, to wit: *Confirmation, Penance, Orders, Matrimony*, and *Extreme Unction*, are not to be accounted Sacraments of the Gospel; being such as have partly grown from corrupt imitation of the Apostles, partly are states of life allowed in the Scriptures, but yet have not like nature of Sacraments with *Baptism* and the *Lord's Supper*, for that they have not any visible sign or ceremony ordained of God, together with a promise of saving grace annexed thereto.

88. The Sacraments were not ordained of Christ to be gazed upon,

or to be carried about, but that we should duly use them. And in such only as worthily receive the same, they have a wholesome effect and operation; but they that receive them unworthily, thereby draw judgment upon themselves.

OF BAPTISM.

89. Baptism is not only an outward sign of our profession, and a note of difference, whereby Christians are discerned from such as are no Christians; but much more a Sacrament of our admission into the Church, sealing unto us our new birth (and consequently our justification, adoption, and sanctification) by the communion which we have with Jesus Christ.

90. The Baptism of Infants is to be retained in the Church, as agreeable to the Word of God.

91. In the administration of Baptism, *exorcism, oil, salt, spittle,* and superstitious *hallowing of the water,* are for just causes abolished; and without them the Sacrament is fully and perfectly administered, to all intents and purposes, agreeable to the institution of our Saviour Christ.[1]

OF THE LORD'S SUPPER.

92. The Lord's Supper is not only a sign of the mutual love which Christians ought to bear one towards another, but much more a Sacrament of our preservation in the Church, sealing unto us our spiritual nourishment and continual growth in Christ.

93. The change of the substance of bread and wine into the substance of the body and blood of Christ, commonly called *Transubstantiation,* can not be proved by holy Writ; but is repugnant to plain testimonies of the Scripture, overthroweth the nature of a Sacrament, and hath given occasion to most gross idolatry and manifold superstitions.

94. In the outward part of the holy Communion, the body and blood of Christ is in a most lively manner *represented ;* being no otherwise present with the visible elements than things signified and sealed are present with the signs and seals—that is to say, symbolically and relatively. But in the inward and spiritual part the same body and blood is really and substantially *presented* unto all those who have grace

---

[1] Comp. *Eleven Articles,* § viii.

to receive the Son of God, even to all those that believe in his name. And unto such as in this manner do worthily and with faith repair unto the Lord's table, the body and blood of Christ is not only signified and offered, but also truly exhibited and communicated.

95. The body of Christ is given, taken, and eaten in the Lord's Supper only after a heavenly and spiritual manner; and the mean whereby the body of Christ is thus received and eaten is Faith.

96. The wicked, and such as want a lively faith, although they do carnally and visibly (as St. Augustine speaketh) press with their teeth the Sacrament of the body and blood of Christ, yet in nowise are they made partakers of Christ; but rather to their condemnation do eat and drink the sign or Sacrament of so great a thing.

97. Both the parts of the Lord's Sacrament, according to Christ's institution and the practice of the ancient Church, ought to be ministered unto God's people; and it is plain sacrilege to rob them of the mystical cup, for whom Christ hath shed his most precious blood.[1]

98. The Sacrament of the *Lord's Supper* was not by Christ's ordinance reserved, carried about, lifted up, or worshiped.

99. The sacrifice of the Mass, wherein the priest is said to offer up Christ for obtaining the remission of pain or guilt for the quick and the dead, is neither agreeable to Christ's ordinance nor grounded upon doctrine Apostolic; but contrariwise most ungodly and most injurious to that all-sufficient sacrifice of our Saviour Christ, offered once forever upon the cross, which is the only propitiation and satisfaction for all our sins.

100. Private mass—that is, the receiving of the *Eucharist* by the priest alone, without a competent number of communicants—is contrary to the institution of Christ.

OF THE STATE OF THE SOULS OF MEN AFTER THEY BE DEPARTED OUT OF THIS LIFE, TOGETHER WITH THE GENERAL RESURRECTION AND THE LAST JUDGMENT.

101. After this life is ended the souls of God's children be presently received into heaven, there to enjoy unspeakable comforts; the souls of the wicked are cast into hell, there to endure endless torments.

---

[1] Comp. *Eleven Articles*, § x.

102. The doctrine of the Church of Rome concerning *Limbus Patrum, Limbus Puerorum, Purgatory, Prayer for the Dead, Pardons, Adoration of Images and Relics*, and also *Invocation of Saints*, is vainly invented without all warrant of holy Scripture, yea, and is contrary unto the same.

103. At the end of this world the Lord Jesus shall come in the clouds with the glory of his Father; at which time, by the almighty power of God, the living shall be changed and the dead shall be raised; and all shall appear both in body and soul before his judgment-seat, to receive according to that which they have done in their bodies, whether good or evil.

104. When the last judgment is finished, Christ shall deliver up the kingdom to his Father, and God shall be all in all.

THE DECREE OF THE SYNOD.

If any minister, of what degree or quality soever he be, shall publicly teach any doctrine contrary to these Articles agreed upon, if, after due admonition, he do not conform himself, and cease to disturb the peace of the Church, let him be silenced, and deprived of all spiritual promotions he doth enjoy.

ARTICULI ARMINIANI sive REMONSTRANTIA.

The Five Arminian Articles. A.D. 1610.

[The official Dutch text is taken from the first edition of 1612, as printed in *De Remonstrantie en het Remonstrantisme*. *Historisch onderzoek door Dr.* Joannes Tideman, *Predikant bij de Remonstrantsch-Gereformeerde Gemeente te Rotterdam* (Te Haarlem, 1851), pp. 17-20. I procured a copy from my friend, Dr. J. J. van Oosterzee, of Utrecht. The Latin translation of Petrus Bertius was literally copied for me by another friend in Holland, Dr. M. Cohen Stuart, from the *Scripta adversaria Collationis Hagiensis*, Lugd. Batav. 1616. The English translation is made for this edition. An older English version, with the Latin (but with several omissions), is given by Peter Heylin, in his *Historia Quinquarticularis*, London, 1660, pp. 50-53. The Preface, the five negative Articles, and Conclusion (see Tideman, pp. 8-27) are omitted.

Niemeyer excludes the Remonstrance from his Collection of Reformed Confessions, but it is necessary to the proper understanding of the Canons of the Synod of Dort. Böckel (pp. 545 sqq.) gives a German translation. Comp. Vol. I. § 65, pp. 508 sqq.]

Art. I.

Dat Godt door een eeuwich, onveranderlyck besluyt, in JESU CHRISTO, *synen Soone, eer des werelts grondt gheleydt was, besloten heeft, uyt het ghevallene sondighe Menschelyck geslachte, die ghene in* CHRISTO, *om* CHRISTUS *wille, ende door* CHRISTUM *salich te maecken, die door de ghenade des heylighen Gheestes, in den selven synen Soone* JESUM *gelooven, ende in den selven gheloove, ende ghoorsaemheyt des gheloofs, door de selve ghenade, totten eynde toe volherden souden: en daer tegens, de onbekeerlycke, en ongelovige in de sonde, en onder de toorne te laten, en te verdoemen, als vreemt van* CHRISTO: *naer 't woordt des H. Evangelij by Johannem* iii. 36: '*Wie in den Sone ghelooft, die heeft het eeuwighe leven, ende wie den Soone ongehoorsaem is, die en sal*

Art. I.

Deus æterno et immutabili decreto in Christo Jesu Filio suo, ante jacta mundi fundamenta, statuit ex genere humano in peccatum prolapso, eos in Christo, propter Christum, et per Christum salvare, qui per gratiam Spiritus Sancti in eundem Filium suum credituri, inque ea ipsa fide et obedientia fidei, per eandem gratiam, usque ad finem essent perseveraturi; contra vero contumacio et incredulos, sub peccato et ira relinquere et condemnare, tanquam a Christo alienos; juxta verbum Evangelii Joh. iii. 36: '*Qui credit in Filium, habet vitam æternam, qui vero Filio non obtemperat, non videbit vitam, sed ira Dei manet super ipsum.*'

Art. I.

That God, by an eternal, unchangeable purpose in Jesus Christ his Son, before the foundation of the world, hath determined, out of the fallen, sinful race of men, to save in Christ, for Christ's sake, and through Christ, those who, through the grace of the Holy Ghost, shall believe on this his Son Jesus, and shall persevere in this faith and obedience of faith, through this grace, even to the end; and, on the other hand, to leave the incorrigible and unbelieving in sin and under wrath, and to condemn them as alienate from Christ, according to the word of the gospel in John iii. 36: 'He that believeth on the Son hath everlasting life: and he that believeth not the Son shall not see life; but the

het leven niet sien, maer de toorne Gods blyft op hem,' ende andere plaetsen der schrifturen meer.

Cui alia quoque Scripturæ dicta respondent.

wrath of God abideth on him,' and according to other passages of Scripture also.

Art. II.

Dat desen volghende, JE-ZUS CHRISTUS de salich-maecker des Werelts, voor alle ende yeder Mensch ghestorven is: alsoo dat hyse alle door den doodt des Cruyces, de versoeninghe ende ver-ghevinghe der sonden ver-worven heeft; alsoo nochtans dat niemandt deselve verghe-vinghe der sonden dadelyck gheniet, dan de Gheloovighe: mede naer 't Woort des Euan-gely by Johannem, Cap. iii. 16 : ' Soo lief heeft Godt de Werelt gehadt, dat hy synen eenighen Soone ghegeven heeft, opdat al, die in hem ghelooft, niet en vergae, maer het eeu-wighe leven hebbe.' Ende in den eersten Brief Johannis int ii. vers 2 : ' Hy is de ver-soeninge voor onse sonden; en niet alleene voor onse, maer voor des gantsche We-relts sonden.

Art. II.

Proinde Jesus Christus, Mundi Salvator, pro omni-bus et singulis hominibus mortuus est, omnibusque per mortem crucis promeritus reconciliationem et remissio-nem peccatorum; ita tamen ut nemo remissionis illius reipsa particeps fiat, præter credentes, idque etiam secun-dum verba Evangelii Joan-nis iii. 16 : ' Ita Deus dilexit Mundum, ut Filium suum unigenitum dederit, ut quis-quis credit in eum, non pe-reat, sed habeat vitam æter-nam.' Et epistola priore Joannis, Cap. ii. v. 2 : ' Ipsa est propitiatio pro peccatis nostris, nec pro nostris tan-tum, sed etiam pro totius Mundi peccatis.'

Art. II.

That, agreeably thereto, Jesus Christ, the Saviour of the world, died for all men and for every man, so that he has obtained for them all, by his death on the cross, redemption and the forgiveness of sins; yet that no one actually enjoys this forgiveness of sins except the believer, according to the word of the Gospel of John iii. 16 : ' God so loved the world that he gave his only-be-gotten Son, that whosoever believeth in him should not perish, but have everlast-ing life.' And in the First Epistle of John ii. 2 : ' And he is the propitiation for our sins; and not for ours only, but also for the sins of the whole world.'

Art. III.

Dat de Mensche 't salich-maeckende Gheloove van hem selven niet en heeft; noch uyt cracht van synen vryen wille, alsoo hy in den stant der afwyckinghe ende der sonden niet goets, dat waer-lyck goet is (gelyck insonder-heyt is het salichmaeckende

Art. III.

Homo salvificam fidem non habet a se, neque ex liberi arbitrii sui viribus, quandoquidem in statu apo-stasiæ et peccati nihil boni (quod quidem vere bonum sit, cujusmodi in primis est fides salvifica) ex se et a se potest cogitare, velle aut

Art. III.

That man has not saving grace of himself, nor of the energy of his free will, in-asmuch as he, in the state of apostasy and sin, can of and by himself neither think, will, nor do any thing that is truly good (such as saving Faith emi-

gheloove) uyt ende van hem selven, can dencken, willen ofte doen. Maar dat het van noode is, dat hy van Godt, in CHRISTO ; *door synen heilighen Geest, werde herboren en vernieut, in verstant, affectie, oft wille, ende alle crachten, opdat hy het ware goet te recht moge verstaen, bedencken, willen, ende volbrenghen, naer 't woordt* CHRISTI, *Johann.* xiii. 5 : '*Sonder my en condt ghy niet doen.*'

facere; sed necessarium est ut a Deo, in Christo, per Spiritum ipsius Sanctum regeneretur atque renovetur, intellectu, affectibus seu voluntate, omnibusque viribus, ut vere bonum recti possit intelligere, meditari, velle atque proficere sicut scriptum est Joh. xv. 5 : '*Sine me nihil potestis facere.*'

nently is); but that it is needful that he be born again of God in Christ, through his Holy Spirit, and renewed in understanding, inclination, or will, and all his powers, in order that he may rightly understand, think, will, and effect what is truly good, according to the Word of Christ, John xv. 5 : 'Without me ye can do nothing.'

ART. IV.

Dat dese ghenade Godts is het beginsel, de voortganck ende volbrenginghe alles goets, oock soo verre, dat de wedergeboren Mensche selfs, sonder dese voorgaende ofte toecommende, opweckende, volgende ende mede-werckende ghenade, noch het goede dencken, willen ofte doen can, noch oock eenighe tentatien ten quade wederstaen : soodat alle goede daden, ofte werckinghen die men bedencken kan de ghenade Godts in CHRISTO *moeten toegeschreven worden. Maer soo vele de maniere van de werckinghe derselver ghenade aengaet, die en is niet onwederstandelyck : want daer staet van velen geschreven, dat sy den heyligen Geest wederstaen hebben. Actor.* vii. *ende elders op vele plaetsen.*

ART. IV.

Hæc Dei gratia est principium, progressus et complimentum omnis boni; adeo quidem ut ne ipse quidem regenitus absque præcedente sive præveniente ista, excitante, prosequente et cooperante gratia, bonum cogitare, velle, aut peragere possit, ullisve ad malum tentationibus resistere, ita ut omnia bona opera actionesque, quas quis cogitando potest adsequi, gratiæ Dei in Christo adscribenda sint. Cæterum, quod ad modum operationis ejus gratiæ attinet, non est ille irresistibilis, quandoquidem scriptum est de multis, quod 'Spiritui Sancto restiterint.' Act. vii. *et alibi locis compluribus.*

ART. IV.

That this grace of God is the beginning, continuance, and accomplishment of all good, even to this extent, that the regenerate man himself, without prevenient or assisting, awakening, following and co-operative grace, can neither think, will, nor do good, nor withstand any temptations to evil; so that all good deeds or movements, that can be conceived, must be ascribed to the grace of God in Christ. But as respects the mode of the operation of this grace, it is not irresistible, inasmuch as it is written concerning many, that they have resisted the Holy Ghost. Acts vii., and elsewhere in many places.

Art. V.

Dat die Jesu Christo, *door een ware gheloove syn inghelyft, ende oversulcx syns levendighmaeckenden Gheestes deelachtig zyn gheworden, overvloedighe cracht hebben, omme teghens den satan, de sonde, de Werelt, ende haer eygen vleesche te stryden, en de overwinninge te vercrygen. Welverstaende altydt, door den bystand van de ghenade des heyligen Geestes: ende dat* Jesus Christus *haer door synen Gheest in alle tentatien bystaet, de handt biet, ende, so sy maer alleene ten stryde bereyt zyn, ende syn hulpe begeeren, ende in geenen ghebreke zyn, staende hout, alsoo dat se door gheene listichheyt noch ghewelt des Satans verleyt, oft uyt* Christi *handen connen ghetrocken worden, naer 't woordt* Christi, *Joh.* x.: '*Niemandt en salse uyt myne handen rucken.' Maer of de selve niet en connen, door naelaticheyt, het beginsel haers Wesens in* Christo *verlaten; de teghenwoordighe Werelt wederom aennemen: van de Heylighe Leere, hen eenmael ghegheven, afwycken: de goede conscientie verliesen: de ghenade verwaerloosen: soude eerst moeten naerder uyt de Heylige Schriftuere*

Art. V.

Ei qui Christo vera fide insiti, ac per consequens vivificantis ejus Spiritus participes facti sunt, abunde instructi sunt viribus, quibus adversus Satanam, peccatum, Mundum, suamque carnem possint pugnare, atque adeo etiam victoriam ab iis referre; semper tamen (quod cautum volumus) auxilio gratiæ Spiritus Sancti; et Jesus Christus ipsis, per Spiritum suum, in omnibus tentationibus adsistit, manum porrigit, ac eosdem (si modo ad pugnam ipsi parati sint, ejusque opem deposcant, sibique ipsis non desint) fulcit ac confirmat, ita ut nulla fraude aut vi Satanæ seduci, aut ex Christi manibus eripi possint, juxta dictum Christi Joh. x.: '*Oves meas nemo rapiet ex manu mea.' Cæterum, utrum iidem non possint per socordiam* τὴν ἀρχὴν τῆς ὑποστάσεως χριστοῦ καταλείπειν,[1] *et præsentem mundum iterum amplecti, a sancta doctrina ipsis semel tradita recedere, bonam conscientiam amittere, gratiamque negligere; esset prius accuratius ex Sacra Scriptura inquirendum quam nos illud posse-*

Art. V.

That those who are incorporated into Christ by a true faith, and have thereby become partakers of his life-giving Spirit, have thereby full power to strive against Satan, sin, the world, and their own flesh, and to win the victory; it being well understood that it is ever through the assisting grace of the Holy Ghost; and that Jesus Christ assists them through his Spirit in all temptations, extends to them his hand, and if only they are ready for the conflict, and desire his help, and are not inactive, keeps them from falling, so that they, by no craft or power of Satan, can be misled nor plucked out of Christ's hands, according to the Word of Christ, John x. 28: 'Neither shall any man pluck them out of my hand.' But whether they are capable, through negligence, of forsaking again the first beginnings of their life in Christ, of again returning to this present evil world, of turning away from the holy doctrine which was delivered them, of losing a good conscience, of be-

---

[1] Heb. iii. 6, 14; 2 Pet. i. 10; Jude 3; 1 Tim. i. 19; Heb. xi. 13.

ondersocht zyn, eer wy 't selve met volle verseeckeringhe onses ghemoets souden connen leeren.

mus alios cum πληροφορία animi nostri docere.[1]

coming devoid of grace, that must be more particularly determined out of the Holy Scripture, before we ourselves can teach it with the full persuasion of our minds.

Dese puncten alsoo voorgedragen ende geleert, houden sy Remonstranten den woorde Godts gelyckformich te wesen, stichtelyck, ende in dese materie ghenoechsaem ter salicheit, sonder dat het van noode zy, oft oock stichtelyck, hooger te climmen, ofte lager te dalen.

Hos igitur articulos ita propositos et traditos censent Remonstrantes divino Verbo conformos, ædificationi idoneos, et in hoc quidem argumento sufficientes ad salutem; ita ut necessarium non sit, aut ædificationi serviens, vel altius conscendere vel inferius subsidere.

These Articles, thus set forth and taught, the Remonstrants deem agreeable to the Word of God, tending to edification, and, as regards this argument, sufficient for salvation, so that it is not necessary or edifying to rise higher or to descend deeper.

---

[1] The here quoted places, or *loca probantia*, are not, like the others in the former articles, written in the text, but in the *margin*.

CANONES SYNODI DORDRECHTANÆ.

The Canons of the Synod of Dort. A.D. 1618 and 1619.

[We give first the full Latin text of the Acts of the Synod of Dort (Dordrecht) on the five controverted heads of doctrine, viz., the Preface, the Articles of Faith, the Errors Rejected, the Names of Subscribers, the Conclusion, the Sentence against the Remonstrants, and the Approval of the States-General, but distinguishing the several parts by different type. They were officially published May 6, 1619, and often since in Latin, Dutch, German, and English. The original is given in the *Corpus et Syntagma Confess.* ed. II. 1654, in the Oxford *Sylloge Confess.* (pp. 397–454), in Niemeyer's *Collectio* (pp. 690–728); the German in Beck's and Böckel's Collections. To the Latin text we append the English abridgment, as adopted by the Reformed Dutch Church in America.]

Judicium Synodi Nationalis Reformatarum Ecclesiarum Belgicarum,

Habitæ Dordrechti Anno MDCXVIII. et MDCXIX. Cui plurimi insignes Theologi Reformatarum Ecclesiarum Magnæ Britanniæ, Germaniæ, Galliæ, interfuerunt, de Quinque Doctrinæ Capitibus in Ecclesiis Belgicis Controversis: promulgatum VI. Maii MDCXIX.

Præfatio.

IN NOMINE DOMINI ET SERVATORIS NOSTRI JESU CHRISTI. AMEN.

Inter plurima, quæ Dominus et Servator noster Jesus Christus militanti suæ Ecclesiæ in hac ærumnosa peregrinatione dedit solatia, merito celebratur illud, quod ei ad Patrem suum in cæleste sanctuarium abiturus reliquit: Ego, inquiens, sum vobiscum omnibus diebus usque ad consummationem sæculi. *Hujus suavissimæ promissionis veritas elucet in omnium temporum Ecclesia, quæ quum non solum aperta inimicorum violentia, et hæreticorum impietate, sed etiam operta seductorum astutia inde ab initio fuerit oppugnata, sane, si unquam salutari promissæ suæ præsentiæ præsidio eam destituisset Dominus, pridem aut vi tyrannorum fuisset oppressa, aut fraude impostorum in exitium seducta. Sed bonus ille Pastor, qui gregem suum, pro quo animam suam posuit, constantissime diligit, persecutorum rabiem tempestive semper, et exserta sæpe dextera, miraculose repressit, et seductorum vias tortuosas, ac consilia fraudulenta detexit atque dissipavit, utroque se in Ecclesia sua præsentissimum esse demonstrans. Hujus rei illustre documentum exstat in historiis piorum imperatorum, regum, et principum, quos Filius Dei in subsidium Ecclesiæ suæ toties excitavit, sancto domus suæ zelo accendit, eorumque opera, non tantum tyrannorum furores compescuit, sed etiam Ecclesiæ cum falsis doctoribus religionem varie adulterantibus conflictanti, sanctarum synodorum remedia procuravit, in quibus fideles Christi servi conjunctis precibus, consiliis, et laboribus pro Ecclesia et veritate Dei fortiter steterunt, Satanæ ministris, licet in angelos lucis se transformantibus, intrepide se opposuerunt, errorum et discordiæ semina sustulerunt, Ecclesiam in religionis puræ concordia conservarunt, et sincerum Dei cultum ad posteritatem illibatum transmiserunt.*

Simili beneficio fidelis noster Servator Ecclesiæ Belgicæ, annos aliquam multos afflictissimæ, gratiosam suam præsentiam hoc tempore testatus est. Hanc enim Ecclesiam a Romani antichristi tyrannide et horribili papatus idolatria potenti Dei manu vindicatam, in belli diuturni periculi toties miraculose custoditam, et in veræ doctrinæ atque disciplinæ concordia ad Dei sui laudem, admirabile reipub. incrementum, totiusque reformati orbis gaudium efflorescentem, JACOBUS ARMINIUS ejusque sectatores, nomen Remonstrantium præ se ferentes, variis, tam veteribus, quam novis erroribus, primum tecte, deinde aperte tentarunt, et scandalosis dissensionibus ac schismatibus pertinaciter turbatam, in tantum discrimen adduxerunt, ut florentissimæ Ecclesiæ, nisi Servatoris nostri miseratio opportune intervenisset, horribili dis-

ridiorum et schismatum incendio tandem conflagrassent.   Benedictus autem sit in sæcula Dominus, qui postquam ad momentum faciem suam a nobis (qui multis modis iram et indignationem ejus provocaveramus) abscondisset, universo orbi testatum fecit, se fœderis sui non oblivisci, et suspiria suorum non spernere.   Cum enim vix ulla remedii spes humanitus appareret, illustrissimis et præpotentibus Belgii fœderati ordinibus generalibus hanc mentem inspiravit, ut consilio et directione illustrissimi et fortissimi principis Arausicani legitimis mediis, quæ ipsorum apostolorum, et quæ eos secutæ Ecclesiæ Christianæ exemplis longo temporum decursu sunt comprobata, et magno cum fructu in Ecclesia etiam Belgica antehac usurpata, sævientibus hisce malis obviam ire decreverint, synodumque ex omnibus, quibus præsunt, provinciis, authoritate sua, Dordrechtum convocarint, expetitis ad eam et favore serenissimi ac potentissimi Magnæ Britanniæ regis JACOBI, *et illustrissimorum principum, comitum, et rerumpublicarum, impetratis plurimis gravissimis theologis, ut communi tot Reformatæ Ecclesiæ theologorum judicio, ista* ARMINII *ejusque sectatorum dogmata accurate, et ex solo Dei verbo, dijudicarentur, vera doctrina stabiliretur, et falsa rejiceretur, Ecclesiisque Belgicis concordia, pax et tranquillitas, divina benedictione, restitueretur.   Hoc est illud Dei beneficium, in quo exultant Ecclesiæ Belgicæ, et fidelis Servatoris sui miserationes humiliter agnoscunt, ac grate prædicant.*

Hæc igitur veneranda Synodus (prævia per summi magistratus authoritatem in omnibus Belgicis Ecclesiis, ad iræ Dei deprecationem et gratiosi auxilii implorationem, precum et jejunii indictione et celebratione) in nomine Domini Dordrechti congregata, divini Numinis et salutis Ecclesiæ accensa amore, et post invocatum Dei nomen, sancto juramento obstricta, se solam Scripturam sacram pro judicii norma habituram, et in caussæ hujus cognitione et judicio, bona integraque conscientia versaturam esse, hoc egit sedulo magnaque patientia, ut præcipuos horum dogmatum patronos, coram se citatos, induceret ad sententiam suam de Quinque notis doctrinæ Capitibus, sententiæque rationes, plenius exponendas.   Sed cum Synodi judicium repudiarent, atque ad interrogatoria, eo, quo æquum erat, modo respondere detrectarent, neque Synodi monitiones, nec generosorum atque amplissimorum ordinum generalium Delegatorum mandata, imo ne ipsorum quidem illustrissimorum et præpotentum DD. ordinum generalium imperia, quicquam apud illos proficerent, aliam viam eorundem Dominorum jussu, et ex consuetudine jam olim in synodis antiquis recepta, ingredi coacta fuit; atque ex scriptis, confessionibus, ac declarationibus, partim antea editis, partim etiam huic Synodo exhibitis, examen illorum quinque dogmatum institutum est.   Quod cum jam per singularem Dei gratiam, maxima diligentia, fide, ac conscientia, omnium et singulorum consensu absolutum sit, Synodus hæc ad Dei gloriam, et ut veritatis salutaris integritati, conscientiarum tranquillitati, et paci ac saluti Ecclesiæ Belgicæ consulatur, sequens judicium, quo et vera verboque Dei consentanea de prædictis Quinque Doctrinæ Capitibus sententia exponitur, et falsa verboque Dei dissentanea rejicitur, statuit promulgandum.

SENTENTIA, DE DIVINA PRÆDESTINATIONE, ET ANNEXIS EI CAPITIBUS,

Quam Synodus Dordrechtana Verbo Dei consentaneam, atque in Ecclesiis Reformatis hactenus receptam esse, judicat, quibusdam Articulis exposita.

PRIMUM DOCTRINÆ CAPUT, DE DIVINA PRÆDESTINATIONE.

ARTICULUS PRIMUS.

Cum omnes homines in Adamo peccaverint, et rei sint facti maledictionis et mortis æternæ, Deus nemini fecisset injuriam, si universum genus humanum in peccato et maledictione relinquere, ac propter pec-

catum damnare voluisset, juxta illa Apostoli, *Totus mundus est ob-*
noxius condemnationi Dei. Rom. iii. 19. *Omnes peccaverunt et de-*
stituuntur gloria Dei. Ver. 23. Et, *Stipendium peccati mors est.*
Rom. vi. 23.

II.

Verum in hoc manifestata est charitas Dei, quod Filium suum unigenitum in mundum misit, ut omnis qui credit in eum, non pereat, sed
habeat vitam æternam. 1 Johan. iv. 9; Johan. iii. 16.

III.

Ut autem homines ad fidem adducantur, Deus clementer lætissimi
hujus nuntii præcones mittit, ad quos vult, et quando vult, quorum
ministerio homines ad resipiscentiam et fidem in Christum crucifixum
vocantur. *Quomodo enim credent in eum, de quo non audierint?*
quomodo autem audient absque prædicante? quomodo prædicabunt,
nisi fuerint missi? Rom. x. 14, 15.

IV.

Qui huic Evangelio non credunt, super eos manet ira Dei. Qui
vero illud recipiunt, et Servatorem Jesum vera ac viva fide amplectuntur, illi per ipsum ab ira Dei et interitu liberantur, ac vita æterna donantur.

V.

Incredulitatis istius, ut et omnium aliorum peccatorum, caussa seu
culpa neutiquam est in Deo, sed in homine. Fides autem in Jesum
Christum et salus per ipsum, est gratuitum Dei donum, sicut scriptum
est: *Gratia salvati estis per fidem, et hoc non ex vobis, Dei donum*
est. Ephes. ii. 8. Item: *Gratis datum est vobis in Christum credere.*
Phil. i. 29.

VI.

Quod autem aliqui in tempore fide a Deo donantur, aliqui non donantur, id ab æterno ipsius decreto provenit; *Omnia enim opera sua*
novit ab æterno: Actor. xv. 18; Ephes. i. 11; secundum quod decretum
electorum corda, quantumvis dura, gratiose emollit, et ad credendum
inflectit, non electos autem justo judicio suæ malitiæ et duritiæ relin-
quit. Atque hic potissimum sese nobis aperit profunda, misericors
pariter et justa hominum æqualiter perditorum discretio; sive decre-

tum illud *electionis* et *reprobationis* in verbo Dei revelatum. Quod ut perversi, impuri, et parum stabiles in suum detorquent exitium, ita sanctis et religiosis animabus ineffabile præstat solatium.

VII.

Est autem electio immutabile Dei propositum, quo ante jacta mundi fundamenta ex universo genere humano, ex primæva integritate in peccatum et exitium sua culpa prolapso, secundum liberrimum voluntatis suæ beneplacitum, ex mera gratia, certam quorundam hominum multitudinem, aliis nec meliorum, nec digniorum, sed in communi miseria cum aliis jacentium, ad salutem elegit in Christo, quem etiam ab æterno Mediatorem et omnium electorum caput, salutisque fundamentum constituit; atque ita eos ipsi salvandos dare, et ad ejus communionem per verbum et Spiritum suum efficaciter vocare ac trahere; seu vera et ipsum fide donare, justificare, sanctificare, et potenter in Filii sui communione custoditos tandem glorificare decrevit, ad demonstrationem suæ misericordiæ, et laudem divitiarum gloriosæ suæ gratiæ, sicut scriptum est: *Elegit nos Deus in Christo, ante jacta mundi fundamenta, ut essemus sancti et inculpati in conspectu ejus, cum charitate; qui prædestinavit nos quos adoptaret in filios, per Jesum Christum, in sese, pro beneplacito voluntatis suæ, ad laudem gloriosæ suæ gratiæ, qua nos gratis sibi acceptos fecit in illo dilecto.* Ephes. i. 4, 5, 6. Et alibi: *Quos prædestinavit, eos etiam vocavit; et quos vocavit, eos etiam justificavit; quos autem justificavit, eos etiam glorificavit.* Rom. viii. 30.

VIII.

Hæc electio non est multiplex, sed una et eadem omnium salvandorum in Vetere et Novo Testamento, quandoquidem Scriptura unicum prædicat beneplacitum, propositum, et consilium voluntatis Dei, quo nos ab æterno elegit et ad gratiam et ad gloriam; et ad salutem et ad viam salutis, quam præparavit ut in ea ambulemus.

IX.

Eadem hæc electio facta est non ex prævisa fide, fideique obedientia, sanctitate, aut alia aliqua bona qualitate et dispositione, tanquam caussa seu conditione in homine eligendo prærequisita, sed ad fidem, fideique obedientiam, sanctitatem, etc. Ac proinde electio est fons omnis salutaris boni : unde fides, sanctitas, et reliqua dona salvifica, ipsa denique vita æterna, ut fructus et effectus ejus profluunt, secundum illud Apostoli : *Elegit nos* (non quia eramus, sed) *ut essemus sancti et inculpati in conspectu ejus in charitate.* Ephes. i. 4.

X.

Caussa vero hujus gratuitæ electionis, est solum Dei beneplacitum, non in eo consistens, quod certas qualitates seu actiones humanas, ex omnibus possibilibus, in salutis conditionem elegit; sed in eo, quod certas quasdam personas ex communi peccatorum multitudine sibi in peculium adscivit, sicut scriptum est : *Nondum natis pueris, cum neque boni quippiam fecissent neque mali,* etc., *dictum est* (nempe Rebeccæ), *Major serviet minori, sicut scriptum est, Jacob dilexi, Esau odio habui.* Rom. ix. 11, 12, 13. Et, *Crediderunt quotquot erant ordinati ad vitam æternam.* Act. xiii. 48.

XI.

Atque ut Deus ipse est sapientissimus, immutabilis, omniscius, et omnipotens : ita electio ab ipso facta nec interrumpi, nec mutari, revocari, aut abrumpi, nec electi abjici, nec numerus eorum minui potest.

XII.

De hac æterna et immutabili sui ad salutem electione, electi suo tempore, variis licet gradibus et dispari mensura, certiores redduntur, non quidem arcana et profunditates Dei curiose scrutando ; sed fructus electionis infallibiles, in verbo Dei designatos, ut sunt vera in Christum fides, filialis Dei timor, dolor de peccatis secundum Deum, esuries et sitis justitiæ, etc., in sese cum spirituali gaudio et sancta voluptate observando.

XIII.

Ex hujus electionis sensu et certitudine, filii Dei majorem indies sese coram Deo humiliandi, abyssum misericordiarum ejus adorandi, seipsos purificandi, et eum, qui ipsos prior tantopere dilexit, vicissim ardenter diligendi, materiam desumunt : tantum abest, ut hac electionis doctrina atque ejus meditatione in mandatorum divinorum observatione segniores, aut carnaliter securi, reddantur. Quod iis justo Dei judicio solet accidere, qui de electionis gratia, vel temere præsumentes, vel otiose et proterve fabulantes, in viis electorum ambulare nolunt.

XIV.

Ut autem hæc de divina electione doctrina sapientissimo Dei consilio per prophetas, Christum ipsum, atque Apostolos, sub Veteri æque atque sub Novo Testamento, est prædicata, et sacrarum deinde literarum monumentis commendata: ita et hodie in Ecclesia Dei, cui ea peculia-riter est destinata, cum spiritu discretionis, religiose et sancte, suo loco et tempore, missa omni curiosa viarum altissimi scrutatione, est pro-ponenda, idque ad sanctissimi nominis divini gloriam, et vividum po-puli ipsius solatium.

XV.

Cæterum æternam et gratuitam hanc electionis nostri gratiam eo vel maxime illustrat, nobisque commendat Scriptura Sacra, quod porro testatur non omnes homines esse electos, sed quosdam non electos, sive in æterna Dei electione præteritos, quos scilicet Deus ex liberrimo, jus-tissimo, irreprehensibili, et immutabili beneplacito decrevit in communi miseria, in quam se sua culpa præcipitarunt, relinquere, nec salvifica fide et conversionis gratia donare, sed in viis suis, et sub justo judicio relictos, tandem non tantum propter infidelitatem, sed etiam cætera omnia peccata, ad declarationem justitiæ suæ damnare, et æternum punire. Atque hoc est decretum *reprobationis*, quod Deum neuti-quam peccati authorem (quod cogitatu blasphemum est) sed tremen-dum, irreprehensibilem, et justum judicem ac vindicem constituit.

XVI.

Qui vivam in Christum fidem, seu certam cordis fiduciam, pacem conscientiæ, studium filialis obedientiæ, gloriationem in Deo per Christum in se nondum efficaciter sentiunt, mediis tamen, per quæ Deus ista se in nobis operaturum promisit, utuntur, ii ad reprobationis mentionem non consternari, nec se reprobis accensere, sed in usu me-diorum diligenter pergere, ac horam uberioris gratiæ ardenter deside-rare et reverenter humiliterque expectare debent. Multo autem minus doctrina de reprobatione terreri debent ii, qui cum serio ad Deum con-verti, ei unice placere, et e corpore mortis eripi desiderant, in via tamen pietatis et fidei eo usque, quo volunt, pervenire nondum possunt, siquidem linum fumigans se non extincturum, et arundinem quassatam se non fracturum, promisit misericors Deus. Iis autem hæc doctrina merito terrori est, qui Dei et Servatoris Jesu Christi obliti, mundi curis et carnis voluptatibus se totos manciparunt, quamdiu ad Deum serio non convertuntur.

XVII.

Quandoquidem de voluntate Dei ex verbo ipsius nobis est judicandum, quod testatur liberos fidelium esse sanctos, non quidem natura, sed beneficio fœderis gratuiti, in quo illi cum parentibus comprehenduntur, pii parentes de electione et salute suorum liberorum, quos Deus in infantia ex hac vita evocat, dubitare non debent.

XVIII.

Adversus hanc gratuitæ electionis gratiam, et justæ reprobationis severitatem, obmurmuranti opponimus hoc apostolicum: *O homo! tu quis es qui ex adverso responsas Deo?* Rom. ix. 20. Et illud Servatoris nostri, *An non licet mihi quod volo facere in meis?* Matt. xx. 15. Nos vero hæc mysteria religiose adorantes, cum Apostolo exclamamus: *O profunditatem divitiarum tum sapientiæ tum cognitionis Dei! Quam imperscrutabilia sunt Dei judicia, et ejus viæ impervestigabiles! Quis enim cognovit mentem Domini? Aut quis fuit ei a consiliis? Aut quis prior dedit ei ut reddatur ei? Nam ex eo, et per eum, et in eum sunt omnia. Ipsi sit gloria in sæcula. Amen.* Rom. xi. 33–36.

REJECTIO ERRORUM,

Quibus Ecclesiæ Belgicæ sunt aliquamdiu perturbatæ. Exposita doctrina Orthodoxa de Electione et Reprobatione, Synodus rejicit Errores eorum:

I.

Qui docent, 'Voluntatem Dei de servandis credituris, et in fide fideique obedientia perseveraturis, esse totum et integrum electionis ad salutem decretum; nec quicquam aliud de hoc decreto in verbo Dei esse revelatum.' Hi enim simplicioribus imponunt, et Scripturæ sacræ manifeste contradicunt, testanti Deum non tantum servare velle credituros, sed etiam certos quosdam homines ab æterno elegisse, quos præ aliis in tempore fide in Christum et perseverantia donaret; sicut scriptum est, *Manifestum feci nomen tuum hominibus, quos dedisti mihi.* Johan. xvii. 6. Item, *Crediderunt quotquot ordinati erant ad vitam æternam.* Act. xiii. 48. Et, *Elegit nos ante jacta mundi fundamenta, ut essemus sancti,* etc. Ephes. 1. 4.

II.

Qui docent, 'Electionem Dei ad vitam æternam esse multiplicem; aliam generalem et indefinitam, aliam singularem et definitam; et hanc rursum vel incompletam, revocabilem, non peremptoriam, sive conditionatam: vel completam, irrevocabilem, peremptoriam, seu absolutam.' Item, 'Aliam electionem esse ad fidem, aliam ad salutem; ita ut electio ad fidem justificantem absque electione peremptoria ad salutem esse possit.' Hoc enim est humani cerebri commentum extra Scripturas excogitatum, doctrinam de electione corrumpens, et auream hanc salutis catenam dissolvens: *Quos prædestinavit, eos etiam vocavit: et quos vocavit, eos etiam justificavit: quos autem justificavit, eos etiam glorificavit.* Rom. viii. 30.

III.

Qui docent, 'Dei beneplacitum ac propositum, cujus Scriptura meminit in doctrina electionis, non consistere in eo, quod Deus certos quosdam homines præ aliis elegerit, sed in eo, quod Deus ex omnibus possibilibus conditionibus (inter quas etiam sunt opera legis) sive ex omnium rerum ordine actum fidei, in sese ignobilem, et obedientiam fidei imperfectam, in salutis conditionem elegerit; eamque gratiose pro perfecta obedientia reputare, et vitæ æternæ præmio dignam censere voluerit.' Hoc enim errore pernicioso beneplacitum Dei et meritum Christi enervatur, et homines inutilibus quæstionibus a veritate justificationis gratuitæ, et simplicitate Scripturarum avocantur; illudque Apostoli falsi arguitur; *Deus nos vocavit vocatione sancta; non ex operibus, sed ex suo proposito et gratia, quæ data est nobis in Christo Jesu ante tempora sæculorum.* 2 Tim. i. 9.

IV.

Qui docent, 'In electione ad fidem hanc conditionem prærequiri, ut homo lumine naturæ recte utatur, sit probus, parvus, humilis, et ad vitam æternam dispositus, quasi ab ipsis electio aliquatenus pendeat.' Pelagium enim sapiunt, et minime obscure falsi insimulant Apostolum scribentem: *Versati sumus olim in cupiditatibus carnis nostræ, facientes quæ carni et cogitationibus libebant, eramusque natura filii iræ, ut et reliqui. Sed Deus, qui dives est misericordia, propter multam charitatem suam, qua dilexit nos, etiam nos cum in offensis mortui essemus, una vivificavit cum Christo, cujus gratia estis servati, unaque suscitavit, unaque collocavit in cœlis in Christo Jesu; ut ostenderet in seculis supervenientibus supereminentes illas opes suæ gratiæ, pro sua erga nos benignitate in Christo Jesu. Gratia enim estis servati per fidem (et hoc non ex vobis, Dei donum est), non ex operibus, ut ne quis glorietur.* Ephes. ii. 3-9.

V.

Qui docent, 'Electionem singularium personarum ad salutem, incompletam et non peremptoriam, factam esse ex prævisa fide, resipiscentia, sanctitate et pietate inchoata, aut aliquamdiu continuata: completam vero et peremptoriam ex prævisæ fidei, resipiscentiæ, sanctitatis, et pietatis finali perseverantia: et hanc esse gratiosam et evangelicam dignitatem, propter quam qui eligitur dignior sit illo qui non eligitur: ac proinde fidem, fidei obedientiam, sanctitatem, pietatem, et perseverantiam non esse fructus sive effectus electionis immutabilis ad gloriam, sed conditiones, et caussas sine quibus non, in eligendis complete prærequisitas, et prævisas, tanquam præstitas.' Id quod toti Scripturæ repugnat, quæ hæc et alia dicta passim auribus et cordibus nostris ingerit: *Electio non est ex operibus, sed ex vocante.* Rom. ix. 11. *Credebant quotquot ordinati erant ad vitam æternam.* Act. xiii. 48. *Elegit nos in semetipso ut sancti essemus.* Ephes. i. 4. *Non vos me elegistis, sed ego elegi vos.* Johan. xv. 16. *Si ex gratia, non ex operibus.* Rom. xi. 6. *In hoc est charitas, non quod nos dilexerimus Deum, sed quod ipse dilexit nos, et misit Filium suum.* 1 Johan. iv. 10.

Vi.

Qui docent, 'Non omnem electionem ad salutem immutabilem esse, sed quosdam electos, nullo Dei decreto obstante, perire posse et æternum perire.' Quo crasso errore et Deum mutabilem faciunt, et consolationem piorum de electionis suæ constantia subvertunt, et Scripturis sacris contradicunt docentibus, *Electos non posse seduci:* Matt. xxiv. 24. Christum *datos sibi a Patre non perdere:* Johan. vi. 39. Deum *quos prædestinavit, vocavit et justificavit, eos etiam glorificare.* Rom. viii. 30.

VII.

Qui docent, 'Electionis immutabilis ad gloriam nullum in hac vita esse fructum, nullum sensum, nullam certitudinem, nisi ex conditione mutabili et contingente.' Præterquam enim quod absurdum sit ponere certitudinem incertam, adversantur hæc experientiæ sanctorum, qui cum Apostolo ex sensu electionis sui exultant, Deique hoc beneficium celebrant, qui *gaudent* cum discipulis, secundum Christi admonitionem, *quod nomina sua scripta sunt in cœlis:* Luc. x. 20; qui sensum denique electionis ignitis tentationum diabolicarum telis opponunt, quærentes, *Quis intentabit crimina adversus electos Dei?* Rom. viii. 33.

VIII.

Qui docent, 'Deum neminem ex mera justa sua voluntate decrevisse in lapsu Adæ et in communi peccati et damnationis statu relinquere, aut in gratiæ ad fidem et conversionem necessariæ communicatione præterire.' Stat enim illud, *Quorum vult, miseretur; quos vult, indurat.* Rom. ix. 18. Et illud, *Vobis datum est nosse mysteria regni cœlorum, illis autem non est datum.* Matt. xiii. 11. Item, *Glorifico te, Pater, Domine cœli et terræ, quod hæc occultaveris sapientibus et intelligentibus, et ea detexeris infantibus: etiam, Pater, quia ita placuit tibi.* Matt. xi. 25, 26.

IX.

Qui docent, 'Caussam cur Deus ad hanc potius, quam ad aliam gentem Evangelium mittat, non esse merum et solum Dei beneplacitum, sed quod hæc gens melior et dignior sit ea, cui Evangelium non communicatur.' Reclamat enim Moses, populum Israeliticum sic alloquens, *En Jehovæ Dei tui sunt cœli, et cœli cœlorum, terra, et quicquid est in ea: Tantum in majores tuos propensus fuit amore Jehova diligendo eos; unde selegit semen eorum post eos, vos inquam, præ omnibus populis, sicut est hodie.* Deut. x. 14, 15. Et Christus: *Væ tibi Chorazin, væ tibi Bethsaida, quia si in Tyro et Sidone factæ essent virtutes illæ quæ in vobis factæ sunt, in sacco et cinere olim pœnitentiam egissent.* Matt. xi. 21.

Ita nos sentire et judicare, manuum nostrarum subscriptione testamur.

Johannes Bogermannus, *Pastor Ecclesiæ Leoverdiensis et Synodi Præses.*
Jacobus Rolandus, *Pastor Ecclesiæ Amstelodamensis et Præsidis Assessor.*
Hermannus Faukelius, *Pastor Ecclesiæ Middelburgensis et Præsidis Assessor.*
Sebastianus Damman, *Pastor Ecclesiæ Zutphaniensis et Synodi Scriba.*
Festus Hommius, *Pastor Ecclesiæ Leydensis et Synodi Scriba.*

Ex Magna Britannia.

Georgius *Episcopus* Landavensis.
Johannes Davenantius, *Presbyter; Doctor ac Sacræ Theologiæ publicus Professor in Academia Cantabrigiensi et Collegii Reginalis ibidem Præses.*
Samuel Wardus, *Presbyter, SS. Theologiæ Doctor, Archidiaconus Fauntonnensis, et Collegii Sidneyani in Academia Cantabrigiensi Præfectus.*
Thomas Goadus, *Presbyter, SS. Theologiæ Doctor, Cathedralis Ecclesiæ Paulinæ Londinensis Præcentor.*
Gualterus Balcanquallus, *Scoto-Britannus, Presbyter, S. Theologiæ Baccalaureus.*

Ex Electorali Palatinatu.

Abrahamus Scultetus, *S. Theologiæ Doctor et Professor in Academia Heydelbergensi.*
Paulus Tossanus, *S. Theologiæ Doctor, et Consiliarius in Senatu Ecclesiastico inferioris Palatinatus.*
Henricus Altingius, *S. Theologiæ Doctor et Professor in Academia Heydelbergensi.*

THE CANONS OF THE SYNOD OF DORT. A.D. 1619. 559

Ex Hassia.

Georgius Cruciger, *S. Theologiæ Doctor, Professor, et pro tempore Rector Academiæ Marpurgensis.*
Paulus Steinius, *Concionator Aulicus et S. Theologiæ in Collegio Nobilitatis Adelphico Mauritiano Professor, Cassellis.*
Daniel Angelocrator, *Ecclesiæ Marpurgensis Pastor, et vicinarum ad Lanum et Æderam Superintendens.*
Rodolphus Goclenius, Senior. *Philosophiæ purioris in Academia Marpurgensi Antecessor primarius, et nunc Decanus.*

Ex Helvetia.

Joannes Jacobus Breytingerus, *Ecclesiæ Tigurinæ Pastor.*
Marcus Rutimeyerus, *S. Theologiæ Doctor et Ecclesiæ Bernensis Minister.*
Sebastianus Beckius, *SS. Theologiæ Doctor, et Novi Testamenti Professor in Academia Basiliensi, ibidemque Facultatis Theologicæ Decanus.*
Wolfgangus Mayerus, *SS. Theologiæ Doctor, Ecclesiæ Basiliensis Pastor.*
Johannes Conradus Kochius, *Ecclesiæ Schaphusianæ Minister.*

A Correspondentia Wedderavica.

Johannes Henricus Alstedius, *in illustri Schola Nassovica, quæ est Herbornæ, Professor ordinarius.*
Georgius Fabricius, *Ecclesiæ Windeccensis in Comitatu Hanovico Pastor, et vicinarum Inspector.*

Ex Republica et Ecclesia Genevensi.

Johannes Deodatus, *in Ecclesia Genevensi Pastor, et in eadem Schola SS. Theologiæ Professor.*
Theodorus Tronchinus, *Divini verbi Minister in Ecclesia Genevensi, et ibidem SS. Theologiæ Professor.*

Ex Republica et Ecclesia Bremensi.

Matthias Martinius, *illustris Scholæ Bremensis Rector, et in ea Divinarum literarum Professor.*
Henricus Isselburg, *SS. Theologiæ Doctor, in Bremensi Ecclesia ad B. Virginis Jesu Christi servus et in Schola Novi Testamenti Professor.*
Ludovicus Crocius, *SS. Theologiæ Doctor, Ecclesiæ Bremensis ad S. Martini Pastor, et in illustri Schola Veteris Testamenti et Philosophiæ practicæ Professor.*

Ex Republica et Ecclesia Emdana.

Daniel Bernardus Eilshemius, *Emdanæ Ecclesiæ Pastor Senior*
Ritzius Lucas Grimershemius, *Emdanæ Ecclesiæ Pastor.*

SS. Theologiæ Professores Belgici.

Johannes Polyander, *SS. Theologiæ Doctor, atque in Academia Leydensi Professor.*
Sibrandus Lubertus, *SS. Theologiæ Doctor, et Professor in Academia Frisiorum.*
Franciscus Gomarus, *Sacrosanctæ Theologiæ Doctor, et Professor in Academia Groningæ et Omlandiæ.*
Antonius Tysius, *Sacræ Theologiæ in illustri Schola Geldro-Velavica, quæ est Hardervici, Professor.*
Antonius Walæus, *Pastor Ecclesiæ Middelburgensis, et ex ejusdem urbis illustri Schola inter Theologos ad Synodum evocatus.*

Ex Ducatu Geldriæ, et Comitatu Zutphaniæ.

Guilielmus Stephani, *SS. Theologiæ Doctor, et Arnhemiensis Ecclesiæ Pastor.*
Ellardus a Mehen, *Ecclesiæ Hardrovicenæ Pastor.*
Johannes Bouillet, *Pastor Ecclesiæ Warnsfeldensis.*
Jacobus Verheyden, Senior, *Ecclesiæ Noviomagensis et Scholæ Rector.*

Ex Hollandia Australi.

Balthasar Lydius, *M. F. Pastor Ecclesiæ Dei in urbe Dordrechto.*
Henricus Arnoldi, *Ecclesiastes Delphensis.*
Gisbertus Voetius, *Ecclesiæ Heusdanæ Pastor.*
Arnoldus Musius ab Holy, *Baillivus Suyd-Hollandiæ Senior Ecclesiæ Dordrechtanæ.*
Johannes de Laet, *Senior Ecclesiæ Leydensis.*

Ex Hollandia Boreali.

Jacobus Triglandius, *Pastor Ecclesiæ Amstelodamensis.*
Abrahamus a Doreslaer, *Pastor Ecclesiæ Enchusanæ.*
Samuel Bartholdus, *Pastor Ecclesiæ Monachodammensis.*
Theodorus Heyngius, *Senior Ecclesiæ Amstelodamensis.*
Dominicus ab Heemskerck, *Senior Ecclesiæ Amstelodamensis.*

Ex Zelandia.

Godefridus Udemannus, *Pastor Ecclesiæ Ziericzeanæ.*
Cornelius Regius, *Ecclesiæ Goesanæ Pastor.*
Lambertus de Rycke, *Ecclesiæ Bergizomianæ Pastor.*
Josias Vosbergius, *Senior Ecclesiæ Middelburgensis.*
Adrianus Hofferus, *urbis Zirizææ Senator, et Ecclesiæ ibidem Senior.*

Ex Provincia Ultrajectina.

Johannes Dibbezius, *Pastor Dordracenus, Synodi Orthodoxæ Ultrajectinæ Deputatus.*
Arnoldus Oortcampius, *Ecclesiæ Amersfortianæ Pastor.*

Ex Frisia.

Florentius Johannes, *Jesu Christi crucifixi Servus in Ecclesia Snecana.*
Philippus Danielis Eilshemius, *Pastor Ecclesiæ Harlingensis.*
Kempo Harinxma a Donia, *Senior Ecclesiæ Leoverdiensis.*
Tacitus ab Aysma, *Senior Ecclesiæ in Buirgirt Hichtum, et Hartwardt.*

Ex Transisalania.

Casparus Sibelius, *Pastor Ecclesiæ Daventriensis.*
Hermannus Wiferdingius, *Ecclesiæ Swollanæ in Evangelio Christi Minister.*
Hieronymus Vogellius, *Hasseltanæ Ecclesiæ Pastor, tempore deputationis inserviens Ecclesia Orthodoxæ Campensi.*
Johannes Langius, *Ecclesiastes Vollenhovianus.*
Wilhelmus a Broeckhuysen ten Doerne, *tanquam Senior deputatus.*
Johannes a Lauwick, *tanquam Senior deputatus.*

Ex Civitate Groningana, et Omlandiis.

Cornelius Hillenius, *Servus Jesu Christi in Ecclesia Groningana.*
Georgius Placius, *Pastor Ecclesiæ Appingadammonensis.*
Wolfgangus Agricola, *Pastor Ecclesiæ Bedumanæ.*
Wigboldus Homerus, *Ecclesiæ Midwoldanæ Pastor.*
Egbertus Halbes, *Ecclesiæ Groninganæ Senior.*
Johannes Rufelaert, *Senior Ecclesiæ Stedumanæ.*

Ex Drentia.

Themo ab Asscheberg, *Pastor Ecclesiæ Meppelensis.*
Patroclus Romelingius, *Pastor Ecclesiæ Rhuinensis.*

Ex Ecclesiis Gallo-Belgicis.

Daniel Colonius, *Pastor Ecclesiæ Leydensis, et Regens Collegii Gallo-Belgici in Academia Leydensi*
Johannes Crucius, *Pastor Ecclesiæ Haerlemensis.*
Johannes Doucher, *Pastor Ecclesiæ Flissinganæ.*
Jeremias de Pours, *Ecclesiæ Gallo-Belgicæ Middelburgensis Pastor.*
Evekardus Beckerus, *Senior Ecclesiæ Gallo-Belgicæ Middelburgensis.*
Petrus Pontanus, *Senior Ecclesiæ Amstelodamensis.*

SECUNDUM DOCTRINÆ CAPUT, DE MORTE CHRISTI, ET HOMINUM PER EAM REDEMPTIONE.

Articulus Primus.

Deus non tantum est summe misericors, sed etiam summe justus. Postulat autem ejus justitia (prout se in verbo revelavit), ut peccata nostra, adversus infinitam ejus majestatem commissa, non tantum temporalibus, sed etiam æternis, tum animi, tum corporis, pœnis puniantur: quas pœnas effugere non possumus, nisi justitiæ Dei satisfiat.

II.

Cum vero ipsi satisfacere, et ab ira Dei nos liberare non possimus, Deus ex immensa misericordia Filium suum unigenitum nobis Sponsorem dedit, qui, ut pro nobis satisfaceret, peccatum et maledictio in cruce pro nobis, seu vice nostra, factus est.

III.

Hæc mors Filii Dei est unica et perfectissima pro peccatis victima et satisfactio, infiniti valoris et pretii, abunde sufficiens ad totius mundi peccata expianda.

IV.

Ideo autem hæc mors tanti est valoris et pretii, quia persona, quæ eam subiit, non tantum est verus et perfecte sanctus homo, sed etiam unigenitus DEI Filius, ejusdem æternæ et infinitæ cum Patre et Spiritu S. essentiæ, qualem nostrum Servatorem esse oportebat. Deinde, quia mors ipsius fuit conjuncta cum sensu iræ Dei et maledictionis, quam nos peccatis nostris eramus commeriti.

V.

Cæterum promissio Evangelii est, ut quisquis credit in Christum crucifixum, non pereat, sed habeat vitam æternam. Quæ promissio omnibus populis et hominibus, ad quos Deus pro suo beneplacito mittit Evangelium, promiscue et indiscriminatim annunciari et proponi debet cum resipiscentiæ et fidei mandato.

VI.

Quod autem multi per Evangelium vocati non resipiscunt, nec in Christum credunt, sed infidelitate pereunt, non fit hoc hostiæ Christi in cruce oblatæ defectu, vel insufficientia, sed propria ipsorum culpa.

VII.

Quotquot autem vere credunt, et per mortem Christi a peccatis, et interitu liberantur ac servantur, illis hoc beneficium, ex sola Dei gratia, quam nemini debet, ab æterno ipsis in Christo data, obtingit.

VIII.

Fuit enim hoc Dei Patris liberrimum consilium, et gratiosissima voluntas atque intentio, ut mortis pretiosissimæ Filii sui vivifica et salvifica efficacia sese exereret in omnibus electis, ad eos solos fide justificante donandos, et per eam ad salutem infallibiliter perducendos: hoc est, voluit Deus, ut Christus per sanguinem crucis (quo novum fœdus confirmavit) ex omni populo, tribu, gente, et lingua, eos omnes et solos, qui ab æterno ad salutem electi, et a Patre ipsi dati sunt, efficaciter redimeret, fide (quam, ut et alia Spiritus Sancti salvifica dona, ipsis morte sua acquisivit) donaret, ab omnibus peccatis, tum originali, tum actualibus, tam post, quam ante fidem commissis sanguine suo mundaret, ad finem usque fideliter custodiret, tandemque absque omni labe et macula gloriosos coram se sisteret.

IX.

Hoc consilium, ex æterno erga electos amore profectum ab initio mundi in præsens usque tempus, frustra obnitentibus inferorum portis, potenter impletum fuit, et deinceps quoque implebitur: ita quidem ut electi suis temporibus in unum colligantur, et semper sit aliqua credentium Ecclesia in sanguine Christi fundata, quæ illum Servatorem suum, qui pro ea, tanquam Sponsus pro sponsa, animam suam in cruce exposuit, constanter diligat, perseveranter colat, atque hic et in omnem æternitatem celebret.

Rejectio Errorum.

Exposita doctrina orthodoxa, rejicit Synodus errores eorum :

I.

Qui docent, 'Quod Deus Pater Filium suum in mortem crucis destinaverit, sine certo ac definito consilio quemquam nominatim salvandi, adeo ut impetrationi mortis Christi sua necessitas, utilitas, dignitas sarta tecta, et numeris suis perfecta, completa atque integra constare potuisset, etiamsi impetrata redemptio nulli individuo unquam actu ipso fuisset applicata.' Hæc enim assertio in Dei Patris sapientiam meritumque Jesu Christi contumeliosa, et Scripturæ contraria est. Sic enim ait Servator : *Ego animam pono pro ovibus, et agnosco eas.* Johan. x. 15, 27. Et de Servatore Esaias propheta : *Cum posuerit se sacrificium pro reatu, videbit semen, prolongabit dies, et voluntas Jehovæ in manu ejus prosperabitur.* Esai. liii. 10. Denique, articulum Fidei, quo Ecclesiam credimus, evertit.

II.

Qui docent, ' Non fuisse hunc finem mortis Christi, ut novum gratiæ fœdus suo sanguine reipsa sanciret, sed tantum, ut nudum jus Patri acquireret, quodcunque fœdus, vel gratiæ, vel operum, cum hominibus denuo ineundi.' Hoc enim repugnat Scripturæ, quæ docet, Christum *melioris,* id est, novi *fœderis Sponsorem et Mediatorem factum esse.* Heb. vii. 22. Et, *Testamentum in mortuis demum ratum esse.* Heb. ix. 15, 17.

III.

Qui docent, 'Christum per suam satisfactionem, nullis certo meruisse ipsam salutem et fidem, qua hæc Christi satisfactio ad salutem efficaciter applicetur, sed tantum Patri acquisivisse potestatem vel plenariam voluntatem, de novo cum hominibus agendi, et novas, quascunque vellet conditiones, præscribendi, quarum præstatio a libero hominis arbitrio pendeat, atque ideo fieri potuisse, ut vel nemo, vel omnes eas implerent.' Hi enim de morte Christi nimis abjecte sentiunt, primarium fructum seu beneficium per eam partum nullatenus agnoscunt, et Pelagianum errorem ab inferis revocant.

IV.

Qui docent, ' Fœdus illud novum gratiæ, quod Deus Pater, per mortis Christi interventum cum hominibus pepigit, non in eo consistere, quod per fidem, quatenus meritum Christi apprehendit, coram Deo justificemur et salvemur ; sed in hoc, quod Deus, abrogata perfectæ obedientiæ legalis exactione, fidem ipsam et fidei obedientiam imperfectam pro perfecta legis obedientia reputet, et vitæ æternæ præmio gratiose dignam censeat.' Hi enim contradicunt Scripturæ, *Justificantur gratis, ejus gratia, per redemptionem factam in Jesu Christo, quem proposuit Deus placamentum per fidem in sanguine ejus.* Rom. iii. 24, 25. Et cum impio Socino, novam et peregrinam hominis coram Deo justificationem, contra totius Ecclesiæ consensum, inducunt.

V.

Qui docent, 'Omnes homines in statum reconciliationis et gratiam fœderis esse assumptos, ita ut nemo propter peccatum originale sit damnationi obnoxius, aut damnandus, sed omnes ab istius peccati reatu sint immunes.' Hæc enim sententia repugnat Scripturæ, affirmanti *nos natura esse filios iræ.* [Ephes. ii. 3.]

VI.

Qui impetrationis et applicationis distinctionem usurpant, ut incautis et imperitis hanc opinionem instillent : Deum, quantum ad se attinet, omnibus hominibus ex æquo ea beneficia voluisse conferre, quæ per mortem Christi acquiruntur ; quod autem quidam præ aliis participes fiant remissionis peccatorum, et vitæ æternæ, discrimen illud pendere ex libero eorum arbitrio, se ad gratiam indifferenter oblatam applicante, non autem ex singulari misericordiæ dono, efficaciter in illis operante, ut præ aliis gratiam illam sibi applicent.   Nam isti, dum simulant se distinctionem hanc sano sensu próponere, populo perniciosum Pelagianismi venenum conantur propinare.

VII.

Qui docent, 'CHRISTUM, pro iis, quos DEUS summe dilexit, et ad vitam æternam elegit, mori nec potuisse, nec debuisse, nec mortuum esse, cum talibus morte CHRISTI non sit opus.' Contradicunt enim Apostolo dicenti : *Christus dilexit me, et tradidit seipsum pro me.* Galat. ii. 20.   Item, *Quis est, qui crimina intentet adversus electos* DEI ? DEUS *est is, qui justificat. Quis est qui condemnet ?* CHRISTUS *est, qui mortuus est.* Rom. viii. 33, 34 : nimirum, pro illis.   Et Salvatori asseveranti, *Ego pono animam meam pro ovibus meis,* Johan. x. 15. Et, *Hoc est præceptum meum, ut diligatis alii alios, sicut ego dilexi vos. Majorem dilectionem nemo habet, quam ut ponat animam suam pro amicis.* Johan. xv. 12, 13.

Huic capiti eadem quæ prius subscribuntur nomina.

TERTIUM ET QUARTUM DOCTRINÆ CAPUT, DE HOMINIS CORRUPTIONE, ET CONVERSIONE AD DEUM EJUSQUE MODO.

Articulus Primus.

Homo ab initio ad imaginem DEI conditus vera et salutari sui Creatoris et rerum spiritualium notitia in mente, et justitia in voluntate et corde, puritate in omnibus affectibus exornatus, adeoque totus sanctus fuit; sed Diaboli instinctu, et libera sua voluntate a Deo desciscens, eximiis istis donis seipsum orbavit: atque e contrario eorum loco cœcitatem, horribiles tenebras, vanitatem, ac perversitatem judicii in mente, malitiam, rebellionem, ac duritiem in voluntate et corde, impuritatem denique in omnibus affectibus contraxit.

II.

Qualis autem post lapsum fuit homo, tales et liberos procreavit, nempe corruptus corruptos; corruptione ab Adamo in omnes posteros [solo Christo excepto] non per imitationem [quod Pelagiani olim voluerunt], sed per vitiosæ naturæ propagationem, justo Dei judicio, derivata.

III.

Itaque omnes homines in peccato concipiuntur, et filii iræ nascuntur, inepti ad omne bonum salutare, propensi ad malum, in peccatis mortui, et peccati servi; et absque Spiritus Sancti regenerantis gratia, ad Deum redire, naturam depravatam corrigere, vel ad ejus correctionem se disponere nec volunt, nec possunt.

IV.

Residuum quidem est post lapsum in homine lumen aliquod naturæ, cujus beneficio ille notitias quasdam de Deo, de rebus naturalibus, de discrimine honestorum et turpium retinet, et aliquod virtutis ac disciplinæ externæ studium ostendit: sed tantum abest, ut hoc naturæ lumine ad salutarem Dei cognitionem pervenire, et ad eum se convertere possit, ut ne quidem eo in naturalibus ac civilibus recte utatur, quinimo qualecumque id demum sit, id totum variis modis contaminet, atque in injustitia detineat, quod dum facit, coram Deo inexcusabilis redditur.

V.

Quæ luminis naturæ, eadem hæc Decalogi per Mosen a Deo Judæis peculiariter traditi est ratio: cum enim is magnitudinem quidem peccati retegat, ejusque hominem magis ac magis reum peragat, sed nec remedium exhibeat, nec vires emergendi ex miseria conferat, adeoque per carnem infirmatus transgressorem maledictione relinquat, non potest homo per eum salutarem gratiam obtinere.

VI.

Quod igitur nec lumen naturæ, nec lex potest, id Spiritus Sancti virtute præstat Deus, per sermonem, sive ministerium reconciliationis, quod est Evangelium de Messia, per quod placuit Deo homines credentes tam in Veteri, quam in Novo Testamento servare.

VII.

Hoc voluntatis suæ mysterium Deus in Veteri Testamento paucioribus patefecit, in Novo Testamento pluribus, sublato jam populorum discrimine, manifestat. Cujus dispensationis caussa, non in gentis unius præ alia dignitate, aut meliore luminis naturæ usu, sed in liberrimo beneplacito, et gratuita dilectione DEI est collocanda. Unde illi, quibus præter et contra omne meritum tanta fit gratia, eam humili et grato corde agnoscere, in reliquis autem, quibus ea gratia non fit, severitatem et justitiam judiciorum DEI cum Apostolo adorare, nequaquam vero curiose scrutari debent.

VIII.

Quotquot autem per Evangelium vocantur, serio vocantur. Serio enim et verissime ostendit Deus verbo suo, quid sibi gratum sit, nimi rum, ut vocati ad se veniant. Serio etiam omnibus ad se venientibus et credentibus requiem animarum, et vitam aeternam promittit.

IX.

Quod multi per ministerium Evangelii vocati, non veniunt et non convertuntur, hujus culpa non est in Evangelio, nec in Christo per Evangelium oblato, nec in Deo per Evangelium vocante, et dona etiam varia iis conferente, sed in vocatis ipsis, quorum aliqui verbum vitae non admittunt securi; alii admittunt quidem, sed non in cor immittunt, ideoque post evanidum fidei temporariae gaudium resiliunt; alii spinis curarum et voluptatibus saeculi semen verbi suffocant, fructusque nullos proferunt; quod Servator noster seminis parabola docet, Matt. xiii.

X.

Quod autem alii, per ministerium Evangelii vocati, veniunt et convertuntur, id non est adscribendum homini, tanquam seipsum per liberum arbitrium ab aliis pari vel sufficiente gratia ad fidem et conversionem instructis discernenti (quod superba Pelagii haeresis statuit), sed Deo, qui ut suos ab aeterno in Christo elegit, ita eosdem in tempore efficaciter vocat, fide et resipiscentia donat, et e potestate tenebrarum erutos in Filii sui regnum transfert, ut virtutes ejus, qui ipsos e tenebris in admirandam hanc lucem vocavit, praedicent, et non in se, sed in Domino, glorientur. Scriptura apostolica passim id testante.

XI.

Caeterum, quando Deus hoc suum beneplacitum in electis exequitur, seu veram in iis conversionem operatur, non tantum Evangelium illis externe praedicari curat, et mentem eorum per Spiritum Sanctum potenter illuminat, ut recte intelligant et dijudicent quae sunt Spiritus Dei, sed ejusdem etiam Spiritus regenerantis efficacia ad intima hominis penetrat, cor clausum aperit, durum emollit, praeputiatum circumcidit, voluntati novas qualitates infundit, facitque eam ex mortua vivam, ex mala bonam, ex nolente volentem, ex refractaria morigeram, agitque et roborat eam, ut, ceu arbor bona, fructus bonarum actionum proferre possit.

XII.

Atque hæc est illa tantopere in Scripturis prædicata regeneratio, nova creatio, suscitatio e mortuis, et vivificatio, quam Deus sine nobis, in nobis operatur. Ea autem neutiquam fit per solam forinsecus insonantem doctrinam, moralem suasionem, vel talem operandi rationem, ut post Dei (quoad ipsum) operationem, in hominis potestate maneat regenerari vel non regenerari, converti vel non converti; sed est plane supernaturalis, potentissima simul et suavissima, mirabilis, arcana, et ineffabilis operatio, virtute sua, secundum Scripturam (quæ ab Authore hujus operationis est inspirata) nec creatione, nec mortuorum resusci tatione minor, aut inferior, adeo ut omnes illi, in quorum cordibus admirando hoc modo Deus operatur, certo, infallibiliter, et efficaciter regenerentur, et actu credant. Atque tum voluntas jam renovata, non tantum agitur et movetur a Deo, sed a Deo acta, agit et ipsa. Quamobrem etiam homo ipse per gratiam istam acceptam credere et resipiscere recte dicitur.

XIII.

Modum hujus operationis fideles in hac vita plene comprehendere non possunt; in eo interim acquiescentes, quod per istam DEI gratiam, se corde credere, et Servatorem suum diligere, sciant ac sentiant.

XIV.

Sic ergo fides Dei donum est, non eo quod a Deo hominis arbitrio offeratur, sed quod homini reipsa conferatur, inspiretur, et infundatur. Non etiam quod Deus potentiam credendi tantum conferat, consensum vero seu actum credendi ab hominis deinde arbitrio expectet, sed, quod et velle credere, et ipsum credere in homine is efficiat, qui operatur et velle et facere, adeoque omnia operatur in omnibus.

XV.

Hanc gratiam DEUS nemini debet. Quid enim debeat ei, qui prior dare nihil potest, ut ei retribuatur? Imo quid debeat ei, qui de suo nihil habet, præter peccatum et mendacium? Qui ergo gratiam illam accipit, soli Deo æternas debet et agit gratias; qui illam non accipit, is aut hæc spiritualia omnino non curat, et in suo sibi placet: aut securus se habere inaniter gloriatur, quod non habet. Porro de iis, qui externe fidem profitentur, et vitam emendant, optime secundum exemplum apostolorum judicandum et loquendum est, penetralia enim cordium nobis sunt incomperta. Pro aliis autem qui nondum sunt vocati, orandus est Deus, qui quæ non sunt vocat tanquam sint. Neutiquam vero adversus eos est superbiendum, ac si nosmetipsos discrevissemus.

XVI.

Sicuti vero per lapsum homo non desiit esse homo, intellectu et voluntate præditus, nec peccatum, quod universum genus humanum pervasit, naturam generis humani sustulit, sed depravavit, et spiritualiter occidit; ita etiam hæc divina regenerationis gratia, non agit in hominibus tanquam truncis et stipitibus, nec voluntatem ejusque proprietates tollit, aut invitam violenter cogit, sed spiritualiter vivificat, sanat, corrigit, suaviter simul ac potenter flectit: ut ubi antea plene dominabatur carnis rebellio et resistentia, nunc regnare incipiat prompta, ac sincera Spiritus obedientia; in quo vera et spiritualis nostræ voluntatis instauratio et libertas consistit. Qua ratione nisi admirabilis ille omnis boni opifex nobiscum ageret, nulla spes esset homini surgendi e lapsu per liberum arbitrium, per quod se, cum staret, præcipitavit in exitium.

XVII.

Quemadmodum etiam omnipotens illa Dei operatio, qua vitam hanc nostram naturalem producit et sustentat, non excludit sed requirit usum mediorum, per quæ Deus pro infinita sua sapientia et bonitate virtutem istam suam exercere voluit: ita et hæc prædicta supernaturalis Dei operatio, qua nos regenerat, neutiquam excludit, aut evertit usum Evangelii, quod sapientissimus Deus in semen regenerationis, et cibum animæ ordinavit. Quare, ut Apostoli, et qui eos secuti sunt doctores, de gratia hac Dei ad ejus gloriam et omnis superbiæ depressionem, pie populum docuerunt, neque tamen interim sanctis Evangelii monitis, sub verbi, sacramentorum, et disciplinæ exercitio eum continere neglexerunt: sic etiamnum, absit, ut docentes aut discentes in Ecclesia Deum tentare præsumant, ea separando, quæ Deus pro suo beneplacito voluit esse conjunctissima. Per monita enim confertur gratia, et quo nos officium nostrum facimus promptius, hoc ipso Dei in nobis operantis beneficium solet esse illustrius, rectissimeque ejus opus procedit. Cui soli omnis, et mediorum, et salutaris eorum fructus atque efficaciæ debetur gloria in sæcula. Amen.

REJECTIO ERRORUM.

Exposita doctrina orthodoxa, Synodus rejicit errores eorum :

I.

Qui docent, 'Proprie dici non posse, quod peccatum originis per se sufficiat toti generi humano condemnando, aut temporales et æternas pœnas promerendo.' Contradicunt enim Apostolo, dicenti, Rom. v. 12 : *Per unum hominem peccatum in mundum introiit, ac per peccatum mors, et ita in omnes homines mors transiit, in quo omnes peccaverunt.* Et vers. 16 : *Reatus ex uno introiit ad condemnationem.* Item, Rom. vi. 23 : *Peccati stipendium mors est.*

II.

Qui docent, 'Dona spiritualia, sive habitus bonos, et virtutes, ut sunt bonitas, sanctitas, justitia, in voluntate hominis, cum primum crearetur, locum habere non potuisse, ac proinde nec in lapsu ab ea separari.' Pugnat enim hoc cum descriptione imaginis Dei, quam Apostolus ponit Ephes. iv. 24 ; ubi illam describit ex justitia et sanctitate, quæ omnino in voluntate locum habent.

III.

Qui docent, 'Dona spiritualia non esse in morte spirituali ab hominis voluntate separata, cum ea in sese nunquam corrupta fuerit, sed tantum per tenebras mentis, et affectuum inordinationem impedita ; quibus impedimentis sublatis, liberam suam facultatem sibi insitam exerere, id est, quodvis bonum sibi propositum ex se, aut velle, sive eligere, aut non velle, sive non eligere possit.' Novum hoc et erroneum est, atque eo facit ut extollantur vires liberi arbitrii, contra Jeremiæ prophetæ dictum, cap. xvii. 9 : *Fraudulentum est cor ipsum supra omnia et perversum.* Et Apostoli, Ephes. ii. 3 : *Inter quos* (homines contumaces) *et nos omnes conversati sumus olim in cupiditatibus carnis nostræ, facientes voluntates carnis ac cogitationum.*

IV.

Qui docent, 'Hominem irregenitum non esse proprie nec totaliter in peccatis mortuum, aut omnibus ad bonum spirituale viribus destitutum, sed posse justitiam vel vitam esurire ac sitire, sacrificiumque Spiritus contriti, et contribulati, quod Deo acceptum est, offerre.' Adversantur enim hæc apertis Scripturæ testimoniis, Ephes. ii. 1, 5 : *Eratis mortui in offensis et peccatis.* Et Gen. vi. 5 et viii. 21 : *Imaginatio cogitationum cordis hominis tantummodo mala est omni die.* Adhæc liberationem ex miseria et vitam esurire ac sitire, Deoque sacrificium Spiritus contriti offerre, regenitorum est, et eorum qui beati dicuntur. Psa. li. 19 et Matt. v. 6.

V.

Qui docent, 'Hominem corruptum et animalem gratia communi, quæ ipsis est lumen naturæ, sive donis post lapsum relictis, tam recte uti posse, ut bono isto usu majorem gratiam, puta evangelicam, sive salutarem, et salutem ipsam gradatim obtinere possit. Et hac ratione DEUM se ex parte sua paratum ostendere, ad Christum omnibus revelandum, quandoquidem media ad Christi revelationem, fidem, et resipiscentiam necessaria, omnibus sufficienter et efficaciter administret.' Falsum enim hoc esse præter omnium temporum experientiam Scriptura testatur. Psa. cxlvii. 19, 20 : *Indicat verba sua Jacobo, statuta sua et jura sua Israeli, non fecit ita ulli genti, et jura ista non noverunt.* Act. xiv. 16 : *Deus sivit præteritis ætatibus omnes gentes suis ipsarum viis incedere.* Act. xvi. 6, 7 : *Prohibiti sunt* (Paulus cum suis) *a Spiritu Sancto loqui sermonem DEI in Asia.* Et, *Quum venissent in Mysiam, tentabant ire versus Bithyniam, sed non permisit eis Spiritus.*

VI.

Qui docent, 'In vera hominis conversione, non posse novas qualitates, habitus, seu dona in voluntatem ejus a Deo infundi, atque adeo fidem, qua primum convertimur, et a qua fideles

nominamur, non esse qualitatem seu donum a Deo infusum; sed tantum actum hominis, neque aliter donum dici posse, quam respectu potestatis ad ipsam perveniendi.' Contradicunt
enim hæc sacris literis, quæ testantur DEUM novas qualitates fidei, obedientiæ, ac sensus
amoris sui cordibus nostris infundere. Jer. xxxi. 33: *Indam legem meam menti eorum, ac
cordi eorum inscribam eam.* Esa. xliv. 3: *Effundam aquas super sitientem, et fluenta super
aridam; effundam Spiritum meum super semen tuum.* Rom. v. 5: *Charitas Dei effusa est
in cordibus nostris per Spiritum Sanctum, qui datus est nobis.* Repugnant etiam continuæ
praxi Ecclesiæ, sic apud prophetam orantis: *Converte me, Domine, et convertar.* Jer. xxxi. 18.

VII.

Qui docent, 'Gratiam, qua convertimur ad Deum, nihil aliud esse quam lenem suasionem;
seu' (ut alii explicant) 'nobilissimum agendi modum in conversione hominis, et naturæ humanæ convenientissimum esse, qui fiat suasionibus; nihilque obstare quo minus vel sola moralis gratia homines animales reddat spirituales; imo Deum non aliter quam morali ratione
consensum voluntatis producere: atque in eo consistere operationis divinæ efficaciam, qua
Satanæ operationem superet, quod Deus æterna bona, Satan autem temporaria promittat.'
Omnino enim hoc Pelagianum est, et universæ Scripturæ contrarium, quæ præter hunc etiam
alium, et longe efficaciorem ac diviniorem Spiritus Sancti agendi modum, in hominis conversione agnoscit. Ezech. xxxvi. 26: *Dabo vobis cor meum, et spiritum novum dabo in medio
vestri, et auferam cor lapideum, daboque cor carneum,* etc.

VIII.

Qui docent, 'Deum in hominis regeneratione eas suæ omnipotentiæ vires non adhibere,
quibus voluntatem ejus ad fidem et conversionem potenter et infallibiliter flectat; sed positis
omnibus gratiæ operationibus, quibus Deus ad hominem convertendum utitur, hominem tamen
Deo, et Spiritui regenerationem ejus intendenti, et regenerare ipsum volenti, ita posse resistere, et actu ipso sæpe resistere, ut sui regenerationem prorsus impediat, atque adeo in
ipsius manere potestate, ut regeneretur vel non regeneretur.' Hoc enim nihil aliud est, quam
tollere omnem efficaciam gratiæ Dei in nostri conversione, et actionem Dei omnipotentis sub-
jicere voluntati hominis, idque contra Apostolos, qui docent, *Nos credere pro efficacitate
fortis roboris Dei.* Ephes. i. 19. Et, *Deum bonitatis suæ gratuitam benevolentiam et opus
fidei potenter in nobis complere.* 2 Thess. i. 11. Item, *Divinam ipsius vim omnia nobis do-
nasse, quæ ad vitam et pietatem pertinent.* 2 Pet. i. 3.

IX.

Qui docent, 'Gratiam et liberum arbitrium esse causas partiales simul concurrentes ad conversionis initium; nec gratiam ordine causalitatis efficientiam voluntatis antecedere;' id est,
'Deum non prius hominis voluntatem efficaciter juvare ad conversionem. quam voluntas ipsa
hominis se movet ac determinat.' Hoc enim dogma Ecclesia prisca in Pelagianis jam olim
condemnavit, ex Apostolo Rom. ix. 16: *Non est volentis nec currentis, sed Dei miserentis.*
Et, 1 Cor. iv. 7: *Quis te discernit?* Et, *Quid habes quod non acceperis?* Item, Phil. ii. 13:
Deus est qui in vobis operatur ipsum velle et perficere pro suo beneplacito.

Huic capiti eadem quæ prius subscribuntur nomina.

Quintum Doctrinæ Caput, de Perseverantia Sanctorum.

Articulus Primus.

Quos Deus secundum propositum suum, ad communionem Filii sui Domini nostri Jesu Christi, vocat, et per Spiritum Sanctum regenerat, eos quidem et a peccati dominio et servitute, non autem a carne, et corpore peccati, penitus in hac vita liberat.

II.

Hinc quotidiana infirmitatis peccata oriuntur, et optimis etiam sanctorum operibus nævi adhærescunt: quæ illis perpetuam sese coram Deo humiliandi, ad Christum crucifixum confugiendi, carnem magis ac magis per Spiritum precum et sancta pietatis exercitia mortificandi, et ad perfectionis metam suspirandi, materiam suggerunt; tantisper dum hoc mortis corpore soluti, cum Agno Dei in cœlis regnent.

III.

Propter istas peccati inhabitantis reliquias, et mundi insuper ac Satanæ tentationes, non possent conversi in ista gratia perstare, si suis viribus permitterentur. Sed fidelis est Deus, qui ipsos in gratia semel collata misericorditer confirmat, et in eadem usque ad finem potenter conservat.

IV.

Etsi autem illa potentia Dei vere fideles in gratia confirmantis et conservantis, major est, quam quæ a carne superari possit; non semper tamen conversi ita a Deo aguntur et moventur, ut non possint in quibusdam actionibus particularibus a ductu gratiæ, suo vitio, recedere, et a carnis concupiscentiis seduci, iisque obsequi. Quapropter ipsis perpetuo est vigilandum et orandum, ne in tentationes inducantur. Quod cum non faciunt, non solum a carne, mundo, et Satana, in peccata etiam gravia et atrocia abripi possunt, verum etiam interdum justa Dei permissione abripiuntur. Quod tristes Davidis, Petri, aliorumque sanctorum lapsus, in sacra Scriptura descripti, demonstrant.

V.

Talibus autem enormibus peccatis Deum valde offendunt, reatum mortis incurrunt, Spiritum S. contristant, fidei exercitium interrumpunt, conscientiam gravissime vulnerant, sensum gratiæ nonnunquam ad tempus amittunt: donec per seriam resipiscentiam in vitam revertentibus paternus Dei vultus rursum affulgeat.

VI.

Deus enim, qui dives est misericordia, ex immutabili electionis proposito, Spiritum Sanctum, etiam in tristibus lapsibus, a suis non prorsus aufert, nec eousque eos prolabi sinit, ut gratia adoptionis, justificationis statu excidant, aut peccatum ad mortem, sive in Spiritum Sanctum committant, et ab eo penitus deserti in exitium æternum sese præcipitent.

VII.

Primo enim in istis lapsibus conservat in illis semen illud suum immortale, ex quo regeniti sunt, ne illud pereat aut excutiatur. Deinde per verbum et Spiritum suum, eos certo et efficaciter renovat ad pœnitentiam, ut de admissis peccatis ex animo secundum Deum doleant, remissionem in sanguine Mediatoris, per fidem, contrito corde, expetant, et obtineant, gratiam Dei reconciliati iterum sentiant, miserationes per fidem ejus adorent, ac deinceps salutem suam cum timore et tremore studiosius operentur.

VIII.

Ita non suis meritis, aut viribus, sed ex gratuita Dei misericordia id obtinent, ut nec totaliter fide et gratia excidant, nec finaliter in lapsibus maneant aut pereant. Quod quoad ipsos non tantum facile fieri posset, sed et indubie fieret; respectu autem Dei fieri omnino non potest: cum nec consilium ipsius mutari, promissio excidere, vocatio secundum propositum revocari, Christi meritum, intercessio, et custodia irrita reddi nec Spiritus Sancti obsignatio frustranea fieri aut deleri possit.

IX.

De hac electorum ad salutem custodia, vereque fidelium in fide perseverantia, ipsi fideles certi esse possunt, et sunt pro mensura fidei, qua certo credunt se esse et perpetuo mansuros vera et viva Ecclesiæ membra, habere remissionem peccatorum, et vitam æternam.

X.

Ac proinde hæc certitudo non est ex peculiari quadam revelatione præter aut extra verbum facta, sed ex fide promissionum Dei, quas in verbo suo copiosissime in nostrum solatium revelavit: ex testimonio *Spiritus Sancti testantis cum spiritu nostro nos esse Dei filios et hæredes.* Rom. viii. 16. Denique ex serio et sancto bonæ conscientiæ et bonorum operum studio. Atque hoc solido obtinendæ victoriæ solatio, et infallibili æternæ gloriæ arrha, si in hoc mundo electi Dei destituerentur, omnium hominum essent miserrimi.

XI.

Interim testatur Scriptura fideles in hac vita cum variis carnis dubitationibus conflictari, et in gravi tentatione constitutos hanc fidei plerophoriam, ac perseverantiæ certitudinem, non semper sentire. Verum Deus, Pater omnis consolationis, *supra vires tentari eos non sinit, sed cum tentatione præstat evasionem.* 1 Cor. x. 13. Ac per Spiritum Sanctum perseverantiæ certitudinem in iisdem rursum excitat.

XII.

Tantum autem abest, ut hæc perseverantiæ certitudo vere fideles superbos, et carnaliter securos reddat, ut e contrario humilitatis, filialis reverentiæ, veræ pietatis, patientiæ in omni lucta, precum ardentium, constantiæ in cruce et veritatis confessione, solidique in Deo gaudii vera sit radix: et consideratio istius beneficii sit stimulus ad serium et continuum gratitudinis et bonorum operum exercitium, ut ex Scripturæ testimoniis et sanctorum exemplis constat.

XIII.

Neque etiam in iis, qui a lapsu instaurantur, lasciviam aut pietatis injuriam procreat rediviva perseverantiæ fiducia; sed multo majorem curam de viis Domini solicite custodiendis, quæ præparatæ sunt ut in illis ambulando perseverantiæ suæ certitudinem retineant, ne propter paternæ benignitatis abusum propitii Dei facies (cujus contemplatio piis vita dulcior, subductio morte acerbior) denuo ab ipsis avertatur, et sic in graviores animi cruciatus incidant.

XIV.

Quemadmodum autem Deo placuit, opus hoc suum gratiæ per prædicationem Evangelii in nobis inchoare; ita per ejusdem auditum, lectionem, meditationem, adhortationes, minas, promissa, nec non per usum sacramentorum illud conservat, continuat, et perficit.

XV.

Hanc de vere credentium ac sanctorum perseverantia, ejusque certitudine, doctrinam, quam Deus ad nominis sui gloriam, et piarum animarum solatium, in verbo suo abundantissime revelavit, cordibusque fidelium imprimit, caro quidem non capit, Satanas odit, mundus ridet, imperiti et hypocritæ in abusum rapiunt, spiritusque erronei oppugnant; sed sponsa Christi ut inæstimabilis pretii thesaurum tenerrime semper dilexit, et constanter propugnavit: quod ut porro faciat procurabit Deus, adversus quem nec consilium valere, nec robur ullum prævalere potest. Cui soli Deo, Patri, Filio, et Spiritui Sancto sit honor et gloria in sempiternum. Amen.

REJECTIO ERRORUM CIRCA DOCTRINAM DE PERSEVERANTIA SANCTORUM.

Exposita doctrina orthodoxa, Synodus rejicit errores eorum:

I.

Qui docent, 'Perseverantiam vere fidelium non esse effectum electionis, aut donum Dei morte Christi partum, sed esse conditionem novi fœderis, ab homine ante sui electionem ac justificationem' (ut ipsi loquuntur) 'peremtoriam, libera voluntate præstandam.' Nam sacra Scriptura testatur eam ex electione sequi, et vi mortis, resurrectionis et intercessionis Christi electis donari. Rom. xi. 7: *Electio assecuta est, reliqui occalluerunt.* Item, Rom. viii. 32: *Qui proprio Filio non pepercit, sed pro omnibus nobis tradidit ipsum, quomodo non cum eo nobis omnia donabit? Quis intentabit crimina adversus electos Dei? Deus est qui justificat. Quis est qui condemnet? Christus in est qui mortuus est, imo qui etiam resurrexit, qui etiam sedet ad dexteram Dei, qui etiam intercedit pro nobis: Quis nos separabit a dilectione Christi?*

II.

Qui docent, 'Deum quidem hominem fidelem sufficientibus ad perseverandum viribus instruere, ac paratum esse eas in ipso conservare si officium faciat: positis tamen illis omnibus, quæ ad perseverandum in fide necessaria sunt, quæque Deus ad conservandam fidem adhibere vult, pendere semper a voluntatis arbitrio, ut perseveret, vel non perseveret' Hæc enim sententia manifestum Pelagianismum continet; et homines, dum vult facere liberos, facit sacrilegos, contra perpetuum evangelicæ doctrinæ consensum, quæ omnem gloriandi materiam homini adimit, et hujus beneficii laudem soli divinæ gratiæ transcribit; et contra Apostolum testantem: *Deum esse qui confirmabit nos usque in finem inculpatos in die Domini nostri Jesu Christi.* 1 Cor. i. 8.

III.

Qui docent, 'Vere credentes et regenitos non tantum posse a fide justificante, item gratia, et salute totaliter et finaliter excidere, sed etiam reipsa non raro ex iis excidere, atque in æternum perire.' Nam hæc opinio ipsam justificationis ac regenerationis gratiam, et perpetuam Christi custodiam irritam reddit. contra diserta Apostoli Pauli verba, Rom. v. 8, 9 : *Si Christus pro nobis mortuus est, quum adhuc essemus peccatores, multo igitur magis, jam justificati in sanguine ejus, servabimur per ipsum ab ira.* Et contra Apostolum Johannem, 1 John iii. 9 : *Omnis qui natus est ex Deo, non dat operam peccato : quia semen ejus in eo manet, nec potest peccare, quia ex Deo genitus est.* Nec non contra verba Jesu Christi, Johan. x. 28, 29 : *Ego vitam æternam do ovibus meis, et non peribunt in æternum, nec rapiet eas quisquam de manu mea ; Pater meus, qui mihi eas dedit, major est omnibus, nec ullus potest eas rapere de manu Patris mei.*

IV.

Qui docent, 'Vere fideles ac regenitos posse peccare peccato ad mortem, vel in Spiritum Sanctum.' Quum idem Apostolus Johan. [Ep. I.] cap. v. postquam vers. 16, 17 peccantium ad mortem meminisset, et pro iis orare vetuisset, statim ver. 18 subjungat: *Scimus quod quisquis natus est ex Deo, non peccat* (nempe illo peccati genere), *sed qui genitus est ex Deo, conservat seipsum, et malignus ille non tangit eum.*

V.

Qui docent, 'Nullam certitudinem futuræ perseverantiæ haberi posse in hac vita, absque speciali revelatione.' Per hanc enim doctrinam vere fidelium solida consolatio in hac vita tollitur, et pontificiorum dubitatio in Ecclesiam reducitur. Sacra vero Scriptura passim hanc certitudinem, non ex speciali et extraordinaria revelatione, sed ex propriis filiorum Dei signis, et constantissimis Dei promissionibus petit. Imprimis Apostolus Paulus, Rom. viii. 39 : *Nulla res creata potest nos separare a charitate Dei, quæ est in Christo Jesu, Domino nostro.* Et Johannes, Epist. I. I. iii. 24 : *Qui servat mandata ejus, in eo manet, et ille in eo : et per hoc novimus ipsum in nobis manere, ex Spiritu quem dedit nobis.*

VI.

Qui docent, 'Doctrinam de perseverantiæ ac salutis certitudine, ex natura et indole sua, esse carnis pulvinar, et pietati, bonis moribus, precibus aliisque sanctis exercitiis noxiam ; contra vero de ea dubitare, esse laudabile.' Hi enim demonstrant se efficaciam divinæ gratiæ, et inhabitantis Spiritus S. operationem ignorare : et contradicunt Apostolo Johanni contrarium disertis verbis affirmanti, Epist. I. iii. 2, 3 : *Dilecti mei, nunc filii Dei sumus ; sed nondum patefactum est id quod erimus : scimus autem fore, ut quum ipse patefactus fuerit, similes ei simus, quoniam videbimus eum, sicuti est. Et quisquis habet hanc spem in eo, purificat seipsum, sicut et ille purus est.* Hi præterea sanctorum tam Veteris quam Novi Testamenti exemplis redarguuntur, qui licet de sua perseverantia et salute essent certi, in precibus tamen, aliisque pietatis exercitiis, assidui fuerunt.

VII.

Qui docent, 'Fidem temporariorum a justificante et salvifica fide non differre nisi sola duratione.' Nam Christus ipse Matt. xiii. 20 et Luc. viii. 13 ac deinceps, triplex præterea inter temporarios et veros fideles discrimen manifesto constituit, quum illos dicit semen recipere in terra petrosa, hos in terra bona, seu corde bono : illos carere radice, hos radicem firmam habere : illos fructibus esse vacuos, hos fructum suum diversa mensura, constanter seu perseveranter proferre.

VIII.

Qui docent, 'Non esse absurdum, hominem priore regeneratione extincta, iterato, imo sæpius renasci.' Hi enim per hanc doctrinam negant seminis Dei, per quod renascimur. incorruptibilitatem: adversus testimonium Apostoli Petri, Epist. I. i. 23: *Renati non ex semine corruptibili, sed incorruptibili.*

IX.

Qui docent, 'Christum nunquam rogasse pro infallibili credentium in fide perseverantia.' Contradicunt enim ipsi Christo, dicenti, Luc. xxii. 32: *Ego rogavi pro te, Petre, ne deficiat fides tua;* et Evangelistæ Johanni, testanti, Johan. xvii. 20, Christum non tantum pro apostolis, sed etiam pro omnibus, per sermonem ipsorum credituris, orasse, ver. 11: *Pater sancte, conserva eos in nomine tuo;* Et ver. 15: *Non oro ut eos tollas e mundo, sed ut conserves eos a malo.*

CONCLUSIO.

Atque hæc est perspicua, simplex, et ingenua Orthodoxæ de Quinque Articulis in Belgio controversis doctrinæ declaratio, et errorum, quibus Ecclesiæ Belgicæ aliquamdiu sunt perturbatæ, rejectio, quam Synodus ex verbo Dei desumptam, et Confessionibus Reformatarum Ecclesiarum consentaneam esse judicat. Unde liquido apparet eos, quos id minime decuit, citra omnem veritatem, æquitatem, et charitatem, populo inculcatum voluisse:

'Doctrinam Ecclesiarum Reformatarum de prædestinatione et annexis ei capitibus, proprio quodam genio atque impulsu, animos hominum ab omni pietate et religione abducere: esse carnis et Diaboli pulvinar, arcemque Satanæ, ex qua omnibus insidietur, plurimos sauciet, et multos tum desperationis, tum securitatis jaculis lethaliter configat: eandem facere Deum authorem peccati, injustum, tyrannum, hypocritam; nec aliud esse quam interpolatum Stoicismum, Manicheismum, Libertinismum, Turcismum: eandem reddere homines carnaliter securos, quippe ex ea persuasos electorum saluti, quomodocunque vivant, non obesse, ideoque eos secure atrocissima quæque scelera posse perpetrare; reprobis ad salutem non prodesse, si vel omnia sanctorum opera vere fecerint: eadem doceri Deum nudo puroque voluntatis arbitrio, absque omni ullius peccati respectu, vel intuitu, maximam mundi partem ad æternam damnationem prædestinasse et creasse: eodem modo, quo electio est fons et caussa fidei ac bonorum operum, reprobationem esse caussam infidelitatis et impietatis: multos fidelium infantes ab uberibus matrum innoxios abripi et tyrannice in gehennam præcipitari, adeo ut iis nec baptismus, nec Ecclesiæ in eorum baptismo preces prodesse queant.'

Et quæ ejus generis sunt alia plurima, quæ Ecclesiæ Reformatæ non solum non agnoscunt, sed etiam toto pectore detestantur. Quare quot

quot nomen Servatoris nostri Jesu Christi pie invocant, eos Synodus hæc Dordrechtana per nomen Domini obtestatur, ut de Ecclesiarum Reformatarum fide, non ex coacervatis hinc inde calumniis, vel etiam privatis nonnullorum, tum veterum tum recentium doctorum dictis, sæpe etiam aut mala fide citatis, aut corruptis, et in alienum sensum detortis, sed ex publicis ipsarum Ecclesiarum Confessionibus, et ex hac orthodoxæ doctrinæ declaratione, unanimi omnium et singulorum totius Synodi membrorum consensu firmata, judicent. Calumniatores deinde ipsos serio monet, viderint quam grave Dei judicium sint subituri, qui contra tot Ecclesias, contra tot Ecclesiarum Confessiones, falsum testimonium dicunt, conscientias infirmorum turbant, multisque vere fidelium societatem suspectam reddere satagunt.

Postremo hortatur hæc Synodus omnes in Evangelio Christi symmystas, ut in hujus doctrinæ pertractatione, in scholis atque in ecclesiis, pie et religiose versentur, eam tum lingua, tum calamo, ad Divini nominis gloriam, vitæ sanctitatem, et consternatorum animorum solatium accommodent, cum Scriptura secundum fidei analogiam non solum sentiant, sed etiam loquantur; a phrasibus denique iis omnibus abstineant, quæ præscriptos nobis genuini sanctarum Scripturarum sensus limites excedunt, et protervis sophistis justam ansam præbere possint doctrinam Ecclesiarum Reformatarum sugillandi, aut etiam calumniandi. Filius Dei Jesus Christus, qui ad dextram Patris sedens dat dona hominibus, sanctificet nos in veritate, eos qui errant adducat ad veritatem, calumniatoribus sanæ doctrinæ ora obstruat, et fidos verbi sui ministros spiritu sapientiæ et discretionis instruat, ut omnia ipsorum eloquia ad gloriam Dei, et ædificationem auditorum, cedant. *Amen.*

Huic capiti eadem quæ prius subscribuntur nomina.

Hæc omnia de Quinque Doctrinæ Capitibus Controversis supra comprehensis, ita esse gesta testatur Illustrissimorum ac Præpotentium DD. Ordinum Generalium ad hanc Synodum Deputati, manuum nostrarum subsignatione.

Ex Geldria.

Martinus Gregorii D., *Consiliarius Ducatus Geldriæ, et Comitatus Zutphaniæ.*
Henricus van Essen, *Consiliarius Ducatus Geldriæ, et Comitatus Zutphaniæ.*

Ex Hollandia.

Walravus de Brederode.
Hugo Muys van Holy.

Jacobus Boelius.
Gerardus de Nieuburch.

Ex Zelandia.

Symon Scotte, *Consiliarius et Secretarius Civitatis Middelburgensis.*
Jacobus Campe, *Ordinum Zelandiæ Consiliarius.*

Ex Provincia Ultrajectina.

Fredericus van Zuylen van Nyevelt.
Wilhelmus van Hardevelt.

Ex Frisia.

Ernestus ab Aylva, *Ordinum Frisiæ Consiliarius, Orientalis Dongriæ Grietmannus.*
Ernestus ab Harinxma, *Consiliarius primarius in Curia Provinciali Frisiæ.*

Ex Transisalania.

Henricus Hagen.

Ex Civitate Groningensi et Omlandiis.

Hieronymus Isbrants, *I. U. D.*
Edvardus Jacobus Clant a Stedum.

Et Illustribus ac Amplissimis DD. Delegatis a Secretis,

Daniel Heinsius.

Sententia Synodi de Remonstrantibus.

Explicata hactenus, et asserta, per Dei gratiam, veritate, erroribus rejectis, et damnatis, abstersis iniquis calumniis; Synodus hæc Dordrechtana (quæ ipsi porro cura superest) serio, obnixe et pro auctoritate, quam ex Dei verbo in omnia suarum Ecclesiarum membra obtinet, in Christi nomine rogat, hortatur, monet, atque injungit omnibus et singulis in Fœderato Belgio Ecclesiarum Pastoribus, academiarum et scholarum Doctoribus, Rectoribus, et Magistris, atque adeo omnibus in universum, quibus vel animarum cura, vel juventutis disciplina est demandata, ut missis quinque notis Remonstrantium Articulis, qui et erronei sunt, et mera errorum latibula, hanc sanam veritatis salutaris doctrinam, ex purissimis verbi divini fontibus haustam, sinceram, et inviolatam, pro viribus et munere suo, conservent: illam populo et juventuti fideliter et prudenter proponant et explicent; usumque ejus suavissimum atque utilissimum, tum in vita, tum in morte, diligenter declarent: errantes ex grege, secus sentientes, et opinionum novitate abreptos, veritatis evidentia mansuete erudiant, si quando det ipsis Deus resipiscentiam, ad agnoscendam veritatem: ut saniori menti redditi, uno spiritu, ore, fide, charitate, Ecclesiæ Dei, et sanctorum communioni, denuo accedant; atque tandem coalescat vulnus Ecclesiæ, et fiat omnium ejus membrorum cor unum et anima una in Domino.

At vero, quia nonnulli e nobis egressi, sub titulo *Remonstrantium* (quod nomen *Remonstrantium* ut et *Contra-Remonstrantium*, Synodus perpetua oblivione delendum censet), studiis et consiliis privatis, modis illegitimis, disciplina et ordine Ecclesiæ violato, atque fratrum suorum monitionibus et judiciis contemptis, Belgicas Ecclesias antea florentissimas, in fide et charitate conjunctissimas, in his Doctrinæ Capitibus, graviter et periculose admodum turbarunt: errores noxios et veteres revocarunt, et novos procuderunt, publice et privatim, voce ac scriptis, in vulgus sparserunt, et acerrime propugnarunt: doctrinam, hactenus in Ecclesiis receptam, calumniis et contumeliis enormibus insectandi, nec modum nec finem fecerunt: scandalis, dissidiis, conscientiarum scrupulis, et exagitationibus, omnia passim compleverunt: quæ certe gravia in fidem, in charitatem, in bonos mores, in Ecclesiæ unitatem et pacem, peccata, cum in nullo homine tolerari juste possint, in Pastoribus censura severissima ab omni ævo in Ecclesia usurpata, necessario animadverti debent; SYNODUS, invocato Dei sancto nomine, suæ auctoritatis ex verbo Dei probe conscia, omnium legitimarum tum veterum tum recentium Synodorum vestigiis insistens, et illustrissimorum DD. Ordinum Generalium auctoritate munita, declarat atque judicat, Pastores illos, qui partium in Ecclesia ductores, et errorum doctores sese præbuerunt, corruptæ religionis, scissæ Ecclesiæ unitatis, et gravissimorum scandalorum, citatos vero ad hanc Synodum, intolerandæ insuper adversus supremi magistratus in hac Synodo publicata decreta, ipsamque hanc venerandam Synodum, pervicaciæ, reos et convictos teneri. Quas ob causas, primo Synodus prædictis citatis omni ecclesiastico munere interdicit, eosque ab officiis suis abdicat, et academicis functionibus etiam indignos esse judicat, donec per seriam resipiscentiam, dictis, factis, studiis contrariis abunde comprobatam, Ecclesiæ satisfaciant, et cum eadem vere et plene reconcilientur, atque ad ejus communionem recipiantur: quod nos in ipsorum bonum, et totius Ecclesiæ gaudium unice in Christo Domino nostro exoptamus. Reliquos autem, quorum cognitio ad Synodum hanc Nationalem non devenit, Synodus Provincialibus, Classibus, et Presbyteriis, ex ordine recepto, committit: quæ omni studio procurent ne quid Ecclesia detrimenti vel in præsens capere, vel in posterum metuere possit. Errorum istorum sectatores spiritu prudentiæ discriminent: refractarios, clamosos, factiosos, turbatores, quam primum officiis ecclesiasticis, et scholasticis, quæ sunt suæ cognitionis et curæ, abdicent: eoque nomine monentur, ut nulla interjecta mora, post acceptum hujus Synodi Nationalis judicium, impetrata ad hoc magistratus auctoritate, conveniant, ne lentitudine malum invalescat et roboretur. Ex infirmitate, et vitio temporum lapsos, vel abreptos, et in levioribus forte hæsitantes, aut etiam dissentientes, modestos tamen, sedatos, vitæ inculpatæ, dociles, omni lenitate, charitatis officiis, patientia, ad veram atque perfectam concordiam cum Ecclesia provocent: ita tamen, ut diligenter sibi caveant, ne quemquam ad sacrum ministerium admittant, qui doctrinæ hisce synodicis constitutionibus declaratæ subscribere, eamque docere recuset: neminem etiam retineant, cujus manifesta dissensione, doctrina in hac Synodo tanto consensu comprobata violari. et Pastorum concordia, Ecclesiarumque tranquillitas denuo turbari queat. Præterea veneranda hæc Synodus serio monet ecclesiasticos omnes cœtus, ut invigilent diligentissime in greges sibi commissos, omnibus subnascentibus in Ecclesia novitatibus mature obviam eant, easque tanquam zizania ex agro Domini evellant: attendant scholis et scholarum moderatoribus ne qua ex privatis sententiis et pravis opinionibus juventuti instillatis, postmodum Ecclesiæ et reipub. pernicies denuo creetur. Denique illustrissimis et præpotentibus DD. Fœderati Belgii Ordinibus Generalibus, gratiis reverenter actis, quod tam necessario et opportuno tempore, afflictis et labentibus Ecclesiæ rebus, Synodi remedio clementer succurrerint, probos et fideles DEI servos in suam tutelam receperint, pignus omnis benedictionis et præsentiæ divinæ, verbi nempe ipsius veritatem, in suis ditionibus sancte et religiose conservatam voluerint: nulli labori, nullis sumptibus ad tantum opus promovendum et perficiendum pepercerint: pro quibus eximiis officiis largissimam a Domino et publice et privatim, et spiritualem et temporalem, remunerationem toto pectore SYNODUS comprecatur: Eosdem porro Dominos clementissimos obnixe et demisse rogat, ut hanc salutarem doctrinam, fidelissime ad verbum Dei et Reformatarum Ecclesiarum consensum a Synodo expressam, in suis regionibus solam et publice audiri velint et jubeant: arceant suborientes omnes hæreses et errores, spiritus inquietos et turbulentos compescant: veros et benignos Ecclesiæ nutritios ac tutores sese probare pergant: in personas supra dictas sententiam pro jure ecclesiastico, patriis legibus confirmato, ratam esse velint, et auctoritatis suæ adjecto calculo, synodicas constitutiones immotas et perpetuas reddant.

NOMINE ET JUSSU SYNODI,

SEBASTIANUS DAMMAN, *Synodi Scriba.*
FESTUS HOMMIUS, *Eccl. Leydensis Pastor, et Synodi Nat. Actuarius.*

In testimonium Actorum, DANIEL HEINSIUS.

Approbatio Illustrissimorum ac Præpotentium Dominorum, DD. Ordinum Generalium.

Ordines Generales Fœderati Belgii omnibus, qui hasce visuri aut lecturi sunt, salutem.
Notum facimus, Quum ad tollendas tristes et noxias illas controversias, quæ aliquot abhine
annis cum magno reipubl. detrimento, et pacis Ecclesiarum perturbatione, exortæ sunt super
quinque notis Doctrinæ Christianæ Capitibus, eorumque appendicibus, visum nobis fuerit, ex
ordine in Ecclesia Dei, ipsaque adeo Belgica, Dordrechtum convocare Synodum Nationalem
omnium Ecclesiarum Fœderati Belgii; utque illa maximo cum fructu et reipubl. emolumento
celebrari posset, non sine gravi molestia, magnisque impensis, ad eandem expetiverimus et im-
petraverimus complures præstantissimos, doctissimos, et celeberrimos Reformatæ Ecclesiæ
Theologos exteros, uti ex prædictæ Synodi Decretorum subscriptione, post singula doctrinæ
Capita videre est; delegatis insuper ex singulis provinciis ad ejusdem directionem nostris
deputatis, qui in eadem ab initio usque ad finem præsentes curam gererent, ut omnia ibidem in
timore Dei, et recto ordine, ex solo Dei verbo, sinceræ nostræ intentioni congruenter, possent
pertractari: Cumque prædicta hæc Synodus singulari Dei benedictione tanto omnium et singu-
lorum, tam exterorum quam Belgicorum, consensu, de prædictis quinque Doctrinæ Capitibus,
eorumque doctoribus jam judicarit, nobisque consultis et consentientibus sexto Maii proxime
præterito decreta et sententiam hisce præfixa promulgarit; Nos, ut exoptati fructus ex magno
et sancto hoc opere (quale nunquam antehac Ecclesiæ Reformatæ viderunt), ad Ecclesias harum
regionum redundare queant, quandoquidem nihil nobis æque cordi et curæ est, quam gloria
Sanctissimi Nominis Divini, quam conservatio et propagatio veræ Reformatæ Christianæ Re-
ligionis (quæ fundamentum est prosperitatis et vinculum unionis Fœderati Belgii), quam con-
cordia, tranquillitas, et pax Ecclesiarum; itemque conservatio concordiæ et communionis Ec-
clesiarum, quæ sunt in hisce regionibus, cum omnibus exteris Reformatis Ecclesiis, a quibus
nos separare nec debuimus, nec potuimus, Visis, cognitis, et mature examinatis atque expensis,
prædicto judicio et sententia Synodi, ista plene in omnibus approbavimus, confirmavimus, et
rata habuimus, approbamus, confirmamus, et rata habemus per præsentes: Volentes ac statu-
entes, ut nulla alia doctrina de quinque prædictis Doctrinæ Capitibus in Ecclesiis harum re-
gionum doceatur aut propagetur, præter hanc, quæ prædicto judicio sit conformis atque con-
sentanea; Mandantes atque imperantes omnibus ecclesiasticis cœtibus, Ecclesiarum Ministris,
Sacrosanctæ Theologiæ Professoribus et Doctoribus, Collegiorum Regentibus, omnibusque in
universum et singulis, quos hæc aliquatenus concernere queant aut attingere, ut in suorum mi-
nisteriorum et functionum exercitio eadem in omnibus fideliter et sincere sequantur, iisque con-
venienter sese gerant. Utque bonæ nostræ intentioni plene ac per omnia ubique possit satisfieri,
Denunciamus et mandamus Ordinibus, Gubernatoribus, Deputatis Ordinum, Consiliariis et
Ordinibus Deputatis provinciarum Geldriæ, et comitatus Zutphaniæ, Hollandiæ, et Westfrisiæ,
Zelandiæ, Ultrajecti, Frisiæ, Transisalaniæ, civitatis Groningæ et Omlandiarum, omnibusque
aliis Officiariis, Judicibus, et Justitiariis, ut prædicti Judicii Synodici, eorumque quæ inde
dependent, observationem promoveant et tueantur, ac promovere et tueri faciant, adeo ut nullam
in hisce mutationem aut ipsi faciant, aut ab aliis ullo modo fieri permittant: Quoniam ad
promovendam Dei gloriam, securitatem et salutem status harum regionum, tranquillitatem et
pacem Ecclesiæ, ita fieri debere judicamus.

Actum sub nostro sigillo, signatione Præsidis, et subscriptione nostri Graphiarii, Hagæ-
Comitis, secundo Julii, anno millesimo, sexcentesimo et decimo nono, signatum erat.

A. Ploos, ut
Et inferius

Ex mandato prædictorum Præpotentium Dominorum Ordinum Generalium
Subscriptum
C. Aerssen.
Eratque spatio impressum prædictum sigillum in cera rubra.

THE CANONS OF THE SYNOD OF DORT,

As held by the Reformed [Dutch] Church in America.

[We append the English text of the Canons of Dort from the *Constitution of the Reformed* (formerly *Reformed Dutch*) *Church in America*, published in New York. It contains only the positive articles on the Five Points, and omits the Preface and Conclusion, the rejection of the opposite errors, and the Sentence against the Remonstrants. In this abridged form the Canons of Dort are still in force in said Church, together with the Belgic Confession and the Heidelberg Catechism, although the name *Dutch* (which had been first formally assumed in 1792) was dropped in 1867 from her ecclesiastical title, the Dutch language being now superseded by the English.]

FIRST HEAD OF DOCTRINE.

Of Divine Predestination.

ART. I. As all men have sinned in Adam, lie under the curse, and are obnoxious to eternal death, God would have done no injustice by leaving them all to perish, and delivering them over to condemnation on account of sin, according to the words of the Apostle (Rom. iii. 19), 'that every mouth may be stopped, and all the world may become guilty before God;' (ver. 23) 'for all have sinned, and come short of the glory of God;' and (vi. 23), 'for the wages of sin is death.'

ART. II. But 'in this the love of God was manifested, that he sent his only-begotten Son into the world,' 'that whosoever believeth on him should not perish, but have everlasting life' (1 John iv. 9; John iii. 16).

ART. III. And that men may be brought to believe, God mercifully sends the messengers of these most joyful tidings to whom he will, and at what time he pleaseth; by whose ministry men are called to repentance and faith in Christ crucified. 'How then shall they call on him in whom they have not believed? And how shall they believe in him of whom they have not heard? And how shall they hear without a preacher? And how shall they preach, except they be sent?' (Rom. x. 14, 15).

ART. IV. The wrath of God abideth upon those who believe not this gospel; but such as receive it, and embrace Jesus the Saviour by a true and living faith, are by him delivered from the wrath of God and from destruction, and have the gift of eternal life conferred upon them.

ART. V. The cause or guilt of this unbelief, as well as of all other sins, is nowise in God, but in man himself: whereas faith in Jesus

Christ, and salvation through him is the free gift of God, as it is written, ' By grace ye are saved through faith, and that not of yourselves: it is the gift of God' (Eph. ii. 8); and, ' Unto you it is given in the behalf of Christ, not only to believe on him,' etc. (Phil. i. 29).

ART. VI. That some receive the gift of faith from God, and others do not receive it, proceeds from God's eternal decree. ' For known unto God are all his works from the beginning of the world' (Acts xv. 18; Eph. i. 11). According to which decree he graciously softens the hearts of the elect, however obstinate, and inclines them to believe; while he leaves the non-elect in his just judgment to their own wickedness and obduracy. And herein is especially displayed the profound, the merciful, and at the same time the righteous discrimination between men, equally involved in ruin; or that decree of *election* and *reprobation*, revealed in the Word of God, which, though men of perverse, impure, and unstable minds wrest it to their own destruction, yet to holy and pious souls affords unspeakable consolation.

ART. VII. Election is the unchangeable purpose of God, whereby, before the foundation of the world, he hath, out of mere grace, according to the sovereign good pleasure of his own will, chosen, from the whole human race, which had fallen through their own fault, from their primitive state of rectitude, into sin and destruction, a certain number of persons to redemption in Christ, whom he from eternity appointed the Mediator and head of the elect, and the foundation of salvation.

This elect number, though by nature neither better nor more deserving than others, but with them involved in one common misery, God hath decreed to give to Christ to be saved by him, and effectually to call and draw them to his communion by his Word and Spirit; to bestow upon them true faith, justification, and sanctification; and having powerfully preserved them in the fellowship of his Son, finally to glorify them for the demonstration of his mercy, and for the praise of the riches of his glorious grace: as it is written, ' According as he hath chosen us in him before the foundation of the world, that we should be holy and without blame before him in love; having predestinated us unto the adoption of children by Jesus Christ to himself, according to the good pleasure of his will, to the praise of the glory of his grace, wherein he hath made us accepted in the Beloved' (Eph. i. 4–6). And elsewhere, 'Whom he did predestinate, them he also called; and whom he called, them he also justified; and whom he justified, them he also glorified' (Rom. viii. 30).

ART. VIII. There are not various decrees of election, but one and the same decree respecting all those who shall be saved both under the Old and New Testament; since the Scripture declares the good pleas-ure, purpose, and counsel of the divine will to be one, according to which he hath chosen us from eternity, both to grace and to glory, to salvation and the way of salvation, which he hath ordained that we should walk therein.

ART. IX. This election was not founded upon foreseen faith, and the obedience of faith, holiness, or any other good quality or disposition in man, as the prerequisite, cause, or condition on which it depended; but men are chosen to faith and to the obedience of faith, holiness, etc. Therefore election is the fountain of every saving good; from which proceed faith, holiness, and the other gifts of salvation, and finally eternal life itself, as its fruits and effects, according to that of the Apostle. 'He hath chosen us [not because we were, but] that we should be holy and without blame before him in love' (Eph. i. 4).

ART. X. The good pleasure of God is the sole cause of this gracious election; which doth not consist herein that God, foreseeing all possi-ble qualities of human actions, elected certain of these as a condition of salvation, but that he was pleased out of the common mass of sin-ners to adopt some certain persons as a peculiar people to himself, as it is written, 'For the children being not yet born, neither having done any good or evil,' etc., 'it was said [namely, to Rebecca] the elder shall serve the younger; as it is written, Jacob have I loved, but Esau have I hated' (Rom. ix. 11–13); and, 'As many as were ordained to eternal life believed' (Acts xiii. 48).

ART. XI. And as God himself is most wise, unchangeable, omnis-cient, and omnipotent, so the election made by him can neither be in-terrupted nor changed, recalled nor annulled; neither can the elect be cast away, nor their number diminished.

ART. XII. The elect, in due time, though in various degrees and in different measures, attain the assurance of this their eternal and un-changeable election, not by inquisitively prying into the secret and deep things of God, but by observing in themselves, with a spiritual joy and holy pleasure, the infallible fruits of election pointed out in the Word of God; such as a true faith in Christ, filial fear, a godly sorrow for sin, a hungering and thirsting after righteousness, etc.

ART. XIII. The sense and certainty of this election afford to the children of God additional matter for daily humiliation before him, for adoring the depth of his mercies, and rendering grateful returns of ardent love to him who first manifested so great love towards them. The consideration of this doctrine of election is so far from encouraging remissness in the observance of the divine commands or from sinking men into carnal security, that these, in the just judgment of God, are the usual effects of rash presumption or of idle and wanton trifling with the grace of election, in those who refuse to walk in the ways of the elect.

ART. XIV. As the doctrine of divine election by the most wise counsel of God was declared by the Prophets, by Christ himself, and by the Apostles, and is clearly revealed in the Scriptures both of the Old and New Testament, so it is still to be published in due time and place in the Church of God, for which it was peculiarly designed, provided it be done with reverence, in the spirit of discretion and piety, for the glory of God's most holy name, and for enlivening and comforting his people, without vainly attempting to investigate the secret ways of the Most High.

ART. XV. What peculiarly tends to illustrate and recommend to us the eternal and unmerited grace of election is the express testimony of sacred Scripture, that not all, but some only, are elected, while others are passed by in the eternal decree; whom God, out of his sovereign, most just, irreprehensible and unchangeable good pleasure, hath decreed to leave in the common misery into which they have willfully plunged themselves, and not to bestow upon them saving faith and the grace of conversion; but permitting them in his just judgment to follow their own way; at last, for the declaration of his justice, to condemn and punish them forever, not only on account of their unbelief, but also for all their other sins. And this is the decree of reprobation which by no means makes God the author of sin (the very thought of which is blasphemy), but declares him to be an awful, irreprehensible, and righteous judge and avenger.

ART. XVI. Those who do not yet experience a lively faith in Christ, an assured confidence of soul, peace of conscience, an earnest endeavor after filial obedience, and glorying in God through Christ, efficaciously wrought in them, and do nevertheless persist in the use of the means which God hath appointed for working these graces in us, ought not to be alarmed at the mention of reprobation, nor to rank themselves among the reprobate, but diligently to persevere in the use of means, and with ardent desires devoutly and humbly to wait for a season of richer grace.   Much less cause have they to be terrified by the doctrine of reprobation, who, though they seriously desire to be turned to God, to please him only, and to be delivered from the body of death, can not yet reach that measure of holiness and faith to which they aspire; since a merciful God has promised that he will not quench the smoking flax, nor break the bruised reed.   But this doctrine is justly terrible to those who, regardless of God and of the Saviour Jesus Christ, have wholly given themselves up to the cares of the world and the pleasures of the flesh, so long as they are not seriously converted to God.

ART. XVII. Since we are to judge of the will of God from his Word, which testifies that the children of believers are holy, not by nature, but in virtue of the covenant of grace, in which they together with the parents are comprehended, godly parents have no reason to doubt of the election and salvation of their children whom it pleaseth God to call out of this life in their infancy.

ART. XVIII. To those who murmur at the free grace of election, and just severity of reprobation, we answer with the Apostle: ' Nay but, O man, who art thou that repliest against God ?' (Rom. ix. 20); and quote the language of our Saviour: ' Is it not lawful for me to do what I will with mine own ?' (Matt. xx. 15).   And therefore with holy adoration of these mysteries, we exclaim, in the words of the Apostle: ' O the depth of the riches both of the wisdom and knowledge of God! how unsearchable are his judgments, and his ways past finding out! For who hath known the mind of the Lord, or who hath been his counselor ? or who hath first given to him, and it shall be recompensed unto him again?   For of him, and through him, and to him are all things: to whom be glory forever.   Amen.'   (Rom. xi. 33–36.)

Of the Death of Christ, and the Redemption of Men thereby.

ART. I. God is not only supremely merciful, but also supremely just. And his justice requires (as he hath revealed himself in his Word) that our sins committed against his infinite majesty should be punished, not only with temporal, but with eternal punishments, both in body and soul; which we can not escape, unless satisfaction be made to the justice of God.

ART. II. Since, therefore, we are unable to make that satisfaction in our own persons, or to deliver ourselves from the wrath of God, he hath been pleased of his infinite mercy to give his only-begotten Son for our surety, who was made sin, and became a curse for us and in our stead, that he might make satisfaction to divine justice on our behalf.

ART. III. The death of the Son of God is the only and most perfect sacrifice and satisfaction for sin; is of infinite worth and value, abundantly sufficient to expiate the sins of the whole world.

ART. IV. This death derives its infinite value and dignity from these considerations; because the person who submitted to it was not only really man and perfectly holy, but also the only-begotten Son of God, of the same eternal and infinite essence with the Father and Holy Spirit, which qualifications were necessary to constitute him a Saviour for us; and because it was attended with a sense of the wrath and curse of God due to us for sin.

ART. V. Moreover the promise of the gospel is, that whosoever believeth in Christ crucified shall not perish, but have everlasting life. This promise, together with the command to repent and believe, ought to be declared and published to all nations, and to all persons promiscuously and without distinction, to whom God out of his good pleasure sends the gospel.

ART. VI. And, whereas many who are called by the gospel do not repent nor believe in Christ, but perish in unbelief; this is not owing to any defect or insufficiency in the sacrifice offered by Christ upon the cross, but is wholly to be imputed to themselves.

ART. VII. But as many as truly believe, and are delivered and saved from sin and destruction through the death of Christ, are indebted for this benefit solely to the grace of God given them in Christ from everlasting, and not to any merit of their own.

ART. VIII. For this was the sovereign counsel and most gracious will and purpose of God the Father, that the quickening and saving efficacy of the most precious death of his Son should extend to all the elect, for bestowing upon them alone the gift of justifying faith, thereby to bring them infallibly to salvation: that is, it was the will of God, that Christ by the blood of the cross, whereby he confirmed the new covenant, should effectually redeem out of every people, tribe, nation, and language, all those, and those only, who were from eternity chosen to salvation, and given to him by the Father; that he should confer upon them faith, which, together with all the other saving gifts of the Holy Spirit, he purchased for them by his death; should purge them from all sin, both original and actual, whether committed before or after believing; and having faithfully preserved them even to the end, should at last bring them free from every spot and blemish to the enjoyment of glory in his own presence forever.

ART. IX. This purpose proceeding from everlasting love towards the elect, has, from the beginning of the world to this day, been powerfully accomplished, and will, henceforward, still continue to be accomplished, notwithstanding all the ineffectual opposition of the gates of hell; so that the elect in due time may be gathered together into one, and that there never may be wanting a Church composed of believers, the foundation of which is laid in the blood of Christ, which may steadfastly love and faithfully serve him as their Saviour, who, as a bridegroom for his bride, laid down his life for them upon the cross; and which may celebrate his praises here and through all eternity.

THIRD AND FOURTH HEADS OF DOCTRINE.

Of the Corruption of Man, his Conversion to God, and the Manner thereof.

ART. I. Man was originally formed after the image of God. His understanding was adorned with a true and saving knowledge of his Creator, and of spiritual things; his heart and will were upright, all his affections pure, and the whole Man was holy; but revolting from God by the instigation of the devil, and abusing the freedom of his

own will, he forfeited these excellent gifts, and on the contrary en
tailed on himself blindness of mind, horrible darkness, vanity, and per-
verseness of judgment; became wicked, rebellious, and obdurate in
heart and will, and impure in [all] his affections.

Art. II. Man after the fall begat children in his own likeness. A
corrupt stock produced a corrupt offspring. Hence all the posterity
of Adam, Christ only excepted, have derived corruption from their
original parent, not by imitation, as the Pelagians of old asserted, but
by the propagation of a vicious nature [in consequence of a just judgment of God].[1]

Art. III. Therefore all men are conceived in sin, and are by nature
children of wrath, incapable of any saving good, prone to evil, dead in
sin, and in bondage thereto; and, without the regenerating grace of
the Holy Spirit, they are neither able nor willing to return to God, to
reform the depravity of their nature, nor to dispose themselves to
reformation.

Art. IV. There remain, however, in man since the fall, the glim-
merings of natural light, whereby he retains some knowledge of God,
of natural things, and of the difference between good and evil, and discovers some regard for virtue, good order in society, and for maintaining an orderly external deportment. But so far is this light of nature
from being sufficient to bring him to a saving knowledge of God, and
to true conversion, that he is incapable of using it aright even in things
natural and civil. Nay farther, this light, such as it is, man in various
ways renders wholly polluted, and holds it [back] in unrighteousness;
by doing which he becomes inexcusable before God.

Art. V. In the same light are we to consider the law of the decalogue, delivered by God to his peculiar people the Jews, by the hands
of Moses. For though it discovers the greatness of sin, and more and
more convinces man thereof, yet as it neither points out a remedy nor
imparts strength to extricate him from misery, and thus being weak
through the flesh, leaves the transgressor under the curse, man can not
by this law obtain saving grace.

Art. VI. What, therefore, neither the light of nature nor the law
could do, that God performs by the operation of his Holy Spirit through

---

[1] 'justo Dei judicio'—omitted in the translation of the Reformed Dutch Church.—Ed.

the word or ministry of reconciliation: which is the glad tidings concerning the Messiah, by means whereof it hath pleased God to save such as believe, as well under the Old as under the New Testament.

Art. VII. This mystery of his will God discovered to but a small number under the Old Testament; under the New, he reveals himself to many, without any distinction of people. The cause of this dispensation is not to be ascribed to the superior worth of one nation above another, nor to their making a better use of the light of nature, but results wholly from the sovereign good pleasure and unmerited love of God. Hence they to whom so great and so gracious a blessing is communicated, above their desert, or rather notwithstanding their demerits, are bound to acknowledge it with humble and grateful hearts, and with the Apostle to adore, not curiously to pry into the severity and justice of God's judgments displayed in others, to whom this grace is not given.

Art. VIII. As many as are called by the gospel are unfeignedly called; for God hath most earnestly and truly declared in his Word what will be acceptable to him, namely, that all who are called should comply with the invitation. He, moreover, seriously promises eternal life and rest to as many as shall come to him, and believe on him.

Art. IX. It is not the fault of the gospel, nor of Christ offered therein, nor of God, who calls men by the gospel, and confers upon them various gifts, that those who are called by the ministry of the Word refuse to come and be converted. The fault lies in themselves; some of whom when called, regardless of their danger, reject the Word of life; others, though they receive it, suffer it not to make a lasting impression on their heart; therefore, their joy, arising only from a temporary faith, soon vanishes, and they fall away; while others choke the seed of the Word by perplexing cares and the pleasures of this world, and produce no fruit. This our Saviour teaches in the parable of the sower (Matt. xiii.).

Art. X. But that others who are called by the gospel obey the call and are converted, is not to be ascribed to the proper exercise of free-will, whereby one distinguishes himself above others equally furnished with grace sufficient for faith and conversion (as the proud heresy of Pelagius maintains); but it must be wholly ascribed to God, who, as he hath chosen his own from eternity in Christ, so he [calls them effectually in time][1] confers upon them faith and repentance, rescues them from the power of darkness, and translates them into the kingdom of his own Son, that they may show forth the praises of him who hath called them out of darkness into his marvelous light; and may glory not in themselves but in the Lord, according to the testimony of the Apostles in various places.

ART. XI. But when God accomplishes his good pleasure in the elect, or works in them true conversion, he not only causes the gospel to be externally preached to them, and powerfully illuminates their minds by his Holy Spirit, that they may rightly understand and discern the things of the Spirit of God, but by the efficacy of the same regenerating Spirit he pervades the inmost recesses of the man; he opens the closed and softens the hardened heart, and circumcises that which was uncircumcised; infuses new qualities into the will, which, though heretofore dead, he quickens; from being evil, disobedient, and refractory, he renders it good, obedient, and pliable; actuates and strengthens it, that, like a good tree, it may bring forth the fruits of good actions.

ART. XII. And this is the regeneration so highly celebrated in Scripture and denominated a new creation: a resurrection from the dead; a making alive, which God works in us without our aid. But this is nowise effected merely by the external preaching of the gospel, by moral suasion, or such a mode of operation that, after God has performed his part, it still remains in the power of man to be regenerated or not, to be converted or to continue unconverted; but it is evidently a supernatural work, most powerful, and at the same time most delightful, astonishing, mysterious, and ineffable; not inferior in efficacy to creation or the resurrection from the dead, as the Scripture inspired by the author of this work declares; so that all in whose hearts God works in this marvelous manner are certainly, infallibly, and effectually regenerated, and do actually believe. Whereupon the will thus renewed is not only actuated and influenced by God, but, in consequence of this influence, becomes itself active. Wherefore, also, man is himself rightly said to believe and repent, by virtue of that grace received.

ART. XIII. The manner of this operation can not be fully comprehended by believers in this life. Notwithstanding which, they rest

---

[1] '*ita eosdem in tempore efficaciter vocat*'—omitted in the translation.

satisfied with knowing and experiencing that by this grace of God they are enabled to believe with the heart and to love their Saviour.

ART. XIV. Faith is therefore to be considered as the gift of God, not on account of its being offered by God to man, to be accepted or rejected at his pleasure, but because it is in reality conferred, breathed, and infused into him; nor even because God bestows the power or ability to believe, and then expects that man should, by the exercise of his own free will, consent to the terms of salvation, and actually believe in Christ; but because he who works in man both to will and to do, and indeed all things in all, produces both the will to believe and the act of believing also.

ART. XV. God is under no obligation to confer this grace upon any; for how can he be indebted to man, who had no previous gift to bestow as a foundation for such recompense? Nay, who has nothing of his own but sin and falsehood. He, therefore, who becomes the subject of this grace owes eternal gratitude to God, and gives him thanks forever. Whoever is not made partaker thereof is either altogether regardless of these spiritual gifts and satisfied with his own condition, or is in no apprehension of danger, and vainly boasts the possession of that which he has not. With respect to those who make an external profession of faith and live regular lives, we are bound, after the example of the Apostle, to judge and speak of them in the most favorable manner; for the secret recesses of the heart are unknown to us. And as to others, who have not yet been called, it is our duty to pray for them to God, who calleth those things which be not as though they were. But we are in no wise to conduct ourselves towards them with haughtiness, as if we had made ourselves to differ.

ART. XVI. But as man by the fall did not cease to be a creature endowed with understanding and will, nor did sin, which pervaded the whole race of mankind, deprive him of the human nature, but brought upon him depravity and spiritual death; so also this grace of regeneration does not treat men as senseless stocks and blocks, nor take away their will and its properties, neither does violence thereto; but spiritually quickens, heals, corrects, and at the same time sweetly and powerfully bends it, that where carnal rebellion and resistance formerly prevailed a ready and sincere spiritual obedience begins to reign; in which the true and spiritual restoration and freedom of our will consist.　Wherefore, unless the admirable Author of every good work wrought in us, man could have no hope of recovering from his fall by his own free will, by the abuse of which, in a state of innocence, he plunged himself into ruin.

Art. XVII. As the almighty operation of God, whereby he prolongs and supports this our natural life, does not exclude, but requires the use of means, by which God of his infinite mercy and goodness hath chosen to exert his influence; so also the before-mentioned supernatural operation of God, by which we are regenerated, in nowise excludes or subverts the use of the gospel, which the most wise God has ordained to be the seed of regeneration and food of the soul.　Wherefore as the Apostles, and the teachers who succeeded them, piously instructed the people concerning this grace of God, to his glory and the abasement of all pride, and in the mean time, however, neglected not to keep them by the sacred precepts of the gospel, in the exercise of the Word, the sacraments and discipline; so, even to this day, be it far from either instructors or instructed to presume to tempt God in the Church by separating what he of his good pleasure hath most intimately joined together.　For grace is conferred by means of admonitions; and the more readily we perform our duty, the more eminent usually is this blessing of God working in us, and the more directly is his work advanced; to whom alone all the glory, both of means and their saving fruit and efficacy, is forever due.　Amen.

FIFTH HEAD OF DOCTRINE.

Of the Perseverance of the Saints.

Art. I. Whom God calls, according to his purpose, to the communion of his Son our Lord Jesus Christ, and regenerates by the Holy Spirit, he delivers also from the dominion and slavery of sin in this life; though not altogether from the body of sin and from the infirmities of the flesh, so long as they continue in this world.

Art. II. Hence spring daily sins of infirmity, and hence spots adhere to the best works of the saints, which furnish them with constant matter for humiliation before God, and flying for refuge to Christ crucified; for mortifying the flesh more and more by the spirit of prayer and by holy exercises of piety; and for pressing forward to the goal of perfection, till being at length delivered from this body of death, they are brought to reign with the Lamb of God in heaven.

ART. III. By reason of these remains of indwelling sin, and the temptations of sin and of the world,[1] those who are converted could not persevere in a state of grace if left to their own strength. But God is faithful, who having conferred grace, mercifully confirms and powerfully preserves them therein, even to the end.

ART. IV. Although the weakness of the flesh can not prevail against the power of God, who confirms and preserves true believers in a state of grace, yet converts are not always so influenced and actuated by the Spirit of God as not in some particular instances sinfully to deviate from the guidance of divine grace, so as to be seduced by, and to comply with, the lusts of the flesh; they must therefore be constant in watching and prayer, that they be not led into temptation. When these are neglected, they are not only liable to be drawn into great and heinous sins by Satan, the world, and the flesh,[2] but sometimes by the righteous permission of God actually fall into these evils. This the lamentable fall of David, Peter, and other saints described in Holy Scriptures, demonstrates.

ART. V. By such enormous sins, however, they very highly offend God, incur a deadly guilt, grieve the Holy Spirit, interrupt the exercise of faith, very grievously wound their consciences, and sometimes lose the sense of God's favor, for a time, until on their returning into the right way by serious repentance, the light of God's fatherly countenance again shines upon them.

ART. VI. But God, who is rich in mercy, according to his unchangeable purpose of election, does not wholly withdraw the Holy Spirit from his own people, even in their melancholy falls; nor suffer them to proceed so far as to lose the grace of adoption and forfeit the state of justification, or to commit the sin unto death;[3] nor does he permit them to be totally deserted, and to plunge themselves into everlasting destruction.

ART. VII. For in the first place, in these falls he preserves in them the incorruptible seed of regeneration from perishing or being totally

---

[1] of the world and Satan (*mundi ac Satanæ*). —Ed.

[2] by the flesh, the world, and Satan (*a carne, mundo, et Satana*).

[3] or against the Holy Ghost (*sive in Spiritum Sanctum*).

lost; and again, by his Word and Spirit, he certainly and effectually renews them to repentance, to a sincere and godly sorrow for their sins, that they may seek and obtain remission in the blood of the Mediator, may again experience the favor of a reconciled God, through faith adore his mercies, and henceforward more diligently work out their own salvation with fear and trembling.

ART. VIII. Thus, it is not in consequence of their own merits or strength, but of God's free mercy, that they do not totally fall from faith and grace, nor continue and perish finally in their backslidings; which, with respect to themselves is not only possible, but would undoubtedly happen; but with respect to God, it is utterly impossible, since his counsel can not be changed, nor his promise fail, neither can the call according to his purpose be revoked, nor the merit, intercession, and preservation of Christ be rendered ineffectual, nor the sealing of the Holy Spirit be frustrated or obliterated.

ART. IX. Of this preservation of the elect to salvation, and of their perseverance in the faith, true believers for themselves may and do obtain assurance according to the measure of their faith, whereby they arrive at the certain persuasion that they ever will continue true and living members of the Church; and that they experience forgiveness of sins, and will at last inherit eternal life.

ART. X. This assurance, however, is not produced by any peculiar revelation contrary to, or independent of the Word of God, but springs from faith in God's promises, which he has most abundantly revealed in his Word for our comfort; from the testimony of the Holy Spirit, witnessing with our spirit, that we are children and heirs of God (Rom. viii. 16); and, lastly, from a serious and holy desire to preserve a good conscience, and to perform good works. And if the elect of God were deprived of this solid comfort, that they shall finally obtain the victory, and of this infallible pledge or earnest of eternal glory, they would be of all men the most miserable.

ART. XI. The Scripture moreover testifies that believers in this life have to struggle with various carnal doubts, and that under grievous temptations they are not always sensible of this full assurance of faith and certainty of persevering. But God, who is the Father of all consolation, does not suffer them to be tempted above that they are able, but will with the temptation also make a way to escape, that they may be able to bear it (1 Cor. x. 13); and by the Holy Spirit again inspires them with the comfortable assurance of persevering.

ART. XII. This certainty of perseverance, however, is so far from exciting in believers a spirit of pride, or of rendering them carnally secure, that, on the contrary, it is the real source of humility, filial reverence, true piety, patience in every tribulation, fervent prayers, constancy in suffering and in confessing the truth, and of solid rejoicing in God; so that the consideration of this benefit should serve as an incentive to the serious and constant practice of gratitude and good works, as appears from the testimonies of Scripture and the examples of the saints.

ART. XIII. Neither does renewed confidence of persevering produce licentiousness or a disregard to piety in those who are recovered from backsliding; but it renders them much more careful and solicitous to continue in the ways of the Lord, which he hath ordained, that they who walk therein may maintain an assurance of persevering; lest by abusing his fatherly kindness, God should turn away his gracious countenance from them (to behold which is to the godly dearer than life, the withdrawing whereof is more bitter than death), and they in consequence thereof should fall into more grievous torments of conscience.

ART. XIV. And as it hath pleased God, by the preaching of the gospel, to begin this work of grace in us, so he preserves, continues, and perfects it by the hearing and reading of his Word, by meditation thereon, and by the exhortations, threatenings, and promises thereof, as well as by the use of the Sacraments.

ART. XV. The carnal mind is unable to comprehend this doctrine of the perseverance of the saints, and the certainty thereof, which God hath most abundantly revealed in his Word, for the glory of his name and the consolation of pious souls, and which he impresses upon the hearts of the faithful. Satan abhors it; the world ridicules it; the ignorant and hypocrite abuse, and heretics oppose it. But the spouse of Christ hath always most tenderly loved and constantly defended it, as an inestimable treasure; and God, against whom neither counsel nor strength can prevail, will dispose her to continue this conduct to the end. Now TO THIS ONE GOD, FATHER, SON, AND HOLY SPIRIT BE HONOR AND GLORY FOREVER. Amen.

Conclusion.

And this is the perspicuous, simple, and ingenuous declaration of the orthodox doctrine respecting the five articles which have been controverted in the Belgic Churches; and the rejection of the errors, with which they have for some time been troubled. This doctrine the Synod judges to be drawn from the Word of God, and to be agreeable to the confession of the Reformed Churches. Whence it clearly appears that some, whom such conduct by no means became, have violated all truth, equity, and charity, in wishing to persuade the public:

'That the doctrine of the Reformed Churches concerning predestination, and the points annexed to it, by its own genius and necessary tendency, leads off the minds of men from all piety and religion; that it is an opiate administered by the flesh and the devil; and the stronghold of Satan, where he lies in wait for all, and from which he wounds multitudes, and mortally strikes through many with the darts both of despair and security; that it makes God the author of sin, unjust, tyrannical, hypocritical; that it is nothing more than an interpolated Stoicism, Manicheism, Libertinism, Turcism; that it renders men carnally secure, since they are persuaded by it that nothing can hinder the salvation of the elect, let them live as they please; and, therefore, that they may safely perpetrate every species of the most atrocious crimes; and that, if the reprobate should even perform truly all the works of the saints, their obedience would not in the least contribute to their salvation; that the same doctrine teaches that God, by a mere arbitrary act of his will, without the least respect or view to any sin, has predestinated the greatest part of the world to eternal damnation, and has created them for this very purpose; that in the same manner in which the election is the fountain and cause of faith and good works, reprobation is the cause of unbelief and impiety; that many children of the faithful are torn, guiltless, from their mothers' breasts, and tyrannically plunged into hell: so that neither baptism nor the prayers of the Church at their baptism can at all profit them;' and many other things of the same kind which the Reformed Churches not only do not acknowledge, but even detest with their whole soul.

Wherefore, this Synod of Dort, in the name of the Lord, conjures as many as piously call upon the name of our Saviour Jesus Christ to judge of the faith of the Reformed Churches, not from the calumnies which on every side are heaped upon it, nor from the private expressions of a few among ancient and modern teachers, often dishonestly quoted, or corrupted and wrested to a meaning quite foreign to their intention; but from the public confessions of the Churches themselves, and from this declaration of the orthodox doctrine, confirmed by the unanimous consent of all and each of the members of the whole Synod. Moreover, the Synod warns calumniators themselves to consider the terrible judgment of God which awaits them, for bearing false witness against the confessions of so many Churches; for distressing the consciences of the weak; and for laboring to render suspected the society of the truly faithful.

Finally, this Synod exhorts all their brethren in the gospe' of Christ to conduct themselves piously and religiously in handling this doctrine, both in the universities and churches; to direct it, as well in discourse as in writing, to the glory of the Divine name, to holiness of life, and to the consolation of afflicted souls; to regulate, by the Scripture, according to the analogy of faith, not only their sentiments, but also their language, and to abstain from all those phrases which exceed the limits necessary to be observed in ascertaining the genuine sense of the Holy Scriptures, and may furnish insolent sophists with a just pretext for violently assailing, or even vilifying, the doctrine of the Reformed Churches.

May Jesus Christ, the Son of God, who, seated at the Father's right hand, gives gifts to men, sanctify us in the truth; bring to the truth those who err; shut the mouths of the calumniators of sound doctrine, and endue the faithful ministers of his Word with the spirit of wisdom and discretion, that all their discourses may tend to the glory of God, and the edification of those who hear them. Amen.

That this is our faith and decision, we certify by subscribing our names.

Here follow the names, not only of PRESIDENT, ASSISTANT PRESIDENT, *and* SECRETARIES *of the Synod, and of the* PROFESSORS OF THEOLOGY *in the Dutch Churches, but of all the* MEMBERS *who were deputed to the Synod as the Representatives of their respective Churches; that is, of the Delegates from* Great Britain, the Electoral Palatinate, Hessia, Switzerland, Wetteraw, the Republic and Church of Geneva, the Republic and Church of Bremen, the Republic and Church of Emden, the Duchy of Gelderland, and of Zutphen, South Holland, North Holland, Zealand, the Province of Utrecht, Friesland, Transisalania, the State of Groningen, and Omland, Drent, and the French Churches.

The Humble
ADVICE
Of the
ASSEMBLY
OF
DIVINES,

Now by Authority of *Parliament*
fitting at WESTMINSTER,

Concerning

A Confeſsion of Faith:

With the QUOTATIONS and TEXTS of
SCRIPTURE annexed.

Preſented by them lately to both Houſes of Parliament.

Printed at LONDON;

AND

Re-printed at EDINBURGH by *Evan Tyler*, Printer to
the Kings moſt Excellent Majeſtie. 1647.

[1]

TO

The Right honorable the Lords and

Commons Affembled in PARLIAMENT.

The humble Advice of the Affembly of Divines
now, by Authority of *Parliament*, fitting
at *WESTMINSTER*.

Concerning a Confeffion of Faith.

CHAP. I.
Of the Holy Scripture.

Lthough the Light of Nature, and the works of Creation and Providence do fo far manifeft the Goodnefs, Wifdom, and Power of God, as to leave men unexcufable *a*; yet are they not fufficient to give that knowledg of God and of his Will, which is neceffary unto falvation *b*. Therefore it pleafed the Lord at fundry times, and in divers manners, to reveal himfelf, and to declare that his Will unto his Church *c*; and afterwards for the better preferving and propagating of the Truth, and for the more fure eftablifhment and comfort of the Church againft the corruption of the flefh, and the malice of Satan and of the world, to commit the fame wholly unto writing *d*: which maketh the Holy Scripture to be moft neceffarye *e*; thofe former ways of Gods revealing his Will unto his people, being now ceafed *f*.

a Rom. 2. 14. 15.
Rom. 1. 19. 20.
Pfa. 19. 1. 2. 3.
Rom. 1. 32.
with chap. 2. 1.
b 1 Cor. 1. 21.
1 Cor. 2. 13. 14.
c Heb. 1. 1.
d Prov. 22. 19. 20. 21.
Luk. 1. 3. 4.
Rom. 15. 4.
Mat. 4. 4. 7. 10.
Ifai. 8. 19. 20.
e 2 Tim. 3. 15.
2 Pet. 1. 19.
f Heb. 1. 1. 2.

A 2

II. Under

THE WESTMINSTER CONFESSION OF FAITH. A.D. 1647.

CONFESSIO FIDEI WESTMONASTERIENSIS.

[The English text is taken from the second edition which appeared under the title, '*The Humble | Advice | of the | Assembly | of | Divines, | now by Authority of Parliament | sitting at Westminster, | concerning | a Confession of Faith : | with the Quotations and Texts of | Scripture annexed. | Presented by them lately to both Houses of Parliament. | Printed at London; | and | reprinted at Edinburgh by Evan Tyler, Printer to | the Kings most Excellent Majestie.* 1647.' The spelling and punctuation are conformed to modern usage.

The changes of the American revision, which occur chiefly in Ch. XXIII., relating to the Civil Magistrate, and in Ch. XXXI., relating to Synods and Councils, are inserted in their proper places, and marked by italics. Minor changes are indicated in foot-notes.

The Latin translation of the Westminster Confession and Catechisms by G. D. (see Preface) appeared first at Cambridge, 1656 (also 1659 ; at Edinburgh, 1694, etc. ; and at Glasgow, 1660), under the title, 'CONFESSIO FIDEI | *in Conventu theologorum authoritate | Parliamenti Anglicani indicto | Elaborata ; | eidem Parliamento postmodum | Exhibita ; | Quin et ab eodem, deindeque ab Ecclesia Scoticana | Cognita et Approbata ; | unâ cum | CATECHISMO | duplici, MAJORI, MINORIQUE ; | E Sermone Anglicano summa cum fide | in Litinum versa. Cantabrigiæ: excudebat Johannes Field, celeberrimæ Academiæ typographus.*']

CONFESSION OF FAITH.	CONFESSIO FIDEI.
### CHAPTER I.	### CAP. I.
Of the Holy Scripture.	De Scriptura Sacro-sancta.

I. Although the light of nature, and the works of creation and providence, do so far manifest the goodness, wisdom, and power of God, as to leave men inexcusable;[1] yet are they not sufficient to give that knowledge of God, and of his will, which is necessary unto salvation;[2] therefore it pleased the Lord, at sundry times, and in divers manners, to reveal himself, and to declare that his will unto his Church;[3] and afterwards, for the better preserving and propagating of the truth, and for the more sure establishment and comfort of the Church against the corruption of the flesh, and the malice

I. *Quanquam naturæ lumen, operaque Dei cum Creationis tum Providentiæ, bonitatem ejus, sapientiam, potentiamque eo usque manifestant, ut homines vel inde reddantur inexcusabiles:*[1] *eam tamen Dei, voluntatisque divinæ cognitionem, quæ porro est ad salutem necessaria, nequeunt nobis ingenerare.*[2] *Quocirca Domino complacitum est, variis quidem modis vicibusque Ecclesiæ suæ semetipsum revelare, suamque hanc voluntatem patefacere ;*[3] *sed et eandem omnem postea literis consignare, quo et veritati suæ tam conservandæ quam propagandæ melius consuleret, nec Ecclesia sua contra carnis corruptelam, contra malitiam mundi*

---

[1] Rom. ii. 14, 15 ; i. 19, 20 ; Psa. xix. 1–3 ; Rom. i. 32 ; ii. 1.

[2] 1 Cor. i. 21 ; ii. 13, 14.
[3] Heb. i. 1.

of Satan and of the world, to commit the same wholly unto writing;[1] which maketh the holy Scripture to be most necessary;[2] those former ways of God's revealing his will unto his people being now ceased.[3]

II. Under the name of holy Scripture, or the Word of God written, are now contained all the Books of the Old and New Testament, which are these:

Satanæque, præsidio foret ac solatio destituta.[1] *Unde factum est, ut, postquam pristini illi modi, quibus olim populo suo Deus voluntatem suam revelabat, jam desiverint,*[2] *Scriptura Sacra sit maxime necessaria.*[3]

II. *Sacræ Scripturæ nomine, seu Verbi Dei scripti continentur hodie omnes illi libri tam Veteris quam Novi Instrumenti,*[4] *nempe quorum inferius subsequuntur nomina.*

Of the Old Testament.

Genesis.	Ecclesiastes.
Exodus.	The Song of Songs.
Leviticus,	Isaiah.
Numbers.	Jeremiah.
Deuteronomy.	Lamentations.
Joshua.	Ezekiel.
Judges.	Daniel.
Ruth.	Hosea.
I. Samuel.	Joel.
II. Samuel.	Amos.
I. Kings.	Obadiah.
II. Kings.	Jonah.
I. Chronicles.	Micah.
II. Chronicles.	Nahum.
Ezra.	Habakkuk.
Nehemiah.	Zephaniah.
Esther.	Haggai.
Job.	Zechariah.
Psalms.	Malachi.
Proverbs.	

Veteris Testamenti.

Genesis.	*Ecclesiastes.*
Exodus.	*Canticum Canticorum.*
Leviticus.	*Isaias.*
Numeri.	*Jeremias.*
Deuteronomium.	*Lamentationes.*
Josua.	*Ezechiel.*
Judices.	*Daniel.*
Ruth.	*Hosea.*
Samuelis 1.	*Joel.*
Samuelis 2.	*Amos.*
Regum 1.	*Obadias.*
Regum 2.	*Jonas.*
Chronicorum 1.	*Micheas.*
Chronicorum 2.	*Nahum.*
Ezra.	*Habucuc.*
Nehemias.	*Zephanias.*
Esther.	*Haggæus.*
Job.	*Zacharias.*
Psalmi.	*Malachias.*
Proverbia.	

Of the New Testament.

The Gospels according to

Matthew,	Luke,
Mark,	John.

Novi autem.

Evangelium secundum

Matthæum,	*Lucam,*
Marcum,	*Johannem.*

---

[1] Prov. xxii. 19–21; Luke i. 3, 4; Rom. xv. 4; Matt. iv. 4, 7, 10; Isa. viii. 19, 20.
[2] 2 Tim. iii. 15; 2 Pet. i. 19.
[3] Heb. i. 1, 2.
[4] [So the Cambridge eds. of 1656 and 1659. The Edinb. ed. reads *Testamenti.*]

The Acts of the Apos-	To Timothy II.	*Acta apostolorum.*	
tles.	To Titus.		*Titum.*
Paul's Epistles to the	To Philemon.	*Pauli epistolæ ad*	*Philemonem.*
Romans.	The Epistle to the He-	*Romanos.*	*Epist. ad Hebræos.*
Corinthians I.	brews.	*Corinthios I. II.*	
Corinthians II.	The Epistle of James.		*Jacobi Epistola.*
Galatians.	The First and Second	*Galatas.*	*Petri Epist. I. II.*
Ephesians.	Epistles of Peter.	*Ephesios.*	
Philippians.	The First, Second, and	*Philippenses.*	*Johan. Epist. I. II.*
Colossians.	Third Epistles of	*Collossenses.*	*III.*
Thessalonians I.	John.	*Thessalonicens I. II.*	
Thessalonians II.	The Epistle of Jude.		*Judæ Epistola.*
To Timothy I.	The Revelation.	*Timotheum I. II.*	*Apocalypsis.*

All which are given by inspiration of God, to be the rule of faith and life.[1]

III. The books commonly called Apocrypha, not being of divine inspiration, are no part of the Canon of the Scripture; and therefore are of no authority in the Church of God, nor to be any otherwise approved, or made use of, than other human writings.[2]

IV. The authority of the holy Scripture, for which it ought to be believed and obeyed, dependeth not upon the testimony of any man or church, but wholly upon God (who is truth itself), the Author thereof; and therefore it is to be received, because it is the Word of God.[3]

V. We may be moved and induced by the testimony of the

Qui omnes divina inspiratione dati sunt in Fidei vitæque regulam.[1]

III. *Libri Apocryphi, vulgo dicti, quum non fuerint divinitus inspirati, Canonem Scripturæ nullatenus constituunt; proindeque nullam aliam authoritatem obtinere debent in Ecclesia Dei, nec aliter quam alia humana scripta, sunt aut approbandi aut adhibendi.*[2]

IV. *Authoritas Scripturæ sacræ propter quam ei debetur fides et observantia, non ab ullius aut hominis aut Ecclesiæ pendet testimonio, sed a solo ejus authore Deo, qui est ipsa veritas: eoque est a nobis recipienda, quoniam est Verbum Dei.*[3]

V. *Testimonium Ecclesiæ efficere quidem potest ut de Scriptura sacra*

---

[1] Luke xvi. 29, 31 ; Eph. ii. 20; Rev. xxii. 18, 19 ; 2 Tim. iii. 16.
[2] Luke xxiv. 27, 44 ; Rom. iii. 2 ; 2 Pet. i. 21.
[3] 2 Pet. i. 19, 21 ; 2 Tim. iii. 16; 1 John v. 9 ; 1 Thess. ii. 13.

Church to an high and reverent esteem of[1] the holy Scripture;[2] and the heavenliness of the matter, the efficacy of the doctrine, the majesty of the style, the consent of all the parts, the scope of the whole (which is to give all glory to God), the full discovery it makes of the only way of man's salvation, the many other incomparable excellencies, and the entire perfection thereof, are arguments whereby it doth abundantly evidence itself to be the Word of God; yet, notwithstanding, our full persuasion and assurance of the infallible truth, and divine authority thereof, is from the inward work of the Holy Spirit, bearing witness by and with the Word in our hearts.[3]

VI. The whole counsel of God, concerning all things necessary for his own glory, man's salvation, faith, and life, is either expressly set down in Scripture, or by good and necessary consequence may be deduced from Scripture: unto which nothing at any time is to be added, whether by new revelations of the Spirit, or traditions of men.[4] Nevertheless we acknowledge the inward illumination of the Spirit of God to be necessary for the sav-

quam honorifice sentiamus;[2] *materies insuper ejus cœlestis, doctrinæ vis et efficacia, styli majestas, partium omnium consensus, totiusque scopus (ut Deo nempe omnis gloria tribuatur), plena denique quam exhibet unicæ ad salutem viæ commonstratio, præter alias ejus virtutes incomparabiles, et perfectionem summam, argumenta sunt quibus abunde se Verbum Dei et luculenter probat; nihilominus tamen plena persuasio et certitudo de ejus tam infallibili veritate, quam authoritate divina non aliunde nascitur quam ab interna operatione Spiritus Sancti, per verbum et cum verbo ipso in cordibus nostris testificantis.*[3]

VI. *Consilium Dei universum de omnibus quæ ad suam ipsius gloriam, quæque ad hominum salutem, fidem, vitamque sunt necessaria, aut expresse in Scriptura continetur, aut consequentia bona et necessaria derivari potest a Scriptura; cui nihil deinceps addendum est, seu novis a spiritu revelationibus, sive traditionibus hominum.*[4] *Internam nihilominus illuminationem Spiritus Dei ad salutarem eorum perceptionem, quæ in Verbo Dei*

---

[1] [Am. ed. *for.*]
[2] 1 Tim. iii. 15.
[3] 1 John ii. 20, 27; John xvi. 13, 14; 1 Cor. ii. 10–12; Isa. lix. 21.
[4] 2 Tim. iii. 15–17; Gal. i. 8, 9; 2 Thess. ii. 2.

ing understanding of such things as are revealed in the Word;[1] and that there are some circumstances concerning the worship of God, and government of the Church, common to human actions and societies, which are to be ordered by the light of nature and Christian prudence, according to the general rules of the Word, which are always to be observed.[2]

VII. All things in Scripture are not alike plain in themselves, nor alike clear unto all;[3] yet those things which are necessary to be known, believed, and observed, for salvation, are so clearly propounded and opened in some place of Scripture or other, that not only the learned, but the unlearned, in a due use of the ordinary means, may attain unto a sufficient understanding of them.[4]

VIII. The Old Testament in Hebrew (which was the native language of the people of God of old), and the New Testament in Greek (which at the time of the writing of it was most generally known to the nations), being immediately inspired by God, and by his singular care and providence kept pure in all ages, are therefore authentical;[5] so as in all controver-

revelantur, agnoscimus esse necessariam:[1] quin etiam nonnullas esse circumstantias cultum Dei spectantes et Ecclesiæ regimen, iis cum humanis actionibus et societatibus communes, quæ naturali lumine ac prudentia Christiana secundum generales verbi regulas (perpetuo quidem illas observandas) sunt regulandæ.[2]

VII. *Quæ in Scriptura continentur non sunt omnia æque aut in se perspicua, aut omnibus hominibus evidentia:[3] ea tamen omnia quæ ad salutem necessaria sunt cognitu, creditu, observatu, adeo perspicue, alicubi saltem in Scriptura, proponuntur et explicantur, ut eorum non docti solum, verum indocti etiam ordinariorum debito usu mediorum, sufficientem assequi possint intelligentiam.[4]*

VIII. *Instrumentum Vetus Hebræa lingua (antiqua Dei populo nempe vernacula) Novum autem Græca (ut quæ apud Gentes maxime omnium tunc temporis, quum scriberetur illud, obtinuerat), immediate a Deo inspirata, ejusque cura et Providentia singulari per omnia huc usque secula pura et intaminata custodita, ea propter sunt authentica.[5] Adeo sane ut ad*

---

[1] John vi. 45; 1 Cor. ii. 9, 10, 12.　　[3] 2 Pet. iii. 16.　　[5] Matt. v. 18.
[2] 1 Cor. xi. 13, 14; xiv. 26, 40.　　[4] Psa. cxix. 105, 130.

sies of religion the Church is finally to appeal unto them.[1] But because these original tongues are not known to all the people of God who have right unto, and interest in the Scriptures, and are commanded, in the fear of God, to read and search them,[2] therefore they are to be translated into the vulgar language of every nation unto which they come,[3] that the Word of God dwelling plentifully in all, they may worship him in an acceptable manner,[4] and, through patience and comfort of the Scriptures, may have hope.[5]

IX. The infallible rule of interpretation of Scripture is the Scripture itself; and therefore, when there is a question about the true and full sense of any Scripture (which is not manifold, but one), it must[6] be searched and known by other places that speak more clearly.[7]

X. The Supreme Judge, by which all controversies of religion are to be determined, and all decrees of councils, opinions of ancient writers, doctrines of men, and private spirits, are to be examined, and in whose sentence we are to rest, can

illa ultimo in omnibus de religione controversiis Ecclesia debeat appellare.[1] Quoniam autem Originales istæ linguæ non sunt toti Dei populo intellectæ (Quorum tamen et jus est ut scripturas habeant, et interest plurimum, quique eas in timore Dei legere jubentur et perscrutari)[2] proinde sunt in vulgarem cujusque Gentis, ad quam pervenerint linguam transferendæ,[3] ut omnes, verbo Dei opulenter in ipsis habitante, Deum grato acceptoque modo colant,[4] et per patientiam ac consolationem Scripturarum spem habeant.[5]

IX. Infallibilis Scripturam interpretandi regula est Scriptura ipsa. Quoties igitur cunque oritur quæstio de vero plenoque Scripturæ cujusvis sensu (unicus ille est non multiplex), ex aliis locis, qui apertius loquuntur, est indagandus et cognoscendus.[7]

X. Supremus judex, a quo omnes de religione controversiæ sunt determinandæ, omnia Conciliorum decreta, opiniones Scriptorum Veterum, doctrinæ denique hominum, et privati quicunque Spiritus sunt examinandi, cujusque sententia te-

---

[1] Isa. viii. 20; Acts xv. 15; John v. 39, 46.
[2] John v. 39.
[3] 1 Cor. xiv. 6, 9, 11, 12, 24, 27, 28.
[4] Col. iii. 16.
[5] Rom. xv. 4.
[6] [Am. ed. may.]
[7] 2 Pet. i. 20, 21; Acts xv. 15; [Am. ed John v. 46 |.

be no other but the Holy Spirit speaking in the Scripture.[1]

nemur acquiescere, nullus alius esse potest, præter Spiritum Sanctum in Scriptura pronunciantem.[1]

CHAPTER II.

Of God, and of the Holy Trinity.

I. There is but one only[2] living and true God,[3] who is infinite in being and perfection,[4] a most pure spirit,[5] invisible,[6] without body, parts,[7] or passions,[8] immutable,[9] immense,[10] eternal,[11] incomprehensible,[12] almighty,[13] most wise,[14] most holy,[15] most free,[16] most absolute,[17] working all things according to the counsel of his own immutable and most righteous will,[18] for his own glory;[19] most loving,[20] gracious, merciful, long-suffering, abundant in goodness and truth, forgiving iniquity, transgression, and sin;[21] the rewarder of them that diligently seek him;[22] and withal most just and terrible in his judgments;[23]

CAP. II.

De Deo et Sacro-sancta Trinitate.

I. *Unus est unicusque,*[2] *vivens ille et verus Deus:*[3] *qui idem est essentia et perfectione infinitus,*[4] *Spiritus purissimus,*[5] *invisibilis,*[6] *sine corpore, sine partibus,*[7] *sine passionibus,*[8] *immutabilis,*[9] *immensus,*[10] *æternus,*[11] *incomprehensibilis,*[12] *omnipotens,*[13] *summe sapiens,*[14] *summe sanctus,*[15] *liberrimus,*[16] *maxime absolutus;*[17] *operans omnia secundum consilium immutabilis suæ ac justissimæ voluntatis,*[18] *ad suam ipsius gloriam;*[19] *idemque summa benignitate,*[20] *gratia, misericordia, et longanimitate; bonitate abundans et veritate; condonans iniquitatem, transgressionem et peccatum;*[21] *studiose quærentium ipsum remunerator;*[22] *sed et in judiciis suis justissimus idem ac tremendus maxime;*[23]

---

[1] Matt. xxii. 29, 31; Eph. ii. 20; Acts xxviii. 25.

[2] Deut. vi. 4; 1 Cor. viii. 4, 6.

[3] 1 Thess. i. 9; Jer. x. 10.

[4] Job xi. 7, 8, 9; xxvi. 14.

[5] John iv. 24.

[6] 1 Tim. i. 17.

[7] Deut. iv. 15, 16; John iv. 24; Luke xxiv. 39.

[8] Acts xiv. 11, 15.

[9] James i. 17; Mal. iii. 6.

[10] 1 Kings viii. 27; Jer. xxiii. 23, 24.

[11] Psa. xc. 2; 1 Tim. i. 17.

[12] Psa. cxlv. 3.

[13] Gen. xvii. 1; Rev. iv. 8.

[14] Rom. xvi. 27.

[15] Isa. vi. 3; Rev. iv. 8.

[16] Psa. cxv. 3.

[17] Exod. iii. 14.

[18] Eph. i. 11.

[19] Prov. xvi. 4; Rom. xi. 56; [Am. ed. Rev. iv. 11].

[20] 1 John iv. 8, 16.

[21] Exod. xxxiv. 6, 7.

[22] Heb. xi. 6.

[23] Neh. ix. 32, 33.

hating all sin,[1] and who will by no means clear the guilty.[2]

II. God hath all life,[3] glory,[4] goodness,[5] blessedness,[6] in and of himself; and is alone in and unto himself all-sufficient, not standing in need of any creatures which he hath made,[7] nor deriving any glory from them,[8] but only manifesting his own glory in, by, unto, and upon them: he is the alone foundation of all being, of whom, through whom, and to whom are all things;[9] and hath most sovereign dominion over them, to do by them, for them, or upon them whatsoever himself pleaseth.[10] In his sight all things are open and manifest;[11] his knowledge is infinite, infallible, and independent upon the creature;[12] so as nothing is to him contingent or uncertain.[13] He is most holy in all his counsels, in all his works, and in all his commands.[14] To him is due from angels and men, and every other creature, whatsoever worship, service, or obedience, he is pleased to require of them.[15]

III. In the unity of the God-

peccatum omne perosus,[1] et qui sontem nullo unquam absolvet modo.[2]

II. *Omnem vitam,[3] omnem gloriam,[4] bonitatem,[5] beatitudinemque[6] omnem in sese habet et a seipso Deus; qui solus in se sibique est ad omnia sufficiens; creaturarum, quas ipse condidit, nullius egens,[7] nec gloriam ab eis derivans ullam,[8] verum in iis, per eas, iis ipsis, ac super eas propriam ipsius gloriam tantummodo manifestans. Is omnis entitatis fons est unicus, a quo, per quem et ad quem omnia;[9] summumque in ea dominium habet, ac per illa, pro illis, in illa pro suo arbitrio quidlibet agendi potestatem.[10] In conspectu ejus aperta sunt omnia ac manifesta;[11] scientia ejus infinita est, infallibilis, atque a creatura independens,[12] adeo ut illi contingens incertumve nihil sit;[13] in omnibus ejus consiliis, operibus et mandatis est sanctissimus.[14] Quicquid cultus, quicquid officii, quicquid obsequii ab Angelis illi, ab hominibus, aut a quavis creatura exigere placet, id illi omne jure optimo debetur.[15]*

III. *In Deitatis unitate personæ*

---

[1] Psa. v. 5, 6.
[2] Nahum i. 2, 3; Exod. xxxiv. 7.
[3] John v. 26.
[4] Acts vii. 2.
[5] Psa. cxix. 68.
[6] 1 Tim. vi. 15 ; Rom. ix. 5.
[7] Acts xvii. 24, 25.
[8] Job xxii. 2, 23.

[9] Rom. xi. 36.
[10] Rev. iv. 11; 1 Tim. vi. 15; Dan. iv. 25. 35.
[11] Heb. iv. 13.
[12] Rom. xi. 33, 34; Psa. cxlvii. 5.
[13] Acts xv. 18 ; Ezek. xi. 5.
[14] Psa. cxlv. 17; Rom. vii. 12.
[15] Rev. v. 12–14.

head there be three persons, of one substance, power, and eternity: God the Father, God the Son, and God the Holy Ghost.[1] The Father is of none, neither begotten nor proceeding; the Son is eternally begotten of the Father;[2] the Holy Ghost eternally proceeding from the Father and the Son.[3]

tres sunt unius ejusdemque essentiæ, potentiæ ac æternitatis; Deus Pater, Deus Filius, ac Deus Spiritus Sanctus.[1] Pater quidem a nullo est, nec genitus nempe nec procedens: Filius autem a Patre est æterne genitus:[2] Spiritus autem Sanctus æterne procedens a Patre Filioque.[3]

CHAPTER III.

Of God's Eternal Decree.[4]

I. God from all eternity did, by the most wise and holy counsel of his own will, freely and unchangeably ordain whatsoever comes to pass;[5] yet so as thereby neither is God the author of sin,[6] nor is violence offered to the will of the creatures, nor is the liberty or contingency of second causes taken away, but rather established.[7]

II. Although God knows whatsoever may or can come to pass upon all supposed conditions,[8] yet hath he not decreed any thing because he foresaw it as future, or as that which would come to pass upon such conditions.[9]

III. By the decree of God, for the manifestation of his glory,

CAP. III.

De æterno Dei Decreto.

I. *Deus, e sapientissimo sanctissimoque consilio voluntatis suæ, libere ac immutabiliter, quicquid unquam evenit, ab omni æterno ordinavit;[5] ita tamen, ut inde nec author peccati evadat Deus,[6] nec voluntati creaturarum sit vis illata, neque libertas aut contingentia causarum secundarum ablata sit, verum potius stabilita.[7]*

II. *Quamvis omnia cognoscat Deus, quæ suppositis quibusvis conditionibus sunt eventu possibilia;[8] non tamen ideo quicquam decrevit quoniam illud præviderat aut futurum, aut positis talibus conditionibus eventurum.[9]*

III. *Deus, quo gloriam suam manifestaret, nonnullos hominum*

---

[1] 1 John v. 7; Matt. iii. 16, 17; xxviii. 19; 2 Cor. xiii. 14.

[2] John i. 14, 18.

[3] John xv. 26; Gal. iv. 6.

[4] [Am. ed. *decrees.*]

[5] Eph. i. 1.; Rom. xi. 33; Heb. vi. 17; Rom. ix. 15, 18.

[6] James i. 13, 17; 1 John i. 5; [Am. ed. Eccl. vii. 29].

[7] Acts ii. 23; Matt. xvii. 12; Acts iv. 27, 28; John xix. 11; Prov. xvi. 33.

[8] Acts xv. 18; 1 Sam. xxiii. 11, 12; Matt. xi. 21, 23.

[9] Rom. ix. 11, 13, 16, 18.

some men and angels[1] are predestinated unto everlasting life,
and others foreordained to everlasting death.[2]

IV. These angels and men, thus
predestinated and foreordained,
are particularly and unchangeably
designed; and their number is so
certain and definite that it can not
be either increased or diminished.[3]

V. Those of mankind that are
predestinated unto life, God, before the foundation of the world
was laid, according to his eternal
and immutable purpose, and the
secret counsel and good pleasure
of his will, hath chosen in Christ,
unto everlasting glory,[4] out of his
mere free grace and love, without
any foresight of faith or good
works, or perseverance in either
of them, or any other thing in the
creature, as conditions, or causes
moving him thereunto;[5] and all
to the praise of his glorious
grace.[6]

VI. As God hath appointed the
elect unto glory, so hath he, by
the eternal and most free purpose
of his will, foreordained all the
means thereunto.[7] Wherefore they
who are elected, being fallen in

*ac Angelorum[1] decreto suo ad æter-
nam vitam prædestinavit, alios
autem ad mortem æternam præordinavit.[2]*

IV. *Prædestinati illi et præor-
dinati homines Angelique, particu-
lariter sunt ac immutabiliter de-
signati, certusque illorum est ac
definitus numerus, adeo ut nec augeri possit nec imminui.[3]*

V. *Qui ex humano genere sunt
ad vitam prædestinati, illos Deus
ante jacta mundi fundamenta, secundum æternum suum ac immutabile propositum, secretumque voluntatis suæ consilium et beneplacitum, elegit in Christo ad æternam
gloriam,[4] idque ex amore suo et
gratia mere gratuita; nec fide, nec
bonis operibus, nec in his illave
perseverantia, sed neque ulla alia
re in creatura, prævisis, ipsum
tanquam causis aut conditionibus
ad id moventibus;[5] quo totum
nempe in laudem cederet gloriosæ
suæ gratiæ.[6]*

VI. *Quemadmodum autem Deus
electos ad gloriam destinavit, sic
omnia etiam quibus illam consequantur media præordinavit, voluntatis suæ proposito æterno simul et
liberrimo.[7] Quapropter electi, post-*

---

[1] 1 Tim. v. 21; Matt. xxv. 41.
[2] Rom. ix. 22, 23; Eph. i. 5, 6; Prov. xvi. 4.
[3] 2 Tim. ii. 19; John xiii. 18.
[4] Eph. i. 4, 9, 11; Rom. viii. 30; 2 Tim. i.
  9; 1 Thess. v. 9.

[5] Rom. ix. 11, 13, 16; Eph. i. 4, 9.
[6] Eph. i. 6, 12.
[7] 1 Pet. i. 2; Eph. i. 4, 5; ii. 10; 2 Thess. ii.
  13.

Adam, are redeemed by Christ,[1] are effectually called unto faith in Christ by his Spirit working in due season; are justified, adopted, sanctified,[2] and kept by his power through faith unto salvation.[3] Neither are any other redeemed by Christ, effectually called, justified, adopted, sanctified, and saved, but the elect only.[4]

VII. The rest of mankind God was pleased, according to the unsearchable counsel of his own will, whereby he extendeth or withholdeth mercy as he pleaseth, for the glory of his sovereign power over his creatures, to pass by, and to ordain them to dishonor and wrath for their sin, to the praise of his glorious justice.[5]

VIII. The doctrine of this high mystery of predestination is to be handled with special prudence and care,[6] that men attending the will of God revealed in his Word, and yielding obedience thereunto, may, from the certainty of their effectual vocation, be assured of their eternal election.[7] So shall this doctrine afford matter of praise, reverence, and admiration of God;[8] and of humility, diligence, and abundant conso-

quam lapsi essent in Adamo, a Christo sunt redempti;[1] *per Spiritum ejus opportuno tempore operantem, ad fidem in Christum vocantur efficaciter; justificantur, sanctificantur,*[2] *et potentia ipsius per fidem custodiuntur ad salutem.*[3] *Nec alii quivis a Christo redimuntur, vocantur efficaciter, justificantur, adoptantur, sanctificantur et salvantur, præter electos solos.*[4]

VII. *Reliquos humani generis Deo placuit secundum consilium voluntatis suæ inscrutabile (quo misericordiam pro libitu exhibet abstinetve) in gloriam supremæ suæ in creaturas potestatis, præterire; eosque ordinare ad ignominiam et iram pro peccatis suis, ad laudem justitiæ suæ gloriosæ.*[5]

VIII. *Doctrina de sublimi hoc prædestinationis mysterio non sine summa cura et prudentia tractari debet,*[6] *quo nimirum homines, dum voluntati Dei in verbo ejus revelatæ advertant animos, eique debitam exhibeant obedientiam, de efficaci sua vocatione certiores facti, ad æternæ suæ electionis assurgere possint certitudinem.*[7] *Ita demum suppeditabit hæc doctrina laudandi, reverendi, admirandique Deum argumentum,*[8] *quin etiam hu-*

---

[1] 1 Thess. v. 9, 10; Tit. ii. 14.
[2] Rom. viii. 30; Eph. i. 5; 2 Thess. ii. 13.
[3] 1 Pet. i. 5.
[4] John xvii. 9; Rom. viii. 28 to the end; John vi. 64, 65; viii. 47; x. 26; 1 John ii. 19.

[5] Matt. xi. 25, 26; Rom. ix. 17, 18, 21, 22; 2 Tim. ii. 19, 20; Jude 4; 1 Pet. ii. 8.
[6] Rom. ix. 20; xi. 33; Deut. xxix. 29.
[7] 2 Pet. i. 10.
[8] Eph. i. 6; Rom. xi. 33.

lation to all that sincerely obey the gospel.[1]

militatis, diligentiæ et consolationis copiosæ omnibus sincere obedientibus evangelio.[1]

Chapter IV.

Of Creation.

I. It pleased God the Father, Son, and Holy Ghost,[2] for the manifestation of the glory of his eternal power, wisdom, and goodness,[3] in the beginning, to create or make of nothing the world, and all things therein, whether visible or invisible, in the space of six days, and all very good.[4]

II. After God had made all other creatures, he created man, male and female,[5] with reasonable and immortal souls,[6] endued with knowledge, righteousness, and true holiness, after his own image,[7] having the law of God written in their hearts,[8] and power to fulfill it;[9] and yet under a possibility of transgressing, being left to the liberty of their own will, which was subject unto change.[10] Beside this law written in their hearts, they received a command not to eat of the tree of the knowledge of good

Cap. IV.

De Creatione.

I. *Deo, Patri, Filio et Spiritui sancto, complacitum est,[2] quo æternæ suæ cum potentiæ tum sapientiæ bonitatisque gloriam manifestaret,[3] mundum hunc, et quæ in eo continentur universa tam visibilia quam invisibilia, in principio intra sex dierum spatium creare, seu ex nihilo condere, atque omnia quidem bona valde.[4]*

II. *Postquam omnes alias creaturas condidisset Deus, creavit hominem marem et fœminam,[5] animabus inditis rationalibus ac immortalibus,[6] imbutos cognitione, justitia, veraque sanctitate, ad suam ipsius imaginem,[7] habentes in cordibus suis inscriptam Divinam legem,[8] simul et eandem implendi vires;[9] non tamen sine quadam violandi possibilitate; libertati siquidem permissi erant voluntatis suæ haud immutabilis.[10] Præter autem hanc in cordibus eorum inscriptam legem de non comedendo ex arbore scientiæ boni malique*

---

[1] Rom. xi. 5, 6, 20 ; 2 Pet. i. 10 ; Rom. viii. 33 ; Luke x. 20.

[2] Heb. i. 2 ; John i. 2, 3 ; Gen. i. 2 ; Job xxvi. 13 : xxxiii. 4.

[3] Rom. i. 20 ; Jer. x. 12 ; Psa. civ. 24 ; xxxiii. 5, 6.

[4] Gen. ch. i. ; Heb. xi. 3 ; Col. i. 16 ; Acts xvii. 24.

[5] Gen. i. 27.

[6] Gen. ii. 7 ; Eccles. xii. 7 ; Luke xxiii. 43 ; Matt. x. 28.

[7] Gen. i. 26 ; Col. iii. 10 ; Eph. iv. 24.

[8] Rom. ii. 14, 15.

[9] Eccles. vii. 29.

[10] Gen. iii. 6 ; Eccles. vii. 29.

and evil; which while they kept they were happy in their communion with God,[1] and had dominion over the creatures.[2]

CHAPTER V.

Of Providence.

God, the great Creator of all things, doth uphold,[3] direct, dispose, and govern all creatures, actions, and things,[4] from the greatest even to the least,[5] by his most wise and holy providence,[6] according to his infallible foreknowledge[7] and the free and immutable counsel of his own will,[8] to the praise of the glory of his wisdom, power, justice, goodness, and mercy.[9]

II. Although in relation to the foreknowledge and decree of God, the first cause, all things come to pass immutably and infallibly,[10] yet by the same providence he ordereth them to fall out, according to the nature of second causes, either necessarily, freely, or contingently.[11]

III. God, in his ordinary providence, maketh use of means,[12] yet is free to work without,[13]

mandatum insuper acceperunt; quod certe quam diu observabant, communione Dei beati erant,[1] dominiumque habebant in creaturas.[2]

CAP. V.

De Providentia.

I. *Magnus ille rerum omnium creator Deus sapientissima sua et sanctissima simul providentia[3] creaturas, actiones, resque[4] a maximis usque ad minimas[5] universas sustentat,[6] dirigit, ordinat, gubernatque secundum infallibilem suam præscientiam,[7] et voluntatis suæ consilium liberum ac immutabile,[8] ad laudem gloriæ sapientiæ suæ, potentiæ, justitiæ, bonitatis, ac misericordiæ.[9]*

II. *Quamvis respectu præscientiæ ac decreti Dei (causæ primæ) omnia immutabiliter atque infallibiliter eveniant,[10] per eandem tamen ille providentiam eadem ordinat evenire necessario, libere, aut contingenter, pro natura causarum secundarum.[11]*

III. *Deus in providentia sua ordinaria mediis utitur,[12] iis tamen non astringitur, quo minus absque eis,[13]*

---

[1] Gen. ii. 27; iii. 8–11, 23.

[2] Gen. i. 26, 28; [Am. ed. Psa. viii. 6–8].

[3] Heb. i. 3.

[4] Dan. iv. 34, 35; Psa. cxxxv. 6; Acts xvii. 25, 26, 28; Job, chaps. xxxviii. xxxix. xl. xli.

[5] Matt. x. 29–31; [Am. ed. Matt. vi. 26, 30].

[6] Prov. xv. 3; [Am. ed. 2 Chron. xvi. 9]; Psa. civ. 24; cxlv. 17.
　　Acts xv. 18; Psa. xciv. 8–11.

[8] Eph. i. 11; Psa. xxxiii. 10, 11.

[9] Isa. lxiii. 14; Eph. iii. 10; Rom. ix. 17; Gen. xlv. 7; Psa. cxlv. 7.

[10] Acts ii. 23.

[11] Gen. viii. 22; Jer. xxxi. 35; Exod. xxi. 13; Deut. xix. 5; 1 Kings xxii. 28, 34; Isa. x. 6, 7.

[12] Acts xxvii. 31, 44; Isa. lv. 10, 11; Hos. ii. 21, 22.

[13] Hos. i. 7; Matt. iv. 4; Job xxxiv. 10.

above,[1] and against them, at his pleasure.[2]

IV. The almighty power, unsearchable wisdom, and infinite goodness of God so far manifest themselves in his providence that it extendeth itself even to the first fall, and all other sins of angels and men,[3] and that not by a bare permission,[4] but such as hath joined with it a most wise and powerful bounding,[5] and otherwise ordering and governing of them, in a manifold dispensation, to his own holy ends;[6] yet so as the sinfulness thereof proceedeth only from the creature, and not from God; who, being most holy and righteous, neither is nor can be the author or approver of sin.[7]

V. The most wise, righteous, and gracious God doth oftentimes leave for a season his own children to manifold temptations and the corruption of their own hearts, to chastise them for their former sins, or to discover unto them the hidden strength of corruption and deceitfulness of their hearts, that they may be humbled;[8] and to raise them to a more close and constant

supra[1] aut etiam contra ea pro arbitrio suo operetur.[2]

IV. Omnipotentem Dei potentiam, sapientiam inscrutabilem, bonitatemque infinitam providentia ejus eo usque manifestat, ut vel ad primum lapsum, omniaque reliqua peccata, seu hominum sint sive angelorum, se extendat;[3] neque id quidem permissione nuda,[4] verum cui conjuncta est sapientissima potentissimaque eorum limitatio,[5] ac aliusmodi ad sanctos sibi propositos fines dispensatione multiplici ordinatio et gubernatio;[6] ita tamen ut omnis eorum vitiositas a sola proveniat creatura, a Deo neutiquam, qui sanctissimus quum sit justissimusque neque est, nec esse quidem potest peccati autor aut approbator.[7]

V. Sapientissimus, justissimus, et gratiosissimus idem Deus, sœpenumero filios suos tentationibus multifariis, suorumque cordium corruptioni ad tempus permittit; quo ob admissa prius peccata castiget eos, vel corruptionis iis detegat vim occultam, cordiumque suorum fraudulentiam ut humilientur;[8] quoque eos excitet ad strictam magis et constantem a seipso proferendis suppetiis

---

[1] Rom. iv. 19–21.
[2] 2 Kings vi. 6; Dan. iii. 27.
[3] Rom. xi. 32–34; 2 Sam. xxiv. 1; 1 Chron. xxi. 1; 1 Kings xxii. 22, 23; 1 Chron. x. 4, 13, 14; 2 Sam. xvi. 10; Acts ii. 23; iv. 27, 28.
[4] Acts xiv. 16.
[5] Psa. lxxvi. 10; 2 Kings xix. 28.
[6] Gen. l. 20; Isa. x. 6, 7, 12.
[7] James i. 13, 14, 17; 1 John. ii. 16; Psa. l. 21.
[8] 2 Chron. xxxii. 25, 26, 31; 2 Sam. xxiv. 1.

dependence for their support unto[1]
himself, and to make them more
watchful against all future occasions of sin, and for sundry other
just and holy ends.[2]

VI. As for those wicked and
ungodly men whom God, as a
righteous judge, for former sins,
doth blind and harden,[3] from
them he not only withholdeth his
grace, whereby they might have
been enlightened in their under-
standings and wrought upon in
their hearts,[4] but sometimes also
withdraweth the gifts which they
had,[5] and exposeth them to such
objects as their corruption makes
occasion of sin;[6] and withal, gives
them over to their own lusts, the
temptations of the world, and the
power of Satan;[7] whereby it comes
to pass that they harden themselves, even under those means
which God useth for the soften-
ing of others.[8]

VII. As the providence of God
doth, in general, reach to all creatures, so, after a most special manner, it taketh care of his Church,
and disposeth all things to the
good thereof.[9]

*dependentiam; Quo denique adversus
omnes occasiones peccati de futuro
reddat cautiores.   Sed et ob alios
etiam varios fines, justos sanctosque
sibi propositos.[2]*

VI. *Quod scelestos illos spectat
impiosque homines, quos Deus, ut
justus judex, ob peccata præceden-
tia excæcat induratque;[3] eis ille
non solum gratiam suam non im-
pertit, qua ipsis cum illuminari
intellectus, tum affici corda potuissent;[4] sed interdum subtrahit eis
quibus imbuti erant dona,[5] et ipsos
exponit illiusmodi objectis, unde
corruptio eorum arripit sibi peccandi occasiones;[6] simulque tradit eos suis ipsorum concupiscentiis
et tentationibus mundi, et potestati
Satanæ;[7] ex quo fit ut seipsos
ipsi indurent, et quidem sub iisdem mediis quibus utitur Deus ad
alios emolliendos.[8]*

VII. *Providentia Dei sicut ad
omnes creaturas universali modo
se extendit; ita modo plane peculiari Ecclesiæ suæ curam gerit,
ac in ejus bonum disponit universa.[9]*

---

[1] [Am. ed. *upon.*]
[2] 2 Cor. xii. 7–9; Psa. lxxiii. throughout;
    lxxvii. 1–10, 12; Mark xiv. 66 to the
    end; John xxi. 15–17.
[3] Rom. i. 24, 26, 28; xi. 7, 8.
[4] Deut. xxix. 4.
[5] Matt. xiii. 12; xxv. 29.

[6] Deut. ii. 30; 2 Kings viii. 12, 13.
[7] Psa. lxxxi. 11, 12; 2 Thess. ii. 10–12.
[8] Exod. vii. 3; viii. 15, 32; 2 Cor. ii. 15, 16;
    Isa. viii. 14; 1 Pet. ii. 7, 8; Isa. vi. 9, 10;
    Acts xxviii. 26, 27.
[9] 1 Tim. iv. 10; Amos ix. 8, 9; Rom. viii
    28: Isa. xliii. 3–5. 14.

CHAPTER VI.

Of the Fall of Man, of Sin, and of the Punishment thereof.

I. Our first parents, being seduced by the subtilty and temptation of Satan, sinned in eating the forbidden fruit.[1] This their sin God was pleased, according to his wise and holy counsel, to permit, having purposed to order it to his own glory.[2]

II. By this sin they fell from their original righteousness and communion with God,[3] and so became dead in sin,[4] and wholly defiled in all the faculties and parts of soul and body.[5]

III. They being the root of all mankind,[6] the guilt of this sin was imputed, and the same death in sin and corrupted nature conveyed to all their posterity descending from them by ordinary generation.[7]

IV. From this original corruption, whereby we are utterly indisposed, disabled, and made opposite to all good,[8] and wholly inclined to all evil,[9] do proceed all actual transgressions.[10]

V. This corruption of nature,

CAP. VI.

De hominis lapsu, de peccato ejusque pœna.

I. *Primi parentes, Satanæ subtilitate ac tentatione seducti, fructus vetiti esu peccaverunt.*[1] *Hoc eorum peccatum secundum sapiens suum sanctumque consilium Deo placuit permittere, non sine proposito illud ad suam ipsius gloriam ordinandi.*[2]

II. *Hoc illi peccato, justitia sua originali et communione cum Deo exciderunt;*[3] *itaque facti sunt in peccato mortui,*[4] *atque in omnibus facultatibus ac partibus animæ corporisque penitus contaminati.*[5]

III. *Quumque illi fuerint radix totius humani*[6] *generis, hujusce peccati reatus fuit imputatus, eademque in peccato mors ac natura corrupta propagata, omnibus illorum posteris, quotquot ab iis ordinaria quidem generatione procreantur.*[7]

IV. *Ab hac originali labe (qua ad omne bonum facti sumus inhabiles prorsus ac impotentes, eique plane oppositi,*[8] *ad malum autem omne proclives penitus)*[9] *proveniunt omnia peccata actualia.*[10]

V. *Hæc naturæ corruptio durante*

---

[1] Gen. iii. 13; 2 Cor. xi. 3.
[2] Rom. xi. 32.
[3] Gen. iii. 6–8; Eccles. vii. 29; Rom. iii. 23.
[4] Gen. ii. 17; Eph. ii. 1; [Am. ed. Rom. v. 12].
  Tit. i. 15; Gen. vi. 5; Jer. xvii. 9; Rom. iii. 10–19.

[6] Gen. i. 27, 28; ii. 16, 17; Acts xvii. 26; Rom. v. 12, 15–19; 1 Cor. xv. 21, 22, 45, 49.
[7] Psa. li. 5; Gen. v. 3; Job xiv. 4; xv. 14.
[8] Rom. v. 6; vii. 18; viii. 7; Col. i. 21; [Am. ed. John iii. 6].
[9] Gen. vi. 5; viii. 21; Rom. iii. 10–12.
[10] James i. 14, 15; Eph. ii. 2, 3; Matt. xv. 19.

during this life, doth remain in those that are regenerated;[1] and although it be through Christ pardoned and mortified, yet both itself and all the motions thereof are truly and properly sin.[2]

VI. Every sin, both original and actual, being a transgression of the righteous law of God, and contrary thereunto,[3] doth, in its own nature, bring guilt upon the sinner,[4] whereby he is bound over to the wrath of God[5] and curse of the law,[6] and so made subject to death,[7] with all miseries spiritual,[8] temporal,[9] and eternal.[10]

Chapter VII.

Of God's Covenant with Man.

I. The distance between God and the creature is so great that although reasonable creatures do owe obedience unto him as their Creator, yet they could never have any fruition of him as their blessedness and reward but by some voluntary condescension on God's part, which he hath been pleased to express by way of covenant.[11]

II. The first covenant made with

hac vita manet etiam in regenitis;[1] *et quamvis per Christum et condonata sit et mortificata; nihilo minus tam ipsa, quam ejus motus universi vere sunt ac proprie peccata.*[2]

VI. *Peccatum omne cum originale tum actuale, quum justæ Dei legis transgressio sit eique contraria,*[3] *peccatori suapte natura reatum infert,*[4] *quo ad iram Dei, ac maledictionem legis*[6] *subeundam obligatur, adeoque redditur obnoxius morti*[7] *simul et miseriis omnibus spiritualibus,*[8] *temporalibus,*[9] *ac æternis.*[10]

Cap. VII.

De fœdere Dei cum homine.

I. *Tanta est inter deum et creaturam distantia, ut licet creaturæ rationales obedientiam illi ut creatori suo debeant, nullam tamen fruitionem ejus tanquam suæ beatitudinis ac præmii habere unquam potuissent, ni voluntaria fuisset aliqua ex parte Dei condescentio; quam ipsi exprimere placuit icto fœdere.*[11]

II. *Primum fœdus cum hominibus*

---

[1] 1 John i. 8, 10; Rom. vii. 14, 17, 18, 23; James iii. 2; Prov. xx. 9; Eccles. vii. 20.

[2] Rom. vii. 5, 7, 8, 25; Gal. v. 17.

[3] 1 John iii. 4.

[4] Rom. ii. 15; iii. 9, 19.

[5] Eph. ii. 3.
Gal. iii. 10.

[7] Rom. vi. 23.

[8] Eph. iv. 18.

[9] Rom. viii. 20; Lam. iii. 39.

[10] Matt. xxv. 41; 2 Thess. i. 9.

[11] Isa. xl. 13–17; Job ix. 32, 33; 1 Sam. ii. 25; Psa. c. 2. 3; cxiii. 5, 6; Job xxii. 2, 3; xxxv. 7, 8; Luke xvii. 10; Acts xvii. 24, 25.

man was a covenant of works,[1] wherein life was promised to Adam, and in him to his posterity,[2] upon condition of perfect and personal obedience.[3]

III. Man by his fall having made himself incapable of life by that covenant, the Lord was pleased to make a second,[4] commonly called the covenant of grace: wherein he freely offered unto sinners life and salvation by Jesus Christ, requiring of them faith in him that they may be saved,[5] and promising to give unto all those that are ordained unto life his Holy Spirit, to make them willing and able to believe.[6]

IV. This covenant of grace is frequently set forth in the Scripture by the name of a testament, in reference to the death of Jesus Christ the testator, and to the everlasting inheritance, with all things belonging to it, therein bequeathed.[7]

V. This covenant was differently administered in the time of the law and in the time of the gospel:[8] under the law it was administered by promises, prophecies,

initum erat fœdus operum,[1] quo vita Adamo promissa erat, ejusque in eo posteris,[2] sub conditione obedientiæ perfectæ ac personalis.[3]

III. *Quum autem homo lapsu suo omnem sibi præstruxisset ad vitam aditum per illud fœdus, complacuit Domino secundum inire,[4] quod vulgo dicimus* Fœdus Gratiæ; *in quo peccatoribus offert gratuito vitam ac salutem per Jesum Christum, fidem in illum ab iis requirens ut salventur;[5] promittensque omnibus qui ad vitam ordinantur se spiritum suum sanctum daturum, qui in illis operetur credendi cum voluntatem tum potentiam.[6]*

IV. *Hoc fœdus Gratiæ in Scriptura sæpe nomine* Testamenti *indigitatur, respectu nimirum mortis Testatoris Jesu Christi, æternæque illius hæreditatis, quam is una cum omnibus eam spectantibus inibi legabat.[7]*

V. *Hoc fœdus sub Lege atque sub Evangelio administratum est modo alio atque alio.[8] Sub Lege quidem per promissiones, prophetias et sacrificia, per circumcisionem, agnum*

---

[1] Gal. iii. 12; [Am. ed. Hos. vi. 7; Gen. ii. 16, 17].

[2] Rom. v. 12–20; x. 5.

[3] Gen. ii. 17; Gal. iii. 10.

[4] Gal. iii. 21; Rom. iii. 20, 21; viii. 3; Gen. iii. 15; Isa. xlii. 6.

[5] Mark xvi. 15, 16; John iii. 16; Rom. x. 6, 9; Gal. iii. 11.   [Am. ed. v. 37].

[6] Ezek. xxxvi. 26, 27; John vi. 44, 45;

[7] Heb. ix. 15–17; vii. 22; Luke xxii. 20; 1 Cor. xi. 25.

[8] 2 Cor. iii. 6–9.

sacrifices, circumcision, the paschal lamb, and other types and ordinances delivered to the people of the Jews, all fore-signifying Christ to come,[1] which were for that time sufficient and efficacious, through the operation of the Spirit, to instruct and build up the elect in faith in the promised Messiah,[2] by whom they had full remission of sins and eternal salvation; and is called the Old Testament.[3]

VI. Under the gospel, when Christ the substance[4] was exhibited, the ordinances in which this covenant is dispensed are the preaching of the word and the administration of the sacraments of Baptism and the Lord's Supper;[5] which, though fewer in number, and administered with more simplicity and less outward glory, yet in them it is held forth in more fullness, evidence, and spiritual efficacy,[6] to all nations, both Jews and Gentiles;[7] and is called the New Testament.[8] There are not, therefore, two covenants of grace differing in substance, but one and the same under various dispensations.[9]

pascalem, aliosque typos ac instituta populo Judaico tradita, quæ omnia Venturum Christum præsignificabant;[1] erantque pro ratione illorum temporum sufficientia, et per operationem spiritus efficacia ad electos instruendum ac ædificandum in fide in promissum Messiam,[2] per quem plenam peccatorum remissionem et salutem æternam sunt consecuti; diciturque Vetus Testamentum.[3]

VI. *Sub evangelio autem, exhibito jam Christo, substantia[4] scilicet ac antitypo, præscriptæ rationes in quibus hoc fœdus dispensatur, sunt prædicatio verbi, et administratio sacramentorum, baptismi nempe ac cœnæ Dominicæ;[5] in quibus quidem utut numero paucioribus, iisque simplicius ac minore cum externa gloria administratis, cum majore tamen plenitudine, evidentia, et efficacia spirituali[6] populis cunctis tam Judæis quam Gentibus[7] exhibetur; Diciturque* Novum Testamentum.[8] *Non sunt ergo duo fœdera gratiæ, re atque natura discrepantia; sed unum idemque, licet non uno modo dispensatum.*[9]

---

[1] Heb., chaps. viii. ix. x.; Rom. iv. 11; Col. ii. 11, 12; 1 Cor. v. 7; [Am. ed. Col. ii. 17].

[2] 1 Cor. x. 1-4; Heb. xi. 13; John viii. 56.

[3] Gal. iii. 7-9, 14.

[4] Gal. ii. 17; [Am. ed. Col. ii. 17].

[5] Matt. xxviii. 19, 20; 1 Cor. xi. 23-25; [Am. ed. 2 Cor. iii. 7-11].

[6] Heb. xii. 22-28; Jer. xxxi. 33, 34.

[7] Matt. xxviii. 19; Eph. ii. 15-19.

[8] Luke xxii. 20; [Am. ed. Heb. viii. 7-9].

[9] Gal. iii. 14, 16; Acts xv. 11; Rom. iii. 21-23, 30; Psa. xxxii. 1; Rom. iv. 3, 6, 16, 17, 23, 24; Heb. xiii. 8.

CHAPTER VIII.

Of Christ the Mediator.

I. It pleased God, in his eternal purpose, to choose and ordain the Lord Jesus, his only-begotten Son, to be the Mediator between God and man,[1] the Prophet,[2] Priest,[3] and King;[4] the Head and Saviour of his Church,[5] the Heir of all things,[6] and Judge of the world;[7] unto whom he did, from all eternity, give a people to be his seed,[8] and to be by him in time redeemed, called, justified, sanctified, and glorified.[9]

II. The Son of God, the second person in the Trinity, being very and eternal God, of one substance, and equal with the Father, did, when the fullness of time was come, take upon him man's nature,[10] with all the essential properties and common infirmities thereof, yet without sin:[11] being conceived by the power of the Holy Ghost in the womb of the Virgin Mary, of her substance.[12] So that two whole, perfect, and distinct natures, the Godhead and the manhood, were inseparably joined to-

CAP. VIII.

De Christo Mediatore.

I. *Complacitum est Deo Filium ejus unigenitum Dominum Jesum in æterno suo proposito eligere atque ordinare ut Mediator esset inter Deum et hominem,[1] Propheta,[2] Sacerdos,[3] et Rex,[4] caput idem et salvator Ecclesiæ suæ;[5] rerum omnium hæres,[6] Mundique Judex;[7] cui ab æterno populum dedit futurum illi in semen,[8] ac per illum stato tempore redimendum, vocandum, justificandum, sanctificandum ac glorificandum.[9]*

II. *Filius Dei persona secunda in Trinitate, verus nempe idem æternusque Deus, substantiæ cum Patre unius ejusdemque, eique coæqualis, cum advenerat temporis plenitudo, assumpsit naturam humanam,[10] una cum omnibus ejus proprietatibus essentialibus, communibusque infirmitatibus, immunem tamen a peccato,[11] conceptus scilicet in utero eque substantia Mariæ Virginis,[12] virtute Spiritus Sancti. Adeo sane ut naturæ duæ, integræ, perfectæ, distinctæque Deitas ac humanitas in una eademque*

---

[1] Isa. xlii. 1; 1 Pet. i. 19, 20; John iii. 16; 2 Tim. ii. 5.

[2] Acts iii. 22; [Am. ed. Deut. xviii. 15].

[3] Heb. v. 5, 6.

[4] Psa. ii. 6; Luke i. 33.

[5] Eph. v. 23.

[6] Heb. i. 2.

[7] Acts xvii. 31.

[8] John xvii. 6; Psa. xxii. 30; Isa. liii. 10.

[9] 1 Tim. ii. 6; Isa. lv. 4, 5; 1 Cor. i. 30.

[10] John i. 1, 14; 1 John v. 20; Phil. ii. 6; Gal. iv. 4.

[11] Heb. ii. 14, 16, 17; iv. 15.

[12] Luke i. 27, 31, 35; Gal. iv. 4.

gether in one person, without conversion, composition, or confusion.[1] Which person is very God and very man, yet one Christ, the only mediator between God and man.[2]

III. The Lord Jesus, in his human nature thus united to the divine, was sanctified and anointed with the Holy Spirit above measure;[3] having in him all the treasures of wisdom and knowledge,[4] in whom it pleased the Father that all fullness should dwell;[5] to the end that, being holy, harmless, undefiled, and full of grace and truth,[6] he might be thoroughly furnished to execute the office of a mediator and surety.[7] Which office he took not unto himself, but was thereunto called by his Father,[8] who put all power and judgment into his hand, and gave him commandment to execute the same.[9]

IV. This office the Lord Jesus did most willingly undertake,[10] which, that he might discharge, he was made under the law,[11] and did perfectly fulfill it;[12] endured most grievous torments immediately in his soul,[13]

persona indissolubili nexu conjunctæ fuerint, sine conversione, compositione, aut confusione.[1] Quæ quidem persona vere Deus est ac vere homo, unus tamen Christus, unicus inter Deum et hominem Mediator.[2]

III. *Dominus Jesus in humana sua natura divinæ hunc modum conjuncta sanctificatus est, ac Spiritu sancto supra mensuram unctus,[3] in se habens omnes sapientiæ notitiæque thesauros;[4] in quo Patri visum est ut omnis plenitudo inhabitaret,[5] atque eo quidem fine ut sanctus, innocuus, intaminatus, plenusque gratiæ ac veritatis existens,[6] ad Mediatoris Vadisque munus exequendum perfecte esset instructus.[7] Quod ille officium non arripuit sibi, verum a Patre erat ad id vocatus,[8] qui omnem ei potestatem ac judicium in manus dedit, unà cum mandato exercendi.[9]*

IV. *Hoc munus promtissima voluntate in se suscepit Dominus Jesus,[10] quod ut expleret factus est sub Lege,[11] eam perfecte implevit,[12] immediate in anima[12] sua gravissimos subiit cruciatus, in cor-*

---

[1] Luke i. 35; Col. ii. 9; Rom. ix. 5; 1 Pet. iii. 18; 1 Tim. iii. 16.
[2] Rom. i. 3, 4; 1 Tim. ii. 5.
[3] Psa. xlv. 7; John iii. 34.
[4] Col. ii. 3.
[5] Col. i. 19.
[6] Heb. vii. 26; John i. 14. Acts x. 38; Heb. xii. 24; vii. 22.
[8] Heb. v. 4, 5.
[9] John v. 22, 27; Matt. xxviii. 18; Acts ii. 36.
[10] Psa. xl. 7, 8; Heb. x. 5–10; John x. 18; Phil. ii. 8.
[11] Gal. iv. 4.
[12] Matt. iii. 15; v. 17.
[13] Matt. xxvi. 37, 38; Luke xxii. 44; Matt. xxvii. 46.

and most painful sufferings in his body;[1] was crucified, and died;[2] was buried, and remained under the power of death, yet saw no corruption.[3] On the third day he arose from the dead,[4] with the same body in which he suffered;[5] with which also he ascended into heaven, and there sitteth at the right hand of his Father,[6] making intercession;[7] and shall return to judge men and angels at the end of the world.[8]

V. The Lord Jesus, by his perfect obedience and sacrifice of himself, which he through the eternal Spirit once offered up unto God, hath fully satisfied the justice of his Father,[9] and purchased not only reconciliation, but an everlasting inheritance in the kingdom of heaven, for all those whom the Father hath given unto him.[10]

VI. Although the work of redemption was not actually wrought by Christ till after his incarnation, yet the virtue, efficacy, and benefits thereof were communicated unto the elect, in all ages successively from the beginning of the world, in and by those promises, types,

pore[1] *vero perpessiones quam maxime dolorificas; crucifixus est, ac mortuus;*[2] *sepultus est, mansitque sub mortis potestate; nec tamen ullam vidit corruptionem.*[3] *Tertio die surrexit a mortuis,*[4] *cum eodem in quo passus fuerat corpore,*[5] *cum quo etiam ascendit in cœlum, ibique sedens ad dextram Patris*[6] *intercedit,*[7] *rediturus inde in consummatione mundi, ad homines angelosque judicandum.*[8]

V. *Dominus Jesus obedientia sua perfecta, suique ipsius sacrificio; quod per æternum Spiritum Deo semel obtulit, justitiæ Patris plene satisfecit,*[9] *ac omnibus ei a Patre datis non modo reconciliationem; verum etiam æternam hæreditatem in regno cœlorum acquisivit.*[10]

VI. *Quamvis redemptionis opus non nisi post incarnationem ejus, a Christo quidem actu effectum fuerit, vis tamen ejus, efficacia, et beneficia per omnia iam inde a mundi primordiis elapsa secula electis sunt communicata, in et per promissiones illas, typos, et sacri-*

---

[1] Matt., chaps. xxvi. xxvii.
[2] Phil. ii. 8.
[3] Acts ii. 23, 24, 27; xiii. 37; Rom. vi. 9.
[4] 1 Cor. xv. 3, 4.
[5] John xx. 25, 27.
[6] Mark xvi. 19.
[7] Rom. viii. 34; Heb. ix. 24; vii. 25.

[8] Rom. xiv. 9, 10; Acts i. 11; x. 42; Matt. xiii. 40–42; Jude 6; 2 Pet. ii. 4.
[9] Rom. v. 19; Heb. ix. 14, 16; x. 14; Eph. v. 2; Rom. iii. 25, 26.
[10] Dan. ix. 24, 26; Col. i. 19, 20; Eph. i. 11, 14; John xvii. 2; Heb. ix. 12, 15.

and sacrifices, wherein he was revealed, and signified to be the seed
of the woman which should bruise
the serpent's head, and the lamb
slain from the beginning of the
world, being yesterday and to-day
the same and forever.[1]

VII. Christ, in the work of mediation, acteth according to both
natures; by each nature doing that
which is proper to itself;[2] yet, by
reason of the unity of the person,
that which is proper to one nature
is sometimes, in Scripture, attributed to the person denominated
by the other nature.[3]

VIII. To all those for whom
Christ hath purchased redemption
he doth certainly and effectually
apply and communicate the same;[4]
making intercession for them,[5] and
revealing unto them, in and by the
Word, the mysteries of salvation;[6]
effectually persuading them by his
Spirit to believe and obey; and
governing their hearts by his Word
and Spirit;[7] overcoming all their
enemies by his almighty power and
wisdom, in such manner and ways
as are most consonant to his wonderful and unsearchable dispensation.[8]

ficia, quibus revelatum erat et sig-
nificatum hunc esse semen illud
mulieris, quod contriturum erat
serpentis caput, agnumque illum
mactatum ab initio mundi; ut qui
heri ac hodie idem est et in sempi-
ternum.[1]

VII. *Christus in opere Media-*
torio agit secundum utramque na-
turam, id agens per utramvis, quod
eidem proprium est,[2] *nonnunquam*
tamen fit propter personæ unita-
tem ut quod uni naturæ propri-
um est, personæ ab altera natura
denominatæ in Scriptura tribua-
tur.[3]

VIII. *Pro quibus Christus re-*
demptionem acquisivit, iis omnibus
certo quidem ac efficaciter eam ap-
plicat impertitque,[4] *pro eis inter-*
cedens,[5] *eisque in verbo et per ver-*
bum revelans mysterium salutis,[6]
per Spiritum suum eis ut credere
velint ac obedire persuadens effica-
citer,[7] *eorumque gubernans corda*
verbo suo spirituque; sed et vi sua
omnipotenti, ac sapientia debellans
omnes eorum hostes, iis autem mo-
dis mediisque quæ admirabili et
inscrutabili ejus dispensationi sunt
maxime consentanea.[8]

---

[1] Gal. iv. 4, 5; Gen. iii. 15; Rev. xiii. 8; Heb. xiii. 8.
[2] Heb. ix. 14; 1 Pet. iii. 18.
[3] Acts xx. 28; John iii. 13; 1 John iii. 16.
[4] John vi. 37, 39; x. 15, 16.
[5] 1 John ii. 1, 2; Rom. viii. 34.
[6] John xv. 13, 15; Eph. i. 7–9; John xvii. 6.
[7] John xiv. 16; Heb. xii. 2; 2 Cor. iv. 13; Rom. viii. 9, 14; xv. 18, 19; John xvii. 17.
[8] Psa. cx. 1; 1 Cor. xv. 25, 26; Mal. iv. 2, 3; Col. ii. 15.

Chapter IX.
Of Free-will.

I. God hath endued the will of man with that natural liberty, that [1] is neither forced nor by any absolute necessity of nature determined to good or evil. [2]

II. Man, in his state of innocency, had freedom and power to will and to do that which is good and well-pleasing to God, but yet mutably, so that he might fall from it. [4]

III. Man, by his fall into a state of sin, hath wholly lost all ability of will to any spiritual good accompanying salvation; [5] so as a natural man, being altogether averse from that good, [6] and dead in sin, [7] is not able, by his own strength, to convert himself, or to prepare himself thereunto. [8]

IV. When God converts a sinner, and translates him into the state of grace, he freeth him from his natural bondage under sin, [9] and by his grace alone enables him freely to will and to do that which is spiritually good; [10] yet so

Cap. IX.
De libero arbitrio.

I. *Eam humanæ voluntati naturalem Deus indidit libertatem, ut nec cogatur unquam, neque absoluta ulla naturæ necessitate ad bonum aut malum determinetur.* [2]

II. *Homo in statu innocentiæ libertatem habuit ac potentiam, quod bonum erat Deoque gratum volendi agendique;* [3] *mutabiliter tamen, ita ut illa potuerit excidere.* [4]

III. *Homo per lapsum suum in statum peccati, potentiam omnem quam habuerat voluntas ejus ad bonum aliquod spirituale et saluti contiguum amisit penitus;* [5] *adeo sane ut naturalis homo, utpote ab ejusmodi bono abhorrens prorsus,* [6] *ac in peccato mortuus,* [7] *non possit unquam suis ipsius viribus convertere semet, sed ne quidem ad conversionem se vel præparare.* [8]

IV. *Quandocunque Deus convertit ac in statum gratiæ transfert peccatorem, eundem eximit naturali sua sub peccato servitute,* [9] *solaque gratia sua potentem reddit ad spirituale bonum volendum præstandumque;* [10] *ita tamen ut propter*

---

[1] [Am. ed. inserts *it.*]
Matt. xvii. 12; James i. 14; **Deut. xxx.** 19; [Am. ed. John v. 40].
[3] Eccles. vii. 29; Gen. i. 26.
[4] Gen. ii. 16, 17; iii. 6.
[5] Rom. v. 6; viii. 7; John xv. 5.

[6] Rom. iii. 10, 12.
[7] Eph. ii. 1, 5; Col. ii. 13.
[8] John vi. 44, 65; 1 Cor. ii. 14; Eph. ii. 2–5; Titus iii. 3–5.
[9] Col. i. 13; John viii. 34, 36.
[10] Phil. ii. 13; Rom. vi. 18, 22.

as that, by reason of his remaining corruption, he doth not perfectly, nor only, will that which is good, but doth also will that which is evil.[1]

V. The will of man is made perfectly and immutably free to good alone, in the state of glory only.[2]

manentem adhuc in eo corruptionem, bonum nec perfecte velit; neque id tantummodo, verum etiam quandoque malum.[1]

V. *Voluntas humana perfecte ac immutabiliter libera ad bonum solum redditur non nisi in statu gloriæ.*[2]

Chapter X.
Of Effectual Calling.

I. All those whom God hath predestinated unto life, and those only, he is pleased, in his appointed and accepted time, effectually to call,[3] by his Word and Spirit,[4] out of that state of sin and death, in which they are by nature, to grace and salvation by Jesus Christ;[5] enlightening their minds, spiritually and savingly, to understand the things of God;[6] taking away their heart of stone, and giving unto them an heart of flesh;[7] renewing their wills, and by his almighty power determining them to that which is good,[8] and effectually drawing them to Jesus Christ;[9] yet so as they come most freely, being made willing by his grace.[10]

II. This effectual call is of God's

Cap. X.
De vocatione efficaci.

I. *Deus quos ad vitam prædestinavit omnes, eosque solos dignatur per verbum suum et spiritum*[3] *constituto suo acceptoque tempore vocare efficaciter*[4] *e statu illo peccati et mortis in quo sunt natura constituti, ad gratiam ac salutem per Jesum Christum;*[5] *idque mentes eorum illuminando, ut modo spirituali et salutari quæ Dei sunt intelligant;*[6] *tollendo eorum cor lapideum, donandoque eis cor carneum;*[7] *voluntates eorum renovando ac pro potentia sua omnipotente ad bonum determinando,*[8] *et ad Jesum Christum trahendo efficaciter;*[9] *ita tamen ut illi nihilominus liberrime veniant, volentes nempe facti per illius gratiam.*[10]

II. *Efficax hæc vocatio est a sola*

---

[1] Gal. v. 17; Rom. vii. 15, 18, 19, 21, 23.
[2] Eph. iv. 13; Heb. xii. 23; 1 John iii. 2; Jude 24.
[3] Rom. viii. 30; xi. 7; Eph. i. 10, 11.
[4] 2 Thess. ii. 13, 14; 2 Cor. iii. 3, 6.
[5] Rom. viii. 2; Eph. ii. 1–5; 2 Tim. i. 9, 10.

[6] Acts xxvi. 18; 1 Cor. ii. 10, 12; Eph. i. 17, 18.
[7] Ezek. xxxvi. 26.
[8] Ezek. xi. 19; Phil. ii. 13; Deut. xxx. 6; Ezek. xxxvi. 27.
[9] Eph. i. 19; John vi. 44, 45.
[10] Cant. i. 4; Psa. cx. 3; John vi. 37; Rom. vi. 16–18.

free and special grace alone, not from any thing at all foreseen in man;[1] who is altogether passive therein, until, being quickened and renewed by the Holy Spirit,[2] he is thereby enabled to answer this call, and to embrace the grace offered and conveyed in it.[3]

III. Elect infants, dying in infancy, are regenerated and saved by Christ through the Spirit,[4] who worketh when, and where, and how he pleaseth.[5] So also are all other elect persons, who are incapable of being outwardly called by the ministry of the Word.[6]

IV. Others, not elected, although they may be called by the ministry of the Word,[7] and may have some common operations of the Spirit,[8] yet they never truly come unto[9] Christ, and therefore can not be saved:[10] much less can men, not professing the Christian religion, be saved in any other way whatsoever, be they never so diligent to frame their lives according to the light of nature and the law of that religion they do profess;[11] and to assert and maintain that they may is

Dei gratia, gratuita illa et speciali; a nulla autem re in homine prævisa;[1] *qui in hoc negotio se habet omnino passive, donec per spiritum sanctum vivificatus ac renovatus,*[2] *potis inde factus sit vocationi huic respondere, gratiamque inibi oblatam et exhibitam amplexari.*[3]

III. *Electi infantes in infantia sua morientes regenerantur salvanturque a Christo per spiritum*[4] (*qui quando et ubi, et quo sibi placuerit modo operatur*),[5] *sicut et reliqui electi omnes, quotquot externæ vocationis per ministerium verbi sunt incapaces.*[6]

IV. *Alii autem, qui non electi sunt, ut ut verbi ministerio vocari possint,*[7] *communesque nonnullas operationes Spiritus experiri,*[8] *nunquam tamen vere ad Christum accedunt, proindeque nec salvari possunt.*[10] *Multo quidem minus poterunt illi, quotquot religionem Christianam non profitentur* (*summam licet operam navaverint moribus suis ad naturæ lumen, istiusque quam profitentur religionis legem componendis*), *extra hanc unicam viam salutem unquam obtinere.*[11] *Atque huic quidem contra-*

---

[1] 2 Tim. i. 9; Titus iii. 4, 5; Eph. ii. 4, 5, 8, 9; Rom. ix. 11.

[2] 1 Cor. ii. 14; Rom. viii. 7; Eph. ii. 5.

[3] John vi. 37; Ezek. xxxvi. 27; John v. 25.

[4] Luke xviii. 15, 16, and Acts ii. 38, 39, and John iii. 3, 5, and 1 John v. 12, and Rom. viii. 9, compared.

[5] John iii. 8.

[6] 1 John v. 12; Acts iv. 12.

[7] Matt. xxii. 14.

[8] Matt. vii. 22; xiii. 20, 21; Heb. vi. 4, 5.

[9] [Am. ed. *to.*]

[10] John vi. 64–66; viii. 24.

[11] Acts iv. 12; John xiv. 6; Eph. ii. 12; John iv. 22; xvii. 3.

very pernicious, and to be detested.[1]

CHAPTER XI.

Of Justification.

I. Those whom God effectually calleth he also freely justifieth;[2] not by infusing righteousness into them, but by pardoning their sins, and by accounting and accepting their persons as righteous: not for any thing wrought in them, or done by them, but for Christ's sake alone; nor[3] by imputing faith itself, the act of believing, or any other evangelical obedience to them, as their righteousness; but by imputing the obedience and satisfaction of Christ unto them,[4] they receiving and resting on him and his righteousness by faith; which faith they have not of themselves, it is the gift of God.[5]

II. Faith, thus receiving and resting on Christ and his righteousness, is the alone instrument of justification;[6] yet is it not alone in the person justified, but is ever accompanied with all other saving graces, and is no dead faith, but worketh by love.[7]

III. Christ, by his obedience and

rium statuere ac defendere, perniciosum admodum est ac detestandum.[1]

CAP. XI.

De Justificatione.

I. Quos Deus vocat efficaciter, eosdem etiam gratis justificat,[2] non quidem justitiam iis infundendo, sed eorum peccata condonando, personasque pro justis reputando atque acceptando; neque id certe propter quicquam aut in iis productum, aut ab iis præstitum, verum Christi solius ergo; eisque ad justitiam non fidem ipsam, non credendi actum, aut aliam quamcunque obedientiam evangelicam, verum obedientiam ac satisfactionem Christi imputando,[4] eum nempe recipientibus, eique ac justitiæ ejus per fidem innitentibus; quam illi fidem ex dono Dei, non a seipsis, habent.[5]

II. Fides hoc modo Christum recipiens, eique innitens ac justitiæ ejus, est justificationis unicum instrumentum;[6] in homine tamen justificato hæc non est solitaria, verum gratiis aliis omnibus salutaribus semper comitata; neque est hæc fides mortua, sed quæ per charitatem operatur.[7]

III. Qui hunc in modum justifi-

---

[1] 2 John 9–11; 1 Cor. xvi. 22; Gal. i. 6–8.
[2] Rom. viii. 30; iii. 24.
[3] [Am. ed. not.]
[4] Rcm. iv. 5–8; 2 Cor. v. 19, 21; Rom. iii. 22, 24, 25, 27, 28; Titus iii. 5, 7; Eph. i.

7; Jer. xxiii. 6; 1 Cor. i. 30, 31; Rom. v. 17–19.
[5] Acts x. 44; Gal. ii. 16; Phil. iii. 9; Acts xiii. 38, 39; Eph. ii. 7, 8.
[6] John i. 12; Rom. iii. 28; v. 1.
[7] James ii. 17, 22, 26; Gal. v. 6.

death, did fully discharge the debt of all those that are thus justified, and did make a proper, real, and full satisfaction to his Father's justice in their behalf.[1] Yet inasmuch as he was given by the Father for them,[2] and his obedience and satisfaction accepted in their stead,[3] and both freely, not for any thing in them, their justification is only of free grace;[4] that both the exact justice and rich grace of God might be glorified in the justification of sinners.[5]

IV. God did, from all eternity, decree to justify all the elect,[6] and Christ did, in the fullness of time, die for their sins, and rise again for their justification:[7] nevertheless, they are not justified until the Holy Spirit doth, in due time, actually apply Christ unto them.[8]

V. God doth continue to forgive the sins of those that are justified;[9] and although they can never fall from the state of justification,[10] yet they may by their sins fall under God's fatherly displeasure, and not have the light of his countenance restored unto them, until they humble them-

cantur, eorum omnium debita Christus per obedientiam suam mortemque prorsus dissolvit; eorumque vice justitiæ Patris sui realem, plenam, et proprie dictam satisfactionem præstitit.[1] Quum tamen non propter in iis quicquam, verum gratuito Pater cum Christum ipsum pro eis dederit,[2] tum obedientiam ejus ac satisfactionem tanquam eorum loco constituti[3] acceptaverit; omnino a gratia gratuita est eorum justificatio;[4] Quo nimirum Dei tum accurata justitia tum locuples gratia glorificata foret in justificatione peccatorum.[5]

IV. *Ab æterno decrevit Deus electos omnes justificare,[6] Christusque in temporis plenitudine mortuus est pro eorum peccatis, et in justificationem eorum resurrexit:[7] nihilo minus tamen justificati prius non sunt, quam Christum eis in tempore suo opportuno Spiritus Sanctus actu applicuerit.[8]*

V. *Perseverat Deus eorum peccata condonare quos semel justificavit,[9] quin et etiamsi excidere statu justificationis nunquam possint;[10] fieri tamen potest ut iræ Dei, paternæ quidem illi, per peccata sua se exponant, nec lumen paterni vultus prius sibi habeant restitutum, quam semet ipsos humiliaverint,*

---

[1] Rom. v. 8–10, 19; 1 Tim. ii. 5, 6; Heb. x. 10, 14; Dan. ix. 24, 26; Isa. liii. 4–6, 10–12.
[2] Rom. viii. 32.
[3] 2 Cor. v. 21; Matt. iii. 17; Eph. v. 2.
[4] Rom. iii. 24; Eph. i. 7.

[5] Rom. iii. 26; Eph. ii. 7.
[6] Gal. iii. 8; 1 Pet. i. 2, 19, 20; Rom. viii. 30.
[7] Gal. iv. 4; 1 Tim. ii. 6; Rom. iv. 25.
[8] Col. i. 21, 22; Gal. ii. 16; Titus iii. 4–7.
[9] Matt. vi. 12; 1 John i. 7, 9; ii. 1, 2.
[10] Luke xxii. 32; John x. 28; Heb. x. 14.

selves, confess their sins, beg pardon, and renew their faith and
repentance.[1]

VI. The justification of believers under the Old Testament was,
in all these respects, one and the
same with the justification of believers under the New Testament.[2]

*peccata agnoverint, imploraverint
veniam, fidem denique et pœnitentiam suam renovaverint.*[1]

*VI. Justificatio fidelium sub Ve-
tere ac Novo*[2] *Testamento quoad
isthæc omnia est una eademque.*[2]

Chapter XII.
Of Adoption.

All those that are justified God
vouchsafeth, in and for his only
Son Jesus Christ, to make partakers of the grace of adoption;[3]
by which they are taken into
the number, and enjoy the liberties and privileges of the children of God;[4] have his name put
upon them;[5] receive the Spirit of
adoption;[6] have access to the
throne of grace with boldness;[7]
are enabled to cry, Abba, Father;[8]
are pitied,[9] protected,[10] provided
for,[11] and chastened by him as by
a father;[12] yet never cast off,[13]
but sealed to the day of redemption,[14] and inherit the promises,[15] as
heirs of everlasting salvation.[16]

Cap. XII.
De Adoptione.

*Deus justificatos omnes dignatur
in filio suo unigenito Jesu Christo,
et propter eundem participes facere
gratiæ Adoptionis;*[3] *per quam in numerum filiorum Dei assumuntur, ta-
liumque immunitatibus ac privilegiis
potiuntur,*[4] *impositum sibi habent nomen Dei,*[5] *Spiritum adoptionis accipiunt,*[6] *aditum habent ad thronum
gratiæ cum confidentia,*[7] *potestatem
consequuntur clamandi Abba Pater,*[8]
commiserationem,[9] *tutelam,*[10] *et providentiam*[11] *sortiuntur; quin et ca-
stigationem Dei paternam experiuntur;*[12] *nunquam tamen abdicantur,*[13]
*verum in diem redemptionis consi-
gnati*[14] *promissiones obtinent hære-
ditario jure,*[15] *ut qui hæredes sunt
æternæ salutis.*[16]

---

[1] Psa. lxxxix. 31–33; li. 7–12; xxxii. 5;
   Matt. xxvi. 75; 1 Cor. xi. 30, 32; Luke
   i. 20.   [xiii. 8.
[2] Gal. iii. 9, 13, 14; Rom. iv. 22–24; Heb.
[3] Eph. i. 5; Gal. iv. 4, 5.
[4] Rom. viii. 17; John i. 12.
[5] Jer. xiv. 9; 2 Cor. vi. 18; Rev. iii. 12.
[6] Rom. viii. 15.
[7] Eph. iii. 12; Rom. v. 2.

[8] Gal. iv. 6.
[9] Psa. ciii. 13.
[10] Prov. xiv. 26.
[11] Matt. vi. 30, 32; 1 Pet. v. 7.
[12] Heb. xii. 6.
[13] Lam. iii. 31.
[14] Eph. iv. 30.
[15] Heb. vi. 12.
[16] 1 Pet. i. 3, 4; Heb. i. 14.

CHAPTER XIII.	CAP. XIII.
Of Sanctification.	*De Sanctificatione.*

I. They who are effectually called and regenerated, having a new heart and a new spirit created in them, are further sanctified, really and personally, through the virtue of Christ's death and resurrection,[1] by his Word and Spirit dwelling in them;[2] the dominion of the whole body of sin is destroyed,[3] and the several lusts thereof are more and more weakened and mortified,[4] and they more and more quickened and strengthened, in all saving graces,[5] to the practice of true holiness, without which no man shall see the Lord.[6]

II. This sanctification is throughout in the whole man,[7] yet imperfect in this life; there abideth still some remnants of corruption in every part,[8] whence ariseth a continual and irreconcilable war, the flesh lusting against the spirit, and the spirit against the flesh.[9]

III. In which war, although the remaining corruption for a time may much prevail,[10] yet, through the continual supply of strength from the sanctifying Spirit of

I. *Quotquot efficaciter vocantur, ac regenerantur, cor novum habentes novumque spiritum in se creatum, sunt virtute mortis et resurrectionis Christi*[1] *per verbum ejus spiritumque in eis inhabitantem*[2] *ulterius sanctificati, realiter quidem ac personaliter : totius corporis peccati dominium in eos destruitur,*[3] *ejusque variæ libidines debilitantur indies magis magisque ac mortificantur ;*[4] *illi interim magis magisque in omni gratia salutari vivificantur et corroborantur indies,*[5] *ad praxim veræ sanctimoniæ, qua quidem destitutus nemo unquam videbit Dominum.*[6]

II. *Universalis est hæc et per totum hominem diffusa sanctificatio,*[7] *verum in hac vita est imperfecta nonnullis corruptionis reliquiis adhuc in omni parte remanentibus,*[8] *unde bellum exoritur perpetuum et implacabile ; hinc carne adversus spiritum, illinc spiritu adversus carnem concupiscente.*[9]

III. *In quo quidem bello licet corruptio residua possit aliquandiu prævalere plurimum,*[10] *pars tamen regenita, sanctificante Christi spiritu perpetuas ferente suppetias,*

---

[1] 1 Cor. vi. 11; Acts xx. 32; Phil. iii. 10; Rom. vi. 5, 6.
[2] John xvii. 17; Eph. v. 26; 2 Thess. ii. 13.
[3] Rom. vi. 6, 14.
[4] Gal. v. 24; Rom. viii. 13.
[5] Col. i. 11; Eph. iii. 16–19.

[6] 2 Cor. vii. 1; Heb. xii. 14.
[7] 1 Thess. v. 23.
[8] 1 John i. 10; Rom. vii. 18, 23; Phil. iii. 12.
[9] Gal. v. 17; 1 Pet. ii. 11.
[10] Rom. vii. 23.

Christ, the regenerate part doth overcome;[1] and so the saints grow in grace,[2] perfecting holiness in the fear of God.[3]

Chapter XIV.
Of Saving Faith.

I. The grace of faith, whereby the elect are enabled to believe to the saving of their souls,[4] is the work of the Spirit of Christ in their hearts,[5] and is ordinarily wrought by the ministry of the Word;[6] by which also, and by the administration of the sacraments and prayer, it is increased and strengthened.[7]

II. By this faith a Christian believeth to be true whatsoever is revealed in the Word, for the authority of God himself speaking therein;[8] and acteth differently upon that which each particular passage thereof containeth; yielding obedience to the commands,[9] trembling at the threatenings,[10] and embracing the promises of God for this life and that which is to come.[11] But the principal acts of saving faith are accepting, receiving, and resting upon Christ alone

evadit victrix);[1] *adeoque sancti in gratia crescunt,*[2] *sanctitatem in timore Domini perficientes.*[3]

Cap. XIV.
De Fide salvifica.

I. *Gratia Fidei, qua electi credere valent ad animarum suarum salutem,*[4] *Spiritus Christi opus est in eorum cordibus operantis,*[5] *effectum plerumque verbi Dei ministerio,*[6] *quo eodem etiam, ut et administratione Sacramentorum atque ⸱⸱⸱ tione robur ei accedit ac incremen- tum.*[7]

II. *Hac Fide credit Christianus verum esse quicquid in verbo revelatur, propter authoritatem ipsius inibi loquentis Dei;*[8] *et varie quidem in illud agit tum obsequendo mandatis,*[9] *tum ad minas contremiscens,*[10] *tum etiam promissa Dei, seu praesentem hanc vitam seu futuram spectent, amplexando,*[11] *pro varia nempe ratione illarum rerum, quae in singulis verbi partibus continentur. Verum fidei salvificae actus illi sunt praecipui, Christi acceptatio et receptio, in eumque solum*

---

[1] Rom. vi. 14; 1 John v. 4; Eph. iv. 15, 16.

[2] 2 Pet. iii. 18; 2 Cor. iii. 18.

[3] 2 Cor. vii. 1.

[4] Heb. x. 39.

[5] 2 Cor. iv. 13; Eph. i. 17–19; ii. 8. Rom. x. 14, 17.

[7] 1 Pet. ii. 2; Acts xx. 32; Rom. iv. 11; Luke xvii. 5; Rom. i. 16, 17.

[8] John iv. 42; 1 Thess. ii. 13; 1 John v. 10; Acts xxiv. 14.

[9] Rom. xvi. 26.

[10] Isa. lxvi. 2.

[11] Heb. xi. 13; 1 Tim. iv. 8.

for justification, sanctification, and eternal life, by virtue of the covenant of grace.[1]

III. This faith is different in degrees, weak or strong;[2] may be often and many ways assailed and weakened, but gets the victory;[3] growing up in many to the attainment of a full assurance through Christ,[4] who is both the author and finisher of our faith.[5]

CHAPTER XV.

Of Repentance unto Life.

I. Repentance unto life is an evangelical grace,[6] the doctrine whereof is to be preached by every minister of the gospel, as well as that of faith in Christ.[7]

II. By it a sinner, out of the sight and sense, not only of the danger, but also of the filthiness and odiousness of his sins, as contrary to the holy nature and righteous law of God, and upon the apprehension of his mercy in Christ to such as are penitent, so grieves for and hates his sins as to turn from them all unto God,[8] purposing and endeavoring

recumbentia pro justificatione, sanctificatione, ipsaque adeo vita æterna, virtute fœderis gratiæ consequendis.[1]

III. *Fides hæc pro diversis ejus gradibus debilior est aut fortior;*[2] *impugnari quidem sæpenumero multisque modis ac debilitari potest, non ita tamen quin victrix evadat;*[3] *et quidem in multis ad plenam usque certitudinem per Christum adolescit,*[4] *qui fidei nostræ idem author est et consummator.*[5]

CAP. XV.

De resipiscentia ad vitam.

I. *Resipiscentia ad vitam est gratia Evangelica,*[6] *cuius quidem doctrina pariter ac illa de fide in Christum est a singulis ministris Evangelii prædicanda.*

II. *Per eam peccator ex inspectu sensuque non solum periculi verum etiam turpitudinis, ac naturæ peccatorum suorum prorsus abominandæ,*[7] *utpote sanctæ Dei naturæ, justæque legi adversantium, atque e perspecta ejus erga pœnitentes in Christo misericordia, ita peccata sua deflet ac detestatur, ut ab eis omnibus ad Deum convertatur*[8] *cum proposito conatuque in cunctis man-*

---

[1] John i. 12; Acts xvi. 31; Gal. ii. 20; Acts xv. 11.
[2] Heb. v. 13, 14; Rom. iv. 19, 20; Matt. vi. 30; viii. 10.
[3] Luke xxii. 31, 32; Eph. vi. 16; 1 John v. 4, 5.
[4] Heb. vi. 11, 12; x. 22; Col. ii. 2.
[5] Heb. xii. 2.
[6] Zech. xii. 10; Acts xi. 18.
[7] Luke xxiv. 47; Mark i. 15; Acts xx. 21.
[8] Ezek. xviii. 30, 31; xxxvi. 31; Isa. xxx. 22; Psa. li. 4; Jer. xxxi. 18, 19; Joel ii. 12, 13; Amos v. 15; Psa. cxix. 128; 2 Cor. vii. 11.

to walk with him in all the ways of his commandments.[1]

III. Although repentance be not to be rested in as any satisfaction for sin, or any cause of the pardon thereof,[2] which is the act of God's free grace in Christ;[3] yet is it of such necessity to all sinners that none may expect pardon without it.[4]

IV. As there is no sin so small but it deserves damnation,[5] so there is no sin so great that it can bring damnation upon those who truly repent.[6]

V. Men ought not to content themselves with a general repentance, but it is every man's duty to endeavor to repent of his particular sins particularly.[7]

VI. As every man is bound to make private confession of his sins to God, praying for the pardon thereof,[8] upon which, and the forsaking of them, he shall find mercy;[9] so he that scandalizeth his brother, or the Church of Christ, ought to be willing, by a private or public confession and sorrow for his sin, to declare his repent-

datorum ejus viis cum eodem ambulandi.[1]

III. *Etsi resipiscentiæ nobis fidendum non sit, ac si ea esset ulla aut pro peccatis satisfactio, aut causa remissionis peccatorum[2] (qui gratiæ Dei in Christo gratuitæ actus est),[3] est nihilominus cunctis peccatoribus usque adeo necessaria, ut sine ea nulla cuivis unquam remissio sit expectanda.[4]*

IV. *Quemadmodum nullum est peccatum adeo exiguum ut damnationem non mereatur,[5] ita neque magnum adeo peccatum ullum est, ut damnationem inferre possit vere pœnitentibus.[6]*

V. *In resipiscentia generali acquiescendum non est, verum ad id contendere tenetur quisque, ut singulorum suorum peccatorum quam particularem agat pœnitentiam.[7]*

VI. *Quemadmodum autem tenetur quivis peccata sua Deo privatim confiteri, et pro remissione illorum precibus contendere:[8] (quod si præstiterit et peccata simul dereliquerit, misericordiam consequetur)[9] ita qui fratri suo, aut Ecclesiæ Christi, scandalo fuerit, promptus et paratus esse debet qua confessione sive privata, sive etiam publica, qua de pec-*

---

[1] Psa. cxix. 6, 59, 106; Luke i. 6; 2 Kings xxiii. 25.
[2] Ezek. xxxvi. 31, 32; xvi. 61–63.
[3] Hos. xiv. 2, 4; Rom. iii. 24; Eph. i. 7.
[4] Luke xiii. 3, 5; Acts xvii. 30, 31.

[5] Rom. vi. 23; v. 12; Matt. xii. 36.
[6] Isa. lv. 7; Rom. viii. 1; Isa. i. 16, 18.
[7] Psa. xix. 13; Luke xix. 8; 1 Tim. i. 13, 15.
[8] Psa. li. 4, 5, 7, 9, 14; lxxii. 5, 6.
[9] Prov. xxviii. 13; 1 John i. 9.

ance to those that are offended,[1] who are thereupon to be reconciled to him, and in love to receive him.[2]

catis suis dolore, resipiscentiam suam eis quibus offendiculo fuerit declarare,[1] quo præstito illi redire cum eo in gratiam debent, eumque denuo cum charitate recipere.[2]

Chapter XVI.
Of Good Works.

I. Good works are only such as God hath commanded in his holy Word,[3] and not such as, without the warrant thereof, are devised by men out of blind zeal, or upon any pretense of good intention.[4]

II. These good works, done in obedience to God's commandments, are the fruits and evidences of a true and lively faith;[5] and by them believers manifest their thankfulness,[6] strengthen their assurance,[7] edify their brethren,[8] adorn the profession of the gospel,[9] stop the mouths of the adversaries,[10] and glorify God,[11] whose workmanship they are, created in Christ Jesus thereunto,[12] that, having their fruit unto holiness, they may have the end, eternal life.[13]

III. Their ability to do good

Cap. XVI.
De bonis operibus.

I. *Bona opera ea tantum sunt quæ in verbo suo sancto præcepit Deus;[3] minime autem ea quæ absque ulla illius authoritate, sunt ab hominibus excogitata, sive e cæco zelo id factum fuerit, seu bonæ intentionis prætextu quoviscunque.[4]*

II. *Bona hæc opera e conscientia mandatorum Dei præstita vivæ veræque fidei fructus sunt ac evidentiæ;[5] per hæc fideles gratitudinem suam manifestant,[6] de salute certitudinem suam augent,[7] fratres suos ædificant,[8] Evangelii professionem ornant,[9] obturant ora adversantibus,[10] ac Deum denique glorificant,[11] cuius opificium sunt in Jesu Christo ad hæc creati,[12] quo fructum habentes ad sanctimoniam, finem consequantur æternam vitam.[13]*

III. *Quod bonis operibus idonei*

---

[1] James v. 16; Luke xvii. 3, 4; Josh. vii. 19; Psa. li. throughout.
[2] 2 Cor. ii. 8; [Amer. ed. Gal. vi. 1, 2].
[3] Micah vi. 8; Rom. xii. 2; Heb. xiii. 21.
[4] Matt. xv. 9; Isa. xxix. 13; 1 Pet. i. 18; Rom. x. 2; John xvi. 2; 1 Sam. xv. 21–23.
[5] James ii. 18, 22.

[6] Psa. cxvi. 12, 13; 1 Pet. ii. 9.
[7] 1 John ii. 3, 5; 2 Pet. i. 5–10.
[8] 2 Cor. ix. 2; Matt. v. 16.
[9] Tit. ii. 5, 9–12; 1 Tim. vi. 1.
[10] 1 Pet. ii. 15.
[11] 1 Pet. ii. 12; Phil. i. 11; John xv. 8.
[12] Eph. ii. 10.
[13] Rom. vi. 22.

works is not at all of themselves, but wholly from the Spirit of Christ.[1] And that they may be enabled thereunto, besides the graces they have already received, there is required an actual influence of the same Holy Spirit to work in them to will and to do of his good pleasure;[2] yet are they not hereupon to grow negligent, as if they were not bound to perform any duty unless upon a special motion of the Spirit; but they ought to be diligent in stirring up the grace of God that is in them.[3]

IV. They who in their obedience attain to the greatest height which is possible in this life, are so far from being able to supererogate and to do more than God requires, as[4] that they fall short of much which in duty they are bound to do.[5]

V. We can not, by our best works, merit pardon of sin, or eternal life at the hand of God, by reason of the great disproportion that is between them and the glory to come, and the infinite distance that is between us and God, whom by them we can neither profit nor satisfy

sint præstandis omnino id a spiritu Christi est, nullatenus autem e seipsis.[1] Et quo eis præstandis pares fiant, præter habitus gratiæ iam infusos, ejusdem Spiritus sancti actualis porro requiritur influentia, qua nempe in iis operetur tum velle tum etiam efficere pro suo ipsius beneplacito:[2] sed neque tamen iis proinde socordiæ sese licet permittere; ac si nisi specialiter eos excitante Spiritu ad nulla pietatis officia præstanda tenerentur; verum sedulam debent navare operam suscitandæ illi quæ in iis est divinæ gratiæ.[3]

IV. Qui gradum obedientiæ summum quidem in hac vita possibilem assequuntur, tantum abest ut supererogare quicquam possint ac plus præstare quam quod Deus requisiverit, ut multum sane subsidant infra illud, quod ex officio præstare obligantur.[5]

V. Peccatorum veniam, aut vitam æternam de Deo mereri non valemus, ne optimis quidem operibus nostris; cum propter summam illam inter ea et futuram gloriam disparitatem; tum etiam propter infinitam distantiam quæ inter nos ac Deum intercedit; cui nos per illa nec pro-

---

[1] John xv. 4-6; Ezek. xxxvi. 26, 27.
[2] Phil. ii. 13; iv. 13; 2 Cor. iii. 5.
[3] Phil. ii. 12; Heb. vi. 11, 12; 2 Pet. i. 3, 5,

10, 11; Isa. lxiv. 7; 2 Tim. i. 6; Acts xxvi. 6, 7; Jude 20, 21.
[4] [Amer. ed. omits *as*.]　　　[Gal. v. 17.
[5] Luke xvii. 10; Neh. xiii. 22; Job ix. 2, 3;

for the debt of our former sins;[1] but when we have done all we can, we have done but our duty, and are unprofitable servants;[2] and because, as they are good, they proceed from his Spirit;[3] and as they are wrought by us, they are defiled and mixed with so much weakness and imperfection that they can not endure the severity of God's judgment.[4]

VI. Yet notwithstanding, the persons of believers being accepted through Christ, their good works also are accepted in him,[5] not as though they were in this life wholly unblamable and unreprovable in God's sight;[6] but that he, looking upon them in his Son, is pleased to accept and reward that which is sincere, although accompanied with many weaknesses and imperfections.[7]

VII. Works done by unregenerate men, although for the matter of them they may be things which God commands, and of good use both to themselves and others;[8]

desse quicquam possumus, neque pro antecedentium peccatorum nostrorum debito satisfacere ;[1] verum cum quantum possumus fecerimus, non nisi quod debemus præstiterimus, ac servi inutiles futuri sumus ;[2] tum denique quoniam a spiritu Dei in quantum bona sunt proficiscuntur,[3] ita vero sunt coinquinata, tantumque imperfectionis ac infirmitas admistum habent, prout a nobis efficiuntur, ut strictum Dei judicium non sint ferendo.[4]

VI. *Nihilominus tamen acceptis in gratiam per Christum fidelium personis, eorum etiam opera bona per eundem accepta sunt ;[5] non quod in hac vita sint omnis culpæ prorsus immunia, quæque in conspectu Dei nullam reprehensionem mereantur ;[6] verum quod illa respiciens in filio suo Deus, quod sincerum est, utcunque multis infirmitatibus ac imperfectionibus involutum, acceptare dignetur ac remunerari.[7]*

VII. *Opera nondum regenitorum, licet, quoad materiam præcepto divino conformia esse possint, sibique ipsis et aliis item utilia ;[8] cum tamen neque a corde profluant per fi-*

---

[1] Rom. iii. 20; iv. 2, 4, 6; Eph. ii. 8, 9; Titus iii. 5–7; Rom. viii. 18; Psa. xvi. 2; Job xxii. 2, 3; xxxv. 7, 8.
[2] Luke xvii. 10.
[3] Gal. v. 22, 23.
[4] Isa. lxiv. 6; Gal. v. 17; Rom. vii. 15, 18; Psa. cxliii. 2; cxxx. 3.

[5] Eph. i. 6; 1 Pet. ii. 5; Exod. xxviii. 38; Gen. iv. 4 with Heb. xi. 4.
[6] Job ix. 20; Psa. cxliii. 2.
[7] Heb. xiii. 20, 21; 2 Cor. viii. 12; Heb. vi. 10; Matt. xxv. 21, 23.
[8] 2 Kings x. 30, 31; 1 Kings xxi. 27, 29; Phil. i. 15, 16, 18.

yet because they proceed not from
a heart purified by faith,[1] nor are
done in a right manner, according
to the Word,[2] nor to a right end,
the glory of God;[3] they are therefore sinful, and can not please God,
or make a man meet to receive
grace from God.[4] And yet their
neglect of them is more sinful and
displeasing unto God.[5]

dem depurato,[1] *nec secundum verbum
eo quo par est præstentur modo,*[2] *sed
neque ad finem debitum, Dei nempe
gloriam, destinentur ;*[3] *sunt proinde
peccata, nec Deo grata esse possunt,
nec reddere quenquam valent idoneum ad gratiam a Deo recipiendum.*[4] *Ejusmodi tamen operum
neglectu, gravius quidem illi peccant Deumque offendunt vehementius.*[5]

CHAPTER XVII.

Of the Perseverance of the Saints.

I. They whom God hath accepted in his Beloved, effectually called and sanctified by his Spirit, can
neither totally nor finally fall away
from the state of grace; but shall
certainly persevere therein to the
end, and be eternally saved.[6]

II. This perseverance of the
saints depends, not upon their own
free-will, but upon the immutability
of the decree of election, flowing
from the free and unchangeable
love of God the Father;[7] upon the
efficacy of the merit and intercession of Jesus Christ;[8] the abiding

CAP. XVII.

De perseverantia Sanctorum.

I. *Quotquot Deus in dilecto suo
acceptavit, vocavit efficaciter ac per
Spiritum suum sanctificavit, non
possunt illi statu gratiæ aut finaliter excidere aut totaliter ; verum in eo ad finem usque certo
perseverabunt, ac salutem æternam
consequentur.*[6]

II. *Hæc autem sanctorum perseverantia, non pendet a libero ipsorum arbitrio, verum a decreti electionis immutabilitate (quod ex amore
Dei Patris fluxit, gratuito illo ac
immutabili),*[7] *a meriti Jesu Christi
ac intercessionis efficacia,*[8] *a Spiritus et seminis Dei in iis perman-*

---

[1] Gen. iv. 3–5 with Heb. xi. 4, 6.
[2] 1 Cor. xiii. 3; Isa. i. 12.
[3] Matt. vi. 2, 5, 16.
[4] Hag. ii. 14; Titus i. 15; Amos v. 21, 22;
	Hos. i. 4; Rom. ix. 16; Titus iii. 5.
[5] Psa. xiv. 4; xxxvi. 3; Job xxi. 14, 15;
	Matt. xxv. 41–45; xxiii. 23.

[6] Phil. i. 6; 2 Pet. i. 10; John x. 28, 29;
	1 John iii. 9; 1 Pet. i. 5, 9; [Am. ed. Job
	xvii. 9].
[7] 2 Tim. ii. 18, 19; Jer. xxxi. 3.
[8] Heb. x. 10, 14; xiii. 20, 21; ix. 12–15;
	Rom. viii. 33, to the end; John xvii. 11,
	24; Luke xxii. 32; Heb. vii. 25.

of the Spirit and of the seed of God within them;[1] and the nature of the covenant of grace:[2] from all which ariseth also the certainty and infallibility thereof.[3]

III. Nevertheless they may, through the temptations of Satan and of the world, the prevalency of corruption remaining in them, and the neglect of the means of their preservation, fall into grievous sins;[4] and for a time continue therein:[5] whereby they incur God's displeasure,[6] and grieve his Holy Spirit;[7] come to be deprived of some measure of their graces and comforts;[8] have their hearts hardened,[9] and their consciences wounded;[10] hurt and scandalize others,[11] and bring temporal judgments upon themselves.[12]

sione;[1] *a natura denique fœderis gratiæ;*[2] *e quibus omnibus etiam emergit certitudo ejusdem et infallibilitas.*[3]

III. *Nihilo tamen minus fieri potest ut iidem illi, qua Satanæ mundique tentatione, qua manentis adhuc in iis corruptionis prævalentia, et neglectu mediorum conservationis suæ, in peccata gravia incidant,*[4] *in eisque ad tempus commorentur;*[5] *unde iram Dei sibi ipsis contrahunt,*[6] *ejusque Spiritum Sanctum contristant,*[7] *gratias suas et consolationes quadantenus et quoad gradus nonnullos amittunt,*[8] *corda sibi habent indurata,*[9] *et vulneratas conscientias;*[10] *aliis nocumento sunt et offendiculo,*[11] *sibimet ipsis denique accersunt judicia Dei temporalia.*[12]

Chapter XVIII.
Of the Assurance of Grace and Salvation.

I. Although hypocrites and other unregenerate men may vainly deceive themselves with false hopes and carnal presumptions of being in the favor of God and estate of salvation,[13] which hope of theirs

Cap. XVIII.
De certitudine gratiæ et salutis.

I. *Quamvis fieri potest ut hypocritæ aliique homines non regeniti spe vana falsisque (pro corruptæ naturæ more) opinionibus præsumptis, se decipiant, favorem Dei, statumque salutis sibi falso arrogantes;*[13] *quæ il-*

---

[1] John xiv. 16, 17; 1 John ii. 27; iii. 9.
[2] Jer. xxxii. 40; [Am. ed. Heb. viii. 10–12].
[3] John x. 28; 2 Thess. iii. 3; 1 John ii. 19; [Am. ed. 1 Thess. v. 23, 24].
[4] Matt. xxvi. 70, 72, 74.
[5] Psa. li. title and verse 14; [Am. ed. 2 Sam. xii. 9, 13].
[6] Isa. lxiv. 5, 7, 9; 2 Sam. xi. 27.
[7] Eph. iv. 30.

[8] Psa. li. 8, 10, 12; Rev. ii. 4; Cant. v. 2, 3, 4, 6.
[9] Isa. xxxvi. 17; Mark vi. 52; xvi. 14; [Am. ed. Psa. xcv. 8].
[10] Psa. xxxii. 3, 4; li. 8.
[11] 2 Sam. xii. 14.
[12] Psa. lxxxix. 31, 32; 1 Cor. xi. 32.
[13] Job viii. 13, 14; Micah iii. 11; Deut. xxix. 9; John viii. 41.

shall perish:[1] yet such as truly believe in the Lord Jesus, and love him in sincerity, endeavoring to walk in all good conscience before him, may in this life be certainly assured that they are in a state of grace,[2] and may rejoice in the hope of the glory of God, which hope shall never make them ashamed.[3]

II. This certainty is not a bare conjectural and probable persuasion, grounded upon a fallible hope;[4] but an infallible assurance of faith, founded upon the divine truth of the promises of salvation,[5] the inward evidence of those graces unto which these promises are made,[6] the testimony of the Spirit of adoption witnessing with our spirits that we are the children of God:[7] which Spirit is the earnest of our inheritance, whereby we are sealed to the day of redemption.[8]

III. This infallible assurance doth not so belong to the essence of faith, but that a true believer may wait long, and conflict with many difficulties before he be partaker of it:[9] yet, being enabled by the Spirit to know the things which are freely given him of God, he

lorum spes peribit:[1] qui tamen in Dominum Jesum vere credunt, eumque sincere diligunt, studentes coram ipso in omni bona conscientia ambulare; evadere possunt in hac vita certi se in statu gratiæ esse constitutos;[2] quin etiam lætari possunt spe gloriæ Dei, quæ quidem spes nunquam eos pudefaciet.[3]

II. Hæc certitudo non est persuasio mere conjecturalis et probabilis, innixa spe fallaci;[4] verum infallibilis quædam fidei certitudo, fundamentum habens divinam promissionum salutis veritatem;[5] gratiarum, quibus promissiones illæ fiunt internam evidentiam;[6] testimonium denique spiritus adoptionis una cum spiritibus nostris testificantis nos esse filios Dei;[7] qui quidem spiritus arrhabo est hæreditatis nostræ, quo in diem redemtionis sigillamur.[8]

III. Hæc certitudo infallibilis, non ita spectat essentiam fidei, quin vere fidelis expectare quandoque diutius, et cum variis difficultatibus confligere prius possit, quam illius compos fiat,[9] verum poterit idem ordinariorum usu debito mediorum, absque revelatione ulla extraordinaria

---

[1] Matt. vii. 22, 23; [Am. ed. Job viii. 13].
[2] 1 John ii. 3; iii. 14, 18, 19, 21, 24; v. 13.
[3] Rom. v. 2, 5.
[4] Heb. vi. 11, 19.
[5] Heb. vi. 17, 18.

[6] 2 Pet. i. 4, 5, 10, 11; 1 John ii. 3; iii. 14; 2 Cor. i. 12.
[7] Rom. viii. 15, 16.
[8] Eph. i. 13, 14; iv. 30; 2 Cor. i. 21, 22.
[9] 1 John v. 13; Isa. l. 10; Mark ix. 24; Psa. lxxxviii. throughout; lxxvii. to ver. 12.

may, without extraordinary revelation, in the right use of ordinary means, attain thereunto.[1] And therefore it is the duty of every one to give all diligence to make his calling and election sure;[2] that thereby his heart may be enlarged in peace and joy in the Holy Ghost, in love and thankfulness to God, and in strength and cheerfulness in the duties of obedience, the proper fruits of this assurance:[3] so far is it from inclining men to looseness.[4]

IV. True believers may have the assurance of their salvation divers ways shaken, diminished, and intermitted; as, by negligence in preserving of it; by falling into some special sin, which woundeth the conscience, and grieveth the Spirit; by some sudden or vehement temptation; by God's withdrawing the light of his countenance, and suffering even such as fear him to walk in darkness and to have no light:[5] yet are they never utterly destitute of that seed of God, and life of faith, that love of Christ and the brethren, that sincerity of heart and conscience of duty, out

eam adipisci,[1] *spiritu nempe quæ Deus illi gratuito donaverit cognoscendi facultatem subministrante. Proindeque tenetur quisque, quo vocationem suam sibi et electionem certam faciat, omnem adhibere diligentiam,*[2] *unde cor suum habeat pace et gaudio in spiritu sancto, in Deum amore et gratitudine, in actibus observantiæ robore et alacritate dilatatum ; qui certitudinus huius fructus proprii sunt ac genuini.*[3] *Tantum abest ut homines inde ad omnem nequitiam discingantur.*[4]

IV. *Certitudo salutis vere fidelibus multifariam concuti potest et imminui imo et quandoque interrumpi ; conservandi scilicet eam incuria ; lapsu in peccatum aliquod insigne, quod conscientiam vulnerat, spiritumque contristat ; tentatione aliqua vehementi ac subitanea ; uti etiam Deo vultus sui lumen subducente, ac permittente ut vel illi qui ipsum timent in tenebris ambulent omni prorsus lumine viduati:*[5] *nunquam tamen destituuntur penitus illo Dei semine vitaque fidei. Christi illa fratrumque dilectione, ea sinceritate cordis et pietatis officia præstandi conscientia ; unde per*

---

[1] 1 Cor. ii. 12 ; 1 John iv. 13 ; Heb. vi. 11, 12 ; Eph. iii. 17–19.

[2] 2 Pet. i. 10.

[3] Rom. v. 1, 2, 5 ; Rom. xiv. 17 ; xv. 13 ; Eph. i. 3, 4 ; Psa. iv. 6, 7 ; cxix. 32.

1 John ii. 1, 2 ; Rom. vi. 1, 2 ; Titus ii. 11, 12,

14 ; 2 Cor. vii. 1 ; Rom. viii. 1, 12· John iii. 2, 3 ; Psa. cxxx. 4 ; 1 John ∧ 6, 7.

[5] Cant. v. 2, 3, 6 ; Psa. li. 8, 12, 14 ; Eph. iv. 30, 31 ; Psa. lxxvii. 1–10 ; Matt. xxvi. 69–72 ; Psa. xxxi. 22 ; lxxxviii. throughout ; Isa. l. 10.

of which, by the operation of the Spirit, this assurance may in due time be revived,[1] and by the which, in the mean time, they are supported from utter despair.[2]

Chapter XIX.
Of the Law of God.

I. God gave to Adam a law, as a covenant of works, by which he bound him and all his posterity to personal, entire, exact, and perpetual obedience; promised life upon the fulfilling, and threatened death upon the breach of it; and endued him with power and ability to keep it.[3]

II. This law, after his fall, continued to be a perfect rule of righteousness; and, as such, was delivered by God upon mount Sinai in ten commandments, and written in two tables;[4] the first four commandments containing our duty towards God, and the other six our duty to man.[5]

III. Beside this law, commonly called moral, God was pleased to give to the people of Israel, as a Church under age, ceremonial laws, containing several typical ordi-

operationem spiritus eadem illa certitudo tempestive possit reviviscere:[1] quibusque interim ne prorsus in desperationem ruant suffulciuntur.[2]

Cap. XIX.
De Lege Dei.

I. *Deus Adamo legem dedit ut fœdus operum, quo cum illum ipsum tum posteros ejus omnes, ad obedientiam personalem, integram, exquisitam simul et perpetuam obligavit, pollicitus vitam si observarent, violatoribus autem mortem interminatus; eundemque potentia et viribus imbuit, quibus par esset illam observando.*[3]

II. *Lex ista post lapsum non desiit esse justitiæ regula perfectissima; quo etiam nomine a Deo est in monte Sinai tradita, tabulis duabus descripta, decem præceptis comprehensa;[4] quorum quatuor prima officium nostrum erga Deum, sex autem reliqua nostrum erga homines officium complectuntur.*[5]

III. *Præter autem hanc legem, quæ moralis vulgo audit, visum est Deo ut populo Israelitico tanquam Ecclesiæ minorenni leges daret ceremoniales instituta typica multifaria*

---

[1] 1 John iii. 9; Luke xxii. 32; Job xiii. 15; Psa. lxxiii. 15; li. 8, 12; Isa. l. 10.

[2] Micah vii. 7–9; Jer. lii. 40; Isa. liv. 7–10; Psa. xxii. 1; lxxxviii. throughout.

[3] Gen. i. 26, 27, with Gen. ii. 17; Rom. ii. 14,

15; x. 5; v. 12, 19; Gal. iii. 10, 12; Eccles. vii. 29; Job xxviii. 28.

[4] James i. 25; ii. 8, 10–12; Rom. xiii. 8, 9; Deut. v. 32; x. 4; Exod. xxxiv. 1; [Am. ed. Rom. iii. 19].

[5] Matt. xxii. 37–40; [Am. ed. Exod. xx. 3–18].

nances, partly of worship, prefigur-
ing Christ, his graces, actions, sufferings, and benefits;[1] and partly
holding forth divers instructions of
moral duties.[2] All which ceremonial laws are now abrogated under
the New Testament.[3]

IV. To them also, as a body politic, he gave sundry judicial laws,
which expired together with the
state of that people, not obliging
any other, now, further than the
general equity thereof may require.[4]

V. The moral law doth forever
bind all, as well justified persons as
others, to the obedience thereof;[5]
and that not only in regard of the
matter contained in it, but also in
respect of the authority of God the
Creator who gave it.[6] Neither doth
Christ in the gospel any way dissolve, but much strengthen, this obligation.[7]

VI. Although true believers be
not under the law as a covenant of
works, to be thereby justified or
condemned;[8] yet is it of great use
to them, as well as to others; in
that, as a rule of life, informing
them of the will of God and their

continentes ; partim de cultu, Christi gratias, actiones, perpessiones ac
beneficia præfigurantia ;[1] partim
autem de moralibus officiis institu-
tiones varias exhibentia.[2] Quæ leges
ceremoniales omnes hodie sub novo
instrumento sunt abrogatæ.[3]

IV. Iisdem etiam tanquam corpori politico leges multas dedit ju-
diciales, quæ una cum istius populi
politeia expirarunt, nullos hodie
alios obligantes supra quod generalis et communis earum æquitas po-
stularit.[4]

V. Lex moralis omnes tam justificatos quam alios quosvis perpetuo li-
gat ad obedientiam illi exhibendam ;[5]
neque id quidem solummodo vi ma-
teriæ quæ in illa continetur, verum
etiam virtute authoritatis eandem
constituentis creatoris Dei ;[6] neque
sane hoc ejus vinculum in evangelio
ulla ratione dissolvit Christus, verum idem plurimum confirmavit.[7]

VI. Quamvis vere fideles non sint
sub lege tanquam sub operum fœdere,
unde aut justificari possint aut condemnari :[8] est tamen ea illis non
minus quam aliis vehementer utilis,
ut quæ quum sit vitæ norma, illos
voluntatem divinam suumque offi-

---

[1] Heb. ix.; x. 1; Gal. iv. 1–3; Col. ii. 17.
[2] 1 Cor. v. 7; 2 Cor. vi. 17; Jude 23.
[3] Col. ii. 14, 16, 17; Dan. ix. 27; Eph. ii. 15, 16.
[4] Exod. xxi.; xxii. 1–29; Gen. xlix. 10, with
   1 Pet. ii. 13, 14; Matt. v. 17, with vers.
   38, 39; 1 Cor. ix. 8–10.

[5] Rom. xiii. 8–10; Eph. vi. 2; 1 John ii. 3, 4,
   7, 8; [Am. ed. Rom. iii. 31, and vi. 15].
[6] James ii. 10, 11.
[7] Matt. v. 17–19; James ii. 8; Rom. iii. 31.
[8] Rom. vi. 14; Gal. ii. 16; iii. 13; iv. 4, 5;
   Acts xiii. 39; Rom. viii. 1.

duty, it directs and binds them to walk accordingly;[1] discovering also the sinful pollutions of their nature, hearts, and lives;[2] so as, examining themselves thereby, they may come to further conviction of, humiliation for, and hatred against sin;[3] together with a clearer sight of the need they have of Christ, and the perfection of his obedience.[4] It is likewise of use to the regenerate, to restrain their corruptions, in that it forbids sin;[5] and the threatenings of it serve to show what even their sins deserve, and what afflictions in this life they may expect for them, although freed from the curse thereof threatened in the law.[6] The promises of it, in like manner, show them God's approbation of obedience, and what blessings they may expect upon the performance thereof;[7] although not as due to them by the law as a covenant of works:[8] so as a man's doing good, and refraining from evil, because the law encourageth to the one, and deterreth from the other, is no evidence of his being under the law, and not under grace.[9]

cium edocendo dirigit simul et obligat ad consentanee ambulandum;[1] ipsisque patere facit naturœ, cordis, vitœque suœ nefaria inquinamenta:[2] adeo ut ad illam semet exigentes, cum peccati ulterius convinci, pro eodem humiliari, ac ejusdem odio inflammari possint;[3] tum vero etiam ut perspicere possint evidentius quam plane necessarius eis Christus, quamque perfecta sit ejusdem obedientia.[4] Verum ulterius etiam regenitis ea utilis esse possit, in quantum nempe corruptiones eorum peccata prohibendo coërcet,[5] graviter autem interminando indicat tum quid vel eorum peccata commeruerint, tum etiam quas ea propter in hac vita afflictiones expectare possint, utcunque ab earum maledictione, quam lex minatur, liberentur.[6] Quinetiam promissiones ejus demonstrant iis obedientia Deo quam accepta sit et approbata; quasque illa prœstita benedictiones[7] (licet non tanquam lege debitas ex operum fœdere)[8] possint illi expectare. Adeo ut quod quis bonum prœstet invitante lege, a malo autem abhorreat lege deterritus, nullo prorsus argumento sit, eum sub lege esse, non vero sub gratia constitutum.[9]

---

[1] Rom. vii. 12, 22, 25; Psa. cxix. 4–6; 1 Cor. vii. 19; Gal. v. 14, 16, 18–23.
[2] Rom. vii. 7; iii. 20.
[3] James i. 23–25; Rom. vii. 9, 14, 24.
[4] Gal. iii. 24; Rom. vii. 24, 25; viii. 3, 4.
[5] James ii. 11; Psa. cxix. 101, 104, 128.
[6] Ezra ix. 13, 14; Psa. lxxxix. 30–34.

[7] Lev. xxvi. 1, 10, 14, with 2 Cor. vi. 16, Eph. vi. 2, 3; Psa. xxxvii. 11 with Matt. v. 5; Psa. xix. 11.
[8] Gal. ii. 16; Luke xvii. 10.
[9] Rom. vi. 12, 14; 1 Pet. iii. 8–12 with Psa. xxxiv. 12–16; Heb. xii. 28, 29.

VII. Neither are the forementioned uses of the law contrary to the grace of the gospel, but do sweetly comply with it :[1] the Spirit of Christ subduing and enabling the will of man to do that freely and cheerfully which the will of God, revealed in the law, requireth to be done.[2]

VII. *Neque interim Legis usus isti iam memorati, Evangelii gratiæ adversantur, sed cum eadem conspirant suaviter,*[1] *voluntatem humanam ita subjugante ac imbuente Christi Spiritu, ut idem illud præstare valeat spontanee ac alacriter, quod ab illa exigit voluntas Dei in lege sua revelata.*[2]

Chapter XX.

Of Christian Liberty, and Liberty of Conscience.

Cap. XX.

De Libertate Christiana deque Libertate Conscientiæ.

I. The liberty which Christ hath purchased for believers under the gospel consists in their freedom from the guilt of sin, the condemning wrath of God, the curse of the moral law ;[3] and in their being delivered from this present evil world, bondage to Satan, and dominion of sin,[4] from the evil of afflictions, the sting of death, the victory of the grave, and everlasting damnation ;[5] as also in their free access to God,[6] and their yielding obedience unto him, not out of slavish fear, but a child-like love and[7] willing mind.[8] All which were common also to believers under the law ;[9] but under the New Testament the liberty of Christians is further enlarged in

I. *Libertas quam Christus acquisivit fidelibus sub Evangelio in eo sita est, quod a reatu peccati, ab ira Dei condemnante, a legis Moralis maledictione immunes fiant,*[3] *quod a præsenti malo seculo, a dura Satanæ servitute, dominioque peccati :*[4] *ab afflictionum malo, ab aculeo mortis, a sepulchri victoria ab æterna denique damnatione*[5] *liberentur ; Quodque libere eis liceat ad Deum accedere :*[6] *eique non e metu servile, verum e filiali dilectione, promtoque animo præbere valeant obedientiam.*[8] *Atque hæc quidem omnia cum fidelibus sub lege habent communia.*[9] *Verum sub Novo Testamento ulterius adhuc se extendit libertas Christiana ; in quantum*

---

[1] Gal. iii. 21 ; [Am. ed. Titus ii. 11–14].

[2] Ezek. xxxvi. 27 ; Heb. viii. 10 with Jer. xxxi. 33.

[3] Titus ii. 14 ; 1 Thess. i. 10 ; Gal. iii. 13.

[4] Gal. i. 4 ; Col. i. 13 ; Acts xxvi. 18 ; Rom. vi. 14.

[5] Rom. viii. 28 ; Psa. cxix. 71 ; 1 Cor. xv. 54–57 ; Rom. viii. 1.

[6] Rom. v. 1, 2.

[7] [Am. ed. inserts a after and.]

[8] Rom. viii. 14, 15 ; 1 John iv. 18.

[9] Gal. iii. 9, 14.

their freedom from the yoke of the ceremonial law, to which the Jewish Church was subjected;[1] and in greater boldness of access to the throne of grace,[2] and in fuller communications of the free Spirit of God, than believers under the law did ordinarily partake of.[3]

II. God alone is Lord of the conscience,[4] and hath left it free from the doctrines and commandments of men which are in any thing contrary to his Word, or beside it in matters of faith or worship.[5] So that to believe such doctrines, or to obey such commands[6] out of conscience, is to betray true liberty of conscience;[7] and the requiring of[8] an implicit faith, and an absolute and blind obedience, is to destroy liberty of conscience, and reason also.[9]

III. They who, upon pretense of Christian liberty, do practice any sin, or cherish any lust, do thereby destroy the end of Christian liberty; which is, that, being delivered out of the hands of our enemies, we might serve the Lord without fear, in holiness and righteousness before him, all the days of our life.[10]

nempe Legis ceremonialis jugo, cui subjecta erat Ecclesia Judaica, eximuntur;[1] majoremque confidentiam ad thronum gratiæ accedendi,[2] sed et effusiorem gratuiti Spiritus Dei communicationem sunt consecuti, quam ordinarie sub Lege fideles participarunt.[3]

II. *Deus solus Dominus est conscientiæ,[4] quam certe exemit doctrinis et mandatis hominum, ubi aut verbo ejus adversantur, aut in rebus fidei et cultus quicquam ei superaddunt.[5] Unde qui ejusmodi aut doctrinas credunt, aut mandatis obtemperant, quasi ad id ex conscientia teneantur, veram ii conscientiæ libertatem produnt.[7] Qui autem vel fidem implicitam, vel obedientiam absolutam cæcamque exigunt, næ illi id agunt, ut cum conscientiæ, tum rationis etiam destruant libertatem.[9]*

III. *Qui sub prætextu Christianæ libertatis, cuivis aut cupiditati indulgent aut peccato assuescunt, eo ipso libertatis Christianæ finem corrumpunt; nempe ut e manibus inimicorum nostrorum liberati, Domino in sanctimonia et justitia coram ipso omnibus diebus vitæ nostræ absque metu serviamus.[10]*

---

[1] Gal. iv. 1–3, 6, 7; v. 1; Acts xv. 10, 11.
[2] Heb. iv. 14, 16; x. 19–22.
[3] John vii. 38, 39; 2 Cor. iii. 13, 17, 18.
[4] James iv. 12; Rom. xiv. 4.
[5] Acts iv. 19; v. 29; 1 Cor. vii. 23; Matt. xxiii. 8–10; 2 Cor. i. 24; Matt. xv. 9.
[6] [Am. ed. *commandments.*]

[7] Col. ii. 20–23; Gal. i. 10; v. 1; ii. 4, 5; Psa. [v. 1.
[8] [Am. ed. omits *of.*]
[9] Rom. x. 17; xiv. 23; Isa. viii. 20; Acts xvii. 11; John iv. 22; Hos. v. 11; Rev. xiii. 12, 16, 17; Jer. viii. 9.
[10] Gal. v. 13; 1 Pet. ii. 16; 2 Pet. ii. 19; John viii. 34; Luke i. 74, 75.

IV. And because the power[1] which God hath ordained, and the liberty which Christ hath purchased, are not intended by God to destroy, but mutually to uphold and preserve one another; they who, upon pretense of Christian liberty, shall oppose any lawful power, or the lawful exercise of it, whether it be civil or ecclesiastical, resist the ordinance of God.[2] And for their publishing of such opinions, or maintaining of such practices, as are contrary to the light of nature, or to the known principles of Christianity, whether concerning faith, worship, or conversation; or to the power of godliness; or such erroneous opinions or practices, as, either in their own nature, or in the manner of publishing or maintaining them, are destructive to the external peace and order which Christ hath established in the Church; they may lawfully be called to account, and proceeded against by the censures of the Church,[3] and by the power of the Civil Magistrate.[4 & 5]

IV. *Quoniam vero potestates quas Deus ordinavit, et libertas quam acquisivit Christus non in eum finem a Deo destinatæ sunt ut se mutuo perimant, verum ut se sustentent ac conservent invicem; Qui itaque sub libertatis Christianæ prætextu potestati cuivis legitimæ (civilis sit sive Ecclesiastica) aut legitimo ejusdem exercitio contraiverint, ordinationi divinæ resistere censendi sunt,[2] Quique vel ejusmodi opiniones publicaverint, praxesve defenderint, quæ lumini naturæ, aut religionis Christianæ de fide, de cultu, aut moribus principiis notis, aut pietatis denique vi ac efficaciæ adversantur; vel ejusmodi opiniones praxesve erroneas, quæ aut sua natura aut publicationis defensionisve modo, externæ paci ac eutaxiæ, quas in Ecclesia sua stabilivit Christus, perniciem minitantur; omnino licitum est tum ab iis facti rationem reposcere, tum in eos qua censuris Ecclesiasticis,[3] qua civilis magistratus potestate animadvertere.[4]*

---

[1] [Am. ed. *powers.*]

[2] Matt. xii. 25; 1 Pet. ii. 13, 14, 16; Rom. xiii. 1–8; Heb. xiii. 17.

[3] Rom. i. 32 with 1 Cor. v. 1, 5, 11, 13; 2 John v. 10, 11; and 2 Thess. iii. 14, and 1 Tim. vi. 3–5, and Titus i. 10, 11, 13 and iii. 10, with Matt. xviii. 15–17; 1 Tim. i. 19, 20; Rev. ii. 2, 14, 15, 20; iii. 9.

[4] Deut. xiii. 6–12; Rom. xiii. 3, 4, with 2 John v. 10, 11; Ezra vii. 23–28; Rev. xvii. 12, 16, 17; Neh. xiii. 15, 17, 21, 22, 25, 30; 2 Kings xxiii. 5, 6, 9, 20, 21; 2 Chron. xxxiv. 33; xv. 12, 13, 16; Dan. iii. 29; 1 Tim. ii. 2; Isa. xlix. 23; Zech. xiii. 2, 3.

[5] [Am. ed. omits *and by the power of the Civil Magistrate,* also the proof-texts.]

CHAPTER XXI.

Of Religious Worship and the Sabbath-day.

I. The light of nature showeth that there is a God, who hath lordship and sovereignty over all; is good, and doeth good unto all; and is therefore to be feared, loved, praised, called upon, trusted in, and served with all the heart, and with all the soul, and with all the might.[1] But the acceptable way of worshiping the true God is instituted by himself, and so limited to[2] his own revealed will, that he may not be worshiped according to the imaginations and devices of men, or the suggestions of Satan, under any visible representations[3] or any other way not prescribed in the Holy Scripture.[4]

II. Religious worship is to be given to God, the Father, Son, and Holy Ghost; and to him alone:[5] not to angels, saints, or any other creature:[6] and since the fall, not without a Mediator; nor in the mediation of any other but of Christ alone.[7]

III. Prayer with thanksgiving, being one special part of religious worship,[8] is by God required of all

CAP. XXI.

De cultu religioso et de Sabbato.

I. *Constat quidem naturæ lumine esse Deum qui in universa Primatum obtinet ac absolutum Dominium, eundemque bonum esse ac omnibus beneficum, proindeque toto corde, tota anima, totisque viribus timendum esse et diligendum, laudandum ac invocandum, eique fidendum esse ac serviendum.*[1] *At rationem verum Deum colendi acceptabilem ipse instituit, itaque voluntate sua revelata definivit, ut coli non debeat secundum imaginationes ac inventa hominum, aut suggestiones Satanæ, sub specie quavis visibili, aut alia via quaviscunque quam scriptura sacra non præscripsit.*[4]

II. *Cultus religiosus Deo Patri Filio et Spiritui sancto, eique soli est exhibendus,*[5] *non angelis, non sanctis, neque alii cuivis creaturæ,*[6] *nec ipsi Deo quidem post lapsum citra Mediatorem, aut quidem per Mediatorem alium quam Jesum Christum.*[7]

III. *Supplicationem cum gratiarum actione, quæ est inter partes præcipuas divini cultus,*[8] *Deus fieri*

---

[1] Rom. i. 20; Acts xvii. 24; Psa. cxix. 68; Jer. x. 7; Psa. xxxi. 23; xviii. 3; Rom. x. 12; Psa. lxii. 8; Josh. xxiv. 14; Mark xii. 33.

[2] [Am. ed. *by.*]

[3] [Am. ed. *representation.*]

[4] Deut. xii. 32; Matt. xv. 9; Acts xvii. 25

Matt. iv. 9, 10; Deut. iv. 15-20; Exod. xx. 4-6; Col. ii. 23.

[5] Matt. iv. 10 with John v. 23 and 2 Cor. xiii. 14; [Am. ed. Rev. v. 11-13].

[6] Col. ii. 18; Rev. xix. 10; Rom. i. 25.

[7] John xiv. 6; 1 Tim. ii. 5; Eph. ii. 18; Col. Phil. iv. 6. [iii. 17

men;[1] and that it may be accepted, it is to be made in the name of the Son,[2] by the help of his Spirit,[3] according to his will,[4] with understanding, reverence, humility, fervency, faith, love, and perseverance;[5] and, if vocal, in a known tongue.[6]

IV. Prayer is to be made for things lawful,[7] and for all sorts of men living, or that shall live hereafter;[8] but not for the dead,[9] nor for those of whom it may be known that they have sinned the sin unto death.[10]

V. The reading of the Scriptures with godly fear;[11] the sound preaching;[12] and conscionable hearing of the Word, in obedience unto God with understanding, faith, and reverence;[13] singing of psalms with grace in the heart;[14] as, also, the due administration and worthy receiving of the sacraments instituted by Christ; are all parts of the ordinary religious worship of God:[15] besides religious oaths,[16] vows,[17] sol-

iubet ab hominibus universis;[1] *quæ, quo Deo grata sit et accepta, est in nomine Filii,*[2] *subsidio spiritus ejus,*[3] *et secundum ipsius voluntatem,*[4] *cum intellectu, reverentia, humilitate, fervore, fide, amore, ac perseverantia offerenda;*[5] *et quidem, si vocalis sit, in lingua nota est efferenda.*[6]

IV. *Preces pro rebus non nisi licitis sunt faciendæ,*[7] *pro hominibus autem cuiuscunque generis, vivis scilicet, aut etiam victuris aliquando;*[8] *pro mortuis autem neutiquam;*[9] *sed neque pro iis, de quibus constare possit eos peccatum ad mortem perpetrasse.*[10]

V. *Scripturarum lectio cum timore pio;*[11] *verbi prædicatio solida,*[12] *ejusdemque auditio religiosa ex obedientia erga Deum, cum intellectu, fide et reverentia;*[13] *Psalmorum cum gratia in corde cantatio,*[14] *prout etiam Sacramentorum, quæ Christus instituit, debita administratio, et participatio digna, sunt divini cultus religiosi partes, et quidem ordinarii.*[15] *Religiosa insuper juramenta,*[16] *votaque;*[17] *solennia je-*

---

[1] Psa. lxv. 2.
[2] John xiv. 13, 14; 1 Pet. ii. 5.
[3] Rom. viii. 26.
[4] 1 John v. 14.
[5] Psa. xlvii. 7; Eccles. v. 1, 2; Heb. xii. 28; Gen. xviii. 27; James v. 16; i. 6, 7; Mark xi. 24; Matt. vi. 12, 14, 15; Col. iv. 2; Eph. vi. 18.
[6] 1 Cor. xiv. 14.
[7] 1 John v. 14.
 1 Tim. ii. 1, 2; John xvii. 20; 2 Sam. vii. 29; Ruth iv. 12.

[9] 2 Sam. xii. 21–23 with Luke xvi. 25, 26; Rev. xiv. 13.
[10] 1 John v. 16.
[11] Acts xv. 21; Rev. i. 3.
[12] 2 Tim. iv. 2.
[13] James i. 22; Acts x. 33; Matt. xiii. 19; Heb. iv. 2; Isa. lxvi. 2.
[14] Col. iii. 16; Eph. v. 19; James v. 13.
[15] Matt. xxviii. 19; 1 Cor. xi. 23–29; Acts ii. 42.
[16] Deut. vi. 13 with Neh. x. 29.
[17] Isa. xix. 21 with Eccles. v. 4, 5; [Am. ed. Acts xviii. 18.—Am. ed. reads *and vows*].

emn fastings,[1] and thanksgivings upon several[2] occasions;[3] which are, in their several times and seasons, to be used in an holy and religious manner.[4]

VI. Neither prayer, nor any other part of religious worship, is now, under the gospel, either tied unto, or made more acceptable by any place in which it is performed, or towards which it is directed:[5] but God is to be worshiped every where[6] in spirit and[7] truth;[8] as in private families[9] daily,[10] and in secret each one by himself,[11] so more solemnly in the public assemblies, which are not carelessly or willfully to be neglected or forsaken, when God, by his Word or providence, calleth thereunto.[12]

VII. As it is of the law of nature, that, in general, a due proportion of time be set apart for the worship of God; so, in his Word, by a positive, moral, and perpetual commandment, binding all men in all ages, he hath particularly appointed one day in seven for a Sabbath, to be kept holy unto him:[13] which, from the

junia,[1] solennesque gratiarum actiones, pro varietate eventuum[3] suo quæque tempore ac opportunitate sancte quidem ac religiose sunt adhibenda.[4]

VI. *Hodie sub evangelio neque preces, nec ulla pars alia religiosi cultus ita cuivis alligatur loco in quo præstetur aut versus quem dirigatur,[5] ut inde gratior evadat et acceptior; verum ubique Deus colendus est[6] in spiritu ac veritate;[8] quotidie[9] quidem inter privatos parietes a quavis familia,[10] ut etiam a quolibet seorsim in secreto;[11] at solenniter magis in conventibus publicis, qui certe quoties eo nos Deus vocat, seu verbo suo seu providentia, non sunt vel ex incuria vel obstinatione animi aut negligendi aut deserendi.[12]*

VII. *Quemadmodum est de lege naturæ ut indefinite portio quædam temporis idonea divino cultui celebrando sejuncta sit ac assignata; ita in verbo suo Deus (præcepto morali, positivo ac perpetuo, homines omnes cujuscunque fuerint seculi obligante) speciatim e septenis quibusque diebus diem unum in Sabbatum designavit, sancte sibi observandum.[13]* Quod

---

[1] Joel ii. 12; Esth. iv. 16; Matt. ix. 15; 1 Cor. vii. 5.
[2] [Am. ed. has *special.*]
[3] Psalm cvii. throughout; Esth. ix. 22.
[4] Heb. xii. 28.
[5] John iv. 21.
[6] Mal. i. 11; 1 Tim. ii. 8.
[7] [Am. ed. inserts *in.*]
[8] John iv. 23, 24.

[9] Jer. x. 25; Deut. vi. 6, 7; Job i. 5; 2 Sam. vi. 18, 20; 1 Pet. iii. 7; Acts x. 2.
[10] Matt. vi. 11; [Am. ed. Josh. xxiv. 15].
[11] Matt. vi. 6; Eph. vi. 18.
[12] Isa. lvi. 7; Heb. x. 25; Prov. i. 20, 21, 24; viii. 34; Acts xiii. 42; Luke iv. 16; Acts ii. 42.
[13] Exod. xx. 8, 10, 11; Isa. lvi. 2, 4, 6, 7; [Am. ed. Isa. lvi. 6].

beginning of the world to the resurrection of Christ, was the last day of the week; and, from the resurrection of Christ, was changed into the first day of the week,[1] which in Scripture is called the Lord's day,[2] and is to be continued to the end of the world, as the Christian Sabbath.[3]

VIII. This Sabbath is then kept holy unto the Lord, when men, after a due preparing of their hearts, and ordering of their common affairs beforehand, do not only observe an holy rest all the day from their own works, words, and thoughts, about their worldly employments and recreations;[4] but also are taken up the whole time in the public and private exercises of his worship, and in the duties of necessity and mercy.[5]

Chapter XXII.
Of Lawful Oaths and Vows.

I. A lawful oath is a part of religious worship,[6] wherein, upon just occasion, the person swearing solemnly calleth God to witness what he asserteth or promiseth; and to judge him according to the truth or falsehood of what he sweareth.[7]

II. The name of God only is that

quidem ab orbe condito ad resurrectionem usque Christi dies ultimus erat in septimana; deinde autem a Christi resurrectione in septimanœ diem primum transferebatur;[1] qui quidem in Scriptura Dies Dominicus[2] nuncupatur, estque perpetuo ad finem mundi tanquam Sabbatum Christianum celebrandus.[3]

VIII. *Tunc autem hoc Sabbatum Deo sancte celebratur, quum post corda rite præparata, et compositas suas res mundanas, homines non solum a suis ipsorum operibus, dictis, cogitatis; (quæ circa illas exerceri solent) a recreationibus etiam ludicris quietem sanctam toto observant die;[4] verum etiam in exercitiis divini cultus publicis privatisque, ac in officiis necessitatis et misericordiæ toto illo tempore occupantur.[5]*

Cap. XXII.
De Juramentis, votisque licitis.

I. *Juramentum licitum est pars cultus religiosi,[6] qua (occasione justa oblata) qui jurat, Deum, de eo quod asserit aut promittit, solenni modo testatur; eundemque appellat se secundum illius quod jurat veritatem aut falsitatem judicaturum.[7]*

II. *Per solum Dei nomen jurare*

---

[1] Gen. ii. 2, 3; 1 Cor. xvi. 1, 2; Acts xx. 7.
[2] Rev. i. 10.
[3] Exod. xx. 8, 10, with Matt. v. 17, 18.
[4] Exod. xx. 8; xvi. 23, 25, 26, 29, 30; xxxi. 15–17; Isa. lviii. 13; Neh. xiii. 15–22.

[5] Isa. lviii. 13; Matt. xii. 1–13.
[6] Deut. x. 20.
[7] Exod. xx. 7; Lev. xix. 12; 2 Cor. i. 23; 2 Chron. vi. 22, 23.

by which men ought to swear, and therein it is to be used with all holy fear and reverence;[1] therefore to swear vainly or rashly by that glorious and dreadful name, or to swear at all by any other thing, is sinful, and to be abhorred.[2] Yet as, in matters of weight and moment, an oath is warranted by the Word of God, under the New Testament, as well as under the Old,[3] so a lawful oath, being imposed by lawful authority, in such matters ought to be taken.[4]

III. Whosoever taketh an oath ought duly to consider the weightiness of so solemn an act, and therein to avouch nothing but what he is fully persuaded is the truth.[5] Neither may any man bind himself by oath to any thing but what is good and just, and what he believeth so to be, and what he is able and resolved to perform.[6] Yet it is a sin to refuse an oath touching any thing that is good and just, being imposed by lawful authority.[7]

IV. An oath is to be taken in the plain and common sense of

debent homines, quod quidem cum omni timore sancto ac reverentia est inibi usurpandum.[1] Proindeque per nomen illud gloriosum ac tremendum jurare leviter, aut temere, vel etiam omnino jurare per rem aliam quamviscunque, sceleratum est et quam maxime perhorrescendum.[2] Veruntamen sicut in rebus majoris ponderis et momenti secundum verbum Dei licitum est jusjurandum non minus quidem sub Novo quam sub Vetere Testamento:[3] ita sane jusjurandum licitum, authoritate legitima si exigatur, non est in rebus ejusmodi declinandum.[4]

III. *Quicunque juramentum præstat eum pondus actionis tam solennis rite secum perpendere oportet, atque juratum de nullo asseverare quod verum esse non habeat sibi persuasissimum.[5] Neque licet cuivis ad agendum quicquam obstringere semet jurejurando, nisi quod revera bonum justumque est, quod ille ejusmodi esse credit, quodque ipse præstare potest statuitque.[6] Veruntamen de re bona justaque jusjurandum, legitima authoritate si exigatur, peccat ille qui detrectat.[7]*

IV. *Juramentum præstandum est sensu verborum vulgari quidem ac*

---

[1] Deut. vi. 13.
[2] Exod. xx. 7 ; Jer. v. 7 ; Matt. v. 34, 37 ; James v. 12.
[3] Heb. vi. 16 ; 2 Cor. i. 23 ; Isa. lxv. 16.
[4] 1 Kings viii. 31 ; Neh. xiii. 25 ; Ezra x. 25.

[5] Exod. xx. 7 ; Jer. iv. 2.
[6] Gen. xxiv. 2, 3, 5, 6, 8, 9.
[7] Numb. v. 19, 21 ; Neh. v. 12 ; Exod. xxii 7–11.

the words, without equivocation or mental reservation.[1] It can not oblige to sin; but in any thing not sinful, being taken, it binds to performance, although to a man's own hurt:[2] nor is it to be violated, although made to heretics or infidels.[3]

V. A vow is of the like nature with a promissory oath, and ought to be made with the like religious care, and to be performed with the like faithfulness.[4]

VI. It is not to be made to any creature, but to God alone:[5] and that it may be accepted, it is to be made voluntarily, out of faith and conscience of duty, in way of thankfulness for mercy received, or for the[6] obtaining of what we want; whereby we more strictly bind ourselves to necessary duties, or to other things, so far and so long as they may fitly conduce thereunto.[7]

VII. No man may vow to do any thing forbidden in the Word of God, or what would hinder any duty therein commanded, or which is not in his own power, and for the performance whereof he hath no prom-

manifesto, sine æquivocatione aut reservatione mentali quaviscunque.[1] *Ad peccandum quenquam obligare nequit, verum in re qualibet cui abest peccatum, qui semel illud præstitit, adimplere tenetur, vel etiam cum damno suo;*[2] *neque sane licet, quamvis hæreticis datum aut infidelibus, violare.*[3]

V. *Votum, naturæ consimilis est cum juramento promissorio, parique debet tum religione nuncupari tum fide persolvi.*[4]

VI. *Non est ulli creaturæ, sed Deo soli nuncupandum,*[5] *et quo gratum illi esse possit acceptumque, est quidem lubenter, e fide, officiique nostri conscientia suscipiendum, vel gratitudinis nostræ ob accepta beneficia testandæ causa, vel boni alicujus, quo indigemus, consequendi; per hoc autem nosmet ad officia necessaria arctius obligamus; vel etiam ad res alias quatenus quidem et quamdiu istis subserviunt.*[7]

VII. *Nemini quicquam vovere licet se acturum, quod aut verbo Dei prohibetur; aut officium aliquod inibi præceptum impediret, quodve non est in voventis potestate, et cui præstando vires illi Deus non est polli-*

---

[1] Jer. iv. 2; Psa. xxiv. 4.
[2] 1 Sam. xxv. 22, 32–34; Psa. xv. 4.
[3] Ezek. xvii. 16, 18, 19; Josh. ix. 18, 19, with 2 Sam. xxi. 1.   [lxvi. 13, 14.
[4] Isa. xix. 21; Eccles. v. 4–6; Psa. lxi. 8;

[5] Psa. lxxvi. 11; Jer. xliv. 25, 26.
[6] [Am. ed. omits *the*.]
[7] Deut. xxiii. 21, 23; Psa. l. 14; Gen. xxviii. 20–22; 1 Sam. i. 11; Psa. lxvi. 13, 14; cxxxii. 2–5.

ise or ability from God.[1] In which respect,[2] popish monastical vows of perpetual single life, professed poverty, and regular obedience, are so far from being degrees of higher perfection, that they are superstitious and sinful snares, in which no Christian may entangle himself.[3]

citus.[1] *Unde Pontificiorum illa de perpetuo cœlibatu, de paupertate, deque obedientia regulari vota Monastica, tantum abest ut perfectionis gradus sint sublimiores, ut superstitionis plane sint ac peccati laquei, quibus nulli unquam Christiano semetipsum licet implicare.[3]*

Chapter XXIII.
Of the Civil Magistrate.

I. God, the Supreme Lord and King of all the world, hath ordained civil magistrates to be under him, over the people, for his own glory and the public good, and to this end hath armed them with the power of the sword, for the defense and encouragement of them that are good, and for the punishment of evil-doers.[4]

II. It is lawful for Christians to accept and execute the office of a magistrate when called thereunto;[5] in the managing whereof, as they ought especially to maintain piety, justice, and peace, according to the wholesome laws of each commonwealth,[6] so, for that end, they may lawfully, now under the New Testament, wage war upon just and necessary occasion.[7 & 8]

Cap. XXIII.
De Magistratu Civili.

I. *Supremus totius Mundi Rex ac Dominus Deus, Magistratus Civiles ordinavit qui vices ejus gerant supra populum ad suam ipsius gloriam, ac bonum publicum ; in quem finem eosdem armavit potestate gladii, propter bonorum quidem animationem ac tutamen, animadversionem autem in maleficos.[4]*

II. *Christianis, quoties ad id vocantur, Magistratus munus et suscipere licet et exequi;[5] in quo quidem gerendo, ut pietatem præcipue, justitiam, ac pacem secundum salubres cujusque Reipublicæ leges tueri debent,[6] ita quo illum finem consequantur, licitum est iis vel hodie sub Novo Testamento in causis justis ac necessariis bellum gerere.[7]*

---

[1] Acts xxiii. 12, 14; Mark vi. 26; Numb. xxx. 5, 8, 12, 13.

[2] [Am. ed. has *respects.*]

[3] Matt. xix. 11, 12; 1 Cor. vii. 2, 9; Eph. iv. 28; 1 Pet. iv. 2; 1 Cor. vii. 23.

[4] Rom. xiii. 1–4; 1 Pet. ii. 13, 14.

[5] Prov. viii. 15, 16; Rom. xiii. 1, 2, 4.

[6] Psa. ii. 10–12; 1 Tim. ii. 2; Psa. lxxxii. 3, 4; 2 Sam. xxiii. 3; 1 Pet. ii. 13.

[7] Luke iii. 14; Rom. xiii. 4; Matt. viii. 9, 10; Acts x. 1, 2; Rev. xvii. 14, 16.

[8] [Am. ed. has *occasions.*]

III. The civil magistrate may not assume to himself the administration of the Word and Sacraments, or the power of the keys of the kingdom of heaven:[1] yet he hath authority, and it is his duty to take order, that unity and peace be preserved in the Church, that the truth of God be kept pure and entire, that all blasphemies and heresies be suppressed, all corruptions and abuses in worship and discipline prevented or reformed, and all the ordinances of God duly settled, administered, and observed.[2] For the better effecting whereof he hath power to call synods, to be present at them, and to provide that whatsoever is transacted in them be according to the mind of God.[3]

III. *Magistratui Civili verbi et sacramentorum administrationem, aut clavium regni cœlorum potestatem assumere sibi non est licitum :*[1] *nihilo tamen minus et jure potest ille, eique incumbit providere ut Ecclesiæ unitas ac tranquillitas conservetur, ut veritas Dei pura et integra custodiatur, ut supprimantur blasphemiæ omnes, hæresesque, ut in cultu ac disciplina omnes corruptelæ ac abusus aut præcaveantur aut reformentur, omnia denique instituta divina, ut rite statuminentur, administrentur, observentur.*[2] *Quæ omnia quo melius præstare possit, potestatem habet tum Synodos convocandi, tum ut ipsis intersit, prospiciatque, ut quicquid in iis transigatur sit menti divinæ consentaneum.*[3]

The above section is changed in the American revision, and adapted to the separation of Church and State, as follows :

[III. *Civil magistrates may not assume to themselves the administration of the Word and Sacraments* (2 Chron. xxvi. 18); *or the power of the keys of the kingdom of heaven* (Matt. xvi. 19 ; 1 Cor. iv. 1, 2); *or, in the least, interfere in matters of faith* (John xviii. 36; Mal. ii. 7; Acts v. 29). *Yet as nursing fathers, it is the duty of civil magistrates to protect the Church of our common Lord, without giving the preference to any denomination of Christians above the rest, in such a manner that all ecclesiastical persons whatever*

---

[1] 2 Chron. xxvi. 18 with Matt. xviii. 17 and xvi. 19 ; 1 Cor. xii. 28, 29 ; Eph. iv. 11, 12; 1 Cor. iv. 1, 2 ; Rom. x. 15 ; Heb. v. 4. Isa. xlix. 23 ; Psa. cxxii. 9 ; Ezra vii. 23–28 ; Lev. xxiv. 16 ; Deut. xiii. 5, 6, 12 ;

2 Kings xviii. 4 ; 1 Chron. xiii. 1–9 ; 2 Kings xxiii. 1–26 ; 2 Chron. xxxiv. 33, 2 Chron. xv. 12, 13.
[3] 2 Chron. xix. 8–11 ; chaps. xxix. and xxx. ; Matt. ii. 4. 5.

shall enjoy the full, free, and unquestioned liberty of discharging every part of their sacred functions, without violence or danger (Isa. xlix. 23). *And, as Jesus Christ hath appointed a regular gov ernment and discipline in his Church, no law of any commonwealth should interfere with, let, or hinder, the due exercise thereof, among the voluntary members of any denomination of Christians, accord ing to their own profession and belief* (Psa. cv. 15 ; Acts xviii. 14–16). *It is the duty of civil magistrates to protect the person and good name of all their people, in such an effectual manner as that no person be suffered, either upon pretence of religion or infidelity, to offer any indignity, violence, abuse, or injury to any other person whatsoever : and to take order, that all religious and ecclesiastical assemblies be held without molestation or disturbance* (2 Sam. xxiii. 3; 1 Tim. ii. 1; Rom. xiii. 4).]

IV. It is the duty of people[1] to pray for magistrates,[2] to honor their persons,[3] to pay them tribute and other dues,[4] to obey their lawful commands, and to be subject to their authority, for conscience' sake.[5] Infidelity or difference in religion doth not make void the magistrate's just and legal authority, nor free the people from their due obedience to him :[6] from which ecclesiastical persons are not exempted ;[7] much less hath the Pope any power or jurisdiction over them in their dominions, or over any of their people ; and least of all to deprive them of their dominions or lives, if he shall judge them to be

IV. *Debet populus pro Magistratibus preces fundere,[2] personas eorum honore prosequi,[3] tributa aliaque eis debita persolvere,[4] obtemperare licitis eorum mandatis, ac propter conscientiam subjici illorum authoritati ;[5] quæ si justa sit ac legitima, non eam illorum infidelitas, non religio diversa cassam reddit, neque populum liberat a debita illis obedientiæ præstatione,[6] qua viri quidem Ecclesiastici non eximuntur,[7] multo minus in ipsos magistratus, intra ditionem suam, aut ex eorum populo quemvis potestatem ullam habet aut jurisdictionem Papa Romanus, minime vero omnium vita illos aut principatu exuendi, si ipse*

---

[1] [Am. ed. reads *of the people*.]
[2] 1 Tim. ii. 1, 2.
[3] 1 Pet. ii. 17.
[6] Rom. xiii. 6, 7.

[5] Rom. xiii. 5 ; Tit. i. 3.
[4] 1 Pet. ii. 13, 14, 16.
[7] Rom. xiii. 1 ; 1 Kings ii. 35 ; Acts xxv 9–11 ; 2 Pet. ii. 1, 10, 11 ; Jude 8–11.

heretics, or upon any other pretense whatsoever.[1]

scilicet eos hæreticos esse judicaverit, vel etiam alio prætextu quoviscunque.[1]

CHAPTER XXIV.

Of Marriage and Divorce.

I. Marriage is to be between one man and one woman: neither is it lawful for any man to have more than one wife, nor for any woman to have more than one husband at the same time.[2]

II. Marriage was ordained for the mutual help of husband and wife;[3] for the increase of mankind with a legitimate issue, and of the Church with an holy seed;[4] and for preventing of uncleanness.[5]

III. It is lawful for all sorts of people to marry who are able with judgment to give their consent.[6] Yet it is the duty of Christians to marry only in the Lord.[7] And, therefore, such as profess the true reformed religion should not marry with infidels, Papists, or other idolaters: neither should such as are godly be unequally yoked, by marrying with such as are notoriously wicked in their life, or maintain damnable heresies.[8]

CAP. XXIV.

De Conjugio et Divortio.

I. *Conjugium inter unum virum ac fæminam unam contrahi debet; neque viro ulli uxores plures, nec ulli fæminæ ultra unum maritum eodem tempore habere licet.*[2]

II. *Conjugium erat institutum, cum propter mariti uxorisque auxilium mutuum,[3] tum propter humani generis prole legitima, Ecclesiæqeu sancto semine incrementum,[4] tum vero etiam ad impudicitiam declinandam.*[5]

III. *Matrimonio jungi cuivis hominum generi licitum est, qui consensum suum præbere valent cum judicio;[6] Veruntamen solum in Domino connubia inire debent Christiani;[7] proindeque quotquot religionem veram reformatamque profitentur, non debent Infidelibus, Papistis, aut aliis quibuscunque idololatris connubio sociari; neque sane debent qui pii sunt impari jugo copulari, conjugium cum illis contrahendo qui aut improbitate vitæ sunt notabiles, aut damnabiles tuentur hæreses.*[8]

---

[1] 2 Thess. ii. 4; Rev. xiii. 15-17.
[2] Gen. ii. 24; Matt. xix. 5, 6; Prov. ii. 17; [Am. ed. 1 Cor. vii. 2; Mark x. 6-9].
[3] Gen. ii. 18.
[4] Mal. ii. 15.
[5] 1 Cor. vii. 2, 9.

[6] Heb. xiii. 4; 1 Tim. iv. 3; 1 Cor. vii. 36-38; Gen. xxiv. 57, 58.
[7] 1 Cor. vii. 39.
[8] Gen. xxxiv. 14; Exod. xxxiv. 16; Deut. vii. 3, 4; 1 Kings xi. 4; Neh. xiii. 25-27; Mal. ii. 11, 12; 2 Cor. vi. 14.

IV. Marriage ought not to be within the degrees of consanguinity or affinity forbidden in the Word;[1] nor can such incestuous marriages ever be made lawful by any law of man, or consent of parties, so as those persons may live together, as man and wife.[2] The man may not marry any of his wife's kindred nearer in blood than he may of his own, nor the woman of her husband's kindred nearer in blood than of her own.[3]

V. Adultery or fornication, committed after a contract, being detected before marriage, giveth just occasion to the innocent party to dissolve that contract.[4] In the case of adultery after marriage, it is lawful for the innocent party to sue out a divorce,[5] and after the divorce to marry another, as if the offending party were dead.[6]

VI. Although the corruption of man be such as is apt to study arguments, unduly to put asunder those whom God hath joined together in marriage; yet nothing but adultery, or such willful desertion as can no way be remedied by

IV. *Connubia intra consanguinitatis affinitatisque gradus in verbo Dei vetitos iniri non est licitum;*[1] *neque possunt ejusmodi incesta conjugia quavis aut humana lege, aut consensione partium fieri legitima, adeo ut personis illis ad instar mariti et uxoris liceat unquam cohabitare.*[2] *Non licet viro e cognatione uxoris suæ ducere, quam si æque seipsum attingeret sanguine, ducere non liceret; sicuti nec fœminæ licet viro nubere a mariti sui sanguine minus, quam a suo liceret, alieno.*[3]

V. *Adulterium aut scortatio si admittatur post sponsalia, ac ante conjugium detegatur, personæ innocenti justam præbet occasionem contractum illum dissolvendi;*[4] *quod si adulterium post conjugium admittatur, licebit parti innocenti divortium lege postulare ac obtinere;*[5] *atque quidem post factum divortium conjugio alteri sociari, perinde acsi mortua esset persona illa quæ conjugii fidem violabat.*[6]

VI. *Quamvis ea sit hominis corruptio ut proclivis sit ad excogitandum argumenta, indebite illos quos Deus connubio junxit dissociandi; nihilominus tamen extra adulterium ac desertionem ita obstinatam, ut cui nullo remedio, nec ab Ecclesia nec a*

---

[1] Lev. chap. xviii.; 1 Cor. v. 1; Amos ii. 7.
[2] Mark vi. 18; Lev. xviii. 24–28.
[3] Lev. xx. 19–21.

[4] Matt. i. 18–20.
[5] Matt. v. 31, 32.
[6] Matt. xix. 9; Rom. vii. 2, 3.

the Church or civil magistrate, is cause sufficient of dissolving the bond of marriage;[1] wherein a public and orderly course of proceeding is to be observed; and the persons concerned in it, not left to their own wills and discretion in their own case.[2]

Chapter XXV.
Of the Church.

I. The catholic or universal Church, which is invisible, consists of the whole number of the elect, that have been, are, or shall be gathered into one, under Christ the head thereof; and is the spouse, the body, the fullness of him that filleth all in all.[3]

II. The visible Church, which is also catholic or universal under the gospel (not confined to one nation as before under the law) consists of all those, throughout the world, that profess the true religion,[4] and of [5] their children;[6] and is the kingdom of the Lord Jesus Christ,[7] the house and family of God,[8] out of which there is no ordinary possibility of salvation.[9]

Magistratu civili subveniri possit, sufficiens causa nulla esse potest conjugii vinculum dissolvendi.[1] Atque hac quidem in re procedendi ordo publicus et regularis est observandus, nec personæ illæ, quarum jus agitur, sunt suo arbitrio judiciove in causa propria permittendæ.[2]

Cap. XXV.
De Ecclesia.

I. *Catholica sive Universalis Ecclesia ea quæ est invisibilis constat e toto electorum numero, quotquot fuerunt, sunt, aut erunt unquam in unum collecti, sub Christo ejusdem Capite; estque sponsa, corpus ac plenitudo ejus qui implet omnia in omnibus.[3]*

II. *Ecclesia visibilis (quæ etiam sub Evangelio, Catholica est et universalis, non autem unius gentis finibus, ut pridem sub lege, circumscripta) ex iis omnibus constat, undecunque terrarum sint, qui veram religionem profitentur,[4] una cum eorundem liberis;[6] estque Regnum Domini Jesu Christi,[7] Domus et familia Dei,[8] extra quam quidem ordinarie fieri nequit ut quivis salutem consequatur.[9]*

---

[1] Matt. xix. 8, 9; 1 Cor. vii. 15; Matt. xix. 6.
[2] Deut. xxiv. 1–4; [Am. ed. Ezra x. 3].
[3] Eph. i. 10, 22, 23; v. 23, 27, 32; Col. i. 18.
[4] 1 Cor. i. 2; xii. 12, 13; Psa. ii. 8; Rev. vii. 9; Rom. xv. 9–12.
[5] [Am. ed. *together with,* instead of *and of.*]
[6] 1 Cor. vii. 14; Acts ii. 39; Ezek. xvi. 20,

21; Rom. xi. 16; Gen. iii. 15; xvii. 7; [Am. ed. Gal. iii. 7, 9, 14; Rom. iv. throughout].
[7] Matt. xiii. 47; Isa. ix. 7.
[8] Eph. ii. 19; iii. 15; [Am. ed. **Prov. xxix.** 18].
[9] Acts ii. 47.

III. Unto this catholic visible Church Christ hath given the ministry, oracles, and ordinances of God, for the gathering and perfecting of the saints, in this life, to the end of the world : and doth by his own presence and Spirit, according to his promise, make them effectual thereunto.[1]

IV. This catholic Church hath been sometimes more, sometimes less visible.[2] And particular churches, which are members thereof, are more or less pure, according as the doctrine of the gospel is taught and embraced, ordinances administered, and public worship performed more or less purely in them.[3]

V. The purest churches under heaven are subject both to mixture and error;[4] and some have so degenerated as to become no churches of Christ, but synagogues of Satan.[5] Nevertheless, there shall be always a Church on earth to worship God according to his will.[6]

VI. There is no other head of the Church but the Lord Jesus Christ:[7] nor can the Pope of Rome, in any

III. *Catholicæ huic Ecclesiæ visibili dedit Christus ministrorum ordinem, oracula, ac instituta Dei ad sanctos usque ad finem mundi in hac vita colligendos simul et perficiendos; in quem finem præsentia sua, spirituque secundum ipsius promissionem, eadem reddit efficacia.*[1]

IV. *Ecclesia hæc Catholica extitit quandoque magis quandoque minus visibilis.*[2] *Ecclesiæ autem particulares (quæ sunt illius membra) eo magis minusve puræ sunt, qui majori aut minori cum puritate in iis docetur excipiturque Evangelii doctrina, administrantur divina instituta, cultusque publicus celebratur.*[3]

V. *Purissimæ omnium quæ in terris sunt Ecclesiæ, cum mixturæ tum etiam errori sunt obnoxiæ,*[4] *eousque autem nonnullæ degenerarunt, ut ex Ecclesiis Christi factæ demum sint ipsius Satanæ Synagogæ;*[5] *nihilominus tamen nunquam deerit in terris Ecclesiæ, quæ Deum colat secundum ipsius voluntatem.*[6]

VI. *Ecclesiæ caput extra unum Dominum Jesum Christum nullum est;*[7] *nec ullo sensu caput ejus esse*

---

[1] 1 Cor. xii. 23; Eph. iv. 11–13; Matt. xxviii. 19, 20; Isa. lix. 21.

[2] Rom. xi. 3, 4; Rev. xii. 6, 14; [Am. ed. Acts ix. 31].

[3] Rev. chaps. ii. and iii. ; 1 Cor. v. 6, 7.

[4] 1 Cor. xiii. 12; Rev. chaps. ii. and iii. , Matt. xiii. 24–30, 47.

[5] Rev. xviii. 2; Rom. xi. 18–22.

[6] Matt. xvi. 18; Psa. lxxii. 17; cii. 28; Matt. xxviii. 19, 20.

[7] Col. i. 18; Eph. i. 22.

sense be head thereof; but is that
Antichrist, that man of sin and son
of perdition, that exalteth himself
in the Church against Christ, and
all that is called God.[1]

*potest Papa Romanus, qui est insig-
nis ille Antichristus, homo ille peccati
et perditionis filius; in Ecclesia semet efferens adversus Christum, et
supra quicquid dicitur Deus.*[1]

CHAPTER XXVI.

Of the Communion of Saints.

1. All saints that are united to
Jesus Christ their head, by his
Spirit and by faith, have fellowship with him in his graces, sufferings, death, resurrection, and
glory:[2] and being united to one
another in love, they have communion in each other's gifts and
graces,[3] and are obliged to the
performance of such duties, public and private, as do conduce to
their mutual good, both in the
inward and outward man.[4]

II. Saints, by profession, are
bound to maintain an holy fellowship and communion in the
worship of God, and in performing such other spiritual services as
tend to their mutual edification;[5]
as also in relieving each other in
outward things, according to their
several abilities and necessities.

CAP. XXVI.

De Communione Sanctorum.

I. *Sancti omnes, qui capiti suo
Jesu Christo per Spiritum ejus ac
per fidem uniuntur, gratiarum ejus,
perpessionum, mortis, resurrectionis
ac gloriæ ejus habent communionem;*[2] *atque inde etiam amore conjuncti sibimet invicem mutuam donorum suorum gratiarumque societatem quandam ineunt,*[3] *ac ad ejusmodi officia præstanda publica et
privata obligantur, quæ ad mutuum
eorum bonum conducant, cum quoad
internum tum etiam quoad externum
hominem.*[4]

II. *Qui sanctos sese profitentur
sanctam illi societatem et communionem inire tenentur et conservare,
cum in divino cultu, tum alia officia
spiritualia præstando, quæ ad mutuam eorum ædificationem conferre
possint;*[5] *Quin etiam porro suble-
vando se mutuo in rebus externis,
pro ratione cujusque vel facultatum*

---

[1] Matt. xxiii. 8-10; 2 Thess. ii. 3, 4, 8, 9;
Rev. xiii. 6.
[2] 1 John i. 3; Eph. iii. 16-19; John i, 16;
Eph. ii. 5, 6; Phil. iii. 10; Rom. vi. 5, 6;
2 Tim. ii. 12.

[3] Eph. iv. 15, 16; 1 Cor. xii. 7; iii. 21-23;
Col. ii. 19.
[4] 1 Thess. v. 11, 14; Rom. i. 11, 12, 14;
1 John iii. 16-18; Gal. vi. 10.
[5] Heb. x. 24, 25; Acts ii. 42, 46; Isa. ii. 3;
1 Cor. xi. 20.

Which communion, as God offereth opportunity, is to be extended unto all those who, in every place, call upon the name of the Lord Jesus.[1]

III. This communion which the saints have with Christ, doth not make them in anywise partakers of the substance of his Godhead, or to be equal with Christ in any respect: either of which to affirm is impious and blasphemous.[2] Nor doth their communion one with another, as saints, take away or infringe the title or propriety[3] which each man hath in his goods and possessions.[4]

Chapter XXVII.
Of the Sacraments.

I. Sacraments are holy signs and seals of the covenant of grace,[5] immediately instituted by God,[6] to represent Christ and his benefits, and to confirm our interest in him:[7] as also to put a visible difference between those that belong unto the Church and the rest of the world;[8] and solemnly to engage them to the service of God in Christ, according to his Word.[9]

II. There is in every sacrament

vel indigentiæ.   Quæ quidem communio, prout opportunitatem Deus obtulerit, est ad eos omnes, qui ubivis locorum Domini Jesu nomen invocant, extendenda.[1]

III. *Hæc autem communio qua sancti cum Christo potiuntur, eos substantiæ Deitatis ejus neutiquam reddit participes, nec ullo respectu æquales Christo: Quorum utrumvis affirmare impium est ac blasphemum;*[2] *neque sane communio illa, quæ iis secum mutuo quatenus sanctis intercedit; cujusquam ad bona et possessiones suas jus privatum vel tollit vel imminuit.*[4]

Cap. XXVII.
De Sacramentis.

I. *Sacramenta sunt fœderis gratiæ signa sacra et sigilla,*[5] *immediate a Deo instituta,*[6] *ad Christum ejusque beneficia repræsentandum, ad jus nostrum in illo confirmandum,*[7] *prout etiam ad illos qui Ecclesiam spectant a reliquis illis qui sunt e mundo, visibili discrimine separandum,*[8] *utque ii solenniter devinciantur ad obedientiam et cultum Deo in Christo juxta verbum ejus exhibendum.*[9]

II. *In Sacramento quolibet est in-*

---

[1] Acts ii. 44, 45; 1 John iii. 17; 2 Cor. chaps. viii. and ix.; Acts xi. 29, 30.
[2] Col. i. 18, 19; 1 Cor. viii. 6; Isa. xlii. 8; 1 Tim. vi. 15, 16; Psa. xlv. 7 with Heb. i. 8, 9.
[3] [Am. ed. *property.*]
[4] Exod. xx. 15; Eph. iv. 28; Acts v. 4.

[5] Rom. iv. 11; Gen. xvii. 7, 10.
[6] Matt. xxviii. 19; 1 Cor. xi. 23.
[7] 1 Cor. x. 16; xi. 25, 26; Gal. iii. 27.
[8] Rom. xv. 8; Exod. xii. 48; Gen. xxxiv. 14; [Am. ed. 1 Cor. x. 21].
[9] Rom. vi. 3, 4; 1 Cor. x. 16, 21.

a spiritual relation or sacramental union, between the sign and the thing signified; whence it comes to pass that the names and the [1] effects of the one are attributed to the other.[2]

III. The grace which is exhibited in or by the sacraments, rightly used, is not conferred by any power in them; neither doth the efficacy of a sacrament depend upon the piety or intention of him that doth administer it,[3] but upon the work of the Spirit,[4] and the word of institution, which contains, together with a precept authorizing the use thereof, a promise of benefit to worthy receivers.[5]

IV. There be only two sacraments ordained by Christ our Lord in the gospel, that is to say, Baptism and the Supper of the Lord: neither of which may be dispensed by any but by a minister of the Word lawfully ordained.[6]

V. The sacraments of the Old Testament, in regard of the spiritual things thereby signified and exhibited, were, for substance, the same with those of the New.[7]

ter signum et rem significatam relatio quœdam spiritualis, sive Sacramentalis unio; unde fit ut alterius nomina et effectus alteri quandoque tribuantur.[2]

III. Quœ in Sacramentis sive per ea rite adhibita exhibetur gratia, per vim aliquam iis intrinsecam non confertur, neque ex intentione vel pietate administrantis pendent Sacramenti vis ac efficacia;[3] verum ex operatione Spiritus,[4] ac verbo institutionis, quod complectitur cum prœceptum, unde celebrandi Sacramenti potestas fit, tum etiam promissionem de beneficiis digne percipientibus exhibendis.[5]

IV. Sacramenta duo tantum sunt a Christo Domino nostro in Evangelio instituta, Baptismus scilicet, et cœna Domini; quorum neutrum debet nisi a ministro verbi legitime ordinato dispensari.[6]

V. Sacramenta Veteris Testamenti si res spirituales per ea significatas exhibitasque respiciamus, quoad substantiam eadem fuere cum his sub Novo.[7]

Chapter XXVIII.

Of Baptism.

I. Baptism is a sacrament of the

Cap. XXVIII.

De Baptismo.

I. Baptismus est sacramentum

---

[1] Am. ed. omits the.
[2] Gen. xvii. 10; Matt. xxvi. 27, 28; Tit. iii. 5.
[3] Rom. ii. 28, 29; 1 Pet. iii. 21.
[4] Matt. iii. 11; 1 Cor. xii. 13.

[5] Matt. xxvi. 27, 28; xxviii. 19, 20.
[6] Matt. xxviii. 19; 1 Cor. xi. 20, 23; iv. 1; Heb. v. 4.
[7] 1 Cor. x. 1–4; [Am. ed. 1 Cor. v. 7, 8].

New Testament, ordained by Jesus Christ,[1] not only for the solemn admission of the party baptized into the visible Church,[2] but also to be unto him a sign and seal of the covenant of grace,[3] of his ingrafting into Christ,[4] of regeneration,[5] of remission of sins,[6] and of his giving up unto God, through Jesus Christ, to walk in newness of life:[7] which sacrament is, by Christ's own appointment, to be continued in his Church until the end of the world.[8]

II. The outward element to be used in this sacrament is water, wherewith the party is to be baptized in the name of the Father, and of the Son, and of the Holy Ghost, by a minister of the gospel lawfully called thereunto.[9]

III. Dipping of the person into the water is not necessary; but baptism is rightly administered by pouring or sprinkling water upon the person.[10]

IV. Not only those that do actually profess faith in and obedience unto Christ,[11] but also the infants

Novi Testamenti, a Jesu Christo institutum,[1] *non solum propter solennem personæ baptizatæ in Ecclesiam visibilem admissionem,*[2] *verum etiam ut signum eidem sit, et sigillum cum fœderis gratiæ,*[3] *tum suæ in Christum insitionis,*[4] *regenerationis,*[5] *remissionis peccatorum,*[6] *ac sui ipsius Deo per Christum dedicationis, ad ambulandum in vitæ novitate.*[7] *Quod quidem Sacramentum e Christi ipsius mandato est in Ecclesia ejus ad finem usque mundi retinendum.*[8]

II. *Elementum externum in hoc Sacramento adhibendum est Aqua; qua baptizari debet admittendus, a ministro Evangelii legitime ad hoc vocato, in nomine Patris et filii et Spiritus Sancti.*[9]

III. *Baptizandi in aquam immersio necessaria non est; verum baptismus rite administratur aqua superfusa vel etiam inspersa baptizando.*[10]

IV. *Non illi solum qui fidem in Christum eique se obedientes fore actu quidem profitentur,*[11] *verum*

---

[1] Matt. xxviii. 19; [Am. ed. Mark xvi. 16].
[2] 1 Cor. xii. 13; [Am. ed. Gal. iii. 27, 28].
[3] Rom. iv. 11 with Col. ii. 11, 12.
[4] Gal. iii. 27; Rom. vi. 5.
[5] Tit. iii. 5.
[6] Mark i. 4; [Am. ed. Acts ii. 38; xxii. 16].

[7] Rom. vi. 3, 4.
[8] Matt. xxviii. 19, 20.
[9] Matt. iii. 11; John i. 33; Matt. xxviii. 19, 20; [Am. ed. Acts x. 47; viii. 36, 38].
[10] Heb. ix. 10, 19–22; Acts ii. 41; xvi. 33; Mark vii. 4.
[11] Mark xvi. 15, 16; Acts viii. 37, 38.

of one or both believing parents are to be baptized.[1]

V. Although it be a great sin to contemn or neglect this ordinance,[2] yet grace and salvation are not so inseparably annexed unto it, as that no person can be regenerated or saved without it,[3] or that all that are baptized are undoubtedly regenerated.[4]

VI. The efficacy of baptism is not tied to that moment of time wherein it is administered;[5] yet, notwithstanding, by the right use of this ordinance the grace promised is not only offered, but really exhibited and conferred by the Holy Ghost, to such (whether of age or infants) as that grace belongeth unto, according to the counsel of God's own will, in his appointed time.[6]

VII. The sacrament of baptism is but once to be administered to any person.[7]

CHAPTER XXIX.

Of the Lord's Supper.

I. Our Lord Jesus, in the night wherein he was betrayed, instituted

etiam infantes qui a Parente vel altero vel utroque fideli procreantur, sunt baptizandi.[1]

V. Quamvis grave peccatum sit institutum hoc despicatui habere vel negligere ;[2] non tamen ei salus et gratia ita individue annectuntur, ut absque illo nemo unquam regenerari aut salvari possit,[3] aut quasi indubium omnino sit regenerari omnes qui baptizantur.[4]

VI. Baptismi efficacia ei temporis momento quo administratur non adstringitur.[5] Nihilominus tamen, usu debito hujus instituti non offertur solum promissa gratia, verum etiam omnibus (tam infantibus quam adultis) ad quos gratia illa e consilio Divinæ voluntatis pertinet, per Spiritum Sanctum in tempore suo constituto realiter confertur et exhibetur.[6]

VII. Sacramentum Baptismi eidem personæ non est nisi semel administrandum.[7]

CAP. XXIX.

De Cœna Domini.

I. Dominus noster Jesus eadem qua prodebatur nocte instituit cor-

---

[1] Gen. xvii. 7, 9, with Gal. iii. 9, 14, and Col. ii. 11, 12, and Acts ii. 38, 39, and Rom. iv. 11, 12 ; 1 Cor. vii. 14 ; Matt. xxviii. 19 ; Mark x. 13–16 ; Luke xviii. 15 ; [Am. ed. Acts xvi. 14, 15, 33]. Luke vii. 30 with Exod. iv. 24–26.

[3] Rom. iv. 11 ; Acts x. 2, 4, 22, 31, 45, 47.
[4] Acts viii. 13, 23.
[5] John iii. 5, 8.
[6] Gal. iii. 27 ; Tit. iii. 5 ; Eph. v. 25, 26 ; Acts ii. 38, 41.
[7] Tit. iii. 5.

the sacrament of his body and blood, called the Lord's Supper, to be observed in his Church, unto the end of the world; for the perpetual remembrance of the sacrifice of himself in his death, the sealing all benefits thereof unto true believers, their spiritual nourishment and growth in him, their further engagement in, and to all duties which they owe unto him; and to be a bond and pledge of their communion with him, and with each other, as members of his mystical body.[1]

II. In this sacrament Christ is not offered up to his Father, nor any real sacrifice made at all for remission of sins of the quick or dead,[2] but only a commemoration of that one offering up of himself, by himself, upon the cross, once for all, and a spiritual oblation of all possible praise unto God for the same;[3] so that the Popish sacrifice of the mass, as they call it, is most abominably injurious to Christ's one only sacrifice, the alone propitiation for all the sins of the elect.[4]

poris et sanguinis sui sacramentum, Cœnam Domini quam dicimus, in Ecclesia sua ad finem usque mundi celebrandum, in perpetuam memoriam sacrificii sui ipsius in morte sua oblati, et ad beneficia istius omnia vere fidelibus obsignandum; in eorum item alimentum ac incrementum in Christo spirituale; quoque ad officia cuncta præstanda, prius quidem illi debita, arctiori adhuc nodo tenerentur; ut vinculum denique ac pignus foret communionis illius quæ iis cum Christo et secum ipsis mutuo, tanquam corporis ipsius mystici membris, intercedit.[1]

II. *In hoc Sacramento non Patri suo offertur Christus, sed neque inibi fit reale aliquod sacrificium ad peccatorum remissionem vivis aut mortuis procurandam;[2] verum unicæ istius oblationis, qua Christus semet ipsum ipse in cruce, et quidem omnino semel obtulit, commemoratio solum; una cum spirituali propterea laudis omnimodæ Deo redditæ oblatione.[3] Unde Pontificiorum istud sacrificium Missæ (uti loqui amant) plane detestandum sit oportet, utpote maxime injuriam uni illi unicoque Christi sacrificio, quod quidem unica est pro peccatis electorum universus propitiatio.[4]*

---

[1] 1 Cor. xi. 23-26; x. 16, 17, 21; xii. 13.

[2] Heb. ix. 22, 25, 26. 28.

[3] 1 Cor. xi. 24-26; Matt. xxvi. 26, 27; [Am. ed. Luke xxii. 19, 20].

[4] Heb. vii. 23, 24, 27; x. 11, 12, 14, 18.

III. The Lord Jesus hath, in this ordinance, appointed his ministers to declare his word of institution to the people, to pray, and bless the elements of bread and wine, and thereby to set them apart from a common to an holy use; and to take and break the bread, to take the cup, and (they communicating also themselves) to give both to the communicants;[1] but to none who are not then present in the congregation.[2]

IV. Private masses, or receiving this sacrament by a priest, or any other, alone;[3] as likewise the denial of the cup to the people;[4] worshiping the elements, the lifting them up, or carrying them about for adoration, and the reserving them for any pretended religious use, are all contrary to the nature of this sacrament, and to the institution of Christ.[5]

V. The outward elements in this sacrament, duly set apart to the uses ordained by Christ, have such relation to him crucified, as that truly, yet sacramentally only, they are sometimes called by the name of the things they represent, to wit, the body and blood of Christ;[6] albeit, in substance and nature, they still

III. *In hoc suo instituto præcepit Dominus Jesus Ministris suis, verbum institutionis populo declarare, orare, ac elementis pani scilicet ac vino benedicere, eaque hac ratione a communi ad sacrum usum separare, quinetiam panem accipere et frangere; poculum item in manus accipere; atque (communicantibus una ipsis) utrumque communicantibus exhibere,[1] nemini autem a congregatione tunc absenti.[2]*

IV. *Missæ privatæ, sive perceptio hujusce Sacramenti a solo vel Sacerdote vel alio quovis;[3] prout etiam poculi a populo detensio,[4] elementorum adoratio, quoque adorentur elevatio aut circumgestatio, ut et prætextu religiosi usus cujuscunque asservatio, sunt quidem omnia tum hujusce Sacramenti naturæ tum Christi institutioni plane contraria.[5]*

V. *In hoc Sacramento externa elementa ad usus a Christo institutos rite separata, ita ad eum crucifixum referuntur ut rerum quas repræsentat nominibus (corporis nempe ac sanguinis Christi) vere quidem, at Sacramentaliter tantum, sint nuncupata,[6] manent siquidem adhuc quoad substantiam et naturam vere solum-*

---

[1] Matt. xxvi. 26–28, and Mark xiv. 22–24, and Luke xxii. 19, 20, with 1 Cor. xi. 23–27.

[2] Acts xx. 7; 1 Cor. xi. 20.

[3] 1 Cor. x. 6.

[4] Mark iv. 23; 1 Cor. xi. 25–29.

[5] Matt. xv. 9.

[6] Matt. xxvi. 26–28.

remain truly, and only, bread and wine, as they were before.[1]

VI. That doctrine which maintains a change of the substance of bread and wine, into the substance of Christ's body and blood (commonly called transubstantiation) by consecration of a priest, or by any other way, is repugnant, not to Scripture alone, but even to common-sense and reason; overthroweth the nature of the sacrament; and hath been, and is the cause of manifold superstitions, yea, of gross idolatries.[2]

VII. Worthy receivers, outwardly partaking of the visible elements in this sacrament,[3] do then also inwardly by faith, really and indeed, yet not carnally and corporally, but spiritually, receive and feed upon Christ crucified, and all benefits of his death: the body and blood of Christ being then not corporally or carnally in, with, or under the bread and wine; yet as really, but spiritually, present to the faith of believers in that ordinance, as the elements themselves are, to their outward senses.[4]

VIII. Although ignorant and wicked men receive the outward elements in this sacrament, yet

que panis ac vinum nihilo minus quam antea fuerant.[1]

VI. *Doctrina illa quæ substantiæ panis ac vini in substantiam corporis et sanguinis Christi conversionem (transubstantiatio vulgo dicitur) sive illam per Sacerdotis consecrationem, sive quomodocunque demum fieri statuit, non scripturæ solum, verum etiam communi omnium sensui ac rationi adversatur, sacramenti naturam evertit, superstitionis multifariæ causa extitit atque etiamnum existit, imo vero et crassissimæ idololatriæ.[2]*

VII. *Digne communicantes, Elementa in hoc sacramento visibilia dum participant,[3] una cum iis interne Christum crucifixum et beneficia mortis ejus universa revera et realiter (modo, non carnali quidem aut corporeo, sed spirituali) per fidem recipiunt eisque vescuntur. Corpus siquidem et sanguis Christi non corporeo aut carnali modo in, cum, vel sub pane ac vino; realiter tamen, ac spiritualiter credentium fidei in hoc instituto, non minus quam externis sensibus elementa ipsa, sunt præsentia.[4]*

VIII. *Homines improbi et ignari externa licet in hoc sacramento percipere possint elementa, rem tamen*

---

[1] 1 Cor. xi. 26–28; Matt. xxvi. 29.
[2] Acts iii. 21 with 1 Cor. xi. 24–26; Luke xxiv. 6, 39.
[3] 1 Cor. xi. 28; [Am. ed. 1 Cor. v. 7, 8].
[4] 1 Cor. x. 16; [Am. ed. 1 Cor. x. 3, 4].

they receive not the thing signified thereby; but by their unworthy coming thereunto are guilty of the body and blood of the Lord, to their own damnation. Wherefore all ignorant and ungodly persons, as they are unfit to enjoy communion with him, so are they unworthy of the Lord's table, and can not, without great sin against Christ, while they remain such, partake of these holy mysteries,[1] or be admitted thereunto.[2]

per ea significatam non recipiunt; verum indigne illuc accedendo, rei fiunt corporis ac sanguinis Dominici ad sui ipsorum condemnationem. Quapropter homines impii et ignari prout communioni cum Deo potiundæ nullatenus sunt idonei, ita prorsus indigni sunt qui accedant ad mensam Domini; neque sine gravi in Christum peccato, possunt (quamdiu tales esse non destiterint Sacra hæc mysteria participare;[1] vel ad ea participandum admitti.[2]

Chapter XXX.
Of Church Censures.

I. The Lord Jesus, as king and head of his Church, hath therein appointed a government in the hand of Church officers, distinct from the civil magistrate.[3]

II. To these officers the keys of the kingdom of heaven are committed, by virtue whereof they have power respectively to retain and remit sins, to shut that kingdom against the impenitent, both by the Word and censures; and to open it unto penitent sinners, by the ministry of the gospel, and by absolution from censures, as occasion shall require.[4]

Cap. XXX.
De Censuris Ecclesiasticis.

I. *Dominus Jesus quatenus Rex et caput Ecclesiæ suæ constituit in ea regimen, quod in officiariorum Ecclesiasticorum manu foret, distinctum a civili Magistratu.[3]*

II. *Officiariis hisce claves regni cælorum sunt commissæ, quarum virtute obtinent potestatem peccata vel retinendi vel remittendi pro varia peccantium conditione; impænitentibus quidem regnum illud tam per verbum quam per censuras occludendi, peccatoribus vero pænitentibus tam evangelii ministerio quam absolutione a censuris idem aperiendi, prout occasio postulaverit.[4]*

---

[1] 1 Cor. xi. 27–29; 2 Cor. vi. 14–16; [Am. ed. 1 Cor. x. 21].
[2] 1 Cor. v. 6, 7, 13; 2 Thess. iii. 6, 14, 15; Matt. vii. 6.
[3] Isa. ix. 6, 7; 1 Tim. v. 17; 1 Thess. v. 12;

Acts xx. 17, 28; Heb. xiii. 7, 17, 24; 1 Cor. xii. 28; Matt. xxviii. 18–20; [Am. ed. Psa. ii. 6–9; John xviii. 36].
[4] Matt. xvi. 19; xviii. 17, 18; John xx. 21–23; 2 Cor. ii. 6–8.

III. Church censures are necessary for the reclaiming and gaining of offending brethren; for deterring of others from the[1] like offenses; for purging out of that leaven which might infect the whole lump; for vindicating the honor of Christ, and the holy profession of the gospel; and for preventing the wrath of God, which might justly fall upon the Church, if they should suffer his covenant, and the seals thereof, to be profaned by notorious and obstinate offenders.[2]

IV. For the better attaining of these ends, the officers of the Church are to proceed by admonition, suspension from the Sacrament of the Lord's Supper for a season, and by excommunication from the Church, according to the nature of the crime and demerit of the person.[3]

Chapter XXXI.
Of Synods and Councils.

I. For the better government and further edification of the Church, there ought to be such assemblies as are commonly called synods or councils.[4]

III. *Omnino necessariæ sunt censuræ Ecclesiasticæ, lucrandis fratribus delinquentibus eisque in viam reducendis, reliquis autem a similibus delictis deterrendis, fermento illi malo, ne totam massam inficiat, expurgando ; ad honorem Christi et Sanctam Evangelii professionem vindicandum, ut prævertatur denique ira Dei, quæ merito in Ecclesiam accendi posset, si ipsius fœdus, hujusque sigilla ab insigniter ac pertinaciter delinquentibus impune profanari pateretur.*[2]

IV. *Quo melius autem hosce fines consequantur, procedere debent Ecclesiæ officiarii, admonendo, a Sacramento cœnæ Dominicæ ad tempus aliquod suspendendo, excommunicando denique ab Ecclesia, pro ratione criminis, atque personæ delinquentis merito.*[3]

Cap. XXXI.
De Synodis et Conciliis.

I. *Quo melius gubernari, ac ulterius ædificari possit Ecclesia, conventus ejusmodi fieri debent, quales vulgo Synodi et Concilia nuncupantur.*[4]

---

[1] [Am. ed. omits *the*.]
[2] 1 Cor. chap. v. ; 1 Tim. v. 20; Matt. vii. 6; 1 Tim. i. 20; 1 Cor. xi. 27 to the end, with Jude 23

[3] 1 Thess. v. 12 ; 2 Thess. iii. 6, 14, 15 ; 1 Cor. v. 4, 5, 13 ; Matt. xviii. 17 ; Tit. iii. 10.
[4] Acts xv. 2, 4, 6.

The American edition here adds the following:

[*And it belongeth to the overseers and other rulers of the particular churches, by virtue of their office, and the power which Christ hath given them for edification, and not for destruction, to appoint such assemblies* (Acts xv.); *and to convene together in them, as often as they shall judge it expedient for the good of the Church* (Acts xv. 22, 23, 25).]

II. As magistrates may lawfully call a synod of ministers and other fit persons to consult and advise with about matters of religion;[1] so, if magistrates be open enemies to the Church, the ministers of Christ, of themselves, by virtue of their office, or they, with other fit persons, upon delegation from their churches, may meet together in such assemblies.[2 & 3]

III. [II.] It belongeth to synods and councils, ministerially, to determine controversies of faith, and cases of conscience; to set down rules and directions for the better ordering of the public worship of God, and government of his Church; to receive complaints in cases of maladministration, and authoritatively to determine the same: which decrees and determinations, if consonant to the Word of God, are to be received with reverence and submission, not only for their agreement with the Word, but also for

II. *Quemadmodum licitum est Magistratibus Synodum Ministrorum aliorumque qui sunt idonei convocare, quibuscum de religionis rebus deliberent ac consultent:*[1] *Ita si Magistratus fuerint Ecclesiæ hostes aperti, licebit Christi ministris a seipsis virtute officii, eisve cum aliis idoneis, accepta prius ab Ecclesiis suis delegatione, in istiusmodi conventibus congregari.*[2]

III. *Synodorum et Conciliorum est controversias fidei et conscientiæ casus, ministerialiter quidem, determinare; regulas ac præscripta quo melius publicus Dei cultus ejusque Ecclesiæ regimen ordinentur constituere; Querelas de mala administratione delatas admittere, deque iis authoritative decernere. Quæ quidem decreta et decisiones, modo verbo Dei consenserint, cum reverentia sunt ac summissione excipienda; Non quidem solum quod verbo Dei sint consentanea, verum etiam gratia potestatis ea constituentis, ut quæ*

---

[1] Isa. xlix. 23; 1 Tim. ii. 1, 2; 2 Chron. xix. 8-11; chaps. xxix., xxx.; Matt. ii. 4, 5; Prov. xi. 14.

[2] Acts xv. 2, 4, 22, 23, 25.

[3] [Am. ed. omits this whole section.]

the power whereby they are made, as being an ordinance of God, appointed thereunto in his Word.[1]

IV. [III.] All synods or councils since the apostles' times, whether general or particular, may err, and many have erred; therefore they are not to be made the rule of faith or practice, but to be used as a help in both.[2]

V. [IV.] Synods and councils are to handle or conclude nothing but that which is ecclesiastical: and are not to intermeddle with civil affairs which concern the commonwealth, unless by way of humble petition in cases extraordinary; or by way of advice for satisfaction of conscience, if they be thereunto required by the civil magistrate.[3]

CHAPTER XXXII.

Of the State of Men[4] after Death, and of the Resurrection of the Dead.

I. The bodies of men, after death, return to dust, and see corruption;[5] but their souls (which neither die nor sleep), having an immortal subsistence, immediately return to God who gave them.[6]　The souls of the righteous, being then made perfect in holiness, are received into the highest heavens, where they behold

sit ordinatio Dei id ad in verbo suo designata.[1]

IV. *Synodi omnes sive concilia post Apostolorum tempora, seu generales sive particulares, errori sunt obnoxiæ, quin neque paucæ erraverunt.　Proindeque fidei aut praxeos norma constituendæ non sunt, verum in utrisque auxilii loco adhibendæ.*[2]

V. *Synodi et Concilia id solum quod Ecclesiam spectat tractare debent et concludere; neque civilibus negotiis, quæ rem publicam spectant ingerere se debent, nisi humiliter supplicando in casibus, si qui acciderint, extraordinariis; aut consulendo, quoties id ab eis postulat Magistratus civilis, nempe quo conscientiæ illius satisfiat.*[3]

CAP. XXXII.

De statu hominum post mortem, deque resurrectione mortuorum.

I. *Hominum corpora post mortem ad pulverem rediguntur, et corruptionem vident:*[5] *At animæ illorum (quæ quidem nec morientur nec obdormiunt) ut quæ subsistentiam habent immortalem, ad Deum continuo earum datorem revertuntur.*[6]　*Animæ quidem Justorum iam tum perfecte sanctificatæ, cœlis supremis ac-*

---

[1] Acts xv. 15, 19, 24, 27-31; xvi. 4; Matt. xviii. 17-20.
[2] Eph. ii. 20; Acts xvii. 11; 1 Cor. ii. 5; 2 Cor. i. 24.
[3] Luke xii. 13, 14; John xviii. 36.
[4] [Am. ed. has *Man*.]
[5] Gen. iii. 19; Acts xiii. 36.
[6] Luke xxiii. 43; Eccles. xii. 7.

the face of God in light and glory, waiting for the full redemption of their bodies:[1] and the souls of the wicked are cast into hell, where they remain in torments and utter darkness, reserved to the judgment of the great day.[2] Besides these two places for souls separated from their bodies, the Scripture acknowledgeth none.

II. At the last day, such as are found alive shall not die, but be changed;[3] and all the dead shall be raised up with the self-same bodies, and none other, although with different qualities, which shall be united again to their souls forever.[4]

III. The bodies of the unjust shall, by the power of Christ, be raised to dishonor; the bodies of the just, by his Spirit, unto honor, and be made conformable to his own glorious body.[5]

CHAPTER XXXIII.
Of the Last Judgment.

I. God hath appointed a day wherein he will judge the world in righteousness by Jesus Christ,[6] to

---

cipiuntur, ubi Dei faciem in lumine ac gloria intuentur, corporum suorum plenam redemtionem expectantes:[1] *Animæ vero improborum conjiciuntur in Gehennam, ubi inter diros cruciatus in tenebris exterioribus conclusæ manent, ad judicium magni illius diei asservatæ.*[2] *Locum autem animabus a corpore solutis extra hosce duos Scriptura Sacra non agnoscit ullum.*

II. *Novissimo illo die, qui comperientur in vivis non morientur quidem sed mutabuntur;*[3] *qui mortui fuerint resuscitabuntur omnes, ipsissimis iis corporibus quibus viventes aliquando fungebantur, ac non aliis, utut qualitate differentibus; quæ denuo animabus quæque suis æterno conjugio unientur.*[4]

III. *Injustorum corpora ad dedecus per potentiam Christi suscitabuntur; justorum autem corpora per spiritum ejus ad honorem, fientque hæc conformia corpori ipsius glorioso.*[5]

CAP. XXXIII.
De ultimo judicio.

I. *Diem Deus designavit quo mundum in justitia judicabit per Jesum Christum;*[6] *cui a Patre data est*

---

[1] Heb. xii. 23; 2 Cor. v. 1, 6, 8; Phil. i. 23, with Acts iii. 21 and Eph. iv. 10; [Am. ed. 1 John iii. 2].

[2] Luke xvi. 23, 24; Acts i. 25; Jude 6, 7; 1 Pet. iii. 19.

[3] 1 Thess. iv. 17; 1 Cor. xv. 51, 52.

[4] Job xix. 26, 27; 1 Cor. xv. 42–44.

[5] Acts xxiv. 15: John v. 28, 29; 1 Cor. xv. 42; Phil. iii. 21.

[6] Acts xvii. 31.

whom all power and judgment is given of the Father.[1] In which day, not only the apostate angels shall be judged,[2] but likewise all persons, that have lived upon earth, shall appear before the tribunal of Christ, to give an account of their thoughts, words, and deeds; and to receive according to what they have done in the body, whether good or evil.[3]

II. The end of God's appointing this day, is for the manifestation of the glory of his mercy in the eternal salvation of the elect;[4] and of his justice in the damnation of the reprobate, who are wicked and disobedient.[5] For then shall the righteous go into everlasting life, and receive that fullness of joy and refreshing which shall come from the presence of the Lord:[6] but the wicked, who know not God, and obey not the gospel of Jesus Christ, shall be cast into eternal torments, and be punished with everlasting destruction from the presence of the Lord, and from the glory of his power.[7]

III. As Christ would have us to be certainly persuaded that there shall be a day of judgment, both to deter all men from sin, and for the

omnis potestas et judicium.[1] *Quo quidem die non solum judicabuntur Angeli apostatici,*[2] *verum etiam omnes homines, quotquot uspiam in orbe terrarum aliquando vixerint, coram Christi tribunali comparebunt, ut cogitationum, dictorum, factorumque suorum rationem reddant, recipiantque simul juxta id quod in corpore quisque fecerit, seu bonum fuerit sive malum.*[3]

II. *Eo autem consilio Diem hunc præstituit Deus, quo nempe misericordiæ suæ constaret gloria ex æterna salute electorum, justitiæ autem e damnatione reproborum, qui improbi sunt et contumaces. Tunc enim justi introibunt in vitam æternam, recipientque plenitudinem illam gaudii ac refrigerii, quæ a præsentia Domini ventura sunt: Impii autem, qui Deum ignorant, quique Evangelio Jesu Christi non morem gerunt, in æternos cruciatus detrudentur, æternaque perditione punientur a præsentia Domini et a potentiæ ipsius gloria profligati.*[7]

III. *Quemadmodum Christus nobis, futurum esse aliquando diem judicii, esse velit persuasissimum; tum quo omnes a peccato absterreantur,*

---

[1] John v. 22, 27.
[2] 1 Cor. vi. 3; Jude 6; 2 Pet. ii. 4.
[3] 2 Cor. v. 10; Eccles. xii. 14; Rom. ii. 16; xiv. 10, 12; Matt. xii. 36, 37.
[4] Rom. ix. 23; Matt. xxv. 21.

[5] Rom. ii. 5, 6; 2 Thess. i. 7, 8; Rom. ix. 22.
[6] Matt. xxv. 31-34; Acts iii. 19; 2 Thess. i. 7.
[7] Matt. xxv. 41, 46; 2 Thess. i. 9; [Am. ed. Isa. lxvi. 24].

greater consolation of the godly in their adversity : [1] so will he have that day unknown to men, that they may shake off all carnal security, and be always watchful, because they know not at what hour the Lord will come; and may be ever prepared to say, Come, Lord Jesus, come quickly.[2] Amen.

tum ob majus piorum solatium in rebus adversis : [1] *ita sane diem ipsum vult ab hominibus ignorari, quo securitatem omnem carnalem excutiant, et nunquam non sint vigilantes (quum qua hora venturus sit Dominus ignorant) utque semper sint parati ad dicendum Veni Domine Jesu, etiam cito veni.* [2] Amen.

CHARLES HERLE, *Prolocutor.*
CORNELIUS BURGES, *Assessor.*
HERBERT PALMER, *Assessor.*
HENRY ROBROUGHE, *Scriba.*
ADONIRAM BYFIELD, *Scriba.*

---

[1] 2 Pet. iii. 11, 14; 2 Cor. v. 10, 11; 2 Thess. i. 5-7; Luke xxi. 27, 28; Rom. viii. 23-25.   [2] Matt. xxiv. 36, 42-44; Mark xiii. 35-37; Luke xii. 35, 36; Rev. xxii. 20.

The Humble

ADVICE

Of the

ASSEMBLY

OF

DIVINES,

Now by Authority of *Parliament*

fitting at WESTMINSTER;

Concerning

A Larger Catechism:

Prefented by them lately to both Houses

of PARLIAMENT.

Printed at LONDON;

AND

Re-printed at EDINBURGH by *Evan Tyler*, Printer to
the Kings moft Excellent Majeftie. 1647.

(3)

TO

The Right honorable the Lords and

Commons Aſſembled in PARLIAMENT;

The humble Advice of the Aſſembly of Divines
fitting at WESTMINSTER.

Concerning

A larger Catechiſm.

QUESTION.

Hat is the chief and higheſt end of man?

A. Mans chief and higheſt end is, to glori-
fie God, and fully to enjoy him for ever.

Q. How doth it appear that there is a God?

A. The very light of nature in man, and
the works of God, declare plainly that there is a God: but
his Word and Spirit only do ſufficiently and effectually
reveale him unto men for their ſalvation.

Q. What is the Word of God?

A. The holy Scriptures of the Old and New Teſta-
ment are the Word of God, the only Rule of Faith and
obedience.

A 2 *Q. How*

THE WESTMINSTER SHORTER CATECHISM. A.D. 1647.

Catechismus Westmonasteriensis Minor.

[This Catechism was prepared by the Westminster Assembly in 1647, and adopted by the General Assembly of the Church of Scotland, 1648; by the Presbyterian Synod of New York and Philadelphia, May, 1788; and by nearly all the Calvinistic Presbyterian and Congregational Churches of the English tongue. It was translated into Greek, Hebrew, Arabic, and many other languages, and appeared in innumerable editions. Although little known on the continent of Europe, it is more extensively used than any other Protestant catechism, except perhaps the Small Catechism of Luther and the Heidelberg Catechism. Want of space compels us to omit the Assembly's Larger Catechism, which is easy of access. For the same reason we have omitted the Scripture proofs.

The English original is conformed to the edition of the Presbyterian Board, compared with the London edition of 1658 and other older English and Scotch editions, which present no variations of any account. The Latin translation is from the Cambridge and Edinburgh editions, containing the Confession and both Catechisms, and reprinted in Niemeyer's Appendix.]

The Shorter Catechism.

Question. 1. What is the chief end of man?

Answer. Man's chief end is to glorify God, and to enjoy him forever.

Ques. 2. What rule hath God given to direct us how we may glorify and enjoy him?

Ans. The Word of God, which is contained in the Scriptures of the Old and New Testaments,[1] is the only rule to direct us how we may glorify and enjoy him.

Ques. 3. What do the Scriptures principally teach?

Ans. The Scriptures principally teach what man is to believe concerning God, and what duty God requires of man.

Ques. 4. What is GOD?

Ans. God is a Spirit, infinite, eternal, and unchangeable, in his

Catechismus Minor.

Quæstio. Quis hominis finis est præcipuus?

Responsio. Præcipuus hominis finis est, Deum glorificare, eodemque frui in æternum.

Quæs. Quam nobis regulam dedit Deus, qua nos ad ejus glorificationem ac fruitionem dirigamur?

Resp. Verbum Dei (quod Scripturis Veteris ac Novi instrumenti comprehenditur) est unica regula, qua nos ad ejus glorificationem ac fruitionem dirigamur.

Quæs. Quid est quod Scripturæ præcipue docent?

Resp. Duo imprimis sunt quæ Scripturæ docent, quid homini de Deo sit credendum, quidque officii exigat ab homine Deus.

Quæs. Quid est Deus?

Resp. Deus est Spiritus essentia, sapientia, potentia, sanctitate, justi-

---

[1] The London edition of 1658, Dunlop's Collection of 1719, and other editions read *Testament*.

being, wisdom, power, holiness, justice, goodness, and truth.

Ques. 5. Are there more Gods than one?

Ans. There is but one only, the living and true God.

Ques. 6. How many persons are there in the Godhead?

Ans. There are three persons in the Godhead: the Father, the Son, and the Holy Ghost; and these three are one God, the same in substance, equal in power and glory.

Ques. 7. What are the decrees of God?

Ans. The decrees of God are his eternal purpose according to the counsel of his will, whereby, for his own glory, he hath fore-ordained whatsoever comes to pass.

Ques. 8. How doth God execute his decrees.

Ans. God executeth his decrees in the works of creation and providence.

Ques. 9. What is the work of creation?

Ans. The work of creation is God's making all things of nothing, by the word of his power, in the space of six days, and all very good.

Ques. 10. How did God create man?

Ans. God created man, male and female, after his own image, in knowledge, righteousness, and holi-

tia, bonitate ac veritate infinitus, æternus, ac immutabilis.

Quæs. Suntne plures uno Deo?

Resp. Unus est unicusque, vivens ille verusque Deus.

Quæs. Quot sunt personæ in Deitate?

Resp. In Deitate personæ tres sunt, Pater, Filius, ac Spiritus Sanctus; suntque hæ tres personæ Deus unus, substantia eædem, potentia ac gloria coæquales.

Quæs. Quid sunt decreta Dei?

Resp. Decreta Dei sunt æternum ejus propositum secundum voluntatis suæ consilium, quo quicquid unquam evenit, propter suam ipsius gloriam præordinavit.

Quæs. Quomodo decreta sua exequitur Deus?

Resp. Deus exequitur decreta sua creationis operibus ac providentiæ.

Quæs. Quid est opus creationis?

Resp. Opus creationis est quo Deus per verbum potentiæ suæ omnia sex dierum spatio ex nihilo condidit, atque omnia quidem valde bona.

Quæs. Qualem creavit Deus hominem?

Resp. Deus hominem creavit marem ac fœminam, juxta suam ipsius imaginem, in cognitione, justitia ac

ness, with dominion over the creatures.

Ques. 11. *What are God's works
of providence?*

Ans. God's works of providence
are his most holy, wise, and powerful preserving and governing
all his creatures, and all their actions.

Ques. 12. *What special act of
providence did God exercise towards
man, in the estate wherein he was
created?*

Ans. When God had created
man, he entered into a covenant of
life with him, upon condition of
perfect obedience: forbidding him
to eat of the tree of knowledge
of good and evil, upon pain of
death.

Ques. 13. *Did our first parents
continue in the estate wherein they
were created?*

Ans. Our first parents, being left
to the freedom of their own will, fell
from the estate wherein they were
created, by sinning against God.

Ques. 14. *What is sin?*

Ans. Sin is any want of conformity unto, or transgression of,
the law of God.

Ques. 15. *What was the sin whereby our first parents fell from the estate wherein they were created?*

Ans. The sin whereby our first
parents fell from the estate wherein

sanctitate, dominium habentem in
creaturas.

Quæs. *Quænam sunt opera Divinæ providentiæ?*

Resp. *Providentiæ Divinæ opera
sunt sanctissima Dei, sapientissima
potentissimaque creaturarum suarum omnium, earumque actionum
conservatio et gubernatio.*

Quæs. *Quem peculiarem providentiæ suæ actum exercebat Deus
circa hominem in statu creationis
suæ existentem?*

Resp. *Postquam Deus hominem
condidisset, inibat cum illo fœdus vitæ, sub conditione perfectæ obedientiæ; esu de arbore scientiæ boni
malique sub pœna mortis eidem in-
terdicens.*

Quæs. *An vero Primi nostri Parentes in quo creati fuerant statu
perstitere?*

Resp. *Primi Parentes voluntatis
suæ libertati permissi peccando in
Deum statu in quo creati fuerant
exciderunt.*

Quæs. *Quid est peccatum?*

Resp. *Peccatum est defectus quilibet conformitatis cum lege Divina,
seu quævis ejusdem transgressio.*

Quæs. *Quodnam erat peccatum
istud quo primi parentes statu in
quo creati fuerant exciderunt?*

Resp. *Peccatum istud quo primi
parentes statu in quo creati fuerant*

they were created, was their eating the forbidden fruit.

Ques. 16. *Did all mankind fall in Adam's first transgression ?*

Ans. The covenant being made with Adam, not only for himself, but for his posterity, all mankind descending from him by ordinary generation, sinned in him, and fell with him, in his first transgression.

Ques. 17. *Into what estate did the fall bring mankind ?*

Ans. The fall brought mankind into an estate of sin and misery.

Ques. 18. *Wherein consists the sinfulness of that estate whereinto man fell ?*

Ans. The sinfulness of that estate whereinto man fell, consists in the guilt of Adam's first sin, the want of original righteousness, and the corruption of his whole nature, which is commonly called original sin; together with all actual transgressions which proceed from it.

Ques. 19. *What is the misery of that estate whereinto man fell ?*

Ans. All mankind by their fall lost communion with God, are under his wrath and curse, and so made liable to all the[1] miseries in

exciderunt, erat comestio fructus interdicti.

Quæs. Totumne genus humanum cecidit in prima Adami transgressione ?

Resp. Quandoquidem fœdus cum Adamo ictum fuerat non suo tantum sed et posterorum suorum nomine; exinde factum est ut totum genus humanum ab illo generatione ordinaria procreatum, in eo peccaverit, cumque eo ceciderit, in prima ejus transgressione.

Quæs. In quem vero statum præcipitavit lapsus iste humanum genus?

Resp. Lapsus iste humanum genus in statum peccati ac miseriæ præcipitavit.

Quæs. In quo consistit status illius in quem lapsus est homo peccaminositas ?

Resp. Status in quem lapsus est homo peccaminositas consistit in reatu primi illius peccati quod Adamus admisit, in defectu originalis justitiæ, totiusque naturæ corruptione, quod Peccatum originale *vulgo dicitur; una cum omnibus peccatis actualibus exinde profluentibus.*

Quæs. Quæ miseria est illius status in quem homo lapsus est ?

Resp. Universum genus humanum lapsu suo communionem cum Deo perdidit, sub ira ejus et maledictione est constitutum, adeoque cunctis hu-

---

[1] Older editions omit *the.*

this life, to death itself, and to the pains of hell forever.

Ques. 20. *Did God leave all mankind to perish in the estate of sin and misery?*

Ans. God, having out of his mere good pleasure, from all eternity, elected some to everlasting life, did enter into a covenant of grace, to deliver them out of the estate of sin and misery, and to bring them into an estate of salvation by a Redeemer.

Ques. 21. *Who is the Redeemer of God's elect?*

Ans. The only Redeemer of God's elect is the Lord Jesus Christ, who being the eternal Son of God became man, and so was, and continueth to be, God and man, in two distinct natures, and one person forever.

Ques. 22. *How did Christ, being the Son of God, become man?*

Ans. Christ, the Son of God, became man, by taking to himself a true body, and a reasonable soul, being conceived by the power of the Holy Ghost, in the womb of the Virgin Mary, and born of her, yet without sin.

Ques. 23. *What offices doth Christ execute as our Redeemer?*

Ans. Christ, as our Redeemer, executeth the offices of a Prophet,

jus vitæ miseriis, ipsi morti, infernique cruciatibus in æternum est obnoxium.

Quæs. An vero Deus humanum genus universum in statu peccati ac miseriæ periturum dereliquit?

Resp. Deus cum ex mero suo beneplacito nonnullos ad vitam æternam ab omni retro æternitate elegisset, fœdus gratiæ cum eis iniit; se nempe liberaturum eos e statu peccati ac miseriæ, atque in statum salutis per redemptorem translaturum.

Quæs. Quis est Redemptor electorum Dei?

Resp. Dominus Jesus Christus est electorum Dei Redemptor unicus, qui æternus Dei Filius cum esset, factus est homo; adeoque fuit, est, eritque Θεάνθρωπος, e naturis duabus distinctis persona unica in sempiternum.

Quæs. Qui autem Christus, Filius Dei cum esset, factus est homo?

Resp. Christus Filius Dei factus est homo, dum corpus verum, animamque rationalem assumeret sibi vi Spiritus Sancti in utero eque substantia Virginis Mariæ conceptus, et ex eadem natus, immunis tamen a peccato.

Quæs. Quæ munera Christus ut Redemptor noster obit?

Resp. Christus quatenus Redemptor noster obit munera Prophetæ,

of a Priest, and of a King, both in his estate of humiliation and exaltation.

Ques. 24. *How doth Christ execute the office of a Prophet?*

Ans. Christ executeth the office of a Prophet, in revealing to us by his Word and Spirit, the will of God for our salvation.

Ques. 25. *How doth Christ execute the office of a Priest?*

Ans. Christ executeth the office of a Priest, in his once offering up of himself a sacrifice to satisfy divine justice, and reconcile us to God, and in[1] making continual intercession for us.

Ques. 26. *How doth Christ execute the office of a King?*

Ans. Christ executeth the office of a King, in subduing us to himself, in ruling and defending us, and in[1] restraining and conquering all his and our enemies.

Ques. 27. *Wherein did Christ's humiliation consist?*

Ans. Christ's humiliation consisted in his being born, and that in a low condition, made under the law, undergoing the miseries of this life, the wrath of God, and the cursed death of the cross; in being buried, and continuing under the power of death for a time.

Sacerdotis ac Regis, cum in humiliationis tum in exaltationis suæ statu.

Quæs. Quomodo Prophetæ munere defungitur Christus?

Resp. Christus defungitur Prophetæ munere, voluntatem Dei in salutem nostram nobis per verbum suum spiritumque revelando.

Quæs. Qua ratione exequitur Christus munus Sacerdotale?

Resp. Christus exequitur Sacerdotale munus, semetipsum semel in sacrificium offerendo, quo justitiæ divinæ satisfaceret, nosque Deo conciliaret; prout etiam perpetuo pro nobis intercedendo.

Quæs. Qui exequitur Christus munus Regium?

Resp. Christus exequitur munus Regium nos sibi subjugando, nos gubernando, tuendoque, ut etiam hostes suos nostrosque coërcendo ac debellando.

Quæs. In quo constitit Christi humiliatio?

Resp. Humiliatio Christi in eo constitit quod fuerit natus, et quidem humili conditione, factus sub lege, quodque vitæ hujus miserias, iram Dei mortemque crucis execrabilem subierit; quod sepultus fuerit, et sub potestate mortis aliquandiu commoratus.

---

[1] Older editions omit *in.*

Ques. 28. *Wherein consisteth Christ's exaltation?*

Ans. Christ's exaltation consisteth in his rising again from the dead on the third day, in ascending up into heaven, in sitting at the right hand of God the Father, and in coming to judge the world at the last day.

Ques. 29. *How are we made partakers of the redemption purchased by Christ?*

Ans. We are made partakers of the redemption purchased by Christ, by the effectual application of it to us by his Holy Spirit.

Ques. 30. *How doth the Spirit apply to us the redemption purchased by Christ?*

Ans. The Spirit applieth to us the redemption purchased by Christ, by working faith in us, and thereby uniting us to Christ in our effectual calling.

Ques. 31. *What is effectual calling?*

Ans. Effectual calling is the work of God's Spirit, whereby, convincing us of our sin and misery, enlightening our minds in the knowledge of Christ, and renewing our wills, he doth persuade and enable us to embrace Jesus Christ, freely offered to us in the gospel.

Ques. 32. *What benefits do they*

Quæs. In quo consistit Christi exaltatio?

Resp. Exaltatio Christi consistit in resurrectione ejus a mortuis tertio die, ascensu in cœlum, sessione ad dextram Dei Patris, adventu ejus ad mundum judicandum die novissimo.

Quæs. Qua ratione participes efficimur redemptionis per Christum acquisitæ?

Resp. Redemptionis per Christum acquisitæ participes efficimur ejusdem nobis efficaci per Spiritum ejus Sanctum, applicatione.

Quæs. Quomodo nobis applicat Spiritus redemptionem per Christum acquisitam?

Resp. Spiritus nobis applicat redemptionem per Christum acquisitam fidem in nobis efficiendo, ac per eandem nos Christo in vocatione nostra efficaci uniendo.

Quæs. Quid est vocatio efficax?

Resp. Vocatio efficax est Spiritus Dei opus, quo nos peccati ac miseriæ nostræ arguens, mentes nostras cognitione Christi illuminans, voluntates nostras renovans, prorsus nobis persuadet, et vires sufficit, ut Jesum Christum amplectamur, gratuito nobis oblatum in Evangelio.

Quæs. Quænam beneficia in hac

that are effectually called partake of in this life?

Ans. They that are effectually called do in this life partake of justification, adoption, sanctification, and the several benefits which, in this life, do either accompany or flow from them.

Ques. 33. *What is justification?*

Ans. Justification is an act of God's free grace, wherein he pardoneth all our sins, and accepteth us as righteous in his sight, only for the righteousness of Christ imputed to us, and received by faith alone.

Ques. 34. *What is adoption?*

Ans. Adoption is an act of God's free grace, whereby we are received into the number, and have a right to all the privileges, of the sons of God.

Ques. 35. *What is sanctification?*

Ans. Sanctification is the work of God's free grace, whereby we are renewed in the whole man after the image of God, and are enabled more and more to die unto sin, and live unto righteousness.

Ques. 36. *What are the benefits which in this life do accompany or flow from justification, adoption, and sanctification?*

Ans. The benefits which in this life do accompany or flow from justification, adoption, and sanctification, are, assurance of God's love,

vita consequuntur ii qui sunt vocati efficaciter?

Resp. *Qui vocati sunt efficaciter, justificationem, adoptionem, et sanctificationem in hac vita consequuntur, una cum omnibus iis beneficiis quæcunque solent in hac vita comitari illas, aut ab iisdem promanare.*

Quæs. *Quid est justificatio?*

Resp. *Justificatio est actus gratiæ Dei gratuitæ, quo peccata nobis condonat omnia, nosque tanquam justos in conspectu suo acceptat, propter solam Christi justitiam nobis imputatam, per fidem tantum apprehensam.*

Quæs. *Quid est adoptio?*

Resp. *Adoptio est actus gratiæ Dei gratuitæ, quo in numerum recipimur ac jus obtinemus ad omnia privilegia filiorum Dei.*

Quæs. *Quid est sanctificatio?*

Resp. *Sanctificatio est opus gratiæ Dei gratuitæ, quo in toto homine secundum imaginem Dei renovamur, et potentes efficimur, qui magis in dies magisque peccato quidem moriamur, justitiæ autem vivamus.*

Quæs. *Quænam sunt illa beneficia quæ justificationem, adoptionem et sanctificationem in hac vita vel comitantur, vel ab eis promanant?*

Resp. *Quæ justificationem, adoptionem et sanctificationem in hac vita vel comitantur vel ab eis promanant beneficia, sunt certitudo amoris Dei,*

peace of conscience, joy in the Holy Ghost, increase of grace, and perseverance therein to the end.

Ques. 37. *What benefits do believers receive from Christ at death?*

Ans. The souls of believers are, at their death, made perfect in holiness, and do immediately pass into glory; and their bodies, being still united to Christ, do rest in their graves till the resurrection.

Ques. 38. *What benefits do believers receive from Christ at the resurrection?*

Ans. At the resurrection, believers being raised up in glory, shall be openly acknowledged and acquitted in the day of judgment, and made perfectly blessed in the full enjoying of God to all eternity.

Ques. 39. *What is the duty which God requireth of man?*

Ans. The duty which God requireth of man is obedience to his revealed will.

Ques. 40. *What did God at first reveal to man for the rule of his obedience?*

Ans. The rule which God at first revealed to man, for his obedience, was the moral law.

Ques. 41. *Wherein is the moral law summarily comprehended?*

Ans. The moral law is summarily comprehended in the ten commandments.

pax conscientiæ, gaudium in Spiritu Sancto, gratiæ incrementum, in eaque ad finem usque perseverantia.

Quæs. *Quænam a Christo beneficia in morte percipiunt fideles?*

Resp. *Animæ fidelium in morte fiunt perfecte sanctæ, ac protinus in gloriam transferuntur; corpora vero usque Christo unita in sepulchris ad resurrectionem usque quiescunt.*

Quæs. *Quæ tandem beneficia a Christo percipiunt fideles in resurrectione?*

Resp. *In resurrectione fideles suscitati in gloria, palam agnoscentur et absolventur in die judicii, fientque perfecte beati plena Dei in omne æternum fruitione.*

Quæs. *Quid autem officii ac observantiæ ab homine exposcit Deus?*

Resp. *Officium quod ab homine Deus exposcit, est obedientia voluntati ejus revelatæ exhibenda.*

Quæs. *Quid homini primum revelavit Deus, quod foret ipsi obedientiæ regula?*

Resp. *Obedientiæ regula, quam Deus homini primum revelavit, erat Lex moralis.*

Quæs. *Ubinam summatim comprehenditur lex moralis?*

Resp. *Lex moralis summatim comprehenditur in Decalogo.*

Ques. 42. *What is the sum of the ten commandments ?*

Ans. The sum of the ten commandments is, to love the Lord our God with all our heart, with all our soul, with all our strength, and with all our mind; and our neighbor as ourselves.

Ques. 43. *What is the preface to the ten commandments ?*

Ans. The preface to the ten commandments is in these words: *I am the Lord thy God, which brought thee out of the land of Egypt, out of the house of bondage.*

Ques. 44. *What doth the preface to the ten commandments teach us ?*

Ans. The preface to the ten commandments teacheth us, that because God is the Lord, and our God and Redeemer, therefore we are bound to keep all his commandments.

Ques. 45. *Which is the first commandment ?*

Ans. The first commandment is, *Thou shalt have no other gods before me.*

Ques. 46. *What is required in the first commandment ?*

Ans. The first commandment requireth us to know and acknowledge God, to be the only true God, and our God; and to worship and glorify him accordingly.

Quæs. Dic quænam sit Decalogi summa ?

Resp. Summa Decalogi est ut Dominum nostrum toto corde, tota anima, tota mente, totisque viribus nostris diligamus; proximum vero nostrum sicut nosmetipsos.

Quæs. Quænam est Decalogi præfatio ?

Resp. Decalogi præfatio hisce verbis continetur [Ego sum Dominus Deus tuus, qui te eduxi e terra Ægypti, e domo servitutis].

Quæs. Quid nos edocet Decalogi præfatio ?

Resp. Decalogi præfatio nos docet, quod quoniam Deus est Dominus, nosterque Deus ac redemptor, ea propter præcepta ejus omnia tenemur observare.

Quæs. Quodnam est mandatum primum ?

Resp. Mandatum primum est [Non habebis Deos alios coram me].

Quæs. In mandato primo quid exigitur ?

Resp. In mandato primo exigitur ut Jehovam esse unicum illum verumque Deum, Deumque nostrum cognoscamus simul et agnoscamus, atque ut talem colamus, ac glorificemus.

Ques. 47. *What is forbidden in the first commandment ?*

Ans. The first commandment forbiddeth the denying, or not worshiping and glorifying the true God, as God, and our God ; and the giving that worship and glory to any other which is due to him alone.

Ques. 48. *What are we specially taught by these words,* " before me," *in the first commandment ?*

Ans. These words, *" before me,"* in the first commandment, teach us that God, who seeth all things, taketh notice of, and is much displeased with, the sin of having any other God.

Ques. 49. *Which is the second commandment ?*

Ans. The second commandment is, *Thou shalt not make unto thee any graven image, or any likeness of any thing that is in heaven above, or that is in the earth beneath, or that is in the water under the earth; thou shalt not bow down thyself to them, nor serve them; for I the Lord thy God am a jealous God, visiting the iniquity of the fathers upon the children, unto the third and fourth generation of them that hate me, and showing mercy unto thousands of them that love me and keep my commandments.*

Quæs. Quid est quod prohibetur mandato primo ?

Resp. *In primo mandato prohibetur veri Dei abnegatio, neglectusque ipsum tanquam Deum, Deumque nostrum colendi ac glorificandi ; prout etiam cultum ac gloriam illi soli debita alii cuivis tribuere aut exhibere.*

Quæs. Quid imprimis docemur verbis istis mandati primi [Coram me] ?

Resp. *Verba isthæc* [Coram me] *in mandato primo nos docent, Deum qui omnia intuetur, peccatum alium habendi Deum cum imprimis advertere, tum vero eodem offendi plurimum.*

Quæs. Quodnam est præceptum secundum ?

Resp. *Secundum præceptum est* [Non facies tibi imaginem quamvis sculptilem, aut similitudinem rei cujusvis quæ est in cœlis superne, aut inferius in terris, aut in aquis infra terram; non incurvabis te iis, nec eis servies: siquidem ego Dominus Deus tuus Deus sum Zelotypus, visitans iniquitates patrum in filios ad tertiam usque quartamque progeniem osorum mei, exhibens vero misericordiam ad millenas usque diligentium me, ac mandata mea observantium].

Ques. 50. *What is required in the second commandment?*

Ans. The second commandment requireth the receiving, observing, and keeping pure and entire, all such religious worship and ordinances as God hath appointed in his Word.

Ques. 51. *What is forbidden in the second commandment?*

Ans. The second commandment forbiddeth the worshiping of God by images, or any other way not appointed in his Word.

Ques. 52. *What are the reasons annexed to the second commandment?*

Ans. The reasons annexed to the second commandment are, God's sovereignty over us, his propriety[1] in us, and the[1] zeal he hath to his own worship.

Ques. 53. *Which is the third commandment?*

Ans. The third commandment is, *Thou shalt not take the name of the Lord thy God in vain: for the Lord will not hold him guiltless that taketh his name in vain.*

Ques. 54. *What is required in the third commandment?*

Ans. The third commandment requireth the holy and reverent use of God's names, titles, attributes, ordinances, word, and works.

Quæs. *Quid exigitur in secundo præcepto?*

Resp. *Præceptum secundum exigit, ut cultus omnes ac instituta religionis quæcunque Deus in verbo suo constituit, excipiamus, observemus, pura denique ac integra custodiamus.*

Quæs. *Quid est quod in secundo præcepto prohibetur?*

Resp. *Secundum præceptum interdicit nobis cultu Dei per simulacra, aut alia ratione quaviscunque quam in verbo suo Deus non præscripsit.*

Quæs. *Quænam sunt rationes præcepto secundo annexæ?*

Resp. *Rationes secundo præcepto annexæ sunt, supremum Dei in nos dominium, illius jus in nobis peculiare, zelusque quo suum ipsius cultum prosequitur.*

Quæs. *Age quodnam est tertium mandatum?*

Resp. *Mandatum tertium sic habetur* [Nomen Domini Dei tui inaniter non usurpabis; non enim eum pro insonte habebit Dominus qui nomen ejus inaniter adhibuerit].

Quæs. *Quid exigitur in mandato tertio?*

Resp. *Mandatum tertium exigit ut Dei nomina, titulos, attributa, instituta, verba, operaque sancte summaque cum reverentia adhibeamus.*

---

[1] London ed. of 1658 reads *property*, and *his* zeal.

Ques. 55. *What is forbidden in the third commandment ?*

Ans. The third commandment forbiddeth all profaning or abusing of any thing whereby God maketh himself known.

Ques. 56. *What is the reason annexed to the third commandment ?*

Ans. The reason annexed to the third commandment is, that however the breakers of this commandment may escape punishment from men, yet the Lord our God will not suffer them to escape his righteous judgment.

Ques. 57. *Which is the fourth commandment ?*

Ans. The fourth commandment is, *Remember the Sabbath-day to keep it holy. Six days shalt thou labor, and do all thy work: but the seventh day is the Sabbath of the Lord thy God: in it thou shalt not do any work, thou, nor thy son, nor thy daughter, thy man-servant, nor thy maid-servant, nor thy cattle, nor thy stranger that is within thy gates; for in six days the Lord made heaven and earth, the sea, and all that in them is, and rested the seventh day: wherefore the Lord blessed the Sabbath-day and hallowed it.*

Ques. 58. *What is required in the fourth commandment ?*

Ans. The fourth commandment

Quæs. Quid prohibetur mandato tertio ?

Resp. Mandatum tertium prohibet rei cujusvis qua Deus se notum facit, profanationem omnem ac abusum.

Quæs. Quænam est ratio subnexa mandato tertio ?

Resp. Ratio mandato tertio subnexa est, quod licet hujus præcepti violatores ab hominibus quandoque nil supplicii ferant, nihilominus tamen Dominus Deus noster eos justum ejus judicium neutiquam patietur subterfugere.

Quæs. Recita mandatum quartum ?

Resp. Mandati quarti verba sunt isthæc [Memineris diem Sabbati ut sanctifices eum; sex diebus operaberis et facies omne opus tuum, septimus vero dies sabbatum est Domini Dei tui, opus in eo nullum facies tu, neque filius tuus, neque filia tua, nec servus tuus, nec ancilla tua, neque jumentum tuum, nec hospes tuus quicunque intra portas tuas commoratur: Nam sex diebus perfecit Dominus cœlum terramque, mare, et quicquid in illis continetur, septimo vero die requievit, quamobrem benedixit Dominus diei sabbati, eumque sanctificavit.]

Quæs. Quid a nobis exigit mandatum quartum ?

Resp. Quartum mandatum a no-

requireth the keeping holy to God such set times as he hath appointed in his Word; expressly one whole day in seven, to be a holy Sabbath to himself.[1]

Ques. 59. Which day of the seven hath God appointed to be the weekly Sabbath?

Ans. From the beginning of the world to the resurrection of Christ, God[2] appointed the seventh day of the week to be the weekly Sabbath; and the first day of the week, ever since, to continue to the end of the world, which is the Christian Sabbath.

Ques. 60. How is the Sabbath to be sanctified?

Ans. The Sabbath is to be sanctified by a holy resting all that day, even from such worldly employments and recreations as are lawful on other days; and spending the whole time in the public and private exercises of God's worship, except so much as is to be taken up in the works of necessity and mercy.

Ques. 61. What is[3] forbidden in the fourth commandment?

Ans. The fourth commandment forbiddeth the omission,[4] or careless performance, of the duties required, and the profaning the day

bis exigit, ut statum illud tempus quod in verbo suo designavit Deus, sanctum ei observemus; integrum nempe Diem e septenis unum in sanctum illi sabbatum celebrandum.

Quæs. E septenis autem quem diem sabbato hebdomadario designavit Deus?

Resp. Deus hebdomadario sabbato designavit septimum diem hebdomadæ ab initio mundi usque ad Christi resurrectionem, exinde vero ad finem usque mundi duraturum, diem septimanæ primum, quod est sabbatum Christianum.

Quæs. Qui autum est sabbatum sanctificandum?

Resp. Sabbatum est sanctificandum diem illum integrum sancte quiescendo, etiam a negotiis et recreationibus mundanis, aliis quidem diebus haud illicitis; totumque illud temporis (præterquam quod operibus necessitatis ac misericordiæ insumendum fuerit) cultus Divini exercitiis publicis privatisque impendendo.

Quæs. Quid prohibetur in mandato quarto?

Resp. Mandatum quartum prohibet officiorum quæ inibi requiruntur, cum omissionem tum præstationem negligentem; prout etiam ejus diei

---

[1] London ed. of 1658: *unto the Lord.*
[2] London ed. of 1658 inserts *hath.*
[3] London ed. of 1658: *what are the sins.*
[4] London ed. of 1658: *the omission of careful.*

by idleness, or doing that which is in itself sinful, or by unnecessary thoughts, words, or works about our worldly employments and [1] recreations.

Ques. 62. *What are the reasons annexed to the fourth commandment ?*

Ans. The reasons annexed to the fourth commandment are, God's allowing us six days of the week for our own employments,[2] his challenging a special propriety[3] in the seventh, his own example, and his blessing the Sabbath-day.

Ques. 63. *Which*[4] *is the fifth commandment ?*

Ans. The fifth commandment is, *Honor thy father and thy mother : that thy days may be long upon the land which the Lord thy God giveth thee.*

Ques. 64. *What is required in the fifth commandment ?*

Ans. The fifth commandment requireth the preserving the honor of,[5] and performing the duties belonging to, every one in their several places and relations, as superiors, inferiors, or equals.

profanationem qualemcunque, sive illum otiose consumendo, sive quod in se peccatum est faciendo, seu denique circa mundana negotia vel recreationes cogitationibus, dictis, factisve non necessariis.

Quæs. Quænam sunt quarto præcepto rationes annexæ ?

Resp. Rationes quarto præcepto annexæ sunt istiusmodi ; quoniam e septimana qualibet sex dies concesserit nobis Deus nostris ipsorum negotiis insumendos ; quoniam in septimo jus sibi vendicat peculiare ; quoniam Deus exemplo suo nobis præivit, ac diei sabbati benedixit.

Quæs. Quodnam est præceptum quintum ?

Resp. Quintum præceptum est hujusmodi [Honora patrem tuum ac matrem tuam ut prolongentur dies tui in terra illa quam tibi largitur Dominus Deus tuus].

Quæs. Quid est quod jubemur mandato quinto ?

Resp. Mandatum quintum nos jubet honorem conservare, ac officia persolvere unicuique pro ratione ordinis ac relationis in quibus fuerit exhibenda, seu superior nobis fiet, sive inferior, sive denique æqualis.

---

[1] London ed. of 1658 reads, *or.*
[2] London ed. of 1658 : *employment.*
[3] London ed. of 1658 : *property.*

[4] London ed. of 1658 : *what.*
[5] London ed. of 1658 omits *of.*

Ques. 65. *What is forbidden in the fifth commandment?*

Ans. The fifth commandment forbiddeth the neglecting of, or doing any thing against, the honor and duty which belongeth to every one in their several places and relations.

Ques. 66. *What is the reason annexed to the fifth commandment?*

Ans. The reason annexed to the fifth commandment is, a promise of long life and prosperity (as far as it shall serve for God's glory, and their own good) to all such as keep this commandment.

Ques. 67. *Which is the sixth commandment?*

Ans. The sixth commandment is, *Thou shalt not kill.*

Ques. 68. *What is required in the sixth commandment?*

Ans. The sixth commandment requireth all lawful endeavors to preserve our own life, and the life of others.

Ques. 69. *What is forbidden in the sixth commandment?*

Ans. The sixth commandment forbiddeth the taking away of our own life, or the life of our neighbor unjustly, or whatsoever tendeth thereunto.

Ques. 70. *Which is the seventh commandment?*

Ans. The seventh commandment

Quæs. *Quid est quod mandatum quintum vetat?*

Resp. *Quintum mandatum vetat honorem, officiumque singulis debitum pro ratione ordinis ac relatione in quibus fuerint, aut negligere, aut adversus ea quicquam machinari.*

Quæs. *Quæ ratio subnectitur quinto præcepto?*

Resp. *Ratio quinto præcepto subnexa est promissio longævitatis, prosperitatisque (quatenus nempe Dei gloriæ ipsorumque conducant utilitati) omnibus facta hoc præceptum observantibus.*

Quæs. *Cedo mandatum sextum?*

Resp. *Mandatum sextum hisce verbis comprehenditur* [Non occides].

Quæs. *Quid a nobis exigit mandatum sextum?*

Resp. *Exigit a nobis mandatum sextum, ut vitam cum nostram tum aliorum honestis quibuscunque rationibus tueamur.*

Quæs. *Quid vero prohibet sextum mandatum?*

Resp. *Sextum mandatum prohibet vitam nobismetipsis, aut injuste proximo vitam adimere, aut quidvis quod eo tendat agere.*

Quæs. *Quodnam est mandatum septimum?*

Resp. *Mandatum septimum hæc*

is, *Thou shalt not commit adultery.*

Ques. 71. *What is required in the seventh commandment ?*

Ans. The seventh commandment requireth the preservation of our own and our neighbor's chastity, in heart, speech, and behavior.

Ques. 72. *What is forbidden in the seventh commandment ?*

Ans. The seventh commandment forbiddeth all unchaste thoughts, words, and actions.

Ques. 73. *Which is the eighth commandment ?*

Ans. The eighth commandment is, *Thou shalt not steal.*

Ques. 74. *What is required in the eighth commandment ?*

Ans. The eighth commandment requireth the lawful procuring and furthering the wealth and outward estate of ourselves and others.

Ques. 75. *What is forbidden in the eighth commandment ?*

Ans. The eighth commandment forbiddeth whatsoever doth, or may, unjustly hinder our own, or our neighbor's wealth or outward estate.

Ques. 76. *Which* [1] *is the ninth commandment ?*

Ans. The ninth commandment is, *Thou shalt not bear false witness against thy neighbor ?*

verba complectuntur [Non mœchaberis].

Quæs. Quid exigitur mandato septimo ?

Resp. Mandatum septimum exigit ut tam nostram quam proximorum castitatem animo, sermone, gestuque conservemus.

Quæs. Quid prohibetur mandato septimo ?

Resp. Septimum mandatum prohibet cogitationes, sermones, actionesque omnes impudicas.

Quæs. Quodnam est præceptum octavum ?

Resp. Præceptum octavum hoc est [Non furaberis].

Quæs. Mandatum octavum quid a nobis exigit ?

Resp. Octavum mandatum a nobis exigit, facultates ac rem externam nostri aliorumque ut procuremus ac promoveamus.

Quæs. In octavo præcepto quid prohibetur ?

Resp. Octavum mandatum prohibet quicquid nostris aut proximorum nostrorum opibus rebusque externis injusto aut est aut esse possit impedimento.

Quæs. Quodnam est præceptum nonum ?

Resp. Præceptum nonum sic se habet [Non eris adversus proximum tuum testis mendax].

---

[1] London ed. of 1658 : *what.*

Ques. 77. *What is required in the ninth commandment ?*

Ans. The ninth commandment requireth the maintaining and promoting of truth between man and man, and of our own and our neighbor's good name, especially in witness-bearing.

Ques. 78. *What is forbidden in the ninth commandment ?*

Ans. The ninth commandment forbiddeth whatsoever is prejudicial to truth, or injurious to our own or our neighbor's good name.

Ques. 79. *Which*[1] *is the tenth commandment ?*

Ans. The tenth commandment is, *Thou shalt not covet thy neighbor's house, thou shalt not covet thy neighbor's wife, nor his man-servant, nor his maid-servant, nor his ox, nor his ass, nor any thing that is thy neighbor's.*

Ques. 80. *What is required in the tenth commandment ?*

Ans. The tenth commandment requireth full contentment with our own condition, with a right and charitable frame of spirit toward our neighbor, and all that is his.

Ques. 81. *What is forbidden in the tenth commandment ?*

Ans. The tenth commandment forbiddeth all discontentment with

Quæs. *Quid a nobis exigit præceptum nonum ?*

Resp. *Præceptum nonum id a nobis exigit ut veritatem inter homines mutuo, utque bonum nomen et existimationem cum nostri tum proximorum nostrorum conservemus ac promoveamus, cum primis vero in ferendo testimonio.*

Quæs. *Quid prohibetur nono præcepto ?*

Resp. *Nonum præceptum prohibet quicquid est aut veritati inimicum ; aut existimationi nostri vel proximorum nostrorum injurium.*

Quæs. *Quale est mandatum decimum ?*

Resp. *Mandatum decimum hæc verba exhibent* [Non concupisces proximi tui domum, non concupisces proximi tui uxorem, non servum, non ancillam, non bovem, non asinum, neque aliud denique quicquam quod est proximi tui].

Quæs. *In decimo præcepto quid exigitur ?*

Resp. *Præceptum decimum exigit ut sorti nostræ plane acquiescamus, utque in proximum et quæcunque sunt ejus debite, benevoleque afficiamur.*

Quæs. *Quæ prohibentur decimo mandato ?*

Resp. *Mandatum decimum prohibet rerum nostrarum displicentiam,*

: London ed. of 1658 · *what.*

our own estate, envying or grieving at the good of our neighbor, and all inordinate motions or [1] affections to any thing that is his.

Ques. 82. *Is any man able perfectly to keep the commandments of God?*

Ans. No mere man, since the fall, is able, in this life, perfectly to keep the commandments of God; but doth daily break them, in thought, word, and deed.

Ques. 83. *Are all transgressions of the law equally heinous?*

Ans. Some sins in themselves, and by reason of several aggravations, are more heinous in the sight of God than others.

Ques. 84. *What doth every sin deserve?*

Ans. Every sin deserveth God's wrath and curse, both in this life and that which is to come.

Ques. 85. *What doth God require of us, that we may escape his wrath and curse, due to us for sin?*

Ans. To escape the wrath and curse of God, due to us for sin, God requireth of us faith in Jesus Christ, repentance unto life, with the diligent use of all the outward means whereby Christ communicateth to us the benefits of redemption.

invidiam ac dolorem de bono proximi, una cum animi nostri motibus et affectionibus circa ea quæ proximi sunt inordinatis quibuscunque.

Quæs. Quisquamne potis est mandata Dei perfecte observare?

Resp. Post lapsum nemo extat humana tantum natura constans, qui mandata Dei perfecte in hac vita implere potest, quominus ea quotidie tum cogitatione, tum dictis factisque violet.

Quæs. An vero sunt omnes violationes legis ex æquo graves?

Resp. Peccata sunt nonnulla aliis cum sua natura, tum propter varias eorum aggravationes in conspectu Dei graviora.

Quæs. Quid est quod meretur peccatum unumquodque?

Resp. Unumquodque peccatum iram Dei meretur ac maledictionem cum in vita præsenti, tum in futura.

Quæs. Quid autem exigit a nobis Deus, quo nobis ob peccatum debitas iram ejus ac maledictionem effugiamus?

Resp. Quo iram Dei ac maledictionem ob peccatum nobis debitas effugiamus, exigit a nobis Deus fidem in Jesum Christum, resipiscentiam ad vitam, una cum usu mediorum omnium externorum diligenti, quibus Christus nobis communicat redemptionis suæ beneficia.

---

[1] London ed. of 1658: ana.

Ques. 86. *What is faith in Jesus Christ?*

Ans. Faith in Jesus Christ is a saving grace, whereby we receive and rest upon him alone for salvation, as he is offered to us in the gospel.

Ques. 87. *What is repentance unto life?*

Ans. Repentance unto life is a saving grace, whereby a sinner, out of a[1] true sense of his sin, and apprehension of the mercy of God in Christ, doth, with grief and hatred of his sin, turn from it unto God, with full purpose of, and endeavor after, new obedience.

Ques. 88. *What are the outward and ordinary means whereby Christ communicateth to us the benefits of redemption?*

Ans. The outward and ordinary means whereby Christ communicateth to us the benefits of redemption, are his ordinances, especially the word, sacraments, and prayer; all which are made effectual to the elect for salvation.

Ques. 89. *How is the word made effectual to salvation?*

Ans. The Spirit of God maketh the reading, but especially the preaching of the word, an effectual means of convincing and convert-

Quæs. Quid est fides in Jesum Christum?

Resp. Fides in Jesum Christum est gratia salvifica, qua illum recipimus, eoque solo nitimur, ut salvi simus, prout ille nobis offertur in evangelio.

Quæs. Quid est resipiscentia ad vitam?

Resp. Resipiscentia ad vitam est gratia salvifica, qua peccator e vero peccati sui sensu, ac apprehensione divinæ in Christo misericordiæ, dolens ac perosus peccatum suum ab illo ad Deum convertitur, cum novæ obedientiæ pleno proposito et conatu.

Quæs. Quænam sunt externa media quibus Christus nobis communicat redemptionis suæ beneficia?

Resp. Media externa ac ordinaria quibus Christus nobis communicat redemptionis suæ beneficia sunt ejus instituta, verbum præsertim, sacramenta, et oratio; quæ quidem omnia electis redduntur efficacia ad salutem.

Quæs. Qua ratione fit verbum efficax ad salutem?

Resp. Spiritus Dei lectionem verbi præcipue vero prædicationem ejus reddit medium efficax convincendi, convertendique peccatores, eosdemque

---

[1] London ed. of 1658 omits *a*.

ing sinners, and of building them up in holiness and comfort through faith unto salvation.

Ques. 90. How is the Word to be read and heard, that it may become effectual to salvation?

Ans. That the Word may become effectual to salvation, we must attend thereunto with diligence, preparation, and prayer; receive it with faith and love, lay it up in our hearts, and practice it in our lives.

Ques. 91. How do the sacraments become effectual means of salvation?

Ans. The sacraments become effectual means of salvation, not from any virtue in them, or in him that doth administer them, but only by the blessing of Christ, and the working of his Spirit in them that by faith receive them.

Ques. 92. What is a sacrament?

Ans. A sacrament is a holy ordinance instituted by Christ; wherein, by sensible signs, Christ and the benefits of the new covenant are represented, sealed, and applied to believers.

Ques. 93. Which are the sacraments of the New Testament?

Ans. The sacraments of the New Testament are Baptism and the Lord's Supper.

Ques. 94. What is Baptism?

Ans. Baptism is a sacrament,

in sanctimonia et consolatione ædificandi per fidem ad salutem.

Quæs. Quomodo legi debet ac audiri verbum, ut evadat efficax ad salutem?

Resp. *Quo verbum evadat efficax ad salutem, debemus ei cum præparatione, ac oratione diligenter attendere; idemque fide excipere ac amore, in animis nostris recondere, ac in vita nostra exprimere.*

Quæs. Qui evadunt sacramenta media efficacia ad salutem?

Resp. *Sacramenta evadunt efficacia ad salutem media, non ulla in ipsis vi, nec in eo qui illa administrat; verum Christi solummodo benedictione, ac Spiritus ejus in iis qui illa per fidem recipiunt operatione.*

Quæs. Quid est sacramentum?

Resp. *Sacramentum est ordinatio sacra a Christo instituta, in qua fidelibus per signa in sensus incurrentia Christus novique fœderis beneficia repræsentantur, obsignantur, et applicantur.*

Quæs. Quænam sunt sacramenta Novi Testamenti?

Resp. *Sacramenta Novi Testamenti sunt Baptismus ac cœna Dei.*

Quæs. Quid est baptismus?

Resp. *Baptismus est Sacra-*

wherein the washing with water, in the name of the Father, and of the Son, and of the Holy Ghost, doth signify and seal our ingrafting into Christ and partaking of the benefits of the covenant of grace, and our engagement to be the Lord's.

Ques. 95. *To whom is Baptism to be administered?*

Ans. Baptism is not to be administered to any that are out of the visible Church, till they profess their faith in Christ, and obedience to him; but the infants of such as are members of the visible church, are to be baptized.

Ques. 96. *What is the Lord's Supper?*

Ans. The Lord's Supper is a sacrament, wherein, by giving and receiving bread and wine, according to Christ's appointment, his death is showed forth, and the worthy receivers are, not after a corporal and carnal manner, but by faith, made partakers of his body and blood, with all his benefits, to their spiritual nourishment and growth in grace.

Ques. 97. *What is required to the worthy receiving of the Lord's Supper?*

Ans. It is required of them that would worthily partake of the Lord's Supper, that they examine

mentum, in quo ablutio per aquam in nomine Patris ac Filii ac Spiritus Sancti, nostram in Christum insitionem, et beneficiorum fœderis gratiæ participationem, pactumque nostrum, nos nempe Domini futuros esse totos, significat obsignatque.

Quæs. *Quibus est Baptismus administrandus?*

Resp. *Baptismus non est administrandus quibusdam extra Ecclesiam visibilem constitutis, donec se in Christum credere, eique obedientes fore professi fuerint; verum infantes eorum qui membra sunt Ecclesiæ visibilis sunt baptizandi.*

Quæs. *Quid est cœna Domini?*

Resp. *Cœna Domini est Sacramentum, in quo pane ac vino secundum Christi institutum datis acceptisque, mors ejus ostenditur; quæ qui digne participant, corporis ejus et sanguinis (non quidem corporeo et carnali modo, verum) per fidem fiunt participes, omniumque ipsius beneficiorum ad nutritionem suam spiritualem suumque in gratia incrementum.*

Quæs. *Ut digne quis participet cœnam Dominicam quid requiritur?*

Resp. *Qui cœnam Dominicam digne cupiunt participare, requiritur, ut semet examinent cum de cog-*

themselves of their knowledge to discern the Lord's body, of their faith to feed upon him, of their repentance, love, and new obedience; lest coming unworthily, they eat and drink judgment to themselves.

Ques. 98. *What is prayer?*

Ans. Prayer is an offering up of our desires unto God, for things agreeable to his will, in the name of Christ, with confession of our sins, and thankful acknowledgment of his mercies.

Ques. 99. *What rule hath God given for our direction in prayer?*

Ans. The whole Word of God is of use to direct us in prayer, but the special rule of direction is that form of prayer which Christ taught his disciples, commonly called, *The Lord's Prayer.*

Ques. 100. *What doth the preface of the Lord's Prayer teach us?*

Ans. The preface of the Lord's Prayer, which is, '*Our Father which art in heaven,*' teacheth us to draw near to God with all holy reverence and confidence, as children to a father, able[1] and ready to help us; and that we should pray with and for others.

Ques. 101. *What do we pray for in the first petition?*

Ans. In the first petition, which

---

nitione sua, qua corpus Domini valeant discernere, tum de fide sua, qua vescantur ipso, tum etiam de resipiscentia sua, amore ac obedientia nova; ne forte indigni si advenerint, judicium edant bibantque sibimetipsis.

Quæs. Quid est precatio?

Resp. Precatio est qua petitiones nostras pro rebus divinæ voluntati congruis offerimus Deo, in nomine Christi, una cum peccatorum nostrorum confessione, et grata beneficiorum ejus agnitione.

Quæs. Quam nobis regulum præscripsit Deus precibus nostris dirigendis?

Resp. Totum Dei verbum utile est nobis in oratione dirigendis; specialis vero directionis norma est illa orationis formula quam discipulos suos edocuit Christus, oratio dominica quæ vulgo dicitur.

Quæs. Quid nos docet orationis Dominicæ præfatio?

Resp. Orationis Dominicæ præfatio nempe [Pater noster, qui es in cœlis] *nos docet accedere ad Deum cum omni sancta reverentia ac confidentia, tanquam filios ad patrem, qui et potis est ut paratus nobis opitulari; prout etiam cum aliis atque pro aliis orare.*

Quæs. Quid est quod oramus in petitione prima?

Resp. In petitione prima, scil.

---

[1] London ed. of 1658 omits *able and.*

is, ' *Hallowed be thy name,*' we pray that God would enable us and others to glorify him in all that whereby he maketh himself known, and that he would dispose all things to his own glory.

Ques. 102. *What do we pray for in the second petition ?*

Ans. In the second petition, which is, ' *Thy kingdom come,*' we pray that Satan's kingdom may be destroyed, and that the kingdom of grace may [1] be advanced, ourselves and others brought into it, and kept in it, and that the kingdom of glory may be hastened.

Ques. 103. *What do we pray for in the third petition ?*

Ans. In the third petition, which is, ' *Thy will be done on earth as it is in heaven,*' we pray that God by his grace would make us able and willing to know, obey, and submit to his will in all things, as the angels do in heaven.

Ques. 104. *What do we pray for in the fourth petition ?*

Ans. In the fourth petition, which is, ' *Give us this day our daily bread,*' we pray that of God's free gift we may receive a competent portion of the good things of this life, and enjoy his blessing with them.

[Sanctificetur nomen tuum] *oramus et efficere velit Deus, ut eum nos aliique, in eis, quibuscunque se notum nobis facit, glorificare valeamus ; atque ad suam ipsius gloriam omnia dirigere velit ac disponere.*

Quæs. Quid petimus in secunda petitione ?

Resp. In petitione secunda, quæ hujusmodi est [adveniat regnum tuum] *petimus ut destruatur regnum Satanæ, gratiæ vero regnum ut promoveatur, ut nos aliique in eo simus cum constituti tum conservati ne excidamus, utque regnum gloriæ velit Deus adproperare.*

Quæs. In petitione tertia quid precamur ?

Resp. In petitione tertia, scil. hisce verbis [fiat voluntas tua in terris sicut in cœlis] *precamur efficere velit Deus, ut nos per gratiam voluntatem ejus tum cognoscere, tum ei in omnibus obtemperare, et nos submittere, id quod in cœlis faciunt Angeli, et valeamus et velimus.*

Quæs. Quid oramus in petitione quarta ?

Resp. In quarta petitione quæ sic habetur [Panem nostrum quotidianum da nobis hodie] *oramus ut e donatione Dei gratuita, bonorum quæ hujus vitæ sunt portionem idoneam obtineamus, ejusque una cum iis benedictione perfruamur.*

---

[1] London ed. of 1658 : *might.*

Ques. 105. *What do we pray for in the fifth petition ?*

Ans. In the fifth petition, which is, 'And forgive us our debts as we forgive our debtors,' we pray that God, for Christ's sake, would freely pardon all our sins; which we are the rather encouraged to ask, because by his grace we are enabled from the heart to forgive others.

Ques. 106. *What do we pray for in the sixth petition ?*

Ans. In the sixth petition, which is, 'And lead us not into temptation, but deliver us from evil,' we pray that God would either keep us from being tempted to sin, or support and deliver us when we are tempted.

Ques. 107. *What doth the conclusion of the Lord's Prayer teach us ?*

Ans. The conclusion of the Lord's Prayer, which is, 'For thine is the kingdom, and the power and the glory forever, Amen,' teacheth us to take our encouragement in prayer from God only, and in our prayers to praise him; ascribing kingdom, power, and glory to him; and in testimony of our desire and assurance to be heard, we say, *Amen.*

Quæs. *Quid precamur in petitione quinta ?*

Resp. *In petitione quinta, cujus verba sunt* [Ac remitte nobis debita nostra, sic ut remittimus debitoribus nostris] *precamur ut Deus peccata nostra omnia gratis velit propter Christum condonare, quod quidem ut petamus eo magis animus nobis fit, quod aliis animitus condonare gratia ipsius auxiliante valeamus.*

Quæs. *Quid petimus in sexta petitione ?*

Resp. *In petitione sexta, quam hæc verba complectuntur* [Et ne nos inducas in tentationem, sed libera nos a malo] *oramus ut velit nos Deus aut immunes a tentatione ad peccatum conservare, aut certe tentatos suffulcire ac liberare.*

Quæs. *Quid nos docet orationis Dominicæ conclusio ?*

Resp. *Orationis Dominicæ conclusio* [Quia tuum est regnum, potentia et gloria, in secula, Amen] *Nos docet animos ac confidentiam nobis in orando a solo Deo derivare, eumque in precibus nostris laudare, regnum ei, potentiam, ac gloriam tribuendo ; quoque desiderium nostrum testemur, et exauditionis confidentiam, dicimus, Amen.*

THE TEN COMMANDMENTS.

EXODUS XX.

God spake all these words, saying, I am the Lord thy God, which have brought thee out of the land of Egypt, out of the house of bondage.

I. Thou shalt have no other gods before me.

II. Thou shalt not make unto thee any graven image, or any likeness of any thing that is in heaven above, or that is in the earth beneath, or that is in the water under the earth: thou shalt not bow down thyself to them, nor serve them: for I the Lord thy God am a jealous God, visiting the iniquity of the fathers upon the children unto the third and fourth generation of them that hate me; and showing mercy unto thousands of them that love me and keep my commandments.

III. Thou shalt not take the name of the Lord thy God in vain: for the Lord will not hold him guiltless that taketh his name in vain.

IV. Remember the Sabbath-day to keep it holy. Six days shalt thou labor, and do all thy work; but the seventh day is the Sabbath of the Lord thy God; in it thou shalt not do any work, thou, nor thy son, nor thy daughter, thy manservant, nor thy maid-servant, nor thy cattle, nor thy stranger that is

DECALOGUS.

EXOD. XX.

Locutus est Deus omnia hœc verba, dicendo ; Ego sum Dominus Deus tuus, qui te eduxi e terra Ægypti, e domo servitutis.

I. *Non habebis deos alios coram me.*

II. *Non facies tibi imaginem quamvis sculptilem, aut similitudinem rei cujusvis quœ est in cœlis superne, aut inferius in terris, aut in aquis infra terram ; non incurvabis te iis, nec eis servies : siquidem ego Dominus Deus tuus Deus sum zelotypus, visitans iniquitates patrum in filios ad tertiam usque quartamque progeniem osorum mei, exhibens vero misericordiam ad millenas usque diligentium me ac mandata mea observantium.*

III. *Nomen Domini Dei tui inaniter non usurpabis ; non enim eum pro insonte habebit Dominus qui nomen ejus inaniter adhibuerit.*

IV. *Memineris diem Sabbati ut sanctifices eum ; sex diebus operaberis et facies omne opus tuum, septimus vero dies sabbatum est Domini Dei tui, opus in eo nullum facies tu, neque servus tuus, nec ancilla tua, neque jumentum tuum, neque hospes tuus quicunque intra portas tuas commoratur : Nam sex diebus perfe-*

within thy gates; for in six days the Lord made heaven and earth, the sea, and all that in them is, and rested the seventh day; wherefore the Lord blessed the Sabbath-day, and hallowed it.

V. Honor thy father and thy mother; that thy days may be long upon the land which the Lord thy God giveth thee.

VI. Thou shalt not kill.

VII. Thou shalt not commit adultery.

VIII. Thou shalt not steal.

IX. Thou shalt not bear false witness against thy neighbor.

X. Thou shalt not covet thy neighbor's house, thou shalt not covet thy neighbor's wife, nor his man-servant, nor his maid-servant, nor his ox, nor his ass, nor any thing that is thy neighbor's.

THE LORD'S PRAYER.

MATT. VI.

Our Father which art in heaven, hallowed be thy name. Thy kingdom come. Thy will be done in earth as it is in heaven. Give us this day our daily bread. And forgive us our debts, as we forgive our debtors. And lead us not into temptation, but deliver us from evil. For thine is the kingdom, and the power, and the glory, forever. Amen.

cit Dominus cœlum, terramque, mare et quicquid in illis continetur : septimo vero die requievit ; quamobrem benedixit Dominus diei Sabbati, eumque sanctificavit.

V. *Honora patrem tuum ac matrem tuam, ut prolongentur dies tui in terra illa quam tibi largitur Dominus Deus tuus.*

VI. *Non occides.*

VII. *Non mœchaberis.*

VIII. *Non furaberis.*

IX. *Non eris adversus proximum tuum testis mendax.*

X. *Non concupisces proximi tui domum, non concupisces proximi tui uxorem, non servum, non ancillam, non bovem, non asinum neque aliud denique quicquam quod est proximi tui.*

ORATIO DOMINICA.

MATT. VI.

Pater noster qui es in cœlis, sanctificetur nomen tuum, adveniat regnum tuum, fiat voluntas tua in terris sicut in cœlis, panem nostrum quotidianum da nobis hodie, ac remitte nobis debita nostra, sicut nos remittimus debitoribus nostris, et ne nos inducas in tentationem, sed libera nos a malo, quia tuum est regnum, potentia et gloria in secula. Amen.

THE CREED.

I believe in God the Father almighty, maker of heaven and earth; and in Jesus Christ his only Son, our Lord; who [1] was conceived by the Holy Ghost, born of the Virgin Mary; suffered under Pontius Pilate, was crucified, dead, and buried; he descended into hell: * the third day he rose again from the dead; he ascended into heaven, and sitteth on the right hand of God the Father almighty; from thence he shall come to judge the quick and the dead. I believe in the Holy Ghost; the holy catholic church; the communion of saints; the forgiveness of sins; the resurrection of the body; and the life everlasting. Amen.

SYMBOLUM.

*Credo in Deum Patrem omnipotentem, creatorem cœli ac terræ; et in Jesum Christum filium ejus unicum, Dominum nostrum; qui conceptus est e Spiritu sancto, natus ex Maria Virgine; passus sub Pontio Pilato, crucifixus, mortuus et sepultus; descendit ad inferos: * tertio die resurrexit a mortuis: ascendit in cœlum, et sedet ad dextram Dei patris omnipotentis: unde venturus est ad judicandum vivos et mortuos. Credo in Spiritum Sanctum: Sanctam ecclesiam catholicam: Sanctorum communionem: remissionem peccatorum, resurrectionem corporis et vitam æternam. Amen.*

* *i. e.*, Continued in the state of the dead, and under the power of death, until the third day.

* i. e., *Permansit in statu mortuorum et sub potestate mortis usque ad diem tertium.*

[1] London ed. of 1658: *which.*

[See addition on p. 704.]

The oldest editions of the Westminster Shorter Catechism have the following addendum:

So much of every Question both in the Larger and Shorter Catechism, is repeated in the Answer, as maketh every Answer an entire Proposition, or sentence in itself: to the end the Learner may further improve it upon all occasions, for his increase in knowledge and piety, even out of the course of catechising, as well as in it.

And albeit the substance of the doctrine comprised in that Abridgment commonly called, *The Apostles' Creed*, be fully set forth in each of the Catechisms, so as there is no necessity of inserting the Creed itself, yet it is here annexed, not as though it were composed by the Apostles, or ought to be esteemed Canonical Scripture, as the Ten Commandments, and the Lord's Prayer (much less a Prayer, as ignorant people have been apt to make both it and the Decalogue), but because it is a brief sum of the Christian faith, agreeable to the Word of God, and anciently received in the Churches of Christ.

CORNELIUS BURGES, *Prolocutor pro tempore.*
HENRY ROBOROUGH, *Scriba.*
ADONIRAM BYFIELD, *Scriba.*

E quæstione qualibet utriusque catechismi repetitum dedimus in responsione quantum responsionem quamlibet reddat propositionem integram, sive sententiam absolutam. Eo nempe consilio ut discenti ulterius utilis esse possit, quoties occasio tulerit, ad cognitionis ac pietatis incrementum, vel extra catechisandi rationem.

Et quamvis in alterutro Catechismo substantia doctrinæ in compendio illo (Symbolo apostolico vulgo dicto) comprehensæ plene ac perfecte exhibeatur, adeo quidem ut nulla supersit necessitas symbolum ipsum inserendi: nihilominus tamen hic illud subnectendum esse duximus; non perinde quasi aut ab ipsis Apostolis fuerit concinnatum, aut pariter cum decalogo, ac oratione Dominica pro Scriptura canonica haberi debeat: (nedum certe pro oratione, quo nomine ignara plebecula cum illud tum decalogum in proclivi fuit ut usurparet), verum quod sit fidei Christianæ breve compendium, verbo Dei consentaneum, ac in Ecclesiis Christi antiquitus receptum.

SYMBOLA EVANGELICA.

PARS TERTIA:

MODERN PROTESTANT CREEDS.

SYMBOLA EVANGELICA.

PART THIRD:

MODERN PROTESTANT CREEDS.

THE SAVOY DECLARATION OF THE CONGREGATIONAL CHURCHES. A.D. 1658.

[The SAVOY DECLARATION consists of a lengthy Preface, a Confession of Faith, and a Platform of Discipline. The first and last are given in full; of the second, the chapters and sections in which it differs from the Westminster Confession of Faith. See Vol. I. pp. 829 sqq. The first edition appeared in London in 1658, as printed by John Field and sold by John Allen 'at the Sun Rising in Paul's Church-yard' (a copy of which is in possession of Rev. Dr. H. M. Dexter, of Boston).

The text is an exact reprint (except in spelling and punctuation) of the second edition, which appeared under the following title:

A

DECLARATION

OF THE

FAITH and ORDER

Owned and practifed in the

Congregational Churches

IN

ENGLAND;

Agreed upon and confented unto

By their

ELDERS and *MESSENGERS*

I N

Their Meeting at the *SAVOY*,

Octob. 12. 1658.

LONDON

Printed for *D.L.* And are to be fold in *Paul*'s Church-yard, *Fleet*-Street, and *Weftminfter*-Hall, 1659.]

A PREFACE.

Confession of the *Faith* that is in us, when justly called for, is so indispensable a due all owe to the Glory of the Sovereign GOD, that it is ranked among the Duties of the first Commandment, such as Prayer is; and therefore by *Paul* yoked with Faith itself, as necessary to salvation: *with the heart man believeth unto righteousness, and with the mouth confession is made unto salvation.* Our Lord Christ himself, when he was accused of his Doctrine, considered simply as a matter of fact by Preaching, refused to answer; because, as such, it lay upon evidence, and matter of testimony of others; unto whom therefore he refers himself: But when both the High-Priest and *Pilate* expostulate his Faith, and what he held himself to be; he without any demur at all, cheerfully makes Declaration, That he *was the Son of God;* so to the High-Priest: and that he was a *King*, and *born to be a King;* thus to *Pilate.* Though upon the uttering of it his life lay at the stake; Which holy Profession of his is celebrated for our example, 1 Tim. vi. 13.

Confessions, when made by a company of Professors of Christianity jointly meeting to that end, the most genuine and natural use of such Confessions is, That under the same form of words, they express the substance of the same *common salvation* or *unity of their faith;* whereby *speaking the same things, they show themselves perfectly joined in the same mind, and in the same judgment,* 1 Cor. i. 10.

And accordingly such a transaction is to be looked upon but as a meet or fit *medium* or *means* whereby to express *that* their *common faith and salvation*, and no way to be made use of as an *imposition* upon any: Whatever is of force or constraint in matters of this nature, causeth them to degenerate from the *name* and *nature* of *Confessions*, and turns them from being *Confessions of Faith*, into *Exactions* and *Impositions of Faith*.

And such *common Confessions* of the Orthodox Faith, made in simplicity of heart by any such Body of Christians, with concord among themselves, ought to be entertained by all others that *love the truth as it is in Jesus*, with an answerable *rejoicing:* For if the unanimous opinions and assertions but in some few points of Religion, and that when by two Churches, namely, that of *Jerusalem*, and the *Messengers of Antioch* met, assisted by some of the *Apostles*, were by the Believers of those times received with so much joy, (as it is said, *They rejoiced for the consolation*) much more this is to be done, when the whole substance of Faith, and *form of wholesome words* shall be declared by the Messengers of a multitude of Churches, though wanting those advantages of Counsel and Authority of the *Apostles*, which that *Assembly* had.

Which acceptation is then more specially due, when these shall (to choose) utter and declare their Faith, in the same substance for matter, yea, *words*, for the most part, that other Churches and Assemblies, reputed the *most Orthodox*, have done before them: For upon such a correspondency, all may see *that* actually accomplished, which the Apostle did but exhort unto, and pray for, in those *two* more eminent Churches of the *Corinthians* and the *Romans*, (and so in them for all the Christians of his time) that both *Jew* and *Gentile*, that is, men of different persuasions, (as they were) *might glorify GOD with one mind and with one mouth.* And truly, the very turning of the Gentiles to the owning of the same Faith, in the substance of it, with the Christian Jew (though differing in greater points than we do from our Brethren) is presently after dignified by the Apostle with this style, That it is the *Confession of Jesus Christ himself;* not as the Object only, but as the Author and Maker thereof: *I will confess to thee* (saith Christ to God) *among the Gentiles.* So that in all such accords, *Christ* is the *great and first Confessor;* and we, and all our Faith uttered by Us, are but the *Epistles*, (as *Paul*) and *Confessions* (as *Isaiah* there) of *their Lord and ours;* He, but expressing what is written in his heart, through their hearts and mouths, *to the glory of God the Father:* And shall not we all rejoice herein, when as Christ himself is said to do it upon this occasion: as it there also follows, *I will sing unto thy Name.*

Further, as the *soundness* and *wholesomeness of the matter* gives the *vigor* and *life* to such

Confessions, so the *inward freeness, willingness*, and *readiness* of the Spirits of the *Confessors* do contribute the *beauty* and *loveliness* thereunto: As it is in *Prayer* to God, so in *Confessions* made to men. *If two or three met, do agree*, it renders both, to either the more acceptable. The Spirit of Christ is in himself too *free*, great and generous a Spirit, to suffer himself to be used by any human arm, to whip men into belief; he drives not, but *gently leads into all truth*, and *persuades* men to *dwell in the tents of like precious Faith;* which would lose of its preciousness and value, if that sparkle of freeness shone not in it: The Character of His People, is to be a *willing people in the day of his power* (not Man's) *in the beauties of holiness*, which are the Assemblings of the Saints: one glory of which Assemblings in that first Church, is said to have been, *They met with one accord;* which is there in that Psalm prophesied of, in the instance of that first Church, for all other that should succeed.

And as this great Spirit is in himself free, when, and how far, and in whom to work, so where and when he doth work, he carrieth it with the same freedom, and is said to be a *free Spirit*, as he both is, and works in us: And where this *Spirit of the Lord is, there is liberty*.

Now, as to this *Confession* of ours, besides, that a conspicuous conjunction of the particulars mentioned, hath appeared therein: There are also *four remarkable Attendants* thereon, which added, might perhaps in the eyes of sober and indifferent Spirits, give the whole of this Transaction a room and rank amongst other many good and memorable things of this Age; at least all set together, do cast as clear a gleam and manifestation of God's Power and Presence, as hath appeared in any such kind of *Confessions*, made by so numerous a company these later years.

The first, is the *Temper* (or distemper rather) of the *Times*, during which, these *Churches* have been gathering, and which they have run through. All do (out of a general sense) complain that the times have been *perilous*, or *difficult times* (as the Apostle foretold); and that in respect to danger from *seducing spirits*, more perilous than the hottest seasons of Persecution.

We have failed through an Æstuation, Fluxes and Refluxes of great varieties of Spirits, Doctrines, Opinions and Occurrences, and especially in the matter of Opinions, which have been accompanied in their several seasons, with powerful persuasions and temptations, to seduce those of our way. It is known, men have taken the freedom (notwithstanding what Authority hath interposed to the contrary) to vent and vend their own vain and accursed imaginations, contrary to the great and fixed Truths of the Gospel, insomuch, as take the whole Round and Circle of Delusions, the Devil hath in this small time, ran; it will be found, that every Truth, of greater or lesser weight, hath by one or other hand, at one time or another, been questioned and called to the Bar amongst us, yea, and impleaded, under the pretext (which hath some degree of Justice in it) that all should not be bound up to the Traditions of former times, nor take Religion upon trust.

Whence it hath come to pass, that many of the soundest Professors were put upon a new search and disquisition of such Truths, as they had taken for granted, and yet had lived upon the comfort of: to the end they might be able to convince others, and establish their own hearts against that darkness and unbelief, that is ready to close with error, or at least to doubt of the truth, when error is speciously presented. And hereupon we do professedly account it one of the greatest advantages gained out of the Temptations of these Times, yea the honor of the Saints and Ministers of these Nations, That after they had sweetly been exercised in, and had improved practical and experimental Truths, this should be their further Lot, to examine and discuss, and indeed, anew to learn over every Doctrinal Truth, both out of the Scriptures, and also with a fresh taste thereof in their own hearts; which is no other than what the Apostle exhorts to, *Try all things, hold fast that which is good.* Conversion unto God at first, what is it else than a savory and affectionate application, and the bringing home to the heart with spiritual light and life, all truths that are necessary to salvation, together with other lesser Truths? All which we had afore conversion taken in but notionally from common Education and Tradition.

Now that after this first gust those who have been thus converted should be put upon a new probation and search out of the Scriptures, not only of all principles explicitly ingredients to Conversion; (unto which the Apostle referreth the *Galatians* when they had diverted from them) but of all other superstructures as well as fundamentals; and together therewith, anew to experiment the power and sweetness of all these in their own souls: What is this but *tried Faith* indeed? and equivalent to a new conversion unto the truth? *An Anchor* that is proved to be *sure* and *steadfast*, that will certainly hold in all contrary storms. This was the eminent seal and commendation which those holy Apostles that lived and wrote last (*Peter, John,* and *Jude* in their Epistles) did set and give to the *Christians* of the latter part of those *primitive times*. And besides, it is clear and evident by all the other Epistles, from first to last, that it cost the Apostles as much, and far more care and pains to preserve them they had converted, *in the truth*, than they had taken to turn them thereunto at first: And it is in itself as great a work and instance of the power of God, that *keeps*, yea, *guards us through faith unto salvation*.

Secondly, let this be added (or superadded rather) to give full weight and measure, even to running over, that we have all along this season, held forth (though quarreled with for it by our brethren) this great principle of these times, *That amongst all Christian States and Churches, there ought to be vouchsafed a forbearance and mutual indulgence unto Saints of all persuasions, that keep unto, and hold fast the necessary foundations of faith and holiness*, in all other matters *extra fundamental*, whether of Faith or Order.

This to have been our constant principle, we are not ashamed to confess to the whole Christian world. Wherein yet we desire we may be understood, not as if in the *abstract* we stood indifferent to falsehood or truth, or were careless whether faith or error, in any Truths but fundamental, did obtain or not, so we had our liberty in our petty and smaller differences; or as if to make sure of that, we had cut out this wide cloak for it: No, we profess that the whole, and every particle of that Faith delivered to the Saints (the substance of which we have according to our light here professed) is, as to the propagation and furtherance of it by *all Gospel means*, as precious to us as our lives; or what can be supposed dear to us; and in our sphere we have endeavored to promote them accordingly: But yet withal, we have and do contend (and if we had all the power which any, or all of our brethren of differing opinions have desired to have over us, or others, we should freely grant it unto them all) we have and do contend for this, That *in the concrete*, the persons of all such gracious Saints, they and their errors, as they are in them, when they are but such errors as do and may stand with communion with Christ, though they should not repent of them, as not being convinced of them to the end of their days; that those, with their errors (that are purely spiritual, and intrench and overthrow not civil societies,) as *concrete with their persons*, should for Christ's sake be borne withal by all Christians in the world; and they notwithstanding be permitted to enjoy all Ordinances and spiritual Privileges according to their light, as freely as any other of their brethren that pretend to the greatest Orthodoxy; as having as equal, and as fair a right in and unto Christ, and all the holy things of Christ, that any other can challenge to themselves.

And this doth afford a full and invincible testimony on our behalf, in that whiles we have so earnestly contended for this just liberty of Saints in all the Churches of Christ, *we ourselves have no need of it*: that is, as to the *matter* of the profession of *Faith* which we have maintained together with others: and of this, this subsequent Confession of Faith gives sufficient evidence. So as we have the confidence in Christ, to utter in the words of those two great Apostles, That *we have stood fast in the liberty wherewith Christ hath made us free* (in the behalf of others, rather than ourselves) and having been *free, have not made* use of our *liberty* for *a cloak of error or maliciousness* in ourselves. And yet, lo, whereas from the beginning of the rearing of these Churches, that of the Apostle hath been (by some) prophesied of us, and applied to us, *That while we promised* (unto others) *liberty, we ourselves would become servants of corruption, and be brought in bondage* to all sorts of fancies and imaginations, yet the whole world may now see after the experience of many years ran through (and it is manifest by this Confession) that the great and gracious God hath not only kept us in that common unity of the Faith and Knowledge of the Son of God, which the whole Community of Saints have and shall in their Generations come unto, but also in the same Truths, both small and great, that are built thereupon, that any other of the best and more pure Reformed Churches in their best times (which were their first times) have arrived unto: This Confession withal holding forth a professed opposition unto the common errors and heresies of these times.

These *two considerations* have been taken from *the seasons* we have gone through.

Thirdly, let the *space of time itself*, or days, wherein from first to last the whole of this Confession was framed and consented to by the whole of us, be duly considered by sober and ingenuous spirits: the whole of days in which we had meetings about it (set aside the two Lord's days, and the first day's meeting, in which we considered and debated what to pitch upon) were but 11 days, part of which also was spent by some of us in Prayer, others in consulting; and in the end all agreeing. We mention this small circumstance but to this end (which still adds unto the former) That it gives demonstration, not of our freeness and willingness only, but of our readiness and preparedness unto so great a work; which otherwise, and in other Assemblies, hath ordinarily taken up long and great debates, as in such a variety of matters of such concernment, may well be supposed to fall out. And this is no other than what the Apostle *Peter* exhorts unto, *Be ready always to give an answer to every man that asketh you a reason, or account of the hope that is in you.* The Apostle *Paul* saith of the spiritual Truths of the Gospel, *That God hath prepared them for those that love him.* The inward and innate constitution of the new Creature being in itself such as is suited to all those Truths, as congenial thereunto: But although there be this mutual *adaptness* between these two, yet such is the mixture of ignorance, darkness and unbelief, carnal reason, pre-occupation of judgment, interest of parties, wantonness in opinion, proud adhering to our own persuasions, and perverse oppositions and averseness to agree with others, and a multitude of such like distempers *common to believing man:* All which are not only mixed with, but at times (especially in such times as have passed over our heads) are ready to overcloud our judgments, and to cause our eyes to be double, and sometimes prevail as well as lusts, and do bias our wills and affections: And such is their mixture, that although there may be existent an habitual preparedness in men's spirits, yet not always a present readiness to be found, specially not in such a various multitude of men, to make a solemn and deliberate profession of all truths, it being as great a work to find the spirits of the just (perhaps the best of Saints) ready for every truth, as *to be prepared to every good work.*

It is therefore to be looked at, as a great and special work of the Holy Ghost, that so numerous a company of Ministers, and other principal brethren, should so *readily, speedily,* and *jointly* give up themselves unto such a whole Body of *Truths that are after godliness.*

This argues they had not their faith to seek; but, as is said of *Ezra*, that *they* were *ready Scribes*, and (as Christ) *instructed unto the Kingdom of Heaven*, being as the good *house-holders* of so many families of Christ, *bringing forth of their store and treasury New and Old.* It shows these truths had been familiar to them, and they acquainted with them, as with their *daily food and provision* (as Christ's allusion there insinuates): In a word, that *so they had preached*, and that *so their people had believed*, as the Apostle speaks upon one like particular occasion. And the Apostle *Paul* considers (in cases of this nature) *the suddenness* or *length of the time*, either one way or the other; whether it were in men's *forsaking* or *learning* of the truth. Thus the *suddenness* in the *Galatians'* case in leaving the truth, he makes a wonder of it: *I marvel that you are SO SOON* (that is, in so short a time) *removed from the true Gospel unto another.* Again on the contrary, in the *Hebrews* he aggravates their backwardness, *That when for the time you ought to be Teachers, you had need that one teach you the very first principles of the Oracles of God.* The Parallel contrary to both these having fallen out in this transaction, may have some ingredient and weight with ingenuous spirits in its kind, according to the proportion is put upon either of these forementioned in their adverse kind, and obtain the like special observation.

This accord of ours hath fallen out without having *held any correspondency together*, or pre pared consultation, by which we might come to be advised of one another's minds. We allege not this as a matter of commendation in us; no, we acknowledge it to have been a great neglect: And accordingly one of the first proposals for union amongst us was, That there might be a constant correspondence held among the Churches for counsel and mutual edification, so for time to come to prevent the like omission.

We confess that from the first, every [one], or at least the generality of our Churches, have been in a manner like so many Ships (though holding forth the same general colors) launched singly, and sailing apart and alone in the vast Ocean of these tumultuating times, and they exposed to every wind of Doctrine, under no other conduct than the Word and Spirit, and their particular Elders and principal Brethren, without Associations among ourselves, or so much as holding out common lights to others, whereby to know where we were.

But yet whilst we thus confess to our own shame this neglect, let all acknowledge, that God hath ordered it for his high and greater glory, in that his singular care and power should have so watched over each of these, as that all should be found to have steered their course by the same Chart, and to have been bound for one and the same Port, and that upon this general search now made, that the same holy and blessed truths of all sorts, which are current and warrantable amongst all the other Churches of Christ in the world, should be found to be our Lading.

The whole, and every [one] of these things when put together, do cause us (whatever men of prejudiced and opposite spirits may find out to slight them) with a holy admiration, to say, That this is no other than the Lord's doing; and which we with thanksgiving do take from his hand as a special token upon us for good, and doth show that God is faithful and upright towards those that are planted in his house: And that as the Faith was but once for all, and intentionally first delivered unto the Saints; so the Saints, when not abiding scattered, but gathered under their respective Pastors according to God's heart into an house, and Churches unto the living God, such together are, as *Paul* forespake it, the most steady and firm *pillar* and *seat of Truth* that God hath any where appointed to himself on earth, where his truth is best conserved, and publicly held forth; there being in such Assemblies weekly a rich dwelling of the Word amongst them, that is, a daily open house kept by the means of those good Householders, their Teachers and other Instructors respectively appropriated to them, whom Christ in the virtue of his Ascension, continues to give as gifts to his people, himself dwelling amongst them; to the end that by this, as the most sure standing permanent means, the Saints might be perfected, till we all (even all the Saints in present and future ages) do come by this constant and daily Ordinance of his unto *the unity of the Faith and Knowledge of the Son of God unto a perfect man, unto the measure of the stature of the fullness of Christ* (which though growing on by parts and piecemeal, will yet appear complete, when *that great and general Assembly* shall be gathered, then when this world is ended, and these dispensations have had their fullness and period) and *so that from henceforth* (such a provision being made for us) *we be no more children tossed to and fro, and carried about with every wind of Doctrine.*

And finally, this doth give a fresh and recent demonstration, that the *great Apostle* and *High-priest of our profession* is indeed *ascended* into heaven, and continues there with power and care, *faithful as a son over his own house, whose house are we, if we hold fast the confidence and the rejoicing of the hope firm unto the end:* and shows that he will, as he hath promised, be with his own Institutions to the end of the world.

It is true, that many sad miscarriages, divisions, breaches, fallings off from holy Ordinances of God, have along this time of tentation (especially in the beginning of it) been found in some of our Churches; and no wonder, if what hath been said be fully considered: Many reasons might further be given hereof, that would be a sufficient Apology, without the help of a retortion upon other Churches (that promised themselves peace) how that more destroying ruptures have befallen them, and that in a wider sphere and compass; which though it should not justify us, yet may serve to stop others' mouths.

Let *Rome* glory of the peace in, and *obedience* of her Children, against the Reformed

Churches for their divisions that occurred (especially in the first rearing of them) whilst we all know the causes of their dull and stupid peace to have been carnal interests, worldly correspondencies, and coalitions, strengthened by gratifications of all sorts of men by that Religion, the principles of blind Devotion, Traditional Faith, Ecclesiastical Tyranny, by which she keeps her Children in bondage to this day. We are also certain, that the very same prejudices that from hence they would cast upon the Reformed (if they were just) do lie as fully against those pure Churches raised up by the Apostles themselves in those first times: for as *we have heard of their patience*, sufferings, consolations, and the transcending gifts poured out, and graces shining in them, *so we have heard complaints* of their *divisions* too, of the *forsakings of their Assemblies,* as the custom or *manner of SOME was* (which later were in that respect *felo de se,* and needed no other *delivering up to Satan* as their punishment, than what they executed upon themselves). We read of the *shipwreck* also of *Faith* and a *good Conscience,* and *overthrowings of the faith of SOME;* and still but of *some* not *all,* nor the *most:* which is one piece of an Apology the Apostle again and again inserts to future ages, and through mercy we have the same to make.

And truly we take the confidence professedly to say, that these tentations common to the purest *Churches of Saints separated from the mixture of the world,* though they grieve us (for *who is offended, and we burn not?*), yet they do not at all stumble us, as to the truth of our way, had they been many more: We say it again, these stumble us no more (as to that point) than it doth offend us against the power of Religion itself, to have seen, and to see daily in *particular persons called out and separated from the world* by an effectual work of conversion, that they for *a while do suffer* under disquietments, vexations, turmoils, unsettlements of spirit, that they are tossed with tempests and horrid tentations, such as they had not in their former estate, whilst they *walked according to the course of this world:* For *Peter* hath sufficiently instructed us whose business it is to raise such storms, even the *Devil's;* and also whose design it is, that *after they have suffered a while,* thereby they shall be *settled, perfected, stablished,* that have so suffered, even *the God of all Grace.* And look what course of dispensation God holds to *Saints personally,* he doth the like to *bodies of Saints* in *Churches,* and the Devil the same for his part too: And that consolatory Maxim of the Apostle, *God shall tread down Satan under your feet shortly,* which *Paul* uttereth concerning the Church of *Rome,* shows how both *God* and *Satan* have this very hand therein; for he speaks that very thing in reference unto their divisions, as the coherence clearly manifests; and so you have both designs expressed at once.

Yea, we are not a little induced to think, that the *divisions,* breaches, etc., of those *primitive Churches* would not have been so frequent among the people themselves, and not the Elders only, had not the freedom, liberties, and rights of the Members (the Brethren, we mean) been stated and exercised in those Churches, the same which we maintain and contend for to be in ours.

Yea (which perhaps may seem more strange to many) had not those Churches been constituted of members enlightened further than with notional and traditional knowledge, by a new and more powerful light of the *Holy Ghost,* wherein *they had been made partakers of the Holy Ghost and the heavenly gift, and their hearts had tasted the good Word of God, and the Powers of the world to come,* and of such Members at lowest, there had not fallen out those kinds of divisions among them.

For Experience hath shown, that the common sort of mere *Doctrinal Professors* (such as the most are nowadays), whose highest elevation is but *freedom from moral scandal, joined* with *devotion* to Christ through mere Education, such as in many *Turks* is found towards *Mohammed,* that these finding and feeling themselves not much concerned in the *active part* of *Religion,* so they may have the honor (especially upon a Reformation of a new Refinement) that themselves are approved Members, admitted to the Lord's Supper, and their Children to the Ordinance of Baptism; they *regard not other matters* (as *Gallio* did not), but do easily and readily give up themselves unto their Guides, being like dead fishes carried with the common stream; whereas those that have a further renewed Light by a work of the Holy

Ghost, whether *saving* or *temporary*, are upon the quite contrary grounds apt to be busy about, and inquisitive into, what they are to receive and practice, or wherein their Consciences are professedly concerned and involved : And thereupon they take the freedom to *examine* and *try the spirits, whether of God or no:* And from hence are more apt to dissatisfaction, and from thence to run into division, and many of such proving to be enlightened but with a *temporary*, not saving *Faith* (who have such a work of the Spirit upon them, and profession in them, as will and doth approve itself to the judgment of Saints, and ought to be so judged, until they be otherwise discovered) who at long-run, prove hypocrites, through indulgence unto Lusts, and then out of their Lusts persist to hold up these divisions unto breach of, or departings from, Churches, and the Ordinances of God, and God is even with them for it, *they waxing worse and worse, deceiving and being deceived;* and even many of those that are sincere, through a mixture of darkness and erroneousness in their Judgments, are for a season apt out of Conscience *to be led away with the error of others, which lie in wait to deceive.*

Insomuch as the Apostle upon the example of those first times, forseeing also the like events in following generations upon the like causes, hath been bold to set this down as a *ruled Case,* that likewise in other Churches so constituted and *de facto* emprivileged as that of the Church of *Corinth* was (which single Church, in the Sacred Records about it, is the completest Mirror of Church Constitution, Order, and Government, and Events thereupon ensuing, of any one Church whatever that we have story of), his Maxim is, *There must be also divisions amongst you;* he setly inserts an [*ALSO*] in the case, as that which had been in his own observation, and that which would be ἐπὶ τὸ πολὺ the fate of other Churches like thereunto, *so prophesieth he:* And he speaks this as peremptorily, as he doth elsewhere in that other, *We must through many tribulations enter into the Kingdom of Heaven:* Yea, and that *all that will live godly in Christ Jesus, shall suffer persecution:* There is a [*MUST*] upon both alike; and we bless God, that we have run through both, and do say, and we say no more, *That as it was then, so it is now,* in both respects.

However, such hath been the powerful hand of God's providence in *these*, which have been the worst of our *Trials*, That out of an approved Experience and Observation of the Issue, we are able to add that other part of the Apostle's Prediction, That therefore *such rents must be, that they which are approved may be made manifest among you;* which holy issue God (as having aimed at it therein) doth frequently and certainly bring about in Churches, as he doth bring upon them that other fate of division, Let them therefore look unto it, that are the Authors of such disturbances, as the Apostle warneth, Gal. v. 10. The experiment is this, That we have seen, and do daily see, that multitudes of holy and precious souls, and (in the Holy Ghost's word) *approved Saints*, have been, and are the more rooted and grounded by means of these shakings, and do continue to cleave the faster to Christ, and the purity of his Ordinances, and value them the more by this cost God hath put them to for the enjoying of them, Who having been planted in the House of the Lord, have flourished in the Courts of our God, in these evil times, to show that the Lord is upright. And this experimented event from out of such divisions, hath more confirmed us, and is a louder Apology for us, than all that our opposites are able from our breaches to allege to prejudice us.

We will add a few words for conclusion, and give a more particular account of this our *Declaration.* In drawing up this *Confession of Faith*, we have had before us the *Articles of Religion*, approved and passed by both Houses of Parliament, after advice had with an *Assembly of Divines*, called together by them for that purpose. To which Confession, for the substance of it, we fully assent, as do our Brethren of *New England*, and the Churches also of *Scotland*, as each in their general Synods have testified.

A few things we have added for obviating some erroneous Opinions, that have been more broadly and boldly here of late maintained by the Asserters, than in former times; and made other additions and alterations in *method*, here and there, and some clearer Explanations, as we found occasion.

We have endeavored throughout, to hold to such Truths in this our Confession, as are more properly termed *matters of Faith;* and what is of *Church-order*, we dispose in certain Propositions by itself. To this course we are led by the Example of the Honorable Houses of Parliament, observing what was established, and what omitted by them in that Confession the Assembly presented to them. Who thought it not convenient to have matters of Discipline and Church Government put into a Confession of Faith, especially such particulars thereof, as then were, and still are controverted and under dispute by men Orthodox and found in Faith. The 30th *cap.* therefore of that Confession, as it was presented to them by the Assembly, which is of Church Censures, their Use, Kinds, and in whom placed : As also *cap.* 31, of Synods and Councils, by whom to be called, of what force in their Decrees and Determinations. And the 4th *Paragr.* of the 20th *cap.*, which determines what Opinions and Practices disturb the peace of the Church, and how such Disturbers ought to be proceeded against by the Censures of the Church, and punished by the Civil Magistrate. Also a great part of the 24th *cap.* of Marriage and Divorce. These were such doubtful assertions, and so unsuitable to a Confession of Faith, as the Honorable Houses in their great Wisdom thought fit to lay them aside : There being nothing that tends more to heighten Dissensions among Brethren, than to determine and adopt the matter of their difference, under so high a Title, as to be an Article of our Faith : So that there are two whole Chapters, and some Paragraphs in other Chapters in their Confession, that we have upon this account omitted ; and the rather do we give this notice, because that Copy of the Parl. followed by us, is in few men's hands ; the other as it came from the Assembly, being approved of in *Scotland*, was printed and hastened into the world, before the Parl. had declared their Resolutions about it ; which was not till *June* 20, 1648, and yet hath been, and continueth to be the Copy (ordinarily) only sold, printed, and reprinted for these 11 years.

After the 19th *cap.* of the Law, we have added a *cap.* of the Gospel, it being a Title that may not well be omitted in a Confession of Faith : In which Chapter, what is dispersed, and by intimation in the Assemblies' Confession, with some little addition, is here brought together, and more fully, under one head.

That there are not Scriptures annexed, as in some Confessions (though in divers others it's otherwise), we give the same account as did the *Reverend Assembly* in the same case ; which was this : ' The Confession being large, and so framed, as to meet with the common Errors, ' if the Scriptures should have been alleged with any clearness, and by showing where the strength of the proof lieth, it would have required a Volume.'

We say further, it being our utmost end in this (as it is indeed of a *Confession*) humbly to give an account what we hold and assert in these matters ; that others, especially the Churches of Christ may judge of us accordingly : This we aimed at, and not so much to instruct others, or convince gainsayers. These are the proper works of other Institutions of Christ, and are to be done in the strength of express Scripture. A *Confession* is an Ordinance of another nature.

What we have laid down and asserted about Churches and their Government, we humbly conceive to be the Order which Christ himself hath appointed to be observed, we have endeavored to follow Scripture light ; and those also that went before us according to that Rule, desirous of nearest uniformity with Reforming Churches, as with our Brethren in *New England*, so with others, that differ from them and us.

The Models and Platforms of this subject laid down by learned men, and practiced by Churches, are various : We do not judge it brotherly, or grateful, to insist upon comparisons, as some have done ; but this Experience teacheth, That the variety, and possibly the Disputes and Emulations arising thence, have much strengthened, if not fixed, this unhappy persuasion in the minds of some learned and good men, namely, That there is no settled Order laid down in Scripture ; but it's left to the Prudence of the Christian Magistrate, to compose or make choice of such a Form as is most suitable and consistent with their Civil Government. Where this Opinion is entertained in the persuasion of Governors, there, Churches asserting their Power and Order to be *jure divino*, and the appointment of Jesus Christ, can have no better nor more honorable Entertainment, than a Toleration or Permission.

Yet herein there is this remarkable advantage to all parties that differ, about what in Government is of Christ's appointment; *in that such Magistrates have a far greater latitude in conscience, to tolerate and permit the several forms of each so bound up in their persuasion, than they have to submit unto what the Magistrate shall impose: And thereupon the Magistrate exercising an indulgency and forbearance, with protection and encouragement to the people of God, so differing from him, and amongst themselves: Doth therein discharge as great a faithfulness to Christ, and love to his people, as can any way be supposed and expected from any Christian Magistrate, of what persuasion soever he is. And where this clemency from Governors is shown to any sort of persons, or Churches of Christ, upon such a principle, it will in equity produce this just effect, That all that so differ from him, and amongst themselves, standing in equal and alike difference from the principle of such a Magistrate, he is equally free to give alike liberty to them, one as well as the other.*

This faithfulness in our Governors we do with thankfulness to God acknowledge, and to their everlasting honor, which appeared much in the late Reformation. The Hierarchy, Common Prayer-Book, and all other things grievous to God's People, being removed, they made choice of an Assembly of learned men, to advise what Government and Order is meet to be established in the room of these things; and because it was known there were different opinions (as always hath been among godly men) about forms of Church Government, there was by the Ordinance first sent forth to call an Assembly, not only a choice made of persons of several persuasions, to sit as Members there, but liberty given, to a lesser number, if dissenting, to report their Judgments and Reasons, as well and as freely as the major part.

Hereupon the Honorable House of Commons (an Indulgence we hope will never be forgotten) finding by Papers received from them, that the Members of the Assembly were not like to compose differences amongst themselves, so as to join in the same Rule for Church Government, did order further as followeth: 𝕿𝖍𝖆𝖙 𝖆 𝕮𝖔𝖒𝖒𝖎𝖙𝖙𝖊𝖊 𝖔𝖋 𝕷𝖔𝖗𝖉𝖘 𝖆𝖓𝖉 𝕮𝖔𝖒𝖒𝖔𝖓𝖘, etc., 𝖉𝖔 𝖙𝖆𝖐𝖊 𝖎𝖓𝖙𝖔 𝖈𝖔𝖓𝖘𝖎𝖉𝖊𝖗𝖆𝖙𝖎𝖔𝖓 𝖙𝖍𝖊 𝖉𝖎𝖋𝖋𝖊𝖗𝖊𝖓𝖈𝖊𝖘 𝖔𝖋 𝖙𝖍𝖊 𝕺𝖕𝖎𝖓𝖎𝖔𝖓𝖘 𝖎𝖓 𝖙𝖍𝖊 𝕬𝖘𝖘𝖊𝖒𝖇𝖑𝖞 𝖔𝖋 𝕯𝖎𝖛𝖎𝖓𝖊𝖘 𝖎𝖓 𝖕𝖔𝖎𝖓𝖙 𝖔𝖋 𝕮𝖍𝖚𝖗𝖈𝖍 𝖌𝖔𝖇𝖊𝖗𝖓𝖒𝖊𝖓𝖙, 𝖆𝖓𝖉 𝖙𝖔 𝖊𝖓𝖉𝖊𝖆𝖛𝖔𝖗 𝖆 𝖚𝖓𝖎𝖔𝖓 𝖎𝖋 𝖎𝖙 𝖇𝖊 𝖕𝖔𝖘𝖘𝖎𝖇𝖑𝖊; 𝖆𝖓𝖉 𝖎𝖓 𝖈𝖆𝖘𝖊 𝖙𝖍𝖆𝖙 𝖈𝖆𝖓 𝖓𝖔𝖙 𝖇𝖊 𝖉𝖔𝖓𝖊, 𝖙𝖔 𝖊𝖓𝖉𝖊𝖆𝖛𝖔𝖗 𝖙𝖍𝖊 𝖋𝖎𝖓𝖉𝖎𝖓𝖌 𝖔𝖚𝖙 𝖘𝖔𝖒𝖊 𝖜𝖆𝖞, 𝖍𝖔𝖜 𝖋𝖆𝖗 𝖙𝖊𝖓𝖉𝖊𝖗 𝖈𝖔𝖓𝖘𝖈𝖎𝖊𝖓𝖈𝖊𝖘, 𝖜𝖍𝖔 𝖈𝖆𝖓 𝖓𝖔𝖙 𝖎𝖓 𝖆𝖑𝖑 𝖙𝖍𝖎𝖓𝖌𝖘 𝖘𝖚𝖇𝖒𝖎𝖙 𝖙𝖔 𝖙𝖍𝖊 𝖘𝖆𝖒𝖊 𝕽𝖚𝖑𝖊 𝖜𝖍𝖎𝖈𝖍 𝖙𝖍𝖆𝖙 𝖇𝖊 𝖊𝖘𝖙𝖆𝖇𝖑𝖎𝖘𝖍𝖊𝖉, 𝖒𝖆𝖞 𝖇𝖊 𝖇𝖔𝖗𝖓 𝖜𝖎𝖙𝖍 𝖆𝖈𝖈𝖔𝖗𝖉𝖎𝖓𝖌 𝖙𝖔 𝖙𝖍𝖊 𝖂𝖔𝖗𝖉, 𝖆𝖓𝖉 𝖆𝖘 𝖒𝖆𝖞 𝖘𝖙𝖆𝖓𝖉 𝖜𝖎𝖙𝖍 𝖙𝖍𝖊 𝕻𝖚𝖇𝖑𝖎𝖈 𝕻𝖊𝖆𝖈𝖊.

By all which it is evident, the Parliament purposed not to establish the Rule of Church Government with such rigor, as might not permit and bear with a practice different from what they had established: In persons and Churches of different principles, if occasion were. And this Christian Clemency and indulgence in our Governors, hath been the foundation of that *Freedom and Liberty*, in the managing of Church affairs, which *our Brethren*, as well as *WE*, that differ from them, do now, and have many years enjoyed.

The Honorable Houses by several Ordinances of Parliament after much consultation, having settled Rules for Church Government, and *such an Ecclesiastical Order* as they judged *would best joint with the Laws and Government of the Kingdom*, did publish them, requiring the practice hereof throughout the Nation; and in particular, by the Min. of the Pr. of *Lon.* But (upon the former reason, or the like charitable consideration) these *Rules* were not imposed by them under any *Penalty*, or rigorous enforcement, though frequently urged thereunto by some.

Our Reverend Brethren of the Province of *London*, having considered of these Ordinances, and the Church Government laid down in them, declared their Opinions to be, *That there is not a complete Rule in those Ordinances; also, that there are many necessary things not yet established, and some things wherein their consciences are not so fully satisfied.* These Brethren, in the same Paper, have published also their joint *Resolution to practice in all things according to the Rule of the Word, and according to these Ordinances, so far as they conceive them [to] correspond to it, and in so doing, they trust they shall not grieve the Spirit of the truly godly, nor give any just occasion to them that are contrary minded, to blame their proceedings.*

We humbly conceive that (*WE* being dissatisfied in these things as our Brethren) the like liberty was intended by the Honorable Houses, and may be taken by us of the *Congregational way* (without blame or grief to the spirits of those *Brethren* at least), to resolve, or rather to continue in the same Resolution and Practice in these matters, which indeed were our practices in times of greatest opposition, and before this Reformation was begun.

And as our Brethren *the Ministers of London*, drew up and published their *opinions* and *apprehensions* about Church Government into an entire System ; so we now give the like public account of our Consciences, and the Rules by which we have constantly practiced hitherto ; which we have here drawn up, and do present. Whereby it will appear how much, or how little we differ in these things from our Presbyterian Brethren.

And we trust there is no just cause why any man, either for our differing from the present settlement, it being out of Conscience, and not out of *contempt*, or our differences one from another, being not *willful*, should charge either of us with that odious reproach of *Schism*. And indeed, if not for our differing from the State settlement, much less because we differ from our Brethren, our differences being *in some lesser things, and circumstances* only, as themselves acknowledge. And let it be further considered, that we have not broken from them or their Order by these differences (but rather they from us), and in that respect we less deserve their censure ; our practice being no other than what it was in our breaking from Episcopacy, and long before Presbytery, or any such form as now they are in, was taken up by them ; and we will not say how probable it is, that the yoke of Episcopacy had been upon our neck to this day, if some such way (as formerly, and now is, and hath been termed *Schism*) had not with much suffering been then practiced, and since continued in.

For *Novelty* wherewith we are likewise both charged by the Enemies of both, it is true, in respect of the public and open Profession, either of Presbytery or Independency, this Nation hath been a stranger to each way, it's possible, ever since it hath been Christian ; though for ourselves we are able to trace the footsteps of an Independent Congregational way in the ancientest customs of the Churches ; as also in the Writings of our soundest Protestant Divines, and (that which we are much satisfied in) a full concurrence throughout in all the substantial parts of Church Government, with our Reverend Brethren the *old Puritan Non-conformists*, who being instant in Prayer and much sufferings, prevailed with the Lord, and we reap with joy, what they sowed in tears. Our Brethren also that are for Presbyterial Subordinations, profess what is of weight against *Novelty* for their way.

And now therefore seeing the Lord, in whose hand is the heart of Princes, hath put into the hearts of our Governors, to tolerate and permit (as they have done many years) persons of each persuasion, to enjoy their Consciences, though neither come up to the *Rule established by Authority:* And that which is more, to give us both Protection, and the same encouragement, that the most devoted *Conformists* in those former Superstitious Times enjoyed ; yea, and by a public Law to establish this Liberty for time to come ; and yet further, in the midst of our fears, to set over us a Prince that owns this Establishment, and cordially resolves to secure our Churches in the enjoyment of these Liberties, if we abuse them not to the disturbance of the Civil Peace.

This should be a very great engagement upon the hearts of all, though of different persuasions, to endeavor our utmost, jointly to promote the honor and prosperity of such a Government and Governors by whatsoever means, which in our Callings as Ministers of the Gospel, and as Churches of Jesus Christ the Prince of Peace, we are any way able to do ; as also to be peaceably disposed one towards another, and with mutual toleration to love as brethren, notwithstanding such differences : remembering, as it's very equal we should, the differences that are between *Presbyterians* and *Independents* being differences between fellow-servants, and neither of them having authority given from God or Man, to impose their Opinions, one more than the other. That our Governors after so solemn an establishment, should thus bear with us both, in our greater differences from their Rule : and after this, for any of us *to take a fellow-servant by the throat*, upon the account of a lesser reckoning, and nothing due to *him* upon it, is to forget, at least not to exercise, that compassion and tenderness we have found, where we had less ground to challenge or expect it.

Our prayer unto God is, That whereto we have already attained, we all may walk by the same rule, and that wherein we are otherwise minded, God would reveal it to us in his due time.

A Declaration of Faith.

[As the Savoy Declaration is merely a modification of the Westminster Confession to suit the Congregational polity, it is only necessary to note the principal omissions, additions, and changes, which will be better understood by comparison with the corresponding original and with the more thorough change made by the American Presbyterians in Chap. XXIII. 3.]

Chap. XX. is added to the Westminster Confession (which accounts for the change of numbers of chapters after Chap. XX.), and reads as follows:

CHAPTER XX.

Of the Gospel, and of the Extent of the Grace thereof.

I. The covenant of works being broken by sin, and made unprofitable unto life, God was pleased to give unto the elect the promise of Christ, the seed of the woman, as the means of calling them, and begetting in them faith and repentance. In this promise the gospel, as to the substance of it, was revealed, and was therein effectual for the conversion and salvation of sinners.

II. This promise of Christ, and salvation by him, is revealed only in and by the Word of God; neither do the works of creation or providence, with the light of nature, make discovery of Christ, or of grace by him, so much as in a general or obscure way; much less that men, destitute of the revelation of him by the promise or gospel, should be enabled thereby to attain saving faith or repentance.

III. The revelation of the gospel unto sinners, made in divers times and by sundry parts, with the addition of promises and precepts for the obedience required therein, as to the nations and persons to whom it is granted, is merely of the sovereign will and good pleasure of God, not being annexed by virtue of any promise to the due improvement of men's natural abilities, by virtue of common light received without it, which none ever did make, or can so do: and therefore in all ages the preaching the gospel hath been granted unto persons and nations, as to the extent or straitening of it, in great variety, according to the counsel of the will of God.

IV. Although the gospel be the only outward means of revealing Christ and saving grace, and is as such abundantly sufficient thereunto; yet that men who are dead in trespasses may be born again, quickened, or regenerated, there is moreover necessary an effectual, irresistible work of the Holy Ghost upon the whole soul, for the producing in them [of] a new spiritual life, without which no other means are sufficient for their conversion unto God.

In the chapter on 'Christian Liberty and Liberty of Conscience' slight modifications are made in two sections, as follows:

SAVOY DECLARATION.	WESTMINSTER CONFESSION.
CHAP. XXI.	CHAP. XX.

II. God alone is Lord of the conscience, and hath left it free from the doctrines and commandments of men, which are in any thing contrary to his Word, or not contained in it; so that to believe such doctrines, or to obey such commands out of conscience, is to betray true liberty of conscience; and the requiring of an implicit faith and an absolute and blind obedience is to destroy liberty of conscience, and reason also.

II. God alone is Lord of the conscience, and hath left it free from the doctrines and commandments of men, which are in any thing contrary to his Word, or beside it, in matters of faith or worship; so that to believe such doctrines, or to obey such commandments out of conscience, is to betray true liberty of conscience; and the requiring of an implicit faith and an absolute and blind obedience is to destroy liberty of conscience, and reason also.

III. They who, upon pretense of Christian liberty, do practice any sin, or cherish any lust, as they do thereby pervert the main design of the grace of the gospel to their own destruction; so they wholly destroy the end of Christian liberty, which is, that being delivered out of the hands of our enemies, we might serve the Lord without fear, in holiness and righteousness before him all the days of our life.

III. They who, upon pretense of Christian liberty, do practice any sin, or cherish any lust, do thereby destroy the end of Christian liberty; which is, that being delivered out of the hands of our enemies, we might serve the Lord without fear, in holiness and righteousness before him all the days of our life.

The fourth and last section of Chap. XX. of the Westminster Confession, which gives the civil magistrate the power of punishing heresy, is entirely omitted. The American Revision of the Westminster Confession omits only the last clause (which is really the only objectionable feature), 'and by the power of the civil magistrate.'

SAVOY DECLARATION.	WESTMINSTER CONFESSION.	AMER. PRESB. REVISION OF THE WESTM. CONF.
CHAP. XXIV.—*Of the Civil Magistrate.*	CHAP. XXIII.—*Of the Civil Magistrate.*	CHAP. XXIII.—*Of the Civil Magistrate.*
III. Although the magistrate is bound to encourage, promote, and protect the professors and profession of the gospel, and to manage and order civil administrations in a due subserviency to the interest of Christ in the world, and to that end to take care that men of corrupt minds and conversations do not licentiously publish and divulge blasphemy and errors, in their own nature subverting the faith and inevitably destroying the souls of them that receive them; yet in such differences about the doctrines of the gospel, or ways of the worship of God, as may befall men exercising a good conscience, manifesting it in their conversation, and holding the foundation, not disturbing others in their ways or worship that differ from them, there is no warrant for the magistrate under the gospel to abridge them of their liberty.	III. The civil magistrate may not assume to himself the administration of the Word and Sacraments, or the power of the keys of the kingdom of heaven: yet he hath authority, and it is his duty to take order, that unity and peace be preserved in the Church, that the truth of God be kept pure and entire, that all blasphemies and heresies be suppressed, all corruptions and abuses in worship and discipline prevented or reformed, and all the ordinances of God duly settled, administered, and observed. For the better effecting whereof he hath power to call synods, to be present at them, and to provide that whatsoever is transacted in them be according to the mind of God.	III. Civil magistrates may not assume to themselves the administration of the Word and Sacraments; or the power of the keys of the kingdom of heaven; or, in the least, interfere in matters of faith. Yet as nursing fathers, it is the duty of civil magistrates to protect the Church of our common Lord, without giving the preference to any denomination of Christians above the rest, in such a manner that all ecclesiastical persons whatever shall enjoy the full, free, and unquestioned liberty of discharging every part of their sacred functions, without violence or danger. And, as Jesus Christ hath appointed a regular government and discipline in his Church, no law of any commonwealth should interfere with, let, or hinder the due exercise thereof, among the voluntary members of any denomination of Christians, according to their own profession and belief.

SAVOY DECLARATION.	WESTMINSTER CONFESSION.	AMER. PRESB. REVISION OF THE WESTM. CONF.
		It is the duty of civil magistrates to protect the person and good name of all their people, in such an effectual manner as that no person be suffered, either upon pretense of religion or infidelity, to offer any indignity, violence, abuse, or injury to any other person whatsoever: and to take order that all religious and ecclesiastical assemblies be held without molestation or disturbance.

In Chap. XXV., 'Of Marriage,' the Savoy Declaration omits sections 5 and 6, and the last clause of section 4, Chap. XXIV., of the Westminster Confession.

SAVOY DECLARATION.	WESTMINSTER CONFESSION.
CHAP. XXVI.—*Of the Church.*	CHAP. XXV.—*Of the Church.*
I. The catholic or universal Church, which is invisible, consists of the whole number of the elect, that have been, are, or shall be gathered into one under Christ, the Head thereof; and is the spouse, the body, the fullness of him that filleth all in all.	I. The catholic or universal Church, which is invisible, consists of the whole number of the elect, that have been, are, or shall be gathered into one, under Christ the Head thereof; and is the spouse, the body, the fullness of him that filleth all in all.
II. The whole body of men throughout the world, professing the faith of the gospel, and obedience unto God by Christ according unto it, not destroying their own profession by any errors everting the foundation, or unholiness of conversation, are and may be called the visible	II. The visible Church, which is also catholic or universal under the gospel (not confined to one nation as before under the law), consists of all those, throughout the world, that profess the true religion, and of their children; and is the kingdom of the Lord Jesus Christ, the house and fam-

catholic Church of Christ, although as such it is not intrusted with the administration of any ordinances, or hath any officers to rule or govern in or over the whole body.

III. The purest churches under heaven are subject both to mixture and error, and some have so degenerated as to become no churches of Christ, but synagogues of Satan. Nevertheless, Christ always hath had, and ever shall have a visible kingdom in this world, to the end thereof, of such as believe in him, and make profession of his name.

ily of God, out of which there is no ordinary possibility of salvation.

III. Unto this catholic visible Church Christ hath given the ministry, oracles, and ordinances of God, for the gathering and perfecting of the saints, in this life, to the end of the world: and doth by his own presence and Spirit, according to his promise, make them effectual thereunto.

IV. This catholic Church hath been sometimes more, sometimes less visible. And particular churches, which are members thereof, are more or less pure, according as the doctrine of the gospel is taught and embraced, ordinances administered, and public worship performed more or less purely in them.

V. The purest churches under heaven are subject both to mixture and error; and some have so degenerated as to become no churches of Christ, but synagogues of Satan. Nevertheless, there shall be always a Church on earth to worship God according to his will.

IV. There is no other head of the Church but the Lord Jesus Christ; nor can the Pope of Rome in any sense be head thereof; but it [he] is that Antichrist, that man of sin and son of perdition that exalteth himself in the Church against Christ, and all that is called God, whom the Lord shall destroy with the brightness of his coming.

V. As the Lord is in care and love towards his Church, hath in his infinite wise providence exercised it with great variety in all ages, for the good of them that love him, and his own glory; so, according to his promise, we expect that in the latter days, Antichrist being destroyed, the Jews called, and the adversaries of the kingdom of his dear Son broken, the churches of Christ being enlarged and edified through a free and plentiful communication of light and grace, shall enjoy in this world a more quiet, peaceable, and glorious condition than they have enjoyed.

VI. There is no other head of the Church but the Lord Jesus Christ: nor can the Pope of Rome, in any sense, be head thereof; but is that Antichrist, that man of sin and son of perdition that exalteth himself in the Church against Christ, and all that is called God.

These Savoy modifications and changes of the Westminster Confession were approved and adopted by American Congregationalists in the Synod of Boston, 1680, and in the Synod at Saybrook, 1708.

Of the Institution of Churches, and the Order appointed in them by Jesus Christ.

I. By the appointment of the Father, all Power for the Calling, Institution, Order, or Government of the Church is invested in a Supreme and Sovereign manner in the Lord Jesus Christ, as King and Head thereof.

II. In the execution of this Power wherewith he is so intrusted the Lord Jesus calleth out of the World unto Communion with himself those that are given unto him by his Father, that they may walk before him in all the ways of Obedience which he prescribed to them in his Word.

III. Those thus called (through the Ministry the Word by his Spirit) he commandeth to walk together in particular Societies or Churches, for their mutual edification and the due performance of that public Worship which he requireth of them in this world.

IV. To each of these Churches thus gathered, according unto his mind declared in his Word, he hath given all that Power and Authority which is any way needful for their carrying on that Order in Worship and Discipline which he hath instituted for them to observe with Commands and Rules for the due and right exerting and executing of that Power.

V. These particular Churches thus appointed by the Authority of Christ, and intrusted with power from him for the ends before expressed, are each of them as unto those ends the seat of that Power which he is pleased to communicate to his Saints or Subjects in this World, so that as such they receive it immediately from himself.

VI. Besides these particular Churches, there is not instituted by Christ any Church more extensive or Catholic intrusted with power for the administration of his Ordinances or the execution of any authority in his Name.

VII. A particular Church gathered and completed according to the mind of Christ consists of Officers and Members: The Lord Christ having given to his called ones (united according to his appointment in Church order) Liberty and Power to choose Persons fitted by the

Holy Ghost for that purpose, to be over them, and to minister to them in the Lord.

VIII. The Members of these Churches are Saints by Calling, visibly manifesting and evidencing (in and by their profession and walking) their Obedience unto that Call of Christ, who being further known to each other by their confession of the Faith wrought in them by the power of God, declared by themselves, or otherwise manifested, do willingly consent to walk together according to the appointment of Christ, giving up themselves to the Lord and to one another by the Will of God, in professed subjection to the Ordinances of the Gospel.

IX. The Officers appointed by Christ to be chosen and set apart by the Church so called, and gathered for the peculiar administration of Ordinances and execution of Power or Duty which he intrusts them with, or calls them to, to be continued to the end of the World, are Pastors, Teachers, Elders, and Deacons.

X. Churches thus gathered and assembling for the Worship of GOD are thereby visible and public, and their Assemblies (in what place soever they are, according as they have liberty or opportunity) are therefore Church or Public Assemblies.

XI. The way appointed by Christ for the calling of any person, fitted and gifted by the Holy Ghost, unto the Office of Pastor, Teacher, or Elder, in a Church, is that he be chosen thereunto by the common suffrage of the Church itself, and solemnly set apart by Fasting and Prayer, with Imposition of Hands of the Eldership of that Church, if there be any before constituted therein: And of a Deacon, that he be chosen by the like suffrage, and set apart by Prayer and the like Imposition of Hands.

XII. The Essence of this Call of a Pastor, Teacher, or Elder unto Office consists in the Election of the Church, together with his acceptation of it, and separation by Fasting and Prayer: And those who are so chosen, though not set apart by Imposition of Hands, are rightly constituted Ministers of Jesus Christ, in whose Name and Authority they exercise the Ministry to them so committed. The Calling of Deacons consisteth in the like Election and acceptation, with separation by Prayer.

XIII. Although it be incumbent on the Pastors and Teachers of the

Churches to be instant in Preaching the Word, by way of Office, yet the work of Preaching the Word is not so peculiarly confined to them but that others also gifted and fitted by the Holy Ghost for it, and approved (being by lawful ways and means in the Providence of God called thereunto), may publicly, ordinarily, and constantly perform it, so that they give themselves up thereunto.

XIV. However, they who are engaged in the work of Public Preaching, and enjoy the Public Maintenance upon that account, are not thereby obliged to dispense the Seals to any other than such as (being Saints by Calling, and gathered according to the Order of the Gospel) they stand related to, as Pastors or Teachers; yet ought they not to neglect others living within their Parochial Bounds, but besides their constant public Preaching to them, they ought to inquire after their profiting by the Word, instructing them in and pressing upon them (whether young or old) the great Doctrines of the Gospel, even personally and particularly, so far as their strength and time will admit.

XV. Ordination alone, without the Election or precedent consent of the Church, by those who formerly have been Ordained by virtue of that Power they have received by their Ordination, doth not constitute any person a Church-Officer, or communicate Office-power unto him.

XVI. A Church furnished with Officers (according to the mind of Christ) hath full power to administer all his Ordinances; and where there is want of any one or more Officers required, that Officer, or those which are in the Church, may administer all the Ordinances proper to their particular Duty and Offices; but where there are no Teaching Officers, none may administer the Seals, nor can the Church authorize any so to do.

XVII. In the carrying on of Church administrations, no person ought to be added to the Church but by the consent of the Church itself; that so love (without dissimulation) may be preserved between all the Members thereof.

XVIII. Whereas the Lord Jesus Christ hath appointed and instituted as a means of Edification that those who walk not according to the Rules and Laws appointed by him (in respect of Faith and Life, so that just offense doth arise to the Church thereby) be censured in his Name and Authority: Every Church hath power in itself to exercise and execute all those Censures appointed by him, in the way and Order prescribed in the Gospel.

XIX. The Censures so appointed by Christ are Admonition and Excommunication; and whereas some offenses are or may be known only to some, it is appointed by Christ that those to whom they are so known do first admonish the offender in private (in public offenses where any sin, before all), and in case of non-amendment upon private admonition, the offense being related to the Church, and the offender not manifesting his repentance, he is to be duly admonished in the Name of Christ by the whole Church, by the Ministry of the Elders of the Church; and if this Censure prevail not for his repentance, then he is to be cast out by Excommunication, with the consent of the Church.

XX. As all Believers are bound to join themselves to particular Churches, when and where they have opportunity so to do, so none are to be admitted unto the Privileges of the Churches who do not submit themselves to the Rule of Christ in the Censures for the Government of them.

XXI. This being the way prescribed by Christ in case of offense, no Church-members, upon any offenses taken by them, having performed their duty required of them in this matter, ought to disturb any Church order, or absent themselves from the public Assemblies or the Administration of any Ordinances, upon that pretense, but to wait upon Christ in the further proceeding of the Church.

XXII. The Power of Censures being seated by Christ in a particular Church, is to be exercised only towards particular members of each Church respectively as such; and there is no power given by him unto any Synods or Ecclesiastical Assemblies to Excommunicate, or by their public Edicts to threaten Excommunication or other Church Censures against Churches, Magistrates, or their people, upon any account, no man being obnoxious to that Censure but upon his personal miscarriage as a Member of a particular Church.

XXIII. Although the Church is a Society of men assembling for the celebration of the Ordinances according to the appointment of Christ, yet every Society assembling for that end or purpose, upon the account of cohabitation within any civil Precincts or Bounds, is not thereby constituted a Church, seeing there may be wanting among them what is essentially required thereunto; and therefore a Believer living with others in such a Precinct may join himself with any Church for his edification.

XXIV. For the avoiding of differences that may otherwise arise, for the greater Solemnity in the Celebration of the Ordinances of Christ, and the opening a way for the larger usefulness of the Gifts and Graces of the Holy Ghost, Saints living in one City or Town, or within such distances as that they may conveniently assemble for divine Worship, ought rather to join in one Church for their mutual strengthening and edification than to set up many distinct Societies.

XXV. As all Churches and all the members of them are bound to pray continually for the good or prosperity of all the Churches of Christ in all places, and upon all occasions to further it (Every one within the bounds of their Places and Callings, in the exercise of their Gifts and Graces), So the Churches themselves (when planted by the Providence of God so as they may have opportunity and advantage for it) ought to hold communion amongst themselves for their peace, increase of love, and mutual edification.

XXVI. In Cases of Difficulties or Differences, either in point of Doctrine or in Administrations, wherein either the Churches in general are concerned, or any one Church, in their Peace, Union, and Edification, or any Member or Members of any Church are injured in or by any proceeding in Censures not agreeable to Truth and Order, it is according to the mind of Christ that many Churches holding communion together do by their Messengers meet in a Synod or Council to consider and give their advice in or about that matter in difference, to be reported to all the Churches concerned: Howbeit, these Synods so assembled are not intrusted with any Church Power properly so called, or with any Jurisdiction over the Churches themselves, to exercise any Censures, either over any Churches or Persons, or to impose their determinations on the Churches or Officers.

XXVII. Besides these occasioned Synods or Councils, there are not instituted by Christ any stated Synods in a fixed Combination of Churches or their Officers in lesser or greater Assemblies, nor are there any Synods appointed by Christ in a way of Subordination to one another.

XXVIII. Persons that are joined in Church-fellowship, ought not lightly or without just cause to withdraw themselves from the communion of the Church whereunto they are so joined : Nevertheless, where any person can not continue in any Church without his sin, either for want of the Administration of any Ordinances instituted by Christ, or by his being deprived of his due Privileges, or compelled to any thing in practice not warranted by the Word, or in case of Persecution, or upon the account of conveniency of habitation ; he, consulting with the Church, or the Officer or Officers thereof, may peaceably depart from the communion of the Church wherewith he hath so walked, to join himself with some other Church where he may enjoy the Ordinances in the purity of the same, for his edification and consolation.

XXIX. Such reforming Churches as consist of Persons sound in the Faith, and of Conversation becoming the Gospel, ought not to refuse the communion of each other, so far as may consist with their own Principles respectively, though they walk not in all things according to the same Rules of Church Order.

XXX. Churches gathered and walking according to the mind of Christ, judging other Churches (though less pure) to be true Churches, may receive unto occasional communion with them such Members of those Churches as are credibly testified to be godly and to live without offense.

THE DECLARATION OF THE CONGREGATIONAL UNION OF ENGLAND AND WALES. A.D. 1833.

[This is printed annually in the *Congregational Year-Book*, London. See Vol. I. p. 730.]

DECLARATION OF THE FAITH, CHURCH ORDER, AND DISCIPLINE OF THE CONGREGATIONAL OR INDEPENDENT DISSENTERS.

Adopted at the Annual Meeting of the Congregational Union, May, 1833.

The CONGREGATIONAL Churches in England and Wales, frequently called INDEPENDENT, hold the following doctrines, as of divine authority, and as the foundation of Christian faith and practice.   They are also formed and governed according to the principles hereinafter stated.

PRELIMINARY NOTES.

1. It is not designed, in the following summary, to do more than to state the leading doctrines of faith and order maintained by Congregational Churches in general.

2. It is not proposed to offer any proofs, reasons, or arguments, in support of the doctrines herein stated, but simply to declare what the Denomination believes to be taught by the pen of inspiration.

3. It is not intended to present a scholastic or critical confession of faith, but merely such a statement as any intelligent member of the body might offer, as containing its leading principles.

4. It is not intended that the following statement should be put forth with any authority, or as a standard to which assent should be required.

5. Disallowing the utility of creeds and articles of religion as a bond of union, and protesting against subscription to any human formularies as a term of communion, Congregationalists are yet willing to declare, for general information, what is commonly believed among them, reserving to every one the most perfect liberty of conscience.

6. Upon some minor points of doctrine and practice, they, differing among themselves, allow to each other the right to form an unbiased judgment of the Word of God.

7. They wish it to be observed, that, notwithstanding their jealousy of subscription to creeds and articles, and their disapproval of the imposition of any human standard, whether of faith or discipline, they are far more agreed in their doctrines and practices than any Church which enjoins subscription and enforces a human standard of orthodoxy; and they believe that there is no minister and no church among them that would deny the substance of any one of the following doctrines of religion, though each might prefer to state his sentiments in his own way.

PRINCIPLES OF RELIGION.

I. The Scriptures of the Old Testament, as received by the Jews, and the books of the New Testament, as received by the Primitive Christians from the Evangelists and Apostles, Congregational Churches believe to be divinely inspired, and of supreme authority. These writings, in the languages in which they were originally composed, are to be consulted, by the aids of sound criticism, as a final appeal in all controversies; but the common version they consider to be adequate to the ordinary purposes of Christian instruction and edification.

II. They believe in One God, essentially wise, holy, just, and good; eternal, infinite, and immutable in all natural and moral perfections; the Creator, Supporter, and Governor of all beings and of all things.

III. They believe that God is revealed in the Scriptures, as the Father, the Son, and the Holy Spirit, and that to each are attributable the same divine properties and perfections.   The doctrine of the divine existence, as above stated, they cordially believe, without attempting fully to explain.

IV. They believe that man was created after the divine image, sinless, and, in his kind, perfect.

V. They believe that the first man disobeyed the divine command, fell from his state of innocence and purity, and involved all his posterity in the consequences of that fall.

VI. They believe that, therefore, all mankind are born in sin, and that a fatal inclination to moral evil, utterly incurable by human means, is inherent in every descendant of Adam.

VII. They believe that God, having, before the foundation of the world, designed to redeem fallen man, made disclosures of his mercy, which were the grounds of faith and hope from the earliest ages.

VIII. They believe that God revealed more fully to Abraham the covenant of his grace, and, having promised that from his descendants should arise the Deliverer and Redeemer of mankind, set that patriarch and his posterity apart, as a race specially favored and separated to his service: a peculiar Church, formed and carefully preserved, under the divine sanction and government, until the birth of the promised Messiah.

IX. They believe that, in the fullness of the time, the Son of God was manifested in the flesh, being born of the Virgin Mary, but conceived by the power of the Holy Spirit; and that our Lord Jesus Christ was both the Son of Man and the Son of God; partaking fully and truly of human nature, though without sin—equal with the Father and 'the express image of his person.'

X. They believe that Jesus Christ, the Son of God, revealed, either personally in his own ministry, or by the Holy Spirit in the ministry of his apostles, the whole mind of God for our salvation; and that, by his obedience to the divine law while he lived, and by his sufferings unto death, he meritoriously 'obtained eternal redemption for us;' having thereby vindicated and illustrated divine justice, 'magnified the law,' and 'brought in everlasting righteousness.'

XI. They believe that, after his death and resurrection, he ascended up into heaven, where, as the Mediator, he 'ever liveth' to rule over all, and to 'make intercession for them that come unto God by him.'

XII. They believe that the Holy Spirit is given, in consequence of Christ's mediation, to quicken and renew the hearts of men; and that his influence is indispensably necessary to bring a sinner to true repentance, to produce saving faith, to regenerate the heart, and to perfect our sanctification.

XIII. They believe that we are justified through faith in Christ, as 'the Lord our righteousness,' and not 'by the works of the law.'

XIV. They believe that all who will be saved were the objects of God's eternal and electing love, and were given by an act of divine sovereignty to the Son of God; which in no way interferes with the system of means, nor with the grounds of human responsibility; being wholly unrevealed as to its objects, and not a rule of human duty.

XV. They believe that the Scriptures teach the final perseverance of all true believers to a state of eternal blessedness, which they are appointed to obtain through constant faith in Christ and uniform obedience to his commands.

XVI. They believe that a holy life will be the necessary effect of a true faith, and that good works are the certain fruits of a vital union to Christ.

XVII. They believe that the sanctification of true Christians, or their growth in the graces of the Spirit, and meetness for heaven, is gradually carried on through the whole period during which it pleases God to continue them in the present life, and that, at death, their souls, perfectly freed from all remains of evil, are immediately received into the presence of Christ.

XVIII. They believe in the perpetual obligation of Baptism and the Lord's Supper; the former to be administered to all converts to Christianity and their children, by the application of water to the subject, 'in the name of the Father, and of the Son, and of the Holy Ghost;'

and the latter to be celebrated by Christian churches as a token of faith in the Saviour, and of brotherly love.

XIX. They believe that Christ will finally come to judge the whole human race according to their works; that the bodies of the dead will be raised again; and that as the Supreme Judge, he will divide the righteous from the wicked, will receive the righteous into 'life everlasting,' but send away the wicked into 'everlasting punishment.'

XX. They believe that Jesus Christ directed his followers to live together in Christian fellowship, and to maintain the communion of saints; and that, for this purpose, they are jointly to observe all divine ordinances, and maintain that church order and discipline which is either expressly enjoined by inspired institution, or sanctioned by the undoubted example of the apostles and of apostolic churches.

PRINCIPLES OF CHURCH ORDER AND DISCIPLINE.

I. The Congregational Churches hold it to be the will of Christ that true believers should voluntarily assemble together to observe religious ordinances, to promote mutual edification and holiness, to perpetuate and propagate the gospel in the world, and to advance the glory and worship of God, through Jesus Christ; and that each society of believers, having these objects in view in its formation, is properly a Christian Church.

II. They believe that the New Testament contains, either in the form of express statute, or in the example and practice of apostles and apostolic churches, all the articles of faith necessary to be believed, and all the principles of order and discipline requisite for constituting and governing Christian societies; and that human traditions, fathers and councils, canons and creeds, possess no authority over the faith and practice of Christians.

III. They acknowledge Christ as the only Head of the Church, and the officers of each church under him, as ordained to administer his laws impartially to all; and their only appeal, in all questions touching their religious faith and practice is to the Sacred Scriptures.

IV. They believe that the New Testament authorizes every Christian church to elect its own officers, to manage all its own affairs, and to stand independent of, and irresponsible to, all authority, saving that only of the supreme and divine Head of the Church, the Lord Jesus Christ.

V. They believe that the only officers placed by the apostles over individual churches are the bishops or pastors and the deacons; the number of these being dependent upon the numbers of the Church; and that to these, as the officers of the Church, is committed respectively the administration of its spiritual and temporal concerns—subject, however, to the approbation of the Church.

VI. They believe that no persons should be received as members of Christian churches but such as make a credible profession of Christianity, are living according to its precepts, and attest a willingness to be subject to its discipline; and that none should be excluded from the fellowship of the church but such as deny the faith of Christ, violate his laws, or refuse to submit themselves to the discipline which the Word of God enforces.

VII. The power of admission into any Christian church, and rejection from it, they believe to be vested in the church itself, and to be exercised only through the medium of its own officers

VIII. They believe that Christian churches should statedly meet for the celebration of public worship, for the observance of the Lord's Supper, and for the sanctification of the first day of the week.

IX. They believe that the power of a Christian church is purely spiritual, and should in no way be corrupted by union with temporal or civil power.

X. They believe that it is the duty of Christian churches to hold communion with each other, to entertain an enlarged affection for each other, as members of the same body, and to co-operate for the promotion of the Christian cause; but that no church, nor union of churches, has any right or power to interfere with the faith or discipline of any other church, further than to separate from such as, in faith or practice, depart from the gospel of Christ.

XI. They believe that it is the privilege and duty of every church to call forth such of its members as may appear to be qualified by the Holy Spirit to sustain the office of the ministry; and that Christian churches unitedly ought to consider the maintenance of the Christian ministry in an adequate degree of learning as one of their especial cares; that the cause of the gospel may be both honorably sustained and constantly promoted.

XII. They believe that church officers, whether bishops or deacons, should be chosen by the free voice of the church; but that their dedication to the duties of their office should take place with special prayer, and by solemn designation, to which most of the churches add the imposition of hands by those already in office.

XIII. They believe that the fellowship of every Christian church should be so liberal as to admit to communion in the Lord's Supper all whose faith and godliness are, on the whole, undoubted, though conscientiously differing in points of minor importance; and that this outward sign of fraternity in Christ should be co-extensive with the fraternity itself, though without involving any compliances which conscience would deem to be sinful.

DECLARATION OF FAITH OF THE NATIONAL COUNCIL OF CONGREGA-
TIONAL CHURCHES, HELD AT BOSTON, MASS., JUNE 14–24, 1865.

[This Declaration was adopted at Plymouth, Massachusetts, on the spot where the first meeting-house of the 'Pilgrim Fathers' stood. The text is taken from the *Debates and Proceedings of the National Council of Congregational Churches* (Boston, 1866), pp. 401–403, as compared with the Congregational Manual on *Ecclesiastical Polity*, published by the Congregational Board, Boston, 1872. pp. 76–80.]

Standing by the rock where the Pilgrims set foot upon these shores, upon the spot where they worshiped God, and among the graves of the early generations, we, Elders and Messengers of the Congregational churches of the United States in National Council assembled—like them acknowledging no rule of faith but the Word of God—do now declare our adherence to the faith and order of the apostolic and primitive churches held by our fathers, and substantially as embodied in the confessions and platforms which our Synods of 1648 and 1680 set forth or reaffirmed. We declare that the experience of the nearly two and a half centuries which have elapsed since the memorable day when our sires founded here a Christian Commonwealth, with all the development of new forms of error since their times, has only deepened our confidence in the faith and polity of those fathers. We bless God for the inheritance of these doctrines. We invoke the help of the

Divine Redeemer, that, through the presence of the promised Comforter, he will enable us to transmit them in purity to our children.

In the times that are before us as a nation, times at once of duty and of danger, we rest all our hope in the gospel of the Son of God. It was the grand peculiarity of our Puritan fathers that they held this gospel, not merely as the ground of their personal salvation, but as declaring the worth of man by the incarnation and sacrifice of the Son of God, and therefore applied its principles to elevate society, to regulate education, to civilize humanity, to purify law, to reform the Church and the State, and to assert and deford liberty; in short, to mold and redeem, by its all-transforming energy, every thing that belongs to man in his individual and social relations.

It was the faith of our fathers that gave us this free land in which we dwell. It is by this faith only that we can transmit to our children a free and happy, because a Christian, commonwealth.

We hold it to be a distinctive excellence of our Congregational system that it exalts that which is more above that which is less important, and by the simplicity of its organization facilitates, in communities where the population is limited, the union of all true believers in one Christian church, and that the division of such communities into several weak and jealous societies, holding the same common faith, is a sin against the unity of the body of Christ, and at once the shame and scandal of Christendom.

We rejoice that, through the influence of our free system of apostolic order, we can hold fellowship with all who acknowledge Christ, and act efficiently in the work of restoring unity to the divided Church, and of bringing back harmony and peace among all who love our Lord Jesus Christ in sincerity.'

Thus recognizing the unity of the Church of Christ in all the world, and knowing that we are but one branch of Christ's people, while adhering to our peculiar faith and order, we extend to all believers the hand of Christian fellowship upon the basis of those great fundamental truths in which all Christians should agree.

With them we confess our faith in God, the Father, the Son, and the Holy Ghost [the only living and true God];[1] in Jesus Christ, the

[1] The words in brackets were inadvertently omitted in the volume of *Proceedings*, but inserted in the text of the *Manual*. See *Cong. Quarterly*, Vol. X. p. 377, where Dr. Quint shows that they belong to the original MS.—*Ed.*

incarnate Word, who is exalted to be our Redeemer and King; and in the Holy Comforter, who is present in the Church to regenerate and sanctify the soul.

With the whole Church, we confess the common sinfulness and ruin of our race, and acknowledge that it is only through the work accomplished by the life and expiatory death of Christ that believers in him are justified before God, receive the remission of sins, and through the presence and grace of the Holy Comforter are delivered from the power of sin and perfected in holiness.

We believe also in the organized and visible Church, in the ministry of the Word, in the sacraments of Baptism and the Lord's Supper, in the resurrection of the body, and in the final judgment, the issues of which are eternal life and everlasting punishment.

We receive these truths on the testimony of God, given through prophets and apostles, and in the life, the miracles, the death, the resurrection of his Son, our Divine Redeemer—a testimony preserved for the Church in the Scriptures of the Old and New Testaments, which were composed by holy men, as they were moved by the Holy Ghost.

Affirming now our belief that those who thus hold 'one faith, one Lord, one baptism,'[1] together constitute the one catholic Church, the several households of which, though called by different names, are the one body of Christ, and that these members of his body are sacredly bound to keep 'the unity of the Spirit in the bond of peace,' we declare that we will co-operate with all who hold these truths. With them we will carry the gospel into every part of this land, and with them we will go into all the world, and 'preach the gospel to every creature.' May He to whom 'all power is given in heaven and earth' fulfill the promise which is all our hope: 'Lo, I am with you alway, even to the end of the World.' Amen.

---

[1] The Apostle puts 'Lord' before 'faith'—Eph. iv. 5.—*Ed.*

THE OBERLIN DECLARATION OF THE NATIONAL CONGREGATIONAL COUNCIL. A.D. 1871.

[The National Council of Congregational churches, which was organized at Oberlin, Ohio, Nov. 17 1871, and which holds triennial sessions, adopted a Constitution with the following declaration of principles concerning faith and Church polity.]

The Congregational churches of the United States, by elders and messengers assembled, do now associate themselves in National Council:

To express and foster their substantial unity in doctrine, polity, and work; and

To consult upon the common interests of all the churches, their duties in the work of evangelization, the united development of their resources, and their relations to all parts of the kingdom of Christ.

They agree in belief that the Holy Scriptures are the sufficient and only infallible rule of religious faith and practice; their interpretation thereof being in substantial accordance with the great doctrines of the Christian faith, commonly called Evangelical, held in our churches from the early times, and sufficiently set forth by former General Councils.

They agree in belief that the right of government resides in local churches, or congregations of believers, who are responsible directly to the Lord Jesus Christ, the One Head of the Church universal and of all particular churches; but that all churches, being in communion one with another as parts of Christ's catholic Church, have mutual duties subsisting in the obligations of fellowship.

The churches, therefore, while establishing this National Council for the furtherance of the common interests and work of all the churches, do maintain the scriptural and inalienable right of each church to self-government and administration; and this National Council shall never exercise legislative or judicial authority, nor consent to act as a council of reference.

THE BAPTIST CONFESSION OF 1688.

(THE PHILADELPHIA CONFESSION.)

[This is the most generally accepted Confession of the Regular or Calvinistic Baptists in England and in the Southern States of America. It appeared first in London, 1677, then again in 1688 and 1689, under the title '*A Confession of Faith put forth by the Elders and Brethren of many Congregations of Christians, Baptized upon Profession of their Faith in London and the Country. With an Appendix concerning Baptism.* It was adopted early in the eighteenth century by the Philadelphia Association of Baptist churches, and is hence called also the PHILADELPHIA CONFESSION OF FAITH.

It is a slight modification of the Confession of the Westminster Assembly (1647) and the Savoy Declaration (1658), with changes to suit the Baptist views on Church polity and on the subjects and mode of baptism. Having given the Westminster Confession in full, I present here only the distinctive features of the Baptist Confession, which my friend, the Rev. Dr. Howard Osgood, Professor in the Baptist Theological Seminary at Rochester, N. Y., has kindly selected for this work.]

In Chapter XX., 'Of Christian Liberty and Liberty of Conscience,' Art. 4 of the Westminster Conf. (Ch. XXI. B. C.) is omitted. In Chapter XXIII., 'Of the Civil Magistrate,' Arts. 3 and 4 of the Westminster Conf. are omitted and the following inserted (Ch. XXIV. B. C.):

Civil Magistrates being set up by God for the ends aforesaid, subjection in all lawful things commanded by them ought to be yielded by us in the Lord, not only for wrath, but for conscience' sake; and we ought to make supplications and prayers for kings and all that are in authority, that under them we may live a quiet and peaceable life, in all godliness and honesty.

In the Chapter 'Of the Church' (Ch. XXV. W. C.; Ch. XXVI. of the Bapt. Conf. and Savoy Declaration), the changes are so great that we give the whole:

1. The Catholic or Universal Church which (with respect to the internal work of the Spirit and truth of grace) may be called invisible, consists of the whole number of the elect, that have been, are, or shall be gathered into one, under Christ, the head thereof: and is the spouse, the body, the fullness of him that filleth all in all.

2. All persons throughout the world, professing the faith of the gospel, and obedience unto God by Christ according unto it, not destroying their own profession by any errors, everting the foundation, or unholiness of conversation, are and may be called visible saints; and of such ought all particular congregations to be constituted.

3. The purest churches under heaven are subject to mixture and error; and some have so degenerated as to become no churches of Christ, but synagogues of Satan; nevertheless, Christ always hath had and ever shall have a kingdom in this world to the end thereof, of such as believe in him, and make professions of his name.

4. The Lord Jesus Christ is the head of the Church, in whom, by the

appointment of the Father, all power for the calling, institution, order, or government of the Church is invested in a supreme and sovereign manner; neither can the Pope of Rome, in any sense, be head thereof, but is no other than Antichrist, that man of sin and son of perdition, that exalteth himself in the Church against Christ, and all that is called God: whom the Lord shall destroy with the brightness of his coming.

5. In the execution of this power wherewith he is so intrusted, the Lord Jesus calleth out of the world unto himself, through the ministry of his Word, by his Spirit, those that are given unto him by his Father, that they may walk before him in all the ways of obedience which he prescribeth to them in his Word. Those thus called he commandeth to walk together in particular societies or churches, for their mutual edification, and the due performance of that public worship which he requireth of them in the world.

6. The members of these churches are saints by calling, visibly manifesting and evidencing (in and by their profession and walking) their obedience unto that call of Christ; and do willingly consent to walk together according to the appointment of Christ, giving up themselves to the Lord and one to another, by the will of God, in the professed subjection to the ordinances of the gospel.

7. To each of these churches thus gathered, according to his mind declared in his Word, he hath given all that power and authority which is any way needful for their carrying on that order in worship and discipline which he hath instituted for them to observe, with commands and rules for the due and right exerting and executing of that power.

8. A particular church gathered and completely organized, according to the mind of Christ, consists of officers and members; and the officers appointed by Christ to be chosen and set apart by the Church (so-called and gathered) for the peculiar administration of ordinances, and execution of power and duty, which he intrusts them with or calls them to, to be continued to the end of the world, are bishops or elders and deacons.

9. The way appointed by Christ for the calling of any person, fitted and gifted by the Holy Spirit, unto the office of bishop or elder in the church is that he be chosen thereunto by the common suffrage of the church itself, and solemnly set apart by fasting and prayer, with im-

position of hands of the eldership of the church, if there be any before constituted therein; and of a deacon, that he be chosen by the like suffrage, and set apart by prayer, and the like imposition of hands.

10. The work of pastors being constantly to attend the service of Christ in his churches, in the ministry of the Word and prayer, with watching for their souls, as they that must give an account to him, it is incumbent on the churches to whom they minister, not only to give them all due respect, but also to communicate to them of all their good things, according to their ability, so as they may have a comfortable supply, without being themselves entangled with secular affairs; and may also be capable of exercising hospitality towards others; and this is required by the law of nature, and by the express order of our Lord Jesus, who hath ordained that they that preach the gospel should live of the gospel.

11. Although it be incumbent on the bishops or pastors of the churches to be instant in preaching the Word by way of office, yet the work of preaching the Word is not so peculiarly confined to them but that others also, gifted and fitted by the Holy Spirit for it, and approved and called by the Church, may and ought to perform it.

12. As all believers are bound to join themselves to particular churches, when and where they have opportunity so to do, so all that are admitted unto the privileges of a church are also under the censures and government thereof, according to the rule of Christ.

13. No church members, upon any offense taken by them, having performed their duty required of them towards the person they are offended at, ought to disturb any church order, or absent themselves from the assemblies of the church or administration of any ordinances upon the account of such offense at any of their fellow-members, but to wait upon Christ in the further proceeding of the church.

14. As each church, and all the members of it, are bound to pray continually for the good and prosperity of all the churches of Christ, in all places, and upon all occasions to further it (every one within the bounds of their places and callings, in the exercise of their gifts and graces), so the churches (when planted by the providence of God so as they may enjoy opportunity and advantage for it) ought to hold communion among themselves for their peace, increase of love, and mutual edification.

15. In cases of difficulties or differences, either in point of doctrine

or administration, wherein either the churches in general are concerned or any one church, in their peace, union, and edification; or any member or members of any church are injured, in or by any proceedings in censures not agreeable to truth and order: it is according to the mind of Christ that many churches, holding communion together, do by their messengers meet to consider and give their advice in or about that matter in difference, to be reported to all the churches concerned; howbeit these messengers assembled are not intrusted with any church power properly so called, or with any jurisdiction over the churches themselves, to exercise any censures either over any churches or persons, to impose their determination on the churches or officers.

Instead of Chapter XXVII., 'Of the Sacraments,' of the Westminster Confession, the following is given (Ch. XXVIII. B. C.):

OF BAPTISM AND THE LORD'S SUPPER.

1. Baptism and the Lord's Supper are ordinances of positive and sovereign institution, appointed by the Lord Jesus, the only Lawgiver, to be continued in his Church to the end of the world.

2. These holy appointments are to be administered by those only who are qualified, and thereunto called, according to the commission of Christ.

Similarly (Ch. XXVIII. W. C.; Ch. XXIX. B. C.):

OF BAPTISM.

1. Baptism is an ordinance of the New Testament ordained by Jesus Christ to be unto the party baptized a sign of his fellowship with him in his death and resurrection; of his being engrafted into him; of remission of sins; and of his giving up unto God, through Jesus Christ, to live and walk in newness of life.

2. Those who do actually profess repentance towards God, faith in and obedience to our Lord Jesus, are the only proper subjects of this ordinance.

3. The outward element to be used in this ordinance is water, wherein the party is to be baptized in the name of the Father, and of the Son, and of the Holy Spirit.

4. Immersion, or dipping of the person in water, is necessary to the due administration of this ordinance.

Chapters XXX., 'Of Church Censures,' and XXXI., 'Of Synods and Councils,' of the Westminster Confession are omitted. On the other hand, a chapter 'Of the Gospel and the Extent of the Grace thereof' is added from the Savoy Declaration, making Chapter XXX. of the Baptist Confession and the Savoy Declaration.

THE NEW HAMPSHIRE BAPTIST CONFESSION. A.D. 1833.

(THE NEW HAMPSHIRE CONFESSION.)

[This Confession was drawn up by the Rev. JOHN NEWTON BROWN, D.D., of New Hampshire (b. 1803, d. 1868), about 1833, and has been adopted by the N͞e͞w Hampshire Convention, and widely accepted by Baptists, especially in the Northern and Western States, as a clear and concise statement of their faith, in harmony with the doctrines of older confessions, but expressed in milder form. The text is taken from the *Baptist Church Manual*, published by the American Baptist Publication Society, Philadelphia.]

DECLARATION OF FAITH.

I. OF THE SCRIPTURES.

We believe that the Holy Bible was written by men divinely inspired, and is a perfect treasure of heavenly instruction;[1] that it has God for its author, salvation for its end,[2] and truth without any mixture of error for its matter;[3] that it reveals the principles by which God will judge us;[4] and therefore is, and shall remain to the end of the world, the true centre of Christian union,[5] and the supreme standard by which all human conduct, creeds, and opinions should be tried.[6]

II. OF THE TRUE GOD.

We believe that there is one, and only one, living and true God, an infinite, intelligent Spirit, whose name is JEHOVAH, the Maker and Supreme Ruler of heaven and earth;[7] inexpressibly glorious in holiness,[8] and worthy of all possible honor, confidence, and love;[9] that in the unity of the Godhead there are three persons, the Father, the Son, and the Holy Ghost;[10] equal in every divine perfection,[11] and executing distinct and harmonious offices in the great work of redemption.[12]

---

[1] 2 Tim. iii. 16, 17; 2 Pet. i. 21; 1 Sam. xxiii. 2; Acts i. 16; iii. 21; John x. 35; Luke xvi. 29–31; Psa. cxix. 111; Rom. iii. 1. 2.

[2] 2 Tim. iii. 15; 1 Pet. i. 10–12; Acts xi. 14; Rom. i. 16; Mark xvi. 16; John v. 38, 39.

[3] Prov. xxx. 5, 6; John xvii. 17; Rev. xxii. 18, 19; Rom. iii. 4.

[4] Rom. ii. 12; John xii. 47, 48; 1 Cor. iv. 3, 4; Luke x. 10–16; xii. 47, 48.

[5] Phil. iii. 16; Eph. iv. 3–6; Phil. ii. 1, 2; 1 Cor. i. 10; 1 Pet. iv. 11.

[6] 1 John iv. 1; Isa. viii. 20; 1 Thess. v. 21; 2 Cor. xiii. 5; Acts xvii. 11; 1 John iv. 6; Jude iii. 5; Eph. vi. 17; Psa. cxix. 59, 60; Phil. i. 9–11.

[7] John iv. 24; Psa. cxlvii. 5; lxxxiii. 18; Heb. iii. 4; Rom. i. 20; Jer. x. 10.

[8] Exod. xv. 11; Isa. vi. 3; 1 Pet. i. 15, 16; Rev. iv. 6–8.

[9] Mark xii. 30; Rev. iv. 11; Matt. x. 37; Jer. ii. 12, 13.

[10] Matt. xxviii. 19; John xv. 26; 1 Cor. xii. 4–6; 1 John v. 7.

[11] John x. 30; v. 17; xiv. 23; xvii. 5, 10; Acts v. 3, 4; 1 Cor. ii. 10, 11; Phil. ii. 5, 6.

[12] Eph. ii. 18; 2 Cor. xiii. 14; Rev. i. 4, 5; comp. ii., vii.

III. OF THE FALL OF MAN.

We believe that man was created in holiness, under the law of his Maker;[1] but by voluntary transgression fell from that holy and happy state;[2] in consequence of which all mankind are now sinners,[3] not by constraint, but choice;[4] being by nature utterly void of that holiness required by the law of God, positively inclined to evil; and therefore under just condemnation to eternal ruin,[5] without defense or excuse.[6]

IV. OF THE WAY OF SALVATION.

We believe that the salvation of sinners is wholly of grace,[7] through the mediatorial offices of the Son of God;[8] who by the appointment of the Father, freely took upon him our nature, yet without sin;[9] honored the divine law by his personal obedience,[10] and by his death made a full atonement for our sins;[11] that having risen from the dead, he is now enthroned in heaven;[12] and uniting in his wonderful person the tenderest sympathies with divine perfections, he is every way qualified to be a suitable, a compassionate, and an all-sufficient Saviour.[13]

V. OF JUSTIFICATION.

We believe that the great gospel blessing which Christ[14] secures to such as believe in him is Justification;[15] that Justification includes the pardon of sin,[16] and the promise of eternal life on principles of righteousness;[17] that it is bestowed, not in consideration of any works of

---

[1] Gen. i. 27; i. 31; Eccles. vii. 29; Acts xvi. 26; Gen. ii. 16.

[2] Gen. iii. 6–24; Rom. v. 12.

[3] Rom. v. 19; John iii. 6; Psa. li. 5; Rom. v. 15–19; viii. 7.

[4] Isa. liii. 6; Gen. vi. 12; Rom. iii. 9–18.

[5] Eph. ii. 1–3; Rom. i. 18; i. 32; ii. 1–16; Gal. iii. 10; Matt. xx. 15.

[6] Ezek. xviii. 19, 20; Rom. i. 20; iii. 19; Gal. iii. 22.

[7] Eph. ii. 5; Matt. xviii. 11; 1 John iv. 10; 1 Cor. iii. 5–7; Acts xv. 11.

[8] John iii. 16; i. 1–14; Heb. iv. 14; xii. 24.

[9] Phil. ii. 6, 7; Heb. ii. 9; ii. 14; 2 Cor. v. 21.

[10] Isa. xlii. 21; Phil. ii. 8; Gal. iv. 4, 5; Rom. iii. 21.

[11] Isa. liii. 4, 5; Matt. xx. 28; Rom. iv. 25; iii. 21–26; 1 John iv. 10; ii. 2; 1 Cor. xv. 1–3; Heb. ix. 13–15.

[12] Heb. i. 8; i. 3; viii. 1; Col. iii. 1–4.

[13] Heb. vii. 25; Col. ii. 9; Heb. ii. 18; vii. 26; Psa. lxxxix. 19; xiv.

[14] John i. 16; Eph. iii. 8.

[15] Acts xiii. 39; Isa. iii. 11, 12; Rom. viii. 1.

[16] Rom. v. 9; Zech. xiii. 1; Matt. ix. 6; Acts x. 43.

[17] Rom. v. 17; Titus iii. 5, 6; 1 Pet. iii. 7; 1 John ii. 25; Rom. v. 21.

righteousness which we have done, but solely through faith in the Redeemer's blood;[1] by virtue of which faith his perfect righteousness is freely imputed to us of God;[2] that it brings us into a state of most blessed peace and favor with God, and secures every other blessing needful for time and eternity.[3]

VI. OF THE FREENESS OF SALVATION.

We believe that the blessings of salvation are made free to all by the gospel;[4] that it is the immediate duty of all to accept them by a cordial, penitent, and obedient faith;[5] and that nothing prevents the salvation of the greatest sinner on earth but his own inherent depravity and voluntary rejection of the gospel;[6] which rejection involves him in an aggravated condemnation.[7]

VII. OF GRACE IN REGENERATION.

We believe that, in order to be saved, sinners must be regenerated, or born again;[8] that regeneration consists in giving a holy disposition to the mind;[9] that it is effected in a manner above our comprehension by the power of the Holy Spirit, in connection with divine truth,[10] so as to secure our voluntary obedience to the gospel;[11] and that its proper evidence appears in the holy fruits of repentance, and faith, and newness of life.[12]

VIII. OF REPENTANCE AND FAITH.

We believe that Repentance and Faith are sacred duties, and also inseparable graces, wrought in our souls by the regenerating Spirit of God;[13] whereby being deeply convinced of our guilt, danger, and help-

---

[1] Rom. iv. 4, 5; v. 21; vi. 23; Phil. iii. 7–9.

[2] Rom. v. 19; iii. 24–26; iv. 23–25; 1 John ii. 12.

[3] Rom. v. 1, 2; v. 3; v. 11; 1 Cor. i. 30, 31; Matt. vi. 33; 1 Tim. iv. 8.

[4] Isa. lv. 1; Rev. xxii. 17; Luke xiv. 17.

[5] Rom. xvi. 26; Mark i. 15; Rom. i. 15–17.

[6] John v. 40; Matt. xxiii. 37; Rom. ix. 32; Prov. i. 24; Acts xiii. 46.

[7] John iii. 19; Matt. xi. 20; Luke xix. 27; 2 Thess. i. 8.

[8] John iii. 3; iii. 6, 7; 1 Cor. i. 14; Rev. viii. 7–9; xxi. 27.

[9] 2 Cor. v. 17; Ezek. xxxvi. 26; Deut. xxx. 6; Rom. ii. 28, 29; v. 5; 1 John iv. 7.

[10] John iii. 8; i. 13; James i. 16–18; 1 Cor. i. 30; Phil. ii. 13.

[11] 1 Pet. i. 22–25; 1 John v. 1; Eph. iv. 20–24; Col. iii. 9–11.

[12] Eph. v. 9; Rom. viii. 9; Gal. v. 16–23; Eph. iii. 14–21; Matt. iii. 8–10; vii. 20; 1 John v. 4, 18.

[13] Mark i. 15; Acts xi. 18; Eph. ii. 8; 1 John v. 1.

lessness, and of the way of salvation by Christ,[1] we turn to God with unfeigned contrition, confession, and supplication for mercy;[2] at the same time heartily receiving the Lord Jesus Christ as our Prophet, Priest, and King, and relying on him alone as the only and all-sufficient Saviour.[3]

IX. OF GOD'S PURPOSE OF GRACE.

We believe that Election is the eternal purpose of God, according to which he graciously regenerates, sanctifies, and saves sinners;[4] that being perfectly consistent with the free agency of man, it comprehends all the means in connection with the end;[5] that it is a most glorious display of God's sovereign goodness, being infinitely free, wise, holy, and unchangeable;[6] that it utterly excludes boasting, and promotes humility, love, prayer, praise, trust in God, and active imitation of his free mercy;[7] that it encourages the use of means in the highest degree;[8] that it may be ascertained by its effects in all who truly believe the gospel;[9] that it is the foundation of Christian assurance;[10] and that to ascertain it with regard to ourselves demands and deserves the utmost diligence.[11]

X. OF SANCTIFICATION.

We believe that Sanctification is the process by which, according to the will of God, we are made partakers of his holiness;[12] that it is a progressive work;[13] that it is begun in regeneration;[14] and that it is carried on in the hearts of believers by the presence and power of the Holy Spirit, the Sealer and Comforter, in the continual use of the ap-

---

[1] John xvi. 8; Acts ii. 37, 38; xvi. 30, 31.

[2] Luke xviii. 13; xv. 18–21; James iv. 7–10; 2 Cor. vii. 11; Rom. x. 12, 13; Psa. li.

[3] Rom. x. 9–11; Acts iii. 22, 23; Heb. iv. 14; Psa. ii. 6; Heb. i. 8; viii. 25; 2 Tim. i. 12.

[4] 2 Tim. i. 8, 9; Eph. i. 3–14; 1 Pet. i. 1, 2; Rom. xi. 5, 6; John xv. 15; 1 John iv. 19; Hos. xii. 9.

[5] 2 Thess. ii. 13, 14; Acts xiii. 48; John x. 16; Matt. xx. 16; Acts xv. 14.

[6] Exod. xxxiii. 18, 19; Matt. xx. 15; Eph. i. 11; Rom. ix. 23, 24; Jer. xxxi. 3; Rom. xi. 28, 29; James i. 17, 18; 2 Tim. i. 9; Rom. xi. 32–36.

[7] 1 Cor. iv. 7; i. 26–31; Rom. iii. 27; iv. 16; Col. iii. 12; 1 Cor. iii. 5–7; xv. 10; 1 Pet. v. 10; Acts i. 24; 1 Thess. ii. 13; 1 Pet. ii. 9; Luke xviii. 7; John xv. 16; Eph. i. 16; 1 Thess. ii. 12.

[8] 2 Tim. ii. 10; 1 Cor. ix. 22; Rom. viii. 28–30; John vi. 37–40; 2 Pet. i. 10.

[9] 1 Thess. i. 4–10.

[10] Rom. viii. 28–30; Isa. xlii. 16; Rom. xi. 29.

[11] 2 Pet. i. 10, 11; Phil. iii. 12; Heb. vi. 11.

[12] 1 Thess. iv. 3; 1 Thess. v. 23; 2 Cor. vii. 1; xiii. 9; Eph. 1. 4.

[13] Prov. iv. 18; 2 Cor. iii. 18; Heb. vi. 1; 2 Pet. i. 5–8; Phil. iii. 12–16.

[14] John ii. 29; Rom. viii. 5; John iii. 6; Phil. i. 9–11; Eph. i. 13, 14.

pointed means—especially the Word of God, self-examination, self-de-
nial, watchfulness, and prayer.[1]

XI. OF THE PERSEVERANCE OF SAINTS.

We believe that such only are real believers as endure unto the
end;[2] that their persevering attachment to Christ is the grand mark
which distinguishes them from superficial professors;[3] that a special
Providence watches over their welfare;[4] and they are kept by the
power of God through faith unto salvation.[5]

XII. OF THE HARMONY OF THE LAW AND THE GOSPEL.

We believe that the Law of God is the eternal and unchangeable
rule of his moral government;[6] that it is holy, just, and good;[7] and
that the inability which the Scriptures ascribe to fallen men to fulfill
its precepts arises entirely from their love of sin;[8] to deliver them
from which, and to restore them through a Mediator to unfeigned
obedience to the holy Law, is one great end of the Gospel, and of the
means of grace connected with the establishment of the visible Church.[9]

XIII. OF A GOSPEL CHURCH.

We believe that a visible Church of Christ is a congregation of baptized believers,[10] associated by covenant in the faith and fellowship of
the gospel;[11] observing the ordinances of Christ;[12] governed by his
laws,[13] and exercising the gifts, rights, and privileges invested in them

---

[1] Phil. ii. 12, 13; Eph. iv. 11, 12; 1 Pet. ii. 2; 2 Pet. iii. 18; 2 Cor. xiii. 5; Luke xi. 35; ix. 23; Matt. xxvi. 41; Eph. vi. 18; iv. 30.

[2] John viii. 31; 1 John ii. 27, 28; iii. 9; v. 18.

[3] 1 John ii. 19; John xiii. 18; Matt. xiii. 20, 21; John vi. 66–69; Job xvii. 9.

[4] Rom. viii. 28; Matt. vi. 30–33; Jer. xxxii. 40; Psa. cxxi. 3; xci. 11, 12.

[5] Phil. i. 6; ii. 12, 13; Jude 24, 25; Heb. i. 14; 2 Kings vi. 16; Heb. xiii. 5; 1 John iv. 4.

[6] Rom. iii. 31; Matt. v. 17; Luke xvi. 17; Rom. iii. 20; iv. 15.

[7] Rom. vii. 12; vii. 7, 14, 22; Gal. iii. 21; Psa. cxix.

[8] Rom. viii. 7, 8; Josh. xxiv. 19; Jer. xiii. 23; John vi. 44; v. 44.

[9] Rom. viii. 2, 4; x. 4; 1 Tim. i. 5; Heb. viii. 10; Jude 20, 21; Heb. xii. 14; Matt. xvi. 17, 18; 1 Cor. xii. 28.

[10] 1 Cor. i. 1–13; Matt. xviii. 17; Acts v. 11; viii. 1; xi. 31; 1 Cor. iv. 17; xiv. 23; 3 John 9; 1 Tim. iii. 5.

[11] Acts ii. 41, 42; 2 Cor. viii. 5; Acts ii. 47; 1 Cor. v. 12, 13.

[12] 1 Cor. xi. 2; 2 Thess. iii. 6; Rom. xvi. 17–20; 1 Cor. xi. 23; Matt. xviii. 15–20; 1 Cor. v. 6; 2 Cor. ii. 7; 1 Cor. iv. 17.

[13] Matt. xxviii. 20; John xiv. 15; xv. 12; 1 John iv. 21; John xiv. 21; 1 Thess. iv. 2; 2 John 6; Gal. vi. 2; all the Epistles.

by his Word;[1] that its only scriptural officers are Bishops, or Pastors, and Deacons,[2] whose qualifications, claims, and duties are defined in the Epistles to Timothy and Titus.

XIV. OF BAPTISM AND THE LORD'S SUPPER.

We believe that Christian Baptism is the immersion in water of a believer,[3] into the name of the Father, and Son, and Holy Ghost;[4] to show forth, in a solemn and beautiful emblem, our faith in the crucified, buried, and risen Saviour, with its effect in our death to sin and resurrection to a new life;[5] that it is prerequisite to the privileges of a Church relation; and to the Lord's Supper,[6] in which the members of the Church, by the sacred use of bread and wine, are to commemorate together the dying love of Christ;[7] preceeded always by solemn self-examination[8]

XV. OF THE CHRISTIAN SABBATH.

We believe that the first day of the week is the Lord's Day, or Christian Sabbath;[9] and is to be kept sacred to religious purposes,[10] by abstaining from all secular labor and sinful recreations;[11] by the devout observance of all the means of grace, both private[12] and public;[13] and by preparation for that rest that remaineth for the people of God.[14]

XVI. OF CIVIL GOVERNMENT.

We believe that civil government is of divine appointment, for the interests and good order of human society;[15] and that magistrates are

---

[1] Eph. iv. 7; 1 Cor. xiv. 12; Phil. i. 27; 1 Cor. xii. 14.

[2] Phil. i. 1; Acts xiv. 23; xv. 22; 1 Tim. iii.; Titus i.

[3] Acts viii. 36–39; Matt. iii. 5, 6; John iii. 22, 23; iv. 1, 2; Matt. xxviii. 19; Mark xvi. 16; Acts ii. 38; viii. 12; xvi. 32–34; xviii. 8.

[4] Matt. xxviii. 19; Acts x. 47, 48; Gal. iii. 27, 28.

[5] Rom. vi. 4; Col. ii. 12; 1 Pet. iii. 20, 21; Acts xxii. 16.

[6] Acts ii. 41, 42; Matt. xxviii. 19, 20; Acts and Epistles.

[7] 1 Cor. xi. 26; Matt. xxvi. 26–29; Mark xiv. 22–25; Luke xxii. 14-20.

[8] 1 Cor. xi. 28; v. 1, 8; x. 3–32; xi. 17–32; John vi. 26–71.

[9] Acts xx. 7; Gen. ii. 3; Col. ii. 16, 17; Mark ii. 27; John xx. 19; 1 Cor. xvi. 1, 2.

[10] Exod. xx. 8; Rev. i. 10; Psa. cxviii. 24.

[11] Isa. lviii. 13, 14; lvi. 2–8.

[12] Psa. cxiii. 15.

[13] Heb. x. 24, 25; Acts xi. 26; xiii. 44; Lev. xix. 30; Exod. xlvi. 3; Luke iv. 16; Acts xvii. 2, 3; Psa. xxvi. 8; lxxxvii. 3.

[14] Heb. iv. 3–11.

[15] Rom. xiii. 1–7; Deut. xvi. 18; 1 Sam. xxiii. 3; Exod. xviii. 23; Jer. xxx. 21.

to be prayed for, conscientiously honored and obeyed;[1] except only in things opposed to the will of our Lord Jesus Christ,[2] who is the only Lord of the conscience, and the Prince of the kings of the earth.[3]

XVII. OF THE RIGHTEOUS AND THE WICKED.

We believe that there is a radical and essential difference between the righteous and the wicked;[4] that such only as through faith are justified in the name of the Lord Jesus, and sanctified by the Spirit of our God, are truly righteous in his esteem;[5] while all such as continue in impenitence and unbelief are in his sight wicked, and under the curse;[6] and this distinction holds among men both in and after death.[7]

XVIII. OF THE WORLD TO COME.

We believe that the end of the world is approaching;[8] that at the last day Christ will descend from heaven,[9] and raise the dead from the grave to final retribution;[10] that a solemn separation will then take place;[11] that the wicked will be adjudged to endless punishment, and the righteous to endless joy;[12] and that this judgment will fix forever the final state of men in heaven or hell, on principles of righteousness.[13]

---

[1] Matt. xxii. 21; Titus iii. 1; 1 Pet. ii. 13; 1 Tim. ii. 1–8.

[2] Acts v. 29; Matt. x. 28; Dan. iii. 15–18; vi. 7–10; Acts iv. 18–20.

[3] Matt. xxiii. 10; Rom. xiv. 4; Rev. xix. 16; Psa. lxxii. 11; ii.; Rom. xiv. 9–13.

[4] Mal. iii. 18; Prov. xii. 26; Isa. v. 20; Gen. xviii. 23; Jer. xv. 19; Acts x. 34, 35; Rom. vi. 16.

[5] Rom. i. 17; vii. 6; 1 John ii. 29; iii. 7; Rom. vi. 18, 22; 1 Cor. xi. 32; Prov. xi. 31; 1 Pet. iv. 17, 18.

[6] 1 John v. 19; Gal. iii. 10; John iii. 36; Isa. lvii. 21; Psa. x. 4; Isa. lv. 6, 7.

[7] Prov. xiv. 32; Luke xvi. 25; John viii. 21–24; Prov. x. 24; Luke xii. 4, 5; ix. 23–26; John xii. 25, 26; Eccl. iii. 17; Matt. vii. 13, 14.

[8] 1 Pet. iv. 7; 1 Cor. vii. 29–31; Heb. i. 10–12; Matt. xxiv. 35; 1 John ii. 17; Matt. xxviii. 20; xiii. 39, 40; 2 Pet. iii. 3–13.

[9] Acts i. 11; Rev. i. 7; Heb. ix. 28; Acts iii. 21; 1 Thess. iv. 13–18; v. 1–11.

[10] Acts xxiv. 15; 1 Cor. xv. 12–59; Luke xiv. 14; Dan. xii. 2; John v. 28, 29; vi. 40; xi. 25, 26; 2 Tim. i. 10; Acts x. 42.

[11] Matt. xiii. 49; xiii. 37–43; xxiv. 30, 31; xxv. 31–33.

[12] Matt. xxv. 35–41; Rev. xxii. 11; 1 Cor. vi. 9, 10; Mark ix. 43–48; 2 Pet. ii. 9; Jude 7; Phil. iii. 19; Rom. vi. 32; 2 Cor. v. 10, 11; John iv. 36; 2 Cor. iv. 18.

[13] Rom. iii. 5, 6; 2 Thess. i. 6–12; Heb. vi. 1, 2; 1 Cor. iv. 5; Acts xvii. 31; Rom. ii. 2–16; Rev. xx. 11, 12; 1 John ii. 28; iv. 17.

CONFESSION OF THE FREE-WILL BAPTISTS. A.D. 1834, 1868.

[This Confession was adopted and issued by the General Conference of the FREE-WILL BAPTISTS of America in 1834, revised in 1848, and again in 1865 and 1868.

The text is taken from the *Treatise on the Faith and Practice of the Free-will Baptists, written under the direction of the General Conference*, Dover, N. H. Published by the Free-will Baptist Printing Establishment, 1871. The sections in which this Confession differs from the preceding Baptist Confessions have been put in italics, viz., Ch. III., 2 and 3, and Ch. VIII. and XIII.]

CHAPTER I.

The Holy Scriptures.

These are the Old and New Testaments; they were written by holy men, inspired by the Holy Spirit, and contain God's revealed will to man. They are a sufficient and infallible guide in religious faith and practice.

CHAPTER II.

Being and Attributes of God.

The Scriptures teach that there is only one true and living God, who is a Spirit, self-existent, eternal, immutable, omnipresent, omniscient, omnipotent, independent, good, wise, holy, just, and merciful; the Creator, Preserver, and Governor of the universe; the Redeemer, Saviour, Sanctifier, and Judge of men; and the only proper object of Divine worship.

The mode of his existence, however, is a subject far above the understanding of man—finite beings can not comprehend him. There is nothing in the universe that can justly represent him, for there is none like him. He is the fountain of all perfection and happiness. He is glorified by the whole inanimate creation, and is worthy to be loved and served by all intelligences.

CHAPTER III.

Divine Government and Providence.

1. God exercises a providential care and superintendence over all his creatures, and governs the world in wisdom and mercy, according to the testimony of his Word.

2. *God has endowed man with power of free choice, and governs*

*him by moral laws and motives ; and this power of free choice is the
exact measure of his responsibility.*

3. *All events are present with God from everlasting to everlasting ;
but his knowledge of them does not in any sense cause them, nor does
ne decree all events which he knows will occur.*

CHAPTER IV.

Creation, Primitive State of Man, and his Fall.

SECTION I.—CREATION.

1. *Of the world.* ' God created the world, and all things that it
contains, for his own pleasure and glory, and the enjoyment of his
creatures.

2. *Of the angels.* The angels were created by God to glorify him,
and obey his commandments. Those who have kept their first estate
he employs in ministering blessings to the heirs of salvation, and in
executing his judgments upon the world.

3. *Of man.* God created man, consisting of a material body and a
thinking, rational soul. He was made in the image of God to glorify
his Maker.

SECTION II.—PRIMITIVE STATE OF MAN AND HIS FALL.

Our first parents, in their original state of probation, were upright ;
they naturally preferred and desired to obey their Creator, and had no
preference or desire to transgress his will till they were influenced and
inclined by the tempter to disobey God's commands. Previously to
this the only tendency of their nature was to do righteousness. In
consequence of the first transgression, the state under which the posterity of Adam came into the world is so far different from that of
Adam that they have not that righteousness and purity which Adam
had before the fall ; they are not naturally willing to obey God, but
are inclined to evil. Hence, none, by virtue of any natural goodness
and mere work of their own, can become the children of God ; but
they are all dependent for salvation upon the redemption effected
through the blood of Christ, and upon being created anew unto obedience through the operation of the Spirit ; both of which are freely
provided for every descendant of Adam.

CHAPTER V.

Of Christ.

SECTION I.

Jesus Christ, the Son of God, possesses all divine perfections. As he and the Father are one, he, in his divine nature, filled all the offices and performed the works of God to his creatures that have been the subjects of revelation to us. As man, he performed all the duties toward God that we are required to perform, repentance of sin excepted.

His divinity is proved from his titles, his attributes, and his works.

1. *His titles.*—The Bible ascribes to Christ the titles of Saviour, Jehovah, Lord of Hosts, the First and the Last, God, true God, great God, God over all, mighty God, and the everlasting Father.

2. *His attributes.*—He is eternal, unchangeable, omnipresent, omniscient, omnipotent, holy, and is entitled to Divine worship.

3. *His works.*—By Christ the world was created; he preserves and governs it; he has provided redemption for all men, and he will be their final judge.

SECTION II.—THE INCARNATION OF CHRIST.

The Word, which in the beginning was with God, and which was God, by whom all things were made, condescended to a state of humiliation in being united with human nature, and becoming like us, pollution and sin excepted. In this state, as a subject of the law, he was liable to the infirmities of our nature; was tempted as we are; but lived our example, and rendered perfect obedience to the Divine requirements. As Christ was made of the seed of David according to the flesh, he is called 'The Son of Man;' and as the Divine existence is the fountain from which he proceeded, and was the only agency by which he was begotten, he is called the Son of God, being the only begotten of the Father, and the only incarnation of the Divine Being.

CHAPTER VI.

The Holy Spirit.

1. The Scriptures ascribe to the Holy Spirit the acts and attributes of an intelligent being. He is said to guide, to know, to move, to give information, to command, to forbid, to send forth, to reprove, and to be sinned against.

2. The attributes of God are ascribed to the Holy Spirit: such as eternity, omnipresence, omniscience, goodness, and truth.

3. The works of God are ascribed to the Holy Spirit: creation, inspiration, giving of life, and sanctification.

4. The same acts which in one part of the Bible are attributed to the Holy Spirit are in other parts said to be performed by God.

5. The apostles assert that the Holy Spirit is Lord and God.

From the foregoing, the conclusion is that the Holy Spirit is in reality God, and one with the Father in all Divine perfections. It has also been shown that Jesus Christ is God, one with the Father. Then these three, the Father, Son, and Holy Spirit, are one God.

The truth of this doctrine is also proved from the fact that the Father, the Son, and the Holy Ghost are united in the authority by which believers are baptized, and in the benedictions pronounced by the apostles, which are acts of the highest religious worship.

CHAPTER VII.

The Atonement and Mediation of Christ.

1. THE ATONEMENT.—As sin can not be pardoned without a sacrifice, and the blood of beasts could never wash away sin, Christ gave himself a sacrifice for the sins of the world, and thus made salvation possible for all men. He died for us, suffering in our stead, to make known the righteousness of God, that he might be just in justifying sinners who believe in his Son. Through the redemption effected by Christ, salvation is actually enjoyed in this world, and will be enjoyed in the next by all who do not, in this life, refuse obedience to the known requirements of God. The atonement of sin was necessary. For present and future obedience can no more blot out our past sins than past obedience can remove the guilt of present and future sins. Had God pardoned the sins of men without satisfaction for the violation of his law, it would follow that transgression might go on with impunity; government would be abrogated, and the obligation of obedience to God would be, in effect, removed.

2. MEDIATION OF CHRIST.—Our Lord not only died for our sins, but he arose for our justification, and ascended to heaven, where, as Mediator between God and man, he will make intercession for men till the final judgment.

CHAPTER VIII.

The Gospel Call.

The call of the gospel is co-extensive with the atonement to all men, both by the word and the strivings of the Spirit; so that salvation is rendered equally possible to all; and if any fail of eternal life, the fault is wholly their own.

CHAPTER IX.

Repentance.

The repentance which the gospel requires includes a deep conviction, a penitential sorrow, an open confession, a decided hatred and an entire forsaking of all sin. This repentance God has enjoined on all men; and without it in this life the sinner must perish eternally.

CHAPTER X.

Faith.

Saving faith is an assent of the mind to the fundamental truths of revelation; an acceptance of the gospel, through the influence of the Holy Spirit; and a firm confidence and trust in Christ. The fruit of faith is obedience to the gospel. The power to believe is the gift of God; but believing is an act of the creature, which is required as a condition of pardon, and without which the sinner can not obtain salvation. All men are required to believe in Christ; and those who yield obedience to this requirement become the children of God by faith.

CHAPTER XI.

Regeneration.

As man is a fallen and sinful being, he must be regenerated in order to obtain salvation. This change is an instantaneous renewal of the heart by the Holy Spirit, whereby the penitent sinner receives new life, becomes a child of God, and disposed to serve him. This is called in Scripture being born again, born of the Spirit, being quickened, passing from death unto life, and a partaking of the divine nature.

CHAPTER XII.

Justification and Sanctification.

1. JUSTIFICATION.—Personal justification implies that the person justified has been guilty before God; and in consideration of the atonement of Christ, accepted by faith, the sinner is pardoned and absolved from the guilt of sin, and restored to the divine favor. Though Christ's atonement is the foundation of the sinner's redemption, yet without repentance and faith it can never give him justification and peace with God.

2. SANCTIFICATION is a work of God's grace, by which the soul is cleansed from all sin, and wholly consecrated to Christ. It commences at regeneration, and the Christian can and should abide in this state to the end of life, constantly growing in grace and in the knowledge of our Lord Jesus Christ.

CHAPTER XIII.

Perseverance of the Saints.

There are strong grounds to hope that the truly regenerate will persevere unto the end and be saved, through the power of divine grace which is pledged for their support; *but their future obedience and final salvation are neither determined nor certain; since, through infirmity and manifold temptations, they are in danger of falling; and they ought therefore to watch and pray, lest they make shipwreck of faith, and be lost.*

CHAPTER XIV.

The Sabbath.

This is one day in seven, which, from the creation of the world, God has set apart for sacred rest and holy service. Under the former dispensation, the seventh day of the week, as commemorative of the work of creation, was set apart for the Sabbath. Under the gospel, the first day of the week, in commemoration of the resurrection of Christ, and by authority of the apostles, is observed as the Christian Sabbath. On this day all men are required to refrain from secular labor, and devote themselves to the worship and service of God.

CHAPTER XV.

The Church.

A CHRISTIAN CHURCH is an organized body of believers in Christ, who statedly assemble to worship God, and sustain the ordinances of the gospel agreeably to his Word. In a more general sense it is the whole body of Christians throughout the world, and only the regenerate are real members. Believers are admitted to a particular church, on giving evidence of faith, and receiving baptism and the hand of fellowship.

CHAPTER XVI.

The Gospel Ministry.

1. QUALIFICATIONS OF MINISTERS.—They must possess good natural and acquired abilities, deep and ardent piety, be specially called of God to the work, and ordained by the laying on of hands.

2. DUTIES OF MINISTERS.—These are, to preach the Word, administer the ordinances of the gospel, visit their people, and otherwise perform the work of faithful pastors.

CHAPTER XVII.

Ordinances of the Gospel.

1. CHRISTIAN BAPTISM.—This is the immersion of believers in water in the name of the Father, the Son, and the Holy Spirit, in which are represented the burial and resurrection of Christ, the death of Christians to the world, the washing of their souls from the pollution of sin, their rising to newness of life, their engagement to serve God, and their resurrection at the last day.

2. THE LORD'S SUPPER.—This is a commemoration of the death of Christ for our sins, in the use of bread, which he made the emblem of his broken body, and the cup, the emblem of his shed blood; and by it the believer expresses his love for Christ, his faith and hope in him, and pledges to him perpetual fidelity.

It is the privilege and duty of all who have spiritual union with Christ thus to commemorate his death; and no man has a right to forbid these tokens to the least of his disciples.[1]

---

[1] [This last clause commits the Free-will Baptists to the principle and practice of *open* communion.—Ed.]

CHAPTER XVIII.

Death and the Intermediate State.

1. DEATH.—As a result of sin, all mankind are subject to the death of the body.

2. THE INTERMEDIATE STATE.—The soul does not die with the body; but immediately after death enters into a conscious state of happiness or misery, according to the moral character here possessed.

CHAPTER XIX.

Second Coming of Christ.

The Lord Jesus, who ascended on high and sits at the right hand of God, will come again to close the gospel dispensation, glorify his saints, and judge the world.

CHAPTER XX.

The Resurrection.

The Scriptures teach the resurrection of the bodies of all men at the last day, each in its own order; they that have done good will come forth to the resurrection of life, and they that have done evil to the resurrection of damnation.

CHAPTER XXI.

The General Judgment and Future Retributions.

1. THE GENERAL JUDGMENT.—There will be a general judgment, when time and man's probation will close forever. Then all men will be judged according to their works.

2. FUTURE RETRIBUTIONS.—Immediately after the general judgment, the righteous will enter into eternal life, and the wicked will go into a state of endless punishment.

THE CONFESSION OF THE WALDENSES. A.D. 1655.

[This Confession belongs to the Calvinistic family, and is in part an abridgment of the Gallican Confession of 1559. It is still in force, or at least highly prized among the Waldenses in Italy. The occasion which called it forth entitles it to special consideration. It was prepared and issued in 1655, together with an appeal to Protestant nations, in consequence of one of the most cruel persecutions which Romish bigotry could inspire. For no other crime but their simple, time-honored faith, the Waldenses in Piedmont were betrayed, outraged, mutilated, massacred, driven into exile, and utterly impoverished by the confiscation of their property and the burning of their villages. (See the frightful pictures of sufferings in the second vol. of Leger, an eye-witness.) The report of these barbarous atrocities roused the indignation of the Christian world. Oliver Cromwell, then Lord Protector of England, ordered a day of humiliation and fasting, sent Sir Samuel Morland as a special commissioner to the Duke of Savoy (Charles Emanuel II.), opened a subscription with £2000 from his private purse, and brought Protestant governments to a sense of their duty, and Roman sovereigns (even the proud bigot Louis XIV.) to a sense of shame. The dispatches were written by his foreign secretary, the great Puritan poet, in classical Latin and in the lofty spirit of his immortal sonnet, composed at that time,

> 'Avenge, O Lord, thy slaughtered saints, whose bones
> Lie scattered on the Alpine mountains cold.'

Cromwell died too soon to finish this noble work of intervention in behalf of humanity and religious liberty. Of the more than £38,000 then raised by public subscription in England alone for the poor Waldenses, only £22,000 reached them; the remaining £16,333 Charles II. unscrupulously wasted on his private pleasures under the pretext, worthy of a Stuart, that 'he was not bound by any of the engagements of an usurper and tyrant, nor responsible for his *debts.*' A fit illustration of the spirit of the Restoration.

The Confession was probably composed by JEAN LEGER, who was at that time the Moderator of the churches in Piedmont, and became afterwards their historian (d. in exile, '*un martyr sans sang,*' as pastor at Leyden, about 1684); although he does not say so, and inserts the Confession simply with the remark, '*la derniere confession de leur Foy qu'ils publierent après leurs massacres de l'an* 1655' (Vol. I. p. 112). It was brought to England by Morland, together with many valuable MSS., which he received from pastors Antoine and Leger, and deposited in the University library at Cambridge, in Aug., 1658.

The French text is found in LEGER, *Histoire des Églises Vaudoises* (Leyde, 1669, 2 vols. fol.), Vol. I. pp. 112–116 (where the Athanasian Creed is added in Vaudois and French, as a part of their creed taught to the children): in C. U. HAHN, *Geschichte der Ketzer im Mittelalter*, Vol. II. pp. 668–673; BERT (Pastor of La Tour), *Livre de Famille* (Geneva, 1830). A Latin text, together with an English version, is given in PEYRAN, *An Histor. Defence of the Waldenses or Vaudois, with Introd. and Appendixes by* TH. SIMS (Lond. 1826), pp. 445–456, from the MSS. of Peyran, the Moderator of the Wald. Churches in 1819. The English text alone is printed in Dr. E. HENDERSON's *The Vaudois* (London, 1845), pp. 251–259, and in WILLIAM HAZLITT's translation of Dr. ALEXIS MUSTON, *The Israel of the Alps: a History of the Persecutions of the Waldenses* (London, 1852), pp. 300–306. I have taken the French original from Leger, with the old spelling. The English translation of Hazlitt is very imperfect, and has been corrected.

The older Confessions of the Waldenses, published by Perrin, Leger (Vol. I.), and Hahn (Vol. II. p. 647 sqq.), are partly of doubtful origin, and have merely historical interest. See Vol. I. pp. 568 sqq.]

BRIÈVE CONFESSION DE FOY DES ÉGLISES REFORMÉES DE PIÉMONT.

Publiée avec leur Manifeste à l'occasion des effroyables massacres de l'an 1655.

Parce que nous avons apris que nos Adversaires ne se contentans pas de nous avoir persecutés, et dépoüillés de tous nos biens, pour nous rendre tant plus odieux, vont encore semans beaucoup de faus bruits, qui tendent non seulement à fletrir nos per-

A BRIEF CONFESSION OF FAITH OF THE REFORMED CHURCHES OF PIEDMONT.

Published with their Manifesto on the occasion of the frightful massacres of the year 1655.

Having understood that our adversaries, not contented to have most cruelly persecuted us, and robbed us of all our good, and estates, have yet an intention to render us odious to the world by spreading abroad many false reports, and so not only to de-

sonnes, mais sur tout à noircir par des in-
fames calomnies la sainte et salutaire Doctrine, dont nous faisons profession, nous sommes obligés, pour desabuser l'esprit de ceux
qui pourroient avoir esté preoccupés de ces
sinistres impressions, de faire une briéve Declaration de nôtre Foy, comme nous l'avons
fait par le passé et conformement à la Parole de Dieu, afin que tout le monde voye la
fausseté de ces Calomnies, et le tort qu'on a
de nous haïr, et de nous persecuter pour une
Doctrine si innocente.

fame our persons, but likewise to asperse
with most shameful calumnies that holy and
wholesome doctrine which we profess, we
feel obliged, for the better information of
those whose minds may perhaps be preoc-
cupied by sinister opinions, to make a short
declaration of our faith, such as we have
heretofore professed as conformable to the
Word of God; and so every one may see
the falsity of those their calumnies, and also
how unjustly we are hated and persecuted
for a doctrine so innocent.

Nous Croyons.

I. Qu'il y a un seul Dieu, qui
est une essence spirituelle, eternelle, infinie, tout sage, tout misericordieuse, et tout juste ; en un
mot tout parfaite ; et qu'il y a
trois Personnes en cette seule et
simple essence, le Pere, le Fils, et
le S. Esprit.

II. Que ce Dieu s'est manifesté
aux hommes par ses œuvres, tant
de la Creation, que de la Providence, et par sa Parole, revelée
au commencement par Oracles
en diverses sortes, puis redigée
par écrit és Livres qu'on appelle
l'Escriture Sainte.

III. Qu'il faut recevoir, comme
nous reçevons cette Sainte Ecriture pour Divine, et Canonique,
c'est-à-dire pour regle de nôtre
Foy, et de nôtre vie, et qu'elle est
contenüe pleinement és Livres de
l'Ancien et du Nouveau Testament : que dans l'Ancien Testa-

We believe,

I. That there is one only God,
who is a spiritual essence, eternal, infinite, all-wise, all merciful,
and all-just, in one word, all-per-
fect; and that there are three
persons in that one only and simple essence : the Father, Son, and
Holy Spirit.

II. That this God has manifested himself to men by his works of
Creation and Providence, as also
by his Word revealed unto us, first
by oracles in divers manners, and
afterwards by those written books
which are called the Holy Scripture.

III. That we ought to receive
this Holy Scripture (as we do) for
divine and canonical, that is to
say, for the constant rule of our
faith and life : as also that the
same is fully contained in the Old
and New Testament; and that by
the Old Testament we must un-

ment doivent estre compris seulement les Livres que Dieu a commis à l'Église Judaïque, et qu'elle
a toûjours approuvé ou reconnü
pour Divins, à sçavoir les cinq
Livres de Moise, Josuê, les Juges,
Ruth, le 1 et 2 de Samuel, le 1 et
2 des Rois, le 1 et 2 des Chroniques ou Paralipomenon, le 1
d'Esdras, Nehemie, Esther, Job, les
Pseaumes, les Proverbes de Salomon, l'Ecclesiaste, le Cantique des
Cantiques, les 4 grands Prophetes
et les 12 petits : et dans le Nouveau les 4 Evangiles, les Actes des
Apôtres, les Epîtres de S. Paul,
une aux Romains, deux aux Corinthiens, une aus Galates, une
aus Ephesiens, une aux Philippiens, une aux Colossiens [deux
aux Thessaloniciens, deux à Timothée, une à Tite, une à Philé-
mon],[1] l'Epître aux Hébreux, une
de S. Jacques, deux de S. Pierre,
trois de S. Jean, une de S. Jude,
et l'Apocalypse.

IV. Que nous reconnoissons la
Divinité de ces Livres Sacrés, non
seulement par le témoignage de
l'Église, mais principalement par
l'eternelle et indubitable verité de
la Doctrine qui y est contenüe,
par l'excellence, sublimité, et majesté du tout Divine qui y paroît,
et par l'opération du S. Esprit,

derstand only such books as God
did intrust the Jewish Church with,
and which that Church has always approved and acknowledged
to be from God : namely, the five
books of Moses, Joshua, the Judges,
Ruth, 1 and 2 of Samuel, 1 and 2
of the Kings, 1 and 2 of the
Chronicles, one of Ezra, Nehemiah,
Esther, Job, the Psalms, the Proverbs of Solomon, Ecclesiastes, the
Song of Songs, the four great and
the twelve minor Prophets : and
the New Testament containing the
four gospels, the Acts of the Apostles, the Epistles of St. Paul—1 to
the Romans, 2 to the Corinthians,
1 to the Galatians, 1 to the Ephesians, 1 to the Philippians, 1 to the
Colossians [2 to the Thessalonians,
2 to Timothy, 1 to Titus, 1 to
Philemon],[1] and the Epistle to the
Hebrews ; 1 of St. James, 2 of St.
Peter, 3 of St. John, 1 of St. Jude,
and the Revelation.

IV. We acknowledge the divinity of these sacred books, not only
from the testimony of the Church,
but more especially because of the
eternal and indubitable truth of
the doctrine therein contained, and
of that most divine excellency, sub-
limity, and majesty which appears
therein ; and because of the opera-

---

[1] [Omitted by Leger and Hahn, no doubt inadvertently.]

qui nous fait recevoir avec defe-
rance le témoignage que l'Église
nous en rend, qui ouvre nos yeux
pour découvrir les rayons de la
lumiere celeste qui éclattent en
l'Ecriture, et rectifie nôtre goût
pour discerner cette viande par
la saveur Divine qu'elle a.

V. Que Dieu a fait toutes
choses de rien, par sa volonté toute
libre, et par la puissance infinie
de sa Parole.

VI. Qu'il les conduit et gou-
verne toutes par sa Providence,
ordonnant et adressant tout se
qui arrive au monde, sans qu'il
soit pourtant ni autheur, ni cause
du mal que les créatures font, ou
que la coulpe luy en puisse, ou
doive en aucune façon estre im-
putée.

VII. Que les Anges ayant esté
creés purs et saints, il y en a qui
sont tombés dans une corruption
et perdition irreparable, mais que
les autres ont perseveré par un
effet de la bonté Divine, qui les a
soûtenus et confirmés.

VIII. Que l'homme qui avoit
esté creé pur et saint, à l'Image de
Dieu, s'est privé par sa faute de
cét estat bienheureux, donnant ses
assentimens aux discours captieus
du Diable.

tion of the Holy Spirit, who causes
us to receive with reverence the
testimony of the Church in that
point, who opens our eyes to discover the beams of that celestial
light which shines in the Scripture, and corrects our taste to discern the divine savor of that spiritual food.

V. That God made all things
of nothing by his own free will,
and by the infinite power of his
Word.

VI. That he governs and rules
all by his providence, ordaining
and appointing whatsoever happens in this world, without being
the author or cause of any evil
committed by the creatures, so
that the guilt thereof neither can
nor ought to be in any way imputed unto him.

VII. That the angels were all
in the beginning created pure and
holy, but that some of them have
fallen into irreparable corruption
and perdition; and that the rest have
persevered in their first purity by
an effect of divine goodness, which
has upheld and confirmed them.

VIII. That man, who was created
pure and holy, after the image of
God, deprived himself through his
own fault of that happy condition
by giving credit to the deceitful
words of the devil.

IX. *Que l'homme a perdu par sa transgression, la justice et la sainteté qu'il avoit receüe, encourant avec l'indignation de Dieu, la mort et la captivité, sous la puissance de celuy qui a l'empire de la mort, assavoir le Diable, à ce point que son franc arbitre est devenu serf et éclave du peché, tellement que de nature tous les hommes, et Juifs et gentils, sont Enfans d'Ire, tous morts en leurs fautes et pechés, et par conséquant incapables d'avoir aucun bon movement pour le salut, ni même former aucune bonne pensée sans la grace ; toutes leurs imaginations et pensées n'estant que mal en tout tems.*

X. *Que toute la posterité d'Adam, est coûpable en luy de sa desobeïssance, infectée de sa corruption, et tombée dans la même calamité jusques aus petits Enfans dés le ventre de leur Mere, d'où vient le nom de Peché orginel.*

XI. *Que Dieu retire de cette corruption et condamnation, les personnes qu'il a éleües par sa misericorde en son Fils Jesus Christ, y laissant les autres par un droit irreprochable de la liberté et justice.*

IX. That man by his transgression lost that righteousness and holiness which he had received, and thus incurring the wrath of God, became subject to death and bondage, under the dominion of him who has the power of death, that is, the devil; insomuch that our free will has become a servant and a slave to sin: and thus all men, both Jews and Gentiles, are by nature children of wrath, being all dead in their trespasses and sins, and consequently incapable of the least good motion to any thing which concerns their salvation: yea, incapable of one good thought without God's grace, all their imaginations being wholly evil, and that continually.

X. That all the posterity of Adam is guilty in him of his disobedience, infected by his corruption, and fallen into the same calamity with him, even the very infants from their mothers' womb, whence is derived the name of original sin.

XI. That God saves from this corruption and condemnation those whom he has chosen [from the foundation of the world, not for any foreseen disposition, faith, or holiness in them, but]¹ of his

---

¹ [The words in brackets are given by Hazlitt and Henderson (perhaps from Morland), but are not found in the French of Leger and Hahn.]

mercy in **Jesus Christ** his Son ;
passing by all **the** rest, according
to the irreprehensible **reason of his**
freedom and justice.

XII. *Que Jesus Christ ayant
esté ordonné de Dieu en son decret
eternel, pour estre le seul Saveur,
et l'unique Chef de son Corps, qui
est l'Église, il l'a rachetée par son
propre Sang, dans l'accomplissement des tems, et luy offre et
communique tous ses benefices par
l'Evangile.*

XIII. *Qu'il y a deux natures
en Jesus Christ, la Divine et
l'humaine vrayement en une
même personne, sans confusion,
sans division, sans separation,
sans changement ; châque nature
gardant ses proprietés distinctes,
et que Jesus Christ est vray
Dieu et vray homme tout ensemble.*

XIV. *Que Dieu a tant aimé le
monde, qu'il a donné son Fils
pour nous sauver par son obeïs-
sance tres-parfaite, nommement
par celle qu'il a montré en souf-
frant la mort maudite de la
Croix, et par les victoires qu'il a
remporté sur le Diable, le péché,
et la mort.*

XV. *Que Jesus Christ ayant
fait l'entiere expiation de nos
pechés par son sacrifice tres-par-*

XII. That Jesus Christ having
been ordained by the eternal decree of God to be the only Saviour and only head of his body
which is the Church, he redeemed
it with his own blood in the fullness of time, and communicates
unto the same all his benefits by
means of the gospel.

XIII. That there are two natures
in Jesus Christ, viz., divine and human, truly united in one and the
same person, without confusion,
division, separation, or alteration ;
each nature keeping its own distinct proprieties ; and that Jesus
Christ is both true God and true
man.

XIV. That God so loved the
world, that is to say, those whom
he has chosen out of the world,
that he gave his own Son to save
us by his most perfect obedience
(especially that obedience which
he manifested in suffering the
cursed death of the cross), and also
by his victory over the devil, sin,
and death.

XV. That Jesus Christ having
made a full expiation for our sins
by his most perfect sacrifice once

fait, une fois offert en la Croix, il ne peut, ni ne doit estre reiteré sous quelque pretexte que ce soit.

XVI. *Que le Seigneur Jesus nous ayant pleinement reconcilié à Dieu par le Sang de sa Croix, c'est par son seul merite, et non par nos œuvres, que nous sommes absous et justifiés devant luy.*

XVII. *Que nous avons union avec Jesus Christ, et communion à ses benefices par la Foy, qui s'appuye sur les promesses de vie, qui nous sont faites en son Evangile.*

XVIII. *Que cette Foy vient de l'operation gracieuse et efficace du S. Esprit, qui éclaire nos ames, et les porte à s'appuyer sur la misericorde de Dieu, pour s'appliquer le merite de Jesus Christ.*

XIX. *Que Jesus Christ est nôtre vray et unique Mediateur : non seulement de Redemption, mais aussi d'Intercession, et que par ses merites et sa mediation, nous avons accés au Pere, pour l'invoquer avec la sainte confiance d'estre exaucés, sans qu'il soit besoin d'avoir recours à aucun autre intercesseur que luy.*

XX. *Que comme Dieu nous promet la regeneration en Jesus*

offered on the cross, it neither can nor ought to be repeated upon any pretext whatsoever, as they pretend to do in the mass.

XVI. That the Lord Jesus having fully reconciled us unto God, through the blood of his cross, it is by virtue of his merits only, and not of our works, that we are absolved and justified in his sight.

XVII. That we are united to Jesus Christ and made partakers of his benefits by faith, which rests upon those promises of life which are made to us in his gospel.

XVIII. That this faith is the gracious and efficacious work of the Holy Spirit, who enlightens our souls, and persuades them to lean and rest upon the mercy of God, and so to apply the merits of Jesus Christ.

XIX. That Jesus Christ is our true and only Mediator, not only redeeming us, but also interceding for us, and that by virtue of his merits and intercession we have access unto the Father, to make our supplications unto him, with a holy confidence that he will grant our requests, it being needless to have recourse to any other intercessor besides himself.

XX. That as God has promised us regeneration in Jesus Christ, so

Christ, ceus qui sont unis à luy par une vive Foy, doivent s'adonner, et s'adonnent en effét, à bonnes œuvres.

XXI. *Que les bonnes œuvres sont si necessaires aus fideles, qu'ils ne peuvent parvenir au Royaume des Cieux sans les faire, estant vray que Dieu les a preparées afin que nous y cheminoins, qu'ainsi nous devons fuir les vices, et nous adonner aux vertus Chrêtiennes, employant les jûnes et tous autres moyens, qui peuvent nous servir à une chose si sainte.*

XXII. *Que bien que nos œuvres ne puissent pas meriter, nôtre Seigneur ne laissera pas de les recompenser de la Vie Eternelle, par une continuation misericordieuse de sa grace, et en vertu de la constance immuable des promesses qu'il nous en fait.*

XXIII. *Que ceux qui possedent la Vie Eternelle en suite de leur Foy, et de leurs bonnes œuvres, doivent estre confiderés comme Saints, et glorifiés, loüés pour leurs vertus, imités en toutes les belles actions de leur vie, mais non adorés, ni invoqués, puis qu'on ne doit prier qu'un seul Dieu par Jesus Christ.*

XXIV. *Que Dieu s'est recüeilli*

those who are united to him by a living faith ought to apply, and do really apply themselves, unto good works.

XXI. That good works are so necessary to the faithful that they can not attain the kingdom of heaven without the same, seeing that God hath prepared them that we should walk therein; and therefore we ought to flee from vice, and apply ourselves to Christian virtues, making use of fasting, and all other means which may conduce to so holy a thing.

XXII. That, although our good works can not merit any thing, yet the Lord will reward or recompense them with eternal life, through the merciful continuation of his grace, and by virtue of the unchangeable constancy of his promises made unto us.

XXIII. That those who are already in the possession of eternal life in consequence of their faith and good works ought to be considered as saints and glorified persons, and to be praised for their virtue and imitated in all good actions of their life, but neither worshiped nor invoked, for God only is to be prayed unto, and that through Jesus Christ.

XXIV. That God has chosen

une Église dans le monde, pour le salut des hommes, quelle n'a qu'un seul Chef, et fondament, qui est Jesus Christ.

XXV. Que cette Église est la compagnie des fideles, qui ayans esté éleus de Dieu, devant la fondation du monde, et appellés par une sainte vocation, s'unissent pour suivre la Parole de Dieu, croyans ce qu'il nous y enseigne, et vivans en sa crainte.

XXVI. Que cette Église ne peut defaillir, ou estre aneantie, mais qu'elle doit estre perpetuelle.

XXVII. Que tous s'y doivent ranger, et se tenir dans sa communion.

XXVIII. Que Dieu ne nous y instruit pas seulement par sa Parole, mais que de plus il a institué des Sacremens pour les joindre à cette Parole, comme des moyens pour nous unir à Jesus Christ, et pour communiquer à ses benefices, et qu'il n'y en a que deux communs à tous les membres de

one Church in the world for the salvation of men, and that this Church has one only head and foundation, which is Jesus Christ.

XXV. That this Church is the company of the faithful, who, having been elected by God before the foundation of the world, and called with a holy calling, unite themselves to follow the Word of God, believing whatsoever he teaches them therein, and living in his fear.

XXVI. That this Church can not fail, nor be annihilated, but must endure forever [and that all the elect are upheld and preserved by the power of God in such sort that they all persevere in the faith unto the end, and remain united in the holy Church, as so many living members thereof].[1]

XXVII. That all men ought to join with that Church, and to continue in the communion thereof.

XXVIII. That God does not only instruct us by his Word, but has also ordained certain sacraments to be joined with it, as means to unite us to Jesus Christ, and to make us partakers of his benefits; and that there are only two of them belonging in common to all the members of the

---

[1] The words in brackets are not represented in the French text of Leger, and are taken from Henderson and Hazlitt.

l'Église sous le Nouveau Testa-
ment, assavoir le Baptéme, et la
Sainte Cene.

XXIX. *Qu'il a institué celuy*
du Baptéme pour un témoignage
de nôtre adoption, et que nous y
sommes lavés de nos pechés au
Sang de Jesus Christ, et renou-
vellés en sainteté de vie.

XXX. *Qu'il a institué celuy de*
la Sainte Cene ou Eucharistie,
pour la nourriture de nôtre ame,
afin que par une vraye, et vive
Foy, par la vertu incomprehensi-
ble du S. Esprit, mangeans ef-
fectivement sa Chair, et beuvans
son Sang, et nous unissans tres-
étroitement et inseparablement à
Christ, en luy, et par luy, nous
ayons la vie spirituelle et eter-
nelle.

Et afin que tout le monde voye
clairement nôtre croyance sur ce
point, nous adjoûtons icy les mé-
mes termes qui sont couchés en
nôtre Priere avant la Commu-
nion, dans nôtre liturgie, ou ma-
niere de celebrer la Sainte Cene,
et dans nôtre Catechisme public,
qui sont pieces qu'on peut voir à
la fin de nos Pseaumes : voicy les
termes de nôtre Priere :

'Et comme nôtre Seigneur non
seulement a une fois offert son
Corps et son Sang pour la remission de nos pechés, mais aussi nous

Church under the New Testament
—to wit, Baptism and the Lord's
Supper.

XXIX. That Christ has instituted
the sacrament of Baptism to be a
testimony of our adoption, and that
therein we are cleansed from our
sins by the blood of Jesus Christ,
and renewed in holiness of life.

XXX. That he has instituted
the Holy Supper, or Eucharist, for
the nourishment of our souls, to
the end that eating effectually the
flesh of Christ, and drinking effectually his blood, by a true and
living faith, and by the incomprehensible virtue of the Holy Spirit,
and so uniting ourselves most
closely and inseparably to Christ,
we come to enjoy in him and by
him the spiritual and eternal life.

Now to the end that every one
may clearly see what our belief is
as to this point, we here insert
the very expressions of that prayer
which we make use of before the
Communion, as they are written in
our Liturgy or form of celebrating
the Holy Supper, and likewise in
our public Catechism, which are to
be seen at the end of our Psalms ;
these are the words of the prayer:

'*Seeing our Lord has not only*
once offered his body and blood
for the remission of our sins, but
is willing also to communicate the

les veut communiquer pour nourriture en vie eternelle, fais nous cette grace que de vraye sinceritè de cœur, et d'un zele ardant nous recevions de luy un si grand benefice, c'est qu'en certaine Foy nous jouïssions de son Corps et de son Sang, voire de luy entierement,' etc.

Les termes de nôtre Liturgie sont : 'Premierement donc, croyons à ces promesses, que Jesus Christ qui est la veritè même a prononcées de sa bouche, assavoir qu'il nous veut vrayement faire participans de son Corps et de son Sang, afin que nous le possedions entierement en telle sorte qu'il vive en nous, et nous en luy.'

Ceus de nôtre Catechisme public sont de même en la Section 53.

XXXI. *Qu'il est necessaire que l'Église aye des Pasteurs, jugés biens instruits, et de bonne vie, par ceux qui en ont le droit, tant pour prêcher la Parole de Dieu, que pour administrer les Sacremens, et veiller sur le troupeau de Jesus Christ, suivant les regles d'une bonne et sainte Discipline, conjointement avec les Anciens et Diacres, selon la pratique de l'Église ancienne.*

XXXII. *Que Dieu a établi les Rois et les Magistrats, pour la conduite des peuples, et que les*

same unto us as the food of eternal life, we humbly beseech thee to grant us this grace that in true sincerity of heart and with an ardent zeal we may receive from him so great a benefit ; that is, that we may be made partakers of his body and blood, or rather of his whole self, by a sure and certain faith.'

The words of the Liturgy are these: '*Let us then believe first of all the promises which Christ (who is the infallible truth) has pronounced with his own mouth, viz., that he will make us truly partakers of his body and blood, that so we may possess him entirely, in such a manner that he may live in us and we in him.*'

The words of our Catechism are the same, *Nella Dominica* 53.

XXXI. That it is necessary the Church should have pastors known by those who are employed for that purpose to be well instructed and of a good life, as well to preach the Word of God as to administer the sacraments, and wait upon the flock of Christ (according to the rules of a good and holy discipline), together with elders and deacons, after the manner of the primitive Church.

XXXII. That God hath established kings and magistrates to govern the people, and that the

peuples leur doivent estre sujets et obeïssans en vertu de cét ordre, non seulement pour l'ire, mais pour la conscience, *en toutes les choses qui sont conformes à la Parole de Dieu, qui est le Roy des Rois, et Seigneur des Seigneurs.*

XXXIII. *Enfin, qu'il faut recevoir le Symbole des Apôtres, l'Oraison Dominicale, et le Decalogue, comme pieces fondamentales de nôtre creance, et de nos devotions.*

Et pour plus ample declaration de nôtre creance, nous reïterons icy la protestation que nous fimes imprimer l'an 1603 assavoir que nous consentons à la saine Doctrine, avec toutes les Églises Reformées de France, d'Angleterre, du Païs-Bas, d'Allemagne, de Suisse, de Boheme, de Pologne, d'Hongrie, et autres, ainsi qu'elle est exprimée en leur Confession d'Ausbourg, selon la declaration qu'en a donné l'Autheur. Et promettons d'y perseverer Dieu aidant, inviolablement en la vie et en la mort, estans prets de signer cette verité eternelle de Dieu de nôtre propre sang, comme l'ont fait nos predecesseurs depuis le tems des Apôtres, particulierement en ces derniers siecles.

people ought to be subject and obedient unto them, by virtue of that ordination, *not only for fear, but also for conscience' sake,* in all things that are conformable to the Word of God, who is the King of kings and the Lord of lords.

XXXIII. Finally, that we ought to receive the symbol of the Apostles, the Lord's Prayer, and the Decalogue as fundamentals of our faith and our devotion.

And for a more ample declaration of our faith we do here reiterate the same protestation which we caused to be printed in 1603, that is to say, that we do agree in sound doctrine with all the Reformed Churches of France, Great Britain, the Low Countries, Germany, Switzerland, Bohemia, Poland, Hungary, and others, as it is set forth by them in their confessions; as also in the Confession of Augsburg, as it was explained by the author,[1] promising to persevere constantly therein with the help of God, both in life and death, and being ready to subscribe to that eternal truth of God with our own blood, even as our ancestors have done from the days of the Apostles, and especially in these latter ages.

---

[1] Viz., the editio variata of 1540, which Calvin subscribed at Strasburg.

Et pourtant nous prions bien humblement toutes les Églises Evangeliques et Protestantes, de nous tenir, nonobstant nôtre pauvreté et petitesse, pour vrais membres du corps mystique de Jesus Christ, soufrans pour son Saint Nom ; et de nous continuer l'assistance de leurs prieres envers Dieu, et tous autres bons offices de leurs charités, comme nous les avons déja abondamment experimentés, dont nous les remerçions avec toute l'humilité, qui nous est possible, et suplions de tout nôtre cœur le Seigneur qu'il en soit luy même le remunerateur, versant sur elles les plus precieuses benedictions de sa grace et de sa gloire, et en cette vie, et en celle qui est à venir. Amen.

Therefore we humbly **entreat** all the Evangelical and Protestant Churches, notwithstanding our poverty and lowness, to look upon us as true members of the mystical body of Christ, suffering for his name's sake, and to continue unto us the help of their prayers to God, and all other effects of their charity, as we have heretofore abundantly experienced, for which we return them our most humble thanks, entreating the Lord with all our heart to be their rewarder, and to pour upon them the most precious blessings of grace and glory, both in this life and in that which is to come. Amen.

ADDITIONS À LA SUS-DITE CONFESSION.

Briéve justification touchant les points, ou articles de Foy, que nous imputent les Docteurs de Rome, en commun avec toutes les Églises Reformées. Nous accusans de croire,

1. *Que Dieu soit autheur du Peché.*
2. *Que Dieu n'est pas tout Puissant.*
4.[2] *Que Jesus Christ s'est desesperé en la Croix.*
5. *Que dans les œuvres du salut, où l'home est mû par l'Esprit de Dieu, il n'y coopere non plus qu'une piece de bois, ou une pierre.*
6. *Qu'en vertu de la Predestination, il n'importe que l'on face bien ou mal.*

ADDITIONS TO THIS CONFESSION.[1]

Brief justification concerning the points or articles of faith which the doctors of Rome impute to us and to all the Reformed Churches. They accuse us of believing the following articles :

1. That God is the author of sin ;
2. That God is not omnipotent ;
3. That Jesus Christ fell into despair upon the cross ;
4. That man, in the work of salvation, where he is moved by the Spirit of God, is no more active than a log or a stone ;
5. That, according to our notion on the subject of predestination, it is of no consequence whether we do good or evil ;

---

[1] Omitted by Henderson and Hazlitt.   [2] The error in numbering (4 for 3, etc.) is Leger's.

7. *Que les bonnes œuvres ne sont pas necessaires au salut.*

8. *Que nous rejettons absolument la Confession des pechés, et la Penitence.*

9. *Qu'il faut rejetter les Jûnes, et autres mortifications de la chair, pour vivre dans la dissolution.*

10. *Que châcun peut expliquer l'Ecriture Sainte comme il luy plait, et selon les inspirations de son esprit particulier.*

11. *Que l'Église peut de tout defaillir, et estre anneantie.*

12. *Que le Baptéme n'est d'aucune necessité.*

13. *Que dans le Sacrement de l'Eucharistie, nous n'avons aucune reelle communion avec Jesus Christ, mais seulement en figure.*

14. *Qu'on n'est pas obligé d'obeïr aux Magistrats, Rois, Princes, etc.*

15. *Parce que nous n'invoquons pas la Sainte Vierge, et les hommes déja glorifiés, on nous accuse de les mépriser, au lieu que nous les publions bienheureus, dignes, et de loüange, et d'imitation, et tenons sur tout la Sainte Vierge* Bienheureuse entre toutes les Femmes.

Or tous ces Chefs qui nous sont ainsi malicieusement imputés, bien loin de les croire ou enseigner parmi nous, que nous les tenons pour heretiques et damnables, et denonçons de tout nôtre cœur anatheme contre quiconque les voudroit soûtenir.

6. That good works are not necessary to salvation;

7. That we entirely reject confession of sins and repentance;

8. That fasting and other mortifications of the flesh must be rejected, in order to lead a dissolute life;

9. That any one may explain the Holy Scripture as he pleases, and according to the fanciful suggestions of his own mind;

10. That the Church can entirely fail and be destroyed;

11. That baptism is not necessary;

12. That in the sacrament of the eucharist we have no communion with Christ in fact, but in a figure only;

13. That obedience is not due to magistrates, kings, princes, etc.;

14. That we despise, because we do not invoke, the most holy Virgin and glorified saints; while in fact we pronounce them blessed and worthy both of praise and imitation, and hold above all the holy Virgin Mary to be 'blessed amongst women.'

All these articles maliciously imputed to us, far from believing or teaching them, we hold to be heretical and damnable, and we denounce from all our heart every one who would maintain them.

THE CONFESSION OF THE CUMBERLAND PRESBYTERIAN CHURCH. A.D. 1829 (1813).

[The Confession of the CUMBERLAND PRESBYTERIAN CHURCH IN THE UNITED STATES (which was organized in 1810, and embraces a large and active membership in the Western and Southern States), is a semi-Arminian revision of the Westminster Confession of Faith. It was adopted in 1813, and finally revised in 1829. It retains the thirty-three chapters in the same order, with the American alterations of Chaps. XXIII. and XXXI., and a few immaterial omissions and additions. The only serious change is in the chapter on Predestination, while even the chapter on Perseverance is essentially retained. We present both texts in parallel columns.

See *The Confession of Faith of the Cumberland Presbyterian Church, revised and adopted by the General Assembly, at Princeton, Ky., May,* 1829, published by its Board of Publication in Nashville, Tenn. Comp. Vol. I. pp. 813 sqq.]

CUMBERLAND CONFESSION.

CHAPTER III.—*The Decrees of God.*

I. God did, by the most wise and holy counsel of his own will, determine to act or bring to pass what should be for his own glory.[1]

II. God has not decreed any thing respecting his creature man, contrary to his revealed will or written word,[2] which declares his sovereignty over all his creatures,[3] the ample provision he has made for their salvation,[4] his determination to punish the finally impen-

[1] Eph. i. 11.
[2] Rev. xx. 12; Rom. ii. 15; Acts xx. 27; Psa. ii. 7.
[3] Dan. iv. 34, 35; Psa. cxxxv. 6; Matt. x. 29-31.
[4] Heb. ii. 9; Matt. xxii. 4; Isa. xlv. 22; 1 Tim. ii. 4, 5, 6; Rev. xxii. 17; Isa. lv. 1; John iii. 16; Rom. viii. 25; 1 John ii. 24, 10.

WESTMINSTER CONFESSION.

CHAPTER III.—*Of God's Eternal Decree* [Am. ed. *Decrees*].

I. God from all eternity did, by the most wise and holy counsel of his own will, freely and unchangeably ordain whatsoever comes to pass;[1] yet so as thereby neither is God the author of sin,[2] nor is violence offered to the will of the creatures, nor is the liberty or contingency of second causes taken away, but rather established.[3]

II. Although God knows whatsoever may or can come to pass upon all supposed conditions;[4] yet hath he not decreed any thing because he foresaw it as future, or as that which would come to pass upon such conditions.[5]

[1] Eph. i. 11; Rom. xi. 33; Heb. vi. 17; Rom. ix. 15, 18.
[2] James i. 13, 17; 1 John i. 5; [Am. ed. Eccl. vii. 29].
[3] Acts ii. 23; Matt. xvii. 12; Acts iv. 27, 28; John xix. 11; Prov. xvi. 33.
[4] Acts xv. 18; 1 Sam. xxiii. 11, 12; Matt. xi. 21, 23.
[5] Rom. ix. 11, 13, 16, 18.

itent with everlasting destruction,[1]
and to save the true believer with
an everlasting salvation.

NOTE.—The remaining six sections of the Westminster Confession, which contain the
knotty points of Calvinism, are entirely omitted. Instead of them an official explanation is
attached, as follows:

'We think it better, under the head of Decrees, to write what we know to be incontro-
vertible from the plain Word of God, than to darken counsel by words without knowledge.
We have elsewhere acknowledged the doctrine of predestination to be a high mystery. We
are free to acknowledge that in our judgment it is easier to fix the limits which man should
not transcend, on either hand, than to give an intelligent elucidation of the subject. We believe that both Calvinists and Arminians have egregiously erred on this point: the former
by driving rational, accountable man into the asylum of fate; the latter by putting too much
stress on man's *works*, and leaving too much out of view the grace that bringeth salvation,
and thereby cherish[ing] those legal principles that are in every human heart. We think
the *intermediate plan* on this subject is nearest the WHOLE truth; for surely, on the one
hand, it must be acknowledged, the love of God, the merits of Christ, and the operation of
the Holy Spirit are the moving, meritorious, and active causes of man's salvation; that God
is a sovereign, having a right to work when, where, how, and on whom he pleases; that salvation, in its device, in its plan, and in its application, is of the Lord; and that without the
unmerited agency and operation of the Spirit of God not one of Adam's race would or could
ever come to the knowledge of the truth—for God is the author as well as the finisher of our
faith. Therefore God, as a sovereign, may, if he pleases, elect a nation, as the Jews, to preserve his worship free from idolatry; many nations for a time, as Christendom, in which to
spread his gospel; individuals, as Cyrus and others, to answer a particular purpose; Paul
and others for apostles; Luther and Calvin to promote the Reformation. But as it respects
the salvation of the soul, God as a sovereign can only elect or choose fallen man in Christ,
who is the end of the law for righteousness to every one that believeth. But it appears to us
incontestible, from God's Word, that God has reprobated *none* from eternity. That all mankind become legally reprobated by transgression is undeniable, and continue so until they
embrace Christ. "Examine yourselves," etc. "Know ye not your own selves, how that
Jesus Christ is in you, except ye be reprobates?" (2 Cor. xiii. 5). Now this can not mean
eternal reprobates, or all who have not Christ in them would be such, the absurdity of which
will at once appear to every common capacity. Reprobation is not what some have supposed
it to be, viz., a sovereign determination of God to create millions of rational beings, and for
his own glory damn them eternally in hell, without regard to moral rectitude or sin in the
creature. This would tarnish the divine glory, and render the greatest, best, and most lovely
of all Beings most odious in the view of all intelligences. When man sinned he was legally
reprobated, but not damned: God offered, and does offer, the law-condemned sinner mercy
in the gospel, he having from the foundation of the world so far chosen mankind in Christ as
to justify that saying in 1 Tim. iv. 10, "Who is the Saviour of all men, especially of them
that believe." This is a gracious act of God's sovereign electing love, as extensive as the
legal condemnation, or reprobation, in which all mankind are by nature. But, in a particular
and saving sense, none can be properly called God's elect till they be justified and united to
Christ, the end of the law for righteousness (none are justified from eternity), as appears evident from the following passages of God's Word: "Who shall lay any thing to the charge of
God's elect? Who is he that condemneth?" (Rom. viii. 33, 34). Now it is certain [that] the
unbeliever is chargeable and condemned. Again, "If it were possible, they shall deceive the
very elect" (Matt. xxiv. 24). It is evident that a man must be enlightened in the knowledge

---

[1] 1 Thess. v. 9; v. 3; Mark xvi. 16.

of God and his Son Jesus, which is eternal life, before he can have spiritual wisdom to discern and detect the deceiver. If, then, by perverting the gracious provision of the gospel in refusing to submit to the righteousness of God, the sinner finally grieves the Spirit of God, to depart from him, he becomes doubly and eternally reprobated; or like the chemist's mineral, which will not coin into pure metal, or the potter's clay, which marred upon the wheel. But if the creature fall into this deplorable situation, he was not *bound* by any revealed or *secret* decree of God to do so: it is his own fault. For God declares in his Word that Christ died for the *whole* world; that he offers pardon to all; that the Spirit operates on *all;* confirming by an oath that he has no pleasure in the death of sinners. Every invitation of the gospel either promises or implies aid by the Divine Spirit. The plan of the Bible is grace and duty. God calls (grace); sinners hearken diligently (duty); God reproves (grace); sinners turn (duty); God pours out his Spirit (grace); sinners resist not the light, but improve it (duty); God makes known his Word, or reveals the plan of salvation (grace); God invites (grace); wicked men, forsake your ways (duty), your thoughts (duty), and turn to the Lord (duty), and God will have mercy on you (grace), and God will abundantly pardon (grace).'

In Chap. IX., *Of Free Will,* the first three and the fifth sections are retained with an addition at the close of Sect. 3, 'without Divine aid.' In the fourth section the last words, 'but [the sinner] doth also will that which is evil,' are omitted.

In Chap. X., *Of Effectual Calling,* the fourth section is omitted, and the third section concerning infant salvation is liberalized and made to embrace all infants as follows:

CUMBERLAND CONFESSION, CHAP. X.	WESTMINSTER CONFESSION, CHAP. X.
III. *All* infants dying in infancy are regenerated and saved by Christ through the Spirit,[1] who worketh when, and where, and how he pleaseth;[2] so also are others *who have never had the exercise of reason,* and who are incapable of being outwardly called by the ministry of the Word.	III. *Elect* infants, dying in infancy, are regenerated and saved by Christ through the Spirit,[1] who worketh when, and where, and how he pleaseth.[2] So also are all other *elect* persons, who are incapable of being outwardly called by the ministry of the Word.[3]

In Chap. XI., *Of Justification,* Sect. 1, 'Those whom God *effectually* calleth,' is changed into 'Those whom God calleth (*and who obey the call*).' In Sect. 4, 'God *did, from all eternity, decree* to justify all *the elect,*' is changed into 'God, before the foundation of the world, *determined* to justify all *true believers.*'

---

[1] Luke xviii. 15, 16; Acts ii. 38, 39.
[2] John iii. 8.

[1] Luke xviii. 15, 16; Acts ii. 38, 39; John iii. 3, 5; 1 John v. 12; Rom. viii. 9.
[2] John iii. 8.
[3] 1 John v. 12; Acts iv. 12.

CUMBERLAND CONFESSION.

CHAPTER XVII.—*The Perseverance of the Saints.*

I. They whom God hath justified and sanctified he will also glorify;[1] consequently, the truly regenerated soul will never totally nor finally fall away from the state of grace, but shall certainly persevere therein to the end, and be eternally saved.[2]

II. This perseverance depends on the unchangeable love and power of God;[3] the merits, advocacy,[4] and intercession of Jesus Christ;[5] the abiding of the Spirit and seed of God within them;[6] and the nature of the covenant of grace;[7] from all which ariseth also the certainty and infallibility thereof.[8]

III. Although there are examples in the Old Testament of good men having egregiously sinned, and some of them continuing for a

WESTMINSTER CONFESSION.

CHAPTER XVII.—*Of the Perseverance of the Saints.*

I. They whom God hath accepted in his Beloved, effectually called and sanctified by his Spirit, can neither totally nor finally fall away from the state of grace; but shall certainly persevere therein to the end, and be eternally saved.[1]

II. This perseverance of the saints depends not upon their own free-will, but upon the immutability of the decree of election, flowing from the free and unchangeable love of God the Father;[2] upon the efficacy of the merit and intercession of Jesus Christ;[3] the abiding of the Spirit and of the seed of God within them;[4] and the nature of the covenant of grace:[5] from all which ariseth also the certainty and infallibility thereof.[6]

III. Nevertheless they may, through the temptations of Satan and of the world, the prevalency of corruption remaining in them,

---

[1] Rom. viii. 38, 39.
[2] John iii. 16; x. 28, 29; Phil. i. 6.
[3] 2 Tim. ii. 19; Jer. xxxi. 3; 1 Pet. i. 5.
[4] 1 John ii. 1.
[5] Heb. vii. 25; x. 10, 14.
[6] John xiv. 16, 17; 1 John iii. 9.
[7] Jer. xxxii. 40; Heb. viii. 10; x. 16, 17.
[8] Job xvii. 9; John xvii. 21, 22; 1 John ii. 19; 2 Thess. iii. 3; Zeph. iii. 17; Mal. iii. 6; Numb. xxii. 19; Rom. v. 9; 2 Cor. i. 21, 22; John iv. 14; Psa. xii. 5; John xvii. 12; 1 Cor. i. 8, 9.

[1] Phil. i. 6; 2 Pet. i. 10; John x. 28, 29; 1 John iii. 9; 1 Pet. i. 5, 9; [Am. ed. Job xvii. 9].
[2] 2 Tim. ii. 18, 19; Jer. xxxi. 3.
[3] Heb. x. 10, 14; xiii. 20, 21; ix. 12–15; Rom. viii. 33–39; John xvii. 11, 24; Luke xxii. 32; Heb. vii. 25.
[4] John xiv. 16, 17; 1 John ii. 27; iii. 9.
[5] Jer. xxxii. 40; [Am. ed. Heb. viii. 10–12].
[6] John x. 28; 2 Thess. iii. 3; 1 John ii. 19; [Am. ed. 1 Thess. v. 23, 24].

time therein;[1] yet now, since life and immortality are brought clearer to light by the gospel,[2] and especially since the effusion of the Holy Ghost on the day of Pentecost,[3] we may not expect the true Christian to fall into such gross sins.[4] Nevertheless they may, through the temptations of Satan, the world, and the flesh, the neglect of the means of grace, fall into sin, and incur God's displeasure, and grieve his Holy Spirit;[5] come to be deprived of some measure of their graces and comforts, and have their consciences wounded; but the real Christian can never rest satisfied therein.*

and the neglect of the means of their preservation, fall into grievous sins;[1] and for a time continue therein:[2] whereby they incur God's displeasure,[3] and grieve his Holy Spirit;[4] come to be deprived of some measure of their graces and comforts;[5] have their hearts hardened,[6] and their consciences wounded;[7] hurt and scandalize others,[8] and bring temporal judgments upon themselves.[9]

---

[1] 2 Sam. xii. 9, 13, 14.
[2] 2 Tim. i. 10.
[3] Luke xxiv. 49; Acts ii. 4.
[4] Acts xvii 30, 31; Matt. xi. 11.
[5] Eph. iv. 30; Rev. ii. 4.

[1] Matt. xxvi. 70, 72, 74.
[2] Psa. li. title and verse 14; [Am. ed. 2 Sam. xii. 9, 13].
[3] Isa. lxiv. 5, 7, 9; 2 Sam. xi. 27.
[4] Eph. iv. 30.
[5] Psa. li. 8, 10, 12; Rev. ii. 4; Cant. v. 2, 3, 4, 6.
[6] Isa. xxxvi. 17; Mark vi. 52; xvi. 14; [Am. ed. Psa. xcv. 8].
[7] Psa. xxxii. 3, 4; li. 8.
[8] 2 Sam. xii. 14.
[9] Psa. lxxxix. 31, 32; 1 Cor. xi. 32.

* NOTE.—To this section the following note is attached in the official edition:

'This doctrine, although it is certainly supported by incontestable proof from the Word of God, as well as by the reason and nature of the union between Christ and his people, yet, like all other truths, has been and may be perverted. The idea of eternal justification and consequent perseverance is unscriptural: the way perseverance is insisted on by some preachers in connection with the preceding parts of their sermons is certainly dangerous. Example: First preach a superficial experience, then make a great many more allowances for weakness and wickedness, stumbling, straying, etc., than God's Word admits, then press perseverance, and you have the formalist or hypocrite confirmed.

'On the other hand, press the doctrines of final apostasy, if the creature does not so and so, making the perseverance of the creature depend chiefly upon his *doings:* you raise in the mind of the *unregenerate* professor the fear of hell, as a high excitement to duty; confirm him in his legality; prepare his mind, indirectly at least, to give glory to himself for his perseverance; settle him down in a self-confident and deplorable situation. What God's Word hath joined together, let not his ministers put asunder; but first let them give a clear, definite description of the new birth, and then let them press the doctrine of heart and practical holiness as the sure consequence ("For by their fruit ye shall know them"), and daily evidences (not the cause) of that gracious state which will insure their final perseverance.

'Then this true and comfortable doctrine will not be perverted, neither will it have a tendency to licentiousness in him "whom the love of Christ constraineth," or the real Christian: no, he serves and desires to serve God with more zeal, and from pure evangelical principles, still laying the foundation in his own mind, and cherishing the principle of ascribing *all* the glory to God for his conversion, his perseverance, and his final and complete redemption.'

THE AUBURN DECLARATION. A.D. 1837.

[The Auburn Declaration, so called from the place of its adoption, belongs to the history of American Presbyterianism, and although it never aspired to the dignity of an authoritative Confession of Faith, it may claim a place here for its intrinsic value and importance before and after the disruption. It originated during the conflict which preceded the division of the Presbyterian Church into Old and New School, A.D. 1837, and was prepared by the Rev. Baxter Dickinson, D.D. (d. 1876). It had been charged, on one side, that sixteen errors, involving considerable departures from true Calvinism and the Westminster standards, had become current in that Church. (They are printed in the *Presbyterian Quarterly and Princeton Review* for 1876, pp. 7, 8.) In answer to this charge, the New School party were led to embody their belief on these points in a corresponding series of 'True Doctrines,' which were incorporated in their Protest, as presented to the General Assembly of 1837. These doctrinal statements were subsequently considered and adopted by an important representative convention at Auburn, New York, Aug., 1837, as expressing their matured views, and those of the churches and ministry represented by them, on the several topics involved. The Declaration thus adopted became, not indeed a creed, but an authoritative explanation of the interpretation given to the Westminster Symbols by the leading minds in the New School Church, as organized in 1838. It was in 1868 indorsed by the General Assembly (O. S.) as containing 'all the fundamentals of the Calvinistic Creed,' and this indorsement was one among the most effectual steps in bringing about the reunion of the two Churches in 1870. The document is rather a disavowal of imputed error than an exposition of revealed truth, and must be understood from the anthropological and soteriological controversies of that period of division now happily gone by.

Both the Errors and the True Doctrines may be found in the *Minutes* of the Assembly for 1837; also, in the *New Digest*, pp. 227-230. See also Art. on *The Auburn Declaration* by Prof. E. D. Morris, D.D., of Lane Seminary, in the *Presbyterian Quarterly and Princeton Review*, Jan. 1876, pp. 5-40.

The original document is deposited in the library of Lane Theol. Sem., Cincinnati, O. The text here given is an accurate copy from it, and was kindly furnished for this work by the Rev. E. D. Morris, D.D. The headings in brackets have been supplied by the editor.]

[PERMISSION OF SIN.]

1. God permitted the introduction of sin, not because he was unable to prevent it consistently with the moral freedom of his creatures, but for wise and benevolent reasons which he has not revealed.

[ELECTION.]

2. Election to eternal life is not founded on a foresight of faith and obedience, but is a sovereign act of God's mercy, whereby, according to the counsel of his own will, he has chosen some to salvation: 'yet so as thereby neither is violence offered to the will of the creatures, nor is the liberty or contingency of second causes taken away, but rather established;' nor does this gracious purpose ever take effect independently of faith and a holy life.

[FALL OF ADAM.]

3. By a divine constitution Adam was so the head and representative of the race that, as a consequence of his transgression, all mankind became morally corrupt, and liable to death, temporal and eternal.

[HEREDITARY SIN.]

4. Adam was created in the image of God, 'endued with knowledge, righteousness, and true holiness.' Infants come into the world not only destitute of these, but with a nature inclined to evil, and only evil.

[INFANTS INVOLVED IN THE MORAL RUIN.]

5. Brute animals sustain no such relation to the moral government of God as does the human family. Infants are a part of the human family, and their sufferings and death are to be accounted for on the ground of their being involved in the general moral ruin of the race, induced by the apostasy.

[UNIVERSAL NEED OF REDEMPTION.]

6. Original sin is a natural bias to evil, resulting from the first apostasy, leading invariably and certainly to actual transgression. And all infants, as well as adults, in order to be saved, need redemption by the blood of Christ, and regeneration by the Holy Ghost.

[IMPUTATION OF SIN AND RIGHTEOUSNESS.]

7. The sin of Adam is not imputed to his posterity in the sense of a literal transfer of personal qualities, acts, and demerit; but by reason of the sin of Adam, in his peculiar relation, the race are treated as if they had sinned. Nor is the righteousness of Christ imputed to his people in the sense of a literal transfer of personal qualities, acts, and merit; but by reason of his righteousness in *his* peculiar relation they are treated as if they were righteous.

[ATONEMENT OF CHRIST.]

8. The sufferings of Christ were not symbolical, governmental, and instructive only; but were truly vicarious, *i. e.*, a substitute for the punishment due to transgressors. And while Christ did not suffer the literal penalty of the law, involving remorse of conscience and the pains of hell, he did offer a sacrifice which infinite wisdom saw to be a full equivalent. And by virtue of this atonement, overtures of mercy are sincerely made to the race, and salvation secured to all who believe.

[MORAL INABILITY.]

9. While sinners have all the faculties necessary to a perfect moral agency and a just accountability, such is their love of sin and opposition to God and his law, that, independently of the renewing influence or almighty energy of the Holy Spirit, they never will comply with the commands of God.

[INTERCESSION OF CHRIST.]

10. The intercession of Christ for the elect is previous, as well as subsequent, to their regeneration, as appears from the following Scripture, viz.: 'I pray not for the world, but for them which thou hast given me, for they are thine. Neither pray I for these alone, but for them also which shall believe on me through their word' (John XVII. 9, 20).

[SAVING FAITH.]

11. Saving faith is an intelligent and cordial assent to the testimony of God concerning his Son, implying reliance on Christ alone for pardon and eternal life; and in all cases it is an effect of the special operations of the Holy Spirit.

[REGENERATION.]

12. Regeneration is a radical change of heart, produced by the special operations of the Holy Spirit, 'determining the sinner to that which is good,' and is in all cases instantaneous.

[SALVATION BY GRACE.]

13. While repentance for sin and faith in Christ are indispensable to salvation, all who are saved are indebted, from first to last, to the grace and Spirit of God. And the reason that God does not save all is not that he wants the *power* to do it, but that in his wisdom he does not see fit to exert that power further than he actually does.

[LIBERTY OF THE WILL.]

14. While the liberty of the will is not impaired, nor the established connection betwixt means and end broken, by any action of God on the mind, he can influence it according to his pleasure, and does effectually determine it to good in all cases of true conversion.

[JUSTIFICATION.]

15. All believers are justified, not on the ground of personal merit, but solely on the ground of the obedience and death, or, in other words, the righteousness of Christ. And while that righteousness does not become theirs, in the sense of a literal transfer of personal qualities and merit, yet from respect to it God can and does treat them as if they were righteous.

[FREEDOM IN FAITH AND UNBELIEF.]

16. While all such as reject the Gospel of Christ do it, not by coercion, but freely, and all who embrace it do it not by coercion, but freely, the reason why some differ from others is that *God* has made them to differ.

CONFESSION OF THE EVANGELICAL FREE CHURCH OF GENEVA. A.D. 1848.

[The FREE CHURCH OF GENEVA seceded from the established Church of the city of Calvin, and issued in 1848 the following Confession of Faith. It fairly represents the doctrinal position of other Free Churches which have been organized in Switzerland and France in opposition to the degenerate Reformed State Churches. It exhibits the Calvinism of the nineteenth century—a Calvinism moderated, simplified, and separated from connection with the civil government.

The French text is taken from the *Notice Historique sur l'église évangélique libre de Genève par* E. GUERS, Genève, 1875, pp. 86–90. It is also found, together with a Presbyterian constitution and a hymn-book, in *Église évangélique a Genève; Recueil de Cantiques pour les assemblées de culte*, etc. Genève and Lyon, 1864.

The English translation was prepared for this work by my friend, Professor ELIE CHARLIER, of New York.]

PROFESSION DE FOI	CONFESSION OF FAITH
de l'église évangélique libre de Genève.	of the Evangelical Free Church of Geneva.

I. Nous croyons que la sainte Écriture est pleinement inspirée de Dieu dans toutes ses parties, et qu'elle est la seule et infaillible règle de la foi.

II. Nous recevons comme Écritures canoniques, pour l'Ancien Testament, tous les livres qui nous sont transmis à ce titre par l'universalité du peuple juif, auquel les oracles de Dieu ont été confiés sous la surveillance du Seigneur ; et nous recevons également comme Écritures canoniques, pour le Nouveau Testament, tous les livres qui, sous l'action de la même Providence, nous ont été transmis à ce titre par l'universalité des Églises de la chrétienté.

III. Nous adorons le Père, le Fils et le Saint-Esprit, un seul

I. We believe that the Holy Scriptures are entirely inspired of God in all their parts, and that they are the only and infallible Rule of Faith.

II. We receive as canonical Scriptures of the Old Testament, all the books which have been transmitted to us, under that title, by the universal consent of the Jewish people, to whom the oracles of God were confided under the guidance of Jehovah ; and we receive equally as canonical Scriptures of the New Testament, all the books which, under the guidance of the same Providence, have been transmitted to us as such by the universal consent of the Churches of the Christian world.

III. We worship the Father, the Son, and the Holy Ghost, one only

Dieu en trois personnes, créateur et conservateur de tout ce qui existe.

IV. Nous croyons que le premier homme, Adam, fut créé à l'image de Dieu, dans une justice et une sainteté véritables; mais que, séduit par Satan, il tomba, et que dès lors la nature humaine fut entièrement corrompue; en sorte que tous les hommes naissent pécheurs, incapables de faire le bien selon Dieu, assujettis au mal, attirant sur eux, par un juste jugement, la condamnation et la mort.

V. Nous croyons que la Parole, qui était de toute éternité avec Dieu et qui était Dieu, a été faite chair, et que, second Adam, né pur d'une vierge par la puissance du Très-Haut, Jésus, seul entre les hommes, a pu rendre à Dieu une parfaite obéissance.

VI. Nous croyons que Jésus, le Christ, Dieu et homme en une seule personne, unique Médiateur entre Dieu et les hommes, est mort à notre place en victime expiatoire, qu'il est ressuscité, et que, élevé dans la gloire, il comparaît maintenant pour nous devant Dieu, en même temps qu'il demeure avec nous par son Esprit.

VII. Nous croyons que nul homme ne peut entrer dans le royaume de Dieu s'il n'a subi dans son âme, par la vertu du Saint-

God in three persons, the Creator and Preserver of all things.

IV. We believe that the first man, Adam, was created, after the image of God, perfectly just and holy; but that, tempted by Satan, he fell, and that, from that time, human nature has been entirely corrupt; so that all men are born sinners, unable to do good before God, inclined to evil, bringing condemnation and death on themselves by a just judgment.

V. We believe that the Word, which was of all eternity with God, and which was God, was made flesh, and that, alone among men, Jesus, a second Adam, born from a virgin by the power of the Most High, has been able to obey God in a perfect way.

VI. We believe that Jesus, the Christ, God and man in one, only Mediator between God and men, died in our place as an expiatory victim, that he rose from the dead, and that, having ascended into glory, he intercedes for us before God, at the same time dwelling with us by the Holy Ghost.

VII. We believe that no man can enter into the kingdom of heaven unless he has felt in his soul, through the virtue of the Holy

Esprit, le changement surnaturel que l'Écriture appelle nouvelle naissance, régénération, conversion, passage de la mort à la vie.

VIII. Nous croyons que nous sommes justifiés devant Dieu, non par des œuvres de justice que nous ayons faites, mais uniquement par grâce et par le moyen de la foi en Christ, dont la justice nous est imputée. C'est pourquoi nous sommes assurés qu'en Lui nous avons la vie éternelle, et que nul ne nous ravira de sa main.

IX. Nous croyons que sans la sanctification personne ne verra le Seigneur, et que, rachetés à grand prix, nous devons le glorifier par nos œuvres. Et quoique le combat entre l'esprit et la chair demeure en nous jusqu'à la fin, toutefois nous ne perdons pas courage, mais ayant reçu une volonté nouvelle, nous travaillons à notre sanctification dans la crainte de Dieu.

X. Nous croyons que le commencement et la fin du salut, la nouvelle naissance, la foi, la sanctification, la persévérance, sont un don gratuit de la miséricorde divine; le vrai croyant ayant été élu en Christ avant la fondation du monde, selon la préconnaissance de Dieu le Père, dans la sanctification de l'Esprit, pour

Ghost, the supernatural change which, in the Holy Scriptures, is called new birth, regeneration, conversion, passing from death to life.

VIII. We believe that we are justified before God, not by righteous works which we may accomplish, but only by grace and through faith in Christ, whose righteousness is ascribed to us. On that account we are assured that in Him we have eternal life, and that no one can pluck us out of his hand.

IX. We believe that without sanctification no man will see the Lord, and that, ransomed at a great price, we must glorify him by our works. And although the battle between the Spirit and the flesh exists unto the end, still we are not discouraged, but, having received a new will, we work for our sanctification in the fear of the Lord.

X. We believe that the beginning and the end of our salvation, our new birth, faith, sanctification, and perseverance are a gratuitous gift of the divine mercy; the true believer having been elected in Christ before the foundation of the world, according to the foreknowledge of God, the Father, in the sanctification of the Holy Ghost,

obéir à Jésus-Christ et pour être arrosé de son sang.

XI. Nous croyons que Dieu, qui à tant aimé le monde que de donner son fils unique, ordonne présentement à tout homme, en tout lieu, de se convertir ; que chacun est responsable de ses péchés et de son incrédulité ; que Jésus ne repousse aucun de ceux qui vont à lui, et que tout pécheur qui invoque sincèrement son Nom sera sauvé.

XII. Nous croyons que le Saint-Esprit applique aux élus, par le moyen de la Parole, le salut que le Père leur a destiné et que le Fils leur a acquis ; de telle sorte que, les unissant à Jésus par la foi, il habite en eux, les affranchit de l'empire du péché, leur fait comprendre les Écritures, les console et les scelle pour le jour de la rédemption.

XIII. Nous attendons des cieux le Seigneur Jésus-Christ, qui transformera le corps de notre humiliation pour le rendre conforme au corps de sa gloire, et nous croyons qu'en cette journée-là, les morts qui sont en Christ sortant à sa voix de leurs tombeaux, et les fidèles qui vivront alors sur la terre, transmués par sa puissance, seront enlevés tous ensemble dans les nuées à sa rencontre, et qu'ainsi nous serons toujours avec le Seigneur.

to obey Jesus Christ and to be bathed in his blood.

XI. We believe that God, who so loved the world that he gave his only Son, now orders every man, in every place, to be converted ; that every one is responsible for his sins and his unbelief ; that Jesus repels none who go to him ; and that every sinner who sincerely appeals to him will be saved.

XII. We believe that the Holy Ghost applies to the chosen ones, by means of the Word, the salvation which the Father has destined for them and which the Son has bought, so that, uniting them to Jesus by faith, he dwells in them, delivers them from the sway of sin, makes them understand the Scriptures, consoles them and seals them for the day of redemption.

XIII. We expect from heaven our Saviour Jesus Christ, who will change our body of humiliation and make it conform to his own body of glory ; and we believe that, in that day, the dead who are in Christ, coming out from their tombs at his voice, and the faithful then living on the earth, all transformed through his power, will be taken up together into the clouds to meet him, and that thus we shall always be with our Saviour.

XIV. Nous croyons qu'il y aura une résurrection des injustes comme des justes; que Dieu a arrêté un jour où il jugera le monde universel par l'homme qu'il a destiné à cela; et que les méchants iront aux peines éternelles, pendant que les justes jouiront de la vie éternelle.

XV. Nous croyons que les églises particulières, établies en divers lieux et plus ou moins mélangées de régénérés et d'inconvertis, doivent se faire connaître au monde par la profession de leur espérance, les actes de leur culte, et le travail de leur charité. Mais nous croyons aussi que, au-dessus de toutes ces églises particulières qui ont été, qui sont et qui seront, il existe devant Dieu une sainte Église universelle, composée de tous les régénérés, et formant un seul corps invisible dont Jésus-Christ est la tête et dont les membres ne seront entièrement manifestés qu'au dernier jour.

XVI. Nous croyons que le Seigneur a institué le baptême et la Cène comme symboles et gages du salut qu'il nous a acquis: le baptême, qui est le signe de la purification par le sang et par l'Esprit de Jésus: la Cène, dans laquelle nous recevons par la foi sa chair et son

XIV. We believe that there will be a resurrection of the unjust as well as of the just; that God has decided upon a day in which he shall judge the whole world by the man chosen for that purpose; that the unjust will go to everlasting punishment, while the just will rejoice in life everlasting.

XV. We believe that individual churches, established in different places, composed more or less of converted and unconverted persons, must make themselves known to the world by the confession of their hope, the acts of their worship, and the works of their charity. But we also believe that, above all these individual churches which have been, are, and will be, there exists before God a holy universal Church, composed of all the redeemed ones, forming one invisible body of which Jesus Christ is the head, and whose members will be entirely known only at the last day.

XVI. We believe that the Saviour has instituted Baptism and the Lord's Supper as symbols and pledges of the salvation which he has acquired for us: Baptism, which is the sign of the purification by the blood and spirit of Jesus Christ: the Eucharist, in

sang, et nous annonçons sa mort jusqu'à ce qu'il vienne.

which we receive by faith his body and his blood, and announce his death until his coming.

XVII. Nous déclarons que, tout en voulant devant Dieu maintenir parmi nous la saine prédication de toutes ces vérités, nous reconnaissons pour frères tous ceux qui, en quelque lieu que se soit, invoquent Jésus-Christ comme leur unique Sauveur et comme leur Dieu; nous voulons les aimer, et nous désirons apprendre du Seigneur à leur donner en toute occasion des témoignages du lien qui nous unit tous en Lui pour l'éternité.

XVII. We declare that, while wishing before God to maintain among ourselves the sound preaching of all these truths, we receive as brethren all such as, in any place whatsoever, pray to Jesus Christ as their only Saviour and their God; we wish to love them, and to learn from our Lord to give them on all occasions tokens of the bonds which unite us all together in Him for eternity.

CREED OF THE FREE CHRISTIAN CHURCH IN ITALY.
(LA CHIESA CRISTIANA LIBERA IN ITALIA.)

Declaration of Principles, adopted unanimously in General Assembly at Milan, June, 1870.

[From the *Fifth Evangelization Report of the Free Italian Church in Italy.* Florence, 1876.]

I. Iddio, Padre, Figliuolo e Spirito Santo, ha manifestato la sua Volontà nella Rivelazione, ch' è la Bibbia, sola regola perfetta ed immutabile di fede e di condotta.

I. God the Father, Son, and Holy Ghost has manifested his will in Revelation, which is the Bible, the alone perfect and immutable rule of faith and conduct.

II. Dio creò l' uomo diritto a sua immagine e similitudine; ma Adamo disobbedendo alla Parola di Dio, peccò, e così per un uomo il peccato è entrato nel mondo, e per lo peccato la morte. Per la qual cosa l' umana natura in

II. God created man perfect in his own image and likeness, but Adam, disobeying the Word of God, sinned, and thus by one man sin has entered into the world, and death by sin. On this account human nature in Adam and by

Adamo, e per Adamo, è divenuta corrotta e peccatrice; e tutti in Adamo nasciamo con l' inclinazione al mal fare, e l' incapacità di fare il bene da Dio comandato; epperciò, naturalmente, siamo tutti peccatori e sotto condannazione.

III. Iddio non vuole la morte del peccatore, ma che venga alla conoscenza della Verità e sia salvato.

IV. La salvezza viene dall' amore eterno e gratuito del Padre; — È acquistata pel sacrificio espiatorio, per la risurrezione e per la intercessione del Figlio, che ci giustifica; — Vien comunicata dallo Spirito Santo, il quale, rigenerando il peccatore, lo unisce a Cristo per la fede, viene ad abitare in lui, produce la pace nel suo cuore, dandogli la sicurezza dell' intera remissione dei suoi peccati, lo rende libero, lo guida e lo consola per mezzo della Parola ch' Egli stesso ha data, lo suggella e lo custodisce, per il giorno della gloriosa apparizione del Signor nostro e Salvatore Gesù Cristo.

V. Il Cristiano, riscattato a gran prezzo, deve glorificare Iddio nel corpo, nell' anima e nello Spirito, che a Dio stesso appartengono, camminando nella santificazione, senza la quale niuno può vedere il Signore. A ciò fare, egli trova

Adam has become corrupt and sinful; and we are all born in Adam with the inclination to do evil, and the inability of doing well what God has commanded; therefore, naturally, we are all sinners under condemnation.

III. God does not desire the death of the sinner, but that he should come to the knowledge of the truth and be saved.

IV. Salvation comes from the eternal and gratuitous love of the Father; it is obtained through the expiatory sacrifice, resurrection, and intercession of the Son; it is communicated by the Holy Spirit, who regenerates the sinner, unites him to Christ by faith, comes and dwells in him, produces peace in his heart, giving him the assurance of the entire remission of his sins, making him free, guiding and consoling him by means of the Word which he himself has given, sealing and guarding him until the day of the glorious appearing of our Lord and Saviour Jesus Christ.

V. The Christian, redeemed with a great price, ought to glorify God in his body, soul, and spirit which belong to God, walking in holiness, without which no man can see the Lord. In order to this, he finds strength in com

forza nella Comunione di Colui, che gli dice: 'La mia grazia ti basta.'

VI. I credenti, rigenerati in Cristo, formano la Chiesa, la quale non può perire nè apostatare, essendo il corpo del Signore Gesù.

VII. Oltre al Sacerdozio Universale, cui appartengono tutti i Cristiani, Dio stesso ha stabilito nella Chiesa diversi ministeri speciali, per lo perfetto adunamento dei Santi e per l' edificazione del Corpo di Cristo : i quali ministeri debbono essere riconosciuti dalla Chiesa medesima.

VIII. Il Signore Gesù Cristo verrà dai Cieli, e trasformerà il nostro corpo di umiliazione in corpo glorioso. In quel giorno i morti, che sono in Cristo, risorgeranno i primi, ed i viventi, trovati fedeli, saranno trasformati, e così tutti insieme saremo rapiti nelle nuvole a scontrare il Signore nell' aria, per esser sempre con Lui : e, dopo il suo regno, risorgeranno anche gli altri tutti per essere giudicati in giudizio.

" *L' Assemblea generale delle Chiese Cristiane Libere in Italia reputa questi articoli l' espressione del Cristianesimo biblico, senza però pretendere che oltre ad essi non ci sieno altre dottrine da credersi nella Bibbia.* . .

" *Essa non pretende all' infallibilità. La sola parola di Dio è infallibile ed immutabile. La Dichiarazione dei principii nella Chiesa non è la causa, od il titolo della salvezza, ma è il legame esterno dell' unità della fede, è la bandiera della Chiesa stessa.*"

munion with him who says to him, 'My grace is sufficient for thee.'

VI. Believers, regenerated in Christ, form the Church, which can not perish nor apostatize, being the body of the Lord Jesus.

VII. In addition to the universal priesthood of believers, God himself has established in the Church various special ministries for the perfecting of the saints and the edifying of the body of Christ, which ministries ought to be recognized by the Church itself.

VIII. The Lord Jesus Christ will come from heaven and transform our body of humiliation into a glorious body. In that day the dead in Christ shall rise first, and the living who are found faithful shall be transformed, and thus together shall we be caught up in the clouds, to meet the Lord in the air, to be forever with the Lord; and, after his Kingdom, all the rest shall rise to be judged in judgment.

These articles are held to suffice as a testimony of a Christianity purely evangelical, without pretending that there are no other doctrines in the Bible to be believed. . .

It is also clearly asserted that this 'Declaration of Principles' does not pretend to infallibility. The Word of God is alone infallible and immutable. Nor is it looked upon as the cause or title to salvation, but simply as the outward bond of unity in the faith and the banner of the Church.

THE CONFESSION OF THE SOCIETY OF FRIENDS, COMMONLY CALLED QUAKERS. A.D. 1675.

[The fifteen Theological Theses or Propositions of ROBERT BARCLAY, which are the text of his 'Apology,' contain the most authoritative summary of the principles and doctrines of the RELIGIOUS SOCIETY OF FRIENDS, commonly called QUAKERS. The 'Apology' appeared first in Latin, 1676, and then repeatedly in English and other languages, and was widely distributed by the Society as a standard doctrinal treatise. I have taken the text from the magnificent copy of the 8th English edition, Birmingham, 1765, 4to. On this and other Quaker Confessions, see Vol. I. pp. 864 sqq.]

THESES THEOLOGICÆ.

TO THE CLERGY, OF WHAT SORT SOEVER, UNTO WHOSE HANDS THESE MAY COME;

BUT MORE PARTICULARLY

To the Doctors, Professors, and Students of Divinity in the Universities and Schools of Great Britain, whether Prelatical, Presbyterian, or any other;

ROBERT BARCLAY, a Servant of the Lord God, and one of those who in derision are called Quakers, wisheth unfeigned repentance, unto the acknowledgment of the Truth.

FRIENDS,—Unto you these following propositions are offered; in which, they being read and considered in the fear of the Lord, you may perceive that simple, naked truth, which man by his wisdom hath rendered so obscure and mysterious that the world is even burthened with the great and voluminous tractates which are made about it, and by their vain jangling and commentaries, by which it is rendered a hundredfold more dark and intricate than of itself it is : which great learning, so accounted of—to wit, your school divinity, which taketh up almost a man's whole lifetime to learn, brings not a whit nearer to God, neither makes any man less wicked, or more righteous than he was. Therefore hath God laid aside the wise and learned, and the disputers of this world; and hath chosen a few despicable and unlearned instruments, as to letter-learning, as he did fishermen of old, to publish his pure and naked truth, and to free it of those mists and fogs wherewith the clergy hath clouded it, that the people might admire and maintain them. And among several others, whom God hath chosen to make known these things—seeing I also have received, in measure, grace to be a dispenser of the same gospel—it seemed good unto me, according to my duty, to offer unto you these propositions; which, though short, yet are weighty, comprehending much, and declaring what the true ground of knowledge is, even of that knowledge which leads to Life Eternal; which is here witnessed of, and the testimony thereof left unto the Light of Christ in all your consciences.   Farewell,   R. B.

THE FIRST PROPOSITION.

Concerning the true Foundation of Knowledge.

Seeing the height of all happiness is placed in the true knowledge of God ('This is life eternal, to know thee the only true God, and Jesus Christ whom thou hast sent '),[1] the true and right understanding

---

[1] John xvii. 3.

of this foundation and ground of knowledge is that which is most necessary to be known and believed in the first place.

Concerning Immediate Revelation.

Seeing 'no man knoweth the Father but the Son, and he to whom the Son revealeth him;' [1] and seeing the revelation of the Son is in and by the Spirit; therefore the testimony of the Spirit is that alone by which the true knowledge of God hath been, is, and can be only revealed; who as, by the moving of his own Spirit, he converted the chaos of this world into that wonderful order wherein it was in the beginning, and created man a living soul, to rule and govern it, so by the revelation of the same Spirit he hath manifested himself all along unto the sons of men, both patriarchs, prophets, and apostles; which revelations of God by the Spirit, whether by outward voices and appearances, dreams, or inward objective manifestations in the heart, were of old the formal object of their faith, and remain yet so to be; since the object of the saints' faith is the same in all ages, though set forth under divers administrations. Moreover, these divine inward revelations, which we make absolutely necessary for the building up of true faith, neither do nor can ever contradict the outward testimony of the Scriptures, or right and sound reason. Yet from hence it will not follow that these divine revelations are to be subjected to the examination, either of the outward testimony of the Scriptures or of the natural reason of man, as to a more noble or certain rule or touchstone; for this divine revelation and inward illumination is that which is evident and clear of itself, forcing, by its own evidence and clearness, the well-disposed understanding to assent, irresistibly moving the same thereunto; even as the common principles of natural truths move and incline the mind to a natural assent: as, that the whole is greater than its part; that two contradictory sayings can not be both true, nor both false: which is also manifest, according to our adversaries' principle, who—supposing the possibility of inward divine revelations—will nevertheless confess with us that neither Scripture nor sound reason will contradict it: and yet it will not follow, according to them, that

---

[1] Matt. xi. 27.

the Scripture or sound reason should be subjected to the examination of the divine revelations in the heart.

THE THIRD PROPOSITION.

Concerning the Scriptures.

From these revelations of the Spirit of God to the saints have proceeded the Scriptures of truth, which contain: 1. A faithful historical account of the actings of God's people in divers ages, with many singular and remarkable providences attending them. 2. A prophetical account of several things, whereof some are already past, and some yet to come. 3. A full and ample account of all the chief principles of the doctrine of Christ, held forth in divers precious declarations, exhortations, and sentences, which, by the moving of God's Spirit, were at several times, and upon sundry occasions, spoken and written unto some churches and their pastors: nevertheless, because they are only a declaration of the fountain, and not the fountain itself, therefore they are not to be esteemed the principal ground of all truth and knowledge, nor yet the adequate primary rule of faith and manners. Nevertheless, as that which giveth a true and faithful testimony of the first foundation, they are and may be esteemed a secondary rule, subordinate to the Spirit, from which they have all their excellency and certainty; for as by the inward testimony of the Spirit we do alone truly know them, so they testify that the Spirit is that guide by which the saints are led into all truth: therefore, according to the Scriptures, the Spirit is the first and principal Leader.[1] And seeing we do therefore receive and believe the Scriptures, because they proceeded from the Spirit, therefore also the Spirit is more originally and principally the rule, according to that received maxim in the schools, *Propter quod unumquodque est tale, illud ipsum est magis tale.* Englished thus: 'That for which a thing is such, that thing itself is more such.'

THE FOURTH PROPOSITION.

Concerning the Condition of Man in the Fall.

All Adam's posterity, or mankind, both Jews and Gentiles, as to the first Adam, or earthly man, is fallen, degenerated, and dead, deprived

---

[1] John xvi. 13; Rom. viii. 14.

of the sensation or feeling of this inward testimony or seed of God, and is subject unto the power, nature, and seed of the Serpent, which he sows in men's hearts, while they abide in this natural and corrupted state;[1] from whence it comes that not their words and deeds only, but all their imaginations are evil perpetually in the sight of God, as proceeding from this depraved and wicked seed. Man, therefore, as he is in this state, can know nothing aright; yea, his thoughts and conceptions concerning God and things spiritual, until he be disjoined from this evil seed, and united to the Divine Light, are unprofitable both to himself and others: hence are rejected the Socinian and Pelagian errors, in exalting a natural light; as also of the Papists, and most Protestants, who affirm that man, without the true grace of God, may be a true minister of the gospel. Nevertheless, this seed is not imputed to infants, until by transgression they actually join themselves therewith; for they are by nature the children of wrath, who walk according to the power of the prince of the air.

THE FIFTH AND SIXTH PROPOSITIONS.

Concerning the Universal Redemption by Christ, and also the Saving and Spiritual Light, wherewith every man is enlightened.

THE FIFTH PROPOSITION.

God, out of his infinite love, who delighteth not in the death of a sinner, but that all should live and be saved, hath so loved the world that he hath given his only Son a Light, that whosoever believeth in him should be saved; who enlighteneth every man that cometh into the world, and maketh manifest all things that are reprovable, and teacheth all temperance, righteousness, and godliness:[2] and this Light enlighteneth the hearts of all in a day,[3] in order to salvation, if not resisted: nor is it less universal than the seed of sin, being the purchase of his death, who tasted death for every man; 'for as in Adam all die, even so in Christ shall all be made alive.'[4]

---

[1] Rom. v. 12, 15; Eph. ii. 1.
[2] Ezek. xviii. 23; Isa. xlxix. 6; John iii. 16; i. 9; Titus ii. 11; Eph. v. 13; Heb. ii. 9.
[3] Pro tempore: for a time.
[4] 1 Cor. xv. 22.

THE SIXTH PROPOSITION.

According to which principle (or hypothesis), all the objections against the universality of Christ's death are easily solved; neither is it needful to recur to the ministry of angels, and those other miraculous means which, they say, God makes use of, to manifest the doctrine and history of Christ's passion unto such, who, living in those places of the world where the outward preaching of the gospel is unknown, have well improved the first and common grace; for hence it well follows, that as some of the old philosophers might have been saved, so also may now some—who by providence are cast into those remote parts of the world where the knowledge of the history is wanting—be made partakers of the divine mystery, if they receive and resist not that grace, 'a manifestation whereof is given to every man to profit withal.'[1]   This certain doctrine then being received, to wit, that there is an evangelical and saving light and grace in all, the universality of the love and mercy of God towards mankind—both in the death of his beloved Son, the Lord Jesus Christ, and in the manifestation of the light in the heart—is established and confirmed against all the objections of such as deny it.   Therefore 'Christ hath tasted death for every man:'[2] not only for all kinds of men, as some vainly talk, but for every one, of all kinds; the benefit of whose offering is not only extended to such, who have the distinct outward knowledge of his death and sufferings, as the same is declared in the Scriptures, but even unto those who are necessarily excluded from the benefit of this knowledge by some inevitable accident; which knowledge we willingly confess to be very profitable and comfortable, but not absolutely needful unto such, from whom God himself hath withheld it; yet they may be made partakers of the mystery of his death—though ignorant of the history—if they suffer his seed and light—enlightening their hearts—to take place; in which light communion with the Father and Son is enjoyed, so as of wicked men to become holy, and lovers of that power by whose inward and secret touches they feel themselves turned from the evil to the good, and learn to do to others as they would be done by; in which Christ himself affirms all to be included.   As they then

---

[1] 1 Cor. xii. 7.   [2] Heb. ii. 9.

have falsely and erroneously taught who have denied Christ to have died for all men, so neither have they sufficiently taught the truth, who, affirming him to have died for all, have added the absolute necessity of the outward knowledge thereof in order to the obtaining its saving effect; among whom the Remonstrants of Holland have been chiefly wanting, and many other asserters of Universal Redemption, in that they have not placed the extent of this salvation in that divine and evangelical principle of light and life wherewith Christ hath enlightened every man that comes into the world, which is excellently and evidently held forth in these Scriptures: Gen. vi. 3; Deut. xxx. 14; John i. 7–9; Rom. x. 8; Titus ii. 11.

THE SEVENTH PROPOSITION.
Concerning Justification.

As many as resist not this light, but receive the same, in them is produced an holy, pure, and spiritual birth, bringing forth holiness, righteousness, purity, and all those other blessed fruits which are acceptable to God; by which holy birth, to wit, Jesus Christ formed within us, and working his works in us, as we are sanctified, so we are justified in the sight of God, according to the apostle's words, 'But ye are washed, but ye are sanctified, but ye are justified, in the name of the Lord Jesus, and by the Spirit of our God.'[1]   Therefore it is not by our works wrought in our will, nor yet by good works, considered as of themselves, but by Christ, who is both the gift and the giver, and the cause producing the effects in us; who, as he hath reconciled us while we were enemies, doth also in his wisdom save us, and justify us after this manner, as saith the same apostle elsewhere, 'According to his mercy he saved us, by the washing of regeneration, and the renewing of the Holy Ghost.'[2]

THE EIGHTH PROPOSITION.
Concerning Perfection.

In whom this holy and pure birth is fully brought forth the body of death and sin comes to be crucified and removed, and their hearts united and subjected unto the truth, so as not to obey any suggestion

---

[1] 1 Cor. vi. 11.   [2] Titus iii. 5.

or temptation of the evil one, but to be free from actual sinning and transgressing of the law of God, and in that respect perfect. Yet doth this perfection still admit of a growth; and there remaineth a possibility of sinning where the mind doth not most diligently and watchfully attend unto the Lord.[1]

THE NINTH PROPOSITION.

Concerning Perseverance, and the Possibility of Falling from Grace.

Although this gift and inward grace of God be sufficient to work out salvation, yet in those in whom it is resisted it both may and doth become their condemnation. Moreover, in whom it hath wrought in part, to purify and sanctify them, in order to their further perfection, by disobedience such may fall from it, and turn it to wantonness, making shipwreck of faith; and 'after having tasted of the heavenly gift, and been made partakers of the Holy Ghost, again fall away.'[2] Yet such an increase and stability in the truth may in this life be attained, from which there can not be a total apostasy.

THE TENTH PROPOSITION.

Concerning the Ministry.

As by this gift, or Light of God, all true knowledge in things spiritual is received and revealed; so by the same, as it is manifested and received in the heart, by the strength and power thereof, every true minister of the gospel is ordained, prepared, and supplied in the work of the ministry; and by the leading, moving, and drawing hereof ought every evangelist and Christian pastor to be led and ordered in his labor and work of the gospel, both as to the place where, as to the persons to whom, and as to the times when he is to minister. Moreover, those who have this authority may and ought to preach the gospel, though without human commission or literature; as, on the other hand, those who want the authority of this divine gift, however learned or authorized by the commissions of men and churches, are to be esteemed but as deceivers, and not true ministers of the gospel. Also, who have received this holy and unspotted gift, 'as they have freely

---

[1] Rom. vi. 14; viii. 13; 1 John iii. 6.
[2] 1 Tim. i. 6; Heb. vi. 4–6.

received, so are they freely to give,'[1] without hire or bargaining, far less to use it as a trade to get money by it: yet if God hath called any from their employments or trades, by which they acquire their livelihood, it may be lawful for such, according to the liberty which they feel given them in the Lord, to receive such temporals— to wit, what may be needful to them for meat and clothing—as are freely given them by those to whom they have communicated spirituals.

THE ELEVENTH PROPOSITION.

Concerning Worship.

All true and acceptable worship to God is offered in the inward and immediate moving and drawing of his own Spirit, which is neither limited to places, times, or persons; for though we be to worship him always, in that we are to fear before him, yet as to the outward signification thereof in prayers, praises, or preachings, we ought not to do it where and when we will, but where and when we are moved thereunto by the secret inspirations of his Spirit in our hearts, which God heareth and accepteth of, and is never wanting to move us thereunto, when need is, of which he himself is the alone proper judge. All other worship then, both praises, prayers, and preachings, which man sets about in his own will, and at his own appointment, which he can both begin and end at his pleasure, do or leave undone, as himself sees meet, whether they be a prescribed form, as a liturgy, or prayers conceived extemporarily, by the natural strength and faculty of the mind, they are all but superstitions, will-worship, and abominable idolatry in the sight of God; which are to be denied, rejected, and separated from, in this day of his spiritual arising: however it might have pleased him— who winked at the times of ignorance, with respect to the simplicity and integrity of some, and of his own innocent seed, which lay as it were buried in the hearts of men, under the mass of superstition—to blow upon the dead and dry bones, and to raise some breathings, and answer them, and that until the day should more clearly dawn and break forth.[2]

---

[1] Matt. x. 8.
[2] Ezek. xiii.; Matt. x. 20; Acts ii. 4; xviii. 5; John iii. 6; iv. 21; Jude 19; Acts xvii. 23.

THE TWELFTH PROPOSITION.
Concerning Baptism.

As there is one Lord and one faith, so there is ' one baptism; which is not the putting away the filth of the flesh, but the answer of a good conscience before God, by the resurrection of Jesus Christ.' And this baptism is a pure and spiritual thing, to wit, the baptism of the Spirit and Fire, by which we are buried with him, that, being washed and purged from our sins, we may ' walk in newness of life;' of which the baptism of John was a figure, which was commanded for a time, and not to continue forever.[1]

As to the baptism of infants, it is a mere human tradition, for which neither precept nor practice is to be found in all the Scripture.

THE THIRTEENTH PROPOSITION.
Concerning the Communion, or Participation of the Body and Blood of Christ.

The communion of the body and blood of Christ is inward and spiritual, which is the participation of his flesh and blood, by which the inward man is daily nourished in the hearts of those in whom Christ dwells;[2] of which things the breaking of bread by Christ with his disciples was a figure, which they even used in the Church for a time, who had received the substance, for the cause of the weak; even as ' abstaining from things strangled, and from blood;' the washing one another's feet, and the anointing of the sick with oil;[3] all which are commanded with no less authority and solemnity than the former; yet seeing they are but the shadows of better things, they cease in such as have obtained the substance.

THE FOURTEENTH PROPOSITION.
Concerning the Power of the Civil Magistrate, in matters purely religious, and pertaining to the conscience.

Since God hath assumed to himself the power and dominion of the conscience, who alone can rightly instruct and govern it, therefore it

---

[1] Eph. iv. 5; 1 Pet. iii. 21; Rom. vi. 4; Gal. iii. 27; Col. ii. 12; John iii. 30; 1 Cor. i. 17.
[2] 1 Cor. x. 16, 17; John vi. 32, 33, 35; 1 Cor. v. 8.
[3] Acts xv. 20; John xiii. 14; James v. 14.

is not lawful for any whatsoever, by virtue of any authority or princi-
pality they bear in the government of this world, to force the consciences of others; and therefore all killing, banishing, fining, impris-
oning, and other such things, which men are afflicted with, for the
alone exercise of their conscience, or difference in worship or opinion,
proceedeth from the spirit of Cain, the murderer, and is contrary to
the truth; provided always that no man, under the pretense of conscience, prejudice his neighbor in his life or estate, or do any thing
destructive to, or inconsistent with, human society; in which case the
law is for the transgressor, and justice to be administered upon all,
without respect of persons.[1]

THE FIFTEENTH PROPOSITION.

Concerning Salutations and Recreations, etc.

Seeing the chief end of all religion is to redeem man from the spirit
and vain conversation of this world, and to lead into inward communion
with God, before whom, if we fear always, we are accounted happy,
therefore all the vain customs and habits thereof, both in word and
deed, are to be rejected and forsaken by those who come to this fear;
such as the taking off the hat to a man, the bowings and cringings of
the body, and such other salutations of that kind, with all the foolish
and superstitious formalities attending them; all which man has invented in his degenerate state, to feed his pride in the vain pomp and
glory of this world; as also the unprofitable plays, frivolous recreations, sportings, and gamings which are invented to pass away the
precious time, and divert the mind from the witness of God in the
heart, and from the living sense of his fear, and from that evangelical
Spirit wherewith Christians ought to be leavened, and which leads
into sobriety, gravity, and godly fear; in which, as we abide, the blessing of the Lord is felt to attend us in those actions in which we are
necessarily engaged, in order to the taking care for the sustenance of
the outward man.[2]

---

[1] Luke ix. 55, 56; Matt. vii. 12, 29; Titus iii. 10.
[2] Eph. v. 11; 1 Pet. i. 14; John v. 44; Jer. x. 3; Acts x. 26; Matt. xv. 13; Col. ii. 8.

EASTER LITANY OF THE MORAVIAN CHURCH. A.D. 1749.

[This is the chief Confession of the Church of the UNITED BRETHREN, commonly called the MORA-
VIANS. It was originally composed in German, and was translated and slightly modified in 1749.
The text is taken from the *Liturgienbuch der Evangelischen Brüdergemeine*, Gnadau, 1873. It has been
kindly prepared in both languages for this work by my friend, the Rt. Rev. EDMUND DE SCHWEINITZ,
S.T.D., Bishop of the Moravian Church, Bethlehem, Pa.]

Litaney am Ostermorgen.

Ich glaube an den Einigen Gott, Vater, Sohn, und heiligen Geist, der alle Dinge geschaffen hat durch Jesum Christ, und war in Christo, und versöhnete die Welt mit ihm selber.

Ich glaube an Gott, den Vater unsers Herrn Jesu Christi, der uns erwählet hat durch denselbigen, ehe der Welt Grund geleget war;

Der uns errettet hat von der Obrigkeit der Finsterniß, und hat uns versetzet in das Reich Seines lieben Sohnes;

Der uns gesegnet hat mit allerlei geistlichem Segen in himmlischen Gütern durch Christum;

Und hat uns tüchtig gemacht zu dem Erbtheil der Heiligen im Licht, da Er uns verordnet hat zur Kindschaft gegen ihn selbst durch Jesum Christ, nach dem Wohlgefallen seines Willens, zu Lobe seiner herrlichen Gnade, durch welche er uns hat angenehm gemacht in dem Geliebten.

Das ist gewißlich wahr!

Wir preisen dich, Vater und Herr Himmels und der Erden, daß du sol-

EASTER MORNING LITANY.

I believe in the One only God, Father, Son, and Holy Ghost, who created all things by Jesus Christ, and was in Christ, reconciling the world unto himself.

I believe in God, the Father of our Lord Jesus Christ, who hath chosen us in him before the foundation of the world;

Who hath delivered us from the power of darkness, and hath translated us into the kingdom of his dear Son;

Who hath blessed us with all spiritual blessings in heavenly places in Christ;

Who hath made us meet to be partakers of the inheritance of the saints in light: having predestinated us unto the adoption of children by Jesus Christ to himself, according to the good pleasure of his will, to the praise of the glory of his grace, wherein he hath made us accepted in the Beloved.

This I verily believe.

We thank thee, O Father, Lord of heaven and earth, because thou

ches den Weisen und Klugen verborgen hast, und hast es den Unmündigen offenbaret. Ja, Vater! denn es ist also wohlgefällig gewesen vor dir.

Vater! verkläre deinen Namen!

Unser Vater in dem Himmel! dein Name werde geheiliget; dein Reich komme; dein Wille geschehe auf Erden wie im Himmel; unser täglich Brod gieb uns heute; und vergieb uns unsre Schulden wie wir unsern Schuldigern vergeben; und führe uns nicht in Versuchung, sondern erlöse uns von dem Bösen; denn dein ist das Reich und die Kraft und die Herrlichkeit in Ewigkeit, Amen.

Vater! habe uns lieb, darum, daß wir deinen Sohn lieben, und glauben, daß er von dir ausgegangen ist.

Ich glaube an den Namen des Eingebornen Sohnes Gottes, durch welchen alle Dinge sind, und wir durch ihn.

Ich glaube, daß er Fleisch ward und wohnete unter uns; und nahm Knechtsgestalt an:

Durch den heiligen Geist empfangen von Maria der Jungfrau; wie die Kinder Fleisch und Blut haben, ist er's gleichermaßen theilhaftig worden, geboren von einem Weibe;

Und an Geberden wie ein Mensch erfunden; ist versucht worden allenthalben, gleich wie wir, doch ohne Sünde:

hast hid these things from the wise and prudent, and hast revealed them unto babes. Even so, Father: for so it seemed good in thy sight.

Father, glorify thy name.

Our Father which art in heaven, hallowed be thy name; thy kingdom come; thy will be done in earth, as it is in heaven; give us this day our daily bread; and forgive us our trespasses, as we forgive them that trespass against us; and lead us not into temptation, but deliver us from evil: for thine is the kingdom, and the power, and the glory, for ever and ever: Amen.

I believe in the name of the only-begotten Son of God, by whom are all things, and we through him;

I believe that he was made flesh, and dwelt among us; and took on him the form of a servant;

By the overshadowing of the Holy Ghost was conceived of the Virgin Mary; as the children are partakers of flesh and blood, he also himself likewise took part of the same; was born of a woman;

And being found in fashion as a man, was tempted in all points like as we are, yet without sin:

Denn er war der Herr, der Engel des Bundes, deß wir begehrten; der Herr und sein Geist hatten ihn gesandt, zu predigen das angenehme Jahr des Herrn.

Er redete, was er wußte, und zeugte, was er gesehen hatte; die ihn aufnahmen, denen gab er Macht, Gottes Kinder zu werden.

Sehet! das ist Gottes Lamm, das der Welt Sünde getragen hat: gelitten unter Pontio Pilato, gekreuziget, gestorben und begraben; ist im Geiste hingegangen, und hat geprediget den Geistern im Gefängniß;

Am dritten Tage wieder auferstanden von den Todten, und mit ihm viele Leiber der Heiligen, die da schliefen;

Aufgefahren gen Himmel, sitzet auf des Vaters Stuhle;

Wird wiederkommen, wie man ihn gesehen hat gen Himmel fahren.

Es spricht der Geist und die Braut: Ach komm!

Und wer es höret, der spreche: Komm!

Amen! ja, Herr Jesu! komm, bleib nicht lange!
Wir warten deiner, uns wird fast bange.
Komm, komm doch, komm!

Auch wird er mit einem Feldgeschrei und Stimme des Erzengels, und mit der Posaune Gottes hernieder kommen vom Himmel, zu richten die Lebendigen und die Todten.

For he is the Lord, the Messenger of the covenant, whom we delight in. The Lord and his Spirit hath sent him to proclaim the acceptable year of the Lord;

He spoke that which he did know, and testified that which he had seen: as many as received him, to them gave he power to become the sons of God.

Behold the Lamb of God, which taketh away the sin of the world;

Suffered under Pontius Pilate, was crucified, dead, and buried;

The third day rose again from the dead, and with him many bodies of the saints which slept;

Ascended into heaven, and sitteth on the throne of the Father; whence he will come, in like manner as he was seen going into heaven.

The Spirit and the bride say, Come.

And let him that heareth say, Come.

Amen! come, Lord Jesus! come we implore thee!
With longing hearts we now are waiting for thee.
Come soon, O come!

The Lord will descend from heaven with a shout, with the voice of the archangel, and with the trump of God, to judge both the quick and the dead.

Das iſt mein Herr, der mich verlornen und verdammten Menſchen erlöſet
hat, erworben, gewonnen, von allen
Sünden, vom Tode und von der Gewalt des Teufels;

Nicht mit Gold oder Silber, ſondern
mit ſeinem heiligen theuren Blute und
mit ſeinem unſchuldigen Leiden und
Sterben;

Auf daß ich ſein eigen ſei, und in
ſeinem Reiche unter ihm lebe und ihm
diene in ewiger Gerechtigkeit, Unſchuld
und Seligkeit;

Gleichwie er iſt auferſtanden vom
Tode, lebet und regieret in Ewigkeit.

Das iſt gewißlich wahr!

Ich glaube an den heiligen Geiſt,
der vom Vater ausgehet, und den uns
unſer Herr Jeſus Chriſtus geſandt hat,
nach ſeinem Hingange, daß er ewiglich
bei uns bleibe;

This is my Lord, who redeemed
me, a lost and undone human creature, purchased and gained me from
sin, from death, and from the power of the devil;

Not with gold or silver, but with
his holy precious blood, and with
his innocent suffering and dying;

To the end that I should be his
own, and in his kingdom live under him and serve him, in eternal
righteousness, innocence, and happiness;

Even as he, being risen from the
dead, liveth and reigneth, world
without end.

This I most certainly believe.

I believe in the Holy Ghost, who
proceedeth from the Father, and
whom our Lord Jesus Christ sent,
after he went away, that he should
abide with us forever;

That he should comfort us, as a
mother comforteth her children;

That he should help our infirmities, and make intercession for us
with groanings which can not be
uttered;

That he should bear witness with
our spirit, that we are the children
of God, and teach us to cry, Abba,
Father;

That he should shed abroad in
our hearts the love of God, and
make our bodies his holy temple;

Und daß er Alles in Allem wirke,
und theile einem Jeglichen mit, nach=
dem er will.

Dem sei Ehre in der Gemeine, die
in Christo Jesu ist, der allgemeinen
heiligen christlichen Kirche, in Gemein=
schaft der Heiligen, zu aller Zeit, und
von Ewigkeit zu Ewigkeit. Amen.

Ich glaube, daß ich nicht aus eige=
ner Vernunft noch Kraft an Jesum
Christum, meinen Herrn, glauben oder
zu ihm kommen kann;

Sondern daß mich der heilige Geist
durch's Evangelium berufet, mit seinen
Gaben erleuchtet, im rechten Glauben
heiliget und erhält;

Gleichwie er die ganze Christenheit
auf Erden berufet, sammlet, erleuchtet,
heiliget, und bei Jesu Christo erhält,
im rechten einigen Glauben;

In welcher Christenheit er mir und
allen Gläubigen täglich alle Sünden
reichlich vergiebt.

Das ist gewißlich wahr.

Ich glaube, daß ich durch die heilige
Taufe, welche ist das Bad der Wieder=
geburt und Erneuerung des heiligen
Geistes, der Gemeine Jesu Christi ein=
verleibt worden bin, welche er geliebet
hat, und hat sich selbst für sie gegeben,
auf daß er sie heiligte, und hat sie ge=
reiniget durch das Wasserbad im Wort.
Amen.

In dieser Gemeinschaft der Gläubi=

And that he should work all in
all, dividing to every man severally as he will.

To him be glory in the Church,
which is in Christ Jesus, the holy,
universal Christian Church, in the
communion of saints, at all times,
and from eternity to eternity.
Amen.

I believe that by my own reason
and strength I can not believe in
Jesus Christ my Lord, or come to
him;

But that the Holy Ghost calleth
me by the gospel, enlighteneth me
with his gifts, sanctifieth and pre-
serveth me in the true faith;

Even as he calleth, gathereth,
enlighteneth, and sanctifieth the
whole Church on earth, which he
keepeth by Jesus Christ in the only
true faith;

In which Christian Church God
forgiveth me and every believer all
sin daily and abundantly.

This I assuredly believe.

I believe that by holy baptism
I am embodied a member of the
Church of Christ, which he hath
loved, and for which he gave himself, that he might sanctify and
cleanse it with the washing of water by the Word.   *Amen.*

In this communion of saints **my**

gen getröste ich mich meines lieben
Herrn und Heilandes Jesu Christi,
welcher ist für mich gestorben, und hat
sein Blut am Kreuze für mich vergossen zur Vergebung der Sünden, und
hat mir seinen Leib und sein Blut im
Sakrament zum Pfande gegeben. Wie
dann die Schrift sagt: Unser Herr
Jesus Christus, in der Nacht, da er
verrathen ward, nahm er das Brod,
dankete und brach es, und gab es seinen Jüngern, und sprach: Nehmet,
esset, das ist mein Leib, der für euch
gegeben wird. Solches thut zu meinem Gedächtniß. Desselbigen gleichen
nahm er auch den Kelch nach dem
Abendmahl, dankete, und gab ihnen
den, und sprach: Nehmet hin, trinket
alle daraus: dieser Kelch ist das
neue Testament in meinem Blut, das
für euch vergossen wird, zur Vergebung der Sünden. Solches thut, so
oft ihr es trinket, zu meinem Gedächtniß.

Darum bleibet er in mir und ich in
ihm, und ich habe das ewige Leben,
und er wird mich auferwecken am jüngsten Tage. Amen.

Ich begehre, aufgelöst und bei
Christo zu sein, welches auch viel besser wäre: ich werde den Tod nicht
schmecken ewiglich, und entgegen kommen zur Auferstehung der Todten;
denn meine Hütte, die ich ablege, das
Korn der Verwesung, wird anziehen
die Unverweslichkeit: das Fleisch ru-
het in Hoffnung;

faith is placed upon my Lord and
Saviour Jesus Christ, who died for
us, and shed his blood on the cross
for the remission of sins, and who
hath granted unto me his body and
blood in the Lord's Supper, as a
pledge of grace; as the Scripture
saith: Our Lord Jesus Christ, the
same night in which he was betrayed, took bread: and when he
had given thanks, he brake it, and
gave it to his disciples, and said,
Take, eat; this is my body which
is given for you; this do in remembrance of me. After the same
manner, also, our Lord Jesus Christ,
when he had supped, took the cup,
gave thanks, and gave it to them,
saying, Drink ye all of it; this is
my blood, the blood of the New
Testament, which is shed for you,
and for many, for the remission
of sins. This do ye, as oft as ye
drink it, in remembrance of me.

Therefore he abideth in me and
I in him, and I have eternal life,
and he will raise me up on the
last day. *Amen.*

I have a desire to depart, and to
be with Christ, which is far better;
I shall never taste death; yea, I
shall attain unto the resurrection
of the dead; for the body which I
shall put off, this grain of corrupti-
bility, shall put on incorruption:
my flesh shall rest in hope;

Und auch dich, du sterbendes Ge=
beine, wird Gott lebendig machen, um
deßwillen, daß sein Geist in dir ge=
wohnet hat.

Amen.

Ich glaube, daß unsre Brüder und
Schwestern, so sie im Herrn entschla=
fen sind, zur oberen Gemeine gefahren
und eingegangen sind in ihres Herrn
Freude; der Leib ist hier begraben:

Den wird Jesus Christus einst beim Erwachen
Seinem verklärten Leib ähnlich machen:
Hallelujah!

**Wir armen Sünder bitten,
du wollest uns erhören, lieber
Herr und Gott!**

Und uns mit der vollendeten Ge=
meine, und insonderheit mit deinen
dieses Jahr über heimberufenen Die=
nern und Dienerinnen, in ewiger Ge=
meinschaft erhalten, und uns dereinst
bei dir zusammen ausruhen lassen von
unsrer Arbeit.

Amen.

Sein' Augen, seinen Mund
Den Leib für uns verwund't,

And the God of peace, that
brought again from the dead our
Lord Jesus, that great Shepherd of
the sheep, through the blood of
the everlasting covenant, shall also
quicken these our mortal bodies, if
so be that the Spirit of God hath
dwelt in them.

Amen.

*We poor sinners pray,
Hear us, gracious Lord and God;*

And keep us in everlasting fellowship with our brethren, and
with our sisters, who have entered
into the joy of their Lord;

Also with the servants and hand-
maids of our Church, whom thou
hast called home in the past year,
and with the whole Church triumphant; and let us rest together
in thy presence from our labors.

Amen.

They are at rest in lasting bliss,
    Beholding Christ our Saviour:
Our humble expectation is
    To live with him forever.

Lord, grant me thy protection,
    Remind me of thy death

Da wir so fest d'rauf bauen,
Das werd'n wir alles schauen,
Und innig herzlich grüßen
Die Maal' an Händ' und Füßen.

Wir grüß'n uns ehrerbietiglich,
Als Glieder seiner Braut,
Die theils allhier noch sehnet sich
Und theils schon dort ihn schaut.

Wenn ich einst werd' erblassen
In seinem Arm und Schooß,
Will ich das Blut auffassen,
Das er für mich vergoß:

Das wird auch mein Gebeine
Mit Lebenskraft durchgehn;
Dann fahr' ich zur Gemeine;
Mein Leib wird aufersteh'n.

And glorious resurrection,
    When I resign my breath:
Ah! then, though I be dying,
    'Midst sickness, grief, and pain,
I shall, on thee relying,
    Eternal life obtain.

Ehre sei dem, der da ist die Auferstehung und das Leben!

Glory be to him who is the Resurrection and the Life; he was dead, and behold, he is alive for evermore;

Wer an ihn glaubet, der wird leben, ob er gleich stürbe.

And he that believeth in him, though he were dead, yet shall he live.

Ehre sei ihm in der Gemeine, die auf ihn wartet, und die um ihn her ist!

Glory be to him in the Church which waiteth for him, and in that which is around him:

Von Ewigkeit zu Ewigkeit.

Forever and ever.

Amen.

Amen.

Die Gnade unsers Herrn Jesu Christi, und die Liebe Gottes, und die Gemeinschaft des Heiligen Geistes, sei mit uns Allen.

The grace of our Lord Jesus Christ, and the love of God, and the communion of the Holy Ghost, be with us all.

Amen.

Amen.

METHODIST ARTICLES OF RELIGION. A.D. 1784.

[The Twenty-five Articles of Religion were drawn up by JOHN WESLEY for the American Methodists, and adopted at a Conference in 1784. They underwent some changes, chiefly verbal, and Art. 23d, acknowledging the sovereignty of the people of the United States, was adopted by the Methodist Episcopal Church in 1804. They are a liberal and judicious abridgment of the Thirty-nine Articles of the Church of England, the Calvinistic and other features being omitted (Arts. 3, 8, 13, 15, 17, 18, 20, 21, 26, 29, 31, 33, 34, 36, and 37).

The text is taken from the official manual of *The Doctrines and Discipline of the Methodist Episcopal Church*, ed. by Bishop HARRIS, New York, 1872.]

I. OF FAITH IN THE HOLY TRINITY.

There is but one living and true God, everlasting, without body or parts, of infinite power, wisdom, and goodness; the Maker and Preserver of all things, visible and invisible. And in unity of this Godhead there are three persons, of one substance, power, and eternity, the Father, the Son, and the Holy Ghost.

II. OF THE WORD, OR SON OF GOD, WHO WAS MADE VERY MAN.

The Son, who is the Word of the Father, the very and eternal God, of one substance with the Father, took man's nature in the womb of the blessed Virgin; so that two whole and perfect natures—that is to say, the Godhead and manhood—were joined together in one person, never to be divided, whereof is one Christ, very God and very man, who truly suffered, was crucified, dead and buried, to reconcile his Father to us, and to be a sacrifice, not only for original guilt, but also for the actual sins of men.

III. OF THE RESURRECTION OF CHRIST.

Christ did truly rise again from the dead, and took again his body, with all things appertaining to the perfection of man's nature, wherewith he ascended into heaven, and there sitteth until he return to judge all men at the last day.

IV. OF THE HOLY GHOST.

The Holy Ghost, proceeding from the Father and the Son, is of one substance, majesty, and glory with the Father and the Son, very and eternal God.

VOL. III.—F F F

V. THE SUFFICIENCY OF THE HOLY SCRIPTURES FOR SALVATION.

The Holy Scriptures contain all things necessary to salvation; so that whatsoever is not read therein, nor may be proved thereby, is not to be required of any man that it should be believed as an article of faith, or be thought requisite or necessary to salvation. In the name of the Holy Scripture we do understand those canonical books of the Old and New Testament of whose authority was never any doubt in the Church. The names of the canonical books are—

Genesis, Exodus, Leviticus, Numbers, Deuteronomy, Joshua, Judges, Ruth, The First Book of Samuel, The Second Book of Samuel, The First Book of Kings, The Second Book of Kings, The First Book of Chronicles, The Second Book of Chronicles, The Book of Ezra, The Book of Nehemiah, The Book of Esther, The Book of Job, The Psalms, The Proverbs, Ecclesiastes or the Preacher, Cantica or Songs of Solomon, Four Prophets the greater, Twelve Prophets the less.

All the books of the New Testament, as they are commonly received, we do receive and account canonical.

VI. OF THE OLD TESTAMENT.

The Old Testament is not contrary to the New; for both in the Old and New Testament everlasting life is offered to mankind by Christ, who is the only Mediator between God and man, being both God and man. Wherefore they are not to be heard who feign that the old fathers did look only for transitory promises. Although the law given from God by Moses, as touching ceremonies and rites, doth not bind Christians, nor ought the civil precepts thereof of necessity be received in any commonwealth, yet, notwithstanding, no Christian whatsoever is free from the obedience of the commandments which are called moral.

VII. OF ORIGINAL OR BIRTH SIN.

Original sin standeth not in the following of Adam (as the Pelagians do vainly talk), but it is the corruption of the nature of every man, that naturally is engendered of the offspring of Adam, whereby man is very far gone from original righteousness, and of his own nature inclined to evil, and that continually.

VIII. OF FREE WILL.

The condition of man after the fall of Adam is such that he can not turn and prepare himself, by his own natural strength and works, to faith and calling upon God; wherefore we have no power to do good works, pleasant and acceptable to God, without the grace of God by Christ preventing us, that we may have a good will, and working with us, when we have that good will.

IX. OF THE JUSTIFICATION OF MAN.

We are accounted righteous before God only for the merit of our Lord and Saviour Jesus Christ by faith, and not for our own works or deservings. Wherefore, that we are justified by faith only is a most wholesome doctrine, and very full of comfort.

X. OF GOOD WORKS.

Although good works, which are the fruits of faith, and follow after justification, can not put away our sins, and endure the severity of God's judgments; yet are they pleasing and acceptable to God in Christ, and spring out of a true and lively faith, insomuch that by them a lively faith may be as evidently known as a tree is discerned by its fruit.

XI. OF WORKS OF SUPEREROGATION.

Voluntary works—besides, over, and above God's commandments —which are called works of supererogation, can not be taught without arrogancy and impiety. For by them men do declare that they do not only render unto God as much as they are bound to do, but that they do more for his sake than of bounden duty is required: whereas Christ saith plainly, When ye have done all that is commanded you, say, We are unprofitable servants.

XII. OF SIN AFTER JUSTIFICATION.

Not every sin willingly committed after justification is the sin against the Holy Ghost, and unpardonable. Wherefore, the grant of repentance is not to be denied to such as fall into sin after justification: after we have received the Holy Ghost, we may depart from grace given, and fall into sin, and, by the grace of God, rise again and amend our lives. And therefore they are to be condemned who say they can no more sin as long as they live here; or deny the place of forgiveness to such as truly repent.

XIII. OF THE CHURCH.

The visible Church of Christ is a congregation of faithful men, in which the pure Word of God is preached, and the sacraments duly administered, according to Christ's ordinance, in all those things that of necessity are requisite to the same.

XIV. OF PURGATORY.

The Romish doctrine concerning purgatory, pardon, worshiping, and adoration, as well of images as of relics, and also invocation of saints, is a fond thing, vainly invented, and grounded upon no warrant of Scripture, but repugnant to the Word of God.

XV. OF SPEAKING IN THE CONGREGATION IN SUCH A TONGUE AS THE PEOPLE UNDERSTAND.

It is a thing plainly repugnant to the Word of God, and the custom of the primitive Church, to have public prayer in the Church, or to minister the sacraments, in a tongue not understood by the people.

XVI. OF THE SACRAMENTS.

Sacraments ordained of Christ are not only badges or tokens of Christian men's profession, but rather they are certain signs of grace, and God's good will toward us, by the which he doth work invisibly in us, and doth not only quicken, but also strengthen and confirm our faith in him.

There are two sacraments ordained of Christ our Lord in the Gospel; that is to say, Baptism and the Supper of the Lord.

Those five commonly called sacraments, that is to say, confirmation, penance, orders, matrimony, and extreme unction, are not to be counted for sacraments of the gospel, being such as have partly grown out of the *corrupt* following of the apostles; and partly are states of life allowed in the Scriptures, but yet have not the like nature of Baptism and the Lord's Supper, because they have not any visible sign or ceremony ordained of God.

The sacraments were not ordained of Christ to be gazed upon, or to be carried about, but that we should duly use them. And in such only as worthily receive the same they have a wholesome effect or operation; but they that receive them unworthily purchase to themselves condemnation, as St. Paul saith, 1 Cor. xi. 29.

XVII. OF BAPTISM.

Baptism is not only a sign of profession, and mark of difference, whereby Christians are distinguished from others that are not baptized; but it is also a sign of regeneration, or the new birth. The baptism of young children is to be retained in the Church.

XVIII. OF THE LORD'S SUPPER.

The Supper of the Lord is not only a sign of the love that Christians ought to have among themselves one to another, but rather is a sacrament of our redemption by Christ's death; insomuch that, to such as rightly, worthily, and with faith receive the same, the bread which we break is a partaking of the body of Christ; and likewise the cup of blessing is a partaking of the blood of Christ.

Transubstantiation, or the change of the substance of bread and wine in the Supper of our Lord, can not be proved by Holy Writ, but is repugnant to the plain words of Scripture, overthroweth the nature of a sacrament, and hath given occasion to many superstitions.

The body of Christ is given, taken, and eaten in the Supper only after a heavenly and spiritual manner. And the means whereby the body of Christ is received and eaten in the Supper is faith.

The sacrament of the Lord's Supper was not by Christ's ordinance reserved, carried about, lifted up, or worshiped.

XIX. OF BOTH KINDS.

The cup of the Lord is not to be denied to the lay people; for both the parts of the Lord's Supper, by Christ's ordinance and commandment, ought to be administered to all Christians alike.

XX. OF THE ONE OBLATION OF CHRIST, FINISHED UPON THE CROSS.

The offering of Christ, once made, is that perfect redemption, propitiation, and satisfaction for all the sins of the whole world, both original and actual; and there is none other satisfaction for sin but that alone. Wherefore the sacrifice of masses, in the which it is commonly said that the priest doth offer Christ for the quick and the dead, to have remission of pain or guilt, is a blasphemous fable and dangerous deceit.

XXI. OF THE MARRIAGE OF MINISTERS.

The ministers of Christ are not commanded by God's law either to vow the estate of single life or to abstain from marriage: therefore it is lawful for them, as for all other Christians, to marry at their own discretion, as they shall judge the same to serve best to godliness.

XXII. OF THE RITES AND CEREMONIES OF CHURCHES.

It is not necessary that rites and ceremonies should in all places be the same, or exactly alike; for they have been always different, and may be changed according to the diversity of countries, times, and men's manners, so that nothing be ordained against God's Word. Whosoever, through his private judgment, willingly and purposely doth openly break the rites and ceremonies of the Church to which he belongs, which are not repugnant to the Word of God, and are ordained and approved by common authority, ought to be rebuked openly, that others may fear to do the like, as one that offendeth against the common order of the Church, and woundeth the consciences of weak brethren.

Every particular Church may ordain, change, or abolish rites and ceremonies, so that all things may be done to edification.

XXIII. OF THE RULERS OF THE UNITED STATES OF AMERICA.

The President, the Congress, the General Assemblies, the Governors, and the Councils of State, *as the delegates of the people*, are the rulers of the United States of America, according to the division of power made to them by the Constitution of the United States, and by the Constitutions of their respective States. And the said States are a sovereign and independent nation, and ought not to be subject to any foreign jurisdiction.[1]

---

[1] As far as it respects civil affairs, we believe it the duty of Christians, and especially all Christian ministers, to be subject to the supreme authority of the country where they may reside, and to use all laudable means to enjoin obedience to the powers that be; and therefore it is expected that all our preachers and people who may be under the British or any other government will behave themselves as peaceable and orderly subjects.

XXIV. OF CHRISTIAN MEN'S GOODS.

The riches and goods of Christians are not common, as touching the right, title, and possession of the same, as some do falsely boast. Notwithstanding, every man ought, of such things as he possesseth, liberally to give alms to the poor, according to his ability.

XXV. OF A CHRISTIAN MAN'S OATH.

As we confess that vain and rash swearing is forbidden Christian men by our Lord Jesus Christ and James his apostle, so we judge that the Christian religion doth not prohibit but that a man may swear when the magistrate requireth, in a cause of faith and charity, so it be done according to the prophet's teaching, in justice, judgment, and truth.

ARTICLES OF RELIGION OF THE REFORMED EPISCOPAL CHURCH IN AMERICA. A.D. 1875.

[These Articles were adopted by the third General Council of the REFORMED EPISCOPAL CHURCH in America, held in Chicago, May 18, 1875. They are based on the Thirty-nine Articles of the Protestant Episcopal Church in the United States, from which the Reformed Episcopal Church has sprung under the lead of Bishop CUMMINS (d. June, 1876). See Vol. I., pp. 665 sqq. They resemble Wesley's abridgment of the English Articles, but retain more of the original. The text is taken from the *Minutes of the Third General Council.* It is also published in pamphlet form.]

ARTICLE I.

Of the Holy Trinity.

There is but one living and true God, who is a spirit, everlasting; of infinite power, wisdom, and goodness; the Maker and Preserver of all things, both visible and invisible. And in unity of this Godhead there be three persons, of one substance, power, and eternity: the Father, the Son, and the Holy Ghost.

ARTICLE II.

Of the Word, or Son of God, which was made very man.

The Son, who is the Word of the Father, begotten from everlasting of the Father, the very and eternal God, of one substance with the Father, took man's nature in the womb of the blessed Virgin, of her substance: so that two whole and perfect natures, that is to say, the Godhead and manhood, were joined together in one person, never to be divided, whereof is one Christ, very God and very man; who truly suffered, was crucified, dead and buried, to satisfy Divine justice, and to reconcile us to his Father, and to be a sacrifice, not only for original sin, but also for actual sins of men.

ARTICLE III.

Of the Resurrection of Christ, and his Second Coming.

Christ did truly rise from death, and took again his body, with flesh, bones, and all things appertaining to the perfection of man's nature, wherewith he ascended into heaven, and there sitteth, our High-Priest and Advocate, at the right hand of the Father, whence he will return to judge the world in righteousness. This Second Coming is the blessed hope of the Church. The heavens have received him, till the times of the restitution of all things. To those who look for him he shall appear a second time without sin unto salvation. Then shall he change the body of our humiliation that it may be fashioned like unto his glorious body. He will take to himself his great power, and shall reign till he have put all enemies under his feet.

ARTICLE IV.

Of the Holy Ghost.

The Holy Ghost, proceeding from the Father and the Son, is of one substance, majesty, and glory with the Father and the Son, very and eternal God.

It is the work of the Holy Ghost to reprove and convince the world of sin, and of righteousness, and of judgment; to take of the things of Christ and show them to men; to regenerate—making men willing, leading them to faith in Christ, and forming Christ in them the hope of glory; to strengthen them with might in their inner man, that Christ may dwell in their hearts by faith; and to secure in them that walking in the ways of God which is called the Fruit of the Spirit. The true Church is thus called out of the world, and is builded together for an habitation of God, through the Spirit.

ARTICLE V.

Of the Sufficiency of the Holy Scriptures for Salvation.

All Scripture is given by inspiration of God. Holy men of God spake as they were moved by the Holy Ghost: Holy Scripture is therefore the Word of God; not only does it contain the oracles of God, but it is itself the very oracles of God. And hence it containeth all things necessary to salvation: so that whatsoever is not read therein, nor may be proved thereby, is not to be required of any man, that it should be believed as an article of faith, or be thought requisite or necessary to salvation. In the name of the Holy Scripture we do understand the canonical books of the Old and New Testament, viz.:

Of the Old Testament:

Genesis,	Deuteronomy,	The 1st Book of Samuel,
Exodus,	Joshua,	The 2d Book of Samuel,
Leviticus,	Judges,	The 1st Book of Kings,
Numbers,	Ruth,	The 2d Book of Kings.

The 1st Book of Chronicles,	Song of Solomon,	Obadiah,
The 2d Book of Chronicles,	Isaiah,	Jonah,
The Book of Ezra,	Jeremiah,	Micah,
The Book of Nehemiah,	Lamentations of Jeremiah,	Nahum,
The Book of Esther,	Ezekiel,	Habakkuk,
The Book of Job,	Daniel,	Zephaniah,
The Psalms,	Hosea,	Haggai,
The Proverbs,	Joel,	Zechariah,
Ecclesiastes,	Amos,	Malachi.

Of the New Testament :

Matthew,	Ephesians,	Hebrews,
Mark,	Philippians,	James,
Luke,	Colossians,	1st Peter,
John,	1st Thessalonians,	2d Peter,
Acts of the Apostles,	2d Thessalonians,	1st John,
Romans,	1st Timothy,	2d John,
1st Corinthians,	2d Timothy,	3d John,
2d Corinthians,	Titus,	Jude,
Galatians,	Philemon,	The Revelation.

The Book[1] commonly called "The Apocrypha" is not a portion of God's Word, and is not therefore to be read in churches, nor to be used in establishing any doctrine.

ARTICLE VI.

Of the Old Testament.

The Old Testament is not contrary to the New: for both in the Old and New Testament everlasting life is offered to mankind by Christ, who is the only Mediator between God and man, being both God and Man. Wherefore they are not to be heard, which feign that the old Fathers did look only for transitory promises; and although the Law given from God by Moses, as touching Ceremonies and Rites, does not bind Christian men, nor the civil precepts thereof ought of necessity to be received in any commonwealth, yet notwithstanding, as a rule of right living, no Christian man whatsoever is free from the obedience of the commandments which are called moral.

ARTICLE VII.

Of Original or Birth Sin.

Original sin standeth not in the following of Adam, as the Pelagians do vainly talk; but it is the fault and corruption of the nature of

---

[1] [Books ?]

every man, that naturally is engendered of the offspring of Adam, whereby man is wholly gone from original righteousness, and is of his own nature inclined to evil, so that the flesh lusteth always contrary to the spirit; and therefore in every person born into this world it deserveth God's condemnation. Men are, as the Apostle speaks, 'by nature the children of wrath.' And this infection of nature doth remain—yea, in them that are regenerated. And although there is no condemnation for them that are in Christ Jesus, yet the Apostle doth confess that concupiscence or lust in such hath of itself the nature of sin.

ARTICLE VIII.

Of Man's Condition by Nature.

The condition of man after the fall of Adam is such that he can not turn and prepare himself, by his own natural strength and good works, to faith and calling upon God. Wherefore we have no power to do good works pleasant and acceptable to God without the grace of God by Christ first inclining us, that we may have a good will, and working with us when we have that good will.

ARTICLE IX.

Of Works before Justification.

Works commonly called good before the grace of Christ and the inspiration of his Spirit, have not the nature of obedience to God, forasmuch as they spring not of faith in Jesus Christ, neither do they make men meet to deserve or to receive grace.

ARTICLE X.

Of Regeneration or the New Birth.

Regeneration is the creative act of the Holy Ghost, whereby he imparts to the soul a new spiritual life.

And whosoever believeth in Christ is born again, for, saith the Scripture, 'ye are all the children of God by faith in Christ Jesus.'

ARTICLE XI.

Of Faith.

The faith which brings justification is simply the reliance or dependence on Christ which accepts him as the sacrifice for our sins, and as our righteousness.

We may thus rely on Christ, either tremblingly or confidingly; but in either case it is saving faith. If, though tremblingly, we rely on him in his obedience for us unto death, instantly we come into union with him, and are justified. If, however, we confidingly rely on him, then have we the comfort of our justification. Simply by faith in Christ are we justified and saved.

ARTICLE XII.

Of the Justification of Man.

We are pardoned and accounted righteous before God, only for the merit of our Lord and Saviour Jesus Christ, by faith; and not for our own works or deservings. He who knew no sin was made sin for us, that we might be made the righteousness of God in him. He bare our sins in his own body. It pleased our heavenly Father, of his infinite mercy, without any our desert or deserving, to provide for us the most precious sacrifice of Christ, whereby our ransom might be fully paid, the law fulfilled, and his justice fully satisfied. So that Christ is himself the righteousness of all them that truly do believe in him. He for them paid their ransom, by his death. He for them fulfilled the law, in his life. So that now in him, and by him, every true Christian man may be called a fulfiller of the law. Wherefore, that we are justified by faith only is a most wholesome doctrine, and very full of comfort.

ARTICLE XIII.

Of Repentance.

The repentance required by Scripture is a change of mind toward God, and is the effect of the conviction of sin, wrought by the Holy Ghost.

The unconverted man may have a sense of remorse, or of shame and self-reproach, and yet he may have neither a change of mind toward God nor any true sorrow; but when he accepts Christ as his Saviour, therein he manifests a change of mind, and is in possession of repentance unto life. The sinner comes to Christ through no labored process of repenting and sorrowing; but he comes to Christ and repentance both at once, by means of simply believing. And ever afterwards his repentance is deep and genuine in proportion as his faith is simple and childlike.

ARTICLE XIV.
Of the Sonship of Believers.

Believers in Christ are born of God, through the regenerating power of his Spirit, and are partakers of the Divine nature; for if 'that which is born of the flesh is flesh,' so 'that which is born of the Spirit is spirit.'

And all who are thus born of God are sons of God, and joint heirs with Christ; and therefore, without distinction of name, brethren with Christ and with one another.

ARTICLE XV.
Of Good Works.

Good works, which are the fruits of faith, and follow after justification, are pleasing and acceptable to God in Christ, and do spring out, necessarily, of a true and lively faith; insomuch that by them a lively faith may be as evidently known as a tree discerned by the fruit. They who truly believe will seek to do the will of God, and they who do not thus seek are not to be accounted true believers.

ARTICLE XVI.
Of Works of Supererogation.

Voluntary works, besides, over, and above God's commandments, which they call works of supererogation, can not be taught without arrogancy and impiety. For by them men do declare that they do not only render unto God as much as they are bound to do, but that they do more for his sake than of bounden duty is required. Whereas Christ saith plainly: 'When ye have done all that are commanded to you,[1] say, We are unprofitable servants.'

ARTICLE XVII.
Salvation only in Christ.

Holy Scripture doth set out unto us the name of Jesus Christ only, whereby men must be saved. His was a finished work and completely sufficient. Without any merit or deserving on our part he has secured

---

[1] [The Eng. Vers. reads: 'all those things which are commanded you' (Luke xvii. 10).—Ed.]

to believers in him pardon, acceptance, sonship, sanctification, redemption, and eternal glory. Those who believe in him are in him complete. They are even now justified and have a present salvation; though they may not at all times have the sense of its possession.

ARTICLE XVIII.

Of Election, Predestination, and Free Will.

While the Scriptures distinctly set forth the election, predestination, and calling of the people of God unto eternal life, as Christ saith: 'All that the Father giveth me shall come to me;' they no less positively affirm man's free agency and responsibility, and that salvation is freely offered to all through Christ.

This Church, accordingly, simply affirms these doctrines as the Word of God sets them forth, and submits them to the individual judgment of its members, as taught by the Holy Spirit; strictly charging them that God commandeth all men every where to repent, and that we can be saved only by faith in Jesus Christ.

ARTICLE XIX.

Of Sin after Conversion.

The grant of repentance is not to be denied to such as fall into sin after conversion: that is to say, after, by the quickening into life by the Holy Ghost, they have turned to God by faith in Christ, and have been brought into that change of mind which is repentance unto life. For after we have received the Holy Ghost we may, through unbelief, carelessness, and worldliness, fall into sin, and by the grace of God we may arise again, and amend our lives; but every such fall is a grievous dishonor to our Lord, and a sore injury to ourselves.

ARTICLE XX.

Of Christ alone, without Sin.

Christ, in the truth of our nature, was made like unto us in all things, sin only excepted, from which he was clearly void, both in his flesh, and in his spirit. He came to be the Lamb without spot, who, by sacrifice of himself, made *once forever*, should take away the sin of the world; and sin (as St. John saith) was not in him. But all we the rest, although born again in Christ, yet offend in many things; and if we say we have no sin, we deceive ourselves, and the truth is not in us.

ARTICLE XXI.

Of the Church.

The souls dispersed in all the world, who adhere to Christ by faith, who are partakers of the Holy Ghost, and worship the Father in spirit and in truth, are the body of Christ, the house of God, the flock of the Good Shepherd—the holy, universal Christian Church.

A visible Church of Christ is a congregation of believers in which the pure Word of God is preached and Baptism and the Lord's Supper are duly ministered according to Christ's ordinance, in all those things that of necessity are requisite to the same. And those things are to be considered requisite which the Lord himself did, he himself commanded, and his apostles confirmed.

As the Church of Jerusalem, Alexandria, Antioch,[1] and Rome have erred, so also others have erred and may err, not only in their living and manner of ceremonies, but also in matters of faith.

ARTICLE XXII.

Of the Authority of a Church.

A Church hath power to decree ceremonies and to establish forms of worship and laws for the government and discipline of its members, and to declare its own faith; yet it is not lawful for any Church to ordain or decide any thing that is contrary to God's Word written, neither may it so expound one place of Scripture that it be repugnant to another. And as the Church ought not to decree any thing against the same, so besides the same ought it not to enforce any thing to be believed for necessity of salvation. The Nicene Creed, as set forth in the Prayer-Book of this Church, and that which is commonly called the Apostles' Creed, ought to be received and believed; for they may be proved by Holy Scripture.

---

[1] [As in the Anglican and the Protestant Episcopal Articles, so here Constantinople—the great rival of Rome and chief representative of the Eastern Church—is omitted, no doubt undesignedly; but some Anglo-Catholics, zealous for intercommunion with the Greek Church, derive comfort from the omission.]

ARTICLE XXIII.

Of the Authority of General Councils.

General Councils (forasmuch as they be an assembly of men, whereof all be not governed with the Spirit and Word of God) may err, and sometimes have erred, not only in worldly matters, but also in things pertaining to God. Wherefore things ordained by them as necessary to salvation are not binding, as such, on a Christian man's conscience unless it may be proved that they be taken out of Holy Scripture. No law or authority can override individual responsibility, and therefore the right of private judgment. For the individual Christian, as Christ distinctly affirms, is to be judged by the Word. The only rule of faith is God's Word written.

ARTICLE XXIV.

Of Ministering in the Congregation.

Those who take upon themselves the office of public preaching, or ministering the ordinances in the congregation, should be lawfully called thereunto, and sent to execute the same. And those we ought to judge lawfully called and sent which be moved to this work by the Holy Ghost, and are duly accredited by the Lord's people.

That doctrine of 'Apostolic Succession,' by which it is taught that the ministry of the Christian Church must be derived through a series of uninterrupted ordinations, whether by tactual succession or otherwise, and that without the same there can be no valid ministry, no Christian Church, and no due ministration of Baptism and the Lord's Supper, is wholly rejected as unscriptural and productive of great mischief.

This Church values its historic ministry, but recognizes and honors as equally valid the ministry of other Churches, even as God the Holy Ghost has accompanied their work with demonstration and power.

ARTICLE XXV.

Of the Sacraments.

By the word Sacrament this Church is to be understood as meaning only a symbol or sign divinely appointed.

Our Lord Jesus Christ hath knit together his people in a visible company by sacraments, most few in number, most easy to be kept, most excellent in signification, viz., Baptism and the Lord's Supper.

Those five so-called Sacraments—that is to say, Confirmation, Penance, Orders, Matrimony, and Extreme Unction—are not to be counted for Sacraments of the gospel, being such as have grown partly of the corrupt following of the Apostles, partly are states of life allowed by the Scriptures; but yet have not like nature of Sacraments with Baptism and the Lord's Supper, for that they have not any visible sign or ceremony ordained of God.

And in such only as worthily receive Baptism and the Lord's Supper are they of spiritual benefit, and yet not that of the work wrought (*ex opere operato*), as some men speak. Which word, as it is strange and unknown to Holy Scripture, so it gendereth no godly, but a very superstitious sense. In such as receive them rightly, faith is confirmed and grace increased by virtue of prayer to God. But they that receive them unworthily purchase to themselves judgment, as St. Paul saith; while it is equally true that none, however conscious of unworthiness, are debarred from receiving them, if they are trusting in the Lord Jesus Christ alone for salvation.

ARTICLE XXVI.

Of Baptism.

Baptism represents the death of believers with Christ, and their rising with him to newness of life. It is a sign of profession, whereby they publicly declare their faith in him. It is intended as a sign of regeneration or new birth. They that are baptized are grafted into the visible Church: the promises of the forgiveness of sin and of adoption to be the sons of God by the Holy Ghost are visibly set forth. The baptism of young children is retained in this Church, as agreeable to ancient usage and not contrary to Holy Writ.

ARTICLE XXVII.

Of the Lord's Supper.

The Supper of the Lord is a memorial of our Redemption by Christ's death, for thereby we do show forth the Lord's death till he come. It is also a symbol of the soul's feeding upon Christ. And it is a sign of the communion that we should have with one another.

VOL. III.—G G G

Transubstantiation (or the change of the substance of bread and wine into the very body and blood of Christ) in the Supper of the Lord can not be proved by Holy Writ, is repugnant to the plain words of Scripture, overthroweth the nature of a sacrament, and hath given occasion to many and idolatrous superstitions.

Consubstantiation (or the doctrine that Christ is veiled under the unchanged bread and wine, and that his very body and blood are present therein and separate the one from the other) is utterly without warrant of Scripture, is contradictory of the fact that Christ, being raised, dieth no more, and is productive equally with transubstantiation of idolatrous errors and practices.

We feed on Christ only through his Word, and only by faith and prayer; and we feed on him, whether at our private devotions, or in our meditations, or on any occasion of public worship, or in the memorial symbolism of the Supper.

The elements of the Lord's Supper were not by Christ's ordinance designed to be reserved, carried about, lifted up, or worshiped.

ARTICLE XXVIII.
Of Both Kinds.

The Cup of the Lord is not to be denied to any of his people, for both the bread and the wine, by Christ's ordinance and commandment, ought to be ministered to all Christian men alike.

ARTICLE XXIX.
Of Unworthy Persons Ministering in the Congregation.

Although in the visible Church the evil be ever mingled with the good, and sometimes the evil have chief authority in the ministration of the Word and ordinances: yet, forasmuch as they do not the same in their own name, but in Christ's, the believer is not deprived of the benefits of God's ordinances; because, though they be ministered by evil men, yet are they Christ's institution, and set forth his promise.

Nevertheless, it appertaineth to the discipline of the Church that inquiry be made of evil ministers, and that they be accused by those that have knowledge of their offences: and finally, being found guilty by just judgment, be deposed.

ARTICLE XXX.

Of the one Oblation of Christ finished upon the Cross.

The offering of Christ once made is that perfect redemption, propitiation, and satisfaction for all the sins of the whole world, both original and actual; and there is none other satisfaction for sin but that alone.   And as there is only this one sacrifice in the Christian Church, once made, never to be repeated, so there is but the one Priest, even Jesus Christ, the Apostle and High-Priest of our profession.   Wherefore the sacrifices of masses, in the which it is commonly said that the priest offers Christ for the quick and the dead, for the remission of pain or guilt, or any representations of the Lord's Supper as a sacrifice, are blasphemous fables and dangerous deceits.

ARTICLE XXXI.

Of Certain Erroneous Doctrines and Practices.

The Romish doctrines concerning purgatory, penance, and satisfaction have no support from the Word of God, and are, besides, contradictory of the completeness and sufficiency of the redemption in Christ Jesus, of justification by faith, and of the sanctifying efficacy of God the Holy Ghost.   Praying for the dead is man's tradition, vainly invented, and is in violation of the express warnings of Almighty God to the careless and unconverted.   The adoration of relics and images, and the invocation of saints, besides that they are grounded upon no warranty of Scripture, are idolatrous practices, dishonoring to God, and compromising the mediatorship of Christ.   It is also repugnant to the Word of God to have public prayer in the Church, or to minister the ordinances, in a tongue not understood by the people.

ARTICLE XXXII.

Of Confession and Absolution.

Private confession of sins to a priest, commonly known as Auricular Confession, has no foundation in the Word of God, and is a human invention.   It makes the professed penitent a slave to mere human authority, entangles him in endless scruples and perplexities, and opens the way to many immoralities.

If one sin against his fellow-man, the Scripture requires him to make confession to the offended party; and so if one sin and bring scandal upon the Christian society of which he is a member. And Christians may often, with manifest profit, confess to one another their sins against God, with a view solely to instruction, correction, guidance, and encouragement in righteousness. But in any and every case confession is still to be made to God; for all sins are committed against him, as well such as offend our fellow-man as those that offend him alone.

Priestly absolution is a blasphemous usurpation of the sole prerogative of God. None can forgive sins as against God but God alone.

The blood of Jesus Christ only can cleanse us from our sins, and always we obtain forgiveness directly from God, whenever by faith in that blood we approach him with our confessions and prayers.

ARTICLE XXXIII.

Of the Marriage of Ministers.

Christian ministers are not commanded by God's law either to vow the estate of single life or to abstain from marriage; therefore it is lawful for them, as for all other Christian men, to marry at their own discretion.

ARTICLE XXXIV.

Of the Power of the Civil Authority.

The power of the civil magistrate extendeth to all men, as well ministers as people, in all things temporal; but hath no authority in things purely spiritual. And we hold it to be the duty of all men who are professors of the gospel to pay respectful obedience to the civil authority, regularly and legitimately constituted.

ARTICLE XXXV.

Of Christian Men's Goods.

The riches and goods of Christian men are not common, but their own, to be controlled and used according to their Christian judgment. Every man ought, of such things as he possesseth, liberally to give alms to the poor, according to his ability; and as a steward of God, he should use his means and influence in promoting the cause of truth and righteousness to the glory of God.

THE DOCTRINAL BASIS OF THE EVANGELICAL ALLIANCE. A.D. 1846.

Adopted at the Organization of the American Branch of the Evangelical Alliance, in January, 1867.

[The Nine Articles were adopted by the first meeting of the Evangelical Alliance, in London, 1846, and published in the *Report of the Proceedings of the Conference, held at Freemasons' Hall, London, from Aug. 19th to Sept. 2d, 1846. Published by order of the Conference.* London, 1847.

The preamble, which we print in small type, was added by the American Branch of the Alliance, organized in the Bible House, New York, Jan., 1867, and, with this qualifying preamble, the doctrinal articles were used at the General Conference of the Alliance held in New York, Oct., 1873.

The Evangelical Alliance is no Church, and has no authority to issue and enforce an ecclesiastical creed. It is simply a voluntary association of individual Christians for the promotion of Christian union and religious liberty; but as such it may declare on what doctrinal basis it proposes to labor for its end, and how much or how little of the traditional faith it takes for granted among its members.]

Resolved, That in forming an Evangelical Alliance for the United States, in co-operative union with other Branches of the Alliance, we have no intention or desire to give rise to a new denomination or sect; nor to affect an amalgamation of Churches, except· in the way of facilitating personal Christian intercourse and a mutual good understanding; nor to interfere in any way whatever with the internal affairs of the various denominations; but, simply, to bring individual Christians into closer fellowship and co-operation, on the basis of the spiritual union which already exists in the vital relation of Christ to the members of his body in all ages and countries.

Resolved, That in the same spirit we propose no new creed; but, taking broad, historical, and evangelical catholic ground, we solemnly reaffirm and profess our faith in all the doctrines of the inspired Word of God, and the consensus of doctrines as held by all true Christians from the beginning. And we do more especially affirm our belief in the Divine-human person and atoning work of our Lord and Saviour Jesus Christ, as the only and sufficient source of salvation, as the heart and soul of Christianity, and as the centre of all true Christian union and fellowship.

Resolved, That, with this explanation, and in the spirit of a just Christian liberality in regard to the minor differences of theological schools and religious denominations, we also adopt, as a summary of the consensus of the various Evangelical Confessions of Faith, the Articles and Explanatory Statement set forth and agreed on by the Evangelical Alliance at its formation in London, 1846, and approved by the separate European organizations; which articles are as follows:[1]

'1. The Divine inspiration, authority, and sufficiency of the Holy Scriptures.

'2. The right and duty of private judgment in the interpretation of the Holy Scriptures.

'3. The Unity of the Godhead, and the Trinity of the persons therein.

---

[1] In the original form the Articles are introduced by the following sentence:

'The parties composing the Alliance shall be such persons only as hold and maintain what are usually understood to be evangelical views in regard to the matters of doctrine under-stated, namely—'

'4. The utter depravity of human nature in consequence of the Fall.

'5. The incarnation of the Son of God, his work of atonement for the sins of mankind,[1] and his mediatorial intercession and reign.

'6. The justification of the sinner by faith alone.

'7. The work of the Holy Spirit in the conversion and sanctification of the sinner.

'8. The immortality of the soul, the resurrection of the body, the judgment of the world by our Lord Jesus Christ, with the eternal blessedness of the righteous, and the eternal punishment of the wicked.

'9. The divine institution of the Christian ministry, and the obligation and perpetuity of the ordinances of Baptism and the Lord's Supper.

'It is, however, distinctly declared: First, that this brief summary is not to be regarded in any formal or ecclesiastical sense as a creed or confession, nor the adoption of it as involving an assumption of the right authoritatively to define the limits of Christian brotherhood, but simply as an indication of the class of persons whom it is desirable to embrace within the Alliance; Second, that the selection of certain tenets, with the omission of others, is not to be held as implying that the former constitute the whole body of important truth, or that the latter are unimportant.'

---

[1] The official *Report of Proceedings* (both on pp. 77 and 189) reads 'for *sinners* of mankind,' which is probably a typographical error. All other issues of the Articles in the Alliance publications read *sins*.

APPENDIX:

THE SECOND HELVETIC CONFESSION
IN ENGLISH.

APPENDIX.

ENGLISH VERSION OF

THE SECOND HELVETIC CONFESSION, A.D. 1566.

(Comp. Vol. III. pp. 233–306.)

[In view of the full summary of this important Confession in Vol. I. 396–420, a translation was omitted in the previous editions of Vol. III. But as the volumes are now sold separately, it is herewith added in the third edition. Several c⸺ .:ers are taken, with slight changes, from the old English translation in *The Harmony of Reformed Confessions*, Cambridge, 1586; 2d ed. London, 1643; and again, ibid. 1842. The division of chapters into sections is conformed to the Latin text, pp. 233–306.]

CHAPTER I.—OF THE HOLY SCRIPTURE BEING THE TRUE WORD OF GOD.

We believe and confess the Canonical Scriptures of the holy prophets and apostles of both Testaments to be the true Word of God, and to have sufficient authority of themselves, not of men. For God himself spake to the fathers, prophets, apostles, and still speaks to us through the Holy Scriptures.

And in this Holy Scripture, the universal Church of Christ has all things fully expounded which belong to a saving faith, and also to the framing of a life acceptable to God; and in this respect it is expressly commanded of God that nothing be either put to or taken from the same (Deut. iv. 2; Rev. xxii. 18, 19).

We judge, therefore, that from these Scriptures are to be taken true wisdom and godliness, the reformation and government of churches; as also instruction in all duties of piety; and, to be short, the confirmation of doctrines, and the confutation of all errors, with all exhortations; according to that word of the Apostle, 'All Scripture given by inspiration of God is profitable for doctrine, for reproof,' etc. (2 Tim. iii. 16, 17). Again, 'These things write I unto thee,' says the Apostle to Timothy, 'that thou mayest know how thou oughtest to behave thyself in the house of God,' etc. (1 Tim. iii. 14, 15). Again, the selfsame Apostle to the Thessalonians: 'When,' says he, 'ye received the word of us, ye received not the word of men, but as it was indeed, the Word of God,' etc. (1 Thess. ii. 13). For the Lord himself has said in the Gospel, 'It is not ye that speak, but the Spirit of my Father speaketh in you;' therefore 'he that heareth you, heareth me; and he that despiseth you, despiseth me' (Matt. x. 20; Luke x. 16; John xiii. 20).

Wherefore when this Word of God is now preached in the church by preachers lawfully called, we believe that the very Word of God is preached, and received of the faithful; and that neither any other Word of God is to be feigned, nor to be expected from heaven: and that now the Word itself which is preached is to be regarded, not the minister that preaches; who, although he be evil and a sinner, nevertheless the Word of God abides true and good.

Neither do we think that therefore the outward preaching is to be thought as fruitless because the instruction in true religion depends on the inward illumination of the Spirit, or because it is written 'No man shall teach his neighbor; for all men shall know me' (Jer. xxxi. 34), and 'He that watereth, or he that planteth, is nothing, but God that giveth the increase' (1 Cor. iii. 7). For albeit 'No man can come to Christ, unless he be drawn by the Heavenly Father' (John vi. 44), and be inwardly lightened by the Holy Spirit, yet we know un- doubtedly that it is the will of God that his word should be preached even outwardly. God could indeed, by his Holy Spirit, or by the min- istry of an angel, without the ministry of St. Peter, have taught Corne- lius in the Acts; but, nevertheless, he refers him to Peter, of whom the angel speaking says, 'He shall tell thee what thou oughtest to do' (Acts x. 6).

For he that illuminates inwardly by giving men the Holy Spirit, the self-same, by way of commandment, said unto his disciples, 'Go ye into all the world, and preach the Gospel to every creature' (Mark xvi. 15). And so Paul preached the Word outwardly to Lydia, a purple- seller among the Philippians; but the Lord inwardly opened the wom- an's heart (Acts xvi. 14). And the same Paul, upon an elegant grada- tion fitly placed in the tenth chapter to the Romans, at last infers, 'Therefore faith cometh by hearing, and hearing by the Word of God' (Rom. x. 14–17).

We know, in the mean time, that God can illuminate whom and when he will, even without the external ministry, which is a thing appertaining to his power; but we speak of the usual way of instructing men, delivered unto us from God, both by commandment and examples.

We therefore detest all the heresies of Artemon, the Manichæans, the Valentinians, of Cerdon, and the Marcionites, who denied that the Scriptures proceeded from the Holy Spirit; or else received not, or interpolated and corrupted, some of them.

And yet we do not deny that certain books of the Old Testament were by the ancient authors called *Apocryphal*, and by others *Ecclesiastical;* to wit, such as they would have to be read in the churches, but not alleged to avouch or confirm the authority of faith by them. As also Augustine, in his *De Civitate Dei*, book xviii., chapter 38, makes mention that 'in the books of the Kings, the names and books of certain prophets are reckoned;' but he adds that 'they are not in the canon,' and that 'those books which we have suffice unto godliness.'

CHAPTER II.—OF INTERPRETING THE HOLY SCRIPTURES; AND OF FATHERS, COUNCILS, AND TRADITIONS.

The Apostle Peter has said that 'the Holy Scriptures are not of any private interpretation' (2 Pet. i. 20). Therefore we do not allow all kinds of exposition. Whereupon we do not acknowledge that which they call the meaning of the Church of Rome for the true and natural interpretation of the Scriptures; which, forsooth, the defenders of the Romish Church do strive to force all men simply to receive; but we acknowledge only that interpretation of Scriptures for orthodox and genuine which, being taken from the Scriptures themselves (that is, from the spirit of that tongue in which they were written, they being also weighed according to the circumstances and expounded according to the proportion of places, either of like or of unlike, also of more and plainer), accords with the rule of faith and charity, and makes notably for God's glory and man's salvation.

Wherefore we do not despise the interpretations of the holy Greek and Latin fathers, nor reject their disputations and treatises as far as they agree with the Scriptures; but we do modestly dissent from them when they are found to set down things differing from, or altogether contrary to, the Scriptures. Neither do we think that we do them any wrong in this matter; seeing that they all, with one consent, will not have their writings matched with the Canonical Scriptures, but bid us allow of them so far forth as they either agree with them or disagree.

And in the same order we also place the decrees and canons of councils.

Wherefore we suffer not ourselves, in controversies about religion or matters of faith, to be pressed with the bare testimonies of fathers or decrees of councils; much less with received customs, or with the multitude of men being of one judgment, or with prescription of long time. Therefore, in controversies of religion or matters of faith, we can not admit any other judge than God himself, pronouncing by the Holy Scriptures what is true, what is false, what is to be followed, or what to be avoided. So we do not rest but in the judgment of spiritual men, drawn from the Word of God. Certainly Jeremiah and other prophets did vehemently condemn the assemblies of priests gathered against the law of God; and diligently forewarned us that we should not hear the fathers, or tread in their path who, walking in their own inventions, swerved from the law of God (Ezek. xx. 18).

We do likewise reject human traditions, which, although they be set out with goodly titles, as though they were divine and apostolical, delivered to the Church by the lively voice of the apostles, and, as it were, by the hands of apostolical men, by means of bishops succeeding in their room, yet, being compared with the Scriptures, disagree with them; and that by their disagreement bewray themselves in no wise to be apostolical. For as the apostles did not disagree among themselves in doctrine, so the apostles' scholars did not set forth things contrary to the apostles. Nay, it were blasphemous to avouch that the apostles, by lively voice, delivered things contrary to their writings. Paul affirms expressly that he taught the same things in all churches (1 Cor. iv. 17). And, again, 'We,' says he, 'write none other things unto you than what ye read or acknowledge' (2 Cor. i. 13). Also, in another place, he witnesses that he and his disciples—to wit, apostolic men—walked in the same way, and jointly by the same Spirit did all things (2 Cor. xii. 18). The Jews also, in time past, had their traditions of elders; but these traditions were severely confuted by the Lord, showing that the keeping of them hinders God's law, and that God is in vain worshiped of such (Matt. xv. 8, 9; Mark vii. 6, 7).

CHAPTER III.—OF GOD; THE UNITY AND THE TRINITY.

We believe and teach that God is one in essence or nature, subsisting by himself, all-sufficient in himself, invisible, without a body, infinite, eternal, the Creator of all things both visible and invisible, the chief good, living, quickening and preserving all things, almighty and supremely wise, gentle or merciful, just and true.

And we detest the multitude of gods, because it is expressly written, 'The Lord thy God is one God' (Deut. vi. 4). 'I am the Lord thy God; thou shalt have no strange gods before my face' (Exod. xx. 2, 3). 'I am the Lord, and there is none other; beside me there is no God. Am not I the Lord, and there is none other beside me alone? a just God, and a Saviour; there is none beside me' (Isa. xlv. 5, 21). 'I the Lord, Jehovah, the merciful God, gracious and long-suffering, and abundant in goodness and truth,' etc. (Exod. xxxiv. 6).

We nevertheless believe and teach that the same infinite, one, and indivisible God is in person inseparably and without confusion distinguished into the Father, the Son, and the Holy Spirit: so, as the Father has begotten the Son from eternity, the Son is begotten in an unspeakable manner; and the Holy Spirit proceeds from them both, and that from eternity, and is to be worshiped with them both. So that there are not three Gods, but three persons, consubstantial, coeternal, and coequal; distinct, as touching their persons; and, in order, one going before another, yet without any inequality. For, as touching their nature or essence, they are so joined together that they are but one God; and the divine essence is common to the Father, the Son, and the Holy Spirit.[1]

For the Scripture has delivered unto us a manifest distinction of persons; the angel, among other things, saying thus to the Blessed Virgin, 'The Holy Spirit shall come upon thee, and the power of the Highest shall overshadow thee; and that holy thing which shall be born shall be called the Son of God' (Luke i. 35). Also, in the baptism of Christ, a voice was heard from heaven, saying, 'This is my beloved

---

[1] Lest any man should slander us, as though we did make the persons all existing together, but not all of the same essence, or else did make a God of divers natures joined together in one, you must understand this joining together so as that all the persons (though distinct one from the other in properties) be yet but one and the same whole Godhead, or so that all and every of the persons have the whole and absolute Godhead.

Son' (Matt. iii. 17). The Holy Spirit also appeared in the likeness of a dove (John i. 32). And when the Lord himself commanded to baptize, he commanded to baptize 'in the name of the Father, and of the Son, and of the Holy Spirit' (Matt. xxviii. 19). In like manner, elsewhere in the Gospel he said, 'The Father will send the Holy Spirit in my name' (John xiv. 26). Again he says, 'When the Comforter shall come, whom I will send unto you from the Father, the Spirit of Truth, who proceedeth from the Father, he shall bear witness of me,' etc. (John xv. 26). In short, we receive the Apostles' Creed, because it delivers unto us the true faith.

We therefore condemn the Jews and the Mohammedans, and all those who blaspheme that sacred and adorable Trinity. We also condemn all heresies and heretics who teach that the Son and the Holy Spirit are God only in name; also, that there is in the Trinity something created, and that serves and ministers unto another; finally, that there is in it something unequal, greater or less, corporeal or corporeally fashioned, in manners or in will diverse, either confounded or sole by itself: as if the Son and Holy Spirit were the affections and proprieties of one God the Father—as the Monarchists, the Novatians, Praxeas, the Patripassians, Sabellius, Samosatenus, Aëtius, Macedonius, the Anthropomorphites, Arius, and such like, have thought.

CHAPTER IV. — OF IDOLS; OR OF IMAGES OF GOD, OF CHRIST, AND OF SAINTS.

And because God is an invisible Spirit, and an incomprehensible Essence, he can not, therefore, by any art or image be expressed. For which cause we fear not, with the Scripture, to term the images of God mere lies.

We do therefore reject not only the idols of the Gentiles, but also the images of Christians. For although Christ took upon him man's nature, yet he did not therefore take it that he might set forth a pattern for carvers and painters. He denied that he came 'to destroy the law and the prophets' (Matt. v. 17), but images are forbidden in the law and the prophets (Deut. iv. 15; Isa. xliv. 9). He denied that his bodily presence would profit the Church, but promised that he would by his Spirit be present with us forever (John xvi. 7; 2 Cor. v. 5).

Who would, then, believe that the shadow or picture of his body doth any whit benefit the godly? And seeing that he abideth in us by the Spirit, 'we are therefore the temples of God' (1 Cor. iii. 16); but 'what agreement hath the temple of God with idols?' (2 Cor. vi. 16). And seeing that the blessed spirits and saints in heaven, while they lived here, abhorred all worship done unto themselves (Acts iii. 12, and xiv. 15; Rev. xix. 10, and xxii. 9), and spake against images, who can think it likely that the saints in heaven, and the angels, are delighted with their own images, whereunto men do bow their knees, uncover their heads, and give such other like honor?

But that men might be instructed in religion, and put in mind of heavenly things and of their own salvation, the Lord commanded to preach the Gospel (Mark xvi. 15)—not to paint and instruct the laity by pictures; he also instituted sacraments, but he nowhere appointed images.

Furthermore, in every place which way soever we turn our eyes, we may see the lively and true creatures of God, which if they be marked, as is meet, they do much more effectually move the beholder than all the images or vain, unmovable, rotten, and dead pictures of all men whatsoever; of which the prophet spake truly, 'They have eyes, and see not,' etc. (Psa. cxv. 5).

Therefore we approve the judgment of Lactantius, an ancient writer, who says, 'Undoubtedly there is no religion where there is a picture.' And we affirm that the blessed bishop Epiphanius did well, who, finding on the church-doors a veil, that had painted on it the picture, as it might be, of Christ or some saint or other, he cut and took it away; for that, contrary to the authority of the Scriptures, he had seen the picture of a man to hang in the Church of Christ: and therefore he charged that from henceforth no such veils, which were contrary to religion, should be hung up in the Church of Christ, but that rather such scruple should be taken away which was unworthy of the Church of Christ and all faithful people. Moreover, we approve this sentence of St. Augustine, 'Let not the worship of men's works be a religion unto us; for the workmen themselves that make such things are better, whom yet we ought not to worship' (*De Vera Religione*, cap. 55).

CHAPTER V. — OF THE ADORATION, WORSHIP, AND INVOCATION OF GOD THROUGH THE ONLY MEDIATOR JESUS CHRIST.

We teach to adore and worship the true God alone. This honor we impart to none, according to the commandment of the Lord, 'Thou shalt adore the Lord thy God, and him alone shalt thou worship,' or 'him only shalt thou serve' (Matt. iv. 10). Surely all the prophets inveighed earnestly against the people of Israel whensoever they did adore and worship strange gods, and not the only true God.

But we teach that 'God is to be adored and worshiped,' as himself has taught us to worship him—to wit, 'in spirit and in truth' (John iv. 24); not with any superstition, but with sincerity, according to his word, lest at any time he also say unto us, 'Who hath required these things at your hands?' (Isa. i. 12; Jer. vi. 20). For Paul also says, 'God is not worshiped with men's hands, as though he needed any thing,' etc. (Acts xvii. 25).

We, in all dangers and casualties of life, call on him alone, and that by the mediation of the only Mediator, and our Intercessor, Jesus Christ. For it is expressly commanded us, 'Call upon me in the day of trouble: I will deliver thee, and thou shalt glorify me' (Psa. l. 15). Moreover, the Lord has made a most large promise, saying, 'Whatsoever ye shall ask of my Father, he shall give it you' (John xvi. 23); and again, 'Come unto me, all ye that labor and are heavy laden, and I will give you rest' (Matt. xi. 28). And seeing it is written, 'How shall they call upon him in whom they have not believed?' (Rom. x. 14), and we do believe in God alone; therefore we call upon him only, and that through Christ. For 'there is one God,' says the apostle, 'and one mediator between God and men, Christ Jesus' (1 Tim. ii. 5). Again, 'If any man sin, we have an advocate with the Father, Jesus Christ the righteous,' etc. (1 John ii. 1).

Therefore we do neither adore, worship, nor pray unto the saints in heaven, or to other gods; neither do we acknowledge them for our intercessors or mediators before the Father in heaven. For God and the mediator Christ do suffice us; neither do we impart unto others the honor due to God alone and to his Son, because he has plainly said, 'I will not give my glory to another' (Isa. xli. 8); and because Peter has said, 'There is no other name given unto men, whereby they must be saved, but the name of Christ' (Acts iv. 12). Those, doubtless, who rest in him by faith do not seek any thing without Christ.

Yet, for all that, we do neither despise the saints nor think basely of them; for we acknowledge them to be the lively members of Christ, the friends of God, who have gloriously overcome the flesh and the world. We therefore love them as brethren, and honor them also; yet not with any worship, but with an honorable opinion of them, and with just praises of them. We also do imitate the saints, for we desire, with the most earnest affections and prayers, to be followers of their faith and virtues; to be partakers, also, with them of everlasting salvation; to dwell together with them everlastingly with God, and to rejoice with them in Christ. And in this point we approve that saying of St. Augustine, in his book *De Vera Religione*, 'Let not the worship of men departed be any religion unto us; for, if they have lived holily, they are not so to be esteemed as that they seek such honors, but they will have us to worship Him by whose illumination they rejoice that we are fellow-servants as touching the reward. They are therefore to be honored for imitation, not to be worshiped for religion's sake,' etc.

And we much less believe that the relics of saints are to be adored and worshiped. Those ancient holy men seemed sufficiently to have honored their dead if they had honestly committed their bodies to the earth after the soul was gone up into heaven; and they thought that the most noble relics of their ancestors were their virtues, doctrine, and faith; which as they commended with the praise of the dead, so they did endeavor to express the same so long as they lived upon earth.

Those ancient men did not swear but by the name of the only Jehovah, as it is commanded by the law of God. Therefore, as we are forbidden to 'swear by the name of strange gods' (Exod. xxiii. 13; Josh xxiii. 7), so we do not swear by saints, although we be requested there unto. We therefore in all these things do reject that doctrine which gives too much honor unto the saints in heaven.

CHAPTER VI.—OF THE PROVIDENCE OF GOD.

We believe that all things, both in heaven and in earth and in all creatures, are sustained and governed by the providence of this wise, eternal, and omnipotent God. For David witnesses and says, 'The Lord is high above all nations, and his glory above the heavens. Who is like unto the Lord, who dwelleth on high, and yet humbleth himself to behold the things that are in heaven and earth?' (Psa. cxiii. 4–6). Again, he says, 'Thou hast foreseen all my ways; for there is not a word in my tongue which thou knowest not wholly, O Lord,' etc. (Psa. cxxxix. 3, 4). Paul also witnesses and says, 'By him we live, move, and have our being' (Acts xvii. 28); and 'of him, and through him, and from him are all things' (Rom. xi. 36).

Therefore Augustine both truly and according to the Scripture said, in his book *De Agone Christi,* cap. 8, 'The Lord said, "Are not two sparrows sold for a farthing? and one of them shall not fall to the ground without the will of your Father." By speaking thus he would give us to understand whatsoever men count most vile, that also is governed by the almighty power of God. For the truth, which said that all the hairs of our head are numbered, says also that the birds of the air are fed by him, and the lilies of the field are clothed by him.'

We therefore condemn the Epicureans, who deny the providence of God, and all those who blasphemously affirm that God is occupied about the poles of heaven, and that he neither sees nor regards us or our affairs. The princely prophet David also condemned these men when he said, 'O Lord, how long shall the wicked, how long shall the wicked triumph? They say the Lord doth not see, neither doth the God of Jacob regard it. Understand, ye unwise among the people; and ye fools, when will ye be wise? He that planted the ear, shall he not hear? and he that hath formed the eye, shall he not see?' (Psa. xciv. 3, 7–9).

Notwithstanding, we do not condemn the means whereby the providence of God works as though they were unprofitable; but we teach that we must apply ourselves unto them, so far as they are commended unto us in the Word of God. Wherefore we dislike the rash speeches of such as say that if all things are governed by the providence of God, then all our studies and endeavors are unprofitable; it shall be sufficient if we leave or permit all things to be governed by the providence of God; and we shall not need hereafter to behave or act with carefulness in any matter. For though Paul did confess that he did sail by the providence of God, who had said to him, 'Thou must testify of me also at Rome' (Acts xxiii. 11); who, moreover, promised and said, 'There shall not so much as one soul perish, neither shall a hair fall from your heads' (Acts xxvii. 22, 34); yet, the mariners devising how they might find a way to escape, the same Paul says to the centurion and to the soldiers, 'Unless these remain in the ship, ye can not be safe' (Acts xxvii. 31). For God, who has appointed every thing his end, he also has ordained the beginning and the means by which we must attain unto the end. The heathens ascribe things to blind fortune and uncertain chance; but St. James would not have us say, 'To-day or to-morrow we will go into such a city, and there buy and sell;' but he adds, 'For that which ye should say, If the Lord will, and if we live, we will do this or that' (James iv. 13, 15). And Augustine says, 'All those things which seem to vain men to be done advisedly in the world, they do but accomplish his word because they are not done by his commandment. And, in his exposition of the 148th Psalm, 'It seemed to be done by chance that Saul, seeking his father's asses, should light on the prophet Samuel;' but the Lord had before said to the prophet, 'To-morrow I will send unto thee a man of the tribe of Benjamin,' etc. (1 Sam. ix. 16).

CHAPTER VII.—OF THE CREATION OF ALL THINGS; OF ANGELS, THE DEVIL, AND MAN.

This good and almighty God created all things, both visible and invisible, by his eternal Word, and preserves the same also by his eternal Spirit: as David witnesses, saying, 'By the word of the Lord were the heavens made, and all the host of them by the breath of his mouth' (Psa. xxxiii. 6); and, as the Scripture says, 'All things that the Lord created were very good' (Gen. i. 31), and made for the use and profit of man.

Now, we say, that all those things do proceed from one beginning: and therefore we detest the Manichees and the Marcionites, who did wickedly imagine two substances and natures, the one of good, the other of evil; and also two beginnings and two gods, one contrary to the other—a good and an evil.

Among all the creatures, the angels and men are most excellent. Touching angels, the Holy Scripture says, 'Who maketh his angels spirits, his ministers a flaming fire' (Psa. civ. 4); also, 'Are they not all ministering spirits sent forth to minister for them who shall be heirs of salvation?' (Heb. i. 14).

And the Lord Jesus himself testifies of the devil, saying, 'He that hath been a murderer from the beginning, and abode not in the truth, because there is no truth in him. When he speaketh a lie, he speaketh of his own: for he is a liar and the father of lies' (John viii. 44).

We teach, therefore, that some angels persisted in obedience, and were appointed unto the faithful service of God and men; and that others fell of their own accord, and ran headlong into destruction, and so became enemies to all good, and to all the faithful, etc.

Now, touching man, the Spirit says that in the beginning he was 'created according to the image and likeness of God' (Gen. i. 27); that God placed him in paradise, and made all things subject unto him; which David doth most nobly set forth in the 8th Psalm. Moreover, God gave unto him a wife, and blessed them.

We say, also, that man doth consist of two, and those divers substances in one person; of a soul immortal (as that which being separated from his body doth neither sleep nor die), and a body mortal, which, notwithstanding, at the last judgment shall be raised again from the dead, that from henceforth the whole man may continue forever in life or in death.

We condemn all those who mock at, or by subtle disputations call into doubt, the immortality of the soul, or say that the soul sleeps, or that it is a part of God. To be short, we condemn all opinions of all men whatsoever who think otherwise of the creation of angels, devils, and men than is delivered unto us by the Scriptures in the Apostolic Church of Christ.

CHAPTER VIII.—OF MAN'S FALL; SIN, AND THE CAUSE OF SIN.

Man was from the beginning created of God after the image of God, in righteousness and true holiness, good and upright; but by the instigation of the serpent and his own fault, falling from the goodness and uprightness, he became subject to sin, death, and divers calamities; and such a one as he became by his fall, such are all his offspring, even subject to sin, death, and sundry calamities.

And we take sin to be that natural corruption of man, derived or spread from our first parents unto us all, through which we, be ing drowned in evil concupiscence, and clean turned away from God, but prone to all evil, full of all wickedness, distrust, contempt, and hatred of God, can do no good of ourselves—no, not so much as think any (Matt. xii. 34, 35).

And, what is more, even as we do grow in years, so by wicked thoughts, words, and deeds, committed against the law of God, we bring forth corrupt fruits, worthy of an evil tree: in which respect we, through our own desert, being subject to the wrath of God, are in danger of just punishment; so that we had all been cast away from God, had not Christ, the Deliverer, brought us back again.

By death, therefore, we understand not only bodily death, which is once to be suffered of us all for our sins, but also everlasting punishments due to our corruption and to our sins. For the Apostle says, ' We were dead in trespasses and sins, and were by nature the children of wrath, even as others; but God, who is rich in mercy, even when we were dead in sins, quickened us together with Christ' (Eph. ii. 1–5). Again, ' As by one man sin entered into the world, and by sin, death, and so death passed upon all men, forasmuch as all men have sinned,' etc. (Rom. v. 12).

We therefore acknowledge that original sin is in all men; we acknowledge that all other sins which spring therefrom are both called and are indeed sins, by what name soever they may be termed, whether mortal or venial, or also that which is called sin against the Holy Spirit, which is never forgiven.

We also confess that sins are not equal (John v. 16, 17), although they spring from the same fountain of corruption and unbelief, but that some are more grievous than others (Mark iii. 28, 29); even as the Lord has said, ' It shall be easier for Sodom' than for the city that despises the word of the Gospel (Matt. x. 15). We therefore condemn all those that have taught things contrary to these; but especially Pelagius, and all the Pelagians, together with the Jovinianists, who, with the Stoics, count all sins equal. We in this matter agree fully with St. Augustine, who produced and maintained his sayings out of the Holy Scriptures. Moreover, we condemn Florinus and Blastus (against whom also Irenæus wrote), and all those who make God the author of sin; seeing it expressly written, ' Thou art not a God that loveth wickedness; thou hatest all them that work iniquity, and wilt destroy all that speak leasing' (Psa. v. 4-6). And, again, 'When the devil speaketh a lie, he speaketh of his own; because he is a liar, and the father of lies' (John viii. 44). Yea, there are even in ourselves sin and corruption enough, so that there is no need that God should infuse into us either a new or greater measure of wickedness.

Therefore, when God is said in the Scripture to harden (Exod. vii. 13), to blind (John xii. 40), and to deliver us up into a reprobate sense (Rom. i. 28), it is to be understood that God does it by just judgment, as a just judge and revenger. To conclude, as often as God in the Scripture is said and seems to do some evil, it is not thereby meant that man does not commit evil, but that God does suffer it to be done, and does not hinder it; and that by his just judgment, who could hinder it if he would: or because he makes good use of the evil of men, as he did in the sin of Joseph's brethren; or because himself rules sins, that they break not out and rage more violently than is meet. St. Augustine, in his *Enchiridion*, says, 'After a wonderful and unspeakable manner, that is not done beside his will which is done contrary to his will; because it could not be done if he should not suffer it to be done; and yet he doth not suffer it to be done unwillingly; neither would he, being God, suffer any evil to be done, unless, being also almighty, he could make good of evil.' Thus far Augustine.

Other questions, as whether God would have Adam fall, or whether he forced him to fall, or why he did not hinder his fall, and such like, we account among curious questions (unless perchance the frowardness of heretics, or of men otherwise importunate, do compel us to open these points also out of the Word of God, as the godly doctors of the Church have oftentimes·done); knowing that the Lord did forbid that man should eat of the forbidden fruit, and punished his transgression; and also that the things done are not evil in respect of the providence, will, and power of God, but in respect of Satan, and our will resisting the will of God.

CHAPTER IX.—OF FREE-WILL, AND SO OF MAN'S POWER AND ABILITY.

We teach in this matter, which at all times has been the cause of many conflicts in the Church, that there is a triple condition or estate of man to be considered. First, what man was before his fall—to wit, upright and free, who might both continue in goodness and decline to evil; but he declined to evil, and has wrapped both himself and all mankind in sin and death, as has been shown before.

Secondly, we are to consider what man was after his fall. His understanding, indeed, was not taken from him, neither was he deprived of his will, and altogether changed into a stone or stock. Nevertheless, these things are so altered in man that they are not able to do that now which they could do before his fall. For his understanding is darkened, and his will, which before was free, is now become a servile will; for it serveth sin, not nilling, but willing—for it is called a will, and not a nill. Therefore, as touching evil or sin, man does evil, not compelled either by God or the devil, but of his own accord; and in this respect he has a most free will. But whereas we see that oftentimes the most evil deeds and counsels of man are hindered by God, that they can not attain their end, this does not take from man liberty in evil, but God by his power does prevent that which man otherwise purposed freely: as Joseph's brethren did freely purpose to slay Joseph; but they were not able to do it, because it seemed otherwise good to God in his secret counsel.

But, as touching goodness and virtues, man's understanding does not of itself judge aright of heavenly things. For the evangelical and apostolical Scripture requires regeneration of every one of us that will be saved. Wherefore our first birth by Adam does nothing profit us to salvation. Paul says, 'The natural man receiveth not the things of the Spirit,' etc. (1 Cor. ii. 14). The same Paul elsewhere denies that we are 'sufficient of ourselves to think any thing as of ourselves' (2 Cor. iii. 5).

Now, it is evident that the mind or understanding is the guide of the will; and, seeing the guide is blind, it is easy to be seen how far the will can reach. Therefore man, not as yet regenerate, has no free-will to good, no strength to perform that which is good. The Lord says in the Gospel, 'Verily, verily, I say unto you, whosoever committeth sin is the servant of sin' (John viii. 34). And Paul the Apostle says, 'The carnal mind is enmity against God; for it is not subject to the law of God, neither indeed can be' (Rom. viii. 7).

Furthermore, there is some understanding of earthly things remaining in man after his fall. For God has of mercy left him wit, though much differing from that which was in him before his fall. God commands us to garnish our wit, and therewithal he gives gifts and also the increase thereof. And it is a clear case that we can profit very little in all arts without the blessing of God. The Scripture, no doubt, refers all arts to God; yea, and the Gentiles also ascribe the beginnings of arts to the gods, as the authors thereof.

Lastly, we are to consider whether the regenerate have free-will, and how far they have it. In regeneration the understanding is illuminated by the Holy Spirit, that it may understand both the mysteries and will of God. And the will itself is not only changed by the Spirit, but it is also endued with faculties, that, of its own accord, it may both will and do good (Rom. viii. 4). Unless we grant this, we shall deny Christian liberty, and bring in the bondage of the law. Besides, the prophet brings in God speaking thus: 'I will put my laws into their minds, and write them in their hearts' (Jer. xxxi. 33; Ezek. xxxvi. 27). The Lord also says in the Gospel, 'If the Son make you free, ye shall be free indeed' (John viii. 36). Paul also to the Philippians, 'Unto you is given for Christ, not only to believe in him, but also to suffer for his sake' (Phil. i. 29). And, again, 'I am persuaded that he that began this good work in you will perform it until the day of Jesus Christ' (ver. 6). Also, 'It is God that worketh in you the will and the deed' (Phil. ii. 13).

Where, nevertheless, we teach that there are two things to be observed—first, that the regenerate, in the choice and working of that which is good, do not only work passively, but actively; for they are moved of God that themselves may do that which they do. And Augustine does truly allege that saying that 'God is said to be our helper; but no man can be helped but he that does somewhat.' The Manichæans did bereave man of all action, and made him like a stone and a block.

Secondly, that in the regenerate there remains infirmity. For, seeing that sin dwells in us, and that the flesh in the regenerate strives against the Spirit, even to our lives' end, they do not readily perform in every point that which they had purposed. These things are confirmed by the apostle (Rom. vii. 13–25; Gal. v. 17).

Therefore, all free-will is weak by reason of the relics of the old Adam remaining in us so long as we live, and of the human corruption which so nearly cleaves to us. In the meanwhile, because the strength of the flesh and the relics of the old man are not of such great force that they can wholly quench the work of the Spirit, therefore the faithful are called free, yet so that they do acknowledge their infirmity, and glory no whit at all of their free-will. For that which St. Augustine does repeat so often out of the apostle ought always to be kept in mind by the faithful: 'What hast thou that thou didst not receive? and if thou didst receive it, why dost thou glory, as if thou hadst not received it?' (1 Cor. iv. 7). Hitherto may be added that that comes not straightway to pass which we have purposed, for the events of things are in the hand of God. For which cause Paul besought the Lord that he would prosper his journey (Rom. i. 10). Wherefore, in this respect also, free-will is very weak.

But in outward things no man denies but that both the regenerate and the unregenerate have their free-will; for man hath this constitution common with other creatures (to whom he is not inferior) to will some things and to nill other things. So he may speak or keep silence, go out of his house or abide within. Although herein also God's power is evermore to be marked, which brought to pass that Balaam could not go so far as he would (Numb. xxiv. 13), and that Zacharias, coming out of the Temple, could not speak as he would have done (Luke i. 22).

In this matter we condemn the Manichæans, who deny that the beginning of evil unto man, being good, came from his free-will. We condemn, also, the Pelagians, who affirm that an evil man has free-will sufficiently to perform a good precept. Both these are confuted by the Scripture, which says to the former, 'God made man upright' (Eccles. vii. 29); and to the latter, 'If the Son make you free, then ye shall be free indeed' (John viii. 36).

CHAPTER X.—OF THE PREDESTINATION OF GOD AND THE ELECTION OF THE SAINTS.

God has from the beginning freely, and of his mere grace, without any respect of men, predestinated or elected the saints, whom he will save in Christ, according to the saying of the apostle, 'And he hath chosen us in him before the foundation of the world' (Eph. i. 4); and again, 'Who hath saved us, and called us with an holy calling, not according to our works, but according to his own purpose and grace, which was given unto us, through Jesus Christ, before the world was, but is now made manifest by the appearance of our Saviour Jesus Christ' (2 Tim. i. 9, 10).

Therefore, though not for any merit of ours, yet not without a means, but in Christ, and for Christ, did God choose us; and they who are now ingrafted into Christ by faith, the same also were elected. But such as are without Christ were rejected, according to the saying of the apostle, 'Prove yourselves, whether ye be in the faith. Know ye not your own selves, how that Jesus Christ is in you, except ye be reprobates?' (2 Cor. xiii. 5).

To conclude, the saints are chosen in Christ by God unto a sure end, which end the apostle declares when he says, 'He hath chosen us in him, that we should be holy and without blame before him through love; who has predestinated us to be adopted through Jesus Christ unto himself, for the praise of his glorious grace' (Eph. i. 4–6).

And although God knows who are his, and now and then mention is made of the small number of the elect, yet we must hope well of all, and not rashly judge any man to be a reprobate: for Paul says to the Philippians, 'I thank my God for you all' (now he speaks of the whole Church of the Philippians), 'that ye are come into the fellowship of the Gospel; and I am persuaded that he that hath begun this work in you will perform it as it becometh me to judge of you all' (Phil. i. 3–7).

And when the Lord was asked whether there were few that should be saved, he does not answer and tell them that few or many should be saved or damned, but rather he exhorts every man to 'strive to enter in at the strait gate' (Luke xiii. 24): as if he should say, It is not for you rashly to inquire of these matters, but rather to endeavor that you may enter into heaven by the strait way.

Wherefore we do not allow of the wicked speeches of some who say, Few are chosen, and seeing I know not whether I am in the number of these few, I will not defraud my nature of her desires. Others there are who say, If I be predestinated and chosen of God, nothing can hinder me from salvation, which is already certainly appointed for me, whatsoever I do at any time; but if I be in the number of the reprobate, no faith or repentance will help me, seeing the decree of God can not be changed: therefore all teachings and admonitions are to no purpose. Now, against these men the saying of the apostle makes much, 'The servants of God must be apt to teach, instructing those that are contrary-minded, proving if God at any time will give them repentance, that they may come to amendment out of the snare of the devil, which are taken of him at his pleasure' (2 Tim. ii. 24–26).

Besides, Augustine also teaches, that both the grace of free election and predestination, and also wholesome admonitions and doctrines, are to be preached (*Lib. de Bono Perseverantiæ*, cap. 14).

We therefore condemn those who seek otherwhere than in Christ whether they be chosen from all eternity, and what God has decreed of them before all beginning. For men must hear the Gospel preached, and believe it. If thou believest, and art in Christ, thou mayest undoubtedly hold that thou art elected. For the Father has revealed unto us in Christ his eternal sentence of predestination, as we even now showed out of the apostle, in 2 Tim. i. 9, 10. This is therefore above all to be taught and well weighed, what great love of the Father toward us in Christ is revealed. We must hear what the Lord does daily preach unto us in his Gospel: how he calls and says, 'Come unto me all ye that labor and are burdened, and I will refresh you' (Matt. xi. 28); and, 'God so loved the world, that he gave his only-begotten Son, that whosoever believeth in him should not perish, but have everlasting life' (John iii. 16); also, 'It is not the will of your Father in heaven that any of these little ones should perish' (Matt. xviii. 14).

Let Christ, therefore, be our looking-glass, in whom we may behold our predestination. We shall have a most evident and sure testimony that we are written in the Book of Life if we communicate with Christ, and he be ours, and we be his, by a true faith. Let this comfort us in the temptation touching predestination, than which there is none more dangerous: that the promises of God are general to the faithful; in that he says, 'Ask, and ye shall receive; every one that asketh receiveth' (Luke xi. 9, 10). And, to conclude, we pray, with the whole Church of God, 'Our Father which art in heaven' (Matt. vi. 9); and in baptism, we are ingrafted into the body of Christ, and we are fed in his Church, oftentimes, with his flesh and blood, unto everlasting life. Thereby, being strengthened, we are commanded to 'work out our salvation with fear and trembling,' according to that precept of Paul, in Phil. ii. 12.

CHAPTER XI.—OF JESUS CHRIST, BEING TRUE GOD AND MAN, AND THE ONLY SAVIOUR OF THE WORLD.

Moreover, we believe and teach that the Son of God, our Lord Jesus Christ, was from all eternity predestinated and foreordained of the Father to be the Saviour of the world. And we believe that he was begotten, not only then, when he took flesh of the Virgin Mary, nor yet a little before the foundations of the world were laid; but before all eternity, and that of the Father after an unspeakable manner. For Isaiah says (liii. 8), 'Who can tell his generation?' And Micah says (v. 2), 'Whose egress hath been from everlasting.' And John says (i. 1), 'In the beginning was the Word, and the Word was with God, and the Word was God,' etc.

Therefore the Son is coequal and consubstantial with the Father, as touching his divinity: true God, not by name only, or by adoption, or by special favor, but in substance and nature (Phil. ii. 6). Even as the apostle says elsewhere, 'This is the true God, and life everlasting' (1 John v. 20). Paul also says, 'He hath made his Son the heir of all things, by whom also he made the worlds; the same is the brightness of his glory and the express image of his person, bearing up all things by his mighty word' (Heb. i. 2, 3). Likewise, in the Gospel, the Lord himself says, 'Father, glorify thou me with thyself, with the glory which I had with thee before the world was' (John xvii. 5). Also elsewhere it is written in the Gospel, 'The Jews sought how to kill Jesus, because he said that God was his Father, making himself equal with God' (John v. 18).

We therefore do abhor the blasphemous doctrine of Arius, and all the Arians, uttered against the Son of God; and especially the blasphemies of Michael Servetus, the Spaniard, and of his complices, which Satan through them has, as it were, drawn out of hell, and most boldly and impiously spread abroad throughout the world against the Son of God.

We also teach and believe that the eternal Son of the eternal God was made the Son of man, of the seed of Abraham and David (Matt. i. 25); not by the means of any man, as Ebion affirmed, but that he was most purely conceived by the Holy Spirit, and born of Mary, who was always a virgin, even as the history of the Gospel does declare. And Paul says, 'He took not on him the nature of angels, but of the seed of Abraham' (Heb. ii. 16). And John the apostle says, 'He that believeth not that Jesus Christ is come in the flesh is not of God' (1 John iv. 3). The flesh of Christ, therefore, was neither flesh in show only, nor yet flesh brought from heaven, as Valentinus and Marcion dreamed.

Moreover, our Lord Jesus Christ had not a soul without sense and reason, as Apollinaris thought; nor flesh without a soul, as Eunomius did teach; but a soul with its reason, and flesh with its senses, by which senses he felt true griefs in the time of his passion, even as he himself witnessed when he said, 'My soul is heavy, even to death' (Matt. xxvi. 38); and, 'My soul is troubled,' etc. (John xii. 27).

We acknowledge, therefore, that there be in one and the same Jesus Christ our Lord two natures—the divine and the human nature; and we say that these two are so conjoined or united that they are not swallowed up, confounded, or mingled together; but rather united or joined together in one person (the properties of each nature being safe and remaining still), so that we do worship one Christ our Lord, and not two. I say one, true God and man, as touching his divine nature, of the same substance with us, and 'in all points tempted like as we are, yet without sin' (Heb. iv. 15).

As, therefore, we detest the heresy of Nestorius, which makes two Christs of one and dissolves the union of the person, so do we abominate the madness of Eutyches and of the Monothelites and Monophysites, who overthrow the propriety of the human nature.

Therefore we do not teach that the divine nature in Christ did suffer, or that Christ, according to his human nature, is yet in the world, and so in every place. For we do neither think nor teach that the body of Christ ceased to be a true body after his glorifying, or that it was deified and so deified that it put off its properties, as touching body and soul, and became altogether a divine nature and began to be one substance alone; therefore we do not allow or receive the unwitty subtleties, and the intricate, obscure, and inconstant disputations of Schwenkfeldt, and such other vain janglers, about this matter; neither are we Schwenkfeldians.

Moreover, we believe that our Lord Jesus Christ did truly suffer and die for us in the flesh, as Peter says (1 Pet. iv. 1). We abhor the most impious madness of the Jacobites, and all the Turks, who execrate the passion of our Lord. Yet we deny not but that 'the Lord of glory,' according to the saying of Paul, was crucified for us (1 Cor. ii. 8); for we do reverently and religiously receive and use the communication of properties drawn from the Scripture, and used of all antiquity in expounding and reconciling places of Scripture which at first sight seem to disagree one from another.

We believe and teach that the same Lord Jesus Christ, in that true flesh in which he was crucified and died, rose again from the dead; and that he did not rise up another flesh, but retained a true body. Therefore, while his disciples thought that they did see the spirit of their Lord Christ, he showed them his hands and feet, which were marked with the prints of the nails and wounds, saying, ' Behold my hands and my feet, that it is I myself: handle me, and see; for a spirit hath not flesh and bones, as ye see me have' (Luke xxiv. 39).

We believe that our Lord Jesus Christ, in the same flesh, did ascend above all the visible heavens into the very highest heaven, that is to say, the seat of God and of the blessed spirits, unto the right hand of God the Father. Although it do signify an equal participation of glory and majesty, yet it is also taken for a certain place; of which the Lord, speaking in the Gospel, says, that ' He will go and prepare a place for his' (John xiv. 2). Also the Apostle Peter says, ' The heavens must contain Christ until the time of restoring all things' (Acts iii. 21).

And out of heaven the same Christ will return unto judgment, even then when wickedness shall chiefly reign in the world, and when Antichrist, having corrupted true religion, shall fill all things with superstition and impiety, and shall most cruelly waste the Church with fire and bloodshed. Now Christ shall return to redeem his, and to abolish Antichrist by his coming, and to judge the quick and the dead (Acts xvii. 31). For the dead shall arise, and those that shall be found alive in that day (which is unknown unto all creatures) ' shall be changed in the twinkling of an eye' (1 Cor. xv. 51, 52). And all the faithful shall be taken up to meet Christ in the air (1 Thess. iv. 17); that thenceforth they may enter with him into heaven, there to live forever (2 Tim. ii. 11); but the unbelievers, or ungodly, shall descend with the devils into hell, there to burn forever, and never to be delivered out of torments (Matt. xxv. 41).

We therefore condemn all those who deny the true resurrection of the flesh, and those who think amiss of the glorified bodies, as did

Joannes Hierosolymitanus, against whom Jerome wrote. We also condemn those who have thought that both the devils and all the wicked shall at length be saved and have an end of their torments; for the Lord himself has absolutely set it down that 'Their worm dieth not, and the fire is not quenched' (Mark ix. 44).

Moreover, we condemn the Jewish dreams, that before the day of judgment there shall be a golden age in the earth, and that the godly shall possess the kingdoms of the world, their wicked enemies being trodden under foot; for the evangelical truth (Matt. xxiv. and xxv., Luke xxi.), and the apostolic doctrine (in the Second Epistle to the Thessalonians ii., and in the Second Epistle to Timothy iii. and iv.) are found to teach far otherwise.

Furthermore, by his passion or death, and by all those things which he did and suffered for our sakes from the time of his coming in the flesh, our Lord reconciled his heavenly Father unto all the faithful (Rom. v. 10); purged their sin (Heb. i. 3); spoiled death, broke in sunder condemnation and hell; and by his resurrection from the dead brought again and restored life and immortality (Rom. iv. 25; 1 Cor. xv. 17; 2 Tim. i. 10). For he is our righteousness, life, and resurrection (John vi. 44); and, to be short, he is the fullness and perfection, the salvation and most abundant sufficiency, of all the faithful. For the apostle says, 'So it pleaseth the Father that all fullness should dwell in him' (Col. i. 19), and 'In him ye are complete' (Col. ii. 10).

For we teach and believe that this Jesus Christ our Lord is the only and eternal Saviour of mankind, yea, and of the whole world, in whom all are saved before the law, under the law, and in the time of the Gospel, and so many as shall yet be saved to the end of the world. For the Lord himself, in the Gospel, says, 'He that entereth not in by the door into the sheepfold, but climbeth up the other way, he is a thief and a robber' (John x. 1). 'I am the door of the sheep' (ver. 7). And also in another place of the same Gospel he says, 'Abraham saw my day, and rejoiced' (John viii. 56). And the Apostle Peter says, 'Neither is there salvation in any other, but in Christ; for among men there is given no other name under heaven whereby they might be saved' (Acts iv. 12). We believe, therefore, that through the grace of our Lord Jesus Christ we shall be saved, even as our fathers were. For Paul says, that 'All our fathers did eat the same spiritual meat, and drink the same spiritual drink: for they drank of the spiritual Rock that followed them: and that Rock was Christ' (1 Cor. x. 3, 4). And therefore we read that John said, that 'Christ was that Lamb which was slain from the foundation of the world' (Rev. xiii. 8); and that John the Baptist witnesseth, that Christ is that 'Lamb of God, that taketh away the sin of the world' (John i. 29).

Wherefore we do plainly and openly profess and preach, that Jesus Christ is the only Redeemer and Saviour of the world, the King and High Priest, the true and looked-for Messiah, that holy and blessed one (I say) whom all the shadows of the law, and the prophecies of the prophets, did prefigure and promise; and that God did supply and send him unto us, so that now we are not to look for any other. And now there remains nothing, but that we all should give all glory to him, believe in him, and rest in him only, contemning and rejecting all other aids of our life. For they are fallen from the grace of God, and make Christ of no value unto themselves, whosoever they be that seek salvation in any other things besides Christ alone (Gal. v. 4).

And, to speak many things in a few words, with a sincere heart we believe, and with liberty of speech we freely profess, whatsoever things are defined out of the Holy Scriptures, and comprehended in the creeds, and in the decrees of those four first and most excellent councils—held at Nicæa, Constantinople, Ephesus, and Chalcedon—together with blessed Athanasius's creed and all other creeds like to these, touching the mystery of the incarnation of our Lord Jesus Christ; and we condemn all things contrary to the same.

And thus we retain the Christian, sound, and Catholic faith, whole and inviolable, knowing that nothing is contained in the aforesaid creeds which is not agreeable to the Word of God, and makes wholly for the sincere declaration of the faith.

CHAPTER XII.—OF THE LAW OF GOD.

We teach that the will of God is set down unto us in the law of God; to wit, what he would have us to do, or not to do, what is good and just, or what is evil and unjust. We therefore confess that 'The law is good and holy' (Rom. vii. 12); and that this law is, by the finger of God, either 'written in the hearts of men' (Rom. ii. 15), and so is called the law of nature, or engraven in the two tables of stone, and more largely expounded in the books of Moses (Exod. xx. 1–17; Deut. v. 22). For plainness' sake we divide it into the moral law, which is contained in the commandments, or the two tables expounded in the books of Moses; into the ceremonial, which does appoint ceremonies and the worship of God; and into the judicial law, which is occupied about political and domestic affairs.

We believe that the whole will of God,[1] and all necessary precepts, for every part of this life, are fully delivered in this law. For otherwise the Lord would not have forbidden that 'any thing should be either added to or taken away from this law' (Deut. iv. 2, and xii. 32); neither would he have commanded us to go straight forward in this, and 'not to decline out of the way, either to the right hand or to the left' (Josh. i. 7).

We teach that this law was not given to men, that we should be justified by keeping it; but that, by the knowledge thereof, we might rather acknowledge our infirmity, sin, and condemnation; and so, despairing of our strength, might turn unto Christ by faith. For the apostle says plainly, 'The law worketh wrath' (Rom. iv. 15); and 'by the law cometh the knowledge of sin' (Rom. iii. 20); and, 'If there had been a law given which would have justified and given us life, surely righteousness should have been by the law. But the Scripture (to wit, of the law) has concluded all under sin, that the promise by the faith of Jesus Christ should be given to them which believe' (Gal. iii. 21, 22). 'Therefore, the law was our schoolmaster to bring us to Christ, that we might be justified by faith' (ver. 24). For neither could there ever, neither at this day can any flesh satisfy the law of God, and fulfill it, by reason of the weakness in our flesh,[2] which remains and sticks fast in us, even to our last breath. For the apostle says again, 'That which the law could not perform, inasmuch as it was weak through the flesh, that did God perform, by sending his own Son in the likeness of sinful flesh' (Rom. viii. 3). Therefore, Christ is the perfecting of the law, and our fulfilling of it; who, as he took away the curse of the law, when he was made a curse for us (Gal. iii. 13), so does he communicate unto us by faith his fulfilling thereof, and his righteousness and obedience are imputed unto us.

---

[1] Understand, as concerning those things which men are bound to perform to God, and also to their neighbors.

[2] That is, any man, although he be regenerate.

The law of God,[1] therefore, is thus far abrogated; that is, it does not henceforth condemn us, neither work wrath in us; 'for we are under grace, and not under the law' (Rom. vi. 14). Moreover, Christ did fulfill all the figures of the law; wherefore the shadow ceased when the body came, so that, in Christ, we have now all truth and fullness. Yet we do not therefore disdain or reject the law. We remember the words of the Lord, saying, 'I came not to destroy the law and the prophets, but to fulfill them' (Matt. v. 17). We know that in the law[2] are described unto us the kinds of virtues and vices. We know that the Scripture of the law,[3] if it be expounded by the Gospel, is very profitable to the Church, and that therefore the reading of it is not to be banished out of the Church. For although the countenance of Moses was covered with a veil, yet the apostle affirms that 'the veil is taken away and abolished by Christ' (2 Cor. iii. 14). We condemn all things which the old or new heretics have taught against the law of God.

CHAPTER XIII. — OF THE GOSPEL OF JESUS CHRIST: ALSO OF PROMISES; OF THE SPIRIT AND OF THE LETTER.

The Gospel, indeed, is opposed to the law: for the law works wrath, and does announce a curse; but the Gospel does preach grace and blessing. John also says, 'The law was given by Moses, but grace and truth came by Jesus Christ' (John i. 17). Yet, notwithstanding, it is most certain that they who were before the law, and under the law, were not altogether destitute of the Gospel. For they had notable evangelical promises, such as these: 'The seed of the woman shall bruise the serpent's head' (Gen. iii. 15). 'In thy seed shall all the nations of the earth be blessed' (Gen. xlix. 10). 'The Lord shall raise up a Prophet from among his own brethren,' etc. (Deut. xviii. 15; Acts iii. 22, and vii. 37).

And we do acknowledge that the fathers had two kinds of promises revealed unto them, even as we have. For some of them were of present and transitory things: such as were the promises of the land of Canaan, and of victories; and such as are nowadays concerning our daily bread. Other promises there were then, and are now, of heavenly and

---

[1] To wit, the moral law, comprehended in the Ten Commandments.
[2] To wit, in the moral law.   [3] To wit, the ceremonial law.

everlasting things; as of God's favor, remission of sins, and life ever-lasting, through faith in Jesus Christ. Now, the fathers had not only outward or earthly, but spiritual and heavenly promises in Christ. For the Apostle Peter says that 'the prophets, which prophesied of the grace that should come to us, have searched and inquired of his salva-tion' (1 Pet. i. 10). Whereupon the Apostle Paul also says, that 'the Gospel of God was promised before by the prophets of God in the Holy Scriptures' (Rom. i. 2). Hereby, then, it appears evidently that the fathers were not altogether destitute of all the Gospel.

And although, after this manner, our fathers had the Gospel in the writings of the prophets, by which they attained salvation in Christ through faith, yet the Gospel is properly called 'glad and happy tidings;' wherein, first by John Baptist, then by Christ the Lord him-self, and afterwards by the apostles and their successors, is preached to us in the world, that God has now performed that which he prom-ised from the beginning of the world, and has sent, yea, and even given unto us, his only Son, and, in him, reconciliation with the Father, re-mission of sins, all fullness, and everlasting life. The history, there-fore, set down by the four evangelists, declaring how these things were done or fulfilled in Christ, and what he taught and did, and that they who believe in him have all fullness—this, I say, is truly called the Gospel. The preaching, also, and Scripture of the apostles, in which they expound unto us how the Son was given us of the Father, and, in him, all things pertaining to life and salvation, is truly called the doc-trine of the Gospel; so as even at this day it loses not that worthy name, if it be sincere.

The same preaching of the Gospel is by the apostle termed the Spir-it, and 'the ministry of the Spirit' (2 Cor. iii. 8): because it lives and works through faith in the ears, yea, in the hearts, of the faithful, through the illumination of the Holy Spirit. For the letter, which is opposed unto the Spirit, does indeed signify every outward thing, but more especially the doctrine of the law, which, without the Spirit and faith, works wrath, and stirs up sin in the minds of them that do not truly believe. For which cause it is called by the apostle 'the min-istry of death' (2 Cor. iii. 7); for hitherto pertains that saying of the apostle, 'the letter killeth, but the Spirit giveth life' (ver. 6). The false apostles preached the Gospel, corrupted by mingling of the law therewith; as though Christ could not save without the law. Such, also, were the Ebionites said to be, who came of Ebion the heretic; and the Nazarites, who beforetime were called Mineans. All whom we do condemn, sincerely preaching the word, and teaching that believers are justified through the Spirit (or Christ) only, and not through the law. But of this matter there shall follow a fuller exposition, under the title of justification.

And although the doctrine of the Gospel, compared with the Pharisees' doctrine of the law, might seem (when it was first preached by Christ) to be a new doctrine (which thing also Jeremiah prophesied of the New Testament); yet, indeed, it not only was, and as yet is (though the papists call it new, in regard of popish doctrine, which has of long time been received), an ancient doctrine, but also the most ancient in the world. For God from all eternity foreordained to save the world by Christ, and this his predestination and eternal counsel has he opened to the world by the Gospel (2 Tim. i. 9, 10). Whereby it appears that the evangelical doctrine and religion was the most ancient of all that ever were or are; wherefore we say, that all they [the papists] err foully, and speak things unworthy the eternal counsel of God, who term the evangelical doctrine and religion a newly concocted faith, scarce thirty years old: to whom that saying of Isaiah does very well agree—'Woe unto them that call evil good, and good evil; that put darkness for light, and light for darkness; that put bitter for sweet, and sweet for bitter' (v. 20).

CHAPTER XIV.—OF REPENTANCE, AND THE CONVERSION OF MAN.

The Gospel has the doctrine of repentance joined with it; for so said the Lord in the Gospel, 'In my name must repentance and remission of sins be preached among all nations' (Luke xxiv. 47).

By repentance we understand the change of the mind in a sinful man stirred up by the preaching of the Gospel through the Holy Spirit, and received by a true faith: by which a sinful man does acknowledge his natural corruption, and all his sins, seeing them convinced by the Word of God, and is heartily grieved for them; and does not only bewail and freely confess them before God with shame, but also does loathe and abhor them with indignation, thinking seriously of present amendment, and of a continual care of in nocency and virtue, wherein to exercise himself holily all the rest of his life.

And surely this is true repentance—namely, an unfeigned turning unto God and to all goodness, and a serious return from the devil and from all evil. Now we do expressly say, that this repentance is the mere gift of God, and not the work of our own strength. For the apostle directs the faithful minister diligently to 'instruct those who oppose the truth, if so be at any time the Lord may give them repentance, that they may acknowledge the truth' (2 Tim. ii. 25). Also the sinful woman in the Gospel, who washed Christ's feet with her tears; and Peter, who bitterly wept and bewailed his denial of his Master—do manifestly show what mind the penitent man should have, to wit, very earnestly lamenting his sins committed. Moreover, the prodigal son, and the publican in the Gospel, that is compared with the Pharisee, do set forth unto us a most fit pattern of confessing our sins to God. The prodigal son said, 'Father, I have sinned against heaven, and against thee: I am not worthy to be called thy son; make me as one of thy hired servants' (Luke xv. 18, 19). The publican, also, not daring to lift up his eyes to heaven, but smiting his breast, cried, 'God be merciful unto me a sinner' (Luke xviii. 13). And we doubt not but the Lord received them to mercy. For John the apostle says, 'If we confess our sins, he is faithful and just to forgive us our sins, and purge us from all iniquity. If we say we have not sinned, we make him a liar, and his word is not in us' (1 John i. 9, 10).

We believe that this sincere confession, which is made to God alone, either privately between God and the sinner, or openly in the church, where that general confession of sins is rehearsed, is sufficient; and that it is not necessary for the obtaining of remission of sins that any man should confess his sins unto the priest, whispering them into his ears, that, the priest laying his hands on his head, he might receive absolution: because we find no commandment nor example thereof in the Holy Scripture. David protests and says, 'I made my fault known to thee, and my unrighteousness did I not hide from thee. I said, I will confess my wickedness to the Lord against myself, and thou hast forgiven the heinousness of my sin' (Psa. xxxii. 5). Yea, and the Lord, teaching us to pray, and also to confess our sins, said, 'So shall ye pray: Our Father which art in heaven, forgive us our debts, even as we forgive our debtors' (Matt. vi. 9, 12). It is requisite, therefore, that we should confess our sins unto God, and be reconciled with our neighbor, if we have offended him. And the Apostle James, speaking generally of confession, says, 'Confess each of you your sins to one another' (James v. 16). If so be that any man, being overwhelmed with the burden of his sins, and troublesome temptations, will privately ask counsel, instruction, or comfort, either of a minister of the Church, or of any other brother that is learned in the law of God, we do not mislike it. Like as also we do fully allow that general and public confession which is wont to be rehearsed in the church, and in holy meetings (whereof we spake before), being, as it is, agreeable with the Scripture.

As concerning the keys of the kingdom of heaven, which the Lord committed to his apostles, they [the papists] prate many strange things; and of these keys they make swords, spears, scepters, and crowns, and full power over mighty kingdoms, yea, and over men's souls and bodies. But we, judging uprightly, according to the Word of God, do say that all ministers, truly called, have and exercise the keys, or the use of them, when they preach the Gospel; that is to say, when they teach, exhort, reprove, and keep in order the people committed to their charge. For they do open the kingdom of God to the obedient, and shut it against the disobedient. These keys did the Lord promise to the apostles, in Matt. xvi. 19; and delivered them, in John xx. 23; Mark xvi. 15, 16; Luke xxiv. 47, when he sent forth his disciples, and commanded them to preach the Gospel in all the world, and to remit sins. The apostle, in the epistle to the Corinthians, says that the Lord 'gave to his ministers the ministry of reconciliation' (2 Cor. v. 18). And what this was he straightway makes plain and says, 'The word or doctrine of reconciliation' (ver. 19). And yet more plainly expounding his words, he adds, that the ministers of Christ do, as it were, go an embassage in Christ's name, as if God himself should by his ministers exhort the people to be reconciled to God (ver. 20); to wit, by faithful obedience. They use the keys, therefore, when they persuade to faith and repentance. Thus do they reconcile men to God; thus they forgive sins; thus they open the kingdom of heaven and bring in the believers; much differing herein from those of whom the Lord spake in the Gospel, 'Woe unto you, lawyers! for ye have taken away the key of knowledge: ye have not entered in yourselves, and those that would have entered ye forbade' (Luke xi. 52).

Rightly, therefore, and effectually do ministers absolve, when they preach the Gospel of Christ, and thereby remission of sins; which is promised to every one that believes, even as every one is baptized; and to testify of it that it does particularly appertain to all. Neither do we imagine that this absolution is made any whit more effectual for that which is mumbled into some priest's ear, or upon some man's head particularly; yet we judge that men must be taught diligently to seek remission of sins in the blood of Christ, and that every one is to be put in mind that forgiveness of sins does belong unto him.

But how diligent and careful every penitent man ought to be in the endeavor of a new life, and in slaying the old man and raising up the new man, the examples in the Gospel do teach us. For the Lord said to him whom he had healed of the palsy, 'Behold, thou art made whole: sin no more, lest a worse thing come unto thee' (John v. 14). Likewise to the woman taken in adultery he said, 'Go thy way, and sin no more' (John viii. 11). By which words he did mean that any man could be free from sin while he lived in this flesh; but he does commend unto us diligence and an earnest care, that we (I say) should endeavor by all means, and beg of God by prayer, that we fall not again into sins, out of which we are risen after the manner, and that we may not be overcome of the flesh, the world, or the devil. Zacchæus, the publican, being received into favor by the Lord, cried out, in the Gospel, 'Behold, Lord, the half of my goods I give to the poor; and if I have taken from any man any thing by false accusation, I restore him fourfold' (Luke xix. 8). After the same manner we preach that restitution and mercy, yea, and giving of alms, are necessary for them who truly repent. And, generally, out of the apostle's words we exhort men, saying, 'Let not sin reign in your mortal body, that ye should obey it through the lusts thereof. Neither give ye your members as weapons of unrighteousness to sin; but give yourselves unto God' (Rom. vi. 12, 13).

Wherefore we condemn all the ungodly speeches of those who abuse the preaching of the Gospel, and say, To return unto God is very easy, for Christ has purged all our sins. Forgiveness of sins is easily obtained; what, therefore, will it hurt to sin? And, We need not take any great care for repentance, etc.   Notwithstanding, we always teach that an entrance unto God is open for all sinners, and that this God does forgive all the sins of the faithful, only that one sin excepted which is committed against the Holy Ghost (Mark iii. 28, 29).

And, therefore, we condemn the old and new Novatians and Catharists; and especially we condemn the Pope's painful doctrine of penance.   And against his simony and simoniacal indulgences we use that sentence of Simon Peter, 'Thy money perish with thee, because thou hast thought that the gift of God might be bought with money. Thou hast no part or fellowship in this matter: for thy heart is not upright before God' (Acts viii. 20, 21).

We also disallow those who think that themselves, by their own satisfactions, can make recompense for their sins committed.   For we teach that Christ alone, by his death and passion, is the satisfaction, propitiation, and purging of all sins (Isa. liii. 4).   Nevertheless, we cease not to urge, as was before said, the mortification of the flesh; and yet we add further, that it must not be proudly thrust upon God for a satisfaction of our sins (1 Cor. viii. 8); but must humbly, as it becomes the sons of God, be performed, as a new obedience, to show thankful minds for the deliverance and full satisfaction obtained by the death and satisfaction of the Son of God.

CHAPTER XV.—OF THE TRUE JUSTIFICATION OF THE FAITHFUL.

To justify, in the apostle's disputation touching justification, does signify to remit sins, to absolve from the fault and the punishment thereof, to receive into favor, to pronounce a man just.   For the apostle says to the Romans, 'God is he that justifieth.   Who is he that can condemn?' (Rom. viii. 33, 44).   Here to justify and to condemn are opposed.   And in the Acts of the Apostles the apostle says, 'Through Christ is preached unto you forgiveness of sins: and from all things (from which ye could not be justified by the law of Moses) by him every one that believes is justified' (Acts xiii. 38, 39).   For in the law, also, and in the prophets, we read, that 'If a controversy were risen among any, and they came to judgment, the judge should judge them; that is, justify the righteous, and condemn the wicked' (Deut. xxv. 1). And in Isa. v. 22, 23, 'Woe to them which justify the wicked for reward.'

Now, it is most certain that we are all by nature sinners, and before the judgment-seat of God convicted of ungodliness, and guilty of death. But we are justified—that is, acquitted from sin and death—by God the Judge, through the grace of Christ alone, and not by any respect or merit of ours. For what is more plain than that which Paul says?— 'All have sinned, and are destitute of the glory of God, and are justified freely by grace, through the redemption which is in Christ Jesus' (Rom. iii. 23, 24).

For Christ took upon himself and bare the sins of the world, and did satisfy the justice of God. God, therefore, is merciful unto our sins for Christ alone, that suffered and rose again, and does not impute them unto us. But he imputes the justice of Christ unto us for our own; so that now we are not only cleansed from sin, and purged, and holy, but also endued with the righteousness of Christ; yea, and acquitted from sin, death, and condemnation (2 Cor. v. 19–21); finally, we are righteous, and heirs of eternal life. To speak properly, then, it is God alone that justifieth us, and that only for Christ, by not imputing unto us our sins, but imputing Christ's righteousness unto us (Rom. iv. 23–25).

But because we do receive this justification, not by any works, but by faith in the mercy of God and in Christ; therefore, we teach and believe, with the apostle, that sinful man is justified only by faith in Christ, not by the law or by any works. For the apostle says, 'We conclude that man is justified by faith, without the works of the law' (Rom. iii. 28). 'If Abraham were justified by works, he hath whereof to boast; but not with God. For what saith the Scripture? Abraham believed God, and it was counted unto him for righteousness; but to him that worketh not, but believeth on him that justifieth the ungodly, his faith is counted for righteousness' (Rom. iv. 2, 3, 5; Gen. xv. 6). And again, 'Ye are saved by grace, through faith; and that not of yourselves: it is the gift of God; not by works, lest any might have cause to boast,' etc. (Eph. ii. 8, 9). Therefore, because faith does apprehend Christ our righteousness, and does attribute all the praise of God in Christ; in this respect justification is attributed to faith, chiefly because of Christ, whom it receives, and not because it is a work of ours; for it is the gift of God. Now, that we do receive Christ by faith the Lord shows at large (John vi. 27, 33, 35, 48–58), where he puts eating for believing, and believing for eating.   For as by eating we receive meat, so by believing we are made partakers of Christ.

Therefore, we do not divide the benefit of justification, giving part to the grace of God or to Christ, and part to ourselves, our charity, works, or merit; but we do attribute it wholly to the praise of God in Christ, and that through faith.   Moreover, our charity and our works can not please God if they be done of such as are not just; wherefore, we must first be just before we can love or do any just works.   We are made just (as we have said) through faith in Christ, by the mere grace of God, who does not impute unto us our sins, but imputes unto us the righteousness of Christ; yea, and our faith in Christ he imputes for righteousness unto us.   Moreover, the apostle does plainly derive love from faith, saying, 'The end of the commandment is love, proceeding from a pure heart, a good conscience, and faith unfeigned' (1 Tim. i. 5).

Wherefore, in this matter we speak not of a feigned, vain, or dead faith, but of a lively and quickening faith; which, for Christ (who is life, and gives life), whom it apprehends, both is indeed, and is so called, a lively faith, and does prove itself to be lively by lively works.   And, therefore, James does speak nothing contrary to this doctrine; for he speaks of a vain and dead faith, which certain bragged of, but had not Christ living within them by faith.   And also James says that works do justify (chap. ii. 14–26), yet he is not contrary to Paul (for then he were to be rejected); but he shows that Abraham did declare his lively and justifying faith by works.   And so do all the godly, who yet trust in Christ alone, not to their own works.   For the apostle said again, 'I live no longer myself, but Christ liveth in me.   And the life which I now live in the flesh, I live through the faith of the Son of God, who loved me, and gave himself for me.   I do not frustrate the grace of God; for if righteousness be by the law, then Christ died without cause' (Gal. ii. 20, 21).

CHAPTER XVI.—OF FAITH AND GOOD WORKS; OF THEIR REWARD, AND OF MAN'S MERIT.

Christian faith is not an opinion or human persuasion, but a sure trust, and an evident and steadfast assent of the mind; it is a most sure comprehension of the truth of God, set forth in the Scriptures and in the Apostles' Creed; yea, and of God himself, the chief blessedness; and especially of God's promise, and of Christ, who is the consummation of all the promises. And this faith is the mere gift of God, because God alone of his power does give it to his elect, according to measure; and that when, to whom, and how much he will; and that by his Holy Spirit, through the means of preaching the Gospel and of faithful prayer. This faith has also its measures of increase; which, unless they were likewise given of God, the apostles would never have said, 'Lord, increase our faith' (Luke xvii. 5).

Now, all these things which we have hitherto said of faith, the apostles taught them before us, even as we set them down. For Paul says, 'Faith is the ground,' or sure subsistence, 'of things hoped for, and the evidence,' or clear and certain comprehension, 'of things which are not seen' (Heb. xi. 1). And again he says that 'all the promises of God in Christ are yea, and in Christ are amen' (2 Cor. i. 20). And the same apostle says to the Philippians that 'it was given them to believe in Christ' (Phil. i. 29). And also, 'God doth distribute unto every man a measure of faith' (Rom. xii. 3). And again, 'All men have not faith' (2 Thess. iii. 2); and, 'All do not obey the Gospel' (2 Thess. i. 8). Besides, Luke witnesses and says, 'As many as were ordained to life, believed' (Acts xiii. 48). And therefore Paul also calls faith 'the faith of God's elect' (Tit. i. 1). And, again, 'Faith cometh by hearing, and hearing by the word of God' (Rom. x. 17). And in other places he oftentimes wills men to pray for faith. And the same also called faith powerful, and that showeth itself by love (Gal. v. 6). This faith pacifies the conscience, and opens to us a free access unto God; that with confidence we may come unto him, and may obtain at his hands whatsoever is profitable and necessary. The same faith keeps us in our duty which we owe to God and to our neighbor, and fortifies our patience in adversity; it frames and makes a true confession, and (in a word) it brings forth good fruit of all sorts; and good works (which are good indeed) proceeds from a lively faith by the Holy Spirit, and are done of the faithful according to the will or rule of God's word. For Peter the Apostle says, 'Therefore, giving all diligence thereunto, add, moreover, to your faith virtue; and to virtue, knowledge; and to knowledge, temperance,' etc. (2 Pet. i. 5, 6).

It was said before that the law of God, which is the will of God, did prescribe unto us the pattern of good works. And the apostle says, 'This is the will of God, even your sanctification, that ye abstain from all uncleanness, and that no man oppress or deceive his brother in any matter' (1 Thess. iv. 3, 6). But as for such works and worships of God as are taken up upon our own liking, which St. Paul calls 'will-worship' (Col. ii. 23), they are not allowed nor liked of God. Of such the Lord says in the Gospel, 'They worship me in vain, teaching for doctrine the precepts of men' (Matt. xv. 9).

We therefore disallow all such manner of works, and we approve and urge men unto such as are according to the will and commandment of God. Yea, and these same works that are agreeable to God's will must be done, not to the end to merit eternal life by them; for 'life everlasting,' as the apostle says, 'is the gift of God' (Rom. vi. 23), nor for ostentation's sake, which the Lord does reject (Matt. vi. 1, 5, 16), nor for lucre, which also he mislikes (Matt. xxiii. 23), but to the glory of God, to commend and set forth our calling, and to yield thankfulness unto God, and also for the profit of our neighbors. For the Lord says again in the Gospel, 'Let your light so shine before men that they may see your good works, and glorify your Father which is in heaven' (Matt. v. 16). Likewise the Apostle Paul says, 'Walk worthy of your calling' (Eph. iv. 1). Also, 'Whatsoever ye do,' says he, 'either in word or in deed, do all in the name of the Lord Jesus, giving thanks to God the Father by him' (Col. iii. 17). 'Let no man seek his own, but every man his brother's' (Phil. ii. 4). And, 'Let ours also learn to show forth good works for necessary uses, that they be not unprofitable' (Tit. iii. 14).

Notwithstanding, therefore, that we teach with the apostle that a man is justified by faith in Christ, and not by any good works (Rom. iii. 28), yet we do not lightly esteem or condemn good works; because we know that a man is not created or regenerated through faith that he should be idle, but rather that without ceasing he should do those things which are good and profitable. For in the Gospel the Lord says, 'A good tree bringeth forth good fruit' (Matt. xii. 33); and, again, 'Whosoever abideth in me, bringeth forth much fruit' (John xv. 5). And, lastly, the apostle says, 'We are the workmanship of God, created in Christ Jesus to good works, which God hath prepared, that we should walk in them' (Eph. ii. 10). And again, 'Who gave himself for us, that he might deliver us from all iniquity, and purge us to be a peculiar people to himself, zealous of good works' (Tit. ii. 14). We therefore condemn all those who do contemn good works, and do babble that they are needless and not to be regarded. Nevertheless, as was said before, we do not think that we are saved by good works, or that they are so necessary to salvation that no man was ever saved without them. For we are saved by grace and by the benefit of Christ alone. Works do necessarily proceed from faith; but salvation is improperly attributed to them, which is most properly ascribed to grace. That sentence of the apostle is very notable: 'If by grace, then not of works; for then grace were no more grace: but if of works, then is it not of grace; for then works were no more works' (Rom. xi. 6).

Now the works which we do are accepted and allowed of God through faith; because they who do them please God by faith in Christ, and also the works themselves are done by the grace of God through his Holy Spirit. For St. Peter says that 'of every nation he that feareth God, and worketh righteousness, is accepted with him' (Acts x. 35). And Paul also, 'We cease not to pray for you, that you may walk worthy of the Lord, and in all things please him, being fruitful in every good work' (Col. i. 9, 10). Here, therefore, we diligently teach, not false and philosophical, but true virtues, true good works, and the true duties of a Christian man. And this we do with all the diligence and earnestness that we can inculcate and beat into men's minds; sharply reproving the slothfulness and hypocrisy of all those who with their mouths praise and profess the Gospel, and yet with their shameful life do dishonor the same; setting before their eyes, in this case, God's horrible threatenings, large promises, and bountiful rewards, and that by exhorting, comforting, and rebuking.

For we teach that God does bestow great rewards on them that do good, according to that saying of the prophet, 'Refrain thy voice from weeping, because thy works shall have a reward' (Jer. xxxi. 16). In the Gospel also the Lord said, 'Rejoice, and be glad, because your reward is great in heaven' (Matt. v. 12). And, 'He that shall give to one of these little ones a cup of cold water, verily I say unto you, he shall not lose his reward' (Matt. x. 42). Yet we do not attribute this reward, which God gives, to the merit of the man that receives it, but to the goodness, or liberality, and truth of God, which promises and

gives it; who, although he owe nothing to any, yet he has promised to
give a reward to those that faithfully worship him, notwithstanding
that he do also give them grace to worship him.   Besides, there are
many things unworthy the majesty of God, and many imperfect things
are found in the works even of the saints; and yet because God does
receive into favor and embrace those who work them for Christ's sake,
therefore he performs unto them the promised reward.   For otherwise
our righteousness is compared to a menstruous cloth (Isa. lxiv. 6); yea,
and the Lord in the Gospel says, 'When ye have done all things that
are commanded you, say, We are unprofitable servants: we have done
that which was our duty to do' (Luke xvii. 10).   So that though we teach
that God does give a reward to our good deeds, yet withal we teach,
with Augustine, that 'God doth crown in us, not our deserts, but his
own gifts.'   And, therefore, whatsoever reward we receive, we say that
it is a grace, and rather a grace than a reward: because those good
things which we do, we do them rather by God than by ourselves;
and because Paul says, 'What hast thou that thou hast not received?
but if thou hast received it, why dost thou boast, as though thou hadst
not received it?' (1 Cor. iv. 7).   Which thing also the blessed martyr
Cyprian does gather out of this place, that 'we must not boast of any-
thing, seeing nothing is our own.'   We therefore condemn those who
defend the merits of men, that they may make frustrate the grace of
God.

CHAPTER XVII. —— OF THE CATHOLIC AND HOLY CHURCH OF GOD, AND OF
THE ONE ONLY HEAD OF THE CHURCH.

Forasmuch as God from the beginning would have men to be
saved, and to come to the knowledge of the truth (1 Tim. ii. 4), therefore it is necessary that there always should have been, and should be
at this day, and to the end of the world, a Church—that is, a company
of the faithful called and gathered out of the world; a communion (I
say) of all saints, that is, of them who truly know and rightly worship
and serve the true God, in Jesus Christ the Saviour, by the word of the
Holy Spirit, and who by faith are partakers of all those good graces
which are freely offered through Christ.   These all are citizens of one
and the same city, living under one Lord, under the same laws, and in
the same fellowship of all good things; for the apostle calls them

'fellow-citizens with the saints, and of the household of God' (Eph. ii. 19); terming the faithful upon the earth saints (1 Cor. iv. 1), who are sanctified by the blood of the Son of God. Of these is that article of our Creed wholly to be understood, 'I believe in the holy Catholic Church, the communion of saints.'

And, seeing that there is always but 'one God, and one mediator between God and men, the man Jesus Christ' (1 Tim. ii. 5); also, one Shepherd of the whole flock, one Head of this body, and, to conclude, one Spirit, one salvation, one faith, one Testament, or Covenant,—it follows necessarily that there is but one Church, which we therefore call CATHOLIC because it is universal, spread abroad through all the parts and quarters of the world, and reaches unto all times, and is not limited within the compass either of time or place. Here, therefore, we must condemn the Donatists, who pinned up the Church within the corners of Africa; neither do we assent to the Roman clergy, who vaunt that the Church of Rome alone is in a manner Catholic.

The Church is divided by some into divers parts or sorts; not that it is rent and divided from itself, but rather distinguished in respect of the diversity of the members that are in it. One part thereof they make to be the Church Militant, the other the Church Triumphant. The Militant wars still on earth, and fights against the flesh, the world, and the prince of the world, the devil; against sin and against death. The other, being already set at liberty, is now in heaven, and triumphs over all those things overcome, and continually rejoices before the Lord. Yet these two churches have, notwithstanding, a communion and fellowship between themselves.

Moreover, the Church Militant upon the earth has evermore had many particular churches, which must all, notwithstanding, be referred to the unity of the Catholic Church. This Militant Church was otherwise ordered and governed before the Law, among the patriarchs; otherwise under Moses, by the Law; and otherwise of Christ, by the Gospel. There are but two sorts of people, for the most part, mentioned: to wit, the Israelites and the Gentiles; or they who, of the Jews and Gentiles, were gathered to make a Church. There are also two Testaments, the Old and the New. Yet both these sorts of people have had, and still have, one fellowship, one salvation, in one and the same Messiah; in whom, as members of one body, they are all joined together under one head, and by one faith are all partakers of one and the same spiritual meat and drink. Yet here we do acknowledge a diversity of times, and a diversity in the pledges and signs of Christ promised and exhibited; and that now, the ceremonies being abolished, the light shines unto us more clearly, our gifts and graces are more abundant, and our liberty is more full and ample.

This holy Church of God is called 'the house of the living God' (2 Cor. vi. 16), 'builded of living and spiritual stones' (1 Pet. ii. 5), 'founded upon a rock' (Matt. xvi. 18), 'which can not be moved' (Heb. xii. 28), 'upon a foundation besides which none can be laid' (1 Cor. iii. 11). Whereupon it is called 'the pillar and ground of the truth' (1 Tim. iii. 15), that does not err, so long as it relies upon the rock Christ, and upon the foundation of the prophets and apostles. And no marvel if it do err, so often as it forsakes Him who is the alone truth. This Church is also called 'a virgin' (1 Cor. xi. 2), and 'the spouse of Christ' (Cant. iv. 8), and 'his only beloved' (Cant. v. 16). For the apostle says, 'I have espoused you to one husband, that I may present you as a chaste virgin to Christ' (2 Cor. xi. 2). The Church is called 'a flock of sheep under one shepherd,' even Christ (Ezek. xxxiv. 22, 23, and John x. 16); also, 'the body of Christ' (Col. i. 24), because the faithful are the lively members of Christ, having him for their head.

It is the head which has the pre-eminence in the body, and from whence the whole body receives life; by whose spirit it is governed in all things; of whom, also, it receives increase, that it may grow up. Also, there is but one head to the body, which has agreement with the body; and therefore the Church can not have any other head besides Christ. For as the Church is a spiritual body, so must it needs have a spiritual head like unto itself. Neither can it be governed by any other spirit than by the Spirit of Christ. Wherefore Paul says, 'And he is the head of the body, the Church: who is the beginning, the first-born from the dead; that in all things he might have the pre-eminence' (Col. i. 18). And in another place, 'Christ,' saith he, 'is the head of the Church: and he is the Saviour of the body' (Eph. v. 23). And again, 'Who is the head of the Church, which is his body, the fullness of him that filleth all in all' (Eph. i. 22, 23). Again, 'Let us grow up into him in all things, which is the head, even Christ;

by whom all the body being knit together, receiveth increase' (Eph. iv. 15, 16). And therefore we do not allow of the doctrine of the Romish prelates, who would make the Pope the general pastor and supreme head of the Church Militant here on earth, and the very vicar of Jesus Christ, who has (as they say) all fullness of power and sovereign authority in the Church. For we hold and teach that Christ our Lord is, and remains still, the only universal pastor, and highest bishop, before God his Father; and that in the Church he performs all the duties of a pastor or bishop, even to the world's end; and therefore stands not in need of any other to supply his room. For he is said to have a substitute, who is absent; but Christ is present with his Church, and is the head that gives life thereunto. He did straitly forbid his apostles and their successors all superiority or dominion in the Church. They, therefore, that by gainsaying set themselves against so manifest a truth, and bring another kind of government into the Church, who sees not that they are to be counted in the number of them of the apostles of Christ prophesied? as in Peter, 2 Epist. ii. 1, and Paul, Acts xx. 29; 2 Cor. xi. 13; 2 Thess. ii. 8, 9, and in many other places.

Now, by taking away the Romish head we do not bring any confusion or disorder into the Church. For we teach that the government of the Church which the apostles set down is sufficient to keep the Church in due order; which, from the beginning, while as yet it wanted such a Romish head as is now pretended to keep it in order, was not disordered or full of confusion. The Romish head doth maintain indeed his tyranny and corruption which have been brought into the Church; but in the mean time he hinders, resists, and, with all the might he can make, cuts off the right and lawful reformation of the Church.

They object against us that there have been great strifes and dissensions in our churches since they did sever themselves from the Church of Rome; and that therefore they can not be true churches. As though there were never in the Church of Rome any sects, any contentions and quarrels; and that, in matters of religion, maintained not so much in the schools as in the holy Chairs, even in the audience of the people. We know that the apostle said, 'God is not the author of confusion, but of peace' (1 Cor. xiv. 33), and, 'Seeing there is

among you emulation and contention, are ye not carnal?' (1 Cor. iii.
3, 4). Yet may we not deny that God was in that Church planted
by the apostle; and that the Apostolic Church was a true Church,
howsoever there were strifes and dissensions in it. The Apostle Paul
reprehended Peter, an apostle (Gal. ii. 11), and Barnabas fell at variance with Paul (Acts xv. 39). Great contention arose in the Church
of Antioch between them that preached one and the same Christ, as
Luke records in the Acts of the Apostles, chap. xv. 2. And there have
at all times been great contentions in the Church, and the most excellent doctors of the Church have, about no small matters, differed in
opinion; yet so as, in the mean time, the Church ceased not to be the
Church for all these contentions. For thus it pleases God to use the
dissensions that arise in the Church, to the glory of his name, to the
setting forth of the truth, and to the end that such as are not approved
might be manifest (1 Cor. xi. 19).

Now, as we acknowledge no other head of the Church than Christ,
so do we not acknowledge every church to be the true Church which
vaunts herself so to be; but we teach that to be the true Church indeed in which the marks and tokens of the true Church are to be
found. Firstly and chiefly, the lawful and sincere preaching of the
word of God as it is left unto us in the writings of the prophets and
the apostles, which do all seem to lead us unto Christ, who in the Gospel has said, 'My sheep hear my voice, and I know them, and they follow me; and I give unto them eternal life. A stranger they do not
hear, but flee from him, because they know not his voice' (John x. 5,
27, 28).

And they that are such in the Church of God have all but one faith
and one spirit; and therefore they worship but one God, and him
alone they serve in spirit and in truth, loving him with all their hearts
and with all their strength, praying unto him alone through Jesus
Christ, the only Mediator and Intercessor; and they seek not life or
justice but only in Christ, and by faith in him; because they do acknowledge Christ the only head and foundation of his Church, and,
being surely founded on him, do daily repair themselves by repentance,
and do with patience bear the cross laid upon them; and, besides, by
unfeigned love joining themselves to all the members of Christ, do
thereby declare themselves to be the disciples of Christ, by continuing

in the bond of peace and holy unity. They do withal communicate in the sacraments ordained by Christ, and delivered unto us by his apostles, using them in no other manner than as they received them from the Lord himself. That saying of the Apostle Paul is well known to all, 'I received from the Lord that which I delivered unto you' (1 Cor. xi. 23). For which cause we condemn all such churches, as strangers from the true Church of Christ, which are not such as we have heard they ought to be, howsoever, in the mean time, they brag of the succession of bishops, of unity, and of antiquity. Moreover, we have in charge from the apostles of Christ 'to shun idolatry' (1 Cor. x. 14; 1 John v. 21), and 'to come out of Babylon,' and to have no fellowship with her, unless we mean to be partakers with her of all God's plagues laid upon her (Rev. xviii. 4; 2 Cor. vi. 17).

But as for communicating with the true Church of Christ, we so highly esteem it that we say plainly that none can live before God who do not communicate with the true Church of God, but separate themselves from the same. For as without the ark of Noah there was no escaping when the world perished in the flood; even so do we believe that without Christ, who in the Church offers himself to be enjoyed of the elect, there can be no certain salvation: and therefore we teach that such as would be saved must in no wise separate themselves from the true Church of Christ.

But as yet we do not so strictly shut up the Church within those marks before mentioned, as thereby to exclude all those out of the Church who either do not participate of the sacraments (not willingly, nor upon contempt; but who, being constrained by necessity, do against their will abstain from them, or else do want them), or in whom faith does sometimes fail, though not quite decay, nor altogether die: or in whom some slips and errors of infirmity may be found. For we know that God had some friends in the world that were not of the commonwealth of Israel. We know what befell the people of God in the captivity of Babylon, where they were without their sacrifices seventy years. We know what happened to St. Peter, who denied his Master, and what is wont daily to happen among the faithful and chosen of God who go astray and are full of infirmities. We know, moreover, what manner of churches the churches in Galatia and Corinth were in the apostles' time: in which St. Paul condemns many and heinous crimes; yet he calls them holy churches of Christ (1 Cor. i. 2; Gal. i. 2).

Yea, and it happens sometimes that God in his just judgment suffers the truth of his Word, and the Catholic faith, and his own true worship, to be so obscured and defaced that the Church seems almost quite razed out, and not so much as a face of a Church to remain ; as we see fell out in the days of Elijah (1 Kings xix. 10, 14), and at other times.   And yet, in the mean time, the Lord has in this world, even in this darkness, his true worshippers, and those not a few, but even seven thousand and more (1 Kings xix. 18; Rev. vii. 4, 9).   For the apostle cries, ' The foundation of the Lord standeth sure, and hath this seal, The Lord knoweth who are his,' etc. (2 Tim. ii. 19).   Whereupon the Church of God may be termed invisible; not that the men whereof it consists are invisible, but because, being hidden from our sight, and known only unto God, it cannot be discerned by the judgment of man.

Again, not all that are reckoned in the number of the Church are saints, and lively and true members of the Church.   For there are many hypocrites, who outwardly do hear the word of God, and publicly receive the sacraments, and do seem to pray unto God alone through Christ, to confess Christ to be their only righteousness, and to worship God, and to exercise the duties of charity to the brethren, and for a while through patience to endure in troubles and calamities.   And yet they are altogether destitute of the inward illumination of the Spirit of God, of faith and sincerity of heart, and of perseverance or continuance to the end.   And these men are, for the most part, at length laid open in their true character.   For the Apostle John says, ' They went out from among us, but they were not of us: for if they had been of us, they would have remained with us' (1 John ii. 19).   Yet these men, while they do pretend religion, are accounted to be in the Church.   Even as traitors in a commonwealth, before they be detected, are accounted in the number of good citizens; and as the cockle and darnel and chaff are found among the wheat; and as wens and swellings are in a perfect body, when they are rather diseases and deformities than true members of the body.   And therefore the Church is very well compared to a drag-net, which draws up fishes of all sorts; and to a field, wherein is found both darnel and good corn (Matt. xiii. 26, 47).   Hence we must be very careful not to judge rashly before the time, nor to exclude, and cast off or cut away, those whom the Lord would not have excluded nor cut off, or whom, without some damage to the Church, we can not separate from it. Again, we must be very vigilant lest the godly, falling fast asleep, the wicked grow stronger, and do some mischief in the Church.

Furthermore, we teach that it is carefully to be marked, wherein especially the truth and unity of the Church consists, lest that we either rashly breed or nourish schisms in the Church. It consists not in outward rites and ceremonies, but rather in the truth and unity of the Catholic faith. This Catholic faith is not taught us by the ordinances or laws of men, but by the holy Scriptures, a compendious and short sum whereof is the Apostles' Creed. And, therefore, we read in the ancient writers that there were manifold diversities of ceremonies, but that those were always free; neither did any man think that the unity of the Church was thereby broken or dissolved. We say, then, that the true unity of the Church does consist in several points of doctrine, in the true and uniform preaching of the Gospel, and in such rites as the Lord himself has expressly set down. And here we urge that saying of the apostle very earnestly, 'Let us, as many as are perfect, be thus minded: and if in any thing ye be otherwise minded, God shall reveal even this unto you. Nevertheless, whereunto we have already attained, let us walk by the same rule, let us mind the same thing' (Phil. iii. 15, 16).

CHAPTER XVIII.—OF THE MINISTERS OF THE CHURCH, THEIR INSTITUTION AND OFFICES.

God has always used his ministers for the gathering or erecting of a Church to himself, and for the governing and preservation of the same; and still he does, and always will, use them so long as the Church remains on earth. Therefore, the first beginning, institution, and office of the ministers is a most ancient ordinance of God himself, not a new device appointed by men. True it is that God can, by his power, without any means, take unto himself a Church from among men; but he had rather deal with men by the ministry of men. Therefore ministers are to be considered, not as ministers by themselves alone, but as the ministers of God, by whose means God does work the salvation of mankind. For which cause we give counsel to beware that we do not so attribute the things appertaining to our conversion and instruction unto the secret virtue of the Holy Spirit as to make void the ecclesiastical ministry. For it behooves us always to have in mind the words of the apostle, 'How shall they believe in him, of whom they have not heard? and how shall they hear without a preacher? Therefore faith is by hearing, and hearing by the word of God' (Rom. x. 14, 17). And that also which the Lord says, in the Gospel, 'Verily, verily, I say unto you, he that receiveth whomsoever I send receiveth me; and he that receiveth me receiveth him that sent me' (John xiii. 20). Likewise what a man of Macedonia, appearing in a vision to Paul, being then in Asia, said unto him; 'Come over into Macedonia, and help us' (Acts xvi. 9). And in another place the same apostle says, 'We are laborers together with God; ye are God's husbandry, ye are God's building' (1 Cor. iii. 9).

Yet, on the other side, we must take heed that we do not attribute too much to the ministers and ministry: herein remembering also the words of our Lord in the Gospel, 'No man can come to me, except the Father which hath sent me draw him' (John vi. 44), and the words of the apostle, 'Who then is Paul, and who is Apollos, but ministers by whom ye believed, even as the Lord gave to every man? So then neither is he that planteth any thing, nor he that watereth, but God that giveth the increase' (1 Cor. iii. 5, 7). Therefore let us believe that God does teach us by his word, outwardly through his ministers, and does inwardly move and persuade the hearts of his elect unto belief by his Holy Spirit; and that therefore we ought to render all the glory of this whole benefit unto God. But we have spoken of this matter in the First Chapter of this our Declaration.

God has used for his ministers, even from the beginning of the world, the best and most eminent men in the world (for, although some of them were inexperienced in worldly wisdom or philosophy, yet surely in true divinity they were most excellent)—namely, the patriarchs, to whom he spake very often by his angels. For the patriarchs were the prophets or teachers of their age, whom God, for this purpose, would have to live many years, that they might be, as it were, fathers and lights of the world. They were followed by Moses and the prophets renowned throughout all the world.

Then, after all these, our heavenly Father sent his only-begotten Son, the most perfect teacher of the world; in whom is hidden the wisdom of God, and from whom we derive that most holy, perfect, and pure doctrine of the Gospel. For he chose unto himself disciples, whom he made apostles; and they, going out into the whole world, gathered together churches in all places by the preaching of the Gospel. And afterward they ordained pastors and teachers in all churches, by the commandment of Christ; who, by such as succeeded them, has taught and governed the Church unto this day. Therefore, as God gave unto his ancient people the patriarchs, together with Moses and the prophets, so also to his people under the new covenant he sent his only-begotten Son, and, with him, the apostles and teachers of this Church.

Furthermore, the ministers of the new covenant are termed by divers names; for they are called apostles, prophets, evangelists, bishops, elders, pastors, and teachers (1 Cor. xii. 28; Eph. vi. 11). The apostles remained in no certain place, but gathered together divers churches throughout the whole world: which churches, when they were once established, there ceased to be any more apostles, and in their places were particular pastors appointed in every Church. The prophets, in old time, did foresee and foretell things to come; and, besides, did interpret the Scriptures; and such are found some among us at this day. They were called evangelists, who were the penmen of the history of the Gospel, and were also preachers of the Gospel of Christ; as the Apostle Paul gives in charge unto Timothy, 'to fulfill the work of an Evangelist' (2 Tim. iv. 5). Bishops are the overseers and watchmen of the Church, who distribute food and other necessities to the Church. The elders are the ancients and, as it were, the senators and fathers of the Church, governing it with wholesome counsel. The pastors both keep the Lord's flock, and also provide things necessary for it. The teachers do instruct, and teach the true faith and godliness. Therefore the Church ministers that now are may be called bishops, elders, pastors, and teachers.

But in process of time there were many more names of ministers brought into the Church. For some were created patriarchs, others archbishops, others suffragans; also, metropolitans, archdeacons, deacons, subdeacons, acolytes, exorcists, choristers, porters, and I know not what others, as cardinals, provosts, and priors; abbots, greater and lesser; orders, higher and lower. But touching all these, we little heed

what they have been in times past, or what they are now; it is sufficient for us that, so much as concerns ministers, we have the doctrine
of the apostles.

We, therefore, knowing certainly that monks, and the orders or sects
of them, are instituted neither by Christ nor by his apostles, we teach
that they are so far from being profitable that they are pernicious and
hurtful unto the Church of God.   For, although in former times they
were tolerable (when they lived solitarily, getting their livings with
their own hands, and were burdensome to none, but did in all places
obey their pastors, even as laymen), yet what kind of men they be now
all the world sees and perceives.   They pretend I know not what vows;
but they lead a life altogether disagreeing from their vows: so that the
very best of them may justly be numbered among those of whom the
apostle speaks: 'We hear that there are some among you which walk
inordinately, working not at all, but are busybodies,' etc. (2 Thess. iii.
11).   Therefore, we have no such in our churches; and, besides, we
teach that they should not be suffered to rout in the churches of
Christ.

Furthermore, no man ought to usurp the honor of the ecclesiastical
ministry; that is to say, greedily to pluck it to himself by bribes, or
any evil shifts, or of his own accord.   But let the ministers of the
Church be called and chosen by a lawful and ecclesiastical election and
vocation; that is to say, let them be chosen religiously by the Church,
and that in due order, without any tumult, seditions, or contention.
But we must have an eye to this, that not every one that will should
be elected, but such men as are fit and have sufficient learning, especially in the Scriptures, and godly eloquence, and wise simplicity; to
conclude, such men as are of good report for moderation and honesty
of life, according to that apostolic rule which St. Paul gives in the 1st
Epistle to Timothy iii. 2–7, and to Titus i. 7–9.   And those who are
chosen let them be ordained by the elders with public prayer, and laying on of hands.   We do here, therefore, condemn all those who run
of their own accord, being neither chosen, sent, nor ordained.   We do
also utterly disallow unfit ministers, and such as are not furnished with
gifts requisite for a pastor.

In the mean time we are not ignorant that the innocent simplicity
of certain pastors in the primitive Church did sometimes more profit

the Church than the manifold, exquisite, and nice learning of some others that were over-lofty and high-minded. And for this cause we also, at this day, do not reject the honest simplicity of certain men, who yet are not destitute of all knowledge and learning.

The apostles of Christ do term all those who believe in Christ 'priests;' not in regard to their ministry, but because that all the faithful, being made kings and priests, may, through Christ, offer up spiritual sacrifices unto God (Exod. xix. 6; 1 Pet. ii. 5, 9; Rev. i. 6). The ministry, then, and the priesthood are things far different one from the other. For the priesthood, as we said even now, is common to all Christians; not so is the ministry. And we have not taken away the ministry of the Church because we have thrust the popish priesthood out of the Church of Christ. For surely in the new covenant of Christ there is no longer any such priesthood as was in the ancient Church of the Jews; which had an external anointing, holy garments, and very many ceremonies which were figures and types of Christ, who, by his coming, fulfilled and abolished them (Heb. ix. 10, 11). And he himself remains the only priest forever; and we do not communicate the name of priest to any of the ministers, lest we should detract any thing from Christ. For the Lord himself has not appointed in the Church any priests of the New Testament, who, having received authority from the suffragan, may offer up the host every day, that is, the very flesh and the very blood of our Saviour, for the quick and the dead; but ministers, who may teach and administer the sacraments. Paul declares plainly and shortly what we are to think of the ministers of the New Testament, or of the Church of Christ, and what we must attribute unto them : ' Let a man,' says he, ' so account of us, as of the ministers of Christ, and stewards of the mysteries of God' (1 Cor. iv. 1). So that the apostle wants us to esteem ministers as ministers. Now the apostle calls them ὑπηρέτας, as it were under-rowers, who have an eye only to their pilot; that is to say, men that live not unto themselves, nor according to their own will, but for others—to wit, their masters, at whose commandment and beck they ought to be. For the minister of the Church is commanded wholly, and in all parts of his duty, not to please himself, but to execute that only which he has received in commandment from his Lord. And in this place it is expressly declared who is our Master, even Christ; to whom the ministers are in subjection in all the functions of their ministry. He adds further that the ministers of the Church are 'stewards, and dispensers of the mysteries of God' (1 Cor. iv. 1). Now the mysteries of God Paul in many places, and especially in Eph. iii. 4, does call 'the Gospel of Christ.' And the sacraments of Christ are also called mysteries by the ancient writers. Therefore for this purpose are the ministers called—namely, to preach the Gospel of Christ unto the faithful, and to administer the sacraments. We read, also, in another place in the Gospel, of 'the faithful and wise steward,' whom 'his Lord shall make ruler over his household, to give them their portion of meat in due season' (Luke xii. 42). Again, in another place of the Gospel, a man goes into a strange country, and, leaving his house, gives unto his servants authority therein, commits to them his substance, and appoints every man his work (Matt. xxv. 14).

This is now a fit place to speak somewhat also of the power and office of the ministers of the Church. And concerning their power some have disputed over busily, and would bring all things, even the very greatest, under their jurisdiction; and that against the commandment of God, who forbade unto his disciples all dominion, and highly commended humility (Luke xxii. 26; Matt. xviii. 3). Indeed, there is one kind of power which is mere and absolute power, called the power of right. According to this power all things in the whole world are subject unto Christ, who is Lord of all: even as he himself witnesses, saying, 'All power is given unto me in heaven and in earth' (Matt. xxviii. 18), and again, 'I am the first and the last, and behold I live forever, and I have the keys of hell and death' (Rev. i. 17, 18); also, 'He hath the key of David, which openeth, and no man shutteth; and shutteth, and no man openeth' (Rev. iii. 7).

This power the Lord reserves to himself, and does not transfer it to any other, that he might sit idly by, and look on his ministers while they wrought. For Isaiah says, 'I will put the key of the house of David upon his shoulder' (Isa. xxii. 22), and again, 'Whose government shall be upon his shoulders' (Isa. ix. 6). For he does not lay the government on other men's shoulders, but does still keep and use his own power, thereby governing all things. Furthermore, there is another power, that of office, or ministerial power, limited by him who has full and absolute power and authority. And this is more like a service than a dominion. For we see that a master does give unto the steward of his house authority and power over his house, and for that cause delivers him the keys, that he may admit or exclude such as his master will have admitted or excluded. According to this power does the minister, by his office, that which the Lord has commanded him to do; and the Lord does ratify and confirm that which he does, and will have the deeds of his ministers to be acknowledged and esteemed by his own deeds. Unto which end are those speeches in the Gospel: 'I will give unto thee the keys of the kingdom of heaven; and whatsoever thou bindest or loosest in earth shall be bound or loosed in heaven' (Matt. xvi. 19). Again, 'Whose sins soever ye remit, they shall be remitted; and whose sins soever ye retain, they shall be retained' (John xx. 23). But if the minister deal not in all things as the Lord has commanded him, but pass the limits and bounds of faith, then the Lord does make void that which he does. Wherefore the ecclesiastical power of the ministers of the Church is that function whereby they do indeed govern the Church of God, but yet so do all things in the Church as he has prescribed in his Word: which thing being so done, the faithful do esteem them as done of the Lord himself. But touching the keys we have spoken somewhat before.

Now the power, or function, that is given to the ministers of the Church is the same and alike in all. Certainly, in the beginning, the bishops or elders did, with a common consent and labor, govern the Church; no man lifted up himself above another, none usurped greater power or authority over his fellow-bishops. For they remembered the words of the Lord, 'He that is chief among you, let him be as he that doth serve' (Luke xxii. 26); they kept themselves by humility, and did mutually aid one another in the government and preservation of the Church. Notwithstanding, for order's sake, some one of the ministers called the assembly together, propounded unto the assembly the matters to be consulted of, gathered together the voices or sentences of the rest, and, to be brief, as much as lay in him, provided that there might arise no confusion.

So did St. Peter, as we read in the Acts of the Apostles, xi. 4–18, who yet for all that neither was above the rest, nor had greater authority than the rest. Very true, therefore, is that saying of Cyprian the martyr, in his book *De Simplicitate Clericorum:* 'The same doubtless

were the rest of the apostles that Peter was, having an equal fellowship with him both in honor and power: but the beginning hereof proceedeth from unity, to signify unto us that there is but one Church.'
St. Jerome also, in his commentary upon the Epistle of Paul to Titus,
has a saying not much unlike this: ' Before that, by the instinct of the
devil, there arose parties in religion, the churches were governed by the
common advice of the elders; but after that every one thought that
whom he had baptized were his own, and not Christ's, it was decreed that
one of the elders should be chosen, and set over the rest, who should
have the care of the whole Church laid upon him, and by whose means
all schisms should be removed.' Yet Jerome does not avouch this as an
order set down of God; for straightway he adds, ' Even as the elders
knew, by the continual custom of the Church, that they were subject
to him that is set over them, so the bishops must know that they are
above the elders rather by custom than by the prescript rule of God's
truth, and that they ought to have the government of the Church in
common with them.' Thus far Jerome. Now, therefore, no man can
forbid by any right that we may return to the old appointment of God,
and rather receive that than the custom devised by men.

The offices of the ministers are divers; yet, notwithstanding, most
men do restrain them to two, in which all the rest are comprehended:
to the teaching of the Gospel of Christ, and to the lawful administration of the sacraments. For it is the duty of the ministers to gather
together a holy assembly, therein to expound the Word of God, and
also to apply the general doctrine to the state and use of the Church;
to the end that the doctrine which they teach may profit the hearers,
and may build up the faithful. The minister's duty, I say, is to teach
the unlearned, and to exhort; yea, and to urge them to go forward in
the way of the Lord who do stand still, or linger and go slowly on:
moreover, to comfort and to strengthen those which are faint-hearted,
and to arm them against the manifold temptations of Satan; to rebuke
offenders; to bring them home that go astray; to raise them that are
fallen; to convince the gainsayers; to chase away the wolf from the
Lord's flock; to rebuke wickedness and wicked men wisely and severely; not to wink at nor to pass over great wickedness. And, besides,
to administer the sacraments, and to commend the right use of them,
and to prepare all men by wholesome doctrine to receive them; to

keep together all the faithful in a holy unity; and to encounter schisms. To conclude, to catechise the ignorant, to commend the necessity of the poor to the Church, to visit and instruct those that are sick, or entangled with divers temptations, and so keep them in the way of life. Besides all this, to provide diligently that there be public prayers and supplications made in time of necessity, together with fastings, that is, a holy abstinency, and most carefully to look to those things which belong to the tranquillity, peace, and safety of the Church.

And to the end that the minister may perform all these things the better, and with more ease, it is required of him that he be one that fears God, prays diligently, gives himself much to the reading of the Scripture, and, in all things, and at all times, is watchful, and does show forth a good example unto all men of holiness of life.

And seeing that there must be discipline in the Church, and that, among the ancient Fathers, excommunication was in use, and there were ecclesiastical judgments among the people of God, wherein this discipline was exercised by godly men; it belongs also to the minister's duty, for the edifying of the Church, to moderate this discipline, according to the condition of the time and public estate, and according to necessity. Wherein this rule is always to be holden, that 'all things ought to be done to edification, decently, and in order' (1 Cor. xiv. 40), without any oppression or tumult. For the apostle witnesses, that 'power was given to him of God, to edify and not to destroy' (2 Cor. x. 8). And the Lord himself forbade the cockle to be plucked up in the Lord's field, because there would be danger lest the wheat also be plucked up with it (Matt. xiii. 29).

But as for the error of the Donatists, we do here utterly detest it; who esteem the doctrine and administration of the sacraments to be either effectual or not effectual, according to the good or evil life of the ministers. For we know that the voice of Christ is to be heard, though it be out of the mouths of evil ministers; forasmuch as the Lord himself said, 'Observe and do whatsoever they bid you observe, but do ye not after their works' (Matt. xxiii. 3). We know that the sacraments are sanctified by the institution, and through the word of Christ; and that they are effectual to the godly, although they be administered by ungodly ministers. Of which matter Augustine, that blessed servant of God, did reason diversely out of the Scriptures against the Donatists. Yet, notwithstanding there ought to be a discipline among the ministers—for there should be intelligent inquiry in the synods touching the life and doctrine of the ministers—those that offend should be rebuked of the elders, and be brought into the way, if they be not past recovery; or else be deposed, and, as wolves, be driven from the Lord's flock by the true pastors if they be incurable. For, if they be false teachers, they are in no wise to be tolerated. Neither do we disallow of general councils, if that they be taken up according to the example of the apostles, to the salvation of the Church, and not to the destruction thereof.

The faithful ministers also are worthy (as good workmen) of their reward; neither do they offend when they receive a stipend, and all things that be necessary for themselves and their family. For the apostle shows that these things are for just cause given by the Church, and received by the ministers, in Cor. ix. 14, and in 1 Tim. v. 17, 18, and in other places also.

The Anabaptists likewise are confuted by this apostolical doctrine, who condemn and rail upon those ministers who live upon the ministry.

CHAPTER XIX.—OF THE SACRAMENTS OF THE CHURCH OF CHRIST.

God even from the beginning added unto the preaching of the Word his sacraments, or sacramental signs, in his Church. And to this does the holy Scripture plainly testify. Sacraments are mystical symbols, or holy rites, or sacred actions, ordained by God himself, consisting of his Word, of outward signs, and of things signified: whereby he keeps in continual memory, and recalls to mind, in his Church, his great benefits bestowed upon man; and whereby he seals up his promises, and outwardly represents, and, as it were, offers unto our sight those things which inwardly he performs unto us, and therewithal strengthens and increases our faith through the working of God's Spirit in our hearts; lastly, whereby he does separate us from all other people and religions, and consecrates and binds us wholly unto himself, and gives us to understand what he requires of us.

These sacraments are either of the Old Church or of the New. The sacraments of the Old were Circumcision, and the Paschal Lamb, which was offered up; under which name, reference is made to the sacrifices which were in use from the beginning of the world. The sacraments of the New Church are Baptism and the Supper of the Lord.

Some there are who reckon seven sacraments of the New Church. Of which number we grant that Repentance, Matrimony, and the Ordination of ministers (we mean not the popish, but the apostolical ordination) are very profitable, but no sacraments. As for confirmation and extreme unction, they are mere devices of men, which the Church may very well spare, without any damage or inconvenience at all; and, therefore, we have them not in our churches, because there are certain things in them which we can by no means allow of.[1] As for that merchandise which the Romish prelates use in ministering their sacraments, we utterly abhor it.

The author and institutor of all sacraments is not any man, but God alone: for man can by no means ordain sacraments; because they belong to the worship of God, and it is not for man to appoint and prescribe a service of God, but to embrace and retain that which is taught unto him by the Lord. Besides, the sacramental signs have God's promises annexed to them, which necessarily require faith: now faith stays itself only upon the Word of God; and the Word of God is resembled to writings or letters, the sacraments to seals, which the Lord alone sets to his own letters. And as the Lord is the author of the sacraments, so he continually works in that Church where they are rightly used; so that the faithful, when they receive them from the ministers, do know that the Lord works in his own ordinance, and therefore they receive them as from the hand of God; and the minister's faults (if there be any notorious in them) can not hurt them, seeing they do acknowledge the goodness of the sacraments to depend upon the ordinance of the Lord. For which cause they put a difference, in the administration of the sacraments, between the Lord himself and his minister; confessing that the substance of the sacraments is given them by the Lord, and the outward signs by the ministers of the Lord.

But the principal thing, which in all sacraments is offered by the Lord, and chiefly regarded by the godly of all ages (which some have called the substance and matter of the sacraments), is Christ our Sa-

---

[1] [Confirmation, with preparatory catechetical instruction, has afterwards been introduced in many Reformed churches in Europe, to supplement infant baptism.]

viour—that only sacrifice (Heb. x. 12); and that Lamb of God slain from the foundation of the world (Rev. xiii. 8); that rock, also, of which all our fathers drank (1 Cor. x. 4), by whom all the elect are circumcised with the circumcision made without hands, through the Holy Spirit (Col. ii. 11, 12), and are washed from all their sins (Rev. i. 5), and are nourished with the very body and blood of Christ unto eternal life (John vi. 54).

Now, in respect of that which is the chief thing, and the very matter and substance of the sacraments, the sacraments of both covenants are equal. For Christ, the only Mediator and Saviour of the faithful, is the chief thing and substance in them both: one and the same God is author of them both: they were given unto both churches as signs and seals of the grace and promises of God; which should call to mind and renew the memory of God's great benefits to them, and should distinguish the faithful from all the religions in the world; lastly, which should be received spiritually by faith, and should bind the receivers unto the Church, and admonish them of their duty. In these, I say, and such like things, the sacraments of both churches are not unequal, although in the outward signs they are diverse.

And, indeed, we do yet put a greater difference between them; for ours are more firm and durable, as those which are not to be changed to the end of the world. Again, ours testify that the substance and promise is already fulfilled and performed in Christ, whereas the other did only signify that they should be fulfilled. And again, ours are more simple, and nothing so painful, nothing so sumptuous, nor so full of ceremonies. Moreover, they belong to greater people, that is dispersed through the face of the whole earth; and because they are more excellent, and do by the Spirit of God stir up in us a greater measure of faith, therefore a more plentiful measure of the spirit does follow them.

But now, since Christ the true Messiah is exhibited unto us, and the abundance of grace is poured forth upon the people of the New Testament, the sacraments of the Old Law are surely abrogated and have ceased; and in their stead the sacraments of the New Testament are placed—namely, for Circumcision, Baptism; and for the Paschal Lamb and sacrifices, the Supper of the Lord.

And as in the old Church the sacraments consisted of the word, the sign, and the thing signified; so even at this day they are composed, as it were, of the same parts. For the Word of God makes them sacraments, which before were none: for they are consecrated by the Word, and declared to be sanctified by him who first ordained them. To sanctify or consecrate a thing is to dedicate it unto God, and unto holy uses; that is, to take it from the common and ordinary use, and to appoint it to some holy use. For the signs in the sacraments are drawn from common use, things external and visible. As in Baptism, the outward sign is the element of water, and that visible washing which is done by the minister; but the thing signified is regeneration and the cleansing from sins. Likewise, in the Lord's Supper, the outward sign is bread and wine, taken from things commonly used for meat and drink; but the thing signified is the body of Christ which was given, and his blood which was shed for us, or the communion of the body and blood of the Lord. Wherefore, the water, bread, and wine, considered in their own nature, and out of this holy use and institution of the Lord, are only that which they are called, and which we find them to be. But let the Word of God be added to them, together with invocation upon his holy name, and the renewing of their first institution and sanctification, and then these signs are consecrated, and declared to be sanctified by Christ. For Christ's first institution and consecration of the sacraments stands yet in force in the Church of God, in such sort that they who celebrate the sacraments no otherwise than the Lord himself from the beginning has appointed, have still, even to this day, the use and benefit of that first and most excellent consecration. And for this cause, in the administration of the sacraments, the very words of Christ are repeated.

And as we learn out of the Word of God that these signs were appointed unto another end and use than the common one, therefore we teach that they now, in this their holy use, do take upon them the names of things signified, and are not still called bare water, bread, or wine; but that the water is called 'regeneration, and washing of the new birth' (Tit. iii. 5), and the bread and wine 'the body of the Lord' (1 Cor. x. 16), or the pledges and sacraments of his body and blood. Not that the signs are turned into the things signified, or cease to be that which in their own nature they are (for then they could not be sacraments, which should consist only of the thing signified, and have no signs); but therefore do the signs bear the names of things, be. cause they are mystical tokens of holy things, and because the signs and the things signified are sacramentally joined together; joined together, I say, or united by a mystical signification, and by the purpose and will of him who first instituted them. For the water, bread, and wine are not common, but holy signs. And he that instituted water in Baptism did not institute it with that mind and purpose that the faithful should only be dipped in the water of Baptism; and he which commanded the bread to be eaten and the wine to be drunk in the Supper did not mean that the faithful should only receive bread and wine without any further mystery, as they eat bread at home in their houses: but that they should spiritually be partakers of the things signified, and by faith be truly purged from their sins, and be partakers of Christ also.

And, therefore, we can not allow of them who attribute the consecration of the sacraments to I know not what syllables; to the rehearsal of certain words pronounced by him that is consecrated,[1] and that has an intent of consecrating; or to some other accidental things, which are not left unto us either by the word, or by the example, of Christ or his apostles. We do also mislike the doctrine of those that speak no otherwise of the sacraments than of common signs, not sanctified, nor effectual. We condemn them also who, because of the invisible things, do despise the visible, and think the signs superfluous, because they do already enjoy the things themselves; such were the Messalians, as it is recorded. We do disallow their doctrine also who teach that grace and the things signified are to be so tied to and included in the signs that whosoever do outwardly receive the signs must needs inwardly participate in the grace, and in the things signified, what manner of men soever they be.

Notwithstanding, as we esteem not the goodness of the sacraments by the worthiness or unworthiness of the ministers, so likewise we do not weigh them by the condition of the receivers. For we know that the goodness of the sacraments does depend upon the faithfulness, or truth, and the mere goodness of God. For even as God's Word remains the true Word of God; wherein not only bare words are uttered when it is preached, but therewithal the things signified by the words

---

[1] [According to the reading, *a consecrato*. But other editions read *a consecratore*, by him who consecrates. See p. 288.]

are offered of God, although the wicked and unbelievers hear and understand the words, yet enjoy not the things signified, because they receive them not by a true faith; even so the sacraments, consisting of the Word, the signs, and the things signified, continue true and perfect sacraments, not only because they are holy things, but also because God offers the things signified, howsoever the unbelievers receive not the things which are offered. This comes to pass, not by any fault in God, the author and offerer of them, but by the fault of men, who do receive them without faith, and unlawfully: 'whose unbelief can not make the truth of God of none effect' (Rom. iii. 3).

Now, forasmuch as in the beginning, where we showed what the sacraments were, we did also, by the way, set down to what end they were ordained, it will not be necessary to trouble ourselves with repeating any thing which has been already handled. Next, therefore, in order, it remains to speak severally of the sacraments of the Christian Church.

CHAPTER XX.—OF HOLY BAPTISM.

Baptism was instituted and consecrated by God; and the first that baptized was John, who dipped Christ in the water in Jordan. From him it came to the apostles, who also did baptize with water. The Lord, in plain words, commanded them to preach the Gospel and to 'baptize in the name of the Father, the Son, and the Holy Spirit' (Matt. xxviii. 19). And Peter also, when divers demanded of him what they ought to do, said to them, in the Acts, 'Let every one of you be baptized in the name of Jesus Christ for the remission of sins, and ye shall receive the gift of the Holy Spirit' (Acts ii. 38). Hence baptism is called by some a sign of initiation for God's people, whereby the elect of God are consecrated unto God.

There is but one baptism in the Church of God; for it is sufficient to be once baptized or consecrated unto God. For baptism once received does continue all a man's life, and is a perpetual sealing of our adoption unto us. For to be baptized in the name of Christ is to be enrolled, entered, and received into the covenant and family, and so into the inheritance, of the sons of God; yea, and in this life to be called after the name of God; that is to say, to be called a son of God; to be purged also from the filthiness of sins, and to be endued with the manifold grace of God, in order to lead a new and innocent life. Baptism, therefore, does call to mind and keep in remembrance the great benefit of God performed to mankind. For we are all born in the pollution of sin and are the children of wrath. But God, who is rich in mercy, does freely purge us from our sins by the blood of his Son, and in him does adopt us to be his sons, and by a holy covenant does join us to himself, and does enrich us with divers gifts, that we might live a new life. All these things are sealed up unto us in baptism. For inwardly we are regenerated, purified, and renewed of God through the Holy Spirit; and outwardly we receive the sealing of most notable gifts by the water, by which also those great benefits are represented, and, as it were, set before our eyes to be looked upon. And therefore are we baptized, that is, washed or sprinkled with visible water. For the water makes clean that which is filthy, and refreshes and cools the bodies that fail and faint. And the grace of God deals in like manner with the soul; and that invisibly and spiritually.

Moreover, by the sacrament of baptism God does separate us from all other religions and nations, and does consecrate us a peculiar people to himself. We, therefore, by being baptized, do confess our faith, and are bound to give unto God obedience, mortification of the flesh, and newness of life; yea, and we are soldiers enlisted for the holy warfare of Christ, that all our life long we should fight against the world, Satan, and our own flesh. Moreover, we are baptized into one body of the Church, that we might well agree with all the members of the Church in the same religion and mutual duties.

We believe that the most perfect form of baptism is that by which Christ was baptized, and which the apostles did use. Those things, therefore, which by man's device were added afterwards and used in the Church we do not consider necessary to the perfection of baptism. Of this kind is exorcism, the use of lights, oil, spittle, and such other things; as, namely, that baptism is twice every year consecrated with divers ceremonies. But we believe that the baptism of the Church, which is but one, was sanctified in God's first institution of it, and is consecrated by the Word, and is now of full force, by the first blessing of God upon it.

We teach that baptism should not be ministered in the Church by women or midwives. For Paul secludes women from ecclesiastical callings; but baptism belongs to ecclesiastical offices.

We condemn the Anabaptists, who deny that young infants, born of faithful parents, are to be baptized. For, according to the doctrine of the Gospel, 'theirs is the kingdom of God' (Luke xviii. 16), and they are written in the covenant of God (Acts iii. 25). Why, then, should not the sign of the covenant of God be given to them? Why should they not be consecrated by holy baptism, who are God's peculiar people and are in the Church of God? We condemn also the Anabaptists in the rest of those peculiar opinions which they hold against the Word of God. We therefore are not Anabaptists, neither do we agree with them in any point that is theirs.[1]

CHAPTER XXI.—OF THE HOLY SUPPER OF THE LORD.

The Supper of the Lord (which is called the Lord's Table, and the Eucharist, that is, a Thanksgiving) is, therefore, commonly called a supper, because it was instituted by Christ at his last supper, and does as yet represent the same, and because in it the faithful are spiritually fed and nourished. For the author of the Supper of the Lord is not an angel or man, but the very Son of God, our Lord Jesus Christ, who did first of all consecrate it to his Church. And the same blessing and consecration does still remain among all those who celebrate no other but that very Supper, which the Lord did institute, and at that do recite the words of the Supper of the Lord, and in all things look unto the one Christ by a true faith; at whose hands, at it were, they do receive that which they do receive by the ministry of the ministers of the Church.

The Lord, by this sacred rite, would have that great benefit to be kept in fresh remembrance which he procured for mankind; to wit, that by giving up his body to death and shedding his blood he has forgiven us all our sins, and redeemed us from eternal death and the power of the devil, and now feeds us with his flesh, and gives us his blood to drink: which things, being apprehended spiritually by a true faith, do nourish us up to life everlasting. And this so great a benefit

---

[1] [It should be remembered that the Anabaptists who are so often condemned in the Lutheran and Reformed Confessions of the sixteenth century were fanatical and revolutionary in their opinions, and must not be confounded with the English and American Baptists, who arose in the seventeenth century and have grown to be one of the largest and most respectable Protestant denominations.—Ed.]

is renewed so oft as the Supper is celebrated.   For the Lord said, 'Do this in remembrance of me' (Luke xxii. 19).

By this holy Supper also it is sealed unto us, that the very body of Christ was truly given up for us, and his blood shed for the remission of our sins, lest our faith might somewhat waver.   And this is outwardly represented unto us by the minister in the sacrament, after a visible manner, and, as it were, laid before our eyes to be seen, which is inwardly in the soul invisibly performed by the Holy Spirit.   Outwardly, bread is offered by the minister, and the words of the Lord are heard : 'Take, eat; this is my body;' and, 'Drink ye all of it; this is my blood' (Matt. xxvi. 26–28; Luke xxii. 17–20).   Therefore the faithful do receive that which is given by the ministers of the Lord, and do eat the bread of the Lord, and do drink of the Lord's cup.   And at the same time inwardly, by the working of Christ through the Holy Spirit, they receive also the flesh and blood of the Lord, and do feed on them unto life eternal.   For the flesh and blood of Christ is true meat and drink unto life eternal : yea, Christ himself, in that he was delivered for us, and is our Saviour, is that special thing and substance of the Supper ; and therefore we suffer nothing to be put in his place.

But that it may the better and more plainly be understood how the flesh and blood of Christ are the meat and drink of the faithful, and are received by the faithful unto life eternal, we will add, moreover, these few things :

Eating is of divers sorts.   (1.) There is a *corporeal* eating, whereby meat is taken into a man's mouth, chewed with the teeth, swallowed down, and digested.   After this manner did the Capernaites in times past think that they should eat the flesh of the Lord; but they are confuted by him (John vi. 30–63).   For as the flesh of Christ could not be eaten bodily, without great wickedness and cruelty, so is it not food for the body, as all men do confess.   We therefore disallow that canon in the Pope's decrees, *Ego Berengarius* (*De Consecrat. Dist.* 2).   For neither did godly antiquity believe, neither yet do we believe, that the body of Christ can be eaten corporeally and essentially, with a bodily mouth.

(2.) There is also a *spiritual* eating of Christ's body; not such a one whereby it may be thought that the very meat is changed into the spirit, but whereby (the Lord's body and blood remaining in their own essence and property) those things are spiritually communicated unto us, not after a corporeal, but after a spiritual manner, through the Holy Spirit, who does apply and bestow upon us those things (to wit, remission of sins, deliverance, and life eternal) which are prepared for us by the flesh and blood of our Lord, sacrificed for us; so that Christ does now live in us, as we live in him; and does cause us to apprehend him by true faith to this end, that he may become unto us such a spiritual meat and drink, that is to say, our life. For even as corporeal meat and drink do not only refresh and strengthen our bodies, but also do keep them in life; even so the flesh of Christ delivered for us, and his blood shed for us, do not only refresh and strengthen our souls, but also do preserve them alive, not so far as they be corporeally eaten and drunken, but so far as they are communicated unto us spiritually by the Spirit of God, the Lord saying, 'The bread that I will give is my flesh, which I will give for the life of the world' (John vi. 51): also it is the spirit that gives life: 'the flesh' (to wit, corporeally eaten) 'profiteth nothing; the words which I speak unto you, they are spirit and they are life' (John vi. 63). And as we must by eating receive the meat into our bodies, to the end that it may work in us, and show its efficacy in us (because, while it is without us, it profiteth us not at all); even so it is necessary that we receive Christ by faith, that he may be made ours, and that he live in us, and we in him. For he says, 'I am the bread of life; he that cometh to me shall not hunger, and he that believeth in me shall not thirst any more' (John vi. 35); and also, 'He that eateth me, shall live through me; and he abideth in me, and I in him' (John vi. 50).

From all this it appears manifestly, that by spiritual meat we mean not any imaginary thing, but the very body of our Lord Jesus, given to us; which yet is received by the faithful not corporeally, but spiritually by faith: in which point we do wholly follow the doctrine of our Lord and Saviour Christ, in the 6th chapter of John. And this eating of the flesh and drinking of the blood of the Lord is so necessary to salvation that without it no man can be saved. But this spiritual eating and drinking takes place also without the Supper of the Lord, even so often as, and wheresoever, a man does believe in Christ. To which purpose that sentence of St. Augustine does happily belong, 'Why dost thou prepare thy teeth and belly? Believe, and thou hast eaten.'

(3.) Besides that former spiritual eating, there is a *sacramental* eating of the body of the Lord ; whereby the believer not only is partaker, spiritually and internally, of the true body and blood of the Lord, but also, by coming to the Table of the Lord, does outwardly receive the visible sacraments of the body and blood of the Lord.   True it is, that by faith the believer did before receive the food that gives life, and still receives the same; but yet, when he receives the sacrament, he receives something more.   For he goes on in continual communication of the body and blood of the Lord, and his faith is daily more and more kindled, more strengthened and refreshed, by the spiritual nourishment.   For while we live, faith has continual increasings ; and he that outwardly does receive the sacrament with a true faith, the same does not only receive the sign, but also does enjoy (as we said) the thing itself.   Moreover, the same does obey the Lord's institution and commandment, and with a joyful mind gives thanks for his redemption and that of all mankind, and makes a faithful remembrance of the Lord's death, and does witness the same before the Church, of which body he is a member.   This also is sealed to those who receive the sacrament, that the body of the Lord was given, and his blood shed, not only for men in general, but particularly for every faithful communicant, whose meat and drink he is, to life eternal.

But as for him that without faith comes to this Holy Table of the Lord, he is made partaker of the outward sacrament only; but the matter of the sacrament, from whence comes life unto salvation, he receives not at all; and such men do unworthily eat of the Lord's Table.   'Now they who do unworthily eat of the Lord's bread and drink of the Lord's cup, they are guilty of the body and blood of the Lord, and they eat and drink it to their judgment' (1 Cor. xi. 26–29). For when they do not approach with true faith, they do despite unto the death of Christ, and therefore eat and drink condemnation to themselves.

We do not, therefore, so join the body of the Lord and his blood with the bread and wine, as though we thought that the bread is the body of Christ, more than after a sacramental manner; or that the body of Christ does lie hid corporeally under the bread, so that it ought to be worshiped under the form of bread; or yet that whosoever he be who receives the sign, receives also the thing itself.   The body of

Christ is in the heavens, at the right hand of his Father; and therefore our hearts are to be lifted up on high, and not to be fixed on the bread, neither is the Lord to be worshiped in the bread. Yet the Lord is not absent from his Church when she celebrates the Supper. The sun, being absent from us in the heavens, is yet, notwithstanding, present among us effectually: how much more Christ, the Sun of Righteousness, though in body he be absent from us in the heavens, yet is present among us, not corporeally, but spiritually, by his lively operation, and so as he himself promised, in his Last Supper, to be present among us (John xiv. xv. and xvi.). Whereupon it follows that we have not the Supper without Christ, and yet that we may have meanwhile an unbloody and mystical supper, even as all antiquity called it.

Moreover, we are admonished, in the celebration of the Supper of the Lord, to be mindful of the body whereof we are members; and that, therefore, we should be at concord with our brethren, that we live holily, and not pollute ourselves with wickedness and strange religions; but, persevering in the true faith to the end of our life, give diligence to excel in holiness of life. It is therefore very requisite that, purposing to come to the Supper of the Lord, we do examine ourselves, according to the commandment of the apostle: first, with what faith we are indued, whether we believe that Christ is come to save sinners and to call them to repentance, and whether each man believes that he is in the number of them that are delivered by Christ and saved; and whether he has purposed to change this wicked life, to live holily, and to persevere through God's assistance, in the true religion, and in concord with his brethren, and to give worthy thanks to God for his delivery.

We think that rite, manner, or form of the Supper to be the most simple and excellent which comes nearest to the first institution of the Lord and to the apostles' doctrine: which does consist in declaring the Word of God, in godly prayers, in the action itself that the Lord used, and the repeating of it; in the eating of the Lord's body and drinking of his blood; in the wholesome remembrance of the Lord's death, and faithful giving of thanks; and in a holy fellowship in the union of the body of the Church.

We therefore disallow those who have taken from the faithful one part of the sacrament, to wit, the Lord's cup. For these do very grievously offend against the institution of the Lord, who says, 'Drink ye *all* of this' (Matt. xxvi. 27); which he did not so plainly say of the bread.

What manner of mass it was that the fathers used, whether it were tolerable or intolerable, we do not now dispute. But this we say freely, that the mass which is now used throughout the Roman Church is quite abolished out of our churches for many and just causes, which, for brevity's sake, we will not now particularly recite. Truly we could not approve of it, because they have changed a most wholesome action into a vain spectacle; also because the mass is made a meritorious matter, and is said for money; likewise because in it the priest is said to make the very body of the Lord, and to offer the same really, even for the remission of the sins of the quick and the dead. Add this also, that they do it for the honor, worship, and reverence of the saints in heaven (and for the relief of souls in purgatory), etc.

CHAPTER XXII.—OF HOLY AND ECCLESIASTICAL MEETINGS.

Although it be lawful for all men privately at home to read the Holy Scriptures, and by instruction to edify one another in the true religion, yet that the Word of God may be lawfully preached to the people, and prayers and supplications publicly made, also that the sacraments may be lawfully administered, and that collections may be made for the poor, and to defray all necessary charges, or to supply the wants of the Church, it is very needful that there should be holy meetings and ecclesiastical assemblies. For it is manifest that, in the apostolic and primitive Church, there were such assemblies, frequented of godly men. So many, then, as do despise them, and separate themselves from them, they are contemners of true religion, and are to be urged by the pastors and godly magistrates to abstain from stubbornly absenting themselves from sacred assemblies. Now, ecclesiastical assemblies must not be hidden and secret, but public and common; except persecution by the enemies of Christ and the Church will not suffer them to be public; for we know what manner of assemblies the primitive Church had formerly in secret corners, being under the tyranny of Roman emperors. But let those places where the faithful meet together be decent, and in all respects fit for God's Church. Therefore, let houses be chosen for that purpose, or churches, that are large and fair, so that they be purged from all such things as do not beseem the Church. And let all things be ordered as is most meet for comeliness, necessity, and godly decency, that nothing be wanting which is requisite for rites and orders, and the necessary uses of the Church.

And as we believe that God does not dwell in temples made with hands, so we know that by reason of the Word of God, and holy exercises therein celebrated, places dedicated to God and his worship are not profane, but holy; and that therefore such as are conversant in them ought to behave themselves reverently and modestly, as they who are in a sacred place, in the presence of God and his holy angels. All excess of apparel, therefore, is to be abandoned in churches and places where Christians meet for prayer, together with all pride and whatsoever else does not beseem Christian humility, discipline, and modesty. For the true ornament of churches does not consist in ivory, gold, and precious stones; but in the sobriety, godliness, and virtues of those who are in the church. 'Let all things be done decently and in order' in the church (1 Cor. xiv. 26). To conclude, 'Let things be done unto edifying' (ver. 40). Therefore, let all strange tongues keep silence in the holy assemblies, and let all things be uttered in the vulgar tongue, which is understood of all men in the company.

CHAPTER XXIII.—OF THE PRAYERS OF THE CHURCH, OF SINGING, AND OF CANONICAL HOURS.

True it is that a man may lawfully pray privately in any tongue that he does understand; but public prayers ought, in the holy assemblies, to be made in the vulgar tongue, or such a language as is known to all. Let all the prayers of the faithful be poured forth to God alone, through the mediation of Christ only, out of a true faith and pure love. As for invocation of saints, or using them as intercessors to entreat for us, the priesthood of our Lord Christ and true religion will not permit us. Prayer must be made for the magistracy, for kings, and all that are placed in authority, for ministers of the Church, and for all necessities of churches; and especially in any calamity of the Church prayer must be made, both privately and publicly, without ceasing.

Moreover, we must pray willingly, and not by constraint, nor for any reward; neither must we superstitiously tie prayer to any place, as though it were not lawful to pray but in the church. There is no necessity that public prayers should be in form and time the same or alike in all churches. Let all churches use their liberty. Socrates, in his *History*, says, 'In any country or nation whatsoever, you shall not find two churches which do wholly agree in prayer.' The authors of this difference, I think, were those who had the government of the churches in several ages. But if any do agree, it deserves great commendation, and is to be imitated by others.

Besides this, there must be a mean and measure, as in every other thing, so also in public prayers, that they be not over-long and tedious. Let, therefore, most time be given to the teaching of the Gospel in such holy assemblies; and let there be diligent heed taken that the people in the assemblies be not wearied with over-long prayers, so that, when the preaching of the gospel should be heard, they, through wearisomeness, either desire to go forth themselves or to have the assembly wholly dismissed. For unto such the sermons seem to be over-long which otherwise are brief enough. Yea, and the preachers ought to keep a mean.

Likewise the singing in sacred assemblies ought to be moderated where it is in use. That song which they call the Gregorian Chant has many gross things in it; wherefore it is upon good cause rejected by our Church, and most other Reformed churches. If there be any churches which have faithful prayer in good manner, without any singing, they are not therefore to be condemned, for all churches have not the advantage and opportunity of sacred music.[1] And certain it is by testimonies of antiquity that, as the custom of singing is very ancient in the Eastern churches, so it was long ere it was received in the Western churches.

In ancient times there were no such things as canonical hours; that is, fixed prayers framed for certain hours in the day, and therein chanted or often repeated, as the Papists' manner is: which may be proved by many of their lessons, appointed in their hours, and divers other arguments. Moreover, they have many absurd things (of which I say no more) that are well omitted by our churches and replaced by matters more wholesome for the universal Church of God.

---

[1] [Zwingli, although himself a friend of poetry and music, went too far at first in excluding both from the Church in Zurich; but the Reformed churches of Switzerland have long since been distinguished for excellent congregational singing in connection with poetical versions of Psalms and Christian hymns.—Ed.]

CHAPTER XXIV.—OF HOLYDAYS, FASTS, AND CHOICE OF MEATS.

Although religion be not tied unto time, yet can it not be planted and exercised without a due dividing and allotting-out of time. Every Church, therefore, does choose unto itself a certain time for public prayers, and for the preaching of the Gospel, and for the celebration of the sacraments; and it is not lawful for any one to overthrow this appointment of the Church at his own pleasure. For except some due time and leisure were allotted to the outward exercise of religion, without doubt men would be quite drawn from it by their own affairs.

In regard hereof, we see that in the ancient churches there were not only certain set hours in the week appointed for meetings, but that also the Lord's Day itself, ever since the apostles' time, was consecrated to religious exercises and to a holy rest; which also is now very well observed by our churches, for the worship of God and the increase of charity. Yet herein we give no place unto the Jewish observation of the day, or to any superstitions. For we do not account one day to be holier than another, nor think that mere rest is of itself acceptable to God. Besides, we do celebrate and keep the Lord's Day, and not the Jewish Sabbath, and that with a free observation.

Moreover, if the churches do religiously celebrate the memory of the Lord's Nativity, Circumcision, Passion, Resurrection, and of his Ascension into heaven, and the sending of the Holy Spirit upon his disciples, according to Christian liberty, we do very well approve of it. But as for festival days, ordained for men or saints departed, we can not allow of them. For, indeed, festival days must be referred to the first table of the law, and belong peculiarly unto God. To conclude, those festival days which are appointed for saints, and abrogated by us, have in them many gross things, unprofitable and not to be tolerated. In the mean time, we confess that the remembrance of saints, in due time and place, may be to good use and profit commended unto the people in sermons, and the holy examples of holy men set before their eyes to be imitated by all.

Now, the more sharply the Church of Christ does condemn surfeiting, drunkenness, and all kinds of lusts and intemperance, so much the more earnestly does it commend unto us Christian fasting. For fasting is nothing else than the abstinence and temperance of the godly, and a watching and chastising of our flesh, taken up for present necessity, whereby we are humbled before God, and withdraw from the flesh those things with which it is cherished, to the end that it may the more willingly and easily obey the Spirit. Wherefore they do not fast at all that have no regard for those things, but imagine that they fast if they stuff their bellies once a day, and for a set or prescribed time do abstain from certain meats, thinking that by this very work wrought they please God and acquire merit. Fasting is a help of the prayers of the saints and all virtues; but the fasts wherein the Jews fasted from meat, and not from wickedness, pleased God nothing at all, as we may see in the books of the Prophets.

Now, fasting is either public or private. In olden times they celebrated public fasts in troublesome times and in the afflictions of the Church; wherein they abstained altogether from meat till the evening, and bestowed all that time in holy prayers, the worship of God, and repentance. These differed little from mournings and lamentations; and of these there is often mention made in the Prophets, and especially in the 2d chapter of Joel. Such a fast should be kept at this day, when the Church is in distress. Private fasts are used by every one of us, according as every one feels the spirit weakened in him; for so he withdraws that which might cherish and strengthen the flesh.

All fasts ought to proceed from a free and willing spirit, and such a one as is truly humbled, and not framed to win applause and the liking of men, much less to the end that a man might merit righteousness by them. But let every one fast to this end, that he may deprive the flesh of that which would cherish it, and that he may the more zealously serve God.

The fast of Lent has testimony of antiquity, but none out of the apostles' writings; and therefore ought not, nor can not, be imposed on the faithful. It is certain that in old time there were divers manners and uses of this fast; whereupon Irenæus, a most ancient writer, says, 'Some think that this fast should be observed one day only, others two days, but others more, and some forty days. This diversity in keeping this fast began not in our times, but long before us; by those, as I suppose, who, not simply holding that which was delivered them from the beginning, fell shortly after into another custom, either through negligence or ignorance.' Moreover, Socrates, the historian, says, 'Because no ancient record is found concerning this matter, I think the apostles left this to every man's own judgment, that every one might work that which is good, without fear or constraint.'

Now, as concerning the choice of meats, we suppose that, in fasting, all things should be denied to the flesh whereby the flesh is made more lusty, wherein it does most immoderately delight, and whereby it is most of all pampered, whether they be fish, spices, dainties, or excellent wines. Otherwise we know that all the creatures of God were made for the use and service of men. All things which God made are good (Gen. i. 31), and are to be used in the fear of God, and with due moderation, without putting any difference between them. For the apostle says, 'To the pure all things are pure' (Tit. i. 15), and also, 'Whatsoever is sold in the shambles, that eat, asking no question for conscience' sake' (1 Cor. x. 25). The same apostle calls the doctrine of those who teach to abstain from meats 'the doctrine of demons;' for that 'God created meats to be received with thanksgiving of them which believe and know the truth. For every creature of God is good, and nothing to be refused, if it be received with thanksgiving' (1 Tim. iv. 1, 3, 4). The same apostle, in the Epistle to the Colossians, reproves those who, by an overmuch abstinence, will get unto themselves an opinion of holiness (Col. ii. 20–23). Therefore we do altogether mislike the Tatians and the Encratites, and all the disciples of Eustathius (of Sebaste), against whom the Gangrian Synod was assembled.

CHAPTER XXV.—OF CATECHISING, OF COMFORTING AND VISITING THE SICK.

The Lord enjoined his ancient people to take great care and diligence in instructing the youth well, even from their infancy; and, moreover, commanded expressly in his Law that they should teach them, and declare the mystery of the sacrament unto them. Now, forasmuch as is evident by the writings of the evangelists and apostles, that God has no less care of the youth of his new people (seeing he says, 'Suffer little children to come unto me; for of such is the kingdom of heaven' (Matt. xix. 14), therefore the pastors do very wisely who do diligently and betimes catechise their youth, laying the first grounds of faith, and faithfully teaching the rudiments of our religion, by expounding the Ten Commandments, the Apostles' Creed, the Lord's Prayer, and the doctrine of the sacraments, with other like principles and chief heads of our religion. And here let the Church perform her faithfulness and diligence in bringing the children to be catechised, as being desirous and glad to have her children well instructed.

Seeing that men do never lie open to more grievous temptations than when they are exercised with infirmities, or else are sick and brought low by diseases, it behooves the pastors of the churches to be never more vigilant and careful for the safety of the flock than in such diseases and infirmities. Therefore let them visit the sick betimes, and let them be quickly sent for by the sick, if the matter shall so require; let them comfort and confirm them in the true faith; finally, let them strengthen them against the dangerous suggestions of Satan. In like manner, let them pray with the sick person at home in his house; and, if need be, let them make prayers for the sick in the public meeting; and let them be careful that they have a happy passage out of this life. As for Popish visiting with the extreme unction, we have said before that we do not like it, because it has many absurd things in it, and such as are not approved by the canonical Scriptures.

CHAPTER XXVI. — OF THE BURIAL OF THE FAITHFUL, AND OF THE CARE WHICH IS TO BE HAD FOR SUCH AS ARE DEAD; OF PURGATORY, AND THE APPEARING OF SPIRITS.

The Scripture directs that the bodies of the faithful, as being temples of the Holy Spirit, which we truly believe shall rise again at the last day, should be honorably, without any superstition, committed to the earth; and, besides, that we should make honorable mention of those who died in the Lord, and perform all duties of love to those they leave behind, as their widows and fatherless children. Other care for the dead we do not enjoin. Therefore, we do greatly mislike the Cynics, who neglected the bodies of the dead, or did carelessly and disdainfully cast them into the earth, never speaking so much as a good word of the deceased, nor any whit regarding those whom they left behind them.

Again, we disapprove of those who are too much and preposterously officious to the dead; who, like the heathen, do greatly lament and bewail their dead (although we do not censure that moderate mourning which the apostle does allow [1 Thess. iv. 13], since it is unnatural not to be touched with sorrow); and who do sacrifice for the dead, and mumble certain prayers, not without their penny for their pains; thinking by these prayers to deliver their friends from torments, wherein, being wrapped by death, they suppose they may be rid of them again by such lamentable songs.

For we believe that the faithful, after bodily death, do go directly unto Christ, and, therefore, do not stand in need of helps or prayers for the dead, or any other such duty of them that are alive. In like manner, we believe that the unbelievers are cast headlong into hell, from whence there is no return opened to the wicked by any offices of those who live.

But as touching that which some teach concerning the fire of purgatory, it is directly contrary to the Christian faith ('I believe in the forgiveness of sins, and the life everlasting'), and to the absolute purgation of sins made by Christ, and to these sayings of Christ our Lord: 'Verily, verily, I say unto you, He that heareth my word, and believeth on him that sent me, hath everlasting life, and shall not come into condemnation; but is passed from death unto life' (John v. 24). Again, 'He that is washed, needeth not save to wash his feet, but is clean every whit: and ye are clean' (John xiii. 10).

Now, that which is recorded of the spirits or souls of the dead sometimes appearing to them that are alive, and craving certain duties of them whereby they may be set free: we count those apparitions among the delusions, crafts, and deceits of the Devil, who, as he can transform himself into an angel of light, so he labors tooth and nail either to overthrow the true faith, or else to call it into doubt. The Lord, in the Old Testament, forbade us to inquire the truth of the dead, and to have any thing to do with spirits (Deut. xviii. 10, 11). And to the glutton, being bound in torments, as the truth of the Gospel does declare, is denied any return to his brethren on earth; the oracle of God pronouncing and saying, 'They have Moses and the Prophets, neither will they be persuaded, if one arose from the dead' (Luke xvi. 29, 31).

CHAPTER XXVII.—OF RITES, CEREMONIES, AND THINGS INDIFFERENT.

Unto the ancient people were given in old time certain ceremonies, as a kind of schooling to those who were kept under the law, as under a schoolmaster or tutor. But Christ, the deliverer, being once come, and the law taken away, we who believe are no more under the law (Rom. vi. 14), and the ceremonies have vanished out of use. And the apostles were so far from retaining them, or repairing them, in the Church of Christ, that they witnessed plainly that they would not lay any burden upon the Church (Acts xv. 28). Wherefore we should seem to bring in and set up Judaism again if we should multiply ceremonies or rites in the Church according to the manner of the Jewish Church. And thus we are not of their judgment who would have the Church of Christ bound by many and divers rites, as it were by a certain schooling. For if the apostles would not thrust upon the Christian people the ceremonies and rites which were appointed by God, who is there, I pray you, that is well in his wits, that will thrust upon it the inventions devised by man? The greater the heap of ceremonies in the Church, so much the more is taken, not only from Christian liberty, but also from Christ, and from faith in him; while the people seek those things in ceremonies which they should seek in the only Son of God, Jesus Christ, through faith. Wherefore a few moderate and simple rites, that are not contrary to the Word of God, do suffice the godly.

And in that there is found diversity of rites in the churches, let no man say, therefore, that the churches do not agree. Socrates says, in his Church History, 'It were not possible to set down in writing all the ceremonies of the churches which are observed throughout cities and countries. No religion does keep every where the same ceremonies, although they admit and receive one and the self-same doctrine touching them; for even they who have one and the self-same faith do disagree among themselves about ceremonies.' Thus much says Socrates; and we, at this day, having diversities in the celebration of the Lord's Supper, and in certain other things, in our churches, yet we do not disagree in doctrine and faith; neither is the unity and society of our churches rent asunder. For the churches have always used their liberty in such rites, as being things indifferent; which we also do at this day.

But yet, notwithstanding, we admonish men to take heed that they count not among things indifferent such as are not indeed indifferent; as some used to count the mass and the use of images in the Church for things indifferent. 'That is indifferent' (says Jerome to Augustine) 'which is neither good nor evil; so that, whether you do it or do it not, you are never the more just or unjust thereby.' Therefore, when things indifferent are wrested to the confession of faith, they cease to be free; as Paul does show that it is lawful for a man to eat flesh if no man do admonish him that it was offered to idols (1 Cor. x. 27, 28); for then it is unlawful, because he that eats it does seem to approve idolatry by eating of it (1 Cor. viii. 10).

CHAPTER XXVIII. — OF THE GOODS OF THE CHURCH, AND THE RIGHT USE OF THEM.

The Church of Christ has riches through the bountifulness of princes, and the liberality of the faithful, who have given their goods to the Church. For the Church has need of such goods; and has had goods from ancient time for the maintenance of things necessary for the Church. Now, the true use of the ecclesiastical goods was, and now is, to maintain learning in schools and in holy assemblies, with all the service, rites, and buildings of the Church; finally, to maintain teachers, scholars, and ministers, with other necessary things, and chiefly for the succor and relief of the poor. But for the lawful dispensing of these ecclesiastical goods let men be chosen that fear God: wise men, and such as are of good report in the government of their families.

But if the goods of the Church, by injury of the time, and the boldness, ignorance, or covetousness of some, be turned to any abuse, let them be restored again, by godly and wise men, unto their holy use; for they must not connive at so impious an abuse. Therefore, we teach that schools and colleges, whereinto corruption is crept in doctrine, in the service of God, and in manners, must be reformed; and that there provision should be made, piously, faithfully, and wisely, for the relief of the poor.

CHAPTER XXIX.—OF SINGLE LIFE, WEDLOCK, AND HOUSEHOLD GOVERNMENT.

Such as have the gift of chastity given unto them from above, so that they can with the heart or whole mind be pure and continent, and not be grievously burned with lust, let them serve the Lord in that calling, as long as they shall feel themselves endued with that heavenly gift; and let them not lift up themselves above others, but let them serve the Lord daily in simplicity and humility. For such are more apt for attending to heavenly things than they who are distracted with the private affairs of a family. But if, again, the gift be taken away, and they feel a continual burning, let them call to mind the words of the apostle, 'It is better to marry than to burn' (1 Cor. vii. 9).

For wedlock (which is the medicine of incontinency, and continency itself) was ordained by the Lord God himself, who blessed it most bountifully, and willed man and woman to cleave one to the other inseparably, and to live together in great concord (Gen. ii. 24; Matt. xiv. 5, 6). Whereupon we know the apostle said, 'Marriage is honorable in all, and the bed undefiled' (Heb. xiii. 4). And again, 'If a virgin marry, she hath not sinned' (1 Cor. vii. 28). We therefore condemn polygamy, and those who condemn second marriages. We teach that marriages ought to be contracted lawfully, in the fear of the Lord, and not against the laws which forbid certain degrees to join in matrimony, lest the marriages should be incestuous. Let marriages be made with consent of the parents, or such as are instead of parents; and for that end especially for which the Lord ordained marriages. And let them be confirmed publicly in the Church, with prayer and blessing. Moreover, let them be kept holy, with peace, faithfulness, dutifulness, love, and purity of the persons coupled together. Therefore let them take heed of brawlings, debates, lusts, and adulteries. Let lawful judgments and holy judges be established in the Church, who may maintain marriages, and may repress all dishonesty and shamefulness, and before whom controversies in matrimony may be decided and ended.

Let children also be brought up by the parents in the fear of the Lord; and let parents provide for their children, remembering the saying of the apostle, 'He that provideth not for his own, hath denied the faith, and is worse than an infidel' (1 Tim. v. 8). But especially let them teach their children honest arts and occupations, whereby they may maintain themselves. Let them keep them from idleness, and plant in them a true confidence in God in all these things; lest they, through distrust, or overmuch careless security, or filthy covetousness, wax loose, and in the end come to no good.

Now, it is most certain that those works which parents do in true faith, by the duties of marriage, and government of their families, are, before God, holy and good works indeed, and do please God no less than prayers, fastings, and alms-deeds. For so the apostle has taught in his epistles, especially in those to Timothy and Titus. And with the same apostle we account the doctrine of such as forbid marriage, or do openly dispraise or secretly discredit it as not holy or clean, among the ' doctrines of demons' (1 Tim. iv. 1).

And we do detest unclean single life, licentious lusts, and fornications, both open and secret, and the continency of dissembling hypocrites, when they are, of all men, most incontinent. All these God will judge. We do not disallow riches, nor contemn rich men, if they be godly and use their riches well; but we reprove the sect of the Apostolicals, etc.

CHAPTER XXX.—OF THE MAGISTRACY.

The magistracy, of what sort soever it be, is ordained of God himself, for the peace and quietness of mankind; and so that he should have the chief place in the world. If the magistrate be an adversary to the Church, he may hinder and disturb it very much; but if he be a friend and a member of the Church, he is a most useful and excellent member thereof; he may profit it very much, and finally may help and further it very excellently.

The chief duty of the civil magistrate is to procure and maintain peace and public tranquillity: which, doubtless, he shall never do more happily than when he shall be truly seasoned with the fear of God and true religion—namely, when he shall, after the example of the most holy kings and princes of the people of the Lord, advance the preaching of the truth, and the pure and sincere faith, and shall root out lies and all superstition, with all impiety and idolatry, and shall defend the Church of God. For indeed we teach that the care of religion does chiefly appertain to the holy magistrate.

Let him, therefore, hold the Word of God in his hands, and look that nothing be taught contrary thereunto. In like manner, let him govern the people, committed to him of God, with good laws, made according to the Word of God in his hands, and look that nothing be taught contrary thereunto. Let him hold them in discipline and in duty and in obedience. Let him exercise judgment by judging uprightly: let him not respect any man's person, or receive bribes. Let him protect widows, fatherless children, and those that be afflicted, against wrong; let him repress, yea, and cut off, such as are unjust, whether in deceit or by violence. 'For he hath not received the sword of God in vain' (Rom. xiii. 4). Therefore let him draw forth this sword of God against all malefactors, seditious persons, thieves, murderers, oppressors, blasphemers, perjured persons, and all those whom God has commanded him to punish or even to execute. Let him suppress stubborn heretics (who are heretics indeed), who cease not to blaspheme the majesty of God, and to trouble the Church, yea, and finally to destroy it.

And if it be necessary to preserve the safety of the people by war, let him do it in the name of God; provided he have first sought peace by all means possible, and can save his subjects in no way but by war. And while the magistrate does these things in faith, he serves God with those works which are good, and shall receive a blessing from the Lord.

We condemn the Anabaptists, who, as they deny that a Christian man should bear the office of a magistrate, deny also that any man can justly be put to death by the magistrate, or that the magistrate may make war, or that oaths should be administered by the magistrate, and such like things.

For as God will work the safety of his people by the magistrate, whom it is given to be, as it were, a father of the world, so all subjects are commanded to acknowledge this benefit of God in the magistrate. Therefore let them honor and reverence the magistrate as the minister of God; let them love him, favor him, and pray for him as their father; and let them obey all his just and equal commandments. Finally, let them pay all customs and tributes, and all other duties of the like sort, faithfully and willingly. And if the common safety of the country and justice require it, and the magistrate do of necessity make war, let them even lay down their life, and spend their blood for the common safety and defense of the magistrate; and that in the name of God, willingly, valiantly, and cheerfully. For he that opposes himself against the magistrate does provoke the wrath of God against him.

We condemn, therefore, all contemners of magistrates, rebels, enemies of the commonwealth, seditious villains, and, in a word, all such as do either openly or closely refuse to perform those duties which they owe.

The Conclusion.—We beseech God, our most merciful Father in heaven, that he will bless the rulers of the people, and us, and his whole people, through Jesus Christ, our only Lord and Saviour; to whom be praise and glory and thanksgiving, both now and forever. Amen.

SYMBOLA EVANGELICA.

PARS QUARTA:

RECENT CONFESSIONAL DECLARATIONS AND TERMS OF CORPORATE CHURCH UNION.

I. RECENT CONFESSIONAL DECLARATIONS.

During the last fifty years a strong impulse has been manifested within parts of Protestant Christendom to formulate new creeds or so to modify the creeds of the sixteenth and seventeenth centuries as to give adequate recognition to the love and fatherhood of God and the duty to carry on Christian missions, to restate such doctrines as the divine predestination, to properly emphasize the duties of human brotherhood, and also to erase polemic statements directed against Christian bodies. The impulse has been the product of modern studies of the New Testament and a reconsideration of the biblical system of doctrine, of historic research, and above all of an irenic spirit which has to a large extent displaced the habit of controversy and polemics among Christians on the matters that have divided them. The Eastern Orthodox Churches are pledged to a strict adherence to the Nicene Creed and ecclesiastical tradition as fixed by the seven councils which they accept as œcumenical: the Roman Church to the primitive creeds, tradition, and also the papal declarations so far as they bear on faith and morals. On the other hand, it is quite consistent with Protestant principles and the XXXIX Articles, the Westminster Confession, XXXI, 4, and other formulas of the sixteenth century for Protestants to modify and revise their creeds, if found necessary in the interest of truth and Christian fellowship and co-operation in the effort to spread the Gospel.

AMERICAN CONGREGATIONAL DECLARATIONS OF FAITH.

The following Statement of Doctrine was issued, 1883, by a commission of the National Council of the Congregational Churches of the U. S., appointed in St. Louis, 1880. Among the members of the commission of twenty-five were President Seelye of Amherst, Dr. Henry M. Dexter, and Professor George P. Fisher of Yale. Its duty was defined to be the preparation 'in the form of a Creed or Catechism, or both, of a simple, clear, and comprehensive exposition of the truths of the Glorious Gospel of the Blessed God, for the instruction and edification of our churches,' not to be adopted by the Council but to be sent out 'to the churches and to the world through the public press, to carry such weight of authority as the character of the Commission and the intrinsic merit of their exposition of truth may command.' See Walker: *Creeds and Platforms of Congregationalism*, 576–84.

STATEMENT OF DOCTRINE.

I. We believe in one God, the Father Almighty, Maker of heaven and earth, and of all things visible and invisible;

And in Jesus Christ, His only Son, our Lord, who is of one substance with the Father; by whom all things were made;

And in the Holy Spirit, the Lord and Giver of life, who is sent from the Father and Son, and who together with the Father and Son is worshipped and glorified.

II. We believe that the Providence of God, by which He executes His eternal purposes in the government of the world, is in and over all events; yet so that the freedom and responsibility of man are not impaired, and sin is the act of the creature alone.

III. We believe that man was made in the image of God, that he might know, love, and obey God, and enjoy Him forever; that our first parents by disobedience fell under the righteous condemnation of God; and that all men are so alienated from God that there is no salvation from the guilt and power of sin except through God's redeeming grace.

IV. We believe that God would have all men return to Him; that to this end He has made Himself known, not only through the works of nature, the course of His providence, and the consciences of men, but also through supernatural revelations made especially to a chosen people, and above all, when the fulness of time was come, through Jesus Christ His Son.

V. We believe that the Scriptures of the Old and New Testaments are the record of God's revelation of Himself in the work of redemption; that they were written by men under the special guidance of the Holy Spirit; that they are able to make wise unto salvation; and that they constitute the authoritative standard by which religious teaching and human conduct are to be regulated and judged.

VI. We believe that the love of God to sinful men has found its highest expression in the redemptive work of His Son; who became man, uniting His divine nature with our human nature in one person, who was tempted like other men, yet without sin; who, by His humiliation, His holy obedience, His sufferings, His death on the cross, and His resurrection, became a perfect Redeemer; whose sacrifice of Himself for the sins of the world declares the righteousness of God, and is the sole and sufficient ground of forgiveness and of reconciliation with Him.

VII. We believe that Jesus Christ, after He had risen from the dead, ascended into heaven, where, as the one Mediator between God and man, He carries forward His work of saving men; that He sends the Holy Spirit to convict them of sin, and to lead them to repentance and faith; and that those who through renewing grace turn to righteousness, and trust in Jesus Christ as their Redeemer, receive for His sake the forgiveness of their sins, and are made the children of God.

VIII. We believe that those who are thus regenerated and justified grow in sanctified character through fellowship with Christ, the indwelling of the Holy Spirit, and obedience to the truth; that a holy life is the fruit and evidence of saving faith; and that the believer's hope of continuance in such a life is in the preserving grace of God.

IX. We believe that Jesus Christ came to establish among men the kingdom of God, the reign of truth and love, righteousness and peace; that to Jesus Christ, the Head of this kingdom, Christians are directly responsible in faith and conduct; and that to Him all have immediate access without mediatorial or priestly intervention.

X. We believe that the Church of Christ, invisible and spiritual, comprises all true believers, whose duty it is to associate themselves in churches, for the maintenance of worship, for the promotion of spiritual growth and fellowship, and for the conversion of men; that these churches, under the guidance of the Holy Scriptures and in fellowship with one another, may determine—each for itself—their organization, statements of belief, and forms of worship; may appoint and set apart their own ministers; and should co-operate in the work which Christ has committed to them for the furtherance of the gospel throughout the world.

XI. We believe in the observance of the Lord's day as a day of holy rest and worship; in the ministry of the Word; and in the two sacraments, which Christ has appointed for His church: Baptism, to be administered to believers and their children, as the sign of cleansing from sin, of union to Christ, and of the impartation of the Holy Spirit; and the Lord's Supper as a symbol of His atoning death, a seal of its efficacy, and a means whereby He confirms and strengthens the spiritual union and communion of believers with Himself.

XII. We believe in the ultimate prevalence of the kingdom of Christ over all the earth; in the glorious appearing of the great God and our Saviour Jesus Christ; in the resurrection of the dead; and in a final judgment, the issues of which are everlasting punishment and everlasting life.

The following 'Statement of Faith' was adopted by the National Council of the Congregational Churches of the U. S., in session at Kansas City, 1913, and is sometimes called the Kansas City Creed. Of the six clauses, four are given, the last two being concerned with the 'purpose' and 'membership' of the National Council. See Barton: *Congregational Creeds and Covenants*, 1917, p. 203 sq., often reprinted in the Year Book of the Congregational Churches. According to Dr. Barton, the Statement 'is not a series of creedal articles, but is an inclusive statement of the essential things most surely believed by Christians.'

The Congregational Churches of the United States, by delegates in National Council assembled, reserving all the rights and cherished memories belonging to this organization under its former constitution and declaring the steadfast allegiance of the churches composing the Council to the faith which our fathers confessed, which from age to age has found its expression in the historic creeds of the Church universal and of this communion, and affirming our loyalty to the basic principles of our representative democracy, hereby set forth the things most surely believed among us concerning faith, polity, and fellowship.

FAITH: We believe in God the Father, infinite in wisdom, goodness and love; and in Jesus Christ, his Son, our Lord and Saviour, who, for us and our salvation, lived and died, rose again, and liveth evermore; and in the Holy Spirit, who taketh of the things of Christ and revealeth them to us, renewing, comforting and inspiring the souls of men. We are united in striving to know the will of God as taught in the Holy Scriptures, and in our purpose to walk in the ways of the Lord, made known or to be made known to us. We hold it to be the mission of the Church of Christ to proclaim the gospel to all mankind, exalting the worship of the one true God, and laboring for the progress of knowledge, the promotion of justice, the reign of peace, and the realization of human brotherhood. Depending, as did our fathers, upon the continued guidance of the Holy Spirit to lead us into all truth, we work and pray for the transformation of the world into the kingdom of God; and we look with faith for the triumph of righteousness and the life everlasting.

POLITY: We believe in the freedom and responsibility of the individual soul and the right of private judgment. We hold to the autonomy of the local church and its independence of all ecclesiastical control. We cherish the fellowship of the churches united in district, state, and national bodies for counsel and co-operation in matters of common concern.

THE WIDER FELLOWSHIP: While affirming the liberty of our churches, and the validity of our ministry, we hold to the unity and catholicity of the Church of Christ, and will unite with all its branches in hearty co-operation; and will earnestly seek, so far as in us lies, that the prayer of our Lord for His disciples may be answered, that 'they all may be one.'

THE PRESBYTERIAN CHURCH OF ENGLAND.

In 1890, the Presbyterian Synod of England adopted the XXIV. Articles of the Faith, prepared by a committee, appointed 1885. In 1892, it further adopted an Appendix of six chapters, dealing with church polity and membership, worship on the Lord's Day, civil government, and church discipline. In a letter to the editor, 1900, Dr. J. Oswald Dykes, who had a leading part in the preparation of the Articles, said that 'in drawing up the Articles, the aim has been to retain the essentials of the Reformed or Calvinistic divinity, but at the same time, to alter the point of view by placing, not the decree of election but the love of God in His Gospel in the centre, and by reverting to the Trinitarian arrangement of the older creeds.' By action of the Synod, 1892, the question is put to office-bearers, 'whether they sincerely own and believe the body of Christian doctrine set forth in the Westminster Confession and the other subordinate standards of the Church, and now more briefly expressed in the XXIV Articles, approved by the Synod, 1890.' The Articles were adopted by the Presbyterian Church of South Africa, 1897.

THE ARTICLES OF THE FAITH.

I. OF GOD. We believe in, and adore, one living and true God, Who is spirit, personal, infinite, and eternal, present in every place, the almighty Author and sovereign Lord of all; most blessed, most holy, and most free; perfect in wisdom, justice, truth and love; to us most merciful and gracious: unto Whom only we must cleave, Whom only we must worship and obey. To Him be glory for ever. Amen.

II. OF THE TRINITY. We acknowledge, with the ancient Church, the mystery of the Holy Trinity as revealed in Scripture, and believe that in the unity of the ever blessed Godhead there are three Persons, the Father, the Son, and the Holy Spirit, of one substance, equal in power and glory.

III. Of Creation. We believe that Almighty God, for His own glory and loving ends, was pleased in the beginning to create the heavens and the earth, by the Son, the Eternal Word; and, through progressive stages, to fashion and order this world, giving life to every creature; and to make man in His own image, that he might glorify and enjoy God, occupying and subduing the earth and having dominion over the creatures, to the praise of his Maker's name.

IV. Of Providence. We believe that God the Creator upholds all things by the word of His power, preserving and providing for all His creatures, according to the laws of their being; and that He, through the presence and energy of His Spirit in nature and history, disposes and governs all events for His own high design: yet is He not in any wise the author or approver of sin, neither are the freedom and responsibility of man taken away, nor have any bounds been set to the sovereign liberty of Him Who worketh when and where and how He pleaseth.

V. Of the Fall. We believe and confess that our first father, Adam, the representative head as well as common ancestor of mankind, transgressed the commandment of God through temptation of the devil, by which transgression he fell from his original state of innocence and communion with God; and so all mankind, being in him, have come under just condemnation, are subject to the penalty of death, and inherit a sinful nature, estranged from God, from which proceed all actual transgressions: and we acknowledge that out of this condition no man is able to deliver himself.

VI. Of Saving Grace. We believe and proclaim that God, Who is rich in mercy as well as of perfect justice, was moved by His great love to man to hold forth from the first a promise of redemption, which from age to age He confirmed and unfolded, and that, in the fulness of the time, He accomplished His gracious purpose by sending His Son to be the Saviour of the world: wherefore our salvation out of sin and misery is ever to be ascribed to free and sovereign grace.

VII. Of the Lord Jesus Christ. We believe in and confess, with the ancient Church, the Lord Jesus Christ, Who, being the eternal Son of God, became man by taking to Himself a true body and soul, yet without sin, being conceived by the power of the Holy Ghost, and born of the Virgin Mary; so that He is both God and Man, two whole perfect and distinct natures, the divine and the human, being inseparably joined together in one person, that He might be the Mediator between God and man, by Whom alone we must be saved.

VIII. Of the Work of Christ. We believe that the Mediator, the Lord Jesus Christ, being anointed with the Holy Spirit to proclaim and set up the Kingdom of God among men, did by His perfect life on earth, through words and deeds of grace, and by His death upon the cross, declare the Father, Whose image He is; and did fully satisfy divine justice, and obtain for us forgiveness of sins, reconciliation to God, and the gift of eternal life, through His obedience on our behalf to the law and will of His Father, even unto death, wherein, bearing our sins, He offered Himself up a sacrifice without spot to God.

IX. Of the Exaltation of Christ. We believe that Jesus Christ, being for our offences crucified, dead, and buried, saw no corruption, but was raised again on the third day, in Whose risen life we live anew, and have the pledge of a blessed resurrection; that in the same body in which He rose He ascended into heaven, where, as our High Priest, He maketh continual intercession for us; and that He sitteth at the right hand of God, Head of the Church, clothed with authority and power as Lord over all.

X. Of the Gospel. We hold fast and proclaim that God, Who willeth that all men should be saved and come to the knowledge of the truth, has, by His Son our Saviour, given commission to the Church to preach unto all nations the Gospel of His grace, wherein He freely offers to all men forgiveness and eternal life, calling on them to turn from sin, and to receive and rest by faith upon the Lord Jesus Christ.

XI. Of the Holy Spirit. We believe in the Holy Spirit, the Lord, the Giver of life, Who worketh freely as He will, without Whose quickening grace there is no salvation, and Whom the Father never withholds from any who ask for Him; and we give thanks that He has in every age moved on the hearts of men; that He spake by the prophets; that through our exalted Saviour He was sent forth in power to convict the world of sin, to enlighten the minds of men in the knowledge of Christ, and to persuade and enable them to obey the call of the Gospel; and that He abides with the Church, dwelling in every believer as the Spirit of truth, of holiness, and of comfort.

XII. Of Election and Regeneration. We humbly own and believe that God the Father, before the foundation of the world, was pleased of His sovereign grace to choose unto Himself in Christ a people, whom He gave to the Son, and to whom the Holy Spirit imparts spiritual life by a secret and wonderful operation of His power, using as His ordinary means, where years of understanding have been reached, the truths of His Word in ways agreeable to the nature of man; so that, being born from above, they are the children of God, created in Christ Jesus unto good works.

XIII. Of Justification by Faith. We believe that every one, who through the grace of the Holy Spirit repents and believes the Gospel, confessing and forsaking his sins, and humbly relying upon Christ alone for salvation, is freely pardoned and accepted as righteous in the sight of God, solely on the ground of Christ's perfect obedience and atoning sacrifice.

XIV. Of Sonship in Christ. We believe that those who receive Christ by faith are united to Him, so that they are partakers in His life, and receive of His fulness; and that they are adopted into the family of God, are made heirs with Christ, and have His Spirit abiding in them, the witness to their sonship, and the earnest of their inheritance.

XV. Of the Law and New Obedience. We believe and acknowledge that the Lord Jesus Christ has laid His people by His grace under new obligation to keep the perfect Law of God, and has by precept and example enlarged our knowledge of that Law, and illustrated the spirit of filial love in which the divine will is to be obeyed; and we bless God that the obedience of Christians, though in this life always imperfect, yet being the fruit of their union to Christ, is accepted for His sake and well-pleasing to God.

XVI. Of Sanctification and Perseverance. We believe that the Holy Spirit dwelling in all Christ's people purifies their hearts, enabling them to do freely and cheerfully that which the will of God requires, so that in measure as they surrender themselves to the Spirit of Christ, and follow the guidance of His Word, they receive strength for daily service, and grow in holiness after the image of their Lord; or if, departing from God through unwatchfulness and neglect of prayer, any of them lapse into spiritual languor, or fall into grievous sins, yet by the mercy of God Who abideth faithful they are not cast off, but are chastened for their backsliding, and through repentance restored to His favour, so that they perish not.

XVII. Of the Church. We acknowledge one holy catholic Church, the innumerable company of saints of every age and nation, who, being united by the Holy Spirit to Christ their Head, are one body in Him, and have communion with their Lord and with one another: further, we receive it as the will of Christ that His Church on earth should exist as a visible and sacred brotherhood, consisting of those who profess faith in Jesus Christ and obedience to Him, together with their children, and organized for the confession of His name, the public worship of God, the upbuilding of the saints, and the proclamation of the Gospel; and we acknowledge, as a part, more or less pure, of this universal brotherhood, every particular Church throughout the world which professes this faith in Jesus Christ and obedience to Him, as Divine Lord and Saviour.

XVIII. Of Church Order and Fellowship. We believe that the Lord Jesus Christ, the sole Head of His Church, has appointed its worship, teaching, discipline and government to be administered according to His will revealed in Holy Scripture, by officers chosen for their fitness, and duly set apart to their office; and although the visible Church, even in its purest branch, may contain unworthy members, and is liable to err, yet believers ought not lightly to separate themselves from its communion, but are to live in fellowship with their brethren: which fellowship is to be extended, as God gives opportunity, to all who in every place call upon the name of the Lord Jesus.

XIX. Of Holy Scripture. We believe that God, Who manifests Himself in creation and providence, and especially in the spirit of man, has been pleased to reveal His mind and will for our salvation at successive periods and in various ways; and that this Revelation has been, so far as needful, committed to writing by men inspired of the Holy Spirit, in the Scriptures of the Old and New Testaments, which are therefore to be devoutly studied by all as God's written Word or message to mankind: and we reverently acknowledge the Holy Spirit speaking in the Scriptures to be the Supreme Judge in questions of faith and duty.

XX. Of the Sacraments. We acknowledge Baptism and the Lord's Supper, the two Sacraments instituted by Christ, to be of perpetual obligation, as signs and seals of the new covenant, ratified in His precious blood; through the observance of which His Church is to confess her Lord and to be visibly distinguished from the rest of the world: Baptism with water into the name of the Father and of the Son and of the Holy Ghost being the sacrament of admission into the visible Church, in which are set forth our union to Christ and regeneration by the Spirit, the remission of our sins, and our engagement to be the Lord's; and the Lord's Supper, the sacrament of communion with Christ and with His people, in which bread and wine are given and received in thankful remembrance of Him and of His sacrifice on the cross, and in which they who in faith receive the same do, after a spiritual manner, partake of the body and blood of the Lord Jesus Christ, to their comfort, nourishment, and growth in grace.

XXI. Of the Second Advent. We assuredly believe that on a day known only to God, the Lord Jesus Christ will suddenly come again from heaven with power and great glory; and we look for this second appearing of our Saviour as the blessed hope of His Church, for which we ought always to wait in sober watchfulness and diligence, that we may be found ready at His coming.

XXII. Of the Resurrection. We believe that the souls of the righteous enter at death upon a state of rest and felicity at home with the Lord; that there shall be a resurrection of the dead, both of the just and of the unjust, through the power of the Son of God; and that the bodies of all who are fallen asleep in Christ, as well as of the faithful who are alive at His coming, shall be fashioned anew and conformed to the body of His glory.

XXIII. Of the Last Judgement. We believe that God will judge the world in righteousness by Jesus Christ, before Whom all men must appear, Who shall separate the righteous from the wicked, make manifest the secrets of the heart, and render to every man according to the deeds which he hath done in the body, whether good or evil, when the wicked shall go away into eternal punishment but the righteous into eternal life.

XXIV. Of the Life Everlasting. Finally, we believe in and desire the life everlasting in which the redeemed shall receive their inheritance of glory in the kingdom of their Father, and be made fully blessed in the presence and service of God, Whom they shall see and enjoy for ever and ever. Amen.

THE PRESBYTERIAN CHURCH IN THE UNITED STATES OF AMERICA.

The Westminster Confession underwent a limited revision, 1903, in the Presbyterian Church North, as it is popularly called. In the last period of the nineteenth century, a demand arose within the Church for such ecclesiastical action as would relieve objections to its statements on the salvation of infants and divine predestination. In 1887, the clause forbidding the marriage of a deceased wife's sister or a deceased husband's brother was struck out. The right to make changes was exercised as early as 1729, when the Synod struck out or altered the chapters on civil government. The report made by a Committee on Revision created by the General Assembly, 1891, was vetoed by the presbyteries. In 1901, the Assembly for the second time appointed a committee stipulating that its work should be 'either by modification of the text or by Declaratory Statement, it being understood that the revision shall in no wise impair the integrity of the system of doctrine set forth in our Confession of Faith and taught in the Holy Scriptures.' The committee was also instructed to prepare a Brief Statement of the Reformed Faith 'expressed, so far as possible, in untechnical terms' for the purpose 'of giving information and a better understanding of our beliefs and not with a view to its becoming a substitute or an alternative of our Confession of Faith.' It was sent forth by the Assembly. In 1906, the Assembly denied an appeal that the Brief Statement be 'used as the Creed of our Church.'[1]

The Revision of the Westminster Confession, 1903, consists of a Declaratory Statement bearing on the subjects of God's decrees and the salvation of infants, changes in three chapters and two new chapters.

DECLARATORY STATEMENT.

While the ordination vow of ministers, ruling elders, and deacons, as set forth in the Form of Government, requires the reception and adoption of the Confession of Faith only as containing the System of Doctrine taught in the Holy Scriptures, nevertheless, seeing that the desire has been formally expressed for a disavowal by the Church of certain inferences drawn from statements in the Confession of Faith, and also for a declaration of certain aspects of revealed truth which appear at the present time to call for more explicit statement, therefore the Presbyterian Church in the United States of America does authoritatively declare as follows:

First, With reference to Chapter III. of the Confession of Faith: that concerning those who are saved in Christ, the doctrine of God's eternal decree is held in harmony with the doctrine of His love to all mankind, His gift of His Son to be the propitiation for the sins of the whole world, and His readiness to bestow His saving grace on all who seek it. That concerning those who perish, the doctrine of God's eternal decree is held in harmony with the doctrine that God desires not the death of any sinner, but has provided in Christ a salvation sufficient for all, adapted to all, and freely offered in the Gospel to all; that men are fully responsible for their treatment of God's gracious offer; that His decree hinders no man from accepting that offer; and that no man is condemned except on the ground of his sin.

---

[1] *Min. of the Gen. Assembly*, 1902, pp. 93–96; 1903, pp. 123–26. Also B. B. Warfield: six artt. in *Presb. Rev.*, 1901, 1902; P. Schaff: *Creed Revision in the Presb. Ch.*, N. Y., 1889, 2d ed., 1890, pp. 75. In the preface, Dr. Schaff said, 'I take my stand on the side of a revision of the Westm. Creed, in accordance with the advanced stage of theology and Christianity.'

Second, With reference to Chapter X., Section 3, of the Confession of Faith, that it is not to be regarded as teaching that any who die in infancy are lost. We believe that all dying in infancy are included in the election of grace, and are regenerated and saved by Christ through the Spirit, who works when and where and how He pleases.

CHANGES IN CHAPTERS.

XVI., 7. Works done by unregenerate men, although for the matter of them they may be things which God commands, and in themselves praiseworthy and useful, and although the neglect of such things is sinful and displeasing unto God; yet, because they proceed not from a heart purified by faith; nor are done in a right manner, according to His Word; nor to a right end, the glory of God; they come short of what God requires and do not make any man meet to receive the grace of God.

XXII., 3. Whosoever taketh an oath ought duly to consider the weightiness of so solemn an act, and therein to avouch nothing but what he is fully persuaded is the truth. Neither may any man bind himself by oath to any thing but what is good and just, and what he believeth so to be, and what he is able and resolved to perform.

XXV., 6. The Lord Jesus Christ is the only head of the Church, and the claim of any man to be the vicar of Christ and the head of the Church, is unscriptural, without warrant in fact, and is a usurpation dishonoring to the Lord Jesus Christ.[1]

THE ADDED CHAPTERS.

XXXIV. Of the Holy Spirit.—I. The Holy Spirit, the third person in the Trinity, proceeding from the Father and the Son, of the same substance and equal in power and glory, is, together with the Father and the Son, to be believed in, loved, obeyed, and worshiped throughout all ages.

II. He is the Lord and Giver of life, everywhere present in nature, and is the source of all good thoughts, pure desires, and holy counsels in men. By Him the Prophets were moved to speak the Word of God, and all writers of the Holy Scriptures inspired to record infallibly the mind and will of God. The dispensation of the Gospel is especially committed to Him. He prepares the way for it, accompanies it with His persuasive power, and urges its message upon the reason and conscience of men, so that they who reject its merciful offer are not only without excuse, but are also guilty of resisting the Holy Spirit.

III. The Holy Spirit, whom the Father is ever willing to give to all who ask Him, is the only efficient agent in the application of redemption. He convicts men of sin, moves them to repentance, regenerates them by His grace, and persuades and enables them to embrace Jesus Christ by faith. He unites all believers to Christ, dwells in them as their Comforter and Sanctifier, gives to them the spirit of Adoption and Prayer, and performs all those gracious offices by which they are sanctified and sealed unto the day of redemption.

IV. By the indwelling of the Holy Spirit all believers being vitally united to Christ, who is the Head, are thus united one to another in the Church, which is His body. He calls and anoints ministers for their holy office, qualifies all other officers in the Church for their special work, and imparts various gifts and graces to its members. He gives efficacy to the Word, and to the ordinances of the Gospel. By Him the Church will be preserved, increased until it shall cover the earth, purified, and at last made perfectly holy in the presence of God.

XXXV. Of the Love of God and Missions.—I. God, in infinite and perfect love, having provided in the covenant of grace, through the mediation and sacrifice of the Lord Jesus Christ, a way of life and salvation, sufficient for and adapted to the whole lost race of man, doth freely offer this salvation to all men in the Gospel.

---

[1] The original runs, 'nor can the Pope of Rome in any sense be head thereof: but is that anti-Christ, that man of sin and son of perdition, that exalteth himself in the Church against Christ and all that is called God.'

II. In the Gospel God declares His love for the world and His desire that all men should be saved, reveals fully and clearly the only way of salvation; promises eternal life to all who truly repent and believe in Christ; invites and commands all to embrace the offered mercy; and by His Spirit accompanying the Word pleads with men to accept His gracious invitation.

III. It is the duty and privilege of every one who hears the Gospel immediately to accept its merciful provisions: and they who continue in impenitence and unbelief incur aggravated guilt and perish by their own fault.

IV. Since there is no other way of salvation than that revealed in the Gospel, and since in the divinely established and ordinary method of grace faith cometh by hearing the Word of God, Christ hath commissioned His Church to go into all the world and to make disciples of all nations. All believers are, therefore, under obligation to sustain the ordinances of religion where they are already established, and to contribute by their prayers, gifts, and personal efforts, to the extension of the kingdom of Christ throughout the whole earth.

BRIEF STATEMENT OF THE REFORMED FAITH, 1902.

Art. I. *Of God.*—We believe in the ever-living God, who is a Spirit and the Father of our spirits; infinite, eternal, and unchangeable in His being and perfections; the Lord Almighty, most just in all His ways, most glorious in holiness, unsearchable in wisdom and plenteous in mercy, full of love and compassion, and abundant in goodness and truth. We worship Him, Father, Son, and Holy Spirit, three persons in one Godhead, one in substance and equal in power and glory.

Art. II. *Of Revelation.*—We believe that God is revealed in nature, in history, and in the heart of man; that He has made gracious and clearer revelations of Himself to Men of God who spoke as they were moved by the Holy Spirit; and that Jesus Christ, the Word made flesh, is the brightness of the Father's glory and the express image of His person. We gratefully receive the Holy Scriptures, given by inspiration, to be the faithful record of God's gracious revelations and the sure witness to Christ, as the Word of God, the only infallible rule of faith and life.

Art. III. *Of the Eternal Purpose.*—We believe that the eternal, wise, holy, and loving purpose of God embraces all events, so that while the freedom of man is not taken away nor is God the author of sin, yet in His providence He makes all things work together in the fulfillment of His sovereign design and the manifestation of His glory; wherefore, humbly acknowledging the mystery of this truth, we trust in His protecting care and set our hearts to do His will.

Art. IV. *Of the Creation.*—We believe that God is the creator, upholder, and governor of all things; that He is above all His works and in them all; and that He made man in His own image, meet for fellowship with Him, free and able to choose between good and evil, and forever responsible to his Maker and Lord.

Art. V. *Of the Sin of Man.*—We believe that our first parents, being tempted, chose evil, and so fell away from God and came under the power of sin, the penalty of which is eternal death; and we confess that, by reason of this disobedience, we and all men are born with a sinful nature, that we have broken God's law, and that no man can be saved but by His grace.

Art. VI. *Of the Grace of God.*—We believe that God, out of His great love for the world, has given His only begotten Son to be the Saviour of sinners, and in the Gospel freely offers His all-sufficient salvation to all men. And we praise Him for the unspeakable grace wherein He has provided a way of eternal life for all mankind.

Art. VII. *Of Election.*—We believe that God from the beginning, in His own good pleasure, gave to His Son a people, an innumerable multitude, chosen in Christ unto holiness, service, and salvation; we believe that all who come to years of discretion can receive this salvation only through faith and repentance; and we believe that all who die in infancy, and all others given by the Father to the Son who are beyond the reach of the outward means of grace, are regenerated and saved by Christ through the Spirit, who works when and where and how He pleases.

Art. VIII. *Of our Lord Jesus Christ.*—We believe in and confess the Lord Jesus Christ, the only Mediator between God and Man, who being the Eternal Son of God, for us men and for our salvation became truly man, being conceived by the Holy Ghost and born of the Virgin Mary, without sin; unto us He has revealed the Father, by His Word and Spirit making known the perfect will of God; for us He fulfilled all righteousness and satisfied eternal justice, offering Himself a perfect sacrifice upon the cross to take away the sin of the world; for us He rose from the dead and ascended into heaven, where He ever intercedes for us; in our hearts, joined to Him by faith, He abides forever as the indwelling Christ; over us, and over all for us, He rules; wherefore, unto Him we render love, obedience, and adoration as our Prophet, Priest, and King forever.

Art. IX. *Of Faith and Repentance.*—We believe that God pardons our sins and accepts us as righteous solely on the ground of the perfect obedience and sacrifice of Christ received by faith alone; and that this saving faith is always accompanied by repentance, wherein we confess and forsake our sins with full purpose of, and endeavour after, a new obedience to God.

Art. X. *Of the Holy Spirit.*—We believe in the Holy Spirit, the Lord and Giver of Life, who moves everywhere upon the hearts of men, to restrain them from evil and to incite them unto good, and whom the Father is ever willing to give unto all who ask Him. We believe that He has spoken by holy men of God in making known His truth to men for their salvation; that, through our exalted Saviour, He was sent forth in power to convict the world of sin, to enlighten men's minds in the knowledge of Christ, and to persuade and enable them to obey the call of the Gospel; and that He abides with the Church, dwelling in every believer as the spirit of truth, of holiness, and of comfort.

Art. XI. *Of the New Birth and the New Life.*—We believe that the Holy Spirit only is the author and source of the new birth; we rejoice in the new life, wherein He is given unto us as the seal of sonship in Christ, and keeps loving fellowship with us, helps us in our infirmities, purges us from our faults, and ever continues His transforming work in us until we are perfected in the likeness of Christ, in the glory of the life to come.

Art. XII. *Of the Resurrection and the Life to Come.*—We believe that in the life to come the spirits of the just, at death made free from sin, enjoy immediate communion with God and the vision of His glory; and we confidently look for the general resurrection at the last day, when the bodies of those who sleep in Christ shall be fashioned in the likeness of the glorious body of their Lord, with whom they shall live and reign forever.

Art. XIII. *Of the Law of God.*—We believe that the law of God, revealed in the Ten Commandments, and more clearly disclosed in the words of Christ, is forever established in truth and equity, so that no human work shall abide except it be built on this foundation. We believe that God requires of every man to do justly, to love mercy, and to walk humbly with his God; and that only through this harmony with the will of God shall be fulfilled that brotherhood of man wherein the kingdom of God is to be made manifest.

Art. XIV. *Of the Church and the Sacraments.*—We believe in the Holy Catholic Church of which Christ is the only Head. We believe that the Church Invisible consists of all the redeemed, and that the Church Visible embraces all who profess the true religion together with their children. We receive to our communion all who profess and obey Christ as their divine Lord and Saviour, and we hold fellowship with all believers in Him. We receive the sacraments of Baptism and the Lord's Supper, alone divinely established and committed to the Church, together with the Word, as means of grace; made effectual only by the Holy Spirit, and always to be used by Christians with prayer and praise to God.

Art. XV. *Of the Last Judgment.*—We believe that the Lord Jesus Christ will come again in glorious majesty to judge the world and to make a final separation between the righteous and the wicked. The wicked shall receive the eternal award of their sins, and the Lord will manifest the glory of His mercy in the salvation of His people and their entrance upon the full enjoyment of eternal life.

Art. XVI. *Of Christian Service and the Final Triumph.*—We believe that it is our duty, as servants and friends of Christ, to do good unto all men, to maintain the public and private worship of God, to hallow the Lord's Day, to preserve the sanctity of the family, to uphold the just authority of the state, and so to live in all honesty, purity, and charity, that our lives shall testify of Christ. We joyfully receive the word of Christ, bidding His people go into all the world and make disciples of all nations, and declare unto them that God was in Christ reconciling the world unto Himself, and that He will have all men to be saved and to come to the knowledge of the truth. We confidently trust that by His power and grace, all His enemies and ours shall be finally overcome, and the kingdoms of this world be made the kingdom of our God and His Christ. In this faith we abide; in this service we labor; and in this hope we pray. Even so, come, Lord Jesus.

THE CONFESSIONAL STATEMENT OF THE UNITED PRESBYTERIAN CHURCH OF NORTH AMERICA.

In 1925, the United Presbyterian Church of North America adopted a Confessional Statement which stands for the boldest official attempt within the Presbyterian family of Churches to restate the Reformed theology of the sixteenth century. It contains forty-four articles, whereas the Westminster Confession contains thirty-three articles. Some of the Westminster headings are omitted, such as 'of effectual calling,' of 'God's eternal decree,' and 'of the perseverance of saints,' and statements of similar or the same import are given under such headings as 'of the divine purpose,' 'of the Gospel call,' and 'of the security of believers.' The Confessional Statement omits for the most part distinctly theological and technical language, but accompanies all its articles with elaborate Scripture texts. Such expressions as elect persons, elect infants, foreordained, imputed, decree of election, covenant of works, covenant of grace, are not repeated, but in their stead such expressions are used as believers, children of God, chosen of God. The Assembly's act making the Statement law provides that 'wherever the Confession deviates from the Westminster standards, its declarations are to prevail.' The Preamble is as follows:

The United Presbyterian Church of North America declares afresh its adherence to the Westminster Confession of Faith and Catechisms, Larger and Shorter, as setting forth the system of doctrine taught in the Scriptures, which are the only infallible and final rule of faith and practice. Along with this it affirms the right and duty of a living Church to restate its faith from time to time so as to display any additional attainments in truth it may have made under the guidance of the Holy Spirit. Accordingly, by constitutional action consummated June 2, 1925, it adopted the following Confessional Statement. This Statement contains the substance of the Westminster symbols, together with certain present-day convictions of the United Presbyterian Church.

The articles treat of God, divine revelation, Holy Scripture, the divine purpose, creation, providence, angels, the sin of man, salvation, election, God the Father, the Lord Jesus Christ, the Holy Spirit, the atonement, the Gospel call, regeneration, saving faith, repentance, justification, adoption, sanctification, union with Christ, the security of believers, assurance, the law of God, the study of God's Word, prayer, praise, Sabbath observance, the sacraments, lawful oaths and vows, the Church, Church order, the ministry, Church fellowship, the family, civil government, the social order, the intermediate state, the second advent, the resurrection, the judgment, the life everlasting, Christian service and the final triumph. The following statements are given in full:

Art. X. *Of Election.*—We believe that the Eternal Father, before the foundation of the world, in His own good pleasure gave to His Son a people, an innumerable multitude, chosen in Christ unto salvation, holiness, and service; that all of these who come to years of discretion receive this salvation through faith and repentance; and that all who die in infancy, and all others who are given by the Father to the Son and are beyond the reach of the outward means of grace, are regenerated and saved by Christ through the Holy Spirit, Who works when and where and how He pleases.

Art. XV. *Of the Gospel Call.*—We believe that the gospel is a revelation of grace to sinners as such, and that it contains a free and unconditional offer of salvation through Christ to all who hear it, whatever may be their character or condition; that the offer is in itself a proper motive to obedience; and that nothing but a sinful unwillingness prevents its acceptance.

Art. XVII. *Of Saving Faith.*—We believe that saving faith is the gift of God; that in it there is not merely an assent to the truth that the Lord Jesus Christ is the Saviour of sinners, but also a cordial acceptance and appropriation of Him, and a fixed reliance upon Him, as our Saviour; that this faith, which involves the conviction of the mind, the trust of the heart, and the obedience of the will, rests solely upon the free and unlimited offer of Christ made in the gospel to sinners of mankind; and that such faith is the necessary and all-sufficient condition and channel for the communication of every spiritual gift and the progressive realization of salvation.

Art. XXXIV. *Of the Ministry.*—We believe that Jesus Christ as the Head of the Church has appointed therein the official ministry of reconciliation; that He calls men to this ministry through the working of the Holy Spirit in their hearts and by the orderings of providence; and that those thus called are to be set apart by ordination, whereby they are solemnly invested with the authority, powers, and duties of their sacred office.

Art. XL. *Of the Second Advent.*—We believe that the Lord Jesus Christ, Who at His ascension was received up into heaven, will come again to earth in person, visibly, with power and great glory; that His coming marks the consummation of the Kingdom of God; that the time thereof is reserved in the Divine counsels; and that this blessed hope is to be cherished as an incentive to watchful living and faithful witness-bearing on the part of Christ's followers.

PROTESTANT AND ROMAN CATHOLIC CATECHISMS.

Luther's Small Catechism, the Heidelberg Catechism, the Catechism of the Book of Common Prayer, and the Westminster Shorter Catechism, all having ecclesiastical authorization, are printed in full in this volume. Calvin's Catechism, which had 372 questions and answers, is treated in Volume I, pp. 467–70. The author of the first Roman Catholic catechisms, Peter Canisius, 1521–97, has recently been canonized and made a doctor of the Church. Leo XIII.'s encyclical on Canisius, 1897, included a severe condemnation of the Protestant Reformation and Reformers. The following Protestant catechisms of recent origin have had Church approval.

1. The Evangelical Free Church Catechism for Use in Home and School, 1898, was prepared by a committee under the direction of the National Council of the Evangelical Free Churches of England. The committee consisted of Congregationalists, Baptists, Wesleyan Methodists, Primitive Methodists, representatives of the Methodist New Connexion, and United Methodist Free Church, Presbyterians, and Bible Christians. The object of the catechism was 'to express the Christian doctrines held in common by all Evangelical Free Churches.' It consists of fifty-two questions and answers, the first question being "What is the Christian Religion?"

2. The School Catechism, 1904, was prepared by a "Conference of Members of the Reformed Churches in Scotland" namely ministers of the Wesleyan Methodist Church, the Congregational Union, the Episcopal Church in Scotland, the Church of Scotland and the United Free Church of Scotland. The conference convened at the invitation of the Church of Scotland. The catechism was "designed not to supersede the distinctive catechisms officially recognized by the several Churches" but to serve in schools where "the children of various Churches are taught together." It has 64 questions and answers, followed by the Apostles Creed, its first question being "Who created the heavens and the earth?"

3. The Intermediate Catechism, 1913, prepared by a committee appointed by the General Assembly of the Presbyterian Church in the U. S. A., was approved by the Assembly of 1913 in so far as it 'directed the Board of Publication to print the catechism for distribution in the

hope that it will be the means of advancing the cause of religious instruction in the home and in our churches.' It contains seventy-two questions and answers, with proof texts. The first question is "What do we most need to know?"

Roman Catholic catechisms of high authority are:

1. A Catechism of Christian Doctrine, prepared and enjoined by order of the Third Plenary Council of Baltimore, 1884, has appeared in several forms adapted to different ages and bears the imprimatures of Cardinals McCloskey, Gibbons, Hayes, and other high American dignitaries. It opens with the question, "Who made the world?"

2. *Catechismo della dottrina cristiana*—Catechism of Christian Doctrine,—1912, contains 433 questions and answers and opens with the question, 'Who created us?' It is 'published by the order of his Holiness, Pope Pius X.' In a letter, dated Oct. 18, 1912, Pius X., after declaring that from the first days of his pontificate he had cherished the greatest concern for the religious instruction of Christian people and in particular children, 'approved and prescribed the catechism for the dioceses and ecclesiastical province of Rome' and called upon priests, teachers, and Christian parents to teach it with all zeal. In 1924, it was ordered by the Italian government taught in the primary schools of Italy. A number of Italian manuals have appeared explaining the answers by historic illustrations and doctrinal explanations. The Manual issued in Turin, 1914, containing 590 pages, is dedicated to Pius X.

The definitions of the Church given in these five catechisms are the following:

The Evangelical Free Church Catechism:[1]

The Holy Catholic Church is that Holy Society of believers in Christ Jesus which He founded, of which He is the only Head, and in which He dwells by His Spirit; so that, though made up of many communions, organized in various modes, and scattered throughout the world, it is yet One in Him.

The School Catechism:

The Church of God is the whole body and brotherhood of Christian People of all countries and all times united by the Holy Spirit to the one Head, the Lord Jesus Christ.

---

[1] Rev. William Price Hughes, *Cont. Rev.*, Jan., 1899, expressed this high expectation which has not been fulfilled: 'Before we are twenty years older, all men will realize that this little catechism is one of the most wonderful and far-reaching facts of the wonderful century now hastening to its close.'

The Intermediate Catechism defines the Church in two answers:

There is only one Church, in which all the saved, in heaven and on earth, are included, and of which Jesus Christ is the Head. The Church on earth is the whole body of those who confess Christ as Lord and Saviour, together with their children.

The catechism of the Baltimore Plenary Council repeats the customary Roman Catholic definition and devotes a number of questions to the nature and authority of the Church:

The Church is the congregation of all those who profess the faith of Christ, partake of the same Sacraments, and are governed by their lawful pastors under one visible Head.

This definition is followed by the statement that 'Our Holy Father the Pope, the Bishop of Rome, is the Vicar of Christ on earth and the visible Head of the Church.'

The Catechism of Pius X.:

The Church is the company of true Christians, that is the baptized who profess the faith and doctrine of Jesus Christ, participate in his sacraments, and obey the pastors instituted by him. . . . The Church of Jesus Christ is the Catholic-Roman Church because it alone is one, holy, catholic, and apostolic, as He wanted it to be.

II. THE CORPORATE UNION OF CHURCH BODIES: BASES AND TERMS.

Lit. A selection is here given of the many works, larger and smaller, on the subject of Church reunion: G. J. Slosser: *Christian Unity*, N. Y., 1929, 425 pp.—G. K. A. Bell, Bp. of Chichester: *Documents on Christian Unity*, 2 vols., Oxf., 1924–30, 382, 225 pp.—P. Schaff: *The Reunion of Christendom*, N. Y., 1893, 46 pp. The enlargement of a paper read before the Chicago Parliament on Religions and his last literary work.—C. H. Briggs: *Church Unity*, N. Y., 1909, 459 pp.—W. R. Huntington: *The Peace of the Ch.*, N. Y., 1891, 240 pp.—Newman Smyth: *Passing Protestantism and Coming Catholicism*, N. Y., 1908, 209 pp.; A Story of Ch. Unity, etc., New Haven, 1923, 87 pp.—Glover: *The Free Churches and Reunion*, Cambr., 1921, 56 pp.—W. T. Manning, Bp. of N. Y.: *The Call to Unity*, N. Y., 1920, 162 pp.—Headlam, Bp. of Gloucester: *Doctr. of the Ch. and Church Reunion*, London, 1920, 326 pp.—Bp. Söderblom: *Christ. Fellowship*, N. Y., 1923, 212 pp.—Rowley, Baptist: *Aspects of Reunion*, N. Y., 1924, 182 pp.—Hayes, Prof. Evanston: *The Heights of Christ. Unity*, Cin., 1927, 271 pp.—Marchant: *The Reunion of Christendom*. A Survey, 1929.—P. Ainslie: *Towards Christ. Unity*, Balt., 1918; *The Scandal of Christianity*, 1929.

During the last fifty years the movement towards the active co-operation or full union of Church bodies has called forth much amicable discussion in religious assemblies, in books, and in proposals looking to that goal, and has issued in the actual consolidation of certain Protestant communions. Historically, it received a mighty impetus from the Evangelical Alliance, whose articles showed the agreement of all Protestant bodies in the fundamental matters of doctrine and whose General Conferences, beginning with the conference in London, 1846, and especially the notable gathering in New York, 1873, gave exhibition of the fellowship between the individual members of the Protestant Churches throughout the world. The spirit of Christian fellowship and co-operation have shown themselves in various ways. The Revision of the English Scriptures was carried on by committees of British and American scholars composed of representative scholars of many denominations for fifteen years. The International Conventions of the Y. M. C. A. and the Sunday School Union and the Missionary Conferences of Edinburgh, 1910, and Jerusalem, 1928, have superseded the barriers of race and nationality and borne witness to common Christian aims. The work of the Salvation Army, ministering to the daily needs of mankind, has an important place in this connection. The consolidations of Churches in mission lands, Japan, China, North and South India, the Philippines, have set an example for the Churches at home to follow.

The unionistic movement has taken the forms of organic union, proposals of such union, and federation for the purpose of co-operation in practical work; and all with the purpose of more effectually furthering the progress of Christ's kingdom by conserving the forces of men and expenditures and avoiding the waste arising from the unwise multiplication of local churches and Church agencies.[1] Such union and federation also serves to exhibit the substantial agreement within Protestantism in answer to the unjust attack from Roman Catholic sources that Protestant denominations are at discord in matters of essential Christian

---

[1] Washington in his address to the bishops, clergy, and laity of the Protestant Episcopal Church, 1789, among other things said: 'It would ill become me to conceal the joy I have felt in perceiving the fraternal affection which appears to increase every day among the friends of genuine religion. It affords edifying prospects indeed to see Christians of different denominations dwell together in more active charity, and conduct themselves in respect to each other, with a more Christian-like spirit, than ever they have done in any former age or in any other nation.'

belief. Denominational divisions have been the natural if not inevitable result of the principle of Protestantism, the right of private judgment. A source of weakness, they have also been an evidence of inherent strength, serving a providential purpose by developing freedom and thoroughness in the study of the New Testament and the early and mediæval history of the Christian Church, by quickening individual effort through competition, and by preventing the stagnation of religious thought and sameness of ritual, such as have marked certain parts of the Christian world. The amicable co-operation of Christian bodies is imperative. Organic union between them is desirable as a means of extending the message of the Gospel. Spiritual unity and fellowship are a mandate of the New Testament. Such unity is nobly expressed in the Anglican Bidding Prayer, by which ministers are bidden to 'pray for Christ's Holy Catholic Church, that is for the whole congregation of Christian people dispersed throughout the whole world.' A bidding prayer offered by the General Convention of the Protestant Episcopal Church, 1919, speaks 'of the blessed company of all faithful people.' In all Protestant churches prayer is made for the Holy Catholic Church, meaning thereby the Holy Christian Church, as Luther would have altered the wording of the Apostles' Creed.

A list of the consolidations which have taken place between Church communions—which is not intended to be exhaustive—and the terms on which such consolidations have been effected seem to be in harmony with the purpose of these volumes and the mind of the author. It must not be forgotten that the first creed formulated in America, the Cambridge Platform, 1648, gave as one of its two ends 'the holding forth of the Unity and Harmony, both amongst and with other Churches,' and its authors declared that 'the more they discerned the unkind and unbrotherly and un-Christian contentions of our godly brethren and countrymen, in matters of church-government, the more they did earnestly desire to see them joyned together in one common faith, and ourselves with them,' and that they did not 'desire to vary from the doctrine of faith, and truth held forth by the churches of our native country.' It may seem that the authors of the Platform took a strange way to show their regard for the unity for which they manifested concern, but it will not be forgotten that, in asserting the independence of the New England churches, they were also concerned for 'peace of con-

science,' which the Platform declared 'more desirable than the peace of
the outward man; and freedom from scruples of conscience more comfortable to a sincere heart than freedom from persecution.'

THE REUNION OF THE CUMBERLAND PRESBYTERIAN CHURCH WITH THE PRESBYTERIAN CHURCH, U. S. A., 1906.

The revision of the Westminster Confession of Faith by the Presbyterian Church North, 1903, modifying the definitions of the divine election and free will, opened the way for the return of the Cumberland
Presbyterian Church, which had existed as an independent body for
nearly a century, to the parent communion. A committee on 'Presbyterian fraternity and union' was appointed by the Cumberland Assembly, 1903, to 'confer with such like committees as may be appointed
by other Presbyterian bodies in regard to the desirability and practica-
bility of closer affiliation and organic union among the members of the
Presbyterian family in the United States.' An immediate reply was
given by the Presbyterian Church North in the appointment of a committee and a Basis of Union was favorably acted upon by a large
majority of the presbyteries of both bodies. In 1906, 'the Union and
Reunion' of the two bodies was declared to be 'in full force and effect.'
At the same time the General Assembly of the Church North made the
declaration that 'no acceptance of the doctrines of the Church is required of any communicant beyond a personal faith in Jesus Christ as
the Son of God and the Saviour of the world and a sincere acceptance
of him' and also that 'ministers, elders, and deacons, in approving the
Confession as Revised, 1903, are required to assent only to the system
of doctrine contained therein and not to every particular statement in
it.' The representatives of the united bodies met in one General Assembly, 1907. At the time of the reunion, the Cumberland Presbyterian
Church had 200,000 members, a number of whom chose to reorganize
or continue an independent organization. The terms of the Basis of
Union are as follows. See Min. of the Gen. Assembly of the U. S. A.,
1903, p. 122; 1904, p. 119; 1905, p. 67; 1906, p. 211:[1]

---

[1] In 1920 the Calvinistic Methodist (or Welsh Presbyterian Church in the U. S.) was
received into corporate union with the Presbyterian Church in the U. S. A. on the basis
of the Westminster Confession and the Scriptures as the inspired Word of God and the
infallible rule of faith and practice.

"The union shall be effected on the doctrinal basis of the Confession of Faith of the Presbyterian Church in the United States of America, as revised in 1903, and of its other doctrinal and ecclesiastical Standards; and the Scriptures of the Old and New Testaments shall be acknowledged as the inspired Word of God, the only infallible rule of faith and practice."

The Basis of the United Lutheran Church in the United States.

Organized Lutheranism in the American colonies dates from the Lutheran ministeriums of Philadelphia and New York formed respectively by Henry Melchior Mühlenberg, 1748, and his son, Frederick Augustus, 1786. Divided in part on account of degrees of doctrinal attachment to the Lutheran Standards and ritual observances, in part on matters of practical import such as membership in lodges and in part on account of national origins, Swedish, Norwegian, etc., groups have within the last twenty years entered into important consolidations and confederations. The consolidations are: 1. The United Lutheran Church in America, 1918, with 971,187 members, composed of the General Synod of the Evangelical Lutheran Church of the United States in America, organized 1820, the General Council of the Evangelical Lutheran Church in North America, organized 1867, and the United Synod of the Evangelical Lutheran Church in the South, organized 1886. To the General Synod belonged the Hartwick, Gettysburg, and other theological seminaries, and to the General Council the Mt. Airy and other seminaries. 2. The American Lutheran Church, 1930, with 340,809 members, composed of the independent Joint Ohio, Iowa and Buffalo Synods.[1] The American Lutheran Conference, constituted 1930, is a federation and includes the American Lutheran Church just mentioned, the Swedish Augustana Synod, the Norwegian and United Danish Churches, and the Lutheran Free Church. The Synodical Conference, numbering 873,454 members, 1930, is a federation of the Missouri Lutherans, the Joint Wisconsin Synod, and several small bodies. The Doctrinal Basis of Union of the United Lutheran Church in America is the following:

---

[1] An impetus was given to the unionistic spirit by the 400th celebration of the XCV Theses, 1917, and the spirit has shown itself most recently in the celebration of the 400th anniversary of the reading of the Augsburg Confession, during the summer of 1930 in Augsburg.

1. The United Lutheran Church in America receives and holds the canonical Scriptures of the Old and New Testaments as the inspired Word of God and as the only infallible rule and standard of faith and practice, according to which all doctrines and teachers are to be judged.

2. The United Lutheran Church in America accepts the three ecumenical creeds—namely, the Apostles', the Nicene, and the Athanasian—as important testimonies drawn from the Holy Scriptures, and rejects all errors which they condemn.

3. The United Lutheran Church in America receives and holds the Unaltered Augsburg Confession as a correct exhibition of the faith and doctrine of the Evangelical Lutheran Church, founded upon the Word of God, and acknowledges all churches that sincerely hold and faithfully confess the doctrines of the Unaltered Augsburg Confession to be entitled to the name of Evangelical Lutheran.

4. The United Lutheran Church in America recognizes the Apology of the Augsburg Confession, the Smalkald Articles, the Large and Small Catechisms of Luther, and the Formula of Concord as in the harmony of one and the same pure scriptural faith.

THE BASIS OF UNION OF THE UNITED CHURCH OF CANADA.

The United Church of Canada was constituted, 1925, by the consolidation of the Congregational, Methodist and Presbyterian bodies, and represents the boldest act, thus far, resulting in organic Church union. An impetus as well as a challenge was given to the union of Church forces by the formation of the Dominion of Canada, 1867, comprising all the British territories of North America except Newfoundland, and a pressing ground for union was given by the waste of means and men in the attempt of the denominations separately to reach the people and to prevent overlapping in the widely scattered and small communities of the Western provinces. The union of 1925 was preceded by consolidations within the Methodist and Wesleyan Canadian communions, 1833–83, and of the four Presbyterian groups, 1875, under a single General Assembly.

The larger movement,[1] resulting in the United Church, had its formal beginning in the appointment of committees on union by the Congregationalists, Methodists, and Presbyterians in 1902, 1903. The exact event to be looked for as the starting-point of the union was the suggestion made by Principal Patrick of Winnipeg College as a fraternal delegate of the Presbyterian Church before the Methodists' meeting in

---

[1] E. L. Morrow: *Ch. Unity in Canada*, Toronto, 1923, 426 pp. Opposed to the United Church movement. J. T. McNeill, Professor in Knox College: *Ch. Union in Canada*, Toronto, 15 pp. An answer to Morrow—*Basis of Union of the Un. Ch. of Canada*. An. Hist. Statement, Toronto, 1924, 34 pp.—R. J. Wilson: *Ch. Union in Canada after Three Years*, Toronto, 1929, 52 pp. Also McNeill: *The Presb. Ch. in Canada*, Toronto, 1925, 226 pp.

General Conference in Winnipeg, 1902. In response, the Conference appointed a committee 'for finding and formulating a Basis of Union with the Congregational and Presbyterian Churches.' In 1903 the Presbyterian General Assembly pronounced 'organic union both desirable and practicable' and placed Principal Caven as head of a committee appointed by it. The Congregationalists also having appointed a committee, the three committees met as a Joint Committee, 1904, in Toronto, and, 1909, it presented its report. Previously, 1906, the Joint Committee invited the Episcopal prelates in Canada and the Baptists to join in the movement, but the invitation was declined. The Methodist and Congregational Churches were almost unanimous in favoring the union. Within the Presbyterian Church a noticeable difference of opinion shewed itself from the beginning and grew more impressive as the movement progressed. The first vote on the Basis of Union, 1910, was as follows:

Congregationalists: Of 10,689 members, 2,933 voted for and 813 against.

Methodists: Of 293,967 members of eighteen years or over, 150,841 voted for and 24,357 against.

Presbyterians: Of 287,944 members, 106,755 voted for and 48,278 against. Upon the Basis of Union as amended—the call for amendment having come from the Presbyterian General Assembly—the vote in the Presbyterian Church, 1915, was as follows: Of the 76 presbyteries, 53 voted for, 13 against, the other 10 being either tied or sending no return. Of the members, 106,534 voted for and 69,913 against.

The Congregational and Methodist Churches having accepted the union, the Presbyterian General Assembly voted, 1922, to proceed 'to organic union as expeditiously as possible.' By act of July 19, 1924, "The United Church of Canada was authorized by 'his Majesty, by and with the advice and consent of the Senate and House of Commons of Canada.'" At the first meeting of the General Council, 1925, 150 delegates represented the former Methodist Church, 150 the Presbyterian, and 40 the Congregational churches. To this number were added 10 delegates from the Council of the Union Churches of Western Canada, which represented Christian communities that had united for worship or been amalgamated.

The Boards and Committees of the three constituent bodies, numbering twenty-six, have been merged into six agencies, the three denominational newspapers into the *New Outlook,* and the three missionary periodicals into one.[1]

The Basis of Union contains sections on doctrine and polity and includes a statement of the qualifications and training for the ministry and on administration, together with an Appendix on legislation. The polity of the Church calls for three superintending bodies, the presbytery, the conference and the General Council, the last meeting every two years. The Basis of Union is as follows:

GENERAL.—1. The name of the Church formed by the union of the Presbyterian, Methodist and Congregational Churches in Canada, shall be "The United Church of Canada." 2. It shall be the policy of The United Church to foster the spirit of unity in the hope that this sentiment of unity may in due time, so far as Canada is concerned, take shape in a Church which may fittingly be described as national.

DOCTRINE.—We, the representatives of the Presbyterian, the Methodist, and the Congregational branches of the Church of Christ in Canada, do hereby set forth the substance of the Christian faith, as commonly held among us. In doing so, we build upon the foundation laid by the apostles and prophets, Jesus Christ himself being the chief cornerstone. We affirm our belief in the Scriptures of the Old and New Testaments as the primary source and ultimate standard of Christian faith and life. We acknowledge the teaching of the great creeds of the ancient Church. We further maintain our allegiance to the evangelical doctrines of the Reformation, as set forth in common in the doctrinal standards adopted by the Presbyterian Church in Canada, by the Congregational Union of Ontario and Quebec, and by the Methodist Church. We present the accompanying statement as a brief summary of our common faith and commend it to the studious attention of the members and adherents of the negotiating Churches, as in substance agreeable to the teaching of the Holy Scriptures.

Art. I. *Of God.*—We believe in the one only living and true God, a Spirit infinite, eternal and unchangeable, in His being and perfections; the Lord Almighty, who is love, most just in all His ways, most glorious in holiness, unsearchable in wisdom, plenteous in mercy, full of compassion, abundant in goodness and truth. We worship Him in the unity of the Godhead and the mystery of the Holy Trinity, the Father, the Son, and the Holy Spirit, three persons of the same substance, equal in power and glory.

Art. II. *Of Revelation.*—We believe that God has revealed Himself in nature, in history, and in the heart of man; that He has been graciously pleased to make clearer revelation of Himself to men of God who spoke as they were moved by the Holy Spirit; and that in the fulness of time He has perfectly revealed Himself in Jesus Christ, the Word made flesh, who is the brightness of the Father's glory and the express image of His person. We receive the Holy Scriptures of the Old and New Testaments, given by inspiration of God, as containing the only infallible rule of faith and life, a faithful record of God's gracious revelations, and as the sure witness to Christ.

Art. III. *Of the Divine Purpose.*—We believe that the eternal, wise, holy, and loving purpose of God so embraces all events that, while the freedom of man is not taken away,

---

[1] The Presbyterian element opposing the consolidation and continuing an independent organization has its main strength in Ontario and had, 1929, 179,530 members, the United Church 650,989. In a third poll, 1924–25, 113,773 Presbyterians voted for the union and 114,367 against it.

nor is God the author of sin, yet in His providence He makes all things work together in the fulfilment of His sovereign design and the manifestation of His glory.

Art. IV. *Of Creation and Providence.*—We believe that God is the creator, upholder and governor of all things; that He is above all His works and in them all; and that He made man in His own image, meet for fellowship with Him, free and able to choose between good and evil, and responsible to his Maker and Lord.

Art. V. *Of the Sin of Man.*—We believe that our first parents, being tempted, chose evil, and so fell away from God and came under the power of sin, the penalty of which is eternal death; and that, by reason of this disobedience, all men are born with a sinful nature, that we have broken God's law and that no man can be saved but by His grace.

Art. VI. *Of the Grace of God.*—We believe that God, out of His great love for the world, has given His only begotten Son to be the Saviour of sinners, and in the Gospel freely offers His all-sufficient salvation to all men. We believe also that God, in His own good pleasure, gave to His Son a people, an innumerable multitude, chosen in Christ unto holiness, service and salvation.

Art. VII. *Of the Lord Jesus Christ.*—We believe in and confess the Lord Jesus Christ, the only Mediator between God and man, who, being the eternal Son of God, for us men and for our salvation became truly man, being conceived of the Holy Spirit and born of the Virgin Mary, yet without sin. Unto us He has revealed the Father, by His word and Spirit, making known the perfect will of God. For our redemption He fulfilled all righteousness, offered Himself a perfect sacrifice on the cross, satisfied Divine justice and made propitiation for the sins of the whole world. He rose from the dead and ascended into Heaven, where He ever intercedes for us. In the hearts of believers He abides forever as the indwelling Christ; above us and over us all He rules; wherefore, unto Him we render love, obedience and adoration as our Prophet, Priest and King.

Art. VIII. *Of the Holy Spirit.*—We believe in the Holy Spirit, the Lord and Giver of life, who proceeds from the Father and the Son, who moves upon the hearts of men to restrain them from evil and to incite them unto good, and whom the Father is ever willing to give unto all who ask Him. We believe that He has spoken by holy men of God in making known His truth to men for their salvation; that, through our exalted Saviour, He was sent forth with power to convict the world of sin, to enlighten men's minds in the knowledge of Christ, and to persuade and enable them to obey the call of the Gospel; and that He abides with the Church, dwelling in every believer as the spirit of truth, of power, of holiness, of comfort and of love.

Art. IX. *Of Regeneration.*—We believe in the necessity of regeneration, whereby we are made new creatures in Christ Jesus by the Spirit of God, who imparts spiritual life by the gracious and mysterious operation of His power, using as the ordinary means the truths of His word and the ordinances of Divine appointment in ways agreeable to the nature of men.

Art. X. *Of Faith and Repentance.*—We believe that faith in Christ is a saving grace whereby we receive Him, trust in Him and rest upon Him alone for salvation as He is offered to us in the Gospel, and that this saving faith is always accompanied by repentance, wherein we confess and forsake our sins with full purpose of and endeavor after a new obedience to God.

Art. XI. *Of Justification and Sonship.*—We believe that God, on the sole ground of the perfect obedience and sacrifice of Christ, pardons those who by faith receive Him as their Saviour and Lord, accepts them as righteous, and bestows upon them the adoption of sons, with a right to all the privileges therein implied, including a conscious assurance of their sonship.

Art. XII. *Of Sanctification.*—We believe that those who are regenerated and justified grow in the likeness of Christ through fellowship with Him, the indwelling of the Holy Spirit, and obedience to the truth; that a holy life is the fruit and evidence of saving faith;

and that the believer's hope of continuance in such a life is in the persevering grace of God. And we believe that in this growth in grace Christians may attain that maturity and full assurance of faith whereby the love of God is made perfect in us.

Art. XIII. *Of Prayer.*—We believe that we are encouraged to draw near to God, our Heavenly Father, in the name of His Son, Jesus Christ, and on our own behalf and that of others to pour out our hearts humbly yet freely before Him, as becomes His beloved children, giving Him the honor and praise due His holy name, asking Him to glorify Himself on earth as in heaven, confessing unto Him our sins and seeking of Him every gift needful for this life and for our everlasting salvation. We believe also that, inasmuch as all true prayer is prompted by His Spirit, He will in response thereto grant us every blessing according to His unsearchable wisdom and the riches of His grace in Jesus Christ.

Art. XIV. *Of the Law of God.*—We believe that the moral law of God, summarized in the Ten Commandments, testified to by the prophets and unfolded in the life and teachings of Jesus Christ, stands forever in truth and equity, and is not made void by faith, but on the contrary is established thereby. We believe that God requires of every man to do justly, to love mercy, and to walk humbly with God; and that only through this harmony with the will of God shall be fulfilled that brotherhood of man wherein the kingdom of God is to be made manifest.

Art. XV. *Of the Church.*—We acknowledge one holy Catholic Church, the innumerable company of saints of every age and nation, who being united by the Holy Spirit to Christ their Head are one body in Him and have communion with their Lord and with one another. Further, we receive it as the will of Christ that His Church on earth should exist as a visible and sacred brotherhood, consisting of those who profess faith in Jesus Christ and obedience to Him, together with their children, and other baptized children, and organized for the confession of His name, for the public worship of God, for the administration of the sacraments, for the upbuilding of the saints, and for the universal propagation of the Gospel; and we acknowledge as a part, more or less pure, of this universal brotherhood, every particular Church throughout the world which professes this faith in Jesus Christ and obedience to Him as divine Lord and Saviour.

Art. XVI. *Of the Sacraments.*—We acknowledge two sacraments, Baptism and the Lord's Supper, which were instituted by Christ, to be of perpetual obligation as signs and seals of the covenant ratified in His precious blood, as means of grace, by which, working in us, He doth not only quicken, but also strengthen and comfort our faith in Him, and as ordinances through the observance of which His Church is to confess her Lord and be visibly distinguished from the rest of the world. 1. Baptism with water into the name of the Father and of the Son and of the Holy Spirit is the sacrament by which are signified and sealed our union to Christ and participation in the blessings of the new covenant. The proper subjects of baptism are believers, and infants presented by their parents or guardians in the Christian faith. In the latter case, the parents or guardians should train up their children in the nurture and admonition of the Lord, and should expect that their children will, by the operation of the Holy Spirit, receive the benefits which the sacrament is designed and fitted to convey. The Church is under the most solemn obligation to provide for their Christian instruction. 2. The Lord's Supper is the sacrament of communion with Christ and with His people, in which bread and wine are given and received in thankful remembrance of Him and His sacrifice on the cross; and they who in faith receive the same, after a spiritual manner, partake of the body and blood of the Lord Jesus Christ to their comfort, nourishment and growth in grace. All may be admitted to the Lord's Supper who make a credible profession of their faith in the Lord Jesus Christ and of obedience to His law.

Art. XVII. *Of the Ministry.*—We believe that Jesus Christ, as the Supreme Head of the Church, has appointed therein a ministry of the word and sacraments, and calls men to this ministry; that the Church, under the guidance of the Holy Spirit, recognizes and chooses those whom He calls, and should thereupon duly ordain them to the work of the ministry.

Art. XVIII. *Of Church Order and Fellowship.*—We believe that the Supreme and only Head of the Church is the Lord Jesus Christ; that its worship, teaching, discipline and government should be administered according to His will by persons chosen for their fitness and duly set apart to their office, and that although the visible Church may contain unworthy members and is liable to err, yet believers ought not lightly to separate themselves from its communion, but are to live in fellowship with their brethren, which fellowship is to be extended, as God gives opportunity, to all who in every place call upon the name of the Lord Jesus.

Art. XIX. *Of the Resurrection, the Last Judgment and the Future Life.*—We believe that there shall be a resurrection of the dead, both of the just and of the unjust, through the power of the Son of God, who shall come to judge the living and the dead; that the finally impenitent shall go away into eternal punishment and the righteous into life eternal.

Art. XX. *Of Christian Service and the Final Triumph.*—We believe that it is our duty as disciples and servants of Christ, to further the extension of His kingdom, to do good unto all men, to maintain the public and private worship of God, to hallow the Lord's Day, to preserve the inviolability of marriage and the sanctity of the family, to uphold the just authority of the State, and so to live in all honesty, purity and charity that our lives shall testify of Christ. We joyfully receive the word of Christ, bidding His people go into all the world and make disciples of all nations, declaring unto them that God was in Christ reconciling the world unto Himself, and that He will have all men to be saved, and come to the knowledge of the truth. We confidently believe that by His power and grace all His enemies shall finally be overcome, and the kingdoms of this world be made the kingdom of our God and of His Christ.

Church Union in Scotland.

In 1929, the "rents" within the Reformed Church of Scotland were healed by the union of the Church of Scotland and the United Free Church of Scotland.[1] The most notable of the ecclesiastical divisions of Scotland occurred, 1843, over the question of patronage by a secession from the Church of Scotland, led by Thomas Chalmers, and the organization of the Free Church of Scotland. Three years later, the United Church of Scotland was formed. These two bodies, 1900, were merged under the name of the United Free Church of Scotland, a small number dissenting and popularly known as the Wee Frees. Declara-

---

[1] *The Proceedings and Debates of the General Assembly of the Un. Free Church of Scotland, May and Oct., 1929,* together with the *Proceedings and Debates of the Assembly, Nov. 1928,* 371 pp., Edinb., 1929. Includes notable addresses on union by the moderator, Alexander Martin of New College.—*Report of the Committee for Conference with the Ch. of Scotland,* Nov., 1928, 106 pp.—*Proceedings of the Union Assembly, Church of Scotland, Oct., 1929,* 120 pp., giving addresses of Cosmo Lang, Abp. of Canterbury, Lord Davidson, former Abp. of Canterbury, President Henry Sloane Coffin, Union Seminary, New York, Rev. Dr. John Hutton, etc.—Buchan and Principal Geo. Adam Smith: *The Kirk in Scotland 1560–1929,* 244 pp., London, 1930, gives a brief history of the Church of Scotland and an account by Principal Smith of the Union Assembly, of which he was a member.

tory Statements were issued by the United Presbyterian Church, 1879, the Church of Scotland, 1889, the Free Church, 1892, and the United Free Church, 1906, modifying or explaining certain sections of the Westminster Confession bearing on the universal intent of the atonement, the real offer of the Gospel to all men, and the salvation of infants dying in infancy unbaptized.

The movement looking towards the consolidation of the Church of Scotland and the United Free Church started in 1909 in an agreement 'to enter into unrestricted conference on the ecclesiastical situation in Scotland and the main causes which keep the Churches apart, in the earnest hope that by God's blessing, misunderstandings and hindrances may be removed and the great object of Presbyterian union in Scotland be thereby advanced.' The war interrupted conferences but did not quench the spirit of union. In nine articles drafted, 1921, the Church of Scotland asserted the separate and independent jurisdiction of the Church and the Church's right to legislate for itself. The same year, the United Free Church Assembly adopted a Brief Statement of the Church's Faith, being 'an expression of the great Christian certainties and of the Christian ideal of Life.' In 1896, all obstacles being removed, a Basis of Union or Uniting Act, was agreed upon by committees of the two communions and, under the so-called Barrier Act of 1697,[1] adopted by their presbyteries. A group of only 22 out of the 1,200 ministers of the United Free Church refused to go into the union.

The consolidation was consummated May, 1929. The two Assemblies met separately in the forenoon of Oct. 2. for 'services of thanksgiving and dedication,' and at 10.20 the members, passing out from their own halls, marched in procession to St. Giles'—the building in which John Knox preached, speaking to the entire Scottish nation—where they joined in singing the 100th Psalm, the reading of the Scriptures, prayer, the recitation of the Apostles' Creed and the Te Deum and other services preparatory to the formal declaration, in the afternoon, of the union, as consummated by the following resolution:

The General Assembly of the Church of Scotland and the General Assembly of the United Free Church of Scotland having been regularly constituted and meeting together

---

[1] The Barrier Act provided that no 'rules or constitutions' should be binding upon the Church unless proposed to the Assembly as an overture, then passed by the presbyteries and finally reported to the Assembly and approved by it.

in joint session this 2nd day of October, 1929 years; devoutly acknowledging the mercy and long-suffering shown by Almighty God to themselves and to their fathers, rendering humble and hearty thanks for the gracious guidance bestowed upon them in this their endeavour to heal the divisions in His Church and to promote His glory, and entreating Him to pour out His Spirit upon His servants and upon those who shall come after them, that as good stewards of the manifold grace of God they may with growing power minister to the people of this land and to the nations that have not yet received the Gospel; do now as in the presence of God adopt the Uniting Act, including the Basis of Union and the accompanying Plan of Union with the Questions and Formula for use at the Ordination and Induction of a Minister, and do hereby, in terms and in pursuance of Deliverances of their respective General Assemblies, with approval of the Presbyteries of the respective Churches in accordance with the provisions of the Barrier Act, Enact and Declare in the name of the Lord Jesus Christ, the great Head of the Church, that these Churches, being historic branches of the Reformed Church in Scotland, do and shall henceforth constitute one Church, and that the name of the united Church shall be The Church of Scotland.

The Moderators of the two Assemblies, Dr. Joseph Mitchell and Principal Alexander Martin, then announced the union in the following words: 'In the faith of Jesus Christ, our Divine King and Head, I do now in the name of the Church of Scotland'—or in the name of the United Free Church of Scotland—'seal and ratify the Union betwixt us made, in token whereof I offer you the right hand of fellowship.' Dr. Mitchell then said, 'And here in the presence of God Most High, we pledge ourselves together in solemn covenant,' to which Dr. Martin added, 'In the name of the Father, and of the Son, and of the Holy Ghost, we invoke the divine blessing upon our act.' In the united Assembly the Duke of York, as commissioner, represented the King of England who, in a letter addressed to the body, bound himself to maintain the rights of the Church of Scotland in these words: 'We assure you of our unwavering concern for the maintenance of the rights and privileges of the Church of Scotland as happily secured and with our earnest prayer that now and in the years to come, you may be filled with the power of the Spirit and that the grace of God may bless and sanctify your labors.' The Duke of York further announced that 'it was His Majesty's determination to uphold the use of Presbyterian government in Scotland.' The Prime Minister, Ramsay MacDonald, wrote to the Assembly that 'all Scotsmen will join with me in the fervent hope that the reunited Church will use its power and influence to make religion a continuing strength in the Scottish character and Presbyterianism a vital form of national worship.' At the time of the union, the Church of Scotland had 759,625 communicants, the Free Church 539,192.

The Basis of Union or Uniting Act includes four articles, together with two statements bearing on Matters Spiritual and the Spiritual Independence of the Church, adopted respectively by the two Churches, 1906 and 1926, which form an integral part of the uniting agreement.

The four articles are as follows:

I. The various matters of agreement between the Churches with a view to union are accepted and enacted without prejudice to the inherent liberty of the united Church as a branch of the Church of God to determine and regulate her own constitution and laws as duty may require, in dependence on the grace of God and under the guidance of His Word and Spirit, all as more particularly set forth in the after-mentioned Act, 1906, and Articles, 1926.

II. The following are leading documents setting forth the constitution, rules and methods of the united Church. [The list includes the Westminster Standards, the Scots Confession, 1560, First Book of Discipline, 1560, Book of Common Order, 1564, and a number of other documents of historic or binding import, as also the Acts on Matters Spiritual, 1926, and the Spiritual Independence of the Church, 1906.]

As this Union takes place on the footing of maintaining the liberty of judgment and action heretofore recognised in either of the Churches uniting, so in particular it is hereby declared that members of both Churches shall have full right, as they shall see cause, to assert and maintain the views of truth and duty which they had liberty to maintain in the said Churches.

The Churches, in entering into Union, under a sense of responsibility as a branch of the Church of God, acknowledge afresh the obligation resting on the Church to provide the ordinances of religion to the people of Scotland through a territorial ministry and to labour for the universal diffusion of the Gospel, and the duty of her members to contribute, according to their ability, both by their service and their means, for the support of the ordinances of religion in this land and the extension of the Kingdom of Christ throughout the world.

III. The General Assembly of the Church of Scotland and the General Assembly of the United Free Church of Scotland enact and ordain that all previous enactments and regulations of the General Assemblies of either uniting Church in force at the passing of this Act, unless in so far as modified by the Basis and Plan of Union, shall continue in force in the same manner as prior to the passing of this Act, so long as they shall not have been repealed or amended in accordance with the law of the united Church: provided always that where any such enactments or regulations are found in conflict or where the former practice of the two Churches is materially different and has not been adjusted by the Basis and Plan of Union any necessary legislation to which the procedure of the Barrier Act is appropriate shall be by interim Act only, which shall be transmitted to Presbyteries in accordance with the provisions of the Barrier Act for consent or suggestions before its adoption as a standing law of the Church.

IV. The General Assembly of the Church of Scotland and the General Assembly of the United Free Church of Scotland enact and ordain that the General Assembly of the Church of Scotland and the General Assembly of the United Free Church of Scotland, when they have met for the purpose of consummating the Union, and have adopted the Uniting Act, shall thereafter have the powers of a General Assembly of the united Church, and may do and authorise all things necessary or proper and lawful to be done with a view to the orderly inauguration and conduct of the affairs of the united Church, and in consistency with the terms of Union agreed upon.

ARTICLES DECLARATORY OF THE CONSTITUTION OF THE CHURCH OF SCOTLAND IN MATTERS SPIRITUAL, 1926.

I. The Church of Scotland is part of the Holy Catholic or Universal Church; worshipping one God, Almighty, all-wise, and all-loving, in the Trinity of the Father, the Son, and the Holy Ghost, the same in substance, equal in power and glory; adoring the Father, infinite in Majesty, of whom are all things; confessing our Lord Jesus Christ, the Eternal Son, made very man for our salvation; glorying in His Cross and Resurrection, and owning obedience to Him as the Head over all things to His Church; trusting in the promised renewal and guidance of the Holy Spirit; proclaiming the forgiveness of sins and acceptance with God through faith in Christ, and the gift of Eternal Life; and labouring for the advancement of the Kingdom of God throughout the world. The Church of Scotland adheres to the Scottish Reformation; receives the Word of God which is contained in the Scriptures of the Old and New Testaments as its supreme rule of faith and life; and avows the fundamental doctrines of the Catholic faith founded thereupon.

II. The principal subordinate standard of the Church of Scotland is the Westminster Confession of Faith approved by the General Assembly of 1647, containing the sum and substance of the Faith of the Reformed Church. Its government is Presbyterian, and is exercised through Kirk Sessions, Presbyteries, Provincial Synods, and General Assemblies. Its system and principles of worship, orders, and discipline are in accordance with "The Directory for the Public Worship of God," "The Form of Presbyterial Church Government," and "The Form of Process," as these have been or may hereafter be interpreted or modified by Acts of the General Assembly or by consuetude.

III. This Church is in historical continuity with the Church of Scotland which was reformed in 1560, whose liberties were ratified in 1592, and for whose security provision was made in the Treaty of Union of 1707. The continuity and identity of the Church of Scotland are not prejudiced by the adoption of these Articles. As a national Church representative of the Christian Faith of the Scottish people it acknowledges its distinctive call and duty to bring the ordinances of religion to the people in every parish of Scotland through a territorial ministry.

IV. This Church, as part of the Universal Church wherein the Lord Jesus Christ has appointed a government in the hands of Church office-bearers, receives from Him, its Divine King and Head, and from Him alone, the right and power subject to no civil authority to legislate, and to adjudicate finally, in all matters of doctrine, worship, government, and discipline in the Church, including the right to determine all questions concerning membership and office in the Church, the constitution and membership of its Courts, and the mode of election of its office-bearers, and to define the boundaries of the spheres of labour of its ministers and other office-bearers. Recognition by civil authority of the separate and independent government and jurisdiction of this Church in matters spiritual, in whatever manner such recognition be expressed, does not in any way affect the character of this government and jurisdiction as derived from the Divine Head of the Church alone, or give to the civil authority any right of interference with the proceedings or judgments of the Church within the sphere of its spiritual government and jurisdiction.

V. This Church has the inherent right, free from interference by civil authority, but under the safeguards for deliberate action and legislation provided by the Church itself, to frame or adopt its subordinate standards, to declare the sense in which it understands its Confession of Faith, to modify the forms of expression therein, or to formulate other doctrinal statements, and to define the relation thereto of its office-bearers and members, but always in agreement with the Word of God and the fundamental doctrines of the Christian Faith contained in the said Confession, of which agreement the Church shall be sole judge, and with due regard to liberty of opinion in points which do not enter into the substance of the Faith.

VI. This Church acknowledges the divine appointment and authority of the civil magistrate within his own sphere, and maintains its historic testimony to the duty of the nation acting in its corporate capacity to render homage to God, to acknowledge the Lord Jesus Christ to be King over the nations, to obey His laws, to reverence His ordinances, to honour His Church, and to promote in all appropriate ways the Kingdom of God. The Church and the State owe mutual duties to each other, and acting within their respective spheres may signally promote each other's welfare. The Church and the State have the right to determine each for itself all questions concerning the extent and the continuance of their mutual relations in the discharge of these duties and the obligations arising therefrom.

VII. The Church of Scotland, believing it to be the will of Christ that His disciples should be all one in the Father and in Him, that the world may believe that the Father has sent Him, recognises the obligation to seek and promote union with other Churches in which it finds the Word to be purely preached, the sacraments administered according to Christ's ordinance, and discipline rightly exercised; and it has the right to unite with any such Church without loss of its identity on terms which this Church finds to be consistent with these Articles.

VIII. The Church has the right to interpret these Articles, and, subject to the safeguards for deliberate action and legislation provided by the Church itself, to modify or add to them; but always consistently with the provisions of the first Article hereof, adherence to which, as interpreted by the Church, is essential to its continuity and corporate life. Any proposal for a modification of or addition to these Articles which may be approved of by the General Assembly shall, before it can be enacted by the Assembly, be transmitted by way of overture to Presbyteries in at least two immediately successive years. If the Overture shall receive the approval, with or without suggested amendment, of two-thirds of the whole of the Presbyteries of the Church, the Assembly may revise the Overture in the light of any suggestions by the Presbyteries, and may transmit the overture when so revised to Presbyteries for their consent. If the overture as transmitted in its final form shall receive the consent of not less than two-thirds of the whole of the Presbyteries of the Church, the General Assembly may, if it deems it expedient, modify or add to these Articles in terms of the said Overture. But if the Overture as transmitted in its final form shall not receive the requisite consent, the same or a similar proposal shall not be again transmitted for the consent of Presbyteries until an interval of five years after the failure to obtain the requisite consent has been reported to the General Assembly.

IX. Subject to the provisions of the foregoing Articles and the powers of amendment therein contained, the Constitution of the Church of Scotland in matters spiritual is hereby anew ratified and confirmed by the Church.

UNITED FREE CHURCH ACT ANENT SPIRITUAL INDEPENDENCE OF THE CHURCH, 1906.

Whereas the General Assembly judged it necessary in the circumstances of the Church to pass the following Act, and although the principles set forth therein involve no new departure and are not in any sense a constitutional novation, but have been always accepted and maintained by this Church, yet in respect of the importance of making manifest to all that the whole Church explicitly adheres to these principles, the General Assembly deemed it right to send it down as an Overture under the Barrier Act: the General Assembly hereby, with consent of a majority of Presbyteries, declare and enact, as follows:—

Considering the situation created by the decisions of the House of Lords on 1st August 1904, in the Cases of *Bannatyne and Others* v. *Lord Overtoun and Others*, and *Young and Others* v. *Macalister and Others*, and the grounds on which these decisions were based; considering also the Resolutions relative thereto of the Commission of Assembly at its ordinary Meeting on 10th August 1904, of which Resolutions the Assembly hereby approve; and considering that it is needful to make clear the position in which the United Free Church of Scotland stands in reference to the questions thus raised, the General Assembly resolve and declare as follows:—

1. They assert and protest that those branches of the Church of Christ in Scotland now united in this Church have always claimed, and this Church continues to claim, that the Church of Christ has under Him as her only Head independent and exclusive jurisdiction and power of legislating in all matters of doctrine, worship, discipline, and government of the Church, including therein the right from time to time to alter, change, add to or modify, her constitution and laws, Subordinate Standards, and Church Formulas, and to determine and declare what these are.

2. The General Assembly accordingly declare anew and enact that it is a fundamental principle and rule of this Church that, in dependence on the grace of God, recognising the authority of the Word of God, contained in the Scriptures of the Old and New Testaments, as the supreme unchangeable Standard, and looking to the Head of the Church for the promised guidance of the Holy Spirit, this Church has the sole and exclusive right and power from time to time, as duty may require, through her Courts to alter, change, add to, or modify, her constitution and laws, Subordinate Standards and Formulas, and to determine and declare what these are, and to unite with other Christian Churches; always in conformity with the Word of God, and also with the safeguards for deliberate action and legislation in such cases provided by the Church herself—of which conformity the Church herself, acting through her Courts, shall be the sole judge—and under a sense of direct responsibility to the ever-living Head of the Church, and of duty towards all the Church's members.

3. The General Assembly also declare and enact that in all the Courts of the Church a decision of the Court given either unanimously, or by a majority of its members present and voting, is the decision of the Court, and the decision of the General Assembly so reached is final. With respect to Acts which are to be binding Rules and Constitutions of the Church, the Assembly shall have regard to the safeguards referred to in the foregoing resolution.

4. The General Assembly further declare that the Church holds her funds and property, present and future, in conformity with these principles; the Church reserving her right to accept and hold benefactions, subject to specific conditions attached to them by the donor, when and so long as she judges these conditions to be consistent with her liberty and her principles, and to be expedient in the circumstances of the time.

THE CONGREGATIONAL AND CHRISTIAN CHURCHES.

The organic union of these two bodies was favorably acted upon by the National Council of Congregational Churches meeting in Detroit, May, 1929, and the General Convention of the Christian Church at Piqua, October 25, 1929. Under the name of the Congregational and Christian Churches, the two communions alike maintain the independence of the local congregation, subject to no higher judicial church body and at the same time the duty of the congregations to take counsel together and co-operate together. The history of the Congregational churches in the United States goes back to Plymouth, 1620; the Christian Church to the last years of the eighteenth century. The "Principles" of the latter body are expressed in the statement: 'The Church of Christ is One; it embraces all those who have been accepted by Christ as his real disciples; and, in its whole and in its parts, it should be so organized, named and governed as to include all and exclude none of those whom Christ has so accepted.' As for fixed formulas, its position is set forth in the words, 'The Holy Scriptures are our only creed.' In 1929 its membership was 99,749 and in union with the Congregationalists the membership is more than 1,000,000. The Plan of Union provides for 'immediate practical unity' and 'complete union into a single body' to be consummated at a joint meeting of the National Congregational Council and the General Convention of the Christian Church at Seattle, 1931. At that time, it is proposed 'to adopt a constitution and organize.' In the meantime a volume has been issued, 1930, in New York and Dayton, the headquarters of the Christian Church, combining the *Congregational Year Book* and the *Christian Annual* with 427 pages, and giving statistics of both bodies. The book is pronounced 'an evidence of the reality of the union.'

The Plan of Union issued by the General Council made up of members of the two bodies sets forth the basis of union in these words:

The basis of this new relation shall be the recognition by each group that the other group is constituted of the followers of Jesus Christ. Each individual church and each group of churches shall be free to retain and develop its own form of expression. Finding in the Bible the supreme rule of faith and life, but recognizing that there is wide room for differences of interpretation among equally good Christians, this union shall be conditioned upon the acceptance of Christianity as primarily a way of life, and not upon uniformity of theological opinion or any uniform practice of ordinances.

METHODIST CHURCH UNION IN ENGLAND.

The union of the English Wesleyan Methodist Church, the Primitive Methodist Church, and the United Methodist Church is confidently expected to be consummated, 1932, under the name, The Methodist Church. The movement is under the direction of The Methodist Union Committee. The United Methodist Church is itself the product of the merging of three bodies, 1907—the Methodist New Connection, the Bible Christians, and the United Methodist Free Churches, organized, respectively, 1797, 1815, 1836. The larger union now under way has been voted upon twice by the three uniting bodies and received from all the necessary three-fourths majority. The final and determining vote is to be taken, 1931, and, if favorable, the first United Conference will be held, 1932. In the meantime, preparation for the organic union is being made by the interchange of pulpits, inter-communion services at the Lord's Table, and gatherings for prayer. The necessary legislation has been passed in Parliament and recognizes that 'the religious doctrines held by each of the Churches or denominations are in substance identical' and that their differences concern matters of organization, procedure, and the tenure and disposition of property. The three denominations have together a membership of 850,000. The main object of the union is announced to be 'the more effective evangelization of the world and service of the age.'

Under the head of Doctrine, the Scheme of Union refers to the articles held in common by the three bodies, without designating them. They are given in this volume, pp. 807–813. The Scheme as it affects 'Doctrine' runs thus:

1. The Methodist Church claims and cherishes its place in the holy Catholic Church, which is the Body of Christ. It rejoices in the inheritance of the Apostolic faith, and loyally accepts the fundamental principles of the historic creeds and of the Protestant Reformation. It ever remembers that in the Providence of God Methodism was raised up to spread Scriptural Holiness through the land by the proclamation of the Evangelical Faith, and declares its unfaltering resolve to be true to its Divinely appointed mission.

The Doctrines of the Evangelical Faith, which Methodism has held from the beginning, and still holds, are based upon the Divine revelation recorded in the Holy Scriptures. The Methodist Church acknowledges this revelation as the supreme rule of faith and practice. These Evangelical Doctrines to which the preachers of the Methodist Church, Ministerial and Lay, are pledged are contained in Wesley's Notes on the New Testament and the first four volumes of his Sermons.

The Notes on the New Testament and the forty-four Sermons are not intended to impose a system of formal or speculative theology on Methodist Preachers, but to set up standards of preaching and belief which should secure loyalty to the fundamental truths of the Gospel of Redemption and ensure the continued witness of the Church to the realities of the Christian experience of salvation.

2. The Conference shall be the final authority within the Church with regard to all questions concerning the interpretation of its doctrines. In any necessary Act of Parliament provision shall be made to secure the recognition of this power.

3. Christ's ministers in the Church are stewards in the household of God, and shepherds of His flock. Some are called and ordained to this sole occupation, and have a principal and directing part in these great duties; but they hold no priesthood differing in kind from that which is common to the Lord's people, and they have no exclusive title to the preaching of the gospel or the care of souls. These ministries are shared with them by others, to whom also the Spirit divides His gifts severally as He wills.

4. It is the universal conviction of the Methodist people that the office of the Christian Ministry depends upon the call of God, Who bestows the gifts of the Spirit, the grace, and the fruit which indicate those whom He has chosen.

5. Those whom the Church recognises as called of God, and therefore receives into its

Ministry, shall be ordained by the imposition of hands, as expressive of the Church's recognition of the Minister's personal call.

6. The Methodist Church holds the doctrine of the priesthood of all believers and consequently believes that no priesthood exists which belongs exclusively to a particular order or class of men.

But in the exercise of its corporate life and worship special qualifications for the discharge of special duties are required and thus the principle of representative selection is recognised.

The preachers, itinerant and lay, are examined, tested, and approved before they are authorised to minister in holy things. For the sake of Church order, and not because of any priestly virtue inherent in the office, the Ministers of the Church are set apart by ordination to the Ministry of the Word and Sacraments.

The general usage of the three uniting Churches whereby the Sacrament of the Lord's Supper is administered by Ministers shall continue to be observed.

III. PROPOSALS LOOKING TOWARDS CHURCH UNIONS.

The most widely discussed of the proposals for Church union has come from the Lambeth Conferences and includes invitations to the Orthodox Churches of the East, the Roman Catholic communion, and the non-episcopal communions of the world. Within the Protestant bodies of the United States definite movements of union are proceeding, and also within Church groups in South India and other lands.

THE LAMBETH PROPOSALS.

I. *The Lambeth Quadrilateral.*—The series of Lambeth Conferences began, 1867, with 76 bishops present from different parts of the world, and ended, 1930, with 308 bishops in attendance. The intervening conferences have been held, 1878, 1888, 1898, 1908, 1920. Their object, to use the words of Archbishop Longley of Canterbury, 1867, is 'not to assume the functions of a general synod, but merely to discuss matters of practical interest and pronounce what we deem expedient in resolutions which may serve as safe guides to future action.' The action taken, 1888, bearing on the reunion of Christendom, is known as the Lambeth Quadrilateral. Its four articles, reaffirmed by succeeding Conferences, were pronounced 'a basis on which approach may be made by God's blessing towards Church Reunion.' The Quadrilateral is as follows:

A. The Holy Scriptures of the Old and New Testaments as containing all things necessary to salvation and as being the rule and ultimate standard of faith.

B. The Apostles' Creed as the Baptismal Symbol; and the Nicene Creed as the sufficient statement of the Christian faith.

C. The two Sacraments ordained by Christ himself—Baptism and the Supper of the Lord—ministered with unfailing use of Christ's words of Institution and of the elements ordained by Him.

D. The Historic Episcopate locally adapted, in the methods of its administration, to the varying needs of the nations and peoples called of God into the unity of His Church.

The Lambeth Quadrilateral was a reaffirmation, with changes in language but not purport, of four articles proposed in the General Convention of the Protestant Episcopal Church, meeting in Chicago, 1886[1], in response to a thousand requests from clergymen bearing on 'the restoration of Christian unity.' The Convention declared it to be

(1) their earnest desire that the Saviour's prayer 'that they all may be one' may in the deepest and truest sense be speedily fulfilled; (2) we believe that all who have been duly baptized with water in the name of the Father and of the Son and of the Holy Ghost are members of the Holy Catholic Church; (3) that in all things of human ordering or human choice relating to modes of worship and discipline, or traditional customs, this Church is ready in the spirit of love and humility, to forego all preferences of her own; (4) that this Church does not seek to absorb other communions but rather, co-operating with them on the basis of a common Faith and Order, discountenance schism, to heal the wounds of the Body of Christ, and to promote the charity which is the chief of Christian graces and the visible manifestation of Christ to the world. But furthermore we do affirm that the Christian unity so earnestly desired by the memorialists can be restored only by the return of all Christian communions to the principles of unity exemplified by the undivided Catholic Church during the first age of its existence, which principles we believe to be the substantial deposit of Christian faith and order committed by Christ and his Apostles to the Church unto the end of the world, and therefore incapable of compromise or surrender by those who have been ordained to be its stewards and trustees, for the common and equal benefit of all men. As inherent parts of this sacred deposit, and therefore as essential to the restoration of unity among the divided branches of Christendom, we account the following, to wit:

1. The Holy Scriptures of the Old and New Testaments as the revealed Word of God.

2. The Nicene Creed as the sufficient statement of the Christian faith.

3. The two Sacraments—Baptism and the Supper of the Lord—ministered with unfailing use of Christ's words of institution and of the elements ordained by Him.

4. The Historic Episcopate locally adapted in the methods of its administration to the varying needs of the nations and peoples called of God into the unity of His Church.

At the Lambeth Conference of 1920, Church reunion was the prominent subject of discussion and an impressive invitation to such union, called An Appeal to all Christian People, was sent forth by its members—'the archbishops and bishops of the Holy Catholic Church in full communion with the Church of England.' The document opened with a

---

[1] These four articles were referred to by the Lambeth Conference, 1888, as 'the important and practical step taken by our brethren of the American Church, 1886.' See Abp. Davidson: *The Three Lambeth Conferences*, London, 1896, 414 pp.

recognition 'of all those who believe in our Lord Jesus Christ and have
been baptized into the name of the Holy Trinity, as sharing with them
membership in the universal Church of Christ which is His body.' The
bishops then proceeded to say that they believed that God wills fellowship and that 'it is God's purpose to manifest this fellowship, so far as
this world is concerned, in an outward, visible, and united society, holding one faith, having its own recognized officers, using God-given means
of grace, and inspiring all its members to the world-wide service of the
Kingdom of God. This is what we mean by the Catholic Church.'
Then, after referring to the ancient episcopal Communions in East and
West to whom 'the Anglican Communion is bound by many ties of
common faith and tradition,' they addressed 'the great non-episcopal
Communions standing for rich elements of truth, liberty and life which
otherwise might have been obscured or neglected, with whom we are
closely linked by many affinities, racial, historical and spiritual.' Expressing the judgment that 'none can doubt that self-will, ambition, and
lack of charity among Christians have been the principal factors in the
mingled process of division, and that these, together with the blindness
to the sin of disunion, are still mainly responsible for the breaches of
Christendom,' they confessed that they 'shared in the guilt of crippling
the Body of Christ and hindering the activity of His Spirit.' Looking
forward to a united Church in which the bodies, now separated, 'will
retain much that has long been distinctive in their methods of worship
and service,' the bishops affirmed that the 'visible unity of the Church
will be found to involve the whole-hearted acceptance' of the following
articles:

The holy Scriptures, as the record of God's revelation of Himself to man, and as being
the rule and ultimate standard of faith; and the Creed commonly called Nicene, as the
sufficient statement of the Christian faith, and either it or the Apostles' Creed as the
Baptismal confession of belief.

The divinely instituted sacraments of Baptism and the Holy Communion, as expressing
for all the corporate life of the whole fellowship in and with Christ.

A ministry acknowledged by every part of the Church as possessing not only the inward
call of the Spirit, but also the commission of Christ and the authority of the whole body.

The question is then asked, 'May we not reasonably claim that the
Episcopate is the one means of providing such a ministry,' but coupled
with the 'thankful acknowledgment' that the ministries of the communions not possessing· the episcopate 'have been manifestly blessed

and owned by the Holy Spirit as effective means of grace.' The judgment is then expressed that, in accepting episcopal ordination, 'no one could possibly be taken to repudiate his past ministry.'

II. *The Lambeth Quadrilateral and the Free Churches of England.*— The Appeal, reaching the Federal Council of the Free Churches of England, was primarily acted upon 1921–25 by a Joint Conference between the Council's representatives of the Baptist, Congregational, Moravian, Presbyterian, Primitive Methodist, United Methodist, and Wesleyan bodies and a committee appointed by the two archbishops of England, the archbishops themselves being included. The deliberations were suspended by the Archbishop of Canterbury, 1925, that 'full opportunity might be given to the Churches to study and understand the documents already submitted' and the Federal Council's committee dismissed.[1] The Free Churches then individually discussed the Quadrilateral and replied to it. In general, objection was made to the Lambeth condition of episcopal ordination as essential, to the limitations put upon the dispensation of the Lord's Supper, and to creeds as of perpetually binding force. The Baptists declared that there is 'no separated body of priests.' The Congregational Union of England and Wales denied that 'the existence of separated Churches is necessarily contrary to the mind of Christ' and affirmed that the view that the validity of the ministry depends on episcopal ordination 'ran counter to their deepest convictions.'

III. *The Lambeth Conference and the Union of Churches in South India.*—The most important subject connected with Church union taken up at the Lambeth Conference of 1930 was the proposed merging of Church bodies in Southern India. Before the Conference assembled, there was much expectation that a large amount of attention would be given to the general subject of Church union. A resolution was presented

---

[1] A memorandum presented June 19, 1925, by the representatives of the Anglican Church in the Joint Conference called the ministries of the Free Churches 'real ministries,' but declared, at the same time, that, though they 'may possess spiritual reality and efficacy, due authority' did not follow. 'This matter of due authority,' it added, 'is to us one of highest importance. Spiritual efficacy is one thing, due authority is another.' See Bell. Documents II., 79. The Churches of Scotland took no part in negotiations, as they were engaged in discussions over their own consolidation. The Rev. C. C. Starbuck, writing years ago, said, 'the impression given him by the consensus of Episcopal judgment on the Historic Episcopate is that it is rather a demand for submission than a solicitation of brotherly union.'

to the Archbishop of Canterbury by the Congregationalists of England, July, 1930, praying 'for the day when the differences in the way of complete fellowship shall be removed.' The preceding April the Oxford-Cheltenham Conference of evangelical Churchmen 'reiterated its conviction that the ministries of the organized non-episcopal Churches are real ministries of the Word and the sacraments' and prayed that the Lambeth Conference 'do all in its power to facilitate the scheme of Church union in India and actively promote intercommunion between the Anglican and non-episcopal communions.' King George, in a communication to the Convocation of Canterbury, pronounced 'the progress made with the promotion of Christian unity very gratifying,' and expressed the hope that the Lambeth Conference 'would contribute to a further advance.' However, no advanced action in the direction of general Church union was taken in 1930.[1]

The Scheme of Union of the Churches of South India came before the Conference by the act of the (Anglican) Church of India, Burma, and Ceylon, with the request for 'advice.' The Scheme, the result of negotiations begun 1919, contemplates the consolidation of the (Anglican) Church of India, Burma, and Ceylon, the South India United Church, and the South India Wesleyan Methodist Church. As formulated, 1929, the Scheme has the following distinctive features: 1. The adoption of episcopacy with modifications in the methods of election and administration. 2. The effectual maintenance of 'the continuity of the historic episcopate,' no particular interpretation of the historic episcopate 'being required.' 3. The validity of the ministrations of clergymen, not episcopally ordained, for at least thirty years after the declaration of the union. 4. The right of such ministers to exercise intercommunion and intercelebration with non-episcopal Churches as before the union. 5. 'The intention that eventually every minister in the united Church will be an episcopally ordained minister.' 6. The forms of worship used in the uniting Churches may be continued.

The three Indian communions, when the Scheme of Union reached them from the Joint Committee, all made conditions to its acceptance. The non-episcopal bodies required that it be made plain that no theory of the episcopate should be regarded as official and that their constitu-

---

[1] The Conference ordered negotiations resumed with the Free Churches of England and opened with the Scotch Churches.

encies should continue to have full liberty of communion with non-episcopal Churches after the lapse of the term of thirty years. On the other hand, the General Council of the Anglican body voted that, in adopting the Scheme (1) it did not commit itself to the principle of the equal validity of all ministries, while at the same time requiring from the other bodies no endorsement of any particular theory of ordination; (2) that the Anglican rule for Anglican ministers in regard to the celebration of the eucharist should continue to be binding; (3) that as 'a measure of great importance, the rite of confirmation should be adopted as early as possible by the United Church.'

The position taken by the Lambeth Conference was set forth by a set of resolutions, in the Encyclical Letter sent out by the Bishops and in the Report of the Committee on the Unity of the Church, and was favorable to the inauguration of the movement. The movement the bishops pronounced a 'venture' and 'an experiment on behalf of the whole body of the Anglican Churches, made by our brethren of South India.' The Committee on the Unity of the Church—whose findings are printed in full but were not adopted by the Conference—approved the conditions proposed by the Anglican Church of India, Burma, and Ceylon, including the ultimate use of confirmation as a general practice of the united Church. The resolutions passed by the Conference gave 'its general approval to the suggestions contained in the Report of its Committee on the Unity of the Church,' and commended them to the General Synod of India, Burma, and Ceylon. They spoke of the Scheme as 'bringing together the distinctive elements of different Christian Communions, on a basis of sound doctrine and episcopal order, in a distinct Province of the Universal Church,' a province not subject to the jurisdiction of Canterbury.[1]

IV. *The Anglican and Protestant Episcopal Churches and the Orthodox Eastern and Old Catholic Churches.* Communications between these

---

[1] The Anglo-Catholic party in England, through Bishop Gore as its spokesman, demands as an essential condition of the union the acceptance of the doctrine of Apostolic succession and the rite of confirmation. In the new edition of his *Church and the Ministry* Dr. Gore says that 'the adoption of the Scheme as it is, would go far to break up the Anglican Communion,' p. 224. See also Gore: *Proposed Scheme of Union in S. India*, 8 pp., London, 1930; Bell: Documents, II., 143–210, and especially the *Lambeth Conference 1930*, a volume of 200 pp. issued by the S. P. C. K., giving the encyclical letter of the bishops, the resolutions passed by the Conference, and the report of the Com. on the Unity of the Ch., and other reports.

communions and friendly approaches have been increasing since the meetings of the General Convention, 1886, and the Lambeth Conference, 1888.[1] Unofficial efforts to bring them together are to be dated from 1863, when the Anglican and Eastern Churches Association was formed in London and, 1864, when the Church Unity Society was formed by Protestant Episcopalians. American and English delegations have visited Eastern prelates—as also the Archbishop of Canterbury, 1929— and prelates of the Eastern Churches have been present at meetings of the General Convention and Lambeth Conferences and have joined in Church services in America and England. The most notable gathering was, 1925, in Westminster Abbey at the services in commemoration of the sixteen hundredth anniversary of the Nicene Council and Creed, when the Archbishop of Canterbury preached the sermon and the East was represented by 'His Holiness and Beatitude and Pope and Patriarch of Alexandria,' the Patriarch of Jerusalem, the Metropolitans of Kieff and Nubia, and other dignitaries.

A commission on relations with the Eastern Churches, appointed by the General Convention, 1910, having completed the work assigned to it, was dismissed, 1925. In the meantime, 1920, the commission, meeting in New York with delegates from the East, formulated a 'Concordat or Terms of Agreement as a basis of restoration of corporate unity and intercommunion,' which were later accepted by the General Convention and by the Patriarch and Holy Synod of Constantinople and other Eastern prelates and ecclesiastical bodies. The basis included (1) the 'authority of the Catholic Church to teach what is necessary to be believed and practised for salvation'; (2) the Scriptures as interpreted by the Catholic Church; (3) the Nicene Creed and the 'decrees of faith' of the œcumenically-called Councils. The two parties also declared their acceptance of 'the sacramental acts of each other.'

As a result of the communications, the validity of Anglican orders has received recognition from the Old Catholics of Holland, Germany and Switzerland, and by the Patriarchs of Constantinople and Jerusalem and other Eastern prelates, the latter with limitations given below.

---

[1] See the Journals of the General Convention and the Reports of the Lambeth Conferences. Canon Douglas: *The Relations of the Angl. Ch. with the Churches of the East*, London, 1921; the "Eastern Ch. books" issued by the Faith Press, London; Bell Doc. on Christ. Unity.

The Lambeth Conference of 1930 was visited by 'the most weighty delegation ever sent by the Orthodox Eastern Church to any Western Church,'[1] and it was agreed to appoint a Joint Theological Commission to consider their differences and agreements in the hope—to use the words of the Lambeth Encyclical Letter of 1930—that 'restoration of communion may become possible as soon as the assemblies of the various Churches can meet.' At a meeting in Lambeth Palace, July 15–18, 1930, between bishops of the English Church and Eastern prelates, seventeen articles were agreed upon as a basis of further discussion by the Joint Theological Commission and promise made that a pro-synod should be convened in the East to discuss the matter. The articles embrace limitations laid down by the Easterners. 1. In regard to the ministry. The demand that the statements of the XXXIX Articles be interpreted by the Book of Common Prayer and that ordination be accepted as a *mysterion*—that is, as being sacramental in its nature and conferring a *charisma*—was agreed to by the Anglicans. 2. In regard to the eucharist. The Anglicans granted that it is a sacrifice in the sense defined in the archbishops' letter to Leo XIII., 1897, and 'as including the whole company of faithful people, living and departed.'[2]

V. *The Church of England and the Roman Catholic Church.*—In volume II. a brief account is given of the 'Malines Conversations' between Cardinal Mercier and an unofficial delegation of Anglican clergymen, 1921–25, also Leo XIII.'s encyclical on Anglican orders and Pius XI.'s encyclical, 1928, setting forth the Vatican's attitude to the movement toward Church unity brought to its attention by the Appeal of the Lambeth Conference, 1920, a copy of which was sent to Rome, and by the invitation to take part in the Lausanne Convention. Pius demanded unconditional submission to the Roman see from all Protestants, including Anglicans.

PROPOSALS OF CHURCH UNION WITHIN THE PROTESTANT CHURCHES OF THE UNITED STATES.

1. *The Protestant Episcopal Proposals.*—Following the action of the General Convention of 1886 proposing four articles as a basis of Church

---

[1] A quotation from the Report of the Com. on the Unity of the Church. A final judgment on the 'weight' of the delegation would require a comparison with the delegations sent from the East to the Councils of Lyons, 1274, and Ferrara, 1439.

[2] The articles and the archbishops' letter, so far as it bore on the eucharistic sacrifice,' are given in the Lambeth Conf., vol. 136–140.

union, the House of Bishops declared 'their desire and readiness to enter into brotherly conference with all or any Christian bodies seeking the restoration of the organic unity of the Church with a view to the earnest study of the conditions under which so priceless a blessing might happily be brought to pass,' and appointed a Commission on Christian Unity 'to open communications with various bodies of Christians in this land.' Prolonged communications were had with the Congregational and Presbyterian Churches. The Synod of the Evangelical Lutheran Church forthwith declared that it could not agree to the historic episcopate or to the Nicene Creed 'as the sufficient statement of the Christian faith.' The Baptists made no official reply, but insisted on the principle of Church independence. The Methodists also made no official reply except to declare its readiness to fraternize with other Churches.

The National Council of Congregational Churches, 1889, responding 'to the courteous and fraternal appeal of the House of Bishops of 1886,' pronounced the 'declaration of the episcopate indispensable' a barrier to union. The effort to secure co-operation or union between the two bodies has been continued, measures now originating with the one and now with the other. In 1910, the National Council 'voiced the earnest hope of closer fellowship with the Episcopal Church in work and worship.' A notable episode in the dealings between the two bodies was opened with an unofficial discussion between members of the two meeting together, the results of which were brought before the General Convention, 1919, in the shape of 'proposals for an approach toward unity.' The proposals were not adopted by the National Council. Three years later, the Bishops at the General Convention adopted a canon recognizing clergymen of other Churches with the right to perform clerical ministrations in the Protestant Episcopal Church and at the same time to continue 'their fellowship or ministry in the communions,' from which they came and, in case such ministers became settled over Episcopal parishes, they were to 'conform to the doctrine, discipline, and worship of this Church and thus become for all purposes ministers of this Church.' For such ordination, while subscription to the historic episcopate was not explicitly mentioned, the acceptance of 'the historic faith of the Church as contained in the Apostles' Creed and the Nicene Creed' was required. The act of the Convention went beyond the resolution of the Lambeth Conference of 1920, which permitted a bishop to give 'occasional authorization to ministers, not episcopally ordained, to preach in churches in his diocese.'[1] The Conference at the same time refused to allow ministers not episcopally ordained to celebrate the communion for Anglican congregations, and declared as the general rule 'that Anglican communicants should only receive the communion at the hands of ministers of their own Church' or a minister otherwise episcopally ordained. The action of the American Bishops, 1922, was found not to have been ratified by the House of Deputies, when Dean Brown and Professor Bainton of Yale University appeared before the Bishop of Connecticut and on that account were denied ordination.

The Communications between the Presbyterian Church in the U. S. A. and the Protestant Episcopal Church were prolonged, lasting from 1887 to 1896, and involved a clear statement of the ecclesiastical principle on which they differed, the principle of Church polity or the relative standing of bishops and presbyters.[2] In accepting the Episcopal invitation and appointing its Committee, 1887, the Presbyterian General Assembly expressed 'its own sincere desire that the conference may lead, if not to a formal oneness of organization, yet to such a vital and essential unity of faith and spirit as shall bring all the followers of our common Lord into hearty fellowship and to mutual recognition and affection and to ministerial reciprocity in the branches of the one visible Church of Christ.' At the same time, the Assembly set forth its conception of the terms of Christian unity in the following words, 'proclaiming them to the world': 1. All believers in Christ constitute one body, mystical yet real, and destined to grow into the fulness of Him who filleth all in all. 2. The Universal Visible Church consists of all those throughout the whole world who profess the true religion, together with their children. 3. Mutual recognition and reciprocity between the different bodies, who profess the true religion, is the first and essential step toward practical Christian unity. With regard to the historic episcopate, the Assembly declared that, although it accepted another origin of the Christian ministry, it 'would find no difficulty with those who interpret the

---

[1] See Newman Smyth: *A Story of Christ. Unity, including the Lamb. Conf. and the Cong.-Episc. Approaches.* New Haven, 1923, 87 pp.

[2] The communications are found in a pamphlet *Church Unity* giving the 'progress and suspension of the negotiations between the two bodies,' 45 pp., Philadelphia, 1899. See Journals of the General Convention, 1895, Appendix XI., pp. 595–613, "Negotiations with the Presbyterians," and Journals, 1892, Appendix X., pp. 545 sqq.

bishops of the New Testament and the primitive Church differently from ourselves, provided our own liberty of interpretation is not infringed.' The reply of the Protestant Episcopal commission was that, so far as the historic episcopate went, the Church in whose name it acted was bound by the words of the Ordinal of the Book of Common Prayer, namely, 'it is evident unto all men, diligently reading Holy Scripture and ancient authors that from the Apostles' time there have been three orders of ministers in Christ's Church, bishops, priests and deacons.' On the question of original historic fact, the two bodies were thus placed in irreconcilable conflict. In one of its communications the Commission stated that 'in days gone by it was the habit of men to glorify divisions, now the great evil of them is generally conceded and the sin of them acknowledged and deplored.' Without replying to the statement, which it certainly would have accepted only with modifications, the Presbyterian committee pronounced that 'external unity' did not seem possible at that time and expressed the hope that measures might be devised to bring the two Churches together in practical Church work, especially on the mission field.

Correspondence with the General Convention was declared stopped by the General Assembly, 1894, until such time as the Convention took action on the Assembly's resolutions of 1887 and had expressed itself 'upon the doctrine of mutual recognition and reciprocity.' In reply to further action of the Episcopal commission, the General Assembly of 1896 declared it 'impossible for it to negotiate with another Christian body on the subject of Christian unity except on terms of parity and the explicit acknowledgement of the Presbyterian Church to be a Church of Christ and its ministry a divinely authorized ministry.' In 1929, the Assembly received from the Episcopal commission an invitation to confer with it and other like commissions in the study of Christian morality, looking toward organic unity—a proposal which it adopted unanimously.

2. *Congregational Proposals of Union.*—The Congregational and Presbyterian Churches have repeatedly affirmed their fellowship with one another and with other Christian bodies on the basis of the Scriptures and the profession and practice of Christian faith. They likewise have made distinct proposals to other ecclesiastical bodies for federation or corporate union. In 1871, the National Council of the Congregational Churches made a notable deliverance—frequently reprinted in issues

of the Biennial Minutes—expressing its desire to co-operate with all the Churches of the Lord and declaring that 'as little as did our fathers in their day, do we in ours make any pretension to be the only Churches of Christ. We believe in the Holy Catholic Church and it is our prayer and endeavor that the unity of the Church may be more and more apparent and that the prayer of our Lord for his disciples may be speedily and completely answered and all be one, that by consequence of this Christian unity in love the world may believe in Christ as sent of the Father to save the world.' The fine report of 1889, made by its chairman, Professor George P. Fisher, in answering the invitation of the General Convention of 1886, pronounced in favor of closer relations with the Presbyterians as desirable and natural in these words: 'The Connecticut Congregationalists and Presbyterians since the settlement of the country have been so close and the points of contact and sympathy so numerous that in endeavoring to secure inter-denominational comity, we are especially concerned to adjust our relations to them.'

The organic union of the Congregationalists, the Church of the United Brethren in Christ, and the Methodist Protestant Church was the subject of discussion from 1898 to 1907. A Joint Committee of the three bodies formulated an Act of Union and a Declaration of Faith. The National Council of Congregational Churches, 1907, referred the Act back to the commission, whereupon the other two Churches withdrew from further negotiations. Later, the Council denied intending by its action opposition to the movement of union.[1]

3. *Presbyterian Proposals of Union.*—Fruitless efforts have several times been made officially to reunite the Presbyterian Church in the U. S. A.—commonly known as the Presbyterian Church North—and the Presbyterian Church in the United States—commonly known as the Presbyterian Church South—as also to reunite the Northern and Southern Methodist bodies, divided on civil union or slavery. Both Presbyterian bodies have proposed union with the United Presbyterian Church of North America, and a plan of consolidation between the United Presbyterian Church and the Presbyterian Church South has actually been agreed upon. The Presbyterian Church North has also at times officially joined with the two Reformed Church bodies in the

---

[1] See Barton, pp. 198, 199, and Minutes of the Nat. Council, 1907, p. 286, and 1910, p. 259.

United States in seeking an agreement which would lead to their coalescence, but without practical result.

At an early time, 1887, the General Assembly of the Church North declared 'its cordial sympathy with the growing desire among Evangelical Christian Churches for practical unity and co-operation in the practical work of spreading the Gospel throughout all the earth.' In 1903, it made the far-reaching deliverance that 'whereas the Presbyterian Church holds Christian fellowship with all who confess and obey Jesus Christ as their Saviour and Lord and acknowledge the duty of all Churches that recognize Him as the only Head of the Church Universal to work in harmony and love for the extension of His kingdom and the good of the world, and whereas this Assembly earnestly desires to commend and promote this Christian co-operation and also practically to advance the cause of Church union by federation and, where possible, by consolidation, be it resolved that a committee be appointed to consider the whole subject of co-operation, confederation and consolidation with other Churches.' In 1918, expressing the 'profound conviction that the time had come for organic union of the evangelical Churches of America,' it overtured 'the National bodies of the Evangelical Communions of America to meet with its representatives for the purpose of formulating a Plan of Union.'[1] The Assembly's earnestness in the cause was shown by the elevation of its committee on Church Comity and Union, 1923, to the Department of Church Co-operation and Union. In 1929 it received with applause a communication from the Methodist Episcopal Church North looking toward union; and conferences are being held between its commissions and commissions from the Presbyterian Church South and the Methodist Episcopal Churches North and South with the Protestant Episcopal commission instructed by the General Convention of 1929 to hold a common conference on co-operation in matters affecting Christian morals.

The most important movement within the Presbyterian or Reformed family of Churches of the United States was begun 1929, when five of them, namely, the Presbyterian Churches North and South, the United Presbyterian Church, the Reformed Church in the U. S.—German Re-

---

[1] The Plan of Union proposed as the name of the united body 'The United Churches of Christ in America.' See Min. of the Gen. Assembly, 1919, pp. 97–123; 1920, pp. 118–122; Min. of the Nat. Council of Cong. Churches, 1920, pp. 48–54

formed—and the Reformed Church in America—Dutch Reformed—
agreed to discuss a plan for their organic union. Through their committees these bodies have been holding meetings and have agreed upon
articles which will be presented to the various representative assemblies
and synods in 1931. In 1930, the Assembly of the United Presbyterian
Church took the initiative in voting for the consolidation. The bodies,
if they unite, will accept the Westminster Confession and Catechisms,
the Heidelberg Catechism, the Canons of Dort, and the Belgic Confession, all of which are accepted by one or more of the bodies concerned
and set forth the Calvinistic type of theology, so called. The following
declarations are also proposed as the fundamentals of Church polity:

1. That the Lord Jesus Christ is the supreme and sole Head of the Church.
2. That the Word of God is the ultimate source and authority in Church government.
3. That the Church's nature, relation and function are spiritual, and spiritual only.
4. That witnessing for Christ is the continuous business of the Church.
5. That the evangelization and Christianization of the world is the aim of the Church.
6. We accept and practice the Presbyterian system as the method or form of Church
organization and government, believing it to be in harmony with the Scriptures.

IV. CHURCH ALLIANCES AND FEDERATIONS OF CHURCHES.

The impulse towards fellowship and co-operation in Christian activi-
ties have also found notable expression within the Protestant world in
œcumenical gatherings of Churches belonging to the same family and
the confederate associations of Protestant Churches here and abroad.
In both cases, proof has been given of the unity of the Protestant
Churches and the possibility of hearty agreement in action without
solidarity of denominational control.

The alliances of Churches belonging to the same families have been
constituted on the basis of the primitive truths of the Gospel and agreement in distinctive denominational principles. They began with the
Alliance of the Reformed Churches, which held its first meeting in Edinburgh, 1876, and are the following: 1. The Baptist World Alliance,
with meetings, London, 1905, Philadelphia, 1911, and Stockholm, 1923.
Among the principles emphasized at Stockholm were the 'universal
priesthood of believers as the basis of the New Testament teaching as

to the Church and the ministry,' and that 'Christian unity can only come through obedience to the will of Christ, as revealed in the New Testament, which Baptists must ever take as their sole, sufficient, certain and authoritative guide.'[1] 2. The International Congregational Council with four meetings, London, 1891, with Rev. Dr. R. W. Dale as president; Boston, 1899, with President Angell of Michigan University as president; Edinburgh, 1908, and Boston, 1920.[2] 3. The Lutheran World Convention, with meetings in Eisenach, 1923, and Copenhagen, 1929, and based on the statement that 'the Lutheran World Convention acknowledges the Holy Scriptures of the Old and New Testament as the only source and infallible norm of all Church teaching and practice, and sees in the Lutheran Confessions especially in the Unaltered Augsburg Confession and Luther's Small Catechism, the pure exposition of the Word of God.' 4. The Œcumenical Methodist Conference, with meetings in London, 1901, Toronto, 1911, London, 1921. 5. The Alliance of the Reformed Churches throughout the World holding the Presbyterian system, whose last three meetings were held in Pittsburgh, 1920, Cardiff, 1925, and Boston, 1929. Its object is to consider questions of general interest to the Presbyterian community, to seek the welfare of Churches, especially such as are weak or persecuted, and disseminate information concerning the kingdom of Christ throughout the world.[3] 6. The Unitarians have also had world conferences under the title, the International Congress of Religious Liberals, beginning in London, 1901. The meeting was held in Prag, 1927.

To these world alliances of Churches affiliated by denominational origins and agreements should be added the congresses uniting representatives of all the Christian bodies of the world except the Roman Catholic Church, namely, the Universal Christian Conference on Life and Work, held in Stockholm, 1925, and the World Conference on

---

[1] See the Report of the Bapt. World Alliance, Stockholm, 223 pp.

[2] The proceedings have been published in separate vols.

[3] These œcum. councils are in line with the words of Dr. Philip Schaff, 1875. Writing of the London gathering which arranged for the Council of 1876, he said: 'We have the Christian union of individual believers in the Ev. Alliance, and now this is a confederation of Churches of all Presb. and Reformed bodies. The last step would be the organic union in one body which will hardly appear till the millennium. In the mean time the Lutheran Churches should have a Luth. Alliance, and the Episcopalians, Methodists, and other eccles. families should have their alliances. In this way, union would be simplified.' (*Life of P. Schaff*, p. 318.)

Faith and Order, Lausanne, 1927. The latter[1] 'disavowed emphatically any attempt to define the conditions of future reunion,' but at the same time considered among other subjects the sacraments, the ministry, and the extent of the authority of Scripture, all of which have an essential bearing on the consolidation of the Churches. Both conferences were attended by representatives from the Eastern Orthodox Churches, who also took part in the proceedings.

The Federation of Churches is represented by the Federal Council of the Evangelical Free Churches of England, formed 1917, and the Federal Council of the Churches of Christ in America, 1905. The English Federation is based upon a Declaratory Statement of Common Faith and Practice which includes the evangelical doctrines of the Trinity, incarnation, 'the Only Headship' of Christ in the Church, sin, the final judgment, the Scriptures, the sacraments, and the ministry, the last defined as 'not a sacerdotal order but as comprising all who are called to it by an inward call of the Holy Spirit authenticated by the call of the Church.'

The Federal Council of the Churches of Christ in America has for its object, as its Plan of Federation states, 'more fully to manifest the essential oneness of the Christian Churches of America in Jesus Christ as their divine Lord and Saviour, to express the fellowship and catholic unity of the Christian Church and to bring the Christian bodies of America into united service, for Christ and the world.'

The Holy Church throughout all the world
Doth acknowledge Thee, the Father everlasting
Thine adorable, true, and only Son
Also the Holy Ghost, the Comforter.
—*Te Deum.*

---

[1] See the *Univ. Christ. Conf. on Life and Work, Stockholm, 1925,* ed. by Bp. Bell, Oxf., 1926, 787 pp. For the Lausanne Conf., Bell: *Documents on Christ. Unity,* I., 377 sqq.; II., 220 sqq.; and *Proceedings of the Conference,* N. Y., 1928, 541 pp. In 1930 a committee appointed by the two English archbishops to 'consider the findings of the Lausanne Conf.' in a long report announced that 'it would never abandon the principle of a ministry conferred by episcopal ordination.' The Report, with statements by Bishops Gore and Palmer on the South India Scheme, 158 pp., publ. Westminster, 1930.

INDEX TO VOL. III.